Law for Business

Twelfth Edition

A. James Barnes, J.D.

Terry Morehead Dworkin, J.D.

Eric L. Richards, J.D.

All of Indiana University

Mc Graw Hill Education

LAW FOR BUSINESS TWELTH EDITION

Published by McGraw-Hill Education, 2 Penn Plaza, New York, NY, 10121.

Some ancillaries, including electronic and print components, may not be available to customers outside the United States.

This book is printed on acid-free paper.

1 2 3 4 5 6 7 8 9 0 QVS/QVS 1 0 9 8 7 6 5 4

ISBN 978-0-07-802381-1
MHID 0-07-802381-5

Senior Vice President, Products & Markets: *Kurt L. Strand*
Vice President, Content Production & Technology Services: *Kimberly Meriwether David*
Director of Development: *Ann Torbert*
Brand Manager: *Tim Vertovec*
Development Editor: *Rebecca Mann*
Marketing Manager: *Michelle Nolte*
Director, Content Production: *Terri Schiesl*
Content Project Manager: *Jolynn Kilburg*
Buyer: *Debra Sylvester*
Media Project Manager: *Shawn Coenen*
Compositor: *Laserwords Private Limited*
Typeface: *10/12 Times New Roman*
Printer: *Quad/Graphics*

Library of Congress Cataloging-in-Publication Data

Barnes, A. James, author.
Law for business / A. James Barnes, J.D., Terry Morehead Dworkin, J.D., Eric L. Richards, J.D., all of Indiana University.—Twelfth Edition.
pages cm
ISBN 978-0-07-802381-1 (alk. paper)
1. Commercial law—United States. 2. Trade regulation—United States. I. Dworkin, Terry Morehead, author. II. Richards, Eric L., author. III. Title.
KF889.B28 2015
346.7307—dc23

2013033985

The Internet addresses listed in the text were accurate at the time of publication. The inclusion of a website does not indicate an endorsement by the authors or McGraw-Hill Education, and McGraw-Hill Education does not guarantee the accuracy of the information presented at these sites.

www.mhhe.com

Preface

For more than 30 years, *Law for Business* has set the standard as an easy-to-read textbook that provides students with the tools for understanding the legal environment of business. This, the 12th edition, has not strayed from that winning formula. The text goes well beyond merely identifying the current legal rules and regulations affecting business by offering insights into new developments and trends that promise to greatly affect the future of both domestic and international businesses. The result is a comprehensive, yet concise, treatment of the legal issues of fundamental importance to business students and the business profession.

We are extremely pleased with the number of institutions and instructors that continue to adopt *Law for Business.* They represent a wide range of programs in business in both two-year and four-year colleges and universities throughout the country and the world. Feedback from faculty and students alike confirms that they particularly like the clear exposition, the careful selection and editing of high-interest cases, and the text's attractive and readable design.

What's New in the Twelfth Edition?

In preparing this latest edition of *Law for Business,* we have tried to maintain the strengths of the past editions while updating the material and cases.

The following changes have been made to the 12th edition of *Law for Business:*

CHAPTER 1

- Replaced the chapter opener case with an abbreviated version of the *Twisdale* case
- Added three new cases: *United States v. Farinella; Coach v. Goodfellow;* and *Lozman v. City of Riviera Beach*
- Edited the *Lawrence v. Texas, Bowles v. Russell,* and *United States v. Stewart* cases for conciseness
- Removed the *Yahoo v. La Ligue Contre* and *United States v. Ressam* cases
- Edited and updated questions and problem cases

CHAPTER 2

- Added 1 new case: *Wal-Mart Stores, Inc. v. Dukes*
- Removed the *Wong v. T-Mobile USA Inc.* case
- Edited and updated questions and problem cases

CHAPTER 3

- Added new section on conscious capitalism
- Moved Foreign Corrupt Practices Act material to Securities Regulation chapter
- Added 3 new cases: *Hart v. Electronic Arts; Everson v. Michigan Department of Corrections* case; *Jane Doe v. Wal-Mart Stores*
- Removed *Virginia v. Black; United States v. Virginia; Midwest Motor Sports* cases
- Edited *Dewitt v. Proctor* case for conciseness
- Edited and updated questions and problem cases

CHAPTER 4

- New chapter opener case
- Added new section on time, place, or manner restrictions

- Added 4 new cases: *U.S. Smokeless Tobacco Manufacturing Co. v. City of New York; Florida Transportation Service v. Miami-Dade County; R.J. Reynolds Tobacco v. Food & Drug Administration; McCullen v. Coakley*
- Removed *Wyeth v. Levine; Granholm v. Heald; Gonzalez v. Raich; National Council of Resistance of Iran v. Albright; Ashcroft v. American Civil Liberties Union; Mainstream Marketing v. Federal Trade Commission; Solis v. Summit Contractors* cases
- Edited *Kelo v. City of New London* case and *Picca* case for conciseness
- Edited and updated questions and problem cases

CHAPTER 5

- Added three new cases: *Lock v. State; United States v. Jones; United States v. Nosal*
- Removed *Chaffee v. Roger; Clark v. Arizona; United States v. Mann; United States v. Hong* cases
- Edited and updated questions and problem cases

CHAPTER 6

- Added three new cases: *Roberts v. McAfee, Inc.; Stickdorn v. Zook; Kimes v. Grosser*
- Removed *Avila v. Citrus Community College; Amrak Productions, Inc. v. Morton; Gates v. Discovery Communications, Inc.; Stevenson v. DuPont*
- Edited and updated questions and problem cases

CHAPTER 7

- Added three new cases: *Putnam County Sheriff v. Price; McDougal v. Lamm; Steigman v. Outrigger Enterprises, Inc.*
- Removed *Sigler v. Kobinsky; Izquierdo v. Ricitelli; Power v. Metropolitan Entertainment Co.* cases
- Edited and updated questions and problem cases

CHAPTER 8

- New chapter opener case
- New section and learning objective on intellectual property aspects of social media
- New Ethics in Action box
- Edited text to account for the patent law changes dictated by the America Invents Act
- Removed Key Contractual Provisions material from the Licensing section
- Edited section on copyright infringement, fair use, and first sale doctrine
- Added 4 new cases: *Association for Molecular Pathology v. Myriad Genetics; Bowman v. Monsanto; Kirtsaeng v. John Wiley & Sons;* and *PhoneDog v. Kravitz*
- Edited *Schwan's v. Kraft Pizza Company* case for conciseness
- Removed *In re Stephen v. Comiskey; Grupo Gigante S.A. de C.V. v. Dallo & Co.; BMG Music v. Gonzalez; Perfect 10 v. Google; Arista Records v. Flea World; DuPont de Nemours & Co. v. Christopher;* and *MedImmune v. Genentech* cases
- Edited and updated questions and problem cases

CHAPTER 9

- Added 2 new cases: *Dodd v. American Family Mutual Insurance Co.* and *Anderson v. Hannaford Brothers Co.*
- Removed *Race v. Fleetwood Retail Corp. of Washington; Staley v. Taylor* cases
- Edited and updated questions and problem cases

CHAPTER 10

- Added 3 new cases: *Allen v. Clarian Health Partners; Permison v. Comcast Holdings Corporation; Alexander v. Lafayette Crime Stoppers, Inc.*
- Removed *Leonard v. Pepsico, Inc.* and *Giovo v. McDonald* cases
- Edited and updated questions and problem cases

CHAPTER 11

- Added 2 new cases: *Trademark Properties, Inc. v. A&E Television Networks* and *Teter v. Glass Onion, Inc.*
- Removed *Basis Technology Corp. v. Amazon.com, Inc.* and *Aetna Life Insurance Co. v. Montgomery* cases
- Edited and updated questions and problem cases

CHAPTER 12

- Added 3 new cases: *Bob Acres, LLC v. Schumacher Farms, LLC; Tasini v. AOL, Inc.; Dixon v. Wells Fargo Bank, NA*
- Removed *McBee v. Nance* and *Duncan v. Duncan* cases
- Edited and updated questions and problem cases

CHAPTER 13

- Added 2 new cases: *Woodman v. Kera, LLC* and *Sexton v. Sexton*
- Removed *Cooper v. The Aspen Skiing Company* and *Willard v. Peak* cases
- Edited and updated questions and problem cases

CHAPTER 14

- Added 2 new cases: *Koehlinger v. State Lottery Commission* and *Gomez-Jimenez v. New York Law School*
- Removed *Morehouse v. Behlman Pontiac-GMC Truck Service, Inc.; Columbia/HCA Healthcare Corp. et al v. Cottey;* and *David D. Murray v. Dianne E. Murray* cases
- Edited and updated questions and problem cases

CHAPTER 15

- Added 3 new cases: *Grigsby v. Russell; Home Paramount Pest Control Companies, Inc. v. Shaffer;* and *Lhotka v. Geographic Expeditions, Inc.*
- Removed *Neiman v. Provident Life & Accident Insurance Co.; Central Indiana Podiatry, P.C. v. Krueger;* and *Alexander v. Anthony Int'l, L.P.* cases
- Edited and updated questions and problem cases

CHAPTER 16

- Added 3 new cases: *East Lynn Fertilizers, Inc. v. CHS, Inc.; MEMC Electronic, Inc. v. BP Solar Int'l, Inc.;* and *State Automobile Mutual Insurance Company v. Flexdar, Inc.*
- Removed *Conner v. Lavaca Hospital Dist.; Wehry v. Daniels;* and *Knight v. Indiana Insurance Company* cases
- Edited and updated questions and problem cases

CHAPTER 17

- Added two new cases: *Allan v. Nersesova* and *Huff v. FirstEnergy Corp.*
- Removed *Caba v. Barker* case
- Edited and updated questions and problem cases

CHAPTER 18

- Added three new cases: *Sargon Enterprises v. University of Southern California; Dean v. Kruse Foundation, Inc.;* and *Equal Employment Opportunity Commission v. Dresser Rand Co.*
- Removed *Dupont Flooring Sys. v. Discovery Zone, Inc.; American Car Rental, Inc. v. Commissioner;* and *Manuma v. Blue Hawaii Adventures, Inc.* case
- Edited and updated questions and problem cases

CHAPTER 19

- Replaced *Heart of Texas Dodge, Inc. v. Star Coach, LLC.* case with *Janke v. Brooks*
- Edited and updated questions and problem cases

CHAPTER 20

- Replaced *Klein v. Sears Roebuck & Co.* case with *Ram Head Outfitters, Ltd. v. Mecham*
- Added *Baba v. Hewlett Packard Co.* case
- Deleted *Thacker v. Menard's* case
- Edited and updated questions and problem cases

CHAPTER 21

- Replaced *Rochester Gas and Electric Corporation v. Delta Star, Inc.* case with *Vasaturo Brothers, Inc. v. Alimenta Trading-USA, LLC.*
- Edited and updated questions and problem cases

CHAPTER 22

- Added 2 new cases: *Beer v. Bennett* and *Cahaba Disaster Recovery, LLC v. Rogers* case about the fire and explosion of the Deepwater Horizon drilling rig in the Gulf of Mexico in 2010
- Deleted *Moore v. Coachmen Industries, Inc.* and *KGM Harvesting Co. v. Fresh Network* cases
- Edited and updated questions and problem cases

CHAPTER 23

- Added new section on moonlighting
- Added 3 new cases: *Wesco Autobody Supply v. Ernest; American Family Mutual Insurance v. Roth; AA Sales & Associates v. Coni-Seal*
- Removed *Kakides v. King Davis Agency; Cameco v. Gedicke; Pacific Aerospace & Electronics v. Taylor;* and *Christensen Sales Agency v. General Time Corporation* cases
- Edited and updated questions and problem cases

CHAPTER 24

- Added 2 new cases: *Opthalmic Surgeons v. Paychex* and *Roberts v. Danner*
- Edited the *NCP* and *TGM* cases for conciseness
- Removed *CSX Transportation v. Recovery Express* and *Freeman v. Busch* cases
- Edited and updated questions and problem cases

CHAPTER 25

- Added two new cases: *Glatt v. Fox Searchlight Pictures, Inc.* and *Mauerhan v. Wagner Corporation*

- Removed *Media General Operations, Inc. v. National Labor Relations Board; Karl Knauz Motors, Inc. and Robert Becker; General Dynamics Land Systems, Inc. v. Cline; Akers v. Kindred Nursing Ctrs. Ltd. P'ship D/B/A Southwood Health* cases
- Edited and updated questions and problem cases

CHAPTER 26

- Added three new cases: *North American Steel Connection v. Watson Metal Products; McCann v. McCann, Jr.;* and *Katris v. Carroll*
- Removed the *La Montagne Builders v. Bowman Brook Purchase Group; Brooks v. Hill;* and *Estate of Countryman v. Farmers Cooperative* cases
- Edited the *In re Garrison-Ashburn, LC* and *Boulanger v. Dunkin' Donuts* cases for conciseness
- Edited and updated questions and problem cases

CHAPTER 27

- Added two new cases: *McGregor v. Crumley* and *In the Matter of Hardwood*
- Removed *Chen v. Wang* and *Gregg v. S. R. Investors, Ltd.* cases
- Edited the *Long v. Lopez* case for conciseness
- Edited and updated questions and problem cases

CHAPTER 28

- Added two new cases: *Keene v. Brookhaven Academy* and *Kertesz v. Korn*
- Removed the *Bridas v. Government of Turkmenistan* and *Balsamides v. Perle* cases
- Edited and updated questions and problem cases

CHAPTER 29

- Added two new cases: *Kirschner v. K&L Gates* and *Sarei v. Rio Tinto*
- Edited the *In re Walt Disney Derivative Litigation; Gantler v. Stephens;* and *SEC v. Gemstar-TV Guide International* cases for conciseness
- Removed the *MM Companies v. Liquid Audio; Omnicare v. NCS Healthcare;* and *Southern Management Corporation v. Taha* cases
- Edited and updated questions and problem cases

CHAPTER 30

- Added two new cases: *Barasch v. Williams Real Estate* and *Lerner v. Immelt*
- Edited *Levco Alternative Fund Ltd. v. The Reader's Digest Association; Accipiter Life Sciences Fund v. Helfer; American Federation v. American International Group;* and *Pirelli Armstrong Tire Corporation v. Raines* cases for conciseness
- Removed *Seinfeld v. Verizon Communications; Lohnes v. Level 3 Communications;* and *In re Oracle Corporation Derivative Litigation* cases
- Edited and updated questions and problem cases

CHAPTER 31

- Added learning objective and new section on Foreign Corrupt Practices Act
- Added new Ethics in Action box
- Removed the sections on Regulation of Proxy Solicitations and International Cooperation
- Added four new cases: *Gibbons v. Malone; Morrison v. National Australia Bank; Matrixx Initiatives v. Siracusano;* and *USA v. Lindsey*

- Edited the *SEC v. Charles Edwards* and *SEC v. Rocklage* cases for conciseness
- Removed the *Credit Suisse Securities v. Glen Billing; Roth v. Perseus L.L.C.; Stoneridge Investment Partners v. Scientific-Atlanta; Greenhouse v. MCG Captial Corporation;* and *South Ferry LP #2 v. Killinger* cases
- Edited and updated questions and problem cases

CHAPTER 32

- Added four new cases: *Delollis v. Friedberg, Smith & Co.; Stephenson v. PriceWaterhouseCoopers; Knappe v. United States; Bennett v. Sprint Nextel Corporation*
- Edited the *APA Excelsior III L.P. v. Premiere Technologies* and *Arthur Anderson v. United States* cases for conciseness
- Removed the *Thabault v. Chait; Tricontinental Industries v. PricewaterhouseCoopers LLP; Ernst & Young L.L.P. v. Pacific Mutual Life Insurance Co.; McCurdy v. SEC;* and *United States v. Roxworthy* cases
- Edited and updated questions and problem cases

CHAPTER 33

- Replaced *Jasphy v. Osinsky* case with *Weissman v. City of New York*
- Edited and updated questions and problem cases

CHAPTER 34

- Replaced *Rothermich v. Union Planters National Bank* case with *Chevron U.S.A., Inc. v. Sheikhpour*
- Edited and updated questions and problem cases

CHAPTER 35

- Replaced *Hemmings v. Pelham Wood Limited Liability Limited Partnership* with *Tan v. Arnel Management Company*

CHAPTER 36

- Modified and expanded the Learning Objectives
- Replaced *In re Estate of Kathleen Lee Meade* case with *Estate of Abshire*
- Edited and updated questions and problem cases

CHAPTER 37

- Added new section on affordable health care
- Added three new cases: *Nationwide Insurance v. Central Laborers' Pension Fund; ISBA Mutual Insurance v. Frank M. Greenfield;* and *Kutlenios v. Correa*
- Edited the *State Farm Mutual Automobile Insurance Company v. Kastner; Terra Nova Insurance v. Fray-Witzer;* and *Mayo v. Hartfield Life Insurance Co.* cases for conciseness
- Removed *Medical Mutual Insurance v. Indian Harbor Insurance; Knight v. Indiana Insurance Company; Phillips v. Saratoga Harness Racing, Inc.; SR International Business Insurance v. World Trade Center Properties;* and *Amex Life Assurance Company v. Superior Court* cases
- Edited and updated questions and problem cases

CHAPTER 38

- Rewrote chapter introduction and made other changes throughout the chapter to reflect recent changes in the law
- Replaced *Chung v. New York Racing Association* case with *Scott v. Zimmerman*
- Edited and updated questions and problem cases

CHAPTER 39

- Added *E & G Food Corp. v. Cumberland Farms, Inc.* case
- Deleted *Griffith v. Mellon Bank, N.A.* case
- Edited and updated questions and problem cases

CHAPTER 40

- Added new material relating to counterfeit checks
- Added new material relating to recent changes in Article 3 of the UCC.
- Replaced *Lawyers Fund for Client Protection of the State of New York v. Bank Leumi Trust Co. of New York* case with *Jones v. Wells Fargo Bank, N.A.*
- Edited and updated questions and problem cases

CHAPTER 41

- Added *Cincinnati Insurance Company v. Wachovia Bank National Association* case
- Deleted *Union Planter's Bank, N.A. v. Rogers* case
- Made changes to text relating to Check 21 and electronic transfers
- Edited and updated questions and problem cases

CHAPTER 42

- Added *Swift, Inc. v. Sheffey* case
- Moved *In re Borden* case to chapter 43
- Updated the text material concerning foreclosures
- Edited and updated questions and problem cases

CHAPTER 43

- Added new material to text concerning recent amendments to Article 9 of the UCC.
- Replaced *Charter One Auto Finance v. Inkas Coffee Distributors Realty* case with *In re Borden* case moved from Chapter 42
- Edited and updated questions and problem cases

CHAPTER 44

- Updated all the dollar values currently in use in the Bankruptcy Code to reflect recent changes in those values
- Replaced *In re Gerhardt* case with *Kreiger v. Educational Credit Management Corporation* case
- Edited and updated questions and problem cases

CHAPTER 45

- Removed the *F. Hoffman, Bell Atlantic, Continental, Weyerhaeuser,* and *Illinois Tool* cases
- Edited the *Valuepest, Leegin, Texaco,* and *Water Craft* case for conciseness
- Added section on reverse settlement marketing agreements
- Added 2 cases: *Federal Trade Commission v. Actavis* and *In re Vitamin C Antitrust Litigation*
- Removed the paragraph on the Act of State doctrine
- Edited and updated questions and problem cases

CHAPTER 46

- Edited section on Consumer Financial Protection Bureau
- Added 3 new cases: *Cline v. Bank of America, NA, Long v. Tommy Hilfiger U.S.A., Inc.;* and *Dunham v. Portfolio Recovery Associates, LLC*

- Removed *Roberts v. Fleet Bank; Chuway v. National Action Financial Services, Inc.; Cannon v. Newmar Corp.* cases
- Edited and updated questions and problem cases

CHAPTER 47

- Made a number of changes in the text to reflect recent developments in the law
- Replaced *United States v. Dean* case with *United States v. Southern Union Co.* case

Pedagogy

We have employed a number of proven pedagogical devices to aid students in their comprehension and critical analysis of the often complex topics raised in any business law course.

Chapter Openers—Most chapters begin with high-interest vignettes that provide a context for the law in the upcoming chapter. They generally take the form of a real-life case and are followed by a list of questions or issues that introduce the reader to the concepts presented in the chapter.

Learning Objectives—Succinct, crisply written learning objectives follow the chapter openers at the beginning of each chapter. The numbered objectives describe what the students can expect to learn as a result of completing the chapter. Each objective is identified by a unique symbol in the margin where the material appears in the text.

Concept Summaries—Each chapter contains numerous outlines, figures, or drawings that reinforce important or complex legal rules, issues, or concepts.

Visual Illustrations—Flowcharts and other visual illustrations are inserted in each chapter to facilitate student comprehension of key topics.

Cases

Textual material is supplemented by recent, high-interest cases decided by state and federal courts. Cases have been selected to illustrate practical applications of the important legal concepts introduced in each chapter. Although the cases are brief, they provide sufficient facts and analysis to clearly explain the law in action. To enhance understanding of the material, each case is placed immediately after the textual point it discusses.

E-Commerce

Most chapters contain one or more e-commerce boxes, cases, or sections that introduce important e-commerce and Internet law topics related to the chapter material. This key feature should enable students to more accurately identify future regulatory efforts and their implications for business.

Ethics in Action

Ethics in Action boxes are interspersed throughout each chapter. Appearing in the form of questions or commentaries, they should assist students in recognizing the ethical issues confronting businesspeople on a daily basis. In many chapters, these features introduce and explore various features of the *Sarbanes-Oxley Act of 2002*. These supplements to the regular textual material will permit students to more fully appreciate the complex and pervasive nature of ethical issues they will encounter in their professional lives. Finally, our increased focus on ethics is demonstrated by the continued inclusion of Chapter 3—"Business Ethics and Corporate Social Responsibility." This chapter clearly explains the predominant theories of ethical reasoning and provides guidelines for making ethical decisions.

International Focus

Where relevant, the authors have inserted cases and textual material introducing the legal and business risks that often attend global operations. Through this global approach, students are taught that international issues are an integral part of business.

AACSB Standards

McGraw-Hill Companies is a proud corporate member of AACSB International. Understanding the importance and value of AACSB accreditation, the authors of *Law for Business* have sought to recognize the curricula guidelines detailed in the AACSB standards for business accreditation by connecting selected questions in the Test Bank to the general knowledge and skill guidelines found in the AACSB standards.

The statements contained in *Law for Business* are provided only as a guide for the users of this text. The AACSB leaves content coverage and assessment clearly within the realm and control of the individual school, the mission of the school, and the faculty. The AACSB does charge schools with the obligation of doing assessment against their own content and learning goals. While *Law for Business* and the teaching package make no claim of any specific AACSB qualification or evaluation, we have, within the book, labeled selected questions according to the six general knowledge and skill areas. The labels or tags within *Law for Business* are as indicated. There are, of course, many more within each Test Bank, the text, and the teaching package that may be used as a standard for your course.

Online Learning Center at www.mhhe.com/barnes12e

The Online Learning Center (OLC) is a website that follows the text chapter by chapter. The 12th edition OLC contains resources for both instructors and students:

- *PowerPoint Slides.* PowerPoint slide sets for every chapter are for use in the classroom or for studying. These slides refer back to figures and concept summaries from the text as well as introduce original material not found anywhere else.
- *Instructor's Manual.* The authors of *Law for Business* have prepared an instructor's manual providing insights into the major topics introduced in each chapter. Each case is briefly summarized and accompanied by a "Points for Discussion" section that poses ideas for stimulating classroom dialogue. This manual also includes the answers to all of the Questions and Problem Cases that appear in the text, as well as references to appropriate places within the chapter to discuss particular end-of-chapter cases.
- *Test Bank.* The Test Bank consists of true/false, multiple choice, and short essay questions in each chapter. We've aligned our Test Bank with new AACSB guidelines, tagging each question according to its learning objective, knowledge, and skill areas.
- *EZ Test Online.* McGraw-Hill's EZ Test Online is a flexible and easy-to-use electronic testing program. The program allows instructors to create tests from book-specific items, accommodates a wide range of question types, and enables instructors to add their own questions. Multiple versions of the test can be created, and any test can be exported for use with course management systems such as WebCT, Blackboard, or any other course management system. EZ Test Online is accessible to busy instructors virtually anywhere via the Web, and the program eliminates the need for them to install test software. Utilizing EZ Test Online also allows instructors to create and deliver multiple-choice or true/false quiz questions using iQuiz for iPod. For more information about EZ Test Online, please see the website at www.eztestonline.com.

- *The Business Law Newsletter, Proceedings.* We have developed this resource to help keep your classes interesting and current. One electronic newsletter is e-mailed to you per month. Instructors across the country have told us they are looking for ways to include current examples and cases, and we hope this newsletter provides you with just that. It is meant to be an easy and effective place to turn for some new discussion topics for your business law courses. Each edition includes:
  - Article abstracts with critical thinking questions
  - Video links with discussion questions and answers
  - Case hypotheticals and ethical dilemmas (with answers)
  - Teaching tips to help you incorporate this newsletter into your class
  - Chapter key that integrates all of the above with each of our McGraw-Hill Business Law texts

Acknowledgments

We wish to thank the many adopters of our prior editions; we have greatly profited from their suggestions. Of course, we have had to use our judgment in determining which ones to follow. Accordingly, responsibility for any shortcomings in this edition remain ours. We do solicit the comments and criticism of instructors and students who use this edition.

The following reviewers provided ideas and insights for this edition. We appreciate their contributions.

Rodney Chrisman
Liberty University

Peter Churchill
Diablo Valley College

Richard Fountain
University of West Florida

Patrick Griffin
Lewis University

Robert Kenagy
Indiana University–South Bend

Russell Meade
Tidewater Community College, Chesapeake

Susanne Ninassi
Marymount University

Kathy Seeberger
Kansas State University

John Shelapinsky
Westmoreland County Community College

We also acknowledge the assistance of the following individuals at Indiana University who facilitated the preparation of the manuscript: Sarah Jane Hughes and Dennis Long of the Indiana University Maurer School of Law; Desma Jones, Lori Kale, and Thomas Snider; as well as Winfield Martin of Seattle University Law School and Andy Dworkin of OHSU.

A. James Barnes, J.D.

Terry Morehead Dworkin, J.D.

Eric L. Richards, J.D.

About the Authors

A. James Barnes, J.D.

Professor of Public and Environmental Affairs and Professor of Law at Indiana University, Bloomington. He previously served as Dean of the School of Public and Environmental Affairs and has taught business law at Indiana University and Georgetown University. His teaching interests include commercial law, environmental law, alternative dispute resolution, law and public policy, and ethics and the public official. He is the co-author of several leading books on business law.

From 1985 to 1988, Professor Barnes served as the deputy administrator of the U.S. Environmental Protection Agency. From 1983 to 1985, he was the EPA general counsel, and in the early 1970s served as chief of staff to the first administrator of EPA. Professor Barnes also served as a trial attorney in the U.S. Department of Justice and as general counsel of the U.S. Department of Agriculture. For six years, from 1975 to 1981, he had a commercial and environmental law practice with the firm of Beveridge and Diamond in Washington, D.C.

Professor Barnes is a member of the Department of Energy's Environmental Management Board, a Fellow in the American College of Environmental Lawyers, and a Fellow of the National Academy of Public Administration. From 1992 to 1998, he was a member of the Board of Directors of the Long Island Lighting Company (LILCO). From 2004 to 2010, he chaired the Environmental Protection Agency's Environmental Finance Advisory Board.

Terry Morehead Dworkin, J.D.

The Jack R. Wentworth Emerita Professor, Business Law, Kelley School of Business, and Visiting Professor, Seattle University School of Law. She previously served as Dean of the Office of Women's Affairs, Indiana University, and as President of the Academy of Legal Studies in Business. She also served as the co-director of the I.U. Center for International Business Education and Research (CIBER) and as the Director for the Program in European Studies at the Center for European Studies, Rijksuniversiteit Limburg in Maastricht, The Netherlands.

Professor Dworkin's primary research interests focus on employment and women's issues, particularly discrimination, whistleblowing, privacy, and leadership. She is the author of numerous articles on employment law, corporate compliance, and product liability law, and of books on business law and whistleblowing. Several of her publications have an international focus.

Professor Dworkin has significant international experience, including invited lectures on international ethics and management in various countries, teaching in Germany and The Netherlands, being a scholar at the Institute for Advanced Legal Studies in England, and presenting a workshop at the UN/NGO Forum on Women in Beijing. In 2010, she was a Fulbright Senior Specialist in Australia. She has also presented papers at a variey of international conferences.

Eric L. Richards, J.D.

Professor of Business Law at Indiana University's Kelley School of Business and Chair of Kelley Direct, the Kelley School's online graduate business program. He also has served as the Resident Director for the Program in European Studies at the Center for European Studies, Rijksuniversiteit Limburg in Maastricht, The Netherlands.

Professor Richards teaches a wide variety of law courses at both the graduate and undergraduate levels, including personal law, international business law, the legal environment of business, commercial law, and business ethics. His research interests have resulted in scholarly publications exploring antitrust law, the First Amendment and campaign finance law, international trade law, and environmental issues. For the past 30 years, he has been on the faculty of the Kelley School of Business at Indiana University. Prior to that, he was on the faculty of the Kansas University School of Business for two years.

During his academic career, Professor Richards has been awarded numerous school, university, and national awards for both his teaching and his research. He also is a martial arts grand master who has taught martial arts for more than 35 years.

Contents in Brief

Table of Contents

Chapter 35
Landlord and Tenant 659

Chapter 36
Estates and Trusts 682

Chapter 40
Liability of Parties 776

Chapter 41
Checks and Electronic Fund Transfers 802

PART 8
CREDIT TRANSACTIONS 823

Chapter 42
Introduction to Security 824

APPENDIXES

Case List

A

B

C

D

E

F

G

H

I

J

K

T

U

V

W

Y

Z

Part 1

Introduction to the Law

Chapter 1

Law, Legal Reasoning, and the Legal Profession

LO

Learning Objectives

After you have studied this chapter, you should be able to:

1. Identify the basic functions of law.
2. List the various sources of law.
3. Analyze a case using the four steps in the process of legal interpretation.
4. Make a legal decision by applying the three-step, *stare decisis* process.
5. Explain how law is able to change despite *stare decisis.*
6. Read a judicial decision and identify which school of legal jurisprudence the judge has followed.
7. Explain when the attorney–client privilege and work product privilege arise and when they are lost.

When a female employee complained of discrimination, her supervisor, James Twisdale, participated in the investigation by giving information to the investigating officials. Twisdale told them that he was skeptical of the woman's claim. After the complaint was resolved in her favor, Twisdale claims that the employer retaliated against him by reducing his responsibilities. He sued the employer under *Title VII of the Civil Rights Act of 1964*. That federal statute outlaws various forms of employment discrimination and makes it unlawful to retaliate against an employee who "has made a charge, testified, assisted, or participated in any manner in an investigation, proceeding, or hearing under" the statute. *Twisdale v. Snow,* 325 F.3d 950 (7th Cir. 2003).

- Which of the basic functions of law are furthered by this federal statute?
- How will the court determine if Twisdale is protected by this law?
- Is Twisdale protected by the statute?

Introduction

What is law? What roles does it play in our lives? These are important questions to consider as you read this first chapter. People view law in many different ways. Some think of the police, while others think of any rules governing day-to-day behavior. Each perception is partially correct. To truly comprehend law and a legal system, one must understand the nature of the underlying society. Law is a reflection of the people, organizations, and values it simultaneously serves and controls. Never lose sight of the dynamic nature of any legal system. To survive and effectively guide, it must draw from the past, reflect the present, and pave the way for the future.

Law in Business

Effective managers and employees must develop knowledge of both law and business because people involved in business also are involved in, and greatly affected by, the law concerning business. With each passing day, this link between law and business grows even stronger.

Chapter Overview

This introductory chapter begins by investigating the essential features of law and the U.S. legal system. Then, after consideration of several fundamental classifications of law, attention turns to the constitutional underpinnings of the legal system. This discussion is followed by an introduction to the primary sources of law and legal reasoning (how courts decide cases). Next, there is a discussion of the important concept called *stare decisis,* which promotes orderly change within the legal system. The chapter then provides a brief look at the predominant schools of legal philosophy (legal jurisprudence) that provide a context for legal decision making. Then, after looking at the role of the legal profession, the chapter closes by introducing students to the importance of practicing preventive law.

The Nature of Law

Law is much more than a set of rules. Our legal system involves processes for social control. It consists of institutions such as legislatures and government agencies for the creation of rules of behavior. It also includes police forces and courts to enforce the rules and resolve disputes. In short, the U.S. legal system encompasses a process and structure for creating, enforcing, and interpreting those rules. This section looks at the idea of rules, the reasons for having rules, and the structure that manages them.

Legal Rules

At its most basic level, law can be seen as rules that limit people's freedom of action. These rules may be called "laws," "statutes," or "ordinances." The label doesn't really matter. The important thing they have in common is that they require people to conform their behavior to some particular standard. This concept of law may be viewed as a **set of principles** that

1. Have **general application** to society.
2. Were developed by a **legitimate authority** within society.
3. May threaten **sanctions** against those who fail to comply with the principles.

Functions of Law

The basic functions of law are

LO1

1. Keeping the peace.
2. Enforcing to maintain order.
3. Facilitating planning.
4. Promoting social justice.

For instance, laws against underage consumption of alcoholic beverages establish certain standards of conduct in an attempt to maintain order and, perhaps, keep the peace. Those functions—*keeping the peace* and *enforcing standards of conduct to maintain order*—help further another function of law that is especially important: *facilitating planning.* Contract law is an example of this function. In making the courts available to enforce contracts, the legal system ensures that parties to contracts either carry out their promises or pay for the damages they cause. For example, through contracts, a manufacturing company can count on either receiving the raw materials and machinery it has ordered or else getting money from the contracting supplier to cover the extra expense of buying substitutes.

While all societies use law to keep peace and maintain order, societies such as ours also use the law to achieve additional goals. The tax laws, for example, seek not only to raise revenue for government expenditure but also to redistribute wealth by imposing higher inheritance and income taxes on wealthy people. The government also may tax certain activities in order to discourage them. Taxes on tobacco products have this intent. The antitrust laws seek to prevent certain practices that might reduce competition and thus increase prices. The Civil Rights Act is designed to promote social justice.

Concept Summary: The Nature of Law

Definition	Functions of Law
A set of principles, rules, and standards of conduct that	Keeping the peace
1. Have general application in the society	Enforcing standards of conduct to maintain order
2. Have been developed by an authority for that society	Facilitating planning
3. Have an associated penalty imposed upon violations	Promoting social justice

The function of these statutes is to *promote social justice* by protecting the disadvantaged. Courts, in applying the law, also seem to be seeking to balance the scales to benefit the "little guy" in dealing with big business, big labor, and big government. Helping the ordinary citizen to deal with a very complex and quite impersonal economy also is the objective of federal legislation establishing social security, welfare, housing, and medical programs.

Classifications of Law

There are many ways to subdivide the law. One is to distinguish between substantive law and procedural law. Another important distinction is between criminal and civil law. This section examines these legal classifications.

Substantive versus Procedural Law

Substantive law sets out the rights and duties governing people as they act in society. *Duties* tend to take the form of a command: "Do this!" or "Don't do that!" An example is the Civil Rights Act of 1964. It tells employers that they must not discriminate among people in hiring and employment on the basis of race, color, religion, sex, or national origin.

Substantive law also establishes *rights and privileges.* An example is the freedom of speech granted by the U.S. Constitution. Another is the right you have to defend yourself if physically attacked—the so-called right of self-defense. A slightly different example is the privilege of receiving food stamps if you meet the qualifications set up by the government.

Procedural law establishes the rules under which the substantive rules of law are enforced. Rules as to what cases a court can decide, how a trial is conducted, and how a judgment by a court is to be enforced are all part of procedural law.

Ethics in Action

Can you think of an example of a duty imposed by substantive law that might violate some moral or ethical belief of an individual? How should such conflicts be resolved? Consider the following case: Two clinics operated in Fargo, North Dakota. One performed abortions while the other provided only pregnancy tests and antiabortion counseling services. However, the antiabortion clinic used a name similar to that of the abortion clinic in order to confuse the public into mistakenly contacting the wrong clinic. Further, it misled the public into believing that it performed abortions, and then, when women seeking abortions arrived, they were given antiabortion materials. After the antiabortion clinic started these tactics, there was a considerable decline in the abortion clinic's business. The jury found that the antiabortion clinic violated the state's false advertising statute.[1]

Criminal versus Civil Law

Criminal law defines breaches of duty to society at large. It is society, through government employees called *prosecutors* (such as district attorneys), that brings court action against violators. If you are found guilty of a crime such as theft, you will be punished by imprisonment or a fine. When a fine is paid, the money generally goes to the state, not to the victim of the crime. A criminal conviction generally is not possible unless it can be shown that an individual violated the terms of a published statute. This is because it is not believed to be fair to punish people unless they should have known that their behavior was illegal. Consider the next case which involves an unsuccessful criminal prosecution.

Private duties owed by one person (including corporations) to another are established by **civil law.** For example, we have a duty to carry out our contractual promises. Tort law defines a host of duties people owe to each other. One of the most common is a duty to exercise reasonable care with regard to others. Failure to do so is the tort of negligence.

[1] *Fargo Women's Health Organization v. FM Women's Help and Caring Connection,* 444 N.W.2d 683 (N.D. Sup. Ct. 1989).

United States v. Farinella

558 F.3d 695 (7th Cir. 2009)

FACTS

Farinella bought 1.6 million bottles of "Henri's Salad Dressing" produced by Unilever. The label on each bottle said "best when purchased by" followed by a date that had been picked by Unilever. Because the "best when purchased by" date was approaching, Farinella pasted on each bottle a new label that displayed a later date. He then resold the salad dressing to discount stores. As a result, he was charged with the crime of introducing into interstate commerce misbranded food with the intent to mislead. Selling salad dressing after the "best when purchased by" date does not endanger human health. Henri's Salad Dressing is edible a decade or more after it is manufactured. There also is no evidence of any regulation by any government body that defines "best purchased by" or forbids a wholesaler or retailer to change the date. However, at the trial an official from the Food and Drug Administration (FDA) testified that FDA approval is necessary to change labels and that no such approval was given to Farinella.

ISSUE

Should Farinella be convicted of the crime of misbranding food?

DECISION

No. The testimony by the FDA official should not have been admitted into evidence. If there is a requirement that the FDA's approval must be obtained before a "best when purchased by" date may be changed, it would, to be a lawful predicate of a criminal conviction, have to be found in some statute or regulation, or at least in some written interpretive guideline or opinion, and not just in the oral testimony of an agency employee. It is a denial of due process of law to convict a person of a crime because he violated some bureaucrat's secret understanding of the law. The idea of secret laws is repugnant. People cannot comply with laws the existence of which is concealed. We do not suggest that a novel fraud can never be punished as a crime. But to prove a person guilty of having made a fraudulent representation, a jury must be given evidence about the meaning (unless obvious) of the representation claimed to be fraudulent, and that was not done here.

Suit for the breach of a civil duty must be brought by the person wronged. Generally, the court does not seek to punish the wrongdoer but rather to make the wronged party whole through a money award called *damages*. For example, if someone carelessly runs a car into yours, that person has committed the civil wrong (tort) of negligence. If you have suffered a broken leg, you will be able to recover damages from the driver (or his or her insurance company). The damages will be an amount of money sufficient to repair your auto, to pay your medical bills, to pay for wages you have lost, and to give you something for any permanent disability such as a limp. Damages for "pain and suffering" also may be awarded.

Although the civil law generally does not aim to punish, there is an exception. If the behavior of someone who commits a tort is outrageous, that person can be made to pay *punitive* damages (also called *exemplary damages*). Unlike a fine paid in a criminal case, punitive damages go to the injured party. (Some states require that a portion of a punitive damage award be placed in a public fund to assist various social causes.)

Sometimes, the same behavior can violate both the civil law and the criminal law. For instance, a person whose drunken driving causes the death of another may face both a criminal prosecution by the state and a civil suit for damages by the survivors of the victim. If both suits are successful, the driver would pay back society for the harm done with a criminal fine and/or prison sentence and compensate the survivors with the payment of money damages.

Concept Summary: Criminal versus Civil Law

	Criminal Case	Civil Case
Elements	Intentional violation of a statute	Harm to another person or property (tort) or breach of a contract
Actors	Prosecutor (government) v. Defendant (accused)	Plaintiff (wronged party) v. Defendant (party causing harm)
Punishment	Fines, imprisonment, execution	Defendant may have to pay the plaintiff compensatory and punitive damages

Constitutional Foundations

Although law is made and enforced by the government, it also defines and organizes the government. To understand the American legal system, you need to be familiar with the constitutional foundation of American government. A very brief review is presented here.

Checks and Balances

The original 13 colonies became sovereign (independent) nations after they won independence from England. Although people in each state were fearful their state might be dominated by other states with different interests, they came to realize the federal government needed more power than had been given to the Continental Congress. So, the founders set up a system of **checks and balances** between the powers of the states and those of the federal government. However, they also wrote the *supremacy clause* into the Constitution. It declares that where state laws conflict with legitimate federal laws, federal law shall prevail.

The founders also devised a system of checks and balances within the federal government. They established three equal branches of government—the legislative, executive, and judicial branches—which have different but complementary functions. As a check on the passage of statutes that might be ill advised, proposals will not become law unless the president and both houses of Congress approve them. A two-thirds majority is required in each house to override a veto by the president. Furthermore, Congress itself cannot enforce a statute; that is left to the executive and judicial branches. The initiative for enforcement must be taken by the executive branch—originally the attorney general.

Today, regulatory agencies take the lead in enforcing certain statutes. However, the executive must go to the judicial branch to punish violations of a statute. Also, it is this branch—the judicial—that interprets statutes and other sources of law.

Constitutional Powers

Under the Constitution, laws enacted by Congress are invalid if the Constitution does not give Congress the power to pass that kind of legislation or if the Constitution prohibits such a law. These restraints are also a part of the system of checks and balances.

Most federal regulations are based on power given to Congress under the Constitution's **Commerce Clause,** which permits Congress to regulate interstate and foreign commerce. Supreme Court decisions since the 1930s generally have interpreted that power very broadly. For example, the Civil Rights Acts were passed under the Commerce Clause power; so was the Clean Air Act.

The federal **taxing power** has been used to regulate business activities. For example, high import duties can be used to shut off the importation of certain foreign goods. In addition, the income tax laws (the Internal Revenue Code) are used to regulate behavior. When the government wishes to encourage certain kinds of investments, it offers tax credits.

Constitutional Limitations

Many prohibitions against government regulation are contained in the **Bill of Rights** (the first 10 amendments to the Constitution). These amendments guarantee certain rights to the people, including the familiar rights of free speech, freedom of religion, and the privilege against unreasonable search and seizure.

Judicial interpretations of the protections offered by the Constitution have varied throughout history. At one time the **Due Process Clause** of the Fourteenth Amendment was construed to prohibit many types of business regulation by state governments. Its statement that a person's liberty shall not be taken without due process was interpreted to be a guaranty of almost total freedom of contract. Under this approach, judges regularly held state and federal regulations unconstitutional. Interpretations of the law change over time, however, and today few statutes regulating business activity are found to violate the Due Process Clause.

Federalism

Under the notion of **federalism,** the United States is composed of 51 different legal systems. The Constitution established a federal government with limited powers rather than a national government. This variety of legal systems is part of the concept of checks and balances. There is a federal legal system, and each state has its own system. However, as noted earlier, when there is conflict between the two systems, the federal rules prevail. This, of course, assumes the federal government is acting under one of the powers granted to it by the Constitution.

Sources of Law

There are numerous sources of law within each of the 51 systems. The primary sources are

LO2

1. Constitutions
2. Treaties
3. Statutes
4. Administrative rules and decisions
5. Executive orders
6. Judicial decisions
7. Private law

Constitutions

The U.S. Constitution is the highest source of law in the United States. Every other form of law must be consistent with the Constitution or it will be struck down by the courts. Each state also has a constitution that is similar to the U.S. Constitution in the design of the government it provides. However, many of them are much more specific and detailed. As a result, they are not as adaptable to changing conditions as the U.S. Constitution, and many have been completely rewritten one or more times. The U.S. Constitution, on the other hand, has had only 17 additional amendments in the more than 200 years since the adoption of the Bill of Rights.

Although state constitutions are subordinate to the U.S. Constitution, they are superior to law derived from other sources within the state. The importance of this will become clearer when the power of judicial review is discussed later in this chapter.

Treaties

The Constitution declares that treaties made by the president with foreign governments and ratified by at least two-thirds of the Senate are "the supreme law of the land." They therefore may override acts of Congress or state legislatures and other laws that are inconsistent. However, conflicts of this sort seldom arise since the states may not make treaties with foreign countries.

Statutes

Within each legal system, federal or state, statutes stand next in the hierarchy. A statute is the product of the lawmaking of a legislature. Statutes may add details to the government framework by establishing a regulatory agency or an agency to provide a public service. Or statutes may establish rules that govern certain kinds of activities, such as the use of automobiles on highways. The entire criminal law, the law applicable to sales of goods, and almost all law limiting or regulating business activities make up **statutory law.**

Both Congress and the state legislatures enact a large number of statutes at every session. The Civil Rights Act mentioned in the chapter opener is a federal statute enacted by Congress. People tend to turn to Congress and/or the state legislatures to urge the passage of "a law" (statute) whenever they recognize a problem. This seems to be true whether it is primarily an economic problem (such as the dwindling availability of petroleum), a moral problem (such as sexual practices), or a health problem (such as misuse of drugs). Because there are 50 state legislatures, statutory law varies from state to state. There is a trend, however, to pass uniform laws in areas such as business where uniformity is seen as particularly important. The Uniform Commercial Code (UCC), which regulates a wide variety of commercial transactions, is the most widely adopted uniform law. The legislatures of all 50 states have enacted the Code in some form.

Governmental units within the states, such as cities and counties, also have the power to legislate. Their enactments are called **ordinances.** Local legislation regulating zoning and noise levels are examples of ordinances.

Administrative Rules and Decisions

Congress and the state legislatures can delegate some of their lawmaking power to a government agency. During the 20th century many administrative agencies were established to regulate particular areas of activity. Businesses are heavily regulated in this manner. While states also establish agencies, our discussion focuses on the federal regulatory agencies.

Independent Agencies

The first federal regulatory agency was the Interstate Commerce Commission (ICC), which was organized by a statute passed in 1887. Congress has followed this model often in establishing other agencies. These are called **independent agencies** because they are not really part of the executive branch of the government under the control of the president. Rather, they are headed by a board or commission. Although the members are nominated by the president, approximately half of them must be from each major political party, and their appointment is confirmed by the Senate for fixed terms.

This type of regulatory agency is given authority by Congress both to make rules and to enforce them. Congress grants rule-making power to the agency instead of establishing detailed rules in statutes. It was believed that the agency members and staff would have greater expertise than Congress and would develop it further through regulatory experience. In addition, it was hoped that continuous regulatory supervision by the agency would be more adaptive to specific needs than reliance on legislation. An example of an agency that relies primarily on rule-making is the Securities and Exchange Commission, which issues rules and may go to the federal courts to enforce them.

Concept Summary: Independent Agencies

Creation	Congress passes enabling legislation specifying the powers of the agency
Features	Headed by a board or commission Members nominated by president Appointments confirmed by Senate Appointees drawn from the two major political parties
Powers	Investigative Rule-making Adjudicatory

Constitutionality of Agency Rules

To make its delegation of power constitutional, Congress must provide adequate standards or guidelines in the statute creating the agency. However, the Supreme Court has upheld some very broad delegations of rule-making power that contain extremely vague guidelines. If adequate guidelines are provided, rules issued by an agency have the same force as statutes passed by Congress.

Judicial Functions

A number of agencies also make law by deciding cases. Some of them regulate primarily on a case-by-case basis through their decisions. Here, the agency performs a quasi-judicial function. It is also, in effect, the prosecutor, since the agency staff decides whether or not to begin an enforcement action. If the agency enforces one of its own rules, it also is performing an executive function. This concentration of functions in a single agency was much criticized until passage of the Administrative Procedure Act of 1946, which requires a separation of the functions within the agency. Now, independent administrative law judges (ALJs) hear the evidence and make preliminary decisions. The agency board or commission then issues a final order. Such orders are appealable to, and enforced by, the federal courts.

Executive Orders

Congress or a state legislature also may delegate rule-making power to the president or a governor. Again, guidelines must be furnished. An example of an important **executive order** was President Franklin D. Roosevelt's 1943 order requiring all contracts for war supplies to include a clause prohibiting race discrimination. Like agency rules, executive orders have the force of law if they are within the authority granted by statute.

Judicial Decisions

Most people do not realize that courts also make law. They do so in three ways: (1) through interpretation they give meaning and effect to the other sources of law, (2) through the common law they find law when no other source offers a solution to a legal dispute, and (3) through judicial review they determine the legitimacy of the actions of other branches of government.

We now look at the common law and then at the process of judicial review. The notion of judicial lawmaking through statutory interpretation is examined in a following section as part of a more comprehensive discussion of legal reasoning.

Common Law

Court-created law is called **common law.** It arises when courts are called upon to resolve disputes for which there is no statute or other source of law establishing a rule. The idea of a common law (or *decisional law*) springs from early English history. After the Normans conquered England in 1066, William the Conqueror and his successors attempted to unite the country by dispatching royal judges to hold court in each of the cities. This practice served to replace the varying customs and rules of each locality with a uniform (or common) system of laws.

The law evolved as more and more disputes were heard by the judges. Uniformity was furthered by the practice of following *precedents.* This meant that whenever the facts of a dispute were similar to those of an earlier case, the judge generally would follow the earlier decision. (This doctrine, known as *stare decisis,* is discussed later in the chapter.) When the American colonies won their freedom from England, they adopted the large body of English common law.

The notion of **equity** is another source of common law. The early English legal system provided a court of chancery, which provided equitable remedies not available to the common law courts. Equity was more flexible than early common law. Rather than adhering blindly to past precedents, the court of chancery sought fundamental fairness. While most states have dispensed with a separate court of chancery, their courts are free to seek equitable solutions when strict adherence to established law would bring about a grave injustice.

Courts also may create common law when they interpret statutes. Some judges are willing to expand the reach of statutes when they believe that doing so furthers important societal goals. (This is a form of legal sociology, which is discussed later in the chapter.) Consider the following case where the court finds a statutory remedy that is not expressly mentioned in the statute.

Coach v. Goodfellow

2013 U.S. App. LEXIS 10976 (6th Cir. 2013)

FACTS

Coach Services designs, markets, and sells a variety of trademarked products. Goodfellow owns and operates a flea market and collects rent from 75 to 100 booth vendors who sell various products there. On numerous occasions, Coach sent letters to Goodfellow, notifying him of counterfeit sales of Coach trademarked products at many of the booths. On several occasions, law enforcement officers raided the flea market and seized thousands of counterfeit products. Despite all of this, Goodfellow made no real effort to prevent the booth vendors from violating Coach's trademark. Coach then sued Goodfellow for violation of its trademark. Goodfellow defended on the grounds that the Lanham Act (which protects trademark rights) allows recovery against

(continued)

an infringer who used the mark in commerce without authorization. The statute says nothing about liability for contributory infringement—the liability of persons who permit or induce others to infringe a trademark.

ISSUE

Can Goodfellow be held liable for contributory trademark infringement?

DECISION

Yes. There is no dispute in this case as to whether infringement occurred. The legal question presented is whether Goodfellow is properly held liable for the infringing acts of others. Although the Lanham Act only refers to direct trademark infringement, our past cases have made clear that contributory liability may also be imposed on those who facilitate the infringement. We hold that Goodfellow is properly held liable for contributory trademark infringement because he knew or had reason to know of the infringing activities and yet continued to facilitate those activities by providing space and storage units to vendors without undertaking a reasonable investigation or taking other appropriate remedial measures.

Judicial Review

Courts also make law through their authority to interpret the meaning of the other sources of law (constitutions, statutes, etc.). Under the power of **judicial review,** a judge may render a legal rule unenforceable by declaring it in conflict with a constitution. Similarly, higher courts may decide that lower court decisions are invalid. Most of the decisions presented in this text are examples of courts engaging in judicial review.

Private Law

Private persons also may create legally binding obligations on one another through their power to contract. When people enter into contractual agreements, the courts generally enforce their terms. But **private law** is subordinate to the other sources of law. As such, contracts are unenforceable when they conflict with the other sources of law or public policy.

Legal Reasoning

Much of law school is spent learning how to "think like a lawyer." Many nonlawyers view this thought process with suspicion as if it were somehow a distortion of reality. However, that is far from the truth. **Legal reasoning** is a useful tool for understanding and persuading. It combines basic analytical thinking with recognition of the special features of the underlying legal system. Legal reasoning is a type of critical thinking that proves useful in both legal and nonlegal situations.

The next three sections introduce three components of legal reasoning. The first section looks at how judges and lawyers interpret the words in statutes and other legal rules. This is followed by an examination of the doctrine of *stare decisis* that underlies our common law system. The section on jurisprudence briefly explores how our legal philosophy (jurisprudence) affects the form and content of our decisions.

Legal Interpretation

LO3

Courts determine law through a process of **legal interpretation.** Many words are ambiguous by nature. Further, most statutes are written in very broad and general language. Thus, the court's power to interpret is an important one. It is especially important when a case involves a situation the legislature did not foresee when it passed the law. Through such interpretation judges can broaden or narrow the reach of a law. In interpreting legal rules, courts generally

1. Look to the plain meaning of the language.
2. Examine the legislative history of the rule.
3. Consider the purpose to be achieved by the rule.
4. Try to accommodate public policy.

Where a statute has been interpreted by a government agency, the courts traditionally defer to that interpretation if it seems reasonable.

Plain Meaning

Generally, the first step in interpreting a statute or other source of law is to look at the **plain meaning** of the words. A judge would not say the legislature meant to establish a 65-mile-per-hour speed limit when the statute says 55. Some courts refuse to go beyond this step. They claim that they should apply a rule according to its literal language and not concern themselves with anything else. To do otherwise, in their minds, would result in their imposing their will on the legislature.

Legislative History

Most courts refer to a statute's **legislative history** when the language is unclear. This involves an examination of investigative committee reports, legislative hearings, and press announcements. They also may look at discrepancies between how a bill was first introduced and how it finally was enacted for guidance on how to interpret its meaning.

Purpose

Part of the court's investigation into a law's legislative history is to determine the **purpose** of the rule. This is because judges generally do not wish to interpret a law in a manner that conflicts with the objectives of the original lawmakers.

Remember the *Twisdale* case in the chapter opener? Read literally, the plain meaning of the statute would protect an employee like Twisdale who participates in an investigation on the side of the employer rather than on the side of the employee who made the charge of discrimination. However, the court did not believe that this interpretation would promote the purpose of the law. The court noted that, under Twisdale's interpretation, he could not be fired if the reason he opposed the woman's discrimination claim was because he was a sexist and a racist. It believed that the purpose of the law was to prevent certain forms of discrimination and could find nothing in the statute's legislative history that supported protecting employees whose resistance to charges of discrimination made by their co-workers provokes the employer's ire. Accordingly, the Title VII did not protect Twisdale from retaliation by his employer.

Public Policy

Judges also may look to general concepts of **public policy** when interpreting legal rules. Of course, there is no firm and fast definition of what constitutes public policy. Some judges may believe the public policy is what the majority of the population thinks is best. Others may question if society really knows what is best and will consider public policy to be what the judge thinks is best for society. It is precisely because of this ambiguity that some courts refrain from using public policy analysis altogether when interpreting laws. However, other courts boldly venture into the public policy realm.

In the next case, the U.S. Supreme Court uses the process of legal interpretation to decide that a floating home is not a "vessel" for purposes of a maritime statute. Notice how the Court examines the purpose (statutory) intent and, in the final two sentences, employs a public policy argument to support its conclusion.

Lozman v. City of Riviera Beach

133 S.Ct. 735 (U.S. Sup. Ct. 2013)

FACTS

Lozman owned a 60-foot by 12-foot floating home that contained a sitting room, bedroom, closet, bathroom, and kitchen, along with a stairway leading to a second level with office space. Unlike a houseboat, Lozman's floating home had no steering mechanism and no means of self-propulsion. Lozman kept it docked in a marina owned and operated by the city of Riviera Beach, Florida. After several unsuccessful attempts to evict Lozman from the marina, the City brought a federal admiralty lawsuit against the floating home, seeking over $3 million for dockage fees. The City argued that the floating home was a "vessel" under admiralty law because it was capable of movement over water.

ISSUE

Is the floating home a "vessel" that is governed by admiralty law?

DECISION

No. A "vessel," for purposes of maritime law statute and admiralty jurisdiction, includes "every description of watercraft or other artificial contrivance used, or capable of being used, as a means of transportation on water." The City's interpretation is too broad. Not *every* floating structure is a "vessel." To state the obvious, a wooden washtub, a swimming platform on pontoons, or a door taken off its hinges are not "vessels," even if they are "artificial contrivances" capable of floating, moving under tow, and incidentally carrying even a fair-sized item or two when they do so. Rather, the statutory intent applies to an "artificial contrivance capable of being used *as a means of transportation on water.*" Consequently, in our view a structure does not fall within the scope of this statutory phrase unless a reasonable observer, looking to the home's physical characteristics and activities, would consider it designed to a practical degree for carrying people or things over water. Lozman's home differs significantly from an ordinary houseboat in that it has no ability to propel itself. Our examination of the purposes of major federal maritime statutes reveals little reason to classify floating homes as "vessels." Admiralty law, for example, provides special attachment procedures lest a vessel avoid liability by sailing away. Lozman, however, cannot easily escape liability by sailing away in his home. He faces no special sea dangers. He does not significantly engage in port-related commerce. Finally, there are policy reasons for adopting a narrower definition of the word "vessel." Adopting a version of the "anything that floats" test would place unnecessary and undesirable inspection burdens upon the Coast Guard.

Law and Orderly Change

People cannot comply with the law unless they know and understand its requirements. This means it must be predictable. On the other hand, in a society in which technological and social change are rapid, law must adapt to changing conditions. This is especially true when basic values are shifting. A fundamental dilemma faced by any legal system is the need to promote certainty and stability while simultaneously accommodating flexibility and change. In short, if a legal system is to stand the test of time, it must have some method of permitting *orderly change.*

Procedural Safeguards

There are several procedural requirements imposed by law on legislatures that help to make statutes knowable to the people. For example, all bills that are introduced are published so citizens as well as legislators can become aware of them. A bill is assigned to a committee, which may hold a public hearing on it. If reported out of the committee, the bill is discussed on the floor of the house that originated it. Amendments are likely both in committee and on the floor. The same process is then followed in the other house. If signed by the chief executive, the bill becomes law. It is then published in its final form.

The Constitution prohibits ***ex post facto* laws.** This means a new statute applies only to actions taken after it becomes effective. Since one cannot adjust one's conduct to a statute not yet passed, this requirement is essential to justice.

The Administrative Procedure Act requires federal rule-making agencies to publish notices of intent to issue regulations and the text of final ones in the *Federal Register.* It also requires agencies to hold hearings or consider comments from interested parties about the proposed rules. The new rules then are printed in the Code of Federal Regulations (CFR), where all administrative rules are published.

Stare Decisis

Stare decisis is the feature of decisional law in common law systems that is most important in permitting orderly change. (The Latin phrase *stare decisis* means "to adhere to decided cases.") This doctrine says that a court, in making a decision, should follow the rulings of prior cases that have similar facts (*precedents*). Three steps are involved in applying *stare decisis:*

LO4

1. Finding an earlier case or cases with similar facts.
2. Deriving a rule of law.
3. Applying that rule to the case at hand.

Predictability

Stare decisis lends predictability to decisional law by relying on prior decisions. This promotes a degree of consistency among judicial decisions. Of course, there are some limits to this certainty. State court decisions are binding only within the same state. Hence, the common law differs from state to state. A court in California may follow a precedent established by a court in Arizona. However, it is not bound to do so.

Adaptability

Stare decisis does not render law rigid and unchanging. To understand how flexibility in the common law is possible, one must understand more about the operation of *stare decisis.*

Concept Summary: Methods of Ensuring Predictability in the Law

Statutes	Public hearings Publication of enacted statutes No *ex post facto* laws
Administrative rules	Notice of intent to issue rules Public hearings Publication of final rules
Court decisions	*Stare decisis* (following past precedent)

LO5

First, a court has considerable freedom in picking precedent cases. Seldom are all of the facts in a case exactly the same as in an earlier case. Therefore, the judge or lawyer can choose, within limits, which facts to emphasize and which to disregard in seeking precedent cases. Certainly a lawyer for the plaintiff (the party bringing the lawsuit) will choose as precedent those cases in which the decision favors the plaintiff's position. He seeks to persuade the judge they are the precedents that should be followed. The defendant likewise argues for precedents favorable to her position.

There also is flexibility at the second step; the lawyer or judge can state the rule to be applied from the precedent cases broadly or narrowly. A difference of a few words in the way the rule is phrased may either include or exclude the case in dispute. The third step—application—follows the first two almost automatically. If the analysis appears acceptable in the first step and the description of the rule seems reasonable in the second step, the third step is convincing.

Furthermore, the highest appeals court in a jurisdiction can **overrule** a precedent case. This does not occur frequently; more commonly a court will **distinguish** the case before it from the precedent by finding differences in facts between the current case and the precedent cases. The constitutional prohibition of *ex post facto* laws does not apply to common or decisional law. Therefore, precedent determined to be in error or out-of-date may be overruled without prior notice, and the new rule may be applied to the current case. Finally, a legislature may override *stare decisis* and change a common law rule by enacting a statute. The rule established by the statute applies thereafter.

Concept Summary: How *Stare Decisis* Permits Change

1. Courts have broad discretion in selecting appropriate precedent.
2. Courts may choose which facts to stress and which to ignore in selecting precedent.
3. The rule of law from the precedent case may be interpreted broadly or narrowly.
4. Courts may distinguish the precedent case.
5. Appellate courts may overrule a precedent case.

Consider the following decision. Notice how the court, using the process of *stare decisis,* examines past precedents to formulate its decision. Ultimately, what was the Supreme Court's rationale for overruling the *Bowers v. Hardwick* case?

Lawrence v. Texas

123 S.Ct. 2472 (U.S. Sup. Ct. 2003)

FACTS

Police officers were dispatched to a private residence in response to a reported weapons disturbance. When they entered an apartment where John Geddes Lawrence resided, the officers observed Lawrence and another man, Tyron Garner, engaging in a sexual act. The two men were arrested, charged, and convicted under a state law prohibiting sodomy. When Lawrence and Garner challenged the constitutionality of the state law, Texas cited *Bowers v. Hardwick,* a previous U.S. Supreme Court decision that upheld the constitutionality of a similar sodomy statute in Georgia.

ISSUE

Does *stare decisis* require that the Texas statute be upheld?

DECISION

No. The Court in *Bowers* failed to appreciate the extent of the liberty at stake. The laws involved in *Bowers* and here seek to control a personal relationship that is within the liberty of persons to choose without being punished as criminals. Over the course of the last decade, states with same-sex prohibitions have moved toward abolishing them. In the United States, criticism of *Bowers* has been substantial and continuing, disapproving of its reasoning in all respects, not just as to its historical assumptions. When a Court is asked to overrule a precedent recognizing a constitutional liberty interest, individual or societal reliance on the existence of that liberty cautions with particular strength against reversing course. The holding in *Bowers,* however,

(continued)

Lawrence v. Texas *(concluded)*

has not induced detrimental reliance. The rationale of *Bowers* does not withstand careful analysis. *Bowers* was not correct when it was decided, and it is not correct today. *Bowers v. Hardwick* should be and now is overruled. The Texas statute furthers no legitimate state interest which can justify its intrusion into the personal and private life of the individual.

Jurisprudence

LO6

Law is much more than a set of rules. It is a dynamic, living institution that reflects the ideas and events of the day. Yet, an often overlooked aspect of law is the legal philosophy of judges and, when applicable, jurors. Their individual values and philosophies can greatly shape the decisions they render. This section discusses four schools of **jurisprudence** (legal philosophy) that are predominant today: legal positivism, natural law, sociological jurisprudence, and legal realism.

Legal Positivism

Legal positivists are unlikely to consider public policy and their own sense of morality when interpreting the law. They see law as the command of legitimate political institutions and, as such, believe it must be enforced to the letter. Legal positivist judges confine their analysis to the plain meaning of the words and, when necessary, to the legislative history in order to strictly follow the will of the lawmakers. While **legal positivism** often creates harsh results by refusing to recognize equitable exceptions, it provides a great sense of predictability to the enforcement of legal rules.

Bowles v. Russell

127 S.Ct. 2360 (U.S. Sup. Ct. 2007)

FACTS

A jury convicted Keith Bowles of murder and sentenced him to 15 years to life imprisonment. Although Bowles had 30 days to file a notice of appeal, he failed to do so. Bowles then moved to reopen the period during which he could file his notice of appeal pursuant to a federal statute, which allows district courts to extend the filing period for 14 days from the day the district court grants the order to reopen. The court granted Bowles's motion, but rather than extending the time period by 14 days, the court inexplicably gave Bowles 17 days to file his notice of appeal. Bowles filed his notice within the 17 days allowed by the court's order, but after the 14-day period allowed by statute. It then was argued that Bowles's notice of appeal should be rejected because it was untimely.

ISSUE

Does the appellate court have jurisdiction to hear Bowles's appeal?

DECISION

No. It has been long and repeatedly held that the time limits for filing a notice of appeal are mandatory and jurisdictional in nature. Accordingly, the petitioner's untimely notice—even though filed in reliance upon a court's order—deprived the court of appeals of jurisdiction. Like the initial 30-day period for filing a notice of appeal, the limit on how long a district court may reopen that period is set forth in a statute. Bowles contends that we should excuse his untimely filing because of the unique circumstances of this case. However, the Court has no authority to create equitable exceptions to jurisdictional requirements. If rigorous rules like the one applied are thought to be inequitable, Congress may authorize courts to promulgate rules that excuse compliance with the statutory time limits.

Natural Law

Natural law thinkers recognize a higher set of rules that override the legitimacy of laws promulgated by political institutions. They disagree with the idea that law and morality are separate. Thus, natural law judges consider their own sense of morality and may refuse to enforce statutes they believe are unjust. A major criticism of natural law jurisprudence is that it does not provide the level of predictability attained by legal positivism because each judge's sense of morality may differ.

For instance, in *Rochin v. California,* 342 U.S. 165 (1952), the U.S. Supreme Court held that police violated a suspected drug dealer's due process rights when they had a hospital pump his stomach after observing him swallow capsules they believed were morphine. The Court found there to be a denial of due process because the conduct of the police "shocks the conscience." Still, it cautioned that the decision was not a "revival" of natural law. The court obviously feared that the public might suspect that it was not exercising sufficient detachment and objectivity. Thus, it was careful to explain: "In each case due process of law requires an evaluation based on a disinterested inquiry pursued in the spirit of science, on a balanced order of facts exactly and fairly stated, on the detached consideration of conflicting claims on a judgment not *ad hoc* and episodic but duly mindful of reconciling the needs both of continuity and of change in a progressive society."

Sociological Jurisprudence

Legal sociologists have a vision for where society is going or should be going and make decisions that promote this social agenda. When interpreting statutes they look beyond the plain meaning of the words and fully consider the legislative purpose as well as their perceptions of the prevailing public policies. Unlike legal positivists, legal sociologists stress the need for law to change and keep pace with the evolution of society. Under **sociological jurisprudence,** each case and legal decision is viewed as a piece of a much bigger and more important puzzle.

Most of the decisions you have seen thus far and will see in later chapters illustrate a legal sociologist orientation. When a court speaks in terms of public policies and their effect on the case at hand, this is the clue that legal sociology is at work. However, some people wrongly conclude that legal positive decisions always lead to harsh results while legal sociology brings about positive consequences. This is not necessarily the case. Consider the *Buck v. Bell* case, 274 U.S. 200 (1927). There, the U.S. Supreme Court permitted Virginia to sterilize women that the state found to be mentally defective. Virginia justified its actions on the grounds that mentally defective persons would become a menace to society; if they were incapable of procreating however, they might benefit themselves and society. In upholding the actions of the state, the Court reasoned that "the public welfare may call upon the best citizens for their lives. It would be strange if it could not call upon those who already sap the strength of the state for these lesser sacrifices in order to prevent our being swamped with incompetence. It is better for all the world, if instead of waiting to execute degenerate offspring for crime, or to let them starve for their imbecility, society can prevent those who are manifestly unfit from continuing their kind."

In the sterilization case, the Supreme Court sacrificed an individual's personal rights in favor of what it regarded as the best interests of society. Would you expect to see such a decision today? No, because our concept of public policy has changed.

Legal Realism

Legal realism focuses on *law in action* rather than on the theoretical rules themselves. It stresses that law must be considered in light of its day-to-day application. Legal realists suggest that decision makers often mask the true basis for their decision behind the rhetoric of the law. They believe that decisions are often more attributable to the biases and moods of decision makers than they are to the formal legal rules that are supposed to determine the outcome.

The problem with legal realism is that it is hard to objectively prove. A judge is unlikely to admit to having any ulterior motives when stating the reason for a particular decision. In fact, a decision maker may be acting on biases that she never has entertained at a conscious level.

Consider the *State in Interest of Gray v. Hogan* case, 613 So.2d 681 (5th Cir. La. 1993). There a woman claimed to have had sexual relations with a man she met while jogging. After becoming pregnant, a blood test indicated a 99.99 percent probability he was the baby's father. State law, however, required that scientific testing alone was not sufficient to prove paternity. But, it would be upheld as reliable where there was other sufficient corroborating evidence of paternity introduced at trial. The woman knew many details about the man's family, employment, and residence, including several details about the inside of his apartment. The man testified he did not know the woman, had never seen her before, did not date her, and never had sexual relations with her. The court ruled that the woman had not provided sufficient evidence of his paternity. Did the judge really believe that the law compelled this result or was he acting on a bias against women who engage in extramarital sexual relations?

The Legal Profession

Lawyers and legal advice are not only necessary when being sued or contemplating litigation. The complexities of modern life confront businesses and their managers with important legal questions on a daily basis. Thus, lawyers provide important assistance to people who wish to avoid legal emergencies and to plan business strategies and tactics.

The Adversary System

Unlike many foreign legal systems where lawyers play a relatively minor role in resolving conflicts, lawyers are key participants in the U.S. judicial process. This is because of this country's reliance on an **adversary system.** The adversary system is premised on the notion that the ultimate truth and, consequently, justice will prevail if each party to a legal dispute is represented by competent legal counsel. Each attorney is then expected to provide the strongest legal representation for her client.

Of course, the adversary system does not give attorneys free reign. In fact, they may be sanctioned if they violate legal and ethical rules designed to ensure the fair operation of the judicial process. In the next case, both the client and the attorney were sanctioned because of the attorney's misconduct.

Lasar v. Ford Motor Company

399 F.3d 1101 (9th Cir. 2005)

FACTS

Steven Lasar was severely injured when he was ejected from his Ford Ranger during a rollover accident. Lasar filed suit against Ford alleging that Ford had designed the Ranger's door-latch mechanism defectively. Before the jury trial began, the court issued a ruling that prohibited Ford from introducing evidence that Lasar had consumed alcohol on the day of the accident. In his opening statements, Ford's attorney, Lawrence Sutter, told the jury: "At about 5:00 that morning, Mr. Lasar got out of bed and went hunting for the morning. Some time in the afternoon, he met up with some of his friends and spent the day playing pool, visiting some local establishments. Somewhere around 10:00 that night, he made the decision to drive himself home. He got into his car and he began his way back to his homestead." Lasar's attorney objected, explaining to the court that Sutter's reference to Lasar "visiting some local establishments" violated the evidentiary rulings. The court ruled that Sutter's statement was an absolutely unacceptable violation of his ruling. Ultimately, the court declared a mistrial and

Lasar v. Ford Motor Company *(concluded)*

discharged the jury. Further, the court imposed monetary sanctions against Ford and Sutter because Sutter "intentionally and in bad faith" violated the ruling.

ISSUE
Did the court err in declaring a mistrial and levying sanctions against Ford and its counsel?

DECISION
No. Ford's attorney clearly made a calculated attempt to introduce evidence that Lasar was drinking before the accident. Sutter's words could reasonably be construed as conveying the message that Lasar had been drinking at a bar (or bars) and then made the dangerous and unlawful decision to drive himself home while intoxicated. In light of the hardship that Sutter's bad faith violation of the order caused to Lasar, the court, and other litigants, the court's decision to impose monetary sanctions against both Sutter and Ford is reasonable.

Professional Responsibilities

Attorneys are required to act in the best interests of their clients. This is because a fiduciary relationship exists between the lawyer and her client. Because of her special training and skills, the legal system grants the attorney a great deal of discretion in precisely how to represent the client's interests. However, as the previous case makes clear, there are limits to the actions an attorney may take in the course of representing her client. These limits arise from the fact that in addition to being an agent of her client, she also is considered to be a servant of the court.

Earlier in the chapter we looked at the *Farinella* case where a man was charged with a crime for changing the "best when purchased by" labels on the salad dressing. In the trial, the prosecutor said to the jury: "Ladies and gentlemen, don't let the defendant and his high-paid lawyer buy his way out of this." Immediately, after the judge sustained the defense attorney's objection to that statement, the prosecutor looked at the jurors and said: "Black and white in our system of justice, ladies and gentlemen. You have to earn justice. You can't buy it." The judge sustained an objection to that statement too. When reviewing the case, the Court of Appeals complained that the judge's response to the first statement was too weak. It believed that he should have made clear to the prosecutor after sustaining the first objection that one more false step and he would declare a mistrial. The appellate court then stressed that the prosecutor's second statement was worse than the first, because it could be understood by the jurors as a warning that the defendant might try to obtain an acquittal by bribery. In this case, had the government presented enough evidence to sustain a conviction, the Court of Appeals stated that it would have reversed the judgment and ordered a new trial on the basis of the prosecutor's misconduct.

Confidentiality

Attorney–Client Privilege

LO7

The **attorney–client privilege** is an important feature of the U.S. legal profession. This rule prevents an attorney from divulging confidential information communicated to the lawyer by a client or potential client in the course of seeking to retain the attorney or otherwise seeking legal advice. The privilege is derived from the notion that the effective functioning of the judicial system will be undermined if a client does not feel free to speak fully and honestly with his attorney.

The existence of the privilege is not dependent upon the attorney actually being retained since it may be necessary to disclose confidential information in the course of persuading a lawyer to take a case. The privilege also covers information divulged to an attorney's subordinates (secretaries or paralegals). There are exceptions to the privilege. For instance, a lawyer has a duty to report a client's statement that he intends to commit a crime. Further, the attorney–client privilege generally does not cover statements made in the presence of people other than the lawyer or her subordinates.

Work Product Privilege

LO7

Like the attorney–client privilege, the **work product privilege** is equally fundamental to the justice system. A lawyer is an officer of the court and is bound to work for the advancement of justice while faithfully protecting the rightful interests of his clients. In performing his various duties, however, it is essential that a lawyer work with a certain degree of privacy, free from unnecessary intrusion by opposing parties and their counsel. Proper preparation of a client's case demands that he assemble information, sift what he considers to be the relevant from the irrelevant facts, prepare his legal theories, and plan his strategy without undue and needless interference. That is the necessary way in which lawyers act within the framework of our system of jurisprudence to promote justice and to protect their clients' interests. This work is reflected, of course, in interviews, statements, memoranda, correspondence, briefs, mental impressions, personal beliefs, and countless other tangible and intangible ways. Were such materials open to opposing counsel on mere demand, much of what is now put down in writing would remain unwritten. Accordingly, the legal system provides a broad privilege against compelled disclosure of the attorney's work product.

Now consider the following case in which Martha Stewart's claim for protection of her e-mail message under the attorney–client privilege is denied. However, the court does ultimately extend her the protections of the attorney's work product privilege.

Ethics in Action

Both the adversary system and the attorney–client privilege may place a lawyer in a position where he knows he is defending a guilty person. Would you represent a murderer under those circumstances?

United States v. Stewart

287 F.Supp.2d 461 (S.D.N.Y. 2003)

FACTS

Martha Stewart sold 3,928 shares of ImClone stock after allegedly learning from her stockbroker that the corporation's chief executive office was seeking to sell his shares. It was suspected that Stewart was acting on inside information that the Food and Drug Administration was going to reject the company's application for approval to market a lead product. While these charges were being investigated by various government agencies, Stewart composed an e-mail that contained her account of the facts relating to her sale of the stock. After sending the e-mail to one of her lawyers, Stewart forwarded a copy to her daughter. In preparation for trial, the U.S. Attorney sought access to the e-mail as part of the discovery process.

ISSUE

Is Stewart required to produce the e-mail for government inspection?

DECISION

No. While Stewart's e-mail to her lawyer was originally protected by her attorney–client privilege, she waived that privilege when she forwarded a copy to her daughter. This is because subsequent disclosure to a third party by a client of a communication with his attorney eliminates whatever privilege the communication may have originally possessed. However, the work product doctrine protects against invading the privacy of an attorney's course of preparation. Most courts have found waiver only when the disclosure substantially increased the opportunities for potential adversaries to obtain the information. By forwarding the e-mail to a family member, Stewart did not substantially increase the risk that the government would gain access to materials prepared in anticipation of litigation. For the foregoing reasons, Stewart's e-mail is work product protected from production in response to the government's subpoena.

Competence and Care

By accepting employment as the client's lawyer, an attorney agrees to exercise the skill, prudence, and diligence expected of lawyers of ordinary skill and competence in the community. The lawyer does not guarantee that the client will win a lawsuit. Thus, he is not necessarily liable for **malpractice** when the client loses. In fact, a lawyer is not liable for every mistake he might make. Lawyers are given a great deal of discretion in selecting an appropriate strategy for handling a legal dispute. As long as an attorney has a rational basis for the strategy he chooses, the courts are not likely to second-guess his professional judgment.

However, a client may successfully bring a malpractice claim when his attorney fails to draft court-related documents properly or in a timely manner, appear at a hearing, or assert a possible claim or defense. And important tactical decisions should be made only after the lawyer consults with his client.

Preventive Law

In the past quarter century there has been a qualitative as well as a quantitative change in the concern of business managers with law. In earlier times, business managers generally employed lawyers only in emergencies. A lawyer might be hired if a business was sued, if a debt could not be collected, or if a supplier's goods were defective and no settlement could be reached. Today, business managers also retain lawyers to help them plan to avoid such emergencies and to comply with the rapidly growing mass of legal rules imposed on business operations by government bodies. This use of lawyers by businesspeople is called **preventive law.**

Objectives of Preventive Law

The objectives of preventive law are to arrange business plans and methods to increase profits by (1) avoiding losses through fines and damage judgments and (2) reaching business goals through enforceable contracts while avoiding government prohibitions. By involving a lawyer in the business-planning process, a desired business objective can be reached with less legal risk. Preventive law further aims to minimize the possibility of failure if the business has to go to court to enforce its rights.

Roles of Lawyers and Clients

Almost every business activity involves legal risks and consequences. To avoid costly judgments and to get that to which they are legally entitled, businesspeople generally need to be familiar with the law applicable to their activities. Studying this book will aid in this, but it will not prepare you to be your own lawyer. Consider an analogy from the field of medicine. While there are times when you need a doctor, you still need a good knowledge of first aid to deal with the most common problems. Such knowledge also will help you to know when you should call a doctor—or in this case, a lawyer.

The practice of preventive law requires a knowledgeable client as well as a knowledgeable lawyer. The client needs to understand the legal system and the applicable law well enough to be able to communicate with the lawyer. The client needs to know what information is relevant and necessary to the lawyer's opinion. Too often clients get into trouble because they have not fully informed their lawyers. A legal opinion is no better than the information on which it is based. Problems also arise when clients apply legal advice to situations not contemplated by the lawyer. This can lead to a lawsuit, or it may discourage the client from doing something that is clearly legal.

Concept Summary: Preventive Law

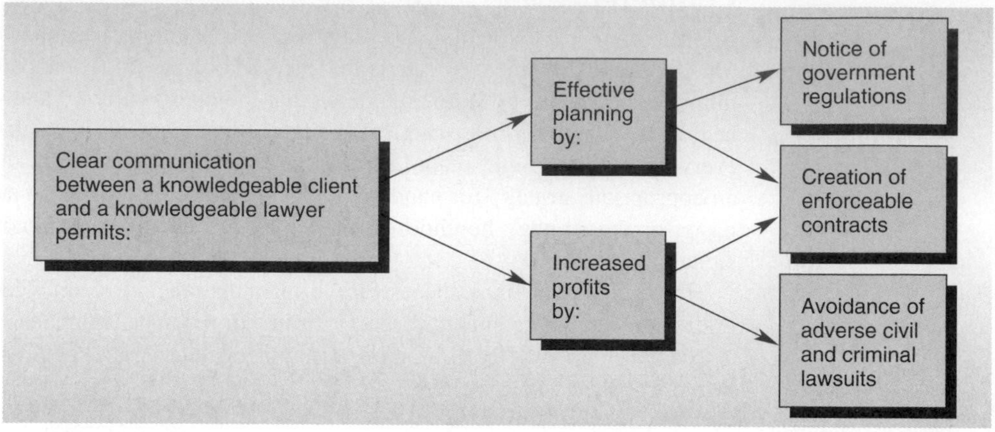

Questions and Problem Cases

1. What are the primary functions of law?
2. Describe the various ways in which the courts *make* law.
3. On Matchmaker's Internet dating service, an unknown person using a computer in Berlin posted a false personal profile of Christianne Carafano. The posting was without the knowledge, consent, or permission of Carafano, who is a popular actress who acts under the stage name of Chase Masterson. The false profile contained several pictures of her. In response to the Matchmaker questionnaire, the profile stated that Carafano was looking for a one-night stand as well as a hard and dominant man with a strong sexual appetite. The profile included Carafano's home address, e-mail address, and her telephone number. Unaware of the improper posting, Carafano soon began to receive sexually explicit messages responding to the profile as well as a threatening fax. Ultimately, Carafano sued Matchmaker for invasion of privacy. Matchmaker moved to dismiss the lawsuit on the grounds that it was immune from liability because it is an Internet service provider. The court agreed with Matchmaker. It cited the Communications Decency Act, which grants most Internet services immunity from liability for publishing false or defamatory material so long as the information was provided by another party. The court admitted that its conclusion results in "serious and utterly deplorable consequences." However, it felt constrained by the statutory language. Which school of legal jurisprudence does this court appear to be following? Explain.
4. RealNetworks offers free basic versions of two products, RealPlayer and RealJukebox, for users to download from RealNetworks' site on the World Wide Web. These products allow users to see and hear audio and video available on the Internet and to download, record, and play music. Before a user can install either of these software packages, he or she must accept the terms of RealNetworks' End User License Agreement, which specifically requires that any unresolved disputes arising from the agreement must be submitted to arbitration in the state of Washington. After using RealNetworks' products and consenting to the terms of the License Agreement, Michael Lieschke read a *New York Times* article, which stated that RealNetworks' products collected personal information about users' listening habits and places they had visited on the World Wide Web and sent the information to RealNetworks via the Internet. Lieschke then filed a lawsuit in Illinois against RealNetworks for trespass to property and privacy, alleging that the

company's products allowed it to access and intercept his electronic communications and stored information without his knowledge or consent. RealNetworks asserted that the court lacked jurisdiction to decide the case because the License Agreement required the dispute to be arbitrated in Washington. However, Lieschke argued that the arbitration clause was not binding because federal law requires that agreements to arbitrate be written in order to be enforced. According to Lieschke, the License Agreement is an electronic agreement and electronic agreements do not satisfy the "written" agreements provisions of the Federal Arbitration Act. Does the electronic License Agreement constitute a writing? Explain the process by which a court would answer this question.

5. One wheel on an automobile manufactured by Buick Motor Company was defectively made. Buick would have discovered the defective condition if it had made a reasonable inspection of the wheel. Buick sold the car to an automobile dealer who in turn sold it to MacPherson. MacPherson was injured when the wheel collapsed. MacPherson sued Buick for negligent failure to inspect the wheel. Buick's main defense was that it had not dealt directly with MacPherson and thus owed him no duty. The general rule governing such suits at the time of this action was that a buyer could not sue a manufacturer for negligence unless there was a contract between the buyer and the manufacturer. However, there had been a previous case, *Thomas v. Winchester,* where a manufacturer falsely labeled a poison that was sold to a druggist, who in turn sold it to a customer. The customer was able to recover against the manufacturer. Further, in *Devlin v. Smith,* a contractor was held liable when he improperly built a scaffold for a painter and the painter's employees were injured when it collapsed. On the basis of this information, explain how the court could permit MacPherson to recover from Buick.
6. Alan Howard is a subscriber of America Online (AOL), an Internet service provider that provides Internet access, electronic mail, and numerous other services to its users. Howard filed a lawsuit against AOL, alleging that the company violated the Communications Act by making unreasonable charges, practices, classifications, or regulations; by unreasonably prejudicing some subscribers by favoring others; and by failing to protect subscriber privacy. AOL defended on the grounds that the Communications Act regulates only common carriers and, since it was not a common carrier, it was not governed by that statute. Carefully explain the process by which the court will determine if AOL is a common carrier.
7. Zerlene Rico sued Mitsubishi Motors for negligence and strict liability. Rico's attorney, Raymond Johnson, somehow obtained the notes of one of the defense attorneys, James Yukevich, after a deposition with Yukevich and a defense expert. The document provided a summary of a defense conference between attorneys and defense experts in which the participants discussed the strengths and weaknesses of Mitsubishi's technical evidence. Johnson made a copy for himself before returning the original to the court reporter. Johnson then made additional copies and sent them to Rico's experts and other members of her legal team. Johnson made no effort to notify defense counsel of his possession of the document and instead used the notes to impeach the testimony of a Mitsubishi expert during his deposition. Yukevich, after discovering that Johnson had a copy of his personal notes, filed a motion to disqualify Rico's legal team. Should the court disqualify Rico's legal team and experts from representing her? Explain.
8. After noticing that Jennifer's baby was not eating well and was small for his age, doctors tested him for drugs. When the test results proved positive, Jennifer admitted to police that she had regularly smoked crack cocaine during her pregnancy. Jennifer was charged with *delivery of a controlled substance to a minor* by delivering the crack to her baby via the umbilical cord. Has Jennifer violated this statute? Carefully explain the process by which a court will analyze this statute.

Chapter 2

Dispute Settlement

Learning Objectives

After you have studied this chapter, you should be able to:

1. Describe the various ways to settle disputes.
2. Define jurisdiction and explain the jurisdictional limits of small claims, trial, and appellate courts.
3. Explain why all cases can't be appealed all the way to the Supreme Court.
4. Explain the advantages and disadvantages of the adversary system.
5. Identify the different stages of a lawsuit.
6. Discuss how an appeal works and why most appeals fail.

Plastix shipped five cases of decorative boxes to Trendco, Inc., for which Trendco had agreed to pay $10,000. Trendco sent Plastix a check for $8,000, claiming that the boxes in one of the cases were defective. Plastix has strict quality control procedures and is sure the boxes were not defective when they left its plant. Plastix wants the $2,000 but is concerned about maintaining good relations with Trendco, which has been a valued customer for several years.

- What alternative does Plastix have to pursuing a lawsuit for the additional $2,000?
- If Plastix decides to sue, where must it file its lawsuit?
- If Plastix decides to sue, what procedures will be followed in the suit?

Means of Dispute Settlement

LO1 Negotiation

Disputes arise in business for many reasons: goods may be defective; customers may not carry out their promises; government regulators may be unreasonable. The courts are the most visible and familiar vehicle for dispute settlement, but most disputes are, and should be, settled by negotiation.

In an earlier day, most businesspeople shunned lawyers and the courts. Typically, a lawsuit was filed only as a last resort after the parties had decided not to do business with each other again. Avoidance of lawyers and the courts is certainly not the rule today. Indeed, we are now a more litigious society. Many of us are quick to go to court. There are many more lawyers, and as indicated in the preceding chapter, businesspeople call on them frequently.

The cost of bringing or defending a lawsuit is rising. The fees of lawyers have increased; however, the biggest increases in costs have come because discovery procedures (discussed later in this chapter) and the trials themselves have become much more time consuming, involving the time of both businesspeople and lawyers.

Settlement of disputes through negotiation is, therefore, even more attractive than it was earlier. If this can be done by the businesspeople themselves, good! However, many attorneys are skilled negotiators, and having a competent advocate speak as an intermediary is often more effective than speaking for oneself. If negotiations fail, there are many ways to pursue a resolution.

Alternative Dispute Resolution

Because of the time, money, and personal resources that get tied up in litigation, businesses and individuals are increasingly turning to alternatives to trials to settle disputes. Courts, also, often require parties involved in certain kinds of disputes to try alternatives in an effort to get the parties to settle before trial. These **alternative dispute resolution (ADR)** mechanisms share many advantages over trials: They are generally quicker, cheaper, and less complicated procedurally, and they receive less publicity. In addition, because they are not as adversarial, they facilitate a continuation of business between the parties after settlement of the dispute. Finally, unlike at trial where there must be a winner and a loser, ADR more readily adapts to compromise solutions.

A new and growing trend is the use of *collaborative counselors* to help facilitate settlements. They are specially trained people (usually lawyers) who are engaged in settlement negotiations. The idea is to encourage the free exchange of information by barring its use in court if a settlement cannot be reached. It is most often used in family law cases but is expanding to other types of cases.

Mediation

A voluntary process that is increasingly used when negotiation seems to be failing is **mediation.** The parties to the dispute choose a third party to assist them in settling it. This **mediator** often tries first to communicate the positions of the parties to each other. Frequently, the areas of serious disagreement are narrower than the parties think. The mediator then usually proposes a basis or several bases for settlement. A mediator merely facilitates negotiation; no award or opinion on the merits of the dispute is given by the mediator. If the mediation is successful, it can result in a *mediation agreement.*

The Federal Mediation and Conciliation Service makes experienced mediators available to serve in labor disputes. When the president declares a "cooling off" period after finding that a strike endangers the national safety or health, the Service is called in. It is available in other cases as well at the request of the union or the employer. Either arbitration or court action may follow unsuccessful mediation.

Mediation is especially useful in situations in which the parties have some continuing relationship because it allows them to compromise and to reach a solution themselves. As a result, they are more likely to be able to constructively work within the agreement. Thus, mediation would be a good method for Plastix and Trendco to use to settle their dispute. Mediation is also often used in interpersonal disputes such as divorce, where child custody arrangements will require the parents to deal with each other for several years. Court-annexed mediation is commonly provided or compelled in these cases.

Arbitration

Arbitration is another widely used alternative to settling disputes in court. It can be used after mediation fails, or instead of it. Arbitration differs from mediation in that the third party to whom the dispute is submitted decides the outcome. Contracts involving securities and commodity trading, casualty insurance, and other kinds of commercial contracts often contain arbitration clauses. Most union–management contracts and many employment contracts also have them.

A particular advantage of arbitration is that an arbitrator who is familiar with the technical or social setting of the dispute may be chosen. This may be particularly important in an international trade dispute or a labor dispute. While arbitration is often provided for in a contract, parties who have not so provided can also choose to have their dispute arbitrated after it has arisen. Many courts now order or provide court-annexed arbitration for certain kinds of cases such as those with limited dollar amounts in dispute. Additionally, many consumer-related disputes now go to arbitration. Despite strong Supreme Court support for arbitration, courts examine contracts requiring arbitration to make sure they are fair and that public interests are adequately protected.

Usually there is only one arbitrator. The parties may select the arbitrator in any way they desire. They may ask the American Arbitration Association to provide a list of available arbitrators. The parties can then alternate in eliminating names from that list until a single name remains. Sometimes a board of three arbitrators is chosen by having each party choose one person; the two chosen arbitrators then select the third.

Most states have passed the Uniform Arbitration Act, which makes both the agreement of parties to arbitrate and the arbitration award enforceable in court. A court will not review the wisdom of the decision of an arbitrator. It may, however, hold that the dispute was not arbitrable under the agreement of the parties, or that the arbitrator exceeded his or her authority, or acted arbitrarily, capriciously, or in a discriminatory manner. The parties may or may not require an opinion (reasons for the award) from the arbitrator. Arbitration awards are usually not published, although many labor dispute awards have been.

International Alternative Dispute Resolution

The increasing volume of international trade, coupled with the complex nature of these relationships, has led to greater reliance on arbitration to resolve contractual disputes. This settlement of disputes by a nonjudicial third party is increasingly called for in international contracts because it is cheaper, quicker, and more private than resolving disputes through litigation. Equally important, however, is the fact that it can take place in a neutral location. The increase in trade with countries such as China, Japan, and Korea, where mediation rather than litigation of disputes is traditional, has given added impetus to this trend.

The growing attractiveness of arbitration has resulted in the establishment of arbitration centers in world capitals such as London, Paris, Cairo, Hong Kong, and Stockholm, and in major cities such as Geneva and New York. Recognition and enforcement of international arbitration agreements and awards are generally controlled through multilateral treaties, such as the 1958 **United Nations Convention on the Recognition and Enforcement of Foreign Arbitral Awards.** The United States and most of its trading partners are signatories to this treaty, which is the legal framework by which the international community regulates the enforcement of arbitral agreements and awards. This convention broadly construes the authority of arbitral panels and severely limits the power of a party to overturn an arbitral award. However, the United States will recognize the enforceability of an award only where the nation of the other party has ratified the convention and only where the dispute is commercial in nature.

Indeed, several global organizations have produced their own set of formal rules and procedures governing international arbitration. These include ADR mechanisms outlined by the **World Trade Organization** (WTO) and the North American Free Trade Agreement. The system envisions that most trade disputes among its member nations will be resolved through consultations. However, it also has established a permanent dispute settlement body (DSB) to coordinate a formal dispute resolution process when informal consultations are unsuccessful. If the parties are unable to resolve their dispute, they may request the formation of a hearing panel made up of independent experts who make findings of fact and issue binding rulings. The DSB also has a standing appellate body.

A losing party is given a reasonable time to comply with its trade obligations or to somehow compensate the winning party. If this does not occur, the winning party may petition the DSB for permission to retaliate against the noncomplying nation. This is usually in the form of increased tariffs.

The **North American Free Trade Agreement** (NAFTA) has established a mechanism for resolving trade disputes through the use of binational panels. The treaty contains elaborate provisions for settling two distinct types of disputes: (1) antidumping and countervailing duty matters and (2) conflicts over a country's interpretation or application of the treaty. The dispute settlement procedures are subject to strict time limits designed to prevent the lengthy delays that have characterized many international dispute mechanisms.

Minitrial and Summary Jury Trial

The **minitrial** is designed to refocus the dispute as a business problem. Executives of the disputing companies, who have settlement authority, hear a shortened presentation of the case by the lawyers for each side. The executives, who now have a better understanding of the strengths and weaknesses of their case and know how a settlement would fit in with their business objectives, meet with the lawyers to negotiate a settlement. The minitrial often involves a neutral third-party advisor. If a settlement is not reached, she or he will render a nonbinding opinion regarding how the dispute is likely to be resolved if it goes to trial, and how the court is likely to rule on factual and evidentiary issues. After this, the parties again try to negotiate a settlement.

A **summary jury trial** has many similarities to the minitrial. However, it is conducted under court guidance, while the minitrial is voluntarily conducted by the parties themselves. In the summary jury trial, a six-member mock jury empaneled by the court hears a shortened presentation of the case by the lawyers for each side and renders an advisory verdict. The presiding court official, who is either a judge or a magistrate, then meets with the parties to help them reach a settlement. Because summary jury trials have been effective in encouraging settlement and court dockets are so clogged, some courts, such as the U.S. Court of Claims, routinely use the procedure in appropriate cases.

Private Judging

Some parties are able to avoid trial while engaging in a process similar to a formal court proceeding by hiring their own judge to settle their dispute. In this **private judging,** or "rent-a-judge," method of dispute resolution, the hired judge (who is often a retired judge) renders a binding opinion after hearing the proofs and arguments of the parties. Many states, such as Ohio, have adopted rules for the handling of these cases.

Other Dispute Resolution Mechanisms

While the ADR systems discussed above are the most commonly used alternatives to trial, especially in business disputes, there are many others. These range from an **ombudsperson,** who is an individual appointed within an organization to settle disputes, to private panels, to small claims court (discussed later in the chapter). **Med/arb** (a combination of mediation and arbitration where the third party first serves as a mediator, then as an arbitrator) and early neutral evaluation (a court-annexed procedure where a neutral private attorney with expertise in the area of the dispute objectively evaluates the case) are emerging ADR approaches. Online dispute resolution (ODR) is another fast growing ADR procedure. It takes place at least partially online and outside courts and is especially effective in long-distance disputes involving technology or minor issues. It is fortunate that disputants are increasingly trying to settle disagreements through alternative means, for our court system is incapable of handling the large number of disputes that occur. However, there is a price to be paid for the speed, economy, informality, and other benefits gained from these alternatives. The most important trade-off involves the traditional procedural safeguards used during litigation to guarantee that every person has his or her "fair day in court." These procedural safeguards are discussed in the following section.

Concept Summary: Alternative Dispute Resolution*

Form	Decision Maker	Advantages	Conductor
Mediation	Disputants	Parties can better work within jointly reached solution.	Mediator
Arbitration	Arbitrator	Arbitrator often has expertise in area of dispute.	Arbitrator
Minitrial	Executives of disputing companies	Companies are more likely to settle.	Neutral third party
Summary Jury Trial	Six-member mock jury	Disputants are more likely to settle.	Judge or magistrate
Private Judge	Hired judge	Circumstances are like a trial, but without a waiting period.	Hired judge

*All these forms of ADR are usually quicker, cheaper, and more private than formal trial litigation. Other advantages are listed within.

The Courts

The dispute resolution mechanism of last resort (short of the use of force) is the courts. Either party to a dispute can bring the lawsuit. If the party brings it to the proper court, the court must decide it. The court cannot wait for the legislature to pass a statute or suggest that the parties go to a different or higher court. However, there are some general kinds of cases that American courts do not consider. Courts do not decide a case if the issue has become **moot.** A case is moot when events occurring after the filing of the lawsuit have made a decision beside the point. An example was a case brought by a white applicant to a law school.[1] At first he was not admitted and claimed reverse racial discrimination; however, he was later admitted before his case had been decided on appeal to the U.S. Supreme Court. The Court refused to rule on the case because it was moot, even though other similar cases were being brought.

Federal courts and most state courts hear only real controversies—concrete disputes between actual parties. *They do not give advisory opinions, nor do they make rulings on hypothetical cases.* This saves the time of judges and avoids the danger that the arguments for one side might not be vigorously pressed because no one as yet has been truly hurt.

LO2

Jurisdiction

As we said above, a court must decide a case if it is brought to the proper court. A court can only hear a case over which it has **jurisdiction.** Jurisdiction is the authority of a court to hear and determine disputes. Jurisdiction can be limited in several ways. Some courts are limited by subject matter jurisdiction. They can hear only cases involving certain types of controversies, such as tax disputes or juvenile matters. Other courts are limited by the amount of damages being sought or the penalty to be assessed. The small claims courts discussed later in this chapter are limited by such jurisdiction. The jurisdiction of all courts is limited geographically.

A court may not decide a legal dispute unless it has **personal jurisdiction** over the defendant. Personal jurisdiction generally does not exist unless the defendant has some close connection with the territory where the suit is brought. Personal jurisdiction is likely to exist if the defendant is a resident of the territory where the court is located or if a nonresident defendant is physically present in that territory. However, the situation becomes much more complicated when a lawsuit is filed against a nonresident who was not physically present in the territory served by the court. In those instances, the court is unlikely to have personal jurisdiction unless it can be shown that the nonresident defendant has certain minimum contacts (a close connection) with the territory where the suit is brought. Courts have developed a three-part test to determine whether they have jurisdiction over nonresident defendants. First, the nonresident defendant must do some act or transaction within the territory or perform some act by which she purposefully avails herself of the privilege of conducting activities within the territory. Second, the claim that is the basis of the lawsuit must be one that arises out of or results from the nonresident defendant's territory-related activities. Third, the exercise of jurisdiction must be reasonable.

The following case, *Attaway v. Omega,* illustrates how the Internet has created new problems in determining jurisdiction. Courts are recognizing a sliding scale for determining whether the operation of an Internet site can support the minimum contacts necessary for the exercise of personal jurisdiction. A passive website, one that merely allows the owner to post information on the Internet, is at one end of the scale. It will not be sufficient to establish personal jurisdiction. At the other end are sites whose owners engage in repeated online contacts with forum residents over the Internet, and in these cases, personal jurisdiction may be proper. In between are those sites with some interactive elements, through which a site allows for bilateral information exchange with its visitors.

Just as the "borderless" Internet has created special problems for personal jurisdiction, so too has the increasing flow of people across national boundaries. Nowhere is this jurisdiction dilemma more marked than when it comes to acts of terrorism. For example,

[1] *DeFunis v. Odegard,* 416 U.S. 312 (1974).

Attaway v. Omega

WL690296 (Ind. Ct. App. 2009)

FACTS

Omega, an Indiana resident, sold a Porsche on eBay to the Attaways, who were Idaho residents. They paid for it through PayPal. The Attaways hired CarHop USA, a Washington auto transporter, to pick up the car. After taking delivery, the Attaways filed a claim with PayPal for a refund, claiming the Porsche was significantly not as described on eBay. PayPal later denied the refund. The Attaways then convinced MasterCard to rescind the payment. Omega then sued the Attaways in small claims court for $5,900. The Attaways defended by asserting, among other things, that the court lacked personal jurisdiction.

ISSUE

Did the Indiana court have personal jurisdiction over the Idaho buyers?

DECISION

Yes. Personal jurisdiction is related to the defendant's contacts with the forum. Courts in other states have found that the usual online auction transaction does not give the purposeful contact necessary for personal jurisdiction because they are random and attenuated contacts. However, there is sufficient contact here because the Attaways: (1) could see the seller's location before bidding on the car; (2) agreed to appear in Indiana by submitting the eBay bid; and (3) hired a shipping company to enter Indiana as their representative to retrieve the car. These contacts exceeded a single online purchase and amounted to a purposeful availment. Additionally, justice is served because imposing an Indiana forum is no more burdensome on the buyers than an Idaho forum would impose on the sellers.

the U.S. District Court held that under the Foreign Sovereign Immunities Act, it had personal jurisdiction over seven Libyans convicted in France of bombing a plane over Niger while it was traveling from Chad to France in September 1989. Seven U.S. citizens were killed on the flight. The families of the deceased brought a civil suit in the District of Columbia. The seven defendants argued that the court did not have personal jurisdiction over them. Using the "minimum contacts" test, the court held that because the plane they chose to destroy was on an international flight and expected to stop in several nations before reaching its final destination, the individual defendants could and should have reasonably assumed that passengers of many nationalities would be on board, from which they could also expect they might be hauled into the courts of those nations whose citizens would die.[2]

Having examined the concept and complexities of jurisdiction, you will find that the notion of venue is somewhat simpler. **Venue** concerns where within a jurisdiction a suit must be heard. Venue rules are established by the states. These rules tell the county where the plaintiff must file suit. For example, a criminal case must usually be filed in the county where the crime took place. Parties who feel they cannot get a fair trial in the designated area can ask the court for a **change of venue.**

State Courts

The names of the various courts and the way jurisdiction is divided between them vary from state to state. We will use the courts of California as an example: They are typical of most states (see Figure 2.1). In general, the state courts have jurisdiction to hear almost any sort of dispute except those involving certain federal laws and issues. Most disputes between citizens of the state and disputes arising from events occurring within the state, such as automobile accidents, are tried in state courts.

[2] *Pugh v. Socialist People's Libyan Arab Jamahirya et al.*, 290 F.Supp.2d 54 (2003).

FIGURE 2.1
The California Court System

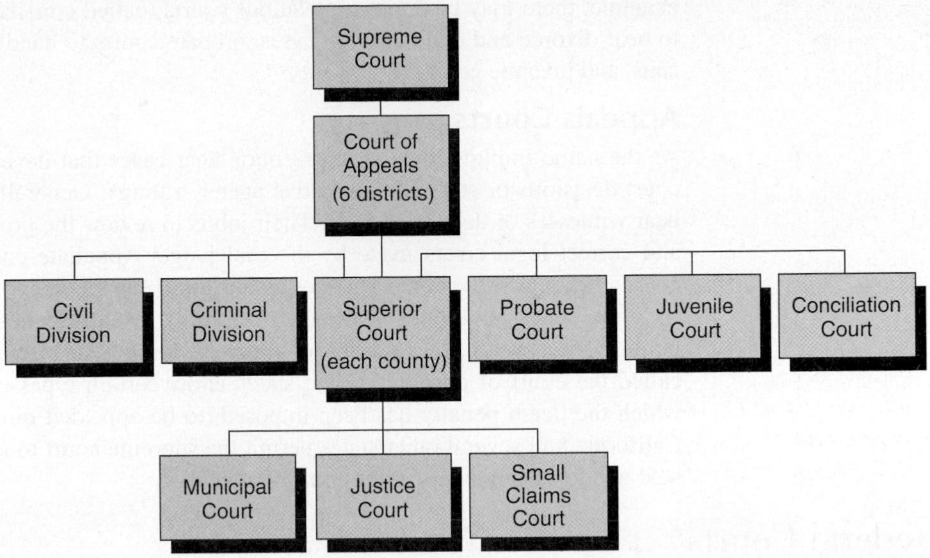

Inferior Courts

Most minor criminal violations and civil disputes involving small amounts of money are handled by courts that keep no record (transcript) of the testimony or proceedings. They are, therefore, not **courts of record.** Without a record there can be no appeal. Usually a dissatisfied party claiming error in such a court may have a new trial (a **trial *de novo***) in a court of record. Inferior courts may be called **municipal courts** in urban areas and **justice of the peace** courts in rural areas. In many states, as in California, justice of the peace courts have been replaced by minor courts such as the justice courts, which operate in less populated counties.

Many cities also have **small claims courts.** These courts handle civil matters involving a limited amount of money. In these courts, the procedures are informal, the parties may argue their own cases, and the judicial officer, who may not be a lawyer, determines both the facts and the law and renders a decision. These courts therefore offer a quick, inexpensive, and easily accessible forum for the settlement of minor disputes.

Trial Courts

Trial courts, like inferior courts, perform the same basic functions: finding the relevant facts, identifying the appropriate rule of law, and combining the facts and the law to reach a decision in settlement of the dispute. Trial courts differ from inferior courts in that the trial courts are courts of general jurisdiction; they are not limited by the amount of civil damages that can be awarded or the criminal penalties that can be imposed. Their geographic jurisdiction is often a county. They also differ in that the judge must be a lawyer, and juries are provided for. The juries decide the facts and, under instructions from the judge about the applicable law, reach a verdict. In addition, trial courts are courts of record. Thus, an appeal can be taken from a trial court decision.

The name of the trial courts that have general jurisdiction varies greatly among states. These courts may be called circuit, district, county, or, as in California, superior courts. Trial courts may be divided into those that hear criminal cases and those that hear only civil cases. Where there is a large population, specialized courts may be established. For example, there may be domestic relations courts (called conciliation courts in California) to hear divorce and child custody cases, probate courts to handle estates of deceased persons, and juvenile courts.

Appeals Courts

As the name implies, state appeals courts hear cases that have been appealed from trial court decisions or state administrative agency rulings. Generally, appellate courts do not hear witnesses or determine facts. Their job is to review the proceedings in the trial court and correct legal errors made by the trial judge. Appellate courts must accept the trial court's findings of fact unless it goes against all the evidence.

Some states have only one court of appeals, usually called the supreme court. The majority, however, have two levels of appellate courts. The intermediate court is frequently called the court of appeals.[3] Some states allow certain types of cases, such as those in which the death penalty has been imposed, to be appealed directly to the highest court. California and several other states permit the supreme court to select the cases it wants to hear and to assign others to the court of appeals.

Federal Courts

Cases heard in the federal courts fall into one of two classes: They are either cases involving a federal question or cases in which there is diversity of citizenship between the parties. Federal questions include cases in which a federal statute is involved, such as a violation of a federal criminal law, or a violation of a right granted by the Constitution. Federal courts have exclusive jurisdiction over patents, copyrights, bankruptcy, crimes defined by federal statutes, and a few other matters. One of these areas involves maritime cases, which are decided under admiralty law. See Figure 2.2 for a diagram of the types of courts in the federal court system.

FIGURE 2.2
The Federal Court System

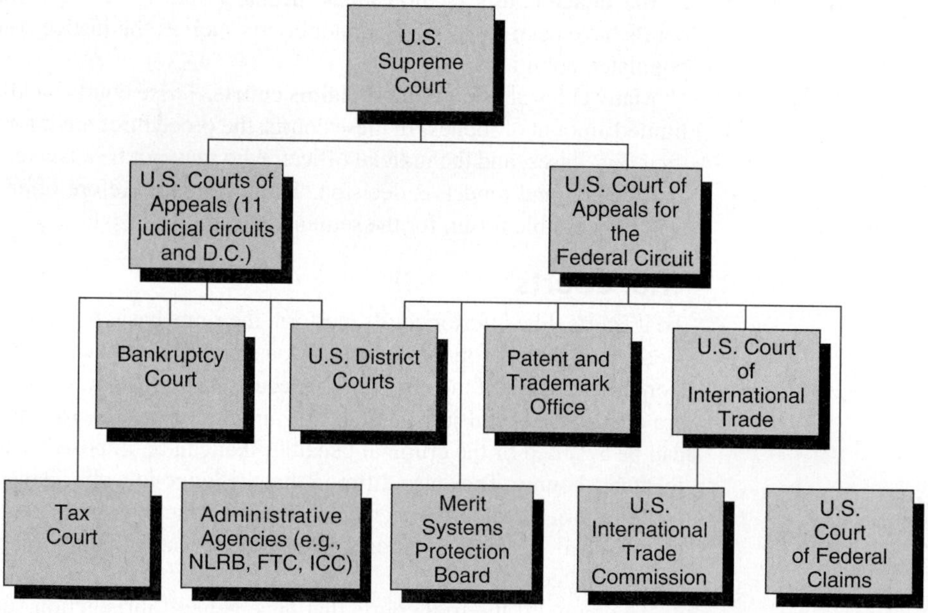

[3]In New York and Maryland the highest court is called the court of appeals. New York's intermediate court is called the supreme court.

Diversity cases are those in which the parties to the dispute are citizens of different states. If the parties are from different states, and the amount involved in the dispute is $75,000 or more, the plaintiff may choose to bring suit in either state or federal court. If the plaintiff chooses to bring suit in state court, the defendant may petition to **remove** the case to federal court. Federal judges tend to have more prestige, so the federal courts attract, on the average, more competent judges. Another common reason for choosing a federal court is to obtain certain procedural advantages that may be available. This may make it easier to get jurisdiction over the defendant and force witnesses to testify. Lack of local bias is also more certain in federal court.

The federal courts generally apply state law in diversity cases. Where a state court has not developed a rule, the federal court will guess, based on past decisions in similar cases, how the highest court of that state would decide the case. There is a body of procedural law called **conflict of laws** that provides rules for a court to follow in deciding which state's law to apply.

District Court

With few exceptions, lawsuits brought in federal courts must be started in district courts. These are the federal trial courts. Like state trial courts, they have both fact-finding (by the judge or jury) and law-finding (by the judge) functions. There is at least one U.S. district court in each state. Most states have two districts; some have more. The number of judges assigned to a district depends on the caseload; some districts have only one judge. Almost all cases are heard by a single judge.

Special Courts

As Figure 2.2 shows, there are several specialized courts in the federal court system. Although the district courts may also hear such cases, contract claims against the United States may be brought in a special U.S. Claims Court. A U.S. Court of International Trade hears disputes over duties imposed on imported goods. The Tax Court hears appeals from decisions of the Internal Revenue Service, and bankruptcy cases are heard by the U.S. Bankruptcy Court, which is divided into the same districts as the district courts. Chapter 44 discusses in greater detail the work of the bankruptcy court.

Court of Appeals

An appeal from a district court is taken to a U.S. court of appeals. The appeal is ordinarily taken to the court of appeals for the region in which the district court is located (see Figure 2.3). Like state intermediate appellate courts, the U.S. courts of appeals generally do not have a fact-finding function. They only review the legal conclusions reached by lower federal courts. The courts of appeal also hear appeals from many federal administrative agency decisions.

There are 13 U.S. courts of appeal. Twelve of the circuit courts have general federal appellate jurisdiction. One of these serves the District of Columbia alone because so many appeals involving the federal regulatory agencies arise there. The other 11, as shown on the map, cover several states. Usually a case is heard by a panel of three judges, but some cases may be heard ***en banc,*** that is, by all the judges of that circuit. The 13th circuit, the U.S. Court of Appeals for the Federal Circuit, hears a wide variety of specialized appeals, including patent, copyright, and trademark matters; Claims Court decisions; and decisions by the Court of International Trade.

FIGURE 2.3
The Federal Judicial Circuits

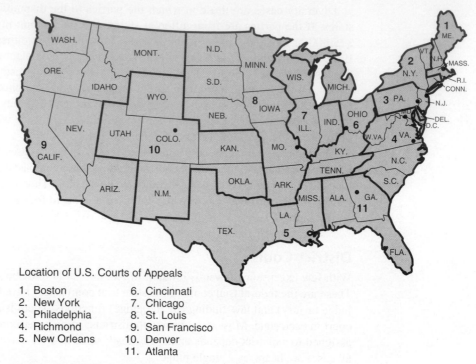

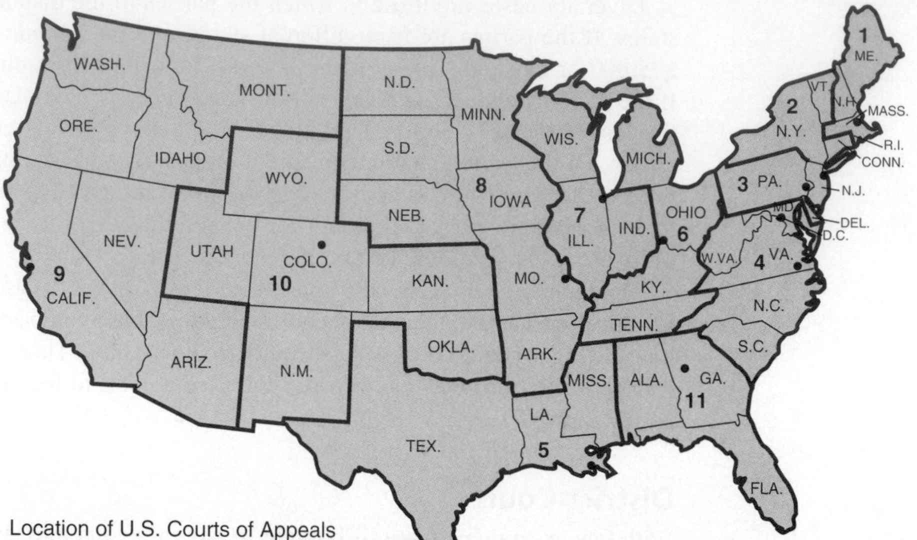

Location of U.S. Courts of Appeals

1. Boston
2. New York
3. Philadelphia
4. Richmond
5. New Orleans
6. Cincinnati
7. Chicago
8. St. Louis
9. San Francisco
10. Denver
11. Atlanta

District of Columbia: D.C. Circuit and Court of Appeals for Federal Circuit.

LO3

The Supreme Court

As the name implies, the U.S. Supreme Court is the highest court of the land. It has final responsibility for interpretation of the Constitution and federal statutes. However, the idea that a party who is dissatisfied with the decision of a lower court can always "take it all the way to the Supreme Court" is erroneous.

The primary way a case can be appealed to the Supreme Court is through **writ of certiorari (cert.).** Hearing such cases is entirely discretionary with the Court. If there have been conflicting decisions in similar cases by different courts of appeals, the Court may grant *cert.* It may also grant *cert.* in a case from the highest court of a state where a right is claimed under the Constitution or where the validity of a federal statute is in question.

Because most appeals to the Court involve its *certiorari* jurisdiction, and relatively few of these are heard, the Court decides only a small percentage of the cases appealed to it. If the Court does hear a case, a long opinion is usually published. In most cases the justices do not all agree. Then there may be a **concurring opinion,** which states the reasoning of those who agree with the result but not the rationale of the majority, and/or a **dissenting** (minority) **opinion.** These opinions do not have the force of the law and cannot be cited as precedent.

The Adversary System

American courts, following the British practice, operate on the **adversary system**—trial through a battle of words between two lawyers. The adversary system represents the idea that truth is best discovered through the presentation of competing ideas. Each lawyer acts as the advocate of his or her client. It is the lawyer's job to present the client's view of the sfacts to the judge, or to the jury if one is used. The lawyer tries to persuade them not only that the client's version is correct but also that the other party's view of the facts, to the extent that it is inconsistent, is in error. The lawyer also seeks to persuade the judge that the law favors the party he or she represents. Trickery or dishonesty by the lawyer in carrying out the advocacy role is improper and may result in disbarment or fines against the wrongdoing lawyer.

The Function of the Judge

The judge's role, under the adversary system, is viewed as not only unbiased but also essentially passive. The trial judge is to keep order in the court and, when a jury is present, to see that the lawyers do not use improper methods to influence the jury. In essence, a trial judge acts as a referee. Generally, the judge stops questions from lawyers or orders witnesses to change their behavior only when asked to do so by one of the lawyers. He or she need not be totally passive, however. The judge is responsible for the correct application of the law to the facts of the case and instructs the jury regarding the law.

This differs from the judge's role in most European countries and other jurisdictions that originally derived their law from the Roman Code. In these systems, judges have a duty to direct the search for truth rather than expecting it to emerge from the efforts of the lawyers for the parties. Therefore, they assume a much more active role in directing proceedings in the court, in requesting certain evidence, and in questioning witnesses.

LO4

Advantages and Disadvantages

Advocates of the adversary system believe that truth is most effectively determined as a result of each lawyer presenting his or her client's "case" through witnesses, and that deception and misperception are best exposed through cross-examination. In addition, the system makes it more difficult for a dishonest or biased judge to control the outcome of a case. Critics argue that honest witnesses can be confused by hostile questioning. They say that the system does not work when the opposing lawyers are of unequal skill. This gives an advantage to the wealthy, who can hire better lawyers. Furthermore, the competition to win can encourage suppression of unfavorable facts and overstatement, if not misstatement, of the truth.

Procedure

The Functions of Procedure

Procedural law is the body of legal rules governing the conduct of a case. Rules of procedure are complex and technical. The basic purpose of procedure is fairness. The nonlawyer needs to know only enough of this body of law to be able to understand the progress of a case through the courts. The procedure in criminal cases differs somewhat from that in civil cases. Here we will focus on civil procedure.

LO5

Pleadings

The complaint, answer, and reply, each of which is discussed below, are known as the **pleadings.** These are the first documents filed with the court, and they start and define the lawsuit. They serve two major functions: They inform the parties of each other's claims, and they form the basis for a trial. Only those matters that are disputed in the pleadings are tried in court. If a fact material to the case has been omitted from the pleadings, a court may permit a party to amend the pleading. Many courts, including federal courts, allow the documents to be filed electronically.

Wal-Mart Stores, Inc. v. Dukes

131 S.Ct. 2541 (U.S. Sup. Ct. 2011)

FACTS

A class made up of 1.5 million current or former employees of Wal-Mart sued the company for sex discrimination. They alleged the managers of individual stores exercised their discretion over pay and promotions disproportionately in favor of men, and the company's refusal to control the discretion was a violation of Title VII of the Civil Rights Act of 1964. The lower courts founds that there was sufficient commonality of the claims that a class action was appropriate, and allowing it would not deny Wal-Mart of its ability to defend itself.

ISSUE

Is there sufficient commonality to allow a class action?

DECISION

No. A party seeking class certification must show that the class has common questions of law or fact. The truth or falsity of the claim must be able to be resolved so that it goes to the central issue of each one of the claims in one stroke. Here, the commonality claim is that Wal-Mart engages in a pattern of discrimination. This necessitates that it be proved in each of the millions of employment decisions at once. There is insufficient proof that the employer operated under a general policy of discrimination. Wal-Mart's announced policy forbids discrimination and the company has penalties for denials of equal opportunity. In a company of Wal-Mart's size and geographic scope, it is unlikely that all managers would exercise their discretion in a common way without some common direction. There is insufficient evidence of that here.

Lawsuits can have more than one plaintiff and/or defendant. Sometimes, when a defendant's actions have injured many plaintiffs, their claims may be consolidated into a **class action** lawsuit. Class actions protect against repetitious claims that could result in inconsistent results if tried individually. Also, it allows individual plaintiffs to redress claims that might otherwise be too small to pursue.

One or more members of a class may sue or be sued as representative of a class if (1) the class is so numerous that joinder of all members is impracticable, (2) there are questions of law or fact common to the class, (3) the claims or defenses of the representative parties are typical of the claims or defenses of the class, and (4) the representative parties will fairly and adequately protect the interests of the class. Some of these issues are involved in the *Wal-Mart* case.

There have been numerous complaints that many class action lawsuits have harmed both class members with legitimate claims and defendants that have acted responsibly. For instance, in many cases the class's attorneys were awarded large fees while the class members received only coupons or other awards of little or no value. Further, state and local courts have been accused of keeping cases of national importance out of federal court, sometimes acting in ways that demonstrated bias against out-of-state defendants. In 2005, Congress passed the **Class Action Fairness Act** (CAFA) in response to these concerns and concerns that the actions were undermining the national judicial system, the free flow of interstate commerce, and the concept of diversity jurisdiction.

The CAFA addresses the concern that plaintiffs' attorneys have abused the class action mechanism to the detriment of class members by limiting the amount of fees the attorneys may receive in cases where a proposed settlement provides for recovery of coupons by class members to the amount of coupons actually redeemed by plaintiffs. Additionally, the judge must hold a hearing and make a written finding that the settlement is fair, reasonable, and adequate for class members. Courts may also require the distribution of unclaimed coupons to charitable or governmental organizations. CAFA also bans favoritism to certain plaintiffs through greater payments to some based on geographic proximity. Finally, CAFA generally requires that the suits be heard in federal court if there is diversity of citizenship and the amount in controversy exceeds $5 million.

In order to save court resources, consolidated arbitration is also being implemented. The arbitrator must decide if consolidation was within the intent of the arbitration clause.

The Complaint

The first step in starting a lawsuit is the filing of a **complaint** with the court. Information about the claim of the plaintiff and the remedy requested, usually damages of a certain amount, are listed in numbered paragraphs (see Figure 2.4). The complaint must contain sufficient facts to show that the plaintiff is entitled to some legal relief and to give the defendant reasonable notice of the nature of the plaintiff's claim. No evidence will be permitted to be given at a trial that is not related to a material fact stated in the complaint.

Summons

The serving of a **summons** on the defendant gives notice to the defendant of the suit, informs him or her who the plaintiff is, and states the time within which the defendant must make an **appearance** (see Figure 2.5). In most states the complaint must be served with the summons.

The rules regarding the service of the summons vary widely. Generally, it is served by the sheriff or other appropriate public official, and only within the geographic limits of the court's jurisdiction. In state courts this is normally a county. In some types of cases, service by mail or by leaving the summons at the defendant's residence or place of business is allowed.

The defendant usually makes an appearance by filing an **answer** to the complaint. This is ordinarily done by defendant's attorney. If the defendant fails to appear, the plaintiff is entitled to a **default judgment.** This has the same effect as if the plaintiff had won in court everything requested in the complaint.

The Answer

The answer generally responds to the complaint paragraph by paragraph. Each **allegation** (statement) of the complaint is admitted or denied, or the defendant may disclaim knowledge and leave the plaintiff to prove the allegations made (see Figure 2.6).

The answer may also state an **affirmative defense.** An affirmative defense is a rule of law enabling the defendant to win even if all of the plaintiff's allegations are true. For example, the plaintiff may allege that the defendant breached their contract. The defendant might respond by admitting that the contract had been breached but that he or she should not be held liable because the contract had been induced by the plaintiff's fraudulent misrepresentations. The defendant's affirmative defense must be supported by facts presented in the same manner as in a complaint.

The defendant can also **counterclaim** for damages. A counterclaim is a new claim stating that plaintiff owes defendant damages because of harm resulting from the incident alleged in the complaint. In the above example, defendant might claim that plaintiff's fraud caused several hundred dollars' worth of damages for which the plaintiff should be liable.

The defendant may make a **motion to dismiss** the case rather than give an answer. If it is clear that the plaintiff has no case, it would be wasteful for the case to continue, and the motion would be granted. The ground for such a motion might be that the facts given in the plaintiff's complaint are not legally sufficient to "state a cause of action"—that is, even if the facts alleged can be proved, the law does not give a remedy for the type of injury alleged. For example, Bill sues the local school system because it gave him a high school diploma but

FIGURE 2.4 **Complaint**

UNITED STATES DISTRICT COURT
SOUTHERN DISTRICT OF INDIANA
INDIANAPOLIS DIVISION

JOHN SMITH	)	
	)	
Plaintiff	)	
	)	
v.	)	CIVIL ACTION NO. IP 79-53-C
	)	
WORLD PRESS, INC.,	)	
and HERBERT MILLER	)	
	)	
Defendants	)	

PLAINTIFF'S COMPLAINT

Plaintiff, for his complaint, states:

1. Plaintiff is a citizen of the State of Indiana. Defendant World Press, Inc., is a Delaware corporation incorporated under the laws of the State of Delaware having its principal place of business in New York, N.Y. Defendant Herbert Miller is the author of the book *40 Seconds and Death* and is a citizen of the State of New York. The matter in controversy exceeds, exclusive of interests and costs, Seventy-Five Thousand Dollars ($75,000.00). Jurisdiction is based upon diversity of citizenship.
2. Defendant World Press, Inc., owns, operates, and publishes books under the name of World Press.
3. During 2003, defendant World Press, Inc., published without plaintiff's prior knowledge or consent, and expressly against plaintiff's permission, in excess of one million copies of the book *40 Seconds and Death*, authored by defendant, Herbert Miller, which contained within Chapter Four (4) a section entitled "Weekend Tryst." This book unnecessarily exposed to the public the private affairs of the plaintiff, John Smith. A copy of said chapter is attached hereto as Exhibit One (1).
4. Said chapter disclosed private facts that would be offensive to a reasonable person and were not of legitimate public interest or concern. Defendant World Press, Inc., and defendant Herbert Miller knew that the plaintiff did not want the matters contained in the chapter to be exposed to the general public and published said chapter over the expressed warnings of the plaintiff.
5. Defendant Herbert Miller was personally told by the plaintiff that he did not want to be quoted by defendant Herbert Miller nor did plaintiff want any reference to plaintiff's family or relatives to appear in any publication. The matters published were culled from a private conversation and amount to an unwarranted intrusion into the plaintiff's private life.
6. Defendant Herbert Miller misled the plaintiff to his detriment by publishing matters of a personal nature without securing the plaintiff's consent. The article exposed private matters concerning plaintiff's marital difficulties and his intimate relationships with family members.
7. The identity of the plaintiff was altered in the book, but the name used in the publication made the plaintiff's true identity readily apparent to neighbors, friends, relatives, business associates, and other members of the community who read the book.
8. As a direct and proximate result of the publication of said book the plaintiff has suffered great mental anguish and humiliation. Relatives of the plaintiff who had been purposely kept unaware of the marital difficulties existent between plaintiff and his wife were notified of same upon reading the book. The plaintiff has become the subject of public curiosity and gossip in his community, and his business affairs have been adversely affected. The plaintiff is a reasonable person of ordinary sensibilities who has been justifiably aggrieved by virtue of having his private life exposed by this publication in a manner constituting an actionable invasion of privacy.

(continued)

FIGURE 2.4 *(concluded)*

9. Defendant World Press, Inc., and defendant Herbert Miller maliciously intended to injure and aggrieve the plaintiff by thrusting on him unwarranted and undesirable publicity and notoriety, knowing that the plaintiff did not wish the matters contained in the chapter to be published. The plaintiff seeks punitive damages of Five Hundred Thousand Dollars ($500,000.00).

WHEREFORE, plaintiff prays for judgment against the defendant World Press, Inc., and Herbert Miller as follows:

1. General damages of One Million Dollars ($1,000,000.00);
2. Special damages as may hereafter be ascertained;
3. Punitive damages of Five Hundred Thousand Dollars ($500,000.00);
4. Costs of this action;
5. Compensation for reasonable attorneys' fees;
6. Such other and further relief as the Court may deem proper in the premises.

QUIK & BONO

By: Quik and Bono

Attorneys for Plaintiff,
John Smith

taught him to read only at a fifth-grade level. Even if this is true, the law does not allow suits for educational malpractice, so the case would be dismissed.

Reply

In some jurisdictions, the plaintiff is allowed or required to **reply** to the defendant's affirmative defense or counterclaim. The reply answers paragraph by paragraph the affirmative defense or counterclaim of the defendant.

Discovery

The **discovery** phase of a lawsuit is the time during which the parties gather the evidence they will use at trial to prove or disprove the allegations made in the pleadings. Modern rules of discovery are designed to ensure that both parties have equal access to the facts so that the case can be judged on its merits. Thus, an attorney can request a copy of almost any relevant document, electronic file, photograph, or other type of evidence that the opposite party might rely on or that, if available, would help the lawyer's case. The limits of discovery are set by the trial judge according to the procedural rules of the jurisdiction.

There are many kinds of discovery. For example, in a claim for physical or emotional injuries, the plaintiff can be required to undergo physical or mental examinations. A party may also take depositions from the opposite party and key witnesses. A *deposition* is an examination under oath, much like the questioning at a trial, in the presence of the attorney for the other party. Or a party may be required to answer written questions called *interrogatories,* which are answered in writing, under oath. New rules regarding e-discovery are being developed.

FIGURE 2.5 **Summons**

UNITED STATES DISTRICT COURT
SOUTHERN DISTRICT OF INDIANA
INDIANAPOLIS DIVISION

JOHN SMITH)
)
Plaintiff)
)
v.) CIVIL ACTION NO. IP 79-53-C
)
)
WORLD PRESS, INC.,)
and HERBERT MILLER)
)
Defendants)

SUMMONS

To Above Named Defendants ____________________

You have been sued by the person(s) named "plaintiff" in the court stated above.

The nature of the suit against you is stated in the complaint which is attached to this document. It also states the demand which the plaintiff has made and wants from you.

You must answer the complaint in writing, by you or your attorney, within twenty (20) days, commencing the day after you receive this summons, or judgment will be entered against you for what the plaintiff has demanded. You have twenty-three (23) days to answer if this summons was received by mail. Such Answer Must Be Made in Court.

If you have a claim for relief against the plaintiff arising from the same transaction or occurrence, you must assert it in your written answer.

Date November 12, 2005

Oliver M. Jones
Clerk (Seal)

Guik and Bono
Attorneys for Plaintiff

430 S. Walnut St.

Bloomington, IN 47401

Telephone 812-336-0000

FIGURE 2.6 **Answer**

UNITED STATES DISTRICT COURT
SOUTHERN DISTRICT OF INDIANA
INDIANAPOLIS DIVISION

JOHN SMITH	)	
	)	
Plaintiff	)	
	)	
v.	)	CIVIL ACTION NO. IP 79-53-C
	)	
WORLD PRESS, INC.,	)	
and HERBERT MILLER	)	
	)	
Defendants	)	

DEFENDANTS' ANSWER

Defendants World Press, Inc., and Herbert Miller make the following answer to Complaint of plaintiff John Smith.

First Defense

1. They admit the allegations of paragraph 1, except deny that Herbert Miller is a citizen of New York. He is a citizen of Maine.
2. They admit that World Press, Inc., publishes books under the name World Press. They deny all other allegations of paragraph 2.
3. They admit that during 2003 World Press, Inc., published a book entitled *40 Seconds and Death* authored by Herbert Miller and that the book contained in its Chapter 4 a section entitled "Weekend Tryst." They admit that Exhibit One (attached to plaintiff's Complaint) is a copy of that section of the book. They deny all other allegations of paragraph 3.

4, 5, 6. They deny the allegations of paragraphs 4, 5, and 6.

7. They admit that plaintiff's real name was not used in the book. They are without knowledge or information sufficient to form a belief as to the truth of the remaining allegations of paragraph 7.

8, 9. They deny the allegations of paragraphs 8 and 9.

Second Defense

Plaintiff John Smith consented to the publication of the information complained of.

Third Defense

The information published by defendants relates to an event and topic of general and public interest. Defendants' publication of the information complained of was privileged by the First and Fourteenth Amendments to the United States Constitution and by Article I, Section 9, of the Indiana Constitution.

(continued)

FIGURE 2.6 *(concluded)*

Fourth Defense

The information published by defendants is true or substantially true in all relevant respects.

WHEREFORE, defendants World Press, Inc., and Herbert Miller pray that plaintiff John Smith take nothing by his complaint, for their costs, and for all other proper relief.

Roger P. Rogers
Attorney for Defendants
World Press, Inc., and Herbert Miller

Pretrial Conference

A procedural device that is designed to narrow issues to be proved at trial or to facilitate a settlement is the **pretrial conference.** It was created to help deal with the increasing congestion in most civil courts. The conference is held in the judge's chambers. The parties themselves and their witnesses are not present because the conference is likely to go better if the parties are represented by intermediaries.

At the conference the judge tries to get the parties' attorneys to **stipulate to** (agree to) as many of the material facts as possible. The judge may find that, in spite of the appearance of the pleadings, there is no true disagreement on some important facts. For example, in an automobile accident case there may be no real issue as to whether the defendant was negligent; the only real question may be whether the plaintiff has suffered permanent disability and what value should be put on it. It saves much court time if the parties stipulate to the facts about the collision.

The judge may also try to persuade the parties to settle the case before trial. By suggesting the difficulty of proving some of the facts alleged in the pleadings and the uncertainty of what decision the jury will render, the judge may get the parties to conclude that they would rather settle than fight in court.

The Trial

Setting the Case for Trial

Once the pleadings are complete, the case is set for trial on the court calendar. Because of congestion, there may be a delay of several months or even years before the trial occurs. Fortunately, most cases are settled before trial, or the congestion would be much worse. Frequently, cases have to be **continued** (postponed) and another date set for any one of several reasons. For example, it may be that another trial has lasted longer than expected or a necessary witness is unavailable.

If a jury is requested, arrangements must be made to have prospective jurors present at the time the trial is scheduled to begin. The jury list is drawn by chance from a list of eligible citizens. Judges differ as to their willingness to accept excuses from prospective jurors who desire to avoid this duty of citizenship. If neither party requests a jury, the judge will hear the case, making separate findings of fact and law in reaching a judgment.

Opening the Case

After the jury, if any, is selected and sworn, the attorneys make **opening statements,** with plaintiff's attorney going first. The attorneys explain the nature of the case and what they intend to prove. The opening statements are more elaborate and probably more dramatically presented when a jury is present than if the case is tried before only a judge.

Presentation of Testimony

The plaintiff's attorney then presents the evidence through witnesses and exhibits. Each witness is sworn and then examined by the plaintiff's attorney; this is called **direct examination.** The defendant's attorney may **cross-examine** each witness, trying to raise doubts as to the person's credibility or trustworthiness. The plaintiff's attorney may then conduct a **redirect examination** to clarify the plaintiff's view of the facts and perhaps to minimize whatever negative effect was created in the cross-examination.

During a witness's testimony, the opposing attorney may object to the presentation of certain evidence. The judge then decides whether the evidence is admissible under the rules of evidence. These rules are designed to ensure that evidence is accurate, nonprejudicial, and legally relevant.

Following the end of testimony by witnesses for the plaintiff, the defendant's lawyer frequently makes a motion for a **directed verdict.** The judge grants the motion only if the plaintiff's evidence is clearly insufficient to support his or her allegations. If the motion is granted, the trial ends. Usually the motion is denied, however, and the trial continues. There is then direct examination of the defendant's witnesses by the defendant's attorney, followed by cross-examination. This is again usually followed by a motion for a directed verdict.

Closing the Case

The attorneys then make closing arguments that sum up the case. Normally the defendant's attorney goes first. This gives the plaintiff, who has the **burden of proof,** the last word. The burden of proof for a criminal case is different from that for a civil case. In a criminal case the state, as plaintiff, must convince the fact finder—jury or judge—**beyond a reasonable doubt** of the defendant's guilt. In a civil case the plaintiff need only have the **preponderance of the evidence** on his or her side. This means that the plaintiff must have shown that it is more likely than not that what was alleged is true.

If there is a jury, the judge instructs it on the law applicable to the case. The attorneys for the parties suggest instructions, tailoring them to the facts as they hope the jury will find them. The judge need not use the proposed instructions since giving proper instructions is her or his responsibility. In many states standard instructions have been developed for common types of cases.

After being instructed, the jury goes to the jury room, where it discusses the case, determines the facts, and applies the law to these facts as instructed by the judge. Ballots are taken until a verdict is reached. In important criminal cases involving much public interest and discussion, the jury may be **sequestered.** This means that jurors are not permitted to leave the supervision of the court, day or night, until excused. This is to keep outside influences away. Once there is unanimous agreement (or whatever majority is required by law) on a verdict, the jury foreperson reports this to the judge. If the jury cannot come to a verdict, there is a **hung jury.** Then a decision must be made by the plaintiff (or the prosecutor in a criminal case) whether to bring the case to trial again.

Whichever way the jury finds, the losing party in a civil case can make a motion for **judgment notwithstanding the verdict (judgment n.o.v.).** This is a claim that no reasonable jury could come to that verdict on the basis of the evidence presented at the trial. Such a motion is rarely granted. The state cannot make such a motion if the defendant is acquitted in a criminal case.

Enforcing the Judgment

At the conclusion of the trial (or after the appeal, if one is taken), the party who wins a remedy is entitled to receive it. In a civil case, this is usually an award of money damages. If the loser does not pay the judgment, the winner can get the court's help to enforce it through the issuance of a writ of execution or a writ of garnishment. A **writ of execution** orders the sheriff to seize and sell enough of the defendant's property to satisfy the judgment. All states have *exemption laws* that exempt certain classes and amounts of a debtor's property from execution. A **writ of garnishment** is designed to reach things belonging to the debtor that are in the hands of third parties, such as wages, bank accounts, and accounts receivable. Garnishment proceedings, like execution sales, are highly regulated by statute. When the property needed to satisfy the judgment is in another state, the plaintiff will have to use the garnishment or execution procedures of that state. Under the U.S. Constitution, the second state is required to give "full faith and credit" to the judgment of the state in which the trial occurred.

Where the court has awarded an equitable remedy such as an injunction, the losing party may be found in **contempt of court** and subjected to a fine or imprisonment if he or she fails to obey the court's orders.

Appellate Procedure

LO6

Basis for Appeal

Being dissatisfied with the judgment of the court is not a sufficient ground for an appeal. To be able to appeal, a party must claim that the court made an *error of law* or that the evidence in the trial did not support the trial court's decision. For example, if an attorney objects to a question asked of a witness by the other attorney, the judge must rule on it. This ruling can serve as a basis for appeal by the party against whom the ruling was made. Or the losing party might claim the judge misstated the law in the instructions to the jury. In order to serve as a basis for appeal, the attorney must have *objected* to the judge's action at the time the alleged error was made. This is to give the trial judge a chance to correct the error and avoid the possible expense of a new trial.

The Appeal

To appeal, the party must file an appeal with the proper appellate court within the period of time established by statute. A **transcript** of the entire trial proceeding, including the testimony of all the witnesses and any discussions between the judge and the attorneys, must be prepared and forwarded to the appeals court. The attorneys for each party also submit a **brief,** or written argument supporting their claims. *Citations* (references) are made to precedent cases and perhaps to *treatises* (textbooks) or articles written by legal scholars. When people or groups other than the parties involved are interested in the outcome of a certain appeal, they may request to be permitted to file *amicus curiae* (friend of the court) briefs.

The appellate process is essentially based on written documents. The appellate courts hear no witnesses and gather no new evidence. Although attorneys for the parties often ask to make oral arguments to supplement the written briefs, permission is not always granted. If the court allows the attorneys to argue orally, they are given only a limited amount of time in which to do so, and the judges frequently interrupt to ask questions. The facts as found by the jury (or judge) at the trial are accepted as true. An exception occurs when it is claimed that there was no competent evidence at the trial to support a finding of fact or the granting or refusal of a motion by the court. For example, an appellate court would have to review the evidence presented at the trial when the error by the trial judge is alleged to be a failure to grant a motion for a directed verdict. The transcript of the trial is used for this purpose. If there is doubt, it is assumed that the trial judge who heard the witnesses made the correct assessment.

Results of Appeal

In order to successfully appeal, the party must show that the errors that were made were **material,** that is, important enough to possibly change the trial outcome. The large majority of appeals are not successful. This is primarily because most errors made at trial are not material; the result would have been the same even if the error had not been made.

Decisions of the appellate courts are based on majority rule. Once a decision is reached, the judges generally write an opinion explaining their legal reasoning. These opinions are published and form the basis of our legal system of precedent. The appeals court may **affirm** (uphold) the judgment of the trial court, or it may **reverse** it. Sometimes a court may reverse and **remand.** This sends the case back to the trial court for further proceedings, and a new trial is then required. It may be remanded on a very narrow question of fact, or it may be a complete retrial of the case. Frequently the parties settle their controversy at this point rather than going through another trial.

Concept Summary: Stages of a Lawsuit

Pleading Stage	Discovery Stage	Trial Stage	Appellate Stage
Complaint	Types of discovery:	Selection of jury	Filing of appeal
Answer	Deposition	Opening statements	Transcript and briefs filed
Reply	Request for admissions	Cases in chief	Oral argument if permitted
	Written interrogatories	Closing arguments	Opinion rendered
	Production of documents	Instructions to jury	
	Request for physical examination	Verdict	
	Request for mental examination	Judgment	
	Electronic discovery	Enforcement (writ of execution of garnishment)	
	Pretrial conference		

Court Problems and Proposed Solutions

Some Criticisms

Like most institutions, the courts are the subject of much criticism. As mentioned earlier, one of the greatest problems is delay. It is often said, "Justice delayed is justice denied." A victim of an automobile collision who cannot get a trial on his or her claim for damages for two, three, or five years may be financially ruined before the losses can be recovered.

Another major criticism is that today courts are trying to deal with cases that they are ill equipped to handle. Examples are cases that involve solving social problems such as racial discrimination in the public schools and inhumane conditions in state prisons or mental institutions. A lawsuit is filed because a person claims his constitutional or other legal rights have been invaded. However, many people question whether the adversary process is the best way of dealing with these complicated problems. Should judges serve as school superintendents? Not in an ideal world; but what if the school board fails or refuses to end the discrimination? A traditional role of the courts is to prevent violence by providing an alternative, peaceful, and more just means of resolving disputes. Critics may well be asked how else or better the interests of the weak and powerless, whether minorities, prisoners, or others, can be protected.

Proposals

One proposal to solve the problems of congestion and delay is to remove whole classes of cases from courts. In most states this has been done for automobile accidents, which used a large proportion of court time. They are now handled on a "no fault" basis in most circumstances. Product liability cases (involving injuries and losses caused by defective products) and malpractice claims against doctors and other professionals are rapidly growing in number. Often the cost of bringing suit, including attorneys' fees, eats up more than half the damage award in these kinds of cases. It has been suggested that these cases could be handled as well or better by administrative agencies, much as workers' compensation cases now are. It has also been proposed (and implemented in many states) that noncontested divorces and distributions of the property of deceased persons be handled administratively.

Other devices have been developed to speed trials and make courts more efficient. These range from computerizing the court, to electronic filing, to severely limiting postponements and/or discovery, to limits on expert witnesses. These devices have some beneficial effects, but they cannot solve the basic problem as long as our society continues to be litigious and inadequate resources are allocated to the courts. One thing seems certain—people will increasingly resort to the use of alternatives to the courts as long as litigation remains so slow and expensive.

Questions and Problem Cases

1. What are the main differences between a trial and an appellate court?
2. Describe two types of discovery.
3. Explain the difference between the judge's role in the adversary system and the role in a code system common in Europe.
4. Explain the difference between mediation and arbitration.
5. What is the plaintiff's burden of proof in a civil case? Who decides whether the plaintiff has met this burden?
6. Wong signed a cell phone contract with T-Mobile. It contained an arbitration clause and a waiver of class action suits. He later filed a class action suit against T-Mobile alleging that the company overcharged for services in violation of the Michigan Consumer Protection Act. Wong's damages were $19.74. However, when other T-Mobile users are included, the alleged amount that was improperly collected could be millions. T-Mobile asked the court to compel arbitration and not allow a class action because of the contract clause. Must Wong arbitrate his claim and thus be barred from bringing a class action?
7. Connie, a resident of Michigan, was visiting her grandmother in California. While dining at a restaurant, a light fixture fell and severely cut Connie's arm. Connie required surgery and several months of physical therapy before she was able to use her arm properly, and she still has residual damage. She sues the restaurant, asking for $500,000 to reimburse medical expenses, lost wages, and the permanent damage, and $500,000 for pain and suffering. Where can the lawsuit be heard, and why?

Chapter 3

Business Ethics and Corporate Social Responsibility

Learning Objectives

After you have studied this chapter, you should be able to:

1. Read an ethical argument and identify which of the four predominant ethical theories it characterizes.
2. Make an ethical argument according to each of the predominant ethical theories.
3. Clearly explain the four major limits on the ability of law to control corporate behavior.
4. Describe the weaknesses of each of the suggested ways in which one might define ethical behavior.
5. List three recommendations for making corporations more sensitive to outside concerns and explain the arguments against each reform.
6. Make an ethical decision by employing the four-step model for ethical decision making.

An explosion and fire on the oil-drilling rig, Deepwater Horizon, killed 11 workers and unleashed the world's worst oil spill. Oil pouring from the ruptured, undersea well devastated wildlife, fishing, and tourism across the U.S. Gulf Coast. As the country reeled from the enormity of the disaster, its initial shock gave way to outrage as investigations revealed the parade of failures that precipitated and/or exacerbated the catastrophe.

For instance, it appears that the explosion was caused by a methane gas surge when workers were temporarily capping the well. Normally, engineers would have

(continued)

used a heavy mud pack to protect against that risk. Questions thus arose as to why British Petroleum, the well's owner and overall operator, substituted much lighter (and less expensive) seawater for the mud compound. Further, British Petroleum's oil spill response plan (a requirement for governmental approval for deepwater drilling) was riddled with glaring omissions and errors. In essence, the plan simultaneously understated the risks of a deepwater leak and overstated the company's capability for containing such an event. Ultimately, the public wondered why the federal Minerals Management Service—the agency that regulates oil rigs—approved a plan that was so severely flawed.

- What ethical responsibilities do businesses owe to society?
- How does one determine whether conduct is or is not ethical?
- Why might a company understate the risks involved in its activities?
- What limits are there to the effectiveness of governmental regulation of corporate behavior?

Introduction

Scarcely a day goes by without some large-scale, corporate scandal headlining the news. The villains may change—from Enron to Lehman Brothers to Toyota to British Petroleum—but the underlying story is the same: Corporations and their executives race to line their pockets with cash at the expense of an unwitting world. Critics of capitalism and Corporate America shout that corporations maximize profits to the detriment of society. They demand a new corporate culture, arguing that businesses should follow a standard of ethical and socially responsible behavior much higher than that imposed by the existing rules of law. They want corporations to behave ethically and responsibly in their relations with consumers, employees, the communities in which they operate, and society generally. In short, they assert that businesses should go beyond the law and make their products safer than the law requires, only terminate employees for good cause, and not arbitrarily abandon communities that are economically dependent on them.

On the other side are those who argue that profit maximization should be the main goal of corporations and that the only ethical norms corporations should feel bound to follow are those embodied in society's laws. By maximizing profits, they say corporations ensure that scarce economic resources (e.g., iron ore, beef, oil) will be allocated to the uses society values most highly (e.g., automobiles, hamburgers, gasoline). The end result is that society as a whole benefits because its total economic welfare is maximized.

This chapter considers the range of difficult issues posed by the claim that corporations should act responsibly and ethically. The aim throughout this chapter is to present the most significant issues involved in the corporate social responsibility debate, not to resolve them. As you will quickly see, the corporate social responsibility question is exceedingly complex, and thus it is not easily resolvable. The debate is likely to continue for as long as private corporations form the backbone of our economic system.

Chapter Overview

This chapter begins by introducing four ethical theories that might guide decision makers in making ethical choices. It then focuses on one of those approaches—profit maximization—and balances it against arguments that corporate managers should look beyond the profit motive and consciously pursue socially responsible paths. As a part of this debate, the chapter looks at arguments why the law alone is not up to the task of curbing corporate abuses. Next, assuming that corporations should behave ethically, the chapter reinforces its earlier discussion of ethical theories by examining various opinions over how to identify what constitutes ethical conduct. That section is followed by an overview of three recommendations designed to make corporations more sensitive to outside values and concerns. Finally, the chapter sketches guidelines that managers might use when making important decisions.

Predominant Ethical Theories

This section examines four predominant theories of ethical conduct. In reading this material, please remember two things. First, this text in no way intends to endorse any particular theory. Second, it is unlikely that any level of argument will change the mind of someone who subscribes to a different ethical viewpoint. Still, it is important that you have a basic understanding of these approaches to ethical decision making. If you wish to be understood by and to influence someone from a different ethical underpinning than you have, you must be able to speak in the ethical language understood and accepted by that person.

Four ethical theories are presented in this chapter: rights theory, justice theory, utilitarianism, and profit maximization. Rights theory is known as a **deontological** ethical theory because it focuses on the actions or process, rather than the consequences. The other three approaches are **teleological** ethical theories because they focus on the consequences of a decision when deciding if it is ethical.

Consider the *Buck v. Bell* case briefly mentioned in the "Sociological Jurisprudence" section of Chapter 1. The Supreme Court decided that it was permissible to sterilize Carrie Buck because it believed the world would benefit from such an action. The Court said that "the public welfare may call upon the best citizens for their lives." This is an example of a teleological ethical theory. If any of you believed that the focus should have been Carrie Buck and that her bodily integrity could not be violated under any circumstances, you are espousing a deontological ethical theory.

Rights Theory

LO1 LO2

Rights theory subscribes to the view that certain human rights are fundamental and must be respected by other people. Thus, its primary focus is on each individual member of society and his or her rights. There are two primary categories of rights theory: Kantianism and the modern rights theories.

Kantianism

Unlike most rights theorists, Immanuel Kant was a strict deontologist. He viewed humans as moral actors that are free to make choices. Under his approach the morality of any action was determined by applying his *categorical imperative.* His first formulation of the categorical imperative is as follows: "Act only on that maxim whereby at the same time you can will that it shall become universal law." (Judge an action by applying it universally.)

Applying the first categorical imperative, you might avoid stealing from other people. This is because your theft could only pass the first categorical imperative if you were willing to have all people feel free to steal as well. Since this would threaten your future security, you would believe that your act of stealing would be ethically wrong. Would the court have sterilized Carrie Buck if it believed that, as a result, the states could freely sterilize any member of society?

Kant also developed a second categorical imperative. It states: "Always act to treat humanity, whether in yourself or in others, as an end in itself, never merely as a means." In short, this means that we should not manipulate others for our own self-interest.

Modern Rights Theories

The problem with Kantianism is that it believes that duties are absolute. Thus, lying or killing would be perceived as never ethically justifiable. Modern rights theorists believe that there may be circumstances when actions like lying and killing could be morally acceptable (i.e., self-defense). The modern rights theories respond to these perceived weaknesses in Kantianism. One popular theory believes that you should abide by a moral rule unless a more important rule conflicts with it. (Our moral compulsion is not to compromise a person's right unless a greater right takes priority over it.)

Of course, the modern rights theorists have choices to make. They must determine what the fundamental rights are and how they are ranked in importance. Much of the constitutional law analysis employed by U.S. courts in protecting individual rights from governmental interference engages in just this sort of analysis. Consider the following case. What are the competing rights? How does the court balance them?

Hart v. Electronic Arts

2013 U.S. App. LEXIS 10171 (3d Cir. 2013)

FACTS

Ryan Hart, a former quarterback for Rutgers University's football team, sued Electronic Arts for violating his right to publicity by using his likeness and biographical information in its NCAA Football series of videogames. Electronic Arts defended on the basis that, even if it had violated Hart's right to publicity, its actions were encompassed within its free speech rights which were protected by the First Amendment.

ISSUE

Should the court dismiss the right to publicity claim on First Amendment grounds?

DECISION

No. The protection afforded to videogames can be limited in situations where the right of free expression necessarily conflicts with other protected rights. This requires that we balance the interests underlying the right to free expression against the interests in protecting an individual's right to exploit his or her identity for commercial purposes. Basically, the balance between the right of publicity and First Amendment interests turns on whether the celebrity likeness is one of the "raw materials" from which an original work is synthesized, or whether the depiction or imitation of the celebrity is the very sum and substance of the work in question. We ask, in other words, *whether the product containing a celebrity's likeness is so transformed that it has become primarily the defendant's own expression rather than the celebrity's likeness.* Applying this test to the case at hand, we find that—based on the combination of both the digital avatar's appearance and the biographical and identifying information—the digital avatar does closely resemble the genuine article. The digital Ryan Hart does what the actual Ryan Hart did while at Rutgers: he plays college football, in digital recreations of college football stadiums, filled with all the trappings of a college football game. This is not transformative. We therefore hold that the videogames do not sufficiently transform Hart's identity to escape his right of publicity claim.

Justice Theory

LO1 LO2

Justice theory is derived from John Rawls's book *A Theory of Justice,* which argued for a just distribution of society's resources. This called for a fair allocation of society's benefits and burdens among all members of society. Under the *greatest equal liberty principle,* each person has an equal right to basic rights and liberties. The *difference principle* holds that social inequalities are acceptable only if they cannot be eliminated without making the worst-off class even worse off.

Under the justice theory, the decision maker's choices are to be guided by fairness and impartiality; however, the focus is on the outcome of the decision. Consider a company faced with a decision to continue its operations in the United States or to move production to India. In deciding on the course that allocates benefits and burdens most fairly, the company may move to India because the workers have fewer opportunities and safety nets there than do the workers in the United States.

Consider the following case where the court upholds an employment policy that discriminates against men. Why was this discrimination permitted? Can you think of a situation where the court would permit discrimination against women and in favor of men?

Everson v. Michigan Department of Corrections

391 F.3d 737 (6th Cir. 2004)

FACTS

The Michigan Department of Corrections (MDOC) barred males from working in certain positions at its female prisons. MDOC designated approximately positions in housing units at female prisons as "female only." The duties of COs and RUOs in the housing units include patrolling the sleeping, shower, and bathroom areas, attending to the basic needs of women prisoners (including the provision of sanitary supplies), monitoring activity in the living quarters, enforcing housing rules and procedures, and assuring that proper standards of care and hygiene are maintained.

ISSUE

Has MDOC illegally discriminated by refusing to consider male applicants for the positions in the female housing units?

DECISION

No. Federal law permits overt gender discrimination where sex is a bona fide occupational qualification (BFOQ) reasonably necessary to the normal operation of that particular business or enterprise. However, the defense is to be read narrowly and the burden is on an employer to establish a BFOQ defense. MDOC made a considered decision that a BFOQ was necessary to address the grave problem of sexual abuse of female inmates. MDOC's plan will significantly enhance the safety of inmates. Males perpetrate most of the sexual abuse in the female facilities. Given the endemic problem of sexual abuse in female prisons, MDOC's plan is reasonably necessary to the normal operation of its female prisons.

Utilitarianism

LO1 LO2

Under utilitarianism, an ethical decision is one that maximizes utility for society as a whole. Thus, in our individual decisions we should always calculate their costs and benefits for every member of society. An action is ethical only if the benefits to society outweigh their costs. This means that sometimes decision makers must sacrifice their own individual interests if doing so gives greater benefit to society.

Derived from the writings of Jeremy Bentham and John Stuart Mill, utilitarianism is a teleological theory that suggests that "the ends justify the means." Bentham phrased maximizing utility as achieving the greatest overall balance of pleasure over pain. Mill believed Bentham's characterization to be too narrow. He described it in broader terms, believing the definition of utility should include satisfactions such as health, knowledge, friendship, and aesthetic delights. He also believed that some satisfactions were more important than others.

Under *act utilitarianism,* the decision maker considers each action separately, assessing its costs and benefits to society. Under *rule utilitarianism* the action is viewed as part of a rule or habit. The appropriate balancing of costs and benefits is made in reference to the long-run consequences of the rule.

Many of the cases we have read, particularly in Chapter 1, where the judges considered public policy in issuing their decisions, appear utilitarian in nature. In fact, much of sociological jurisprudence, which involves framing a decision as part of a bigger puzzle, looks to be a utilitarian approach. Consider the discussion of the oil spill in the chapter opener. During the ensuing congressional investigation, Senator Lisa Murkowski of oil-rich Alaska asserted that the disaster "reminded us of a cold reality, the production of energy will never be without risk or environmental consequence." Is she calling for a utilitarian balancing?

Consider the next case. Can the employer make a reasonable argument that its actions were justified under utilitarianism?

Dewitt v. Proctor Hospital

517 F.3d 944 (7th Cir. 2008)

FACTS

Phillis Dewitt was a valuable employee at Proctor Hospital. Dewitt and her husband, Anthony, were covered under Proctor's health insurance plan. Throughout Dewitt's tenure at Proctor, Anthony suffered from prostate cancer and received expensive medical care. His covered medical expenses were paid by Proctor, which was partially self-insured. It paid for members' covered medical costs up to $250,000 per year. Anything above this "stop-loss" figure was covered by an insurance policy. Proctor confronted Dewitt about Anthony's high medical claims because they were unusually high. (Over a three-year period, his medical claims averaged over $100,000 per year.) Soon thereafter, Proctor fired Dewitt and designated her as "ineligible to be rehired in the future." Dewitt sued, alleging "association discrimination" under the Americans with Disabilities Act (ADA). Specifically, she alleges that Proctor fired her to avoid having to continue to pay for the substantial medical costs that were being incurred by her husband under Proctor's self-insured health insurance plan.

ISSUE

Has Dewitt stated a claim for association discrimination under the ADA?

DECISION

Yes. Because Proctor's unusually high "stop-loss" coverage didn't kick in until claims exceeded $250,000, it personally felt the heavy bite of Dewitt's expenses. That the powers-that-be at Proctor were interested specifically in the high cost of Anthony's medical treatment is obvious. Finally, the timing of Dewitt's termination suggests that the financial albatross of Anthony's continued cancer treatment was an important factor in Proctor's decision. One could reasonably conclude that Proctor, which faced a financial struggle of indeterminate length, was concerned that Anthony—a multi-year cancer veteran—might linger on indefinitely. Because Dewitt has established that direct evidence of association discrimination may have motivated Proctor in its decision to fire her, a jury should be allowed to consider her claim.

Profit Maximization

LO1 LO2

Profit maximization is a teleological theory that is based on the *laissez-faire* theory of capitalism first espoused by Adam Smith in the 18th century. It contends that business managers should maximize a business's long-run profits within the limits of the law. Unlike utilitarianism, profit maximization focuses exclusively on making a decision that maximizes profits for the manager and/or the organization. It believes that this focus ultimately will optimize total social utility.

Allocational Efficiency

Under this theory, the primary objective of a business corporation is to maximize profits. (As a general rule, management may consider objectives other than profit only if they do not interfere with the ultimate profit objective.) This objective has been promoted by economists on the grounds that it results in an *efficient allocation of society's scarce resources.* Firms that most efficiently use resources generally will be able to undersell their competitors and, due to the greater sales that should result, reap higher profits. As a result, they often will be able to outbid less-efficient resource users. Hence, scarce resources will be allocated efficiently—that is, to the users and uses most highly valued by consumers and most capable of giving consumers a maximum return on their expenditures. If corporate managers choose to pursue goals other than profit maximization, they claim that resources will not be put to their most efficient uses, and society's total wealth will be reduced.

To illustrate the last point, assume for the sake of argument that all the firms in the American steel industry spontaneously decide to observe pollution standards stricter than those now imposed by law. In addition, assume that they do so even though they know that their buyers may not automatically buy "responsibly" produced steel or be willing to pay more for such steel. Since socially responsible behavior of this sort costs money, the firms in question face a dilemma. They can attempt to pass on the increased costs to buyers in the form of higher prices, thus reducing the buyers' return per dollar spent and (possibly) their ability to purchase other goods and services. Or the firms can refuse to increase their prices and accept lower profits. In this case, dividends and employee salaries may have to be reduced, and the firms' ability to bid for scarce resources, like iron ore, may also suffer. The likely result is a flow of employees, investment funds, and resources away from these firms. This, in turn, may mean lower steel production and lower overall social wealth than would otherwise be the case. In either case, socially responsible behavior imposes unmistakable costs on society. Imagine the added costs that might befall the socially responsible companies (as well as society) if foreign steel producers refused to follow the responsible course taken by their American counterparts.

Criticism of Allocational Efficiency Rationale

Critics claim that allocational efficiency is not society's only (or even its most important) goal and that sometimes it must be sacrificed for other social concerns. This argument stresses that profit maximization can result in harm to employees, consumers, communities, the environment, and society as a whole. For example, corporations that leave a community when they find cheaper labor, favorable tax rates, and/or low-interest loans in another community may thereby enjoy increased profits, aid in the efficient allocation of scarce resources, and maximize total economic welfare. But this obviously is small consolation to the abandoned community, which may be left with little more than an empty factory shell. Even less likely to be consoled by these results are former employees who cannot find work or schoolchildren whose schools may be underfunded as a consequence of the erosion of the community's tax base.

Some defenders of profit maximization might agree that other social values sometimes outweigh allocational efficiency, or at least they might concede that the question is debatable. They would argue, however, that corporate managers need not concern themselves with questions of social responsibility because market forces and other private activity usually force business to behave in a responsible fashion.

The central point of this argument is that in a free society with a free economy people can organize to make their grievances felt. If a sufficient number do so, corporate behavior can be made more responsible without having managers abandon their basic profit maximization orientation. If such efforts fail because they do not attract sufficient support, this suggests that the complaints were not too valid in the first place. Or it may indicate that the consumers who did not "join up" decided that the costs of achieving success outweighed the benefits accruing from success.

It can be argued, therefore, that a way to motivate corporate behavior is to create compelling financial incentives for the desired conduct. For instance, the European Union, out of a concern over global warming, assesses heavy monetary fines against companies that exceed the cap it has placed on carbon emissions. As a result, company accountants began to view carbon as a liability that must be factored into share prices. However, EU rules grant each company tradable allowances for each ton of carbon it emits. Accordingly, companies may profit by selling their unused allowances to other firms that would otherwise be forced to refit their plants or shut down. Carbon emissions have thus become a measurable risk of doing business—similar to currency and interest rates. If they are not effectively managed, companies suffer where it hurts the most—at the bottom line. EU banks and insurance companies, recognizing this fact of business life, now factor climate risk into their decisions to extend loans or insurance coverage. Some banks actually loan money to companies that reduce emissions, take their tradable allowances, and sell them to other clients. This EU measure is based on the assumption that what it takes to ensure that corporations and their managers engage in ethical conduct is to give such action a measurable price.

Concept Summary: Ethical Theories

Deontological Theories (focus is on the decision itself)	Rights Theory (duty not to harm the fundamental rights of others)	Kantianism (strict deontology)
		Modern Rights Theories (mixed deontology)
Teleological Theories (focus is on the consequences of a decision)	Justice Theory (decisions are guided by fairness and impartiality)	
	Utilitarianism (maximize utility for society as a whole)	
	Profit Maximization (maximize a business's long-run profits)	

The Law as a Corporate Control Device

Profit maximization advocates often respond to complaints that they have no social responsibility agenda by pointing out that if irresponsible corporate behavior creates sufficient public dissatisfaction, the legal system will prohibit undesirable conduct. Just as a free society permits individuals and groups to put moral and economic pressure on corporations, it also allows them to make their desires felt in the political arena. Passage of the Sarbanes-Oxley Act seems to affirm this position. (That legislation has increased fines and civil damages for corporate wrongdoing by both U.S. and foreign businesses that register their securities on a stock exchange in the United States.) And while critics of such legislation may complain about particular forms of regulation, defenders of profit maximization always recognize that corporations have an obligation to obey the laws established by the legal system.

In fact, most of the scandals that dominated business news during the past few years would have been avoided if the executives involved had merely complied with the law. Further, recent survey data, as well as a string of court decisions involving corporations, their officers, and legal counsel, reveal a judicial willingness to more carefully scrutinize corporate decision making.

However, there are limits on the law's ability to control irresponsible corporate behavior. Four of these limitations are discussed in the next sections:

LO3

1. Corporate influence on the content of law.
2. Conscious lawbreaking.
3. Unknown harms.
4. Irrational corporate behavior.

To the extent that these weaknesses exist, they undermine the argument that profit maximization brings about the best interests of society and perhaps suggest that managers should consciously engage in socially responsible behavior.

Corporate Influence on the Content of the Law

One problem with the idea that the law is an effective corporate control device stems from the fact that business has a significant voice in determining the content of society's rules and regulations. Thus, the law frequently tends to reflect corporate interests. As a result, corporations are sometimes free to engage in behavior that noncorporate segments of society would find unethical.

The political influence exerted by large corporations is a familiar subject. Because of their size, resources, and sophistication, they have (or can purchase) the ability to influence legislation. Even if Congress or the state legislatures enact hostile regulatory legislation, corporations sometimes can blunt its impact. For example, they may use their political influence to reduce the funding received by the agency enforcing the legislation. Or they may *co-opt* the agency by persuading it to take a probusiness view. This commonly occurs through the frequent exchange of personnel between the agency and the industry it is intended to regulate.

More and more businesses are taking an active approach to government regulation. They have discovered that by initiating legislation they can

1. Head off the risk of later unpredictable lawsuits.
2. Influence the nature of the legislation—minimizing the risk of more extensive and costly regulations.
3. Ensure that all of their competitors are subject to the same constraints.

Refer back to the chapter opener and its discussion of the environmental disaster in the Gulf of Mexico. The Minerals Management Service—the government watchdog for oil-drilling safety—was discovered to have ceded most safety oversight to the drilling industry. In part, this was because the complexity of the offshore operations rendered the poorly funded regulators unable to competently carry out the oversight task. However, the agency also operated under a glaring conflict of interest. At the same time that it was supposed to police safety, it was charged with generating revenue from drilling on the outer continental shelf. In contrast, the United Kingdom has two separate governmental agencies involved in its offshore-drilling industry: One handles the safety oversight functions and another promotes revenue-generating aspects. The results seem to be that the United Kingdom has a far better safety record in the drilling industry.

Conscious Lawbreaking

Even where the legal rules do not reflect business interests, corporations may consciously decide that it makes sense to violate those rules. As rational actors with a desire to maximize profits, corporations may conclude that breaking the law poses acceptable risks if the benefits gained by doing so are great, the penalties for violation are relatively light, and/or the chances of being sued or prosecuted are low.

In recognition of this phenomenon, the Sarbanes-Oxley Act attempts to increase the likelihood of detection and prosecution and raises the penalties for illegal behavior. Specifically, it creates a five-member Public Company Accounting Oversight Board with the authority to regulate CPA firms that audit publicly traded corporations. (Two members of the board are certified public accountants.) The law also broadly defines obstruction of justice and makes obstruction of audit work papers a felony. Further, the law increases the penalties for illegal behavior. For instance, the maximum sentence for violations of securities laws has been doubled. It now is 20 years in prison. Further, the maximum criminal fine for individuals has been increased to $5 million, and the fine for companies is $25 million.

Corporate Disregard for Unpopular Laws

Several other factors increase the likelihood that corporations will engage in conscious or semiconscious lawbreaking. The "let's take the risk" mentality may be reinforced when the law is (or is perceived to be) uncertain. Corporate or industry norms may regard a measure of illegal (or borderline) behavior as morally acceptable. This is especially likely to be true when corporate managers regard the relevant legal rules as misguided.

For instance, an extremely controversial law, the Family and Medical Leave Act, provides covered employees with up to 12 weeks of unpaid family and medical leave each year. It has been estimated that at least 40 percent of employers have refused to comply with its terms. However, in recent years, courts have more strictly enforced the statute and have even held that supervisors may be held personally liable for violations of the law.

Ethics in Action

Are corporations the only persons who refuse to comply with unpopular laws? What about underage college students who use fake IDs in bars and liquor stores? From an ethical standpoint, is their behavior more or less ethical than people who profit from selling fake IDs? Students may wish to read *Millenium Club v. Avila,* 809 N.E.2d 906 (Ind. Ct. App. 2004), where the court permits a bar owner who had been fined for serving alcohol to underage drinkers (the drinkers had fake IDs) to sue the minors for fraud.

Unknown Harms

Exclusive reliance on market forces to control corporate behavior rests on the assumption that consumers always know when the environment is being degraded or their health is being threatened. Reliance on the law as a corporate control device involves a similar assumption, namely, that legislators and regulators possess similar knowledge. Clearly legal action to control socially harmful corporate behavior will not be forthcoming until the need for such action is apparent. Yet hardly a month goes by when we fail to learn that a product that we have used with perfect confidence for years has some newly discovered harmful side effects, or that some chemical commonly used in production processes poses risks to workers, consumers, or the environment.

In some such cases, after-the-fact legal action may simply be incapable of compensating for harms that have already occurred. Also, it is fairly obvious that corporate managers are often equally ignorant of the effects of their products or production processes. In some instances, however, corporate managers' intimate familiarity with their own products or production processes may make them aware of such dangers long before they are apparent to society in general.

This may have been the case with asbestos. We now know that repeated exposure to asbestos may bring on asbestosis and mesothelioma, a cancer of the mesothelial cells with a poor prognosis for recovery. Yet both of these medical conditions have a long latency period, perhaps as long as 50 years. When its former employees, suffering from these ailments, began bringing claims against Johns-Manville, an asbestos manufacturer, the company initially responded that any lawsuits were barred by statutes of limitations requiring claims to be brought within three years of exposure. The courts disagreed and permitted the claims to go through, ultimately bankrupting the company.

Still, by the time the dangers of exposure became apparent to the public and the lawsuits began to accumulate, the managers, directors, and shareholders of the company had long since retired or died. Thus, it is conceivable that the company, had it been fully aware of the danger lurking on the distant horizon, under a profit maximization philosophy, may have been willing to withhold this information from employees and customers.

Irrational Corporate Behavior

The final argument against the law's ability to control corporations contends that much of today's irresponsible behavior results from corporations' *inability* to *respond sensibly* to legal threats. The law's ability to affect business behavior depends on a clear perception of the penalties for illegal actions and a rational response to the resulting risk. To the extent that corporations fail these tests of clear perception and rational response, the law's ability to control them suffers.

Supporters of the view that corporations often act irrationally generally begin by noting that, as a rule, people are not especially perceptive and clearheaded. Everyone "blocks out" certain aspects of the external world, and the tendency to do so is much greater when the excluded information is troubling. Thus, for example, corporate managers planning a highly profitable venture may downplay potential legal problems because recognition of such potential problems would make the venture less attractive. In the chapter opener case, it appears that British Petroleum was behind schedule on its drilling rig and incurring heavy lease costs each day. Could this delay have led to a decision to minimize the risk of a methane surge when it substituted seawater for heavy mud during the packing procedure?

By combining the perceptual abilities of many people, it would seem that organizations should be able to correct individuals' deficiencies. But while this is often true, there are also certain features of organizational life that make accurate perception and rational response *less* likely. We will mention three such phenomena: risky shift, groupthink, and the tendency of bad news not to rise.

Risky Shift

Social psychologists and students of organizational behavior have long been aware of a phenomenon called **risky shift.** This means that a group of people who must reach a consensus on an acceptable level of risk often decide on a level of risk higher than the risk they would accept as individuals. Thus, the decisions made by a team of managers may create greater legal problems than decisions made by an isolated manager. Refer back to the chapter opener. Why didn't the engineers use the heavy mud pack that is standard for capping a well?

Groupthink

Also relevant here is the familiar phenomenon of **groupthink:** the tendency for members of a group to internalize the group's values and perceptions and to suppress critical thought. As a result, if our team of managers is planning a highly profitable venture to which the success of each team member is tied, each may minimize the venture's legal problems because these conflict with the group's goals.

Ethics in Action

GlaxoSmithKline, a British drug company, was accused of consumer fraud for allegedly withholding negative information and misrepresenting data about the effectiveness of prescribing the antidepressant drug Paxil to children. The company is charged with suppressing the results of four studies that indicated that the drug not only was ineffective in treating children but also increased the risk of suicidal thoughts. Glaxo-SmithKline claims that all of its studies were made available to the public. However, the lawsuit asserts that an internal company memorandum indicated that GlaxoSmithKline intended to "manage the dissemination of the data in order to minimize any potential negative commercial impact." Glaxo's revenue for Paxil prescriptions to children totaled $55 million. The government is seeking the return of all profits on those sales in its civil lawsuit. Was the company acting in a morally responsible manner? Could this case be an example of groupthink?

Concept Summary: Limitations on Legal Control of Corporate Behavior

Limitation	Cause	Result
Corporate Influence	Many corporations possess tremendous political power.	• Corporations blunt the effectiveness of many regulations. • They "capture" regulatory agencies.
Conscious Lawbreaking	• Many criminal penalties are too low. • Often the risk of detection and prosecution is low.	Breaking the law may pose an acceptable risk when: • Benefits from illegal activity are great. • Penalties are light. • Chance of being punished is small.
Unknown Harms	We are not always aware of what is dangerous.	After-the-fact legal action is incapable of compensating for many harms that have already occurred.
Irrational Corporate Behavior	• *Risky shift*—groups often accept higher risks than do individuals. • *Groupthink*—tendency to internalize group values and suppress critical thought. • *Bad news doesn't rise*—subordinates may hesitate to speak against actions favored by superiors.	Sanctions are ineffective if a corporation does not respond to them sensibly.

Consider the case of *Sperau v. Ford Motor Company,* 674 So.2d 24 (Ala. Sup. Ct. 1995). Ford officials, under pressure to comply with the company's minority dealer recruitment program, tried to persuade two African Americans to leave their construction business and open a Ford dealership. Ford falsely told them the vast majority of black dealers were successful in making a profit. It also withheld data that made clear that the return on investment for black dealers was substantially lower than the average for all dealers. Ford routinely withheld this information from black dealer candidates. Ultimately, when the men's dealership went bankrupt, they successfully sued Ford for fraud and deceit. Was the company's behavior rational?

Bad News Doesn't Rise

Somewhat similar to groupthink is another familiar feature of organizational life: the tendency "for bad news not to get to the top." When subordinates know that top managers are strongly committed to a particular course of action, they may not report problems for fear of angering their superiors. Ideally, of course, managers should desire to be fully informed of potential legal risks, but occasionally their response is to penalize the bearer of bad news instead.

In the next case, it is not clear if subordinates were intentionally failing to keep Acme's president up to date regarding sanitary conditions or if he was remiss in following through. However, in this landmark case on corporate officer liability, the U.S. Supreme Court makes it clear that the law demands that corporate officers erect organizational structures that ensure that important information rises to the top.

United States v. Park

421 U.S. 658 (U.S. Sup. Ct. 1975)

FACTS

Acme Markets is a national retail food chain with approximately 36,000 employees, 874 retail outlets, 12 general warehouses, and four special warehouses. Its headquarters, including the office of the president, Park, who is chief executive officer of the corporation, are located in Philadelphia, PA. The government charged Acme and Park with violations of the federal Food, Drug, and Cosmetic Act because food that was being held in Acme's Baltimore warehouse had been contaminated by rodents. Acme pleaded guilty; however, Park claimed that he was not guilty. Evidence at trial demonstrated that the FDA advised Park by letter of unsanitary conditions in Acme's Philadelphia warehouse. Soon thereafter, the FDA found that similar conditions existed at the company's Baltimore warehouse. A follow-up inspection, several months later, found that there had been improvement in the sanitary conditions, but that there was still evidence of rodent activity. Park related that, upon receipt of the FDA letter, he conferred with Acme's vice president for legal affairs, who informed him that the Baltimore vice president was investigating the situation immediately and would be taking corrective action to reply to the letter.

ISSUE

Is Park criminally liable for the violations of the act?

DECISION

Yes. Park testified in his defense that he had employed a system in which he relied upon his subordinates, and that he was ultimately responsible for this system. He testified further that he had found these subordinates to be "dependable" and had "great confidence" in them. By this and other testimony Park evidently sought to persuade the court that, as the president of a large corporation, he had no choice but to delegate duties to those in whom he reposed confidence, that he had no reason to suspect his subordinates were failing to ensure compliance with the act, and that, once violations were unearthed, acting through those subordinates he did everything possible to correct them. However, this demonstrates that Park was on notice that he could not rely on his system of delegation to subordinates to prevent or correct unsanitary conditions at Acme's warehouses, and that he must have been aware of the deficiencies of this system before the Baltimore violations were discovered.

Defining Ethical Corporate Behavior

Even if a corporation makes a conscious decision to behave in an ethical manner, the debate does not end. As the first section of this chapter indicated, there is diversity of opinion over what exactly is meant by ethical behavior. However, some corporate social responsibility advocates argue that ethical guidance for corporate managers may come from three sources:

1. Values that find wide acceptance.
2. Corporate or industry codes of conduct.
3. Constituency values.

E-Commerce

In *U-Haul International v. Whenu.com,* 279 F.Supp.2d 723 (E.D. Va. 2003), the court refused to hold that a company engaging in "pop-up" advertising on the Internet engaged in trespass or trademark infringement. The plaintiff complained that the pop-up ads crowd a computer user's screen and block out its business website display. The court held for the defendant because computer users unknowingly consent to the pop-up ads when they download certain free screen savers and other free software from the Internet. The judge ended his opinion by lamenting, "Alas, we computer users must endure pop-up advertising along with her ugly brother unsolicited bulk email, spam, as a burden of using the Internet." Do you agree? How do pop-up advertisers ethically justify their intrusions?

Values That Find Wide Acceptance

One theory suggests that ethical corporate behavior should be based on *values that actually find wide acceptance today.* However, corporations and managers adopting this course will immediately confront an unfortunate fact of modern life: its *bewildering array of conflicting ethical views.* On some moral questions affecting the corporation, there is admittedly a general consensus. Almost everyone, for example, would agree that assassination and industrial sabotage are reprehensible means of dealing with competitors. But on many other questions there is considerable disagreement.

LO4

For companies transacting business across the globe, the identification of such common values may be even more daunting. This is because culture may have strong influences on ethical attitudes of business managers. (Some other studies dispute this assertion and suggest instead that business managers are forced to adopt industry attitudes if they are to survive in the business world.) If we assume that culture does shape ethical attitudes, we may have difficulty identifying a comprehensive list of accepted values. For instance, managers in collectivist societies may be more inclined to commit software piracy or to engage in insider trading than members of more individualist societies. In addition, managers' attitudes toward ethical behavior may be even more related to their own personal integrity than to most other factors.

Corporate or Industry Codes of Ethical Conduct

Many large corporations and several industries have adopted codes of conduct to guide executive decision making. The Sarbanes-Oxley Act requires public corporations to disclose whether they have adopted a code of ethics for senior financial officers and to report any change in the code or waiver of their application. A new SEC rule requires fund companies and other investment advisors that register with the SEC to adopt and enforce an ethics code, which outlines general standards to avoid conflicts of interest and requires managers to report any code violations to the fund's chief compliance officer.

Common provisions in industry codes define as unethical certain types of advertising or hiring practices. Some corporate codes prohibit employees from accepting gifts from suppliers of the corporation. The Organization for Economic Cooperation and Development (OECD), an international institution created for the purpose of promoting harmonized rules where multilateral cooperation is necessary, monitors the institutional and policy framework of corporations and company law. An OECD report—*Business Approaches to Combating Corrupt Practices*—looks at websites of the top multinational corporations to gain insight into the global business community's anticorruption efforts. It asserts that most corporate anticorruption programs are voiced in the enterprises' codes of conduct or corporate mission statements. However, after reviewing these statements, the report concluded that these statements tend to speak in positive terms (i.e., commitment to integrity or honesty) rather than expressly publishing policies that deal directly with corruption.

LO4 Thus, there are two popular views of such codes. One view sees them as genuine attempts to foster ethical behavior within a corporation or an industry. The other view regards them as thinly disguised attempts to mislead the public into believing that business behaves ethically in order to head off legislation that might impose more severe constraints on it. For instance, at the time the Enron scandal was unfolding, the corporation had a 64-page code of conduct reinforced by videos by its chief executive (who was subsequently indicted for his part in the conspiracy to defraud investors). No matter which view is correct, there is no guaranty that these codes will accurately reflect the values of society.

Jane Doe v. Wal-Mart Stores

572 F.3d 677 (9th Cir. 2009)

FACTS

Wal-Mart developed a code of conduct which it incorporated into its contracts with foreign suppliers. The Standards require foreign suppliers to adhere to local laws and local industry standards regarding working conditions like pay, hours, forced labor, child labor, and discrimination. They also include a paragraph which states: *"Wal-Mart will undertake affirmative measures, such as on-site inspection of production facilities, to implement and monitor said standards. Any supplier which fails or refuses to comply with these standards or does not allow inspection of production facilities is subject to immediate cancellation of any and all outstanding orders with Wal-Mart."* Employees of Wal-Mart's foreign suppliers in countries including China, Bangladesh, Indonesia, Swaziland, and Nicaragua sued the company, alleging that Wal-Mart does not adequately monitor its suppliers and that Wal-Mart knows its suppliers often violate the Standards. They claim that Wal-Mart represents to the public that it improves the lives of its suppliers' employees and that it does not condone any violation of the Standards. The lawsuit claims that the employees are third-party beneficiaries of the Standards and therefore have the right to sue to ensure that they are enforced.

ISSUE

Should the lawsuit against Wal-Mart be dismissed?

DECISION

Yes. A promise in a contract creates a duty in the promisor to any intended beneficiary to perform the promise, and the intended beneficiary may enforce the duty. However, a beneficiary is only "an intended beneficiary" if recognition of a right to performance in the beneficiary is appropriate to effectuate the intention of the parties. However, this language does not create a duty on the part of Wal-Mart to monitor the suppliers, and does not provide Plaintiffs a right of action against Wal-Mart as third-party beneficiaries. The language and structure of the agreement show that Wal-Mart reserved the right to inspect the suppliers, but did not adopt a duty to inspect them. Wal-Mart made no promise to monitor the suppliers and, accordingly, no such promise flows to plaintiffs as third-party beneficiaries.

Constituency Values

Today it is widely recognized that the large modern corporation interacts with a number of important constituencies—for example, employees, unions, suppliers, customers, and the community in which it operates. Related to this perception is a view of corporate responsibility that holds the corporation should attempt to act in the best interests of all of its various constituencies. To the extent possible, for example, the corporation should treat its employees fairly, bargain honestly with unions, make its products as safe as possible, be a good citizen of the local community, and so forth.

LO4

The major problem with this conception of ethical corporate behavior is that the values (or interests) of these various constituencies may conflict. What is beneficial to one constituency may be harmful to another. For example, although one community will suffer when a corporation moves its plant to another community, the second community will generally benefit. How are corporate managers to balance such claims? Are they qualified to do so?

Refer again to the chapter opener. In the immediate aftermath of the oil spill, the government announced a six-month moratorium on further deepwater drilling until the safety issues could be explored. A petroleum service company immediately sued to block the moratorium. Obviously, petroleum service companies and, perhaps, British Petroleum employees did not have the same values as environmentalists and adjacent homeowners.

Even where there is widespread agreement on particular values, moreover, people disagree on the weight to be given each value when they conflict. Almost everyone, for example, agrees that material abundance and environmental protection are worthwhile goals, but there is seldom agreement on the inevitable trade-offs that must be made between them. Consider the following case. Do you agree with the Court's conclusion that decisions about the welfare of employees' future children are not a legitimate concern for an employer?

International Union v. Johnson Controls

499 U.S. 187 (U.S. Sup. Ct. 1991)

FACTS

Johnson Controls manufactures batteries. In the manufacturing process, lead is a primary ingredient. Occupational exposure to lead entails health risks, including the risk of harm to any fetus carried by a female employee. After discovering that eight employees became pregnant while maintaining blood levels in excess of 30 micrograms per deciliter (the critical level for someone hoping to have children), Johnson Controls responded by announcing a broad exclusion of women from jobs that exposed them to lead. Several female employees sued the company, claiming that its policy was illegal sex discrimination.

ISSUE

Does the fetal-protection policy illegally discriminate on the basis of sex?

DECISION

Yes. Johnson Controls' fetal-protection policy explicitly discriminates against women on the basis of their sex. Johnson Controls argues that its fetal-protection policy falls within the so-called safety exception to the BFOQ. However, the unconceived fetuses of Johnson Controls' female employees are not third parties whose safety is essential to the business of battery manufacturing. No one can disregard the possibility of injury to future children; however, the BFOQ is not so broad that it transforms this deep social concern into an essential aspect of battery making. Our case law makes clear that the safety exception is limited to instances in which sex or pregnancy actually interferes with the employee's ability to perform the job. Fertile women participate in the manufacture of batteries as efficiently as anyone else. Johnson Controls' professed moral and ethical concerns about the welfare of the next generation do not suffice to establish a BFOQ of female sterility. Decisions about the welfare of future children must be left to the parents who conceive, bear, support, and raise them rather than to the employers who hire those parents.

Concept Summary: What Is Ethical Behavior?

Source	Dilemma
1. Values that find wide acceptance	• Wide array of conflicting values • Weight to be given such values
2. Corporate or industry codes of conduct	• Unilateral action may penalize the actor. • Codes may be mere pretext to head off necessary regulation. • Codes may not reflect society's values.
3. Constituency values	• Conflicting values among different constituents • How to balance conflicting claims

The Corporate Governance Agenda

LO5

Numerous proposals designed to make corporations more sensitive to outside concerns have been offered throughout the past few decades. Generally these recommendations are of a *procedural* nature. That is, they do not attempt to define ethical corporate behavior in detail. Instead, they try to restructure the corporate decision-making process so that it will be more likely to accommodate a variety of values. Following are three such recommendations:

1. Giving shareholders greater power.
2. Changing the composition of the corporate board.
3. Changing the management structure.

Greater Shareholder Power

Under the traditional model of the corporation, the shareholders are supposed to be in control of the organization. Thus, some proposals for modifying internal corporate governance have stressed that shareholders be given a greater voice in shaping corporate policy. Two such recommendations are (1) giving shareholders greater power to nominate directors and (2) giving them the power to adopt resolutions binding the corporate directors.

However, it is highly unlikely that greater control by shareholders will lead to greater corporate social responsibility. Consider the following three arguments against their success.

1. Many, if not most, shareholders have a considerable interest in profit maximization and are not likely to initiate or approve corporate actions contrary to profit maximization.
2. Many shareholders will not have access to the information necessary to closely monitor the noneconomic performance of corporations.
3. There is no guaranty that the values of "ethical" shareholders would be representative of society as a whole. Fewer than 5 percent of all Americans own 60 percent of all corporate shares held by individuals. Many shareholders within this group have sufficient wealth to isolate themselves from many of the socially undesirable effects of corporate actions.

In the wake of the recent corporate scandals, the OECD's 30 member countries approved a revised version of the organization's *Principles of Corporate Governance,* offering recommendations on how to rebuild and maintain investor confidence. The revised *Principles* insist on greater transparency and disclosure within corporate structures, in part to ensure that directors and managers are more accountable to shareholders. However, this recommendation is also designed to protect against the types of conflicts of interest at the root of the most recent corporate scandals. Institutional investors are specifically urged to disclose their corporate governance policies so the public can better understand how they are using their voting rights.

Rating agencies and financial analysts are called upon to avoid conflicts of interest to ensure that their advice is not compromised. In the same vein, it is recommended that auditors be wholly independent from the companies they review and that their legal duties extend to shareholders. Finally, a new principle was added that advocates greater protection for whistle-blowers, including the creation of institutional structures through which they can report corporate wrongdoing.

Changing the Composition of the Board

Critics of the corporation have made numerous recommendations for changing the composition of the corporate board of directors so it might better force management to assume a more responsible posture. Many proposals focus on ensuring greater involvement of outside directors as a check on management power. (Sarbanes-Oxley requires publicly traded corporations to have board audit committees comprising only independent directors.) Others call for board representation for constituencies of all sorts (e.g., labor, government, creditors, local communities, minorities, environmentalists) and that certain directors be assigned special areas of concern (e.g., consumer protection, environmental affairs) or that special committees of the board be assigned similar functions.

New federal sentencing guidelines, implemented as part of Sarbanes-Oxley, provide greater incentives for directors to ensure their corporations are not breaking the law. Previous standards for board oversight were too vague to be effective. While they demanded that corporations implement compliance plans, they failed to designate who must have oversight authority. In contrast, the new guidelines assign specific oversight responsibilities to directors in an attempt to curb the largely unrestrained powers accumulated by management over the years. Prior to these most recent guidelines, the U.S. Sentencing Commission already instructed judges to increase the fines for companies if their directors did not take reasonable steps to monitor managerial conduct in order to discover and prevent criminal activity.

However, there are problems with such measures. For instance, while the new guidelines require board members to attend briefings and take real steps to prevent criminal behavior, the sanctions apply only to the corporations themselves, not to individual board members. While shareholders might be able to sue directors who fail to ensure that compliance programs are working, any damages are likely to be paid by insurers. More generally, such proposals are criticized on the grounds that they fail to recognize the limited time, information, and expertise directors can bring to bear when considering corporate affairs. These problems would be exacerbated by the difficulty many corporations might have in attracting highly qualified directors if personal legal liability were attached to such positions. Finally, a proposal designed to greatly broaden the background of the board might result in an unwieldy body incapable of making substantive decisions.

Changes in Management Structure

Some reformers argue that the best way to produce more responsible corporate behavior is to squarely confront the shift in power away from shareholders and directors to the corporation's managers. This requires making fundamental changes in the corporation's internal management structure. Some specific proposals for accomplishing this end include the following:

1. Specified offices within certain corporations (e.g., offices for environmental affairs, worker safety, and product safety).
2. Licensing requirements for holding certain corporate positions (e.g., certain educational requirements for safety engineers).

3. Offices for ensuring that relevant external information is received by the corporation (e.g., data from auto repair shops for car manufacturers or data from doctors for drug companies).
4. Internal information flow procedures for ensuring that relevant external information gets to the proper internal corporate departments (to guaranty, for instance, that bad news will get to the top).
5. Documentation of certain internal findings before undertaking various activities (e.g., drug companies might be required to produce a document resembling an environmental impact statement before marketing a new product).

In cases in which irresponsible corporate behavior is less the product of profit seeking than of failed perceptions, many of these proposals could have a beneficial effect. However, such benefits probably would be obtained only at the cost of further bureaucratic complexity within the corporate structure. Their implementation might greatly reduce the corporation's ability to make quick responses to changing business conditions.

Corporate Reward Structure

There is one other criticism of the structure of management that deserves attention. This theory suggests that most profit maximizers actually are doing a poor job of maximizing profits because they generally try to maximize only *short-term* profits. Such firms, in other words, sacrifice the future to the present and thus do not promote long-term allocational efficiency.

Concept Summary: Corporate Governance Reforms

Rationale: Make Corporations More Sensitive to Outside Concerns		
Theory	**Proposals**	**Flaws**
Greater shareholder power	• Power to nominate directors • Ability to adopt binding resolutions	• Many shareholders favor profit maximization • Limited access to information on noneconomic performance • Shareholders don't represent broad cross-section of society
Change composition of corporate board	• More outside directors • Constituency directors • Special interest committees	• Limited time, information, and expertise • Increased risk of legal liability for directors • Unwieldy boards
Change the management structure	• Constituency offices • Licensure of certain corporate positions • Require corporate offices that ensure receipt of external information • Procedures to ensure the flow of internal information • Documentation of planning process required before corporate actions permitted • Lengthen the focus of management	• Increasing bureaucratization of corporate structure • Loss of flexibility to respond to emergencies • Is society willing to pay for social responsibility?

The reward structures that exist in many corporations are said to further this tendency. For example, salary, bonus, and promotion decisions frequently are tied to year-end profitability, and top executives often have relatively brief terms of office. Thus, the interests of managers may not always be synonymous with the long-range interests of their corporate employers. In such cases, the corporation may be more inclined toward illegal or irresponsible behavior due to the short-term orientation of its managers. The prospect of legal trouble "down the road" may not make much of an impression on such managers. These critics argue that some means must be found that will effectively encourage managers to lengthen their focus when making corporate decisions.

A quick look at the corporate scandals of the past few years makes several things clear: The corporate wrongdoers acted in their own selfish interests; the corporate reward system encouraged them to act selfishly, illegally, and unethically; and the wrongdoers acted without effective supervision. Of equal importance, the wrongdoers knew that they were violating the law and that their behavior was not ethically defensible. These facts certainly suggest the types of structural changes that should be made in corporate management.

To the extent that stock options motivated executives to inflate reports of corporate profits, the Sarbanes-Oxley Act of 2002 offers a partial remedy. It attempts to recover fraudulently obtained stock option profits by requiring the chief executive officer and chief financial officer to reimburse the company when the corporation is required to restate its financial statements filed with the Securities and Exchange Commission. Both the CEO and the CFO must disgorge any bonus or stock compensation that was received within 12 months after a false financial report was filed with the SEC.

Conscious Capitalism

A resolution of the debate between profit maximization theorists and those who advocate the corporate social responsibility path may not require an either/or choice. In a recently published book, *Conscious Capitalism*, the authors suggest that the two approaches can be reconciled. (See John Mackey and Raj Sisodia, *Conscious Capitalism,* Harvard Business Review Press, 2013.) They argue that corporate critics have highjacked the conversation and created the fallacy that the underlying nature of business is somehow contrary to socially responsible behavior. Even corporate efforts to engage in socially responsible activities are viewed as mere window dressing designed to mask a more sinister profit motivation.

Conscious capitalists don't distinguish making profits from ethical behavior. Instead, they believe that business is good because it creates economic value and is ethical because it derives its strength from voluntary exchange that ultimately benefits all of society. The book's authors point out that most entrepreneurs did not initially create their businesses to maximize profits. While they certainly had a profit motivation, they generally are driven more by a sincere desire to do something that needed to be done—to benefit society in some way.

The crux of conscious capitalism is for businesses and their leaders to tap into that higher purpose throughout the life of the enterprise. Ultimately, they will share the journey with stakeholders (customers, shareholders, employees, suppliers, distributors, and communities) who have a similar vision. Basically, by creating and perpetuating value for those constituents, the business is acting in a socially responsible way.

This does not mean that profit is not important. Conscious capitalists still must deliver strong financial results or they will fail to meet an important shareholder demand. Thus, if any corporate philanthropy does not provide value to investors, the managers should be held accountable. However, it is argued that the conscious capitalism approach will bring about long-term value and, in the short term, the overriding shared values will greatly assist companies in reconciling otherwise competing concerns of their constituents.

Guidelines for Ethical Decision Making

We have seen that the market may be ineffective for a number of reasons in forcing corporations to behave in an ethical manner. Among other things, the relative ignorance and powerlessness of consumers, the isolation of some corporations from the discipline of the market, and the failure of some corporations to respond to signals from the market in a rational manner indicate the necessity for some other control device. Yet it is not clear that the law is up to the task of forcing corporations to engage in ethical behavior. First, it is not certain that all corporations will respond to the threat of financial penalties. (They may be in a position to pass these costs on to the consumer in the form of higher prices for the products and services they sell.) Second, corporations are powerful forces in determining the content and enforcement of laws. Third, the law can respond only to dangers that are apparent to society as a whole. Fourth, sometimes corporations seem to behave irrationally, thereby destroying the deterrent value of legal restrictions.

The shortcomings inherent in these control devices are not the whole problem. We have seen that even if corporations voluntarily elect to pursue ethical ends, the debate is not over. We are still confronted with the immense task of determining whose ethics should prevail. Until this fundamental question can be answered, none of the proposals for reforming the corporate structure is likely to satisfy all critics.

Finally, one may properly ask whether we as a society really want corporations to engage in the difficult task of resolving conflicting social claims. Legislatures were designed for this important social function and, given the current structure of corporations, are probably better suited for it. Until corporate critics are able to convince the public that other corporate forms are more likely to provide significant reductions in socially undesirable corporate behavior without reducing the benefits we all derive from the current system, the legislatures, along with the marketplace, are likely to remain the primary regulators of corporate conduct. Likewise, until corporate critics are able to construct an ethical system capable of earning a broad social consensus, a corporate manager seeking ethical guidance unavailable from either the law or the marketplace must rely on his or her individual conscience.

Model for Making Ethical Decisions

LO6

This chapter first outlined the predominant theories of ethical decision making and then presented the long-running debate between profit maximizers and those who believe that managers should make conscious ethical choices in guiding their corporations. While this may (or may not) make interesting reading, managers still walk away with a fundamental dilemma: How do I make the crucial decisions that can so greatly affect the lives of people inside and outside my corporation?

The following decision-making model is drawn heavily from the thoughts of Joseph L. Badaracco Jr. He has developed a set of four questions that he recommends should be asked by managers confronted by seemingly insoluble problems. However, we agree with his warning against relying solely on any one of them. Instead, because they balance and correct one another, they must be asked and answered together.

Which Course of Action Does the Most Good and the Least Harm?

This question is teleological in nature in that it focuses on the morality of the consequences of the decision. More precisely, it is utilitarian if it encompasses the full range of consequences to society at large. However, it could be consistent with profit maximization if the focus is narrowed to the manager's business organization. As with any sound decision-making model, this question requires a thorough gathering of all facts relevant to the decision. Specifically, this investigation is designed to identify all groups and individuals who will benefit from the various choices available to the decision maker and to measure how great each benefit is likely to be. Simultaneously, it must find out who will be put at risk or otherwise suffer from each course of action, measure the extent of that risk or suffering, and determine if the risk or suffering can be otherwise alleviated. Ultimately, this should assist in discovering which managerial decision is likely to do the most good and least harm.

Which Alternative Best Serves Others' Rights?

Borrowing from both the modern rights theories and justice theory, this question identifies which particular rights are at stake. Initially, at least, it examines the rights of everyone who will be affected by the particular decision. Thus, it may be construed as extending beyond the inquiry one might expect from a profit maximizer because it is likely to extend the manager's focus beyond the traditional boundaries of his corporation, community, or nation.

What Course Is Consistent with Personal Morality and the Basic Values of the Company?

This question draws from the decision maker's personal philosophy (the morality of private life), as well as the commitments she owes to the corporation and its shareholders. It may extend beyond the traditional perception of such duties if the manager views her commitment to the organization as an end unto itself and seeks to ensure that it has a place in the future as well as the present. Further, it might well extend outwardly to a wide range of constituencies such as suppliers, customers, unions, and communities. In short, this question forces the decision maker to examine her own personal values while simultaneously considering the values that guide her company and the purposes it serves.

Which Course of Action Is Feasible?

Drawing from Machiavellian thought, this question recognizes that ethics and morality must be practical. This requires the decision maker to honestly assess his actual power within the organization. He also must consider the company's competitive, financial, and political strength, as well as any potential costs and risks. Further, the decision maker must calculate the time available for any possible action. Finally, even if a particular option is believed to be feasible, the manager's work is not done. He then must decide how best to implement the course of action. This should include back-up plans in case things go badly or conditions change.

Using the Guidelines

Strict adherence to these guidelines in no way guaranties that all moral dilemmas will have entirely happy endings. As former Supreme Court Justice Benjamin Cardozo recognized, the quest for justice is frequently reduced to "seeking the least erroneous solution to an insoluble problem." Similarly, managing a business is much more than determining what is right. Many times the choice does not come down to doing what is ethical rather than what is unethical. Instead, decision makers often must choose between competing responsibilities.

Concededly, these guidelines are not practical in every circumstance. Time constraints frequently make sophisticated analysis impractical. Still, they can prove quite useful for important decisions that are likely to present legal and/or ethical problems. Of course, this requires decision makers to recognize those types of situations. This insight, generally, can be cultivated by people willing to honestly reflect on their past, present, and future behavior. Such introspection is crucial to sound decision making.

More important, as Professor Michael Metzger, of Indiana University's Kelley School of Business, has observed, people must realize "that they are their life's work—nothing should be more important to themselves than the kind of person they make themselves. They need to understand that every day, with every decision they make, they are both shaping themselves and writing their life's story."

Concept Summary: Ethical Decision-Making Model

1. Which course of action does the most good and the least harm?
2. Which alternative best serves others' rights?
3. What course is consistent with my personal morality and the basic values of the company?
4. Which course of action is feasible?

Questions and Problem Cases

1. Profit maximizers sometimes argue that corporate abuses are adequately controlled by legal rules. Specifically, explain how the social responsibility advocates respond to this assertion.
2. Richmond Plasma Corporation (RPC) is a wholly owned subsidiary of Automated Medical Laboratories, Inc. (AML). The Food and Drug Administration (FDA) had closed RPC twice before because of problems with overbleeding of donors (removing more blood from a donor than federal regulations allow). Following the first closing, RPC made Partucci, a regional manager, the responsible head of RPC and charged him with ensuring compliance with FDA regulations. Partucci established a special compliance office that supervised a compliance team. Just prior to an FDA inspection, the compliance team ordered RPC employees to falsify records and, in some instances, the compliance team members falsified records themselves. After several RPC employees reported these activities to the FDA, AML was indicted for engaging in a criminal conspiracy to falsify records. AML argued that there was no evidence that any officer or director at AML knowingly and willfully participated in or authorized the unlawful practices at RPC or that the criminal acts were undertaken to benefit AML. The court disagreed. It held that the company may be criminally liable for the unlawful practices at RPC if its agents were acting within the scope of their employment. The fact that many of their actions were unlawful or against company policy did not absolve AML from legal responsibility. Specifically, how might an advocate of corporate social responsibility use this case to attack the arguments in favor of relying on profit maximization?
3. Leta Fay Ford's supervisor in the purchasing department of Revlon, Inc., Karl Braun, made numerous sexual advances toward her. At Revlon's annual service award picnic on May 3, 1980, Braun grabbed Ford, restrained her in a chokehold with his right arm, and ran his hand over her breasts, stomach, and crotch. That

same month, Ford began a series of meetings with various members of Revlon's management to report her complaints about Braun. During this time, he continued to harass her. Despite Ford's numerous meetings and complaints, no action was taken by Revlon until nine months after her initial complaint. It was not until this meeting that Braun was finally confronted by the company and told that he would be closely monitored. Three months after this meeting (one year after Ford's initial complaints), Revlon's personnel manager submitted a report confirming Ford's charges and issuing Braun a letter of censure. During the time of her harassment, Ford developed high blood pressure, a nervous tic in her left eye, rapid breathing, and other symptoms of emotional stress. She ultimately attempted suicide. Particularly disturbing is the fact that Revlon knew of the supervisor's outrageous conduct, was aware of Ford's growing emotional and physical distress, and still totally disregarded its own company policy for protecting its employees from such harassment. Specifically, how might this case be used to undermine the profit maximization arguments?

4. One of this country's richest commercial fishing areas was devastated by a massive oil spill when an oil tanker, the *Exxon Valdez,* ran aground. The ship's captain had been treated for alcoholism and returned to work. After the oil spill, his blood test showed a high level of alcohol in his blood. Following the wreck of the tanker, Exxon announced that, even after treatment, known alcohol and drug abusers won't be allowed to return to so-called critical jobs such as piloting a ship, flying a plane, or operating a refinery, although they will be given other jobs. Exxon Chairman Lawrence Rawl defended the new policy by stating: "Even with close follow-up, there are certain things you can't have people do." United Airlines, on the other hand, has a corporate policy of regularly returning pilots to the job after they have received treatment for alcoholism. It believes that not reinstating them would be short-sighted because such a policy would discourage alcoholics from seeking help. Profit maximizers base their arguments against the social responsibility model on several grounds. Specifically, describe the criticism of social responsibility revealed by these conflicting approaches to the alcoholism problem.
5. Managers at Russia's largest industrial enterprises have been reluctant to embrace all that capitalism seems to offer. Many argue that it is unethical to adopt Western practices such as mass layoffs and aggressive pricing policies. Are they correct? Discuss.
6. U.S. tobacco companies have discovered an eager market for tobacco products in Eastern Europe. However, of the developed world, life expectancy is shortest in that region of the world and antismoking groups say that in middle age, one-third of all male deaths in Eastern Europe are caused by tobacco. How can tobacco company executives ethically justify targeting this market?
7. After someone laced Tylenol capsules with cyanide, killing seven people, Johnson & Johnson (the maker of Tylenol) recalled and destroyed 31 million capsules at a cost of over $100 million. Within six weeks, Tylenol was back on store shelves in new, triple-sealed safety packages. Within three months, Tylenol had recovered 95 percent of its leading market share. In weathering this storm, the company credited its corporate philosophy, which held that the company had four responsibilities: customers, employees, communities, and shareholders. Was Johnson & Johnson assuming a profit maximization or social responsibility posture in responding to this crisis? Explain.
8. After toxic fumes leaked from Union Carbide's pesticide plant in Bhopal, India, over 3,300 people were killed and another 30,000 injured. Two sources later

indicated that Union Carbide had conducted feasibility studies on whether to build the plant in Bhopal. Both sources claimed there was concern inside the company whether such a complex facility could be safely maintained in India. A former Union Carbide engineer who worked on one of the studies claimed that the company was fully aware of the risk. In fact, the company's final liability—a $465 million settlement—was described as a bargain. This amounted to only a few thousand dollars apiece for families of the dead and injured. Had the disaster occurred in the United States, Union Carbide probably would have had to pay several billion dollars. Would it be ethical for Union Carbide to accept the greater risk of a disaster by locating the plant in India because such a risk would be more than offset by the lower damages it would have to pay there? Explain.

Chapter 4

Business and the Constitution

Learning Objectives

After you have studied this chapter, you should be able to:

1. Look at proposed legislation and explain whether or not a state government has constitutional authority to enact it.
2. Look at proposed legislation and explain whether or not the federal government has constitutional authority to enact it.
3. Examine a case involving governmental interference with property rights and explain whether the property owner is entitled to compensation under the Takings Clause.
4. Review a situation involving governmental action and describe whether or not procedural due process has been met.
5. Review a situation involving governmental action and describe whether or not substantive due process has been met.
6. Clearly distinguish between the constitutional protection to commercial speech and that accorded noncommercial speech.
7. Explain the three types of powers that may be vested in administrative agencies.

John Gilmore refused the request to show his identification at the Southwest Airlines ticketing counter. The clerk informed Gilmore that he could opt to be screened at the gate in lieu of presenting the requisite identification. The clerk then issued Gilmore a new boarding pass, which indicated that he was to be searched before boarding the airplane. At the gate, Gilmore again refused to show identification. The identification policy is part of a Transportation Security Administration (TSA) security directive. Gilmore argued that the identification policy violated his due process rights. *Gilmore v. Gonzales*, 435 F.3d 1125 (9th Cir. 2006).

- What are our due process rights? How do they arise?
- Who owes us due process rights?
- Does the identification policy violate an air traveler's due process rights?

Introduction

We live in an era when disenchantment with elected officials is rampant. Yet while the public demonstrates against regulatory intrusions, it also clamors for governmental action to reverse the financial meltdown or save us from environmental disasters. Despite complaints about regulation, we can safely say that regulation is here to stay. Today we are witnessing a "deregulation" movement aimed at reducing numerous "friendly" regulations that in the past operated to shield some businesses from the forces of competition. In other areas conflicting or overlapping regulations may need to be reworked. Nonetheless, as long as the United States continues to be a highly complex and industrialized society, regulation will be an important fact of life.

State Regulation of Business

State Power

State governments have very broad powers. They have the power to tax, to own and operate businesses, and to take private property for public purposes by the power of eminent domain. They also have broad "police powers" to legislate to promote the health, safety, and general welfare of their citizens.

LO1 The states retain the exclusive power to regulate **intrastate commerce**—economic activities that have no significant effect on commerce outside their own borders. Their power to regulate **interstate commerce** (commerce among the states) is limited because the Commerce Clause of the U.S. Constitution gives the federal government the power to regulate commerce "with foreign nations" and "among the several states." This, combined with the Supremacy Clause of the Constitution, which holds federal laws superior to state laws in cases of conflict, restricts the states' powers.

Federal Preemption

The federal government has the exclusive right to regulate all **foreign commerce** of the United States and all aspects of interstate commerce when there is an essential need for

Concept Summary: The Balance between Federal and State Power

Exclusive Federal Power	Foreign commerce. Interstate commerce where there is a need for national uniformity. Interstate commerce where there is a federal statute preempting the area.
Concurrent Power	States may regulate incidental, not direct, aspects of interstate commerce if: The state is furthering a legitimate local interest. There is no discrimination against interstate commerce in favor of local commerce. The costs to interstate commerce do not exceed the benefits to local health, safety, and welfare.
Exclusive State Power	Purely local (intrastate) functions. Recent decisions have cast great doubt on the continued viability of this restriction on federal power.

nationwide regulation. Thus, if Congress enacts valid legislation dealing with foreign or interstate commerce and state law conflicts with that legislation, the state law will be unconstitutional. In such cases, the state law is said to be **expressly preempted.** State legislation may also be preempted when Congress has demonstrated an intent to exclusively regulate an entire regulatory area. Accordingly, pervasive regulation of an activity by the federal government may prevent state regulation through **implied preemption.**

U.S. Smokeless Tobacco Manufacturing Co. v. City of New York

708 F.3d 428 (2d Cir. 2013)

FACTS

A New York City ordinance prohibits the sale in the city of any flavored tobacco product except in a tobacco bar. The U.S. Smokeless Tobacco Manufacturing Company challenged the validity of the ordinance, arguing that it is preempted by the Family Smoking Prevention and Tobacco Control Act. That federal statute authorizes the Food and Drug Administration (FDA) to establish standards "respecting the construction, components, ingredients, additives, constituents, including smoke constituents, and properties of . . . tobacco products." Although the statute prohibited the FDA from banning all tobacco products, it banned the use of flavoring additives in cigarettes and authorized the FDA to prohibit the use of other ingredients in tobacco products if it deems them particularly harmful to the public health. The federal statute contains a preemption clause that cautions that it should not be construed to limit the authority of states or their political subdivisions to enact rules more stringent than the federal requirements.

ISSUE

Is the city ordinance preempted by the federal statute?

DECISION

No. U.S. Smokeless Tobacco asks us to imply that local governments may not make it impossible or impracticable for adults to purchase tobacco products whose contents comply with the federal standards. Significantly, however, no provision explicitly embodying such a restriction on state authority can be found in the text of the statute. While the federal statute prohibits the FDA from banning entire categories of tobacco products throughout the country, it does not extend that prohibition to state and local governments. It reserves regulation at the manufacturing stage exclusively to the federal government but allows states and localities to continue to regulate sales and other consumer-related aspects of the industry in the absence of conflicting federal regulation. We are therefore not persuaded that the City is infringing on the role reserved for the federal government.

Dormant Commerce Clause

The Commerce Clause in the U.S. Constitution has two dimensions. First, as will be discussed in the next section, it is an affirmative grant of power to the federal government. Second, however, it has a negative sweep as well. Specifically, in what may be described as its "negative" or "dormant" aspect, the Commerce Clause limits the authority of the states to interfere with the flow of interstate commerce in two ways: (1) it prohibits discrimination aimed directly at interstate commerce and (2) it prohibits state legislation that unduly burdens interstate commerce.

Accordingly, the states are free to regulate aspects of interstate commerce that have not been preempted by the federal government as long as their efforts do not run afoul of the negative commerce clause. Four factors generally are considered in determining the validity of state legislation under this analysis. To be constitutional, the state statute must (1) further a legitimate state interest; (2) not discriminate in favor of local interests and against out-of-state interests; (3) allow only incidental, not direct, regulation of interstate commerce; and (4) not impose costs on interstate commerce that are more excessive than necessary to bring about the state interests.

Florida Transportation Service v. Miami-Dade County

703 F.3d 1230 (11th Cir. 2012)

FACTS

A Miami-Dade County ordinance required that stevedores (workers who load and unload cargo) working in the Port of Miami have a license. Stevedore permits expired annually and a county ordinance required each stevedore company each year to reapply and be reassessed, along with any new applicants, as to competency, safety record, financial strength, and need. Historically, the licensing body did not engage in the required review process. Instead, the licenses of current stevedore companies were automatically renewed while those of new applicants were automatically rejected.

ISSUE

Do the actions of the licensing body violate the dormant commerce clause?

DECISION

Yes. We need not decide if the license practice discriminates against interstate commerce because we conclude that it unduly burdened interstate commerce. The rubber-stamp process employed by the licensing authority demonstrates that the sole factor that determined if a stevedore license would be granted each year was whether the applicant already had a permit. These permitting practices were aimed at preventing competition against incumbent stevedores. This clearly burdened interstate commerce. New entrants were effectively shut out, even if they could have provided better service, better equipment, or lower prices than the incumbent stevedores. It does not matter that some of the stevedore companies who received licenses were incorporated out-of-state. For dormant commerce clause purposes, the important point is that all of the permit holders were operating locally at the Port or were otherwise entrenched at the Port as a cargo terminal operator or as co-owner of an operating stevedore company. The asserted goals of ensuring that stevedores were skilled, experienced, and safe were in no way furthered by the practice of rubber-stamping the applications of currently licensed companies.

Federal Regulation of Business

LO2

Early interpretations of the Commerce Clause focused primarily on its negative power to restrict state regulation of interstate commerce. With the increase in federal regulation that followed the Civil War, the courts tended to focus on the Commerce Clause as a limitation on the federal government's power to regulate business. Federal statutes were invalidated on the ground that they were not sufficiently related to interstate commerce.

Later decisions took a broader view of the Commerce Clause, recognizing federal power to regulate activities that have a "substantial relationship" to interstate commerce. In today's highly interdependent economy, most important economic activity is within the reach of federal regulation under the current expansive view of the Commerce Clause.

Constitutional Checks on Governmental Power

State Action

Certain constitutional checks on governmental power apply to both Congress and the states. These protections are included in the various amendments to the Constitution. However, the Constitution protects the individual only against governmental activity, usually called **state action.** As a result, unless such interference is prohibited by statute, private deprivation of individual liberties is permitted. In determining whether state action exists, and therefore whether the constitutional checks apply, courts examine the degree of governmental involvement in the challenged activity. In the chapter opening example, state action was involved because the identification policy was mandated by federal law.

E-Commerce Cyber Promotions provided advertising services for companies by sending unsolicited e-mail via the Internet to members of America Online (AOL). Because it was upset with Cyber's dissemination of the unsolicited e-mail to its members, AOL sent a number of e-mail bombs to Cyber's Internet service providers. These e-mail bombs occurred when AOL gathered all unsolicited e-mail sent by Cyber to undeliverable AOL addresses, altered the return path of such e-mail, and then sent the altered e-mail in a bulk transmission to Cyber's service providers in order to disable the service providers. As a result of the e-mail bombing, two of Cyber's Internet service providers terminated their relationship with the company. Cyber sued, claiming that AOL's action violated its First Amendment rights. The court disagreed. Why? AOL is a private online company. Because there was no state action, AOL did not owe Cyber any constitutional rights.

The Takings Clause

LO3

The U.S. Constitution, in both the Fifth and the Fourteenth Amendments, prohibits the government (federal, state, and local) from taking real or personal property for public use without paying just compensation. This *Takings Clause* is triggered by the power of **eminent domain,** whereby the government forces private property holders to sell their land so it may be dedicated to public use. The Takings Clause has three primary components: (1) there must be a taking, (2) it must be for a public purpose, and (3) the private property owner is then entitled to just compensation.

Taking

Not every governmental interference with property ownership constitutes a taking. For example, the zoning ordinances enacted by many cities and counties interfere with a landowner's use of the property. However, because the interference is limited, no compensation is required. Of course, if the government physically invades the property or, in some other manner, greatly limits its value or usefulness to the owner, a taking has occurred and compensation must be paid. Anytime a landowner is denied all economically beneficial use of the property, a compensable taking has occurred.

Public Use

The government may not constitutionally take someone's property unless it is for a public purpose. These might include seizing land to build highways, water control projects, or some type of public building. The public purpose is not always so clear. For instance, in many cases cities have used their power of eminent domain in furtherance of an urban renewal project. This certainly may be a permissible public use. However, if the city turns the land over to private developers who profit from the enterprise, the taking may well be unconstitutional.

Kelo v. City of New London

545 U.S. 469 (U.S. Sup. Ct. 2005)

FACTS

After decades of economic decline, city officials in New London targeted the city for economic revitalization. To this end, New London Development Corporation (NLDC), a private nonprofit entity established some years earlier to assist the city in planning economic development, was reactivated. The city council authorized the NLDC to purchase property or to acquire property by exercising eminent domain in the city's name. When negotiations to purchase the home of Susette Kelo failed, the NLDC initiated condemnation proceedings,

(continued)

Kelo v. City of New London *(concluded)*

attempting to use the power of eminent domain to acquire their property in exchange for just compensation.

ISSUE

Does the city's decision to take property satisfy the "public use" requirement of the Takings Clause?

DECISION

Yes. The disposition of this case turns on the question whether the city's development plan serves a "public purpose." The city has carefully formulated an economic development plan that it believes will provide appreciable benefits to the community, including—but by no means limited to—new jobs and increased tax revenue. As with other exercises in urban planning and development, the city is endeavoring to coordinate a variety of commercial, residential, and recreational uses of land, with the hope that they will form a whole greater than the sum of its parts. Because that plan unquestionably serves a public purpose, the takings challenged satisfy the public use requirement. Promoting economic development is a traditional and long accepted function of government.

Property-rights advocates immediately attacked the *Kelo* decision. They argued that condemnations should be used only for roads, bridges, reservoirs, and other purely public projects. Further, they complained that the decision opened the door for cities to routinely uproot low-income families by seizing their homes and handing them over to private businesses under the premise that this would maximize overall tax revenues. Alarmed by these complaints, state lawmakers throughout the country have been changing their eminent domain laws. Some states now prevent condemnation for economic development unless it is designed to eliminate urban blight. Others are considering constitutional amendments that would bar the government from taking private property for economic development.

Just Compensation

In the case of a zoning ordinance in which no taking has occurred, the government need not compensate the property owner despite the inconvenience caused by the governmental action. However, when an actual taking for public use does occur, the government must provide just compensation to the dispossessed landowner. Generally, this entails calculating the fair market value of the property involved in the taking. Of course, this does not provide complete satisfaction for many property owners. They frequently argue that the fair market value is insufficient because it fails to properly consider goodwill or future profits or that it disregards people's emotional attachments to their land.

The Due Process Clause

Historically, among the most important of the constitutional restraints on governmental power have been the Due Process Clauses of the Fifth and Fourteenth Amendments. The Fifth Amendment Due Process Clause prohibits the federal government from depriving any person "of life, liberty, or property, without due process of law." The Fourteenth Amendment applies the same standard to the states. Corporations have long been considered "persons" protected by these constitutional guaranties.

Procedural Due Process

LO4

As originally interpreted, the Due Process Clause was viewed as a guarantee of **procedural due process.** This meant that the government could accomplish its objectives only by following fair procedures. Reasonable notice, the right to a hearing before an impartial tribunal, and adherence to any established procedures were required whenever the government interfered with the rights of people.

In the chapter opening example, Gilmore argued that the airline identification policy violated his procedural due process rights because he was penalized for failing to comply with a law that he has never seen. The court rejected this argument, noting that several airline personnel asked him for identification and told him that in order to board the aircraft he must either present identification or be subject to a "selectee" search. Although Gilmore was not given the text of the identification policy, he was nonetheless accorded adequate notice. The court did not believe that he was entitled to elaborate notification requirements because the identification policy did not impose any criminal sanctions. Rather, it simply prevents noncomplying individuals from boarding commercial flights.

Substantive Due Process

LO5

Government actions that are procedurally fair may still be unconstitutional if they are substantively unfair. This notion, **substantive due process,** protects people from arbitrary or unreasonable governmental interference with their life, liberty, or property rights. However, as we will see below, when governmental regulations restrict only economic rights (property rights), the government is granted great discretion. However, when life or highly valued liberty interests are at stake, the governmental action will be struck down unless it passes rigorous judicial scrutiny (discussed below).

Equal Protection

The states are prohibited from arbitrarily discriminating against persons by the **Equal Protection Clause** of the Fourteenth Amendment, which prohibits any state from arbitrarily discriminating against persons. A similar restraint against the federal government also exists because the courts have interpreted the Fifth Amendment Due Process Clause as including an equal protection component. As a result, neither the states nor the federal government may unfairly discriminate. Specifically, the Equal Protection Clause holds that the government must treat like cases alike. However, there are many times when the government provides benefits to, or imposes burdens on, some groups and not others. The constitutionality of such discrimination turns on the nature of the disfavored group and the government's reasons for making the distinction. This analysis is explained below.

Concept Summary: Procedural Due Process

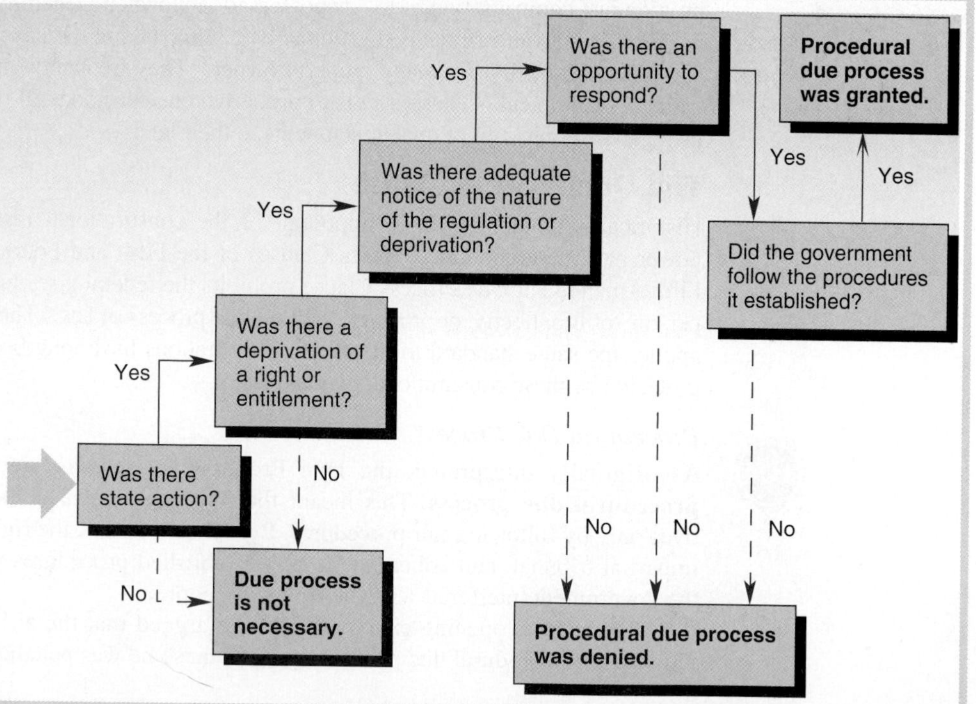

Due Process and Equal Protection Scrutiny

Whenever regulatory programs discriminate they trigger equal protection analysis. Likewise, when they interfere with the exercise of individual rights, they are subject to both a substantive and a procedural due process challenge. When courts are called upon to decide if there has been a constitutional violation, they must balance the individual rights that are restricted (or the disfavored group in an equal protection case) against the governmental purposes served by the regulation.

The judicial tests for examining Due Process and Equal Protection challenges share a common premise. When the government interferes with highly valued rights or discriminates on the basis of highly suspicious classifications, its actions will not be permitted unless they further an extremely important objective. However, when the intrusion into individual rights is slight, judicial oversight is lenient. There are three general types of analysis employed by the courts in Due Process and Equal Protection cases: rational basis, strict scrutiny, and intermediate scrutiny.

Rational Basis Analysis

Courts use **rational basis analysis** when reviewing legislation restricting economic interests (property) or discriminating on the basis of nonsuspect classifications (categories other than race, national origin, gender, or illegitimacy). This is an extremely lenient level of scrutiny that presumes the regulation is constitutional. As long as the governmental action has a reasonable relationship to the achievement of a legitimate purpose, it is declared constitutional. Even foolish and misdirected provisions are generally valid if they are subject only to rational basis review. Basically, courts will uphold the governmental action if there is any reasonably conceivable state of facts that could provide a rational basis. Thus, those seeking to invalidate a statute using rational basis analysis must negate every conceivable basis that might support it.

Strict Scrutiny Analysis

Courts generally presume that governmental action is unconstitutional when it denies people fundamentally important constitutional rights. In determining whether a **fundamental right** exists, the inquiry is whether the right involved is such that it cannot be denied without violating the fundamental principles of liberty and justice. The fundamental rights generally are those liberties spelled out for protection in the Bill of Rights (speech, religion, association, right to vote, privacy, etc.). Further, if the government discriminates on the basis of certain **suspect classifications** (race or national origin), courts also place a burden on the government to justify its action.

When the government restricts the exercise of fundamental rights or discriminates on the basis of a suspect class, courts require more than a mere rational relationship between the statutory ends and means. Instead, the legislation is reviewed under **strict scrutiny.** Under this analysis, the statute is unconstitutional unless the government demonstrates that it is pursuing a *compelling governmental interest* in the *least intrusive manner.*

E-Commerce

In *United States v. American Library Association,* 539 U.S. 194 (U.S. Sup. Ct. 2003), the U.S. Supreme Court upheld provisions of the *Children's Internet Protection Act* (CIPA), which forbids public libraries to receive federal assistance for Internet access unless they install filtering software that prevents minors from accessing material deemed harmful to them. The Court avoided strict scrutiny analysis by reasoning that "CIPA does not 'penalize' libraries that choose not to install blocking software, or deny them the right to provide patrons with unfiltered Internet access. Rather, CIPA simply reflects Congress' decision not to subsidize their doing so."

Concept Summary: Substantive Due Process/ Equal Protection Analysis

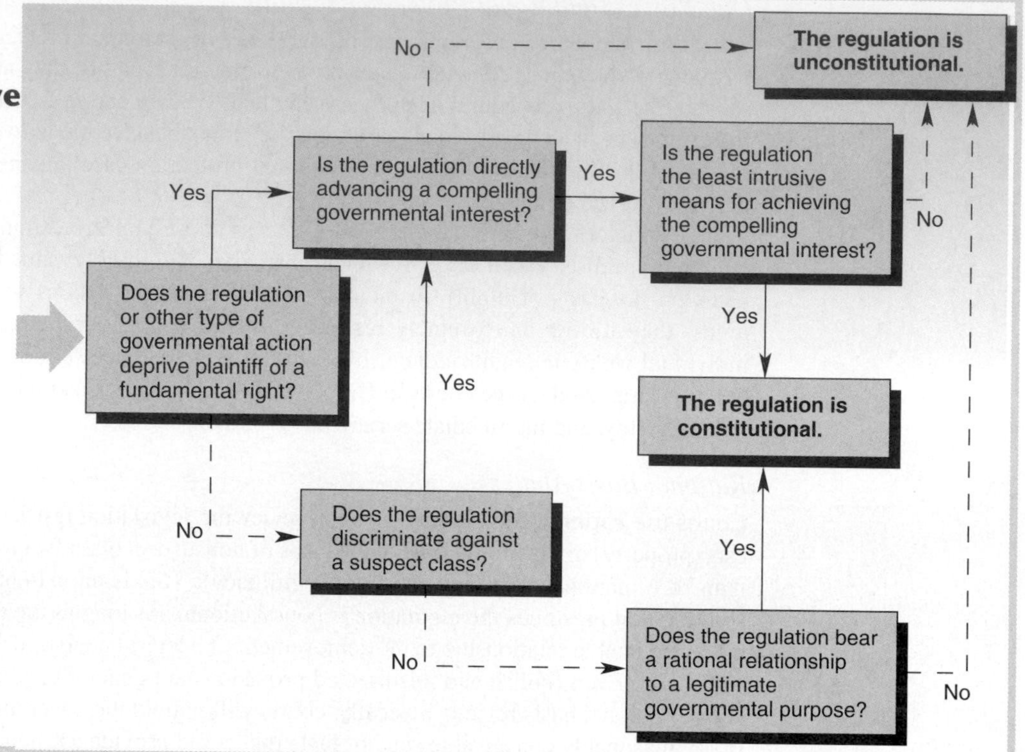
Does the regulation or other type of governmental action deprive plaintiff of a fundamental right?
Yes
Is the regulation directly advancing a compelling governmental interest?
No
Yes
Is the regulation the least intrusive means for achieving the compelling governmental interest?
No
The regulation is unconstitutional.
Yes
The regulation is constitutional.
No
Does the regulation discriminate against a suspect class?
Yes
No
Does the regulation bear a rational relationship to a legitimate governmental purpose?
Yes
No

Intermediate Scrutiny Analysis

Courts also recognize several types of **intermediate scrutiny** lying somewhere between rational basis and strict scrutiny analysis. This test generally is used to evaluate restrictions on commercial speech or discrimination on the basis of certain suspect classifications (gender or a person's illegitimate birth). This level of scrutiny generally requires that the classification serves important governmental objectives and is substantially related to the achievement of those objectives. (The intermediate scrutiny used for restrictions on commercial speech is discussed later in the chapter.)

The First Amendment

The First Amendment to the U.S. Constitution prohibits the government from abridging freedom of speech. Thus, speech is a fundamental right, and governmental action that limits such expression is subject to strict scrutiny analysis. However, the courts have historically distinguished between noncommercial and commercial speech when reviewing the constitutionality of governmental restrictions.

Noncommercial Speech

LO6

The courts have consistently given the highest degree of constitutional protection to **noncommercial speech** (also known as *pure* or *political speech*). Thus, governmental restrictions on noncommercial speech must undergo strict scrutiny analysis. As such, they will be upheld only if the government can show that (1) the regulation is furthering a *compelling governmental interest* and (2) the regulation is no broader than absolutely necessary (*least intrusive means*) to promote that governmental interest.

Commercial Speech

While constitutional safeguards have always been extended to noncommercial speech, it was long thought that **commercial speech,** such as advertising, enjoyed no First Amendment protection. However, in the mid-1970s the Supreme Court held that purely commercial speech was entitled to some constitutional protection. This protection was justified primarily by the public's interest in the free flow of accurate commercial information. Therefore, only truthful commercial speech was entitled to First Amendment protection. False, misleading, or deceptive advertising might be lawfully suppressed.

LO6

Beyond the need for commercial speech to be truthful (there is no such precondition for protection for noncommercial speech), the courts also analyze commercial speech regulations with an **intermediate scrutiny** that falls between strict scrutiny and rational basis analysis. This requires the government to establish that it has a *substantial interest* (something less than a compelling interest) and that it is *directly advancing* that interest in a manner *no more extensive than necessary* to serve that interest.

R.J. Reynolds Tobacco v. Food & Drug Administration

696 F.3d 1205 (D.C. Cir. 2012)

FACTS

Federal law required that all cigarette packages manufactured or sold in the United States bear color graphics depicting the negative health consequences of smoking. The statute mandates that the new warning labels comprise the top 50 percent of the front and rear panels of cigarette packages and 20 percent of the area of each cigarette advertisement. Pursuant to this authority, the Food and Drug Administration (FDA) selected nine images that would accompany the statutorily prescribed warnings. These included images of cancerous lungs and dead bodies.

ISSUE

May the FDA require that tobacco companies place graphic images on tobacco packages?

DECISION

No. The primary objective of this FDA rule was to both discourage nonsmokers from initiating cigarette use and to encourage current smokers to consider quitting. Assuming FDA's interest in reducing smoking rates is substantial, we next evaluate whether FDA has offered substantial evidence showing that the graphic warning requirements directly advance that governmental interest. The government bears the burden of justifying its attempt to restrict commercial speech, and its burden is not light. A restriction that provides only ineffective or remote support for the government's purposes is not sufficient, and the government cannot satisfy its burden by mere speculation or conjecture. The requirement that a restriction directly advance the asserted interest is critical, because without it, the government could interfere with commercial speech in the service of other objectives that could not themselves justify a burden on commercial expression. Here, the FDA has not provided a shred of evidence showing that the graphic warnings will directly advance its interest in reducing the number of Americans who smoke.

Time, Place, or Manner Restrictions

Constitutional questions arise when people seek access to public property for the purpose of communicating with others. The government generally may impose reasonable restrictions on the **time, place, or manner** of such expression. For instance, a city may prohibit the use of loudspeakers in residential neighborhoods if the restriction applies equally to all types of expression (music, political speech, advertising). Courts employ a three-part test in deciding whether a law is a reasonable time, place, and manner restriction. First, they ask whether the speech restrictions are content neutral. Second, they must be narrowly tailored to serve a significant government interest. Finally, such laws must leave open ample alternative channels for the communication of information.

McCullen v. Coakley

708 F.3d 1 (1st Cir. 2013)

FACTS

The Massachusetts legislature passed legislation that created a 35-foot buffer zone around the entrances, exits, and driveways of abortion clinics. Four categories of people are permitted to be in those areas: (1) persons entering or leaving the facility; (2) employees/agents of the facility acting within the scope of their employment; (3) law enforcement or other emergency or repair personnel acting within the scope of their employment; and (4) persons using the public sidewalk or street to the facility to reach a destination other than such facility. Pro-life advocates challenged the constitutionality of the statute, claiming that it prevents them from gaining close personal contact with women that they wish to dissuade from seeking abortions.

ISSUE

Does this statute violate first amendment rights of the pro-life advocates?

DECISION

No. This statute is viewpoint-neutral in that it does not advocate for or against abortion rights. In addition, the legislation is a narrowly tailored effort by the state to take reasonable steps to ensure the safe passage of persons wishing to enter health care facilities. Importantly, the statute leaves open adequate alternative means of communication. To begin, the demonstrators and their placards are visible to their intended audience. Their voices are audible. To be sure, the statute curtails their ability to carry on gentle discussions with prospective patients at a conversational distance, embellished with eye contact and smiles. But as long as a speaker has an opportunity to reach her intended audience, the Constitution does not ensure that she always will be able to employ her preferred method of communication. The statute is, therefore, a valid time-place-manner regulation.

Administrative Agencies

The explosion of government regulation in the United States has witnessed an accompanying social phenomenon of great importance: the creation and widespread use of administrative agencies. Courts and legislatures often are not well suited to deal with many of the complex problems continually arising in our rapidly changing environment. Administrative agencies, on the other hand, possess the ability to develop a reservoir of expertise in various areas of regulation. They are better suited to bring about a continuous and rapid development of regulatory policy without resorting to the slower, case-by-case approach followed by the courts and the cumbersome law-making process that frequently characterizes legislation. Allowing such agencies to hear and adjudicate disputes speeds up problem solving and reduces the burdens placed on an already overworked judicial system. While there are numerous administrative agencies at both the state and federal levels, our discussion focuses on federal regulatory agencies.

Breadth of Agency Regulation

The goods we buy, the advertising of those goods, the interest rates we pay on loans, the rates we pay for utilities, and the availability and cost of public transportation are only a few of the many aspects of our lives that administrative agencies regulate. In the workplace, agencies regulate wages and hours of work, working conditions, unemployment and retirement benefits, and workers' compensation. Most people will never enter a court in their entire lifetime, but the actions of administrative agencies directly affect all our lives on a daily basis.

Characteristics of Agencies

Administrative agencies are, in theory, part of the executive branch of government. However, they may also perform legislative and judicial functions. In addition to investigating and prosecuting violations of statutes and regulations, many agencies have the power to issue regulations that have the force of law. They may also adjudicate disputes involving alleged violations of their regulations and the statutes they are charged with enforcing. There are two primary types of agencies: executive and independent.

Executive Agencies

Some administrative agencies reside exclusively within the executive branch of government. The Occupational Safety and Health Administration (OSHA), the Food and Drug Administration (FDA), and the Internal Revenue Service (IRS) are examples of these executive agencies. The president appoints the heads of the executive agencies and may remove them at his will.

Independent Agencies

Some agencies are called independent agencies because they are not really part of the executive branch of the government and under the control of the president. Instead, they are headed by a board or commission. Although the members are nominated by the president, approximately half of them must be from each major political party and their appointment is confirmed by the Senate for fixed terms.

This type of regulatory agency is given authority by Congress both to make rules and to enforce them. Congress grants rule-making power to the agency instead of establishing detailed rules in statutes. It is believed that the independent agency members and staff have greater expertise than Congress and, accordingly, will better understand the issues that arise within their area of responsibility. In addition, it is hoped that continuous regulatory supervision by the agency would be more adaptive to specific needs than reliance on legislation.

Agency Powers

LO7

The authority of some agencies is confined to the performance of largely routine duties. However, the independent agencies frequently are granted wide-ranging authority to act. There are three primary powers that fall within this broad discretion: investigative power, rule-making power, and adjudicatory power.

Investigative Power

Agencies often are given broad investigative power so they can effectively regulate. They need to uncover much information about various practices so they can detect and prosecute regulatory violations. Because many people will not voluntarily cooperate with information requests, these agencies often exercise a *subpoena power* to gain access to witnesses and documentary evidence.

Courts place limits on the subpoena power in order to protect individual privacy interests. Investigations are not permitted unless they are authorized by law and conducted for a legitimate agency purpose. Even then, subpoena requests must be specific and not unreasonably burdensome. For instance, while investigating a man for suspicious securities trading activities, the Commodity Futures Trading Commission (CFCT) issued a subpoena requiring him to produce copies of his federal income tax returns. A federal court ruled that he need not comply with the demand. It held that the self-reporting, self-assessing character of the income tax system would be compromised were tax returns freely disclosed to agencies enforcing regulatory programs unrelated to tax collection itself. The court stressed that the CFCT issued the subpoena as a matter of rote, merely hoping the tax returns might contain information germane to the investigation. (See *Commodity Futures Trading Commission v. Collins,* 997 F.2d 1230 (7th Cir. 1993).)

Rule-Making Power

An agency's rule-making power is derived from the enabling legislation enacted by Congress for the creation of the agency. That statute may be an unconstitutional delegation of legislative power if it does not set out adequate guidelines for agency action. Further, courts will overturn agency actions when the agency acts contrary to the authority it has been granted by its enabling statute.

When an agency's rulemaking does not exceed its regulatory authority, the courts generally do not substitute their judgment for that of an agency, even if they believe an agency's rules to be unwise. Only agency decisions that are *arbitrary and capricious* are overturned by the courts.

Under what is known as the **Chevron Doctrine,** courts conduct a two-part inquiry to determine whether to sustain an agency's interpretation of the statutory scheme it is charged with administering. First, they look to see whether Congress has directly spoken to the precise question at issue. If the intent of Congress is clear, that is the end of the matter; the court, as well as the agency, must give effect to the unambiguously expressed intent of Congress. However, if the statute is silent or ambiguous with respect to the specific issue, the question for the court is whether the agency's answer is based on a permissible construction of the statute. Under this second step of the analysis, any reasonable construction of the statute is a permissible construction. In fact, the agency's interpretation need not be the only reasonable interpretation or even the most reasonable interpretation. Rather, a court will defer to an agency's reasonable interpretation of a statute even if the court might have preferred another.

Adjudicatory Power

A number of agencies also exercise adjudicatory powers by deciding cases. Some of them regulate primarily on a case-by-case basis through their decisions. Agency hearings are much less formal than court trials, since they never involve juries, and rules of evidence are less strictly observed. Those who are unhappy with an agency's decision must exhaust all administrative remedies before appealing the decision to a court of law. On appeal, the scope of judicial review of administrative agencies' actions is fairly limited.

When an agency decides a case, it is carrying out a judicial function. It is also, in effect, the prosecutor, since the agency staff decides whether or not to begin an enforcement action. Further, the agency serves as a legislature when making a rule and an executive when enforcing it. This concentration of functions in a single agency was much criticized until passage of the *Administrative Procedure Act of 1946,* which requires a separation of the functions within the agency. Now, independent administrative law judges (ALJs) hear the evidence and make *preliminary decisions.* The agency board or commission then issues a *final order.* Such orders are appealable to, and enforced by, the federal courts.

Although courts grant broad discretion to agencies to carry out their adjudicatory functions, they will overturn agency decisions that violate fundamental procedural protections. Consider the following case. As you read it, note its similarity to the procedural due process concept discussed earlier in the chapter.

Picca v. Mukasey

512 F.3d 75 (2d Cir. 2008)

FACTS

Arturo Picca, a citizen of Italy, lived in the United States without incident for 35 years. After Picca was convicted of attempted sale of a controlled substance, the Department of Homeland Security served Picca with a "Notice to Appear," charging him with removability under a federal statute. The Notice to Appear included a list of qualified attorneys and organizations who were available to represent him at no cost. Picca appeared at several hearings, each time represented by an attorney. However, when Picca appeared at the fourth hearing, his counsel informed the immigration judge (IJ) that he was withdrawing from his representation of Picca. The IJ then granted a continuance in order for Picca to "get another lawyer." Picca appeared before an IJ one final time. In advance of that hearing, Picca's wife submitted a letter stating that their family did "not have the funds to keep paying the large sums of money that are needed for each hearing." Despite the fact that Picca was not represented by an attorney, the IJ proceeded with the hearing and entered an order of removal.

ISSUE

Was Picca denied due process of law?

DECISION

Yes. At the final hearing, the IJ, upon learning that Picca's attorney had resigned, proceeded to adjudicate Picca's claims without telling Picca that he had a right to be represented or informing him of the existence of free legal services. The IJ's failure to do so was especially notable because the letter from Picca's wife indicated that Picca likely would have taken advantage of free legal services if made aware of their existence. The fact that the Notice to Appear included a list of qualified organizations and attorneys that provide free legal services does not remedy this flaw. That regulation specifically states that the immigration judge shall advise the respondent of the availability of free legal services and ascertain that the respondent has received a list of such programs.

Questions and Problem Cases

1. In response to numerous human rights violations perpetrated by the government of Burma (Myanmar), Massachusetts adopted a statute generally barring state entities from buying goods or services from any person (defined to include a business organization) identified on a restricted purchase list of those doing business with that country. The restricted list includes any business (domestic or foreign) that either is currently doing business in Burma or transacts such business at some future date. Three months later, Congress passed a statute (Burma Act) imposing a set of mandatory and conditional sanctions on Burma. This federal law has five basic parts. First, it imposes sanctions directly on Burma. Second, it authorizes the president to impose further sanctions subject to certain conditions. This second section makes clear that the sanctions apply only to U.S. persons or businesses and to new investment in Burma; foreign businesses or U.S. companies already doing business there are exempt from its coverage. Third, the statute directs the president to work to develop a comprehensive, multilateral strategy to bring democracy to and improve human rights practices and quality of life in Burma. Fourth, it requires to the president to periodically report to Congress any progress toward democratization and better living conditions in Burma. And fifth, the president is authorized to waive, temporarily or permanently, any sanctions under the law if he determines and certifies to Congress that the application of such sanction would be contrary to the national security interests of the United States. The National Foreign Trade Council, a nonprofit corporation representing many companies doing business in Burma, argued that the Massachusetts statue was preempted by the federal Burma Act. Is the Massachusetts statute preempted by the federal Burma Act? Explain.

2. A city passed an ordinance prohibiting people from camping and/or storing personal possessions on public streets and other public property. The law was challenged as a violation of the constitutional rights of homeless people. Clearly explain the analysis a court will use in determining the constitutionality of the ordinance.
3. The Maryland Department of Human Resources revoked a child care center's license on findings that a number of preschool-age children were victims of physical and sexual abuse while in the center's care. None of the alleged victims of child abuse testified in any of the proceedings. Instead, the agency acted entirely on hearsay through the parents and others who had spoken with the children. The child care center requested an opportunity to conduct psychological examinations of the alleged victims prior to the hearing. This request was denied. The child care center argued that the decision to revoke its license in the absence of such an examination was a denial of procedural due process. Was the decision to revoke the license a denial of procedural due process?
4. Nebraska voters adopted an article to their state constitution that prohibited nonfamily farm corporations from owning and operating Nebraska farm land. MSM Farms, a Nebraska corporation with unrelated shareholders, challenged the family farm measure on the grounds that it violated the equal protection clause of the U.S. Constitution. Specifically, MSM Farms argued that the state's prohibition of nonfamily corporate farming denied it equal protection because it was not rationally related to achieving any legitimate state purpose. Does the family farm measure discriminate in violation of the equal protection clause?
5. Ridge Line owned a large shopping center. The U.S. government purchased property to build a postal facility next to a shopping center owned by Ridge Line. When the postal facility was completed, storm water runoff sharply increased by at least 70 percent. Accordingly, Ridge Line built a storm water detention pond to handle the increased runoff. It asked the Postal Service to share in the cost of constructing the detention facilities. However, the government refused to pay anything. Ridge Line then sued, claiming the additional water flow caused by the development of the Postal Service facility constituted a taking, entitling it to compensation under the Takings Clause of the U.S. Constitution. The Postal Service argued there was no compensable taking because Ridge Line did not suffer a permanent and exclusive occupation by the government that destroyed its possession, use, or disposal of its property. Is the Postal Service correct? Explain.
6. Under the Anti-Terrorism and Effective Death Penalty Act (AEDPA), the secretary of state is empowered to designate an entity as a "foreign terrorist organization," which results in blocking any funds that the organization has on deposit in the United States. The administrative process requires the secretary to compile an administrative record and based upon that record to make findings. However, at no point in the proceedings establishing the administrative record is the alleged terrorist organization afforded notice of the materials used against it, or a right to comment on such materials or the developing administrative record. Nothing in the statute forbids the use of third-hand accounts, press stories, materials on the Internet, or other hearsay regarding the organization's activities. In fact, the secretary may base the findings on classified material, to which the organization has no access at any point during or after the proceeding to designate it as terrorist. Is this statute constitutional? Explain.
7. A Minnesota statute banned the retail sale of milk in plastic nonreturnable containers that are not biodegradable but permitted such sales in other nonreturnable containers, such as paperboard cartons. The statute stated that the purpose of the ban was to

promote resource conservation, ease solid waste disposal problems, and conserve energy. The Clover Leaf Creamery Company challenged the statute on equal protection grounds. It argued that the true purpose of the statute was to promote the interests of certain segments of the local dairy and pulpwood industries at the expense of other segments of those same industries. It also argued that paperboard containers had environmental drawbacks, that they required more energy to produce than did plastic containers, and that plastic containers took up less space at landfills and presented fewer solid waste disposal problems than did paperboard containers. Did the statute violate the Equal Protection Clause?

8. Jason Heckel, an Oregon resident, regularly sent unsolicited commercial e-mail, or spam, over the Internet. The Washington State Attorney General's Office received complaints from Washington recipients of Heckel's unsolicited e-mail. They alleged that his messages contained misleading subject lines and false transmission paths. The Consumer Protection Division immediately notified Heckel that Washington state law made it illegal to use a third party's domain name without permission, misrepresent or disguise in any other way the message's point of origin or transmission path, or use a misleading subject line. Despite this warning, Heckel continued to send his unsolicited commercial e-mails using misleading subject lines, false or unusable return e-mail addresses, and false or misleading transmission paths. Finally, the state sued Heckel for civil damages, asking for a permanent injunction against his business practices. In response, Heckel argued that the Washington statute violated the Commerce Clause. Does the Washington statute unconstitutionally burden interstate commerce?

Chapter 5

Crimes

Learning Objectives

After you have studied this chapter, you should be able to:

1. Describe the elements essential for a criminal conviction.
2. Understand the various types of capacity, particularly the insanity and irresistible impulse defenses.
3. Explain the exclusionary rule and the reasoning behind it.
4. Describe the types of violations encompassed by Sarbanes-Oxley, and who has liability under the law.
5. Articulate the scope of RICO and the main things that have to be proved for a conviction.

Hartley was accused of conspiring to defraud the U.S. government by supplying breaded shrimp that did not conform to military specifications, of committing mail fraud by sending the government invoices through the mail seeking payment for the shrimp, and of interstate transportation of money obtained by fraud by obtaining U.S. Treasury checks for the invoices for the shrimp. He and his company were also charged with violating the Racketeer Influenced and Corrupt Organizations Act (RICO) because these crimes allegedly established a pattern of racketeering.

- What constitutional protections does Hartley have as one who has been accused of a crime?
- What are the essentials of a crime that the government must show in order to obtain a conviction?
- Can these related acts flowing from one incident committed by a legitimate business establish a pattern of racketeering activity?

The Nature of Crimes

Crimes are **public wrongs**—acts prohibited by the *state* or *federal government.* Criminal prosecutions are brought by the prosecutor in the name of the government. Those who are convicted of committing criminal acts are subject to punishment established by the state or federal government in the form of fines, imprisonment, or execution.

Crimes are usually classed as felonies or misdemeanors, depending on the seriousness of the offense. **Felonies** are serious offenses such as murder, rape, and arson that are generally punishable by confinement in a penitentiary for substantial periods of time. Conviction of a felony may, in some cases, also result in **disenfranchisement** (loss of the right to vote) and bar a person from practicing certain professions such as law or medicine. **Misdemeanors** are lesser crimes such as traffic offenses or disorderly conduct that are punishable by fines or confinement in a city or county jail. Those convicted of crimes must also bear the **stigma** or social condemnation that accompanies a criminal conviction.

Whether a given act is classified as criminal or not is a social question. Our definitions of criminal conduct change with time. Behavior that was once considered criminal (e.g., blasphemy) is no longer treated as such. Today, we see many proposals to decriminalize certain kinds of behavior such as marijuana, gambling, prostitution, and consensual sex. Those who argue for decriminalization maintain that attempts to treat such "victimless crimes" criminally are ineffective, cause corruption, overburden the courts and police, and cause a loss of respect for the law. We also see calls for increased criminal penalties as a way to control corporate behavior. Deciding how to treat unwanted behavior is one of the more difficult problems facing society today.

The Essentials of Crime

LO1

In order for a person to be convicted of criminal behavior, the state must (1) demonstrate a prior statutory prohibition of the act, (2) prove beyond a reasonable doubt that the defendant committed every element of the criminal offense prohibited by the statute, and (3) prove that the defendant had the capacity to form a criminal intent. Figure 5.1 gives an overview of these steps.

Prior Statutory Prohibition

Before behavior can be treated as criminal, the legislature must have passed a statute making it criminal. Both Congress and the state legislatures can make an act a crime, and individuals are subject to the criminal laws of both systems. The Constitution protects against ***ex post facto*** **laws**—statutes that would punish someone for an act that was not considered criminal when the act was committed. Only those who commit the prohibited act *after* the effective date of the statute may be prosecuted.

The power of Congress and the state legislatures to make behavior criminal is constitutionally limited in other ways. Congress and state legislatures cannot make behavior criminal that is protected by the U.S. Constitution. For example, they would be prohibited from enforcing laws that unreasonably restrict the First Amendment right to freedom of speech and expression. Criminal statutes must also define the prohibited behavior clearly, so that an ordinary person would understand what behavior is prohibited. This requirement comes from the Due Process Clauses in the Fifth and Fourteenth Amendments to the U.S. Constitution. These limits are illustrated by the *Lock* case.

Lock v. State

971 N.E. 2d 71 (Ind. Sup. Ct. 2012)

FACTS

Lock was convicted of operating a vehicle as a habitual traffic violator. Indiana's motor vehicle statute provided that individuals whose driving privileges are suspended, as were Lock's, can still commute so long as the device they use is designed to have a maximum speed of 25 miles per hour. Lock was driving his motorized bicycle at 43 miles per hour on a flat surface when apprehended. Lock challenged his conviction, arguing that his bicycle was not encompassed by the statute because it had a maximum designed speed of 25 miles per hour. He argued that the law was unconstitutionally vague and that he did not know his speed was possible until he was pulled over.

ISSUE

Was the statute unconstitutionally vague?

DECISION

No. While the statute looks to the original manufacturer's maximum design speed, it also encompasses any subsequent modification or redesigns. Lock's vagueness argument is equivalent to a drunk driver's argument that a drunk driving statute is vague because he did not know until he was pulled over how many beers would render him impaired. This clearly would be unsuccessful. Lock's conviction stands. His driving privileges are revoked for life.

Proof Beyond a Reasonable Doubt

In view of the fact that in criminal cases we are dealing with the life and liberty of the accused person, as well as the stigma accompanying conviction, the legal system places strong limits on the power of the state to convict a person of a crime. Criminal defendants are *presumed innocent.* The state must overcome this presumption of innocence by proving every element of the offense charged against the defendant **beyond a reasonable doubt** to the satisfaction of all (or in some cases, a majority of) the jurors. This requirement is the primary way our system minimizes the risk of convicting an innocent person.

The state must prove its case within a framework of procedural safeguards, discussed later in this chapter, that are designed to protect the accused. The state's failure to prove any

FIGURE 5.1
A Criminal Case

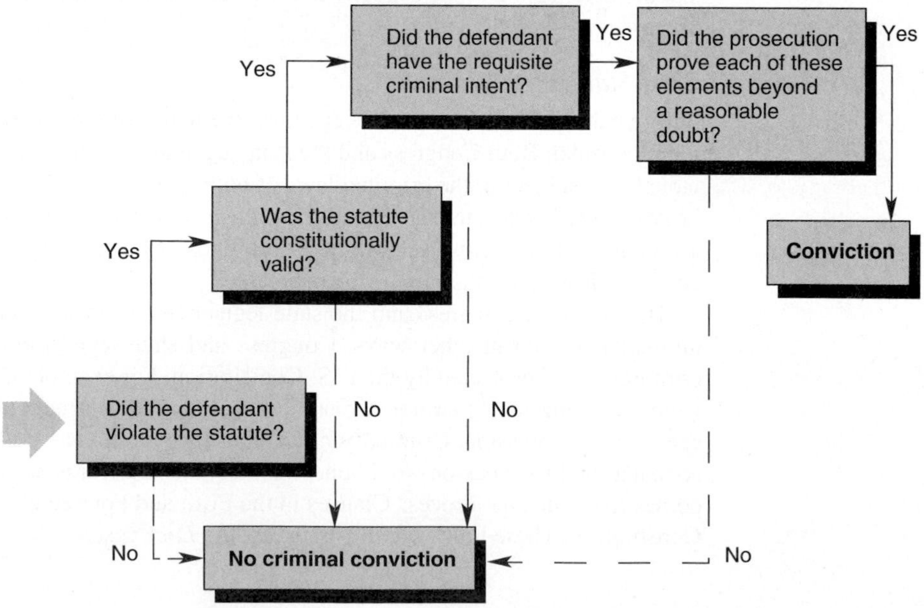

material element of its case results in the accused being acquitted or found not guilty, even though he or she may actually have committed the crime charged.

LO2

The Defendant's Capacity

Mens rea (criminal intent) is an element of most serious crimes. The basic idea behind requiring intent is that the criminal law generally seeks to punish *conscious* wrongdoers. Criminal intent may be inferred from the nature of the defendant's acts, but the defendant must be capable of forming the required criminal intent. Generally, a person can be incapable of forming the required intent due to intoxication, infancy, or insanity.

Voluntary intoxication is generally not a complete defense to criminal liability. It can, in some cases, diminish the extent of a defendant's liability if it prevents the formation of a specific criminal intent. For example, many first-degree murder statutes require proof of **premeditation,** a conscious decision to kill. A highly intoxicated defendant may not be capable of premeditation and may therefore be convicted of only second-degree murder, which does not generally require premeditation.

In common law, children under the age of 7 were incapable of forming a criminal intent, children between the ages of 7 and 14 were presumed incapable, and children between the ages of 14 and 21 were presumed capable. This is the concept of **infancy.** The **presumptions** relating to **capacity** were **rebuttable** by specific evidence about the intellectual and moral development of the accused. Today, most states have statutes that treat defendants below a stated age (usually 16 or 17) differently from adult offenders. The focus of these laws is rehabilitation rather than capacity, and they provide for special juvenile court systems and separate detention facilities. Repeat offenders, or those charged with very serious offenses, may be treated as adults. In 2005 the Supreme Court forbade the imposition of the death penalty for juveniles, citing the evolving U.S. ethical standards and the weight of international opinion.

Insanity on the part of a criminal defendant can affect a criminal trial in three ways. If the accused is incapable of assisting in the defense of the case, trial may be delayed until the accused regains sanity. An accused who becomes insane after trial but before sentencing is not sentenced until sanity has been regained. Insanity at the time the criminal act was committed absolves the defendant of criminal liability.

The states have adopted various insanity tests for criminal responsibility. These tests are not medical tests. They are legal tests designed to punish conscious, willful wrongdoers. A person may have been medically insane at the time of the criminal act but still legally responsible. Until recently, the trend was to broaden the legal definition of insanity by using such tests as the **irresistible impulse** rule or the test proposed by the American Law Institute, which says that defendants are not criminally responsible if, due to a mental disease or defect, they lack the substantial capacity to appreciate the wrongfulness of the act or to conform their conduct to the requirements of the law. Recent well-publicized cases have caused some jurisdictions to return to a narrower standard. For example, the standard adopted for federal criminal cases absolves only those defendants who cannot understand the nature and wrongfulness of their acts. In addition, some states have instituted a "guilty, but mentally ill" verdict as an alternative to the traditional "not guilty by reason of insanity" verdict. This alternative allows jurors to convict rather than acquit mentally ill defendants, with the assurance that they will be given treatment after conviction.

A criminal defendant is presumed to be sane. The defendant must introduce evidence that creates a reasonable doubt as to his or her sanity. Juries are often hostile toward insanity pleas, fearing that defendants are only trying to avoid punishment. Recent legislative changes in some jurisdictions have made it more difficult to successfully raise the insanity defense by requiring defendants to prove their insanity beyond a reasonable doubt.

Criminal Procedure

In addition to the presumption of innocence, our legal system has several other built-in safeguards to protect the accused. These safeguards are designed to prevent innocent people from being convicted of crimes they did not commit. They also represent an ideal of the proper role of government in a democracy. As Justice Oliver Wendell Holmes once said, "I think it less evil that some criminals should escape than that the government should play an ignoble part."

Table 5.1 illustrates some of the safeguards enjoyed by criminal defendants in our legal system.

Many of these safeguards are based on the Fourth and Fifth Amendments to the U.S. Constitution. The Fourth Amendment safeguards are designed to protect individuals from arbitrary and unreasonable governmental intrusion on their right to privacy, as the *Jones* case illustrates. The Fifth Amendment safeguards protect against compulsory self-incrimination and multiple prosecutions for the same offense. None of these protections is absolute. For example, while people cannot be compelled to testify against themselves, **nontestimonial** evidence such as fingerprints, hair samples, bodily fluids, and cells can be obtained through compulsion.

In determining whether a governmental action has unconstitutionally infringed on an individual's right, the court must balance the governmental need to do the action against the intrusion on the individual's rights. The assistance of computers and other electronic devices makes the balancing even harder for the courts.

Many of the safeguards discussed in Table 5.1, such as the exclusionary rule, the *Miranda* warning, and the places where one can reasonably expect to be protected from unreasonable warrantless searches, are being narrowed through recent Supreme Court interpretations. In times of rising crime rates, we frequently hear the argument that the incidence of crime is somehow related to our treatment of criminal defendants. While it is

United States v. Jones

132 S.Ct. 945 (U.S. Sup. Ct. 2012)

FACTS

Jones was a suspect being investigated by a joint FBI and District of Columbia drug task force. The investigators obtained a warrant to attach a global positioning device (GPS) to Jones's Jeep Grand Cherokee. The warrant later expired but the investigators went ahead and attached a magnetic GPS device to Jones's Jeep when it was parked in a public place. Investigators used the data it collected to link Jones to a cocaine stash house. That data was admitted as evidence in his trial, and he was convicted of federal drug offenses. He challenged his conviction, arguing that the use of the device constituted a search, and a valid warrant was needed if the evidence was to be used.

ISSUE

Did the investigators need a warrant to use a tracking device on defendant's car?

DECISION

Yes. The Fourth Amendment provides that people have a right to be secure in their "persons, houses, papers, and effects" against unreasonable searches and seizures. It is beyond dispute that a vehicle is an "effect." Jones had a reasonable expectation of privacy regarding it. When the government obtains information by physically intruding on a constitutionally protected area, a search has occurred. The installation of a GPS device and the use of that device to monitor the vehicle's movement constituted a search. The location information gathered by the GPS falls within the Fourth Amendment's limits on government searches and seizures.

LO3 **TABLE 5.1 Criminal Procedural Protection**

Description	Common Identification	Amendment
1. Illegally gained evidence (evidence resulting from "unreasonable searches and seizures" prohibited by the Fourth Amendment) cannot be used in criminal prosecutions.	Exclusionary rule	Fourth Amendment
2. A warrant for a search or arrest cannot be issued without probable cause.	Probable cause requirement	Fourth Amendment
3. Acquitted defendants can't be tried twice for the same crime.	Prohibition against double jeopardy	Fifth Amendment
4. Defendants in criminal cases have the right to remain silent and can't be compelled to testify against themselves.	Part of the *Miranda* warning	Fifth Amendment
5. When persons are taken into custody, the police must inform them of the right to remain silent, the right to counsel (which will be provided if they can't pay), and that anything they say can be used against them in court. Confessions made without these warnings cannot be used to convict a person.	*Miranda* warning	Fifth Amendment
6. Persons charged with crimes have a right to be represented by effective counsel if imprisonment can result from conviction.	Part of the *Miranda* warning	Sixth Amendment
7. Accused persons have a right to a speedy, public trial by a jury of their peers.	Trial by jury	Sixth Amendment
8. Persons accused of crimes have the right to confront and cross-examine their accusers.	Right of confrontation	Sixth Amendment
9. Excessive bail or fines and cruel and unusual punishment are prohibited.	No cruel and unusual punishment	Eighth Amendment

no doubt true that criminal safeguards allow some guilty persons to go free, attacking the root causes of criminal behavior is likely to do more to reduce crime than any reformation of the constitutional mandates. Some of the protections discussed in Table 5.1 have also been eroded due to terrorism concerns and for people suspected of being terrorists.

After the World Trade Center and Pentagon attacks on September 11, 2001, Congress enacted legislation designed to protect the public against future terrorist acts. The Uniting and Strengthening America by Providing Appropriate Tools Required to Intercept and Obstruct Terrorism Act of 2001 (USA PATRIOT Act) was signed into law on October 26, 2001. The purpose of the law is to protect against possible future terrorist threats within the United States by expanding the government's use of wiretapping and electronic surveillance power, clamping down on illegal immigration and money laundering, providing swift relief to victims of terrorism, and increasing information-sharing power between investigative agencies.

The USA PATRIOT Act allows law enforcement to use increased surveillance techniques, including the ability to conduct covert searches, obtain sensitive personal records, and track e-mail and Internet usage with minimal judicial and congressional oversight. It requires that deposits exceeding $10,000 and any suspicious monetary deposits be reported to the CIA, the Treasury Department, and other intelligence agencies. Authorities can also obtain a person's credit, medical, and student records after seeking a Surveillance Court warrant. Some critics of the law worry that the USA PATRIOT Act compromises the public's Fourth Amendment rights. While the safeguarding of the public against terrorism is important, they contend that the law tips the balance too heavily in the government's favor.

The discussion so far has focused on the rights of those accused of crimes. In recent years, legislatures have begun to accord rights to the victims of crime. Congress passed the *Crime Victims' Rights Act* to give victims the right to be "reasonably heard" at public sentencing proceedings in federal district court, among other things. Some courts have interpreted this to mean the right to be heard in person; others that victims can be limited to written impact statements in meeting the statutory requirement. Many states have equivalent statutes for crimes prosecuted in state courts. They can also include, among other things, a right to be notified when a felon is to be released from prison.

Crime and People in Business

People in business today are more likely than ever before to have some unpleasant contact with the criminal justice system. There is a trend today to get tough with white-collar crime. *White-collar crime* is the term used to describe various nonviolent criminal offenses committed by businesspersons and organizations. The focus of this trend is on business-related acts that primarily harm people outside the corporation. Such crime costs the public billions of dollars a year. A part of this trend is to make violations of regulatory statutes criminal offenses punishable by fines and/or imprisonment.

Many prosecutors and judges are demonstrating a "get tough" attitude about white-collar crimes that have often been treated leniently in the past. Today, corporate officials and agents may be held liable for crimes that they personally commit, for crimes they aid or abet, and for crimes they fail to prevent by neglecting to control the misconduct of those subject to their control. The last category of liability is sometimes known as the **responsible corporate officer doctrine.** Under this doctrine officials are even being tried for homicide and related crimes because prosecutors feel that the officials' actions (or lack thereof) are responsible for the deaths or serious injuries of employees and consumers. The idea of the responsible corporate officer has been integrated into many state and federal laws. It is argued that personal liability for corporate executives is necessary to **deter** corporations from violating laws and from viewing any fines imposed on the corporation as merely a cost of doing business. Those who may be held responsible include corporate officers who had the authority to make decisions regarding the operation of the regulated facility and failed to implement measures that would have prevented the violations from occurring. A corporate officer may be found liable even when the officer had no actual knowledge of, or control over, the activities in question.

Problems with Individual Liabilities

The get-tough attitude on the part of law enforcement officials is probably the result of several factors. There has been a long-standing public outcry against the lenient treatment of white-collar crime. This has been aggravated by statistics indicating the tremendous cost of such crime, by the atmosphere of public hostility toward people in positions of power and authority, by the Enron and similar corporate fraud scandals, and by the financial crisis that began in 2007.

Imposing individual criminal responsibility on persons in business poses difficult problems for prosecutors, however. The criminal law was developed with individual wrongdoers in mind. Corporate decisions are often the product of the inputs of numerous individuals. "Bad news" about corporate activities may not reach upper-level managers. As a result, it is often difficult to prove criminal intent on the part of individual managers. One legislative response to this problem of difficulty of proof has been the creation of regulatory statutes that impose liability without proof of the level of intent or knowledge traditionally required for criminal liability.

Most criminal offenses of regulatory laws are based on violations codified by the Health Care Finance Administration, the Occupational Health and Safety Administration, the

Consumer Products Safety Commission, and many environmental agencies. Many of these laws came into existence in response to the Industrial Revolution and are aimed at protecting public health, welfare, and safety. Under these "public welfare" offenses, ignorance of the law is no excuse.

Sentencing Guidelines

Another illustration of the get-tough attitude is contained in the *Federal Sentencing Guidelines* designed to establish consistent sentences for federal crimes. In order to arrive at the sentence, judges are supposed to use a formula based on issues such as the seriousness of the crime, the defendant's criminal record, and the circumstances of the crime. They specifically mandate stiffer penalties for white-collar crime. For example, crimes such as price-fixing, bid rigging, and insider trading carry a minimum two-month prison term, and the likelihood of a prison term for tax fraud is more than doubled. In 2005, the Supreme Court held that the *Guidelines* are advisory and that sentences can be reviewed for reasonableness using the factors set out in the *Guidelines.*

In addition to individual penalties, the *Corporate Sentencing Guidelines* establish penalties for organizations, including *corporate probation.* Under corporate probation, federal courts can monitor convicted companies and force them to establish programs to prevent and deter wrongdoing. The *Guidelines* also provide that corporations can reduce penalties by cooperating with investigations, making good faith efforts to self-police, establishing whistleblowing procedures, and self-reporting wrongdoing.

LO4 The Sarbanes-Oxley Act of 2002

The public outrage sparked by Enron, WorldCom, and other widely publicized corporate scandals generated strong support to crack down on white-collar criminals when it comes to accounting practices. The Sarbanes-Oxley Act of 2002 includes civil, criminal, and accounting reforms that drastically expand the accountability demanded of corporate officers and directors. Sarbanes-Oxley requires executives to pay close attention to the "quality of their companies' financial reporting" and requires them to take steps to discover deficiencies in reporting systems and make necessary changes. The criminal provisions of the act are found in sections titled the *Corporate and Criminal Fraud Accountability Act* and the *White-Collar Crime Penalty Enhancement Act.* These sections of the act create new federal offenses, increase the penalties for existing offenses, and call for a reexamination of the *Federal Sentencing Guidelines* to ensure that white-collar criminals are being adequately punished. Under the law:

- It is a crime for anyone to knowingly alter or destroy documents with the intent to impede, obstruct, or influence a government investigation.
- The chief executive officer (CEO) and chief financial officer (CFO) must certify reports submitted to the Securities and Exchange Commission (SEC). It is a crime for a CEO or CFO to certify a report he or she knows to be false.
- CEOs and CFOs must reimburse the company for any bonuses or other incentive compensation if any financial reporting is misleading due to misconduct, even if the misconduct was not attributable to the CEO or CFO.
- It is a felony to defraud shareholders of a publicly traded company.
- Procedures for whistleblowing, including anonymous reporting, must be established, and employees who "blow the whistle" on their employers for fraud are offered legal protection.

LO5 RICO

Numerous crimes are encompassed within the term *white-collar crime,* from bribery to fraud to price-fixing to regulatory violations such as environmental pollution. A statute increasingly being used to prosecute white-collar crime is the Racketeer Influenced and

Corrupt Organizations Act (RICO).[1] Much of the current activity and controversy in the area of criminal laws affecting business surrounds this act.

RICO was passed by Congress as part of the Organized Crime Control Act of 1970 and, as the name suggests, was designed to stop the entry of organized crime into legitimate business enterprises. The broad language of the RICO statute, however, has resulted in its application to legitimate businesses in cases involving white-collar crimes such as securities fraud, mail fraud, and wire fraud. This development has made RICO one of the most controversial pieces of legislation affecting business in our legal history. Supporters of RICO argue that the law is not abused when it is used against those not involved in organized crime because the conduct prohibited by the statute is harmful no matter who engages in it. These supporters view RICO as an effective and much-needed weapon against unethical business practices. Critics of RICO, on the other hand, assert that it is an overbroad statute that has needlessly hurt business reputations and that it ought to be amended by Congress so that it cannot be used against legitimate businesses. As the *Boyle* case illustrates, the Supreme Court has generally refused to narrow the reach of RICO. Thus, any change in this controversial legislation will likely come from Congress.

RICO prohibits (1) using income derived from "a pattern of racketeering activity" to acquire an interest in an enterprise, (2) acquiring or maintaining an interest in an enterprise through a pattern of racketeering activity, (3) conducting or participating in the affairs of an enterprise through a pattern of racketeering activity, or (4) conspiring to do the preceding. *Racketeering activity* includes the commission of any of over 30 federal or state crimes that include bribery; mail, wire, and securities fraud; and extortion. To show a pattern of activity, the prosecution must prove, at a minimum, the commission of two offenses within a 10-year period.

Companies also face civil liability under RICO. The government can seek civil penalties, and individuals injured by RICO violations can recover treble damages (three times their actual loss) plus attorneys' fees. The treble damages provision has caused a growing number of individuals to bring RICO claims for a wide range of activities, from abortion protests to tobacco advertising. This has contributed to the controversy surrounding the act.

In addition to growing criminal liability, businesses are increasingly being asked to help fight crime. This is evident in money-laundering rules. The USA Patriot Act, discussed earlier, broadens the types of businesses involved in the fight against money laundering well beyond the banks that were traditionally involved. The law includes organizations such as securities and commodities brokers; travel agencies; dealers in precious metals or jewels; car, boat, and airplane dealers; casinos; and those involved in real estate closings and settlements. Among other things, these businesses must report suspicious activity, including large cash transactions.

Boyle v. United States

200 U.S. 321 (U.S. Sup. Ct. 2009)

FACTS

Boyle and others participated in a series of bank robberies in New York, New Jersey, Ohio, and Wisconsin in the 1990s. There was a core group, and others were recruited from time to time. Boyle joined the group after it had been operating for three years. The group was informally organized, without

(continued)

[1] 18 U.S.C. Secs. 1961–1968 (1976).

a hierarchy or leader. They usually targeted cash-laden night-deposit boxes and split the proceeds. The participants met to plan each crime, gather tools, and assign the roles to be played. There was not any long-term master plan or agreement. In 2003 Boyle was indicted for participating in a racketeering activity. Boyle argued that there was no structure or hierarchy, and therefore there was no enterprise. Without an "enterprise" there could be no liability under RICO.

ISSUE

Must there be an ascertainable structure beyond that inherent in the pattern of the racketeering activity in order to qualify as an "enterprise" under RICO?

DECISION

No. RICO makes it unlawful for any person employed by or associated with any enterprise to conduct or participate, directly or indirectly, in the conduct of the enterprise's affairs through a pattern of racketeering activity. The statute does not define the outer boundaries of the word "enterprise" but does state that it can include "any group of individuals associated in fact though not a legal entity." Use of the word "any" ensures a wide reach, and the statute provides that it is to be liberally construed to achieve its purposes. Thus, an enterprise can be a group of individuals associated together for a common purpose of engaging in a course of conduct. An associated-in-fact enterprise must have a purpose, longevity sufficient to pursue the purpose, and relationships among those associated with the enterprise. Boyle was part of an enterprise for RICO purposes; the existence of an association-in-fact is often more readily proven by what it does rather than by an abstract analysis of its structure.

Concept Summary: RICO

Prohibited Acts	1. To use income from racketeering activity to purchase an interest in an enterprise 2. To acquire or maintain an interest in an enterprise through racketeering activity 3. To conduct or participate in the affairs of an enterprise through racketeering activity 4. To conspire to do 1–3		
Requirements	1. Two listed offenses within a 10-year period 2. Threat of continued criminal activity (pattern of racketeering activity)		
Common Business Violations	Mail fraud Securities fraud Wire fraud Bribery		
Penalties	**Criminal**	**Civil**	
	Fine up to $25,000 Imprisonment up to 20 years Forfeiture	In government suit: Divestiture Dissolution Other forfeiture	In private suit: Treble damages Attorneys' fees

The Foreign Corrupt Practices Act

Just as white-collar crime includes fraud and bribery within national boundaries, it also includes bribery that reaches beyond national borders. In 1977, Congress enacted the Foreign Corrupt Practices Act (FCPA). The FCPA makes it a crime for any American firm to offer, promise, or make payments or gifts of anything of value to foreign officials and certain others. It also establishes recordkeeping and internal-control requirements for firms subject to the Securities Exchange Act of 1934. Individuals who violate the FCPA can be fined $100,000 and/or imprisoned up to five years, while corporations that violate the antibribery provisions may be fined up to $2 million.

Global Anticorruption Initiatives

Since the 1990s, the world has experienced a rapid increase in trade and international business transactions. As a result, the international community has become even more concerned with corruption in international business dealings. In 2000, the United States ratified the Inter-American Convention Against Corruption (IACAC). The IACAC was initiated by the Organization for American States (OAS) and criminalizes transnational bribery in the Western Hemisphere. Twenty-three members of the OAS have signed the pact. In 1997, the Organization for Economic Development and Cooperation adopted the Convention on Combating Bribery of Officials in International Business Transactions. The Convention requires that all 35 participating nations make it a crime to bribe foreign officials, designate appropriate punishments for violations, and agree to extradite those charged with bribery. Similarly, both the European Union and the Pacific Basin Economic Council have adopted resolutions addressing bribery and corruption. Lastly, several international financial and development institutions, such as the World Trade Organization, the World Bank, and the International Monetary Fund, have implemented policies and procedures aimed at preventing corruption by fostering transparency and accountability. As business transactions increasingly cross national borders, cooperative antibribery efforts such as these are vital.

Cybercrime

It is obvious that electronic communication has reshaped the way we do business. However, with the increased use of Internet communications, including e-mail and social media sites such as Twitter, comes new and more complex ways for lawbreakers to commit crimes. It is important to note that while a corporation may face liability based on its own use of electronic communication, a corporation may also face potential liability for the online activities of its employees.

Both federal and state laws spell out the specifics of computer crime. It is a crime to access or use a computer without authorization. It also is a crime for people to access the services of commercial service providers without paying their fees. And it is illegal for hackers to alter or destroy data stored in another person's computer. In fact, there is a whole host of criminal statutes outlawing a range of online activities such as theft, distribution of obscene materials, destruction of property, and trespass. Of course, computers also broaden the ways in which evidence of crimes can be obtained. This evidence includes information gained from social networking sites like Facebook, MySpace, and Twitter.

Two federal laws address computer privacy and are worth examining here: the Electronic Communications Privacy Act (ECPA) and the Computer Fraud and Abuse Act (CFAA).

The Electronic Communications Privacy Act

The ECPA broadly imposes privacy obligations on those who process and handle electronic communications, as well as on those who intercept such messages. It is a derivative of the original federal wiretap law, enacted in 1968. Congress believed an update was necessary in light of the dramatic changes in computer and telecommunications technologies in recent years. The ECPA actually contains two major provisions: (1) its Wiretap Act protects against unauthorized interception of electronic communications and (2) its Stored Communication Act protects against unauthorized access and disclosure of electronic communication while it is in electronic storage.

The wiretap provisions make it unlawful for an electronic communication provider to intentionally disclose or use the contents of electronic communications. However, there are exceptions to these proscriptions. For instance, it would be permissible to intercept, use, or disclose such communications if such action were necessary to protect the provider's property rights or if the actions were taken in cooperation with law enforcement or intelligence officials as part of government-authorized surveillance.

Electronically stored data are protected by the Stored Communication provision. This part of the statute prohibits access to and disclosure of such information by third parties both when they had no authority and when they have exceeded their authority. However, this specific application of the ECPA applies only to third-party senders, and recipients of stored communication are not covered.

The Computer Fraud and Abuse Act

The CFAA civilly and criminally prohibits certain access to computers. Specifically, it bars a person without authorization from knowingly transmitting a program, information, code, or command with the intent of causing damage to a computer that is used in interstate or foreign commerce or communications. Other provisions in the statute prohibit interference with computers used by, or for the benefit of, the government or financial institutions. In general, the CFAA seeks to protect the privacy of information and communications as well as the national security of the United States. Simultaneously, it prohibits acts of sabotage or vandalism to protected computers or networks.

United States v. Nosal

642 F.3d 781 (9th Cir. Ct. App. 2011)

FACTS

When Nosal resigned from his job at Korn/Ferry, he signed an agreement promising not to compete with the company for a year and also agreed to serve as an independent contractor for them. It agreed to pay him $25,000 a month for a year, and also to give him two lump-sum payments. A few months later, Nosal recruited three Korn/Ferry employees to help him start a business. Before leaving, those employees downloaded a large amount of information from Korn/Ferry computers such as source lists, names, and contact information for executives. Nosal was subsequently indicted on a variety of counts including violations of the Computer Fraud and Abuse Act. The government alleged Nosal knowingly and with intent to defraud aided and abetted the employees to exceed their authorized access to Korn/Ferry computers. Nosal challenged the indictment, alleging that the law was aimed at computer hackers and not at people who access computers with authorization but then misuse the information.

ISSUE

Did Nosal violate the CFAA?

DECISION

No. Computers have become an indispensable part of our daily lives. We use them for work, for play, and sometimes play at work. Many employers have adopted policies prohibiting the use of their computers for nonbusiness purposes. The CFAA defines the phrase, "exceeds authorized access" as "to access a computer with authorization and to use such access to obtain or alter information" that he or she is not entitled to. A broad interpretation would transform the CFAA from an antihacking statute into a broad misappropriation statute. If Congress meant to broadly expand criminal liability to everyone who uses a computer in violation of use restrictions—which may well include everyone who uses a computer—we would expect it to say so more clearly. A plausible interpretation is that the language encompasses both external hackers and inside hackers who access unauthorized files or information. The computer gives employees new ways to procrastinate. These ways are routinely prohibited by many company use policies but employers seldom take action. These should not be turned into crimes. While some courts have chosen to read the statute broadly, we do not follow them. The phrase "exceed authorized access" does not apply to violations of use restrictions. This gives citizens fair notice of the criminal laws.

Recent Developments in Cybercrime

Congress has increasingly taken a "get tough" approach to cybercrime. Below are a few of the most recent developments in computer crime legislation.

- Enacted in response to the events of September 11, 2001, the Cyber Security Enhancement Act of 2002 (CSEA) and the USA PATRIOT Act make it easier for the government to collect personal electronic information and substantially stiffen the penalties for computer criminals. For example, the USA PATRIOT Act lowers the standards for governmental surveillance of foreign nationals, permits the government to gather information about e-mail messages, and dispenses with the probable cause standard needed to search one's person or property, as discussed earlier in this chapter. The act also changed the Computer Fraud and Abuse Act by making it easier to charge computer criminals with a felony and by increasing maximum punishments. Similarly, the CSEA reduces the amount of privacy in stored communication by allowing an Internet service provider (ISP) to disclose private information to a government agent, not just law enforcement officials, if the ISP has a "good faith" belief that the information concerns a serious crime. The new law also authorizes life sentences for individuals who knowingly or recklessly commit a computer crime that results in death and 20-year sentences for individuals who knowingly or recklessly commit a computer crime that results in serious bodily injury.
- The Controlling the Assault of Non-Solicited Pornography and Marketing Act (CAN-SPAM) took effect on January 1, 2004, and attempts to address the glut of "junk e-mail" commonly known as "spam." The statute requires that unsolicited commercial e-mail messages be labeled and include opt-out instructions and the senders' physical address. It prohibits the use of deceptive subject lines and false headers. The Federal Trade Commission was authorized to establish a "do-not-e-mail" registry. State laws that require labels on unsolicited commercial e-mail or prohibit such messages entirely are preempted. The doctrine of preemption is based on the Supremacy Clause of the U.S. Constitution and invalidates state laws that interfere with, or are contrary to, federal law.

International Efforts to Combat Cybercrime

The global nature of computer systems has led to an international effort to fight computer-related crime. Drafted under U.S. influence, the Council of Europe's "Convention on Cybercrime" aims to harmonize computer crime laws around the world by obliging participating countries to outlaw computer intrusion, child pornography, commercial copyright infringement, and online fraud. The treaty also requires each country to pass laws that permit the government to search and seize e-mail and computer records, perform Internet surveillance, and order ISPs to preserve logs in connection with an investigation. The United States is 1 of 38 nations that have signed on to the treaty, which the U.S. Senate ratified in 2006. Other transnational groups, such as the G-8, have developed task forces to address high-tech crime. Many nongovernmental organizations and private corporations have also joined in the effort to fight cybercrime by harmonizing national legislation.

Because of the increased liability faced by businesses and businesspeople in recent years, knowledge of the criminal law is an essential element of a contemporary business education.

Questions and Problem Cases

1. What are the differences between felonies and misdemeanors?
2. What is the Foreign Corrupt Practices Act and what are its penalties?
3. Describe two laws designed to fight cybercrime.
4. While working as a lifeguard, Mann secretly installed a video camera in the women's locker room. The police discovered it was Mann who installed it because he had accidentally filmed himself during the installation. They got a warrant to search Mann's computer and hard drives for evidence of voyeurism. During the search, the officer discovered evidence of child pornography. Mann challenged the use of this evidence because it exceeded the scope of the warrant. The state argued that it fell within the "plain-view" doctrine. Is the state correct? Why?
5. Hong bought a wastewater treatment plant and named it Avion. He carefully avoided any formal association with the company and was not an officer. However, he did control its assets and played a substantial role in its operations. Hong investigated a water treatment system and was told it was not for treating completely untreated wastewater. It was purchased anyway. It did not work well and untreated water was discharged into the city's sewer system in violation of Avion's discharge permit. Hong was found guilty of violating the Clean Water Act, fined $1.3 million, and sentenced to 36 months in prison. Hong challenged the conviction, claiming that since he was not a formally designated officer, he could not be held responsible under the corporate officer doctrine. Is this correct? Why?
6. Sult challenged his conviction under a Florida law that made it a crime to wear or display law enforcement insignia without authorization. He argued that the statute was overly broad because it did not have an intent-to-deceive element and therefore could penalize innocent behavior. Should the conviction be overturned? Explain why or why not.
7. Congress passed the Marine Transportation Act after 9/11 to boost security. Under it, ferries were considered at high risk of a "maritime security incident" and had to adopt security plans. The company that runs the ferry across Lake Champlain planned to visually search carry-on baggage and vehicle trunks. A commuter on the ferry challenged the searches because they were suspicionless and done without a warrant. Were the searches constitutional? Why?
8. The complainant was a convicted sex offender. After his conviction, Massachusetts passed a law that would require him to wear a satellite-based monitoring device. He challenged the law's application to him as unconstitutional because it would, *expost facto*, apply a punishment that was not in existence when he committed the crime. Should this argument be successful? Explain.

Chapter 6

Intentional Torts

Learning Objectives

After you have studied this chapter, you should be able to:

1. Explain what a tort is and what it is designed to do.
2. Define preponderance of the evidence and indicate who has the burden of proof.
3. Identify the differences between assault and battery.
4. Describe the differences among slander, libel, and invasion of privacy, and describe the interests they are designed to protect.
5. Explain the differences between trespass and conversion.
6. Identify the torts protecting economic relations.

Stevens was leaving a local department store when an armed security guard grabbed her arm and asked her to accompany him to an office in the back of the store. Once there, she was accused of shoplifting, and security personnel searched her, her purse, and the contents of a bag she was carrying. They found nothing incriminating. The store personnel kept her there for over two hours, badgering her to sign a release admitting her guilt in exchange for an agreement by the store not to prosecute her.

- What intentional torts has the store committed against Stevens?
- What elements would Stevens have to show in order to prove these torts?
- Is Stevens likely to get punitive damages?

Introduction Torts

LO1

Torts are private (civil) wrongs against persons or property. Persons who are injured by the tortious act of another may file a civil suit for actual **(compensatory)** damages to compensate them for their injuries. Injury in tort can include much more than physical injury (and resulting direct injuries such as loss of pay and medical benefits). It also encompasses such intangible harms as loss of privacy, emotional distress, and injury to reputation. In some cases, **punitive damages** in excess of the plaintiff's actual injuries may be recovered. Punitive damages are used to punish the defendant and deter the defendant and others from repeating behavior that is particularly offensive.

In recent years the Supreme Court has narrowed the amounts and circumstances under which punitive damages can be awarded. For example, the Court held in 2003 that in general, punitive awards are more likely to be excessive when the ratio of punitive to compensatory damages exceeds single digits.

Exxon Shipping Co. v. Baker

(U.S. Sup. Ct. 2008)

FACTS

In 1989, an Exxon supertanker ran aground on a reef off Alaska, spilling millions of gallons of crude oil into Prince William Sound. The captain had a history of alcohol abuse, and his blood alcohol level was still high 11 hours after the spill. He had "inexplicably exited the bridge" before the accident, leaving a tricky course correction to unlicensed subordinates. Exxon pleaded guilty to criminal violations and was fined. It settled a civil action by the United States and Alaska for at least $900 million and paid $303 million in voluntary payments to private parties. Additionally, it spent $2.1 billion on cleanup. Other civil cases brought by fishermen and other interests whose businesses were disrupted by the spill were consolidated into this lawsuit. They were awarded $287 million in compensatory damages and $5 billion in punitive damages. The court of appeals reduced the punitive award to $2.5 billion. This award was appealed as excessive, among other issues.

ISSUE

Were the punitive damages excessive?

DECISION

Yes. In this case, the Court is not deciding under state law, where approaches to punitive damages vary, but under federal maritime law. Thus, we can decide this as we see fit. We believe the punitive damages should not have exceeded the actual damages of $507.5 million. Since 1763 U.S. courts have allowed damages that exceed compensatory damages as a punishment for extraordinary wrongdoing, to deter similar actions in the future, and to compensate for intangible injuries for which compensation is otherwise unavailable. The consensus today is that they are for retribution and deterring harmful conduct. Thus, degrees of relative blameworthiness are relevant. Action taken or omitted in order to augment profit represents an enhanced degree of punishable culpability, as does willful or malicious action taken with a purpose to injure. Higher punitive damages are considered appropriate when wrongdoing is hard to detect or when the value of injury and the compensatory award are small. While punitive damages are more frequent and higher in the U.S. than other countries, the most recent studies tend to show that the median ratio of punitive damages to compensatory awards has been less than 1:1. Thus, despite audible criticism, punitive awards are not increasing in the percentage of cases awarding them nor in the amounts awarded. The real problem is the stark unpredictability of such awards. Using a ratio would help address this. In this case, defendant's action was worse than negligence but less than malicious. It was reckless, but not for profit. A ratio of 1:1 in maritime cases such as this is appropriate.

The same behavior may give rise to both civil (tort) and criminal liability. For example, a rapist is criminally liable for the crime of rape and is also civilly liable for the torts of assault, battery, false imprisonment, and intentional infliction of emotional distress. The

TABLE 6.1
Crimes versus Intentional Torts

	Crimes	Intentional Torts
Nature	Criminal	Civil
Elements	(1) Violation of a statute (2) Intent	(1) Harm to another person or property (2) Intent
Actors	Government prosecutor v. defendant	Plaintiff v. defendant (victim) (tortfeasor)
Burden of Proof	Prosecutor must establish defendant's guilt beyond a reasonable doubt.	Plaintiff must establish defendant's liability by a preponderance of the evidence.
Punishment	Fines, imprisonment, execution	Defendant may have to pay the plaintiff compensatory and punitive damages.

reason more victims of crimes do not file civil lawsuits against their attackers is simply that most criminal defendants are financially unable to pay a damage award. Some of the important differences between torts and crimes are shown in Table 6.1.

LO2 The plaintiff's burden of proof in a tort case is proof by a **preponderance of the evidence.** This simply means that when both sides have presented their evidence, the greater weight of the believable evidence must be on the plaintiff's side. This standard of proof is applied in all civil cases, in which only money is at stake, in contrast to criminal cases, in which the defendant's life or liberty may be at stake.

In tort law, society is engaged in a constant balancing act between individual rights and duties. What kinds of behavior should a person have to tolerate in his or her fellow citizens, and what kinds of behavior should be considered intolerable? Historically, our legal system seems to be expanding the grounds for tort liability. Torts are generally classified according to the level of fault exhibited by the wrongdoer's behavior. This chapter deals with **intentional torts:** types of behavior that indicate either the wrongdoer's conscious desire to cause harm or the wrongdoer's knowledge that such harm was substantially certain to result. **Negligence** and **strict liability** torts will be discussed in Chapter 7.

LO1

Interference with Personal Rights

LO3

Battery

The basic personal interest that any legal system can protect is a person's right to be free from injurious or unpleasant physical contact with others. Battery, an intentional, unconsented-to touching that is harmful or offensive, protects that interest. The least touching can be a battery if it produces injury or would be considered offensive to a *person of ordinary sensibilities.*

The defendant need not actually touch the plaintiff's body to be liable for battery. It is sufficient to touch anything connected to the plaintiff's body. For example, if Bob snatches Mary's purse off her shoulder, or kicks her dog while she is walking it on a leash, he is liable for battery even though he has not touched her body. In addition, a battery can be committed by setting something in motion that touches the plaintiff.

Consent must be freely and intelligently given to be a defense to battery. Consent may in some cases be inferred from a person's voluntary participation in an activity. For example, a boxer could hardly complain about normal injuries suffered in a fight. However, a quarterback who is knifed on the 50-yard line clearly has a battery claim. What about a hockey player who is hit by a hockey stick in a fight that erupts during a game? Should his claim be barred on account of his voluntary participation in an admittedly violent sport? Such cases raise difficult issues about the scope of consent; there are no easy answers. The court in the case above makes the call in favor of the team.

LO3

Assault

The tort of assault is designed to protect people from threats of battery. **Assault** is putting another in apprehension of an imminent (immediate) threat to his or her physical safety. No contact is necessary. Assault focuses on the well-grounded apprehension in the mind of the plaintiff.

Would an ordinary person in the plaintiff's situation have thought that battery was imminent? Most courts say that "mere words are not enough" for assault and require some affirmative act, like a threatening gesture by the defendant. Threats of battery in the future ("I'll get you next week") or attempts at battery that the plaintiff is not aware of at the time, like a bullet fired from a great distance that misses the plaintiff, are not grounds for a civil assault suit.

False Imprisonment

The tort of false imprisonment protects both physical (freedom of movement) and mental (freedom from knowledge of confinement) interests. **False imprisonment** is the intentional confinement of a person for an appreciable time (a few minutes is enough) without the person's consent. *Confinement* occurs when a person substantially restricts another person's freedom of movement. A partial obstruction of a person's progress is not false imprisonment. Two examples of partial obstruction are standing in a person's path and locking the front door of a building a person is in without locking the back door.

If escape from confinement is possible but involves an unreasonable risk of harm or affront to the person's dignity, false imprisonment has occurred. Traditionally, a person must know that he or she is confined, and any consent to confinement must be freely given. Consent given in the face of an implied or actual threat of force by the confiner or an assertion of legal authority by the confiner is not freely given.

Most false imprisonment cases today probably involve shoplifting. Under common law, the store owner who stopped a suspected shoplifter was liable for any torts committed in the process if the plaintiff was innocent of any wrongdoing. Today, many states have passed statutes giving store owners a **conditional privilege** to stop persons they reasonably believe are shoplifting, as long as the owner acts in a reasonable manner and detains the suspect only for a reasonable length of time. The store in the example at the beginning of the chapter probably exceeded its statutory privilege because it kept Stevens for over two hours after determining that she did not have any stolen items, and it badgered her to sign a release. Thus, Stevens could sue the store for false imprisonment, as well as other torts such as battery and intentional infliction of emotional distress. The store may also be liable for punitive damages.

Intentional Infliction of Mental Distress

The courts have traditionally been reluctant to grant recovery for purely mental injuries for fear of opening the door to fictitious claims. Developments in modern medicine have, however, made such injuries more provable. As a result, most courts have moved away from the traditional "impact" rule, which allowed recovery for mental injuries only if a battery had occurred, and are allowing recovery solely for severe emotional distress. Some courts still require physical manifestation of the emotional distress, such as a tic or an ulcer, before they allow a suit to be brought. All courts require that the defendant's conduct be **outrageous**—that is, substantially certain to produce severe emotional distress in a person of ordinary sensibilities.

Chesher v. Neyer

477 F.3d 784 (6th Cir. 2007)

FACTS

The coroner of Hamilton County, Ohio, asked a photographer to work on an autopsy training video. The photographer obtained permission to work on an art project using bodies in the morgue, often with props. For example, one photo involved a dollhouse ladder placed against a body's open skull, and another corpse had sheet music put on her body, a snail near her groin, and other items pressed into her hand and mouth. He took 317 photos over six months. A photo-developing studio reported the photos to the Cincinnati police, and the case gained wide publicity. Plaintiffs, relatives of the deceased, sued for intentional infliction of emotional distress.

ISSUE

Can the coroner be sued for intentional infliction of emotional distress?

DECISION

Yes. The coroner has a duty to protect the integrity of bodies in his custody and see that they are treated in a safe and respectful manner. Yet, he gave the photographer free reign in the morgue over a long period of time, contrary to legal advice. The bodies were used for other than a proper government purpose without the permission of the legal representatives of the deceased. The morgue left the photographer alone with autopsy subjects after seeing the offending photos. The actions were clearly outside the scope of official duties. Defendant can be found to have acted in an extreme and outrageous manner, recklessly causing the relatives emotional distress.

Defamation

LO4

Since injury to a person's reputation can cause that person considerable anguish and harm, the torts of **libel** (written defamation) and **slander** (oral defamation) were designed to protect against such injury. The basis of both torts is the publication of an untrue statement that injures a person's reputation or character. *Publication* in this context means communication of the statement to at least one person other than the defamed party. If that statement exposes a person to hatred, contempt, or ridicule, it is defamatory. It is usually up to the jury to decide if a given statement is defamatory.

Because it is the *individual's* reputation that is being protected, the defamatory statement must be "of and concerning" the plaintiff to be actionable. Thus, the plaintiff could not sue for defamation when slanderous statements such as ethnic slurs are made about a group, even though she is a member of that group. Courts recognize a limited right of corporations and other business entities to protect their reputations. They can bring claims for defamatory statements that harm them in conducting their business or that deter others from dealing with them. False statements about the quality of a company's products or services may give rise to a cause of action for **disparagement,** which is discussed later in this chapter.

Damages are presumed in libel cases, unless the written statement is not defamatory on its face. For example, an announcement in the newspaper that Bob married Sue is not defamatory on its face even though Bob was married to Mary at the time, because the average reader would not think there was anything wrong with Bob marrying Sue. A similar analysis occurs in the following case.

Because slander is oral, and therefore considered less damaging, a person may not recover for it without proving actual damages, unless the nature of the defamatory statement is so serious that the law has classified it as *slander per se.* Classic forms of slander per se are statements that a person has a "loathsome" disease, has committed a serious crime, is professionally incompetent or guilty of professional improprieties, or is guilty of serious sexual misconduct. Broadcast defamation, which involves both oral and visual impressions, is generally considered to be libel.

Truth is a complete defense to a defamation suit. No matter how embarrassing or terrible the statement, if it is true, the person who communicated it cannot be held liable. False statements may also not be the basis for a successful defamation suit if they are communicated in a privileged situation. The law recognizes that in certain kinds of situations, the necessity to speak without fear of liability is more important than protecting reputation or character. The greater the necessity, the broader the privilege. Therefore, statements communicated in some situations are granted **absolute privilege**—they can never serve as a basis for a successful defamation suit. Statements by members of Congress on the floor of Congress, statements by participants in judicial proceedings, and private statements between spouses are absolutely privileged. Other statements are only **conditionally privileged**—they can serve as a basis for a successful suit if the person publishing the statement abuses the privilege. Statements made in the furtherance of legitimate business interests, such as providing employee references or credit reports, are often conditionally privileged.

Williams v. Tharp

915 N.E.2d 980 (Ind. Sup. Ct. 2009)

FACTS

Williams and Kelsey went to a Papa John's restaurant to pick up an order. Kelsey had on a rectangular fanny pack with silver reflective material that he wore in front. Kelsey took money out of the pack to help pay for the order and handed it to Williams, who paid with a credit card, and started home. Tharp, a delivery driver, came in while Williams and Kelsey were paying. He went outside and told a passerby that he thought a customer had a gun. The passerby called the police. Tharp told another employee there was a customer with a gun, but the employee did not see any evidence of it. When Officer Frolick arrived, Tharp gave him the license number of Williams's car. Tharp said the customer pulled a handgun out of his waistband or a holster, and then put it back. He described the gun as a medium-sized silver gun with a brown wooden handle with two small silver circles. Williams and Kelsey were ordered out of the car at gunpoint when they arrived home, ordered to their knees, handcuffed, and held for over an hour while family and neighbors looked on. They did not have a gun; the store employees said there had been no robbery and they saw no evidence of a gun. In the meantime, Tharp fled because he had outstanding warrants for his arrest and had obtained his job under a false identity. Williams and Kelsey sued for defamation, false imprisonment, and intentional infliction of emotional distress. Tharp defended that there was a qualified privilege to report to the police, and therefore there was no liability.

ISSUE

Was there a qualified privilege that insulates Tharp from liability?

DECISION

Yes. A qualified privilege exists to make a good faith communication to the police for the public interest of enhancing public safely and investigating crime. Indeed, the Indiana Department of Homeland Security provides a toll-free number, mail address, and e-mail address to encourage citizens to report suspicious activity. However, this is a qualified privilege, and citizens also have an interest in avoiding false accusations of criminal misconduct. The privilege is lost if the communication was motivated by ill will, there was excessive publication, or the statement was made without belief or grounds for belief in its truth. It is best to foster open communication between citizens and law enforcement, and leave the task of investigation and appropriate response to trained professionals. There is insufficient evidence to conclude Tharp's statement was knowingly false and, since he did not know Williams or Kelsey, no evidence of ill will. While the statement was false, the privilege protects Tharp from liability.

The U.S. Supreme Court has given the media an almost absolute privilege when discussing public officials by requiring that the official prove **actual malice** when suing for false and defamatory statements. This means that the official must prove that the statement was made with knowledge of falsity, or with reckless disregard for the truth, which is usually very difficult to do. The Court felt that the public interest in the "free and unfettered debate" of important social issues justified this limitation on a public official's rights.[1] **Public figures** (private persons who are famous or have involved themselves in some public controversy) face a similar burden of proof for similar reasons.[2] The courts have also recognized a conditional privilege protecting fair and accurate media reporting of public proceedings.

Hatfill v. New York Times Co.

(4th Cir. 2008)

FACTS

Dr. Steven Hatfill was identified as a "person of interest" in the fatal anthrax mailings in the wake of the September 11 terrorist attacks. He sued *The New York Times* for defamation after a *Times* columnist, Kristof, wrote a series of columns in 2002. With each column Kristof identified new evidence that suggested Hatfill as a prime suspect, noting that he had access to anthrax, knew how to make it, and had a motive. He also criticized the FBI for not adequately investigating the evidence against Hatfill. Hatfill said that the columns defamed him by falsely alleging he engaged in terrorist and homicidal activity and that it was defamation per se because it linked him to the anthrax mailings. The *Times* argued that Hatfill was a "limited purpose public figure" and therefore was required to show actual malice.

ISSUE

Is Hatfill a limited purpose public figure?

DECISION

Yes. A public figure, when suing for defamation, must prove that the alleged defamatory statement was made with malice, or with knowledge that it was false or with reckless disregard for the truth. This requirement fosters society's interest in uninhibited, robust, and wide-open public debate on public issues. Also, public figures have greater access to channels of effective communication and thus can better counter false statements than can private citizens. While some public figures have assumed roles of such persuasive power and influence that they are public figures for all purposes, others have the public figure designation because they have thrust themselves into a particular public controversy. The latter are public figures for only those limited purposes that pertain to that controversy. Dr. Hatfill was a research scientist who was a respected figure in the bioterrorism community, giving public lectures, writing articles, and involving himself in preparedness training for bioterrorist attacks. Hatfill had access to channels of effective communication, and he had assumed a role of special prominence in a public controversy about bioterrorist attacks. Hatfill cannot show malice because Kristof's columns were, above all, concerned with the government's efforts to protect the nation from a bioterrorist attack.

As we saw in Chapter 5, law enforcement officials are now actively policing cyberspace to deter and punish misconduct by computer users. Just as the number of computer crimes are increasing, so too are the number of "cybertorts." Two of the most prevalent intentional torts for which computer users might be found liable are defamation and trespass (discussed later in this chapter).

Perhaps because of the spontaneous nature of so much activity in cyberspace, incidents of defamation seem particularly frequent on the Internet. Because such messages may reach millions of people throughout the world in a matter of seconds, malicious statements may have tremendous capacity to injure innocent victims.

[1] *New York Times v. Sullivan,* 376 U.S. 254 (1964).

[2] *Curtis Publishing Co. v. Butts,* 388 U.S. 130 (1967).

Roberts v. McAfee, Inc.

http://pub.bna.com/w/1036012.pdf
9th Cir. Ct. App. (2011)

FACTS

Roberts allowed McAfee's controller and senior vice president to backdate 20,000 stock options the company had given him several months earlier when he was promoted. This increased the value of Roberts's options by about $10/share. Backdating is not illegal *per se;* it is illegal if done without company authorization or reported as a compensation expense. In 2006, government agencies began a nationwide investigation into backdating and identified McAfee as one of 17 companies suspected of backdating. The backdating of Roberts's stock was revealed. McAfee told its lawyers and the investigating agencies that Roberts admitted what he had done was wrong. Roberts said he told the company, as did the controller, that they thought the original date was wrong and therefore they had the authority to change it. Roberts was subsequently fired and also indicted by the government. Soon after the firing, McAfee posted on its webpage a press release that Roberts had been fired because of an "improper" incident related to employee stock options. It remained on the site for 3½ years.

During his trial, evidence emerged that tended to show the backdating in Roberts's case was not illegal and that the company had evidence of this. The jury found Roberts not guilty on two charges and prosecutors dismissed other charges on which the jury could not reach agreement. Roberts then sued McAfee for defamation. Although the statute of limitations had run, Roberts claimed that McAfee's failure to take down the press release once it had substantial indications of its falsity amounted to a republication, thereby keeping the defamation claim alive.

ISSUE

Was leaving the press release on the website a republication of defamatory material?

DECISION

No. Under California law, a publication in a mass communication format such as a newspaper, a magazine, or a computer, accrues upon the first publication of the communication, thereby sparing the courts from litigation of stale claims arising from such things as when a book or magazine is resold years later. Information is generally considered "published" within the meaning of this single-publication rule when it is first made available to the public. Likewise, the publication on the Internet is considered a single publication no matter how long it remains. Failure to remove a libel from a building or a site can subject one to a successful defamation claim, but the claim must be brought within the statute of limitations, which did not occur here. It would be different if the publication were out of print for some time or unavailable in digital form and the publisher made a conscious decision to reissue it or again make it available for download. Then, a republication would have occurred. The need to protect Web publishers from almost perpetual liability for statements they make available to the hundreds of million people who have access to the Internet is greater even than the need to protect the publishers of conventional hard copy newspapers, magazines, and books.

Efforts to prevent defamatory statements on the Internet have been thwarted to some degree by the ability of computer users to operate under an alias. However, some online service companies have been willing to reveal an author's true identity when confronted by a court subpoena. One potential remedy is to sue the online service companies that operate the bulletin boards where the defamatory statement appears. However, this remedy is rarely made available to injured plaintiffs. The federal Communications Decency Act immunizes service providers from liability for messages that originated with third parties.

LO4 Invasion of Privacy

The recognition of a **right of privacy** is a relatively recent development in tort law. This area is still undergoing considerable development and has currently expanded to include several kinds of behavior that infringe on a person's "right to be left alone." Intrusion on a person's solitude or seclusion is a widely recognized form of invasion of privacy. Phone harassment of debtors by creditors, illegal searches of a person or a person's property, and obscene phone calls are examples of this form of invasion of privacy.

Publishing true but private facts about a person can also be an invasion of privacy. Acts like putting an ad in the paper saying that a person does not pay his or her bills, publishing embarrassing details of a person's illnesses, or publishing pictures of a parent's deformed child are examples of this form of invasion of privacy. Putting a person in a false light in the public eye by signing his or her name to a public letter or telegram, or using a person's photo to illustrate an article with which that person has no real connection, have also been held to be invasions of privacy. These forms of invasion of privacy are based on **publicity.** Therefore, some widespread dissemination of the information is necessary for liability. It should also be noted that truth is not a defense to "publication of private facts." Publication of matters of public record, or of newsworthy items (items of legitimate public interest), cannot be the basis of a successful suit for invasion of privacy.

Public figures cannot complain about publicity that is reasonably related to their public activities. Since the right of privacy is a personal right, corporations cannot rely on it.

A final form of invasion of privacy involves using a person's name or likeness for commercial purposes without that person's consent. For example, using a person's name or image in an ad to imply that he or she endorses the product or service, if done without permission, would be an invasion of privacy. This form of privacy protects a property interest one has in oneself. This is a developing area of privacy, and exactly what is protected, how long it is protected, and whether the right is inheritable vary greatly from state to state.

Misuse of Legal Proceedings

Malicious prosecution, wrongful use of civil proceedings, and abuse of process are three tort theories that protect people from harms resulting from wrongfully brought lawsuits. **Malicious prosecution** gives a remedy for the financial, emotional, and reputational harm that can result when criminal proceedings are wrongfully brought. An action for **wrongful use of civil proceedings** compensates for similar damages arising from wrongfully brought civil suits. In both instances, the plaintiff must show that the wrongfully brought suit *terminated in his favor*, that the suit was brought *without probable cause* to believe the suit was justified, and that it was brought *for an improper purpose.*

Roberts v. McAfee

9th Cir. Ct. App. (2011)

FACTS

(This is the same case as discussed earlier in the chapter. In this suit, as happens in a large number of lawsuits, plaintiffs sue under more than one theory and decisions are made about each of those theories.) In addition to suing for defamation, Roberts sued for malicious prosecution, claiming that McAfee failed to disclose exculpatory evidence and fabricated evidence which made him look guilty, and this was available to the government. Additionally, it fired him because of the backdating. All of this made him look guilty and led to his prosecution.

ISSUE

Did McAfee wrongfully cause prosecution to be brought against Roberts?

DECISION

No. To succeed on a malicious prosecution claim, a plaintiff must prove that the prior action: (1) was commenced by or at the direction of the defendant and was pursued to a legal termination in the plaintiff's favor; (2) was brought without probable cause; and (3) was initiated with malice. Roberts cannot show a lack of probable cause. Probable cause exists where it is objectively reasonable for the defendant to suspect the plaintiff had committed a crime. Here McAfee had probable cause to accuse Roberts of participating in illegal backdating. Even if McAfee withheld some evidence so that Roberts seemed more culpable, that is not enough to destroy probable cause. There was enough other evidence to give probable cause. Despite the fact that Roberts was able to beat the criminal and civil charges against him, it does not mean there was no probable cause to bring them.

Abuse of process does not require that the suit terminate in the defendant's favor or that there be no probable cause in order for the person wrongfully sued to win. What is required is proof that the suit was brought for a primary purpose other than the one for which such proceedings are designed. This requirement often involves situations in which the person bringing the suit is trying to force the defendant to take an action unrelated to the subject of the suit. For example, assume Craig wants to buy Andrew's business but Andrew refuses to sell. If Craig then brings a *nuisance* suit against the business in order to force the sale, Craig may be liable to Andrew for abuse of process. See Table 6.2 for a summary of the misuse of legal proceedings.

Interference with Property Rights

Property rights have traditionally occupied an important position in our legal system. Suits for tortious interference with property rights are generally brought by the party with the right to *possess* the property rather than its owner. However, the owner of land that has been leased to another may bring a suit if the interference also results in lasting damage to the property. Trespass to land, trespass to personal property, and conversion are the traditionally recognized torts against property.

Trespass to Land

Any entry by a person onto land in the possession of another is a **trespass,** unless the entry is done with the possessor's permission or is privileged. The same is true for causing anything to enter the land in the possession of another. A person who remains on the land of another, as in the case of a tenant who stays after the lease has expired, or who allows anything to remain on another's property, is trespassing. No actual harm to the property is necessary for trespass. However, if no actual losses result, the plaintiff usually will recover only nominal damages.

TABLE 6.2
Misuse of Legal Proceedings

	Requirements			
Type	**Malice**	**Wrongful Suit Ended in Plaintiff's Favor**	**No Probable Cause**	**Wrongful Motive**
1. Malicious prosecution	Yes	Yes	Yes	Yes
2. Wrongful use of civil proceedings	Yes	Yes	Yes	Yes
3. Abuse of process	No	No	No	Yes

Stickdorn v. Zook

957 N.E.2d 1014 (Ind. Ct. App. 2011)

FACTS

The defendants built a milking facility on their farm that was 15 feet from the Stickdorn's house. When they emptied a manure pit on the farm, which they did many times over several years, the stench of rotten eggs and raw sewage permeated the plaintiffs' home. They became physically ill and a stream that crossed their property became polluted. The Stickdorns told defendants how sick they were made and that emptying manure onto snow-covered ground could cause pollution, but they refused to do anything. This remained so even after the state department of environment advised them they were polluting and they had to change their practices. The situation became so bad that the Stickdorns had to move out of their house. Eventually the Stickdorns sued for trespass and nuisance.

ISSUE

Could the emptying of the manure pit in such a manner that the runoff and fumes caused injury to the Stickdorn's property and themselves create a trespass and a nuisance?

DECISION

Yes. An intermittent, nonabated nuisance is a new and separate injury that gives rise to a new cause of action for each incident. Here, the nuisance was not abated and its continuance caused further injury. The odors, the contaminated streams from the defendants' repeated manure spills, the improper spreading of the waste on the fields, and the refusal to put a cover on the manure pit as recommended by the department of environment was an intermittent, abatable nuisance for which defendants can be liable under theories of trespass and nuisance.

LO5

Trespass to Personal Property

Intentional interference with personal property in the possession of another is a trespass if it (1) harms the property or (2) deprives the possessor of its use for an appreciable time. Consent and privilege are defenses to trespass to personal property.

Kimes v. Grosser

195 Cal. App. 4th 1556 (2011)

FACTS

Kimes adopted a stray cat, named it Pumpkin, and kept it as his pet. The cat was perched on the fence between the yards of Kimes and Grosser when the cat was shot off. Kimes spent $6,000 for the surgery required to save Pumpkin's life. Pumpkin was partially paralyzed and Kimes spent another $30,000 on care for the cat. Kimes sued Grosser for the willful and malicious shooting of the cat and sought damages for the expenses incurred for Pumpkin's care.

ISSUE

Are pets personal property for which damages can be recovered?

DECISION

Yes. Pets are considered the property of their owners. When personal property is injured, the owner can recover for the lesser of (1) the diminution of the property's market value caused by the injury or (2) the reasonable cost of repairing the property. While stray cats have no market value, it does not follow that plaintiff must be turned out of court with nominal damages. For example, scrap books may have no market value, but they are of great value to the owner. Here, Kimes is not plucking a number out of the air for the sentimental value of his damaged property. He seeks compensation for Pumpkin's care and treatment because of the shooting. This is a rational way of demonstrating damages apart from the cat's market value. Kimes is entitled to recover the reasonable and necessary costs relating to Pumpkin's care and treatment resulting from the person who wrongfully injured the cat. In addition, Kimes can recover punitive damages if he can show the shooting was willful. Other states such as Kansas and New York have similarly held.

Internet service providers are beginning to bring trespass actions against spam distributors who flood the Internet with unsolicited advertisements. This practice of mailing unsolicited bulk e-mail causes serious problems for the service providers. Although a source of controversy, cybertrespass is commonly considered to be a trespass on personal property, not on real property. As such, most courts have held that a trespasser is liable when the trespass diminishes the value of personal property. Where no damage occurs, no trespass is found. For example, the California Supreme Court recently held that a corporation could not sue for trespass to personal property based on the mass sending of e-mails to the employees of the corporation because the e-mails neither damaged nor impaired the functioning of the recipient computer.[3]

Conversion

Conversion is the unlawful taking of or exercise of control over the personal property of another person. The essence of conversion is the wrongful deprivation of a person's personal property rights. One who unlawfully takes goods from the possession of another is liable for conversion even though the taker mistakenly believes he or she is entitled to possession. The same is true of those who wrongfully sell, mortgage, lease, or use the goods of another. A plaintiff's remedy for conversion is the reasonable value of the property. Some courts reduce the plaintiff's damages when the property can be returned unharmed and the defendant's conversion was the result of an honest mistake.

The difference between conversion and trespass to personal property is based on the degree of interference with another's property rights. Courts consider such factors as the extent of the harm to the property, the extent and duration of the interference with the other's right to control the property, and whether the defendant acted in good faith. The greater the interference and lack of good faith, the more likely the act will be considered to be conversion, for which the defendant must pay the reasonable value of the property.

Interference with Economic Relations

LO6

The tort law protecting persons against unreasonable interference with their economic relations with others is a more recent development than the previously discussed areas. Three classic torts in this area are disparagement, interference with contract, and interference with economic expectations.

Disparagement

False statements about the personal behavior of persons in business are covered by the tort of defamation. False statements about the quality of a seller's product or services, or the seller's ownership of goods offered for sale, may give rise to the tort of **disparagement.** Proof of actual damage (e.g., lost sales or other opportunities) is necessary for a successful disparagement action.

Interference with Contract

One who intentionally induces a person to breach a contract with another or who prevents performance of another's contract may be liable in damages to the party deprived of the benefits of the contract. This tort, **interference with contract,** seeks to protect the sanctity of private contractual relationships. Some courts do not hold a person liable whose conduct merely caused a breach of contract (as opposed to actively inducing the breach). Inducing a breach of contract may be justifiable in some cases.

[3] *Intel Corp. v. Hamidi,* 71 P.3d 296 (Cal. Sup. Ct. 2003).

Interference with Economic Expectations

Early examples of this tort, **interference with economic expectations,** involved the use of force to drive away a person's customers or employees. Today, liability has been broadened to include nonviolent forms of intentional interference as well.

Allison v. Union Hospital, Inc.

2008 WL 732424 (Ind. Ct. App. 2008)

FACTS

Allison, a Certified Registered Nurse Anesthetist, had worked as an independent contractor for Union Hospital since 1991. In 2001, a new contract was negotiated that said the contract could be terminated by either party without cause. In 2005 Allison determined that the contract was causing her financial difficulty and sent a letter to the hospital providing 90-day notice of her decision to terminate the contract. She also expressed a desire to renegotiate the contract in a previously scheduled meeting the following month. In the meantime, the hospital tried to find a replacement for Allison but found no one. At the scheduled meeting they started contract negotiation, and the next month, they reached an agreement that eliminated the termination-without-cause clause. When the hospital's attorney drafted the formal agreement, he provided a different contract, which was then rejected by Allison. The hospital was negotiating with another group to provide anesthesia services even though it had a contract with Allison. Allison sued for tortious interference with contract.

ISSUE

Is there evidence that Union Hospital tortiously interfered with the contract with Allison?

DECISION

Yes. Interference with a contract is an actionable tort that reflects the public policy that contract rights are property rights that should be protected from unjustified interference by third parties. In order to succeed, a plaintiff must prove (1) the existence of a valid contract; (2) defendant's knowledge of the contract; (3) defendant's intentional inducement of the breach of the contract; (4) the absence of justification; and (5) damages from the breach. A contracting party cannot normally tortiously interfere with its own contract. However, liability can arise when it conspires with another party to do so. Here, Union negotiated a contract with another group even though it had a contract with Allison. The group, though, thought Allison's contract was terminable at will and therefore is not liable for tortuous interference.

Concept Summary: Intentional Torts

	Type	Main Elements	Common Defense
Interference with Personal Rights	Battery	Unconsented-to harmful or offensive touching	Consent
	Assault	Putting in immediate apprehension for physical safety	
	False imprisonment	Unconsented-to confinement for appreciable time	Privilege
	Infliction of mental distress	Outrageous conduct that causes emotional distress	

(continued)

Concept Summary: Intentional Torts *(concluded)*

	Type	Main Elements	Common Defense
	Defamation	Publications of untrue statements injurious to reputation or character	Truth
	Invasion of privacy	Unwarranted publicity; commercial use of identity; intrusion; false light	Newsworthy
	Malicious prosecution; wrongful use of civil proceedings	Malice; no probable cause; plaintiff's success in wrongful suit	Probable cause
	Abuse of process	Wrongful motive	
Interference with Property Rights	Trespass to land	Entry on other's land without permission	Privilege
	Trespass to personal property	Interference with another's personal property	
	Conversion	Unlawful dominion over other's property	
Interference with Economic Relations	Disparagement	False, harmful statements about products or services	Truth
	Interference with contract	Inducing breach or preventing performance of another's contract	Privilege
	Interference with economic expectations	Unreasonable interference with another's business	

Questions and Problem Cases

1. Explain the elements necessary to show false imprisonment.
2. Describe the different kinds of invasion of privacy and what their main elements are.
3. Explain punitive damages and describe how they are determined.
4. Robert B. represented to Kathleen K. that he was free from venereal disease when he knew or should have known he had herpes. Relying on this representation, Kathleen K. had sexual intercourse with him and contracted the disease. She sued him, in part basing her case on battery. Her suit was dismissed because the trial court found that there was not a cause of action for this type of private sexual conduct. On appeal, can Kathleen K. show the elements of battery?
5. During an intercollegiate community college baseball game a batter was hit by a pitch. In the next inning, that batter's team's pitcher hit the other team's batter, Avila, in the head with an inside pitch and injured him. Avila sued for an intentional battery. Will he be successful? Explain why.
6. Albright was hired to be a bodyguard for Madonna. He became romantically involved with her for two years. Several years later he contracted to sell information about Madonna for a biography. One chapter featured his relationship with her. The book

had 48 pages of photos, one of which showed Madonna accompanied by two men. One of the men was identified as Albright and the caption said that he was her secret lover and one-time bodyguard. In fact, the photo was of Jose Guiterez. *People* magazine and *News of the World* reprinted the photo and caption. Albright sued for defamation because Guiterez was an "outspoken homosexual" who "often dressed as a woman" and engages in allegedly "homosexually graphic, lewd, lascivious, offensive and possibly illegal conduct." Will he be successful? Explain why.

7. Gates pleaded guilty to being an accessory after the fact to a murder. He served his 3-year sentence and lived an obscure private life for the next 10 years. Then Discovery Communications produced a documentary about the crime. Gates sued Discovery for invasion of privacy, arguing that due to his quiet, lawful life for 10 years his activities were no longer newsworthy and that his privacy was invaded. Was it? Why?
8. Rosa Parks was a civil rights icon who became famous in 1955 when she refused to give up her bus seat for a white passenger. This act prompted Martin Luther King's legendary bus boycott. In 1998 the rap group Outkast released an album whose first single was a profanity-laced song titled "Rosa Parks." A transcript of the rap lyrics suggests that the song has nothing to do with Rosa Parks but is a self-congratulatory anthem to Outkast's stardom. Parks claimed that since the song had nothing to do with her, her name was used only to exploit her celebrity to sell records. Thus, the song was an unauthorized, commercial appropriation of her name that tarnished her legacy and violated her right to privacy. Explain why this claim is or is not correct.
9. Roach, who used the name Debbie Tay, was a tattooed topless dancer who often was a guest on Howard Stern's show. He labeled her "Space Lesbian" because of her stories of sexual encounters with female aliens. When Roach died, she was cremated. Her sister gave part of her cremains to a close friend of Roach's. Stern persuaded the friend to appear on the show and bring them. Roach's brother told the station he objected to this. Nonetheless, the friend came and Stern, the friend, and other participants made comments about the cremains while handling bone fragments. Stern encouraged a participant to taste some of the cremains and describe what they tasted like, encouraged the friend to wear some around his neck, speculated about what various parts were, and said, "Wow, she was a piece of ash." Roach's brother sued for intentional infliction of emotional distress. Were Stern's actions sufficiently outrageous for such a claim?
10. Mr. and Mrs. Bhattal checked into the Grand Hyatt in New York, sent their luggage to their room, and, after stopping briefly at their room, locked the door and went to lunch. When they returned, their luggage was gone. Due to a computer error, the hotel had shipped their luggage to the airport along with the luggage of a Saudi Arabian flight crew who had previously occupied the Bhattals's room. The Bhattals filed a conversion suit against the hotel. Will they recover from the hotel? Why?

Chapter 7

Negligence and Strict Liability

Learning Objectives

After you have studied this chapter, you should be able to:

1. Explain how the purpose of negligence differs from that of intentional tort.
2. Explain duty and causation.
3. Define the reasonable person standard and why it is an objective standard.
4. Identify the limitations on negligent infliction of emotional distress.
5. Discuss the differences between the two kinds of comparative fault.
6. Describe the factors a court considers when determining whether strict liability should be applied.

Mr. Property Management owned the Chalmette Apartments. Over a two-year period police investigated numerous serious crimes committed at the apartment complex. Soon thereafter, a man abducted a 10-year-old girl from the sidewalk in front of her house, dragged her across the street to a vacant apartment in the complex, and raped her. The apartment's front door was off its hinges, the windows were broken, and the apartment was filthy and full of debris. A city ordinance required property owners to keep the doors and windows of vacant structures securely closed to prevent unauthorized entry.

- Could the owner of the apartments foresee that a crime of this type was likely to happen and therefore should have taken steps to protect against it?
- Does the statutory requirement establish the standard of conduct that the owner must follow in order not to be negligent?
- Can the owner be held liable for acts of violence that are committed by others?

Negligence

LO1

The Industrial Revolution, which began in the early part of the 19th century, created serious problems for the law of torts. Railroads, machinery, and newly developed tools were contributing to a growing number of injuries to people and property that simply did not fit within the framework of intentional torts since most of these injuries were unintended. The legal system was forced to develop a new set of rules to deal with these situations, and the result was the law of negligence, which requires people to take reasonable care to avoid injuring others.

Basically, **negligence** is an unintentional breach of duty by the defendant that results in harm to another. A plaintiff in a negligence suit must prove several things to recover (see Table 7.1):

1. That the defendant had a duty not to injure the plaintiff.
2. That the defendant breached that duty.
3. That the defendant's breach of duty was the actual and legal (proximate) cause of the plaintiff's injuries.

To be successful, the plaintiff must also overcome any defenses to negligence liability raised by the defendant.

TABLE 7.1
Requirements for a Negligence Case

Duty	Breach of duty	Injury	Cause in fact / Proximate cause

LO2

LO3

Duty

The basic idea of negligence is that every member of society has a duty to conduct his or her affairs in a way that avoids injury to others. The law of negligence holds our behavior up to an **objective** standard of conduct: We must conduct ourselves like a "reasonable person of ordinary prudence in similar circumstances." This standard is *flexible,* since it allows consideration of all circumstances surrounding a particular accident, but it is still objective, since the "reasonable person" is a hypothetical being who is always thoughtful and careful never to endanger others unreasonably.

Whether a person owes a particular duty to another person is determined by the court. Often the court will look at the *relationship* of the parties. For example, a contractual relationship can give rise to duties that would not otherwise exist. Likewise, common carriers, innkeepers, and today even landlords have special duties to protect those who use their facilities from harm. In the following case, relationships of a government entity and a duty to the public are examined.

Putnam County Sheriff v. Price

954 N.E.2d 551 (Ind. Sup. Ct. 2011)

FACTS

A driver lost control of his car early in the early morning on an icy road and a sheriff's department deputy responded. He contacted the county highway department and told them about the icy condition. He then left without doing anything to alleviate the icy condition or warn the public of it. A few hours, later Price lost control of his car at the same

(continued)

Putnam County Sheriff v. Price *(concluded)*

location and suffered injuries. He sued the sheriff's department for negligence.

ISSUE

Did the sheriff's department have a duty to alleviate the icy condition or warn of it?

DECISION

No. Governmental bodies have a common law duty to exercise reasonable care and diligence to keep streets in a reasonably safe condition for travelers. This duty requires the entity to adopt appropriate precautions—including warning of hazardous road conditions or temporarily closing roads—to prevent persons using due care from suffering injury. This is based on premises liability law and this, in turn, presupposes that the government agency owns, maintains, or controls the roadway. This was not the case here, so the sheriff did not owe a duty to the motorist in this case.

Statutes can also establish duties. Generally, people who do not do what a statute requires are considered to be **negligent per se** because they are not acting as the "reasonable person" would. If the actions cause injury of the kind the statute was designed to protect against, and if the person who is injured is within the group of people the statute was designed to protect, then the defendant is presumed negligent.

The ordinance in the Mr. Property Management summary at the beginning of this chapter set a standard from which the apartment owner deviated. The statute was designed to deter criminal activity by removing conspicuous and easily accessible opportunities for criminal conduct. It was designed to protect the general public. Since the rape victim is within this class of people, and the harm she suffered was the type the statute was designed to prevent, she can rely on the doctrine of negligence per se. See Table 7.2.

TABLE 7.2
Negligence Per Se: The Elements

Statute prohibits or requires action.	Defendant's actions violate statute.	Plaintiff's injuries are the kind the statute was designed to protect against.	Plaintiff is within the group the statute was designed to protect.

Breach of Duty

A person is guilty of breach of duty if he or she exposes another person to a foreseeable, unreasonable risk of harm, something the "reasonable person" would never do. The courts ask whether the defendant did something the reasonable person would not have done or failed to do something the reasonable person would have done. If the defendant guarded against all foreseeable harms and exercised reasonable care, he or she is not liable even though the plaintiff may be injured. So, if Bob is carefully driving his car within the speed limit and a child darts into his path and is hit, Bob is not liable for the child's injuries. In deciding the "reasonableness" of a given risk, the courts ordinarily consider several factors. What is the likelihood that harm will result from a person's actions, and how serious is the potential harm? On the other hand, does the actor's conduct have any social utility? If so, how easy would it be for the actor to avoid or minimize the risk of harm associated with that conduct?

LO2

Causation

Even if the defendant has breached a duty owed to the plaintiff, he or she will not be liable unless the breach actually caused the plaintiff's injury. For example, Bob is speeding down the street, breaching his duty to those in the area, and Frank falls down the front steps of his house and breaks his leg. Bob was negligent, but since there is no causal connection between his breach of duty and Frank's injury, he is not liable for it.

Wells v. SmithKline Beecham Corp.

No. 09-50224 (5th Cir. Ct. App. Mar. 22, 2010)

FACTS

Dr. Wells, a successful pathologist, became ill with Parkinson's disease and took medication for it. Since the 1970s, he had gone to Las Vegas to gamble but had kept his losses under control. In 2004, Wells discussed with his doctor an article he had read that indicated the drug he was on might cause problem gambling. At that time, Wells had lost \$2 million. His doctor switched him to Requip, made by GlaxoSmithKline. Wells's gambling urges subsided initially but then came back even stronger, and he lost \$10 million in five months. He then stopped taking Requip and did not return to Vegas. Wells sued SmithKline for failing to warn that the drug could cause problem gambling.

ISSUE

Is there sufficient evidence that the drug caused Wells's gambling problem?

DECISION

No. Wells must show that the failure to warn caused his injury. Wells engaged three expert witnesses to address causation. Relying on some studies and SmithKline internal documents, as well as the fact that the drug's label now carries a warning about possible gambling side effects, they showed some association. However, the studies were mainly based on anecdotal evidence, not on statistically significant epidemiology. Moreover, each expert conceded that there existed no scientifically reliable evidence of a cause-and-effect relationship between Requip and gambling. Wells failed to adequately prove causation.

In some cases, a person's act may be the **cause in fact**—the actual or direct cause—of an incredible series of losses to numerous people. In intentional tort cases the courts have traditionally held people liable for all the consequences that directly result from their intentional wrongdoing, however bizarre and unforeseeable they may be. With the creation of liability for negligence, the courts began to recognize that negligent wrongdoers (who were less at fault than intentional wrongdoers) should not necessarily be liable for every direct result of their negligence. This idea of placing a legal limit on the extent of a negligent person's liability came to be called **proximate cause.** So, a negligent person is liable for only the *proximate* results of his or her negligence.

The courts have not, however, reached agreement on the test that should be used for proximate cause. The proximate cause question is really one of social policy. In deciding which test to adopt, a court must weigh the possibility that negligent persons will be bankrupted by tremendous liability against the fact that some innocent victims may go uncompensated.

Some courts hold defendants liable only for the reasonably foreseeable results of their negligence. Others hold defendants liable only for injuries to plaintiffs who are within *the scope of* the foreseeable risk. If the defendant could not have reasonably foreseen some injury to the plaintiff, then the defendant is not liable for any injury to the plaintiff that in fact results from his or her negligence. The *Restatement (Second) of Torts,* recognizing the "after the fact" nature of proximate cause determinations, suggests that negligent defendants should not be liable for injuries that, if one looks backward after the accident, appear to be "highly extraordinary."

In the Mr. Property Management case at the beginning of this chapter, the court must decide if the apartment owner should have foreseen the risk that someone might use the empty, easily accessible apartment to commit a crime, or whether the rape that occurred there was "highly extraordinary." The fact that there had been many serious crimes in the apartment complex in the past two years would help lead to a finding that the lack of maintenance was a proximate cause of the injury.

Ethics in Action

Assume that Mr. Property Management is operating its apartment complex in a city without an ordinance requiring the sealing of vacant structures. Does it have an ethical duty to securely close vacant structures in urban, high-crime areas?

Courts also consider whether an intervening force, which happens after the defendant's negligent act and contributes to the plaintiff's injury, should excuse the defendant from liability. For example, suppose Deborah leaves her keys in the car while she runs into the store, and Mary Beth steals the car. While driving recklessly, Mary Beth hits Angela, severely injuring her. Should Deborah be liable for Angela's injuries? Usually, the courts say that if the intervening force was **foreseeable,** it will not excuse the defendant from liability. If it was foreseeable that someone might steal a car with keys left in it, and drive recklessly, then Deborah would be liable for Angela's injuries.

General Causation Rules

Regardless of what test for proximate cause the courts adopt, they generally agree on certain basic principles of causation. One such basic rule is that negligent defendants "take their victims as they find them." This means that if some physical peculiarity of a person aggravates his or her injuries, the defendant is liable for the full extent of the injuries. For example, Jim's head strikes the windshield of his car when Mike's negligently driven truck

Johnson v. Walmart Stores, Inc.

No. 08-4226 (7th Cir. Ct. Of App Dec. 12, 2009)

FACTS

Candace Johnson bought bullets from a Walmart store. The sales clerk did not require her to present a FOID card, as required by the Illinois Firearm Owners Identification Card Act. She would have been unable to get such a card because she had been a mental patient within five years of the incident. When she got home, she loaded a revolver and shot herself. She died from the wound. Her husband, Mark Johnson, sued Walmart for negligence and emotional distress, among other claims. Walmart argued there was no proximate cause.

ISSUE

Was Walmart the proximate cause of Candace Johnson's death?

DECISION

No. Johnson alleges that Walmart was negligent in training the clerk, and that lack of training led to the sale of the bullets, which led to Candace killing herself. A proximate cause is one that produces an injury through a natural and continuous sequence of events unbroken by any effective intervening cause. Suicide is considered by most courts to be an unforeseeable act that breaks the chain of causation required for proximate cause. There is nothing in the evidence to show that the suicide was foreseeable to Walmart. If liability were allowed, every murder or violent crime committed with a gun purchased in violation of the FOIC Act would impose liability on the retailer. Absent a specific legislative direction that establishes strict liability, there is no liability for the suicide. Without proximate cause, there can also be no negligence per se.

runs into him. Due to the fact that Jim's skull was abnormally thin (an "eggshell skull"), he dies from the blow, which would have only slightly injured a normal person. Mike is liable for Jim's death. Likewise, negligent persons are generally held liable for diseases their victims contract while weakened by their injuries, and jointly liable (along with the negligent physician) for negligent medical care their victims receive for their injuries.

Negligent persons are also generally liable for injuries sustained by those who are injured while making reasonable attempts to avoid being injured by the negligent person's acts. So, if Jamie dives out of the path of Howard's negligently driven car and breaks her arm in the process, Howard is liable for her injury. It is also commonly said that "negligence invites rescue," and that negligent persons should be liable to those who are injured while making a reasonable attempt to rescue someone endangered by the negligent person's act.

Res Ipsa Loquitur

In some cases negligence may be difficult to prove because the defendant has superior knowledge of the circumstances surrounding plaintiff's injury. If the defendant was in fact negligent, he or she will be understandably reluctant to disclose facts that prove liability. If the defendant had exclusive control of the thing that caused the injury, and the injury that occurred would not ordinarily happen in the absence of negligence, the doctrine of ***res ipsa loquitur*** ("the thing speaks for itself") creates an inference of negligence. This puts the burden on the defendant to show that the injury was not caused by his or her negligence. If the defendant fails to do so, he or she may be found liable. *Res ipsa* has been used frequently in plane crash and product liability cases in which the cause of the injury may be difficult to prove because important evidence was destroyed in the accident.

LO4 Negligent Infliction of Emotional Distress

In Chapter 6, we discussed the reluctance of the courts to allow recovery for purely mental injuries produced by intentional acts. The courts have been even more reluctant to allow such suits when the emotional injury is the product of negligent behavior. Fearing spurious claims and "opening the floodgates of litigation," courts initially required some "impact" (contact with the plaintiff's person) before recovery would be allowed. As scientific proof of emotional injury became more available, many courts dropped the impact rule but still insisted that plaintiffs show some physical injury or symptoms resulting from their mental distress before allowing recovery. Recently, a growing number of courts have allowed recovery without proof of physical injury if plaintiff suffered serious emotional distress as a foreseeable result of defendant's conduct.

Courts are also increasingly allowing *third parties* to recover for emotional distress resulting from witnessing harm caused to another person by defendant's negligent acts. For example, a mother is watching her child get off the school bus when he is hit by a negligently driven car. In the past, the mother would have been denied recovery unless she suffered some impact as a result of the negligence or was within the "zone of danger" created by the negligent act. Today, an increasing number of courts would allow the mother to recover. Generally, these courts require that the person actually witness the injury, that it be to a close relative, and that he or she suffer serious emotional distress as a result. Many courts also require that this emotional distress result in physical symptoms or injury. (See Table 7.3.) Additionally, an increasing number of courts allow a suit when the people are engaged, or the relationship involves a marital-like relationship even though they are not married. The following case asks the court to expand the category of those who can sue even further.

McDougal v. Lamm

WL 3079207 (N.J. Sup. Ct. 2012)

FACTS

McDougal was walking her Maltipoo dog, Angel, when it was attacked and killed by a neighbor's larger dog. She sued the neighbor for negligence and infliction of emotional distress. She argued that pets have now achieved an elevated status that makes them companions in the lives of human beings, not just property, and the tort of emotional distress should be broadened to encompass this.

ISSUE

Should a person who witnesses the traumatic death of her pet be able to sue for negligent infliction of emotional distress?

DECISION

No. New Jersey recognized the right to recover emotional distress damages arising out of observing the traumatic death of another in 1980. Since that time, it has been narrowly applied and carefully limited. We have never concluded that it can be applied to the observation of a death, however traumatic, by one who did not share a close familial relationship or intimate, marital-like bond with the victim. Although we recognize that many people form close bonds with their pets, we conclude that those bonds do not rise to the level of a close familial or intimate marital-like bond. The bond between humans and animals is often an emotional and enduring one. However, permitting it to support an emotional distress claim would require that we either vastly expand the classes of human relationships that could sue, or that we elevate the relationships with animals above those we share with other human beings. Neither response would be sound. We therefore decline to expand the category to pet owners.

TABLE 7.3
Negligent Infliction of Emotional Distress on Third Parties

Defendant's negligence causes injury to victim.	Witness suffers serious emotional distress.	Witness is a close relative.	Witness saw or in some way perceived the injury when it occurred.	Physical symptoms resulting from emotional distress required by some states.

Defenses to Negligence

The two traditional defenses to negligence are **contributory negligence** and **assumption of risk.** These defenses are based on the idea that everyone has a duty to exercise reasonable care for his or her own safety. Persons who fail to exercise such care should not be able to recover because their own behavior helped cause their injuries. So, if Craig steps into the path of Andy's speeding car without checking to see whether any cars are coming, his contributory negligence would prevent him from receiving damages for his injuries from Andy.

Contributory negligence, however, can produce harsh results. Slightly negligent persons might not recover anything for very serious injuries caused by defendants' greater negligence. To ease the harshness of this result, a number of courts adopted the doctrine of **last clear chance.** This doctrine holds that even though plaintiff was negligent, he or she can still recover if it can be shown that the defendant had the "last clear chance" to avoid the harm. Thus, if Craig is crossing the street not realizing the light has changed, and Andy is speeding down the street, if Andy could have stopped in time to avoid the accident but failed to do so, Craig can still recover for his injuries.

LO5

Recently, most states have abandoned contributory negligence and last clear chance and adopted a **comparative negligence** system. This is seen as fairer because it distributes the cost of the accident according to the degree of both plaintiff's and defendant's fault.

The U.S. Supreme Court affirmed system in a recent case.

Norfolk Southern Railway Co. v. Sorrell

127 S.Ct. 799 (Sup. Ct. 2007)

FACTS

Sorrell was driving a dump truck loaded with asphalt to repair railroad crossings when another Norfolk truck approached. Sorrell claimed he was forced off the road. The truck flipped and he was injured. Sorrell sued Norfolk under the Federal Employer's Liability Act (FELA) for negligently failing to provide a reasonably safe place to work. Norfolk defended by arguing that Sorrell was responsible for his own injuries because he negligently drove into the ditch. The legal question before the Court was whether the FELA was passed to benefit railroad employees and therefore the railroad had a higher burden in proving fault.

ISSUE

Should the same comparative fault standard be applied to the railroad and the worker's claims?

DECISION

Yes. The defenses of contributory negligence and assumption of the risk are no longer viable under the FELA. The standard now is contributory fault whereby a plaintiff's negligence no longer bars a recovery but his recovery is diminished in proportion to his fault. The rules determining fault should be the same for both the plaintiff and defendant. It would be difficult to figure out the appropriate proportion of fault if the standards for determining causation were different for plaintiff and defendant. It is easier if the jury compares like with like—apples with apples.

While comparative negligence systems differ in their details, most states have adopted a "pure" comparative negligence system. This system allows plaintiffs to recover the portion of their losses not attributable to their fault. For example, in the situation described earlier, assume that the jury determined that Craig was 33 percent at fault for his injuries, and Andy was 67 percent at fault, and that Craig suffered $27,000 in damages. Under a pure comparative fault system, Craig could recover $18,000 from Andy. A few states have adopted a "mixed" comparative fault system. Under this system, plaintiffs are barred from recovery if they are as much or more at fault for their injuries as defendant. Thus, if Craig were found to be 55 percent at fault for his injuries, he would not be able to recover anything under a mixed system.

There are some cases in which plaintiffs in negligence suits have voluntarily exposed themselves to a known danger created by another's negligence. For example, Liz voluntarily goes for a ride with Jim, who is obviously drunk. Such plaintiffs have **assumed the risk** of injury and are barred from recovery. The plaintiff must fully understand the nature and extent of the risk to be held to have assumed it. Some of the states that have adopted comparative negligence have also done away with the assumption of risk defense, treating all forms of contributory fault under their comparative negligence scheme.

Steigman v. Outrigger Enterprises, Inc.

267 P.3d 1238 (2011)

FACTS

Steigman got caught in a rainstorm and returned to her room in the Outriggers' Ohana Surf Hotel in Honolulu to dry off. She went out on the lanai (balcony) to get a chair where she slipped, slid across the balcony, and injured her foot when it got trapped under the lanai railing. She sued the hotel for negligence. The hotel defended by arguing that her injury was caused solely by her own negligence

(continued)

because the wet lanai presented a known or obvious danger of being slippery but she went out anyway. Steigman argued the passage of Hawaii's comparative fault statute nullified the hotel's defense.

ISSUE

Did the passage of the comparative negligence statute nullify the common law tort defenses barring recovery for plaintiffs injured by known or obvious dangers?

DECISION

Yes. Prior to the adoption of comparative negligence by the legislature, the courts applied contributory negligence, and an injured plaintiff was denied recovery if it was shown that her negligence contributed to her injury. The unfairness of this led to the passage of the modified comparative statute. The statute provides that an injured plaintiff can recover even if her own negligence contributed to her own injury as long as her negligence is not greater than that of the defendant. This makes the known or obvious danger rule inapplicable. This is consistent with today's values and is consistent with the majority of states that no longer make contributory negligence a complete bar to recovery.

Recklessness

When a defendant's behavior indicates a "conscious disregard for a known high degree of probable harm to another," the defendant is guilty of **recklessness.** Like negligence, recklessness involves posing a foreseeable risk of harm to others. However, that risk of harm must be significantly greater than the degree of risk that would make an act negligent. For example, Bob bets his friends he can drive down a crowded street blindfolded, and he strikes Tom. Recklessness is more morally objectionable than negligence (i.e., than if Bob had been merely speeding) but less objectionable than intentional wrongdoing (i.e., if Bob had driven up on the curb after Tom). Therefore, contributory negligence is not a good defense to recklessness, but assumption of risk is a good defense. So, the fact that Tom did not look before stepping into Bob's path would not defeat his recovery, but evidence that Tom had bet Bob's friends he could run in front of Bob without being hit would bar any recovery by Tom. Since recklessness involves a high degree of fault, the plaintiff stands a good chance of recovering punitive damages in recklessness cases.

E-Commerce

In Chapter 6 we saw that §230 of the Communications Decency Act (CDA) immunizes service providers from certain defamation and injurious falsehood claims. It is worth noting that the CDA may also protect service providers from negligence claims. A California appellate court recently ruled that eBay was protected by CDA immunity when buyers of sports memorabilia complained that the artifacts they bought on eBay bore false autographs. Similar to the *Carafano* case discussed in Chapter 6, the court reasoned that eBay was not a "publisher," but a service provider, and could not be held liable for information provided by a third party who posted false information on its site.[1]

Strict Liability

LO6

The third kind of tort, in addition to negligence and intentional torts, is **strict liability.** Strict liability means that a person who participates in certain kinds of activities is held responsible for any resulting harm to others, despite the use of the utmost care and caution. For this reason, strict liability is commonly described as "liability without fault." The basic

[1] *Gentry v. eBay, Inc.*, 99 Cal. App. 4th 816 (2002).

idea behind strict liability is that the risks associated with certain activities should be borne by the person whose actions created the risk and caused the loss, rather than by an innocent person who has suffered the loss. Traditionally, strict liability was imposed for those activities that were considered abnormally dangerous or *ultrahazardous*. Thus, people who kept animals that were "naturally dangerous" and people who did blasting were subject to strict liability when their activities injured someone, regardless of the precautions they took to avoid injuring others. Generally speaking, assumption of risk is a good defense to strict liability suits.

The most recent major application of strict liability is to the manufacturers of defective products that are "unreasonably dangerous"—that is, defective in a way that endangers life or property and is not readily apparent to buyers. This important topic is discussed in greater detail in Chapter 19.

Phillips v. DuPont de Nemours & Co.

521 F.3d 1028 (9th Cir. 2008)

FACTS

During World War II, the government built the Hanford Nuclear Weapons Reservation to produce plutonium for military purposes. It asked DuPont to run it, which it reluctantly agreed to do to help further the war effort. This facility helped build the atomic bomb that was dropped on Nagasaki, Japan. The plutonium production emitted I-131, known as radioiodine. This was known to have adverse health effects. In the 1980s, over 2,000 people sued, claiming that the emissions caused them thyroid cancer and other forms of cancer. The lead plaintiffs sued under a theory of strict liability under Washington state law. DuPont argued that running the Hanford facility was not an abnormally dangerous activity as required by Washington law for strict liability.

ISSUE

Can plaintiffs rely on a strict liability theory?

DECISION

Yes. The Restatement (Second) of Torts lists six factors to be considered when determining whether an activity is abnormally dangerous:

1. Whether the activity involves a high degree of risk of harm.
2. Whether the gravity of the harm which may result is likely to be great.
3. Whether the risk cannot be eliminated by the exercise of reasonable care.
4. Whether the activity is not a matter of common usage.
5. Whether the activity is inappropriate to the place where it is carried out.
6. The value of the activity to the community.

Not all factors need to be present in order for strict liability to be applied. Defendants need not have known exactly what type of harm might result; it is sufficient that the risk be so unusual, either because of its magnitude or the circumstances surrounding it. There is no question that the defendants should have anticipated some of the many risks associated with operating a nuclear facility, creating plutonium, and releasing I-131 into the atmosphere.

Current Issues

In the last few years, virtually all states have passed tort reform measures. The impetus behind this effort is the assumed "crisis" in the liability insurance area, characterized by dramatically higher premiums, reductions in coverage, and sometimes refusal to cover certain activities. While there is heated debate about whether a crisis actually exists, business and insurance lobbying groups have persuaded legislatures to pass reform bills. Common

Concept Summary: Negligence

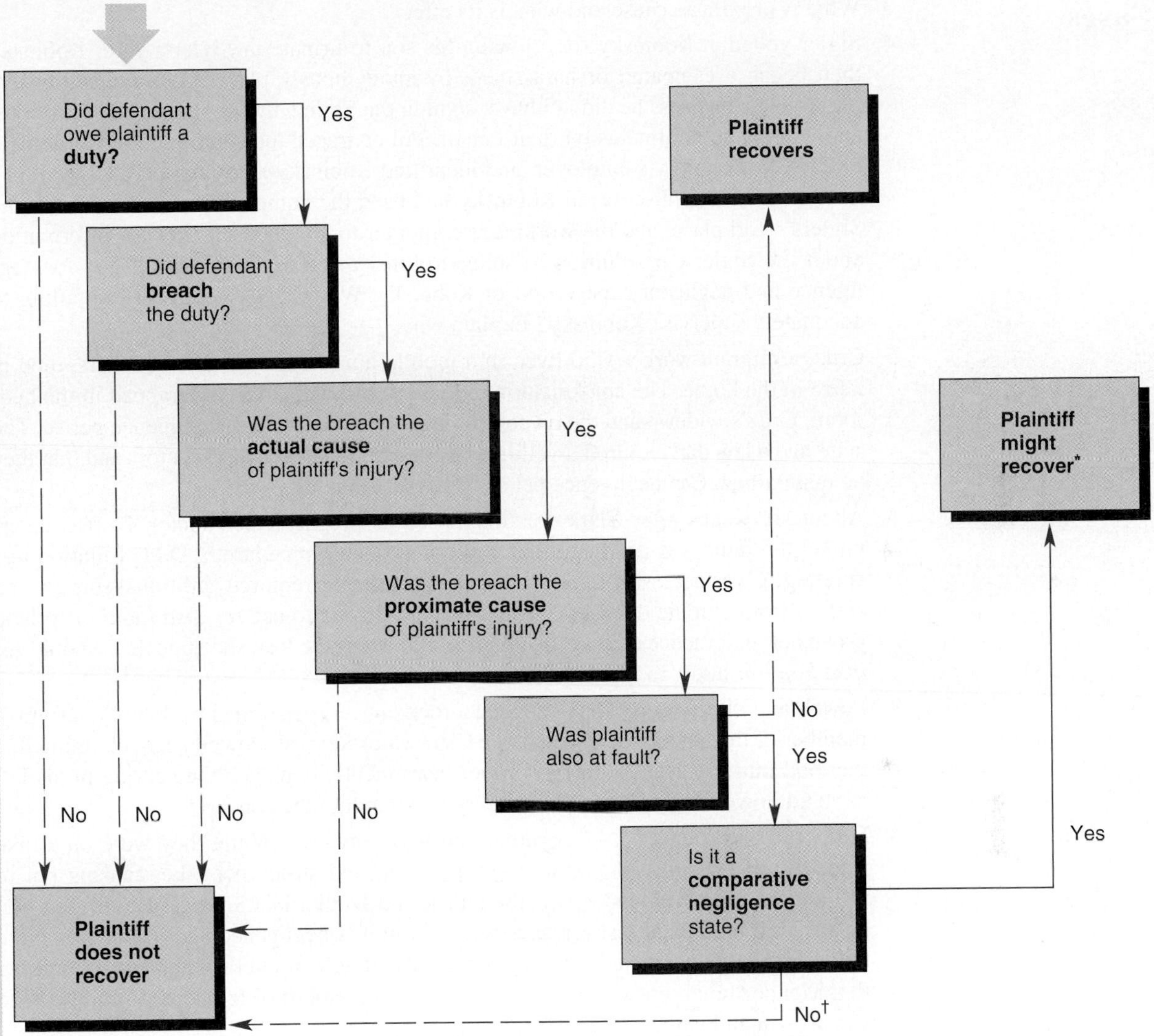

Plaintiff's recovery is contingent on the degree of his or her comparative fault and the type of* ***comparative negligence statute.*
†Plaintiff might still recover under a theory of ***last clear chance*** *or if defendant was* ***reckless.***

reform measures include limits on the amount of noneconomic damages (such as damages for pain and suffering and emotional distress) that can be recovered in a torts suit, and limits on punitive damage amounts and the way they are awarded. Certain defendants such as doctors, the skiing industry, and municipalities have gained limits on their liability and restrictions on the way a case against them can be handled. Sometimes these reform measures are combined with regulation of insurers to help control or reduce premium increases and policy cancellations. In some states the courts have held the reform measures to be unconstitutional under the state constitution because they unfairly limit plaintiffs' right to seek redress in the courts for their injuries. The debate about the need to reform tort law is unlikely to end soon, and legislatures can be expected to continue to be active on the insurance and tort reform front.

Questions and Problem Cases

1. Explain *res ipsa loquitor*.
2. What is negligence per se? Give an example.
3. What is proximate cause and what is its effect?
4. Sigler yelled at Kobinsky for allowing his son to urinate in Sigler's yard. Kobinsky then began a campaign of harassment by anonymously placing ads indicating that Sigler had a business he did not have, signing the Siglers up for various subscriptions, and making commitments on their behalf. Police traced the source of the harassment to CUNA, Kobinsky's employer, and identified Kobinsky as a suspect. CUNA did an internal audit and discovered Kobinsky had used the company cell phone to call the Siglers' workplace, and the workplace computer to conduct searches for information about the Siglers. In addition to suing Kobinsky, the Siglers sued CUNA for negligence and negligent supervision of Kobinsky. Was CUNA negligent for failing to adequately supervise Kobinsky? Explain why.
5. Cruz, a migrant worker who lived in a mobile home with six other workers, died in a fire in the home. The smoke alarm did not go off, and Cruz was trapped in the bedroom. Cruz's widow sued the owner of the mobile home under negligence per se. The state had a law that required dwellings be equipped with smoke detectors and that they be maintained. Can negligence per se be used? Explain.
6. About six weeks after Clark was diagnosed as pregnant, her doctor, Norris, determined the fetus was dead and that a minor surgical procedure, a D&C (dilation and curettage), was necessary to remove it. As a result, she required additional surgery and suffers from chronic diarrhea. Clark was not allowed to use *res ipsa loquitur* to help prove her malpractice case against Norris, and when she lost, she appealed. Should *res ipsa loquitor* apply to this case?
7. Powell and three companions attended a rock concert performed by John Fogertym, a member of the defunct band Credence Clearwater Revival. Powell sued, claiming that the loud music played by the performer permanently damaged the hearing in his left ear. Did Powell assume the risk of injury by attending the concert?
8. Izquierdo and Mendez lived together and were engaged. While they were on a bike ride, one of Ricitelli's dogs ran after Izquierdo and struck her bike, causing her to fall and be injured. Mendez saw the attack and Izquierdo's injuries. He alleged that he suffered emotional distress as a result Ricitelli's negligence and that it was more than would be anticipated by a disinterested witness. Ricitelli defended by arguing that Mendez could not sue because he was not a member of Izquierdo's family. Who should win and why?
9. Donald and Emily Egan took a bike tour with Vermont Bicycle Touring (VBT) of Virginia's horse and wine country. VBT planned the route, rented the bikes, supplied tour guides, and provided a van for people who wanted to ride in it for part of the tour. They warned riders that traffic on part of the ride might be heavy and that the shoulder was narrow, and they could opt to ride in the van. After the Egans had ridden almost a mile on the part warned about, they were hit by a driver, Jenkins, who was legally blind, incompetent, and whose license had been confiscated by his guardian. Donald died and Emily was seriously injured. VBT defended against the Egans' negligence suit by arguing that it was not the proximate cause of the accident. Was Jenkins a sufficient superseding cause of the injuries so that VBT should be held not to be the proximate cause of the injuries?

10. On September 11, 2001, four airliners were hijacked: Two were flown into the World Trade Center in New York, one into the Pentagon, and another crashed in Pennsylvania. Some of those injured and representatives of those who died sued the airlines, the airport security companies, and the airport operators. Among other claims, the plaintiffs alleged the defendants performed negligent screening. The defendants responded that they owed no duty to the victims because the defendants could not reasonably foresee terrorists would hijack several jumbo jets and crash them, killing passengers, crew, thousands on the ground, and themselves. Were the crashes within a foreseeable class of hazards resulting from the negligent performance of security screenings?

Chapter 8

Licensing and Intellectual Property

Learning Objectives

After you have studied this chapter, you should be able to:

1. Explain the rules governing when a patent will be granted, as well as the legal protections afforded by a patent.
2. Explain the rules governing when a trademark will be granted, as well as the legal protections afforded by a trademark.
3. Explain the rules governing when a copyright will be granted, as well as the legal protections afforded by a copyright.
4. Explain the rules governing when a trade secret will be granted, as well as the legal protections afforded by a trade secret.
5. Identify the risks involved in licensing technology, and explain how to use a licensing agreement to minimize those risks.
6. Identify the special intellectual property problems created by the widespread use of social media.

Cecilia Gonzalez downloaded copyrighted music through an online file-sharing network. When she was charged with copyright infringement, Cecilia pointed out that she was not aware that her actions were illegal because she downloaded data rather than discs. All of the copyright notices appeared on the actual CDs and not on the data she accessed online. BMG Music v. Gonzalez, 430 F.3d 888 (7th Cir. 2005).

- What is a copyright? How is it protected?
- What is a proper copyright notice? What effect does it have?
- Will Cecilia avoid copyright liability because she did not actually see the notices?

Introduction

While the U.S. legal system supports competitive markets, it also values private research and development. Recognizing that unbridled competition is likely to undermine incentives to innovate, this country offers legal protection for creative products, processes, and services. Thus, the legal system maintains a careful balance between a competitive marketplace and the need to shield innovators from unfettered competition. As a result, many of the ideas and creations that whet the nation's cultural, educational, and economic appetites are governed by **intellectual property** law. This body of rules grants limited monopolies to creative individuals and businesses.

Many businesses resort to technology licensing to market their intellectual property. In fact, for businesses unwilling to face the economic and political risks associated with direct investment overseas, technology licensing often provides a quick and relatively inexpensive entry into foreign markets. Licensing arrangements allow a firm to license for a fee its intellectual property (patents, copyrights, trademarks, and trade secrets) to companies that may then carry out production, sales, and service activities.

While licensing agreements offer extensive business opportunities, they must be approached cautiously. Businesses that hastily share their core technology risk permanently losing it. Accordingly, business managers must acquaint themselves with the legal and practical issues involved in intellectual property and the licensing of technology.

Chapter Overview

The chapter begins with an introduction to the basic types of intellectual property. This includes a discussion of the legal rules surrounding patents, trademarks, copyrights, and trade secrets. The focus then shifts to the legal aspects of transferring technology. This involves an examination of the basic nature of licensing, including the advantages and risks commonly associated with technology transfers. The chapter closes with a look at special intellectual property issues related to the rise of social media.

Intellectual Property Rights

There are four basic types of intellectual property: patents, trademarks, copyrights, and trade secrets. This section introduces these forms of intellectual property, briefly sketching the legal protection given to each.

LO1

Patents

A patent provides its owner with the exclusive right to make, use, or sell an invention or process during the patent period. The major advantage of a patent is that it deprives competitors of the opportunity to use the invention without the patent holder's consent. This temporary monopoly is expected to encourage the creation and utilization of new products and technologies.

For most of its history, the United States based its patent laws on a "first-to-invent" system, which meant that patentability was determined by the state of the art at the time the process or product was invented. However, beginning in 2013, the United States, pursuant to the *America Invents Act*, joined the rest of the world by switching to a "first-to-file" system. Patent protection generally runs for a period of 20 years, although design patents are protected for 14 years.

Patentable Creations

Most patents involve inventions of commercially useful goods or novel processes for producing such items. However, many developing countries do not extend patent protection for inventions involving food or drugs. Others protect only the processes for producing these articles.

In the United States the following things may be patented: (*a*) processes; (*b*) machines; (*c*) products; (*d*) compositions of elements (new chemical compounds); (*e*) improvements of processes, machines, and compositions; (*f*) ornamental designs for products; and (*g*) plants produced by asexual reproduction. Articles or processes falling within these categories may be patented if they are novel and useful. Excluded from patent protection are laws of nature, physical phenomena, and abstract ideas. Thus, a new mineral discovered in the earth, a plant found in the wild, or a mathematical formula is not patentable. Such discoveries are manifestations of nature, free to all people and reserved exclusively to none.

Association for Molecular Pathology v. Myriad Genetics

2013 U.S. LEXIS 4540 (U.S. Sup. Ct. 2013)

FACTS

Myriad Genetics discovered the precise location and sequence of two human genes, mutations of which can substantially increase the risks of breast and ovarian cancer. It obtained several patents based on this discovery. Those patents gave Myriad the exclusive right to isolate particular genes. Such isolation is necessary to develop tests that are useful in assessing whether a woman has an increased risk of cancer. From its discovery, Myriad also was able to synthetically create DNA, known as complementary DNA (cDNA), which contains the same protein-coding information found in a segment of natural DNA but omits portions within the DNA segment that do not code for proteins. After Myriad discovered that two genetic diagnostic laboratories were violating its patents by conducting genetic testing services for women, it demanded that they stop.

ISSUE

Should the Court uphold Myriad's patents?

DECISION

Yes and no. This case requires the Court to resolve whether a naturally occurring segment of deoxyribonucleic acid (DNA) is patent eligible by virtue of its isolation from the rest of the human genome. We also address the patent eligibility of synthetically created DNA known as complementary DNA (cDNA). We hold that a naturally occurring DNA segment is a product of nature and not patent eligible merely because it has been isolated. Myriad did not create or alter any of the genetic information encoded in the genes it discovered. Instead, Myriad's principal contribution was uncovering the precise location and genetic sequence. However, the synthetically-made cDNA is patent eligible because it is not naturally occurring. Myriad's lab technician's unquestionably created something new when cDNA was made. It is not a product of nature.

Ethics in Action

Prior to the *Myriad Genetics* decision, the biotech company sold the only gene test for detecting the increased risk of breast cancer in women. Myriad was accused of using its patents to impose artificially high prices for its tests and to stifle medical innovation by preventing other researchers from using the gene to develop other tests. How can this sort of behavior be defended on ethical grounds?

Patentability of Incremental Advances

One controversial area within the realm of patent law involves the patentability of incremental advances to already patented products or processes. This issue frequently arises in cases of "business-methods" patents and computer software programs that make small improvements to prior designs. U.S. patent law prohibits patent protection for incremental changes when the differences between the new product or process and the prior art would have been *obvious* to a person having ordinary skill in the art at the time the original product or process was made.

In recent years, there has been a great deal of concern about companies, called **patent trolls,** who purchase patent rights without the intent of directly using them. Instead, these patent-holding firms demand licensing fees from companies who knowingly or unknowingly infringe upon their patent rights. A related problem arises when patent owners fail to use or license their patented goods or processes. Some nations respond to this situation by issuing compulsory licenses when a patent holder does not make patented goods or processes available to the public. This is particularly likely to occur when the unused patents relate to pharmaceutical products.

Patent Exhaustion

A patent holder's rights over the patented product generally end once it is sold to a lawful purchaser. This doctrine, known as **patent exhaustion,** gives the buyer, or anyone to whom she resells the article, the right to freely use or resell the item. However, as the U.S. Supreme Court emphasizes in the next case, there are limits to the doctrine. For instance, after a sale, the buyer may not make new copies of the patented product. In particular, the purchaser does not have the right to reproduce the patented article.

Bowman v. Monsanto

133 S.Ct. 1761 (U.S. Sup. Ct. 2013)

FACTS

Monsanto patented a genetic modification to soybean seeds and marketed it as Roundup Ready seed. It sells the seeds to growers with a special licensing agreement that permits a grower to plant the purchased seeds in one (and only one) season. He can then consume the resulting crop or sell it as a commodity, usually to a grain elevator or agricultural processor. The farmer may not replant the harvested soybeans, nor may he supply them to anyone else for that purpose. (A single Roundup Ready seed can grow a plant containing dozens of genetically identical beans, each of which, if replanted, can grow another such plant—and so on and so on.) A farmer, Bowman, purchased Roundup Ready each year and sold his entire crop to a grain elevator. However, for his second crop of each season, Bowman purchased "commodity soybeans" intended for human or animal consumption from a grain elevator and planted them in his fields. Bowman knew that many of the seeds he purchased would contain Monsanto's patented technology. Bowman saved seed from his late-season planting to use for his second planting in each of the subsequent years.

ISSUE

Is Bowman's practice protected under the patent exhaustion doctrine?

DECISION

No. Under the patent exhaustion doctrine, Bowman could resell the patented soybeans he purchased from the grain elevator; so too he could consume the beans himself or feed them to his animals. Monsanto would have no business interfering with those uses of Roundup Ready beans. But the exhaustion doctrine does not permit Bowman to make additional patented soybeans without Monsanto's permission. That is precisely what Bowman did. Because Bowman reproduced Monsanto's patented invention, the exhaustion doctrine does not protect him.

Patent Infringement

Under U.S. law, patent infringement occurs when a person makes, uses, or sells the patented invention in the United States without the patent holder's authorization. Anyone who assists the infringer in these unlawful activities also may be liable. When an infringement occurs, overseas U.S. businesses may petition the government to block the importation of foreign goods that infringe U.S. patent rights. Further, the patent holder is entitled to monetary damages (up to three times the losses caused by the infringement). Finally, a court may issue an injunction to prevent future violations.

Extraterritorial Reach of U.S. Patent Law

It general, no infringement occurs under U.S. law when a product patented in the United States is made and sold in another country. However, there is an exception. Section 271(f) of the Patent Act provides that infringement does occur when one supplies from the United States, for combination abroad, a patented invention's components.

For instance, AT&T holds a patent on an apparatus for digitally encoding and compressing recorded speech. Microsoft's Windows operating system contains software that enables a computer to process speech in the manner claimed by AT&T's patent. Uninstalled Windows software does not infringe the patent; it is infringed only when a computer is loaded with Windows and thereby capable of performing as the patent speech processor. Thus, if a foreign manufacturer installs a master disk of Windows on the foreign-made computers, it would violate the AT&T patent. Curiously, however, the U.S. Supreme Court has held that the patent is not violated if the foreign manufacturer installs copies of Windows taken from the master disk in the computer (*Microsoft v. AT&T,* 127 S.Ct. 1746 (Sup. Ct. 2007)).

Concept Summary: Patent Protection

Goods (food/drugs)	Patentable if novel and useful	Processes (applications of laws of nature/physical phenomena/abstract ideas)
U.S. approach: First to file	Standard	Most nations: First to file
Exclusive right to make, use, or sell	Patent Rights	If fail to use patent: Loss of patent or compulsory license
Violations in U.S.: Treble damages, injunction, or seizure	Remedies	Violations overseas: Look to foreign court

Trademarks

LO2

A trademark is a distinctive word, name, symbol, or device used by a business to distinguish its goods from those of its competitors. The term *service mark* is used to describe services. Descriptive terms that identify the businesses themselves, rather than their products or services, are called *trade names.* For the purposes of this chapter, both types of identifying marks are referred to as trademarks.

Reasons for Legal Protection

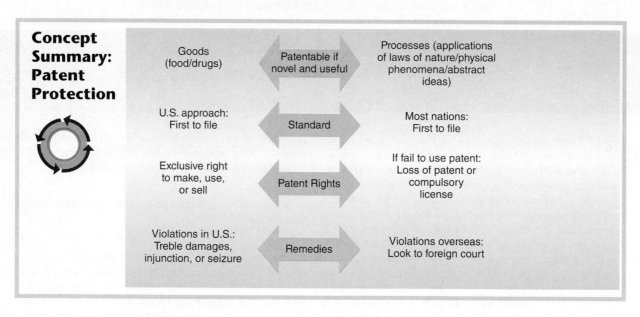

Trademarks are given legal protection to assist purchasers in distinguishing among the many firms, products, and services in existence within a particular market. For this reason, they generally must be *distinctive* to merit legal protection. In fact, a trademark owner can lose its protection if the name or symbol becomes so widely used that it acquires a generic meaning. (This happened to aspirin.)

There are four basic categories of distinctiveness: *arbitrary* (or fanciful) terms, which bear no logical or suggestive relation to the actual characteristics of the goods; *suggestive* terms, which suggest rather than describe the characteristics of the goods; *descriptive* terms, which describe a characteristic or ingredient of the article to which they refer; and *generic* terms, which function as the common descriptive name of a product class. If a term is arbitrary or suggestive, courts treat it as distinctive and automatically qualify it for trademark protection. If a term is descriptive, trademark protection exists only if a claimant proves that the term conveys to consumers a secondary meaning of association with the claimant. Finally, if a term is generic, courts are unwilling to afford it trademark protection.

Schwan's v. Kraft Pizza Company

460 F.3d 971 (8th Cir. 2006)

FACTS

Schwan's introduced Freschetta Brick Oven pizza, a square, fire-baked crust topped with high quality ingredients. Schwan's chose the name *Brick Oven,* hoping to convey gourmet quality and a restaurant-like eating experience. Seven months after Schwan's launched Freschetta Brick Oven pizza, Kraft contacted packaging vendors to create a Tombstone Brick Oven–style pizza to compete directly with Freschetta Brick Oven pizza. When Schwan's filed a trademark infringement suit, Kraft moved for summary judgment on the grounds that the term *Brick Oven* is generic.

ISSUE

Is the term *Brick Oven* pizza entitled to trademark protection?

DECISION

No. Because a generic term denotes the thing itself, it cannot be appropriated by one party from the public domain; it therefore is not afforded trademark protection even if it becomes associated with only one source. We conclude that Brick Oven, as used to identify pizza, is a generic term. This is because Brick Oven pizza is a pizza that is cooked in a brick oven. Accordingly, Schwan's could not acquire a trademark for the term.

The Registration Process

Most countries provide a registration system for trademarks; however, the legal significance of this process varies from nation to nation. For instance, in the United States and most common law countries, a trademark is not eligible for registration in the absence of prior commercial use. And, even after registration, legal protection can be lost if the holder fails to use the trademark. U.S. trademarks are registered for 10-year terms, although the holder generally can renew the registration repeatedly.

Throughout the rest of the world, the first person to register a trademark becomes its legal owner. This legal protection is given to the first person to register even when that individual was not the first person to use the trademark. Many successful U.S. businesses have been surprised to discover when entering foreign markets that local entities already own their trademarks in those countries.

Trademark Rights

A fundamental principle of trademark law is **first in time equals first in right.** Under the principle of first in time equals first in right, priority ordinarily comes with earlier use of a mark in commerce. It is not enough to have invented the mark first or even to have registered it first. This is because of the **territoriality principle,** which says that priority

Concept Summary: Trademark Protection

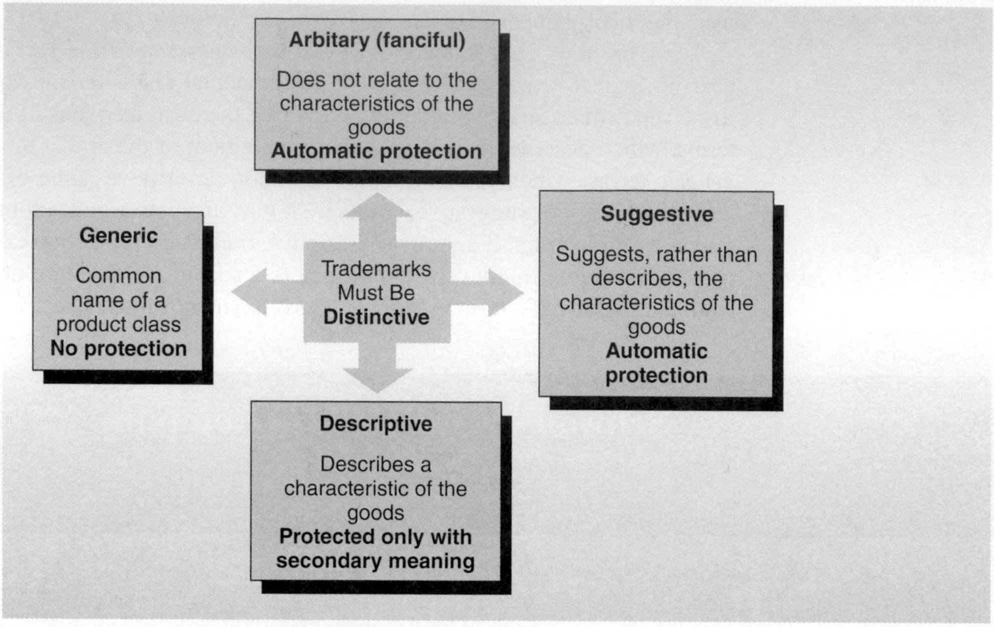

of trademark rights in the United States depends solely upon priority of use in the United States, not on priority of use anywhere in the world. Earlier use in another country usually does not count.

While the territoriality principle is a long-standing and important doctrine within trademark law, it is not absolute. Some courts recognize a **famous mark exception** to the territoriality principle when U.S. consumers identify goods with a trademark that has been used abroad. Courts defend this exception on the grounds that it protects against consumer confusion and fraud.

Trademark Infringement

In order to recover for trademark infringement, a plaintiff generally must show that (1) it possesses the trademark; (2) the defendant used the mark in commerce; (3) the defendant's use of the mark was in connection with a sale, distribution, or advertising of goods and services; and (4) the defendant's use of the trademark is likely to confuse customers. Trademark law was designed to help buyers identify favored goods and services. Thus, it traditionally permitted multiple parties to use the same mark for different classes of goods or services if such use was not likely to confuse consumers.

Remember the *Coach v. Goodfellow* (2013 U.S. App. LEXIS 10976 (6th Cir. 2013)) case in Chapter 1. There, the court read the direct trademark infringement language of the Lanham Act (a law protecting trademark rights) broadly and found it to include a remedy against persons who permit or induce others to infringe a trademark. Thus, it found the owner of a flea market liable for "contributory" trademark infringement for doing nothing to stop vendors in his flea market from selling counterfeit goods when he was aware that rampant trademark infringements were occurring there.

Trademark Dilution

The analysis is different under **trademark dilution** laws. These laws protect "distinctive" or "famous" marks from unauthorized uses even when confusion is not likely to occur.

This is because the trademark dilution laws focus on protecting the investment of trademark owners, while traditional trademark laws were intended to protect consumers. To prevail on a trademark dilution claim, a trademark owner must prove (1) its marks are famous; (2) the defendant is making commercial use of the marks in commerce; (3) the defendant began using the trademarks after they became famous; and (4) the defendant's use of the trademarks dilutes their distinctive quality.

For instance, Netscape employed a practice called "keying" on its Internet search engines. When a person searched for Playboy trademarks, graphic banner ads would appear on the search result pages showing sites owned by other companies. According to a federal court, Netscape was liable for diluting Playboy's trademarks. By keying adult-oriented ads to Playboy's trademarks, Netscape actively created initial interest confusion because users would be confused regarding the sponsorship of the unlabeled banner ads. (See *Playboy Enterprises v. Netscape Communications,* 354 F.3d 1020 (9th Cir. 2004).)

Extraterritorial Reach of U.S. Trademark Laws

U.S. courts issue injunctions and provide monetary damages for trademark holders who prove that another person has used a similar mark in connection with the sale of goods or services where such use is likely to cause confusion. Customs officials may block the importation of foreign goods that are likely to infringe the trademark of a U.S. holder.

Problems arise when U.S. trademark owners find their rights are being violated overseas. While courts have recognized that U.S. trademark law may reach extraterritorial conduct, they have never adopted a precise test to govern such cases. Perhaps the best-known framework for extraterritorial reach, known as the *Vanity Fair* test, is used when U.S. citizens are sued for violating U.S. trademarks abroad. It asks (1) whether the defendant is a U.S. citizen, (2) whether the defendant's actions have a substantial effect on U.S. commerce, and (3) whether relief would create a conflict with foreign law. These three prongs are given an uncertain weight.

Of course, the *Vanity Fair* test is used only when the defendant is a U.S. citizen. Courts use a different framework for determining the extraterritorial reach of the trademark laws when the defendant is a foreign party. Generally, U.S. courts will enforce the trademark laws against noncitizens acting outside of the country if the complained-of activities have a substantial effect on U.S. commerce. If this "substantial effects" question is answered in the negative, the court lacks jurisdiction over the defendant's extraterritorial acts; if it is answered in the affirmative, the U.S. court possesses subject matter jurisdiction.

For instance, Cecil McBee, a U.S. citizen, regularly tours Japan as a jazz musician. Without McBee's consent, Delica—a Japanese clothing retailer—sells a line of clothing under the trade name "Cecil McBee." While Delica sells over $100 million worth of "Cecil McBee" clothing in Japan each year, none of the clothing is sold outside of Japan. Because none of the clothing was sold in the United States, the U.S. federal court refused to hear McBee's trademark claim. His only remedy was to sue Delica in Japan. However, he lost that claim as well because Delica holds the Japanese trademark for "Cecil McBee." (See *McBee v. Delica Co.,* 417 F.3d 107 (1st Cir. 2005).)

Copyrights

LO3

A copyright prohibits the unauthorized reproduction of creative works such as books, magazines, poems, drawings, paintings, musical compositions, sound recordings, films, and DVDs. While most developed countries extend copyright protection to computer software, much of the world offers it little or no protection. In the United States a copyright generally lasts for the life of the author plus 70 years. However, because of various amendments to the rules, the precise life of a copyright may vary. For instance, for works created prior to 1978, the copyright period is 75 years. For works for hire, the period is 95 years from the first publication or 120 years (whichever comes first).

Creation and Notice

In the United States and many other countries, a copyright comes into existence automatically upon the creation of the work. Although owners may register their copyrights with the appropriate governmental office, they are not required to do so. Copyright owners often provide notice of their copyright by indicating its existence on copies of their works. In the United States a copyright infringer generally is prohibited from reducing its liability by claiming innocent infringement if proper notice has been given.

Refer back to the chapter opener where Cecilia Gonzalez was downloading CDs from an online, file-sharing network. She argued that she was not aware of the illegality of her actions because the copyright notices appeared on the actual CDs rather than on the Internet site where she accessed the music. The court was not impressed. It stated that, since the notice appeared on the actual CD, she could have learned of the copyrights if she had inquired. She was assessed damages in the amount of $22,500.

Copyright Infringement

Businesses frequently are unaware of the subtle ways in which copyright issues might arise. For instance, the manuals, specification sheets, and sales literature provided to distributors and franchisees generally are protected by copyrights. Even an inadvertent reproduction of these copyrighted materials can subject a firm to liability for copyright infringement. In the United States a copyright holder may collect its actual damages plus the profits earned by the infringer. In the alternative, the copyright holder may elect to receive statutory damages between $750 and $30,000 for inadvertent violations or $150,000 for willful infringement. Thus, a U.S software company recently paid a $100,000 settlement for violating another company's copyrights by electronically distributing a dozen of its telecommunications newsletters.

To establish **direct copyright infringement,** a plaintiff must prove (1) ownership of a valid copyright and (2) copying of constituent elements of the work that are original. Copyright owners may also have a cause of action in instances of **contributory copyright infringement.** Three elements must be proven for a copyright holder to recover under a theory of contributory copyright infringement: (1) direct infringement by a primary infringer, (2) knowledge of the infringement by the defendant, and (3) material contribution to the infringement by the defendant. This theory of recovery has been used effectively against several suppliers of peer-to-peer file sharing software that has been used to download CDs and DVDs from the Internet.

Finally, copyright owners have recovered a theory of **vicarious copyright infringement.** In order to prevail in such a case, the copyright owner must prove three things: (1) direct infringement by a primary party, (2) a direct financial benefit to the defendant, and (3) the defendant's right and ability to supervise the infringers. This theory of recovery is an outgrowth of the doctrine of *respondeat superior*, which imposes liability on those with the power to supervise the behavior of a lawbreaker. In *Arista Records v. Flea World*, 2006 U.S. Dist. LEXIS 14988 (D. N.J. 2006), this cause of action was successfully employed against a flea market owner who permitted vendors at his flea market to illegally sell copyrighted merchandise.

Despite the promise these theories of recovery seem to suggest, when an infringement occurs abroad, a U.S. exporter may discover that it has little recourse against the infringer. Some countries offer little or no copyright protection and many others lack the will or the resources to enforce their copyright laws. While the U.S. government, trade groups, and individual companies have begun serious efforts to persuade foreign governments to prosecute overseas offenders, the results of these activities have been mixed. Further, in many instances, even when enforcement does occur, the penalties assessed are extremely weak.

Fair Use

Even if copyright infringement has been shown, a defendant might be able to avoid liability if his use of the copyrighted material falls within the **fair use** defense. The copyright act sets out four factors for evaluating whether a use is a fair use: (1) purpose and character of the use (commercial uses are presumptively unfair); (2) nature of the copyrighted work (the scope of fair use is greater for informational work than for creative work); (3) amount and substantiality of portions used (fair use may apply if there are substantial differences between the copyrighted work and the derivative work); and (4) effect on the market (fair use does not apply if the use diminishes the value or marketability of the original work).

For instance, Google indexes websites via software that automatically scans and stores the content of each website into an easily searchable catalog. This search receives a text search string and returns reduced-sized, or "thumbnail" images organized into a grid. Google stores thumbnails in its cache, in order to present the results of the user's query. Some of these thumbnails contained nude photographs that were protected under copyrights owned by Perfect 10. A court found that Google's use of the thumbnails was highly transformative because the search engine puts the images in a different context, thereby transforming them into a new creation. (The original image was created to serve as entertainment while Google's subsequent use transformed the image into a pointer directing a user to a source of information.) The court held that Google's activities were protected under the fair use doctrine. See *Perfect 10 v. Google*, 508 F.3d 1146 (9th Cir. 2007).

First Sale Doctrine

The Copyright Act specifically states that a purchaser of copyrighted material "lawfully made . . . is entitled, without the authority of the copyright, to sell or otherwise dispose of the possession of that copy." This is known as the **first sale** doctrine. Like the patent exhaustion doctrine (discussed above), this means that the copyright owner cannot prevent a lawful purchaser of copyrighted material from reselling that material. Consider the next case where the U.S. Supreme Court rejects the argument that the first sale doctrine does not apply to books lawfully sold overseas and then resold in the United States.

Kirtsaeng v. John Wiley & Sons

133 S.Ct. 1351 (U.S. Sup. Ct. 2013)

FACTS

John Wiley & Sons publishes academic textbooks protected by U.S. copyright laws. When Wiley assigns the right to publish such texts overseas to its foreign subsidiary, the editions generally contain language prohibiting them from being resold in the United States. While Kirtsaeng was studying in the United States, he asked his friends and family in Thailand to buy copies of foreign edition English-language textbooks at Thai book shops, where they sold at low prices, and mail them to him in the United States.

(continued)

Kirtsaeng v. John Wiley & Sons *(concluded)*

Kirtsaeng would then sell them, reimburse his family and friends, and keep the profit.

ISSUE

Does the "first sale" doctrine permit Kirtsaeng to freely sell the foreign-bought books in the United States?

DECISION

Yes. The first sale doctrine permits the owner of a lawfully purchased copyrighted work to resell it without limitations imposed by the copyright holder. The "first sale" doctrine has an impeccable historic pedigree. For centuries, courts and legal scholars have recognized the importance of leaving buyers of goods free to compete with each other when reselling or otherwise disposing of those goods. The doctrine makes no geographical distinctions. Finally, reliance upon the "first sale" doctrine is deeply embedded in the practices of those, such as booksellers, libraries, museums, and retailers, who have long relied upon its protection. Museums, for example, are not in the habit of asking their foreign counterparts to check with the heirs of copyright owners before sending a Picasso on tour.

Concept Summary: Copyright Protection

Coverage	Original and creative works that are set out in a tangible medium of expression from which they can be perceived, reproduced, or communicated.
Creation and Notice	Arises upon creation. Registration is not required, but normally is a prerequisite for infringement suits. Notice often provided, but is not required.
Duration	**Pre-1978 works**—75 years **Post-1978 works**—life of the author plus 70 years **Work-for-Hire**—95 years from first publication or 120 years from creation (whichever comes first)
Ownership Rights	Exclusive rights to reproduce, prepare derivative works, and distribute copies. May be sold or licensed.

Trade Secrets

LO4

A trade secret, generally, is developed by a firm over the course of its business activities. Sometimes called know-how or propriety information, this type of intellectual property includes secret formulas, devices, processes, techniques, and compilations of information (e.g., customer lists). A trade secret usually does not receive legal protection unless its owner took reasonable precautions to keep it a secret. Further, it must be established that the secret product, process, or idea provides its owner with a distinct advantage over competitors.

A business may attempt to maintain a trade secret when it has a process or product that is not novel enough to receive patent protection. Or it may choose to forgo the patent route because the monopoly period for patents is relatively short. Trade secret protection, on the other hand, can last forever if nobody is ever able to independently discover the secret. For example, the formula for Coca-Cola has remained a trade secret for over 100 years. If the formula had been patented, the patent would have expired years ago.

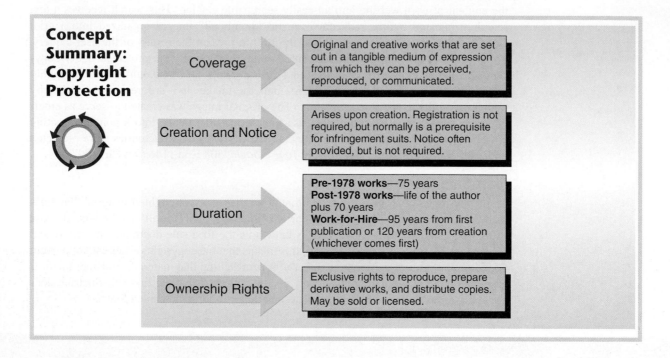

Maintaining Secrecy

As a precondition to receiving trade secret protection, the owner must take reasonable means to maintain secrecy. This may include limiting the number of persons to whom the secret is disclosed, advising employees of the importance of confidentiality, and having those given access sign contracts containing nondisclosure clauses. The reasonableness of precautions varies with the competitive importance of the secret, the costs of the measures, and the likelihood that someone will discover the secret.

Businesses often fail to appreciate the range of things that could be protected as trade secrets. For instance, safety procedures, sources of various raw materials, training programs, and quality control systems all can make substantial contributions to the competitiveness of an enterprise. By placing reasonable limitations on the external flow of information concerning these processes and lists, a company could possibly claim them as trade secrets.

Misappropriation

In the United States an individual is liable for disclosing or using a trade secret if she (1) acquired it by improper means (e.g., theft, trespass, spying, or bribery); (2) obtained it from one who acquired it by improper means; (3) breached a duty of confidentiality regarding the secret; or (4) acquired it from someone who breached a duty of confidentiality regarding the secret. When a misappropriation occurs, the owner generally is entitled to compensatory damages and, in cases of willful misappropriations, punitive damages. An individual may freely use the trade secrets of another if he discovers them through proper means, such as reverse engineering.

Throughout much of the world, trade secret protection is much more limited. Many countries confine liability for misappropriation to individuals who have violated the terms of an agreement to maintain confidentiality. Third parties who did not sign such a contract would not be liable. Further, some underdeveloped nations either refuse to enforce confidentiality provisions or greatly limit the time period during which secrecy must be maintained.

PhoneDog v. Kravitz

2011 U.S. Dist. LEXIS 129229 (N.D. Cal. 2011)

FACTS

PhoneDog is an interactive marketing company that reviews mobile products and services and provides users with resources needed to research, compare prices, and shop from mobile carriers. It uses a variety of social media, including Twitter, Facebook, and YouTube, to market and promote its services to users. Kravitz worked at PhoneDog as a product reviewer and video blogger. He used the company's Twitter accounts to disseminate product information and promote PhoneDog's services to approximately 17,000 followers. After Kravitz ended his employment, he changed his Twitter account handle from "@PhoneDog_Noah" to "@noahkravitz" and continued to interact with his followers. According to PhoneDog, all "@PhoneDog_Name" Twitter accounts used by its employees, as well as the passwords to such accounts, constitute proprietary, confidential information. It therefore sued Kravatz for misappropriation of its trade secrets.

ISSUE

Should the court dismiss the misappropriation of trade secrets claim?

DECISION

No. Kravitz argues that the claim should be dismissed because the account he allegedly misappropriated is not a trade secret. Specifically, he asserts that the followers of the account are not secret because they are and have been publicly available for all to see at all times. With respect to the password to the account, Kravitz contends that passwords to Twitter accounts do not derive any actual or potential

(continued)

PhoneDog v. Kravitz *(concluded)*

independent economic value because they do not provide any substantial business advantage. Rather, he argues that the passwords merely allow the individual logging on to view information already widely known. Kravitz also claims that he—not PhoneDog—initially created the password and that PhoneDog did not make any reasonable efforts to maintain the secrecy of the password. We deny the motion to dismiss this lawsuit. Whether the password and account followers are trade secrets and whether Kravitz's conduct constitutes misappropriation are matters for the court to consider at trial. (The two parties privately settled this dispute soon after this decision was posted.)

Ethics in Action

During mid-2006, federal prosecutors charged three people with stealing trade secrets from Coca-Cola and attempting to sell them to PepsiCo. One of the three, an administrative assistant to a Coke executive, was videotaped stuffing company documents and a product sample into a personal bag. Prosecutors reported that PepsiCo provided Coke with a copy of a letter which offered to sell Pepsi confidential information. That triggered the FBI's video surveillance that led to the arrests. A Pepsi spokesman reported that the company "did what any responsible company would do in cooperating with Coke." He added that "competition can sometimes be fierce, but also must be fair and legal." Coke's chief executive noted that the breach of trust "underscores the responsibility we each have to be vigilant in protecting our trade secrets. Information is the lifeblood of the company."

- If you were a PepsiCo official and were certain that this theft would have gone undetected, would you have contacted Coke?
- Does your answer at all depend on how valuable the information was and how sure you were that the theft would not be uncovered?

Source: "Trio Charged with Selling Coca-Cola Trade Secrets," *The Wall Street Journal*, July 6, 2006, p. B6.

Concept Summary: Liability for Trade Secret Misappropriation

1. Acquired it by improper means (theft, trespass, bribery, spying)
2. Obtained it from one who acquired it by improper means
3. Breached a duty of confidentiality
4. Obtained it from one who breached a duty of confidentiality

Technology Transfer Agreements

A technology transfer occurs when a business licenses its intellectual property to another firm. These contractual agreements generally permit a company to quickly penetrate a market without incurring the substantial financial and legal risks associated with direct investment. This section begins with an examination of the fundamental nature of licensing. It then discusses the advantages and the risks associated with technology transfers. This is followed by a brief look at the issues involved in negotiating a licensing agreement. The section closes with a review of the basic contractual provisions included in a technology transfer agreement.

Nature of Licensing

While intellectual property owners generally have the right to prevent others from exploiting their creations, they may selectively authorize individuals to make use of them. This is the principal purpose of a licensing agreement: It permits an intellectual property owner to grant to another the right to use protected technology in return for some form of compensation. The actual contract may take a variety of forms depending on the needs of the parties, the nature of the intellectual property, and the controlling laws.

Parties to the Licensing Agreement

The person who owns the intellectual property is known as the **licensor.** In return for some type of payment, the licensor permits another, the **licensee,** to produce, use, or sell the intellectual property. Sometimes the licensee is permitted to *sublicense* all or part of its rights in the technology to a sublicensee. Whether this right or others exist is determined by the licensing agreement itself, as well as by the laws of the country where the licensing activities take place.

As a general rule, persons who buy from patent holders or their licensees are not restricted by the original licensing contract. Thus, while a patent holder may prevent its competitors from selling its patented products, a customer who has bought a patented product may freely resell it without fear of violating the original patent.

The Need to License

Frequently, an intellectual property owner has few options other than licensing its technology to others. For instance, many inventors do not have production facilities or marketing networks capable of profitably using or selling their creations. In these cases, an inventor may license a manufacturer or sales representative to produce or sell the product. Further, in some nations it is not legally permissible or practical to do business without some level of participation by a local person or company. Thus, a foreign intellectual property owner may be compelled to license its technology to a local firm.

Advantages of Licensing

Licensing provides numerous benefits for both licensors and licensees. Licensors directly benefit by receiving royalty payments and gaining a presence in a market that might otherwise be inaccessible. As was previously noted, licensing allows a firm to penetrate foreign markets much more quickly than direct investment. Further, by licensing rather than directly investing, a business minimizes its physical and financial presence overseas, thereby reducing the risks of suffering devastating losses in the event of an expropriation. Some firms select licensing over exporting activities because it provides a method of escaping the tariff and nontariff barriers erected by many importing nations.

Licensees also derive benefits from licensing arrangements, which may provide them with access to products and ideas that otherwise might not be available. They may also gain tremendous competitive advantages through close association with a licensor's established reputation.

Risks of Licensing

LO5

Despite its many benefits, technology licensing is not without its drawbacks. Perhaps the greatest risk is that the licensee, after gaining access to the licensor's technology, will sever the licensing relationship and become a competitor. While the licensor may attempt to contain this risk through a carefully constructed contract, many countries refuse to enforce restrictive provisions. In fact, even in the United States, if the restrictions are too severe, they may violate antitrust laws.

If a licensor does not closely monitor the activities of a licensee, it runs the risk that the licensee will produce inferior products or provide inferior service. This could erode goodwill that the licensor has taken years to develop. Further, some licensees cannot be trusted to honestly report their use of the licensed technology. If this occurs, and if royalty payments are based on such use, a licensor may be cheated out of large sums of money. Only by regularly auditing a licensee's business records can a licensor be certain that this is not occurring.

Negotiating the Agreement

Global licensing agreements require meticulous planning and a great deal of flexibility. Businesses generally agree that the key to successful collaboration is the development of trust between the licensor and licensee. However, licensors are justifiably wary about entrusting their intellectual property to overseas companies, especially when the agreement encompasses core technologies or vital markets. Similarly, licensees are reluctant to invest their resources in establishing a foothold if they fear that they will be replaced by the licensor once the venture becomes highly profitable.

Principal Considerations

Licensing agreements require a careful partner selection process that clearly identifies each firm's objectives and details how each plans to meet the other's expectations. Likewise, they necessitate a hands-on, personal interaction during both the negotiation and implementation phases. The actual licensing agreement should be drafted only after identification of areas of potential conflict. Further, it should include provisions detailing the rights and obligations of the licensor and licensee in the event the relationship is terminated. Finally, as with all business agreements, the licensing contract should establish mechanisms for resolving disputes.

Limits on Negotiating Authority

The range of issues that may be governed by the technology transfer agreement is often severely limited. Many developing nations have enacted legislation designed to protect local licensees from the superior bargaining strength possessed by foreign businesses. Much of this legislation is a direct outgrowth of past instances where multinational corporations originally penetrated overseas markets through licensing agreements with local companies. Then, once the foreign operation became a viable concern, the licensor replaced the licensee with one of its own subsidiaries. In response to these practices, host countries frequently refuse to enforce contractual provisions granting liberal termination rights to the licensor. In the United States, many states have laws protecting the rights of licensees.

Concept Summary: Confidentiality Clauses

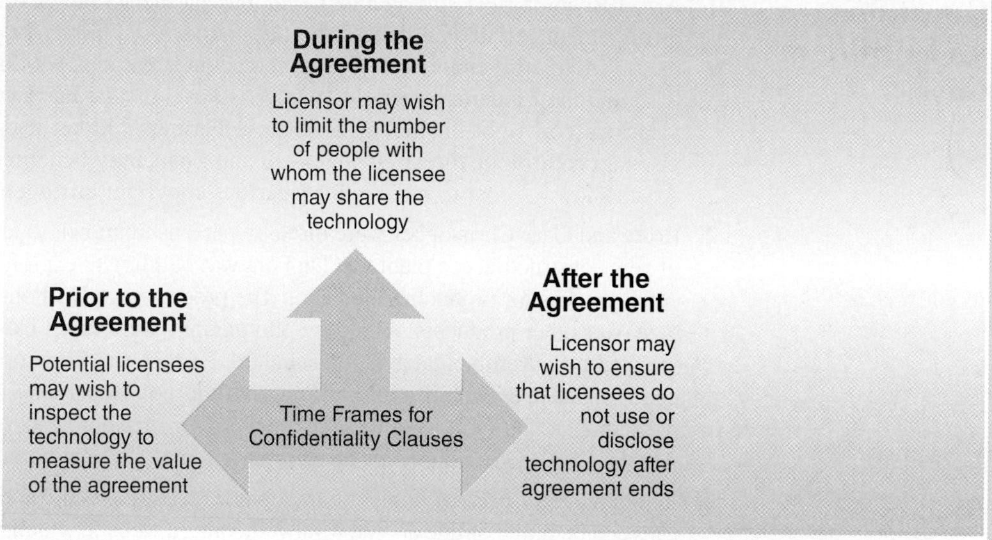

During the Agreement
Licensor may wish to limit the number of people with whom the licensee may share the technology
Prior to the Agreement
Potential licensees may wish to inspect the technology to measure the value of the agreement
Time Frames for Confidentiality Clauses
After the Agreement
Licensor may wish to ensure that licensees do not use or disclose technology after agreement ends

Intellectual Property Aspects of Social Media

LO6

A quick glance around makes clear that social media is a way of life. Facebook, LinkedIn, Twitter, and YouTube are primary avenues for ever-growing numbers of people throughout the world to share all types of information. They enable people to quickly mobilize around ideas or opinions as viewpoints can go viral in a matter of minutes. For these reasons, modern businesses are more and more reliant on social media to take the pulse of their clientele and to publicize new products, services, and ideas.

As managers migrate to social media avenues to communicate with the world, they are cautioned to beware of legal problems that inevitably accompany any new technology. For instance, a business may encourage high levels of interactivity on its own social media sites in order to better understand its customer base. When doing so, it must develop policies for dealing with defamatory statements or postings that may infringe upon the intellectual property rights of others. While the *Communications Decency Act* immunizes online service providers from liability for the information that originated with third persons, a growing number of courts have expressed a willingness to narrow this protection in cases where the service provider exercises active editorial control over the content.

It makes good sense for companies to engage in widespread monitoring of social media content to head off budding complaints or criticisms. However, actions should be carried out in a legally responsible manner. For instance, company employees who conceal their affiliation online and tout their company's products may run afoul of federal rules against unfair and deceptive advertising. Federal Trade Commission guidelines require that people endorsing a product or service must disclose their affiliation with the producer or service provider. In addition, intellectual property owners should survey the horizon to safeguard against dilution or outright infringement of their rights. This is particularly true with trademark rights which can be lost if they are not enforced. For more insight, see Peter Brody and Mariel Goetz, *Ten Things You Need to Know about Social Media and Intellectual Property in 2013,* BNA Insights U.S. Law Week 81 no.30, p. 1159 (February 12, 2013).

Questions and Problem Cases

1. Arista Records filed suit against Columbus Farmers Market for vicarious copyright infringement. Arista claims that the flea market is a "pirate bazaar" where many of the flea market's vendors sell pirated and counterfeit compact discs and cassette tapes in violation of federal copyright laws. Arista claims that Farmers Market is liable for vicarious copyright infringement because Farmers Market had the ability to supervise and control the direct infringement and financially benefited from it. What must Arista show in order to recover for vicarious copyright infringement?
2. Rolfe and Gary Christopher were hired by persons unknown to take aerial photographs of new construction at a plant that Du Pont was building to exploit a highly secret unpatented process for producing methanol. The process gave Du Pont a competitive advantage over other producers. All of the photographs were taken from public airspace and violated no governmental aviation standard. Further, the Christophers did not have any confidential relationship with Du Pont and did not violate any laws while taking the photographs. Du Pont sued the Christophers for misappropriation of its trade secrets. Are the Christophers liable for misappropriation of Du Pont's trade secret? Explain.
3. Reverend Jerry Falwell holds the trademark "Jerry Falwell," and Jerry Falwell Ministries can be found online at "www.falwell.com," a website which receives 9,000 hits per day. Christopher Lamparello created a website at the domain name "www.fallwell.com" to respond to what he believed were Falwell's "untruths about gay people." Although the interior pages of Lamparello's website did not contain a disclaimer, the homepage prominently stated, "This website is NOT affiliated with Jerry Falwell or his ministry"; advised, "If you would like to visit Rev. Falwell's website, you may click here"; and provided a hyperlink to Reverend Falwell's website. Lamparello never sold goods or services on his website. Lamparello's domain name and website at www.fallwell.com received only 200 hits per day and had no measurable impact on the quantity of visits to Reverend Falwell's website. Should Reverend Falwell recover under his trademark infringement claim? Explain.
4. Russ Hardenburgh operated a computer bulletin board service (BBS). For a fee, subscribers received access to certain files which were otherwise off-limits to the general public, and had the right to download a set number of megabytes of electronic information from these files every week. The central BBS grew to 124 computers, with nearly 6,000 subscribers. Approximately 110,000 files were available for downloading, nearly half of which were graphic image files. To increase its stockpile of photographs, Hardenburgh provided an incentive to encourage subscribers to upload information onto the BBS. They were given a "credit" for each megabyte of electronic data that they uploaded onto the system. For each credit, the subscriber was entitled to download 1.5 extra megabytes of electronic information, in addition to the megabytes available under the normal terms of subscription. Many of the photographs contributed by subscribers were Playboy photographs. Is Hardenburgh liable to Playboy for copyright infringement? Explain.
5. Diehr wished to patent his process for molding raw uncured synthetic rubber into cured precision products. The process used a mold for shaping rubber under heat and pressure and then curing it while still in the mold. Previous efforts at curing and molding synthetic rubber had failed because of the inability to accurately measure and control the temperature inside the molding press. Diehr's process constantly measured the temperature inside the mold, feeding the information to a computer that constantly recalculated the curing time, so that the molding press would open at the correct time. A U.S. patent examiner rejected Diehr's patent application, asserting that processes involving the laws of nature and physical phenomena are not eligible for patent protection. Is Diehr's process eligible for patent protection? Explain.

6. Mars Sales Company and Berner International Corporation compete in the production and sale of devices that use a barrier of moving air directed across an open doorway or other opening for temperature and insect control. These devices, which were first manufactured in the United Kingdom under the name *air curtains,* originally were marketed in the United States under that name by Berner. When Mars began selling air curtains, it coined and adopted the term *air door* to distinguish its device from others on the market. When other manufacturers used *air door* in connection with or on their products, Mars objected and the companies refrained from using the name. Soon thereafter, Mars learned that Berner had begun using *air door* in the promotion of its products. How will a court decide whether it should order Berner to refrain from using the term *air door?*
7. WhenU.com (WhenU) distributes a downloadable software program, called SaveNow, that is generally bundled for distribution with other software programs. For example, the pop-up advertisement software is found in many Web-based "free" screensaver programs downloaded by individual computer users. Once a user accepts the license agreement, the SaveNow software is delivered and installed on the user's computer. Using "keying," the SaveNow program determines whether the user's computer should receive a pop-up advertisement which is selected at random from WhenU clients that match the category of the user's activity. The program will then display a pop-up advertisement on the user's computer screen; this pop-up ad will generally appear in front of all the windows the user may have open at the time. Once the pop-up ad is displayed, the user must either move the mouse and click the ad closed or use the keystrokes "Alt-F4" to close the ad. To maintain its business, WhenU sells advertising space and opportunities to merchants that want to take advantage of the SaveNow software. U-Haul complained that WhenU's pop-up advertisements, which crowd the computer user's screen and block out U-Haul's website display, in effect, infringe on U-Haul's registered trademark because the pop-ups often display ads from U-Haul's competitors. Should U-Haul recover for trademark infringement? Explain.
8. Lockheed owns the federally registered SKUNK WORKS service mark for "engineering, technical consulting, and advisory services with respect to designing, building, equipping, and testing commercial and military aircraft and related equipment." Despite this fact, several companies registered domain names such as "skunkwrks.com," "skunkworks.com," "skunkwerks.com," "the-skunkwerks.com," and "theskunkworks.com." Lockheed claims that Network Solutions (NSI) directly infringed its SKUNK WORKS service mark by accepting the domain name registrations. Is Network Solutions liable to Lockheed for direct infringement and dilution of Lockheed's service mark? Explain.

Part 2

Contracts

Chapter 9

The Nature and Origins of Contracts

LO

Learning Objectives

After you have studied this chapter, you should be able to:

1. Define a contract and explain its purposes.
2. Discuss the concept of a "good" and explain why it matters in contract law.
3. Contrast the CISG with the UCC.
4. Explain the differences among valid, unenforceable, voidable, and void contracts.
5. Know the differences between an express and an implied contract.
6. Understand the concept of promissory estoppel and the relevance it has to contract law.

The outline in Figure 9.1 on the following page gives you an overview of what you will be studying in the next 10 chapters, in Part 2 of this book, "Contracts." The outline presents an approach you can use in organizing the material you learn about contract law and in analyzing contract problems. The material is presented in the context of four broad questions. After studying the chapters, you should be able to determine the answers to these questions in the context of specific fact situations. For example, after studying Chapters 10, 11, and 12, you will know how to determine if there was the good offer, acceptance, and consideration necessary for a contract. The four basic organizational questions are:

- Is there a contract?
- Is the contract enforceable?
- Who can enforce the contract?
- Was the contract breached and what are the remedies?

FIGURE 9.1
Contracts

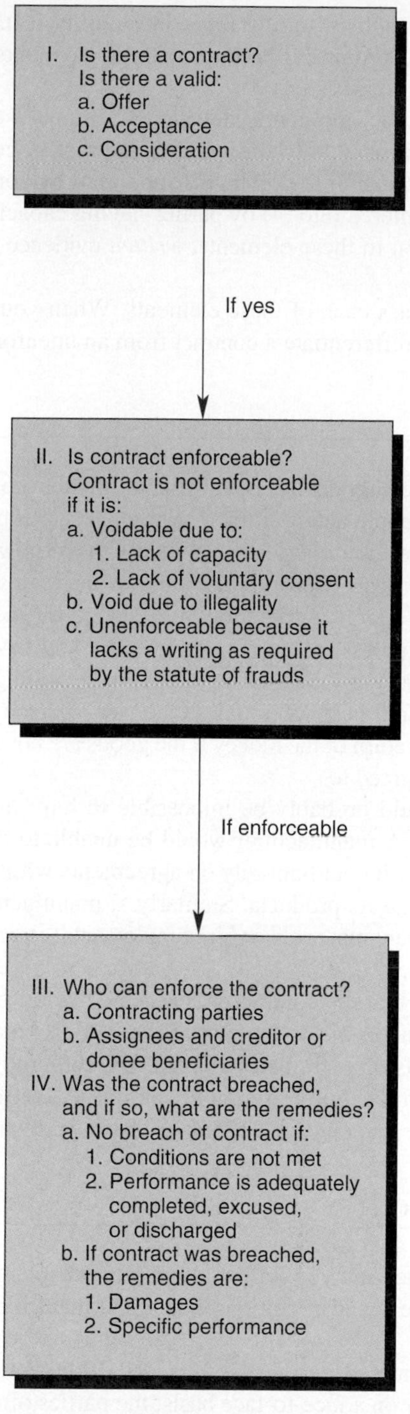

I. Is there a contract?
Is there a valid:
a. Offer
b. Acceptance
c. Consideration
If yes
II. Is contract enforceable?
Contract is not enforceable if it is:
a. Voidable due to:
1. Lack of capacity
2. Lack of voluntary consent
b. Void due to illegality
c. Unenforceable because it lacks a writing as required by the statute of frauds
If enforceable
III. Who can enforce the contract?
a. Contracting parties
b. Assignees and creditor or donee beneficiaries
IV. Was the contract breached, and if so, what are the remedies?
a. No breach of contract if:
1. Conditions are not met
2. Performance is adequately completed, excused, or discharged
b. If contract was breached, the remedies are:
1. Damages
2. Specific performance

What Is a Contract?

LO1

A **contract** is a *legally enforceable promise* or set of promises. However, not all promises are contracts. If Bill promises to take Mary to the movies on Saturday night but takes Judy instead, can Mary successfully sue Bill for breaking his promise? No. If Bill buys a car from Friendly Motors and promises to pay for it in monthly installments, can Friendly Motors force Bill to honor his promise if he stops making payments? Yes. What is the difference between these two promises?

Over the years, the common law courts developed a number of requirements that a promise had to meet before it would be considered a contract. A contract is (1) an agreement (an *offer* and an *acceptance* of the offer) (2) supported by consideration (with some exceptions) (3) voluntarily entered into (4) by parties having capacity to contract (5) to do a legal act or acts. In addition to these elements, *written* evidence of some kinds of contracts is required.

Chapters 10–16 will discuss each of these elements. When you fully understand each element, you will be able to differentiate a contract from an unenforceable promise.

Why Have Contracts?

LO1

Contracts are probably a necessary device in any kind of market economy where goods and services are exchanged by people acting in their own interest. People might not enter into agreements that call for some future performance unless they know some means (the law) exist to force other people to honor their promises. For example, a small business might be afraid to supply its goods to a large corporation in exchange for the corporation's promise to pay for them next month unless the business knows it could have outside help to force the corporation to pay. Similarly, a weak person might not be willing to pay a strong person today for goods to be delivered next week unless the weak person knows there is outside help available to enforce the return of the money if the goods are not delivered or if the goods delivered are not what was agreed to.

It is also true that it would probably be impossible to have an industrialized market economy without contracts. A manufacturer would be unable to do the kind of planning necessary to run a business if it could not rely on agreements with suppliers to furnish the raw materials needed to make its products. Similarly, a manufacturer might not be willing to commit itself to buy raw materials or hire employees if it could not rely on buyers' promises to buy its products.

It is not surprising, then, that the contract was accepted as the basis for business transactions at a very early point in history. Egyptians and Mesopotamians recognized and enforced contracts thousands of years before Christ. By 1603 the common law courts of England recognized the enforceability of simple contracts. To fully understand why our contract law took its present shape, we must look briefly at its historical roots.

How Has Contract Law Developed?

Many of the rules of contract law you will study in later chapters were developed in the 18th and 19th centuries. The social conditions existing at that time played a strong role in shaping contract law.

Most contracts people entered into in the 18th and 19th centuries fit a typical mold. People dealt with each other on a face-to-face basis; the parties often knew each other personally, or at least knew each other's reputation for fair dealing. The kinds of things people bought and sold were relatively simple, and the odds were that the buyer knew enough about the purchase to make an intelligent choice.

The 19th century also saw *laissez-faire* (free market) economic theories treated as a highly important part of public policy. The courts were unwilling to interfere with people's private agreements or to do anything that might interfere with the country's growing industrialization. "Freedom of contract" was the rule of the day. This "hands-off" policy made contracts an ideal device for business. People in business were able to do the kinds of economic planning that increasing industrialization required. They were also able to limit or shift many of their economic risks by placing clauses in their contracts that they could be sure the courts would enforce. For example, manufacturers were commonly allowed to *disclaim* (avoid responsibility for) any liability for injuries caused by their products.

The result of these factors was what may appear to you to be a hard-nosed attitude on the part of the courts. As long as a person voluntarily entered into a contract (within the broad limits discussed in Chapter 15), the courts would generally enforce it even if the results were grossly unfair. It was not uncommon for courts to say things such as, "It is not the business of the courts to relieve fools of the consequences of their folly." The courts were also generally unwilling to consider the argument that a party did not freely enter a contract because the other party had superior bargaining power and used that power to force the weaker party to accept "unfair" contract terms.

The Industrial Revolution that modernized America also changed many of the basic assumptions underlying contract law. The things people bought and sold became more and more complex. Buyers often had little or no knowledge about the goods they bought. People were buying products manufactured hundreds of miles from their homes, from sellers they often did not know.

An increasingly large percentage of agreements were based on *form contracts.* Frequently, people did not sit down and bargain about the terms of their agreement; instead, they used a printed contract form created before their agreement, often doing little more than filling in the blanks. Any student who has signed a lease or taken out a loan has had experience with form contracts. Some people argued that many parts of our economy in fact had imperfect or monopolistic competition and that free-market theories were no longer the correct basis for public policy in modern society.

The legal system began to respond to these changes in our way of life, changing contract law in the process. Many important contractual relationships that had earlier been left to private bargaining began to be controlled to some degree by legislation. Think for a minute about all the state and federal laws that govern employment contracts: minimum wages, maximum hours, workers' compensation, unemployment benefits, nondiscrimination, and so on. The legislatures have also, for example, passed statutes that make manufacturers more responsible for the products they produce. Often, this public interference in private contracts is justified as an attempt to protect those who lack the power to protect themselves by bargaining for fair contract terms.

Many courts also began to shift their emphasis from protecting business and promoting industrialization to protecting consumers and workers. Courts today are generally willing to consider defenses based on inequality of bargaining power between the parties, and they may refuse to enforce or may even rewrite contracts to avoid injustice. Most modern courts also tend to view with great suspicion attempts by manufacturers to limit their responsibility for their products by contract. This is particularly so when the buyer is a consumer. It is probably safe to say that the trend toward more judicial and legislative input into private contracts will continue for some time to come. Despite this trend, however, the idea that a contract is an agreement freely entered into by the parties is still the basis for enforcing most private contracts today.

Contract law continues to change to meet new challenges and conditions. Online commerce is causing many contract rules to be reexamined.

The Uniform Commercial Code

The biggest reform of contract law has resulted from the adoption of the Uniform Commercial Code (UCC) by all the states (except Louisiana, which has adopted only part of the Code). The Uniform Commercial Code was created by the American Law Institute and the National Conference of Commissioners on Uniform State Laws. The drafters had several purposes in mind, including promoting fair dealing and higher standards of behavior in the marketplace. The most obvious purpose was to establish a uniform law to govern commercial transactions that often take place across state lines.

Despite the intentions of the drafters, complete uniformity has not been achieved. This is so for several reasons. Some sections of the Code were drafted with alternatives, giving adopting states two or three versions of a section to choose from. Some states later amended various sections of the Code, and some sections of the Code have been interpreted differently by different state courts. However, much greater uniformity exists now than existed previously. Work is currently under way to revise many of the Code sections to reflect changes that have occurred since the Code was drafted. Some of these include the transition from a goods to a service economy, changes in what creates commercial value, and the increasing use of computers.

The Code is divided into 9 articles that deal with many of the problems that might ordinarily arise in a commercial transaction. Most of these articles are discussed in Parts 3, 7, and 8 of this book. Article 2, the article that applies to contracts for the sale of goods, is discussed in the following contract chapters as well as in Part 3. In May 2003, the American Law Institute approved a revised version of Article 2. At the time of this writing, no states had yet adopted the amendments; therefore, this discussion relies on the former version of the Code, while noting some of the more relevant amendments along the way.

Article 2

LO2

Article 2 applies to all contracts for the **sale of goods** (2-102).[1] Although the Code contains a somewhat complicated definition of *goods* (2-105), the most important thing to understand is that the term *goods* means *tangible personal property.* This means that contracts for the sale of things such as motor vehicles, books, appliances, and clothing are covered by Article 2. Article 2 does not apply to contracts for the sale of real estate or stocks and bonds, information, and other intangibles.

Article 2 also does not apply to service contracts. This can cause confusion because, while contracts for employment or other services are clearly not covered, many contracts involve elements of both goods and services. The test the courts most frequently use to determine whether Article 2 applies to a particular contract is to ask which element—goods or services—*predominates* in the contract. Basically, this means that any agreement calling for services that involve significant elements of personal skill and judgment is probably not governed by Article 2. For example, Lucy suffers an injury due to impurities in a permanent solution for hair. Can she sue for breach of warranty under the Code, or must she sue on some other theory? If Lucy bought the solution ("goods") at a drugstore and applied it herself, the Code applies. If, however, the solution was applied at a beauty shop (the application by a trained professional is a substantial service element), a court would probably not apply the Code. Construction contracts, remodeling contracts, and

[1] The numbers in parentheses refer to specific Uniform Commercial Code sections. The sections appear in the website for this book. Article 2A applies to *leases.*

auto repair contracts are other examples of mixed goods and services contracts that may be considered outside the scope of the Code.

The following case involves such an issue.

Conwell v. Gray Loon Outdoor Marketing Group, Inc.

906 N.E.2d 805 (Ind. Sup. Ct. 2009)

FACTS

Conwell was a partner in a company, Piece of America (POA), which sold one-square-inch parcels of land in each of the 50 states. The company wanted to sell through a website and approached Gray Loon Marketing to design and publish its website. Gray Loon gave POA a website design proposal and an estimated price of $8,080. The proposal stated, "It is Gray Loon's philosophy that clients have purchased goods and services from us and that inherently means ownership of those goods and services as well." POA agreed, the website was created, and POA paid in full. Several months later POA asked for several changes, some of which required major programming work. Gray Loon agreed over the phone and began work on the changes. When the changes were complete, POA said it no longer wanted them and did not pay the $5,224.50 bill sent by Gray Loon. After several failed attempts to collect, Gray Loon took the website offline and sued for nonpayment. POA argued that the contract was for services, and that under the common law, since there was no agreement as to price for the modifications, it is not liable.

ISSUE

Should the common law be applied to this contract?

DECISION

Yes. In order to decide this, the definition of a website must first be examined. A website consists of computer programming that is decoded by an Internet browser to show the "graphic user interface" that ranges from a simple combination of graphics and text to interactive applications. There are essentially two aspects: the content that the pages on a website display and the programming that encodes it so that a browser can interpret it. In this case, Gray Loon provided both the programming and most of the content, and also hosted the website. Article 2 of the UCC applies to transactions in goods. Goods means things which are movable at the time of the contract, excluding money and investment securities. When there is a close question as to whether a transaction involved the transfer of goods or performance of services, what predominates usually controls. Software can be a good if it is contained in a tangible medium, especially if sold on a mass scale. Here, though, the customized software was not a sale for goods. A website created under arrangements calling for the designer to fashion, program, and host its operation on the designer's server is neither tangible nor moveable in the conventional sense. Service predominates, and the UCC does not apply.

The first question you should ask when faced with a contracts problem: *Is this a contract for the sale of goods?* If it is not, apply the principles of common law contracts. If it is, apply the Code rule, *if there is one*. The Code has modified only some of the basic rules of contract law. If there is no specific Code rule governing the problem, apply the relevant common law rule. See Figure 9.2.

Creation of Practical Contract Rules

Article 2 reflects an attitude about contracts that is fundamentally different from that of the common law. The Code is more concerned with rewarding people's legitimate expectations than with technical rules, so it is generally more *flexible* than traditional contract law. A court that applies the Code is more likely to find the parties had a contract than a court that applies contract law (2-204). In some cases, the Code gives less weight to technical requirements such as consideration (discussed in Chapter 12) than is the case in contract law (2-205 and 2-209).

FIGURE 9.2
Choice of Law: Goods vs. Services

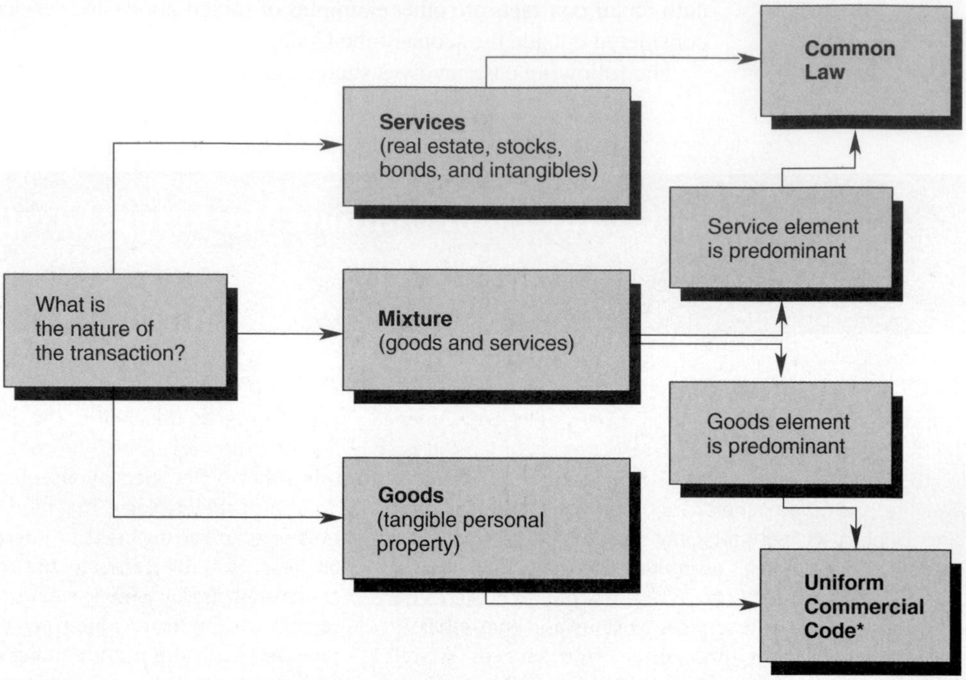

* If there is no specific Uniform Commercial Code provision governing the transaction, use the common law.

The drafters of the Code sought to create practical rules to deal with what people actually do in today's marketplace. We live in the day of the form contract, so some of the Code rules try to deal fairly with that fact (Sections 2-205, 2-207, 2-209, and 2-302). Throughout the Code, the words *reasonable, commercially reasonable,* and *seasonably* (within a reasonable time) are found. This "reasonableness" standard is different from the hypothetical "reasonable person" standard used in tort law. A court that tries to decide what is reasonable under the Code is more likely to be concerned with what people really do in the marketplace than with what a nonexistent reasonable person would do.

Cyber-Contracts

Electronic contracting is becoming increasingly commonplace. More and more people are purchasing goods and services they find advertised on websites, and agreements are frequently made through an exchange of e-mail messages. In large part, most electronic contracting issues may be resolved through a familiarity with traditional contract rules. Initially, the drafters of the Uniform Commercial Code considered adding a new section to the Code to address "information contracts." However, the drafters abandoned this effort and amended the definition of "goods" to *exclude* information (2-103[k]). This means that a transaction such as software downloaded from the Internet would not qualify as a good, whereas a good which incidentally incorporates information, such as a car's computer-controlled antilock braking system, would still be considered a transaction in goods.

The abandoned UCC revisions became part of a proposed statute called the Uniform Computer Information Transaction Act (UCITA). Only a few states have adopted UCITA. We will return to a discussion of the statute in the chapters on contract offers and acceptances.

Good Faith and Fair Dealing

The drafters of the Code also tried to promote fair dealing and higher standards of behavior in the marketplace. They attempted to do this in several ways in Article 2. The Code imposes a duty on everyone making agreements under the Code to act in *good faith* (1-203). It expressly recognizes the concept of an *unconscionable* contract (2-302)—one that is grossly unfair or one-sided—and gives the courts broad powers to remedy such unfairness. Further, the Code imposes certain standards of quality on sellers of goods as a matter of law. These are called *implied warranties* (2-314 and 2-315) (discussed in Chapter 19). Sellers' power to contractually deny (disclaim) responsibility for their goods is also limited (2-316 and 2-302).

Some sections of the Code (Sections 2-201[2], 2-205, 2-207[2], and 2-314), *in some cases,* impose a higher standard of behavior on "merchants" than on nonmerchants in recognition of the fact that buyers tend to place more reliance on professional sellers and that professionals are generally more knowledgeable and better able to protect themselves than nonprofessionals. The Code defines **merchant** (2-104[1]) on a case-by-case basis. If a person *regularly deals in the kind of goods being sold,* or pretends to have some special knowledge about the goods, or employs an agent in the sale who fits either of these two descriptions, that person is a *merchant* for the purposes of the contract in question. So, if you buy a used car from a used-car dealer, the dealer is a merchant for the purposes of your contract. But if you buy a refrigerator from a used-car dealer, the dealer is probably not considered to be a merchant for purposes of that sale.

Because Article 2 exhibits the basic tendencies of contract law discussed earlier in the chapter, many courts apply Code concepts to cases not specifically covered by the Code. In addition, many courts have broadly interpreted the Code to apply to contracts for things one would not normally classify as "goods." The Code concepts of good-faith dealing and unconscionability have also enjoyed wide application. Thus, contract law under the Code and the common law are growing more similar.

Contracts for the International Sale of Goods

Historically, nations have adopted a wide variety of approaches to contract law. Such variety resulted in confusion and impeded global trade. Business lawyers were required to spend a great deal of time researching different legal schemes in order to draft agreements that would protect the parties' expectations throughout the world. Transactions were often delayed or otherwise burdened by disagreements between the parties over the selection of a particular choice of law provision within the contract. In an attempt to overcome these problems, the United Nations Convention on Contracts for the International Sale of Goods (CISG) was created. The fundamental goal of the CISG is to unify and codify an international law of sales in much the same way that the Uniform Commercial Code provides uniformity and stability for transactions among contracting parties from different states in the United States. The CISG provides rules governing the formation of international contracts and regulates the transfer of goods under those contracts. It applies to contracts between parties from signatory countries (countries that have agreed to be bound by the treaty).

LO3

Despite many similarities to the Uniform Commercial Code (UCC), the CISG does differ in several respects. First, the CISG applies only to commercial sales of goods, while the UCC governs both consumer and commercial transactions. Second, while the UCC has some provisions holding merchants to higher standards than those imposed on nonmerchants, the CISG does not. (This is because all parties must be merchants under the CISG since it applies only to commercial sales.) Third, the UCC (with some exceptions) requires contracts for the sale of goods in excess of $500 to be in writing. The CISG has no writing requirement unless the contract contains a written provision requiring that modifications for terminations be in writing. Finally, the CISG generally requires that acceptance be a mirror image of the offer, while the UCC focuses on which terms of the offer and acceptance are the same. See Table 9.1.

The Hague Convention on the Law Applicable to Contracts for the International Sale of Goods (Choice-of-Law Convention) resulted from an attempt to harmonize choice-of-law rules with the CISG. It provides courts in the signatory countries with rules for determining which law applies to contracts for the sales of goods when those contracts involve parties from different countries. It allows contracting parties to specify which country's laws will apply to their transaction but also provides a way for the court to decide if the parties have not so chosen.

If both parties to a contract reside in countries that have adopted the CISG, those terms automatically will control the transaction unless the agreement contains a provision specifically rejecting its applicability. If the buyer and seller are not from countries that have adopted the CISG, it will not govern unless their contract specifically calls for its application. Otherwise, the governing law, when not specified in the contract, will be the law of the country in which the seller's place of business is located.

TABLE 9.1
CISG versus UCC

	CISG	UCC
Application	*International commercial sales* of goods	*Any* sale of goods
Parties	Applies only to merchants	Applies to any party (merchants often held to higher standards)
Acceptance	"Mirror image" rule (certain terms considered material)	Offer and acceptance must contain same terms or Section 2-207 for forms*
Consideration	None needed to modify contract	None needed to modify contract
Writing	No writing needed	Sale of goods in excess of $500 requires a writing

* See Chapter 12 for a discussion of §2-207.

Types of Contracts

Several terms are used to describe the different kinds of contracts our legal system recognizes. These terms will be used throughout the following chapters.

LO4

Valid, Unenforceable, Voidable, and Void Contracts

A **valid contract** is one that meets all the legal requirements for a contract. Valid contracts are therefore enforceable in court.

An **unenforceable contract** is one that meets the basic legal requirements for a contract but will not be enforced due to some other legal rule. For example, in Chapter 16, we will see that the law says some kinds of contracts must be in writing to be enforceable. Contracts for the sale of real estate are one example of a contract required to be in writing. So, Bob may agree to sell his house to Mary and every basic requirement for a contract may be present (a voluntary agreement to do a legal act by parties with the capacity to contract, supported by consideration), but if the agreement is not in writing, the contract will not be enforced by the court.

A **voidable contract** is one that may be canceled by one or both of the parties. It is enforceable against both parties unless a party with the right to cancel the contract has done so. For example, in Chapter 13, we will see that minors have the legal right to cancel their contracts. So, if Frank buys a used car from Honest Bob's Used Cars and Frank is a minor, the parties have a voidable contract. It is binding and enforceable against both parties unless Frank decides to cancel the contract.

The following case is another example of this concept.

Dodd v. American Family Mutual Insurance Co.

956 N.E.2d 769 (Ind. Ct. App. 2011)

FACTS

Michael and Katherine were living in Katherine's house when it was destroyed by fire. The house was insured and she was reimbursed for the loss. A few months later, Michael executed an application for homeowner's insurance from American Family Mutual Insurance Co. (American Mutual) and said on the application that he had not "had any past/current losses at any locations." He also indicated that his "girlfriend/fiancé" Katherine would live in the house. The policy was issued. Michael and Katherine built a new home and were married two years later. Michael renewed the policy every year and his name remained the only one on the policy. Five years after the first fire, the garage and its contents were destroyed by fire. When American Family denied the claim for fire losses, the Dodds sued. The Dodds concede that Michael made a material misrepresentation on the application. However, they argued that the misrepresentation merely made the insurance policy voidable at the option of American Family and that American family did not follow the appropriate steps to void the policy because it did not return the premiums the Dodds had paid on the policy. This, the Dodds argued, left the policy in effect.

ISSUE

Was the contract voidable or void from the outset due to misrepresentation?

DECISION

Voidable. A material misrepresentation on an insurance policy renders the coverage voidable at the insurance company's option. Here, Michael failed to disclose material facts relevant to the insurance coverage. He requested insurance in his name alone and failed to disclose the destruction by fire of Katherine's house in which he lived. The policy was also voidable at American Family's option by the terms of the application. The form stated, "**You** warrant the statements in **your** application to be true . . . . **We** may void this policy if the statements **you** have given us are false and **we** have relied on them." This language clearly makes the policy voidable. In general, when an insurance company seeks to rescind a policy for material misrepresentation, it must first tender the premiums back. We do not have sufficient evidence here to determine if that was done in a timely manner.

The **void contract** lacks one or more of the basic requirements for a contract. Such an agreement has no legal force or effect. An example is an agreement to steal a car. One of the basic requirements for a valid contract is that the thing the parties have agreed to do is legal. Stealing a car is illegal; therefore, such an agreement would be considered void.

Unilateral and Bilateral Contracts

Contracts are called either unilateral or bilateral depending on whether one or both of the parties made a promise. In a **unilateral contract,** only one of the parties makes a promise. The other party performs an act in exchange for that promise. For example, Mary runs an ad in the paper offering a $5 reward for the return of her lost dog, Sparky. Mary has made a promise to pay the person who performs the act of returning Sparky.

In a **bilateral contract,** both parties make a promise. For example, Sue Smith, the owner of Hi-Fi Heaven, orders 100 stereo receivers from Steve Jones, a salesman for Slick Sound Manufacturing Company. Sue has made a promise to pay for the receivers in exchange for

Concept Summary: Types of Contracts by Enforceability

Valid	Contains all elements needed to be enforceable
Unenforceable	Contains basic elements required for a contract but the courts will not enforce it due to a legal rule (such as the statute of frauds)
Voidable	One of the contracting parties can avoid the contract
Void	Lacks basic element(s) necessary for a contract

Slick Sound's promise to deliver them. In the next chapter, you will learn that unilateral contracts create some special problems in the areas of offer and acceptance. This fact causes the courts to treat a contract as bilateral whenever it is possible to do so.

Executed and Executory Contracts

A contract is **executed** when all the parties have fully performed their duties under the contract. A contract is **executory** as long as it has not been fully performed. A contract is partially executory when one person has performed his promise under the contract but the other person has not performed hers.

LO5

Express and Implied Contracts

A contract is **express** when the parties have directly stated its terms at the time the contract was formed. They may have done this orally or in writing. So, when Bill tells Joe, "I'll sell you my 1988 truck for $10,000," and Joe replies, "You've got a deal," an express contract has been created.

There are many cases, however, in which the parties have clearly reached an agreement, even though they have not expressly stated its terms. When the surrounding facts and circumstances indicate that an agreement has in fact been reached, an **implied contract** is created. Suppose you go to your dentist for treatment. Ordinarily you would not expressly state the terms of your mutual agreement beforehand, although it is clear that you do, in fact, have an agreement. A court would infer a promise on the part of your dentist to use reasonable care in treating you and a promise on your part to pay a reasonable fee for the dentist's services.

Anderson v. Hannaford Brothers Co.

80 U.S.L.W. 525 (1st Cir. Ct. App. 2011)

FACTS

Hannaford, a national supermarket chain, had an electronic payment processing system that was hacked. As a result, 4.2 million credit and debit card numbers, expiration dates, and security codes were stolen. Many of the Hannaford customers had thousands of charges to their debit and credit card accounts as a result of the theft. Hannaford customers sued the company for breach of implied contract, among other theories.

(continued)

Anderson v. Hannaford Brothers Co. *(concluded)*

ISSUE

Was there an implied contract?

DECISION

Yes. A contract contains promises set forth in express words as well as implied provisions that are indispensable to carrying out the intent of the parties. Here, the implied contract was that Hannaford would not use the credit card data for other people's purchases, would not sell the data to others, and would take reasonable measures to protect the information. When a customer uses a credit card in a commercial transaction, she intends to provide the data to the merchant only. She does not expect or intend the merchant to allow unauthorized third parties to access the data. A jury could reasonably find there was an implied contract between Hannaford and its customers that the company would take reasonable measures to protect the credit and debit card information.

It is possible to describe any contract by using one or more of the terms discussed earlier in this chapter. Consider this contract: Martha's Beauty Salon sends Hair Affair Manufacturing Company an order for 10 cases of hair spray at $75 a case. Hair Affair sends Martha's an acknowledgment form accepting the order. The parties have a *valid, express, bilateral contract.* The contract is *executory* until Hair Affair has delivered the goods and Martha's has paid for them.

Quasi Contract

As you saw in Chapter 1, the common law as it initially developed was a fairly rigid, inflexible way of dealing with many problems. One aspect of this rigidity was that the courts insisted that all the elements of a contract be present before the courts would find a legally binding agreement between the parties. This attitude caused an injustice in some cases. Sometimes a person might have done something that benefited another person but there were no facts from which a court could infer an agreement between the parties. In such a case, the party who received the benefit could be *unjustly enriched* at the expense of the other party. This unfair result could be avoided if a court created or implied a promise by the benefited party to pay the reasonable value of the benefit.

A **quasi contract** is a legal fiction created by the court to avoid injustice in such cases. It requires the defendant to act as if he had promised to pay for the benefit he voluntarily received. Since there is no factual basis for implying a promise to pay, as we have in an implied contract case, the courts, in effect, create the promise. This promise imposed by law is applied in a wide variety of cases. It is impossible to list all the kinds of cases that may create a liability based on quasi contract. The basic idea is that quasi contract applies where one of the parties *voluntarily receives a benefit* from the other party under circumstances that make it *unfair* to keep the benefit without paying for it. Generally, the person is required to pay the *reasonable value* of the benefit received. A person is not held liable under quasi contract for benefits he or she received unknowingly, or for benefits he or she reasonably believed were given as a gift.

For example, Fred's Painting Company has a contract to paint Walter's house at 525 East Third Street. Fred's painters arrive by mistake at Bob's house at 325 East Third Street and begin painting. Bob sees Fred's painters but does not say anything because his house needs painting. Bob later refuses to pay for the paint job, arguing that the parties have no contract.

There are clearly no facts here to justify implying an agreement between Fred's and Bob. However, the courts would probably hold Bob liable to Fred's on a quasi contract basis. On the other hand, if Bob had come home from vacation to find his home mistakenly painted, he would not be liable to Fred's since he did not knowingly accept the paint job.

Palese v. Delaware State Lottery Office

2006 Del. Ch. LEXIS 126 (Del. Chancery 2006)

FACTS

Palese bought five lottery tickets. He used a "play slip" to select his numbers, then filled his numbers in on the grid. He put the tickets in his pocket, went home, and did laundry. Several days later he heard that someone had won but had not claimed the prize. After failing to find his tickets, he remembered he did the laundry and assumed the tickets had been destroyed in the wash. He checked the play slip, which had not been in his pocket, and discovered he had won. Palese wrote the lottery and explained his dilemma. They responded that he would have to wait a year, and if no one else claimed the prize, they would consider whether the play slip would entitle him to the prize. Eleven months later, Palese read that the unclaimed jackpot had been transferred to the state's general fund. Palese contacted the lottery and again explained what had happened. The lottery said he had to have the ticket and denied his claim. Palese sued the lottery, arguing the state had been unjustly enriched.

ISSUE

Should the court allow recovery under a theory of quasi contract?

DECISION

No. The lottery rules say, "all winning tickets will be validated. A winning ticket must not be counterfeit in whole or in part and must be presented by a person authorized to play the lottery." They also say that the lottery "shall not be responsible for lost, stolen, or mutilated tickets." When he bought the ticket, Palese entered into a contract with the lottery. The terms on the back of the ticket put him on notice that, among other things, "[de]termination of winners and transactions are subject to Delaware State Lottery laws, rules, regulations, and directives. Void if mutilated, altered, illegible or incomplete. Not responsible for torn or stolen tickets." Courts developed unjust enrichment or quasi contract as a theory of recovery to remedy the absence of a formal contract. A party cannot recover under the theory if a contract exists. The lottery had the right to determine the merits of Palese's claim. Its conduct was not wrong or unreasonable. A quasi contract will not be imposed.

Concept Summary: Types of Contracts

Unilateral	An act exchanged for a promise
Bilateral	A promise exchanged for a promise
Executory	A contract that has not been fully performed
Executed	A contract that has been fully performed
Express	Terms are stated orally or in writing
Implied	Terms are indicated by facts and circumstances
Quasi Contract (Implied-in-Law)	Contractlike duties imposed by the court to prevent unjust enrichment

Promissory Estoppel

LO6

Another important idea that the courts developed to deal with the unfairness that sometimes results from the strict application of contract rules is the doctrine of **promissory estoppel.** Traditional contract law is basically designed to protect *bargains* that people make and that satisfy all the legal requirements for a binding contract. Around the turn of this century, however, the courts were confronted with cases in which persons relied on promises made by others that did not amount to contracts because they lacked some element required for a contract. Allowing the person who made such a promise (the promisor) to argue that no contract was created could, in some cases, work an injustice on the person who relied on the promise (the promisee).

In cases where denying enforcement would produce a serious injustice, some courts began to protect promisees by saying that the promisors were *estopped* (prevented) from raising any legal defense they might have to the enforcement of the promise. For example, John's parents told him that they would give the family farm to him when they died. Relying on this promise, John stayed at home and worked on the farm for several years. When they died, John's parents left the farm to his sister Martha. Should Martha and the parents' estate be allowed to defeat John's claim to the farm by arguing that the parents' promise was unenforceable because John gave no consideration for the promise (since the parents did not request that John stay home and work on the farm in exchange for their promise)? Many courts began to say that Martha and the parents' estate were estopped from raising this defense because of the unfairness to John that would result. Out of such cases grew the doctrine of promissory estoppel.

The *Restatement (Second) of Contracts,* an authoritative work on the common law of contracts that is often relied on by the courts, says:

> A promise which the promisor should reasonably expect to induce action or forbearance on the part of the promisee or a third person and which does induce such action or forbearance is binding if injustice can be avoided only by enforcement of the promise. The remedy granted for breach may be limited as justice requires. [Section 90]

While the *Restatement* does not have the force of law, most courts follow the requirements for promissory estoppel stated in it. Thus, they require a *promise* that the promisor should foresee is likely to induce reliance; significant *reliance* on the promise by the promisee; and *injustice* as a result of reliance. Promissory estoppel is fundamentally different from traditional contract theory since it protects *reliance,* not bargains. In the following chapters, you will see promissory estoppel being used to enforce promises that are not supported by consideration and oral promises that would ordinarily be required to be in writing. The growth of this new theory for enforcing promises is one of the most important developments in contract law in this century.

Figure 9.3 summarizes the requirements for promissory estoppel.

FIGURE 9.3
Requirements for Promissory Estoppel

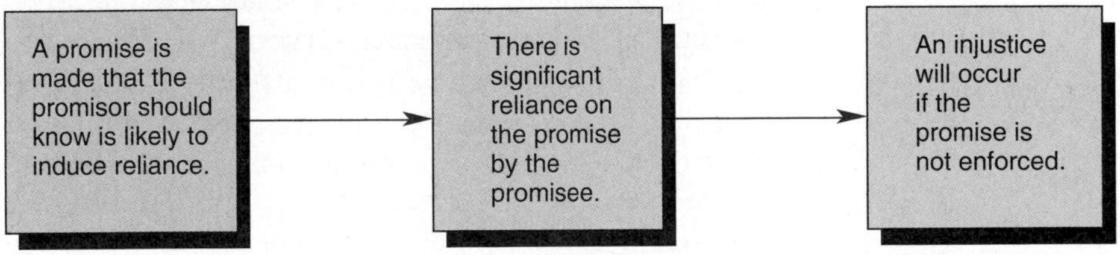

A promise is made that the promisor should know is likely to induce reliance.
There is significant reliance on the promise by the promisee.
An injustice will occur if the promise is not enforced.

Ethics in Action

Contracts are steeped in the idea of a voluntary bargain. However, the concepts of quasi contract and promissory estoppel are aimed at avoiding injustice. How do we explain these exceptions? What are the interests of justice we are concerned with?

Questions and Problem Cases

1. Explain how the court determines whether to apply the UCC or the common law in a contract involving both services and goods.
2. What is the difference between a unilateral and a bilateral contract?
3. Explain the concept of promissory estoppels.
4. Kasim owned a Super 8 Lodge and rented space to Duncan for a bar-lounge. Duncan was responsible for remodeling costs and operating expenses. She put a substantial amount of her personal property in it. Duncan did not reveal she was a convicted felon which, under Florida law, made it illegal for her to be in charge of a bar-lounge. After learning this, Kasim barred her from entering the area and kept all the property she had put there. Can Duncan recover under a theory of unjust enrichment? Why?
5. Sheldorado Aluminum Products sold an aluminum awning to Villette and installed it on the back of his home for use as a carport. There was no formal written contract, but there was a bill of sale. The day after installation, the awning began to leak. Six months later, after a snow storm, the awning collapsed on top of Villette's new Mercedes. Villette sued for the return of the $3,000 paid to Sheldorado. Should this contract be decided under the UCC or the common law? Why?
6. The Races bought a mobile home from Fleetwood Retail Corp. They had a lot in mind, but Fleetwood convinced them to buy a lot from it, telling the Races that lots were scarce, others were looking, and it would be off the market. Fleetwood assured the Races that it had checked with a contractor regarding the feasibility of putting the trailer on the lot. When the Races' contractor tried to get a septic permit, it was denied because the lot was too small for their trailer; it turned out to be smaller than Fleetwood represented. The Races sued for breach of the obligation of good faith and fair dealing. Explain why they should or should not be successful.
7. The Taylors bought an ocean front lot in Oregon. The next year, Staley bought an ocean front lot south of the Taylors and built a home on it. Over the years, Staley often expressed concern that when the Taylors built their house, they could block her view. They said they would not. When they began planning their home, they asked Staley to submit a letter in support of a setback variance they sought. She said she would as long as her view wasn't blocked. They again told her it wouldn't be blocked. When the house was built, it partially blocked her view. She sued for breach of an implied contract. Can an implied contract be inferred from the parties' conduct? Explain.
8. Goff-Hamel, an employee of Hastings Family Planning Services for 11 years, was asked by Obstetricians & Gynecologists, P.C. (O&G), to come work for them. She accepted and agreed to start work two months later. She gave notice at Hastings and got fitted for uniforms at O&G. The day before she was to start, she was told not to come to work because one of the wives of an O&G owner objected to her hiring. Goff-Hamel sued for promissory estoppel. Will she be successful? Why?

Chapter 10

Creating a Contract: Offers

Learning Objectives

After you have studied this chapter, you should be able to:

1. Explain the three main elements of an offer.
2. Describe how the UCC and the common law differ on definiteness.
3. Identify the special rules pertaining to advertisements.
4. Discuss how bids are considered in contract law.
5. Identify the various ways an offer can end.
6. Explain the differences in revocation under the common law and the UCC.

Cagle went to Roy Buckner Chevrolet to discuss buying a 1978 Limited Edition Corvette CP (the "Indy Vette"). The salesman agreed to sell one to Cagle, and signed his name in the middle of the company's form after putting "list price" as the price to be paid. The form was left partially uncompleted. Cagle signed the form and left a deposit of $500. Buckner later refused to deliver the car to Cagle, claiming the agreement was too indefinite to be a good offer.

- How specific must an offer be to form the basis of a contract?
- What do the courts look at to determine whether the offeror intended to make a binding offer?
- What does the court do to fill in missing terms?

FIGURE 10.1
Offers

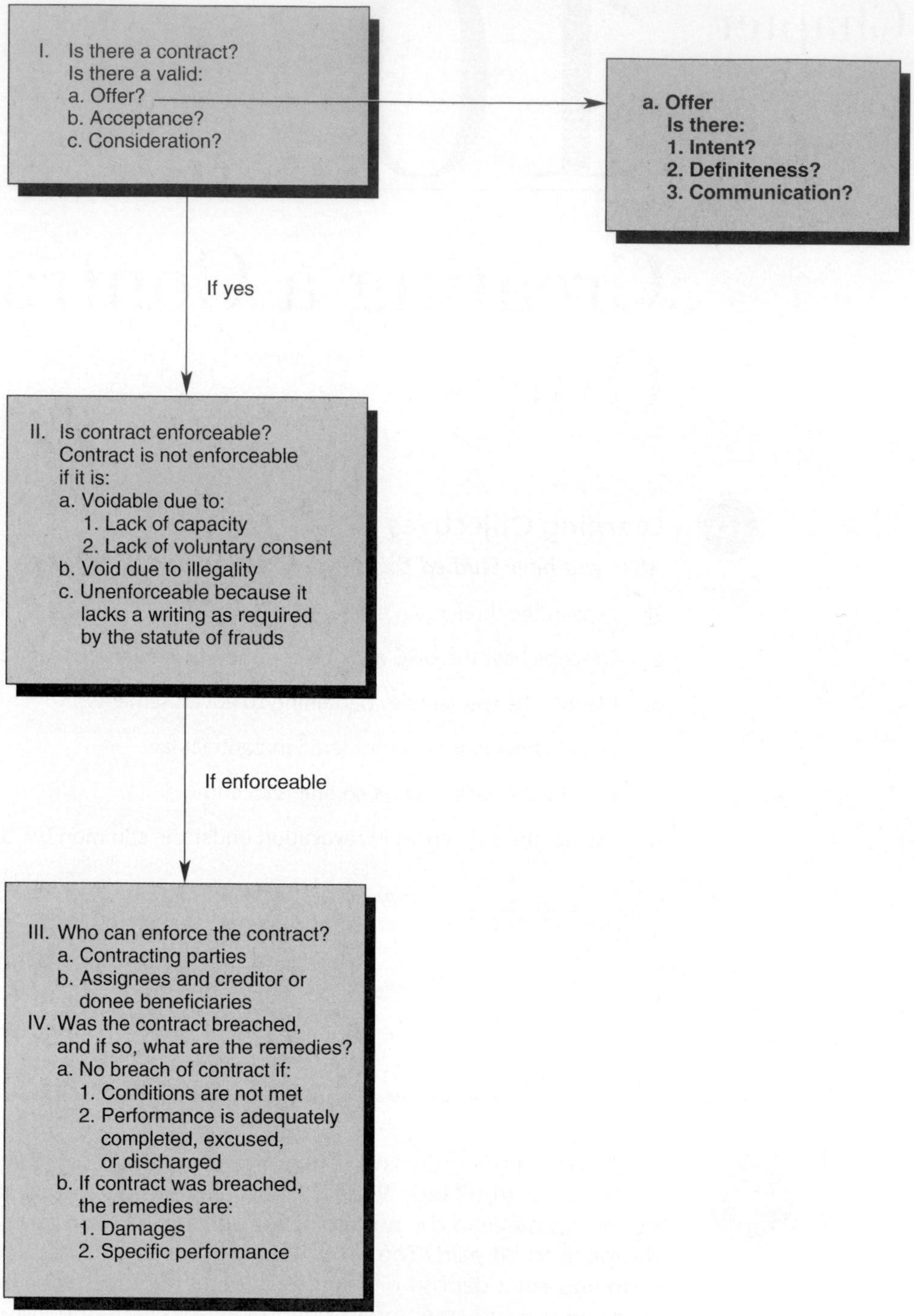
I. Is there a contract?
Is there a valid:
a. Offer?
b. Acceptance?
c. Consideration?
a. Offer
Is there:
1. Intent?
2. Definiteness?
3. Communication?
If yes
II. Is contract enforceable?
Contract is not enforceable
if it is:
a. Voidable due to:
1. Lack of capacity
2. Lack of voluntary consent
b. Void due to illegality
c. Unenforceable because it
lacks a writing as required
by the statute of frauds
If enforceable
III. Who can enforce the contract?
a. Contracting parties
b. Assignees and creditor or
donee beneficiaries
IV. Was the contract breached,
and if so, what are the remedies?
a. No breach of contract if:
1. Conditions are not met
2. Performance is adequately
completed, excused,
or discharged
b. If contract was breached,
the remedies are:
1. Damages
2. Specific performance

Introduction

LO1

When a dispute arises between the parties to a contract, there are two basic questions the court often has to answer: Did the parties in fact have a contract? If they did, what are its terms? The manner in which the court answers these questions is very important in shaping its decision.

The main thing a court looks for in deciding whether the parties entered into a contract is an **agreement,** or a "meeting of the minds" between the parties. This is so because the whole of traditional contract law is based on the idea of enforcing agreements that the parties made freely. At a very early point in the development of contract law, the courts created the basic formula for a contract:

Offer + Acceptance = Agreement

Did one of the parties indicate to the other party that he or she was willing to enter into an agreement on certain terms and conditions? Did the other party indicate that he or she was willing to agree to those terms and conditions? If so, then the parties have indicated the mutual assent necessary for a contract.

There are two things that you should bear in mind while studying contracts. The first is that the courts do not rely on what the parties say they *actually* (subjectively) intended. This can never be known, and after a dispute has arisen, such statements are often unreliable. Instead, the courts look at the intent of the parties *objectively.* Would a reasonable person who knew all the circumstances surrounding the agreement believe that the parties intended to enter into a contract?

The second thing you should bear in mind is that when courts use the words **offer** and **acceptance,** they are using them in their technical, legal sense. This can cause confusion in two ways. *Offer* and *accept* have everyday meanings that are not necessarily the same as their legal meanings. Also, the parties to a dispute may have used these words in their everyday sense, being unaware of their legal meaning. This can lead to the potentially confusing situation where a party says "I accept" but the courts find that he or she, in fact, made an "offer." Therefore, it is very important that you understand the legal meaning of offer and acceptance.

What Is an Offer?

An *offer* is the manifestation of a willingness to enter into a contract if the other person agrees to the terms. The question of what amounts to an offer is important for several reasons. If there is no offer, there is nothing to accept and a contract cannot be created. A person who has made an offer (the **offeror**) has given the party to whom he or she has made the offer (the **offeree**) the power to create a binding contract by accepting. It is also important to know what is included in the terms of the offer, since the offer often contains all the terms of the contract. This is so because in most cases all the offeree does is indicate acceptance of the offer.

Intent

The basic thing the courts require for the creation of an offer is a **present intent to contract** on the part of the offeror. When all the circumstances surrounding the parties' dealings are considered, did the offeror ever, in effect, say: "This is it—agree and we have a contract on these terms"? As the *Republican National Committee* case illustrates, this is objectively determined.

The two main things a court looks for in answering this question are how **definite** the supposed offer is and whether the offeror has **communicated** it to the offeree.

LO2

Definiteness

Did the offeror specifically indicate what he was willing to do and what he wanted the offeree to do or agree to do in return? If not, his behavior will probably be classed as an "invitation to offer" or an "invitation to negotiate," and will have no legal effect. If

Republican National Committee v. Taylor

299 F.3d 887 (D.C. Cir. 2002)

FACTS

In 1995 the Republican National Committee (RNC) ran an advertisement in the newspapers *USA Today* and *Roll Call.* The ad featured a photograph of Haley Barbour, then chair of the RNC, holding an oversized check for $1 million, payable to "your name here." Below the picture was the following message: "Heard the one about Republicans 'cutting' Medicare? The fact is Republicans are increasing Medicare spending by more than half. I'm Haley Barbour, and I'm so sure of that fact I'm willing to give you this check for a million dollars if you can prove me wrong." The advertisement goes on to assert that under the Republican plan, the government would increase Medicare spending over the next seven fiscal years, culminating in a 2002 expenditure 62% higher than that in 1995. The bottom right portion of the ad featured a clip-out coupon, inviting readers who disagreed with the assertion to check a box labeled "I don't believe you, Haley" and return the coupon with their analyses of "why you are wrong" to the RNC's Washington, D.C., address. Approximately 80 people across the country did not believe Haley and mailed in claims for the million-dollar prize. The RNC responded to each claimant by sending him or her a form letter rejecting the claim as incorrect and enclosing a Congressional Budget Office report. Initially, the RNC claimed that the ad was a parody and not binding on the RNC.

ISSUE

Was there sufficient evidence of intent to form a binding contract?

DECISION

Yes. The District Court was correct in finding that the advertised offer of a reward or premium for the performance of a specified act is a proposition submitted to all persons who may accept and comply with its conditions. Until accepted it may be withdrawn; but when accepted, it becomes a binding contract between the proposer and the acceptor who shall have performed the service or done the act required. Here, the ad was an offer for a valid unilateral contract, which anyone could have accepted by submitting a coupon proving Barbour wrong.

the offeror said, "If we're going to trade cars, you'll have to give me some money in addition to your car," this clearly was not an offer. The parties are still negotiating and may never reach a mutually satisfactory agreement. On the other hand, if the offeror said, "I'll trade you my car for your car and $500," this looks like an offer. If the offeree accepts, both parties are bound to a contract. This is what happened in the Cagle case at the beginning of this chapter. The court found that offering to sell a specific car at list price was sufficiently specific to constitute a valid offer.

Allen v. Clarian Health Partners

980 N.E.2d 306 (Ind. Sup. Ct. 2012)

FACTS

Allen sought medical treatment at a Clarian Health Partners (Clarian) hospital. He was uninsured and signed a form contract under which he agreed to pay all charges associated with the treatment but there was no dollar amount indicated. After his treatment, Allen was charged $15,641.64 for medical services and supplies. This amount was more than double what would have been charged to the insurance company if he had been insured. He challenged the contract saying there was no price term and therefore it was not enforceable.

(continued)

Allen v. Clarian Health Partners *(concluded)*

ISSUE

Was the contract definite enough to be enforceable?

DECISION

Yes. In order to be enforceable, a contract must be reasonably definite and certain. Allen claims the agreement lacks this because it lacks a material term—a price—necessary to be enforceable. In order to determine this, the court must consider the facts and circumstances existing at the time the agreement was made. Hospital prices, while imprecise, are not sufficiently indefinite to justify imposition of a reasonable price standard. Precision on price in the health care market is nearly impossible because the exact treatment and supplies cannot be predetermined. A reasonable price, though, can be determined. The agreement is enforceable.

The more specific the proposal, the more likely the court is to call it an offer. Courts have traditionally said they are contract enforcers, not makers. They did not want to force parties to do something they had not agreed to do. While courts today still will not make contracts for parties, the trend is to tolerate more indefiniteness and, consequently, more open and missing terms. Both the Code and the *Restatement,* through doctrines such as good faith and commercial reasonableness, provide ways to fill in the gaps. At a minimum, the terms of the offer, which can be express or implied from the circumstances, must be sufficiently clear so that what was promised can be determined. Without that, the courts could not decide whether the contract was breached, or what the remedy should be in case of breach. The *Conwell* case involves this decision.

No part of Article 2 is a better indication of the Code's desire to dispense with technicalities and protect people's expectations than its general rules governing the creation of sales contracts (2-204). A sales contract can be created "in any manner sufficient to show

Conwell v. Gray Loon Outdoor Marketing Group, Inc.

906 N.E.2d 805 (Ind. Sup. Ct. 2009)

FACTS

(This is the same case that you saw in Chapter 9, in which the court decided the case should be decided under the common law. Most cases that are appealed involve more than one legal issue that the court must decide. That is the case here.) Conwell was a partner in a company, Piece of America (POA), which sold one-square-inch parcels of land in each of the 50 states. The company wanted to sell through a website and approached Gray Loon Marketing to design and publish its website. Gray Loon gave POA a website design proposal and an estimated price of $8,080. The proposal stated, "It is Gray Loon's philosophy that clients have purchased goods and services from us and that inherently means ownership of those goods and services as well." POA agreed, paid a deposit of 50 percent, and design commenced. POA asked for a few minor changes, none of which were written down. When the work was finished, Gray Loon charged $8,500, and POA paid in full.

Several months later, POA asked for several changes, some of which required major programming work. Gray Loon agreed over the phone to make the changes and immediately began work on them. POA did not request a proposal or quote, and Gray Loon did not provide one. Gray Loon did not save a copy of the original website, as was its practice unless the customer asked for it, which POA did not do. When the modifications were complete, Gray Loon contacted POA for approval. At that time, POA said it no longer wanted the changes. Subsequently, Gray Loon sent POA a bill for $5,224.50. After several failed attempts to collect, the head of Gray Loon met with Conwell, who said he had no problem with the invoice, but POA needed more time to collect the funds for payment. During the months this took place, the website remained online at a cost of $75

(continued)

Conwell v. Gray Loon Outdoor Marketing Group, Inc. *(concluded)*

per month. Finally, Gray Loon sent a registered letter saying it would take the site down if POA didn't pay. When POA didn't, Gray Loon took the website offline and sued for nonpayment. POA argued that the contract was for services, and that under the common law, since there was no agreement as to price for the modifications, it is not liable.

ISSUE

Was there a valid offer that could be accepted?

DECISION

Yes. To be valid and enforceable, a contract must be reasonably definite and certain. All that is required is reasonable certainty in the terms and conditions of the promises made, including by whom and to whom. Only essential terms need be included. A court will not find a contract so uncertain as to preclude enforcement where a reasonable and logical interpretation will render the contract valid. Here we see the agreement for modifications was a new contract, separate from the first, which was completed. POA asked for the changes and did not inquire how much it would cost. Gray Loon submitted what it thought was a reasonable price, and Conwell said he had no problem with the invoice. The lack of a prior price does not defeat the contract claim.

agreement, including conduct by both parties which recognizes the existence of a contract" (2-204[1]). So, if the parties are *acting as though they have a contract* (by delivering or accepting goods or payment, for example), this is enough to create a binding agreement, even if it is impossible to point to a particular moment in time when the contract was created (2-204[2]). The fact that the parties did not expressly agree on all the terms of their contract does not prevent its creation. A sales contract does not fail due to "indefiniteness" if the court finds that the parties *intended* to make a contract and that their agreement is complete enough to allow the court to reach a fair settlement of their dispute ("a reasonably certain basis for giving an appropriate remedy," 2-204[3]).

The Code contains several gap-filling rules to fill in the blanks the parties left in their agreement regarding price (2-305), quantity (2-306), delivery (2-307, 2-308, and 2-309), and time for payment (2-310) (these are further discussed in Chapter 19). Of course, if the facts indicate that a term was left out because the parties were unable to reach an agreement about it, this would probably mean that the intent to contract is absent, and no contract was created. The United Nations Convention on Contracts for the International Sale of Goods (CISG) is similar to the UCC in that it requires that an offer be directed to a specific person or persons, be stated with sufficient definiteness, and indicate that the person making the offer intends to be bound by the agreement. However, unlike the UCC, the CISG does not consider an offer sufficiently definite if it lacks price terms. The offer must indicate the goods and expressly or impliedly provide means for determining quantity and price of the goods involved to be valid under the CISG. Thus, like the common law versus the UCC, it can sometimes be important to the parties whether the CISG rather than the UCC will be applied. The first issue involved in the following case is whether the CISG should be applied to settle the contract dispute.

Chateau des Charmes Wines v. Sabate USA

328 F.3d 528 (9th Cir. 2003)

FACTS

Chateau des Charmes Wines Ltd. is a Canadian company. It bought special corks for its wines from Sabate USA, a wholly owned subsidiary of Sabate France. Chateau bought the corks because they were supposed to not cause wines to be spoiled by "cork taint," a distasteful flavor that some

(continued)

Chateau des Charmes Wines v. Sabate USA *(concluded)*

corks produce. The agreement was made over the phone, with the parties agreeing on quantity, price, and shipping and payment terms. Later, Chateau placed a second phone order on the same terms. The corks were sent in 11 shipments. An invoice either accompanied, preceded, or followed each shipment. On the face of each invoice it stated, in French, "Any dispute arising under the present contract is under the sole jurisdiction of the Court of Commerce of the City of Perpignan." Several terms were also printed in French on the back, one of which said, "[A]ny disputes arising out of this agreement shall be brought before the court with jurisdiction to try the matter in the judicial district where Seller's registered office is located." Chateau bottled wines with the corks and subsequently the bottled wines developed cork taint. Chateau sued Sabate in California where the subsidiary is headquartered. Sabate argued that the case could not be tried there.

ISSUE

Does the CISG apply to this contract?

DECISION

Yes. The dispute in this case arises out of an agreement for a sale of goods manufactured by a French party, sold through a United States party, to a Canadian party. Such international sales contracts are ordinarily governed by a multilateral treaty, the United Nations Convention on Contracts for the International Sale of Goods (CISG). It applies to contracts of sales of goods between parties whose places of business are in different countries when those countries are parties to the CISG. The United States, France, and Canada are all signatory states to the CISG. And none agreed to the CISG with reservations that would affect its applicability in this case. Moreover, because the President submitted the Convention to the Senate and the Senate ratified it, there is no doubt that the CISG governs the substantive question of contract formation involved in this case. This agrees with decisions of other U.S. circuit court decisions confronted with the question of what law governs issues of contract formation that are antecedent to determining the validity and enforcement of forum selection clauses.

LO1 Communication to the Offeree

An important factor in determining whether an offeror had the required intent to contract is whether she communicated her offer to the offeree. The act of communicating the offer indicates that the offeror is willing to be bound by its terms. On the other hand, an uncommunicated offer may be evidence that the offeror has not yet decided to enter into a binding agreement. For example, Bill has been discussing the possibility of selling his house to Joan. Bill tells Frank, a mutual friend, that he intends to offer the house to Joan for $35,000. Frank calls Joan and tells her of his conversation with Bill. Joan then calls Bill and says, "I accept your offer" Is this a contract? No; since Bill had not communicated his proposal to Joan, there was no offer for Joan to accept.

Permison v. Comcast Holdings Corporation

WWW.buckleysandler.com/...Permison (Dist. W. Wash. 2013)

FACTS

Permison signed up for cable television and Internet with Comcast over the phone. Comcast's technicians came to his home and installed the services. Comcast's routine business practice is to have its technicians give the subscribers a Welcome Kit which contains Comcast's terms and conditions. The technicians are instructed to tell the customers to read and accept the terms when they are activating the services. Within the terms is a clause mandating arbitration of all disputes. Permison stated that he did not recall seeing

(continued)

Permison v. Comcast Holdings Corporation *(concluded)*

or receiving any such terms or conditions. He did sign work orders and an Equipment User Agreement. Subsequently, Permison sued Comcast for violations of the Telephone Consumer Protection Act, and Comcast sought to compel arbitration.

ISSUE

Was Permison adequately informed about the terms of the contract?

DECISION

No. There is insufficient evidence that Permison received and had an opportunity to review and understand the terms of the offer. Reliance on standard business practices is not sufficient. Comcast must produce business records or testimony that showing that Permison actually received and assented to the terms. This it has not done.

Cyber-Contracts

Websites, like newspaper advertisements, generally will be treated as invitations to buyers to make an offer rather than as offers themselves. Thus, when a computer user orders goods or services he finds advertised on a website, the user is offering to buy the goods or services at the advertised terms. The website owner is then free to accept or reject his offer.

Shrinkwrap and Click-On Contracts

In recent years, a great deal of legal controversy has emerged from the increasing use of shrinkwrap agreements by sellers of computer software. Generally, when a purchaser buys software, the software is in the form of a disk or CD. These disks are encased in plastic shrinkwrap and frequently bear a label stating that by removing the shrinkwrap, the buyer accepts the terms of the software seller's licensing agreement. This is known as "shrinkwrap contracting." However, this practice raises ethical problems similar to those involved in the use of small print, complex, or "hidden" language; some critics point out that some consumers may not understand that by opening the software, they are agreeing to its terms. Indeed, it is likely that many purchasers do not read or understand the agreement. However, shrinkwrap agreements are enforceable unless the terms violate contract rules such as unconscionability. Similar issues can be involved in click-on agreements, as the following case illustrates.

Bragg v. Linden Research, Inc.

487 F.Supp.2d 593 (E.D. Penn. 2007)

FACTS

Mark Bragg (Marc Woebegone in Second Life) engaged in role-playing in the virtual world of Second Life operated by Linden Research. Here people have avatars to represent themselves, and people build and acquire virtual property. In 2003 Linden announced that it would recognize participants' full intellectual property protection for the digital content they created or otherwise owned in Second Life. Thus, avatars could buy virtual land, make improvements to the land, exclude others from entering, and rent or sell it for a profit. Bragg paid Linden real money as "tax" on the properties he owned. He eventually acquired a virtual property, Taessot, for $300. Linden e-mailed Bragg that he had improperly bought the land, took Taessot away, and froze his account, which effectively confiscated all of Bragg's virtual property and currency. It alleged Bragg had violated the Terms of Service by URL-hacking the land auction website to gain access to property that was otherwise unavailable to

(continued)

Bragg v. Linden Research, Inc. *(concluded)*

him. Bragg sued Linden for the value of his property. Linden asserted that the case must go to arbitration because of a clause in the click-on Terms of Service (TOS) agreement.

ISSUE

Can Linden enforce the Terms of Service agreement?

DECISION

No. Arbitration agreements are enforceable unless there are such defenses as fraud, duress, or unconscionability. Unconscionability has both procedural and substantive aspects. The procedural aspect can be satisfied by showing (1) oppression through the existence of unequal bargaining power or (2) surprise through hidden terms common in the context of adhesion contracts. The substantive part can be satisfied by showing overly harsh or one-sided results that "shock the conscience." The more significant one is, the less important is the other. A contract of adhesion is a standardized contract which, imposed and drafted by the party of superior bargaining strength, gives the other party only the opportunity to accept or reject it. The TOS presented by Linden are a contract of adhesion. Linden presented them on a take it-or-leave-it basis. A potential participant could either click assent, or refuse and be denied access. Linden also had superior bargaining power, and there was no reasonably available marketing alternative. Second Life was the only virtual world that specifically granted participants property rights in virtual land. Additionally, the arbitration clause was not clear in the TOS and was one-sided. Linden cannot enforce the click-on TOS.

Special Problems with Offers

There are several common problems for students when they attempt to determine whether an offer exists. These problems involve situations in which the courts have applied special rules to certain types of behavior, or in which there are difficult problems of interpretation.

LO3 Advertisements

The courts have generally held that ads for the sale of goods at a specified price are not offers; instead, they are treated as invitations to negotiate or to make an offer. The same rule is generally applied to catalogs, price lists, price quotations, and goods displayed in stores. This rule probably fairly reflects the intent of the sellers involved, since they probably have only a limited number of items to sell and do not intend to give everyone who sees their ad the power to bind them to a contract. It can cause problems for would-be buyers, however, who may believe they have a legal right to the advertised goods they attempt to buy. In reality, such a buyer is making an offer to purchase the goods on the advertised terms, which the seller (as offeree) is free to accept or reject.

Under certain circumstances, however, courts have held that specific ads were offers. These cases generally involve ads that are highly specific about the goods that are offered and what is requested in return. Still, specific terms, standing alone, are probably not enough to make an ad an offer. Most of the ads that have been treated as offers require the buyer to do something extraordinary to accept. The great potential for unfairness to the offeree in such cases is probably the true basis for the courts' holdings that ads of this sort are offers. For example, Friendly Ford runs the following ad in the newspaper: "We're bananas about the new Mustangs! The first person to bring us five tons of bananas will receive a brand new 1999 Mustang fully equipped with every available option." Mary reads the ad and buys five tons of bananas and presents them to Friendly. Most courts would probably hold that Mary is entitled to the car.

Advertisements are regulated outside of contract law by the Federal Trade Commission and consumer protection laws. These outlaw such things as false advertising and "bait and switch" tactics. Discussion of such regulation is contained in Chapter 46.

Rewards

Ads for rewards for the return of lost property, for information, or for the capture of criminals are generally held to be offers for unilateral contracts. The offeree must perform the requested act to accept—that is, return the lost property, supply the requested information, or capture the wanted criminal.

Alexander v. Lafayette Crime Stoppers, Inc.

28 So. 3d 1253 (La. Ct. App. 2010)

FACTS

Alexander was being attacked in her home in 2002 when her son arrived and chased off the attacker. They reported the crime to the local police and provided a description. The lead investigator on the attack suspected the attacker might be the serial murderer identified as the South Louisiana Serial Killer. He shared the information with a task force set up to capture the killer. On May 22, 2003, a composite sketch was created based on an interview with Ms. Alexander and it was released to the public. An investigator on another crime thought the photo looked like his suspect, and a photo lineup was created that included his suspect. On May 25, Alexander picked the suspect from the other crime from the photo lineup as the man who attacked her. On or about August 14, Alexander sought the rewards totaling $150,000 offered by Baton Rouge Crime Stoppers and the Lafayette Crime Stoppers, which had been widely publicized in various media for the identification of the killer. Both offers had an expiration date of August 1, 2003. They refused to pay because they said she did not qualify for the rewards because she did not notify them until after August 1. She sued.

ISSUE

Is Alexander entitled to the reward?

DECISION

No. Acceptance of a reward occurs when it is received by the offeror. Alexander argues that she accepted when she provided the information to the authorities. She also argued that this is a customary manner to accept reward offers from Crime Stoppers organizations. However, Alexander did not meet the terms of the offer. Acceptance had to be received by the offerors by the time prescribed in the offer in the place where communications of that kind were to be deposited, in this case, the phone numbers cited in the offers. This was not done. Since Alexander did not contact the offerors by the time stated, no contract was created.

Auctions

Sellers at auctions are generally held to be making an invitation to offer. Bidders at such auctions are treated as offerors, making offers the seller is free to accept or reject. Therefore, an item can be withdrawn from sale at any time prior to acceptance. Acceptance occurs when the auctioneer declares the goods sold. Only when the auction is advertised as being "without reserve" is the seller required to accept the final offer—the highest bid. Section 2-328 of the Uniform Commercial Code contains the rules of law that govern an auction of goods.

LO4

Bids

The bidding process in construction work is a source of many legal disputes. People who advertise for such bids (the owner of the project or a general contractor who wants to farm out a portion of a large job to a subcontractor, for example) are generally held to have made an invitation to offer. Those who submit bids are treated as offerors. This causes particular problems in disputes between general contractors and subcontractors.

A general contractor may rely on a subcontractor's bid by using the subcontractor's figures in arriving at the total amount of its bid. Later, the subcontractor may find that the price of the materials or labor needed to do the job has risen, and may wish to revoke the bid. Unfortunately, the subcontractor may find that revocation will not be allowed (see the section on estoppel later in this chapter). The subcontractor may then be especially disturbed to find that when the general contractor's bid is accepted, the general contractor does not have to award the subcontractor the job. This is because the courts usually hold that the general contractor's use of the subcontractor's bid in computing its own is not an acceptance of that bid.

This treatment of subcontractors is probably not so unfair as it seems at first glance. A general contractor whose bid is accepted is bound by contract to do the job at the bid price. If the subcontractor is allowed to revoke, the general contractor may not be able to get anyone else to do the subcontractor's job for the price of the subcontractor's bid. The general contractor's profit on the job will then be reduced, and it may even have to do the job at a loss. On the other hand, the subcontractor who does not get the job generally has lost only the cost of computing the bid, a normal business expense.

Concept Summary: Solicitations of Offers

Ads	Auctions	Bids
1. Solicitations: general ads, price lists, goods displayed in stores.	1. Solicitations: offering the item at auction.	1. Solicitations: advertising for bids.
2. Construed as an offer if specific acts are required of offeree and unfairness would result if not enforced.	2. Becomes an offer if advertised as "without reserve."	2. Even though a subcontractor's bid is an offer, it generally cannot be withdrawn if the general contractor has relied on it.

What Terms Are Included in Offers?

Once a court decides that an offer existed, it must then decide what terms were included in the offer so that it can determine the terms of the parties' agreement. Another way of asking this question is to ask what the offeree agreed to. Is a person going to a show bound by the fine print on the ticket? How about fine print or clauses on the back of a contract?

There are no easy answers to these problems. The courts have generally held that if the offeree actually reads the terms, or if a reasonable person should have been on notice of them, the offeree is bound by them. However, as you saw in the last chapter, judges are increasingly refusing to enforce clauses they think are unconscionable because the offeree did not reasonably know of their existence, they place unfair burdens on the offeree, or they are worded in such a way that the offeree could not reasonably be expected to understand their meaning. Nonetheless, it is still fair to say that people are expected to live up to the agreements they make, as the *Morales* case shows.

Morales v. Sun Constructors, Inc.

541 F.3d 218 (3d Cir. Ct. App. 2008)

FACTS

Morales, a welder in the U.S. Virgin Islands, became an employee of Sun Constructors, Inc. (Sun). He signed an employment agreement that had an arbitration clause. The clause covered nearly 8 of the 13 pages of the agreement. When Sun terminated Morales for allegedly dropping a bottle of urine from a great height on another contractor's employees, he filed a wrongful termination suit against Sun. Sun argued that any dispute had to be arbitrated. Morales argued that he did not understand that the agreement contained an arbitration clause because the agreement was written in English and he speaks Spanish.

ISSUE

Were the terms of the offer sufficiently communicated?

DECISION

Yes. When he was hired, Morales passed a written English exam and, as required, attended a 2½-hour orientation session conducted in English. Langner, a Sun employee conducting the orientation, asked a bilingual applicant who was at the session to tell Morales what was being said and to help Morales fill out the documents. Langner covered the arbitration clause in the session. Morales did not ask the bilingual applicant what he was signing, and he did not specifically explain the arbitration clause to Morales. Mutual assent is necessary for the formation of a contract. However, as the Supreme Court has said, "It will not do for a man to enter into a contract and, when called upon to respond to its obligations, to say that he did not read it when he signed it, or did not know what it contained." We decline to make an exception to this rule in Morales's case. It was incumbent on Morales to acquaint himself with the content of the offer before he signed it. He failed to ask for a translation. Morales is bound by the arbitration clause.

Ethics in Action

Is it ethical for a business to use misleading headings, small print, complex language, or language on the reverse side of the contract to hide terms? Would your answer differ if the other party to the contract were another business instead of a consumer?

How Long Do Offers Last?

LO5

Once you know that an offer existed and what its terms were, you must then decide how long the offer was in effect. This is important because if an offer has been terminated for some reason, the offeree no longer has the power to create a contract by accepting. In fact, an offeree who attempts to accept after an offer has terminated is himself making an offer because he is indicating a present intent to contract on the terms of the original offer. The original offeror is free to accept or reject this new offer.

Terms of the Offer

The offer itself may include terms that limit its life. These may be specific terms such as "this offer good for 10 days" or "you must accept by October 4, 2011," or more general terms such as "by return mail" or "immediate acceptance." Obviously, the more general terms can cause difficult problems for courts in trying to decide whether an offeree accepted in time. This is also true of more specific terms such as "this offer good for 10 days" if the offer does not specify whether the 10-day period begins when the offer is sent or when the offeree receives it. The courts do not agree on this point. It should be clear that wise offerors will protect themselves by being as specific as possible in stating when their offers end.

Lapse of Time

If the offer does not state a time for acceptance, it is valid for a "reasonable time," which depends on the circumstances surrounding the offer.

If the offer covers items that have rapidly changing prices, such as stocks and bonds or commodities, a reasonable time may be measured in minutes. If the offer covers goods that may spoil, such as produce, a reasonable time for acceptance is also fairly short. On the other hand, a reasonable time for the acceptance of an offer to sell real estate may be several days.

If the parties have dealt with each other on a regular basis, the timing of their prior dealings is highly relevant in measuring a reasonable time for acceptance. Also, the nature of the negotiations, whether by letter or telephone, for example, can also influence the reasonable length of an offer.

LO6

Revocation

Offerors generally have the power to revoke their offers at any time prior to acceptance even if they have promised not to revoke for a stated period of time. However, there are several exceptions to the general rule that can take away an offeror's power to revoke.

Firm Offers

The drafters of the Code knew that offerors often promise to hold their offers open and that those who receive such offers are often ignorant of the law and believe them to be irrevocable. So, the Code protects the expectations of offerees in the **firm offer** rule. A firm offer is irrevocable even though the offeree has given no consideration to support the offeror's promise to hold the offer open. For an offer to sell goods to be a firm offer, it must meet three basic requirements:

1. It must have been made in a *signed writing* (no oral firm offers).
2. The offeror must be a *merchant.*
3. It must contain *assurances* that it will be held open (some indication that it will not be revoked).

If any one of these requirements is missing, the common law applies, allowing the offeror to revoke at any time prior to acceptance. Firm offers are irrevocable for the period of time stated in the offer. If none is stated, they are irrevocable for a reasonable time, as determined by the circumstances of the case. The outer limit on the period of irrevocability for firm offers is three months, whatever the terms of the offer may say. So, the offeror who makes a firm offer and promises to hold it open for six months could revoke after three, assuming the offeree has not accepted.

Options

If the offeree gives the offeror something of value in exchange for a promise not to revoke the offer for a stated period of time, an option contract has been created. An **option** is a separate contract for the limited purpose of holding the offer open. The offeree, as with any other offer, is free to accept or reject the offer; he or she has simply purchased the right to accept or reject within the stated period. (See Figure 10.2.)

FIGURE 10.2
Creating an Option

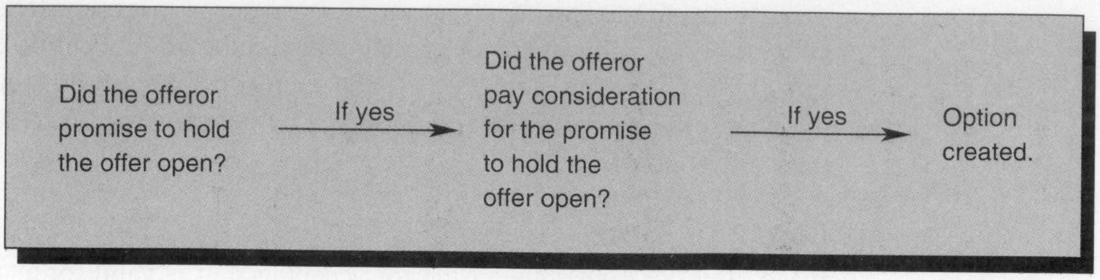

Ethics in Action

Under the common law an offer can be revoked any time prior to acceptance even if the offeror has promised to hold it open longer, unless the offeree has purchased an option. Is it unethical to renege on a gratuitous promise to hold an offer open?

Estoppel

In some cases, the doctrine of promissory estoppel, which was discussed in Chapter 9, can operate to prevent offerors from revoking their offers before acceptance. If the offeror makes her offer in such a way that the offeree might reasonably expect her not to revoke it, and if the offeree in fact does reasonably rely on the offer in such a way that he will suffer some significant loss if she is allowed to revoke it, a court may say she is *estopped* from revoking. This means that the court will deny the offeror the power to revoke in order to avoid unjustly injuring the offeree. As you will recall, promissory estoppel requires a *promise* that the promisor should foresee is likely to induce reliance, *significant reliance* on the promise by the promisee, and *injustice* as a result of reliance. If any one of these three elements is missing, estoppel does not apply.

Consider the subcontractor–contractor dispute discussed earlier in this chapter. Estoppel is frequently applied to such cases. Smith Electrical Supply (a subcontractor) submits a bid of $100,000 to Evans Construction Company (a general contractor) for the electrical work in the new Acme Building. Smith's bid is the lowest Evans receives, and Evans knows Smith to be a reliable firm, so Evans uses Smith's $100,000 figure in computing its bid for the total job. Due to rising costs of electric wiring and conduit, Smith decides it cannot profitably do the job and tries to revoke. Evans is awarded the contract and cannot get anyone to do the electrical work for less than $120,000. Smith will be estopped from revoking. Smith knew Evans was likely to rely on its bid (in fact, it hoped Evans would). Evans relied on Smith's bid by making an offer to perform based, in part, on Smith's price. Evans will lose $20,000 if Smith is allowed to revoke.

What if Evans could get Walters Electric to do the job for $100,000? In this case, estoppel would not apply since no injustice would result to Evans if Smith were allowed to revoke.

Revocation of Offers for Unilateral Contracts

The concept of promissory estoppel is often used to prevent unfairness in unilateral contract offer withdrawals. The general rule that the offeror can revoke at any time prior to acceptance causes special problems when the offer is for a unilateral contract. The common law traditionally held that the offeree must fully perform the requested act to accept an offer for a unilateral contract. What if the offeree intends to accept and starts to perform but the offeror revokes before the performance is complete?

If the offeror benefited from the offeree's attempted performance, some courts may allow the offeror to revoke but require him or her to pay the offeree the reasonable value of the performance under a quasi contract theory. Suppose Bob says to Frank, "I'll give you $800 to plow my 40 acres," and Frank begins to plow, intending to accept. After Frank has plowed 15 acres, Bob says, "I've changed my mind; I revoke." Bob is allowed to revoke but is liable to Frank for the reasonable value of plowing 15 acres.

If the offeror did not benefit from the offeree's attempted performance, most courts hold that the offeree has a reasonable time to complete the performance and that the offeror cannot revoke for that reasonable time. So, if Betty offered Frank a commission for finding her a $10,000 loan at a 10 percent annual rate and Frank has begun to contact lenders about the loan, Frank will have a reasonable time to get a loan commitment. During this time, Betty is not allowed to revoke. This rule prevents unfairness to Frank but may result in unfairness to Betty. If Frank's attempted performance is half-hearted or ineffective, Betty must wait for a reasonable period before making her offer to someone else.

To avoid these kinds of problems, many courts hold a contract to be bilateral whenever possible. This is similar to a view the *Restatement* takes. It holds that once the offeree has begun performance, the offer cannot be withdrawn because the beginning of performance is interpreted to be the offeree's promise to render complete performance. This promise makes the contract bilateral.

The Effectiveness of Revocations

Difficult problems of timing can result when an offeror is trying to revoke and an offeree is attempting to accept. The general rule is that a revocation is not effective until it is *actually received* by the offeree. So, if the offeree accepts before he or she has received a mailed revocation, a contract results. This rule recognizes the possibility that offerees who are unaware of a revocation may act in reliance on their belief that the offer is still open. A few states hold that a revocation is effective when it is sent, however.

A major exception to the general rule involves offers made to the general public in newspapers and on radio and television. Since it would be impossible in most cases to reach every offeree with a revocation, the courts have held that a revocation made in the same manner as the offer is effective when published, without proof of communication to the offeree.

Rejection

An offer is terminated when it is rejected by the offeree. An offeree may *expressly reject* an offer by stating that he will not accept it or by giving some other indication that he does not intend to accept the offer.

An offeree may *impliedly* reject an offer by making a **counteroffer.** Any attempt by the offeree to change the *material* terms of the offer or to add significant new terms to the offer is treated as a counteroffer. This is so because the offeree is showing her unwillingness to accept the offeror's terms. If an offeree merely asks about the terms of the offer without indicating a rejection of it *(an inquiry regarding terms)*, spells out *terms implied* in the offer, or accepts but complains about the terms *(a grumbling acceptance)*, a rejection is not implied. Determining whether an offeree has made a counteroffer, an inquiry regarding terms, a grumbling acceptance, or is merely expressing implied terms is sometimes a difficult matter, to be decided on the facts of each case.

The general rule on effectiveness of rejections is that rejections, like revocations, must be actually received by the offeror to be effective. This means that an offeree who has mailed a rejection can change her mind and accept if she communicates her acceptance to the offeror before the rejection arrives.

Death or Insanity of Either Party

The death or insanity of either party to an offer automatically (without notice) terminates the offer. This is so because no "meeting of the minds" is possible when one of the parties has died or becomes insane.

Destruction of Subject Matter

If the subject matter of a proposed contract is destroyed without the knowledge or fault of either party after the making of an offer but before its acceptance, the offer is terminated. So, if Joan offers to sell Ralph a boat but a storm destroys the boat before Ralph accepts, the offer is terminated when the boat is destroyed.

Intervening Illegality

If the performance of a proposed contract becomes illegal after the offer is made but before it is accepted, the offer is terminated. So, if Johnson Farms has offered to sell its wheat crop to a buyer for Iraq but two days later, before Johnson's offer has been accepted, Congress places an embargo on all grain sales to Iraq, the offer is terminated by the embargo.

Concept Summary: Offer

I. There is a valid offer if there is:
   a. Intent—
      Objectively determined.
   b. Definiteness—
      Sufficiently clear so that what was promised can be determined.
   c. Communication—
      Terms that are not adequately communicated (such as those in fine print) are not part of the offer.

II. The offer is still valid if it has not:
   a. Been terminated by its own time limit.
   b. Lapsed.
   c. Been revoked.
   d. Been rejected.
   e. Been terminated by operation of law due to:
      1. Death or insanity of either party.
      2. Destruction of the subject matter.
      3. Intervening illegality.

Questions and Problem Cases

1. Explain how the intent of an offeror is determined.
2. Explain the difference between firm offers and options.
3. Pepsico ran a contest for "Pepsi Stuff" featuring different prizes that could be bought with Pepsi "points" obtained by buying Pepsi Cola. One ad featured a teenager gloating

over items he had obtained with his points, and ended with his arriving at high school in a Harrier fighter jet obtained with 7 million points. Leonard, who described himself as "typical of the Pepsi Generation," sought to acquire the jet even though it was not listed in the Pepsi Stuff catalogue. He got points plus $700,000 from acquaintances to buy enough points for the jet, filled out the order form, wrote at the bottom, "1 Harrier jet" and enclosed the points and check. He was later informed the jet was unavailable and that its use in the ad was "fanciful" and [was] simply included to create a humorous and entertaining ad." Was the ad an offer that Leonard could accept? Explain why.

4. Giovo was in an accident with McDonald. McDonald's insurer, GEICO, and Giovo's attorney exchanged offers and counteroffers to settle Giovo's negligence claim. GEICO eventually agreed to meet all of Giovo's settlement conditions except her demand to be paid $18/day for the loss of the use of her car. As to that point, GEICO proposed to pay $10/day. Giovo rejected this and filed an action against McDonald. McDonald contended the matter had been settled. Is this correct? Explain.
5. Cornwell was a partner in a company, POA, which sold one-inch parcels of land in each of the 50 states. It approached Gray Loon Marketing (GLM) to design and publish a website through which it would sell the parcels. GLM gave POA a proposed design and an estimated price of $8,080. It stated their philosophy was, "that clients have purchased goods and services . . . and that inherently means ownership of those goods and services as well." POA agreed, paid a deposit, and design commenced. POA asked for a few minor changes, the work was finished, and POA paid the amount asked for, $8,500. Several months later POA asked for several changes, some requiring major programming work. GLM agreed over the phone to make them and began work immediately. When it completed the work, GLM contacted POA for approval. At that time, POA said it no longer wanted the changes. GLM then sent a bill for $5,224. After several attempts to collect, POA asked for more time to collect the funds, stating it had no problem with the work. When POA failed to pay, GLM sued for nonpayment. POA argued that the contract was for services and that under common law, since there was no agreement for the price of the modifications, it was not liable. Is this correct? Why?
6. Plaintiffs downloaded AOL's Version 5.0 software. They alleged the software caused unauthorized changes to the configuration of their computers, such that they could no longer access other Internet service providers, non-AOL e-mail programs, or personal information and files. They filed a class action suit against AOL in Massachusetts. AOL said that under the forum selection clause in the click-on agreement agreed to at the time of downloading, the suit had to be heard in Virginia. Will AOL succeed? Why?
7. Saltarelli worked for Future Ford and had his health insurance under its group plan. He then went to work at a Bob Baker dealership and signed up for its insurance. However, because Baker's policy had a three-month waiting period, this coverage did not start until April 8. Saltarelli therefore continued his coverage with Future through April. On May 4 Saltarelli was diagnosed with stomach cancer, and he died on May 29. When his estate tried to collect for his medical bills, Baker refused to pay, citing a statement in the definitions section of a 43-page booklet describing the plan that excluded preexisting conditions such as cancer. Was the term effectively and fairly communicated?
8. When he was a high school senior, Aronson researched colleges on the Internet. A primary consideration was cost and the nature and types of financial aid. The University of Mississippi's (UM) website had information on a John Waddell Scholarship, which provided $1,000 per year and a waiver of out-of-state tuition. Relying

on this information, Aronson requested an application package. When he received it in October 1997, it had the 1997 catalogue. The catalogue further described the scholarship, including that it was offered to students who score 26–27 on the ACT and have a GPA of 90 percent or higher. Priority consideration was given to those admitted by April 1, 1997. To keep the scholarship, the student had to have a 3.0 or better GPA. Aronson sent in his application and was admitted on November 6, 1997. He sent a check on April 6, 1998, for orientation fees and a room deposit. Before orientation, Aronson's stepfather called UM to ensure that Aronson met the scholarship requirements and was told that he did and that it was for $1,000 per year and waiver of out-of-state tuition. At orientation, the stepfather was told that the criteria had changed, that Aronson did not qualify for the waiver, and that the total had been reduced to $2,000. When UM refused to give him the $4,000 plus the waiver, Aronson sued. Did Aronson and UM have a contract based on the terms in the catalogue? Why?

9. Rodziewicz's tractor-trailer struck a concrete barrier and got stuck on the top. He called Waffco to get it off. When he asked how much it would cost to tow it, he was told $275. He told Waffco to tow it to the local Volvo dealer. Waffco got it off after a few minutes and towed it to its yard a few miles away. It then told Rodziewicz that he would have to pay $4,070 in labor costs, figured at 11 cents a pound, in addition to the towing charge. Will he have to pay it? Why?

Chapter 11

Creating a Contract: Acceptances

LO

Learning Objectives

After you have studied this chapter, you should be able to:

1. Describe the three elements necessary for a valid acceptance.
2. Explain how the Battle of the Forms works.
3. Discuss how the CISG differs from the UCC in terms of form contracting.
4. Explain the rule about silence as acceptance.
5. Understand the effect of a lack of a writing when one is anticipated.
6. Articulate what happens when a nonauthorized means of communication is used.

Stephens sent Horwitz an offer to sell her his house and adjoining orchard for $300,000. Horwitz, after thinking about the offer for a few days, wrote Stephens a letter accepting his offer and asking if he intended to leave his farming equipment with the property. The next day, before Horwitz's letter arrived, Stephens phoned Horwitz and told her he had decided to sell his property to someone else who had offered him $320,000.

- Was Horwitz's letter an effective acceptance or a counteroffer?
- When does acceptance through the mail become effective?
- Was Stephens's phone call an effective revocation?

FIGURE 11.1
Acceptance

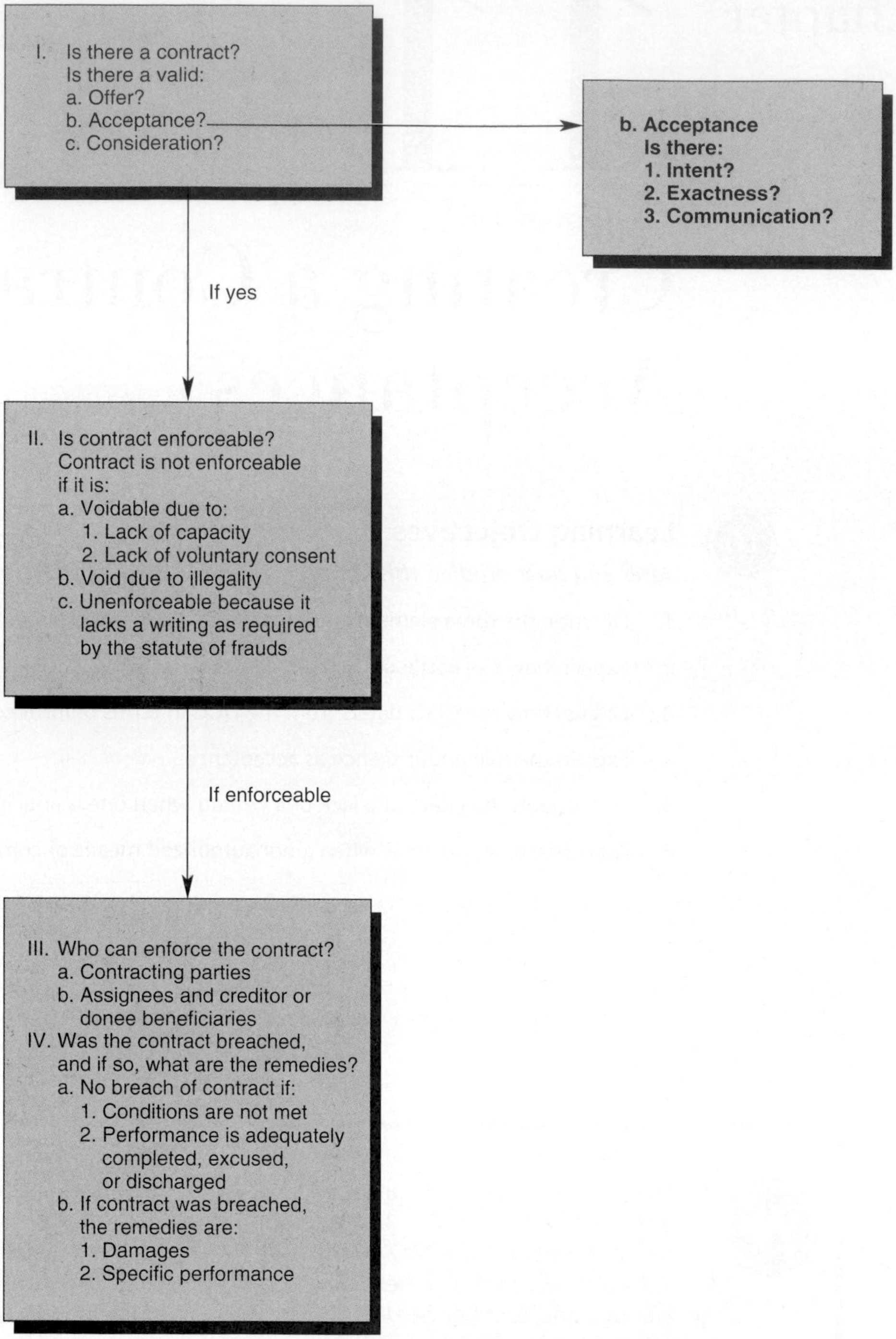
I. Is there a contract?
Is there a valid:
a. Offer?
b. Acceptance?
c. Consideration?
b. Acceptance
Is there:
1. Intent?
2. Exactness?
3. Communication?
If yes
II. Is contract enforceable?
Contract is not enforceable if it is:
a. Voidable due to:
1. Lack of capacity
2. Lack of voluntary consent
b. Void due to illegality
c. Unenforceable because it lacks a writing as required by the statute of frauds
If enforceable
III. Who can enforce the contract?
a. Contracting parties
b. Assignees and creditor or donee beneficiaries
IV. Was the contract breached, and if so, what are the remedies?
a. No breach of contract if:
1. Conditions are not met
2. Performance is adequately completed, excused, or discharged
b. If contract was breached, the remedies are:
1. Damages
2. Specific performance

What Is an Acceptance?

LO1

Once the court has found that one of the parties to a dispute made an *offer,* the next thing it looks for in order to determine whether a contract resulted is whether the offeree **accepted** the offer. The court looks for the same *present intent* to contract on the part of the offeree that it earlier looked for on the part of the offeror. When all the circumstances surrounding the parties' dealings with each other are considered, did the offeree ever, in effect, say: "I'm willing to enter into a binding contract on the terms of your offer?" If so, the offer has been accepted. The offeree may indicate assent expressly or impliedly. The offeree must, however, accept the offer on the offeror's terms. Acceptance, like an offer, is objectively determined.

As the preceding chapter indicated, any attempt by the offeree to materially alter the terms of the offer is treated as a counteroffer and terminates the offer. In the introductory problem to this chapter, Horwitz's letter was an acceptance since she was merely inquiring about Stephens's intentions regarding the machinery. If she had said she accepted on the condition that he include the farm machinery, however, it would have been a counteroffer.

Trademark Properties, Inc. v. A&E Television Networks

2011 U.S. App. LEXIS 7382 (4th Cir. 2011)

FACTS

Davis, a real estate broker, came up with an idea for a reality television show based on buying property at bargain prices, quickly renovating them, and then selling them for a profit, commonly called *flipping.* He pitched it to several networks including A&E. Davis claimed a contract was formed over the phone in June 2004 and included a nonnegotiable term that he and A&E split the revenues. The A&E executive responded to the terms by saying, "Okay, okay, I get it." He also said A&E's board had to approve the show's development. The deal was not reduced to writing, but the show was produced and aired. Subsequently, there was a dispute over compensation and the relationship was ended in 2006. When Davis sued for breach of contract, A&E argued that the executive's statement merely showed that he understood the terms and was not an unambiguous acceptance.

ISSUE

Was the statement of the A&E executive an acceptance?

DECISION

Yes. In general, oral contracts are as enforceable as written contracts. In both, mutual assent is required. There must be a meeting of the minds. There is no contract without assent or acceptance. In an oral contract, though, assent may be harder to prove. It may be proved through an act or conduct that shows the intention to contract. There is objective evidence here of A&E's assent. While "Okay, okay, I get it" is not unambiguous, it can be an acceptance, and Davis clearly thought it was. He was told the board approved the money for the series, and 13 shows were made by A&E. Davis worked hard to get sponsors and ads for the show, and he worked with A&E on product placement opportunities. There is sufficient objective evidence for the jury's decision that there was acceptance and a contract.

The Battle of the Forms

LO2

The Uniform Commercial Code has created an exception to this "mirror image" rule in cases where contracts for the sale of goods are made by exchanging forms (2-207). Since the majority of contracts are form contracts, this rule has wide impact. The seller of goods and the buyer send each other forms that have terms beneficial to their individual interests. Seldom do these forms agree in their entirety, and the parties seldom read the other's form in its entirety. Yet the parties usually assume, and proceed as if there is, a contract. Applying the mirror image rule to such cases would often frustrate the parties' original intent. If a dispute arose before the parties started to perform, a court applying the mirror image rule would hold that the parties did not have a contract. If a dispute arose after the parties started to perform, the court would probably hold that the offeror had impliedly accepted the offeree's counteroffer and was bound by its terms. Neither of these results is very satisfactory.

The Code changes the common law rule by saying that a timely *expression of acceptance* creates a contract even if it includes terms that are *different* from those stated in the offer or states *additional* terms on points the offer did not address (2-207[1]). This controversial rule is known as the "Battle of the Forms." The only exception to this rule occurs when the attempted acceptance is *expressly conditional* on the offeror's agreement to the terms of the acceptance (2-207[1]). In that case, no contract is created.

What are the terms of a contract created by the exchange of nonconforming forms? The Code says that if the parties are both *merchants,* the *additional* terms in the offeree's form are included in the agreement unless:

1. The offer *expressly limited acceptance* to its own terms.
2. The new terms would *materially alter* the offer.
3. The offeror gives *notice of objection* to the new terms within a reasonable time after receiving the acceptance (2-207[2]).

If one or both parties are nonmerchants, the additional terms are treated as "proposals for addition to the contract."

When the acceptance is made expressly conditional on agreement to the new terms, or when the offeree clearly is making a counteroffer by expressly rejecting the offer, no contract is created. However, the Code (2-207[3]) says that if the parties begin performance (or do something else that "recognizes the existence of a contract"), a contract is created. The terms of this contract are those on which the writings of the parties *agree,* supplemented by appropriate gap-filling provisions of the Code (discussed in Chapter 19). Remember that the Battle of the Forms rules apply only when both parties have forms.

It is worth noting that in 2003 the American Law Institute approved an amendment to Section 2-207 of the UCC eliminating the materiality test of the Battle of the Forms. Because courts have struggled over whether a disputed term "materially alters" an agreement or not, the new Section 2-207 shifts the focus from determining which terms are excluded to which terms are agreed upon: the agreed-upon terms form the contract, while all other terms are rejected. This new version of 2-207 promises to be much clearer to understand and apply. However, many states have not incorporated the revamped 2-207 into their version of the UCC.

LO3

The rules under the CISG regarding what terms become part of the contract are somewhat different from the UCC's, as the following case illustrates.

Chateau des Charmes Wines v. Sabate USA

328 F.3d 528 (9th Cir. 2003)

FACTS

(This is the same case, involving the sale of tainted corks, that appeared in the previous chapter. As with most lawsuits, this case involved several legal issues. For illustrative purposes, the textbook authors usually highlight only one issue per case to emphasize a point.)

Chateau des Charmes Wines bought special corks for its wines from Sabate USA, a wholly owned subsidiary of

(continued)

Chateau des Charmes Wines v. Sabate USA *(concluded)*

Sabate France. The corks were not supposed to cause wines to be spoiled by "cork taint." The agreement was made over the phone, with the parties agreeing on quantity, price, shipping, and payment terms. Later, Chateau placed a second phone order on the same terms. More than $500 was involved. The corks were sent in 11 shipments. An invoice accompanied, preceded, or followed each shipment. On the face of each invoice it stated, in French: "Any dispute arising under the present contract is under the sole jurisdiction of the Court of Commerce of the City of Perpignan." Several terms were also printed in French on the back, one of which said, "[A]ny disputes arising out of this agreement shall be brought before the court with jurisdiction to try the matter in the judicial district where Seller's registered office is located." Chateau bottled wines with the corks and subsequently the bottled wines developed cork taint. Chateau sued Sabate in California where the subsidiary is headquartered. Sabate argued that the case could not be tried there.

ISSUE

Are the forum selection clauses on Sabate France's invoices part of the contract?

DECISION

No. The CISG sets out a clear way to analyze international contracts for the sale of goods: A contract of sale need not be concluded or evidenced by writing and is not subject to any other requirements as to form. In this, the CISG differs from the UCC, which requires a contract for the sale of goods of the value involved here to be in writing. A proposal is an offer if it is sufficiently definite to indicate the goods, expressly or implicitly makes provisions for determining the quantity and the price, and demonstrates an intention by the offeror to be bound if the proposal is accepted. In turn, an offer is accepted if the offeree makes a statement or does other conduct that indicates assent to the offer. The CISG further states that the contract is made the moment when an acceptance of an offer becomes effective. In the facts of this case, the oral agreements between Sabate USA and Chateau made on the phone, which spelled out the kind of cork, the quantity, and the price, were sufficient to create a complete and binding contract. The terms of those agreements did not include a forum selection clause. The CISG states that any "additional or different terms relating to the settlement of disputes are considered to alter the terms of the offer materially." There is no indication that Chateau conducted itself in a manner that evidenced any affirmative assent to the forum selection clauses in the invoices. Rather, Chateau merely performed its obligations under the oral contract. Therefore, the proposed material changing forum selection clauses did not become part of the contract.

Concept Summary: Accepting the Exact Offer

Common Law Rule (for sale of real estate and services, primarily)	Acceptance cannot materially vary from the offer.	If it does, it is a rejection of the offer and a counteroffer.
UCC Rule (2-207) (for sale of goods)—when contract made by exchange of forms	Acceptance form can have terms additional to or different from the offer.	A contract can result, but the differing terms may not be part of the contract (see Chapter 17).
UCC Rule—when forms not exchanged	Acceptance cannot materially vary from the offer.	If it does, it is a rejection of the offer and a counteroffer.

Accepting an Offer for a Unilateral Contract

As you saw in Chapter 9, in a unilateral contract a promise is exchanged for an act. To accept an offer to enter into such a contract, the offeree must perform the requested act or make the requested promise. So, if Mary tells Sue, "I'll give you $100 (the promise) if you find my lost dog Sparky (the requested act)," Sue must find the dog to accept Mary's offer.

Accepting an Offer for a Bilateral Contract

The courts, if possible, interpret an offer as proposing a bilateral contract. A bilateral contract is a promise for a promise, and the offeree must make the promise requested in the offer. So, if Tom hands Betty a detailed offer for the purchase of Betty's house and Betty signs the offer without changing any of its terms, both parties are bound on the terms of the offer. Betty has promised to deliver a deed on the agreed-on closing date in exchange for Tom's promise to pay the agreed-on price on that date.

An offeree may expressly accept the offer, as Betty did in the preceding example, or may impliedly accept by doing something that objectively indicates agreement. For example, James, a farmer, leaves three bushels of tomatoes with Roger, the owner of a grocery store. James says, "Look these over. If you want them, they're $20 a bushel." Roger sells the tomatoes to his customers. By treating them as if he owned them, he has impliedly accepted James's offer.

The UCC requires less formality in regard to acceptance under Section 2-204 than the common law. However, acceptance must be sufficiently clear, as the following case shows.

Teter v. Glass Onion, Inc.

723 F. Supp. 2d 1138 (W.D. Mo. 2010)

FACTS

Teter, a renowned artist, sold his pictures through selected galleries including the Spring Street Gallery (SSG). Glass Onion, Inc. (GOI), agreed to purchase SSG and its assets contingent on SSG obtaining an agreement that Teter would continue the existing agreement he had with SSG. GOI's owners met with Teter and he agreed to continue the relationship. He also informed them that his daughter, Shawnee, would be joining his family business and would be handling publication of Teter's work and generally act on his behalf. The sale then went through. GOI entered eight sales transactions of Teter's paintings and prints over the next few months. Then Teter said that GOI would have to sign a dealership agreement in order to continue the relationship. When GOI refused, Teter demanded that all images of his work be removed from GOI's website and ads. When GOI didn't comply, Teter sued for copyright and trademark infringement, and GOI countersued for breach of contract.

ISSUE

Was there an enforceable contract for Teter to continue the relationship it had with SSG with GOI?

DECISION

No. The UCC permits a contract to be formed in any manner and can be found to exist even if the exact moment of creation cannot be determined. It can be based on the conduct of the parties. However, the basic elements of an agreement must still be present. While the purchase of the eight works constituted individual contracts the parties agreed to through their actions, they do not show an ongoing agreement to sell artworks to GOI on the same terms as it sold to the predecessor owner of SST. Their discussions were too indefinite to show consent. Additionally, consideration for such a promise is absent. Lacking these, there is not a contract under the UCC and Teter can refuse to sell his artwork to GOI.

Silence as Acceptance

LO4

Since the basis of contract law is the voluntary agreement of the parties, the law generally requires some affirmative indication of assent from offerees before it binds them to the terms of an offer. This generally means that an offeror is not allowed to word his or her offer so that the offeree must act to avoid being bound to a contract. An offer that said "If you do not object within 10 days, we have a contract" imposes no legal duty on the offeree to respond. It also means that mere silence on the part of the offeree is generally not acceptance.

On the other hand, always bear in mind that the ultimate question of the courts in acceptance cases is this: Did the offeree objectively indicate an intent to be bound by the terms of the offer? Sometimes the circumstances of the case impose on the offeree a duty to reject an offer or be bound by it. This is what the court finds in the following case.

In such a case, the offeree's silence constitutes an acceptance and a contract is created. If the parties have dealt with each other before and silence signaled acceptance in their prior dealings, the offeree who remains silent in the face of an offer may be held to have accepted. Return to the example of the farmer and the grocer. Assume that for the last two years, James has regularly sent Roger certain produce items and Roger has always promptly returned those items he did not want. James sends Roger 10 bushels of green beans, and Roger does not return them. At the end of the month, as is his usual practice, James bills Roger for the beans. Roger sends back the bill, saying, "I don't want the beans; come to the store and pick them up." Was there a contract? Most courts would say that, due to the prior dealings between the parties, Roger accepted the beans by failing to reject them. A similar situation could arise due to trade usage, where the parties are both members of a trade in which failure to reject promptly customarily indicates acceptance. An offeree's silence can also operate as acceptance if the offeree has indicated that it will ("If you don't hear from me in five days, I accept") or if the offeree allows the offeror to perform the offered services without objection.

Lambert v. Don M. Barron Contractor, Inc.

974 So. 2d 198 (La. Ct. App. 2008)

FACTS

Don M. Barron is a commercial construction contractor doing business as Don M. Barron, Inc. (DMB). The company was having financial problems as a result of difficulties on various projects. Barron and Lambert had a long-standing professional relationship based on their public service on the Louisiana State Board of Licensed Contractors. In 1998, they talked by phone about Barron's personal problems and financial difficulties. Barron sent various construction contracts and correspondence for Lambert's review, and Lambert assisted in the arbitrator selection process. A week later, Lambert flew on a DMB plane to meet with Barron and his employee. Lambert contends that, before boarding the plane to return home, Barron contracted with him for consulting services. Lambert told Barron that his customary charge was $3,100 per month, and the minimum term for his services was one year. He also charged 10 percent of any monies recovered for the client. After receiving Lambert's invoice for $53,100, Barron made one payment, thinking it covered Lambert's review of the documents and the trip, and no others. Lambert sent another invoice for $34,100, requesting payment for the services he had performed. Barron responded, "I received your bill last week and was very shocked. I do not know where you are coming from, and what you have done to think you deserve any kind of pay." He pointed out that Lambert had been paid for the trip and document review, and said he did not want to be a part of Lambert's client list, nor had he asked for any advice since the trip. Lambert sued.

ISSUE

Did Barron accept Lambert's offer?

DECISION

No. A contract is bilateral when the parties obligate themselves reciprocally, so that the obligation of each party is correlative to the obligation of the other. Offer and acceptance may be made orally, in writing, or by action or inaction that is clearly indicative under the circumstance of consent. Barron testified he never orally accepted Lambert's offer for consulting services, nor was there a writing reflecting consent. Under the special circumstances here, Barron's silence also did not reasonably lead Lambert to believe a contract had been formed. Rather, there was advice and a trip made on the basis of a prior friendship. Barron provided the documents that Lambert reviewed without any indication that his friend's review would require compensation. There is no tacit evidence that Barron accepted Lambert's offer for consulting services made at the airport.

Ethics in Action

In most circumstances, silence is not acceptance. What ethical problems would arise if silence generally were presumed to constitute acceptance?

Who Can Accept an Offer?

The only person with the legal power to accept an offer and create a contract is the original offeree (or his or her agent). An attempt to accept by anyone other than the offeree is therefore treated as a legal offer, since the party attempting to accept is indicating a willingness to contract on terms of the original offer. The original offeror is free to accept or reject this new offer. For example, Mary offers to sell her business to Jane. Jane tells Mike about the offer, and Mike sends Mary a letter attempting to accept her offer. No contract is created. Since Mike is not the offeree, he has merely made an offer that Mary is free to accept or reject.

Acceptance When a Writing Is Anticipated

Often the parties who are negotiating a contract prepare a written draft of the agreement for both parties to sign. This is a good idea because then there is written evidence of the terms of their agreement if a dispute arises at a later date. If a dispute arises before the writing is signed, however, there may be a question about when or whether the parties in fact reached agreement. One of the parties may want to back out and argue that the parties did not intend a contract to result until the writing was signed. The other party may argue that a contract was created before the writing was signed and that the writing was merely intended to record on paper the agreement the parties had already reached.

LO5 The courts determine the intent of the parties on this point by applying the objective test of what a reasonable person familiar with the circumstances would be justified in believing the parties intended. If it appears that the parties concluded their negotiations and reached agreement on all the material aspects of the transaction, the courts will probably conclude that a contract resulted at the time when agreement was reached. The failure of the parties to sign the writing is therefore unimportant. If, on the other hand, it appears that the parties were still in the process of negotiation at the time the dispute arose, the courts will probably find that no contract was created. The same would be true when the parties have clearly indicated an intent not to be bound until both sign the writing.

Sprout v. Bd. of Educ.

2004 W. Va. LEXIS 31 (2004)

FACTS

Rebecca Sprout, a secretary at Gore Middle School, filed an employment grievance against the school arising out of extra work she performed as a yearbook sponsor and out of alleged entitlement to credit for past work experience. The school board wanted to settle the grievance and asked Sprout how much she wanted in exchange for dropping her grievance. Sprout submitted a written

(continued)

offer to the board requesting $17,000. The board voted to offer Sprout the $17,000 settlement. The following day, board president Sally Cann approached Sprout and made the offer. Sprout found this acceptable and Cann responded that she would "get things started." Cann further told Sprout that Sprout did not need do anything and that the papers were to be prepared and then presented to the board for approval. Sprout understood that the agreement had to be put in writing and voted upon by the board before it become effective. However, when Cann reported Sprout's acceptance to other board members, the board refused to approve the agreement based upon advice from its lawyer. When Sprout contacted the board's lawyer to ascertain the status of the settlement, he told her no agreement had been reached. Sprout sued the board, arguing that she had a valid contract with the board because Cann's proposal constituted a contractual offer that Sprout correspondingly accepted. In response, the board argued that a contract was not formed because both parties believed that the agreement had to be reduced to writing and then reviewed again for further consideration by the board.

ISSUE

Was the agreement between Sprout and the school board a contract?

DECISION

No. When it is shown that the parties intend to reduce a contract to writing this circumstance creates a presumption that no final contract has been entered into. Although an agreement may have been tentatively reached between Sprout and the board, Sprout's letter proposing settlement and the conversation between Sprout and Cann showed that there was no true meeting of the minds. Sprout testified that she understood that the agreement would be effective only once a contract was drawn up and the board voted. Therefore, it is clear that neither party intended to nor expected to be bound by the agreement until the particular terms were provided for in a written contract that would be voted upon at a later date by the board.

Communication of Acceptance

To accept an offer for a unilateral contract, where a promise is exchanged for an act, the offeree must perform the act requested by the offeror. When the act is completed, the contract is created. Notice of this type of acceptance is not necessary for the creation of the contract unless the offer specifically requires notice. In order to accept all other offers, however, the offeree must make the requested promise. The general rule is that such promises must be *communicated* in order to be effective and create a contract.

Manner of Communication

The offeror may specify **(stipulate)** in the offer the time, place, or method of communicating acceptance. In such a case, the offeree must comply fully with the offeror's stipulations. Any material deviation makes the attempt to accept ineffective. If the offer merely suggests a method or place of communication or is silent on these points, the offeree may accept within a reasonable time by any reasonable means of communication.

When Is Acceptance Communicated?

LO1

When acceptance is effective can be critically important. In most instances, the offeror has the power to revoke the offer at any time before acceptance. The offeror may be seeking to revoke an offer at the same time the offeree is trying to accept it. A mailed or telegraphed acceptance may get lost and never be actually received by the offeror. The time limit for accepting the offer may be rapidly approaching. Was the offer accepted before a revocation was received or before the offer expired? Does a lost acceptance create a contract when it is dispatched, or is it totally ineffective?

If the parties are dealing face to face or the offeree is accepting by telephone, these problems are minimized. As soon as the offeree has said, "I accept," or words to that effect, a contract is created (assuming the offer is still in existence). For example, Mary offered to sell

Chuck her 1965 Mustang for $500. While talking on the phone to Bruce, she mentions her offer. Bruce tells her that old Mustangs are in big demand and her car is worth at least $2,500. When she hangs up the phone she sees Chuck walking up her driveway. She opens the window and yells, "I take back my offer!" The startled Chuck then yells, "You can't. I accept!" Is there a contract? Clearly not, since Mary revoked her offer before Chuck accepted.

Problems with the timing of acceptances multiply when the offeree is using a means of communication that creates a time lag between dispatching the acceptance and its actual receipt by the offeror. The offeror can minimize these problems since he or she has the power to control the conditions under which the offer can be accepted. The offeror need only state in the offer that he or she must *actually receive* the acceptance for it to be effective. This is clearly the best thing for an offeror to do since it affords the offeror the maximum amount of protection. It gives the offeror the most time to revoke and ensures that he or she will never be bound to a contract by an acceptance that is not received.

The offeror who does not use the power to require actual receipt of the acceptance will find that the law has developed rules that make some acceptances effective at the moment they are dispatched, regardless of whether the offeror ever actually receives them. These rules generally apply when the offeror has made the offer under circumstances that might reasonably lead the offeree to believe that acceptance by some means other than telephone or face-to-face communication is acceptable.

Authorized Means of Communication

As a general rule, an acceptance is effective *when dispatched* (delivered to the communicating agency) if the offeree uses an **authorized means** of communication. The offeror can expressly or impliedly indicate the authorized means. He or she can expressly authorize a particular means of communication by saying, in effect, "You may accept by mail (telegram, etc.)." In such a case, a contract is created at the moment the acceptance was mailed, even if it was lost and the offeror never received it. Any attempt by the offeror to revoke after the letter was mailed would be ineffective. Likewise, an offer sent by a **stipulated means** is effective when dispatched.

Under traditional contract principles, a given means of communication may also be impliedly authorized in one of two ways. First, if the offer or circumstances do not indicate otherwise, the means the offeror used to communicate the offer is the impliedly authorized means for accepting. So, mailed offers impliedly authorize mailed acceptances, telegraphed offers impliedly authorize telegraphed acceptances, and so on. In the problem case described at the beginning of the chapter, Horwitz used an impliedly authorized means of acceptance. Thus, her acceptance was good when mailed, and a contract was created at that time. Stephens's attempted revocation was therefore ineffective.

Trade usage may also impliedly authorize a given means of acceptance. If both the parties are members of a trade in which acceptances are customarily made by a particular means of communication, the courts assume the offeree is impliedly authorized to accept by that means unless the offer indicates to the contrary. Many courts today are following the lead of the Uniform Commercial Code and the *Restatement Second* by saying that the offeror who remains silent impliedly authorizes the offeree to accept by any **reasonable** means of communication.

Unlike the UCC, the U.N. Convention on Contracts for the International Sale of Goods (CISG) holds acceptances to be effective when they are *received,* not when they are dispatched.

Acceptance by Shipment

Stating that the offeror impliedly authorizes acceptance in any reasonable manner means that in cases in which it is unclear whether the offer calls for acceptance by a return promise or by performance, either manner of acceptance, if reasonable, will be effective to create a contract. So, in some cases a seller may accept a buyer's offer by *shipping* the goods or by *promising* to ship them. Sellers who accept by performing, however, must notify the buyer of their acceptance within a reasonable time. Buyers who have not received such notice may treat the offer as having "lapsed" before acceptance and may contract with another seller (2-206[2]).

The Code specifically says that an order requesting "prompt" or "current" shipment of goods impliedly invites acceptance by either a prompt promise to ship or a prompt shipment of the goods (2-206[1][b]). For example, Mary's Office Supply sends Bob's Business Machines an order for 25 Compaq personal computers, to be shipped "as soon as possible." The day Bob receives Mary's order, he ships the computers. Later that day Mary phones Bob and tries to revoke her offer. She cannot revoke, since a contract was created when Bob shipped the computers.

What if Bob did not have 25 Compaqs in stock and shipped 15 Compaqs and 10 IBM personal computers? The Code says that the seller who ships "nonconforming goods" (something different from what was ordered) has *accepted and breached* the contract, unless the seller reasonably notifies the buyer that such a shipment is intended as an "accommodation" to the buyer. In such a case, shipment is in effect a counteroffer that the buyer is free to accept or reject (2-206[1][b]). This provision is designed to protect buyers against the so-called unilateral contract trick. A dishonest seller who has received a "rush" order may send the wrong goods, hoping that the buyer's necessity will force him to accept. Under common law rules, the seller was making a counteroffer. If the buyer took the goods, she had accepted the seller's counteroffer. If she rejected them, the seller had no liability for sending nonconforming goods. The Code rule forces the seller to give the buyer timely notice of his inability to fill the order, which allows the buyer to accept or the time to seek other goods.

Nonauthorized Means of Communication

LO6

If an authorized means of acceptance is expressly or impliedly present, any attempt by the offeree to accept by a **nonauthorized means** is not effective until the acceptance is actually *received* by the offeror. The following example illustrates these principles: On May 1, 2002, Bob received a telegram from Ralph offering to build Bob a resort cottage for $200,000. On May 5, 2002, at 10:00 AM, Ralph sends Bob a telegram attempting to revoke the offer. At 11:00 AM on the same day, Bob mails Ralph a letter attempting to accept the offer. At 11:30 AM, Bob receives Ralph's revocation. Do the parties have a contract? The answer depends on several factors:

1. Assume Ralph's telegraphed offer said: "Acceptance by mail is advisable." If so, the parties have a contract because Ralph expressly authorized acceptance by mail. Therefore, Bob's mailed acceptance would be effective when dispatched at 11:00 AM and a contract would be created at that time. Ralph's revocation would be ineffective, since it was not actually received (as revocations must be) before the contract was created.
2. Assume Ralph's offer was silent on the question of what means Bob could use to accept. If so, under traditional contract principles, the parties would not have a contract because the impliedly authorized means of communication in this instance was telegram (the means Ralph used to communicate the offer). Bob attempted to accept by a nonauthorized means (mail), so his acceptance would not be effective until Ralph actually received it. Ralph effectively revoked the offer before receiving Bob's acceptance. However, in a state that holds that the offeror impliedly authorizes acceptance by any reasonable means, the parties may have a contract if the court concludes that mail was a reasonable way for Bob to accept Ralph's offer.

3. Assume Bob and Ralph are both construction contractors and the custom in the construction business is to offer by telegram and accept by mail. In this instance, the parties would have a contract because Bob used the means of communication impliedly authorized by trade usage. His acceptance would be effective when mailed, creating a contract before Ralph's revocation was received.

There is one major exception to the rule that acceptances by the authorized means of communication are effective on dispatch. If the offeree has dispatched inconsistent responses to the offer by sending both a rejection and an acceptance, whichever response reaches the offeror first will determine whether a contract is created. So, if Marty sends Frank a letter offering to sell him a condominium in Florida for $150,000 and Frank sends Marty a letter offering $135,000 (a counteroffer), but later changes his mind and sends a letter accepting the original offer for $150,000, no contract will result if Marty receives the counteroffer before he receives the acceptance. This exception is designed to protect offerors like Marty who receive rejections and may rely on them by selling to someone else, being unaware of the fact that the offeree has also sent an acceptance.

Concept Summary: Communication of Acceptance

Stipulated Means of Communication	Time, place, or method of communication spelled out in offer.	Full compliance required for effective acceptance.
Authorized Means of Communication	Spelled out in offer, implied by way offer communicated, or implied by trade usage.	Acceptance effective when dispatched.
Reasonable Means of Communication (rule of UCC and some courts)	Any means deemed reasonable by the court in light of the circumstances.	Acceptance effective when dispatched.
Unauthorized Means of Communication	Generally, a means slower than the way the offer was communicated.	Acceptance not effective until received.

Cyber-Contracts

Browse-Wrap Contracts

Browse-wrap contracts often accompany the sale of software. The use of "click-on" and browse-wrap contracts is becoming common and involves some of the same issues as shrinkwrap contracts. A case involving a click-on contract was included in Chapter 10. Unlike shrinkwrap contracts, which are in paper form, click-on and browse-wrap contracts come in electronic form. In click-on agreements, a user assents to contractual terms by clicking on a button that reads "yes" or "I agree." In browse-wrap agreements, however, the user does not expressly assent to the terms of a contract, but instead, these agreements claim that a user assents to the terms by taking a specified action, such as using a certain website or installing software. Often, the terms of a browse-wrap contract are somewhere on the Web page and begin with a phrase such as "use of this site constitutes acceptance of the terms."

The terms of such contracts must be reasonable to be enforceable. Courts have found that a license agreement that was "hidden" down below a button that activated a software program and below the instructions for downloading was not enforceable.[1] The court found that users were encouraged to download software before manifesting assent to any terms, before being given a reasonable opportunity to view any terms, and before even receiving notice of the existence of any terms. Due to the design of the website, a reasonably prudent user "would not have known or learned" of the existence of the license.[2]

Concept Summary: Acceptance

There is a valid acceptance if there is:

1. **Intent:**
   Objectively manifested.
2. **Exactness:**
   No material changes from the offer.
3. **Communication:**
   a. In the stipulated manner as spelled out in the offer.
   b. By an expressly or impliedly authorized means (effective when dispatched).
   c. By a nonauthorized means (effective when received).

[1] *Specht v. Netscape Communications Corp.,* 150 F.Supp.2d 585 (S.D.N.Y. 2001).
[2] *Specht v. Netscape Communications Corp.,* 306 F.3d 17 (2d Cir. N.Y. 2002).

Questions and Problem Cases

1. What is a *material change* and what impact does it have on an offer?
2. Explain how a court determines if a writing is anticipated.
3. Explain how one can accept a unilateral contract.
4. Jerry Falwell, on his *Old Time Gospel Hour* show number 595, preached about the Second Coming of Christ. As part of this sermon, he talked about God's wrath that would be poured out on false religions. He cited the Metropolitan Community Church, a gay church founded by Jerry Sloan, his former roommate from his seminary days, as one of these false religions, a "vile and satanic system [that] will one day be utterly annihilated and there will be a celebration in heaven." He also spoke of them as immoral and "brute beasts." Falwell later appeared on a TV talk show in California. Sloan, who was in the audience, asked Falwell why he said these things, and Falwell denied ever saying them. When Sloan said he had a tape of the show, Falwell again made a denial and offered to pay $5,000 if the tape could be produced. Sloan, who had the tape at home, later gave it to Falwell and demanded the $5,000. Did Sloan effectively accept Falwell's offer?
5. JOL makes casino gaming chips from palletized polyester resin. It bought the resin from General Electric for eight years and then started buying it from Adell because Adell said the resin was of equal or superior quality and sold it for less. JOL's purchase orders said nothing about warranties or remedies in case of a breach. Adell's forms sent with the shipments did contain terms including a damage limitation clause, which limited damages to the purchase price. JOL's casino customers complained that the new chips were less attractive and durable than the prior ones and JOL had to replace 1 million chips. When JOL sued, Adell argued JOL could not sue for more than the purchase price. Is this correct? Why?

6. Basis entered an agreement with Amazon whereby it would provide services allowing Amazon to create an electronic commerce service in Japan. A few months later, they signed a "Series of Preferred Stock Purchasing Agreement" under which Amazon bought 1,654,412 shares of Basis stock and got a seat on Basis's board. It also got an agreement designed to maintain the percentage of Amazon's ownership of Basis. The agreements became the focus of a dispute between them. Basis sued Amazon. The parties entered into settlement negotiations. Basis counsel sent an e-mail that set out the terms and ended it by saying, "please contact me first thing tomorrow morning if this e-mail does not accurately summarize the settlement terms . . . ." Amazon replied, "Correct." After this they exchanged e-mails and drafts which kept changing. When Basis sought to enforce the settlement agreement, Amazon argued it was incomplete and indefinite. Is Amazon correct? Why?
7. Montgomery was covered under a group life insurance policy and his ex-wife was the beneficiary. When he remarried, Michael designated his new wife, Cynthia, as the beneficiary and she mailed the form to Aetna. When Michael died, Cynthia claimed the benefits, but Aetna denied the claim, stating it did not have the change of beneficiary form in its files. Cynthia argued that when she mailed the form a presumption was raised that Aetna had received the form. Is she correct? Explain.
8. Pearsall and Alexander, friends for over 20 years, met twice a week after work at a liquor store. There they bought what they called a "package"—a half-pint of vodka, orange juice, two cups, and two lottery tickets. They then went to Alexander's home to scratch the tickets, drink, and watch TV. When they won, they bought more tickets. One day Pearsall bought a package, and when he returned to the car, asked Alexander regarding the lottery, "Are you in on it?" Alexander said, "Yes." When Pearsall asked him for half the price, Alexander said he had no money. At his home, Alexander worried that Pearsall might lose the tickets, grabbed them, and scratched them. They were losers. Later Alexander bought another package. This time Pearsall snatched the tickets and he scratched one and Alexander the other. Alexander's won $20,000. He refused to split the money with Pearsall. Does Pearsall have a right to half the winnings?
9. Falbe bought a computer from Dell over the phone. When he received it, it came with Dell's standard "Terms and Conditions of Sale" form. It said: "Please read this document carefully. It contains very important information about your rights and obligations, as well as limitations and exclusions that may apply to you. This document contains a dispute resolution clause. . . . This Agreement contains the terms and conditions that apply to purchases. . . . By accepting delivery of the computer. . . . Customer agrees to be bound by and accepts these terms and conditions." It also contained the return policy, which stated that the computer could be returned in 30 days from the date of invoice, and an arbitration clause. Several months later Falbe sued Dell for fraud, claiming it misrepresented the procedure for obtaining a $200 rebate. Dell argued that the dispute had to be arbitrated. Who will prevail? Why?

Chapter 12

Consideration

LO

Learning Objectives

After you have studied this chapter, you should be able to:

1. Explain why consideration is necessary for a valid contract.
2. Define legal value and tell how it interacts with adequacy of consideration.
3. Discuss the effect of preexisting duties and give some examples.
4. Understand how modification of an existing contract under the UCC is different from the common law.
5. Contrast the treatment of liquidated and unliquidated debts.
6. Explain past consideration and how it operates.

The Carrocias contracted to have Todd build them a log home. Todd used inadequate construction techniques that resulted in structural problems. After a windstorm brought the inadequacies to light, the Carrocias hired Todd to replace tie-rods in the walls to correct the structural problems. They did not pay him for the tie-rod work.

- Was the Carrocias' promise to pay for the tie-rod work enforceable?
- Did Todd give any legally valuable consideration in return for the Carrocias' promise to pay?
- Can Todd recover for the work done under an equitable theory?

FIGURE 12.1
Consideration

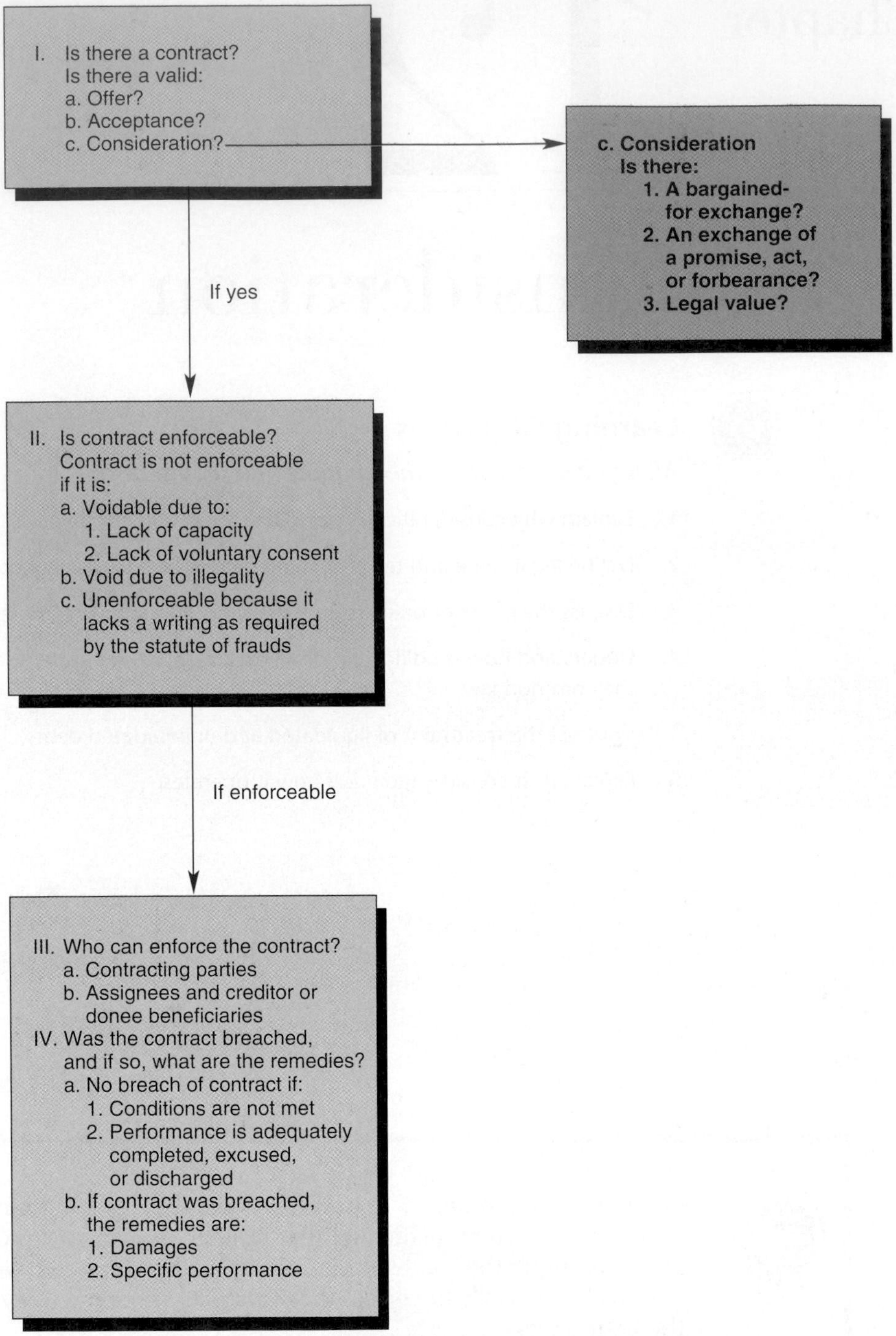
I. Is there a contract?
Is there a valid:
a. Offer?
b. Acceptance?
c. Consideration?
c. Consideration
Is there:
1. A bargained-for exchange?
2. An exchange of a promise, act, or forbearance?
3. Legal value?
If yes
II. Is contract enforceable?
Contract is not enforceable if it is:
a. Voidable due to:
1. Lack of capacity
2. Lack of voluntary consent
b. Void due to illegality
c. Unenforceable because it lacks a writing as required by the statute of frauds
If enforceable
III. Who can enforce the contract?
a. Contracting parties
b. Assignees and creditor or donee beneficiaries
IV. Was the contract breached, and if so, what are the remedies?
a. No breach of contract if:
1. Conditions are not met
2. Performance is adequately completed, excused, or discharged
b. If contract was breached, the remedies are:
1. Damages
2. Specific performance

The Idea of Consideration

LO1

At a fairly early point in the development of contract law, the common law courts decided not to enforce gratuitous (free) promises. Simply put, this means that the courts generally do not enforce a promise against the person who made it (the **promisor**) unless the person the promise was made to (the **promisee**) has given up something in exchange for the promise. In effect, the requirement of **consideration** requires a promisee to pay the "price" the promisor asked for in order to gain the right to enforce the promisor's promise. This idea is consistent with the common law idea that the purpose of contract law was to enforce *bargains.* So, if Mary (the promisor) promises to give Bob (the promisee) a diamond ring and Bob has done nothing in return for her promise, Bob will not be able to enforce Mary's promise against her, since it was *not supported by consideration.* A useful definition of *consideration* is *legal value, bargained for and given in exchange for an act or promise.*

LO2

Legal Value

A promisee's consideration may be an *act* (in the case of some unilateral contracts) or a *promise* (in the case of some unilateral contracts and all bilateral contracts). Consideration can have **legal value** in one of two ways. If the promisee does or agrees to do something he or she had no prior legal duty to do in exchange for the promisor's promise, that provides legal value. If the promisee agrees not to do something he or she has a legal right to do in exchange for the promisor's promise, that also provides legal value.

Under this definition many things can have *legal* value without having *monetary* (economic) value. So, if Frank's grandmother promises to pay Frank $500 if he will quit smoking for one year and Frank quits, he can enforce her promise against her. He has given legal value (by not doing something he had a right to do) in exchange for her promise, despite the fact that his quitting smoking has no everyday value in dollars and cents.

Devaney v. L'Esperance

949 A.2d 743 (N.J. Sup. Ct. 2008)

FACTS

When she was 23, Devaney began working for L'Esperance, who was 51, as a receptionist for his ophthalmology practice. They became involved in an intimate, 20-year relationship. L'Esperance was married to someone else, and he continued to live with his wife. He promised Devaney he would divorce his wife, marry her, and have a child with her. During this time Devaney rented places in her own name and paid for most things herself. They did vacation together but otherwise never cohabited. The relationship eventually ended. Devaney quit her job, pursued educational opportunities, and moved to Connecticut. A year later she moved to Seattle, where she lived for three years. During this time she frequently talked by phone with L'Esperance and asked him for money. He sent her $400 per month to cover incidental expenses. He asked her to move back to the East Coast and promised that if she did, he would "make things right," divorce his wife, marry her, buy a home, and they would have a child. She agreed to move back after she saw a separation agreement signed by the wife. She moved to New Jersey, lived in a condominium bought by L'Esperance, and drove a car he bought. He paid for various expenses, including her undergraduate and graduate education. During the seven years she lived there, L'Esperance only spent the night six or seven times. He changed his mind about having a child with her and finally told her he wanted to discontinue the relationship. She started seeing someone else, and when L'Esperance stopped by the condo one night, he was denied admittance because her boyfriend was there. Shortly thereafter, he had her evicted. She sued him, claiming he promised to support her for life.

ISSUE

Was there consideration of legal value for the promise to support her for life?

DECISION

No. This is essentially a palimony suit, which is a claim for support between unmarried persons. It is a relatively new cause of action and recognizes the changing social mores about living together. To be successful in this type of suit, the couple had to have a marital-type relationship. Entry into such a relationship and then conducting oneself in accordance with its unique character is sufficient consideration to enforce a promise for support. The question is, did they have to cohabit in order to have this type

(continued)

Devaney v. L'Esperance *(concluded)*

of relationship? Devaney claims she devoted herself to L'Esperance for 20 years in reliance on the promise that he would support her for life. She argues that they committed to each other, provided companionship, and met each other's financial, emotional, physical, and social needs. Her actions, she argues, were full consideration for his promise to support. L'Esperance argues that a marital-type relationship requires two people to commit to each other, forgoing other liaisons and opportunities, and since he was married and living with his wife, this did not happen. He further argues there is no public policy interest in promoting childbearing in the context of an adulterous relationship. We find that that there must be a marital-type relationship coupled with an express or implied promise to support, but cohabitation is not necessarily required. Cohabitation is to be considered, but is not determinitive. However, the parties' relationship here was best characterized as a dating relationship.

Adequacy of Consideration

Legal value has nothing to do with *adequacy* of consideration. As long as the consideration given by the parties to an agreement has legal value, the courts generally do not concern themselves with whether parties to a contract received any actual value in exchange for their promises, or whether the promises or performances exchanged were of relatively equal value. Freedom of contract is the freedom to make bad bargains as well as good ones, so promisors' promises are enforceable if they "got what they asked for" in exchange for making their promises, even if "what they asked for" is not nearly so valuable in worldly terms as what they promised in return.

Several qualifications must be made to this general rule. First, if the inadequacy of consideration is apparent *on the face of the agreement,* most courts would not enforce the agreement because they would assume it was a gift disguised to look like a contract. Thus, an agreement by Martha to pay her brother $500 in exchange for $100, with no other terms or conditions, is unenforceable.

Agreements that recite "$1" or "$1 and other valuable consideration" as the consideration for a promise are similarly treated. This **nominal consideration** is generally not recognized by the courts unless it was in fact *truly* bargained for. If it wasn't bargained for, the promise is a disguised gift and unenforceable.

Gross inadequacy of consideration may also give rise to an inference of fraud, duress, lack of capacity, and so on. In addition, gross inadequacy may lead to a finding of unconscionability under the Uniform Commercial Code. Inadequacy of consideration standing alone, however, is not enough to prove lack of reality of consent or capacity.

Courts may refuse to grant **equitable remedies** to those who seek to enforce grossly inadequate bargains on the grounds that such persons are not entitled to the special treatment equity affords. So, if Bob agrees to sell Mary his house (worth $155,000) for $125,000, Mary can probably recover damages for breach of contract if Bob refuses to perform, but she may not be able to get an order for the specific performance of Bob's promise (ordering Bob to give Mary a deed to his house).

Ethics in Action

Is it ethical to insist on a strict enforcement of a contract when you have paid nominal or inadequate consideration?

Bob Acres, LLC v. Schumacher Farms, LLC

979 N.W.2d 723 (2011)

FACTS

Acres agreed to buy 25 acres of land from Schumacher Farms for $70,000. The written agreement, among other things, stated that Schumacher had received $500 "earnest money." Earnest money was never discussed, paid, or demanded at that time. The sale was supposed to close by August 14 but it did not occur. Schumacher's attorney began drafting an easement, and said the deal would close when that was done. After an inquiry about completion of the sale in December, Schumacher said it was no longer interested. When Acres sued, Schumacher said there was no contract because the $500 was not paid and therefore there was no consideration.

ISSUE

Was the agreement unenforceable for lack of consideration?

DECISION

No. To be enforceable, an agreement or promise requires consideration. Acres alleges there was consideration because the parties exchanged mutual promises—Acres's promise to sell and Schumacher's promise to buy. A false recital of $500 earnest money does not mean the agreement fails for lack of consideration. Neither promise was made in reliance on the earnest money. It is merely an assurance that the purchaser is acting in good faith. The false recital cannot be used to avoid the contract.

FIGURE 12.2
The Concept of Consideration

A legally valuable promise, act, forbearance	Bargained for and given in exchange for	A legally valuable promise, act, or forbearance

Bargained for and Given in Exchange

Saying consideration must be bargained for means that, in addition to having legal value, the consideration given by the promisee must be the consideration the promisor *requested in exchange for making his or her promise.* The courts are saying, in effect: "If you [the promisor] got your price for making your promise, we will enforce your promise against you."

See Figure 12.2 for a summary of the concept of consideration.

Solving Consideration Problems

Students often have difficulty with the concept of consideration. One reason is that most disputes about consideration involve *bilateral contracts* (a promise for a promise). This causes confusion in two ways. First, since bilateral contracts by definition include two promises, each party is both a promisor (on the promise he or she made to the other party) and a promisee (on the promise the other party made in return). Second, students often forget that *merely making the requested promise* is enough for consideration in bilateral contracts cases.

Here is a simple problem-solving method to help you in determining whether consideration has been given in a case. Ask yourself:

1. *Which promise is at issue?* This ordinarily is the promise that a court is trying to decide whether to enforce.
2. *Who is the promisee of that promise?* This is the party seeking to enforce the promise.
3. *Has the promisee given consideration?* If so, and if the other elements of a binding contract are present, the promise is enforceable.

If you understand the definition of consideration and use this method, you will be able to work out most consideration problems with ease. Take a simple bilateral contract situation and see how this problem-solving method works.

Facts

On May 15, 2004, Mary enters into an agreement with Apex Painting Company to have Apex paint her house before June 15, 2004, for the sum of $3,000.

Alternative Case A

On May 20, 2004, Mary calls Apex and tells it the deal is off, since Ralph's Painting Company has agreed to paint her house for $2,500. Apex sues Mary, and she argues lack of consideration as a defense.

1. The promise at issue is Mary's promise to pay Apex for painting her house.
2. The promisee on this promise is Apex.
3. Apex has given consideration. Apex agreed to do something it had no prior duty to do—paint Mary's house—in exchange for her promise. Apex can enforce Mary's promise against her.

Alternative Case B

On May 15, 2004, Apex calls Mary and tells her it will not be able to paint her house because it just got a very profitable job painting a new apartment complex. Mary sues Apex, and it argues lack of consideration as a defense.

1. The promise at issue is Apex's promise to paint Mary's house.
2. Mary is the promisee on this promise.
3. Mary has given consideration. She agreed to do something she had no prior duty to do—hire and pay Apex for painting her house—in exchange for Apex's promise. She can enforce Apex's promise against it.

Now that you understand the meaning of consideration and have a method to help you solve consideration problems, you are ready to learn some of the traditional rules about consideration. These are mostly statements about how the requirement of consideration works in various kinds of situations.

Rules of Consideration

LO3

Preexisting Duties

As a general rule, performing or agreeing to perform a preexisting duty is not consideration. This makes sense when you remember the definition of consideration. In order to have given *legal value,* the promisor must either have done (or agreed to do) something he had no duty to do or has agreed not to do something he had a right to do. If the promisor already had a duty to do what he has done or promised to do, the promisor has not given legal value. The same is clearly true if the promisor agreed not to do something he had no right to do. Several examples of this rule follow.

Promises Not to Commit Crimes or Torts

Every member of society has a duty to obey the law and not commit crimes or torts. Therefore, a promisor's promise not to commit such an act can never be consideration.

Tasini v. AOL, Inc.

851 F. Supp. 2d 734 (S.D. N.Y. 2012)

FACTS

The Huffington Post launched www.huffingtonpost.com in 2005. It was designed as a for-profit enterprise. It provides a mix of content that is written by paid staff, collected from other websites, or submitted by unpaid bloggers, the majority of whom are professional or semi-professional writers. Tasini was an unpaid contributor who had contributed content 216 times over five years, Rather than pay, these contributors get exposure while the Post keeps production costs low. The Post also gains exposure by the contributors promoting their own submissions via their social networks. The Post sells advertising, and the rates are based on the number of visitors to the Post's site. In 2011, AOL purchased the Post. Tasini argued that the Post was an attractive target because of its ability to attract high-quality content at no cost. He argued that a significant portion of the purchase price was traceable to him and those similarly situated, and he sued to recover that.

ISSUE

Should Tasini now receive payment for his work?

DECISION

No. Tasini entered into the transactions with the Post with full knowledge of the facts and no expectations of compensation other than exposure, which he did receive. No one forced Tasini to give his work to the Post. There is no good argument for retroactively awarding compensation just because the Post later benefitted from his contributions. You can't change the rules of the game after the game has been played. This case is different from situations where people submit things expecting compensation but under circumstances where they are not sure their contribution will be used. In that case, they would deserve compensation.

For example, Bill promises to pay Mike, the school bully, $2 a week for "protection" in exchange for Mike's promise not to beat Bill up. Bill refuses to pay. Bill's promise is unenforceable because it is not supported by consideration.

Promises by Public Officials to Perform Official Duties

Public officials obviously are bound to perform their official duties, so promises by public officials to perform these duties are not consideration. For example, Harry owns a liquor store that has been robbed several times. He promises to pay Fran, a police officer whose beat includes Harry's store, $50 a week to "keep an eye on the store" while walking her beat. Harry's promise is unenforceable, since it was not supported by consideration.

Promises to Perform Preexisting Contractual Duties

By far the greatest number of preexisting duty cases involve **contractual** duties. These cases usually occur when the parties attempt to modify an existing contract but no new consideration is furnished to support the agreement to modify.

For example, Capucine enters into a contract with Toptex Construction Company to build a new house for her for $175,000. When the construction is partially completed, Jones, the owner of Toptex, calls Capucine and says that due to the rising cost of building materials, Toptex will have to stop work unless she pays an extra $5,000. Capucine agrees but later refuses to pay more than the $175,000 originally agreed on. Toptex sues for $5,000. The promise at issue is Capucine's promise to pay the extra $5,000. Toptex cannot enforce that promise because Toptex has not given consideration. All Toptex has done is build the house, something it already had a legal duty to do under the parties' original contract. Similarly Todd, the builder in the introductory problem, cannot collect for the tie-rods. He was under a duty to construct the house in a workmanlike manner. Providing tie-rods to supplement his defective construction is merely a continuation of that preexisting duty.

Of course, if *new consideration* is provided to support a modification, it is enforceable. So, if Capucine had asked Toptex to add a room that was not called for in the original plans and promised to pay an extra $5,000 for the new room, her promise to pay more would be enforceable. Toptex, in this case, would have done something it had no legal duty to do in exchange for Capucine's promise.

Zhang v. Sorichetti

103 P.3d 20 (Nev. Sup. Ct. 2004)

FACTS

On February 1, Zhang contracted to buy former realtor Sorichetti's home and a few of its furnishings for $532,500. Closing was to be in March. On February 3, Sorchetti told Zhang that he was terminating the sale "to stay in the house a little longer." He stated (incorrectly) that Nevada law allows the rescission of real property purchase agreements within three days of contracting. He said, though, that he would sell the house if Zhang paid more money, and Zhang agreed. The new contract listed the sales price as $578,000. The closing date was April. On February 16 Sorichetti told Zhang that a murder had occurred in the house several years earlier, and that Zhang could cancel the contract if she wished. She declined. Sorichetti later refused to carry out the contract and Zhang sued for damages and specific performance of the original contract.

ISSUE

Can Zhang get the house at the original price?

DECISION

Yes. Where two parties have a contract and one becomes dissatisfied and refuses to perform unless the other party promises to pay more than the contract price, there cannot be a second agreement. As a matter of principle, the second agreement must be held invalid because the dissatisfied party has suffered no legal detriment since at the time of the second agreement he was already bound to do the promised action. This is the preexisting rule. Thus, the February 3 agreement is not enforceable and Sorichetti is bound by the February 1 agreement.

Ethics in Action

Is it ethical to promise to pay a person more to complete a job and then to renege on the promise because the other party had a preexisting obligation to complete the task at the original price?

The parties to a contract can always terminate their old contract and enter into a new one by mutual agreement (called a *novation*) even if the obligations of one party remain the same while the obligations of the other party are increased. The courts, however, are very suspicious of these situations, asking, in effect: Who would voluntarily agree to pay more for what they have a right to for less? Therefore, the courts require clear and convincing evidence that the termination of the old contract and the creation of the new one are free of any elements of coercion or fraud.

The consideration requirement is often criticized as being too formalistic; mechanical application of the rule can lead to significant injustice. Therefore, the modern trend is to relax the requirement by expanding exceptions to the rule and providing substitutes for it. This is the case with some preexisting contractual duties.

Unforeseeable Difficulties

Generally speaking, a court will enforce a modification that is not supported by new consideration if a contracting party has run into **unforeseeable difficulties** that make his or her performance impossible or highly impracticable. In this situation, the party who has run into trouble is neither a bad person trying to take advantage of the promisor nor an imprudent person trying to escape the consequences of a bad bargain. Therefore, the courts enforce the modification in the interest of fairness, although technically no new consideration has been given. You should note, however, that strikes, increases in the costs of raw materials, and bad weather are not considered unforeseeable. A revolution in Central America that caused supplies to be cut off would be foreseeable; a revolution in France would not. A building contractor who, in excavating the foundation of a new building, strikes bedrock in an area where bedrock formations are not usually found so close to the surface could also rely on this exception to the general rule.

Modifications and the Code

LO4

The Code has made a major change in the traditional rule in the case of agreements to modify existing contracts. Agreements to modify contracts for the sale of goods *need no consideration* to be binding (2-209[1]). People often freely agree to modify their agreements and believe that such modifications are binding. The Code chose to reward these people's expectations.

For example, assume Plastex Corporation enters a contract to supply The Picnic Place with plastic dishes and utensils for $3.50 a setting. After the contract is made, the price of oil suddenly rises, and Plastex's manufacturing costs are greatly increased. Plastex notifies Picnic Place that it can no longer afford to supply the articles at $3.50 a setting and is raising the price to $4. Picnic Place can, of course, refuse to pay $4 a setting and hold Plastex liable for breach of contract if it does not deliver the goods at the original price. However, Picnic Place may believe that paying $4 is better than taking a chance that it won't have dishes and utensils in time for the summer season. Picnic Place may therefore agree to pay the new price. If it does, Plastex can enforce the agreement to pay $4 per setting because it was voluntarily entered into, even though no new consideration was given.

Several points should be noted concerning the way this section of the Code operates. First, there is *no duty* to agree to a modification. Picnic Place could have refused to agree to Plastex's increased price and enforced the original contract. Second, the exception applies only to *existing contracts.* Third, only one term of the existing contract was altered. The other terms under the contract remained in force. Finally, modifications are subject to review under the Code's principles of good faith and fair dealing. Unfair agreements or agreements that result from coercion are unlikely to be enforced.

The Code contains two provisions to protect people from fictitious claims that an agreement has been modified. If the original agreement requires any modification to be in writing, an oral modification is unenforceable (2-209[2]). Regardless of what the original contract says, if the price of the goods in the modified agreement is $500 or more, the modification is not enforceable unless it is in writing or other requirements of the Code's statute of frauds are met (2-201).

As we saw in Table 9.1 in Chapter 9, like the Code, the United Nations Convention on Contracts for the International Sale of Goods (CISG) does not require additional consideration to modify a contract. Like the Code, the CISG guards parties' expectations by allowing them to modify contracts by "mere agreement." Also similar to the Code, the CISG requires that where parties originally agree that any modification will be in writing, oral modification is ineffective.

Promises to Discharge Debts for Part Payment

In many cases, a debtor offers to pay a creditor a sum less than the creditor is demanding in exchange for the creditor's promise to accept the part payment as full payment of the debt. If the creditor later sues for the balance of the original debt, is the creditor's promise to take less enforceable? The answer depends on the nature of the debt and the circumstances of the debtor's payment.

LO5

Liquidated Debts

The general rule is that a promise to discharge a **liquidated debt** for part payment of the debt at or after its due date is unenforceable due to lack of consideration. A liquidated debt is one that is *due* and *certain,* which means that there is no dispute about the existence or the amount of the debt. If a debtor does nothing more than agree to pay less than an amount clearly owed, how can that be valid consideration for the creditor's promise to take less? The debtor has actually done less than he or she already had a duty to do, namely, to pay the full amount of the debt.

For example, Beth borrows $2,000 from the First City Bank, payable in six months. When the time for payment arrives, Beth sends the bank a check for $1,800 marked: "In full payment for any and all claims First City has against me." First City cashes the check (impliedly promising to accept it as full payment by cashing it) and later sues Beth for $200. First City can recover the $200, since Beth has given no consideration to support its implied promise to accept $1,800 as full payment.

On the other hand, if Beth had done something she had no duty to do in exchange for First City's promise, she could enforce First City's promise against it and avoid paying the $200. If Beth had *paid early* (before the loan contract called for payment), or *at a different place* from that called for in the loan contract, or *in a different medium of exchange* from that called for in the loan contract (e.g., a car worth $1,800) in exchange for First City's promise, she has given consideration and can enforce the promise.

Unliquidated Debts

An honest dispute about the existence or amount of a debt makes the debt an **unliquidated** one. Assume Tom and Mark are involved in an automobile accident. Tom claims that Mark is at fault and that his total losses from the accident are $9,500. Mark denies responsibility for the accident and argues that Tom's losses are far less than $9,500. There are only two ways to finally settle this dispute: (1) allow a court to determine the nature and extent of the parties' liabilities or (2) reach a private settlement agreement. If Mark offers to pay Tom $2,000 in full payment of all claims Tom has against him and Tom accepts, Tom has entered a binding **accord and satisfaction**—the legal term for settling a disputed

Double H Housing Corp. v. David

947 A.2d 38 (D.C. Ct. App. 38 2008)

FACTS

David leased an apartment from Double H for a period commencing July 29, 1995, and ending July 31, 1996, for $1,473 per month. After that time, David continued to live in the apartment on a month-to-month basis. In May 2003, Double H notified David his rent would be $1,488 if David signed a new lease for a year; otherwise, it would be $1,561 to continue the month-to-month tenancy. In August, David

(continued)

starting paying $1,488, but he never signed a new lease. David testified that he had negotiated with the property manager, who agreed to this. On August 14, Double H sent him a past-due notice for failing to pay $1,561. He received no other notices, and he continued to negotiate with Double H until October 2004. David explained he had lived there for eight years and had always paid his rent on time and thus a long-term commitment was not necessary. In May 2004, Double H sent a letter telling him he could "renew [his] current lease for another 12-month term starting July 1, 2004, at the same lease rate of $1,561. . ." but if he didn't sign, his rent would be $1,611 per month. David wrote a letter stating that his current rent was $1,488 and that the next rent cycle did not commence until a month after the deadline set by Double H. It responded that since he was on a month-to-month tenancy, it could raise the rent after 30-days notice. They stated that there "is no offer to renew for a rate of $1,488 per month." David paid rent for the next four months at $1,488, and Double H cashed each check. After that, they returned his checks and sued him for what they claimed he owed starting from August 2003, plus late fees.

ISSUE

Was the cashing of the rent checks accord and satisfaction?

DECISION

Yes. Double H had the right to negotiate a new rent and charge a discounted rent if he signed a year's lease. While conditioning a rent discount on a signing puts the tenant at a "tremendous disadvantage," David did have a meaningful choice. However, Double H cannot collect for the increased amount in 2003 or 2004. David stayed in the apartment and paid the lower rent, and Double H cashed the checks. He sought to negotiate the lower rent, but held out, hoping Double H would relent and accept the lower amount that he tendered each month. There was an accord and satisfaction. When an amount is in dispute and the debtor sends a check for less as settlement in full, cashing the check is acceptance of the offer operating as full satisfaction.

claim. Both Mark and Tom have given up their right to have a court decide their liability in exchange for the other's promise to settle their dispute for a definite amount. Therefore, their mutual promises are supported by consideration and enforceable.

Code Section 1-207

This section states: "A party who with explicit reservation of rights performs . . . in a manner demanded or offered by the other party does not thereby prejudice the rights reserved." Some courts have interpreted this language to mean that sellers of goods can cash checks marked "payment in full" and still collect for the unpaid amount if they have attempted to reserve their rights through phrases such as "under protest" or "without prejudice." Courts that take this approach thereby avoid the operation of the accord and satisfaction rule. A majority of courts, though, hold that cashing a "payment in full" check discharges the obligation under the Code. Additionally, several states have enacted a new version of 1-207, which specifically states that 1-207 does not apply to accord and satisfaction.

Composition Agreements

Compositions are agreements between a debtor and two or more creditors who agree to accept a stated percentage of their liquidated claims against the debtor at or after the due date, in full satisfaction of their claims. They are generally treated as binding on the parties to the agreement, despite the fact that doing so appears to be contrary to the general rule on liquidated debts. Creditors usually enter compositions when they believe that failure to do so may result in the debtor's bankruptcy, in which case they might ultimately recover a smaller percentage of their claims than that agreed to in the composition.

Concept Summary: Preexisting Duties

Type	Reason	Exception
1. Promises not to commit crimes or torts	Since every member of society has this duty, the promise lacks consideration.	
2. Promises by public officials to perform official duties	Since public officials are bound to perform their official duties, these promises lack consideration.	
3. Promise to perform preexisting contractual duties a. Common law rule	Since the promisee is already under contract to perform the promise, It lacks consideration.	Unforeseeable difficulties that made performance impossible or highly impractical can make promise enforceable.
b. Uniform Commercial Code Rule (2-209)	If commercially reasonable and freely agreed to, promise to alter existing contract for sale of goods is enforceable.	No additional consideration is needed.
4. Promise to pay part of a debt a. Liquidated debt	Since the amount is due and certain, a promise to pay less lacks consideration.	Composition agreements enforced without additional consideration.
b. Unliquidated debt	Since the amount is genuinely in dispute, an agreement resulting in accord and satisfaction is enforceable.	Under UCC Section 1-207, *some courts* allow collection of the remainder if checks marked "payment in full" are cashed with reservation.

LO6

Past Consideration

The courts generally hold that past consideration is no consideration. This rule of consideration basically focuses on the "bargained for and given in exchange" part of our definition of consideration. If a promisee's performance was rendered *before* the promisor's promise was made, then it can never serve as consideration, even though it may meet the "legal value" part of the test. This is so because it was not "bargained for and given in exchange" for the promisor's promise. Return to our earlier example with Frank and his grandmother, but assume that in this case Frank's grandmother says to him, "I'm glad you quit smoking last year, so I'll give you $500 for your birthday." If she later refuses to pay, can Frank enforce her promise? No; he has not given consideration because he did not quit smoking in exchange for her promise.

Moral Obligation

Some courts and legislatures have created an exception to the past consideration rule for **moral obligations.** These cases usually contain promises made by a promisor to pay for board and lodging previously provided to a needy relative or a very close friend, or a promise to pay the debts of a relative. Some courts have found it distressing that such promises would not be enforced and have enforced them despite their lack of consideration. In addition, a few states have passed statutes making promises to pay for past benefits enforceable if the promise is contained in a writing that clearly expresses the promisor's intent to be bound.

Forbearance to Sue

Forbearance occurs when someone promises not to file a legal suit in exchange for a promise to pay a certain sum of money or some other consideration. The promise not to file suit is valid consideration because the promisor has given up a legal right, the right to sue. There are, however, some qualifications on this rule.

The courts clearly do not want to sanction extortion by allowing people to threaten to file spurious (unfounded) claims in the hope that others will agree to some payment to avoid the expense or embarrassment of suit. On the other hand, we have a strong public policy favoring private settlement of disputes and do not want to require people to second-guess the courts. Therefore, it is generally said that in order for forbearance to be valid consideration, the promisee must in *good faith* believe he or she has a valid claim.

Mutuality of Obligation

Generally, a bilateral contract that lacks mutuality is unenforceable due to lack of consideration. As you learned earlier, in a bilateral contract the mutual promises of the parties form the consideration for the agreement. However, the fact that a party made a promise in exchange for the other party's promise is not enough to provide consideration. The promise made must also meet the "legal value" part of our consideration definition. The parties must have bound themselves to do something they had no duty to do, or not to do something they had a right to do.

This issue is raised in some cases because what first looks like a binding promise turns out to be an **illusory promise.** Illusory promises are worded in a way that allows the promisor to decide whether or not to perform the promise. A promise to "buy all the wheat I want" is illusory. A bilateral agreement based on an illusory promise is unenforceable due to lack of mutuality. This means that an illusory promise cannot serve as consideration.

Additional Exceptions to the Requirement of Consideration

Promissory Estoppel

The doctrine of promissory estoppel, which was discussed in Chapters 9 and 10, is increasingly being used to enforce promises that are not supported by consideration. Such liberal use is encouraged by the *Restatement (Second) of Contracts.* If the three elements required for estoppel are present (a *promise* likely to induce reliance, *reliance* on that promise, and *injustice* as a result of reliance), the promisor may be *estopped* from raising the defense of lack of consideration. For example, a tenant tells her landlord that she is considering remodeling her apartment and asks if he intends to allow her to renew her lease. He says yes but later refuses to honor his promise. If the tenant has actually spent a substantial sum remodeling in reliance on the landlord's promise, his promise is probably enforceable against him.

Dixon v. Wells Fargo Bank, NA

798 F. Supp. 236 (D. Mass. 2011)

FACTS

The Dixons had a mortgage with Wells Fargo Bank. The Dixons sought a loan modification. While the bank did not promise this, it did verbally promise to try for a modification so long as the Dixons stopped making their payments. In that case, the unpaid amount would be added to the modified loan. The Dixons stopped their payments but Wells Fargo never followed through on its promise and moved to foreclose. The Dixons sued.

ISSUE

Can the promise be acted on even though there was no consideration?

DECISION

Yes. Usually parties cannot sue for breach of contract unless each has given something of value, or consideration. However, promissory estoppel allows a party to seek damages if there is reasonable reliance on the promise, a loss was suffered, and there is injustice because of the reliance. This is not a vague "agreement to agree" which has been found in other cases. Here the bank acted opportunistically and the decision to foreclose was "unseemly conduct at best." The Dixons incurred costs as a result. They are entitled to sue.

Firm Offer

Remember that under the Code, an offer by a merchant in a signed writing to keep an offer open is good without additional consideration. This concept was discussed in Chapter 10.

Charitable Subscriptions

A promise to make a gift for a charitable or educational purpose is unenforceable unless and until the institution to which the promise was made incurs obligations by relying on the promise. This exception is usually justified on the basis of either estoppel or public policy.

Debts Barred by Bankruptcy Discharge or the Statute of Limitations

Once a bankrupt debtor is granted a discharge (bankruptcy is discussed in Chapter 44), creditors no longer have a legal right to collect the discharged debts. Similarly, a creditor who fails to file suit to collect a debt within the time limit set by the appropriate statute of limitations loses the right to collect it. However, many states enforce *new promises* by debtors to pay these kinds of debts even though technically they are not supported by consideration, since the creditors have no rights to give up in exchange for the debtors' new promises. This is a source of great potential danger to debtors and great temptation for creditors. Many states recognize this fact by requiring such promises to be in writing to be enforceable. The Bankruptcy Act requires a reaffirmation promise to be made prior to discharge; the promise can be revoked within 30 days after it becomes enforceable, and the Bankruptcy Court must approve it. In addition, the Bankruptcy Court must counsel individual debtors about the legal effects of reaffirmation.

Concept Summary: Consideration

There is valid consideration if there is:

1. A bargained-for exchange
2. of a promise, act, or forbearance
3. that had legal value
   a. not preexisting duty
   b. not past consideration
   c. not illusory promise
   or

(continued)

Concept Summary: Consideration (concluded)

4. A recognized exception:
   a. Promise to perform preexisting contractual duties under Section 2-209, or unforeseen difficulties.
   b. Accord and satisfaction of an unliquidated debt.
   c. "Payment in full" check for goods cashed with reservation under Section 1-207.
   d. Composition agreement.
   e. Past consideration recognized as a moral obligation.
   f. Promissory estoppel.
   g. Relied-on charitable subscription.
   h. New promise to pay discharged debt if in writing or meets requirements of Bankruptcy Act.

Questions and Problem Cases

1. Explain the effect of unforeseeable difficulties.
2. What is an illusory promise?
3. Explain why past consideration is not good consideration.
4. After McBee and Nance began dating, McBee had financial difficulties and Nance gave her various cash loans. McBee signed a promissory note for $15,000, secured by a deed of trust on her house. After she failed to make payments, Nance foreclosed on the house. McBee then sued, arguing the consideration was inadequate; that it should be the same as the amount of the note. Is this correct? Explain.
5. Adirondack Community College had a contract to have heating and air conditioning systems in campus buildings replaced. Gold was a subcontractor for part of the work. Due to the unavailability of the basic thermostats which were specified in the original plans, Gold substituted more complicated and expensive ones. Gold sought to recover for the additional work and expense. Can it he?
6. Slattery, an independent, licensed polygraph operator, was employed by law enforcement authorities to question a suspect. During the testing, which was conducted over two days, the suspect confessed to killing a guard in a Wells Fargo robbery, a crime about which the suspect was not being questioned. The suspect was convicted and sentenced for the murder. Slattery claimed a $25,000 reward Wells Fargo had offered for information leading to the arrest and conviction of the person or persons participating in the shooting. Is Slattery entitled to the reward?
7. Joe was a 48-year-old wealthy businessman when he began dating Celeste, 22. He asked her to move in with him, but she refused, saying she didn't want to do it unless they were going to have a long-range, permanent husband/wife type of relationship. She later moved in with him, and they reached an agreement wherein she would prepare meals, manage the home, and arrange for remodeling. Joe earned the income and managed the investments. A key part of the agreement was to try to have children together. She alleged that they understood that all property acquired would be treated as joint property. They had a son a couple of years later. The next year they married. Four years later they had twins. Two years later, Celeste filed for divorce and claimed all property should be equitably divided, including Joe's property before they cohabited. Joe argued that he should not have to share any property because a contract between nonmarital

partners is invalid if sexual acts form part of the consideration, and the promise to bear children necessarily involved sexual intercourse. Will Joe have to divide his property? Explain.

8. Duncan made a will that divided her property among her five children. It stated that if her son died before her, his share should go to his wife. She also made a separate agreement with the children that she would not change the will in exchange for their promise that they would not challenge it or make any claim against the estate. The son died three months after that. Later, Duncan gave two of her children powers of attorney, and they conveyed all of the real property to the surviving children. Duncan then revoked the will and made a new one, leaving her property to her children but not to her son's wife. The son's wife sued. Did the agreement not to revoke the will lack consideration? Why?
9. The Cunninghams contracted with Crites to have him build their house for $105,000. They were to pay their own closing costs and get a credit at closing because they owned the land on which the home was constructed; Crites was to receive a builder's fee of $12,500. The closing date was October 30, but the house was not finished until February. They met in January to discuss the closing and outstanding bills. They agreed the Cunninghams would pay $10,000 of the bills, and Crites would drop the builder's fee. Crites failed to appear at the closing and asked for the builder's fee. Was there an enforceable accord and satisfaction? Explain.

Chapter 13

Capacity to Contract

Learning Objectives

After you have studied this chapter, you should be able to:

1. Explain why capacity is required for contracts.
2. Know the consequences of and the limits on a minor disaffirming a contract.
3. Understand the concept of emancipation.
4. Define *necessaries* and how they are determined.
5. Explain the test and effect of mental incapacity.

Webster Street Partnership leased an apartment to Matt and Pat, both minors, for one year. After paying rent for two months, Pat and Matt were unable to pay the third month's rent, and they were asked to move out. Webster Street was unable to rerent the apartment for two months. It sued the boys for this lost rent, as well as for other fees and damages. Matt and Pat refused to pay and countersued for the return of the rent they had already paid.

- Can Matt and Pat avoid paying damages because they were minors when they made the contract?
- Can Matt and Pat disaffirm the contract and recover what they had already paid while they lived in the apartment?
- Could Webster Street disaffirm the rental contract when it discovers Matt and Pat are minors?

FIGURE 13.1
Capacity

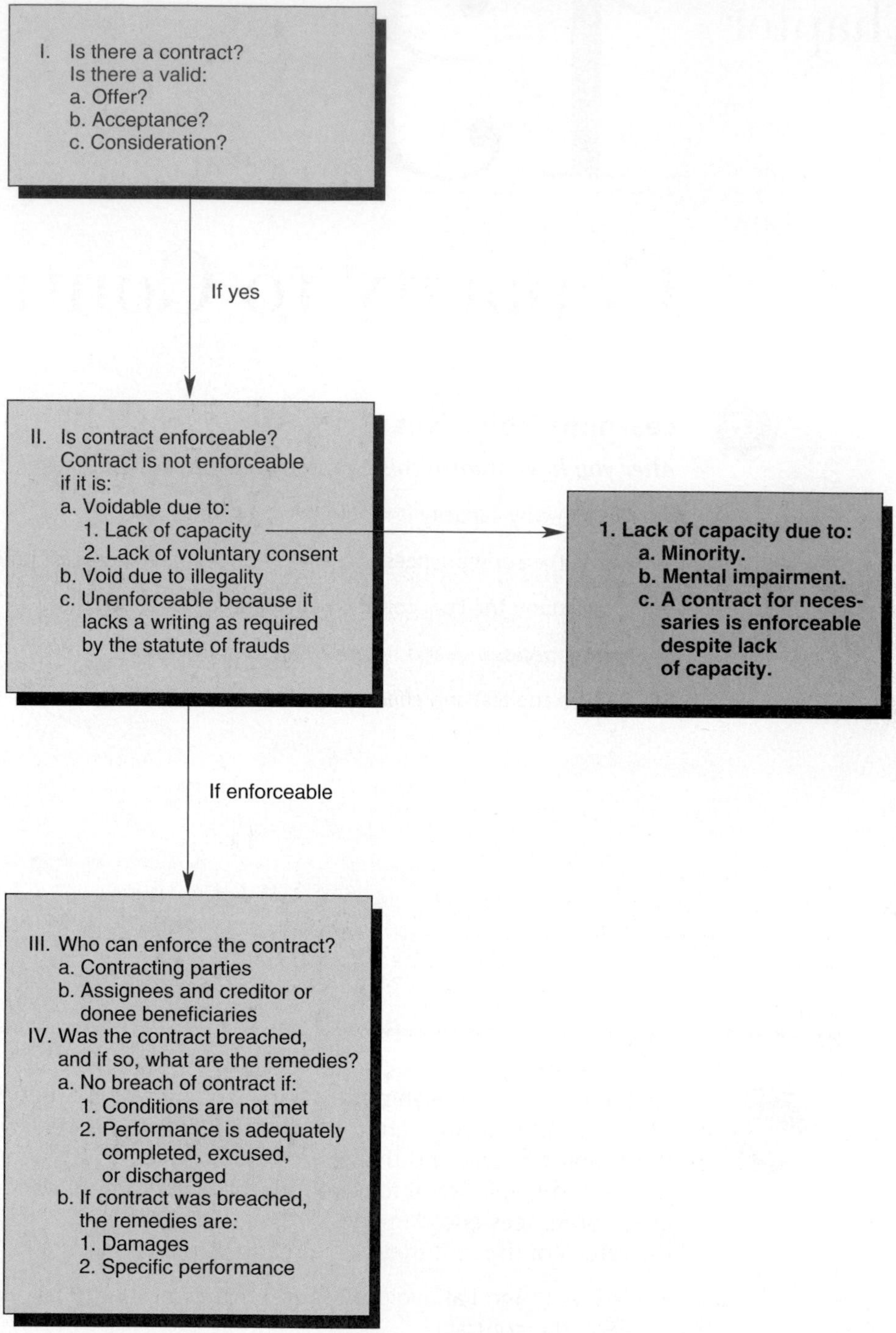
I. Is there a contract?
Is there a valid:
a. Offer?
b. Acceptance?
c. Consideration?
If yes
II. Is contract enforceable?
Contract is not enforceable if it is:
a. Voidable due to:
1. Lack of capacity
2. Lack of voluntary consent
b. Void due to illegality
c. Unenforceable because it lacks a writing as required by the statute of frauds
1. Lack of capacity due to:
a. Minority.
b. Mental impairment.
c. A contract for necessaries is enforceable despite lack of capacity.
If enforceable
III. Who can enforce the contract?
a. Contracting parties
b. Assignees and creditor or donee beneficiaries
IV. Was the contract breached, and if so, what are the remedies?
a. No breach of contract if:
1. Conditions are not met
2. Performance is adequately completed, excused, or discharged
b. If contract was breached, the remedies are:
1. Damages
2. Specific performance

Introduction

LO1

The law uses the word **capacity** to describe the ability of a person to do a legally valid act. Certain classes of persons have traditionally been treated as having a limited capacity to contract because the law sought to protect them in their contractual relations with others.

Three major classes of persons are given this special protection: minors, people who are mentally impaired, and intoxicated persons.

If either party entering a contract lacks the capacity to contract, the contract is **void** or **voidable,** depending on the kind of incapacity involved. Capacity to contract, however, is *presumed,* which means that the party who claims incapacity must prove it.

Minors' Contracts

The Reason for Minors' Incapacity

The idea behind minors' incapacity is that a minor (a person who is not legally considered to be an adult) may not be able to bargain effectively with older, more experienced persons. The courts responded to this idea by making minors' contracts *voidable*—that is, the minor is given the right to **disaffirm** (cancel) his or her contracts. Since the idea is to protect the minor, *only* the minor can disaffirm; adults who contract with minors are bound to the agreement unless the minor chooses to disaffirm. Thus, Webster Street, the landlord in the chapter opening, would not be able to disaffirm its rental contract with Matt and Pat if they wished to continue living in the apartment and continued to pay the rent.

NYC Mgmt. Group Inc. v. Brown-Miller

2004 U.S. Dist. LEXIS 8652 (2004)

FACTS

Jessica Stamm was a 16-year-old aspiring model from Canada. In March 2002, Jessica made a trip to New York City to secure representation in the New York market. During that trip, she entered a modeling contest with a first-place prize of a two-year contract with a guarantee of $100,000 against the winner's modeling earnings. On September 5, 2002, Jessica won the modeling contest. Later that month, an agreement was executed by Jessica, NY Models, and Debbie Stamm, Jessica's mother. The agreement provided that during the term of the contract, Jessica agreed to be represented by NY Models and its affiliates throughout the world and that NY Models was to be her exclusive representative as a print, television, or runway model, or otherwise on an exclusive basis. However, after only a few months relations soured between Jessica and NY Models. Jessica felt that NY Models made poor decisions and was interfering in her relationship with her parents. Thereafter she executed a written statement dated February 21, 2003, disaffirming "any agreement that I may have entered into, or which may have been entered into on my behalf, with New York Model Management." NY Models sued.

ISSUE

Can Jessica disaffirm the contract?

DECISION

Yes. Minors are entitled to disaffirm a contract. Such a disaffirmance functions to rescind the contract. The ability of a child to disaffirm a contract is grounded in the principle that adults contract with children at their peril. Certain exceptions to the right and power of disaffirmance nonetheless exist. For example, in certain circumstances a minor may not disaffirm a contract that a parent or guardian has entered into on the minor's behalf. Usually, the object of these agreements is to alter or limit liability that enables the minor to obtain some benefit, such as medical services or participation in an activity. The agreement Jessica entered is different. The agreement contains no release from liability, but rather resembles a standard service contract spelling out the performance required of each party to the contract—namely, of Jessica and the modeling agency. It is clear that while the contract requires Jessica to perform as a model, no performance is required of Debbie Stamm, who by signing merely signals her assent to her daughter's entry into the agreement without assuming any obligation of her own. Such indications of parental approval are not enough to override the right of the child to disaffirm her own contracts. Indeed, if both the minor and the parent sign a contract under which both are contractually bound to perform, the minor may disaffirm without affecting the parent's contractual obligation. There is nothing about Jessica's agreement with NY Models that appears to take it outside the statutory rubric allowing a minor to disaffirm her contract.

Ability to Disaffirm

LO2

The general rule is that minors may disaffirm their contracts at any time during their minority and for a reasonable time after attaining majority. In most states, a minor becomes an adult at 18 (the age of majority). What constitutes a "reasonable time" after majority depends on the facts and circumstances of each case. Generally, a minor may disaffirm by doing anything that clearly indicates to the other party an intent not to be bound by the terms of the contract. No one but the minor or the minor's personal representative (a guardian or the administrator of a deceased minor's estate) may exercise the right to disaffirm. Since the public policy of protecting minors is the basis of the capacity rule, that policy will influence the court in deciding whether a minor's contract can be disaffirmed when the contract was cosigned by the parent on the minor's behalf. The following case is illustrative.

If the minor's contract involves title to real estate, the minor cannot disaffirm until reaching majority. This is due to the special importance the law has traditionally accorded to ownership of real property. The rule is designed to protect a minor from improvidently disaffirming a transaction involving such property.

Woodman v. Kera LLC

785 N.W.2d 1 (Mich. Sup. Ct. 2010)

FACTS

Trent Woodman's fifth birthday party was held at Bounce Party, an indoor play area with inflatable play equipment operated by Kera LLC. During the party, Trent jumped off the slide and broke his leg. Trent's mother, on his behalf, filed a negligence suit, among other causes of action, against Kera. Before the party, Trent's father, as his guardian, had signed a waiver of liability. The waiver stated that there was some inherent risk in engaging in physical activity and that he acknowledged that he assumed the risk in exchange for being allowed to use Bounce Party. It also stated that he would hold Bounce Party harmless and waived his claim against it. Kera argued the suit must be dismissed on the basis of the waiver.

ISSUE

Was the waiver valid against the suit for the child's injuries?

DECISION

No. A parental preinjury waiver is a contract which Mr. Woodman voluntarily signed on behalf of his son. However, the well-established Michigan common law on this, established 130 years ago, is that a minor lacks the capacity to contract. Had Trent signed the waiver, it would be unenforceable. Likewise, a parent or guardian cannot contractually bind his minor ward. Additionally, a minor cannot empower an agent to contract in his behalf. While the company argues for the upholding of freedom of contract as the basis for upholding the contract, the rules about capacity constrain that freedom. If we changed the law, businesses might have reduced incentives to maintain their property appropriately, leading to increased injuries in children. If the legislature thinks the rule should be changed after considering the costs and benefits to society, we leave it to them to do so.

Ratification

The minor who does not disaffirm within a reasonable time after attaining majority is held to have **ratified** the contract and thereafter loses the right to disaffirm. The idea behind ratification is that adults who indicate an intent to be bound by contracts entered while still minors should be bound to those contracts and denied the right to disaffirm thereafter. As adults, they are assumed to have sufficient knowledge and experience to judge the wisdom of those contracts. By the same reasoning, minors, lacking such traits, cannot ratify contracts while still minors.

Any words or conduct on the part of a minor after reaching majority that clearly indicates an intent to be bound by the contract are enough for ratification. If the minor, after attaining majority, sells or gives away the consideration he or she received under the agreement, this is probably enough for ratification. Performing part of the contract after attaining majority, such as making payments or accepting some performance under the contract, is often treated as evidence of an intent to ratify. However, some states require a formal statement by the minor before they find ratification.

The Consequences of Disaffirming

Minors who successfully disaffirm a contract are entitled to the return of any consideration they have given the adult party to the contract. In return, minors are obligated to return to the adult any consideration still in their possession that they received from the adult.

Under common law, minors are entitled to the return of their property given as consideration, even if that property is possessed by a third party at the time of disaffirmance. Suppose, for example, that Katie trades in her motorcycle on the purchase of a car from B-2 Used Cars. B-2 then sells the motorcycle to Leann. After experiencing several problems with the car, Katie decides to disaffirm the car sales contract. She must return the car but is entitled to reclaim the motorcycle from Leann. Leann, in turn, has to try to get her money back from B-2. In order to protect innocent third parties such as Leann, the Uniform Commercial Code changed the common law. Minors whose contracts involve goods can no longer reclaim those goods from innocent third parties.

A difficult problem arises when the minor is no longer in possession of the consideration the adult gave, or when the consideration has been partially consumed or damaged, or has otherwise declined in value. For example, Rebecca (age 17) buys a 1998 Toyota from B-2 Used Cars. Two months later, she totally wrecks the car. Rebecca then calls B-2 and says she is disaffirming the contract and wants her $300 down payment back, plus the two $125 monthly payments she has made. The question is: Must Rebecca place B-2 in *status quo ante* (the position B-2 would be in if the contract had never come into existence) by paying the reasonable value of the car? The traditional common law answer is that the minor who no longer has the consideration the adult gave does not have any duty to place the adult in status quo. In the context of the case at the beginning of the chapter, Matt and Pat, who have used the apartment for two months, have nothing to return to Webster Street. They can still get their rent back.

Ethics in Action

Is it ethical for minors to disaffirm otherwise fair contracts when they know they will be unable to return the adult to the status quo?

Barriers to Disaffirmance

As you can see, the disaffirmance rule places severe hardship on adults in some cases. It was probably adopted as a deterrent, for what was to prevent adults from contracting with minors if the worst thing that could happen if the minor disaffirmed was that adults would get back whatever consideration they gave under the contract? Many courts today are reacting against the harshness of this rule by requiring the disaffirming minor to place the adult in status quo in some circumstances. This is especially true in cases where the minor is close to 18, the contract is fair, the adult was not at fault in contracting with the minor, and the adult would suffer an important loss if not returned to status quo.

Because of the potential unfairness to adults, a growing number of courts are also creating exceptions to the general rule that minors can disaffirm their contracts. This has happened, for example, in cases where minors have lied about their age. Similarly, state legislatures have passed statutes denying minors the right to disaffirm certain kinds of contracts. These statutes typically involve things such as contracts for medical care, life insurance, bank accounts, loans for college tuition, agreements to support children, contracts made while running a business, and employment contracts of minor professionals such as actors and athletes. Such contracts are usually required to be fair and sometimes require court approval.

In the following case, the singer LeAnn Rimes was represented by attorneys and a guardian ad litem and had approval for the contract from several courts. Thus, the court considered it fair to enforce its terms.

Rimes v. Curb Records

129 F.Supp.2d 984 (N.D. Tex. 2001)

FACTS

On April 17, 1995, LeAnn Rimes, who was 12, signed a recording contract with Curb Records, Inc. The contract had a forum selection clause requiring disputes to be heard in Davidson County, Tennessee. Rimes was represented by attorneys and a guardian ad litem. In June, the parties sought and obtained a court order removing Rimes's disability as a minor for the purposes of entering into the recording contract. Later, a dispute arose and Rimes attempted to avoid the forum selection clause on the basis of her minority.

ISSUE

Can Rimes avoid the forum selection clause on the basis of her minority?

DECISION

No. (The court's decision is in the form of a lyric to be sung to the tune of the LeAnn Rimes song "How Do I Live.")

LeAnn Rimes
A very rich and famous star
Wasn't so rich in times afar
But what a talent she had!
Enter Curb
To sign a contract, they hoped
After her talent they scoped
They saw the cash in her eyes
But LeAnn
Who at 12 was hardly dumb herself
Wanted to retain her future wealth
Oh
If you could have seen
Baby those attorneys changed everything
But so many lines!
They missed one thing.

Chorus
Why did you sign, LeAnn Rimes?
So long ago
Off on that choice of forum?
Your attorneys didn't know?
They made lots of changes, but one thing survived . . .
Forum clause, to that clause, what weight do we give?

Many times
Back and forth from judge to attorney
Both in Texas and in Tennessee
There was so much to review.
And LeAnn
With a guardian to oversee

(continued)

Rimes v. Curb Records *(concluded)*

She disavowed her own minority
Oh
Now she believes
Her age will invalidate everything
She ever signed
We must decide

(The second chorus is omitted, and the court instructs the next part to be sung to LeAnn Rimes's "I Need You." The first part, giving the history of court decisions on forum selection clauses is omitted. The court cites several cases, some of which are named in the following first line.)

Through and through! Mitsui, Amplican, Kessmann
Required proof! She's not met that burden.
While there's freedom as a judge, reinventing the rule
I won't do.

. . .

Although I
Would love to meet LeAnn Rimes
It's gonna have to be another time.
Oh
This case must now leave
Baby you must take away everything
Away from my court

. . .

This case now lives in Tennessee

. . .

Emancipation

LO3

Emancipation is the term used to describe the termination of a parent's right to receive services and wages from a child and to generally control him. Emancipation can occur, for example, when a minor marries or gets a job and moves away from home and the parent does not object. No formalities are required. Emancipation does not usually give the minor the capacity to contract, as is shown by the following case.

Sexton v. Sexton

2012 WL 2054859 (Ind. Ct. App. 2012)

FACTS

The Sextons were divorced in 2007. The mother was awarded custody of the children, K.S. and Ko., and the father was ordered to pay child support. While in high school, K.S. got a CNA license and began working at a nursing home. After she graduated, she began attending classes at the community college. She then learned she was pregnant, and two months later stopped working and attending classes. Her father then sought a court order to have her declared emancipated and that he no longer had to pay child support. He stated that K.S. refused to see him and informed him that he would no longer have a relationship with her or his grandson. K.S. continued to live with her mother, paid no rent, and had her expenses covered. She had a relationship with her son's father, who was employed. She only asked him to provide diapers. The court found that K.S. was emancipated and that her father no longer had to pay support. Her mother challenged this finding.

ISSUE

Was K.S. emancipated?

DECISION

Yes. Parents are required to provide support and protection for the welfare of their children until they reach the statutory age or until they no longer require care and support. Here, K.S., who is 19, has put herself outside her parents' care or control. One factor is that she had a child. Also, she continues to have a romantic relationship with the child's father, who provides the support K.S. requested. In addition, K.S. applied for and received some governmental assistance. She refuses to have a relationship with her father and also denies him a relationship with his grandson. These decisions are those of an adult not under the control and care of either parent. She is emancipated.

LO2

Misrepresentation of Age by Minors

Often, an adult faced with a minor's attempt to disaffirm a contract argues that the minor misrepresented his or her age. If the adult can prove this charge to the court's satisfaction, a question arises about what effect the misrepresentation should have on the minor's right to disaffirm. In theory, the right to disaffirm should not be affected, since one who lacks capacity cannot acquire it merely by claiming to have capacity.

In reality, however, the minor who misrepresents his or her age is not allowed to defraud adults by doing so. The courts have used several different methods to achieve this result. Some courts allow the minor to disaffirm but require the minor to place the adult in status quo. Others hold that the minor is *estopped* from raising the defense of minority and is therefore bound by the terms of the agreement. Many states allow the minor to disaffirm but hold the minor liable to the adult in tort for *deceit.*

LO4

Necessaries

Necessaries are generally defined as those things that are essential to a minor's continued existence and general welfare. Things that have traditionally been treated as necessaries include food, clothing, shelter, medical care, basic educational and/or vocational training, and the tools of a minor's trade. Items sold to a minor are not considered necessaries if the minor's parent or guardian has supplied or is willing to supply similar items. The court in the Webster Street chapter opening found that the apartment rental was not a necessary because the boys' parents were perfectly willing to have them live at home.

Minors are generally held liable on a *quasi contract* basis for the *reasonable value* of necessaries furnished to them. This is so because penalizing adults who supply minors with necessaries would not only produce an unfair result but also discourage other adults from supplying minors with necessaries. Since minors are liable for only the reasonable value of necessaries they actually receive, they do not have to pay the contract price of necessaries if it is greater than their reasonable value. (See Figure 13.2.)

Minors are also not liable for the value of necessaries they have purchased under a contract but have not received at the time they disaffirm. For example, Mary Smith, a minor, rented an apartment in Tudor Village for $800 a month. She signed a one-year lease. After living there three months, Mary decided to move to another apartment complex. Mary can disaffirm her lease because she lacked capacity to contract. She is liable for the reasonable value of three months' rent at Tudor Village, but she is not liable for the remaining nine months' rent (she has not actually received any benefits from the remainder of the lease). If she could convince the court that the reasonable value of living at Tudor Village was less than $800 a month, she would be liable only for the lesser amount.

FIGURE 13.2
Necessaries

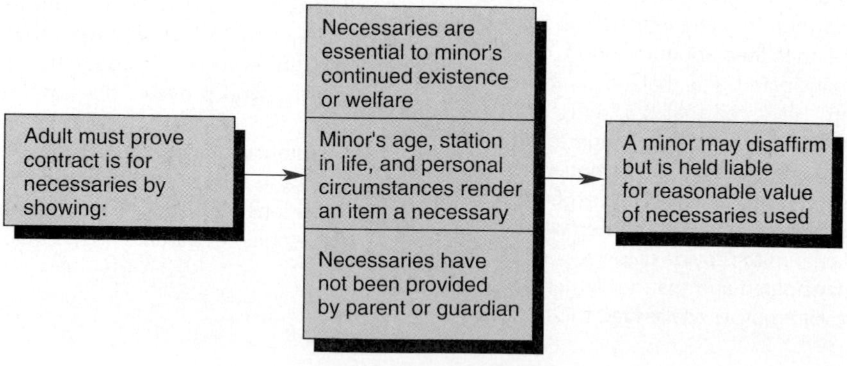

FIGURE 13.3
Minors' Right to Disaffirm

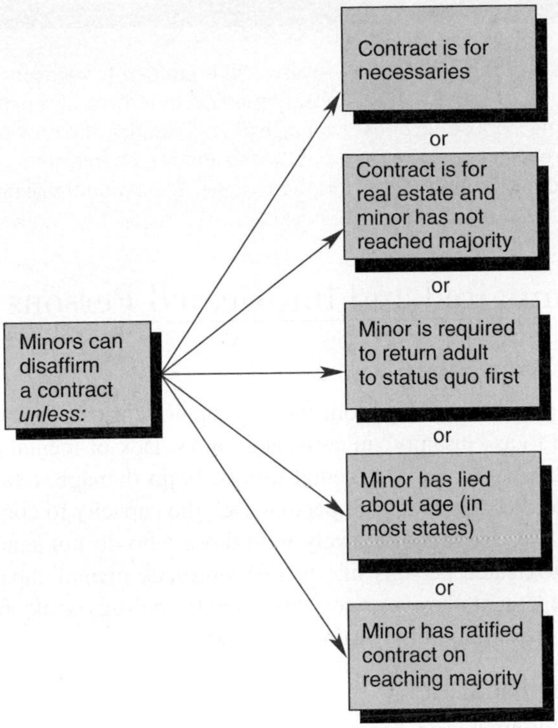

Whether a given item is considered a necessary depends on the facts of the particular case. The minor's age, station in life, and personal circumstances are all relevant to this issue. Thus, a car may be considered a necessary for a minor who needs it to get to work but not for a high school student who merely wishes to avoid riding the school bus. As a general rule, the definition of *necessary* is widening to include things commonly considered important by today's standards. The adult has the burden of proving that an item is a necessary. (See Figure 13.3.)

In re Estate of Reed v. Reed

No. 08CA0146 (Colo. Ct. App. Dec. 24, 2008)

FACTS

Charles Reed was injured in a car accident when he was four years of age. After neurological testing and consultation, he was diagnosed with post-traumatic stress disorder. He was referred to Aylesworth, a psychologist, who treated Charles. Charles, through his mother as legal guardian, filed a negligence action against the car driver. The suit was settled, and $15,000 was to be paid for Charles's claim, including his medical expenses. Aylesworth's bill of $7,703 was the largest portion of that. The parents declared bankruptcy and their bills were discharged, including Charles's medical bills. The $9,366 left from the settlement after attorneys' fees was to be put in a structured annuity to be paid to Charles when he reached maturity. Aylesworth objected, saying he had provided services to Charles pursuant to a signed agreement with the mother that he would be paid out of any settlement.

ISSUE

Did the doctor provide necessaries for which he can recover?

DECISION

Yes. Parents are primarily liable for the medical expenses of their minor children, and when the child sustains an injury, they have a legally recognized claim for reimbursement for those expenses. Here, though, Charles's mother brought the

(continued)

In re Estate of Reed v. Reed *(concluded)*

suit in his name; she did not bring it in her behalf. Thus, she had no right to encumber the amount recovered because children are protected against parents whose actions effectively foreclose a minor's right of recovery, regardless of motive. The agreement is not enforceable. However, Aylesworth is entitled to recovery because he provided necessary medical treatment. If a parent cannot or will not pay for a child's necessaries, the provider who provides them can get the fair and reasonable amount from the child's estate, if is there is one. This amount will be determined by the court.

Contracts of Mentally Impaired and Intoxicated Persons

Theory of Incapacity

Like minors, people suffering from mental impairment can lack the capacity to contract. Often referred to as "insanity" in cases and books, lack of mental capacity can be induced by a variety of causes such as mental illness, brain damage, retardation, or senility. The basic reason for holding that such persons lack the capacity to contract is that we presume they are unable to bargain effectively with those who do not share their disability. Many states treat intoxicated persons like people who lack mental capacity if, at the time they entered the agreement, they were so intoxicated from drugs or alcohol that they were unable to understand the nature of the business at hand.

The Test of Incapacity

LO5

The test usually applied in contract law is whether a party, at the time the contract was entered into, had sufficient mental capacity to understand the nature and effect of the contract. A person could be medically insane (e.g., suffering from paranoid delusions) but still have the legal capacity to contract. A person could be periodically insane but enter a binding contract during a lucid moment. A person could be senile, of less-than-ordinary intelligence, or highly neurotic but still be able to understand the nature of the transaction.

The Effect of Incapacity

If a court later finds that a person lacked mental capacity at the time the contract was entered into, the contract is *voidable* at the election of that person (or his or her guardian or administrator). A distinction is made between such agreements and those made by persons who had been adjudicated insane before entering the agreement. *Adjudicated* in this context means a general hearing was held on the person's mental competency, and the court determined that the person was of unsound mind and appointed a guardian or conservator of the person's estate. In most states, the agreements of persons who have been adjudicated insane are *void.*

Estate of Prickett v. Womersley

905 N.E.2d 1008 (Ind. Sup. Ct. 2009)

FACTS

Margaret Pricket became incapacitated and needed a guardianship. A bank was appointed to oversee her estate, and a daughter Carolyn and Real Services Inc. were appointed co-guardians of her person. Margaret lived with another daughter, Marilyn Womersley, until she died four years later. During the guardianship, Margaret signed an agreement stating that Womersley be paid for her services out

(continued)

of Margaret's estate. The guardian was not a party to this. Womersley filed a claim against Margaret's estate after her death for $546,000 for expenses and personal services she rendered to her mother. The estate objected, arguing that Margaret was incompetent, and that the expenses and services were gratuitous.

ISSUE
Is Margaret's agreement legally enforceable?

DECISION
No. In general, where one accepts valuable services from another, the law implies a promise to pay for them, especially in the case of general creditors. However, when family members living together render services in the family context, there is no implication that they will be paid. To rebut this presumption, there must be evidence of an express or implied contract. Womersley must show an intention on the part of the recipient to pay for the services, and an expectation of pay on the person rendering the services. While there is a signed, written statement that was witnessed by two persons that Marilyn should be paid for her services, no express or implied contract should be found here. Margaret had been legally declared incompetent and therefore was incapable of giving consent.

Necessaries
People lacking mental capacity are liable for the *reasonable value* of necessaries on the same basis and for the same reasons as minors.

The Right to Disaffirm
Like minors, people lacking mental capacity can disaffirm their contracts and, on disaffirmance, must return any consideration they received that they still have. Must they also place the other party in status quo? The answer depends on whether the other party was on notice of the person's lack of capacity. If there was no reason to know of the other party's lack of capacity, the contract cannot be disaffirmed without placing him or her in status quo. If, on the other hand, he or she knew or should have known of the other party's incapacity, the person lacking such capacity is allowed to disaffirm without restoring the status quo. This rule punishes those who may try to take advantage of people who lack capacity but protects those who have no such intent.

Ratification
People who regain their capacity can ratify their contracts just like a minor who attains majority. If the person dies or is adjudicated insane, his or her personal representative may ratify the contract. Ratification has the same effect in this context that it does in minors' contracts.

Concept Summary: Lack of Capacity

A contract is voidable due to:
1. Lack of capacity because of minority.
   Exceptions (i.e., situations where contracts are not voidable):
   a. Contract is for necessaries.
   b. Contract is ratified on reaching majority.
   c. Minor lied about age (in some states).
2. Lack of capacity because of mental impairment.
   Exceptions (i.e., situations where contracts are not voidable):
   a. If adjudicated insane, contract is void.
   b. Contract is for necessaries.
   c. Contract is ratified on regaining capacity.

Questions and Problem Cases

1. What is the effect of ratification on minors' contracts?
2. What are some barriers to disaffirmance?
3. Explain the concept of necessaries and how they are determined.
4. Dodson, 16, bought a truck for $4,900 in cash from Shrader. After driving it for nine months, he took it to a mechanic to check out a problem and was told there was a burned valve in the engine. Dodson drove the truck for two more months without repairs, until the engine "blew up." Later, the inoperable truck was struck while parked and damaged further. Dodson tendered the truck to Shrader and demanded his $4,900 back. Shrader refused to return the money without being paid the difference between the value of the truck as tendered, which was $500, and the $4,900. Must Dodson put Shrader in status quo?
5. Cooper, a minor, was a member of the Aspen Valley Ski Club for many years and was a competitive skier. Cooper and his mother signed a release of liability. It stated that he and his parents assumed all responsibility for risks that may occur. During training for a high-speed event, Cooper fell and hit a tree. He was seriously injured, including the loss of his vision. When Cooper sued the club, it cited the exculpatory clause. Should it be enforced? Why?
6. In 1996, Kobe Bryant was a 17-year-old high school basketball star. He declared his intention to forgo college and enter the NBA draft. Score Board, Inc. (SBI), contacted his agent about making a deal for marketing products relating to Bryant's career. SBI forwarded a signed licensing agreement to Bryant that gave SBI the right to make licensed products, such as trading cards, with Bryant's image. Bryant rejected it and sent a signed counteroffer to SBI. SBI signed it and put it in its files. Six weeks later, Bryant turned 18, and three days after that, he deposited SBI's check for $10,000 in his account. He then began performing his obligations under the agreement, including autograph signing sessions and public appearances. He continued to perform his duties for a year and a half. At that point, SBI entered bankruptcy and Bryant sought to repudiate the contract. Had Bryant ratified the contract? Why?
7. When actress Brooke Shields was 10, she posed nude in a bathtub for a series of photographs taken by Gary Gross for Playboy Press. Shields's mother signed a consent form that gave Gross the right to use the photos at any time for any purpose. The pictures were used several times, including use in a book by Shields about her life. When she was 17, Shields attempted to stop additional use of the photos by disaffirming the consent. Gross defended by citing a New York statute that allowed parents to give consent for minor models. Did New York's statute deny Shields her common law right to disaffirm the contract?
8. Patricia and William had a child, Gabrielle. Patricia had custody and William was ordered to pay child support. When Gabrielle was ready to apply for college, William agreed to provide her with food, shelter, and his financial information necessary to financial aid applications in exchange for his support obligation. Two weeks after moving into his house, Gabrielle moved out because she could not get along with him, and moved into her mother's trailer. She was dropped from the junior college because she did not complete the financial aid forms. Gabrielle next enrolled at a local college and worked there for the catering service. She was then in a car accident and missed too many classes to complete the semester. Her father never provided his tax information, and as a result, Gabrielle was billed $1,689. The debt was turned over to a collection agency. When Gabrielle then moved in with her mother, her father sued to have her declared emancipated. Should the court relieve her father of having to pay because Gabrielle was emancipated? Explain why.

9. The Home Savings and Loan Association loaned Haith money to refinance her mortgage and remodel her home. Haith was later adjudicated incompetent and a guardian was appointed for her. The guardian sought to have the loan set aside on the basis of Haith's incompetency despite the fact that Haith could not return what she had received. Will the guardian succeed?
10. A minor bought an Ernie Banks baseball card from a baseball card store. The card was marked $12, and the inexperienced clerk who sold it did not know the store owner, who was gone at the time of the sale, meant it to be sold for $1,200. Can the owner get the card back because of the minor's lack of capacity? Why?

Chapter 14

Voluntary Consent

Learning Objectives

After you have studied this chapter, you should be able to:

1. Explain the reason voluntary consent is required for an enforceable contract.
2. Understand the remedy for lack of consent and who can assert it.
3. Describe the elements of misrepresentation.
4. Describe the elements of fraud.
5. Explain the difference between duress and undue influence.
6. Contrast mutual and unilateral mistake.

Johnson bought a house from Davis for $310,000. He had noticed peeling plaster and ceiling stains in the family room but the sellers implied they were caused by a minor window problem that had been repaired. A few days later, after a heavy rain, he discovered water gushing into the house and was told that $25,000 in repairs to the roof and walls were required.

- Do buyers have a duty to make their own investigations before entering contracts?
- Do sellers have a duty to disclose latent defects?
- Can Johnson disaffirm the contract?

FIGURE 14.1
Voluntary Consent

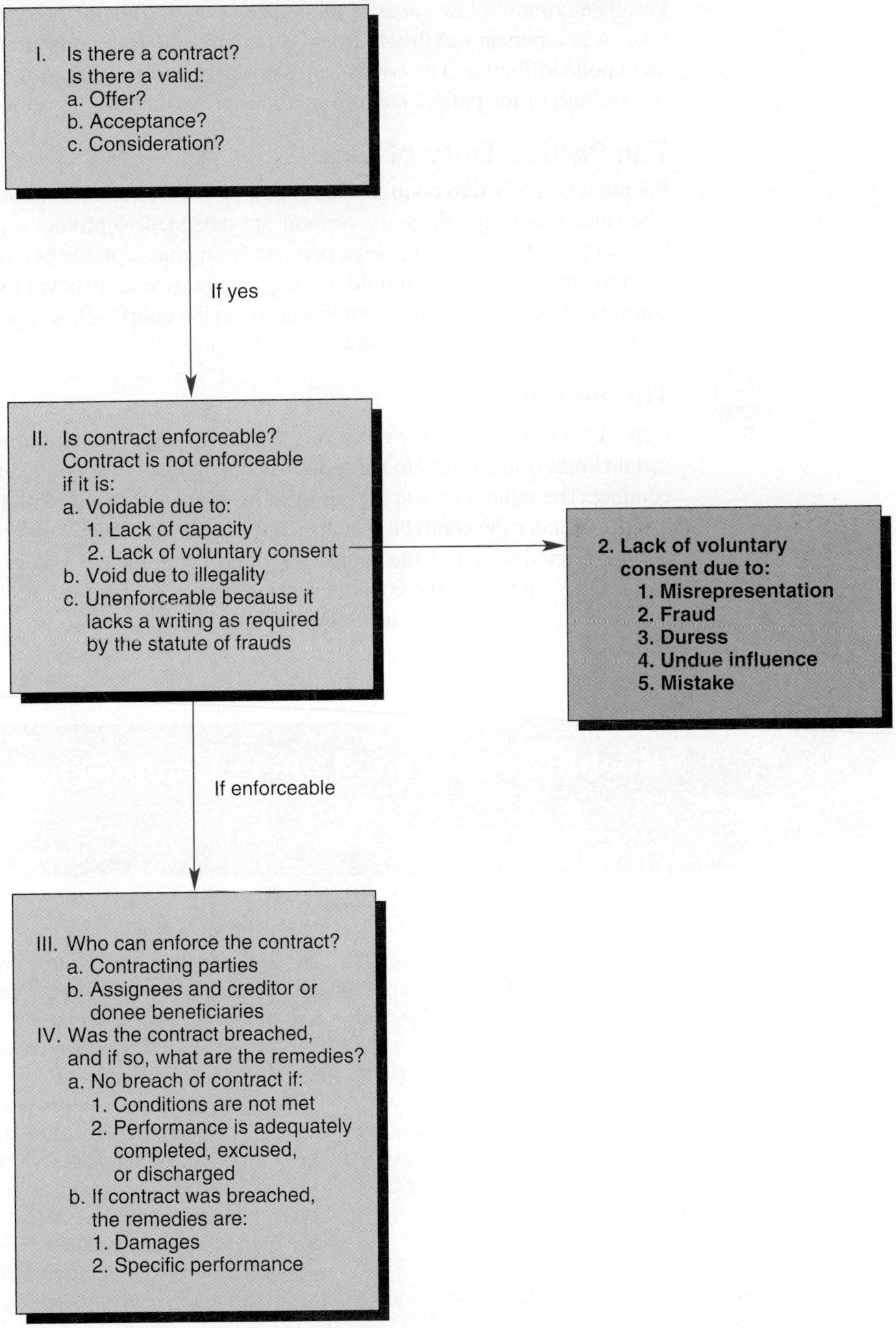
I. Is there a contract?
Is there a valid:
a. Offer?
b. Acceptance?
c. Consideration?
If yes
II. Is contract enforceable?
Contract is not enforceable if it is:
a. Voidable due to:
1. Lack of capacity
2. Lack of voluntary consent
b. Void due to illegality
c. Unenforceable because it lacks a writing as required by the statute of frauds
2. Lack of voluntary consent due to:
1. Misrepresentation
2. Fraud
3. Duress
4. Undue influence
5. Mistake
If enforceable
III. Who can enforce the contract?
a. Contracting parties
b. Assignees and creditor or donee beneficiaries
IV. Was the contract breached, and if so, what are the remedies?
a. No breach of contract if:
1. Conditions are not met
2. Performance is adequately completed, excused, or discharged
b. If contract was breached, the remedies are:
1. Damages
2. Specific performance

Introduction

LO1 The Need for Real Consent

Even if the facts and circumstances surrounding a case indicate that the parties reached an agreement, that agreement must be **voluntary** to be enforceable. This is so because the idea that a contract is a voluntary agreement between the parties is the basis of contract law. The common law came to recognize several kinds of behavior that could operate to take away a person's ability to freely enter into a contract: misrepresentation, fraud, duress, and undue influence. The courts also came to recognize that a mistake of fact on the part of one or both of the parties could sometimes prevent a true agreement from being reached.

The Parties' Duty of Care

People who enter into contracts are required to exercise reasonable caution and judgment. The rules requiring voluntary consent are designed to protect a party to a contract from innocent errors on his or her own part and from unacceptable behavior by the other party to the agreement. A person should use reasonable care to discover everything relevant to the contract he or she is about to enter. Rarely do the courts allow a party to avoid responsibility for a carelessly made promise.

LO2

The Remedy

Contracts entered into as a result of misrepresentation, fraud, duress, undue influence, and certain kinds of mistakes are **voidable.** The injured party (or parties) may **rescind** (cancel) the contract. The injured person returns what he or she has received and recovers what he or she has given under the contract. If no performance has yet been rendered when the grounds for rescission are discovered, the injured party may notify the other party that he or she **disaffirms** (denies the validity of) the contract. If the other party sues for breach of contract, the injured party can use lack of voluntary consent as a defense.

Koehlinger v. State Lottery Commission

933 N.E.2d 534 (Ind. Ct. App. 2010)

FACTS

Indiana has a lottery that included a scratch-off game called Cash Blast. The lottery posted information about the number of prizes not yet claimed on its website. The odds of winning each prize ranging from $10 to $250,000 were one in 3.29. The return-to-player was approximately 73.4 percent of the money spent. In 2005, a computer error caused the website to overestimate the number of unclaimed prizes. Koehlinger and others sued the lottery claiming misrepresentation, among other theories, and they sought rescission of their contract and return of their money.

ISSUE

Should the ticket buyers be able to rescind their contracts?

DECISION

Yes. The plaintiffs entered into a contract when they bought the tickets. It is a well-settled doctrine that where a party to a contract makes a misrepresentation as to a material existing fact, and one justifiably relies and acts on that fact to his detriment, the one who relies can rescind the contract, whether the falsity of the representation was known to the party making it or not. It is undisputed that the lottery misrepresented the number of Cash Blast tickets remaining. The plaintiffs had no means of discovering the true number and thus justifiably relied on it. That misrepresentation was material. There is evidence that some of the players relied to their detriment on the material misrepresentation of the odds. Those that can prove such reliance are entitled to rescission.

Ratification

Those who discover that they have been the victim of misrepresentation, fraud, duress, undue influence, or mistake must act promptly to rescind or disaffirm their contracts. The person who waits for an unreasonable time after discovery to complain may be held to have **ratified** the contract and may lose the power to rescind. The idea behind the doctrine of ratification is simple: One who waits too long to complain has indicated satisfaction with the agreement despite the initial lack of true consent.

Misrepresentation

LO3

The basic idea of misrepresentation is that one of the parties to a contract created in the mind of the other party a mistaken impression about an important fact or facts concerning the subject of the contract. Acting in reliance on this mistaken belief, the victimized party entered into a contract he or she would not otherwise have entered if the full truth had been known. The elements of **misrepresentation** are ordinarily given as *misrepresentation* of a *material fact justifiably relied on* to the *detriment* of (causing harm to) the person relying. Note that a mere untrue assertion is not sufficient. A person seeking to avoid a contract on the ground of misrepresentation must prove all of these elements.

Knowledge of Falsity

Note also that none of the elements listed above requires any proof that persons guilty of the misrepresentation know that their statement is untrue. Misrepresentation can result from an honest mistake or negligence on the part of the misrepresenter. This is so because of the long-standing equitable principle that one who makes a statement bears the risk of its truth.

Materiality

A *material* fact is one that would contribute to a reasonable person's decision to enter the contract. Materiality is determined by the circumstances of each particular case. For example, assume that Bob, who was living in Illinois, bought real estate by mail through Fran, a Florida real estate agent. Fran sent Bob several pictures of the house and a general description of the house and its neighborhood. Included in the description was the statement that the house was "within easy walking distance of schools, churches, and shopping centers." After moving in, Bob discovers that the closest school is four miles away. Is this misrepresentation sufficiently material to justify rescission?

The answer depends on who Bob is. If Bob is a retired, childless widower, the misrepresentation could be judged to be immaterial. On the other hand, if Bob has a child in school, the nearness of schools could well be considered material.

Fact versus Opinion

In addition to being material, an actionable misrepresentation must concern a present or past *fact*. This is another way of saying that the subject of the misrepresentation must be *knowable*. Statements about future events ("This stock will double in price in the next two years") or statements of opinion ("This is the most attractive house in the neighborhood") do not serve as a basis for rescission, although people may, in fact, rely on them. One of the constant problems in this area is whether a given statement was mere *puffing* (a term used to indicate sales talk) or amounted to an actionable misstatement of material fact. For example, the seller who says, "This is a good car" is probably puffing, whereas the seller who says, "This car was owned by an elderly man who drove it only twice a week" is probably guilty of misrepresentation if the car was actually used by a drag racer. Often the result will turn on whether the person making the statement had superior knowledge and bargaining power.

FIGURE 14.2
Misrepresentation

Defendant:	Misrepresented a fact	→	The fact was material			
Plaintiff:	Relied on the fact	→	Reliance was justified	→	Plaintiff was harmed by reliance	

Justifiable Reliance

There are basically two ideas behind making justifiable reliance an element of misrepresentation. The first is the idea that there should be some *causal connection* between a misrepresentation and the complaining party's entry into the contract. If the complaining party knew the truth, or for some other reason did not in fact rely on the misrepresentation, why should it be a basis for canceling the contract? The second idea behind justifiable reliance is that parties who enter a contract must take reasonable steps to discover the facts about the contracts they enter into. So, if the facts are readily discoverable by either party (e.g., by reasonable inspection or because they are a matter of public record), a party generally is not allowed to rely on the other party's statements about them.

The *Restatement (Second) of Contracts* and many courts are placing less stress on the justifiable reliance requirement. However, as a general rule, people are still required to make a reasonable effort to watch out for themselves.

Detriment

The courts do not allow a person who claims to have been victimized by a misrepresentation to cancel the contract unless he or she can show some *detriment* (injury) as a result of the misrepresentation. Ordinarily, however, if one can prove the other elements of misrepresentation (particularly the "material fact" element), it is fairly easy to show injury. All that must be shown is that the complaining party would be in a better position if things were as they had been represented.

Fraud

LO4

In some cases, the complaining party may be able to prove that the party who made the misstatement knew or should have known that it was untrue. **Fraud** is intentional misrepresentation. To prove fraud, one must prove all the elements of misrepresentation plus two additional elements: that the misrepresentation was (1) *knowingly* made with the (2) *intent to deceive* (technically called *scienter*).

What Is a "Knowingly Made" Misstatement?

Clearly, if it can be shown that a defendant actually knew that what he or she said was untrue, a "knowing" misstatement has been proven. It is also sufficient to show that the defendant possessed enough information so that he should have known the truth, even if he actually did not. So, if Acme Used Cars tells Mary that the Pinto is in excellent running order although Acme has not bothered to check out the statement of the previous owner that the car was making strange noises and there might be something wrong with it, Mary could probably show fraud. Acme should have known, based on the prior owner's statements, that something was probably wrong and should have checked it out. Mary could also show that Acme made the statement *recklessly.* Making statements without sufficient information to believe they are true (recklessness) is sufficient to constitute fraud.

In the chapter opening Johnson case, the seller of the home must have known or at least was recklessly ignorant of the fact that there were major problems with the roof. When

Johnson inquired about the stains, and the seller implied the problem was due to a window that had been fixed, the response was sufficient for fraud and Johnson could rescind the contract.

Intent to Deceive

Scienter refers to the mental state of the defendant. The courts generally infer an intent to deceive from the fact that the defendant knowingly made a misstatement to a plaintiff who was likely to rely on it. The defendant's motivation is irrelevant; she may actually believe that she is doing the plaintiff a favor. For example, Beth is trying to sell her friend Mike a car. Beth thinks that the car is a good one and that the price is a real bargain. Beth knows, however, that the car's odometer was disconnected for a year and that the car has much higher mileage on it than the odometer indicates. She tells Mike that the car "has only 20,000 miles on it" (the figure the odometer shows). Beth is guilty of fraud.

Taking action to conceal a fact also indicates *scienter.* So if Beth turned back the odometer from 30,000 to 20,000 miles but said nothing about the mileage to Mike, she would be guilty of fraud. Likewise, concealing something in fine print in the middle of a lengthy document in the reasonable belief that the other party will not read it can be evidence of fraud.

Jordan v. Knafel

378 Ill. App.3d 219 (Ill. Ct. App. 2007)

FACTS

Knafel was performing as a singer in a hotel bar in Indianapolis in 1989 at the same time the Chicago Bulls were playing in the city. An NBA referee introduced her to Michael Jordan over the phone. She and Jordan had phone conversations during the spring and summer. In December 1989, three months after Jordan married his wife, they met in Chicago and had unprotected sex. In November 1990, they again had relations. In early 1991 Knafel learned she was pregnant and was convinced it was Jordan's baby. Knafel alleged Jordan was worried about his image and product endorsements, and after she refused to abort the fetus, he proposed a settlement of $5 million when he retired from professional basketball in exchange for her not filing a paternity suit and keeping their involvement confidential. Jordan paid her hospital and medical costs when the baby was born, plus $250,000 for her "mental pain and anguish arising from her relationship with him." A month later blood samples showed Jordan was not the father. In 1993, Jordan retired, but in 1995, he returned to play. Two years after Jordan retired in 1998, Knafel asked for the $5 million. Jordan alleged it was an extortion attempt, and even if there was an agreement, it was unenforceable due to fraud.

ISSUE

Is there sufficient evidence of intent and justifiable reliance?

DECISION

No. Fraud in the inducement of a contract makes it voidable at the election of the injured party. In order for there to be fraud, he must prove the representation was: (1) one of a material fact; (2) made for the purpose of inducing the other party to act; (3) known to be false or not actually believed by the maker; and (4) was relied on by the other party to his detriment. Knafel represented that she was pregnant with Jordan's child. His paternity was not a subject of discussion at the time of the settlement and the settlement was not contingent on it. Knafel alleges his only motive was to protect his image and his lucrative endorsements. While a general fear of public exposure of their relationship may have been a factor in the settlement, it need not be the decisive factor. Knafel's own statement that Jordan was the father was material and a substantial factor in inducing Jordan to act. If not, her agreement not to file a paternity suit would have been a mere pretext to extort money. Since Jordan was not the father, Knafel must have known at the time that she stated he was that there was uncertainly as to this fact. When a party claims to know a fact with a certainty yet knows that she does not have that certainty, that constitutes a fraudulent misrepresentation. Jordan relied on the misrepresentation, and therefore the agreement is voidable by him.

Fraud by Silence

Does a party to a contract have a duty to disclose to the other party all the material facts he or she knows about the subject of the contract? The original common law position on this issue was *caveat emptor* (let the buyer beware). The seller could remain silent without fear of being found guilty of fraud. Only actual statements by the seller could serve as a basis for fraud. The duty, therefore, was placed on buyers to ask the right questions of the seller, forcing the seller to make statements about the subject of the sale.

Today, however, many courts recognize that *caveat emptor* often produced unfair results. Some buyers simply do not know enough to ask the right questions about the subject of the sale; thus, many courts are recognizing a limited duty on the part of the seller to disclose material facts. Generally, this duty is limited to material facts that the buyer could not have discovered by reasonable inspection and would be unlikely to inquire about.

Gomez-Jimenez v. New York Law School

2012 WL 934387 (N.Y. Sup.)

FACTS

Gomez-Jimenez was a graduate of the New York Law School. He and other students sued the school for fraud and misrepresentation, claiming that the employment and salary information put out by the school was deceptive and that the school inflated its statistics in order to recruit and retain students. They alleged the school concealed or failed to disclose that their data included temporary and part-time positions, including those the school temporarily hired in order to make its statistics look better. Additionally, they claimed the school reported mean salaries that were calculated on information submitted by a deliberately small, specifically selected subset of graduates. This misleading information led them to enroll in law school to obtain, at a very high price, a law degree that proved less valuable in the marketplace than they were led to believe. They sued to get a refund of their tuition, among other damages.

ISSUE

Was there fraudulent concealment?

DECISION

No. To state a claim for fraudulent misrepresentation, plaintiff must show a misrepresentation of a material omission of fact that was false and known to be false by the defendant, made for the purpose of inducing the other party to rely on it, justifiable reliance, and injury. A claim for fraudulent concealment must also include a showing that there was a duty to disclose. This the plaintiffs did not do. Although there is no question that the type of information published by the school left students with an incomplete, if not false, impression of the school's placement success, this statistical "gamesmanship" was not adequately misleading. There was no representation as to whether the work cited was full or part time. Further, the school disclosed that the salary information was based on a small sample of self-reporting graduates. Thus, there is no fraud. Furthermore, plaintiffs have not alleged any special relationship or fiduciary obligation requiring a duty of full and complete disclosure by the defendant. Thus, there was no fraudulent concealment. We are not unsympathetic to plaintiffs' concerns, and we are troubled by the unquestionably less than candid and incomplete disclosures. Defendant had at least an ethical duty of absolute candor, but not a legal duty,

Some courts consider the duty to disclose to be especially important in the consumer real estate sales area. Since the purchase of a home is the largest investment most consumers make, courts are increasingly protecting that investment by holding knowledgeable developers, sellers, and their agents liable when they fail to reveal defects or problems that seriously undermine the value of the home. In the chapter opening case, the seller may have had a duty to disclose major defects in the roof that allowed water to "cascade in" even if Johnson had not inquired about the stains.

Legislatures are also expanding the situations in which persons must make disclosures. For example, the Truth in Lending Act[1] and federal securities laws[2] both mandate that certain information be disclosed. Additionally, several states have passed laws requiring specific disclosures in real estate transactions.

As use of the Internet grows and purchases are increasingly made online, fraud also grows apace. There are several websites giving advice on how to avoid this problem: http://www.fraud.org, www.nclnet.org/shoppingonline, and www.nclnet.org/essentials/security.html. Some of the suggestions include things you learned in other chapters, such as understanding the offer or that a legitimate settler will give you the details about the product or services, the total price, delivery time, warranty information, and refund and cancellation policies. Other examples are that the safest way to pay is by credit card because these charges can be disputed; also, beware of downloads from unfamiliar sites because they can also be accompanied by the theft of your phone number and result in expensive phone charges. Of course, promises of easy money are highly suspect, and requests for personal information when you are not paying for something are unlikely to be legitimate.

Ethics in Action

When does a party have an ethical duty to disclose information to the other party to the contract?

Fraud in the Execution

Fraud in the execution involves misstatements about the content or legal effect of something usually contained in a form or preprinted contract. People who relied on the misstatement rather than reading the document for themselves were seen as not having justifiably relied and thus usually could not claim fraud. While this rule is still true, if the signer was in some way prevented or discouraged from reading the contract, or if a special relationship involving trust and confidence existed between the parties and this led to the person's not understanding the nature of the document she was signing, fraud in the execution resulted. This type of fraud generally prevents a contract from being created.

The Remedy for Fraud

The buyer who can prove fraudulent misstatements or failure to disclose on the part of the seller has a choice of remedies. He or she may *rescind* the contract, like the buyer who can prove only misrepresentation. A defrauded buyer also has the option of *affirming* the contract and suing in tort for damages resulting from the fraud. This is so because the elements of fraud are the same as the elements for the tort of **deceit.** The buyer could recover actual damages resulting from the fraud (usually the difference between the true value of what the buyer bought and its represented value). So, if Bob bought a car from Frank for $500 and Frank told him it was in excellent condition, knowing its transmission was bad, Bob can choose his remedies. He can rescind the contract, return the car, and get back his $500; or he can keep the

[1] See Chapter 46 for further discussion of this act.

[2] See Chapter 31 for further discussion of these laws.

car and sue for $100 (the difference between the purchase price and the true value of the car with a defective transmission). Bob might also be able to get punitive damages since fraud is intentional wrongdoing.

FIGURE 14.3
Fraud

Defendant:	*Intentionally* misrepresented a fact	→	The fact was material				
Plaintiff:	Relied on the fact	→	Reliance was justified	→	Plaintiff was harmed by reliance		

Duress and Undue Influence

LO5

General Nature

Duress and *undue influence* are terms used to describe situations in which one party to an agreement interfered with the other party's ability to resist entering into the agreement. The basic idea of **duress** is that one of the parties, by making some *threat of harm,* forced the other party to enter an agreement he or she would not otherwise have entered. **Undue influence** is closely related to duress, but it exists only when the parties had some confidential relationship at the time of the contract. The basic idea of undue influence is that the dominant person in a confidential relationship took advantage of the other party to the relationship by getting the other party to enter into an unfavorable agreement.

Contracts made under duress and undue influence are *voidable* because the injured party has been deprived of the ability to make a free choice. Their promise is not a voluntary one as required by contract law. Note that both duress and undue influence must be exerted at the time the contract is entered into; exerting such force later will not make the contract voidable.

Duress

The common law courts originally required a threat of physical injury before they would find duress. Modern courts require only that the *threat* be a *wrongful* one.

Whether an act is wrongful depends on the facts and circumstances of the particular case. A threat to breach a contract can be wrongful if it appears that the person making the threat is attempting to extort additional payments when he has no reasonable justification for breaching the contract. Threatening economic harm or withholding someone's property without justification can also be wrongful. To be sufficient for duress, the threatened harm must be such that a disastrous loss would occur if the threat were carried out. It is not wrongful to take advantage of someone's difficult financial condition to drive a hard bargain if the bargainer did not create the difficulty.

The *Restatement* and most courts take the position that a threat of criminal prosecution is wrongful pressure even though the person making the threat has good reason to believe that the other person has committed a crime.

The courts have generally held that the threat of a well-founded civil suit is not duress. If this were not so, every party who settled a suit out of court could later argue duress. If, however, the threat is used to force the party to enter an unfair transaction that is unrelated to the rights involved in the threatened suit, this can be duress. For example, a husband in the process of divorcing his wife may threaten to sue for custody of their children (something he has a legal right to do) unless she gives him stock she owns in his company. The threat of an unfounded civil suit could also constitute duress if the fear of the expense of defending the suit forced the threatened party to enter an agreement against his or her will.

If the act is wrongful, the basic question the courts ask is whether that act effectively deprived the other party of his or her ability to resist entering the agreement. Did the wrongful act leave the person with no reasonable alternative but to enter the contract? See Figure 14.4.

FIGURE 14.4
Duress

Defendant:	Threatened	→	Threat was wrongful
Plaintiff:	Free will was overcome	→	Entered into a contract that would not otherwise have been entered into

David D. Murray v. Dianne E. Murray

2011 Ohio 1546 (Ohio Ct. App. 2011)

FACTS

After 11 years of marriage, David sought a divorce. Over the next three years the parties fought over various issues. After court hearings and hours of mediation, the court held a final hearing to resolve the issues, and an agreement was read into the record. After that, Dianne expressed dissatisfaction with its terms and claimed she had signed the agreement under duress. She claimed she felt pressure during the whole process which she failed to disclose to either her counsel or the mediator.

ISSUE

Was there sufficient evidence of duress to refuse to enforce the agreement?

DECISION

No. Settlement and compromise are highly favored by the law. In a divorce proceeding, neither a change of heart nor poor legal advice is a reason to set aside a settlement agreement. Mediation is, by definition, a procedure by which the parties negotiate a resolution to their dispute with the assistance of a third party mediator. Although a nonbinding process, a settlement agreement reached through a mediation process is as enforceable as any contractual agreement. To avoid a contract on the basis of duress, a party must prove coercion by the other party to the contract and that circumstances permitted no other alternative but to assent. It is not enough to show that one assented merely because of difficult circumstances. Here, the parties spent many hours in mediation with their attorneys present, and there seemed to be an agreement at least twice to which Dianne later objected. Dissatisfaction with or general remorse about signing a consent agreement do not, however, constitute duress. Dianne merely had a change of heart.

Undue Influence

The basic idea behind undue influence is to protect the old, the timid, and the physically or mentally weak from those who gain their confidence and attempt to take advantage of them. Victims of undue influence must have the mental capacity to contract but lack the ability to adequately protect themselves against unscrupulous persons who gain their confidence. In most states, a confidential relationship raises a presumption of undue influence that the benefiting party must disprove.

Most of the cases in which undue influence is charged involve relatives, friends, or longtime advisors (such as lawyers or bankers) of an elderly or sick person, who are alleged to have gotten the victim to make gifts or sales at unfair prices. For example, Marge Johnson, age 84, spent her last five years living with her daughter Joan. Marge had been in poor health and was unable to care for herself. When Marge died, her other heirs discovered that two weeks before her death, Marge had sold her house to Joan for $90,000. The market value of the house at the time of the sale was $300,000. The other heirs may attempt to have the sale set aside, arguing that it is the product of undue influence. Joan will probably argue that Marge knew the true value of the house but sold it to her at the lower price as a reward for taking care of her for so many years. Whether this was, in fact, undue influence depends on Marge's mental state, Joan's behavior, and Marge's knowledge of the value of the property. Each case is very fact-specific, as the following illustrates.

Compton v. First National Bank of Monterrey

No. 66A03-0906-CV249 (Ind. Sup. Ct. Jan. 19, 2010)

FACTS

Stephen Compton had six children. He provided for them in his will to varying degrees. One son, Gregory, was to receive 150 acres of farmland. Stephen also executed a power of attorney naming son Scott his attorney. Three years later, Stephen was hospitalized with end-stage renal disease. While in the hospital, Stephen sold the land that had been set aside for Gregory to Scott and his wife. He also executed a contract purchasing Scott and Angela's house and an adjoining two acres and put that in Gregory's name. He was released from the hospital a week later, and died the next month. The will was admitted to probate. The Monterrey Bank, which was appointed personal representative, noted that the sales had not been completed due to Stephen's death. It then sought completion of the contracts. Three of Stephen's children, including Gregory, challenged the completion of the contracts alleging that they were due to undue influence, that Scott had forged his father's signature, and that Scott had power of attorney over Stephen. The notary testified that Stephen did in fact sign the documents and that he understood what he was doing. Compton talked about changing his will and worked on real estate transactions after he was released from the hospital and outside of Scott's presence.

ISSUE

Was there undue influence?

DECISION

No. A person of sound mind has the right to dispose of property as he sees fit, no matter how inequitable or unjust it may appear to others. However, there is a common law presumption of undue influence when an attorney or someone with power of attorney benefits from the transaction. The power of attorney creates a fiduciary relationship. Undue influence is defined as the exercise of sufficient control over a person to cause that person to do what he would not have done if such control had not been exercised. This presumption can be overcome by evidence. Here, however, Scott did not use the power of attorney to do the transactions. Although Scott used his own attorney to draw up the contracts, and took them to the hospital, there is sufficient evidence that Stephen wanted the actions taken and he was competent to make that decision. The contracts are enforceable.

Ethics in Action

The undue influence rules generally are used to protect the very old or very young. Do we have special ethical duties to these classes of people? Why or why not? Are there other classes to which we owe special duties of care?

Mistake

The Nature of Mistake

The term *mistake* is used in contract law to describe the situation in which one or both of the parties to an agreement acted under an untrue belief about the existence or non-existence of a *material fact.* The things that were said about materiality and fact in the section on misrepresentation hold true in mistake cases. In **mistake** cases, unlike fraud and misrepresentation cases in which the victim is also acting under a mistaken belief about the facts, the mistaken belief about the facts is not the product of a misstatement by the other party. Mistake in this sense does not include errors of judgment, ignorance, or a party's mistaken belief that he or she will be able to fulfill certain obligations under a contract.

The reason behind the idea of mistake is that mistake may prevent the "meeting of the minds" required by contract law. In deciding mistake cases, courts often seem to be trying more obviously to "do justice" than in other kinds of cases. This is why decisions in mistake cases sometimes seem to depart from the announced rules of law dealing with mistake.

LO6

Mutual Mistake

Mistake cases are classed as **mutual** or **unilateral,** depending on whether both or only one of the parties was acting under a mistaken belief about a material fact. Mutual mistake is always a basis for granting rescission of the contract at the request of either party. Clearly, no meeting of the minds took place and therefore no true contract was ever formed.

Mutual mistake can arise in many different ways. The parties may unintentionally use a term in their agreement that is *ambiguous*—capable of being honestly understood in two different ways. For example, on August 13, 2002, Apex Imports, Inc., of New York City, orders a shipment of Oriental rugs from Bristol Carpets, Ltd., of Bristol, England. Apex requests that the carpets be shipped on the *China Seas,* a ship scheduled to leave Liverpool, England, on August 15, 2002, for New York. Bristol accepts Apex's order, thinking Apex means another ship with the same name scheduled to leave Liverpool on December 1, 2002. Since Apex was unaware of the second ship, its order did not specify a shipment date. Neither party to the agreement is at fault, and either may elect to rescind the agreement. The test for determining the existence of a mutual mistake is, however, an *objective* one. This means that objective factors may remove what first looks like ambiguity.

The parties may also be mistaken about the subject matter of their agreement. For example, Kathy owns a Mercedes and a Porsche. Bob has always wanted a Porsche and knows Kathy owns one. Kathy decides to sell her Mercedes and buy a BMW. A mutual friend of Bob and Kathy tells Bob, "Kathy's selling her car." Thinking Kathy is selling the Porsche (he does not know she also has a Mercedes), Bob calls Kathy and says, "I'll give you $9,500 for your car." Kathy, thinking Bob is talking about the Mercedes, says, "You've got a deal." Obviously, there is not meeting of the minds in this case. The *Jordan* case on the next page also involves this issue.

Unilateral Mistake

The basic rule is that if only one of the parties to the agreement is acting under a mistaken belief, this is not grounds for rescission. The reasoning behind the rule is that the law does not want to give all people who want to get out of a contract an easy exit by allowing them to argue

Jordan v. Knafel

378 Ill. App.3d 219 (Ill. Ct. App. 2007)

This is the same case you saw earlier in the chapter. In addition to alleging fraud, Jordan defended against Knafel's claim for $5 million on the basis of mutual mistake.

ISSUE

Is there sufficient evidence to show mutual mistake?

DECISION

Mutual mistake requires a mistake by both parties as to a basic assumption on which the contract was made, and that the assumption had a material effect on the agreed exchange of performances. If this is proved, the contract is voidable by the adversely affected party unless he bears the risk of the mistake. Even if Knafel's representation that Jordan was the father was made in good faith, it was ultimately mistaken. The issue of paternity went to a basic assumption on which the contract was made because it was the consideration for the alleged settlement of her paternity claim. Her certainty had a material effect on the agreed exchange of performances. Jordan did not bear the risk of mistake because he was not obliged to assume that Knafel had another sexual partner at the time of conception in the face of Knafel's categorical representation. Jordan is entitled to rescind the agreement on the basis of mutual mistake.

mistake. It also wants to encourage people to exercise reasonable care to find out all the facts when entering their agreements. Therefore, it is often said that if a person's own negligence is the cause of his or her mistake, relief will not be granted.

However, when one looks at the cases involving unilateral mistake, it appears that the courts often grant rescission if they are convinced that a person was truly mistaken and that a serious injustice would result from enforcing the agreement. This is sometimes true even when the mistaken party was slightly negligent.

Other factors that the courts weigh when deciding whether to grant relief are whether relief can be granted without causing the other party to suffer a material loss and whether the nonmistaken party knew or should have known of the mistake. If the nonmistaken party will not be hurt by allowing rescission, the courts are more inclined to do so. If someone must bear a loss as a result of the agreement, the courts are inclined to impose the loss on the mistaken party by not granting rescission unless it appears that the other party should have known of the mistake. In such a case, the courts are likely to grant rescission rather than allow one party to take advantage of the other's mistake. This is so even if the nonmistaken party must bear a loss as a result of rescission, since he or she could have avoided the loss by acting in good faith (by informing the mistaken party of the error) or by exercising reasonable care (to discover the mistake when the facts should have indicated that the other party was mistaken). See Figure 14.5.

FIGURE 14.5 **Unilateral Mistake**

Plaintiff:	Made mistake nonnegligently or with slight negligence	→	Mistake was of a fact	→	Promptly notified defendant when mistake was discovered	→	Serious injustice would result if contract is enforced
Defendant:	Will not suffer much harm if rescission allowed		or		Knew or should have known of the mistake and instead tried to take advantage of it		

Concept Summary: Voluntary Consent

There is no voluntary consent if there is:

1. Misrepresentation:
   a. Misrepresentation of a material fact.
   b. Justifiably relied on to the plaintiff's harm.
2. Fraud:
   a. Intentional misrepresentation of a material fact.
   b. Justifiably relied on to the plaintiff's harm.
3. Duress:
   a. Wrongful threat.
   b. Plaintiff's free will was overcome.
4. Undue Influence:
   a. Confidential relationship.
   b. Plaintiff was induced to make an unfavorable agreement.
5. Mistake:
   a. Mutual:
      i. Untrue belief by both parties about a material fact.
      ii. Either party can rescind.
   b. Unilateral:
      i. Mistaken party may be able to rescind if meets certain conditions, or
      ii. If other party knew or should have known of the mistake and is trying to take unfair advantage of it.

Questions and Problem Cases

1. What is fraud in the execution?
2. Who has the right to disaffirm a contract?
3. Explain the difference between duress and undue influence.
4. Morehouse went to the Behlman dealership to look at used cars. She told the salesman, Bogosian, who had 42 years of experience selling cars, that she was an inexperienced buyer and was looking for a reliable and lasting van. Bogosian said he had years of experience and he knew what was good. He recommended a van that he said was in excellent condition, had been well-maintained, and would be reliable. She test drove the van, and when she said it felt sluggish and the engine jerked, he said the roughness was standard and that he didn't hear anything wrong with the engine. After buying the van, Morehouse returned it five times with a multitude of complaints, primarily about the engine overheating. When she sued, the dealer said Bogosian's statements were merely expressions of opinion and not material misrepresentations of fact. Is this correct? Explain.
5. Stambovsky, to his horror, discovered that the house he had recently contracted to buy was commonly reputed to be possessed by poltergeists. Ackley, the seller of the house, had widely publicized their presence, including stories in both *Reader's Digest* and the local press, and on a walking tour of the Village of Nyack, New York, where the house was located. Stambovsky sought to rescind the contract of sale. Did the seller have a duty to disclose to the buyer the fact that the house was haunted?
6. Cottey was working for a hospital when it was merged with another company. He was offered an attractive financial package in order to get him to stay. Part of it was a plan that provided a large bonus when the plan fully vested in the sixth year. He was not given a written description of the plan or told that it could be rescinded by the company at its

discretion. It was rescinded three years later, but Cottey continued to work for the company until he was fired for allowing a female dancer to perform for a doctor's birthday party in an operating room. Cottey sued and claimed, among other things, that he was fraudulently induced to enter the employment contract with the company. The company argued that a misrepresentation cannot occur by silence. Who is correct and why?

7. Keith and Cross were employees of CBS. They told their supervisor, Jacobson, about their idea of forming an independent company to provide video promotion spots. Jacobson was in charge of selecting outside vendors and told them he thought they could get a contract with CBS. An exclusive contract was approved by Jacobson and his supervisor. Keith and Cross agreed to remain until their replacements could be hired. The next day Jacobson asked them to "help him out" because he had helped them, and asked for $500 per month. Although distressed and shocked, they agreed because Jacobson could fire them or kill the contract once they left; they felt intimidated and that they had no alternative but to agree. They made three payments and then Jacobson demanded $1,000 per month. When they could not pay, Jacobson raised problems with their work and the contract was likely to be canceled. At this point they told CBS about the demands, and Jacobson was fired. A few months later their contract was canceled on the basis of "admitted wrongdoing." Keith and Cross sued for economic duress. Will they be successful? Why or why not?

8. M.M., 16, gave birth at her home. She had hidden her pregnancy from her parents. She was taken to the hospital, where she stayed two days. Her father told her she could not bring the child home. M.M. was unwed, unemployed, young, and with limited educational means. An adoption agency was contacted by her family, and a representative visited her twice in the hospital, informing M.M. and her family about the adoption process. When she was released from the hospital, the representative met her in the parking lot and received the baby. The next day, the representative went to the home and left the adoption papers to be signed. The day after that, M.M. and her parents went to the agency, signed the papers, and met the adoptive parents. Four years after the adoption was finalized, M.M. sought the return of the child. Was her assent the result of undue influence and therefore not enforceable?

Chapter 15

Illegality

Learning Objectives

After you have studied this chapter, you should be able to:

1. Explain the general approach courts take to illegal contracts and why.
2. Discuss the differences between a regulatory statute and a revenue-raising statue, and their different outcomes.
3. Define an exculpatory clause and tell why it is an issue in contract law.
4. Describe the types of agreements that are exceptions to the rule that contracts in restraint of trade are illegal.
5. Identify the elements that are considered in deciding whether a contract is unconscionable under the common law.
6. Differentiate the UCC's treatment of unconscionability from the common law approach.

Mary Beth Whitehead agreed to be impregnated by William Stern's sperm, to carry the child to term, and to turn the child over to William and his wife when it was born. The Sterns agreed to pay Whitehead $10,000 for her services. After the child was born, Whitehead refused to turn the child over to the Sterns, and they sued to enforce the contract.

- Can a contract be declared illegal if there is no law prohibiting it?
- Should the courts refuse to enforce this type of agreement because it violates public policy?
- If the agreement is declared illegal, can the Sterns recover any payments they may have made to Whitehead?

FIGURE 15.1
Illegality

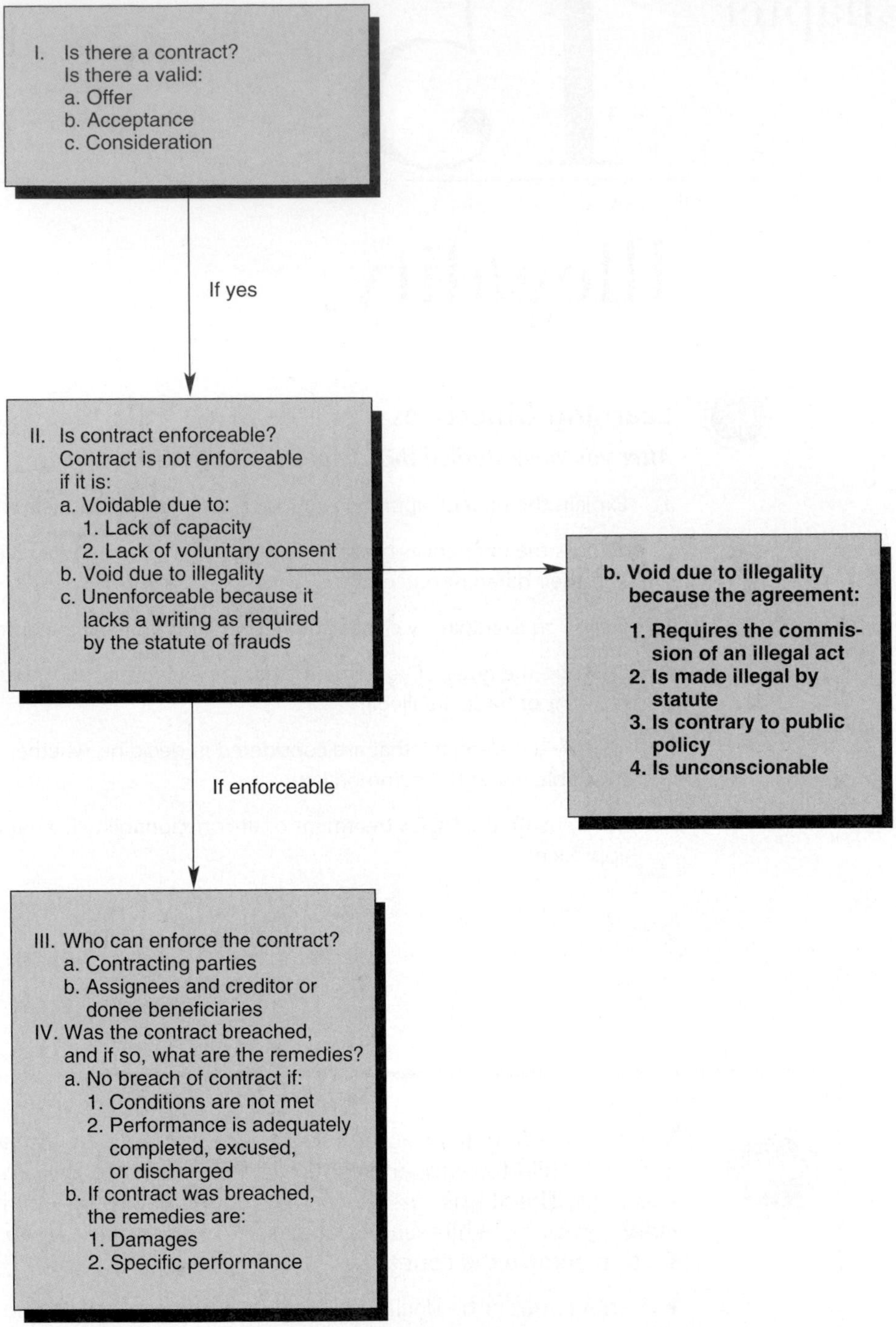
I. Is there a contract?
Is there a valid:
a. Offer
b. Acceptance
c. Consideration
If yes
II. Is contract enforceable?
Contract is not enforceable if it is:
a. Voidable due to:
1. Lack of capacity
2. Lack of voluntary consent
b. Void due to illegality
c. Unenforceable because it lacks a writing as required by the statute of frauds
b. Void due to illegality because the agreement:
1. Requires the commission of an illegal act
2. Is made illegal by statute
3. Is contrary to public policy
4. Is unconscionable
If enforceable
III. Who can enforce the contract?
a. Contracting parties
b. Assignees and creditor or donee beneficiaries
IV. Was the contract breached, and if so, what are the remedies?
a. No breach of contract if:
1. Conditions are not met
2. Performance is adequately completed, excused, or discharged
b. If contract was breached, the remedies are:
1. Damages
2. Specific performance

Introduction

Illegality

LO1

Even if the parties to an agreement have met every other requirement for a valid contract, their agreement is unenforceable if either its formation or its performance is illegal or contrary to the public interest. The public welfare is simply more important than the right of individuals to bargain freely. No sensible legal system would enforce bargains that undermine its authority or its basic objectives.

Types of Illegality

An agreement is illegal if it calls for behavior that violates a statute or a rule of common law. Also, certain kinds of agreements are themselves made illegal by statutes. An agreement that is contrary to a general rule of public policy is also illegal. The Whitehead agreement featured in the chapter opening could be illegal under any of these. It could violate existing laws outlawing the selling of human beings. In addition, some states have passed laws making surrogate mother contracts illegal. Finally, some courts have held surrogacy agreements to be against public policy.

The Presumption of Legality

When determining the legality of an agreement, the courts presume the parties intended a legal result and interpret their agreement accordingly. All doubts are resolved in favor of the legality of the agreement unless the parties clearly intended an illegal bargain.

The Effect of Illegality

General Rule

Hands off illegal agreements is the general position taken by the courts. A court will not enforce illegal agreements but will leave the parties where it finds them. This means that a party to an illegal agreement generally cannot recover damages for breach of the agreement, recover consideration given to the other party, or recover in quasi contract for benefits conferred on the other party. The basic reason for this rule is to further the public interest, not to punish the parties to an illegal agreement. Since the public interest is most important, courts will sometimes allow recovery if this would best serve the public interest in a particular case. Two such exceptions to the hands-off approach are discussed later in this chapter.

Ignorance of Fact or Special Regulation

Even though it is often said that ignorance of the law is no excuse, the courts have sometimes allowed recovery if one or both of the parties to an illegal bargain are ignorant of the facts that made the bargain illegal. Recovery is allowed only for performance rendered before the parties learned of the illegality, and only if the illegality does not involve immoral behavior or present a serious threat to the public welfare.

The same is true where one of the parties to a contract is unaware of the fact that the contract is illegal due to a violation of a special statute regulating the other party's business. For example, Frank enters a contract to perform in a play at Martha's theater. Frank does not know that Martha does not have a license to operate the theater as required by statute. Frank can recover the wages provided for in the agreement for the performances he gave before he learned of the violation.

One of the main reasons for refusing to enforce illegal contracts is to deter people from entering into such contracts. A court is therefore not likely to be disturbed when a person who has knowingly entered such a contract is hurt by the hands-off approach. The same is not true where a party unknowingly enters such a contract, and this accounts for the above exceptions. Similarly, exceptions to the general rule are usually made on behalf of those who have entered illegal agreements due to misrepresentation, fraud, duress, or undue influence.

Rights of Protected Parties

Many regulatory statutes attempt to protect certain classes of the public. In cases in which a person whom a statute seeks to protect enters into an agreement in violation of the statute, the protected person is allowed to enforce the agreement, or at least recover any consideration he or she has parted with. The obvious reason for this exception to the hands-off rule is that public policy is not well served if courts punish the person a statute seeks to protect. For example, most states require foreign corporations (those incorporated outside the state) to obtain a license before doing business in the state. These statutes often specifically provide that an unlicensed corporation cannot enforce contracts it enters into with citizens of the state. Citizens of the licensing state, however, are generally allowed to enforce their contracts with the unlicensed foreign corporation.

Rescission before Performance of Illegal Act

Public policy is clearly served best by any rule that encourages people not to commit illegal acts. Parties who have fully or partially performed their part of an illegal contract have little incentive to raise the question of illegality if they know that, due to the hands-off approach to illegal contracts, they will be unable to recover what they have given. To encourage such people to cancel illegal agreements, the courts allow one who rescinds the contract *before* any illegal act has been performed to recover any consideration given. For example, John, the owner of a restaurant, offers Bob, an employee of a competitor's restaurant, $1,000 for some of his competitor's secret recipes. He gives Bob $500 in advance. If John has second thoughts and tells Bob the deal is off before receiving any recipes, he can recover the $500.

Illegality and Divisible Contracts

A contract may call for the performance of several promises, some legal and some illegal. If the contract is divisible—that is, if the legal parts can be separated from the illegal parts—the courts enforce the legal parts of the contract. If the contract is not divisible, the illegal parts "taint" the entire contract, making it unenforceable.

Similarly, if the main purpose of a contract can be achieved without enforcing an illegal part of the contract, a court will enforce the main part of the agreement. For example, Barbara agrees to buy Kathy's beauty shop and the agreement bars Kathy from operating as a beautician for the rest of her life. The sale is enforceable, but the agreement not to compete is not enforced for reasons discussed later in this chapter.

Contracts to Commit Illegal Acts

Agreements to Commit Crimes

An agreement that calls for the commission of a crime is illegal. If Alice hires Bob to burn down Tom's place of business, such an agreement would be unenforceable, and Alice would be unable to recover any money she paid Bob to do the job. An agreement may be illegal if its net effect is criminal, even though the acts called for are individually lawful. For example, the only newspapers in a city may form a joint agency to sell subscriptions and advertising, acts that are legal in themselves. However, the effect of these acts may be to fix the price of these items, which, as you will see in Chapter 45, is a violation of the antitrust laws.

Agreements to Commit Torts

A contract that cannot be performed without committing a tort is illegal. So, if Mary hires John to throw a pie in her business law professor's face, their agreement is illegal, since John would have to commit the tort of battery (and probably assault) to perform his side of the contract.

Contracts Made Illegal by Statute

Wagering Statutes

All states have statutes that either prohibit or regulate gambling. Agreements in violation of these statutes are illegal. A recurring problem in this area is how to tell an illegal *wagering contract* from legal *risk-shifting* and *speculative bargaining* agreements.

When the parties create a new risk for the sole purpose of bearing it, that is an illegal wager. An example is a $25 bet by Jan that the Dolphins will win the Super Bowl. Jan has no financial interest in a Dolphins victory other than that created by the bet. She created the risk of losing the $25 for the sole purpose of bearing that risk. If, however, the parties agree who shall bear an existing risk, that is a legal risk-shifting agreement. Property insurance contracts are classic examples of risk-shifting agreements. The owner of the property pays the insurance company a fee in return for the company's agreement to bear the risk that the property will be damaged or destroyed. If, however, the person who takes out the policy had no legitimate economic interest in the insured property (called an *insurable interest* in insurance law), the agreement is an illegal wager.

Stock and commodity market transactions are good examples of speculative bargains that are legal. In both cases the purchasers are obviously hoping their purchases will increase in value and the sellers believe they will not. The difference between these transactions and wagers lies in the fact that the parties to stock and commodities transactions are legally bound to the purchase agreement (although the purchaser may never intend to actually take delivery of the stock or commodity). In an illegal wager, such as a bet on the future performance of a stock or commodity, no purchase is involved.

Grigsby v. Russell

222 U.S. 149 (U.S. Sup. Ct. 2011)

FACTS

Burchard needed an operation but couldn't afford it. He asked Dr. Grigsby to buy his life insurance policy in exchange for $100 and Grigsby paying the premiums, which Grigsby did. Burchard later died, but the insurer refused to pay on the policy. It alleged the agreement was against public policy because Grigsby had no insurable interest in the life of Burchard.

ISSUE

Is the agreement unenforceable as against public policy?

DECISION

No. A contract of insurance upon a life in which the insured has no interest is a pure wager that gives the insured a sinister counter interest in having that life come to an end. The chance that in some cases it may prove a sufficient motive for crime is greatly enhanced if the whole world of the unscrupulous are free to bet on what life they choose. The very meaning of an insurable interest is an interest in having the life continue. However, this case is very different. Burchard sought the assignment in order to help his life. The contract was sold in good faith. Life insurance has become in our day one of the best recognized forms of investment and self-compelled saving. It is desirable to give life policies the ordinary characteristics of property.

Statutes Declaring Bargains Void or Voidable

Many states have passed statutes making certain kinds of agreements void or voidable. Two examples of such statutes are usury laws and Sunday laws.

Usury laws prohibit charging more than a stated amount of interest for the use of money. The penalty for violation ranges from forfeiture of excess interest, through forfeiture of all interest, to forfeiture of interest and principal, depending on the state. In several states usury laws do not apply to loans to corporations, and many states allow a higher price to be charged for credit sales than cash sales without counting the price difference as interest.

Perez v. Rent-A-Center Inc.

892 A.2d 1255 (N.J. Sup. Ct. 2006)

FACTS

Over 14 months, Perez signed five rent-to-own contracts with Rent-A-Center Inc. (RAC) to buy used furniture, a used washer, a new dryer, a new computer, a used DVD player and TV, and a used large-screen TV and cabinet. Each contract said that "this is a rental agreement only" and that ownership would not pass unless she had "paid the total of rental payments plus the option payment necessary to acquire ownership." The property had a cash price of $9,301.72, but if she wanted to purchase the items, the total payments would be $18,613.32. The difference was the interest charged for the "privilege of buying the products over time." The range of interest on the items was between 79.7 percent and 82.7 percent. Perez stopped paying after she had made payments of $8,156.72. RAC sued her for money damages and the return of the items. She then filed her own suit alleging that the interest rate exceeded the state's usury statute.

ISSUE

Are rent-to-own contracts sufficiently similar to retail purchase contracts to be covered by the state usury statute?

DECISION

Yes. The vast majority of rent-to-own customers are the working poor whose incomes are on the margin of economic stability; they engage in rent-to-own purchases to get goods they could not otherwise buy. New Jersey's usury statute, which applies to retail credit sales, caps legal interest at 30 percent. It applies to a retail buyer, a retail seller, an agreement to pay the retail price in installments, and goods for personal, family, or household use. The agreements between Perez and RAC meet these requirements. Although the statute does not mention rent-to-own contracts, the legislature meant for the statute to be applied to agreements that are similar to traditional retail installment sales. The fact that Perez did not have an "absolute and unequivocal" contract to buy the goods does not remove the agreements from the statute's coverage, as RAC argued. The legislature meant to protect consumers from overreaching merchants. Finding that these contracts are within the statute does that.

Sunday laws (also called "Blue Laws") prohibit the performance of certain work and the transaction of certain business on Sunday. Such laws vary considerably from state to state. In most states the trend is to allow weekday "ratification" of Sunday contracts. In addition, exceptions are made for acts that must be done to protect health, life, or property.

Regulatory Statutes

LO2

Congress and the state legislatures have passed a variety of statutes regulating numerous kinds of activities. The most common kind of regulatory statute requires persons, partnerships, or corporations to acquire a license before engaging in a regulated activity. The basic purpose of such statutes is to protect the public from dishonest or unskilled persons. Lawyers, doctors, dentists, and other professionals are required to pass examinations to become licensed to practice. In many states real estate brokers, stockbrokers, and insurance agents may also be required to pass an examination and prove they are of good character before being granted a license.

Barbers, beauty operators, building contractors, electricians, plumbers, and others who perform skilled services are usually required to obtain licenses. The same is true for pawnbrokers, retailers, and wholesalers of liquor and tobacco, and sellers of other special items. The purpose of the licensing statute in all of these examples is, again, to protect the public welfare.

It is generally held that agreements by unlicensed persons to perform regulated services or engage in regulated businesses are illegal and therefore unenforceable. For example, an unlicensed person who acts as a real estate broker and sells a house would be unable to recover the agreed-on commission for the sale. Likewise, an unlicensed lawyer cannot collect for his work.

One major exception to this general rule that must be noted is the case of **revenue-raising statutes.** The failure to obtain a license required by a statute whose sole purpose is to raise revenue does not affect the legality of unlicensed persons' agreements. Whether a statute is classed as *regulatory* (for the protection of the public) or *revenue raising* depends on the intent of the legislature, which may not always be clearly expressed. As a general rule, statutes that require proof of character and skill and impose a penalty for violation are considered regulatory. Those that impose a significant license fee and allow anyone who pays the fee to obtain a license are classed as revenue raising.

The reason for making the distinction between the two types of statutes is that the strong societal interest in protecting the public against fraud and incompetence may justify the sometimes harsh measure of denying recovery for services rendered to those who violate regulatory statutes. This strong public interest is absent where the statute violated is merely aimed at raising revenue, and such statutes ordinarily impose a substantial fine for violation in any event.

You should also note that the courts may not deny recovery in every case, even where regulatory statutes are violated. If the amount forfeited would be great and the unlicensed party is neither dishonest nor incompetent, a court may not feel that the public interest is best served by allowing the other party to the agreement to be unjustly enriched at the expense of the unlicensed party. The court chose not to do this in the following case, however.

Alatriste v. Ceasar's Exterior Designs, Inc.

153 Cal. App.4th 656 (Cal. Ct. App. 2010)

FACTS

Alatriste hired Ceasar's Exterior Designs, Inc. (CEDI) to do landscaping work at his new home. After working for five months, CEDI quit after Alatriste refused to continue to pay for work performed. At that time, Altariste had paid CEDI $57,500. Alatriste sued to get his money back because CEDI did not have a landscaping contractor's license as required by state law and did not get one until four months into the project. CEDI argued that Alatriste knew it was not licensed and that it should be paid for the work done during the time it was licensed.

ISSUE

Can CEDI recover for the part of the work it did while it was licensed?

DECISION

No. The licensing requirement provides minimal assurance that all persons offering such services have the requisite skill and character, understand applicable local laws and codes, and know the rudiments of administering a contracting business. They are designed to protect the public from incompetent or dishonest work. The denial encourages licensure by denying payment for work done without a license. This is true even though the person knew the contractor lacked a license, and applies to all work done under the contract and despite the quality of work done.

Concept Summary: Contracts Made Illegal by Statute

Type of Statute	Actions Affected	Remedy
Wagering Statutes	Betting	None
Usury Statutes	Interest charged for the use of money	Forfeiture of excess or all interest, or interest and principal
Sunday or "Blue Laws"	Selling certain goods such as alcohol, or performing certain acts on Sunday	Weekday ratification usual
Contracts with Persons Who:		
1. Have **failed** to obtain a **license**	1. Contracts in jobs that require proof of character or skill	1. None
2. Have **failed** to pay a **licensing fee**	2. Licensing required for revenue-raising purposes	2. Contracts generally enforceable

Contracts Contrary to Public Policy

The Idea of Public Policy

Public policy is a broad concept that is impossible to define precisely. Perhaps the only realistic way to define it is to say that a court's view of public policy is determined by what the court believes is in the best interests of society. Public policy may change with the times; changing social and economic conditions may make behavior that was acceptable in an earlier time unacceptable today, or vice versa.

There is therefore no simple rule for determining when a particular bargain is contrary to public policy and illegal. Public policy is contradicted by immoral and unethical agreements, even though they may not call for the performance of an illegal act. The courts have broad discretion in ruling on questions of public policy, and this discretion can provide the legal system with a degree of healthy flexibility.

Courts may differ in their views of what constitutes desirable public policy—a difference that can make a contract legal in one state and illegal in another. This is true of surrogacy contracts such as that involved in the *Whitehead* case in the chapter opening. The following are additional examples of contracts that courts frequently find to be contrary to public policy.

Contracts Injurious to Public Service

The public interest is best served when public officials fully and faithfully perform their duties. It should come as no surprise, then, that agreements that induce public servants to deviate from their duties are illegal. For example, agreements to pay public employees more or less than their lawful salary are unlawful. Agreements that create a conflict between a public employee's personal interests and public duties are also illegal. A good example of this kind of case would be an agreement between a state highway department employee and a real estate speculator who pays the public employee for advance notice of the planned routes of new highway construction. Agreements to pay public servants to influence their decision making are also illegal.

Contracts to Influence Fiduciaries

Any agreement that tends to induce a **fiduciary** (a person in a position of trust or confidence like a trustee, agent, or partner) to breach his or her fiduciary duties is illegal. This is so because such an agreement operates as a fraud on the principal or beneficiary who is entitled to the fiduciary's loyalty. This applies to agreements by fiduciaries that favor the interests of a third person at the expense of their principals' interests, and agreements that produce a conflict between fiduciaries' personal interests and their principals' interests. The only way a fiduciary may lawfully enter such an agreement is by fully and fairly disclosing the conflict to his or her principal or beneficiary in advance.

Exculpatory Clauses

LO3

An **exculpatory clause** is a provision in a contract that attempts to relieve one party to the contract from liability for the consequences of his or her own negligence. Public policy generally favors holding people responsible for their own behavior. In addition, courts are concerned that a party relieved of liability for his negligence will not have the incentive to be careful to avoid injuring others. On the other hand, if no duty to the public is involved and the parties have freely and knowingly agreed, the exculpatory clause may be enforceable. Exculpatory clauses that seek to avoid liability for willful misconduct or fraud, however, are generally unenforceable.

Johnson v. New River Scenic Whitewater Tours, Inc.

313 F.Supp.2d 621 (2004)

FACTS

In August 1999, the Fort Johnson Baptist Church sponsored a youth trip to Charleston, West Virginia, for the purpose of performing mission work. The trip culminated in a whitewater rafting excursion on the New River. John Peters, Fort Johnson's Associate Pastor for Youth and Education, handled most of the arrangements for the whitewater event on the church's behalf. Prior to the start of the trip, Fort Johnson required the youth participants to obtain "permission slips" from their parents or guardians. Karen Johnson gave verbal permission for her 14-year-old daughter, Lindsay, to participate. Peters subsequently signed two documents on Lindsay's behalf—an indemnity agreement and a release of liability with the rafting company, New River Scenic Whitewater Tours, Inc. (NRS). During the trip, Lindsay's raft flipped over and she drowned before she could be rescued. Johnson brought a wrongful death suit against NRS. NRS subsequently filed a third-party claim against Fort Johnson Baptist Church and Peters, asserting that they were contractually obligated to indemnify New River Scenic based on two documents signed by Peters the morning of the trip that contain language of both release of liability and indemnification. The church responded that such agreements are void as against public policy.

ISSUE

Should the court refuse to enforce the agreement on the ground of public policy?

DECISION

Yes. A clause in an agreement exempting a party from tort liability is unenforceable on grounds of public policy if the agreement would exempt a party from liability arising from that party's failure to comply with a safety statute, as the safety obligation created by the statute for such purpose is an obligation owed to the public at large and is not within the power of any private individual to waive. Under the West Virginia law, a whitewater operator whose conduct fails to conform to the standard of care expected by a member of his profession must bear the burden of risk of injury of those minors who are adversely impacted by his tortious conduct. For this reason, public policy precludes a parent from indemnifying a potential tortfeasor for harm to his/her child. Furthermore, allowing a parent to indemnify a third party for its tortious conduct toward the parent's minor child would result in a serious affront to the doctrine of parental immunity. If a parent could enter into a binding contract of indemnification regarding tort injuries to her minor child, the result would be that the child, for full vindication of his legal rights, would need to seek a recovery from his parent. This would clearly abrogate the strong West Virginia public policy to preserve the peace and tranquility of society and families by prohibiting such intrafamily legal battles. Therefore any release executed either by the victim or a parent on her behalf is unenforceable.

Contracts in Restraint of Trade

LO4

One of the basic assumptions underlying our economic system is that the public interest is, in most cases, best served by free competition. On the other hand, the courts have recognized that there are some situations where limited restrictions on competition are justifiable. The courts therefore look very closely at agreements that attempt to limit competition to see whether the restraint imposed is reasonable or should be struck down for violating public policy. In Chapter 45 you will also learn that some agreements in restraint of trade are specifically made illegal by the antitrust laws.

Agreements whose *sole* purpose is to restrain trade are illegal. However, a restraint that is merely *ancillary to* (supplementary to) a contract may be legal if it is designed to protect interests created by the contract and it is *no broader than is reasonably necessary* to protect those interests. For example, it is common for a contract for the sale of a business to provide that the seller will not compete with the buyer for a specified period of time after the sale. If the restriction covers a reasonable geographic area and a reasonable time period, it will probably be upheld. Similarly, employment contracts often provide that employees will not compete with or work for a competitor of their employer after they have ceased their employment. If such a restriction is reasonably necessary to prevent an employee from disclosing trade secrets or taking away the employer's customers, and it has reasonable geographic and time limitations, it is also likely to be upheld.

Courts also consider the degree of hardship a covenant not to compete would have on the public and on the party who would be restrained from competing. Restrictions on competition work a greater hardship on an employee than on someone who has sold a business. Therefore, employee agreements not to compete are often judged by a stricter standard than are similar agreements that accompany the sale of a business.

The courts do not agree on how to treat a restriction that is unreasonably broad. Some courts enforce the restraint for a reasonable period of time and within a reasonable geographic area. Others strike the entire restriction and refuse to grant the buyer or employer any protection. Some states bar enforcement through a statute.

It also has been traditionally held that agreements restricting the free *alienation* (sale) of land are contrary to public policy, which favors a free market in land.

Home Paramount Pest Control Companies, Inc. v. Shaffer

http://pub.bna.com/lw/1101837.pdf (Va. Sup. Ct. 2011)

FACTS

Shaffer, an employee of Home Paramount Pest Control Companies (Home), signed an agreement containing a provision that prevented him from working or being involved in any manner in any business involving pest control, in any city or county in the state in which he worked for two years after his employment ceased. Six months later he resigned and soon thereafter started working for Connor's Termite and Pest Control. Home sued Shaffer for breach of contract. Shaffer asserted that the noncompete clause was overbroad and therefore unenforceable.

ISSUE

Is the noncompete clause overbroad and therefore unenforceable?

DECISION

Yes. A provision that restricts competition is enforceable if it is narrowly drawn to protect the employer's legitimate business interest, is not unduly burdensome on the employee's ability to earn a living, and is not against public policy. In determining this, we consider the function, geographic scope, and duration of the restriction. The function

(continued)

Home Paramount Pest Control Companies, Inc. v. Shaffer *(concluded)*

element is considered in light of whether the prohibited activity is of the same type as that actually engaged in by the employer. When a former employer seeks to prohibit its former employee from working in any capacity for its competitor, it must prove a legitimate business reason for doing so. Home's clause bars Shaffer from working in the pest control industry in any capacity and from engaging even indirectly, or concerning himself in any manner whatsoever, in the pest control business, even as a passive stockholder of a publicly traded international conglomerate with a pest control subsidiary. This is too broad. It did not further Home's legitimate business interests. Even though the geographic scope and duration are reasonable, the agreement is unenforceable.

Unequal Bargains

As you saw in Chapter 9, the courts were historically unwilling to consider arguments that a contract was the product of unequal bargaining power. As long as all the legal elements of a contract were present and the agreement was free from misrepresentation, fraud, duress, undue influence, or mistake, the common law courts would enforce it, despite the fact that its terms might be grossly unfair to one of the parties. This was justified by the doctrine of *freedom of contract.*

The changing nature of our society, however, has produced many contract situations in which the bargaining power of the parties may be grossly unequal. This may make it possible for one of the parties to effectively dictate the terms of the agreement and to take advantage of this power by dictating terms that are unfair to the other party. The legal system has responded to these changes in two major ways.

First, there has been an increasing "public" input through legislation into many previously private contract situations. Wage and hour laws, workers' compensation laws, usury laws, and rent control laws are just a few of the many kinds of statutes aimed at placing limits on the exercise of private bargaining power.

LO5

Second, today's courts are responding to the problem by recognizing the idea of **unconscionable contracts** and **contracts of adhesion**—contracts in which the only choice for one of the parties is between "adhering" to the terms dictated by the other party or not contracting at all. A court may refuse to enforce such an agreement as contrary to public policy. Clauses in fine print or in such technical language that an ordinary person would not understand their meaning have also been stricken on this basis. Unequal bargaining power standing alone is not enough to justify unenforceability, however. It must also appear that the party with superior power used it to take unfair advantage of the other party to the agreement. The courts are especially likely to find such inequality in cases involving consumer contracts with businesses, although there are also numerous cases in which contracts between small companies and large industrial giants have been held to be adhesion contracts. While courts are increasingly willing to prevent oppression and unfair surprise by finding agreements to be unconscionable or contracts of adhesion, they will not use such doctrines to relieve people of their bad bargains.

Lhotka v. Geographic Expeditions, Inc.

104 Cal. Rptr.3d 844 (Cal. Ct. App. 2010)

FACTS

Lhotka died from an altitude-related illness while he and his mother, Menefee, were on an expedition up Mount Kilimanjaro with Geographic Expeditions, Inc. (GEI). Before going, they signed a waiver of liability and a release form after receiving a letter from GEI that said completion of the

(continued)

Lhotka v. Geographic Expeditions, Inc. *(concluded)*

form was mandatory. It also contained a mediation clause calling for mediation of any dispute in San Francisco and if that failed, binding arbitration, with liability, if any, limited to the cost of the trip. After Lhotka's death, Menefee sued under various theories, including that the arbitration clause was unconscionable.

ISSUE

Was the arbitration clause unconscionable?

DECISION

Yes. Unconscionability is generally recognized to include an absence of meaningful choice on the part of one of the parties along with contract terms that are unreasonably favorable to the other party. There is both a procedural and substantive element. GEI argues that its clause is neither. GEI argues it was not oppressive because Menefee didn't show that there was an industry wide requirement that travel clients must accept such an agreement without modification; they failed to even negotiate about this. However, GEI's own form said they had to sign the agreement without modification. It also said that other travel companies were no different. GEI led Menefee and her son to believe there was no other option. Therefore they lacked bargaining power. We also reject as unsound the argument that, since this was a recreational activity, the parties had the option of not going. We also find substantive unconscionability. The limited liability amount guaranteed that they could not recover anything approaching full recompense for the harm. Additionally, they had to mediate and arbitrate in San Francisco even though they were Colorado residents, which meant they had expenses that GEI did not. Finally, it required them to indemnify GEI for costs and attorney fees. GEI's arbitration scheme provides a potent disincentive for an aggrieved client to pursue a claim and may well guarantee that GEI wins even if it loses. The agreement is unconscionable.

The *Restatement (Second) of Contracts* urges broad powers on the courts to deal with unconscionability. The Uniform Commercial Code specifically grants courts these broad powers.

Ethics in Action

A large bank required customers to sign a signature card. In extremely small type the card stated that the depositor agreed that the account was subject to the bank's present and future rules, regulations, practices, and charges. On the basis of this agreement, the bank charged depositors $6 for each check returned for insufficient funds. The actual cost to the bank for processing each check was 30 cents. Thus, there was a 2,000 percent differential between the bank's actual cost and the fee it charged. Is it ethical for a business to make this kind of return in this manner?

The Code and Unconscionable Contracts

LO6

Section 2-302 recognizes the idea of an **unconscionable contract.** The drafters of the Code knew that many contracts today are not truly consensual, even though the classic forms of lack of voluntary consent (like fraud, duress, undue influence, and mistake) are not present, and that they are often the products of unequal bargaining power between the parties. Many consumer contracts are created on preprinted forms drawn by one party's attorney. These form contracts sometimes contain provisions that are unreasonably favorable to the party whose attorney drafted them. In addition, these contracts are sometimes so filled with legalese (technical legal wording) that consumers in reality do not understand the nature of the contract they have signed.

The Code gives the courts considerable power to deal with these problems by giving them freedom to remedy unconscionable contracts. If a court finds a contract to be unconscionable, it can refuse to enforce it entirely, enforce it without any unconscionable clause, or enforce it in a way that avoids an unconscionable result.

The Code does not define *unconscionable,* leaving it instead for the courts to define. In doing so, the courts have tended to follow the path charted by those earlier courts that refused to enforce "adhesion contracts" on the grounds that they were contrary to public policy. Unconscionable contracts are often described as those that are so unfair that they "shock the conscience of the court." This unfairness may result from the fact that one of the parties did not either notice or truly understand a clause of the contract (because it was too technically worded, in fine print, on the back of the contract, etc.). A finding of unconscionability may also result when a party with superior bargaining power imposes unfair terms on the other party.

Unconscionability will probably not apply to any terms of an agreement that were truly bargained for, even though one of the parties made a "bad deal." Consumers who are dealing with merchants are generally more successful in arguing unconscionability than merchants who are dealing with other merchants because the courts are more likely to assume that, as compared to consumers, merchants have more bargaining power, better access to legal advice, and more knowledge about the nature of the transactions they enter. In those few cases in which merchants have successfully argued unconscionability, they were usually small businesspeople (who in reality had no more bargaining power than a consumer) dealing with large corporations.

Concept Summary: Common Contracts Contrary to Public Policy

Type of Contract	Action Involved	Conditions under Which Contract Sometimes Enforced
Contracts Injurious to Public Service	Bribes	
Contracts to Influence Fiduciaries	Prize, reward, or other inducement	Full disclosure to, and agreement of, beneficiary
Exculpatory Clauses	Release of liability for negligence	No duty to public involved, and free agreement by other party
Contracts in Restraint of Trade	Agreement not to compete	If ancillary to contract for sale of a business, or for employment, and is no broader than necessary and not injurious to public
Contracts Resulting from Unequal Bargaining Power	Unconscionable or adhesion contracts	

Current Issues

Today many illegality issues facing courts involve public policy questions about family relationships. The family has long been considered to be a crucial social institution, and it is therefore protected by the courts. The nature and role of the family in our society are changing, however, and courts are being asked to recognize these changes. You already saw one example of this in the cases dealing with division of property between couples who live together without getting married.

Another example is raised by the Whitehead case in the chapter opening. What are the permissible ways for people to bring children into the family unit? Should the courts

(continued)

Current Issues (concluded)

recognize contracts involving surrogacy, or *in vitro* fertilization? The courts and legislatures are split in their answers to these difficult questions.

Another area in transition involves *antenuptial agreements*. Antenuptial agreements are entered into by a couple before marriage and determine how property should be divided if there is later a divorce. Traditionally, courts held such agreements to be void as against public policy because they might facilitate or induce a divorce and because they usually left the woman financially needy. Many courts are now allowing such agreements, however, because they recognize that attitudes toward divorce have changed, as has the ability of women to support and protect themselves. In addition, rather than encouraging divorce, they recognize that such agreements may actually promote marital stability by making clear the expectations and responsibilities of the parties.

Questions and Problem Cases

1. What is the general rule of recovery under illegal contracts?
2. Discuss the interaction between illegality and divisibility.
3. Explain a contract of adhesion and give an example.
4. Neiman was found guilty of illegally practicing law. Once out of work he suffered from bipolar disorder. He sought disability benefits under a disability insurance policy designed to compensate for loss of income derived entirely from his law practice. Since he was practicing law illegally, can he recover? Why?
5. Todd wanted to have a child but did not want to get married. Straub agreed to have intercourse with her after she signed an agreement stating that she would hold him harmless for emotional and financial support of a child that might result from their relationship. Eleven months later, Todd gave birth to B.M.T. After three years of raising B.M.T. without any support from Straub, Todd filed suit for B.M.T. seeking a declaration of paternity and child support. Is Straub's agreement unenforceable on the basis of public policy?
6. Krueger worked for Central Indiana Podiatry (CIP) under a series of two-year contracts. Each contract had a clause that said that for two years after leaving CIP, he would not divulge the names of patients or contact them regarding podiatry services or solicit CIP employees. He also was prohibited from practicing podiatry in any county in which CIP had an office or any adjacent county. This encompassed 43 counties, or about the middle half of the state. CIP then began investigating Krueger for sexual harassment, at which point Krueger copied the names and addresses of patients of one of the offices. He was soon fired, and two months later he agreed to work for a practice in one of the counties covered by the CIP terms. He gave the new employer the copied names and addresses of CIP patients and sent out an announcement to them about his new employer and the fact that it was only 10 minutes away. Should the restrictive covenant be enforced? Explain your reasoning.
7. Alexander had a seventh-grade education and had worked over 20 years as a heavy equipment operator. He attended an orientation meeting with Anthony, Int'l where he was given a standard form employment contract without a chance to negotiate or reject specific terms. He signed it because he needed the money. There was a mandatory arbitration clause along with a requirement that any claim must be filed within 30 days of the event if a claim was found to be nonarbitrable, the losing party was to

bear the costs, and punitive damages were excluded. After he was fired, Alexander sued the company for age and race discrimination. Was the agreement unconscionable and therefore unenforceable? Why?

8. The Harrises claimed to be victims of a fraudulent home improvement scheme perpetrated by Green Tree Financial Corp. Green Tree recruited home improvement contractors, told the contractors to obtain high-interest second-mortgage contracts on home improvements by targeting relatively unsophisticated, low- to middle-income senior citizens, promising that the work would be performed at an affordable cost and that no payment would be due until the customer was completely satisfied. The form contracts allowed Green Tree to charge exorbitant amounts for collateral protection insurance. They obtained these contracts by using high-pressure sales tactics such as in-home sales and telemarketing. After the Harrises signed the forms, the contractors either did not do the promised work or did it in an unsatisfactory manner. When the Harrises sued, Green Tree sought to enforce an arbitration clause in the contracts. This clause was contained in the secondary mortgage contract which appeared in small print on the back and near the bottom of the one-page form contract. In the clause Green Tree reserved the right to sue but the Harrises did not have that right. Is the clause unconscionable and therefore unenforceable?
9. The University of West Virginia has both intramural and club athletics. The university takes no role in the organization, regulation, or supervision of club sports, but it actively controls the intramural sports and regulates them for safety. Recognition as a club sport entitles the club to get money from the school, to join the sports club federation and get more money, and to use the school's facilities. Students participating in club sports are required to sign a release stating they recognize the hazards involved in the activity and that they waive any claims they may have against the university for injuries or death occurring as a result of their participation in the sport. Kyriazis played the club sport of rugby and was injured. When he sued, the university said the suit was barred by the exculpatory agreement. Should the court refuse to enforce the agreement on the ground of public policy?

Chapter 16

The Form and Meaning of Contracts

Learning Objectives

After you have studied this chapter, you should be able to:

1. Explain the reasoning behind the statute of frauds and the effect of a failure to comply.
2. Describe what debts are covered by the statute of frauds.
3. Discuss the role part performance plays in contracts transferring an interest in land.
4. Define bilateral contracts not capable of being performed in a year, and explain how the courts interpret them.
5. Explain how the UCC's statute of frauds differs from the common law's statute.
6. Explain the parol evidence rule and describe the exceptions to it.

M & M Flying Service, Inc., entered into a written contract with the Andalusia-Opp Airport Authority to run management and commercial activities from January 1, 1983, to December 31, 1987. The Authority came under new management on January 1, 1988. When the new management and M & M failed to agree on the terms of a renewal of M & M's contract, the Authority sought to stop M & M from operating at the airport. M & M argued that at the same time it had signed the management contract in 1983, it had also signed a 10-year lease, and that the Authority had orally promised that M & M could continue to operate commercial activities for the life of the lease.

- Is the oral promise that commercial activities could continue for five years enforceable without a writing?
- Was the fact that M & M operated commercial activities from 1983 to 1988 sufficient evidence that it was promised another five years so that no writing is required for that promise?
- Did the promise about allowing commercial activities for five years have to be in writing because it was to take place on the Authority's land?

FIGURE 16.1
When a Contract Is Unenforceable

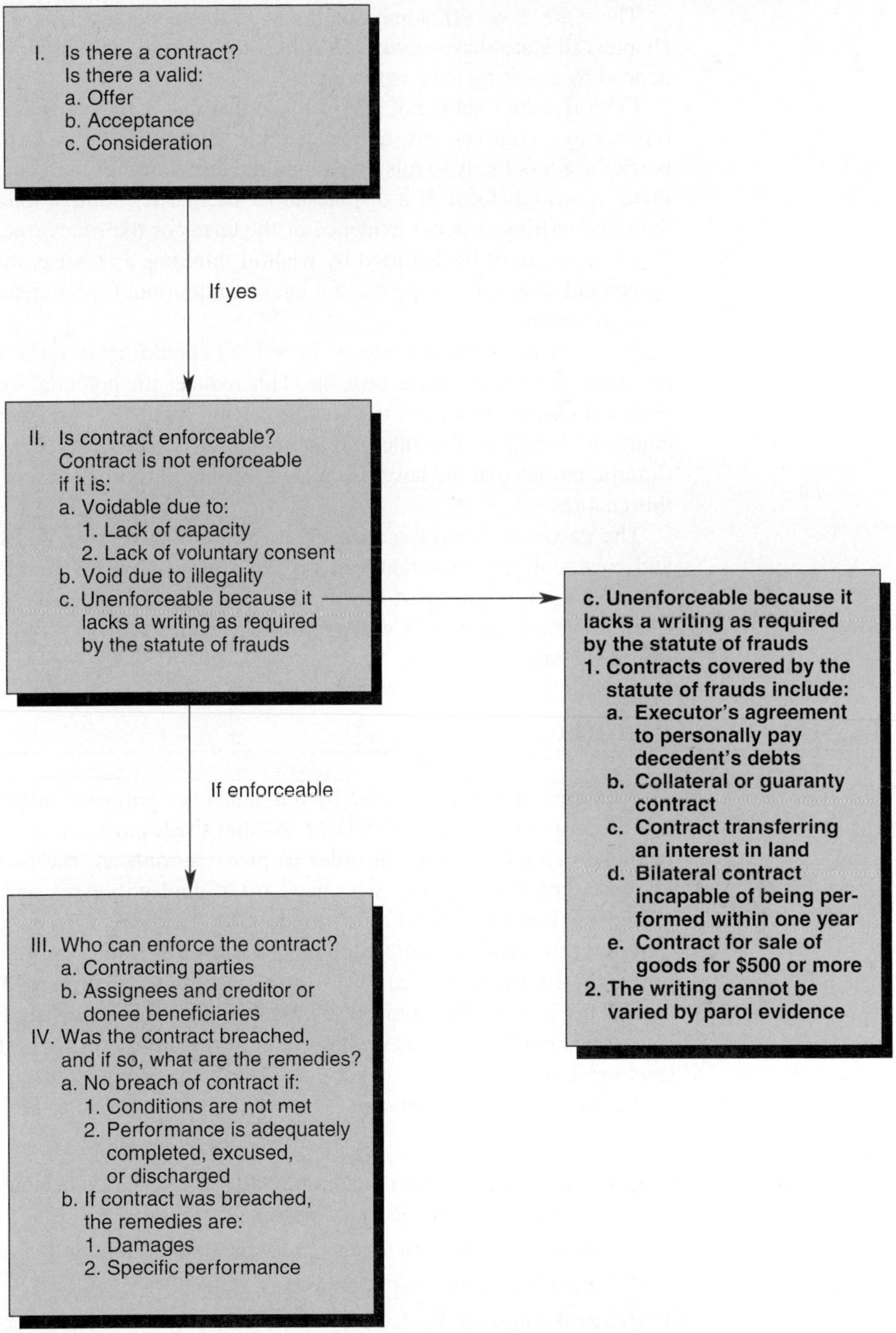

I. Is there a contract?
Is there a valid:
a. Offer
b. Acceptance
c. Consideration
If yes
II. Is contract enforceable?
Contract is not enforceable if it is:
a. Voidable due to:
1. Lack of capacity
2. Lack of voluntary consent
b. Void due to illegality
c. Unenforceable because it lacks a writing as required by the statute of frauds
c. Unenforceable because it lacks a writing as required by the statute of frauds
1. Contracts covered by the statute of frauds include:
a. Executor's agreement to personally pay decedent's debts
b. Collateral or guaranty contract
c. Contract transferring an interest in land
d. Bilateral contract incapable of being performed within one year
e. Contract for sale of goods for $500 or more
2. The writing cannot be varied by parol evidence
If enforceable
III. Who can enforce the contract?
a. Contracting parties
b. Assignees and creditor or donee beneficiaries
IV. Was the contract breached, and if so, what are the remedies?
a. No breach of contract if:
1. Conditions are not met
2. Performance is adequately completed, excused, or discharged
b. If contract was breached, the remedies are:
1. Damages
2. Specific performance

Many people mistakenly believe that oral contracts are not binding and enforceable. How many times have you heard someone say, "I agreed, but they didn't get it in writing"? The truth is that oral contracts are generally every bit as binding and enforceable as written ones.

There are, however, some exceptions to this general rule. As you will see later in this chapter, all states have *statutes of frauds* that require certain kinds of contracts to be evidenced by a writing to be enforceable.

Even if a contract is not one of those that the statute of frauds requires to be in writing, written contracts are more desirable than oral contracts for several reasons. The parties are less likely to misunderstand the terms of their agreement if they have reduced them to written form. If a dispute about the parties' obligations should arise at a later date, the writing is better evidence of the terms of their agreement than their memories, which may fail or be distorted by wishful thinking. Likewise, the existence of a written agreement may provide protection against intentional misstatements about the terms of the agreement.

Parties who put their contracts in writing should try to make the writing as complete and unambiguous (clear) as possible. This reduces the potential for later disagreement and makes it easier for a court to construe, or interpret, the agreement if a dispute arises. A court that is called on to interpret an ambiguous agreement relies on rules of construction (interpretation) that the law has created for this purpose. These will be discussed later in this chapter.

The parties to a written agreement should also be sure that the writing is complete and covers all the important terms of their agreement for another important reason. As you will see in a later part of this chapter, a rule of law called the *parol evidence rule* often prevents a party to a written contract from trying to prove terms that were left out of the writing.

The Statute of Frauds

LO1

The statutes of frauds adopted by the states are patterned after the original statute of frauds adopted in England in 1677. At that time, parties to a lawsuit could not testify in their own cases. Thus, in order to prove a contract, the parties had to rely on the testimony of third persons who were often paid witnesses or friends, and false testimony was common. In an effort to stop the widespread fraud and perjury, Parliament required those contracts in which the potential for fraud was great, or the consequences of fraud were especially serious, to be in writing to be enforceable. A **statute of frauds** essentially says that in some cases, the law will require more evidence (a writing) that the parties had an agreement than the oral testimony of the party claiming that a contract existed.

Among those classes of contracts traditionally required to be in writing by the statute of frauds are:

1. Contracts by the executor or administrator of a deceased person's estate to be personally liable for a debt of the deceased person.
2. Contracts by one person to answer for the debt or default of another.
3. Contracts for the transfer of an interest in land.
4. Bilateral contracts that have not been fully performed by either party and are not capable of being performed within a year of their formation.

Several additional classes of contracts have been added to the traditional categories covered by the statute. For example, the Uniform Commercial Code states that contracts for the sale of goods costing $500 or more are not enforceable without a writing or other specified evidence. Many states also require contracts to pay debts barred by a bankruptcy discharge or the statute of limitations to be evidenced by a writing. In addition, many states require contracts to pay a commission on the sale of real estate to be evidenced by a writing.

The U.N. Convention on the International Sale of Goods, the "international UCC," has decided not to require the formality of a writing. While countries could choose to require a writing and still sign the Convention, most countries throughout the world have opted to do away with strict form requirements. Thus, oral international contracts between companies in signatory countries will be enforced without a writing.

The Effect of Failure to Comply

In most states, the statute of frauds makes oral contracts that come within its provisions **unenforceable,** not void or voidable. This means several things. If the parties to such an oral contract have both fully performed their obligations, neither is allowed to rescind the contract. Their mutual performance is ample evidence that a contract in fact existed. If one of the parties to an executory oral contract files suit to enforce the contract and the other party does not raise the statute of frauds as a defense, the court will enforce the agreement.

If an oral contract is declared to be unenforceable under the statute of frauds, and one of the parties has rendered some performance under the contract that conferred benefits on the other party, he or she can recover the reasonable value of the performance in *quasi contract.* In some instances that will be discussed later, part performance of a contract is sufficient to take the contract outside the scope of the statute or to satisfy the statute's requirement by providing the extra element of proof of a contract's existence beyond the mere oral testimony of a party.

One of the troubling things about the statute is its potential for injustice. It can as easily be used to defeat a contract that was actually made as to defeat a fictitious agreement. In recent years, some courts have begun to try to prevent such injustices by using the equitable doctrine of *promissory estoppel* to allow some parties to recover under oral contracts that the statute of frauds would ordinarily render unenforceable. If the plaintiff has *materially relied* on the oral promise and will suffer *serious losses* if the promise is not enforced, courts in these states hold that the other party is estopped from raising the statute of frauds as a defense. The idea behind these decisions is that the statute, which is designed to prevent injustice, should not be allowed to work an injustice. These cases also impliedly recognize the fact that the reliance required by promissory estoppel to some extent provides evidence of the existence of a contract between the parties, since it is unlikely that a person would materially rely on a nonexistent promise.

Ethics in Action

Is it ethical to challenge the enforceability of an oral contract on statute of frauds grounds when all of the other elements of a contract are clearly in existence?

Contracts Covered by the Statute of Frauds

Executors' Agreements to Personally Pay Their Decedents' Debts

LO2

When a person dies, an executor or administrator is appointed by the probate court to settle the deceased person's (the decedent's) estate. Basically, this involves paying all outstanding claims against the estate and distributing any remainder to the decedent's heirs. The executor or administrator is often a relative or close friend of the decedent.

Creditors of the decedent who fear that the decedent's estate will not be great enough to cover their claims may try to get the executor to agree to be personally responsible for the decedent's debts. Executors who are relatives or close friends may feel morally obligated to make such promises, although they have no legal obligation to do so. In extreme cases, creditors who would otherwise suffer a great loss may be tempted to lie and claim the executor made such a promise. To prevent such fraud and to guard against ill-considered promises by executors, such promises must be in writing to be enforceable.

Contracts to Answer for the Debt of Another

In addition to the executor's contracts just discussed, there are many other common situations in which one person agrees to be responsible for the debts or default of another. Such contracts are called **collateral** or **guaranty contracts.** The essence of such contracts is that a third person (the *guarantor*) agrees to perform the contractual duties another person (the *obligor*) owes under another contract, *if* the obligor does not perform. The person to whom the obligor and the guarantor are contractually liable is called the *obligee.* These situations, then, involve three parties and two promises, one of which is conditional. Only the conditional promise by the guarantor to the obligee to be responsible for the obligor's debt must be in writing.

If, for example, a clothing store (the obligee) that has opened a credit account with Mike, a college student (the obligor), gets Mike's older brother Tom (the guarantor) to agree to pay the amount owed on the account if Mike fails to do so, this is a guaranty contract. Tom's contract must be in writing to be enforceable. (See Figure 16.2.)

FIGURE 16.2
Guaranty Contract

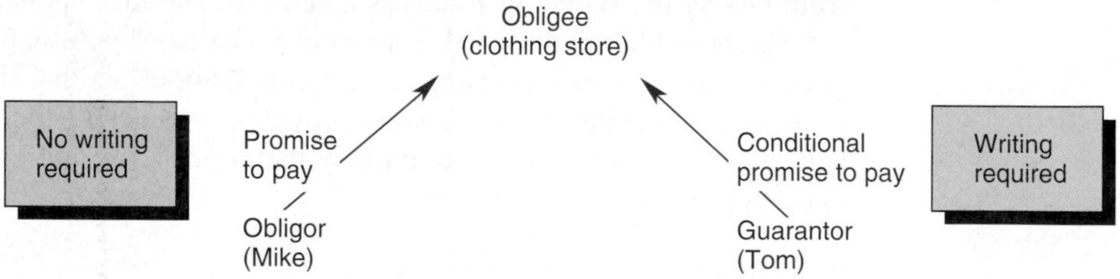

Many three-party transactions are not guaranty contracts but are instead *original contracts* of the third party. The distinction between an original contract and a guaranty contract is important because original contracts do not need to be evidenced by a writing to be enforceable. The major difference between the two is that a party to an original contract is *primarily* liable (absolutely liable under the terms of the contract) to perform his or her contractual duties, while a guarantor is only *secondarily* liable (liable only if the obligor does not perform).

For example, Bob and Joe agree to buy a television set from Frank's TV Service for $189.95, payable over 24 months. Bob and Joe are **co-obligors** on the sales agreement

FIGURE 16.3
Original Contract

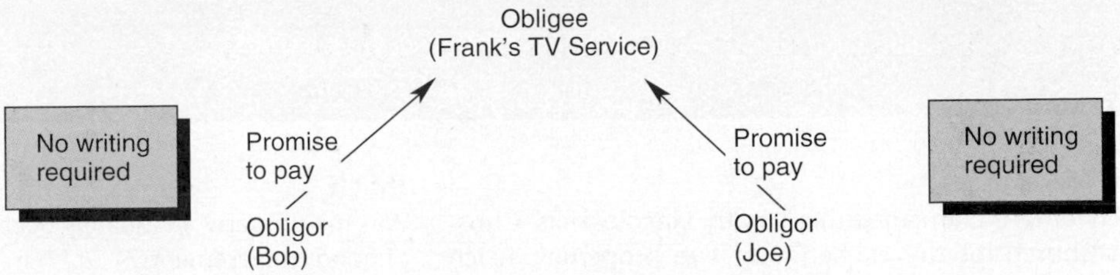

and are both *primarily* liable to make the payments. Frank's TV can collect the amount due under the agreement from *either* Bob or Joe without first showing a demand for payment from the other. Bob and Joe's promises are therefore *original* ones and need not be evidenced by a writing to be enforceable. (See Figure 16.3.)

In some cases, what would at first glance appear to be a guaranty contract within the statute will be treated as an original contract outside the statute's scope. This is due to the **leading object** doctrine, which says that the promises of those who are primarily motivated by a desire to secure some personal benefit fall outside the statute. Thus, if people promising to pay for the debt of another are primarily motivated to make the promise because they expect some personal benefit by so doing, their conditional promise does not need to be in writing to be enforceable.

Contracts Transferring an Interest in Land

LO3

Our legal system has historically treated land as being more important than other forms of property. This special treatment stems from the time when land was the primary basis of wealth. As a result of this special status, contracts transferring ownership rights in real estate must be evidenced by a writing to be enforceable. Therefore, oral contracts to sell or mortgage real estate, to permit the mining and removal of minerals from land, and to grant easement (access) rights to land are generally unenforceable. Most states have a separate statute of frauds covering leases. Generally, these statutes require a writing only for long-term leases (e.g., for leases of a year or longer). A contract to erect a building or to insure a building does not come under the real estate provision of the statute of frauds because such contracts do not involve the transfer of ownership rights.

In some cases, **part performance** of a contract for the sale of land takes the contract out of the coverage of the statute. In order for part performance to have this effect, it must clearly indicate the existence of a contract of sale and not be consistent with any other interpretation. Ordinarily, this requires that the buyer either has made substantial improvements to the property or has taken possession of the property and paid part or all of the purchase price. There are two primary reasons for allowing part performance to substitute for the statute's writing requirement. First, the courts are preventing the injustice that would occur to the party who has acted in reliance on the oral contract. Also, the nature of the reliance required in part performance cases tends to furnish good evidence that the parties did, in fact, have a contract. The only other instance where part performance has this effect is in the case of sales contracts under the Uniform Commercial Code. See the *Reich* case on the next page for further discussion.

Bilateral Contracts Not Capable of Being Performed within One Year

LO4

Long-term bilateral contracts must be in writing because contracts that call for performance over a considerable period of time increase the risk of faulty or willfully inaccurate recollection of their terms in subsequent disputes. Unfortunately, attempts at line drawing such as this can produce apparently silly results in many cases.

Reich v. Lincoln Hills Christian Church

888 N.E.2d 239 (Ind. Ct. App. 2008)

FACTS

Reich entered an agreement with Lincoln Hills Christian Church for the exchange of two properties. Reich had a remainder interest in the property owned by his mother, who had a life interest in it. She did not sign the agreement. The agreement said Lincoln Hills would pay all costs, any back taxes, moving expenses, and attorney fees, plus a payment of $40,000 to Reich. It also stated it would trade the Reich property for the Shuck property, "with property line as discussed with Webster Oglesby: Elders walked onto the property and agreed with the new property line discussed between Mr. Reich and Mr. Oglesby." A year later, Reich sought specific performance of the contract because the church refused to perform.

ISSUE

Was the property adequately described to meet the statute of frauds requirements?

DECISION

No. The statute of frauds provides that a person may not bring an action involving any contract for the sale of land unless the promise, contract, or agreement is signed by the party against whom the contract is to be enforced. It must describe with reasonable certainty each party and the land. At the time the agreement was executed, Reich's mother had a life interest in the property, but the agreement does not mention this and she did not sign it. The agreement also does not describe with reasonable certainty the Reich property. The statute of frauds is not satisfied, and Reich's claim is dismissed.

The first thing to note is that these statutes are generally worded to include only executory bilateral contracts "not to be performed within one year" or "not capable of being performed within one year." This means that if it is *possible* for the contract to be performed within a year, it need not be evidenced by a writing, despite the fact that performance *is not likely to be* or *is not in fact* completed within a year. The M & M Flying Service contract, discussed in the introductory case, was alleged to be for five years. By its terms, then, it could not be performed within a year, and had to be in writing to be enforceable.

Also note that the statutes apply only to *executory bilateral* contracts. Therefore, most courts hold that if a contract has been fully performed by one side, the promise of the other party is enforceable even if it cannot be performed within a year. Thus, if Fran lends Craig $500 and Craig orally promises to repay the loan within 18 months, Fran can enforce the promise even though it is oral.

The one-year period is computed from the time the contract comes into existence, not from the time performance is to begin. Most states begin counting on the day after the contract comes into existence (parts of days are not counted), a few on the day it is formed.

When a contract states an indefinite time for performance, it need not be evidenced by a writing if it is possible to perform the contract within one year. So, oral contracts to perform "for life" are generally enforceable, since one of the parties concerned could die within a year and have thereby fully performed.

What Kind of Writing Is Required?

While the statutes of frauds of all the states are not the same, most states require only a *memorandum* of the parties' agreement; they do not require that the entire contract be in writing or that the writing be in a single document. The writing can be in any form, including letters, telegrams, receipts, or any other writing indicating that the parties had a contract. It can be made any time before the suit is filed.

Although there is a general trend away from requiring complete writings to satisfy the statute of frauds, an adequate memorandum must still contain several things. The identity of the parties to the contract must be indicated in some way, and the subject matter of the contract must be identified with reasonable certainty. These things can be contained in several documents, so long as it is clear that the documents all relate to the same agreement. The requirement that the subject matter be identified with reasonable certainty causes particular problems in contracts for the sale of land, since many states require a detailed description of the property to be sold. The statutes of the states vary on whether the memorandum must state the consideration agreed to by the parties.

One point on which the states generally agree is that the memorandum needs to be signed only by the party to be bound (or his or her agent). This means that both parties' signatures do not have to appear in the writing. The idea here simply is that it is the defendant who needs protection against fraud, so it is his or her signature that is required to satisfy the statute. It is, however, in the best interests of both parties for both signatures to appear on the writing; otherwise, the contract evidenced by the writing is enforceable only against the signing party. In most instances, the signature can appear any place on the memorandum. Any writing, mark, initials, stamp, engraving, or other symbol placed or printed on a memorandum will suffice as a signature if it was intended to authenticate (indicate the genuineness of) the writing.

Cyber-Contracts and E-Signatures

The increasing number of contracts transacted over the Internet has prompted legislative reform at both the state and federal levels to facilitate e-commerce without revising traditional contract rules. Enacted in 2000, the Electronic Signatures in Global and National Commerce Act (E-Sign) pertains to agreements affecting interstate commerce and provides that a contract or signature may not be denied legal effect "solely because it is in electronic form." This gives a digital signature the same effect as one written in ink on paper. E-Sign defines an electronic signature as "any electronic sound, symbol, or process attached to or logically associated with a contract or other record and executed or accepted by a person with the intent to sign the records." Such signatures are already in common use. A PIN number used to access an ATM and a password used to enter a website would meet this definition.

However, E-Sign sets precise rules that businesses must follow when seeking consumer consent to electronic contracts. These include gaining a consumer's "affirmative consent" to receive contractual information electronically, making clear when consent is for more than a single transaction, and spelling out the procedures and price for withdrawing consent in the future. E-businesses must not only make clear to consumers the system's requirements for receiving electronic data but also refrain from imposing consent withdrawal fees if the consumer, at some future date, can no longer receive electronic information because the business has upgraded its system. By creating a uniform national law, Congress intended to promote and foster e-business.

Congress also intended for E-Sign to work in conjunction with the Uniform Electronic Transactions Act (UETA). The UETA is a proposed uniform state law that, like E-Sign, is intended to remove barriers to e-commerce by giving effect to electronic records and signatures. Unlike E-Sign, however, UETA does not offer specific rules governing when consent has been given electronically. At the time of this writing, over 40 states had adopted UETA.

Coca-Cola v. Babyback's International, Inc.

841 N.E.2d 557 (Ind. Sup. Ct. 2006)

FACTS

Coca-Cola Bottling Company of Indianapolis (Coke Indy) had an agreement with Babyback's International, Inc. (BBI), under which Coke Indy would pay BBI to arrange for coolers to display the companies' products side by side in Indianapolis. BBI then began discussions with Coca-Cola Enterprises (CCE) about a similar marketing plan in Louisville. BBI performed pursuant to the discussions but no contract was signed. They continued discussions at CCE's headquarters in Atlanta about nationwide expansion, which would have lasted for more than a year. BBI alleged a memorandum faxed to it by CCE summarized the oral agreement, which was to last more than a year. The day after BBI made the claim, it was denied by CCE. BBI sued to enforce the contract, arguing that its part performance and the memo made CCE's statute of frauds defense invalid.

ISSUE

Is CCE's statute of frauds defense valid?

DECISION

Yes. BBI's argument regarding part performance is not successful. There is no part performance exception to a contract that cannot be performed within a year. The memorandum also is not sufficient to remove the contract from the statute of frauds. It merely shows that the parties had not yet reached an agreement. The memo lacked essential terms such as starting date, amount of up-front payments, the identity and location of stores to be involved, and the allocation of responsibilities for advertising, promotion, and delivery and installation of the coolers. The overall incompleteness unequivocally establishes that no final agreement had been reached.

The Code's Statute of Frauds

LO5

The Code has its own statute of frauds section (2-201), which applies to contracts for the sale of goods for $500 or more. The unique thing about the Code's approach to the statute of frauds issue is that the Code recognizes that the basic purpose of the statute of frauds (to provide more evidence that a contract existed than the mere oral testimony of one of the parties) can be satisfied by several kinds of things *other than a writing.*

East Lynn Fertilizers, Inc. v. CHS, Inc.

2010 WL 5070752 (C.D. Ill. Dec. 30, 2010)

FACTS

Hostetter, an agent for CHS, orally negotiated a deal with Allen in which East Lynn would buy 360 tons of anhydrous ammonia for $1,180/ton, for delivery in April 2009. Hostetter sent an e-mail confirming the terms and stating, "Invoice and contract to follow." A few days later CHS sent a "Crop Nutrient Sales Agreement" which was signed and returned by Allen. Also, Allen paid 10 percent down, or $42,800. Allen wanted to ensure he would have enough inventory for his customers the following spring. CHS did not sign the agreement but filed it. Four months later the price of the chemical had dropped significantly and Allen sent a letter to Hostetter, with whom he had done business for several years, seeking to modify the contract and explaining he needed a lower price in order to remain competitive. The next month he sent a letter stating that he didn't need so much ammonia because he had lost customers due to the price he had to charge and that since CHS had not signed the agreement, it was not binding. He sued for the return of his deposit and CHS sued for breach of contract.

ISSUE

Should Allen be held to the sales agreement?

DECISION

Yes. Through their actions, the parties manifested a present intent to be bound: CHS when it sent the agreement to Allen, and Allen when he signed the agreement. Under the UCC., a sales contract for more than $500 must be in writing and signed by the party to be charged. The statute of frauds was satisfied here because CHS's signature

(continued)

was not required. It was only required of the party to be bound, in this case, Allen, who had signed. Additionally, the agreement stated that acceptance could be in the form of any payment made under the agreement, which Allen did. Therefore, CHS is justified in keeping the deposit.

If the goods are *specially manufactured for the buyer* and "not suitable for sale to others in the normal course of the seller's business," and the seller has made a substantial beginning in manufacturing them or has entered a binding agreement to acquire them for the buyer before learning that the buyer is denying the existence of a contract, the buyer loses the statute of frauds defense (2-201[3][a]).

The Code permits other exceptions to the writing requirement when it has other reliable proof of the existence of a contract. For instance, if a party being sued on a contract *admits the existence* of the contract in testimony in court or in any of the pleadings filed during the course of the lawsuit, that satisfies the statute (2-201[3][b]).

Partial performance also creates an exception. If a party accepts goods or accepts payment for goods, the statute of frauds is satisfied *to the extent of the payment made or the goods accepted* (2-201[3][c]). For example, Mary and John have an oral contract for the sale of 100 pairs of boots at $10 a pair. If Mary delivers the boots and John accepts them, or if John pays for the boots and Mary accepts payment, neither can raise the statute of frauds as a defense. If, however, only some of the boots are delivered (50 pairs) or only a partial payment is made ($500), the remainder of the agreement is unenforceable.

The basic Code writing requirement (2-201[1]) is that there be evidence of the parties' contract in the form of a written memorandum that indicates the existence of a contract between the parties, indicates the quantity of goods sold, and is signed by the party to be charged. So, a letter that said

> I agree to sell to John Smith 200 wrenches.
>
> (Signed)
>
> Steve Jones

would be sufficient to satisfy the Code's writing requirement against Steve.

In most cases, however, John Smith would have a good statute of frauds defense against Steve because John did not sign the writing. The Code provides, however, that if John is a *merchant* and he receives this writing from Steve and does not object in writing within 10 days after receiving it, he loses his statute of frauds defense (2-201[2]). Steve still must convince the court that the parties had a contract, but he is not prevented by the statute of frauds from trying to do so. The idea behind this subsection of the Code is that the natural response of a person who did not have a contract would be to object. John's failure to object satisfies the statute's requirement of some extra proof (beyond Steve's oral testimony) that a contract existed.

MEMC Electronic Materials, Inc. v. BP Solar Int'l, Inc.

9 A.3d 508 (Md. Ct. Spec. App. 2010)

FACTS

MEMC supplied BP Solar with silicon powder used in manufacturing solar panels under a long-standing relationship. Seeking to get a long-term contract, BP Solar e-mailed MEMC to ask for a quote for 300 tons of powder for three years. MEMC replied that it could commit to 150 tons for

(continued)

MEMC Electronic Materials, Inc. v. BP Solar Int'l, Inc. *(concluded)*

the next three years at $3.50/kg for the coming year, with the price for the next two years to be negotiated. There after, they talked by phone. An internal e-mail was circulated, with a copy to BP Solar, stating that it was anticipated that a larger quantity would be available and that pricing would be determined later. BP Solar e-mailed the next day. "I agree with [the] comments below." After a few more e-mail exchanges, MEMC shipped 224 tons. It then discontinued its shipments and BP Solar sued for breach of contract. MEMC argued there was no contract because the parties were still negotiating, particularly regarding the price, and there was no signed writing from BP Solar.

ISSUE

Was there sufficient evidence of a contract to satisfy the UCC. Statute of Frauds?

DECISION

Yes. The purpose of the Statute of Frauds is to prevent fraud, not to prevent enforcement of legitimate transactions. Maryland law recognizes that a series of writings can satisfy the statute. Also, if so intended, a typed name is sufficient for a signature. Here, the e-mail messages indicated an agreement, and the one indicating a minimum of 150 metric tons per year for three years satisfied the quantity requirement. Additionally, a minimum price was established in an e-mail from BP Solar to MEMC which MEMC received and did not object to. This satisfies a UCC. merchant exception to the statute of frauds. Under the exception, even when there is no writing signed by the person against whom the enforcement is sought, the statute of frauds will not bar action if the defendant is a merchant who received but did not object to a written confirmation within 10 days after receipt (UCC. Section 2-201[2]). The contract is enforceable.

Concept Summary: Statute of Frauds

Type of Contract Required to Be in Writing	Exception (besides Promissory Estoppel)
1. Executor's agreements to personally pay decedent's debts.	
2. Collateral guaranty contracts.	Leading object rule.
3. Transfers of interest in land.	Part performance.
4. Bilateral contracts incapable of performance within one year.	(Construe as possible to perform within a year.)
5. Contract for sale of goods for $500 or more.	Specially manufactured goods. Admission. Part performance. Merchant's failure to object to memo within 10 days.

Interpreting Contracts

The Necessity of Interpretation

Many times the parties to a contract disagree about the meaning of one or more terms of their agreement. When this occurs, the courts must interpret or construe the contract to determine the rights and duties of the parties. The interpretation of uncertain or ambiguous terms is a question for the jury. The basic standard of interpretation is objective: The courts attempt to give the agreement the meaning that a reasonable person would be expected to give it in light of the surrounding facts and circumstances.

Rules of Construction

The courts have created certain basic rules to guide them in interpreting contracts. Most of these are simply matters of common sense. The first thing a court does is attempt to determine the *principal objective* of the parties. Every clause of the contract is then interpreted in light of this principal objective. Ordinary words are given their usual meaning and technical words their technical meaning unless a different meaning was clearly intended.

If the parties are both members of the same trade, profession, or community in which certain words are commonly given a particular meaning (this is called *usage*), the courts presume the parties intended the words' meanings to be controlled by that trade usage. For example, if the word *dozen* in the bakery business means 13 rather than 12, a contract between two bakers for the purchase of 10 dozen loaves of bread will be presumed to mean 130 loaves rather than 120. Usage can also add provisions to the parties' agreement. If the court finds that a certain practice is a matter of common usage in the trade, profession, or community of the parties, the court assumes that the parties intended to include that practice in their agreement. Parties who are members of a common business, profession, or community and who intend not to be bound by usage should specifically say so in their agreement.

If the parties used a form contract, or the contract is partly printed and partly written, the *written terms control the printed terms* if the two conflict. If one of the parties drafted the contract, ambiguities are resolved *against the party who drafted the contract.* This is especially true in insurance contracts.

State Automobile Mutual Insurance Company v. Flexdar, Inc.

964 N.E.2d 845 (Ind. Sup. Ct. 2012)

FACTS

Flexdar manufactured rubber stamps and printing plates and, in the process, used the chemical trichloroethylene (TCE). When it was discovered that TCE was present in the groundwater around the plant, the Indiana Department of Environmental Management said Flexdar would be liable for cleanup costs. Flexdat had a general liability policy and an umbrella policy with State Automobile Mutual Insurance (State Auto). There was a pollution exclusion in the policy. Pollutants were defined as "any solid, liquid, gaseous or thermal irritant or contaminant, including smoke, vapor, soot, fumes, acids, alkalis, chemicals, and waste." State Auto said it was not required to cover the costs for the cleanup. Flexdar sued, arguing that the language of the policy was ambiguous and therefore open to interpretation by the court.

ISSUE

Was the exclusion clause sufficiently ambiguous so that interpretation was required?

DECISION

Yes. The clause cannot be read literally because it would negate nearly all coverage. Practically every substance would qualify as a pollutant, rendering the exclusion meaningless. To take a literal approach would yield untenable results. We apply a different approach. Applying basic contract principles, our decisions have consistently held the insurer should specify what falls within its pollution exclusion. We have refused to uphold similar language in previous cases and State Auto should have known this. Where an insurer's failure to be more specific renders its policy ambiguous, we construe the policy in favor of coverage and against the insurer. After all, the insurance company writes the policies, and we buy the forms or we do not buy insurance. Thus, we find that TCE is not a pollutant.

The Parol Evidence Rule

The Purpose of the Rule

LO6

The basic idea behind the parol evidence rule is that when the parties to an agreement have expressed their agreement in a complete, unambiguous writing, the writing is the best evidence of their intent. This is generally true since the terms of the writing are known and irrefutable, whereas oral statements by the parties after a dispute has arisen regarding what they had agreed to may be affected by faulty memory, wishful thinking, or outright bad intent. Even prior writings made by the parties may represent only preliminary subjects of negotiation on which the parties never agreed. So, the **parol evidence rule** says that a party cannot vary the terms of a written contract by introducing evidence of terms allegedly agreed on *prior to, or contemporaneous with* (at the same time as), the writing. (See Figure 16.4.)

FIGURE 16.4
Parol Evidence Rule

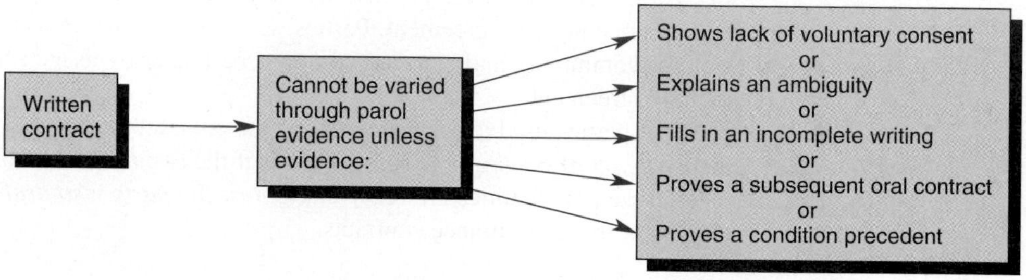

The parol evidence rule is a potential source of danger for parties who reduce their agreements to written form, since it can operate to prevent proof of terms that the parties did, in fact, agree to. For example, Bob buys a house from Susan. They orally agree that Susan will pay for any major repairs the house needs for the first year Bob owns it. The written contract of sale, however, does not include this term, and when the furnace breaks down three months after the sale, Susan refuses to pay the cost of repair. If the written contract is complete and unambiguous, Bob will probably be barred from proving the oral repair term.

The lesson to be learned from this example is that parties who put their agreements in writing should make sure that all the terms of their agreement are included in the writing.

Extra Equipamentos e Exportacao v. Case Corp.

541 F.3d 719 (7th Cir. 2008)

FACTS

Case, an Illinois-based equipment manufacturer, hired Brazilian distributor Extra Equipamentos to distribute its products in that South American nation in 1992. Seven years later, Extra sued subsidiary Case Brazil in Brazilian court, saying that employees there had fradulently overcharged Extra. The president of Extra and a vice president of Case later signed a "Release of Claims and Settlement of Certain Obligations," in which the parties set limits on past due payments and agreed to drop the lawsuit. Case Brazil later quit using Extra as its distributor. In 2001, two years after the release was signed, Extra sued in a U.S. court, claiming that Case's vice president had orally promised, while negotiating the release, that Case Brazil would keep using Extra as a distributor if

(continued)

Extra signed the release. Extra claimed Case had fradulently manipulated its official into signing a release that gave Case benefits, but which Case never intended to honor.

ISSUE

Should Case be bound by its executive's oral agreement to keep employing Extra?

DECISION

No. To prove fraud, a victim must show that he relied on another's fradulent representations. Case and Extra's release states that it "constitutes the entire agreement between the parties, and . . . supersedes all prior negotiations and agreements" on that issue. Another section of the release, entitled "No Reliance On The Other Party," says that "the parties are not relying on representations or statements made by the other party or any person representing them except for the representations and warranties expressed in this Release." These clauses are sometimes called "big boy" clauses, affirming "we're big boys and can look after ourselves." Such clauses let parties rely on the terms of a written contract without worry that parties will later sue over extraneous discussions. In common law, this is codified in the "parol evidence rule," which forbids evidence of discussions in a contract's negotiation from varying the final contract's written terms, if the contract seems clear and complete. The parol evidence rule covers contracts, not tort claims for fraud. But Extra's fraud claim is based solely on an oral statement made during contract negotiations; allowing the claim would make fraud suits a tool for subverting the parol evidence rule. The president of a large company, represented by experienced U.S. and Brazilian lawyers, agreed to the release and its "no-reliance" clause. Extra is a big boy, and the clause is valid and applicable.

Exceptions to the Parol Evidence Rule

There are many situations in which either the writing is not the best evidence of the agreement between the parties, or a party is not challenging the writing but instead is challenging the underlying contractual obligation that the writing represents. These are the bases of thc following exceptions, where oral testimony regarding the meaning of the written contract is allowed.

Lack of Voluntary Consent

A party is always allowed to introduce oral proof that the contract the writing represents was entered into as the result of fraud, misrepresentation, duress, undue influence, or mistake. This sort of proof is allowed because it does not seek to contradict the terms of the writing and because of our strong public policy against enforcing such agreements. For the same reasons, oral testimony that attempts to show that the contract is illegal is also allowed.

Ambiguous Contracts

If the terms of the writing are unclear, oral testimony can be introduced to aid the court in interpreting the writing. A party can introduce testimony about the facts and circumstances surrounding the agreement without contradicting its terms.

Incomplete Writings

If the writing is clearly incomplete, a party can introduce proof of consistent oral terms that "fill the gaps" in the writing. A party is never allowed, however, to use this exception to alter, vary, or contradict the written terms of the contract.

Subsequent Oral Contracts

A party can always introduce proof of an oral agreement made after the writing was created. A writing made on the 5th of the month is plainly not the best evidence of an agreement made on the 10th of the month. You should note, however, that subsequent oral modifications of contracts may sometimes be unenforceable due to lack of consideration or failure to comply with the statute of frauds. In addition, the courts look closely at the evidence of the claimed oral modification.

Conditions Precedent

If the written agreement is silent about the date it is to take effect or about any conditions that must occur before it becomes effective, oral testimony can be introduced to prove these facts. Such proof merely elaborates on, but does not contradict, the terms of the writing.

Contracts controlled by the U.N. Convention on the International Sale of Goods also allow oral testimony about the meaning of the contract. While the CISG does not specifically mention parol evidence, courts are interpreting the convention to allow it.

Concept Summary: Form and Meaning of Contracts

1. A contract is unenforceable if it lacks a writing as required by the statute of frauds. Contracts covered by the statute of frauds include:
   a. Executor's agreement to personally pay decedent's debts.
   b. Collateral or guaranty contract.
   c. Contract transferring an interest in land.
   d. Bilateral contract incapable of being performed within one year.
2. A contract may be enforceable if promissory estoppel or other exception applies.
3. A written contract cannot be varied by parol evidence (unless exception applies).

Questions and Problem Cases

1. What does the statute of frauds say about an executor's agreement to personally pay a decedent's debts?
2. Explain the basic idea behind the statute of frauds
3. Describe three exceptions to the parol evidence rule.
4. Dr. Conner, a family practitioner, worked under one-year contracts at a rural clinic operated by a hospital. During contract negotiations for the coming year, she asked that her time at the clinic be separated from her time at the hospital in order to help with a tax issue. During negotiations, she continued to work without a contract. She finally presented her case to the hospital's board of directors, who entered into an agreement to offer her a three-year contract that spelled out monthly salary and vacation days. They encouraged the administrator, attorneys, and the doctor's representative to work out the changes and to come back to them. Four days later the board met in emergency session and voted to rescind the earlier motion. They then made offers to other doctors for less lucrative contracts while continuing to employ Conner. After several months, she sued. The hospital defended by arguing the statute of frauds was not met. Is this correct? Why?
5. The Fujiis told Nakamura they could not pay their daughter's tuition at USC and asked him to pay "certain tuition invoices" for her. He orally agreed in exchange for their express promise to repay the money on demand. He issued five checks to USC totaling $40,339 over a 15-month period. A year later the Fujiis made the same request for their younger daughter, and he orally agreed on the same conditions. He issued six checks for her tuition over a three-year period, totaling $60,964. When Nakamura

demanded payment, the Fujiis refused to pay, and Nakamura sued them. Will the statute of frauds prevent Nakamura from collecting? Explain.

6. Valentine, an adult, was charged with criminal assault. His parents contacted the Crozier law firm about representing him, and the firm agreed. It claimed the parents orally agreed to guarantee payment for the legal fees incurred by their son. Valentine's mother paid a retainer fee of $250. The firm represented the son until the parents asked it to stop. The firm claimed it was owed $4,200, and sued the parents for that amount. The parents defended by citing the statute of frauds. Is the parents' oral promise enforceable?
7. Popanz, the associate director of Peregrine Corp., was offered the position of director. She refused the position based on the oral promise made by the director when Popanz had been hired that she could retain her current position until she reached age 65, which would happen in several years. Three years later Peregrine terminated Popanz when it eliminated her position. She sued for breach of the promise of employment until 65. Is her claim barred by the statute of frauds? Explain.
8. Daniels sells Formula One memorabilia. He sold an autographed Michael Schumacher helmet to Wehry for $3,500. While in Daniels shop, he saw a reproduction of an Ayrton Senna helmet which he also wanted. He was told it was only sold in a set of three, but that Daniels would see if the distributor would sell it individually. A few days later he told Wehry he would sell it separately. Wehry told him to order it. When it arrived, Wehry also wanted a Ferrari model and told Daniels he would pick it and the helmet up when the Ferrari model arrived. When it arrived, Wehry said he would be in the following week to pick both up. When he didn't come, he told Daniels that he had been busy and would pick them up before Christmas. This didn't happen, and Daniels finally sued. Wehry admitted he had ordered the items. Can Daniels collect even though there is no writing? Why?
9. Indiana University basketball coach Bob Knight had a homeowner's policy with Indiana Insurance Co. The policy had a "business exclusion" that excluded bodily injury which is expected or intended, or which arises out of a business engaged in by the insured. Knight was sued by his assistant coach for pushing him and causing him to fall. Knight settled the suit by agreeing to pay him $25,000 and admitting he had pushed him. Knight then sought indemnification under his homeowner's policy. Does the exclusion apply to Knight's actions? Explain why.

Chapter 17

Third Parties' Contract Rights

Learning Objectives

After you have studied this chapter, you should be able to:

1. Describe an assignment and explain which contracts are assignable.
2. List the rights and duties of assignees.
3. Explain a delegation of duties and its effect.
4. Discuss the difference between a donee beneficiary and a creditor beneficiary.
5. Define an incidental beneficiary and whether he or she has any rights under a contract.

Peterson had a three-year employment contract as a newscaster-anchorman on WTOP-TV. After one year under this contract, the station was sold, and Peterson's contract was assigned to the new owner. Peterson subsequently negotiated a contract with another station and resigned. When he was sued by the new owner for breach of contract, Peterson claimed the new owner had no rights under his contract with the former owners of the station and therefore could not sue him.

- Can someone pursue rights under another person's contract?
- Did Peterson have a right not to have his contract assigned to someone with whom he had not contracted?
- Could Peterson hold the original owners liable if the new owners breached the contract with him?

FIGURE 17.1
Third Parties' Contract Rights

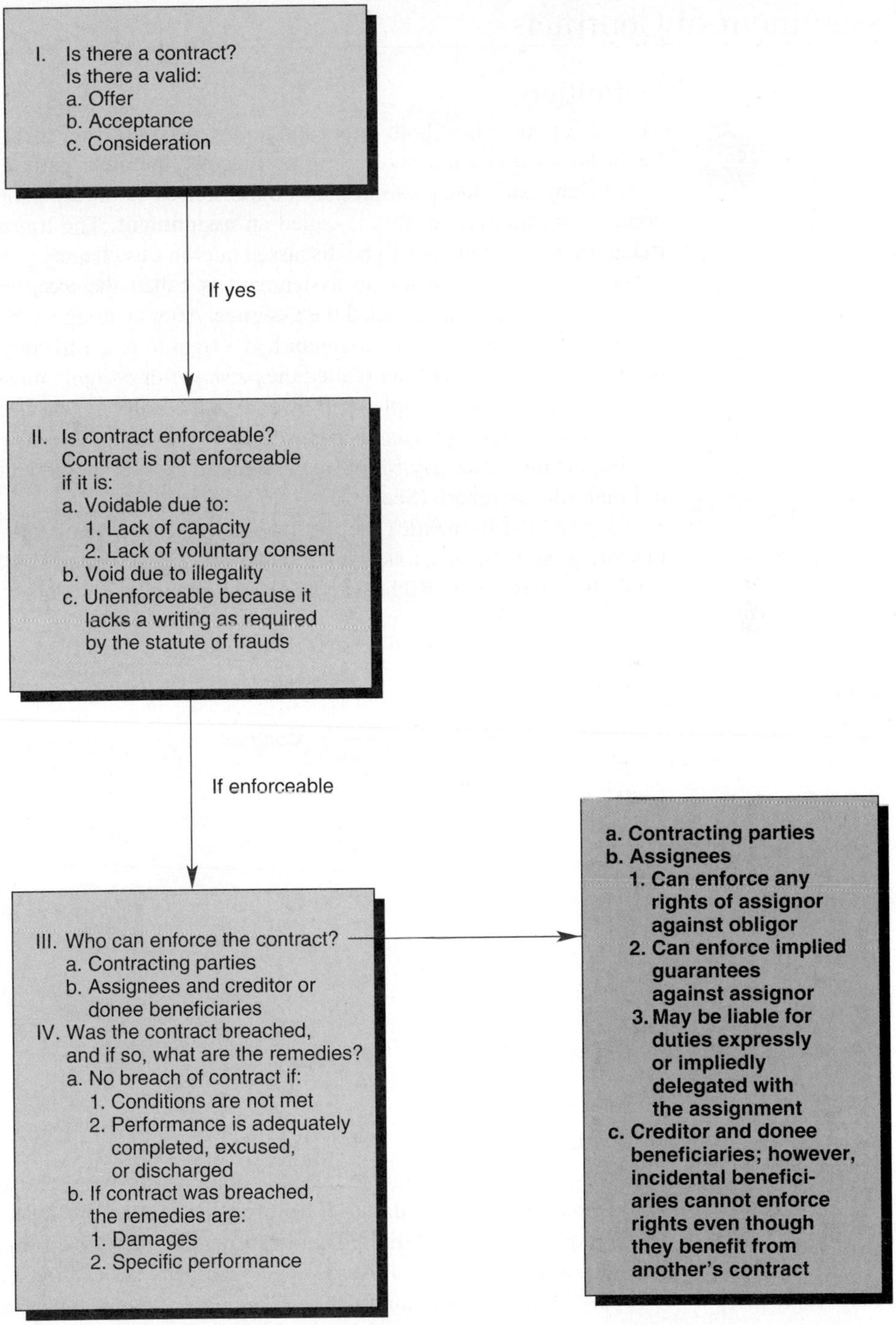

I. Is there a contract?
Is there a valid:
a. Offer
b. Acceptance
c. Consideration
If yes
II. Is contract enforceable?
Contract is not enforceable if it is:
a. Voidable due to:
1. Lack of capacity
2. Lack of voluntary consent
b. Void due to illegality
c. Unenforceable because it lacks a writing as required by the statute of frauds
If enforceable
III. Who can enforce the contract?
a. Contracting parties
b. Assignees and creditor or donee beneficiaries
IV. Was the contract breached, and if so, what are the remedies?
a. No breach of contract if:
1. Conditions are not met
2. Performance is adequately completed, excused, or discharged
b. If contract was breached, the remedies are:
1. Damages
2. Specific performance
a. Contracting parties
b. Assignees
1. Can enforce any rights of assignor against obligor
2. Can enforce implied guarantees against assignor
3. May be liable for duties expressly or impliedly delegated with the assignment
c. Creditor and donee beneficiaries; however, incidental beneficiaries cannot enforce rights even though they benefit from another's contract

Up to this point our discussion of contracts has focused on the rights and duties of the original parties to the contract. There are, however, two kinds of situations in which persons who were not originally parties to a contract may claim some interest in it: These concern assignments of contracts and third-party beneficiaries of contracts.

Assignment of Contracts

Definition

LO1

A contract consists of both rights and duties. A contracting party has the duty to perform his or her own promise and the right to receive the other party's promised performance. These rights and duties can usually be transferred to third persons. When *rights* under a contract are transferred, this is called an **assignment.** The transfer of *duties* is called a **delegation.** Delegations will be discussed later in this chapter.

The person who makes an assignment is called the **assignor,** and the person who accepts the assignment is called the **assignee.** After an assignment, the assignee is entitled to whatever performance the assignor had a right to under the original contract. The other original party to the contract (called the *promisor* or *obligor*) must render all performance to the assignee. For example, Bill owes Frank $100, payable in six months. Frank, who needs money today, assigns his rights to the payment to Mary for $80. Bill (the promisor or obligor) must now pay Mary (the assignee) the $100 he previously owed a duty to pay to Frank (the assignor). (See Figure 17.2.)

No particular formalities are required to create an assignment. It can be done orally or in writing, so long as the assignor's intent to assign is clear. In addition, consideration is generally not required. Rights can be given away as well as sold.

FIGURE 17.2
Assignment Obligations

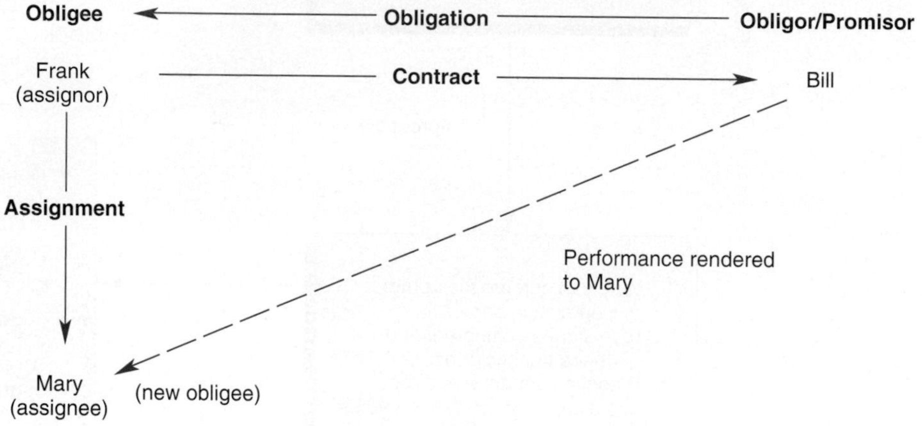

What Contracts Are Assignable?

LO1

Not all contracts are assignable over the objection of the promisor. Any assignment that would *materially alter* the duties of the promisor is unenforceable, since the promisor cannot be required to do something significantly more than, or different from, what he or she originally agreed to do. So, if Acme Sugar Company has entered a "requirements" contract to supply all the sugar requirements of Goody Candy Company, a small candy manufacturer, Goody could not assign its contract rights to Yummy Candy Corporation, a much larger candy manufacturer. Clearly, Yummy's sugar requirements would be much greater than Goody's.

Contracts involving *personal rights* are also generally nonassignable. These are contracts in which some element of personal skill, credit, character, or judgment is an essential part of the agreement. In such a case, the substitution of the assignee for the assignor would materially change the nature of the performance required of the promisor. Employment contracts are therefore generally held nonassignable. In the Peterson case in the chapter opening, however, the court found that Peterson's contract was assignable since his duties did not change and the sale merely substituted one corporate owner for another. The corporate owners did not render personal services to Peterson.

Contracts that *expressly forbid assignment* are also generally nonassignable. However, some states refuse to enforce such clauses where the rights assigned would otherwise be assignable. Other states interpret nonassignment clauses very strictly. For example, a court may say that a clause barring assignment of the contract prohibits only the delegation of duties. The *Restatement* and the Uniform Commercial Code take this latter approach. Bankruptcy filings can also cause a court to assign a contract despite nonassignment clauses.

Travelers Casualty and Surety Co., Inc. v. U.S. Filter Corp.

895 N.E.2d 1172 (Ind. Sup. Ct. 2008)

FACTS

U.S. Filter was one of five companies that sought coverage from Travelers for personal injury claims brought against them. The injuries were due to silica exposure from the operation of Wheelabrator blast machines, now owned by U.S. Filter. Wheelabrator had a complex ownership history spanning nearly 100 years, with different companies owning it and the stock being assigned several times. As a result of this long history, there were over 80 insurance policies that might be applicable. Each of the policies contained a provision that required consent from the insurer for any assignment of policy rights. The insurers argued that the insurance rights did not transfer with the changes in ownership. The companies argued that the policy coverage was assigned with each change in ownership down the line of corporate succession.

ISSUE

Were the contracts assigned when the ownership was transferred?

DECISION

No. The free flow of capital and assets between business entities is important for the vitality of national and international markets. Normally, in mergers and consolidations, assets and liabilities are transferred, including insurance coverage rights, to the new entity. However, the policies here contained a non-assignment-without-consent clause. Consent-to-assignment clauses are virtually boilerplate in most contracts of insurance. Insurers have a legitimate interest in restraining assignment; these provisions protect them from a material increase in risk for which they did not bargain. Courts widely recognize an exception to the enforcement of such clauses for assignments made after the loss has occurred. This is because once the loss occurs, the insurance company's risk is not increased because the claim has now vested.

Assignments *contrary to public policy* are also not effective. *Assignments of future wages* are an example. In order to protect wage earners from unwisely impoverishing themselves, some states prohibit wage assignments by statute. Others allow such assignments but regulate them in various ways, such as limiting the amount that may be assigned.

Generally, all other kinds of assignments that do not involve personal relationships or increase the promisor's burden are enforceable. Promises to pay money, deliver goods, or sell land are generally assignable. Contracts not to compete with a buyer of a business or an employer are also generally assignable with the sale of the business. The purpose of such contracts is to protect the *goodwill* of the business (the value of the business as a going concern), an asset that can be sold with the business.

The Consequences of Assignment

The Rights and Duties of Assignees

LO2

An assignee is entitled to all the rights his or her assignor had under the assigned contract, including the right to the promisor's performance. If the promisor does not perform, the assignee can sue for nonperformance. An assignee, however, cannot acquire any greater rights than the assignor has. Therefore, if the promisor has a good defense against the assignor (e.g., fraud, lack of consideration, lack of capacity), that defense is also good against the assignee.

Assignees should promptly notify the promisor of the assignment. This is necessary because the promisor who renders performance to the assignor without notice of the assignment has no further liability under the contract. Promisors with notice of the assignment who render performance to the assignor or to any third party remain liable to the assignee under the assigned contract. Assignors who accept performance from the promisor after the assignment hold any benefits they receive as trustee for their assignees.

Notice to the promisor may be important in one other situation. If the assignor later wrongfully assigns the contract to a second assignee who pays for it without notice of the first assignment, a question of priority results. Who is entitled to the promisor's performance, and who is stuck with a lawsuit against the assignor? The majority of states follow the *American rule,* which holds that the first assignee has priority. Some states, however, follow the *English rule,* which gives priority to the first assignee to give notice of assignment. In both types of states, a potential assignee should contact the promisor before taking the assignment.

Assignors who are *paid* for making an assignment are potentially liable to assignees for certain **implied guarantees.** These guarantees are imposed by law unless the assignment agreement clearly indicates to the contrary. They are:

1. The assigned claim is valid, which means that:
   a. The promisor has capacity to contract.
   b. The contract is not illegal.
   c. The contract is not voidable for any other reason known to the assignor (such as fraud or misrepresentation).
   d. The contract has not been discharged prior to assignment.
2. The assignor has good title to the rights assigned.
3. The assignor will not do anything to impair the value of the assignment.
4. Any written instrument representing the assigned claim is genuine.

Assignors who wrongfully assign the same claim more than once are therefore liable to an assignee who is later held to have acquired no rights against the promisor. The assignor does not impliedly warrant the solvency of the promisor.

Delegation of Duties

LO3

When a promisor appoints another to perform his duties under a contract, this is called a *delegation.* Like assignments, not all duties are delegable. If the duty to be performed could be performed fully by many different persons, it is delegable. If performance depends on the personal skill, character, or judgment of the promisor, however, it may not be delegated. Thus, in the Peterson case in the chapter opening, Peterson would not have been able to delegate his duties to another newscaster-anchorman since they involved his personal skill. Public policy can also prevent the delegation of duties.

Sometimes it is not clear whether a delegation was intended. Does an assignment of the assignor's rights carry with it an implied delegation of the assignor's duties under the contract? Unless the assignment agreement clearly indicates a contrary intent, courts today tend to interpret assignments as including a delegation of the assignor's duties. A promise on the part of the assignee to perform these duties is implied, and this implied promise is enforceable by *either* the promisor or the assignor. Both the Code and the *Restatement* support this interpretation. If general assignment language is used, such as an assignment of "the contract," or of "all my rights under the contract," courts following the Code or *Restatement* would interpret it as creating both an assignment and a delegation.

The promisor who delegates duties is *still liable* to the promisee if the party to whom the duties were delegated fails to satisfactorily perform them. This rule is necessary to make contracts truly binding; otherwise, a promisor could avoid virtually all liability by merely delegating duties she did not want to perform.

Riegleman v. Krieg

679 N.W.2d 857 (Wis. Ct. App. 2004)

FACTS

Krieg was involved in a work-related automobile accident. He retained the services of the Warshafsky law firm to represent him in his personal injury claim. Riegleman provided chiropractic treatment to Krieg for approximately three years after his accident. Riegleman's total treatment bill exceeded $19,000. Krieg and the law firm both signed a doctor's lien document, which authorized and directed the law firm to pay the chiropractor such sums as might be due for service rendered to Krieg and to withhold that amount from any settlement, judgment, or verdict. After Krieg's personal injury case settled in mediation, Krieg and the firm were advised by another doctor that Riegleman's charges were excessive and they refused to release $5,640 from the settlement funds that was owed to Riegleman. Riegleman sued Krieg and the law firm.

ISSUE

Did Krieg successfully delegate his duty to pay Riegleman to the law firm?

DECISION

Yes. An assignment of rights under a contract is a delegation of performance of the duties of the assignor and its acceptance by the assignee constitutes a promise by the assignee to perform those duties. This promise is enforceable by either the assignor or the other party to the original contract. Here, the document is an unambiguous contract creating an assignment. It shows clear language of its intent: Krieg authorized "my attorney, to pay directly to [Riegleman] such sums as may be due and owing him for service rendered to me, and to withhold such sums from such settlement, judgment, or verdict as may be necessary to protect [Riegleman] adequately." The Warshafsky law firm agreed "to honor the (lien) to protect adequately said above named doctor." An attorney should not assume that he or she can ignore an assignment that he or she has agreed to honor simply because a client changes his or her mind about the assignment. As the Warshafsky law firm executed such an assignment, it is obligated to distribute the proceeds of the claim in accordance with it. Therefore, the Warshafsky law firm and Krieg are jointly and severally liable for the medical fees due and owing Riegleman.

The only exception to this rule is when the parties enter into a novation. A **novation** is a new, separate agreement by the promisee to release the original promisor from liability in exchange for a third party's agreement to assume the promisor's duties. To have a novation requires more than the obligee's consent to having the delegate perform the duties. The language used by the parties or the circumstances surrounding the transaction must show that the obligee consented to the *substitution* of one obligor for another.

Third-Party Beneficiary Contracts

Generally, those who are not parties to a contract have no rights in the contract even though they may benefit from its performance. If the parties to the contract *intended* to benefit a third party, however, the third party can enforce the contract. There are two classes of **third-party beneficiaries** that have such enforcement rights: **donee beneficiaries** and **creditor beneficiaries.** If the third party only incidentally benefits from the contract and was not an intended beneficiary, he or she is an **incidental beneficiary** and cannot enforce it.

A factor that is often considered in determining intent to benefit is whether the person making the promise to perform was to render performance directly to the third party. For example, if Mary contracts with Greetings Galore to have balloons delivered to Joe on his birthday, the fact that the balloons were to be delivered to Joe would be good evidence that the parties intended to benefit Joe. Once a donee or creditor beneficiary has accepted the contract, or relied on it, the original parties cannot cancel or modify the contract without the third party's consent, unless the original contract gives them the right to do so. Generally, life insurance contracts give the insured the right to change the beneficiary without the beneficiary's consent.

Donee Beneficiaries

LO4

A third person is a *donee beneficiary* if the promisee's *primary purpose* in contracting was to make a *gift* of the contracted performance to the third party. Either the promisee or the donee beneficiary can sue the promisor for not performing the promise. The beneficiary can recover the value of the promised performance, while the promisee can recover damages resulting from nonperformance (usually only nominal damages). In the example above, Joe was a donee beneficiary of Greetings Galore and Mary's contract, and he as well as Mary could sue if Greetings Galore failed to perform. (See Figure 17.3.)

FIGURE 17.3
Donee Beneficiary

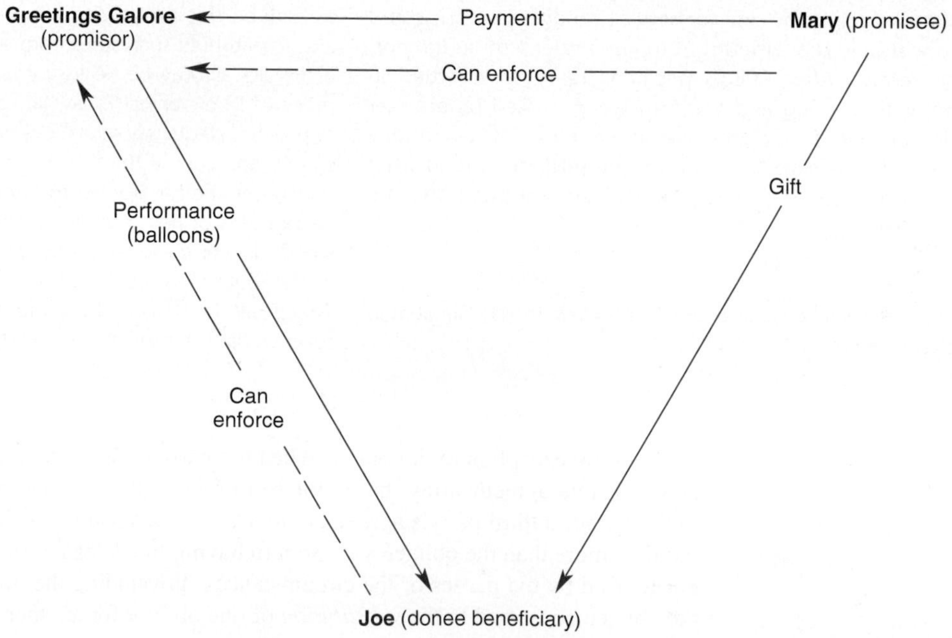

Life insurance contracts are a common form of donee beneficiary contract. The insurance company (the promisor), in return for payment of a premium, contracts with the owner of the policy (the promisee) to pay benefits to a beneficiary on the death of the insured (who may or may not be the promisee). If the insured dies and the company does not pay, the beneficiary can sue for the policy amount.

Creditor Beneficiaries

If the promisor's performance will *satisfy a legal duty* that the promisee owes a third party, the third party is a *creditor beneficiary.* The duty owed can be any kind of legal duty and need not necessarily be the payment of money. The creditor beneficiary has rights against *both* the promisee and the promisor.

For example, Bill buys a car on time from Honest Bob's Motors. Bill then sells the car to Sue, who agrees to make the remaining payments Bill owes Honest Bob's. Honest Bob's is a creditor beneficiary of Bill (the promisee) and Sue's (the promisor) contract and can recover the balance due from either Bill or Sue. (See Figure 17.4)

Allan v. Nersesova

307 S.W.3d 564 (Tex. Ct. App. 2010)

FACTS

Allan and Koraev owned units in a condominium project, with Allan's unit beneath Koraev's. Nersesova managed Koraev's rental unit. Over two years Allan's unit suffered eight incidents of water and sewage incursions as a result of plumbing problems and misuse of appliances in Koraev's unit. Allan sued both Koraev and Nersesova, among other defendants, on a variety of theories including breach of contract. All the defendants except Nersesova and Koraev settled with Allan. At trial, they were found liable for 30 percent of the damages each and the tenants for 40 percent. Koraev challenged the verdict against him, claiming that no contract existed between him and Allan. Allan asserted that the governing documents of the condominium formed a contract between each unit owner and the Owners' Association, and under that Koraev was required to comply with the governing documents and rules and regulations, and these made him liable for any damage caused to another unit.

ISSUE

Was Allan a creditor beneficiary?

DECISION

Yes. Because Allan was not in privity of contract with Koraev, she can only sue for breach of contract if she can show that she was a third-party beneficiary. She must show that the contracting parties entered into the contract directly and primarily for the benefit of the third party. There are three types of beneficiaries—donee, creditor, and incidental. A party is a creditor beneficiary if no intent to make a gift appears from the contract but performance will satisfy a duty of the promisee to the beneficiary. The promisee must have intended that the beneficiary has the right to enforce the contract. The condominium's governing document states that each owner must comply with its provisions, and failure to do so is grounds for an action to recover damages and reimbursement of all attorneys' fees. Koraev's failure to live up to the contract between him and the Association was a breach of his duty not to cause damage. Allan can sue because he was an intended creditor beneficiary of Koraev's contract.

Incidental Beneficiaries

LO5

Occasionally, the performance of a contract intended solely for the benefit of the promisee will also incidentally benefit a third person. These *incidental beneficiaries* acquire no rights under the contract and so cannot sue for nonperformance.

FIGURE 17.4
Creditor Beneficiary

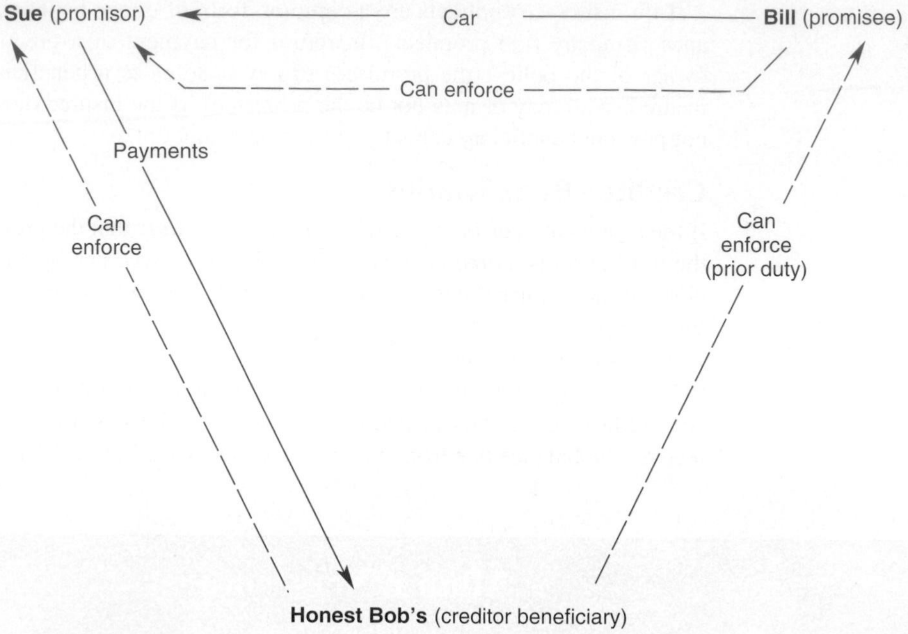

For example, Dave's house is in bad condition. He hires Ace Construction Company to paint and reroof the house. Dave's neighbor Aimee would benefit from this contract, since Dave's house is an eyesore that may affect the value of Aimee's property. Aimee, however, is an incidental beneficiary of Dave's contract with Ace and has no right to sue Ace if it breaches the contract. Members of the general public are generally held to be incidental beneficiaries of contracts such as street repair contracts entered into by municipalities or other government units.

Audler v. CBC Innovis, Inc.

519 F.3d 239 (5th Cir. Ct. App. 2008)

FACTS

Audler filed a class action lawsuit based on a determination by CBC Innovis (CBC) that his and others' property was outside a Special Flood Hazard Area (SFHA). The Flood Disaster Protection Act requires flood insurance for secured loans on homes within SFHA and mandates that banks and other lending institutions determine whether a property is located within the zone. CBC provides such information to the lenders. Audler's property is located in Louisiana, and his property was damaged by floodwaters from hurricane Katrina. He alleged he did not have flood insurance because of CBC's report. Among other things, he sued for breach of warranty and misrepresentation.

ISSUE

Was Audler an intended beneficiary of the contracts between the lenders and CBC?

DECISION

No. The determination of whether a home was in the flood area was undertaken solely for the benefit of the lender. Audler was not a member of the limited group for whom the reports were supplied. While CBC knew Audler would receive a copy of the report, this is not sufficient. The main purpose of the law requiring the lender to get the report was so that lenders would make sure there is insurance so that the cost to the government for flood relief is reduced. Audler was not the intended beneficiary of the flood zone certification.

Huff v. FirstEnergy Corp.

130 Ohio St.3d 196 (Ohio Sup. Ct. 2011)

FACTS

Ohio Edison hired a contractor to inspect trees and vegetation near its power lines. The contract had a clause under which the contractor promised to "safeguard all persons and property from injury" in carrying out its duties under the contract. Huff was walking along a road during a heavy thunderstorm when a branch from a large sugar maple fell and hit her. She sued for her injuries, alleging the tree was within the easement area that was supposed to have been inspected, and that they did not realize and remove the diseased maple tree.

ISSUE

Was Duff an intended beneficiary of the contract between the power company and the tree maintenance company?

DECISION

No. A person is an intended beneficiary of a promise if circumstances indicate the promisee intended to give the beneficiary the benefit of the promised performance. Generally, this is determined by the language of the contract. If the language is ambiguous, we look at the circumstances surrounding the contract formation. Here there is no indication that there was an intent to benefit people walking along public roads. It was made to support Ohio Edison's electrical service. The clause was intended to protect the public while the contractor carried out its work, but the injury happened after the work was completed. Huff cannot sue under the contract.

Concept Summary: Enforcing the Contract

Who can enforce the contract?

1. Contracting parties.
2. Assignees.
   a. Can enforce any rights of assignor against obligor.
   b. Can enforce implied guarantees against assignor.
   c. May be liable for duties expressly or impliedly delegated with the assignment.
3. Donee and creditor beneficiaries.

Incidental beneficiaries cannot enforce rights even though they benefit from another's contract. Members of the general public are usually incidental beneficiaries of governmental contracts for goods and services.

Questions and Problem Cases

1. Explain why personal rights are not assignable.
2. Explain the difference between a donee beneficiary and a creditor beneficiary.
3. What are the duties of an assignee?
4. Carnese was suffering from the effects of a stroke. She had an idea for an estate plan that included residuary bequests to two relatives. An attorney met with her and promised to prepare her will that would be invulnerable to being contested in order to maximize gifts to the residual beneficiaries. She died a few weeks after she signed the will. Soon thereafter, the will was challenged. Settlement of the contest resulted in a depletion of $620,000 from the residual estate. The residual beneficiaries sued, claiming they were donee beneficiaries of the lawyer's promise to prepare a will that wouldn't be subject to challenge. Are they intended donee beneficiaries? Why?

5. Kethan's employment contract with MedEcon contained a noncompetitive clause providing he could not work for a competitor for two years after leaving. It also had geographic restrictions. Kethan worked for several years and established a strong relationship with MedEcon's customers. MHA bought MedEcon's assets, including Kethan's employment contract. A month later Kethan gave notice of his resignation. Soon thereafter, a main customer of MHA quit dealing with it, and Kethan went to work for it. MHA argued it could enforce the noncompetitive clause because the contract had been assigned to it. Is it correct? Explain.
6. Audler filed a class action lawsuit based on a determination that CBC Innovis classified their property as being outside a Special Flood Zone Hazard Area (SFHA). The Flood Disaster Protection Act requires flood insurance for secured loans on homes within a SFHA, and CBC provides that information to the lenders. Audler's and the others' property was flooded by hurricane Katrina. They alleged they did not have flood insurance because of CBC's designation and sued under the contracts between the lenders and CBC, asserting they were intended beneficiaries of those contracts. Is this correct? Explain.
7. Theresa and Ricky LaShelle divorced in 1985. Theresa was awarded the house, where she resided with the couple's two children. She was responsible for paying the first mortgage contract on the home, and Ricky for paying the second mortgage. His assumption of the second mortgage was in lieu of his paying maintenance and child support. At the time of the divorce, Ricky was losing $40,000 per year; Theresa was earning $12,000 per year. Ricky continued to lose money in 1986 and finally sold his tractor to Ostendorf in return for Ostendorf's paying off the second mortgage contract, which he failed to do. Ricky later filed for bankruptcy and sought to be discharged from his duty to pay off the second mortgage. Was Ricky's duty to make the mortgage payments delegable?
8. Anderson went to Monahan Beaches Jewelry Center to look for an engagement ring for his fiancée, Warren. The salesman discussed various attributes of rings to help define what might be pleasing to Warren. Anderson later bought a "diamond" ring and gave it to Warren on Christmas. Shortly thereafter, Warren noticed a chip in the stone and returned it to Monahan, which agreed to replace it with a stone of equal or greater value. Warren then took the ring to another store for appraisal, at which time she discovered the alleged diamond was really cut glass or cubic zirconia. Can Warren sue Monahan for breach of contract under Anderson and Monahan's contract?

Chapter 18

Performance and Remedies

Learning Objectives

After you have studied this chapter, you should be able to:

1. Distinguish between the different types of conditions.
2. Explain the difference between complete and substantial performance.
3. Define the different kinds of impossibility.
4. Explain ways in which performance is discharged.
5. Discuss the theory of damages in contract cases and identify the different types of damages.
6. Tell what kinds of contracts are entitled to specific performance.

Kapenis put in a bid to buy the Gildeases' house. The contract contained a clause stating that the offer was subject to Kapenis's "obtaining suitable financing interest rate no greater than 12¾ percent." Kapenis rejected all loan programs offered to him as having monthly payments that were too high, as not being assumable, or as having terms that were not satisfactory. Kapenis then withdrew his offer. The Gildeases sued him for breach of contract.

- Did the interest rate condition have to be met before there would be an enforceable contract?
- Did Kapenis breach the contract by rejecting all financing programs available?
- If the contract was breached, what are the appropriate remedies?

FIGURE 18.1
Performance and Remedies

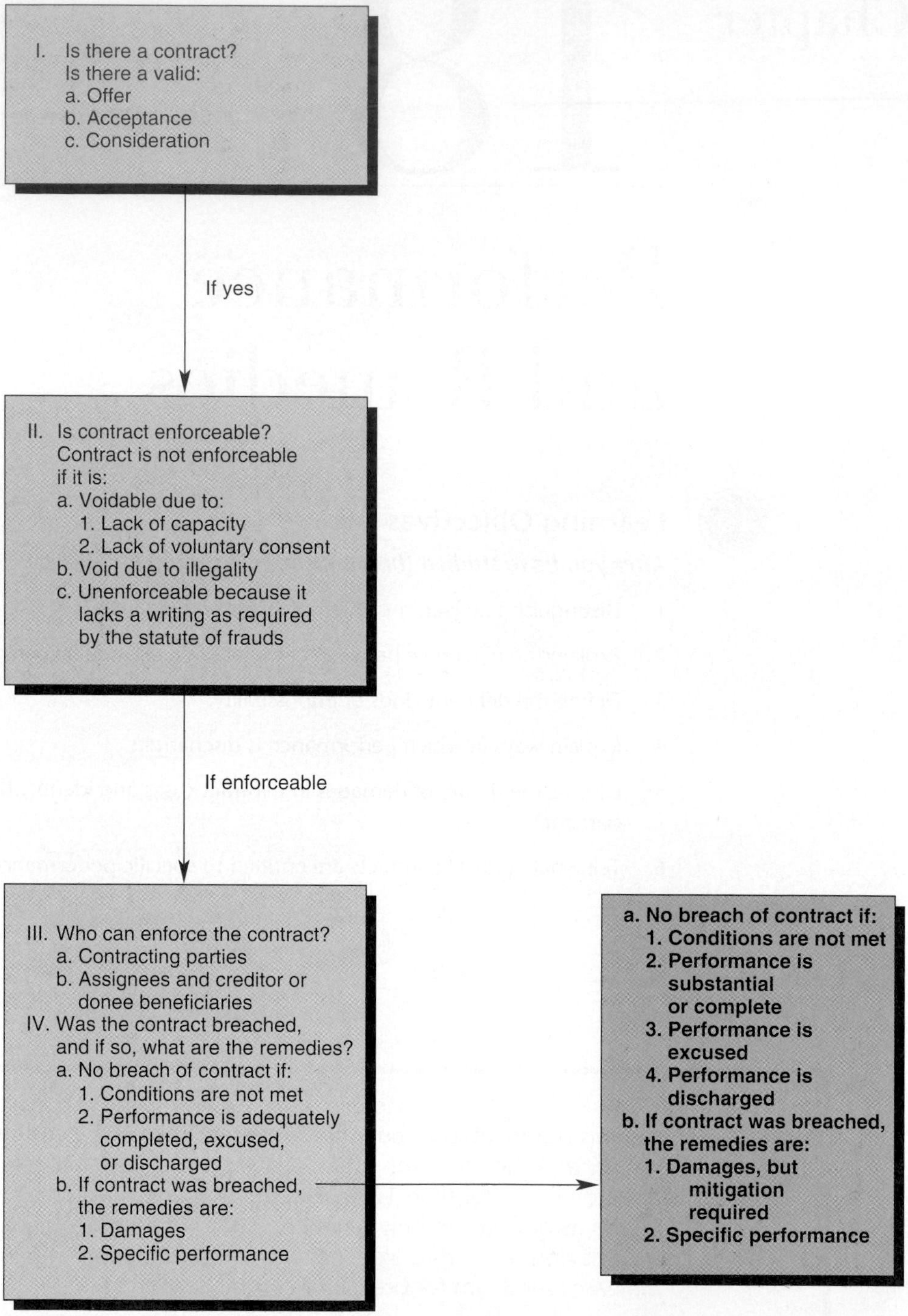
I. Is there a contract?
Is there a valid:
a. Offer
b. Acceptance
c. Consideration
If yes
II. Is contract enforceable?
Contract is not enforceable if it is:
a. Voidable due to:
1. Lack of capacity
2. Lack of voluntary consent
b. Void due to illegality
c. Unenforceable because it lacks a writing as required by the statute of frauds
If enforceable
III. Who can enforce the contract?
a. Contracting parties
b. Assignees and creditor or donee beneficiaries
IV. Was the contract breached, and if so, what are the remedies?
a. No breach of contract if:
1. Conditions are not met
2. Performance is adequately completed, excused, or discharged
b. If contract was breached, the remedies are:
1. Damages
2. Specific performance
a. No breach of contract if:
1. Conditions are not met
2. Performance is substantial or complete
3. Performance is excused
4. Performance is discharged
b. If contract was breached, the remedies are:
1. Damages, but mitigation required
2. Specific performance

In Chapter 9, the introductory chapter to this part of the text, we defined contracts as *legally enforceable agreements.* If an agreement meets all the requirements we have discussed in previous chapters, it is a contract and therefore enforceable. In the majority of contract situations, issues of enforceability never even arise because the parties perform their duties voluntarily and fully.

If a dispute arises between the parties to a contract, however, several important questions may be raised. Many of these questions deal with the parties' duties of performance under the contract. Are there any *conditions* in the contract that affect the parties' duties? If so, have these conditions been met? Have parties who have rendered performance under the contract satisfied their contractual duties, or is their performance so defective that it amounts to a *material breach* of the contract? Does a party who has failed to perform satisfactorily have some legal *excuse* for not performing, or has his or her duty to perform been *discharged* in some way?

Even if it is clear that one of the parties has materially breached the contract, a dispute may still arise about the *remedies* to which the other party is entitled. The answers to these questions can be very important in determining the rights of the parties.

Conditions

Definition

Generally, a party's contractual duty to perform arises at the time the contract is formed, even though the time for performing is set for a future date. The parties may, however, provide that a party's duty to perform is qualified by the happening of some event, or **condition.**

Types of Conditions

LO1

If the event must occur before a party's duty to perform arises, this is called a **condition precedent.** For example, Tom promises to buy Mary's race car for $350,000 if the car wins the Indianapolis 500 race. The car's winning the race is a condition precedent to Tom's duty to buy. If the car does not win, a *failure of condition* has occurred, and Tom has no duty to buy the car. Likewise, Kapenis's condition of suitable financing, described in the introductory case, had to be met before he was obligated to buy the Gildeases' house.

If the happening of a condition discharges an existing duty to perform, this is called a **condition subsequent.** For example, Joan and Mike enter a contract requiring Joan to mow Mike's grass on July 3, the day before his big party on July 4, unless it rains. If it rains, Joan does not have to mow the grass, and Mike's duty to pay Joan is discharged.

If the contract calls for the parties to perform their duties at the same time, each party's duty to perform is conditioned on the other party's performance. These conditions are called **concurrent conditions.** Neither party can enforce the other party's promise without performing or *tendering* (offering) performance. For example, Pete agrees to buy Wendi's cookie store for $150,000. Pete does not have a duty to pay the $150,000 unless Wendi tenders the store. Wendi does not have a duty to give Pete the store unless Pete tenders the $150,000.

Concept Summary: Conditions

	Conditions
Condition precedent	Performance excused *unless* condition occurs.
Condition subsequent	Performance excused *if* condition occurs.
Concurrent conditions	*Tender* of performance precedes right to demand performance.

Rockford Mutual Insurance Company v. Pirtle

911 N.E.2d 60 (Ind. Ct. App. 2009)

FACTS

Pirtle bought a historic building with a mortgage and insured it with Rockford Mutual Insurance Company (RMIC). The building was damaged by an accidental fire, and Pirtle made a claim on his insurance. The independent adjuster hired by RMIC estimated the damage to be $79,907, and RMIC authorized a settlement of $80,000. Pirtle rejected it because it was not enough to satisfy the mortgage or repair the building, and the policy limit was $193,000. Because of the damage, he was not able to continue to lease the building. A contractor hired by Pirtle estimated the damages to be $232,915. A second RMIC claims supervisor accepted that estimate after noticing that no other contractors would do the work for $80,000, and offered Pirtle the $193,000 limit on Pirtle's policy, but he had to repair the building first. When Pirtle hired an attorney, RMIC offered him $69,875, which it considered to be the actual cash value of the building. After further negotiations failed, Pirtle sued for breach of contract, but then accepted $86,147 while continuing to contest the actual cash value.

ISSUE

Is Pirtle bound by condition precedent to repair the building in order to receive payment under the insurance policy?

DECISION

No. The policy provided that for buildings insured at replacement cost, RMIC would pay no more than the actual cash value of the damages until actual repair or replacement was completed. Pirtle used the payment of the actual cash value to pay the mortgage rather to repair the building. Because of the dispute over the amount, Pirtle did not get the payment for six months, was struggling, and trapped in a no-win situation. By the time he took the $86,147, he was behind on the mortgage payments and had no rental income. Only after the foreclosure process had started and the property had been condemned by the city did RMIC offer $69,874 with the balance of the policy limit of $193,000 to be paid when the property was repaired. He had little choice but to use the money to pay the mortgage, and this left him with no money for repairs. In cases where the insurer fails to advance the necessary funds, the condition in the policy that actual replacement is necessary to get full payment is excused. Fairness requires that Pirtle be excused from doing the repairs before getting the full amount of the policy.

The Creation of Conditions

Conditions may be expressly or impliedly created. **Express conditions** are created by oral or written statements in the contract. No special words are necessary to create an express condition, but they are often created by words such as *provided that, on condition that, if, when, while, after,* and *as soon as.*

The nature of the parties' contract may also lead the courts to imply a **constructive (implied) condition** on the parties' duties of performance. For example, in bilateral contracts that call for an exchange of performances at the same date, or that do not state a time for performance, the law infers that each party's performance is a *constructive concurrent condition* of the other party's duty to perform. So, in a contract between Sam and Jan for the sale of a car, Sam's duty to pay for the car is conditioned on Jan's delivery of the car, and Jan's duty to deliver is conditioned on Sam's tender of the purchase price. If, however, their contract had called for Jan to deliver the car on a stated date and Sam to pay for the car two weeks later, Jan's delivery would be a *constructive condition precedent* of Mike's duty to pay.

Standards of Performance

A common source of dispute between contracting parties is whether the parties have fulfilled their duties of performance under the contract. Promisors must perform their contractual duties in the manner they have promised to perform them. If they do not, they are liable for breach of contract, they are not entitled to payment under the contract, and the contract can be terminated. The courts have attempted to create practical, commonsense standards for evaluating the parties' performance. They recognize three basic degrees of performance: *complete or satisfactory performance, substantial performance,* and *material breach* of contract.

Complete or Satisfactory Performance

LO2

Some kinds of contractual duties can be completely and perfectly performed. The payment of money, the delivery of a deed, and the delivery of certain goods are all duties that can be performed to a high degree of perfection. Promisors who completely perform such duties are entitled to receive the full contract price in return. Promisors in complete performance contracts who do not completely perform cannot recover the contract price. They may, however, recover in quasi contract for benefits conferred on the other party.

Substantial Performance

Some kinds of contractual duties are very difficult to perform perfectly due to their nature and the limits of human ability. Examples of these are found in construction projects, agricultural contracts, and many contracts for personal or professional services. Such duties are, however, capable of being substantially performed in most cases. **Substantial performance** is performance that falls short of complete performance in minor respects but does not deprive the promisee of a material part of the consideration that was bargained for. Promisors may make an honest attempt to perform, but due to lack of ability or factors beyond their control, they may fall short of complete performance. If their performance is such that it cannot be returned to them, and there was no express condition for complete performance, they will be held to have substantially performed their duties. This allows the promisor to be compensated for his or her performance.

An example of substantial performance is a building that deviates slightly from the contract's specifications. What constitutes substantial performance depends on the circumstances of each case. The promisor who substantially performs is generally entitled to the contract prices less any damage the other party has suffered as a result of the defective performance. If the promisor willfully failed to completely perform, the doctrine of substantial performance will not apply.

Concept Summary: Complete or Satisfactory Performance

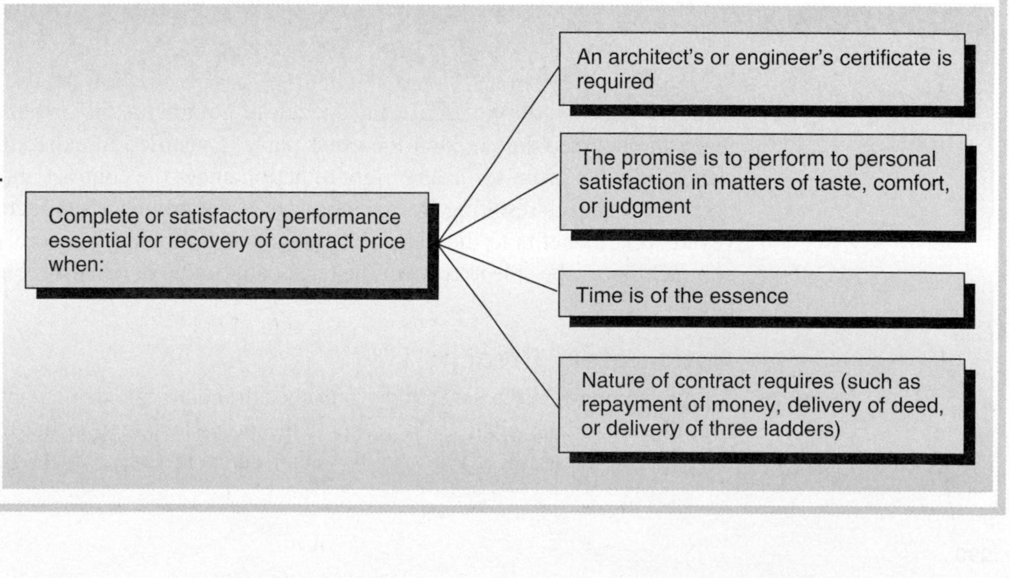
Complete or satisfactory performance essential for recovery of contract price when:
An architect's or engineer's certificate is required
The promise is to perform to personal satisfaction in matters of taste, comfort, or judgment
Time is of the essence
Nature of contract requires (such as repayment of money, delivery of deed, or delivery of three ladders)

Arnhold v. Ocean Atlantic Woodland Corp.

284 F.3d 693 (7th Cir. 2002)

FACTS

Arnhold and Argoudelis farmed 280 acres near a fast-growing suburb of Chicago. They agreed to sell the land to Ocean Atlantic, which planned to develop it into a residential subdivision. The parties agreed to cooperate and make sure that the conditions necessary for the development, such as that the property would be annexed and would be rezoned, would be done before the closing date of November 1, 1997. When that had not happened by November 1 despite their best efforts, the parties agreed to extend the deadline to January 15, 1999. Ocean Atlantic met with planning officials about the planned development during the first half of 1998, but by fall 1998 they still had not presented a petition for annexation. After negotiations and litigation, the parties agreed to reset the date for closing at November 30, 1999. As that date neared, Ocean Atlantic got Arnhold and Argoudelis to agree to an extension to January 25, 2001, and a time-is-of-the-essence clause was put in the new agreement. On January 18 Ocean Atlantic sent a letter demanding a new closing date of May 1 and for Arnhold and Argoudelis to pay $680,000 in development fees, a term they introduced for the first time. This was rejected and the January 25 date was reasserted by the sellers. Ocean Atlantic failed to tender the $7.26 million at the closing and the sellers declared the contract terminated. Ocean Atlantic sued for specific performance.

ISSUE

Did Ocean Atlantic materially breach the contract?

DECISION

Yes. "What a diff'rence a day makes . . . twenty-four little hours." This song lyric emphasizes the time-is-of-the-essence issue. If this clause is in the contract, one party has indicated that the time specified by the contract is essential to him. Of course, time can be of the essence even without the phrase being used if the circumstances of the contract require it. A party that fails to perform its contractual duties is liable for breach, and a material breach will excuse the other party's performance. Materiality focuses on two issues: the intent of the parties and the equitable factors surrounding the breach. Thus, the first question here is whether timely performance by a particular date is of such significance that the contract would not have been made if the provision had not been included. If not, if the breach was minor, and if provided performance was within a reasonable time, there is not a material breach. Even if the parties intended the date to be crucial, equitable considerations can cause it not to be strictly enforced.

It is clear from the last agreement that the sellers intended the January 25 date to be of the essence. The sellers agreed to extend the time and give the buyers one last chance, but not past that date. The sellers displayed the patience of Job in getting what they had bargained for. Even though Ocean Atlantic had spent $1.7 million, this does not change the equities in this case. Although Ocean Atlantic blames its failure to comply on its investment partner and lender, Ocean Atlantic waited until the 11th hour to get the necessary documents for the loan. When parties wait until the last minute to comply with deadlines, they are playing with fire. "Never put off until tomorrow what you can do today." The breach was material.

Material Breach

The promisor is guilty of **material breach** of contract if his or her performance fails to reach the degree of perfection the other party is justified in expecting under the circumstances. Such a promisor has no right of action under the contract and is liable to the other party for damages resulting from the breach. If the promisor's defective performance conveyed some benefits to the party that cannot be returned, the promisor may, under quasi contract theory, be able to recover the reasonable value of benefits conferred from the other party.

Anticipatory Breach

A promisor may also be held to have breached the contract under the doctrine of **anticipatory repudiation** or **anticipatory breach.** If the promisor, prior to the time for performance, indicates an intent not to perform his or her duties under the contract, the other party may treat the contract as breached and sue for that breach immediately if he or she so chooses. Anticipatory repudiation may take the form of an express statement by the promisor, or it may be implied from actions by the promisor that indicate an intent not to perform. For example, John, who has contracted to sell a car to Bill, sells the car to Marla two weeks before the delivery date set by his contract with Bill. Impliedly, John has repudiated his contract with Bill.

Special Performance Problems

There are two special problem areas relating to performance that should be discussed in detail. These are contracts where the promisor agrees to perform to the **personal satisfaction** of the promisee, and construction contracts that condition the property owner's duty to pay on the builder's obtaining an **architect's** or **engineer's certificate** certifying that the builder satisfactorily performed.

When the promisor agrees to perform to the promisee's personal satisfaction in contracts involving matters of personal taste, comfort, or judgment, the promisee who is honestly dissatisfied may reject the performance without liability, even if doing so is unreasonable. If, on the other hand, the contract involves issues of mechanical fitness, utility, or marketability, most courts require the promisee to accept performance that would satisfy a reasonable person.

Building and construction contracts commonly require the builder to give the owner a certificate issued by a specific engineer or architect before the owner has a duty to pay the builder. These certificates, which are often issued at each stage of completion, indicate that the work is done to the satisfaction of the architect or engineer. Contractors who are unable to produce a required architect's or engineer's certificate cannot recover under the contract unless their failure is excused. This may be done by showing that the named architect or engineer is dead, ill, or insane; that the architect or engineer is acting in bad faith; or that the other party has prevented the issuance of the certificate. If the architect or engineer who denies certification is acting in good faith, even if he or she is being unreasonable in doing so, the majority of courts hold that the owner has no duty to pay under the contract. A minority of courts recognize unreasonable refusal as an excuse where the contract has been substantially performed.

The Time for Performance

Failure to perform on time is a breach of the contract. In some cases, the failure may be serious enough to constitute a material breach. If the contract does not expressly or impliedly state a time for performance, performance must be completed within a reasonable time. What constitutes a "reasonable time" depends on the circumstances of each case.

In contracts in which failure to perform on time is a material breach, it is said that **time is of the essence.** A contract may expressly provide that time is of the essence. If so, the courts enforce this provision unless doing so would impose an unjust penalty on the promisor. The courts may also imply that time is of the essence if late performance is of little or no value to the promisee. For example, Ted contracts with the *Morning Tribune* to run an ad for Christmas trees from December 21 to December 24, but the paper does not start running Ted's ad until December 26. Clearly, time is of the essence in this contract and the *Morning Tribune* has materially breached.

If time is not of the essence of a contract, the promisee must accept late performance rendered within a reasonable time of when performance was due. The promisee is then entitled to deduct or set off from the contract price any losses suffered due to the delay.

Excuses for Nonperformance

Promisors who fail to perform satisfactorily may be able to avoid liability for breach of contract if they can show some *legal excuse* for their failure. Prevention of performance and impossibility of performance are the two traditionally accepted forms of excuse.

Prevention

The basic idea of prevention is that the promisee who causes the promisor's failure of performance cannot complain about the failure. Promisees owe promisors a duty of cooperation in the performance of a contract. Promisees who breach this duty by failing to cooperate or actively hindering or delaying performance are themselves guilty of a material breach of the contract. This relieves the promisor of any duty of further performance under the contract.

Impossibility

LO3

If it becomes impossible for a promisor to perform his or her contractual duties, the duty to perform is discharged and the promisor is not liable for material breach. **Impossibility** in the legal sense of the word, however, means "it cannot be done," not "I cannot do it." Promisors who find they have agreed to perform duties that are beyond their capabilities, or that have become unprofitable or difficult to perform, are generally not excused from their duty to perform. However, if some event arises after the formation of the contract that renders performance objectively impossible, nonperformance will be excused. The courts have traditionally recognized three kinds of impossibility: incapacitating illness or death of the promisor in a personal service contract, intervening illegality, and destruction of the subject matter essential to performance. Some courts today also recognize a fourth kind of impossibility called *commercial impracticability* or *commercial frustration.*

Illness or Death of Promisor

Personal service contracts are the only contracts that the promisor's death terminates. For example, if Dave contracts to sell his house to Terry and dies before the closing date, Terry can enforce the contract against Dave's estate. However, if Dave, a concert pianist, dies before giving a concert he has agreed to perform, his estate is not liable for breach of contract.

Illness may also excuse the promisor's failure to perform if the nature of the required performance and the seriousness and duration of the illness make it impossible for the promisor to substantially perform.

Intervening Illegality

If a statute or government regulation enacted after a contract's creation makes performance of a party's contractual duties illegal, the promisor is excused from performing. Statutes or regulations that merely make performance more difficult or less profitable do not excuse nonperformance.

Destruction of Subject Matter

If, through no fault of the promisor, something that is essential to the promisor's performance is destroyed, the promisor is excused from performing. For example, Jill, a skating champion, is hired by the owners of the civic arena to put on a skating demonstration. If the arena is destroyed by fire prior to the date of Jill's performance, Jill's nonperformance will be excused. The destruction of items that the promisor intends to use in performing does not excuse nonperformance if substitutes are available, even though securing them makes performance more difficult or less profitable.

Commercial Impracticability

Some courts are relaxing the strict common law position on impossibility of performance by recognizing as an excuse for nonperformance circumstances that do not amount to impossibility. These courts recognize **commercial impracticability** as an excuse when unforeseeable developments make performance highly or unreasonably expensive, or of little value to the promisee. Assume, for example, that Biggs rented a boat from Maritime, Inc. The contract required Maritime to keep the boat in repair. While Biggs was loading the boat, it was rammed by another boat, causing severe damage. Estimates showed that it would cost more to fix the boat than the boat was worth prior to the collision. The court might well find it was unreasonable to require Maritime to repair the boat under these circumstances.

Commercial impracticability acts as an excuse only if the promisor did not expressly or impliedly assume the risk that the event would occur. The *Restatement* has adopted the commercial impracticability standard, as has the Uniform Commercial Code for contracts involving the sale of goods.

Commercial Frustration

Commercial frustration, or *frustration of venture,* is very similar to impracticability. Under this doctrine, performance is excused when events occur after the formation of the contract that would make the return performance of the other party worthless to the promisor. Like impracticability, the event must not have been foreseeable, and the promisor must not have expressly or impliedly assumed the risk that the event would occur.

East Capitol View Community Development Corp. v. Robinson

941 A.2d 1036 (D.C. Ct. App. 2008)

FACTS

Robinson had a one-year written employment contract with East Capitol. Before the year was out, she was told that East Capitol was terminating her due to lack of funding. There was nothing in the contract that made her employment contingent on funding. Robinson filed suit for breach of contract. East Capitol defended by arguing impossibility.

ISSUE

Can East Capitol rely on the doctrine of impossibility?

DECISION

No. Performance under a contract may be excused if (1) there was an unexpected occurrence of an intervening act; (2) the risk of the unexpected occurrence was not allocated by agreement or custom; and (3) the occurrence makes performance objectively impossible or highly impractical. It only excuses nonperformance in extreme circumstances. A party's financial inability to perform rarely, if ever, excuses performance. Indeed, even insolvency is unlikely to excuse performance. This is because a party generally assumes the risk of its own inability to perform. Of course, parties may contractually reallocate risk. However, they did not do so in this case.

Discharge

The Nature of Discharge

LO4

Parties who have been released from their obligations under a contract are said to be **discharged.** Normally, both parties to a contract are discharged when they have completely performed their contractual duties. There are, however, several other things that can operate to discharge a party's duty of performance.

Earlier in this chapter you saw several situations in which a party's duty to perform could be discharged: the occurrence of a condition subsequent, the nonoccurrence of a condition precedent, material or anticipatory breach by the other party, and excused nonperformance. There are several other ways discharge can occur.

Discharge by Agreement

Since contracts are created by mutual agreement, they may also be discharged by **mutual agreement.** An agreement to discharge must be supported by consideration to be enforceable.

Discharge by Waiver

A party to a contract may **waive** his or her right to insist on complete performance. Waiver occurs when a party accepts incomplete performance without objection, knowing that the defects in performance will not be remedied. In order to avoid waiving their rights, parties who receive incomplete performance should give the other party prompt notice that they expect complete performance and will seek damages if defects are not corrected.

Discharge by Alteration

If the parties' agreement is represented by a written instrument, a material, **intentional alteration** of the instrument by one of the parties discharges the other party. If a party consents to an alteration or does not object to it after learning of it, he or she is not discharged. Alterations by third parties without the knowledge or consent of either contracting party do not affect the parties' rights.

Discharge by Statute of Limitations

Courts have long refused to allow people to sue if they delay an unreasonable time in bringing their lawsuit. All states statutorily establish the reasonable time within which a lawsuit must be brought. These statutory time limits are called **statutes of limitations.**

One who has breached a contractual duty may be discharged from liability for breach if the other party does not bring suit within the statute of limitations for contracts. The time period for enforcing contracts varies from state to state, and many states distinguish between oral and written agreements. The UCC statute of limitations for contracts involving the sale of goods is four years from the time the goods are tendered. The statutory period ordinarily begins to run from the date of the breach, but it may be delayed if the party with the right to sue is incapacitated (e.g., insane).

Remedies

The Theory of Remedies

LO5

If a party does not perform as promised under the contract, and performance has not been excused or discharged, then the other party is entitled to a remedy for the breach of the contractual promise. A court that awards a remedy for breach of contract tries to put the injured party in the same position he or she would have been in if the contract had been performed. Ordinarily, this may be done by awarding the injured person a judgment for money damages. If the loser in the suit does not pay the judgment, the winner is entitled to the court's help in enforcing it, as described in Chapter 2.

Damages in Contract Cases

There are several kinds of damages that may be recoverable in contract cases. The amount and kind of damages that may be recovered in a given dispute depend on the circumstances of the case. However, damages must be proved with reasonable certainty. Losses that are purely speculative are not recoverable.

Sargon Enterprises v. University of Southern California

55 Cal.4th 747 (Cal. Sup. Ct. 2012)

FACTS

Sargon Enterprises (SE) was a small company with annual profits that peaked at $101,000. It contracted with the University of Southern California to do clinical studies of SE's patented implant. SE claimed that USC failed to give it proper reports during the five-year study, and this led to damages including lost profits. SE sued USC. At trial its expert testified that had USC fulfilled its contractual obligations, SE would have become a market leader within 10 years and would have earned profits ranging from $200 million to $ 1 billion. USC challenged this testimony as being too speculative.

ISSUE

Was the evidence about future profits too speculative?

DECISION

Yes. The evidence is too speculative. The damage projections bear no relationship to the company's actual profits. They were not based on data from similarly sized and situated companies. The opinion must be based on a reasonable basis and an opinion based on speculation or conjecture is inadmissible. Speculative, unreliable testimony should be excluded.

Compensatory Damages

A party suing for breach of contract who has suffered actual losses as a result of the breach is entitled to recover **compensatory damages.** These damages are designed to place the plaintiff in the same position as if the contract had been performed. Compensatory damages ordinarily are measured by the loss in value of the promised performance. They are the difference between the value of performance that the plaintiff actually received and the value of the performance he or she had the right to expect. If no performance is rendered, the damages would be the value of the promised performance. The court will subtract from this amount any cost or loss the plaintiff was able to avoid by not having to perform his or her own promises. For example, Don agrees to sell his guitar worth $200 to Jane for $150, but he later refuses to go through with the deal. Jane's loss in value would be $200 less the $150 she did not pay Don, so her damages would be $50. Compensatory damages are normally limited to losses that would ordinarily occur as a result of breaching the contract.

Consequential Damages

In some cases the special circumstances of the plaintiff cause him or her to suffer losses that would not ordinarily be foreseeable as a result of the breach. Normally, such **consequential damages** are not recoverable unless the defendant had reason to foresee them at the time the contract was created. Generally, this means that the defendant must have known of the special circumstances that caused the loss. So, if Speedy Trucking Company contracts to deliver parts to Apex Manufacturing's plant without knowing that Apex is shut down waiting for the parts, Speedy is not liable for the consequential damages Apex suffers as a result of late delivery of the parts.

Rockford Mutual Insurance Company v. Pirtle

911 N.E.2d 60 (Ind. Ct. App. 2009)

FACTS

This is the same case you saw earlier in the chapter, where a condition precedent was not enforced because the insurance company effectively prevented its performance through failing to pay amounts due under the policy. At trial, the jury awarded Pirtle consequential damages of $406,137. RMIC contested that award, arguing its delay in paying was made in good faith because of the dispute over the actual cash value, and that the damages should be capped at the policy limit of $193,000.

ISSUE

Were consequential damages appropriate in this case?

DECISION

Yes. A party injured by a breach of contract may recover consequential damages when the non-breaching party's loss flows naturally and probably from the breach and was contemplated by the parties when the contract was made. This generally limits consequential damages to reasonably foreseeable economic losses. The policy limits restrict the amount the insurer may have to pay in the performance of the contract, not the damages that are recoverable for its breach. RMIC's motive for delayed payment is irrelevant because the promisee will be compensated for all damages proximately resulting from the promisor's breach. RMIC argued that costs such as the utility bills, property taxes, and an increase in the quote were not foreseeable at the time of contracting and were not proximately caused by the delayed payment. The fire occurred on November 11, 2000, and the jury trial concluded on October 17, 2007. The cost of repairs, utilities, and property taxes were likely to increase during the seven-year period between the damage to the building and the jury's award. They flow directly from RMIC's failure to pay. Had Pirtle been able to use the building as a rental property during those years, the rent likely would have increased. RMIC also argues that the award is excessive. In order to justify a reversal on grounds of excessive damages, the amount of damages assessed must appear to be so outrageous as to impress the court as being motivated by passion, prejudice, and partiality. Here, the award was based on evidence presented regarding the reconstruction bid, the utilities and debris removal costs, the loss of rental income, and the loss of personal property. It is not excessive.

Nominal Damages

Nominal damages are very small damages that the court may award the plaintiff when a technical breach of contract has occurred without causing any actual loss. Typically, they are no more than $1.

Liquidated Damages

The parties to a contract may provide in advance that a specific sum shall be recoverable if the contract is breached. Such provisions are called **liquidated damage** provisions. If the amount specified is reasonable and if the nature of the contract is such that actual damages would be difficult to determine, liquidated damage provisions are enforced. When liquidated damage provisions are enforced, the amount of damages agreed on is the injured party's exclusive remedy. If the amount specified is unreasonably great in relation to the probable loss or injury, however, or if the amount of damages could be determined easily in the event of breach, the courts declare the provision to be a *penalty* and refuse to enforce it.

Dean v. Kruse Foundation, Inc.

973 N.E.2d 583 (Ct. App. Ind. 2012)

FACTS

The Kruse Foundation is a charitable organization that operates a World War II and car museum. Kimball International donated a furniture factory with 43 acres to the foundation. However, the foundation had trouble with maintaining the property and paying the property taxes, utility bills, and insurance and trouble with thefts and vandalism. It therefore decided to sell the property. It held an auction and the terms of the purchase agreement were printed in the materials provided to each bidder. Each bidder had to sign the documents in order to participate in the auction. A provision stated that $400,000 of the purchase price would be deposited as earnest money and that if the buyer failed to complete the purchase within a reasonable time, the money would be forfeited and the seller could sue for specific performance. Gates, a professional and experienced real estate developer, was the highest bidder. Gates later found problems with the property's title condition, and when another suitable buyer could not be found, sued for breach of contract, fraud, and conversion and Kruse countersued for breach of contract. Gates claimed the $400,000 was liquidated damages and that was the agreed-to remedy for the breach. Kruse argued it should get damages representing the difference between the purchase price and the price it ultimately had to sell the property for, or $2,468,794.

ISSUE

Was the provision in the agreement a liquidated damage clause?

DECISION

No. A liquidated damage clause provides for the forfeiture of a stated sum of money upon a breach of contract without proof of damages. It is generally enforceable where the nature of the agreement is such that damages for breach would be uncertain, difficult, or impossible to ascertain. However, provisions constituting penalties are not enforceable. The distinction between a penalty provision and one for liquidated damages is that a penalty is imposed to secure performance of the contract and liquidated damages are in lieu of performance. The purchase agreement here does not label the forfeited money as liquidated damages. It only indicates it is part of the purchase price to be forfeited upon breach. Additionally, there is a great disproportionality between the loss and the amount provided for. These factors indicate an intent to penalize the purchaser for a breach of contract. It is not a reasonable forecast of the damages to be paid in full.

Punitive Damages

Ordinarily, **punitive damages** are not recoverable for breach of contract. They are recoverable only when extreme circumstances justify penalizing the defendant, such as if the breach of contract is willful, wanton, or malicious. Punitive damages also are sometimes specifically authorized by statute, as is the case with some consumer protection statutes.

While punitive damages are not ordinarily available in contract cases, they are available if the plaintiff can sue in tort for a bad faith breach, as discussed above. In these cases plaintiffs not only can collect damages for injuries such as emotional distress but also are likely to get large punitive damage awards because defendants' actions have been especially wrongful. Bad faith breach of contract actions have been most commonly allowed in suits against insurers for bad faith nonpayment of legitimate claims, and, more recently, against employers for wrongful firing of employees. Because these types of suits tend to blur the traditional line between tort and contract law, courts are moving cautiously in adopting the reasoning, and a few courts have decided to disallow punitive damages in certain bad faith cases.

The Duty to Mitigate Damages

Plaintiffs who have been injured by a breach of contract have a duty to **mitigate** (avoid or minimize) the damages they suffer if they can do so without undue risk, expense, or humiliation. They are not able to recover damages for injuries they could easily have avoided. For example, an employee who has been wrongfully fired would be entitled to damages equal to his or her wages for the remainder of the employment period. Such an employee, however, has a duty to make reasonable efforts to seek a similar job elsewhere and thereby minimize damages.

Equal Employment Opportunity Commission v. Dresser Rand Co.

http://pub.bna.com/lw/04cv6300.pdf (W.D.N.Y. 2011)

FACTS

Davis, a Jehovah's Witness and a machinist at Dresser Rand (Dresser), refused to work on any implements of war due to his religious beliefs. This presented a problem since Dresser regularly performed manufacturing jobs for the Navy. However, he asked for and was given alternative jobs numerous times. Subsequently, he asked for but was denied an alternative job and was terminated. He sued for religious discrimination. At trial, an expert testified that if Davis has taken eight months of community college training he would have been much more employable. Since he didn't do this to mitigate his damages he wasn't entitled to the damages for back pay that was requested.

ISSUE

Did Davis have a duty to get more training in order to mitigate damages?

DECISION

No. Employees must undertake reasonably diligent efforts to find comparable employment in order to fulfill the duty to mitigate damages. However, they are not required to pursue retraining or alternative education. They also do not have to go into another line of work or take a demotion or a demeaning position in order to receive back pay damages. While it would have been to Davis's advantage to obtain such training, he did not have a duty to do so. He did seek work with the skills he had at the time he was fired and is entitled to back pay for being wrongfully fired.

Equitable Remedies

If the legal remedies for breach of contract (usually money damages) are not adequate to fully remedy a party's injuries, a court has the discretionary right to grant an **equitable remedy.** Whether equitable relief is granted depends on the equities of a particular case. By applying "maxims" of equity such as "He who seeks equity must do equity," and "He who comes to equity must come with clean hands," the courts grant equitable relief only when justice is served by doing so. The two most common equitable remedies are specific performance and injunction. (See Table 18.1.)

Specific Performance

LO6

If the subject matter of a contract is *unique* so that a money damage award will not adequately compensate a buyer whose seller has refused to perform, a court may order the seller to **specifically perform** the contract. Real estate traditionally has been treated as unique and is the most common subject of specific performance decrees. For example, Frank enters a contract to sell his house to Dorothy for $90,000. When he learns that the market value of the house is $95,000, Frank decides not to go through with the sale. Dorothy sues Frank for breach of contract. Her normal legal remedy would be her lost profit on the sale (the market price less the contract price—$5,000 in this example). However, since real estate is generally treated as unique, Dorothy could get the court to order Frank to specifically perform his duties under their contract by giving her a deed to the property.

Personal property is generally not considered unique, but antiques, heirlooms, and works of art may merit specific performance. Specific performance is generally not granted in personal service contracts because it would require a form of involuntary servitude and would probably be ineffective in giving the promisee what was bargained for.

i.Lan Systems, Inc. v. NetScout Service Level Corp.

2002 U.S. Dist. LEXIS 209 (D. Mass. Jan. 2, 2002)

FACTS

i.Lan entered into a Value Added Reseller (VAR) agreement with NetScout to resell NetScout's software to its customers. i.Lan claimed it purchased the unlimited right to use the software, replete with perpetual upgrades and support, whereby it could effectively rent, rather than sell, the software to its customers. It points to the purchase order to support its claim. NetScout points to the VAR agreement and the clickwrap license agreement contained in the software to refute this. The clickwrap license states that "[NetScout's] liability for damages to licensee for any cause whatsoever, regardless of the form of any claim or action, shall be limited to the license fees paid for the licensed product." However, another section states that each party has the right to bring judicial proceedings to enforce its rights under the agreement, and specifically mentions specific performance. i.Lan sought specific performance of the agreement for perpetual upgrades and unlimited support.

ISSUE

Is the subject matter of the contract sufficiently unique to warrant specific performance?

DECISION

No. Specific performance is allowed when the items are unique or not replaceable as a practical matter. i.Lan argues that the software is unique because it is copyrighted and took years to develop. The same could be said of any mass-produced item, and a mass-produced product is the antithesis of the word "unique." More importantly, the software is one of several competing software packages in the market that run on ordinary computers and perform substantially the same functions. They are interchangeable as a practical matter. i.Lan could purchase comparable software on the open market and reconfigure its systems to run that software. Since the software is not unique, i.Lan cannot have specific performance.

TABLE 18.1
Remedies

Damages	
Compensatory	Loss in value of promised performance
Consequential	Foreseeable losses from special circumstances of particular contract
Nominal	Award for purely technical breach of contract (usually $1.00)
Liquidated	Damages specified in contract for breach
Punitive	Usually unavailable—sometimes awarded for bad faith breach
Equitable Remedies	
Specific Performance	Promisor ordered to perform contract where subject matter is unique
Injunction	Ordered to prevent irreparable injury

Injunctions

Injunctions are available when a breach of contract threatens to produce an *irreparable injury.* A court can order a party to do certain acts (a **mandatory injunction**) or to refrain from doing certain acts (a **prohibitory injunction**). For example, an employee with special skills who has agreed not to work for a competitor may be *enjoined* from breaching his or her contract and working for that competitor. Like specific performance, an injunction cannot be used to compel personal service.

Concept Summary: Performance and Remedies

Was the contract breached and what are the remedies?

I. No breach of contract if
- a. Conditions are not met
  - 1. Condition precedent does not occur
  - 2. Condition subsequent occurs
- b. Performance excused due to
  - 1. Prevention by promisee
  - 2. Impossibility due to
    - (a) Illness or death of promisor
    - (b) Intervening illegality
    - (c) Destruction of subject matter
    - (d) Commercial impracticability
    - (e) Commercial frustration
- c. Performance discharged due to
  - 1. Agreement
  - 2. Waiver
  - 3. Alteration
  - 4. Running of statute of limitations
- d. Contract completely or substantially performed

II. If contract was breached, remedies are
- a. Damages
  - 1. Compensatory
  - 2. Consequential
  - 3. Nominal
  - 4. Liquidated
  - 5. Punitive
- b. Equitable remedies
  - 1. Specific performance
  - 2. Injunction

Questions and Problem Cases

1. Explain when time is of the essence.
2. Define anticipatory breach and give an example.
3. Describe briefly the types of conditions.
4. Johnson, a graduate student at Yale, was assigned a committee of faculty advisors co-chaired by Skelly and Schmitz. Johnson developed an idea for his dissertation and recorded his idea in a private journal. Two other students read his journal and explained his idea to Schmitz, and Schmitz asked Johnson to explain it to him. Schmitz told him that in order to complete his dissertation and pass his qualifying exam, he would have to trust the faculty. Reluctantly, Johnson explained his theory. Schmitz and Skelly published Johnson's theory without attribution to Johnson. Johnson sent a letter to the director of doctoral students complaining of academic fraud but did not get a response. Later, Yale stopped delivering his monthly salary supplement and his funding. Johnson then wrote to the dean of the program, who informed him that an inquiry

committee would be formed. Five months later, they found there were no grounds for his fraud allegations. Their investigation consisted of a keyword search to determine originality and did not include any intellectual analysis of Johnson's ideas, nor did they talk to him. He appealed to the provost, who declined to reevaluate his claim. Can Johnson successfully sue Yale for breach of contract? Why?

5. In 1857, the *Central America,* which was loaded with gold from California, sank off Cuba. Thompson organized the Columbus-America Discovery Group, an organization that won the race to locate the sunken ship. In 1983, Thompson, Standefer, and Doering entered a contract contemplating the salvage of the ship. It stated, "It is agreed that a corporation . . . will be formed between [us]. The object of forming [it] is to carry out the duties of the . . . Group under the joint venture with Mr. John." The agreement further provided that if the joint venture discontinued operations for any reason, the corporation or individuals therein would still receive a share of any salvage from the ship. John was to finance the search and salvage procedures. John, however, never signed the contract or the joint venture agreement, and a corporation was never chartered. After the failure of the joint venture, Standefer had virtually no active participation in the location of the ship or the salvage operation. Nonetheless, Standefer sought to assert rights under the contract and share in the treasure that was salvaged by Thompson. Thompson alleged that the creation of the joint venture was a condition precedent to the contract's effectiveness. Is he correct? Explain.
6. Discovery Zone owned and operated more than 300 "pay for play children's entertainment centers" called FunCenters. It contracted with DuPont to install flooring in the centers. When they signed the contract, Discovery was emerging from bankruptcy and realigning its business according to a bankruptcy reorganization plan. DuPont fell behind in laying the floors and Discovery Zone lapsed back into bankruptcy. Discovery Zone sued for $20 million in damages, alleging that if DuPont had completed its work in a timely manner, it would have increasing revenues and would not have reentered bankruptcy. Can it recover the lost profits? Why?
7. Seaboard Lumber contracted with the U.S. Forest Service to cut, remove, and pay for timber on the Forest Service's land, known as the What lot, in two and a half years. Between the time the contract was made and the final performance date, timber prices dropped significantly because of a decline in housing construction due to a rise in interest rates, and Seaboard decided not to cut the timber. When the Forest Service sued for damages, Seaboard defended on the basis of impossibility or commercial impracticality. Will it succeed? Why?
8. American Car Rental (ACR), at the top of its rental agreement, stated, "Vehicles driven in excess of 79 miles per hour will be charged $150 fee per occurrence. All our vehicles are GPS equipped. It charged customers the fee every time the GPS showed that the car's speed was 79 m.p.h. for two or more minutes. When sued, ACR argued that the fee was a liquidated damages charge. Is this correct? Explain.
9. Manuma was to serve as the entertainment director/musician on Blue Hawaii's daily dinner cruise for a guaranteed one-year period. He was fired after eight months due to Blue Hawaii's financial difficulties. Blue Hawaii offered him two other positions, one involving manual labor at a shipyard, and one involving light maintenance and cleaning of a yacht. Manuma declined both offers and sued for his lost pay due under the contract. Did Manuma have a duty to accept one of the positions in order to mitigate the damages? Why?

Part 3

Sales

Chapter 19

Formation and Terms of Sales Contracts

Learning Objectives

After you have studied this chapter, you should be able to:

1. Analyze whether a transaction involves the sale of goods to which the Uniform Commercial Code applies or whether common law contract principles apply to the transaction.
2. Recall the major provisions of the Code that are applicable to the formation of contracts for the sale of goods, including the "gap fillers" that the Code deems part of the contract when the parties omit critical terms or state them in an unclear manner.
3. Explain when title to goods passes from the seller to the buyer.
4. Explain what is meant by a *voidable title* and explain when a buyer can obtain better title to goods than the seller had.
5. Apply the Code's rules concerning risk of loss to determine who had the risk of loss in a given transaction where the goods that were the subject of a contract were lost or destroyed before the buyer took possession.
6. Distinguish between sale or return, sales on approval, and sales on consignment and explain the ramifications those distinctions have for the rights of buyers and sellers.

Paul Reynolds used the Trek website to purchase a racing bike with a frame utilizing a newly developed high-strength but lightweight alloy. He selected the model he wanted and provided the company with the necessary information to place the $2,200 purchase price and $75 shipping costs on his Visa card. The bicycle was damaged during shipment when the box was punctured by a forklift truck that was loading other boxes onto the carrier's truck. Paul took the damaged bicycle to a local bicycle dealer to have it repaired. After the bicycle was repaired, but before Paul could pick it up, a clerk in the store, by mistake, sold the bicycle for $1,500 to Melissa Stevenson, who bought it as a birthday gift for her boyfriend. This situation raises a number of legal issues that, among others, will be covered in this chapter, including:

(continued)

- Can a legally enforceable contract for the sale of goods be formed electronically?
- Between Paul and Trek, who had the risk of loss or damage to the bicycle during the time it was under shipment to him?
- Would Paul be entitled to recover possession of the bicycle from Melissa and her boyfriend?

Introduction

In Part 2, "Contracts," we introduced the common law rules that govern the creation and performance of contracts generally. Throughout much of history, special rules, known as the *law merchant,* were developed to control mercantile transactions in goods. Because transactions in goods commonly involve buyers and sellers located in different states—and even different countries—a common body of law to control these transactions can facilitate the smooth flow of commerce. To address this need, the Uniform Commercial Code (UCC, or Code) was prepared to simplify and modernize the rules of law governing commercial transactions.

This chapter reviews some Code rules that govern the formation of sales contracts previously discussed. It also covers some key terms in sales contracts, such as delivery terms, title, and risk of loss. Finally, it discusses the rules governing sales on trial, such as sales on approval and consignments.

Sale of Goods

LO1

The **sale of goods** is the transfer of ownership to tangible personal property in exchange for money, other goods, or the performance of services. The law of sales of goods is codified in Article 2 of the Uniform Commercial Code. While the law of sales is based on the fundamental principles of contract and personal property, it has been modified to accommodate current practices of merchants. In large measure, the Code discarded many technical requirements of earlier law that did not serve any useful purpose in the marketplace and replaced them with rules that assure merchants and consumers of goods that laws will be applied in keeping with commercial expectations.

In 2003, the American Law Institute approved a series of proposed amendments to Article 2, Sale of Goods, that are intended to modernize and clarify some of its provisions. The amendments are not effective until they have been adopted by a state and incorporated into its version of Article 2 of the Uniform Commercial Code. However, some controversy exists concerning the proposed amendments, and because at the time this book went to press they had not been adopted by any state, they are not incorporated into the discussion of Article 2 that follows.

Article 2 of the Code applies only to *transactions in goods.* Thus, it does not cover contracts to provide services or to sell real property. However, some courts have applied the principles set out in the Code to such transactions. When a contract appears to call for the furnishing of both goods and services, a question may arise as to whether the Code applies. For example, the operator of a hair salon may use a commercial solution intended to be used safely on humans that causes injury to a person's head. The injured person then might

FIGURE 19.1
Choice of Law

*If there is no specific Uniform Commercial Code provision governing the transaction, use the common law.

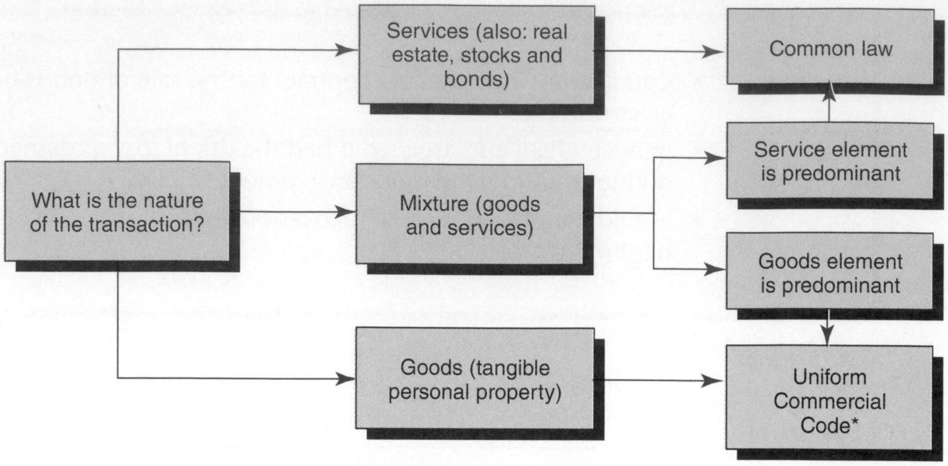

bring a lawsuit claiming that there was a breach of the Code's warranty of the suitability of the solution. In such cases, the courts commonly see whether the sale of goods is the *predominant* part of the transaction or merely an *incidental* part; where the sale of goods predominates, courts normally apply Article 2.

Thus, the first question you should ask when faced with a contracts problem is whether this is a contract for the sale of goods. If it is not, then the principles of common law that were discussed in Part 2, "Contracts," apply. If the contract is one for the sale of goods, then the Code applies (see Figure 19.1).

In the case that follows, *Janke v. Brooks,* the court looked to see whether services or goods were the predominant element in the contract, and then concluded that the UCC was not applicable because the service element was predominant.

Janke v. Brooks

77 UCC Rep.2d 352 (U.S.D.C., D. Col. 2012)

FACTS

Janke was the owner of a classic 1957 Chevrolet Nomad. After seeing a feature on the ESPN program *On The Block,* he contacted Donald and Normandy Brooks about restoring the car. He traveled to the Brookses' shop in Sparks, Nevada, to discuss the project.

He received an estimate that included a series of price quotes and list sheets that contemplated the installation and/or repair of a number of parts as well as a number of items that were to be fabricated by the Brookses' mechanic. If the items could have been fabricated or installed by any competent mechanic, there would not have been any need to ship the prized car to a specialty shop to remodel the vehicle. The parts and materials constituted slightly more than half of the quoted price but was somewhat skewed by the fact there was a 50 percent markup on the price of new parts and materials.

Janke then forwarded a deposit and had the Nomad shipped from his home in Wheatridge, Colorado, in September 2008. He informed Brooks that he wanted the car to be ready in time to be entered in and displayed at the "Hot August Nights" classic car show in Reno, Nevada, in early August 2010. Despite assurances, when he arrived in Nevada on July 28, 2010, he learned that the car was not finished. Subsequently, he was advised that the car's engine block was cracked and would have to be replaced.

(continued)

Donald Brooks assured Janke that the car would be fixed and shipped to him in Colorado.

On November 17, 2010, the car was delivered to Janke in Wheatridge. The car broke down several times in the first 25 miles, after which Janke hired another mechanic to inspect and evaluate the build. He discovered a number of defects in the car, that the Brooks' design strategy was unreasonable, that the car was not built consistently with the build sheet, and that the defects in the car could not have been corrected simply by replacing the defective parts.

Janke brought an action against Brooks for breach of contract as well as for breach of implied warranties under the Uniform Commercial Code.

ISSUE

Was the contract to restore the Nomad a "transaction in goods" to which the UCC implied warranties would be applicable?

DECISION

No. Where a contract contemplates both the sale of goods and the performance of services, the controlling criterion is the primary purpose of the contract. The test for inclusion or exclusion is not whether goods and services are mixed, but granting that they are mixed, whether their predominant fact, their thrust, their purpose, reasonably stated, is the rendition of service with goods incidentally involved (e.g., contract with artist for painting) or is a transaction of sale, with labor incidentally involved (e.g., installation of a water heater in a bathroom).

This case is a mixed contract for goods and services. While Janke technically acquired a property interest in all of the parts and materials incorporated into the car, they were merely incidental to the overarching purpose to craft a wholly remodeled car where the whole was greater than the sum of its parts. Accordingly, this was predominately a contract for services; thus, the warranties under the UCC are inapplicable.

Leases

A lease of goods is a transfer of the right to possess and use goods belonging to another. Although the rights of one who leases goods (a lessee) do not constitute ownership of the goods, leasing is mentioned here because it can be an important way of acquiring the use of many kinds of goods, from automobiles to farm equipment. In most states, Article 2 and Article 9 of the UCC were applied to such leases by analogy. However, rules contained in these articles sometimes were inadequate to resolve special problems presented by leasing. For this reason, a new article of the UCC dealing exclusively with leases of goods, Article 2A, was written in 1987. Article 2A has been adopted by 48 states and the District of Columbia as of the time of this writing. Because of space limitations, it is not covered in detail in this textbook.

Higher Standards for Merchants

The Code recognizes that buyers tend to place more reliance on professional sellers and that professionals are generally more knowledgeable and better able to protect themselves than nonprofessionals. Therefore, the Code distinguishes between merchants and nonmerchants by holding merchants to a higher standard in some cases (Sections 2-201[2], 2-205, 2-207[2], and 2-314).[1] The Code defines **merchant** (2-104[1]) on a case-by-case basis. If a person regularly deals in the kind of goods being sold, or purports to have some special knowledge about the goods, or employs an agent in the sale who fits either of these two descriptions, that person is a merchant for the purposes of the contract in question. So, if you buy a used car from a used-car dealer, the dealer is a merchant for the purposes of your contract. But if you buy a refrigerator from a used-car dealer, the dealer is probably not considered to be a merchant for purposes of that sale.

Code Requirements

The Code requires that parties to sales contracts act in *good faith* and in a *commercially reasonable manner.* Further, when a contract contains an unfair or unconscionable clause,

[1] The numbers in parentheses refer to sections of the Uniform Commercial Code.

or the contract as a whole is unconscionable, the courts have the right to refuse to enforce the unconscionable clause or contract (2-302). The Code's treatment of unconscionability is discussed in detail in Chapter 15, "Illegality."

A number of the Code provisions concerning the sale of goods were discussed in the chapters on contracts. The Concept Summary below lists some of the important provisions discussed earlier, together with the chapters in the text where the discussion can be found.

Concept Summary: Formation of Contracts

LO2

Offer and Acceptance (Chapters 10 and 11)

1. A contract can be formed in any manner sufficient to show agreement, including conduct by both parties that recognizes the existence of a contract.
2. The fact that the parties did not agree on all the terms of their contract does not prevent the formation of a contract.
3. A firm written offer by a merchant that contains assurances it will be held open is irrevocable for a period of up to three months.
4. Acceptance of an offer may be made by any reasonable manner and is effective on dispatch.
5. A timely expression of acceptance creates a contract even if it contains terms different from the offer or states additional terms *unless* the attempted acceptance is expressly conditioned on the offer's agreement to the terms of the acceptance.
6. An offer inviting a prompt shipment may be accepted either by a prompt promise to ship or a prompt shipment of the goods.

Consideration (Chapter 12)

1. Consideration is not required to make a firm offer in writing by a merchant irrevocable for a period of up to three months.
2. Consideration is not required to support a modification of a contract for the sale of goods.

Unconscionability (Chapter 15)

If a court finds a contract for the sale of goods to be unconscionable, it can refuse to enforce it entirely, enforce it without any unconscionable clause, or enforce it in a way that avoids an unconscionable result.

Statute of Frauds (Chapter 16)

1. Subject to several exceptions, all contracts for the sale of goods for $500 or more must be evidenced by a writing signed by the party against whom enforcement of the contract is sought. It is effective only as to the quantity of goods stated in the writing.
2. A signed writing is not required if the party against whom enforcement is sought is a merchant, received a written memorandum from the other party, and did not object in writing within 10 days of his receipt of it.
3. An exception to the statute of frauds is made for specially manufactured goods not suitable for sale to others on which the seller has made a substantial beginning in manufacturing or has entered into a binding contract to acquire.
4. An exception to the statute of frauds is made for contracts that a party admits the existence of in court testimony or pleadings.
5. If a party accepts goods or payment for goods, the statute of frauds is satisfied to the extent of the payment made or the goods accepted.

E-Commerce

ELECTRONIC WRITINGS AND THE STATUTE OF FRAUDS

The Electronic Signatures in Global and National Commerce Act (the "E-Sign" Act) was enacted by Congress and became effective in the United States on October 1, 2000. The E-Sign law covers many everyday transactions including sales transactions even where the law of the state involved still has a version of Article 2 that requires a "signed writing" or another means of satisfying the Article 2 statute of frauds found in Section 2-201. Federal laws "preempt," that is, displace, state laws if the two sets of laws are in conflict. If state law requires a signed writing or another indicator that the purported buyer and seller actually intended to form a contract, E-Sign allows the parties to use electronic authentications instead of signed writings. E-mail messages and online orders sent by the buyer would suffice. States that have adopted the Uniform Electronic Transactions Act (UETA) also allow online communications to satisfy the Section 2-201 statute-of-frauds requirement.

Terms of Sales Contracts

LO2

Gap Fillers

The Code recognizes the fact that parties to sales contracts frequently omit terms from their agreements or state terms in an indefinite or unclear manner. The Code deals with these cases by filling in the blanks with common trade practices or by giving commonly used terms a specific meaning that is applied unless the parties' agreement clearly indicates a contrary intent.

Price Terms

A fixed price is not essential to the creation of a binding sales contract. Of course, if price has been the subject of a dispute between the parties that has never been resolved, no contract is created because a "meeting of the minds" never occurred. However, if the parties omitted a price term or left the price to be determined at a future date or by some external means, the Code supplies a price term (2-305). Under the common law, such contracts would have failed due to "indefiniteness." If a price term is simply omitted, or if the parties agreed to agree on price at a later date but cannot, or if the parties agreed that price would be set by some external agency (like a particular market or trade journal) that fails to set the price, the Code says the price is a *reasonable price at the time for delivery* (2-305[1]). If the agreement gives either party the power to fix the price, that party must do so in *good faith* (2-305[2]). If the surrounding circumstances clearly indicate that the parties did not intend to be bound in the event that the price was not determined in the agreed-on manner, no contract results (2-305[4]).

The hypothetical scenario at the beginning of this chapter poses the situation where a person uses a manufacturer's website to purchase a bicycle and asks whether an enforceable contract for the sale of goods can be formed electronically. Given the information in the E-Commerce box entitled "Electronic Writings and the Statute of Frauds," how would you answer the question?

Quantity Terms

Output/Requirements Contracts

In some cases, the parties may state the quantity of goods covered by their sales contract in an indefinite way. Contracts that obligate a buyer to purchase a seller's *output* of a certain item or all the buyer's *requirements* of a certain item are commonly encountered. These contracts caused frequent problems under the common law because of the indefiniteness of the parties' obligations. If the seller decided to double its output, did the buyer have to accept the entire amount? If the market price of the item soared much higher than the contract price, could the buyer double or triple its demands?

The Code limits quantity in such cases to "such actual output or requirements as may occur in good faith" (2-306[1]). Even good faith amounts may not be tendered or demanded if they are "unreasonably disproportionate" to any stated estimate in the contract or to "normal" prior output or requirements if no estimate is stated (2-306[1]).

In the case that follows, *Noble Roman's, Inc. v. Pizza Boxes, Inc.*, the court looked to the contract and to the parties' course of performance to conclude that the contract was a "requirements" contract and not an order for a specified number of pizza boxes.

Noble Roman's, Inc. v. Pizza Boxes, Inc.

57 UCC Rep.2d 901 (Ct. App. Ind. 2005)

FACTS

Noble Roman's is a franchisor of pizza restaurants, but the company does not own or operate any restaurants. Its franchisees order supplies approved by Noble Roman's. Pizza Boxes is a broker that acts as an intermediary for vendors that manufacture pizza boxes.

In 2002 William Gilbert, director of R&D and distribution for Noble Roman's, e-mailed Michael Rosenberg, vice president of Pizza Boxes, regarding Noble Roman's interest in "clamshell" boxes for use in a new "pizza-by-the-slice" program. Gilbert stated that the estimated usage at this stage is from 400,000 to a million units per year to start. After Noble Roman's approved the box design, the parties worked out the details for the purchase. Gilbert explained that the pizza-by-the-slice program was just getting started at one of its franchise locations, but he anticipated that other locations would implement the program over time. The two agreed that 2.5 million boxes would be needed annually, that Multifoods, Noble Roman's distributor, would submit orders for the boxes and pay the invoices, and that Multifoods would pick up the boxes after the orders were filled.

On November 1, 2002, Rosenberg sent Gilbert a confirming letter, 2002, which stated:

> Dear Bill:
>
> Please sign in the space below to confirm the following order:
>
> Item: 18/6 Slice Box 220/case
> Quantity: 2,500,000
> Print: Two colors
> Price: $101.45/M
> FOB: Bakersfield or Stockton, Ca. (in-trailer load quantity—approx. 230,000 per load)
> To be picked up by Multifoods. PBI remits invoice Multifoods.
>
> Extras for printing preps are included at $4,500 ($1.80/M) and amortized over the entire order. In the event that the total of 2.5 million boxes are not manufactured, Noble Roman's is responsible for any portion of the prep charge remaining.

Gilbert signed and dated the letter and returned it to Rosenberg. On its own initiative, Pizza Boxes, through its vendor, Dopaco, Inc., manufactured 519,200 boxes in anticipation of Multifoods' future orders. Multifoods submitted an initial purchase order to Pizza Boxes for six cases (12,000) boxes, and Multifoods paid Pizza Boxes for that order. However, after the initial order, Multifoods did not order any more boxes. When Rosenberg called Multifoods to inquire why it had not ordered more boxes, he was told that the franchisees were "not using this product."

Pizza Boxes then asked Noble Roman's to pay for approximately 500,000 boxes that Pizza Boxes had made but Multifoods had not ordered. Noble Roman's responded that it was a franchisor and not an operator of restaurants that specifies and arranges for the manufacture of products and supplies sold by its franchisees, and that Noble Roman's does not purchase any supplies or products. Once Noble

(continued)

Roman's includes products or supplies in its specifications, then any purchase order is signed by the distributor, which buys all of the supplies and distributes them to the franchisees who sign purchase orders with the distributor. Pizza Boxes then filed suit against Noble Roman's, alleging breach of contract and seeking $54,901.44 for the unpaid inventory and tooling charges.

ISSUE

Is Noble Roman's liable to Pizza Boxes for the unpaid inventory charges?

DECISION

No. Initially, the court rejected Pizza Boxes' contention that the November 1, 2002, letter was a purchase order—that is, a document authorizing a seller to deliver goods with payment to be made later. Rather, the court determined that the letter was a requirements contract. The letter is not an order for 2.5 million boxes but, on its face, contemplates that not all 2.5 million boxes would be manufactured. Taken together, the letter and the course of performance show the intent of the parties that Multifoods would submit purchase orders against the requirements contract, would be invoiced, and would pay for the boxes supplied by Pizza Boxes. Noble Roman's did not order the boxes in dispute and is entitled to summary judgment on Pizza Boxes' breach of contract claim for the cost of the unused boxes. However, under the terms of the contract, Noble Roman's is liable to Pizza Boxes for the portion of the prep charges still owed for the boxes that were not manufactured.

Exclusive Dealing Contracts

The Code takes a similar approach to *exclusive dealing* contracts that obligate dealers to deal only in one manufacturer's product line. Under the common law, these contracts were sources of difficulty because the parties' duties were indefinite. Did the dealer have to make any effort to sell the manufacturer's products, and did the manufacturer have any duty to supply the dealer? The Code says that unless the parties agree to the contrary, sellers have a duty to use their *best efforts* to supply their buyers, who have a duty to use their *best efforts* to sell the goods (2-306[2]).

Delivery Terms

Unless the parties agree to the contrary, the Code says that the goods ordered are to be delivered in a *single-lot shipment* (2-307). If the contract is silent about the place for delivery, the goods are to be delivered at the *seller's place of business* (2-308[a]). The only exception to this rule is in the case of contracts dealing with identified goods that both parties at the time of contracting know are located someplace other than the seller's place of business. In such a case, the *site of the goods* is the place for delivery (2-308[b]).

Time Terms

The Code takes the same position as the common law when the parties' contract is silent about the time for performance. Performance in such cases must be tendered within a *reasonable time* (2-309[1]). If the parties' contract calls for a number of performances over an indefinite period of time (e.g., an open-ended requirements contract), the contract is valid for a *reasonable time* but may be terminated at any time by either party after giving *reasonable notice* (2-309[2] and [3]).

Finally, the Code also provides for the time and place of payment. Unless the parties agreed on some other payment terms, payment for the goods is due at the "time and place at which the buyer is to receive the goods" (2-310[a]).

Title and the Code

Code Changes

The Code also deals with many important questions about the **ownership (title)** of the goods in sales contracts. This is important for several reasons. If the goods are lost, stolen, damaged, or destroyed, who must bear the **risk of loss,** the seller or the buyer? Whose creditors (the seller's or the buyer's) have the legal right to seize the goods to satisfy their claims? What are the rights of those who buy goods that are subject to the **claims of third parties** (e.g., their rightful owner or secured creditors)? Who has the **insurable interest** that the law requires before a party can purchase insurance protection for the goods?

Under the common law, most problems concerning risk of loss, insurable interest, and the rights of various third parties to the goods were answered by determining who had title to the goods. The Code, to clarify these questions, has specific rules that generally do not depend on who has title.

LO3

General Title Rules

Physical Delivery

The Code does have a general title section. It provides that title passes to the buyer when the seller has completely performed his or her duties concerning *physical delivery* of the goods (2-401[2]). So, if the contract merely requires the seller to *ship* the goods, title passes to the buyer when the seller delivers the goods to the carrier. If the contract requires *delivery* of the goods by the seller, title passes to the buyer when the goods are delivered and tendered to the buyer.

The case that follows, *Butler v. Beer Across America,* illustrates the principle that title to beer passed to the buyer when the seller transferred it to the carrier because the seller was not required to make delivery at the destination.

Butler v. Beer Across America

40 UCC Rep.2d 1008 (U.S.D.C., N.D. Ala. 2000)

FACTS

In April 1999, while his parents were away from home on vacation, Hunter Butler, a minor, used a credit card in his name to order 12 bottles of beer through Beer Across America's Internet site on the World Wide Web. When his mother, Lynda Butler, returned home, she found several bottles from the shipment of beer remaining in the refrigerator. Lynda Butler then filed a civil lawsuit against Beer Across America seeking damages under Section 6-5-70 of the Alabama Civil Damages Act. The Civil Damages Act provides for a civil action by the parent or guardian of a minor against anyone who knowingly sells or furnishes liquor to the minor. A threshold issue in the lawsuit was whether the sale of the beer had taken place in Alabama so that a court in Alabama would have personal jurisdiction over Beer Across America.

Beer Across America was an Illinois corporation involved in the marketing and sale of alcoholic beverages and other merchandise. The beer was brought by carrier from Illinois to Alabama. The sales invoice and shipping documents provided that the sale was FOB the seller, with the carrier acting as the buyer's agent. Moreover, the invoice included a charge for sales tax but no charge for beer tax; Alabama law requires that sales tax be collected for out-of-state sale of goods that are then shipped to Alabama but requires beer tax be collected only on sales within Alabama.

ISSUE

Did the sale of the beer take place in Alabama?

DECISION

No, the sale took place in Illinois. The court noted that under the versions of the Uniform Commercial Code in effect in both Illinois and Alabama, a sale consists in the passing of title from the seller to the buyer. Title to goods passes at the time and place of shipment when the contract does not require the seller to make delivery at the destination. Accordingly, ownership to the beer passed to Hunter Butler upon tender of the beer to the carrier.

(Author's note: The court went on to transfer the case to the U.S. District Court for the Northern District of Illinois.)

Delivery without Moving the Goods

If delivery is to be made without moving the goods, title passes at the *time and place of contracting* if the goods have been identified to the contract. **Identification** occurs when the surrounding circumstances make it clear that the goods are those "to which the contract refers" (2-501). This may result from the contract description of the goods (if they are distinct from other goods in the seller's possession) or from actions of the seller, such as setting aside or marking the goods.

Negotiable Document of Title

Sometimes when the goods are being shipped by a professional carrier, the parties will use a **negotiable document of title.** For instance, a seller may ship the goods to the buyer with payment due on delivery. The document of title (a negotiable bill of lading) serves as the contract between the seller and the shipper as well as identifies who has title and control of the goods. The document of title (signifying the right to control the goods) will not be surrendered to the buyer until she pays for the goods. If the contract calls for the seller to deliver a negotiable document of title to the goods (like a warehouse receipt or a bill of lading) to the buyer, title passes when the document of title is delivered.

Buyer's Rejection

In some instances, the buyer will **reject** the goods, perhaps because he does not believe that they conform to the contractual specifications. Whatever the reason, if the buyer rejects tender of the goods, title will automatically be revested in the seller.

Title and Third Parties

A basic rule of property law is that a person can transfer no greater rights (title) in property than he himself possesses. So, if Bob steals an iPad from Mary and sells it to Mike, Mike has no greater title to the iPad than Bob possessed. Thus, Mary could recover the iPad from Mike just as she could have recovered it from Bob. The Code, however, makes three important exceptions to this rule in order to protect the rights of innocent buyers.

Transfers of Voidable Title

LO4

A seller who has voidable title can pass good title to a **good faith purchaser for value** (2-403[1]). Sellers may obtain voidable title by impersonating another person when acquiring the goods from their rightful owner, paying for the goods with a bad check, failing to pay for goods sold on a "cash sale" basis, or obtaining the goods in some other fraudulent manner. **Good faith** means "honesty in fact in the transaction concerned" (1-201[19]), and a buyer has given "value" if he or she has given any consideration sufficient to support a simple contract (1-201[44]).

The primary reason for this exception is to place the burden of loss on the party who had the best opportunity to avoid the harm. Good faith purchasers can do nothing to avoid injury. However, the rightful owners of goods at least have the opportunity to protect themselves by taking steps to assure themselves of the buyer's identity, accepting only cash or certified checks, refusing to part with the goods until they have cash in hand, or taking steps to discover fraud before parting with the goods. In view of their greater relative fault, the Code requires the original owners of the goods to bear the burden of collecting from their fraudulent buyers. This principle is illustrated in *Alsafi Oriental Rugs v. American Loan Co.*

Alsafi Oriental Rugs v. American Loan Co.

864 S.W.2d 41 (Ct. App. Tenn. 1993)

FACTS

In December 1990, Arlene Bradley entered Alsafi Oriental Rugs and advised the owner that she was an interior decorator and that she was interested in selling some of his rugs to one of her customers. Alsafi did not know Bradley and had never done business with her. However, he allowed her to take three rugs out on consignment with the understanding that she would return them if her customer was not interested. In fact, however, Bradley was not obtaining the rugs for a "customer" but was instead working for another individual, Walid Salaam, a rug dealer.

A friend of Bradley's had introduced her to Salaam earlier. Salaam had advised the two women that he was the owner of a recently closed oriental rug store that he was attempting to reopen. He offered to teach them how to become decorators and told them that when his store reopened, they could operate out of the store. Salaam advised them that until he got his store restocked, however, he wanted them to "check out" rugs on approval from other rug dealers in town. As they had no experience with oriental rugs, Salaam instructed them which rugs to look for. He then instructed them to go to rug dealers in Memphis and advise them that they were interior decorators with customers that wanted to purchase oriental rugs.

After Bradley obtained possession of the three rugs from Alsafi, she turned them over to Salaam, who in turn took them to a pawnshop operated by the American Loan Company. There Salaam pawned the rugs, obtaining approximately $5,000 after filling out the required paperwork. Salaam failed to redeem the rugs. Following the default, the pawnshop gave the appropriate notice that it intended to dispose of them.

In April 1991 Alsafi learned that his rugs were at the pawnshop. After visiting the pawnshop and identifying the three rugs as his, he brought suit to recover possession of them.

ISSUE

Was Alsafi entitled to recover the rugs from the pawnshop?

DECISION

No. Under Section 2-403(1), a person with voidable title has power to transfer a good title to a good faith purchaser for value. Where goods have been delivered under a transaction of purchase, the purchaser has this power even though the delivery was procured through fraud punishable as larcenous under the criminal law. Here, Bradley obtained the goods through a voluntary transfer of possession described as a "consignment"—and not through any wrongful nonpermissive taking of the goods. As such Bradley was a purchaser of the goods—albeit with voidable title to them—and was empowered by her transaction with Alsafi to pass title to Salaam, who in turn passed title to the American Loan Company, which was found by the court to be a good faith purchaser for value, having no actual knowledge or reason to believe that Salaam was not the true owner of the rugs.

Buyers in the Ordinary Course of Business

The second exception made by the Code concerns **buyers in the ordinary course of business.** A "buyer in the ordinary course of business" is one who, in good faith, buys goods from a person dealing in goods of that type without knowing that the sale violates the ownership rights of any third party (1-201[9]). Under the Code, buyers in the ordinary course take goods free of any security interest in the goods that their seller may have given a third party (9-307).

For example, Art's Jeep Sales borrows money from First Financial Services and gives First Financial a security interest in all its inventory of vehicles. The security interest gives First Financial the right to seize Art's inventory if it defaults on the loan. If Bob buys a new Jeep from Art's, he takes the Jeep free and clear of First Financial's security interest if he is a "buyer in the ordinary course." The basic purpose of this exception is to protect those who innocently buy from merchants, thereby promoting confidence in such commercial transactions. Security interests and the rights of buyers in the ordinary course of business are discussed in more detail in Chapter 43, "Security Interests in Personal Property."

Entrusting Goods

The Code's third major exception to the general common law rule on title is the "entrusting rule" (2-403[2] and [3]). Anyone who entrusts goods to a merchant who regularly deals in such goods gives that merchant the power to give good title to a "buyer in the ordinary course." In the scenario presented at the beginning of this chapter, Paul takes his damaged bicycle for repair to a shop that sells and repairs bicycles. By mistake, a clerk in the bicycle shop sells the bicycle to Melissa. The bicycle shop can pass good title to Melissa, a buyer in the ordinary course of business. In such a case, Paul would have to sue the bicycle shop for conversion of the bicycle; he could not get it back from Melissa. The purpose of this exception is to promote commerce by giving buyers the knowledge that they will get good title to goods they purchase in the ordinary course of their sellers' business.

In the case that follows, *Sutton v. Snider,* when the owner of a motorcycle entrusted it to a motorcycle dealer, a buyer in the ordinary course of business from the dealer obtained good title to the motorcycle and the original owner was not entitled to recover it from the buyer.

Sutton v. Snider

33 P.3d 309 (Ct. Civ. App. Okla. 2001)

FACTS

On May 8, 2000, Paul Sutton delivered his 1995 Harley Davidson Model FLF motorcycle to Super Bikes to allow them to display the motorcycle for sale. Sutton retained the keys and the certificate of title to the motorcycle, but the keys were not necessary to drive it. The written consignment agreement provided that Sutton would receive $18,000 on the sale of the motorcycle and that Super Bikes would retain everything over that; there also was a pencil notation of "low dollars 17,000." On August 17, 2000, Mike Snider paid Super Bikes $17,500, the price it asked for the vehicle, and took possession of the motorcycle. He was aware that Super Bikes held it on consignment but was not aware of the consignor or of any of the terms of the consignment. Snider testified that Super Bikes said it would deliver the title to him as soon as his check cleared.

Super Bikes never paid Sutton for the motorcycle. Sutton discovered that Snider had the motorcycle and sent letters to both Snider and the owners of Super Bikes demanding either the return of possession of the motorcycle or the payment of $17,500. Sutton then brought a lawsuit against Snider seeking return of the motorcycle. Snider asserted that he had obtained good title to the motorcycle as a buyer in the ordinary course of business from a dealer in goods of that kind.

ISSUE

Did Snider get good title to the motorcycle as a buyer in the ordinary course of business?

DECISION

Yes. When the owner of the motorcycle entrusted it to a merchant who dealt in goods of that kind and it was sold, the buyer was a buyer in the ordinary course of business. While Sutton retained the certificate of title and the keys, the keys were not necessary to drive the motorcycle. Snider had no knowledge of the identity of the consignor and had no notice of any restrictions on Super Bikes' authority to sell the motorcycle. Accordingly, title to the motorcycle passed to Snider as a buyer in the ordinary course of business when he paid the agreed-upon price to Super Bikes.

Concept Summary: Title and Third Parties

General Rule

A seller cannot pass better title to goods than he has.

Exceptions to General Rule

1. A person who has voidable title to goods can pass good title to a bona fide purchaser for value.
2. A buyer in the ordinary course of a retailer's business takes free of any interests in the goods that the retailer has given to others.
3. A person who buys goods in the ordinary course of a dealer's business takes free of any claims of a person who entrusted those goods to the dealer.

Ethics in Action

Suppose you are the owner of a small jewelry store that sells new and antique jewelry. A customer leaves a family heirloom—an elaborate diamond ring—with you for cleaning and resetting. By mistake a clerk in your store sells it to another customer. What would you do? If you were the buyer of the ring and had given it to your fiancée as a gift and then were informed of the circumstances, what would you do?

Risk of Loss

Overview

LO5

The transportation of goods from sellers to buyers is a risky business. The carrier of the goods may lose, damage, or destroy them; floods, tornadoes, and other natural catastrophes may take their toll; thieves may steal all or part of the goods. If neither party is at fault for the loss, who should bear the risk? If the buyer has the risk when the goods are damaged or lost, the buyer is liable for the contract price. If the seller has the risk, he or she is liable for damages unless substitute performance can be tendered.

The common law placed the risk on the party who had technical title at the time of the loss. The Code rejects this approach and provides specific rules governing risk of loss that are designed to provide certainty and place the risk on the party best able to protect against loss and most likely to be insured against it. Risk of loss under the Code depends on the terms of the parties' agreement, the moment the loss occurs, and whether one of the parties was in breach of contract when the loss occurred.

The Terms of the Agreement

The parties have the power to control who has the risk of loss by specifically saying so in their agreement (2-509[4]). This they may do directly or by using certain commonly accepted shipping terms in their contract. In addition, the Code has certain general rules on risk of loss that amplify specific shipping terms and control risk of loss in cases in which specific terms are not used (2-509).

Shipment Contracts

If the contract requires the seller to ship the goods by carrier but does not require that the seller guarantee their delivery to a specific destination, the risk passes to the buyer when the goods are delivered to the carrier (2-509[1][a]). The following are commonly used shipping terms that create **shipment contracts:**

FOB (free on board). **FOB (free on board)** calls for the seller to deliver the goods free of expense and at the seller's risk to the place designated. So, if the contract term is "FOB Chicago" or some other place of *shipment,* the seller bears the risk and expense of delivering the goods *to the carrier* (2-319[1][a]). If the term is "FOB vessel, car, or other vehicle," the seller must *load* the goods on board at his or her own risk and expense (2-319[1][c]).

FAS (free alongside). **FAS (free alongside)** is commonly used in maritime contracts and is normally accompanied by the name of a specific vessel and port. The seller must deliver the goods alongside the vessel at his or her own risk and expense (2-319[2]).

CIF (cost, insurance, and freight). **CIF (cost, insurance, and freight)** means that the price of the goods includes the cost of shipping and insuring them. The seller bears this expense and the risk of loading the goods (2-320).

C&F (cost and freight). **C&F (cost and freight)** is the same as CIF except that the seller is not obligated to insure the goods.

In the scenario presented at the opening of the chapter, Paul uses the Trek website to order a bicycle from Trek and has it shipped to him with Paul paying the shipping charges. The arrangement creates a "shipment contract" and when the bicycle is damaged en route, Paul has the risk of loss or damage once Trek has put the bicycle in the hands of the carrier and made an appropriate contract for the shipment of the bicycle.

Destination Contracts

If the contract requires the seller to guarantee delivery of the goods to a specific destination, the seller bears the risk and expense of delivery to that destination (2-509[1][b]). The following are commonly used shipping terms that create **destination contracts:**

FOB destination. An **FOB** term coupled with the place of **destination** of the goods puts the expense and risk of delivering the goods to that destination on the seller (2-319[1][b]).

Ex-ship. **Ex-ship** does not specify a particular ship but places the expense and risk on the seller until the goods are *unloaded* from whatever ship is used (2-322).

No arrival, no sale. **No arrival, no sale** places the expense and risk during shipment on the seller. If the goods fail to arrive through no fault of the seller, the seller has no further liability to the buyer (2-324).

Goods in the Possession of Third Parties

When, at the time of contracting, the goods are in the hands of a third-party bailee (like a carrier or warehouseman) and are to be delivered without being moved, the risk passes to the buyer when the buyer has *the power to take possession* of the goods (2-509[2]). If the goods are covered by a document of title (negotiable or nonnegotiable), the risk passes when the buyer *receives the document of title.* When no document of title is involved, the risk passes when the bailee *acknowledges the buyer's right to possession.*

Risk Generally

If none of the special rules that have just been discussed applies, the risk passes to the buyer on receipt of the goods if the seller is a merchant. If the seller is not a merchant, the risk passes to the buyer when the seller tenders (offers) delivery of the goods (2-509[3]). For example, Frank offers to sell Susan a car, and Susan sends an e-mail accepting Frank's offer. When he receives the e-mail, Frank calls Susan and tells her she can "pick up the car anytime." That night, the car is destroyed when a tree falls on it during a storm. If Frank is a used-car salesman, he must bear the loss. If Frank is an accountant, Susan must bear the loss.

The case that follows, *Capshaw v. Hickman,* illustrates another critical issue, that is, whether the seller in fact tendered delivery to the buyer.

Breach of Contract and Risk of Loss

The Code follows the trend set by earlier law of placing the risk of loss on a party who is in breach of contract. There is no necessary reason why a party in breach should bear the risk, however. In fact, shifting the risk to parties in breach sometimes produces results

Capshaw v. Hickman

64 UCC Rep.2d 543 (Ct. App. Ohio 2007)

FACTS

Charles Capshaw entered into a written contract with Rachel Hickman to purchase Hickman's 1996 Honda Civic EX for $5,025. The contract provided, among other things, that "the title will be surrendered upon the new owner's check clearing." Capshaw made a down payment of $80 in cash and gave Hickman a personal check for the balance. She provided Capshaw with the keys to the vehicle and also complied with his request to sign the certificate of title over to his father and placed the certificate in the vehicle's glovebox. They agreed the vehicle was to remain parked in Hickman's driveway until the check cleared.

Unfortunately, before Hickman was notified by her bank that the check had cleared, a hailstorm heavily damaged the vehicle. Due to the damage, Capshaw decided that he no longer wanted the vehicle and asked Hickman to return his money. Hickman refused, believing that the transaction was complete and that the vehicle belonged to Capshaw. She also requested that it be removed from her driveway.

Capshaw brought suit against Hickman, alleging, among other things, conversion, breach of contract, and "quasi-contract and unjust enrichment—promissory estoppel." Capshaw contended that the risk of loss remained with Hickman until the check cleared; because it had not cleared at the time the hail damaged the car, Hickman sustained the loss. Hickman maintained that the risk of loss for a non-merchant seller like her passes to the buyer after the seller tenders delivery to the buyer.

The trial court found that the parties agreed the transfer of title and delivery of the vehicle would occur only after the successful transfer of funds. Because neither had occurred at the time of the hailstorm, the court concluded that the risk of loss remained with the seller. Hickman appealed, arguing that the risk of loss in this instance should depend on whether there had been a tender of delivery and not on whether or not title had passed.

ISSUE

Does the risk of loss in this case depend on whether or not title had passed?

DECISION

No. The appeals court noted that under the UCC, the question of ownership and passage of title is no longer determinative of risk of loss. Rather, risk of loss passes to the buyer on his receipt of the goods if the seller is a merchant; otherwise the risk of loss passes to the buyer on "tender of delivery." Here, Hickman was not a merchant, so the determinative question is whether there had been a tender of delivery. Tender of delivery occurs when the seller has completed its obligations with respect to delivery of the car. The court found that the difficulty in applying the law in this case lies in determining why the car remained in Hickman's driveway where the information available in the case record did not address that question. If Capshaw paid by check but Hickman refused to consider payment for the car made until the check cleared and would not allow it to be moved until that occurred, then there had not be a tender of delivery where the buyer was free to take the vehicle. Consequently, the risk of loss would have remained with the seller. Alternatively, if the car remained in the driveway at the buyer's suggestion in order to induce Hickman to take a personal check, then the risk of loss passed to Capshaw at the time of the transaction, as he would be considered to have taken delivery and simply left the car in the driveway as a means of inducing Hickman to accept payment in the form (a personal check) that was most convenient to Capshaw. The court sent the case back to the trial court to determine why the car remained in the driveway.

contrary to some of the basic policies underlying the Code's general rules on risk by placing the risk on the party who does not have possession or control of the goods. When the seller tenders goods that the buyer could lawfully reject because they do not conform to the contract description, the risk of loss remains on the seller until the defect is cured or the buyer accepts the goods (2-510[1]). When a buyer rightfully revokes acceptance of the goods, the risk of loss is on the seller from the beginning to the extent that it is not covered by the buyer's insurance (2-510[2]).

Buyers who repudiate a contract for identified, conforming goods before risk of loss has passed to them are liable for a commercially reasonable time for any damage to the goods that is not covered by the seller's insurance (2-510[3]). For example, Trendy Shoe Stores contracts to buy 1,000 pairs of shoes from Acme Shoe Manufacturing Company. Acme crates the shoes and stores them in its warehouse pending delivery to Trendy. Trendy then tells Acme it will not honor its contract for the shoes, and they are destroyed by a fire in Acme's warehouse shortly thereafter. If Acme's insurance covers only part of the loss, Trendy is liable for the balance.

Insurable Interest

The Code rules that govern risk of loss are supplemented by rules that give the parties an **insurable interest** in the goods, which allows them to insure themselves against most of the risks they must bear. Buyers may protect their interest in goods before they obtain title to them, since they have an insurable interest in goods at the moment the goods are *identified to the contract* (2-501[1]). Sellers have an insurable interest in their goods as long as they have title to the goods or a security interest in them (2-501[2]).

Concept Summary: Risk of Loss

The point at which the risk of loss or damage to goods identified to a contract passes to the buyer is as follows:

1. If there is an agreement between the parties, the risk of loss passes to the buyer at the time they have agreed to.
2. If the contract requires the seller to ship the goods by carrier but does not require that the seller guarantee their delivery to a specific destination (shipment contract), the risk of loss passes to the buyer when the seller has delivered the goods to the carrier and made an appropriate contract for their carriage.
3. If the contract requires the seller to guarantee delivery of the goods to a specific destination (destination contract), the risk of loss passes to the buyer when the goods are delivered at the designated destination.
4. If the goods are in the hands of a third person and are to be delivered without being moved, the risk of loss passes to the buyer when the buyer has the power to take possession of the goods; for example, when he receives a document of title.
5. In any situation other than those noted above where the seller is a merchant, the risk of loss passes to the buyer on his receipt of goods.
6. In any situation other than those noted above where the seller is not a merchant, the risk of loss passes to the buyer on the tender of delivery to the buyer by the seller.
7. When a seller tenders goods that the buyer could lawfully reject because they do not conform to the contract description, the risk of loss stays on the seller until the defect is cured or the buyer accepts them.
8. When a buyer rightfully revokes acceptance of goods, the risk is on the seller to the extent it is not covered by the buyer's insurance.
9. If a buyer repudiates a contract for identified, conforming goods before risk of loss has passed to the buyer, the buyer is liable for a commercially reasonable time for any loss or damage to the goods that is not covered by the seller's insurance.

Sales on Trial

There are several common commercial situations in which a seller entrusts goods to another person. This may be done to give a potential buyer the chance to decide whether or not to buy the goods or to give the other party a chance to sell the goods to a third party. These cases present difficult questions about who has the risk of loss of the goods and whose creditors may attach the goods. The Code provides specific rules to answer these questions depending on the nature of the parties' agreement.

Sale or Return

LO6

In a **sale or return** contract, the goods are delivered to the buyer *primarily for resale* with the understanding that the buyer has the right to return them (2-326[1][b]). Unless the parties agreed to the contrary, title and risk of loss rest with the buyer. Return of the goods is at the buyer's risk and expense (2-327[2][b]), and the buyer's creditors can attach the goods while they are in the buyer's possession (2-326[2]). Placing the risk on the buyer in these cases recognizes the fact that sale or return contracts are generally *commercial* transactions.

Sale on Approval

In a **sale on approval,** the goods are delivered to the buyer *primarily for the buyer's use* (2-326[1][a]). The buyer is given the opportunity to examine or try the goods so as to decide whether to accept them. Risk of loss and title to the goods do not pass to the buyer until the buyer accepts the goods (2-327[1][a]). Any use of the goods that is consistent with a trial of the goods is not an acceptance, but the buyer who fails to give reasonable notice of an intent to return the goods may be held to have accepted them (2-327[1][b]).

The buyer's creditors cannot reach goods held on approval (2-326[2]), and return of the goods is at the seller's risk and expense (2-327[1][c]). These provisions recognize the fact that sales on approval are primarily *consumer* transactions.

Questions and Problem Cases

1. Star Coach, LLC, is in the business of converting sport utility vehicles and pickup trucks into custom vehicles. Star Coach performs the labor involved in installing parts dealers. Heart of Texas Dodge purchased a new Dodge Durango from Chrysler Motors and entered into an agreement with Star Coach whereby Star Coach would convert the Durango to a Shelby 360 custom performance vehicle and then return the converted vehicle to Heart of Texas Dodge. The manufacturer delivered the dealer's Durango to Star Coach, and over a period of several months, Star Coach converted the vehicle using parts supplied by another company, Performance West. Several months later, Star Coach delivered the vehicle to Heart of Texas Dodge, and Heart of Texas Dodge paid Star Coach the contract price of $15,768 without inspecting the vehicle. Two days later, Heart of Texas Dodge inspected the vehicle and concluded that the workmanship was faulty. It stopped payment on the check and Star Coach filed suit against Heart of Texas Dodge. One of the issues in the litigation was whether the UCC applied to the contract in this case. Does the UCC apply to a contract for the conversion of a van that involves both goods and services?
2. Keith Russell, a boat dealer, contracted to sell a 19-foot Kinsvater boat to Robert Clouser for $8,500. The agreement stipulated that Clouser was to make a down payment of $1,700, with the balance due when he took possession of the boat. According to the contract, Russell was to retain possession of the boat in order to install a new engine and drive train. While the boat was still in Russell's possession, it was completely destroyed when it struck a seawall. Transamerica, Russell's insurance company, refused to honor Russell's claim for the damages to the boat. The insurance policy between Transamerica and Russell covered only watercraft under 26 feet in

length that were not owned by Russell. Transamerica argued that the boat was not covered by the policy since Russell still owned it at the time of the accident. Did Russell have title to the boat at the time of the accident?

3. Club Pro Golf Products was a distributor of golf products. It employed salespeople who called on customers to take orders for merchandise. The merchandise was sent by Club Pro directly to the purchaser, and payment was made by the purchaser directly to Club Pro. A salesman for Club Pro, Carl Gude, transmitted orders for certain merchandise to Club Pro for delivery to several fictitious purchasers. Club Pro sent the merchandise to the fictitious purchasers at the fictitious addresses where it was picked up by Gude. Gude then sold the merchandise, worth approximately $19,000, directly to Simpson, a golf pro at a golf club. Gude then retained the proceeds of sale for himself. Club Pro discovered the fraud and brought suit against Simpson to recover the merchandise. Did Simpson get good title to the merchandise he purchased from Gude even though Gude had obtained it by fraud?
4. Chilla Mitchell decided to sell her Cadillac Concours. She talked to Tommy Thrash, the proprietor of an automobile dealership called "Repro City" and Thrash assured her that he could get $16,500 for the vehicle. Mitchell agreed to leave her car for sale at Thrash's lot, and Thrash agreed to pay her $16,500 on the sale of the vehicle. Mitchell retained the certificate of title to the car. On October 26, Roosevelt Jones bought the car from Repro City for $18,655. Jones received a bill of sale and application for title. Thrash did not pay Mitchell. Mitchell returned to the address where she had left her vehicle but the car lot was gone. She was unable to locate Thrash. When she learned that Jones had the car, she filed a lawsuit against him seeking its return. Does Mitchell have the legal right to recover the car from Jones?
5. Legendary Homes, a home builder, purchased various appliances from Ron Mead T.V. & Appliance, a retail merchant selling home appliances. They were intended to be installed in one of Legendary Homes' houses and were to be delivered on February 1. At 5:00 on that day, the appliances had not been delivered. Legendary Homes's employees closed the home and left. Sometime between 5:00 and 6:30, Ron Mead delivered the appliances. No one was at the home so the deliveryman put the appliances in the garage. During the night, someone stole the appliances. Legendary Homes denied it was responsible for the loss and refused to pay Ron Mead for the appliances. Ron Mead then brought suit for the purchase price. Did Legendary Homes have the risk of loss of the appliances?
6. In June, Ramos entered into a contract to buy a motorcycle from Big Wheel Sports Center. He paid the purchase price and was given the papers necessary to register the cycle and get insurance on it. Ramos registered the cycle but had not attached the license plates to it. He left on vacation and told the salesperson for Big Wheel Sports Center that he would pick up the cycle on his return. While Ramos was on vacation, there was an electric power blackout in New York City and the cycle was stolen by looters. Ramos then sued Big Wheel Sports Center to get the money he had paid for the cycle. Did Big Wheel Sports Center have the risk of loss of the motorcycle?
7. Richard Burnett agreed to purchase a mobile home with a shed from Betty Jean Putrell, Executrix of the Estate of Lena Holland. On Saturday, March 3, 1990, Burnett paid Putrell $6,500 and was given the certificate of title to the mobile home as well as a key to it, but no keys to the shed. At the time the certificate of title was transferred, the following items remained in the mobile home: the washer and dryer, mattress and box springs, two chairs, items in the refrigerator, and the entire contents of the shed. These items were to be retained by Putrell and removed by her. To facilitate removal

she retained one key to the mobile home and the only keys to the shed. On Sunday, March 4, the mobile home was destroyed by fire through the fault of neither party. At the time of the fire, Putrell still had a key to the mobile home as well as the keys to the shed and she had not removed the contents of the mobile home or of the shed. The contents of the shed were not destroyed and were subsequently removed by Putrell. Burnett brought suit against Putrell to recover the $6,500 he had paid for the mobile home and shed. Did the seller, Putrell, have the risk of loss of the trailer?

Chapter 20

Warranties and Product Liability

Learning Objectives

After you have studied this chapter, you should be able to:

1. Explain what is meant by an *express warranty* and how it is created.
2. Describe the *implied warranty of merchantability* and list the six tests of merchantability in a contract for the sale of goods.
3. Explain how the *implied warranty of fitness for a particular purpose* differs from the *implied warranty of merchantability.*
4. Distinguish the *warranty of title* from the other implied warranties.
5. Discuss when and how a merchant can limit or exclude warranties in a contract for the sale of goods.
6. Explain when someone who is not the purchaser of goods may benefit from a warranty.
7. Discuss when a manufacturer may be held liable for *negligence* in the manufacture or sale of goods.
8. Explain what is meant by the term *strict liability* as it is used to hold sellers liable for injuries and discuss the elements that must be present for strict liability to be available to an injured party, as well as the defenses that may be available to the seller.

After seeing an advertisement on television for a small SUV manufactured by Ford, you visit a dealer's showroom, where the salesperson extols its virtues as an ideal vehicle for commuting and for both city and suburban driving. You decide to purchase a used version, and then while you are driving your 16-month-old SUV on an interstate highway, a tire blows out, with the tread separating from the rest of the tire. The SUV, which is susceptible to rollovers, rolls over, the vehicle is badly damaged, and you are seriously injured. Who is responsible for the accident and for the damages you have sustained? You, the manufacturer of the SUV, the manufacturer of the tire, and/or the dealer from whom you purchased the vehicle?

(continued)

If it can be shown that the vehicle and/or tire were defective at the time you purchased the vehicle, liability might be placed on one or both of the manufacturers and/or the dealer based on one or more of a number of legal theories: (1) express warranty, (2) implied warranties that are imposed by law, (3) negligence, or (4) strict liability. In this chapter, we will explore the legal rules for holding manufacturers and sellers liable for product quality.

Introduction: Historical Development of the Law

Prior to 1900, the sale of goods was commonly made in a face-to-face negotiation between the buyer and the seller. The goods were relatively simple and could be examined on the spot. Frequently, the seller was a peddler who would leave for parts unknown as soon as he had sold his wares. The sale was often looked on as a test of wits; the seller did his best to drive a sharp bargain. Similarly, the buyer did everything possible to get a good buy. In this situation, neither the buyer nor the seller placed much faith in the statements of the other. The statements made by the seller were taken by the buyer to be sales talk. These statements were not binding on the seller unless he clearly assumed responsibility for the quality of the goods he was selling.

Business methods have changed over time. Today, sales to businesspeople are frequently made by a salesperson calling on the customer. The salesperson either describes the goods or displays samples of the goods. The selling of many kinds of consumer goods is done through advertising on television, in newspapers and magazines, or on the Internet. These changes in the way sales of goods are made have led to changes in the law providing more protection to buyers of these goods. Manufacturers and sellers are also held much more accountable for the quality and safety of the goods they sell because of changes in society's concept of who can best bear the responsibility for the quality of goods.

In the next section of this chapter, we will cover the obligations and rules concerning seller responsibility for product quality that arise under the Uniform Commercial Code's warranty provisions. Later in the chapter, we will cover obligations that arise under the federal Magnuson-Moss Act, the common law of negligence, and the doctrine of strict liability.

Warranties

In general, a **warranty** is a contractual promise by the seller regarding the quality, character, or suitability of the goods sold. In a product liability suit based on breach of warranty, the plaintiff is claiming that the product did not live up to the seller's promise. If the seller, through words or behavior, makes promises about the goods, he has created an **express warranty.** In addition, certain responsibilities for the quality of goods sold are imposed on the seller by the Uniform Commercial Code. These warranties arise whether or not the seller has made express promises as to the quality of the goods. The warranties imposed by law are known as **implied warranties.**

LO1

Express Warranties

In order to create an express warranty, it does not matter whether the seller uses the words *warranty* or *guarantee* or whether the seller *intends* to make a warranty. The critical elements for creation of an express warranty are that the seller make a *statement of fact or a promise* to the buyer *concerning the goods* that *becomes part of the bargain* between the buyer and seller (2-313[1][a]).[1] Sellers who merely give an opinion or recommend the goods do not create an express warranty. Thus, sellers are not considered to have made an express warranty if they confine their statements to "sales talk." Some examples of sales talk are: "It is a good buy"; "These goods are first class"; or "You should be happy with this."

Whether a statement made by a seller is interpreted as an opinion or as an express warranty often depends on the relative experience and knowledge of the buyer and seller. If the seller deals in the type of goods she is selling and the buyer does not deal in such goods and knows little about them, a statement by the seller about the quality or character of the goods might be interpreted as a warranty. On the other hand, if the buyer is a dealer in such goods and has had experience and knowledge similar to that of the seller, the same statement might be interpreted as an expression of an opinion.

For example, if a used-car dealer who is very familiar with the mechanical operation of cars is selling a car to a person who is not knowledgeable about cars, the dealer's statements about the condition of the car and its performance are likely to be treated as statements of fact or promises creating an express warranty. However, if that same dealer is selling a car to another dealer who is equally knowledgeable about cars, the seller's statements are less likely to be treated as promises on which the dealer would rely in deciding to purchase the car.

In the case that follows, *Bobholz v. Banaszak,* the court found that representations made by the seller in advertisements for a ski boat constituted express warranties.

[1]The numbers in parentheses refer to sections of the Uniform Commercial Code.

Bobholz v. Banaszak

49 UCC Rep.2d 25 (Ct. App. Wisc. 2002)

FACTS

In July 2001, Randall Bobholz purchased a 1998 Glastron GS185 ski boat from John Banaszak. Bobholz discovered the boat while searching the Internet. It was advertised on two different websites, eBay, an Internet auction site, and American Boat Listing. The eBay ad described the boat as "in perfect condition" and American Boat Listing described it as "in excellent condition." Both advertisements noted that Banaszak had used the boat only minimally, approximately 21 to 24 hours since he purchased it.

On the basis of these representations, Bobholz contacted Banaszak to discuss the boat. In the course of their conversation, Banaszak again stated that the boat was in excellent condition, that it had been properly maintained and winterized, and that he had personally winterized the boat the year prior. Accordingly, Bobholz offered to purchase the boat for $12,500, and Banaszak accepted. The following day they met in Madison to transfer the check, boat, and title. Bobholz briefly inspected the boat, which appeared to be in "meticulous" condition.

Two weeks later, Bobholz was operating the boat when the engine started to lose power and then "just died." He took the boat to a marina to investigate the problem and learned that the intake manifold on the boat's engine had two cracks in it, allowing water into the engine, which

(continued)

caused irreparable damage. According to the service manager, the two cracks were the result of improper winterization of the engine. The marina replaced the engine at a cost of $4,220.

Bobholz filed a small claims action to recover that amount. In his complaint, Bobholz argued that because the defect in the engine existed at the formation of the contract, Banaszak had breached his express warranty that the boat was in "excellent" and "perfect" condition. Banaszak argued that the advertisement should not be considered an express warranty. He asserted that he was a "casual seller" so that the doctrine of caveat emptor, or buyer beware, should apply and that any representation as to the quality of the boat was made in the course of the sales negotiation and did not constitute a warranty.

ISSUE

Did the statements in the advertisements constitute express warranties?

DECISION

Yes. Initially, the court noted that where a product is warranted to be without defects, the common law doctrine of caveat emptor, or "buyer beware," does not apply. All representations made in the course of a sales negotiation do not constitute warranties. Sellers are expected to make generalized statements regarding the quality of their products. Puffery is merely an expression of the seller's opinion and the buyer has no right to rely on it. For an express warranty to be created, there must be an "affirmation of fact" relating to the goods that becomes part of the "basis of the bargain." Here Banaszak represented to Bobholz in the eBay advertisement and during the sales negotiation that the ski boat was in "perfect condition." He did not couch the statement as being his opinion or his belief. The statement was an affirmation of fact relating to the goods, and this representation regarding the quality of the boat was a basis of the bargain because it induced Bobholz to purchase the boat.

In negotiating a sale, a seller may use descriptive terms to convey to the buyer an idea of the quality or characteristics of the goods; for example, Brand X is "a skin cream for oily skin." Similarly a seller might use pictures, drawings, blueprints, or technical specifications, or in some cases a sample or model. When a seller uses descriptive terms and the buyer takes them into consideration when making the purchase, the seller has expressly warranted that the goods she delivers will meet that description. If a sample or model is part of the basis of a bargain of a contract, the seller has expressly warranted that the goods delivered will conform to the sample or model (2-313[1][b], [c]).

Implied Warranties

Nature of Implied Warranties

Under present methods of merchandising, the buyer commonly has little or no opportunity to examine goods carefully before making a decision to purchase them. In addition, because of the complexity and nature of many of the goods that are sold today, buyers are often not in a position to test the goods adequately to determine their quality prior to buying them. The merchant dealing in the goods or the manufacturer of such goods is in a much better position to make a thorough examination or test of the goods to determine their adequacy and quality. Therefore, in the interest of promoting higher standards in the marketplace, the law imposes certain responsibilities on the seller for the quality, character, and suitability of the goods sold. This is particularly true where the seller is a merchant dealing in goods of that kind.

Implied warranties imposed by law are not absolute. They arise only under certain circumstances, and the seller may include a clause in the contract that excludes them. The courts, however, favor implied warranties. If the seller wishes to be relieved of the responsibility for implied warranties, the sales contract must clearly provide that the parties did not intend the implied warranties to become part of the contract.

There are two implied warranties of quality imposed under the Code: (1) the implied warranty of merchantability and (2) the implied warranty of fitness for a particular purpose.

These two warranties overlap, and under some circumstances the seller may be held liable for breach of both warranties.

Implied Warranty of Merchantability

LO2

If the seller is a merchant who deals in the kind of goods sold, there is an *implied warranty* that the goods are **merchantable,** or fit for their ordinary purpose. If the person who sells the goods does not deal in goods of that kind, the implied warranty of merchantability is not involved. For example, if your occupation is selling clothing and you sell your used 1994 Chevrolet to a neighbor, there is no implied warranty that the car is merchantable.

The common test for **merchantability** is whether the goods are *fit for the ordinary purpose* for which such goods are used (2-314[2][c]). Thus, a person of normal weight who buys a chair should be able to sit on it without its collapsing. The chair should also withstand other things people commonly do with chairs, such as occasionally standing on them or dragging them across the floor.

The other tests of merchantability for all sales contracts are:

1. The goods conform to any promises or statements of fact made on the container or label.
2. The goods are adequately packaged and labeled.
3. The goods are of the same kind, quality, and quantity within each unit (case, package, carton).
4. Fungible goods (mixed goods that are identical and cannot be separated, such as grain and coal) are of average quality for the kind of goods described in the contract.
5. The goods conform closely enough to the description in the contract to be acceptable to others in the trade or business (2-314[2]).

The case that follows, *Denny v. Ford Motor Co.,* involves a claim that a small sports utility vehicle was not fit for the ordinary purposes for which it was to be used—driving on a highway.

Denny v. Ford Motor Co.

662 N.E.2d 730 (Ct. App. N.Y. 1995)

FACTS

Nancy Denny was severely injured when the Ford Bronco II that she was driving rolled over. The accident occurred when Denny slammed on her brakes in an effort to avoid a deer that had walked directly into her motor vehicle's path. Denny and her husband brought an action against Ford Motor Company, the vehicle's manufacturer, asserting a claim for, among other things, breach of the implied warranty of merchantability.

The evidence at the trial centered on the particular characteristics of utility vehicles, which are generally made for off-road use on unpaved and often rugged terrain. Such use often necessitates climbing over obstacles such as fallen logs and rocks. While utility vehicles are traditionally considerably larger than passenger cars, some manufacturers have created a category of downsized "small" utility vehicles, that are designed to be lighter, to achieve better fuel economy, and to appeal to a wider consumer market. The Bronco II in which Denny was injured falls into this category.

Denny produced evidence showing that small utility vehicles in general, and the Bronco II in particular, present a significantly higher risk of rollover accidents than do ordinary passenger automobiles. She showed that the Bronco II had

(continued)

Denny v. Ford Motor Co. *(concluded)*

a low stability index attributable to its high center of gravity and relatively narrow track width. The vehicle's shorter wheel base and suspension system were additional factors contributing to its instability. Ford had made minor design changes in an effort to achieve a higher stability index, but none of the changes produced a significant improvement in the vehicle's stability.

Ford argued at the trial that the design features of which Denny complained were necessary to the vehicle's off-road capabilities. According to Ford, the vehicle had been intended to be used as an off-road vehicle and had not been designed to be sold as a conventional passenger automobile. Ford's own engineer stated that he would not recommend the Bronco II to someone whose primary interest was to use it as a passenger car, because the features of a four-wheel drive utility vehicle were not helpful for that purpose and the vehicle's design made it inherently less stable.

A Ford marketing manual, however, predicted that many buyers would be attracted because utility vehicles were "suitable to contemporary life styles" and were "considered fashionable" in some suburban areas. According to the manual, the sales presentation should take into account the vehicle's "suitability for commuting and for suburban and city driving." Additionally, the vehicle's ability to switch between two-wheel and four-wheel drive would "be particularly appealing to women who may be concerned about driving in snow and ice with their children." The Dennys testified that the perceived safety benefits of its four-wheel drive capacity were what attracted them to the Bronco II and that they were not at all interested in its off-road use.

ISSUE

Did Ford breach the implied warranty of merchantability when it sold the Bronco II for use as an on-road vehicle when it had a propensity to roll over in such use?

DECISION

Yes. The law implies a warranty by a manufacturer that places its product on the market that the product is reasonably fit for the ordinary purpose for which it was intended. Here the Dennys claim that the Bronco was not fit for its ordinary purpose because of its alleged propensity to roll over and the lack of warnings to the consumer of this propensity. The jury found that Ford had breached the implied warranty of merchantability.

Under the Code, the implied warranty of merchantability applies to the selling of food or drink (2-314[1]). Thus, if food or drink sold in a restaurant is not wholesome, the seller may be held liable for breach of this warranty. The courts, however, disagree on how to judge whether food is wholesome if it contains a naturally occurring but unexpected substance. Some courts, using a "foreign–natural" test, say that the warranty is breached if the substance is "foreign" to the food but not if it is natural to it. Thus, if Carl bought a chicken sandwich with a piece of metal in it that injured his mouth, he would be able to recover. If, however, his mouth were instead injured by a piece of chicken bone in the sandwich, he would not be able to recover. A growing number of courts have adopted a different test. Under this test, plaintiffs can recover if they could not reasonably expect the substance to be in the food, even if it is naturally occurring. Courts using this test would allow Carl to recover if he could show that a reasonable person would not expect to find a chicken bone in a chicken sandwich. These issues are addressed in the *Mexicali Rose* case with the court's majority and the dissenting justices reaching different conclusions.

Mexicali Rose v. Superior Court

16 UCC Rep.2d 607 (Sup. Ct. Cal. 1992)

FACTS

Jack Clark was a customer at the Mexicali Rose restaurant. He ordered a chicken enchilada and sustained throat injuries when he swallowed a one-inch chicken bone. He brought an action for damages based on breach of the implied warranty of merchantability, negligence, and strict liability. He alleged that Mexicali Rose negligently left the bone in the

(continued)

enchilada and the food was unfit for human consumption. He also asserted that he did not expect to find a bone and that it is not common knowledge that there may be bones in a chicken enchilada.

ISSUE

Was Mexicali Rose liable for breach of the implied warranty of merchantability because of the presence of the chicken bone in the enchilada?

DECISION

No. The court applied the foreign–natural test and held that if an injury-producing substance is natural to the preparation of the food served, then it can be said that it was reasonably expected by its very nature and the food cannot be determined unfit or defective. In such a case the injured person does not have a cause of action for breach of implied warranty or for strict liability. The court went on to say that if the presence of the natural substance is the consequence of a restaurateur's failure to exercise due care in food preparation, the injured patron can sue under a negligence theory. Alternatively, if the injury-causing substance is foreign to the food served, then the injured patron may sue on the grounds of breach of warranty and strict liability and the court must determine whether the substance (1) could be reasonably expected by the average consumer and (2) rendered the food unfit or defective.

DISSENT

The dissenting justices took a different view, noting that a majority of the court had held that processed food containing a sharp, concealed bone is fit for consumption, though no reasonable consumer would anticipate finding the bone. They noted that the majority had declared, in effect, that the bone is natural to the dish and therefore the dish is fit for consumption. The rule created by the majority seems bizarre in application to mass producers and distributors of processed food, irrational in differentiating between natural and unnatural contaminants, and unfair in saddling the objectively reasonable—and truthful—consumer with costs he or she had no way of protecting against. In applying the implied warranty of merchantability, courts should consider "natural" to mean that the consumer should anticipate finding the object in the meal. The focus should be on whether the object should reasonably be anticipated in the dish as served.

Implied Warranty of Fitness for a Particular Purpose

At times, the seller may know the *particular purpose* for which the buyer needs the goods and know that the buyer is *relying* on the seller to select goods suitable for that purpose. If these two conditions are met, then the seller makes an **implied warranty** that the goods will be *fit for that particular purpose* (2-315).

LO3

In some instances, the buyer will tell the seller the particular purpose for which the goods are needed. For example, a farmer goes to a feed store and tells the clerk that he needs a pesticide that will kill corn borers. If the clerk knows the farmer is depending on her to pick a suitable pesticide, there is an implied warranty that the product selected will be fit for the farmer's needs. If, when properly used, the product selected kills the farmer's corn or is ineffective against corn borers, the implied warranty is breached.

In other instances, the particular purpose is implied from the circumstances. For example, when a high school football coach orders football helmets from a sporting goods manufacturer, it is implied that the helmet will be used by his players while playing football. Therefore, the helmets are sold with an implied warranty that they will be fit for the particular purpose of protecting players heads from injury while playing football.

While the warranty of merchantability and warranty of fitness for a particular purpose can both accompany the sale of a good, as in Carl's case, they are not the same. The implied warranty of merchantability applies only to merchants, while the warranty of fitness for a particular purpose can also apply to nonmerchants. The warranty of merchantability focuses on whether the goods are fit for the ordinary purposes for which such goods are used; the warranty of fitness, for a particular purpose or the buyer's individual purpose. Thus, if a 350-pound man tells the clerk he needs a chair that will not collapse under his weight and is sold one that will support a person of only average weight, the warranty of fitness for a particular purpose is breached but not the warranty of merchantability.

If the buyer gives the seller technical specifications of the goods she wishes to buy or clearly indicates the particular goods desired, there is no implied warranty of fitness for a particular purpose. Under these circumstances, there is no evidence that the buyer is relying on the seller's judgment or expertise.

In the case that follows, *Ram Head Outfitters, Ltd. v. Mecham,* the seller was found to have made and breached a warranty for a particular purpose.

Ram Head Outfitters, Ltd. v. Mecham

74 UCC Rep.2d 261 (U.S.D.C., D. Arizona 2011)

FACTS

Stan Simpson was the principal of Ram Head Outfitters, Ltd., an outfitting business that took clients hunting and fishing in remote areas of the Canadian wilderness. Ram Head used airplanes to gain access to those areas, and its operation required pilots to take off and land on rough terrain—such as gravel bars or mountainsides—a very challenging type of flying.

Robert Mecham was a retired farmer who, prior to becoming a farmer, owned a crop-dusting business and worked as a crop duster for 18 seasons from 1977 to 1994. Crop dusting requires pilots to perform multiple takeoffs and landings, oftentimes on rough terrain, and is generally more dangerous than flying an airplane under normal conditions. During the time he owned the crop-dusting business, the company owned as many as 12 airplanes but usually owned no more than 4 or 5 airplanes in any given year. Over the course of 25 years, Mecham owned and sold approximately 15 planes. They were purchased and sold in connection with his crop-dusting business as well as for his individual use.

In late 2005, Mecham purchased a Cessna A185E plane through a broker in California for $119,880. The plane had been in an accident in 1993 but had passed two annual inspections since Mecham became its owner, one in 2006 and one in early 2008. The plane was very similar to planes Mecham had flown in his crop-dusting business.

After having owned it for about 27 months and having flown it for approximately 20 hours, Meacham, in March 2008, decided to sell the plane and on March 13 advertised it as for sale in Trade-A-Plane, a national advertising media for aircraft. The advertisement said the plane was a "fast, clean" airplane.

At that same time, Simpson was looking to purchase a plane because his Cessna 185 had incurred substantial damage as a result of a landing gear failure. Simpson saw the advertisement the same day it appeared and immediately contacted Mecham. During several ensuing telephone and in-person conversations, Simpson made it clear to Mecham how Ram Head intended to use the plane, sharing with him the nature of its business and the necessity to make rough landings in inhospitable terrain. The two men discussed the similarities between the flying required for crop dusting and for Ram Head's business.

Simpson inspected the plane's log books and briefly took it for a flight, and conducted a brief inspection. He also contracted with Bob Mace, a mechanic who owned Mace Aviation and had previously worked on the plane for Mecham, to inspect it, but, ultimately, Mace did not have time to conduct a detailed inspection. Simpson agreed to purchase the plane from Mecham for $117,500. The bill of sale did not contain any "as is" or other warranty defeating clause. Simpson also hired the mechanic to do some work on the plane, install some additional equipment to facilitate short and rough field landings, and conduct the annual inspection needed to obtain an Export Certificate of Airworthiness. The mechanic did the requested repair work over a period of about two months but did not perform a complete annual inspection. However, he advised the Federal Aviation Administration that he had done so—and the FAA issued the Export Certificate.

On May 27, 2008, Simpson took possession of the plane and flew the plane from Mesa, Arizona, to Edmonton, Alberta, Canada, stopping along the way in Utah, Idaho, and Montana. Upon arrival in Edmonton, the plane underwent an importation inspection by a Canadian Minister of Transit inspector. The inspector determined that the Export Certificate of Airworthiness was not valid, as the aircraft was not in an airworthy condition due to numerous, serious defects. For instance, the main landing gear box, horizontal stabilizer, door posts, cabin floor and outboard fittings all required significant structural repairs. Additionally, the belly skin under the plane had been corroded by battery acid, and the plane had several cracked brackets and torque tubes and countless loose rivets and oversized rivet holes. The plane also had a number of undocumented and improper previous repairs.

These defects rendered the plane unsafe for flight, that is, not airworthy. The plane was repaired and made airworthy

(continued)

at Ram Head's expense, but because of the extensive nature of the repairs, Ram Head was unable to use the plane for the 2008 hunting season and had to lease another plane at its own expense.

ISSUE

Was there a breach of an implied warranty of fitness for a particular purpose?

DISCUSSION

Yes. The court held that Ram Head has established a breach of the implied warranty of fitness for a particular purpose. Through his conversations with Simpson, Mecham had reason to know of the particular purpose for which Ram Head required the plane. Ram Head also established that Simpson relied on Mecham's skill or judgment to select the plane. The record showed that Mecham was very familiar with airplanes of the type he sold to Ram Head, having owned such planes for both business and pleasure for over 30 years. In addition, due to his time as a crop duster, Mecham possessed specific experience and expertise concerning the type of dangerous and unconventional flying demanded by Ram Head's business. Furthermore, the court found that even though Simpson had some reason to believe a Cessna 185 might be suitable for Ram Head's operation, Simpson relied on Mecham's skill and judgment in deciding to purchase this particular plane.

[Author's note: The court went on to find that Mecham had breached the implied warranty of merchantability as well and that the mechanic had breached his contract with Ram Head to repair and to inspect the plane. The court held that Mecham and the mechanic were jointly and severally liable for the damages established by Ram Head of $120,149.74].

Warranty of Title

LO4

The **warranty of title** differs from other warranties in that it protects the buyer in ownership of the goods bought. In contrast, the other warranties discussed in this chapter relate to the quality of the goods sold. The general rule under the Code is that in any contract for the sale of goods, the seller warrants to the buyer that he has the right to sell them (2-312). If, for example, the seller stole the goods, the seller does not have good title to them, and the warranty of title is breached when he sells them to the buyer.

Under the warranty of title, the seller also warrants that the goods are *free of any liens or claims of other parties* unless the buyer was given notice of the liens or claims at the time the contract was made (2-312). Suppose John puts his car up for sale. John originally borrowed the money to buy the car from his bank, and the bank took a security interest or lien on it to secure John's repayment of the loan. If John still owes $600 to the bank at the time he sells the car to Ann, John must either pay off the bank before he transfers title to Ann or specifically provide in his agreement with Ann that the automobile is being sold subject to the bank's lien.

When the seller of goods is a merchant, the warranty of title also covers a claim by a third party that the sale or use of the goods infringes a patent held by that third party.

The warranty of title is not made where there is specific language in the contract or circumstances giving the buyer reason to know that the seller does not claim to have title—such as a sheriff's sale.

Exclusions and Modifications of Warranties

General Rules

LO5

Under the Code, the parties to a contract have, within certain limits, the right to agree to relieve the seller from all or part of the liability for express or implied warranties. Frequently, sellers try to exclude or limit their responsibility for these warranties; however, such exclusions and modifications are not looked on with favor by the courts. The seller must satisfy a number of strict requirements in order to be successful in excluding or modifying an express or implied warranty. These requirements are designed to make it likely that the buyer is aware of the clause modifying or excluding the warranty and freely consents to it. In a dispute, the court considers the reasonableness of the particular exclusion or modification and will refuse to enforce an exclusion it finds to be unreasonable or unconscionable.

Limitation of Express Warranties

If sellers do not want to be liable for express warranties, they should try to avoid making any. This is difficult, however, because the seller is likely to make statements about the goods or use models or samples. A seller who makes an express warranty and who also tries to disclaim all express warranties by including a disclaimer clause in the contract is not likely to succeed. The disclaimer will probably be disregarded on the ground that it is inconsistent with the express warranty (2-316[1]).

Exclusion of Implied Warranties

In order to exclude the implied warranty of merchantability, the seller must specifically mention *merchantability* in the exclusion. The exclusion does not have to be in writing but if it is in writing, the clause that excludes all or part of the warranty of merchantability must be *conspicuous* (2-316[2]). Thus, the exclusion clause must be printed or written into the contract in large type or letters, or in an ink of a different color, so that the person reading the contract is not likely to overlook it. If the seller is particularly concerned that the exclusion clause be enforced, the seller should have the buyer separately initial the exclusion clause.

To exclude the implied warranty of fitness for a particular purpose, the exclusion must be in *writing* and it must be *conspicuous* (2-316[2]). Thus, a general disclaimer such as, "ALL IMPLIED WARRANTIES ARE HEREBY DISCLAIMED," if sufficiently conspicuous, would disclaim the warranty of fitness for a particular purpose. It would not, however, exclude the warranty of merchantability because the word *merchantability* was not used.

Warranties can also be excluded by the circumstances of the sale. Goods sold "as is" or "with all faults" are sold without the implied warranties of merchantability and fitness for a particular purpose. These phrases, which usually accompany the sale of used or damaged goods, call the buyer's attention to the warranty exclusion and make it clear that there are no warranties (2-316[3][a]). A seller can also limit both implied warranties by making goods available for examination and demanding that the buyer examine them. If the buyer takes the goods without examining them, the buyer has no implied warranty with regard to defects that should have been discovered through inspection (2-316[3][b]).

In the case that follows, *Baba v. Hewlett Packard Co.*, the court found that a disclaimer was effective to relieve the seller of a defective computer from liability for breach of any implied warranty of merchantability.

Baba v. Hewlett Packard Co.

78 UCC Rep.2d 989 (U.S.D.C., N.D. Cal. 2012)

FACTS

Ray Ritz, a resident of Massachusetts, purchased a Hewlett Packard (HP) model tx2000 notebook computer from HP in March 2008. Many of the HP tx2000 computers shipped between January and October 2008 exhibited a problem that caused the cursor to independently migrate to the bottom right corner of the screen. In December 2008, the company that manufactured the computers for HP determined that this "crazy cursor" problem was being caused by electromagnetic interference (EMI) emanating from

(continued)

components on the motherboard and that a foil insert on the keyboard cover would block the EMI and resolve the problem. In January 2009 HP issued advisories to its engineers and service providers describing the problem and its proposed solution. At the same time it posted a notice to customers through its website advising them of the problem and inviting them to contact HP service and support for assistance. The tx2000 computers manufactured after June 1, 2008, were built with a keyboard cover component that already included the corrective foil insert.

Each tx2000 was accompanied by a written limited warranty. The first page of the warranty read in capital letters, "EXCEPT AS EXPRESSLEY SET FORTH IN THIS LIMITED WARRANTY, HP MAKES NO OTHER WARRANTIES OR CONITIONS, EXPRESS OR IMPLIED, INCLUDING ANY IMPLIED WARRANTIES OF MERCHANTABILITY." It continued, "ANY IMPLIED WARRANTIES THAT MAY BE IMPOSED BY LAW ARE LIMITED IN DURATION TO THE LIMITED WARRANTY PERIOD" of one year from the date of purchase.

The computer was not warranted to be "uninterrupted or error free." Rather, the statement indicated, "HP will at its discretion, repair or replace any component or hardware product that manifests a defect in materials or workmanship during the Limited Warranty Period." The warranty clarified, "IF YOUR HP PRODUCT FAILS TO WORK AS WARRANTED ABOVE, YOUR SOLE AND EXCLUSIVE REMEDY (AT THE SOLE DISCRETION OF HP) SHALL BE ONE OF THE FOLLOWING: REPAIR OF THE HP PRODUCT, REPLACEMENT OF THE HP PRODUCT, OR A REFUND OF YOUR PURCHASE PRICE OR LEASE PAYMENTS (LESS INTEREST)." The limited warranty did not cover software problems.

The crazy cursor problem on Ritz's computer emerged a few months after he purchased it in March 2008. It became increasingly problematic and in December 2008 Ritz stopped using the computer for work purposes, but continued to use it for personal e-mail and for games. In June 2009, after the expiration of his one-year limited warranty, he contacted HP service about the cursor on the tx2000. HP service failed to identify the issues correctly as the crazy cursor problem. Ritz was told that he was probably touching the touchscreen accidentally and to desensitize the touchscreen or change the power setting. Ritz declined to pay for an additional level of technical support in order to get further assistance. He again contacted HP service through their website in June 2009 and was directed to change the touchpad settings as well as to verify that the correct touchpad software was installed.

Ritz joined a class action lawsuit against HP along with others who had purchased the tx2000 and had encountered the crazy cursor problem. The plaintiffs asserted claims for breach of the implied warranty of merchantability and breach of express warranty. HP moved for summary judgment of one of the subclasses that included Ritz who were claiming breach of the implied warranty of merchantability.

ISSUE

Was the disclaimer of any implied warranties of merchantability effective to preclude Ritz from asserting a claim of breach of the implied warranty of merchantability against HP?

DECISION

Yes. Under the Uniform Commercial Code as enacted in Massachusetts, such a disclaimer is valid if it includes the word "merchantability" and, if in writing, is "conspicuous." Here, the disclaimer language was in all capital letters and located on the first page of the warranty.

The court went on to note that, no matter how conspicuous, in Massachusetts a disclaimer cannot relieve a seller of "consumer goods" of the implied warranty of merchantability. Under the Massachusetts version of the UCC, a 'consumer good" is one "used or bought for use *primarily* for personal, family, or household purposes." Ritz had testified that he bought his tx2000 for work in March 2008 and had claimed a tax deduction for the computer in light of its claimed use for business purposes. He used it nearly nine hours a day for business purposes through December 2008. After that time, he reduced his use of the tx2000 because of its crazy cursor, utilizing it only to read his "work e-mail" and to play games. Because Ritz's tx200 is "equipment," rather than a consumer good, the disclaimer of the implied warranty of merchantability is enforceable.

Unconscionable Disclaimers

The Code gives the court the authority to refuse to enforce a particular clause or even an entire contract if it finds it is *unconscionable* (2-302). Disclaimers of warranty that are not conspicuous would be seen as unconscionable. Disclaimers of warranty can also be unconscionable if there is a great disparity of bargaining power between the buyer and the seller and if the court believes that the disclaimer was forced on the buyer with no chance to bargain over its form. A court is most likely to find a disclaimer unconscionable in the case of a personally injured consumer, and somewhat less likely to do so when the consumer has suffered only property damage or economic loss. It is least likely to find the disclaimer unconscionable where the plaintiff is a merchant trying to recover for property damage or economic loss.

Limitation of Warranties

Sellers may try to limit their liability for breach of warranty. For example, the seller might agree to be responsible for only repairing or replacing a product that is not as it is warranted to be. Such a limitation may be enforced unless a court finds that it is *unconscionable* or that the limitation causes the warranty to *fail of its essential purpose.* A court is most likely to find a failure of essential purpose where a defect in a small part causes serious injury to a consumer and the seller is claiming that his responsibility is only to replace the defective part. Likewise, most states hold that where a consumer good has caused personal injury to the consumer, a limitation or exclusion of consequential damages is unconscionable.

E-Commerce

CYBERLAW IN ACTION

In Chapter 10, you read about shrinkwrap and click-on contracts, which are often used in sales of computer hardware and licenses of software and in establishing terms of use for access to networks and websites. It is extremely common for these shrinkwrap or clickwrap contracts to contain **warranty disclaimers** and **limitation of remedy** clauses. For some examples of how these disclaimers and limitations of remedy look, see *Warranty and Liability Disclaimer Clauses in Current Shrinkwrap and Clickwrap Contracts,* http://www.cptech.org/ecom/ucita/licenses/liability.html.

The courts that have considered the enforceability of clickwrap or shrinkwrap warranty disclaimers or limitations of remedy have upheld them. For example, in *M. A. Mortenson Company, Inc. v. Timberline Software Corp.,* 998 P.2d 305 (Wash. Sup. Ct. 2000), Mortenson, a general contractor, purchased Timberline's licensed software and used it to prepare a construction bid. Mortenson later discovered that its bid was $1.95 million too low because of a malfunction of the software. When Mortenson sued Timberline and others for breach of warranty, Timberline asserted that the limitation of remedies clause contained in the software license, which limited Mortenson's remedies to the purchase price of the software, prevented Mortenson from recovering any consequential damages caused by a defect in the software. Although Mortenson contended that it never saw or agreed to the terms of the license agreement, the Washington Supreme Court held that the terms of the license became part of the parties' contract. The terms were set forth or referenced in various places, such as the shrinkwrap packaging for the program disks, the software manuals, and the protection devices for the software. Applying the principle that limitations of remedy are generally enforceable unless they are unconscionable, the court found the limitation of remedies clause to be conscionable and enforceable.

Who Benefits from a Warranty?

Purchaser

LO6

When a product is defective and injures someone, the question arises as to whether the injured person can benefit from the warranty and recover from the seller or manufacturer for breach of warranty. For example, suppose Molly buys an electric table saw for her husband, Joe, as a birthday present. She purchases the saw at Ace Hardware. The saw was made by the Blake Manufacturing Company. While Joe was using this saw, the blade flew off, severely injuring Joe's arm. This happened because the saw had been improperly designed. The saw came with a warranty that it was guaranteed against defects in material and workmanship for a period of 90 days.

Suppose Joe tries to sue Ace Hardware, claiming breach of an express warranty or breach of the implied warranty of merchantability. The hardware store might try to claim that Joe should not be able to sue it for breach of warranty because he did not purchase this saw from the hardware store. Remember that warranties arise as part of a contract, and the contract in this case was between Molly and the hardware store.

A similar problem could arise if either Joe or Molly tried to sue Blake to recover for the injuries on the grounds that the manufacturer had breached either an express warranty or the implied warranty of merchantability. The manufacturer might claim that it had sold the saw to the hardware store but that it had not dealt with either Joe or Molly. The manufacturer would say it had no contract or warranty responsibility to either of them.

Privity of Contract

In the past, the courts applied the general rule of contract law that a person who was not a party to the contract has no right to enforce it. A person had to be in **privity of contract** to enforce the contract. Unless a person had purchased the defective goods, he or she had no cause of action for breach of warranty. Furthermore, even the purchaser of defective goods was able to sue only the immediate seller and not the manufacturer, with whom there had been no contract.

Today, most courts allow an injured purchaser to recover directly from the manufacturer of the goods. This is true even though the version of the Code adopted in some states does not expressly authorize such a suit. In most cases, the manufacturer had control over the condition of the product when it reached the buyer's hands and should be held liable for any defects in it. The fact that the consumer may bring suit against the manufacturer in no way relieves the retailer of its responsibility for the fitness or merchantability of the goods. In most states, the buyer is permitted to sue both the retailer and the manufacturer in the same suit. This is true both for implied warranties and for express warranties that may have been made by the manufacturer.

Nonpurchasers

The Code also extends some of the benefits of warranties to persons who did not themselves purchase the particular defective goods. One alternative version of the Code extends warranty protection to "*any natural person who is in the household of the buyer or who is a guest in his house* if it is reasonable to expect that such person may use, consume, or be affected by the goods and who is injured in his person by breach of warranty" (2-318, Alternative A). Moreover, the seller is not permitted to exclude or limit this liability. Thus, in the example involving the table saw, the Code would allow Joe to sue for breach of warranty because he is a member of the buyer's household.

A more difficult question is raised when the injured person is an employee of the buyer of the goods or a bystander. The decisions concerning bystanders and employees are not consistent among all states; however, there is a growing tendency for the courts to allow persons who have been injured as a result of breach of warranties of goods to claim the benefit of the warranties. This problem is directly addressed in an alternative version of the Code that has now been enacted by a significant number of states (2-318, Alternative C). It provides:

> A seller's warranty whether express or implied extends to any person who may reasonably be expected to use, consume, or be affected by the goods and who is injured by breach of the warranty. A seller may not exclude or limit the operation of this section with respect to injury to the person of the individual to whom the warranty extends.

This version of the Code would allow bystanders or employees to recover for breach of warranty if they could have reasonably been expected to be affected by the goods and were in fact injured as a result of the breach.

In the case that follows, *Bryant v. Hoffmann-La Roche, Inc.*, the court held that a patient who had received free samples of a drug from her doctor was not entitled to pursue a claim of breach of warranty against the manufacturer of the drug.

Bryant v. Hofmann-La Roche, Inc.

51 UCC Rep.2d 422 (Ct. App. Ga. 2003)

FACTS

In 1997 Carolyn Bryant was being treated for cardiac problems, including hypertension and atrial fibrillation, by Dr. Harold Carlson. In connection with that treatment, Carlson prescribed a number of medications for Mrs. Bryant, including Betapace, a beta-blocking drug. On August 18, Dr. Carlson increased the Betapace dosage and on August 25 he prescribed Posicor, a heart medication manufactured by Hoffmann-La Roche that recently had been placed on the market. Posicor is a calcium channel blocker medication used to treat high blood pressure and angina.

On August 26, Mrs. Bryant took the Betapace at approximately 7 AM and again at noon, and took Prosicor for the first time at approximately 10 AM that day. That afternoon, her husband found her at the bottom of the stairs in her home and it was later determined that she had suffered severe brain injuries.

Dr. Carlson testified that at the time he prescribed Posicor for her it was his practice to give patients samples of the drug and then write a prescription if the samples were effective. The doctor obtained these samples from a Hoffmann-La Roche sales representative who visited his office to give him a sales pitch on Posicor.

Following her death, Bryant's husband brought a lawsuit against Hoffmann-La Roche asserting claims, among other things, of negligence, breach of express warranty, breach of the implied warranties of merchantability and fitness for a particular purpose, and strict liability. He alleged his wife's injuries were linked directly to the use of Posicor and its interaction with Betapace. One of the questions in the litigation was whether Carolyn Bryant was entitled to the benefit of the implied warranties in the UCC.

ISSUE

Was Mrs. Bryant barred from claiming the benefit of the implied warranties of merchantability and fitness for a particular purpose on the grounds there was no privity between her and Hoffmann-La Roche because she did not purchase the drug directly from the manufacturer?

DECISION

Yes. The court noted that under Section 2-318 of the UCC, a seller's warranty extends to any natural person who is in the family or household of his buyer or who is a guest in his home if it is reasonable to expect that such person may use, consume, or be affected by the goods and who is injured in person by breach of the warranty. Thus, under Georgia's version of the UCC, only a very limited class of individuals who are not in privity with the seller are entitled to the protection of the seller's warranties. Assuming the UCC applies to the transaction between Dr. Carlson and Hoffmann-La Roche, because Mrs. Bryant was not a member of the doctor's household or family, nor was she a guest in his home, she is not entitled to an extension of any implied warranty existing between the drug manufacturer and the doctor.

Concept Summary: Warranties under the UCC

Warranty	Creation	Defense/Disclaimer
Express Warranty (2-313)	An express warranty is created where: 1. Seller makes an *affirmation of fact* or *promise* concerning the goods that becomes part of the *basis of the bargain.*	1. Seller may defend on grounds that statement was an *opinion* or *recommendation,* or that it did *not* become part of the basis of the bargain (e.g., it was made after the sale).

(continued)

Concept Summary: Warranties under the UCC *(concluded)*

Warranty	Creation	Defense/Disclaimer
	2. Descriptive terms, drawings, or technical specifications are used. 3. A sample or model is used as the basis for the contract.	2. Any disclaimer must be consistent with the express warranty made or it may be disregarded.
Implied Warranty of Merchantability (2-314)	The implied warranty of merchantability is an implied warranty of quality imposed by law on *merchants* dealing in goods of that kind. Goods must be fit for the *ordinary purpose* for which such goods are used.	1. Disclaimer may be oral or in writing but must mention *merchantability* and, if in writing, must be *conspicuous.* 2. Disclaimer is effective if the sale is stated to be "as is" or "with all faults." 3. If buyer inspects, or is offered opportunity to inspect, then she is bound by defects that were found, or should have been found. 4. Court may refuse to enforce an unconscionable disclaimer.
Implied Warranty of Fitness for a Particular Purpose (2-315)	The implied warranty of fitness for a particular purpose is imposed by law on sellers (including nonmerchants) who: 1. Know the purpose or use for which the buyer is acquiring the goods. 2. Know that the buyer is relying on the sellers to select goods suitable for that purpose.	1. Disclaimer must be in *writing* and *conspicuous.* 2. Disclaimer is effective if the sale is stated to be "as is" or "with all faults." 3. If buyer inspects, or is offered opportunity to inspect, then she is bound by defects that were found, or should have been found. 4. Court may refuse to enforce an unconscionable disclaimer.
Implied Warranty of Title (2-312)	In any sale of goods, the seller impliedly warrants that she has the right to sell the goods, that buyer will get good title, and that the goods are free of liens or claims by third parties unless buyer is given notice of them.	Warranty may be limited or excluded by specific language or by circumstances (e.g., police auction).

Federal Trade Commission Warranty Rules

Magnuson-Moss Warranty Act

In the late 1960s and early 1970s, Congress conducted a number of investigations into consumer product warranties and their terms. It concluded that the warranties were frequently confusing, misleading, and frustrating to consumers, and that the law governing warranties should be changed to encourage manufacturers to market more reliable products for competitive reasons. Congress based its findings in part on the fact that consumer products are typically sold with a form contract dictated by the seller, that the consumer cannot bargain with the seller over terms, and that the remedies stated in these contracts are sometimes not useful to the consumer. For these reasons, Congress passed the Magnuson-Moss Warranty Act, which became effective in 1975.

Purpose of the Act

The Magnuson-Moss Warranty Act is intended to (1) provide minimum warranty protection for consumers, (2) increase consumer understanding of warranties, (3) ensure warranty performance by providing useful remedies, and (4) encourage better product reliability by making it easier for consumers to choose among products on the basis of their likely reliability. The act applies to all sellers of a "consumer product" that costs more than $5 who give the consumer a written warranty. It does not require the seller to make a warranty. In fact, it may have led to fewer warranties being made.[2]

Requirements of the Act

Under the act and the warranty regulations of the Federal Trade Commission (FTC), the seller is not required to give a written warranty. If the seller does give a warranty, however, it must comply with the act and the regulations. The seller must disclose in a single document, in simple and understandable language, the following items of information:

1. The persons who can enforce or use the warranty (for example, the original purchaser or any subsequent owner of the item during the term of the warranty).
2. A clear description of the products, parts, components, characteristics, and properties covered by the warranty, and, if necessary, the items excluded from the warranty.
3. A statement of what the maker of the warranty will do and what items or services will be paid for if the product is defective, malfunctions, or does not conform to the warranty, and (if needed for clarity) a statement of what the warrantor will not pay for.
4. The time the warranty begins (if it begins on a date other than the purchase date) and its duration.
5. A step-by-step explanation of how to obtain warranty service and information about any *informal dispute settlement mechanisms* (for example, arbitration) made available by the seller.
6. Any limitations on the duration of implied warranties and any exclusions or limitations on relief, such as consequential or incidental damages (for example, not paying to drain the basement after the water heater breaks), and an explanation that under some state laws those exclusions or limitations may not be allowed.
7. A statement that the consumer has certain legal rights under the warranty as well as other rights that may vary from state to state.

[2] The act covers consumer products that cost more than $5, but the regulations adopted by the Federal Trade Commission to implement the act cover only products that cost more than $15.

Full Warranties

The maker of the warranty must state whether the warranty is a **full warranty** or a **limited warranty.** A full warranty means:

1. The warrantor will fix or replace any defective product, including removal and reinstallation if necessary, free of charge.
2. It is not limited in time (say, to one or two years).
3. It does not either exclude or limit payment for consequential damages unless the exclusion or limitation is printed conspicuously on the face of the written warranty.
4. If the product cannot be repaired or has not been repaired after a reasonable number of efforts to repair it, the consumer may choose between a refund and a replacement.
5. The warrantor cannot impose duties on the consumer except reasonable duties (for example, the warranty cannot require the consumer to ship a piano to the factory) or a duty not to modify the product.
6. The warrantor is not required to fulfill the warranty terms if the problem was caused by damage to the product through unreasonable use.

A full warranty does not have to cover the whole product. It may cover only part of the product, such as the picture tube of a television set. Also, anyone who owns the product during the warranty period may invoke or use the warranty.

Limited Warranties

A limited warranty is any other warranty covered by the act that does not meet the standards for a full warranty. For example, a limited warranty may cover only parts, not labor, or may require the purchaser to return a heavy product to the seller or service representative for service. It may also require the purchaser to pay for handling or allow only a pro rata refund or credit, depending on the length of time since the product was purchased. Often, a limited warranty protects only the first purchaser.

Availability of Warranties

The act requires the seller to make the written warranty terms available to the prospective buyer before the sale. For example, the text of the warranty might be displayed next to the product, or on the package in which the product is enclosed. Warranty terms can also be collected in notebooks in the department that sells the goods and may even be microfilmed, so long as the prospective buyer can readily use the microfilm reader. The maker of the warranty is required to make the text of the warranty available to sellers in forms that sellers can readily use, such as providing copies of the written warranty with each product, or on a tag, sticker, label, or other attachment to the product, or on a sign or poster. These warranty requirements also cover catalog and door-to-door sales.

Enforcement

The FTC enforces the disclosure provisions of the warranty act and regulations; for example, it enforces the seller's obligation to make the terms available before the sale and the format requirements imposed on all makers of warranties (manufacturers or sellers). Consumers have the right to sue the maker for failure to fulfill the terms of the warranty. Consumers can sue the manufacturer if the manufacturer offers the warranty, or the retailer if the retailer grants the warranty.

Negligence

Product Liability in General

Liability of a seller based on breach of warranty is only one of the theories of liability that courts have used to impose liability on the manufacturer or seller of goods for personal injury or property damage that results from the use of the goods. Two other legal bases for product liability are negligence and strict liability.

LO7

Negligence

In Chapter 8, you studied the general rules concerning negligence. The basic rule is that a person owes a *duty of care* to avoid *foreseeable injury to others.* As long ago as 1916, courts held that a manufacturer could be liable to a consumer of a defective product on the grounds that the manufacturer was negligent in not adequately *inspecting* the product. Subsequently, courts have held manufacturers liable for negligence not only for failing to inspect but also for:

1. *Improperly manufacturing* the goods.
2. *Misrepresenting* the character of goods or their fitness for a particular purpose.
3. Failing to *disclose known defects,* adequately *warn about known dangers,* or *instruct about proper use.*
4. Failing to use *due care in designing* the goods.

In the case that follows, *Weigl v. Quincy Specialties Company,* a manufacturer was held liable for negligence in the design and testing as well as for failure to warn of danger in using a lab coat that seriously injured a user when it caught fire while she was wearing it.

Weigl v. Quincy Specialties Company

735 N.Y.S.2d 729 (Sup. Ct., N.Y. County., N.Y. 2001), aff'd, 766 N.Y.S.2d 428 (2003)

FACTS

Susan Weigl, 25 years old, was a lab technician. In 1989, while she was preparing materials for a classroom experiment, the substance she was mixing in a blender ignited, causing the lab coat she was wearing to catch fire. The lab coat was manufactured by Quincy Specialties Company. Lab coats marketed by Quincy were made of 65 percent polyester and 35 percent cotton fabric that had a tendency to melt and fuse to the wearer when exposed to a flame. The lab coat worn by Weigl was sold as a lab coat and burned much more readily than flame-retardant coats offered by other manufacturers. Quincy's coats contained no warnings as to their flammability.

Weigl sustained second- and third-degree burns to at least 17 percent of her body in the areas of her face, chest, arms, and hands. While she made a good cosmetic recovery to her face and hands, her chest, breasts, and upper arms were severely and permanently scarred. Her back, sides, and buttocks—the sites from which skin was taken for grafting—were also severely and permanently scarred. The scarred areas from the burns and the skin grafts cover virtually all of Weigl's torso except for her stomach.

She was hospitalized after the fire for approximately one month during which she underwent excruciating debridements and two skin graft surgeries. In 1993, she underwent a third surgery to relieve the pain, burning, and itching associated with very thick scars known as scar contractures, which had developed across her breast. Notwithstanding the surgery, Weigl continued to experience the symptoms and it was undisputed that there was no further treatment available to relieve them.

Weigl brought suit against Quincy Specialties for breach of warranty and negligence in the design, production, and sale of the lab coat. A jury awarded Weigl $20,000,000, including damages for past and future pain and suffering. The trial court reduced the award, and Weigl stipulated to a reduction of damages to $7,992,084. Quincy Specialties appealed.

ISSUE

Was Quincy Specialties liable to Weigl for negligence in the design, testing, and failing to warn of the dangers of the lab coat?

(continued)

Weigl v. Quincy Specialties Company *(concluded)*

DECISION

Yes. The court noted that the lab coats manufactured by Quincy Specialties and marketed as lab coats had a tendency to melt and fuse to the wearer when exposed to a flame and burned much more readily than flame-retardant coats sold by other companies, and that the coat contained no warnings as to its flammability characteristics. Accordingly, Weigl had established Quincy Specialties' liability under the theories of defective design, negligent testing, failure to warn, and breach of warranty.

Duties

Middlemen such as retailers, distributors, and wholesalers have no duty to inspect new, prepackaged goods unless they know of or have reason to know of a defect.

Traditionally, there was no duty to warn of obvious dangers. Thus, a knife manufacturer did not have to put a warning on its knives cautioning users that they could cut themselves. While this is still somewhat true, an increasing number of courts hold that the **obvious danger** rule is no longer a complete defense. To these courts, the obviousness of the danger is merely one of the factors to be considered in determining liability. Courts also hold that there is a duty to warn *after* the sale, where practicable, when a manufacturer learns that the product may be dangerous. For example, the manufacturer of canned vegetables has a duty to warn the public if it discovers that some of its cans are contaminated, even if it does not discover this until several months after the cans have left its plant.

Privity and Disclaimers Do Not Apply

Because liability based on negligence does not involve a contractual relationship, it does not matter whether or not the buyer dealt directly with the manufacturer. The manufacturer's duty of care extends to all persons who might foreseeably be injured if the manufacturer does not exercise its duty of care. It is foreseeable that the ultimate consumer of goods or a bystander might be hurt if goods are not properly designed or built. Likewise, disclaimers in contracts are usually not effective to shield a manufacturer or seller against liability for negligence to consumers. Usually such clauses are held to be against public policy.

Ethics in Action

In recent years, concerns have surfaced about the safety of a wide variety of products, particularly toys containing lead, lead paint, and phthalates, a chemical used to make various kinds of hard plastics flexible. In 2008, Congress, in the Consumer Product Safety Improvement Act of 2008, overhauled the mandate given to the Consumer Product Safety Commission, putting in place federal standards for lead, lead coatings, and phthalates and giving CPSC increased authority concerning reporting, recall, and certification by manufacturers and importers as well as stronger enforcement powers.

In the time period before the new rules were to take effect in 2009, some manufacturers and distributors rushed to distribute toys in this country so they could be sold at discount prices before they would be banned. Others moved to export such products when it became clear they would not pass the U.S. safety standards. Companies are required to give the CPSC 30 days' notice that they plan to export products that do not meet mandatory standards, which would give CPSC time to notify the country to which they are being sent that the goods are coming, but such shipments are not banned by law.

Are these actions ethical? What should a manufacturer, distributor, or retailer do with goods that do not comply with U.S. health or safety standards?

Strict Liability

LO8

Reasons for Development of Strict Liability

Persons injured by defective products were not always able to recover for their injuries under negligence or breach of warranty. Often, contributory negligence on the part of the plaintiff completely barred recovery for injuries sustained as a result of negligence on the part of the defendant. While this is generally not true today because of the adoption of comparative negligence, it was a very important factor at the time strict liability developed. In addition, it was often difficult for the plaintiff to prove negligence because the evidence was in the defendant's control.

Similarly, as you have seen, a person who is injured by a defective product may have trouble in bringing a successful lawsuit based on breach of warranty if he or she was not the buyer, in the buyer's family or household, or the buyer's guest. In addition, warranties were often excluded. As a result of these barriers to recovery, many people were unable to recover when injured by defective products.

In the mid-1960s, courts increasingly took note of the limitations inherent in both breach of warranty and negligence as a means for redressing product-caused injuries, and began to apply strict liability in tort to product liability cases. Under this theory, sellers are held liable regardless of whether or not they exercised reasonable care. If the product is inherently dangerous so that no amount of due care could make it safe, then the manufacturer is required to give the user notice of the unreasonable danger. Privity, disclaimers, and contributory negligence do not bar recovery.

Application of strict product liability has grown until today the theory is the one most commonly used to hold manufacturers liable when products they place on the market are defective and cause injuries to people. The purpose of strict product liability is to ensure that the costs of injuries from defective products are borne by the seller who put the products on the market, rather than by the injured person. The sellers can pass on these costs in the form of higher prices, and thereby socialize the risk by spreading the cost back through society.

Elements of Strict Liability

The essential element for strict product liability is that the product be defective. Generally, to be successful under this theory, the plaintiff must show that:

1. A product has been sold in a *defective condition* that makes it *unreasonably dangerous* to the user or consumer.
2. The seller is engaged in the business of selling such a product.
3. The product is expected to and does reach the consumer without substantial change in the condition in which it is sold.
4. The consumer or other person sustains physical harm or property damage because of the defective condition.

A product can be defective in the same way that it caused harm due to the manufacturer's negligence; that is, it can be defective because it was mismanufactured, misdesigned, lacked proper warnings or instructions, or was misrepresented. The primary difference between the two theories is that negligence focuses on the manufacturer's conduct, and asks whether the manufacturer acted reasonably. Strict liability focuses on the product, and asks whether the product is unreasonably dangerous because of its defect. Often the answer to both questions is the same.

While strict liability is currently accepted by most states, its application varies among the states. Some states may apply it to situations involving the sale of services, used merchandise, or real estate; others may not. Some courts apply strict liability to retailers as well as manufacturers. Other courts will not hold the retailer liable if the manufacturer is available for suit. Several states have passed legislation that absolves a seller from liability if the manufacturer can be held liable. Most states hold that plaintiffs cannot recover for purely economic losses under strict liability. A number of states, however, allow such recovery if the defect caused the product to be unreasonably dangerous, even if it did not result in physical injury.

Ethics in Action

Assume you are the chief executive officer (CEO) of a company that manufactures baby pillows filled with foam pellets. After the pillows have been on the market for about three months and you have sold about 10,000 of them, you receive reports implicating your pillow in the suffocation deaths in their cribs of two infants under the age of three months. What, if anything, would you do about the products already sold? What, if anything, would you do about the products you have in inventory?

State of the Art

In determining whether a product is **inherently dangerous** or has been **defectively designed,** the courts look to the "state of the art" in existence at the time of manufacture. Under the decisions in most states, this does not mean simply what other companies in the industry are doing; rather, the focus is on whether anything else could have been done to make the product safer, given the practical and technological limitations of the time. In some instances, design changes or improvements made subsequently by a manufacturer have been used as evidence of what the manufacturer should have done earlier.

These principles are illustrated in the case that follows, *Uniroyal Goodrich Tire Co. v. Martinez.*

Uniroyal Goodrich Tire Co. v. Martinez

977 S.W.2d 328 (Sup. Ct. Texas 1998)

FACTS

Roberto Martinez was injured while installing a Goodrich tire on a motor vehicle. The injury occurred after the 16-inch tire exploded while Martinez was attempting to mount it on a 16.5-inch rim. He did so despite the presence of a prominent warning label on the tire. The warning specifically stated that one should never mount a 16-inch tire on a 16.5-inch rim and that doing so could cause severe injury or death because the tire would explode.

Martinez sued Goodrich under strict liability. His theory was not that the warning was inadequate, but rather that the exploding tire was defective because Goodrich had failed to use a safer alternative bead design that would have kept it from exploding. Martinez introduced evidence that Goodrich's competitors—and eventually Goodrich itself—had adopted a safer tire bead design. Goodrich argued that the alternative design was not in fact safer because if the tire was matched to a wrong rim size, the bead would not seat on the rim and would inevitably explode during use. Martinez, however, produced counterevidence that the alternative design not only would have prevented the injury he sustained but would not have introduced other dangers of equal or greater magnitude.

(continued)

ISSUE

Is a manufacturer strictly liable for injuries caused by a plaintiff's failure to follow a suitable warning if the manufacturer knows of a safer alternative product design?

DECISION

Yes. To establish a design defect under Section 402A of the *Restatement (Third) of Torts,* a claimant must establish that the defendant could have provided a safer alternative design. This design must be reasonable—that is, it must be able to be implemented without destroying the utility of the product. In determining whether a reasonable alternative design exists, the court can weigh various factors bearing on the risk and utility of the product, including whether the product contains suitable warnings and instructions. However, instructions and warnings may be ineffective because users of the product may not be adequately reached, may be likely to be inattentive, or may be insufficiently motivated to follow the instructions or heed the warnings. Thus, warnings are not a substitute for a reasonably safe design. Here the jury could reasonably find that a reasonable alternative design existed.

Defenses

Most states that have adopted strict liability do not allow the injured party to recover if the injuries resulted from the **misuse** of the product. This means that if the plaintiff used the product in a manner that was not intended or foreseeable, he may not recover. So, for example, if April decides to trim the sides of her hedge with her electric lawn mower and is injured, she would probably not be able to recover.

Plaintiffs are also denied recovery when their injuries result from the alteration of the product after it left the manufacturer. However, if the alteration and the danger it created were foreseeable, the manufacturer can be held liable for not designing the product so that it could not be altered, or for failing to warn against alteration.

Finally, knowingly assuming an obvious risk of injury is a defense to strict product liability in most states.

Industrywide Liability

Industrywide liability is an outgrowth of strict product liability. Like strict liability, it was adopted to allow a larger number of people who were injured by products to recover. It carries out the policies behind strict liability because it is designed to take the risk of product-related injuries off the consumer and place them on the manufacturer, who can spread the cost back through society. The need for the theory of industrywide liability arose because an increasing number of people were being injured by standardized products that did not cause the injury until after a number of years. Because of the time lapse and the fact that different manufacturers' products were interchangeable, plaintiffs were unable to identify which of the manufacturers making that kind of product made the product that injured them.

For example, many manufacturers have produced asbestos. Often, those working with asbestos could not tell which manufacturer processed the asbestos they were working with. Many of the asbestos-related diseases these workers suffered did not occur until 20 to 40 years after they had worked with the asbestos. Thus, they were unable to successfully identify the particular manufacturer that made the asbestos that injured them. In order to overcome such problems, several courts have decided to apportion liability among the firms in that industry that could have produced the product rather than make the plaintiff identify a particular manufacturer. While the details differ from state to state, most courts apportion the liability between the manufacturers on the basis of their market share. Not all courts faced with the issue have chosen to adopt industrywide liability. However, it is possible that more will do so as discoveries grow about widely used products that injure over long periods of time.

Concept Summary: Bases for Product Liability

	Express Warranty	Implied Warranties of Merchantability or Fitness for a Particular Purpose	Negligence	Strict Liability
Basis	Included by parties in the contract of sale.	Imposed by law in the contract of sale.	Duty to use due care to avoid foreseeable injury. Includes duty concerning design, inspection, manufacture, representation, disclosure of defects, and instruction as to safe use.	Liability without fault imposed on manufacturers and sellers of unreasonably dangerous products.
Who Benefits/ Who Can Use	Buyer, members of his family, and, in some states, any person who may reasonably be expected to use, consume, or be affected by the goods and who is injured by the breach.	Buyer, members of his family, and, in some states, any person who may reasonably be expected to use, consume, or be affected by the goods and who is injured by the breach.	Person to whom duty of care is owed and who is injured by breach. Privity of contract is not required.	Person injured by using or consuming product where the defect is the proximate cause of the injury or damage. Privity of contract is not required.
Defenses	Warranty was not made or was effectively disclaimed or limited.	The warranty was effectively disclaimed or limited.	1. Seller exercised reasonable care. 2. Buyer assumed the risk. 3. Buyer was contributorily negligent.	1. Product has been substantially changed since it left the manufacturer or seller. 2. Buyer was adequately warned about the unreasonable danger. 3. Product was state of the art when designed or manufactured. 4. Buyer used product in an unintended or unforeseen manner. 5. Buyer assumed all obvious risk of injury.
Disclaimers	Possible to the degree it is not inconsistent with the express warranty made.	Possible so long as it is not unconscionable.	Generally not effective to shield against liability for negligence to consumers.	Generally not effective.

A manufacturer who is sued on the basis of industrywide liability may try to defend on the grounds that (1) it did not manufacture the product that caused the injury to the plaintiff, (2) its market share was less than alleged by the plaintiff, or (3) the risks from its product were lower than those from other manufacturers.

Possible Limitations on Strict Liability

The broad expansion of seller's liability for defective products has generated claims that the law has gone too far. Some manufacturers and insurance companies contend that product liability law now so favors the consumer that it is stifling the development of new products and putting unreasonable cost burdens on manufacturers—and, in turn, on consumers. As a result, many state legislatures have passed laws limiting the seller's liability. Frequently, these laws have focused on (1) defining what is state of the art, (2) protecting a manufacturer if its products meet government safety standards, (3) protecting subsequent sellers from suit if the manufacturer is available, and (4) using comparative fault to reduce a damage award if the plaintiff contributed to his or her own injury.

Statutes of Repose

The most commonly adopted reform, however, was a statute of repose. A **statute of repose** bars the bringing of a tort-based product liability suit after a certain number of years—usually 10—from the date the product is first sold to a user. This is a significant change in the law for people who are injured by products such as asbestos or DES that do not cause injury until many years later. In most states, the tort statute of limitations gives people one or two years *from the time they discover* their injury in which to bring their suit. People covered by statutes of repose now cannot bring suit if their injury is not discovered within the statutory period. A few state courts have declared their state's statute of repose unconstitutional because it denies people the right to seek redress for their injuries when they had no chance to discover their injuries within the statutory period.

Questions and Problem Cases

1. John Klages, the night auditor at a motel, was working one evening when the motel was held up. When he was unable to open the safe, one of the robbers pointed a gun at Klages's head and pulled the trigger. However, the gun was a starter pistol and he was not seriously injured. Klages decided he needed something to protect himself against future robberies. He went to the Market Supply Company to see about using mace and was shown a leaflet distributed by General Ordnance Equipment Corporation concerning its mace weapons. The leaflet contained this description:

   > Rapidly vaporizes on face of assailant effecting instantaneous incapacitation . . . It will instantly stop and subdue entire groups . . . instantly stops assailants in their tracks . . . an attacker is subdued instantly, for a period of 15 to 20 minutes. . . . Time magazine stated that chemical mace is "for police the first, if not the final, answer to a nationwide need—a weapon that disables as effectively as a gun and yet does no permanent injury." The effectiveness is the result of a unique, incapacitating formulation (patent pending), projected in a shotgun-like pattern of heavy liquid droplets that, upon contact with the face, cause extreme tearing, and a stunned, winded condition, often accompanied by dizziness and apathy.

   On the basis of this description, Klages purchased the weapon. Several months later, some people posing as potential guests held up the motel at gunpoint and ordered Klages to open the safe. Using the cash register as a shield, Klages squirted the mace at one of the robbers, hitting him beside the nose. Klages then ducked but the robber followed him down and shot him in the head, causing Klages to lose the sight in his right eye. He then sued Market Supply Company and General Ordnance, claiming, among other things, breach of express warranty. Were the statements in the leaflet promises or affirmations of fact constituting an express warranty?

2. Custom Concepts designed a product known as the Magic Crystal Ball as a premium for use by McDonald's restaurants in some of its children's selections on its menu. As designed, the Magic Crystal Ball was to be a hollow plastic ball enclosing a paper cube. The child-player was to "ask a question" of the ball, shake it, and turn it upside down to read an answer printed on one of the faces of the paper cube. Plastic Products agreed to manufacture the Magic Crystal Balls for Custom. Working from drawings supplied by Custom, Plastic produced a prototype that was approved by Custom and McDonald's and passed a safety test by U.S. Testing, a laboratory that evaluates consumer products for quality and safety. Plastic then accepted a purchase order to make 1,785,500 of the crystal balls and began production. However, the production-run crystal balls failed the safety test because Plastic had thinned the edges of the walls so that its injection molds would fill uniformly. Custom had Plastic hold production, and then McDonald's canceled its order because of time constraints in the promotional campaign of which the Magic Crystal Ball was to be a part. Custom notified Plastic that the project was off and brought suit against Plastic alleging breach of warranty. Did Plastic breach an express warranty when the production crystal balls did not conform to the prototype?
3. Irma Virgil bought a pint-sized thermos bottle from Kash N' Karry. After a couple of months of use, she poured coffee into it one morning and was adding some milk when it imploded, throwing hot coffee and glass into her face and injuring her eye. Irma testified that she had not dropped the thermos and had not abused it. She sued Kash N' Karry, claiming, among other things, breach of warranty of merchantability. Was the warranty of merchantability breached?
4. Mitchell bought a hamburger from Wendy's. When he began to eat the hamburger, he felt something extremely hard strike his tooth, causing pain that he described as feeling like "someone had shot me in the tooth with a BB. It was painful and got more painful." He immediately stopped chewing, removed the food from his mouth and discovered bone-colored particles that had broken when he bit into them. He reported it to the restaurant manager who subsequently apologized, threw the food away, and asked him to complete a claim form. Mitchell brought an action against Wendy's seeking to recover for personal injuries he sustained when he broke his tooth eating the hamburger. Wendy's moved for summary judgment in its favor on the issues of the warranties of merchantability and fitness for a particular purpose, arguing that the defect was a substance that was "natural" to beef and also that it was not liable for any defect that was discoverable by reasonable prudence on the part of the consumer. Should the court grant summary judgment to Wendy's?
5. Beck, a high school baseball coach, ordered six pairs of flip-type baseball sunglasses from Rayex Corporation. Rayex had advertised the sunglasses as baseball sunglasses that would give "instant eye protection." While one of his baseball players, Michael Filler, was using a pair the glasses were hit by a fly ball. The glasses shattered, and as a result, Filler lost his right eye. Filler then brought a lawsuit against Rayex, claiming, among other things, a breach of the implied warranty of fitness for a particular purpose. Was the manufacturer liable for breach of the implied warranty of fitness for a particular purpose?

6. Paul Brokke purchased a Pentax Super Program camera for $89.95 from Albert Williams, the operator of a pawnshop in Bozeman, Montana. Shortly after the purchase, Brokke was notified by the Bozeman police department that the camera was stolen property; he was directed to surrender it to the police department, which he did. He then returned to the pawnshop and requested a refund for his purchase of the stolen merchandise. Williams denied the request, and Brokke brought suit to recover the purchase price. Williams argued that he had no knowledge that the camera was stolen property and asserted that he disclaimed any warranty of title of goods sold in his business by way of a large sign posted in his store stating that all merchandise is sold "as is." Brokke denied having seen any such sign. Is Williams liable to Brokke for breach of the warranty of good title in the sale of the stolen camera?
7. Jake, a car salesman, is discussing a particular car with Jones, a customer at Jake's dealership. Jake tells Jones, "You won't find a car like this at any price. This car is a crown jewel." Later Jake says that he bought the car at an auction in Kentucky. Influenced by these statements, Jones buys the car. The bill of sale conspicuously says that the car is being sold "AS IS" and that no warranties or representations concerning the car have been made or given, except as stated in the bill of sale. Later, Jones discovers that the car's brakes are so defective that the car is unsafe to drive.

   Which, if any, of Jake's statements are express warranties? Which, if any, have been breached here? Does the language in the bill of sale disclaim any express warranties that might exist? Does the language in the bill of sale disclaim the implied warranty of merchantability? On the assumption that the implied warranty of merchantability has not been disclaimed, is it breached here?
8. Mark Hemphill was a football player for Southern Illinois University. He sustained injuries to his spine when he was hit while wearing a helmet manufactured by Riddell Sporting Goods, Inc. He brought suit against the university's athletic director (Gale Sayers), the football coach, the trainer, the manufacturer of the helmet, and the merchant from whom the helmet was purchased by the university. He sought to recover based on claims of negligence, strict liability, and breach of implied warranties. Riddell sought to have the claim of breach of implied warranties against it dismissed on the grounds there was no privity of contract between it and Hemphill. Should Hemphill's breach of warranty claims against Riddell be dismissed on the grounds there was no privity of contract between it and Hemphill?
9. On October 10, 1985, Zachary Griggs, then 11 months old, sustained serious injuries in a fire at his Pennsylvania home that his three-year-old stepbrother, Kenneth Hempstead, ignited with a disposable butane lighter manufactured by BIC Corporation. Kenneth removed the lighter from his stepfather's pants pocket in the early hours of the morning and set fire with it to Zachary's bedding while the rest of the household slept. Two incidents within six months preceded this fire, in which Kenneth attempted to light either matches or a lighter, of which his parents were aware and for which they disciplined Kenneth. Prior to Zachary's injuries, his mother had seen warnings that BIC placed on the packaging of its lighters to keep them away from children. She was also independently aware that lighters should be kept out of the reach of children. Timothy and Catherine Griggs, as parents and guardians of Zachary, sued BIC alleging that its failure to manufacture a childproof lighter constituted both defective and negligent design. Is BIC potentially liable to the Griggses for failure to manufacture a childproof lighter?
10. Douglas Bratz and Bradley Baughn were injured while riding a Honda mini–trail bike. At the time, they were eight years old. Douglas was driving and Bradley was the

passenger when the bike hit a truck. Douglas had run three stop signs and was looking behind him at a girl riding another mini–trail bike at the time of the accident. Bradley was not wearing a helmet, and while Douglas was wearing one, it flew off when the bike hit the truck because it was not fastened. The minibike contained a warning label prominently posted in front of the operator. It read: READ OWNER'S MANUAL CAREFULLY. THIS VEHICLE WAS MANUFACTURED FOR OFF-THE-ROAD USE ONLY. DO NOT OPERATE ON PUBLIC STREETS, ROADS OR HIGHWAYS. The operator's manual contained a similar admonition as well as a statement urging the user to wear a helmet. The fathers of both boys owned motorcycles and had purchased minibikes for their children. The parents of the injured boys filed suit against Honda, claiming, among other things, that the mini–trail bike was unreasonably dangerous. Honda maintained that it had provided sufficient warning as to the danger of improper operation. Should Honda be held strictly liable for the injuries?

Chapter 21

Performance of Sales Contracts

Learning Objectives

After you have studied this chapter, you should be able to:

1. Explain what is meant by the terms *good faith, course of dealing,* and *usage of trade* as they pertain to the performance of sales contracts.
2. List the basic obligations and rights of the buyer and seller concerning the delivery of and payment for goods.
3. Explain when acceptance of goods occurs, what the effect of accepting goods is, and when a buyer who has accepted goods has the right to revoke such acceptance.
4. Discuss the buyer's rights and duties on improper delivery of goods as well as the seller's right to cure a defective delivery.
5. Indicate when a party to a contract has the right to seek assurances from the other party that it will perform its obligations.
6. Evaluate when a party will have its performance excused on the grounds of commercial impracticability.

Sarah Saunders was interested in purchasing a new sport utility vehicle. Using the Web page of a large-volume dealer in a nearby city, she provided the dealer with the make, model, color, and primary options for the vehicle she was seeking. The dealer indicated that he could obtain a vehicle meeting Sarah's specifications, quoted her a very favorable price, and offered to deliver the vehicle to her at the apartment house where she lived. Sarah accepted the offer and wired a deposit to the dealer. When the vehicle arrived, the truck driver refused to unload it from the car carrier or let Sarah inspect it until she had given him a certified check for the balance due. Then he gave her the title to the vehicle, unloaded it, and drove away. Sarah subsequently discovered a number of scratches in the paint and that

(continued)

some of the options she had bargained for—such as a sunroof—were not on the vehicle. When she complained to the dealer, he offered her a monetary "allowance" to cover the defects. She also discovered that the vehicle had a tendency to stall and have to be restarted when she stopped at intersections. Despite repeated trips to the nearby city to have the dealer remedy the problem, those efforts have been unavailing. Sarah has indicated that she wants to return the vehicle to the dealer and get a vehicle that performs properly, but the dealer insists that she has to give him additional time to try to fix it. This situation raises a number of legal questions that, among others, will be discussed in this chapter, including:

- Did Sarah have the right to inspect the vehicle before she paid the balance of the purchase price?
- When Sarah discovered the scratches on the vehicle and that it did not conform to the contract specifications, could she have refused to accept the car and required the dealer to provide one that met the contract?
- Does Sarah have the right to return the defective vehicle to the dealer and obtain either a new vehicle or her money back, or must she give the dealer the opportunities he wants to try to remedy the defect?

Introduction

In the two previous chapters, we have discussed the formation and terms of sales contracts, including those terms concerning express and implied warranties. In this chapter, the focus is on the legal rules that govern the performance of contracts. Among the topics covered are the basic obligations of the buyer and seller with respect to delivery and payment, the rights of the parties when the goods delivered do not conform to the contract, and the circumstances under which the performance of a party's contractual obligations are excused.

General Rules

The parties to a contract for the sale of goods are obligated to perform the contract according to its terms. The Code gives the parties great flexibility in deciding between themselves how a contract will be performed. The practices in the trade or business as well as any past dealings between the parties are used to supplement or explain the contract. The Code provides both buyer and seller with certain rights. It also sets out what is expected of the buyer and seller on points the parties did not deal with in their contract. Keep in mind that the Code changes basic contract law in a number of respects.

LO1

Good Faith

The buyer and seller must act in *good faith* in the performance of a sales contract (1-203).[1] **Good faith** is defined to mean "honesty in fact" in performing the duties assumed in the contract or in carrying out the transaction (1-201[9]). And, in the case of a merchant, **good**

[1] The numbers in parentheses refer to the sections of the Uniform Commercial Code.

faith means honesty in fact as well as the observance of reasonable commercial standards of fair dealing in the trade (2-103[1][b]). Thus, if the seller is required by the contract to select an assortment of goods for the buyer, the selection must be made in good faith; the seller should pick out a reasonable assortment (2-311). It would not be good faith to include, for example, only unusual sizes or colors.

Ethics in Action

When supplies of goods that are the subject of a contract are in significantly shorter supply than when the agreement was made and the price has risen, the seller may be tempted to look for an excuse to cancel the contract so that he can sell to someone else at a higher profit. Recent examples include changes in the markets for cement, scrap metals, steel, and certain lumber products where the prices rapidly escalated because of growing international demand for those products. Suppliers locked into contracts to sell those products at prices now well below market prices would have a strong incentive to try to get out of their current contract so they might realize the benefit of the higher market price.

Similarly, if the goods are in significantly more plentiful supply than when a contract was made, the buyer might be tempted to create an excuse to cancel so that he can buy elsewhere at a lower price. This commonly arises when crops—such as apples, grapes, popcorn, and oranges—have particularly favorable growing conditions and the supply available to the market is much greater than usual.

When, if ever, is a seller or buyer ethically justified in trying to find a way out of a contractual obligation because the supply or market conditions have so changed that he can make a better deal elsewhere? Concomitantly, are there circumstances under which the other party, acting in an ethically responsible manner, should voluntarily release the disadvantaged party from his or her contractual commitment?

Course of Dealing

The terms in the contract between the parties are the primary means for determining the obligations of the buyer and seller. The meaning of those terms may be explained by looking at any performance that has already taken place. For example, a contract may call for periodic deliveries of goods. If a number of deliveries have been made by the seller without objection by the buyer, the way the deliveries were made shows how the parties intended them to be made. Similarly, if there were any past contracts between the parties, the way they interpreted those contracts is relevant to the interpretation of the present one. If there is a conflict between the express terms of the contract and the past **course of dealing** between the parties, the express terms of the contract prevail (2-208[2]).

In the case that follows, *Grace Label, Inc. v. Kliff,* the court looked to the prior dealing between the parties to explain or supplement the terms of a current contract between the parties.

Usage of Trade

In many kinds of businesses, there are **customs and practices of the trade** that are known by people in the business. These customs and practices are usually assumed by parties to a contract for goods of that type. Under the Code, these trade customs and practices can be used in interpreting a contract (1-205). If there is a conflict between the express terms of the contract and trade usage, the express terms prevail (2-208[2]).

Grace Label, Inc. v. Kliff

355 F.Supp.2d 965 (S.D. Iowa 2005)

FACTS

Steve Kliff, a citizen of California, is a sole proprietor in the business of brokering printing projects. On May 24, 2002, Barcel, S.A. de C.V. (Barcel), a Mexican company, by purchase order contracted with Kliff for at least 47,250,000 foil trading cards bearing the likeness of Britney Spears. Barcel is a large, multinational corporation which sells a variety of food products. It indicated that the cards would be placed in snack food packaging and would come in direct contact with the food contents.

On May 30, Kliff by purchase order contracted with Grace Label to produce the Spears cards. Grace is an Iowa corporation engaged in the business of manufacturing pressure-sensitive labels and flexible packaging. The purchase order described the product as a "Foil Trading Card (Direct Food Contact Compatible)." It also specified the printing process was to use "FDA Varnish," which Grace Label understood it was to use to accomplish the food-contact-compatibility requirement. Grace Label did not have any direct communication with Barcel because Kliff did not want them to be in touch with his customer.

The Spears job was the third or fourth Barcel job Grace Label had worked on with Kliff in about a year's time. Two of the jobs were arranged while Kliff was employed by Chromium Graphics; together they involved 58,000,000 "scratch off" game piece cards where customers rubbed off a coating to determine if they had won a prize. In February 2002, Kliff arranged for Grace Label to do the "Ponte Sobre Ruedas Job," which involved printing about 42,000,000 "peel apart" game piece cards where consumers peeled off a top layer to see if they had won a prize. The Spears card was simply a trading card with no scratch-off or peel-apart feature. The Spears card was varnished on both sides; the others were varnished on one side only. The "direct food compatible" description appeared only in the Spears card purchase order. All of the cards manufactured by Grace Label for the various Barcel projects were inserted in packages of Barcel's snack food products. On several occasions Kliff advised Grace Label that he wanted the same materials used for the Spears cards as had been used on the prior jobs.

The adhesive used on the Chromium Graphics cards was Rad-Cure 12PSFLV, as specificed by Chromium Graphics. This particular adhesive is not listed on the Rad-Cure website as being among Rad-Cure's FDA (Food & Drug Administration) food grade adhesives—but Grace Label was unaware of this. Other than ordering the FDA-approved varnish, Grace Label did nothing to determine if the other materials used to produce the Spears cards were compatible for direct contact with food items. Before its work for Barcel, Grace Label had not produced a product intended to be in direct contact with food—and it assumed that the materials it was told to use had been approved by Chromium Graphics or Barcel.

Grace Label produced prototype cards, using left-over materials from the past Barcel jobs (except for the foil, which has no odor), and submitted them to Barcel, through Kliff, for approval. Grace Label understood that Barcel was interested in the size and weight of the cards to make sure they would fit in the Barcel dispensing units. Kliff was on the Grace Label premises during the first week of production and had many boxes of cards brought to him for inspection. He raised no issues concerning the cards.

On June 28, 2002, Grace Label shipped 17,138,000 production cards directly to Barcel. An additional 7,500,000 cards were shipped to Barcel on July 5, 2002. After receipt of the production cards, Barcel complained to Kliff that the cards emitted a foul odor and were not fit for use in the potato chip bags for which they were intended. Grace Label suggested they be aired out to eliminate the odor. Barcel attempted to do this—but the odor persisted despite Grace Label's contention that the Spears production cards smelled the same as the cards for the other Barcel jobs that Grace Label had printed and which had been accepted by Kliff and Barcel.

Barcel rejected the cards under its contract with Kliff before the final production of cards was shipped from Grace Label. Kliff thereupon canceled the remaining order with Grace Label. Beyond a $90,000 down payment, Kliff did not pay Grace Label the contract amount for the cards. Grace Label then brought suit against Kliff for breach of contract. Kliff contended that the cards smelled bad and that the smell was caused by a chemical (beta-phenoxyethyl acrylate [BPA]) in the adhesive which was not direct-food compatible. Kliff's expert stated that the BPA was undetectable in the prototype cards but that in the production cards, the concentration of BPA far exceeded that in uncured or cured Rad-Cure. Grace Label's response was that Kliff specified and approved of the material components of the cards and it relied on Kliff and Barcel to select appropriate material as it had no expertise in the area. This argument would require the court to consider the course of dealing between the parties; Kliff objected to the introduction of this evidence.

ISSUE

Should the court allow evidence concerning the prior course of dealing between the parties to explain or supplement the terms of the contract between Kliff and Grace Label?

(continued)

Grace Label, Inc. v. Kliff *(concluded)*

DECISION

Yes. The court held that a written contract intended by the parties to be the final expression of their agreement may not be contradicted by evidence of prior agreements, but that it could be explained or supplemented by course of dealing between the parties. Such evidence would be intended not to change or vary the contract terms, but rather to explain what the parties meant by them. At the same time, the court concluded that there were genuine issues of material fact that precluded giving summary judgment at this time. These included (1) whether the parties intended, on the basis of successful use of adhesive and other material on prior jobs, that the trading cards made with the same materials would be "direct food compatible" within the meaning of the contract and (2) whether the odor on the cards was worse than what had been accepted before.

Waiver

In a contract in which there are a number of instances of partial performance (such as deliveries or payments) by one party, the other party must be careful to object to any later deliveries or payments. If the other party does not object, it may be waiving its right to cancel the contract if other deliveries or payments are late (2-208[3] and 2-209[4]).

For example, a contract calls for a fish market to deliver fish to a restaurant every Thursday and for the restaurant to pay on delivery. If the fish market regularly delivers the fish on Friday and the restaurant does not object, the restaurant will be unable later to cancel the contract for that reason. Similarly, if the restaurant does not pay cash but rather sends a check the following week, then the fish market must object if it may want to rely on the late payment as grounds for later canceling the contract.

A party who has waived rights to a portion of the contract not yet performed may *retract the waiver* by giving reasonable notice to the other party that strict performance will be required. The retraction of the waiver is effective unless it would be unjust because of a *material change* of position by the other party in *reliance* on the waiver (2-209[5]).

Assignment

Under the Code, the duties of either the buyer or the seller generally may be delegated to someone else. If there is a strong reason for having the original party perform the acts, such as that the quality of the performance might be different if another party performed them, then duties cannot be delegated. Also, if the parties agree in the contract that there is to be no assignment, then duties cannot be delegated. However, the right to receive performance—such as to receive goods or payment—can be assigned (2-210).

Delivery

LO2

Basic Obligations

The basic duty of the seller is to *deliver* the goods called for by the contract. The basic duty of the buyer is to *accept and pay for the goods* if they conform to the contract (2-301). The buyer and seller may agree that the goods are to be delivered in several lots or installments. If there is no agreement for delivery in installments, then all the goods must be delivered to the buyer in a single delivery.

Place of Delivery

The buyer and seller may agree on the place where the goods will be delivered. If no such agreement is made, then the goods are to be delivered at the seller's place of business. If the seller does not have a place of business, then delivery is to be made at her home.

These rules do not apply if the goods are located somewhere other than the seller's place of business or home. In those cases, the place of delivery is the place where the goods are located (2-308).

Seller's Duty of Delivery

The seller's basic obligation is to tender delivery of goods that conform to the contract with the buyer. **Tender of delivery** means that the seller must make the goods available to the buyer. This must be done during reasonable hours and for a reasonable period of time so that the buyer can take possession of the goods (2-503).

The contract of sale may require the seller merely to ship the goods to the buyer but not to deliver the goods to the buyer's place of business. If it does, the seller must put the goods into the possession of a carrier such as a trucking company or a railroad. The seller must also make a **reasonable contract** with the carrier to take the goods to the buyer. Then the seller is required to **notify** the buyer that the goods have been shipped.

If the seller does not make a reasonable contract for delivery or notify the buyer and a material delay or loss results, the buyer has the right to reject the shipment. For example, suppose the goods are perishable, such as fresh produce, and the seller does not have them shipped in a refrigerated truck or railroad car. If the produce deteriorates in transit, the buyer can reject the produce on the grounds that the seller did not make a reasonable contract for shipment of it (2-504).

In some situations, the goods sold may be in the possession of a bailee such as a warehouse. If the goods are covered by a negotiable warehouse receipt, the seller must indorse the receipt and give it to the buyer (2-503[4][a]). This enables the buyer to obtain the goods from the warehouse. This type of situation exists when grain being sold is stored at a grain elevator. If the goods are with a bailee but no negotiable warehouse receipt was issued, the seller must notify the bailee of the sale. The seller must then obtain the bailee's agreement to hold the goods for the buyer, or the seller must have the goods released to the buyer (2-503[4][b]).

Inspection and Payment

Buyer's Right of Inspection

Normally, the buyer has the right to inspect the goods before she accepts or pays for them. The buyer and seller may agree on the time, place, and manner in which inspection will be made. If no agreement is made, then the buyer may inspect the goods at any reasonable time and place and in any reasonable manner (2-513[1]).

If the shipping terms are **cash on delivery (COD),** then the buyer must pay for the goods before inspecting them unless they are marked "Inspection Allowed." However, if it is obvious even without inspection that the goods do not conform to the contract, the buyer may reject them without paying for them first (2-512[1][a]). For example, if a farmer contracted to buy a bull and the seller delivered a cow, the farmer would not have to pay for it. The fact that a buyer may have to pay for goods before inspecting them does not deprive the buyer of remedies against the seller if the goods do not conform to the contract (2-512[2]).

Payment

The buyer and seller may agree in their contract that the price of the goods is to be paid in money or in other goods, services, or real property. If all or part of the price of goods is payable in real property, then only the transfer of goods is covered by the law of sales of goods. The transfer of the real property is covered by the law of real property (2-304). The contract may provide that the goods are sold on credit to the buyer and that the buyer has a period of time to pay for them. If there is no agreement for extending credit to the buyer, the buyer must pay for them on delivery. The buyer can usually inspect the goods before payment except when they are shipped COD, in which case the buyer must pay for them before inspecting them.

Unless the seller demands cash, the buyer may make payment by personal check or by any other method used in the ordinary course of business. If the seller demands cash, the seller must give the buyer a reasonable amount of time to obtain it. If payment is made by check, the payment is conditional on the check's being honored by the bank when it is presented for payment (2-511[3]). If the bank refuses to pay the check, the buyer has not satisfied the duty to pay for them. In that case, the buyer does not have the right to retain the goods and must give them back to the seller.

Acceptance, Revocation, and Rejection

LO3

Acceptance

Acceptance of goods occurs when a buyer, after having reasonable opportunity to inspect the goods, either indicates that he will take them or fails to reject them. To **reject** goods, the buyer must **notify** the seller of the rejection and **specify** the defect or nonconformity. If a buyer treats the goods as if he owns them, the buyer is considered to have accepted them (2-606).

For example, Ace Appliance delivers a new television set to Beth. Beth has accepted the set if, after trying it and finding it to be in working order, she says nothing to Ace or tells Ace that she will keep it. Even if the set is defective, Beth is considered to have accepted it if she does not give Ace timely notice that she does not want to keep it because it is not in working order. If she takes the set to her vacation home even though she knows it does not work properly, this also is an acceptance. In the latter case, the use of the television set would be inconsistent with its rejection and the return of ownership to the seller.

If a buyer accepts any part of a *commercial unit* of goods, he is considered to have accepted the whole unit (2-606[2]). A **commercial unit** is any unit of goods that is treated by commercial usage as a single whole. It can be a single article (such as a machine), a set of articles (such as a dozen, bale, gross, or carload), or any other unit treated as a single whole (2-105[6]). Thus, if a bushel of apples is a commercial unit, then a buyer purchasing 10 bushels of apples who accepts 8½ bushels is considered to have accepted 9 bushels.

In the case on the next page, *Weil v. Murray,* the buyer was considered to have accepted a painting that he had retained after inspection and had handled inconsistently with ownership of the seller.

Effect of Acceptance

Once a buyer has accepted goods, she cannot later reject them unless at the time they were accepted, the buyer had reason to believe that the nonconformity would be cured. By accepting goods, the buyer does not forfeit or waive remedies against the seller for any nonconformities in the goods. However, if the buyer wishes to hold the seller responsible, she must give the seller **timely notice** that the goods are nonconforming.

The buyer is obligated to pay for goods that are accepted. If the buyer accepts all the goods sold, she is, of course, responsible for the full purchase price. If only part of the goods are accepted, the buyer must pay for that part at the contract rate (2-607[1]).

Weil v. Murray

2001 WL 345222 (U.S.D.C, S.D.N.Y. 2001)

FACTS

On October 19, 1997, Mark Murray, a New York art dealer and gallery owner, traveled to Montgomery, Alabama, to view various paintings in the art collection owned by Robert Weil. Murray examined one of the paintings under ultraviolet light—a painting by Edgar Degas entitled "Aux Courses." Murray discussed the Degas with Ian Peck, another art dealer, who indicated an interest in buying it and asked Murray to arrange to have it brought to New York.

Murray and Weil executed an agreement that provided for consignment of the Degas to Murray's gallery "for a private inspection in New York for a period of a week from November 3" to be extended only with the express permission of the consignor. The director of Murray's Gallery picked up the painting, which was subsequently shown by Murray to Peck. Peck agreed to purchase the painting for $1,225,000 with Murray acting as a broker. On November 8, Murray advised Weil that he had a buyer for the Degas and they orally agreed to the sale. They subsequently entered into a written agreement for the sale of the painting for $1 million that indicated, among other things, that if Weil did not receive full payment by December 8, Murray would disclose the name of the undisclosed principal on whose behalf he was acting.

Neither Murray nor anyone else ever paid Weil the $1 million. Nonetheless, Murray maintained possession of the Degas from November 3, 1997, through March 25, 1998, when Weil requested its return. At some point in mid-November, Weil and Peck took the Degas to an art conservator. A condition report prepared by the conservator and dated December 3, 1997, showed that the conservator had cleaned the painting and sought to correct some deterioration. Weil brought an action to recover the price of the painting from Murray.

ISSUE

Did Murray "accept" the painting and thus become liable for the purchase price?

DECISION

Yes. Goods that a buyer has in his possession necessarily are accepted or rejected by the time a reasonable time for inspecting them passes. Murray first inspected the painting in Montgomery, and then had it in his possession in his gallery and was present when it was examined by an expert. Thus, he not only had a reasonable time to inspect the Degas, he actually did inspect it and is deemed to have accepted it because he did not reject it. Moreover, when Murray permitted the painting to be cleaned and altered, he had committed an act inconsistent with the seller's ownership of the painting. Murray accepted the painting and was liable for the agreed-upon purchase price.

LO3 Revocation of Acceptance

Under certain circumstances, a buyer is permitted to **revoke,** or undo, the acceptance. A buyer may revoke acceptance of nonconforming goods where (1) the nonconformity *substantially impairs the value* of the goods and (2) the buyer accepted them *without knowledge* of the nonconformity due to the difficulty of discovering the nonconformity or the buyer accepted the goods because of *assurances* by the seller (2-608[1]).

The right to revoke acceptance must be exercised within a reasonable time after the buyer discovers or should have discovered the nonconformity. Revocation is not effective until the buyer notifies the seller of the intention to revoke acceptance. After a buyer revokes acceptance, he has the same rights as if the goods had been rejected when delivery was offered (2-608). The *Waddell v. L.V.R.V., Inc.* case, which appears on the next page, illustrates some of the considerations involved in determining whether a buyer acted reasonably to revoke acceptance.

The right to revoke acceptance could arise, for example, where Arnold buys a new car. While driving it home, he discovers that the car has a seriously defective transmission. When Arnold returns the car to the dealer, the dealer promises to repair it, so Arnold decides to keep the car. If the dealer does not fix the transmission after repeated efforts to do so, Arnold could revoke his acceptance on the grounds that the nonconformity substantially impairs the value of the car, that he took delivery of the car without knowledge of the nonconformity, and that his acceptance was based on the dealer's assurances that he would fix the car. Similarly, revocation of acceptance might be involved where a serious problem with the car that was not discoverable by inspection shows up during the first month's use.

Revocation must be invoked prior to any *substantial change in the goods,* however, such as serious damage in an accident or wear and tear from use over a period of time. What constitutes a "substantial impairment in value" and when there has been a "substantial change in the goods" are questions that courts frequently have to decide when an attempted revocation of acceptance results in a lawsuit.

Waddell v. L.V.R.V., Inc.

58 UCC Rep.2d 654 (Sup. Ct. Nev. 2006)

FACTS

In 1996, Arthur and Roswitha Waddell served jointly as president of the Las Vegas area Coachmen Association Camping Club. During the course of one of the group's meetings, they spoke with Tom Pender, the sales manager of Wheeler's Las Vegas RV (Wheeler's), about upgrading the motor home they owned to a "diesel pusher" motor coach. Pender took the Waddells to the Wheeler's lot and showed them a 1996 Coachmen Santara model diesel pusher coach. The Waddells test-drove and eventually agreed to purchase the RV and an extended warranty. Before they took possession of the RV, they requested that Wheeler's perform various repairs, including service on the RV's engine cooling system, new batteries, and alignment of the door frames. Wheeler's told the Waddells that the repairs had been performed as requested, and they took delivery of the RV on September 1, 1997.

The Waddells first noticed a problem with the RV's engine shortly after taking possession of it. They drove the RV from Las Vegas to Hemet, California. On the return trip, the entry door popped open and while they were ascending a moderate grade the RV's engine overheated to such a degree that Mr. Waddell had to pull over to the side of the road and wait for the engine to cool down.

When the Waddells returned from California, they took the RV back to Wheeler's for repairs. Despite Wheeler's attempts to repair the RV, the Waddells continually experienced more problems with the RV, including further episodes of the engine's overheating. Between September 1997 and March 1999, Wheeler's service department spent a total of seven months during different periods of time attempting to repair the RV.

On June 9, 2000, the Waddells brought suit against Wheeler's seeking both equitable relief and monetary damages. The trial court concluded that the RV's nonconformities substantially impaired its value to the Waddells and allowed them to revoke their acceptance of the RV. The court also ordered Wheeler's to return all of the Waddell's out-of-pocket expenses. Wheeler's appealed the judgment.

ISSUE

Were the Waddells justified in revoking their acceptance of the RV?

DECISION

Yes. The Supreme Court noted that under Section 2-608 of the UCC, a buyer may revoke his acceptance if the item suffers from a nonconformity that substantially impairs its value to him and (a) the buyer accepted the goods on the understanding the seller would cure the nonconformity or (b) the buyer was unaware of the nonconformity and the nonconformity was concealed by the difficulty of discovery or by the seller's assurances that the good was conforming. The court adopted a two-part test to determine whether a nonconformity substantially impairs the value of the goods to the buyer. First, it focused on the subjective value of the goods to the Waddells. It noted that they had purchased the RV to enjoy the RV lifestyle. They had owned similar vehicles which they used both as a residence and for camping trips—and they intended to sell their home and spend two to three years traveling around the country. Second,

(continued)

the court focused on whether there was an objective impairment of the value of their particular needs. Here, the evidence showed that the RV's engine would overheat within 10 miles of embarking if the travel involved any climbing. As a result of the overheating, the Waddells were forced to park on the side of the road and wait for the engine to cool down before continuing. Consequently, the RV spent 7 months of the 18 months following its purchase in the repair department at Wheeler's. The problems made the RV unreliable and stressful to the Waddells; it also was unsafe.

The court also addressed the question of whether the Waddells had acted to revoke their acceptance of the vehicle within a reasonable time after purchasing it and concluded that they had acted within a reasonable time. The Waddells promptly brought the problems with the vehicle to Wheeler's attention and gave them more than adequate opportunity to cure them. They had also demanded a full refund of the purchase price in March 1999, more than a year before they filed suit, but Wheeler's never responded to their repeated inquiries until early 2000.

LO4 Buyer's Rights on Improper Delivery

If the goods delivered by the seller do not conform to the contract, the buyer has several options. The buyer can (1) reject all of the goods, (2) accept all of them, or (3) accept any commercial units and reject the rest (2-601). The buyer, however, cannot accept only part of a commercial unit and reject the rest. The buyer must pay for the units accepted at the price per unit provided in the contract.

Where the contract calls for delivery of the goods in separate installments, the buyer's options are more limited. The buyer may reject an installment delivery only if the nonconformity *substantially affects the value of that delivery* and *cannot be corrected* by the seller. If the defect or nonconformity is relatively minor, the buyer must accept the installment. The seller may offer to replace the defective goods or give the buyer an allowance in the price to make up for the nonconformity (2-612).

For example, a produce wholesaler agrees to provide a grocer with 10 crates of lettuce each week for the next year. This would be an installment contract. If one week, about half the lettuce in one of the crates has rotted, the buyer likely would have to accept the shipment and settle for an adjustment in the price for that crate. If six of the crates contained rotten lettuce, the seller would either have to promptly remedy the nonconforming delivery and send six replacement crates or the seller would be able to reject the entire shipment on the grounds that the nonconformity (the six crates of rotten lettuce) substantially affected the value of the entire delivery that week.

Rejection

If a buyer has a basis for rejecting a delivery of goods, the buyer must act within a reasonable time after delivery. The buyer must also give the seller notice of the rejection, preferably in writing (2-602). The buyer should be careful to state all of the defects on which he is basing the rejection, including all that a reasonable inspection would disclose. This is particularly important if the defect is one that the seller might cure (remedy) and the time for delivery has not expired. In that case, the seller may notify the buyer that she intends to redeliver conforming goods.

If the buyer fails to state in connection with his rejection a particular defect that is ascertainable by reasonable inspection, he will not be permitted to use the defect to justify his rejection if the seller could have cured the defect had she been given reasonable notice of it. In a transaction taking place between merchants, the seller has, after rejection, a right to a written statement of all the defects in the goods on which the buyer bases his right to reject, and the buyer may not later assert defects not listed in justification of his rejection (2-605).

In the case that follows, *Fitl v. Strek,* the court addressed the question of whether a buyer had acted in a timely fashion to notify the seller of a significant defect in an otherwise very valuable baseball trading card.

Fitl v. Strek

690 N.W.2d 605 (Sup. Ct. Neb. 2005)

FACTS

In September 1995, James Fitl attended a sports card show in San Francisco where Mark Strek, doing business as Star Cards of San Francisco, was an exhibitor. Fitl purchased from Strek a 1952 Mickey Mantle Topps baseball card for $17,750. According to Fitl, Strek represented that the card was in near mint condition. After Stek delivered the card to Fitl in Omaha, Nebraska, Fitl placed it in a safe-deposit box.

In May 1997, Fitl sent the baseball card to Professional Sports Authenticators (PSA), a leading grading service for sports cards that is located in Newport, California. PSA reported to Fitl that the card was ungradable because it had been discolored and doctored. The expert from the firm stated that any alteration of a card, including the touchup or trimming of a card, would render it valueless. In this case, the edges of the card had been trimmed and reglued. One spot on the front of the card and a larger spot on the back had been repainted, which left the card with no value. He also said that the standard for sports memorabilia was a lifetime guarantee and that a reputable dealer would stand behind what he sold and refund the money if an item was fake or had been altered.

On May 29, 1997, Fitl wrote to Strek and indicated that he planned to pursue "legal methods" to resolve the matter. Strek replied that Fitl should have initiated a return of the baseball card in a timely fashion so that Strek could have confronted his source and remedied the situation. Strek asserted that a typical grace period for the unconditional return of a card was from seven days to one month.

In August 1997, Fitl sent the baseball card to ASA Accugrade, Inc. (ASA), in Longwood, Florida, for a second opinion. ASA also concluded that the baseball card had been refinished and trimmed.

On September 8, 1997, Fitl sued Strek, alleging that Strek knew the baseball card had been recolored or otherwise altered and concealed this fact from him. Fitl claimed he had relied on Strek's status as a reputable dealer.

ISSUE

Did Fitl provide a reasonable notification to Strek of the defective condition of the baseball card when the notification took place 20 months after the purchase?

DECISION

Yes. The trial court found that Fitl had notified Strek as soon as he realized the baseball card was altered and worthless and that Fitl had notified Strek of the defect within a reasonable time after its discovery. The court rejected Strek's theory that Fitl should have determined the authenticity of the baseball card immediately after it had been purchased. On appeal, the Nebraska Supreme Court concluded that Fitl was justified in relying on the representations and was not required to conduct an investigation at the time he purchased the card to determine whether they were false.

Right to Cure

If the seller had some reason to believe the buyer would accept nonconforming goods, then the seller can take a reasonable time to reship conforming goods. The seller has this opportunity even if the original time for delivery has expired. For example, Ace Manufacturing contracts to sell 200 plain red baseball hats to Sam's Sporting Goods, with delivery to be made by April 1. On March 1, Sam's receives a package from Ace containing 200 red baseball hats with blue trim and refuses to accept them. Ace can notify Sam's that it intends to cure the improper delivery by supplying 200 plain red hats, and it has until April 1 to deliver the plain red hats to Sam's. If Ace thought Sam's would accept the red hats with blue trim because on past shipments it did not object to the substitution, then Ace has a reasonable time even after April 1 to deliver the plain red hats.

Wrongful Rejection

If the buyer wrongfully rejects goods, he is liable to the seller for breach of the sales contract (2-602[3]).

Buyer's Duties after Rejection

If the buyer is a merchant, then the buyer owes certain duties concerning the goods that he rejects. First, the buyer must follow any reasonable instructions the seller gives concerning disposition of the goods. The seller, for example, might request that the rejected goods be shipped back to the seller. If the goods are perishable or may deteriorate rapidly, then the buyer must make a reasonable effort to sell the goods. The seller must reimburse the buyer for any expenses the buyer incurs in carrying out the seller's instructions or in trying to resell perishable goods. In reselling goods, the buyer must act reasonably and in good faith (2-603). Question 7 at the end of this chapter illustrates the decisions that a buyer who receives nonconforming, perishable goods must make.

If the rejected goods are not perishable or the seller does not give the buyer instructions, then the buyer has several options. First, the buyer can store the goods for the seller. Second, the buyer can reship them to the seller. Third, the buyer can resell them for the seller's benefit. If the buyer resells the goods, the buyer may keep expenses and a reasonable commission on the sale. Where the buyer stores the goods, the buyer should exercise care in handling them. The buyer must also give the seller a reasonable time to remove the goods (2-604).

If the buyer is not a merchant, then his obligation after rejection is to hold the goods with reasonable care to give the seller an opportunity to remove them. The buyer is not obligated to ship them back to the seller (2-602).

Concept Summary: Acceptance, Revocation, and Rejection

Acceptance

1. Occurs when buyer, having had a reasonable opportunity to inspect goods, either (1) indicates he will take them or (2) fails to reject them.
2. If buyer accepts any part of a commercial unit, he is considered to have accepted the whole unit.
3. If buyer accepts goods, he cannot later reject them *unless* at the time they were accepted the buyer had reason to believe that the nonconformity would be cured.
4. Buyer is obligated to pay for goods that are accepted.

Revocation

1. Buyer may revoke acceptance of nonconforming goods where (1) the nonconformity *substantially impairs the value* of the goods and (2) buyer accepted the goods without knowledge of the nonconformity because of the difficulty of discovering the nonconformity or buyer accepted because of assurances by the seller.
2. Right to revoke must be exercised within a *reasonable* time after buyer discovers or should have discovered the nonconformity.
3. Revocation must be invoked before there is any *substantial change* in the goods.
4. Revocation is not effective until buyer notifies seller of his intent to revoke acceptance.

Rejection

1. Where the goods delivered do not conform to the contract, buyer may (1) reject all of the goods, (2) accept all of the goods, or (3) accept any commercial unit and reject the rest. Buyer must pay for goods accepted.
2. Where the goods are to be delivered in installments, an installment delivery may be rejected *only* if the nonconformity substantially affects the value of that delivery and cannot be corrected by the seller.
3. Buyer must act within a reasonable time after delivery.
4. Buyer must give the seller *notice* of the basis for the rejection.

Assurance, Repudiation, and Excuse

LO5

Assurance

The buyer or seller may become concerned that the other party may not be able to perform required contract obligations. If there is a reasonable basis for that concern, the buyer or seller can demand **assurance** from the other party that the contract will be performed. If such assurances are not given within 30 days, then the party is considered to have repudiated the contract (2-609).

For example, a farmer contracts to sell 1,000 bushels of peaches to a canner, with delivery to be made in September. In March, the canner learns that a severe frost has damaged many of the peach blossoms in the farmer's area and that 50 percent of the crop has been lost. The canner has the right, in writing, to demand assurances from the farmer that she will be able to fulfill her obligation in light of the frost. The farmer must provide those assurances within 30 days. For example, she might advise the canner that her crop sustained only relatively light damage or that she had made commitments to sell only a small percentage of her total crop and expects to be able to fill her obligations. If the farmer does not provide such assurances in a timely manner, then she is considered to have repudiated the contract. The canner then has certain remedies against the farmer for breach of contract. These remedies are discussed in the next chapter.

In the case that follows, *Vasaturo Brothers, Inc. v. Alimenta Trading-USA LLC*, the court held that a buyer had the right to suspend its performance of an installment contract and demand assurances when the seller was in default on several installments, thus impairing the value of the entire contract.

Vasaturo Brothers, Inc. v. Alimenta Trading-USA, LLC

75 UCC Rep.2d 116 (U.S.D.C., D. N.J. 2011)

FACTS

On July 28, 2008, Vasaturo Brothers entered into a contract with Alimenta Trading pursuant to which Vasaturo was to pay Alimenta Trading $380,000 on September 1, 2008, $370,000 on October 1, 2008, and $370,000 on November 1, 2008. In turn, Alimenta Trading was to deliver 50 full container loads of Italian peeled tomatoes in the following installments: 10 full container loads within September 2008; 10 full container loads within October 2008; 10 full container loads within November 2008; 10 full container loads within December 2008; and 10 full container loads within January 2009.

Vasaturo paid Alimenta Trading $380,000 in September 2008 and $370,000 in October 2008. As of November 1, 2008, when the third payment was due, only 5 of the 20 loads of tomatoes had been delivered. As a result, Vasaturo refused to prepay the last installment of $370,000 because it had not received the "containers of tomatoes consistent with its previous payments of $750,000." On November 20, Vasaturo's president e-mailed Alimenta Trading, explaining that they were awaiting the balance of the containers. Alimenta Trading responded saying that all the missing containers would be delivered in the next few days. By November 24, the 15 missing containers had still not been delivered, nor had any of the additional 10 containers that were to be delivered within the month. At that point, Vasaturo's president sent another e-mail, demanding adequate assurance that the shipments would be delivered. Vasaturo did not receive any reply to that e-mail.

On March 20, 2009, Vasaturo filed suit, claiming among other things breach of contract when Alimenta Trading failed to deliver the entirety of two installments of tomatoes by November 1. Alimenta Trading counterclaimed, contending that Vasaturo breached the contract when it failed to make the final payment of $370,000 on November 1.

ISSUE

Was Vasaturo entitled to suspend its performance under the contract and withhold final payment until it received adequate assurance of performance from the seller?

(continued)

DECISION

Yes. The court began by noting that this was an "installment contract" that contemplated delivery of tomatoes in five separate lots to be separately accepted on five different dates. Breach of an installment contract occurs when there is a nonconformity with respect to one or more installments that substantially impairs the value of the whole contract. Here, Alimenta Trading's failure to deliver the tomatoes goes to the essence of the contract which revolves around the purchase and delivery of canned tomatoes. Although Vasaturo had paid $750,000 as of November 1, Alimenta Trading had delivered only 5 containers of the 20 it had agreed to deliver. Furthermore, as of November 24, an additional 10 containers were due to be delivered with only six days remaining in the month. Alimenta Trading refused to explain its reasons for nondelivery or to give adequate assurances that the tomatoes would soon be delivered. As such, its non conformity as to the timing and quantity of its delivery of the first two installments substantially impaired the entire contract, resulting in a contract breach by Alimenta Trading as a matter of law.

As to Alimenta Trading's contention that Vasaturo had breached the contract, it needs to be noted that the UCC provides that

> When reasonable grounds for insecurity arise with respect to the performance of either party, the other may in writing demand adequate assurance of due performance and until he receives such assurance may if commercially reasonable suspend any performance for which he has not already received the agreed return.

Vasaturo had reasonable grounds for insecurity and after demanding and failing to receive adequate assurance of performance, was entitled to suspend its performance under the contract and withhold final payment until it received such assurance.

Anticipatory Repudiation

Sometimes one of the parties to a contract repudiates the contract by advising the other party that he does not intend to perform his obligations. When one party repudiates the contract, the other party may suspend his performance. In addition, he may either await performance for a reasonable time or use the remedies for breach of contract that are discussed in the next chapter (2-610).

Suppose the party who repudiated the contract changes his mind. Repudiation can be withdrawn by clearly indicating that the person intends to perform his obligations. The repudiating party must do this before the other party has canceled the contract or materially changed position by, for example, buying the goods elsewhere (2-611).

LO6

Excuse

Unforeseen events may make it difficult or impossible for a person to perform his contractual obligations. The Code rules for determining when a person is excused from performing are similar to the general contract rules. General contract law uses the test of **impossibility.** However, in most situations, the Code uses the test of **commercial impracticability.**

The Code attempts to differentiate events that are unforeseeable or uncontrollable from events that were part of the risk borne by a party. If the goods required for the performance of a contract are destroyed without fault of either party prior to the time the risk of loss passed to the buyer, then the contract is voided (2-613).

Suppose Jones agrees to sell and deliver an antique table to Brown. The table is damaged when Jones's antique store is struck by lightning and catches fire. The specific table covered by the contract was damaged without fault of either party prior to the time the risk of loss was to pass to Brown. Under the Code, Brown has the option of either canceling the contract or accepting the table with an allowance in the purchase price to compensate for the damaged condition (2-613).

Commercial Impracticability

If unforeseen conditions cause a delay or inability to make delivery of the goods (make performance *impracticable*), the seller is excused from making delivery. However, if a seller's capacity to deliver is only partially affected, then the seller may allocate production among his customers. If the seller chooses to allocate production, notice must be given to the buyers. When a buyer receives this notice, the buyer may either terminate the contract or agree to accept the allocation (2-615).

For example, United Nuclear contracts to sell certain quantities of fuel rods for nuclear power plants to a number of electric utilities. If the federal government limits the amount of uranium United has access to, so that United is unable to fill all its contracts, United is excused from full performance on the grounds of commercial impracticability. However, United may allocate its production of fuel rods among its customers and give them notice of the allocation. Then, each utility can decide whether to cancel the contract or accept the partial allocation of fuel rods.

In the absence of compelling circumstances, courts do not readily excuse parties from their contractual obligations, particularly where it is clear that the parties anticipated a problem and sought to provide for it in the contract.

Questions and Problem Cases

1. Cavenish Farms owns a potato-processing facility. Mathiason Farms and Valley View Farms ("the Growers") are in the business of raising potatoes. In 2005, Cavenish and the Growers entered into contracts whereby each of the Growers agreed to grow 25,000 hundredweight of russet Burbank potatoes on certain designated fields and sell them to Cavenish. The contracts specified that they were for "crop year 2005" and Cavenish agreed to pay a base price of $4.70 per hundredweight for "usable potatoes." The Growers could not sell potatoes grown on the designated fields unless Cavenish first rejected or released them.

   In November 2005, Cavenish made advance payments to the Growers as required by the contracts. It thereafter became apparent that there were problems with the quality of the potatoes, and the Growers attempted to recondition the potatoes by warming the piles. Cavenish refused to make the next scheduled advance payments due on February 15, 2006. Cavenish inspected two loads of potatoes in late February 2006 and determined that they were not acceptable. On March 31, 2006, Cavenish e-mailed the Growers that it was rejecting the potatoes and sent a formal letter of rejection on April 3, 2006. By that time the potatoes had deteriorated and were unmarketable.

   Cavenish sued the Growers, seeking return of the advance payments as well as damages for failure to deliver potatoes as promised. The Growers counterclaimed, arguing among other things, that Cavenish had breached the implied covenant of good faith and acted in bad faith by delaying its notice of rejection of the 2005 crop, thereby precluding the Growers from selling the potatoes to another buyer before they totally deteriorated. Cavenish took the position that it had the right under the contract to accept or reject the potatoes at any time up until July 31, 2006, without breaching the contract. Should the court find that Cavenish acted in bad faith in delaying its notice of rejection for more than a month after it had decided to reject the potatoes?

2. Harold Ledford agreed to purchase three used Mustang automobiles (a 1966 Mustang coupe, a 1965 fastback, and a 1966 convertible) from J. L. Cowan for $3,000. Ledford gave Cowan a cashier's check for $1,500 when he took possession of the coupe, with the understanding he would pay the remaining $1,500 on the delivery of the fastback and the convertible. Cowan arranged for Charles Canterberry to deliver the remaining vehicles to Ledford. Canterberry dropped the convertible off at a lot owned by Ledford and proceeded to Ledford's residence to deliver the fastback. He refused to

unload it until Ledford paid him $1,500. Ledford refused to make the payment until he had an opportunity to inspect the convertible, which he suspected was not in the same condition that it had been in when he purchased it. Canterberry refused this request and returned both the fastback and the convertible to Cowan. Cowan then brought suit against Ledford to recover the balance of the purchase price. Was Ledford entitled to inspect the car before he paid the balance due on it?

3. Spada, an Oregon corporation, agreed to sell Belson, who operated a business in Chicago, Illinois, two carloads of potatoes at "$4.40 per sack, FOB Oregon shipping point." Spada had the potatoes put aboard the railroad cars; however, he did not have floor racks used in the cars under the potatoes as is customary during winter months. As a result, there was no warm air circulating and the potatoes were frozen while in transit. Spada claims that his obligations ended with the delivery to the carrier and that the risk of loss was on Belson. What argument would you make for Belson?

4. James Shelton is an experienced musician who operates the University Music Center in Seattle, Washington. On Saturday, Barbara Farkas and her 22-year-old daughter, Penny, went to Shelton's store to look at violins. Penny had been studying violin in college for approximately nine months. Mrs. Farkas and Penny advised Shelton of the price range in which they were interested, and Penny told him she was relying on his expertise. He selected a violin for $368.90, including case and sales tax. Shelton claimed the instrument was originally priced at $465 but that he discounted it because Mrs. Farkas was willing to take it on an "as is" basis. Mrs. Farkas and Penny alleged that Shelton represented that the violin was "the best" and "a perfect violin for you" and that it was of high quality. Mrs. Farkas paid for it by check. On the following Monday, Penny took the violin to her college music teacher, who immediately told her that it had poor tone and a crack in the body and that it was not the right instrument for her. Mrs. Farkas telephoned Shelton and asked for a refund. He refused, saying that she had purchased and accepted the violin on an "as is" basis. Had Farkas "accepted" the violin so that it was too late for her to "reject" it?

5. On May 23, Deborah McCullough, a secretary, purchased a Chrysler LeBaron from Bill Swad Chrysler-Plymouth. The automobile was covered by both a limited warranty and a vehicle service contract (extended warranty). Following delivery, McCullough advised the salesperson that she had noted problems with the brakes, transmission, air conditioning, paint job, and seat panels, as well as the absence of rust proofing. The next day, the brakes failed and the car was returned to the dealer for the necessary repairs. When the car was returned, McCullough discovered that the brakes had not been properly repaired and that none of the cosmetic work had been done. The car was returned several times to the dealer to correct these problems and others that developed subsequently. On June 26, the car was again returned to the dealer, who kept it for three weeks. Many of the defects were not corrected, however, and new problems with the horn and brakes arose. While McCullough was on a shopping trip, the engine abruptly shut off and the car had to be towed to the dealer. Then, while she was on her honeymoon, the brakes again failed. The car was taken back to the dealer with a list of 32 defects that needed correction. After repeated efforts to repair the car were unsuccessful, McCullough sent a letter to the dealer calling for rescission of the purchase, requesting return of the purchase price, and offering to return the car on receipt of shipping instructions. She received no answer and continued to drive it. McCullough then filed suit. In the following May, the dealer refused to do any further work on the car, claiming that it was in satisfactory condition. By the time of the trial, in June of the next year, it had been driven 35,000

miles, approximately 23,000 of which had been logged after McCullough mailed her notice of revocation. By continuing to operate the vehicle after notifying the seller of her intent to rescind the sale, did McCullough waiver her right to revoke her original acceptance?

6. Haralambos Fekkos purchased from Lykins Sales & Service a Yammar Model 165D, 16-horsepower diesel tractor and various implements. On Saturday, April 27, Fekkos gave Lykins a check for the agreed-on purchase price, less trade-in, of $6,596, and the items were delivered to his residence. The next day, while attempting to use the tractor for the first time, Fekkos discovered it was defective. The defects included a dead battery requiring jump starts, overheating while pulling either the mower or tiller, missing safety shields over the muffler and the power takeoff, and a missing water pump. On Monday, Fekkos contacted Lykins's sales representative, who believed the claims to be true and agreed to have the tractor picked up from Fekkos's residence; Fekkos also stopped payment on his check. Fekkos placed the tractor with the tiller attached in his front yard as near as possible to the front door without driving it onto the landscaped area closest to the house. Fekkos left the tractor on the lawn because his driveway was broken up for renovation and his garage was inaccessible, and because the tractor would have to be jump-started by Lykins's employees when they picked it up. On Tuesday, Fekkos went back to Lykins's store to purchase an Allis-Chalmers tractor and reminded Lykins's employees that the Yammar tractor had not been picked up and remained on his lawn. On Wednesday, May 1, at 6:00 AM, Fekkos discovered that the tractor was missing, although the tiller had been unhitched and remained in the yard. Later that day, Lykins picked up the remaining implements. The theft was reported to the police. On several occasions, Fekkos was assured that Lykins's insurance would cover the stolen tractor, that it was Lykins's fault for not picking it up, and that Fekkos had nothing to worry about. However, Lykins subsequently brought suit against Fekkos to recover the purchase price of the Yammar tractor. Was Fekkos liable for the purchase price of the tractor that had been rejected and was stolen while awaiting pickup by the seller?
7. Walters, a grower of Christmas trees, contracted to supply Traynor with "top-quality trees." When the shipment arrived and was inspected, Traynor discovered that some of the trees were not top quality. Within 24 hours, Traynor notified Walters that he was rejecting the trees that were not top quality. Walters did not have a place of business or an agent in the town where Traynor was. Christmas was only a short time away. The trees were perishable and would decline in value to zero by Christmas Eve. Walters did not give Traynor any instructions, so Traynor sold the trees for Walters's account. Traynor then tried to recover from Walters the expenses he incurred in caring for and selling the trees. Did the buyer act properly in rejecting the trees and reselling them for the seller?
8. Creusot-Loire, a French manufacturing and engineering concern, was the project engineer to construct ammonia plants in Yugoslavia and Syria. The design process engineer for the two plants—as well as a plant being constructed in Sri Lanka—specified burners manufactured by Coppus Engineering Corporation. After the burner specifications were provided to Coppus, it sent technical and service information to Creusot-Loire. Coppus expressly warranted that the burners were capable of continuous operation using heavy fuel oil with combustion air preheated to 260 degrees Celsius. The warranty extended for one year from the start-up of the plant but not exceeding three years from the date of shipment. In January 1989, Creusot-Loire ordered the burners for the Yugoslavia plant and paid for them; in November 1989, the burners were shipped to

Yugoslavia. Due to construction delays, the plant was not to become operational until the end of 1993. In 1991, however, Creusot-Loire became aware that there had been operational difficulties with the Coppus burners at the Sri Lanka and Syria plants and that efforts to modify the burners had been futile. Creusot-Loire wrote to Coppus expressing concern that the burners purchased for the Yugoslavia plant, like those in the other plants, would prove unsatisfactory and asking for proof that the burners would meet contract specifications. When subsequent discussions failed to satisfy Creusot-Loire, it requested that Coppus take back the burners and refund the purchase price. Coppus refused. Finally, Creusot-Loire indicated that it would accept the burners only if Coppus extended its contractual guarantee to cover the delay in the start-up of the Yugoslavia plant and if Coppus posted an irrevocable letter of credit for the purchase price of the burners. When Coppus refused, Creusot-Loire brought an action for breach of contract, seeking a return of the purchase price. Coppus claimed that Creusot-Loire's request for assurance was unreasonable. How should the court rule?

Chapter 22

Remedies for Breach of Sales Contracts

Learning Objectives

After you have studied this chapter, you should be able to:

1. Recall the basic objective of the remedies provided for by the Code for a breach of a contract for the sale of goods.
2. Explain what is meant by the term *liquidated damages* and discuss when the Code allows the enforcement of a liquidated damages clause in a contract for the sale of goods.
3. Recall the statute of limitations provided in the Code that is applicable to lawsuits alleging breach of a contract for the sale of goods.
4. List and describe the remedies that the Code makes available to an injured seller.
5. List and describe the remedies that the Code makes available to an aggrieved buyer.
6. Explain what is meant by the term *cover* in the context of a contract for the sale of goods.
7. Explain what is meant by the terms *incidental damages* and *consequential damages* and indicate when an injured buyer is able to recover consequential damages.
8. Discuss when an aggrieved buyer has a right to specific performance of a contract for the sale of goods.

Suppose that Kathy is engaged to be married. She contracts with the Bridal Shop for a custom-designed bridal gown in size 6 with delivery to be made by the weekend before the wedding. Kathy makes a $500 deposit against the contract price of $2,500. If the dress is completed in conformance with the specifications

(continued)

and on time, then Kathy is obligated to pay the balance of the agreed-on price. But what happens if either Kathy or the Bridal Shop breaches the contract? Consider these examples:

- If Kathy breaks her engagement and tells the Bridal Shop that she is no longer interested in having the dress before the shop has completed making it, what options are open to the Bridal Shop? Can it complete the dress or should it stop work on it?
- If the Bridal Shop completes the dress but Kathy does not like it and refuses to accept it, what can the Bridal Shop do? Can it collect the balance of the contract price from Kathy, or must it try to sell the dress to someone else?
- If the Bridal Shop advises Kathy that it will be unable to complete the dress in time for the wedding, what options are open to Kathy? If she has another dress made by someone else, or purchases a ready-made one, what, if any, damages can she collect from the Bridal Shop?
- If the Bridal Shop completes the dress but advises Kathy it plans to sell it to someone else who is willing to pay more money for it, does Kathy have any recourse?

These questions, and others, will be addressed in this chapter.

Introduction

LO1

Remedies in General

Usually, both parties to a contract for the sale of goods perform the obligations they agreed to in the contract. Occasionally, however, one of the parties to a contract fails to perform his obligations. When this happens, the injured party has a variety of remedies for breach of contract. The objective of these remedies is to put the injured person in the *same position as if the contract has been performed.* The remedies that are made available to the injured party by the Uniform Commercial Code are discussed in this chapter.

LO2

Agreements as to Remedies

The buyer and seller may provide their own remedies, to be applied in the event that one of the parties fails to perform. They can also limit either the remedies that the law makes available or the damages that can be recovered (2-719[1]).[1] If the parties agree on the amount of damages that will be paid to the injured party, this amount is known as **liquidated damages.** An agreement for liquidated damages is enforced if the amount is reasonable and if actual damages would be difficult to prove in the event of breach of the contract. The amount is considered reasonable if it is not so large as to be a penalty or so small as to be unconscionable (2-718[1]).

[1] The numbers in parentheses refer to sections of the Uniform Commercial Code.

For example, Carl Carpenter contracts to sell a display booth for $3,000 to Hank Hawker for Hawker to use at the county fair. Delivery is to be made to Hawker by September 1. If the booth is not delivered on time, Hawker will not be able to sell his wares at the fair. Carpenter and Hawker might agree that if delivery is not made by September 1, Carpenter will pay Hawker $1,750 as liquidated damages. The actual sales Hawker might lose without a booth would be very hard to prove, so Hawker and Carpenter can provide some certainty through the liquidated damages agreement. Carpenter then knows what he will be liable for if he does not perform his obligation. Similarly, Hawker knows what he can recover if the booth is not delivered on time. The amount ($1,750) is probably reasonable. If it were $500,000, it likely would be void as a penalty because it would be way out of line with the damages that Hawker would reasonably be expected to sustain. And if the amount were too small, say, $1, it might be considered unconscionable and therefore not enforceable.

If a liquidated damages clause is not enforceable because it is a penalty or unconscionable, then the injured party can recover the actual damages that were suffered.

Liability for **consequential damages** resulting from a breach of contract (such as lost profits or damage to property) may also be limited or excluded by agreement. The limitation or exclusion is not enforced if it would be unconscionable. Any attempt to limit consequential damages for injury caused to a person by consumer goods is considered prima facie unconscionable (2-719[3]). Suppose an automobile manufacturer makes a warranty as to the quality of the automobile. Then it tries to disclaim responsibility for any person injured if the car does not conform to the warranty and to limit its liability to replacing any defective parts. The disclaimer of consequential injuries in this case would be unconscionable and therefore would not be enforced. Exclusion of or limitation on consequential damages is permitted where the loss is commercial, as long as the exclusion or limitation is not unconscionable.

Statute of Limitations

LO3

The Code provides that a lawsuit for breach of a sales contract must be filed within four years after the breach occurs. The parties to a contract may shorten this period to one year, but they may not extend it to longer than four years (2-725). A breach of warranty normally is considered to have occurred when the goods are delivered to the buyer. However, if the warranty covers future performance of goods (e.g., a warranty on a tire for four years or 40,000 miles), then the breach occurs at the time the buyer should have discovered the defect in the product. If, for example, the buyer of the tire discovers the defect after driving 25,000 miles on the tire over a three-year period, he would have four years from that time to bring any lawsuit to remedy the defect. This principle is illustrated in the case that follows.

Poli v. DaimlerChrysler Corp.

47 UCC Rep.2d 260 (Sup. Ct., App. Div. N.J. 2002)

FACTS

On March 23, 1993, Poli purchased a new 1992 Dodge Spirit manufactured by DaimlerChrysler Corporation. When he made the purchase, Poli elected to obtain a seven-year, 70,000-mile powertrain warranty from DaimlerChrysler.

Over the next few years, the car required a series of repairs and replacements to the engine timing belt, one of the parts covered by the powertrain warranty. On December 16, 1993, after the car had been driven 16,408 miles, Poli had the timing belt replaced. More than three years

(continued)

later, on March 21, 1997, after the car had been driven 36,149 miles, the timing belt was repaired. Poli then had to replace the timing belt on May 16, 1997, on January 5, 1998, and on July 6, 1998. The timing belt again failed on July 31, 1998, causing the destruction of the "short block" of the engine, which the dealer took six months to repair. All of the timing belt repairs and replacements were undertaken by the dealer in accordance with the seven-year, 70,000-mile powertrain warranty.

On December 15, 1998, Poli brought an action against DaimlerChrysler for breach of warranty. The company moved for summary judgment on the grounds that the breach of warranty claim was barred by the four-year statute of limitations in the UCC because it was brought more than four years after the car had been purchased and that is when the breach occurred. Poli claimed that the breach of warranty claim was timely because the seven-year, 70,000-mile powertrain warranty was a "guarantee of performance" that DaimlerChrysler breached by failing to properly repair the timing belt.

ISSUE

Was Poli's breach of warranty claim barred by the four-year statute of limitations?

DECISION

No. The limitations period under the UCC for breach of a sales contract is "four years after the cause of action has accrued" (2-725[1]). The cause of action accrues when the breach occurs, regardless of the aggrieved party's lack of knowledge of the breach; a breach of warranty normally occurs when tender of delivery is made. However, the UCC makes an exception to the general rule if a warranty explicitly extends to future performance of the goods and discovery of the breach must await time of such discovery; in this case, the cause of action accrues when the breach is or should have been discovered. Whether the seven-year, 70,000-mile warranty constituted a warranty of future performance or there was an independent promise to repair defects in the powertrain that appeared within the term of the warranty, the breach did not occur when the car was delivered in 1993, but rather when persistent problems in the engine timing belt appeared in 1997 or when DaimlerChrysler was unable to repair the defect in a timely way in July 1998. Thus, Poli's complaint was timely filed in December 1998 and is not barred by the statute of limitations.

Seller's Remedies

Remedies Available to an Injured Seller

LO4

A buyer may breach a contract in a number of ways; the most common are (1) by wrongfully refusing to accept goods, (2) by wrongfully returning goods, (3) by failing to pay for the goods when payment is due, and (4) by indicating an unwillingness to go ahead with the contract.

When a buyer breaches a contract, the seller has a number of remedies under the Code, including the right to:

1. Cancel the contract.
2. Withhold delivery of any undelivered goods.
3. Resell the goods covered by contract and recover damages from the buyer.
4. Recover from the buyer the profit the seller would have made on the sale or the damages the seller sustained.
5. Recover the purchase price of goods delivered to or accepted by the buyer.
6. Reclaim goods in the possession of an insolvent buyer.

Cancellation and Withholding of Delivery

When a buyer breaches a contract, the seller has the right to cancel the contract and to hold up his own performance of the contract. The seller may then set aside any goods that were intended to fill the seller's obligations under the contract (2-704).

If the seller is in the process of manufacturing the goods, the seller has two choices. The seller may complete manufacture of the goods or stop manufacturing and sell the uncompleted goods for their scrap or salvage value. In choosing between these two alternatives, the seller should choose the one that will minimize the loss (2-704[2]). Thus, the seller would be justified in completing the manufacture of goods that could be resold readily at the contract price. However, a seller would not be justified in completing specially manufactured goods that could not be sold to anyone other than the buyer who ordered them. The purpose of this rule is to permit the seller to follow a reasonable course of action to **mitigate** (minimize) the damages.

The hypothetical case at the beginning of the chapter posits a customer who contracts with the Bridal Shop for the creation of a custom-designed bridal gown in size 6 and then seeks to cancel the order before the Bridal Shop has completed it. What options are open to the Bridal Shop? Can it complete the dress and recover the full contract price from the customer or should it stop work on it? What facts would be important to your decision? As you reflect on these questions, you might consider the facts set out in question 3 at the end of this chapter, when a manufacturer of pool tables stopped work on some customized pool tables. What considerations does it suggest that the Bridal Shop might be advised to take into account in deciding whether or not to continue work on the bridal gown?

Resale of Goods

If the seller sets aside the goods intended for the contract or completes the manufacture of such goods, the seller is not obligated to try to resell the goods to someone else. However, the seller may resell them and recover damages. The seller must make any resale in *good faith* and in a *reasonable commercial manner.* If the seller does so, the seller is entitled to recover from the buyer as damages the *difference* between the *resale price* and the *price the buyer agreed to pay* in the contract (2-706).

If the seller resells, he may also recover incidental damages but must give the buyer credit for any expenses the seller saved because of the buyer's breach of contract. **Incidental damages** include storage charges and sales commissions paid when the goods were resold. Expenses saved might be the cost of packaging and/or shipping the goods to the buyer (2-710).

If the seller intends to resell the goods in a private sale to another buyer, the seller must give the first buyer reasonable notice of the proposed resale. If the resale will be at a public sale such as an auction, the seller generally must give the buyer notice of the time and place of the auction. The seller may make a profit at the resale if the goods bring more than the contract price. If the seller makes a profit, the seller may keep it and does not have to give the profit to the buyer (2-706).

Recovery of the Purchase Price

In the normal performance of a contract, the seller delivers conforming goods (goods that meet the contract specifications) to the buyer. The buyer accepts the goods and pays for them. The seller is entitled to the purchase price of all goods *accepted* by the buyer. The seller is also entitled to the purchase price of all goods that *conformed* to the contract and were *lost or damaged after the buyer assumed the risk for their loss* (2-709). For example, a contract calls for Dell to ship 35 computers to Maxwell's Office Supply with shipment "FOB Dell's manufacturing facility." If the computers are lost or damaged while on their way to Maxwell's, Maxwell's is responsible for paying Dell for them.

The seller may also recover the purchase or contract price from the buyer in one other situation. This is where the seller has made an honest effort to resell the goods and was unsuccessful or where it is apparent that any such effort to resell would be unsuccessful. This might happen where the seller manufactured goods especially for the buyer and the goods are not usable by anyone else. Assume Sally's Supermarket sponsors a bowling team. It orders six green-and-red bowling shirts to be embroidered with "Sally's Supermarket" on the back and the names of the team members on the pocket. After the shirts are completed, Sally's wrongfully refuses to accept them. The seller will be able to recover the agreed-on purchase price if it cannot sell the shirts to someone else.

If the seller sues the buyer for the contract price of the goods, the seller must hold the goods for the buyer. Then the seller must turn the goods over to the buyer if the buyer pays for them. However, if resale becomes possible prior to the time the buyer pays for the goods, the seller may resell them. Then the seller must give the buyer credit for the proceeds of the resale (2-709[2]).

Damages for Rejection or Repudiation

When the buyer refuses to accept goods that conform to the contract or repudiates the contract, the seller does not have to resell the goods. The seller has two other ways of determining the damages that the buyer is liable for because of the buyer's breach of contract: (1) the difference between the contract price and the market price at which the goods are currently selling and (2) the "profit" the seller lost when the buyer did not go through with the contract (2-708).

The seller may recover as damages the *difference* between the *contract price* and the *market price* at the time and place the goods were to be delivered to the buyer. The seller may also recover any incidental damages but must give the buyer credit for any expenses the seller has saved (2-708[1]). This measure of damages is most commonly sought by a seller when the market price of the goods dropped substantially between the time the contact was made and the time the buyer repudiated the contract.

For example, on October 1, Wan Ho Manufacturing contracts with Sports Properties, Inc., to sell the company 100,000 New England Patriot bobble heads at $6.50 each, with delivery to be made in Boston on December 1. By December 1, the market for New England Patriot bobble heads has softened considerably because a competitor flooded the market with them first, and the bobble heads are selling for $3 each in Boston. If Sports Properties repudiates the contract on December 1 and refuses to accept delivery of the 100,000 bobble heads, Wan Ho is entitled to the difference between the contract price of $6.50 and the December 1 market price in Boston of $300,000. Thus, Wan Ho could recover $250,000 in damages plus any incidental expenses, less any expenses it saved by not having to ship the bobble heads to Sports Properties (such as packaging and transportation costs).

If getting the difference between the contract price and the market price would not put the seller in as good a financial position as if the contract had been performed, the seller may choose an alternative measure of damages based on the lost profit and overhead the seller would have made if the sale had gone through. The seller can recover this *lost profit and overhead* plus any incidental expenses. However, the seller must give the buyer credit for any expenses saved as a result of the buyer's breach of contract (2-708[2]).

Using the bobble head example, assume that the direct labor and material costs to Wan Ho Manufacturing of making the bobble heads was $2.75 each. Wan Ho could recover as damages from Sports Properties the profit Wan Ho lost when Sports Properties defaulted on the contract. Wan Ho would be entitled to the difference between the contract price of $650,000 and its direct cost of $275,000. Thus, Wan Ho could recover $375,000 plus any incidental expenses and less any expenses saved, such as the shipping costs to Boston.

This measure of damages is illustrated in the case that follows, *Jewish Federation of Greater Des Moines v. Cedar Forrest Products Co.*

Jewish Federation of Greater Des Moines v. Cedar Forrest Products Co.

52 UCC Rep.2d 422 (Ct. App. Iowa 2003)

FACTS

Cedar Forrest Products Company (CFP) manufactures precut building packages for shelters, pavilions, gazebos, and other structures typically utilized in park, camp, and recreational facilities. The Jewish Federation of Greater Des Moines (Jewish Federation) contracted with CFP for the manufacture of a 3,500-square-foot building with unique and customized features. With the signing of the Purchase and Sales Agreement, Jewish Federation sent CFP a deposit of $53,605; shortly thereafter it prematurely sent the remaining balance of $160,813 for a total contract price of $214,418. After a series of redesign discussions and change orders, Jewish Federation informed CFP it was rescinding the contract and requesting return of all monies paid. CFP returned $160,530.54, but retained $53,887.46 as lost profits it would have made had Jewish Federation not breached the contract.

In anticipation of the building project, CFP purchased cedar paneling, insulation, floor plywood, and cedar timber. It had not begun to assemble the building when Jewish Federation breached the contract. After the breach, CFP was able to sell the purchased items to other customers for the same price as called for in the Jewish Federation contract.

Jewish Federation filed an action for the return of the remaining $53,887.46, claiming there had been no meeting of the minds and the agreement was merely a quote based on a preliminary schematic drawing; CFP counterclaimed for breach of contract. The trial court found the agreement was a completely integrated contract that Jewish Federation had breached and determined that CFP was only entitled to retain $13,470.13 for "incidental damages." CFP appealed.

ISSUE

Was CFP entitled to recover the profit it would have made from full performance of the contract?

DECISION

Yes. The court said that the primary issue was the proper measure of damages for a "lost volume" seller under these circumstances. The basic objective of the remedies provided under the UCC is to put the aggrieved party in as good a position as if the other party had fully performed. The normal measure of damages for nonacceptance or repudiation by the buyer is the difference between the market price at the time and place for tender and the unpaid contract price together with incidental damages but less expenses saved in consequence of the buyer's breach. However, if this measure is inadequate to put the seller in as good a position as performance would have done, then the measure of damages is the profit (including reasonable overhead) that the seller would have made from full performance by the buyer, together with incidental damages, due allowance for costs reasonably incurred, and due credit for payments or proceeds of resale. The trial court was not correct in limiting the recovery to incidental damages on the grounds that CFP had not yet begun to assemble the purchased items. Under the UCC, CFP is entitled to be put in the same position as if the contract had been performed, which means that it is entitled to recover the profit it would have made if it had completed the manufacture of the building.

LO2 Liquidated Damages

If the seller has justifiably withheld delivery of the goods because of the buyer's breach, the buyer is entitled to recover any money or goods he has delivered to the seller over and above the agreed amount of liquidated damages. If there is no such agreement, the seller will not be permitted to retain an amount in excess of $500 or 20 percent of the value of the total performance for which the buyer is obligated under the contract, whichever is smaller. This right of restitution is subject to the seller's right to recover damages under other provisions of the Code and to recover the amount of value of benefits received by the buyer directly or indirectly by reason of the contract (2-718).

Seller's Remedies Where Buyer Is Insolvent

Unless the seller has agreed to extend credit to the buyer, the buyer must pay for the goods at the time they are delivered. When the seller is ready to make delivery of the goods, the seller may withhold delivery until the payment is made (2-511[1]).

Suppose a seller has agreed to extend credit to a buyer, and then before making delivery, the seller discovers, the buyer is insolvent. A buyer is insolvent if he cannot pay his bills when they become due. The seller then has the right to withhold delivery until the buyer pays cash for the goods and for any goods previously delivered for which payment has not been made. The seller also has the right to require the buyer to return any goods the insolvent buyer obtained from the seller within the previous 10 days. If the buyer told the seller she was solvent at any time in the previous three months—and in fact she was not solvent—the seller can reclaim goods received by the buyer even earlier than the last 10 days (2-702).

If a seller discovers a buyer is insolvent, the seller has the right to stop delivery of any goods that are being shipped to the buyer. This would involve notifying the carrier, for example, the trucker or the airline, in time to prevent delivery to the buyer (2-705).

Concept Summary: Seller's Remedies (on Breach by Buyer)

Problem	Remedy
Buyer refuses to go ahead with contract and seller has goods	1. Seller may cancel contract, suspend his performance, and set aside goods intended to fill the contract. a. If seller is in the process of manufacturing, he may complete manufacture or stop and sell for scrap, picking the alternative that in his judgment at the time will minimize the seller's loss. b. Seller can resell goods covered by contract and recover difference between contract price and proceeds of resale. c. Seller may recover purchase price where resale is not possible. d. Seller may recover damages for breach based on difference between contract price and market price, or in some cases based on his lost profits.
Goods are in buyer's possession	1. Seller may recover purchase price. 2. Seller may reclaim goods in possession of insolvent buyer.
Goods are in transit	1. Seller may stop any size shipment if buyer is insolvent. 2. Seller may stop carload, truckload, planeload, or other large shipment for reasons other than buyer's insolvency.

Buyer's Remedies

LO5

Buyer's Remedies in General

A seller may breach a contract in a number of different ways. The most common are (1) failing to make an agreed delivery, (2) delivering goods that do not conform to the contract, and (3) indicating an intention not to fulfill the obligations under the contract.

A buyer whose seller breaks the contract is given a number of remedies:

1. Canceling the contract and recovering damages where the buyer rightfully rejected goods or justifiably revoked acceptance.

2. Buying other goods ("covering") and recovering damages from the seller based on any additional expense the buyer incurs in obtaining the goods.
3. Recovering damages based on the difference between the contract price and the current market price of the goods.
4. Recovering damages for any nonconforming goods accepted by the buyer based on the difference in value between what the buyer got and what the buyer should have gotten.
5. Obtaining specific performance of the contract where the goods are unique and cannot be obtained elsewhere.

In addition, the buyer can in some cases recover consequential damages (such as lost profits) and incidental damages (such as expenses incurred in buying substitute goods).

Buyer's Right to Damages

Where a buyer has rightfully rejected goods or has justifiably revoked acceptance of goods, the buyer may cancel the contract, recover as much of the purchase price as has been paid, and recover damages. Thus, while the Code does not explicitly use the common law contract term *rescission* (discussed in Chapter 17), it does incorporate the concept.

Beer v. Bennett

71 UCC Rep.2d 507 (N.H. Sup. Ct. 2010)

FACTS

Bennett was a registered automobile dealer in New Hampshire doing business under the name the Nickled Stork. He posted an advertisement on his Internet website offering the following for sale:

> 1958 Fiat Osca Spyder 1.5 liter DOHC engine 4 speed trans. Engine and trans are out of the car, but we have most of a spare engine that comes with the car. Body is in very good condition, recently painted robin's egg blue. Top bows will need new top added and some other upholstery work required, but quite rare Pininfarina coachwork, pretty vigorous performance from a well designed DOHC Italian Motor.

Beer restored old cars as a hobby and had been searching for some time for a car like the one Bennett advertised. He contacted him and, after some negotiation, purchased the advertised vehicle for $6,000. He also arranged to have the car shipped to him at a cost of $1,298.

On receipt of the car, Beer discovered that it was missing a number of the parts necessary to make it operable, including "a bell housing starter, generator, distributor, engine mounts, fan, exhaust manifold and the entire handbrake mechanism." He contacted Bennett but they could not resolve the issue, and Beer brought suit against Bennett.

The trial court awarded damages to Beer that included refund of the purchase price and shipping costs plus certain other costs. The court also ordered Beer to return the Fiat to Bennett upon payment of the judgment and the cost of the return shipment. If Bennett failed to make payment and arrangements for return within 60 days, he would forfeit ownership of the Fiat.

Bennett appealed, claiming that the trial court failed to apply the correct measure of damages. He claimed they should have been based on the difference between what Beer paid and the value of what he received. Bennett further argued that since Beer failed to prove the value of what he received, he was not entitled to recover any damages.

ISSUE

Was Beer entitled to a refund of the purchase price or was he limited to damages based on the difference between what he paid and the value of what he received?

DECISION

The New Hampshire Supreme Court found that the terms of the remedy awarded made it clear it was not intended to be an award of actual damages. Rather, the remedy was one of rescission. It then concluded that the remedy was sustainable as enforcement of a revocation of acceptance under the Uniform Commercial Code.

(continued)

Section 2-608 provides for revocation of acceptance of nonconforming goods by a buyer under certain circumstances. Once a valid revocation of acceptance has been made, the proper measure of damages is found in Section 2-711. That section provides that a buyer who justifiably revokes acceptance may recover as much of the price as has been paid. It also provides, in part, that the buyer has a security interest in goods in his possession or control for any payments made on their price, and any expenses reasonably incurred in their inspection, receipt, transportation, care, and custody.

The UCC also states that a buyer who justifiably revokes acceptance has the same rights and duties with regard to the goods involved as if he had rejected them. Therefore, where the buyer has physical possession of the goods, and after the seller has repaid the purchase price, the nonmerchant's only duty with respect to the goods is to hold them with reasonable care at the seller's disposition for a time sufficient to permit the seller to remove them. The remedy here—return of the purchase price to Beer and return of the Fiat to Bennett upon his payment of the judgment and his arrangements for return shipment and payment for the same—is entirely proper under the UCC.

LO6

Buyer's Right to Cover

If the seller fails or refuses to deliver the goods called for in the contract, the buyer can purchase substitute goods; this is known as **cover.** If the buyer does purchase substitute goods, the buyer can recover as damages from the seller the *difference* between the *contract price* and the *cost of the substitute goods* (2-712). For example, Frank Farmer agrees to sell Ann's Cider Mill 1,000 bushels of apples at \$8.00 a bushel. Farmer then refuses to deliver the apples. Cider Mill can purchase 1,000 bushels of similar apples, and if it has to pay \$8.50 a bushel, it can recover the difference (50 cents a bushel) between what it paid (\$8.50) and the contract price (\$8.00). Thus, Cider Mill could recover \$500 from Frank.

The buyer can also recover any incidental damages sustained but must give the seller credit for any expenses saved. In addition, the buyer may be able to obtain consequential damages. The buyer is not required to cover, however. If the buyer does not cover, the other remedies under the Code are still available (2-712[3]).

Incidental Damages

LO7

Incidental damages include expenses the buyer incurs in receiving, inspecting, transporting, and storing goods shipped by the seller that do not conform with those called for in the contract. Incidental damages also include any reasonable expenses or charges the buyer has to pay in obtaining substitute goods (2-715[1]).

Consequential Damages

In certain situations, an injured buyer is able to recover **consequential damages,** such as the buyer's lost profits caused by the seller's breach of contract. The buyer must be able to show that the seller knew or should have known at the time the contract was made that the buyer would suffer special damages if the seller did not perform his obligations. The buyer must also show that he could not have prevented the damage by obtaining substitute goods (2-715[2]).

Suppose Knitting Mill promises to deliver 20,000 yards of a special fabric to Dora Designs by September 1. Knitting Mill knows that Dora Designs wants to acquire the material to make garments suitable for the Christmas season. Knitting Mill also knows that in reliance on the contract with it, Dora Designs will enter into contracts with department stores to deliver the finished garments by October 1. If Knitting Mill delivers the fabric after September 1 or fails completely to deliver it, it may be liable to Dora Designs for any consequential damages she sustains if she is unable to acquire the same material elsewhere in time to fulfill her October 1 contracts.

Consequential damages can also include an injury to a person or property caused by a breach of warranty. For example, an electric saw is defectively made. Hank purchases the saw, and while he is using it, the blade comes off and severely cuts his arm. The injury to Hank is consequential damage resulting from a nonconforming or defective product.

In the hypothetical case presented at the beginning of this chapter, a customer contracts with the Bridal Shop to make a custom-designed bridal gown in size 6 in time for her wedding. The case posits the Bridal Shop advising the customer that it will not be able to complete the production of the gown in time for the wedding, If the customer covers by buying a gown from another wedding shop, what is the measure of damages that the customer would be entitled to? Can you think of incidental damages or consequential damages that might be incurred in this situation and that might be claimed?

Damages for Nondelivery

If the seller fails or refuses to deliver the goods called for by the contract, the buyer has the option of recovering damages for the nondelivery. Thus, instead of covering, the buyer can get the *difference* between the *contract price* of the goods and their *market price* at the time the buyer learns of the seller's breach. In addition, the buyer may recover any incidental damages and consequential damages but must give the seller credit for any expenses saved (2-713).

Suppose Farmer agreed on June 1 to sell and deliver 5,000 bushels of wheat to a grain elevator on September 1 for $7 per bushel and then refused to deliver on September 1 because the market price was then $8 per bushel. The grain elevator could recover $5,000 in damages from Farmer, plus incidental damages that could not have been prevented by cover.

Damages for Defective Goods

If a buyer accepts defective goods and wants to hold the seller liable, the buyer must give the seller *notice* of the defect within a *reasonable time* after the buyer discovers the defect (2-607[3]). Where goods are defective or not as warranted and the buyer gives the required notice, the buyer can recover damages. The buyer is entitled to recover the *difference* between the *value of the goods received* and the *value the goods would have had if they had been as warranted.* The buyer may also be entitled to incidental and consequential damages (2-714).

For example, Al's Auto Store sells Anne an automobile tire, warranting it to be four-ply construction. The tire goes flat when it is punctured by a nail, and Anne discovers that the tire is really only two-ply. If Anne gives the store prompt notice of the breach, she can keep the tire and recover from Al's the difference in value between a two-ply and a four-ply tire.

This remedy is illustrated in the following case, *Cahaba Disaster Recovery, LLC v. Rogers*.

Cahaba Disaster Recovery, LLC v. Rogers

76 UCC Rep.2d 624 (U.S.D.C., S.D. Ala. 2012)

FACTS

On April 20, 2010, the *Deepwater Horizon* drilling rig exploded in the Gulf of Mexico. The resultant oil spill threatened coastal communities from Louisiana to Florida. In an effort to protect their beaches and marshlands, certain of these communities hired emergency response

(continued)

companies to deploy and service offshore "boom"—floating barriers designed to arrest the movement of oil-contaminated water. Among those companies was DRC Emergency Services, LLC, Mobile, an Alabama-based limited liability company that in turn engaged Cahaba Disaster Recovery, LLC, to locate and procure oil boom to be used for DRC's projects.

In April 2010 Cahaba made its first-ever purchases of small quantities of oil containment boom and oil absorbent boom. "Oil containment" boom is designed to keep oil-contaminated water in place whereas "oil absorbent" boom is meant to extract and retain oil while repelling water. The purchases had to conform to certain specifications in DRC's contracts. With respect to containment boom, those specifications were quite detailed. Conversely, the absorbent boom that Cahaba was instructed to order simply had to be either five or eight inches in diameter.

After a telephone exchange with Lenny Rogers, the managing partner of International Lining, LLC, on May 1 in which Cahaba's interest in acquiring absorbent boom was made clear, Cahaba entered into a contract with International Lining for the purchase of 150,000 feet of what it believed would be "eight inch absorbent boom" at a contract price of $200,000 plus $8,100 in freight charges for a total of $208,100.

Cahaba wired the purchase price to International Lining. When the product was delivered to Cahaba on May 7, part of the delivery was accompanied by a shipping statement that referred to 13,000 lineal feet of "FOC 8" boom product. When Cahaba's employees could not identify the type of product that Cahaba had received, they contacted Rogers. He explained that the delivered product, labeled as "Rapid Oil Containment Barrier," but occasionally referred to by International Lining as "Fast Oil Containment" or "FOC," was a revolutionary product that could both absorb and contain oil. During a subsequent telephone conversation, Rogers assured Cahaba that the FOC boom was, in fact, absorbent boom.

Cahaba then attempted, without success, to employ the FOC boom to satisfy its contracts with DRC and also to sell the boom to others responding to the Deepwater Horizon spill.

Six weeks later, on June 15, 2010, Cahaba advised Rogers that the FOC boom did not meet Cahaba's needs and that it wished to return the boom. Rogers quickly responded that International Lining would not accept any return. Subsequently, Cahaba conducted a field test of the FOC boom off the coast of Escambia, Florida—and determined that the FOC boom effectively contained, but did not absorb, oil. When Rogers was advised of the test results, he confirmed that the boom acted like a containment boom but also asserted that it also acted like an absorbent boom because oil is "almost magnetized" to the material and "I promise you that it works." However, he did not offer to, or attempt to, replace Cahaba's stock of FOC boom with absorbent boom. Three months later, Cahaba filed suit against Rogers and International Lining, alleging breach of contract and fraud for delivering containment boom rather than absorbent boom.

In its defense, International Lining contended that it did everything it was required to do under the contract. Moreover, as an affirmative defense International Lining asserted that under the Alabama UCC, a buyer's acceptance of nonconforming goods precludes its right to return the goods to the seller.

ISSUE

Is Cahaba entitled to recover damages for breach of contract and breach of warranty?

DECISION

Yes. The court found that the parties contracted for 150,000 feet of absorbent boom. International Lining's admission that the boom delivered to Cahaba was not absorbent confirmed that the tender of FOC boom did not conform to the terms of the contract and constituted nonperformance on the part of International Lining. The court further found that the delivery of nonabsorbent boom constituted a breach of International Lining's express warranty that the boom would absorb oil.

Cahaba was precluded from returning the boom because it had "accepted" the boom by relying on Rogers's assurances and then waiting seven weeks before assessing the validity of the assessment. However, a buyer who accepts nonconforming goods is not precluded from pursuing other remedies for the seller's breach. To preserve its right to recover damages, the buyer must within a reasonable time after the breach is discovered (or should have been discovered), notify the seller or be barred from any remedy. Here, Cahaba notified International Lining of the nonconformity and gave it an opportunity to cure it or otherwise settle with Cahaba, which International Living did not avail itself of.

The measure of damages for breach of warranty in regard to accepted goods "is the difference at the time and place of acceptance between the value of the goods as accepted and the value they would have had if they had been as warranted." International Lining is liable for the $208,100 purchase price, less the value of the FOC boom as accepted by Cahaba. The purchase price is evidence of the value of the goods as warranted. The FOC boom had no value to Cahaba because it could not be deployed as absorbent boom and did not satisfy any of DRC's specifications for containment boom. Accordingly, the difference between the value of the goods as warranted and the value at the time and place of acceptance is $208,100.

Ethics in Action

Question 7 at the end of this chapter is based on the following situation: Barr purchased from Crow's Nest Yacht Sales a 31-foot Tiara pleasure yacht manufactured by S-2 Yachts. He had gone to Crow's Nest knowing the style and type of yacht he wanted. He was told that the retail price was $102,000 but that he could purchase the model he had in mind for $80,000. When he asked about the reduction in price, he was told that Crow's Nest had to move it because there was a change in the model and they had new ones coming in. He was assured that the yacht was new and that there was nothing wrong with it and that there only 20 hours on the engine. When Barr began to use the boat, he experienced tremendous difficulties with equipment malfunctions. On examination by an expert, it was determined that the yacht had earlier been sunk in salt water, resulting in significant rusting and deterioration in the engine, equipment, and fixtures.

How would you assess the ethicality of the representations made by the salesperson to the purchaser in response to his question? In a case like this, should it be incumbent on a purchaser to ask the right questions in order to protect himself, or should there be an ethical obligation on the seller to disclose voluntarily material facts that may be relevant to the purchaser's making an informed decision?

Concept Summary: Buyer's Remedies (on Breach by Seller)

Problem	Buyer's Remedy
Seller fails to deliver goods or delivers nonconforming goods that buyer rightfully rejects or justifiably revokes acceptance of	1. Buyer may cancel the contract and recover damages. 2. Buyer may "cover" by obtaining substitute goods and recover difference between contract price and cost of cover. 3. Buyer may recover damages for breach based on difference between contract price and market price.
Seller delivers nonconforming goods that are accepted by buyer	Buyer may recover damages based on difference between value of goods received and value they would have had as warranted.
Seller has goods but refuses to deliver them and buyer wants them	Buyer may seek specific performance if goods are unique and cannot be obtained elsewhere.

LO8

Buyer's Right to Specific Performance

Sometimes the goods covered by a contract are **unique** and it is not possible for a buyer to obtain substitute goods. When this is the case, the buyer is entitled to specific performance of the contract. **Specific performance** means that the buyer can require the seller to give the buyer the goods covered by the contract (2-716). Thus, the buyer of an antique automobile such as a 1910 Ford might ask a court to order the seller to deliver the specified automobile to the buyer because it was one of a kind. On the other hand, the buyer of grain in a particular storage bin could not get specific performance if he could buy the same kind of grain elsewhere.

Taylor v. Hoffman Ford, Inc.

57 UCC Rep.2d 805 (Super. Ct. Conn. 2005)

FACTS

On February 5, 2004, Michael Taylor entered into a retail purchase order agreement with Hoffman Ford for the first new 2005 Ford GT 40 allotted and/or delivered to Hoffman Ford. The sales price was listed "MSRP Dealer Prep." MSRP is the manufacturer's suggested retail price and dealer preparation charges are charges associated with getting the car ready for delivery and usually run between $100 and $500. The dealer preparation charge is about the same for all new cars. On March 4, 2004, Taylor paid, and Hoffman accepted, a $5,000 deposit on the purchase.

The Ford GT 40 is a limited-edition car, a re-creation of a 1960s race car, and was first being produced in 2005. There is an extra value associated with the first year of a limited-edition automobile as well as with being the original owner and scarcity also affects market price. Hoffman Ford was allotted one 2005 Ford GT, which was to be delivered sometime in September 2004. The manufacturer's suggested retail price for the car is $156,945. The price necessary to purchase a GT 40 on the open market is substantially greater than the manufacturer's suggested retail price. At the time, some cars were available for sale on the Internet at prices starting at $250,000. The open-market price of such a car was likely to be double the manufacturer's suggested retail price. However, the Ford GT 40 was not readily available on the open market and it was highly unlikely that the car could be purchased from another dealer.

In November 2004 Taylor's lawyer inquired of counsel for Hoffman Ford whether Hoffman would duly perform the contract between them. Hoffman Ford's counsel replied that it stood ready, willing, and able to perform under the contract and that the price of the car, including "dealer prep," is $300,000. Hoffman Ford normally did not charge a "dealer prep" but claimed in this case it was an "availability" surcharge.

As a result of this response, Taylor filed a lawsuit against Hoffman Ford for breach of contract and sought an injunction against transferring ownership or possession to anyone else of the first 2005 GT allotted to Hoffman Ford, as well as specific performance and damages. Subsequently, Hoffman Ford received an offer from another buyer to purchase the car.

ISSUE

Is Taylor entitled to seek specific performance of the contract?

DECISION

Yes. The court issued a temporary injunction against transferring ownership and/or possession of the first 2005 GT 40 allotted and/or delivered to Hoffman Ford pending final resolution of all of the contract issues. The court found that there was a contract for the sale of the 2005 GT 40 and that by demanding a grossly excessive dealer preparation fee, the seller had created an anticipatory repudiation of the contract. Accordingly, under these circumstances, Taylor was entitled to seek specific performance of the contract for the sale of the limited-edition vehicle when the dealer failed to provide due assurance of performance. The court noted that Section 2-716 provides that when the seller has repudiated a contract, the court may decree specific performance where the goods are unique. The court also referenced a similar case where a car sought to be purchased by a buyer was a limited edition, and of short supply, and could not be purchased on the open market without considerable expense, trouble, loss, great delay, and inconvenience, and the court held that specific performance was an appropriate remedy.

In the case above, *Taylor v. Hoffman Ford, Inc.*, the court concluded that specific performance would be available for an aggrieved buyer of a limited-edition car.

Buyer and Seller Agreements as to Buyer's Remedies

As mentioned earlier in this chapter, the parties to a contract may provide for additional remedies or substitute remedies for those expressly provided in the Code (2-719). For example, the buyer's remedies may be limited by the contract to the return of the goods and the repayment of the price or to the replacement of nonconforming goods or parts. However, a court looks to see whether such a limitation was freely agreed to or whether it is unconscionable. In those cases, the court does not enforce the limitation and the buyer has all the rights given to an injured buyer by the Code.

Questions and Problem Cases

1. International Record Syndicate (IRS) hired Jeff Baker to take photographs of the musical group Timbuk-3. Baker mailed 37 "chromes" (negatives) to IRS via the business agent of Timbuk-3. When the chromes were returned to Baker, holes had been punched in 34 of them. Baker brought an action for breach of contract to recover for the damage done to the chromes.

   A provision printed on Baker's invoice to IRS stated: "[r]eimbursement for loss or damage shall be determined by a photograph's reasonable value which shall be no less than $1,500 per transparency." Baker testified that he had been paid as much as $14,000 for a photo session, which resulted in 24 photographs, and that several of them had already been resold. He also had received as little as $125 for a single photograph. He once sold a photograph taken in 1986 for $500 and sold several reproductions of it later for a total income of $1,500. Was the liquidated damages provision enforceable by Baker?

2. Lobianco contracted with Property Protection, Inc., for the installation of a burglar alarm system. The contract provided in part:

   > Alarm system equipment installed by Property Protection, Inc., is guaranteed against improper function due to manufacturing defects or workmanship for a period of 12 months. The installation of the above equipment carries a 90-day warranty. The liability of Property Protection, Inc., is limited to repair or replacement of security alarm equipment and does not include loss or damage to possessions, persons, or property.

   As installed, the alarm system included a standby battery source of power in the event that the regular source of power failed. During the 90-day warranty period, burglars broke into Lobianco's house and stole $35,815 worth of jewelry. First, they destroyed the electric meter so that there was no electric source to operate the system, and then they entered the house. Second, the batteries in the standby system were dead, and thus the standby system failed to operate. Accordingly, no outside siren was activated and a telephone call that was supposed to be triggered was not made. Lobianco brought suit, claiming damage in the amount of her stolen jewelry because of the failure of the alarm system to work properly. Did the disclaimer effectively eliminate any liability on the alarm company's part for consequential damages?

3. Murrey & Sons Company, Inc. (Murrey), was engaged in the business of manufacturing and selling pool tables. Erik Madsen was working on an idea to develop a pool table that, through the use of electronic devices installed in the rails of the table, would produce lighting and sound effects in a fashion similar to a pinball machine. Murrey and Madsen entered into a written contract whereby Murrey agreed to manufacture 100 of its M1 4-by-8-foot six-pocket coin-operated pool tables with customized rails capable of incorporating the electronic lighting and sound effects desired by Madsen. Under the agreement, Madsen would design the rails and provide the drawings to Murrey, who would manufacture them to Madsen's specifications. Madsen was to design, manufacture, and install the electronic components for the tables. Madsen agreed to pay $550 per table or a total of $55,000 for the 100 tables and made a $42,500 deposit on the contract.

   Murrey began the manufacture of the tables while Madsen continued to work on the design of the rails and electronics. Madsen encountered significant difficulties and notified Murrey that he would be unable to take delivery of the 100 tables. Madsen then brought suit to recover the $42,500 he had paid Murrey.

   Following Madsen's repudiation of the contract, Murrey dismantled the pool tables and used salvageable materials to manufacture other pool tables. A good portion of the material was simply used as firewood. Murrey made no attempt to market the 100 pool tables at a discount or at any other price in order to mitigate its damages. It claimed the salvage value of the materials it reused was $7,488. There was evidence that if Murrey had completed the tables, they would have had a value of at least $21,250 and could have been sold for at least that much, and that the changes made in the frame to accommodate the electrical wiring would not have adversely affected the quality or marketability of the pool tables. Murrey said it had not completed manufacture because its reputation for quality might be hurt if it dealt in "seconds" and that the changes in the frame might weaken it and subject it to potential liability. Was Murrey justified in not completing manufacture of the pool tables?

4. Dubrow, a widower, was engaged to be married. In October, he placed a large order with a furniture store for delivery the following January. The order included rugs cut to special sizes for the prospective couple's new house and many pieces of furniture for various rooms in the house. One week later, Dubrow died. When the order was delivered, his only heir, his daughter, refused to take the furniture and carpeting. The furniture store then sued his estate to recover the full purchase price. It had not tried to resell the furniture and carpeting to anyone else. Under the circumstances, was the seller entitled to recover the purchase price of the goods?

5. Catherine Baker purchased a fake fur coat from the Burlington Coat Factory Warehouse store in Scarsdale, New York, paying $127.99 in cash. The coat began shedding profusely, rendering the coat unwearable. The shedding was so severe that Baker's allergies were exacerbated, necessitating a visit to her doctor and to the drugstore for a prescription.

   She returned the coat to the store after two days and demanded that Burlington refund her $127.99 cash payment. Burlington refused, indicating that it would give her a store credit or a new coat of equal value, but no cash refund. Baker searched the store for a fake fur of equal value and found none. She refused the store credit, repeated her demand for a cash refund, and brought a lawsuit against Burlington when it again refused to make a cash refund.

   In its store, Burlington displayed several large signs that state, in part,

   WAREHOUSE POLICY
   Merchandise in New Condition May Be Exchanged Within 7 Days of Purchase for Store Credit and Must Be Accompanied by a Ticket and Receipt. No Cash Refunds or Charge Credits.

   On the front of Baker's sales receipt was the following language:

   Holiday Purchases May Be Exchanged Through January 11th, 1998. In House Store Credit Only. No Cash Refunds or Charge Card Credits.

   On the back of the sales receipt was the following language:

   We Will Be Happy to Exchange Merchandise in New Condition Within 7 Days When Accompanied By Ticket and Receipt. However, Because of Our Unusually Low Prices: No Cash Refunds or Charge Card Credits Will Be Issued. In House Store Credit Only.

   At the trial, Baker claimed that she had not read the language on the receipt and was unaware of Burlington's no-cash-refunds policy. The court found that Burlington had breached the implied warranty of merchantability when it sold the defective coat to Baker. Where the seller breaches the implied warranty of merchantability and the buyer returns the defective goods, is the buyer entitled to a refund of the purchase price paid for the goods?

6. Cohn advertised a 30-foot sailboat for sale in *The New York Times*. Fisher saw the ad, inspected the sailboat, and offered Cohn $4,650 for the boat. Cohn accepted the offer. Fisher gave Cohn a check for $2,535 as a deposit on the boat. He wrote on the check, "Deposit on aux sloop, D'arc Wind, full amount $4,650." Fisher later refused to go through with the purchase and stopped payment on the deposit check. Cohn readvertised the boat and sold it for the highest offer he received, which was $3,000. Cohn then sued Fisher for breach of contract. He asked for damages of $1,679.50. This represented the $1,650 difference between the contract price and the sale price plus $29.50 in incidental expenses in reselling the boat. Was Cohn entitled to recover the difference between the contract price and the resale price plus his incidental expenses?
7. Barr purchased from Crow's Nest Yacht Sales a 31-foot Tiara pleasure yacht manufactured by S-2 Yachts. He had gone to Crow's Nest knowing the style and type yacht he wanted. He was told that the retail price was $102,000 but that he could purchase the model they had for $80,000. When he asked about the reduction in price, he was told that Crow's Nest had to move it because there was a change in the model and they had new ones coming in. He was assured that the yacht was new, that there was nothing wrong with it, and that it had only 20 hours on the engine. Barr installed a considerable amount of electronic equipment on the boat. When he began to use it, he experienced tremendous difficulties with equipment malfunctions. On examination by a marine expert, it was determined that the yacht had earlier been sunk in salt water, resulting in significant rusting and deterioration in the engine, equipment, and fixtures. Other experts concluded that significant replacement and repair were required, that the engines would have only 25 percent of their normal expected life, and that following its sinking, the yacht would have only half of its original value. Barr then brought suit against Crow's Nest and S-2 Yachts for breach of warranty. To what measure of damages is Barr entitled to recover for breach of warranty?
8. De La Hoya bought a used handgun for $140 from Slim's Gun Shop, a licensed firearms dealer. At the time, neither De La Hoya nor Slim's knew that the gun had been stolen prior to the time Slim's bought it. While De La Hoya was using the gun for target shooting, he was questioned by a police officer. The officer traced the serial number on the gun, determined that it had been stolen, and arrested De La Hoya. De La Hoya had to hire an attorney to defend himself against the criminal charges. De La Hoya then brought a lawsuit against Slim's Gun Shop for breach of warranty of title. He sought to recover the purchase price of the gun plus $8,000, the amount of his attorney's fees, as "consequential damages." Can a buyer who does not get good title to the goods he purchased recover from the seller consequential damages caused by the breach of warranty of title?

Part 4

Agency and Employment

Chapter 23

The Agency Relationship—Creation, Duties, and Termination

Learning Objectives

After you have studied this chapter, you should be able to:

1. Look at a fact situation and determine whether or not an agency relationship has been created.
2. List the duties an agent owes her principal and identify when any of the duties has been violated.
3. List the duties a principal owes his agent and identify when any of the duties has been violated.
4. Explain the legal restrictions on a principal's right to terminate an agent.
5. Explain how to end an agent's apparent authority upon termination of an agency.

Stephen Dowell Carter was hired by Sara Lee Corporation to service computers for the company. While working for Sara Lee, Carter formed a company, PC Technologies, that supplied parts to Sara Lee. Part of Carter's job at Sara Lee was to order replacement parts when employees contacted him and reported computer failures. When Sara Lee employees became suspicious of PC Technologies due to difficulties in contacting the company, Carter continually reassured his superiors that he was in contact with PC Technologies and would take care of any problems. When Sara Lee employees suggested that PC Technologies be replaced on

(continued)

the project, Carter told them he was concerned that Sara Lee would be breaching its contract with PC Technologies. However, PC had no recorded contract with Sara Lee. At no time did Carter reveal that he had a financial interest in PC Technologies.[1]

- Was Carter an agent of Sara Lee? How do we tell? Why do we care?
- What duties did Carter owe Sara Lee?
- Did Carter violate any of the duties he owed Sara Lee?

Introduction

An agency relationship arises when one person (the **agent**) acts for the benefit of and under the direction of another (the **principal**). You have no doubt been involved in agencies numerous times. You may have assisted a friend by making some purchase on her behalf. While doing so, you were acting as her agent. If you have ever employed an attorney to represent you in court or to negotiate some claim against someone else, the attorney acted as your agent. Agency law especially focuses on the relations between principals and agents and the third persons with whom agents deal in making contracts on behalf of principals. Because it has developed primarily from the decisions of courts, most agency rules spring from the common law.

Agency law addresses three basic questions:

1. What duties do a principal and agent owe each other?
2. What is the liability of the principal and the agent on contracts made by the agent?
3. When is the principal liable for the torts of the agent?

Answers to the last two questions are deferred until Chapter 24. This chapter focuses on the first question—determining the duties that principals and agents owe each other. This discussion is preceded by an examination of how agency relationships are created. The chapter ends with a discussion of the proper ways of terminating an agency.

Creation of an Agency

Nature of Agency

LO1

Agency relationships are usually formed by contract, although they may be found in the absence of a contractual agreement. An agency may be either written or oral[2] and either compensated or uncompensated. In fact, a court may find that there is an agency relationship even though the parties have expressly agreed that they do not intend to create one. For example, a manufacturer may control the selling activities of a franchised retailer so

[1] *Sara Lee Corporation v. Carter,* 500 S.E.2d 732 (N.C. Ct. App. 1998).

[2] Some states, however, have an "equal dignity rule" that holds that if the contract the agent forms must be in writing, the agency agreement also must be in writing.

closely that the retailer is treated as the agent of the manufacturer. Even a statement in the franchise agreement declaring that the retailer is not an agent of the manufacturer is not binding on the court.

An agency results from any indication of consent by the principal that the agent may act on the principal's behalf and under her control. This can be proven not only by direct evidence between the parties but also by the surrounding circumstances such as the words and conduct of the parties. Consider the following case and the factors the court used in denying the existence of an agency relationship.

Iragorri v. United Technologies

285 F.Supp.2d 230 (D.C. Conn. 2003)

FACTS

Mauricio Iragorri fell to his death down an empty elevator shaft in Cali, Colombia, after a repair person employed by International Elevator, Inc. (International), propped open the elevator door with a screwdriver and left the entranceway unattended and unbarricaded, while the elevator car was not in place. Iragorri's surviving spouse alleges that International (the company that maintained and repaired the elevator in question) and OTESA were negligent in their duties, and that the negligence of International and OTESA is attributable to Otis Elevator on a principal/agent theory.

ISSUE

Were International and OTESA agents of Otis Elevator?

DECISION

No. Three elements are necessary to prove the existence of an agency relationship: (1) a manifestation by the principal that the agent will act for him, (2) acceptance by the agent of the undertaking, and (3) an understanding between the parties that the principal will be in control of the undertaking. In this case, the plaintiff has not presented evidence that Otis provided for International or OTESA to act on Otis's behalf, or that International or OTESA agreed to act on behalf of Otis. Thus, plaintiff has not met her burden as to the first and second requirements for the establishment of an agency relationship. Although OTESA and International were licensees that sold, installed, serviced, and maintained Otis equipment in Colombia, this does not establish that either International or OTESA acted on behalf of Otis. A party that buys goods for resale to a third person is not considered the agent in the transaction unless the parties agree that his duty is to act primarily for the benefit of the ones delivering the goods for him.

Capacity to Be a Principal

Generally, a person can do anything through an agent that he or she could legally do personally. The legal effect of the agent's action on behalf of the principal is usually the same as if the principal had done the act. For example, minors and insane persons are bound by contracts made by their agents only to the extent that they would have been bound if they had taken the action in person. This is true even though the agent has full capacity to contract.

Business organizations and groups of people can also act through an agent. Each partner is an agent of the other partner(s) in carrying on partnership business. A corporation is a legal entity that can act only through agents. An unincorporated association such as a club or neighborhood association is not viewed as a legal entity. Although its members may appoint an agent and will be bound by the agent's acts, the association itself does not become a party to a contract made by an agent.[3]

[3] Many states have enacted statutes making unincorporated associations' assets subject to suit.

Concept Summary: Creation of an Agency

Test	**Is one party (agent) acting:** 1. For the benefit of *and* 2. Under the control of another (principal)?
Evidence	Look at the parties' words, actions, and the surrounding circumstances.
Formalities	Generally, none are required: 1. No contract is necessary. 2. Agreement may be oral. 3. Agent need not be compensated.
Capacity	No legal capacity necessary to serve as an agent (some regulatory exceptions). (Incapacitated agent may avoid agency agreement.) Any "person" with legal capacity may be a principal.
Power	Agent may do anything that the principal could do (with some exceptions).

Capacity to Be an Agent

A person can have the capacity to act as an agent although he or she does not have the legal capacity to contract. For example, Helen, a minor, may serve as an agent to make a contract that is binding on William, the adult principal. Note, however, that while Helen has the capacity to bind William on a contract with a third person, she may be able to release herself from the agency agreement at her option. Partnerships, as well as corporations, may act as agents. Marriage does not automatically establish an agency relationship; however, a person may be appointed as an agent by his or her spouse.

Types of Agents

Commercial Agents

There are several characteristics that commonly distinguish *commercial agents* from distributors and other nonagents. First, agents generally do not maintain their own inventory of goods; instead, they take orders on behalf of their principal. Second, agents usually are compensated through the payment of a commission when a sale is completed. Third, agents seldom bear the financial risk of nonpayment by the purchaser. Fourth, agents often possess the authority to contract on behalf of their principals.

Sometimes courts make a distinction between a commercial agent and a *sales representative.* Both are agents. However, the term "sales representative" often is used to describe an agent who does not possess the authority to contract on behalf of its principal. While a commercial agent can bind its principal to a contract with third persons, a sales representative may only solicit business. The principal must finalize the agreement itself.

Employees

Employees (they are called *dependent agents* throughout much of the world) are under the control of their employer/principal as to both the *objective* of their work and the *means* used to achieve it. Thus, employers generally give detailed directions over their employees' day-to-day activities. Most nations closely regulate employment relationships. Thus, when exporters closely control their agents' hours and working conditions, they run the risk of becoming subject to restrictive labor laws. In some nations, particularly in Latin America, these labor laws apply unless the agent is a corporation.

Independent Contractors

There are wide differences in the level of control that a principal chooses to exercise over its agents. **Independent contractors** (they are called *independent agents* throughout much of the world) are permitted to work according to their own methods. They are under the control of their principals as to the *result* that is to be achieved, but not as to the means used to accomplish that result.

Principals often wish to structure their agreements so as to maintain an independent agency. In most nations there are few restrictions on the right to terminate independent contractors. Further, principals are less likely to be liable for their agents' torts and crimes when they exercise little control over their agents' daily activities.

International *distributors,* unlike agents, typically purchase products directly from the manufacturer and bear the risk of no sale or nonpayment by the ultimate purchaser. They are compensated by the profits they earn on their operations. Distributors generally are not agents and, as a result, manufacturers are less likely to be legally responsible for their contracts, torts, or crimes. Further, many nations place few restrictions on the retention or termination of distributors.

Businesses must be careful not to inadvertently transform their distributors into agents. In many countries, failure to explicitly disavow an agency relationship in a distributorship contract may result in the creation of an agency. Further, notwithstanding the language of the parties' agreement, an exporter's strict control over its distributors' day-to-day activities may persuade local courts to treat the distributors as agents.

Duties of Agents to Principals

LO2

The duties of an agent to the principal normally derive from either the contract, if any, between them or from the common law of agency. While most agency relationships arise out of contract, the agency contract, especially if it is oral, may state little more than the general purpose of the agency. For example, Patrick may merely tell Angie to sell his car after he goes into the army. In such cases, the duties the agent owes to the principal must be found in the common law.

The following duties exist at the common law even when the agency agreement is silent:

1. Duty of loyalty.
2. Duty to obey instructions.
3. Duty to exercise care and skill.
4. Duty to communicate information.
5. Duty to account for funds and property.

Duty of Loyalty

Of all of the common law duties an agent owes the principal, the most important is the fiduciary duty of loyalty. A **fiduciary** is one who is trusted to act in the best interests of another rather than pursuing his or her own interests. While all of the other common law duties can be reduced by agreement, the duty of loyalty cannot be eliminated. In fact, courts are hesitant to enforce an agreement that diminishes this duty in even the slightest way.

Conflicts of Interest

The agent's **duty of loyalty** requires complete honesty from the agent in all dealings with the principal. Further, the duty requires either avoidance of conflicts between the interests of the agent and those of the principal or full disclosure of any such conflict to the principal. If, after such advance disclosure, the principal is willing to continue the agency relationship, the agent is shielded from liability for breach of the duty of loyalty.

Such disclosure should include notification of all compensation that the agent expects to receive in the course of fulfilling the agency functions, because the agent is not permitted to make a secret profit from the agency. Anything of value that comes to the agent because of the agency relationship belongs to the principal. Thus, if Alfred is a purchasing agent for General Electric Company and receives kickbacks or secret gifts from suppliers from whom he purchases goods for GE, the company is entitled to those gifts.

Agents breach their duty of loyalty by buying for the principal from themselves even if they charge a fair price. The duty of loyalty demands that the agent avoid even the **appearance of impropriety.** Such purchases are permissible only when the agent has informed the principal, in advance, of the potential conflict of interest and fully discloses other pertinent facts.

Consider the case that opened this chapter. Carter was an agent of Sara Lee and, as such, owed the company a fiduciary duty with respect to his role in recommending the purchase of, and in actually ordering and purchasing, computer parts. An agent can neither purchase from nor sell to the principal unless the agent, in good faith, fully discloses to the principal all material facts surrounding the transaction, and the principal consents to the transaction. In this case, it is clear that Carter acted in the double capacity of both purchasing agent and vendor. Further, he never disclosed this conflict of interest to his superiors. He thereby breached his fiduciary duty to Sara Lee.

Further, in the course of carrying out her agency duties, an agent is not permitted to seize any opportunities available to her principal. For example, suppose Bill authorizes Alice, who is going to an antique car rally, to buy a car for him if she finds a bargain. She learns of a very good deal but takes it for herself instead of buying it for Bill. Bill would be able to get the car from Alice at her cost. If Alice had already sold the car to someone else, Bill could recover damages for the loss of the bargain. Likewise, an agent is not permitted to enter into any business in competition with the principal.

Wesco Autobody Supply v. Ernest

2010 Ida. LEXIS 146 (Ida. Sup. Ct. 2010)

FACTS

Wesco Autobody Supply bought three autobody supply stores from Paint & Equipment Supply. Several weeks after the purchases, the majority of Wesco's employees at the stores quit and began working for Paint & Supply. Wesco accused five of the employees of soliciting their fellow employees to quit Wesco and work for Paint & Equipment. It was asserted that they also drafted letters of resignation for other employees. Wesco asserts that all of this occurred before any of the employees had left Wesco.

ISSUE

Has Wesco stated a claim for breach of loyalty?

DECISION

Yes. Loyalty to his trust is the first duty that an agent owes to his principal. It follows as a necessary conclusion that the agent must not put himself in such a relationship that his interests become antagonistic to those of his principal. Throughout the duration of an agency relationship, an agent has a duty to refrain from competing with the principal and from taking action on behalf of or otherwise assisting the principal's competitors. During that time, an agent may take action, not otherwise wrongful, to prepare for competition following termination of the agency relationship. By drafting letters of resignation for other

(continued)

Wesco Autobody Supply v. Ernest *(concluded)*

employees and speaking to other employees about quitting, the five employees may have put themselves in such a position that their interests became antagonistic to those of their principal or that they may have been assisting the principal's competitors. If these actions occurred before the five employees terminated their agency relationship with Wesco, they have violated their duty of loyalty.

Moonlighting

It may be possible for an agent/employee to supplement her income by taking on a second job. Whether or not this violates the duty of loyalty may turn on several factors. Courts consider several factors in deciding if the duty of loyalty is breached. One consideration is the possible existence of contractual provisions preventing a second job. For example, the employment contract might permit an employee to seek a second source of income, whether through a second job or an independent business. Conversely, a noncompetition covenant might limit an employee's economic activities both during and after employment.

Another consideration is whether the principal knew of or agreed to the agent's secondary profit-seeking activities. Disclosure of an intention to pursue a second source of income alerts the principal to potential problems and protects the agent from a charge of disloyalty. The status of the agent and her relationship to the principal's business should be considered. For instance, an officer, director, or key executive has a higher duty than does someone stocking shelves in a grocery store.

The nature of the second source of income and its effect on the principal's business must be examined. For example, the duty of loyalty generally precludes acts of direct competition. Further, agents should not engage in conduct that causes their principal to lose customers, sales, or potential sales. Nor should they take advantage of their principal by engaging in secret self-serving activities, such as accepting kickbacks from suppliers or usurping the principal's business opportunities. Agents who defraud their principals or engage in direct competition with them run the risk of discharge, forfeiture of the right to compensation, and other legal and equitable remedies.

Ethics in Action

Suppose that a client contracted for the principal's services specifically because of its desire to draw from the agent's special expertise. Is the agent breaching an ethical duty to the client by allowing it to contract with the principal, knowing that he will soon terminate his relationship with the principal's company?

Dual Agency

Usually one cannot serve as agent for both parties to a transaction; however, the principals may consent to such a dual role if the parties are both fully informed. Suppose Pamela employs Allen as a real estate broker to find a buyer for her residence. Patti wants to buy some houses as rental property and has agreed to pay Allen a commission on those she buys through him. Allen arranges a sale of Pamela's house to Patti. If he has not informed both of them of his dual role, he is not entitled to a commission from either. If only Patti is aware of and approves the arrangement, Allen may collect a commission from her but not from Pamela. A principal who was not informed of the agent's dual role also retains the right to rescind any contract made by the agent in his dual role.

Courts make an exception when the dual agent is employed merely as a **middleman.** If an agent is employed to find a buyer for one party and a seller for the other and the parties intend to and do negotiate their own transaction, the agent is only a middleman. If neither party relies on the agent for advice or negotiation, there is no breach of loyalty. Real estate brokers normally just bring the parties together rather than actually negotiating a contract of sale. However, the party first employing the broker usually expects to and does in fact rely on the broker for advice. Therefore, it is a breach of duty if the agent also purports to advise the other party.

Confidential Information

Another aspect of the duty of loyalty is the duty of agents to avoid disclosing or using the principal's secrets. Agents breach this duty if they either disclose confidential information to others or use it to benefit themselves. Trade secrets such as formulas, processes, and mechanisms are included within this duty; so are customer lists, special selling techniques, and sales manuals. However, agents may use the general knowledge and skills they have acquired while employed by their principal. This is true even when a former agent is competing with her former principal after termination of the agency relationship. A principal claiming a trade secret must be able to show that the information was protected and treated as a secret within the agency. This usually means that only a few people were allowed access to it and that it was never disclosed to anyone else except on a confidential basis.

American Family Mutual Insurance v. Roth

485 F.3d 930 (7th Cir. 2007)

FACTS

American Family Mutual Insurance had an agreement with its agents that required all agents to enter all new business in the company's database. The agreement warned agents that the database contains confidential information and may not be used except in the ordinary course of the agent's business with the company. An agent had access only to the information in the database that concerned the customers whom he served. It might be customer information originated by the agent or information furnished to it by the company when another agent resigned and his customers had therefore to be reassigned. After Roth's agency with American Mutual was terminated, he was accused of soliciting his former customers from a customer list he had compiled separately from the company's database while he had been working for the insurance company.

ISSUE

Has Roth breached a duty he owed his principal?

DECISION

Yes. Once agents enter customer information in the database, the information becomes the exclusive property of the plaintiff, or at least exclusive as against the agent. The information, insofar as it had been developed by the agent rather than supplied to him by the plaintiff, would be his trade secret initially—but only until he uploaded the information into the plaintiff's database, at which point it would become American Family's trade secret. There is nothing unfair about the arrangement. The agents benefited from being able to use the plaintiff's database, as well as from receiving customers from the plaintiff; in exchange they gave the plaintiff the right to keep, after termination of the agency relationship, any customer information that they'd acquired in the course of the relationship.

Concept Summary: The Agent's Duty of Loyalty

Nature	**Fiduciary Duty:** • Action in best interests of principal. • Complete honesty. • Cannot be eliminated by agreement.
Proscriptions	Agent should avoid: • Conflicts of interest: self-dealing. secret profits. usurping principal's opportunities. • Dual agencies. • Misuse of confidential information.
Exception	Agent may engage in otherwise prohibited activity: • With principal's consent. • After full and open disclosure.

E-Commerce

The *Electronic Communications Privacy Act* (ECPA) prohibits "intercepts" of electronic communications such as e-mail. In *Fraser v. Nationwide Mutual,* 352 F.3d 107 (3d Cir. 2003), an insurance company was concerned that one of its insurance agents might be revealing company secrets to its competitors. It therefore searched its main file server—on which all of the agent's e-mail was logged—for e-mail to or from the agent that showed improper behavior. The search confirmed the agent's disloyalty and he was discharged. After the agent sued, the court held that the company's e-mail search did not violate the ECPA because an "intercept" (required by the statute) can only occur contemporaneously with transmission. The company did not access the agent's e-mail at the initial time of the transmission. It also did not violate ECPA provisions forbidding accessing electronic communications in electronic storage without authorization. This is because that provision excepts communications service providers from its coverage. Because the e-mail was stored on the company's computer system, the search fell within that exception.

Duty to Obey Instructions

An agent is not entitled to substitute her personal judgment for that of the principal. The agent may not ignore instructions just because they seem unwise or not truly in the best interests of the principal. If no instruction is given, the agent should exercise her best judgment to further the interests of the principal.

The agent has a duty to obey the principal and will be liable for any loss to the principal caused by failure to follow such instructions. Suppose Joe instructs Alma, a clerk in his store, to sell goods only for cash except to those customers who have previously established accounts with him. While Joe is gone, Alma sells goods on credit to a very well-dressed customer. Later, Joe is unable to collect. Alma is liable to Joe for the price of the goods. The fact that Alma thought Joe would benefit from her action is not a defense since she acted contrary to his instructions.

There are a few situations in which the agent may act contrary to the principal's instructions without incurring liability. Suppose Joe had told Alma not to obligate him for any goods or services during his absence. While he was gone and out of contact with Alma, a tornado damaged the roof of his store. Alma would have implied authority to obligate Joe for any reasonable roof repairs that she might arrange. It is reasonable for Alma to believe that, in the emergency and despite the instructions, Joe would have wanted her to have the roof repaired. (Implied authority will be discussed more fully in Chapter 24.)

Ethics in Action

Suppose that you are a sales representative for a major manufacturer with responsibility over the company's independent (franchised) retail dealers. The manufacturer instructs you to pressure the retailers to adhere to its suggested retail prices. Specifically, you are told to "threaten and cajole" them if that is what it takes to get their compliance. Retail price-fixing agreements between manufacturers and retailers violate the antitrust laws, while voluntary compliance with suggested prices does not. What should you do?

Duty to Exercise Care and Skill

Unless changed by agreement, the agent has a duty to act with ordinary care and with the skill common for the kind of work he is hired to do. An agent who is authorized to receive goods or to make collections has a duty to use customary practices to protect the principal's property. While the agent who makes loans is not an insurer of their collectibility, the agent must use care to investigate the credit standing of any borrowers. If it is usual to require security, the agent must investigate the adequacy of the security.

If the agent is acting without pay—a **gratuitous agent**—that fact is taken into account by the courts. The standard of care and skill required generally is less for a gratuitous agent than it is when the agent is to be compensated.

Duty to Communicate Information

The agent has a duty to inform the principal of knowledge the agent gains in the course of her responsibilities. This duty will be violated if the agent does not promptly notify the principal of anything of relevance to the agency that she knows or should know are of concern to the principal.

Ikola v. Schoene

590 S.E.2d 750 (Ga. Ct. App. 2003)

FACTS

Schoene, a real estate agent, represented Ikola in connection with the purchase of a home. When Ikola first saw the property, she noticed a sump pump in the basement, and Schoene told Ikola that she would never have to worry about flooding because of the pump. The contract provided Ikola with the right to inspect the property and to request that the sellers repair any defects, provided Ikola gave them an inspection report. Ikola raised the issue of a professional inspection, but Schoene told her that she was not entitled to one. In addition, Ikola did not receive a copy of the sellers' property disclosure statement, although the contract stated that one was attached. Ikola then telephoned Schoene to request the sellers' property disclosure statement. Not only did Schoene refuse to answer her calls, she wrote Ikola a memo incorrectly stating that the contract did not require one. The sellers, in fact, had completed two property disclosure statements that made reference to water accumulations. Following the first significant rainfall after closing on the home, Ikola

(continued)

discovered water streaming into the basement through the sump pump and the baseboards. Ikola sued Schoene, asserting that Schoene breached her agency duties.

ISSUE

Should a jury be permitted to determine if Schoene violated her agency duties?

DECISION

Yes. Schoene owed Ikola the duties an agent owes to her principal. Schoene had a duty to disclose material facts of which she had actual knowledge. This necessarily implies a duty to provide the disclosure statement to the buyer. In this case, there is evidence that not only did Schoene fail to provide the statements to Ikola, Schoene intentionally withheld them from her. This evidence raises an issue of fact as to whether Schoene breached the duty to disclose material facts affecting the property. Additionally, the overriding duty of a buyer's agent is to promote the buyer's interests. In this case, there is evidence that Schoene attempted to force Ikola to proceed with an "as-is" sale and actively discouraged her from obtaining a professional inspection. A jury could find that Schoene acted adversely to Ikola's interests and thereby breached the duty to promote them.

Duty to Account for Funds and Property

Property

An agent frequently is given money or property (tools, an automobile, or samples) by the principal. If so, the agent has a duty to return them or to account for his inability to do so on request by the principal. Included among the property for which the agent must account are any secret profits he received in violation of the duty of loyalty as well as any bribes or kickbacks that he might have received from third persons in the scope of the agency.

An Accounting

If the job of the agent includes receiving payments or operating a farm or business for the principal, the agent must periodically give the principal an accurate record of receipts and expenditures. The contract that establishes the agency normally states when such records are due. It may be as often as each day, or it may be only once a year. However, an **accounting** is more than just giving the principal a record of receipts and expenditures. It also involves an agreement, express or implied, between the agent and the principal that the record is correct. The principal may ask a court for a formal accounting if she is dissatisfied with the agent's records.

Commingling

An agent has a duty to keep the principal's property separate from her own. If the agent fails to do this, she is liable for any loss to the principal. If the agent **commingles** goods that are fungible—that is, if she mixes goods that are identical and cannot be separated—the agent bears the risk of any loss. For example, suppose Amy is carrying in her purse $1,000 in expense money that belongs to RCA Corporation, her employer. Mixed with it is $500 of her own money. She is robbed. Later, the thief is caught and the police recover $900. RCA will be entitled to the $900 if Amy cannot identify which of the bills belonged to RCA and which belonged to her.

An agent has the duty to deposit funds of the principal in a separate bank account. This should be either an account in the principal's name or a special account in the form: "Ames, in trust for Parker." Professional agents who serve a number of clients often maintain an account in the form: "Ames's Clients' Trust Fund."

Embezzlement

Agents are often given property of the principal for use in the principal's business. If the agent takes the property with the intent to deprive the principal of it, the agent is guilty of the crime of **embezzlement.** Whether or not the property of the principal is wrongfully used, the agent must return it or be liable for its value in an action for **conversion.**

If an agent uses the money of the principal for the agent's purposes, the principal may choose either to sue for the money or to obtain whatever was purchased with it. Suppose Andrew, as agent, is paid $5,000 owed by a debtor of Perkins, Andrew's principal. Instead of giving it immediately to Perkins, Andrew invests it in the stock of Golden Mining Company. Luckily, the market price of the stock rises to $10,000 before Perkins learns of the wrongdoing. Perkins is entitled to all of the stock. If instead the value of the stock had decreased, Perkins could recover the $5,000.

Duties of Principals to Agents

LO3

A well-drafted agency contract would be expected to set out the duties the principal owes to the agent. However, if the contract is poorly drafted or if there is no contract at all, the courts look to the common law of agency for guidance. The following duties generally are imposed on the principal by the common law:

1. The duty to compensate.
2. The duty to reimburse and indemnify.
3. The duty to keep accounts.

Duty to Compensate

Normally, a duty to pay the agent is implied unless special circumstances or the relationship of the parties suggests that a gratuitous agency was intended. The agency agreement should specify the amount of compensation due the agent and when it has been earned. Many disputes arise because no clear agreement has been reached. In the absence of agreement, the agent is entitled to the customary or reasonable value of the services performed. Custom is sometimes quite clear. For example, in most communities, real estate brokers all charge the same commission rate. If there is no clear custom and the amount is in dispute, expert witnesses may testify as to what a reasonable amount would be.

Contingent Compensation

Compensation is often made contingent on results. Sales agents are frequently paid an agreed-on percentage of the value of the sales they make. Stockbrokers are also usually paid on a commission basis. Lawyers in the United States, especially when serving plaintiffs in tort actions such as automobile claims, often agree to contingent fees. If they win the case for the plaintiff, they get some share (often one-third) of the recovery. The plaintiff has only expenses and court costs to pay if there is no recovery.

An agent is entitled to be paid if the agreed-on result is obtained even though the principal does not benefit. For example, Albert is employed by Pierce Manufacturing Company as a salesperson. As a result of material shortages, Pierce is unable to produce and ship several large orders taken by Albert and accepted by Pierce. Albert is entitled to his commission on those orders. However, if Pierce had informed Albert of the shortage and had stopped approving orders he sent in, Pierce would have no liability to Albert.

It is common to give agents who are compensated on a commission basis a monthly or weekly "draw" against commissions to be earned. This gives the agent money for living expenses. At some longer interval, such as quarterly or once a year, the agent is paid the amount by which the commissions exceed the draw. If it is not clear from the employment contract whether the agent must reimburse the principal if the draw exceeds the commissions, courts generally hold that overpayments cannot be recovered.

Procuring Cause

Generally, agents do not receive commissions on transactions that occur after termination of the agency relationship. However, when an agent was the primary factor in a purchase or sale, the **procuring cause** rule may entitle the procuring agent to her commission regardless of who eventually completes the sale. This rule is designed to permit agents to collect commissions on sales completed after termination of the agency relationship if the sale primarily resulted from the agent's efforts. Without the rule, the principal easily could escape paying the agent's commissions while enjoying the fruits of her labors.

AA Sales & Associates v. Coni-Seal

550 F.3d 605 (7th Cir. 2008)

FACTS

Saltzman worked for Coni-Seal, an automobile parts manufacturer, as a sales agent. They had a written agreement entitling Saltzman to a commission on "all products sold to approved accounts." In turn, "approved accounts" were defined as accounts that Coni-Seal had given Saltzman authorization to solicit. Finally, the agreement stated that after termination, Saltzman would continue to receive commissions on all accounts that had been previously called on and sold by Saltzman. After Coni-Seal gave Saltzman approval to solicit sales from AutoZone, he made approximately 50 trips to the company at his own expense. Later the company authorized a second sales agent to make sales calls on AutoZone but, according to Saltzman, promised him that he still would be entitled to his commission. Soon thereafter, Coni-Seal began selling parts to AutoZone; however, Saltzman was not personally responsible for bringing about those sales. Coni-Seal then asked Saltzman to stop calling on AutoZone. Saltzman now complains that, although Coni-Seal made several million dollars in sales to AutoZone, he received no commissions for any of the sales. Coni-Seal replies that Saltzman is not entitled to commissions because he was not the procuring cause of the sales.

ISSUE

Can Saltzman recover commissions even though he is not the procuring cause of the sales?

DECISION

Yes. Under the "procuring cause" rule, agents are not entitled to commissions unless they show that they actually sold the property in question, were instrumental in bringing the sale, or procured a purchaser who was willing and able to purchase on the stipulated terms. However, the procuring cause rule is merely a default rule and is inapplicable when a contract specifies other bases of fee recovery. Here, the parties' agreement does not require Saltzman to prove that he actually effectuated sales in order to be entitled to a commission. On the contrary, we think the contract means what it says: while the contract remains in effect, Saltzman will be entitled to commissions based on all sales to approved accounts; after the contract has been terminated, however, he will be entitled to commissions only when he can show that he actually brought about sales to the relevant account while the contract was still in effect. Because the parties' contract does not require Saltzman to show that he was the cause of a sale in order to be entitled to pretermination commissions, the procuring cause rule does not apply.

Duration of Employment

Sometimes an agent is expected to incur substantial expenses that are to be recouped through a commission on completion of the agency. When no duration is agreed on and the agent has made the expenditures, a court may hold that the principal cannot terminate the agency until after the agent has had a reasonable time to try to earn the expected commission. Suppose a developer gives Ralph, a real estate broker, an exclusive right to sell residential lots. It is customary for brokers to use extensive advertising and to establish an office in the subdivision. Ralph does this even though the agreement with the developer does not specify its duration. The developer cannot cancel the contract until Ralph has had a reasonable opportunity to recover his costs.

Real Estate Commissions

A real estate broker who represents a seller normally earns the commission when he finds a buyer "ready, willing, and able" to make the purchase on the offered terms. "Able," of course, means that the buyer has or can borrow the asking price for the property. If the seller has not given the broker specific terms of price, closing date, or other important items, then the commission is not earned until the contract of purchase has been made.

Insurance Commissions

In the life insurance business, it is customary for the company to pay the agent a commission on all premiums paid on the insurance contracts sold. This encourages the agent to provide continued service to policyholders and to recognize the fact that the value of the sale is greater than the first payment. In other lines of business, including casualty insurance, the agent is paid a commission on renewals by, or repeated transactions with, a customer first sold by the agent. Such agreements should clearly state whether the agent or the agent's representative is entitled to such payments after the agent's death or termination of employment.

Duty to Reimburse and Indemnify

Sometimes agents make advances from their own funds in conducting the principal's business. If the agent is acting within the scope of her authority, the principal has a duty to reimburse the agent for expenses incurred for the principal. Also, if the agent suffers losses while acting for the principal within the scope of the agent's authority, the principal has a duty to indemnify the agent.

For example, suppose Abby is a salesperson for Pruitt Company. She is in Cleveland when she is asked by Pruitt to go to a foreign trade show. She uses her own funds to pay workers to set up the company's booth at the show. In order to ship the exhibit back to Pruitt, she is required to pay a $500 export fee, again out of her own funds. Pruitt has a duty to reimburse her for her expenses and to indemnify her for the export fee.

However, if some fault of the agent causes a loss, the principal will not be required to indemnify the agent for the amount of the loss. And, of course, the principal is not liable for unauthorized expenses incurred by the agent.

Duty to Keep Accounts

The principal has a duty to keep records from which the compensation due the agent can be determined. This duty is reinforced by tax laws that require such recordkeeping. For example, an employer must keep and make available to a salesperson a record of the sales on which commissions have been earned.

Enforcement of Liabilities between Principals and Agents

Breach of Duty by Agent

When an agent's breach of duty causes harm to the principal, the principal may deduct the loss from the amount due the agent. If no compensation is due the agent, the principal can bring an action in court. If the breach of duty is serious enough, the principal may have no duty to compensate the agent even though the principal can show no actual damages. The agent may even be discharged without liability in spite of an unexpired contract.

Breach of Duty by Principal

In most situations, an agent who is in lawful possession of property that belongs to the principal has a lien on it for the compensation due him for his performance of the agency responsibilities. For example, if a stockbroker has purchased a security for a client, he may hold the certificate until he is paid. Likewise, an attorney has a lien on the documents of the client while they are in the attorney's possession. Of course, the agent may also bring a lawsuit against the principal for any injuries suffered as a result of a breach of duty by the principal.

Concept Summary: Agency Duties

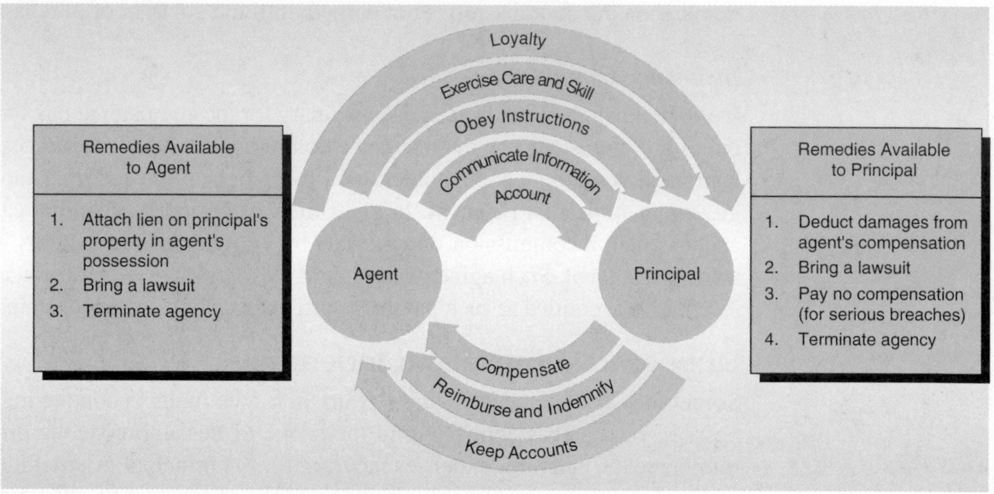

Termination of Agent's Powers

Termination by Will of Parties

LO4

A well-drafted agency agreement usually will discuss when or how the agency is to end. The relationship then will terminate at the time or on the happening of an event stated in the contract. For example, the agency may be for one year, or the principal and agent may agree that the agency is to last until the principal's new plant is complete and ready to operate. If no time or event is specified, then the agency automatically ends when the result for which the agency was created has been accomplished. Of course, both parties may mutually agree to modify their agency contract and accelerate or extend the termination date.

Agency at Will

Notwithstanding the agency agreement, either party generally may terminate the agency at any time, since the relationship is based on mutual consent. This gives each party the **power to terminate** even if there is no contractual right to do so. For example, suppose the agency agreement provides that the agency will continue for five years. Despite this language, either the agent or the principal can end it before then—say, in two years. This doctrine—known as **agency at will**—stems from the judicial reluctance to force people to continue personal relationships against their will. Of course, whenever one party exercises the *power to terminate* in violation of the *right to terminate,* the other party may recover monetary damages in a breach of contract suit.

There are several exceptions to the rule that one possesses the power to terminate the agency at any time. Two such instances will be discussed below: (1) agency coupled with an interest and (2) certain legislative restrictions.

Agency Coupled with an Interest

An **agency coupled with an interest** is one exception to the general rule that either party has the power to terminate an agency. It arises when the power is given as a security. Such an agency is irrevocable without the consent of the agent. A common example of this type of agency is where a creditor is authorized to sell property pledged as security for a loan. Suppose Paula borrows $1,000 from Adam. She gives Adam authority as her agent to sell her diamond ring to satisfy his claim if she does not pay the loan back as promised. Paula cannot revoke Adam's power to sell the ring. Even her death does not terminate the agency so long as the debt remains unpaid.

Concept Summary: Power versus Right to Terminate

Power	Right	Consequence
Yes	Yes	May terminate without penalty
Yes	No right if violation of contract	May terminate but liable for contract damages
No power if agency coupled with interest or violation of law	No right if there is no power	May *not* terminate

Legislative Restrictions

An agency termination based on race, color, sex, religion, national origin, and age generally is prohibited by state and federal legislation. Statutes also may prevent termination of an agent for engaging in labor union activities or reporting unsafe working conditions. These and other public policy exceptions are developed more fully in Chapter 25.

Concept Summary: Events That Properly Terminate the Agency

Operation of Law	Death or insanity of either party. Bankruptcy affecting the agency. Illegality or impossibility of agency objective. Destruction of subject matter of the agency. Material change in business conditions.
Will of the Parties	Terms of the contract. Agency objective is accomplished. Mutual agreement of the parties.

Termination by Operation of Law

The law terminates an agency if certain events occur. Among these are the death or insanity of either party and the bankruptcy of either party if it affects the agency. Where an agent's credit does not affect the agency (e.g., a salesperson in a retail store), the agency is not terminated by bankruptcy. Further, banks generally continue to have the authority to act as a depositor's agent for check-cashing purposes for a limited period of time after the depositor/agent's death. (This exception will be discussed in greater detail in Chapter 41.)

Termination also occurs if the objective of the agency becomes impossible or illegal or if the subject matter of the agency is lost or destroyed. For example, a real estate broker may be hired as a rental agent for a house. If the house burns down, the agency ends.

A substantial change in market values or business conditions that affects the subject of the agency ends it if a reasonable agent would believe that termination is desired by the principal. For example, assume that a broker is authorized to sell a large block of stock in an aircraft manufacturer at a fixed price. If war breaks out and the president announces a large increase in aircraft purchases that would greatly benefit the manufacturer, the agency authority to sell at the original price would terminate.

Notice to Third Persons

LO5

An agent still may be able to bind the principal on contracts with third persons after termination of the agency if the third person is unaware that the agency has ended. This is because an agency continues in existence as to a third person until that person has notice or knowledge of its termination.[4] To avoid being bound by acts of the agent after termination, the principal must give **actual notice** to those who have dealt with the former agent. A written notification generally is most desirable because it is easy to prove its existence. **Constructive notice** is sufficient for persons who may have been aware of the agency but have never formally dealt with it. A notice in a newspaper of general circulation in the area is normally sufficient for such persons. Suppose a husband has permitted his wife to charge things to his account at several stores. He then publishes an advertisement in the local newspaper: "After November 1, I shall no longer accept responsibility for the debts incurred by my wife." This would be effective against stores that had not yet charged him for goods bought by his wife, but he should send letters to stores where he has already paid such bills in order to avoid further liability.

Several exceptions to the notice rules do exist. Notice is not necessary when the agency is terminated due to death of the principal, loss of legal capacity by the principal, or impossibility of performance.

Johnson v. Nationwide Insurance Company

1998 U.S. App. LEXIS 22392 (2d Cir. 1998)

FACTS

Shelly A. Johnson claimed that her brother-in-law, Michael P. Donnelly, a former employee of Nationwide, induced her to invest $70,000 in a Nationwide tax-free mutual fund. At the time she made the investment, Shelly was unaware that Michael was no longer an actual or implied agent of Nationwide. After she discovered that Michael had misappropriated the funds, Shelly sued Nationwide. She contended that Michael still had apparent authority to represent Nationwide because the company had failed to properly notify her of his termination.

ISSUE

Is Nationwide liable to Shelly for her investment?

DECISION

Yes. Nationwide widely advertised Michael's agency and provided him with various indicia of authority which cloaked him with an aura of authority on which Shelly reasonably relied. Because Nationwide did not publicize its termination of Michael to his previous customers, much less to those members of the public who, like Shelly, would be justified in believing the agency still existed, it is liable to Shelly.

[4] This notion—called *apparent authority*—will be developed more fully in Chapter 24.

Concept Summary: Notice of Agency Termination*

Third Person	Type of Notice	Example
Those who dealt with agent before termination	Actual	Direct personal communication (e.g., letter)
Those who knew of agency but had never dealt with it before termination	Constructive	Newspaper announcement
Those who never knew of existence of the agency	None	

*Notification is not necessary when termination is due to principal's death, loss of capacity, or impossibility of performing agency objective.

International Agency Agreements

This chapter has examined the common law rules of agency that supplement any special rights or obligations that the principal and agent may include in an agency contract. In the United States, there are few restrictions on what terms may be included in such an agreement. That is not the case, however, in many countries throughout the world. Those nations reserve special protections for local agents irrespective of any contract entered into with the foreign principal.

Most of the world does not share the United States' notion of agency at will. Accordingly, it may be extremely difficult to terminate an overseas agent without good cause. And, even when such terminations are permitted, the principal may be required to give reasonable notice and offer some amount of severance pay.

Questions and Problem Cases

1. Cameco, a producer of food products, employed Gedicke as a salaried traffic manager at a salary of approximately $38,000 per year. Gedicke's primary duty was arranging transportation of Cameco's food products to retail stores by common carrier. His duties included coordinating Cameco's shipping schedules, negotiating the lowest possible shipping rates, and supervising the warehouse employees who loaded the trucks. Because of his position, Gedicke became familiar with the identity of Cameco's suppliers, customers, and common carriers, as well as its delivery routes and rates. Without telling Cameco, Gedicke and his wife formed Newton Transport Service, which Gedicke operated primarily out of his home. Acting on behalf of distributors or truckers, Gedicke arranged for the transportation of food products to retailers. After several years, Newton Transport's profits exceeded $62,000 a year. Two of the distributors for which Newton Transport arranged transportation sold the same products as Cameco. On over 600 occasions, Gedicke arranged for a trucker transporting Cameco's goods also to transport goods for Newton Transport's customers. However, the addition of Newton Transport freight actually enabled Gedicke to negotiate lower rates for Cameco. Gedicke admitted that he engaged in telephone conversations relating to Newton Transport's business during his scheduled hours with Cameco. However, he took no more than 15 minutes per

day for such matters and used his personal credit card in making such calls. Has Gedicke clearly breached his duty of loyalty? Explain.

2. *Video Case:* See "Martin Manufacturing." Mr. Martin, the president of Martin Manufacturing, fires a purchasing agent named Mitch because Mitch has been taking kickbacks from suppliers. Martin also withholds Mitch's last paycheck until Martin can determine how much Mitch's misbehavior has cost him. Has Mitch breached any fiduciary duties to Martin? If so, identify which ones. Will Mitch be required to give Martin the amount of any kickbacks he has received? Can Martin fire Mitch under these circumstances without incurring liability? Finally, is Martin legally justified in withholding Mitch's paycheck?
3. CP Clare, a manufacturer of electrical components, engaged Industrial Representatives, Inc. (IRI) in April 1991 to solicit orders for its products. By fall 1994, CP Clare's sales in IRI's territory exceeded $6 million annually, a tenfold increase since IRI's engagement. CP Clare decided to take promotion in-house and sent IRI a letter terminating the agency at the end of October 1994. CP Clare gave IRI 42 days' notice (their agency agreement required only 30). The contract contained a further obligation: CP Clare had to pay IRI a commission for all products ordered before the termination date that were delivered in the next 90 days. CP Clare kept this promise. However, IRI believed it had not been paid enough for the work it did in boosting CP Clare's sales. IRI argued that the termination violated public policy because CP Clare was trying to take "opportunistic advantage" of the goodwill IRI's services created for CP Clare's products. In short, IRI felt that it had made a substantial investment in the product sales and that the anticipated future sales were now like an annuity that CP Clare wrongfully decided to capture. Has CP Clare unlawfully terminated the agency relationship?
4. Willis was employed to find buyers for Haveg Industries' wire products. His agency contract permitted either party to terminate the agreement on 30 days' written notice. In the event of such a termination, the agreement entitled Willis to commissions only on orders accepted by Haveg up to and including the termination date. During his employment, Willis convinced Boeing Company to choose Haveg's product as its general-purpose wire. However, before Boeing made any orders, Haveg terminated Willis's contract. Boeing's first major order did not occur until more than a year and a half after his termination and the company continued to make major purchases during the next five years. Willis argued that Haveg terminated him in bad faith in order to avoid paying his commissions on the Boeing orders. He sued Haveg to recover his commissions on all purchases made by Boeing during the five years following his termination. Is Willis entitled to the commissions because his efforts were the procuring cause of the orders?
5. Ronald Chernow is in the business of auditing telephone bills for customers. He determines whether the customer's phone equipment is in place, properly billed, and in working order. He also checks for overcharges and receives half of any overcharge refund the customer receives from the telephone company. Chernow hired Angelo Reyes as an auditor. During his employment, Reyes, without Chernow's knowledge, took various steps to establish a business that competed with Chernow's. He obtained three auditing contracts and performed work under those agreements while still employed by Chernow. He also solicited a fourth account but did no work for that firm until after terminating his employment with Chernow. None of the businesses with whom Reyes contracted was one of Chernow's existing customers. Further, Reyes's personal soliciting and auditing activities did not take place during his regular working

hours. He devoted that time exclusively to Chernow's business. Did Reyes breach the duty of loyalty he owed Chernow?

6. Edward Taylor and James Petri left their employment with Pacific Aerospace & Electronics, Inc. (PAE) to form a competing concern, RAAD Technologies, Inc. (RAAD). After leaving PAE, Taylor and Petri compiled for RAAD a list of prospective customers, projects, and history. The list was derived from their memories of information developed by or available to them at PAE and included customer contacts, information about active projects and engineers, and customers' business and design preferences. Information they could not recall, including telephone numbers and addresses, was obtained from a business card file which Taylor took with him from PAE. Taylor and Petri used customer information they took from PAE to contact and solicit business from PAE customers. For instance, in preparation for a sales trip to southern California, Taylor and Petri prepared a memorandum summarizing their recollections of particular PAE customers' engineers and their histories and attitudes about PAE. Because of this information, RAAD was able to negotiate a lower commission structure with potential customers. Did the former employees violate their duties of loyalty and confidentiality? Explain.
7. Mary Fletcher entered into an exclusive listing agreement with Robert Hicks, a licensed real estate broker, to have him help her sell some land and buildings. During the period of the listing agreement, Hicks was in contact with a number of prospective buyers, including Walter STEERE. When the listing agreement expired and the property was still unsold, Fletcher and Hicks agreed that Hicks would continue to market the property for her. Soon thereafter, Hicks told Fletcher that he had an offer from STEERE to buy the property for $1.1 million. After Fletcher accepted STEERE'S offer, she learned that Hicks and STEERE had purchased the property together as partners. Has Hicks violated his agency duties to Fletcher? Explain.
8. *Video Case:* See "Martin Manufacturing." Immediately after being fired by Martin Manufacturing (see problem case 2), Mitch decided to squeeze one last bit of profit from his relationship with Martin. Thus, he called a customer with whom he had dealt on many occasions and ordered several cases of fasteners on Martin's behalf. Later, he resold the fasteners himself, pocketing the money. Is Martin liable to the supplier for the fasteners? In any event, what should Martin do to protect itself against cases like this?

Chapter 24

Liability of Principals and Agents to Third Parties

Learning Objectives

After you have studied this chapter, you should be able to:

1. Examine an agency fact situation and determine whether or not an agent has authority to bind a principal to a contract.
2. Identify when an otherwise unauthorized act has been ratified by a principal.
3. Describe the circumstances under which an agent is personally liable for a contract negotiated with a third party.
4. Review a fact situation and determine whether or not the principal is liable for the torts or crimes of the agent.

After suffering pain in his chest and left arm, Gilbert visited the emergency room of Sycamore Municipal Hospital. Dr. Frank, the emergency room doctor, ran several tests and informed Gilbert there was no evidence of heart disease. Gilbert was prescribed pain medication and discharged that day. He died later that evening. An autopsy revealed signs of heart disease. The hospital contended it was not liable for the doctor's alleged malpractice because he was not the hospital's agent or employee. It argued that the emergency room staff were independent contractors, although emergency room patients were not advised of this fact. The court held that the hospital could be held vicariously liable for the doctor's alleged malpractice under a doctrine of apparent agency.[1]

- What is meant by vicarious liability? When does it arise?
- What is an apparent agency and how does it arise?
- What is an independent contractor? How does it differ from an agent or employee?

[1] *Gilbert v. Sycamore Municipal Hospital,* 622 N.E.2d 788 (Sup. Ct. Ill. 1993).

Introduction

This chapter examines the various types of liability that principals and agents may owe to third persons who deal with the agency. It begins with a discussion of the contract law issues that generally arise in agency situations. This includes an exploration of the authority that an agent must possess before she may bind her principal to a contract with a third person. Closely related to these authority issues are the principal's contractual liability for an agent's misrepresentations, the agent's knowledge, and the actions of subagents appointed by the agent, which are discussed briefly. The focus then shifts to a discussion of the contractual liability that the agent may incur in carrying out his agency functions. The chapter closes with an examination of the tort and criminal liability that may be imposed on principals and agents for the actions of agents in carrying out their agency responsibilities.

The Agent's Authority to Bind the Principal on Contracts

A principal is bound on a contract entered into on his behalf by an agent if the agent had authority to act for the principal. Such authority may be either actual or apparent. Actual authority may be expressed or implied. Even if no actual authority has been given, the principal may be held liable because he either appeared to give authority to the agent (apparent authority) or ratified the act of the agent (or one posing as an agent).

LO1

Thus, a clear understanding of the contractual liability of a principal to a third person for a contract created by an agent requires an examination of the following concepts:

1. Actual authority
   a. Express authority
   b. Implied authority
2. Apparent authority
3. Ratification

Actual Authority

Actual authority is the true authority granted to the agent by the principal. It is proper authority in the sense that an agent acting within her actual authority is not in violation of her agency duty to the principal. Actual authority may be either express or implied.

Express Authority

Authority is **express** when the principal specifically describes the extent of the agent's powers. Generally, this may be done orally, although some states have statutes that require the authority of an agent who is to buy or sell land to be in writing. An **attorney-in-fact** is the technical label given to an agent whose authority is in writing. Suppose that Paul plans to be in Europe for the summer and wishes to sell his car. He may appoint Anne as his attorney-in-fact to sign the necessary papers on his behalf. Anne is said to possess his **power of attorney.** The test of an agent's express authority is *the specific language the principal used in granting the authority.*

Implied Authority

Often express authority is incomplete and does not cover every contingency because the principal can seldom foresee every circumstance in which the agent may need to act. Therefore, an agent also possesses the **implied authority** to do whatever else is reasonably necessary to accomplish the objectives of the agency. This may include what is customary for agents to do in the particular business of the principal or in similar transactions in the community. However, implied authority is limited by any specific prohibitions or other indications of the principal's wishes.

The test used by a court in determining the extent of the agent's implied authority is the *justifiable belief of the agent.* Suppose that Herb is left in charge of Joe's store while Joe is out of town on business. Joe's instructions to Herb said nothing about the arrival of merchandise. Herb would have implied authority to sign a delivery receipt for any arriving goods if he could reasonably believe that they had in fact been ordered.

Agents also have implied power to act in emergencies (sometimes called *inherent agency power*). If a tornado breaks the windows and tears off part of the roof of the store, Herb has implied authority to make necessary repairs if he cannot reach Joe for further instructions. This is true even if Joe told Herb not to make purchases of any kind. Each of these exercises of implied authority would be binding on Joe as if he had personally performed the acts himself.

The terms *general agent* and *special agent* frequently arise in discussions of implied authority. A general agent is a person who acts for the principal in a number of transactions over a period of time. A special agent, on the other hand, is authorized by the principal to do a specific act or to handle one or a few of certain types of business transactions. Her authority to act is limited to that single transaction. Thus, one might expect general agents to have a broader range of implied authority than special agents.

Apparent Authority

Apparent authority is created by the conduct of the principal that causes a third person reasonably to believe that another has the authority to act for the principal. It may exist if a principal has intentionally or by want of ordinary care induced and permitted third persons to believe a person is her agent even though no actual authority has been conferred on the agent. The source of apparent authority is the principal, just as it is for express and implied authority. Words or acts of an agent alone cannot create apparent authority.

The test used for determining the extent of an agent's apparent authority is the *justifiable belief of a third party* dealing with the agent. Remember, if the agent justifiably believed she had authority, her authority would be *implied, not apparent.* This distinction can be very important because an agent's exercise of apparent authority, in the absence of actual authority, is in violation of the agent's duty to the principal. Thus, a principal who is bound to a contract with a third person based on an agent's apparent authority may sue the agent for damages.

Apparent authority may arise from customs in the trade. Thus, when a principal wishes to impose limitations on an agent's authority that are not customary, it is important that such restrictions be communicated to third persons in order to avoid apparent authority. Former agents also may possess apparent authority if the principal does not notify third persons of the termination of the agency relationship. (Termination and notice were discussed in Chapter 23.)

Apparent Agent

A person may have apparent authority although he never has been appointed an agent by the principal. The apparent authority arises from the principal's failure to inform third persons that the relationship is not what it appears to be. Consider the medical malpractice case that opened this chapter. The hospital considered its emergency room doctors to be independent contractors rather than agents or employees. However, it failed to advise emergency room patients of this arrangement. Although the doctrine of apparent authority normally is applied in contract cases, the court found in this tort suit that the patient's reasonable belief made the doctor an **apparent agent** of the hospital. Specifically, the court held that the hospital and its doctors behaved in a manner that would lead a reasonable person to believe an agency existed.

Duty of Third Persons to Determine Agent's Authority

Generally, people who deal with an agent or a purported agent have a duty to determine the extent, if any, of the agent's authority. The fact that an agent may have some implied or apparent authority does not end the inquiry. The specific question is whether the agent or purported agent had implied or apparent authority to make the particular agreement.

Ophthalmic Surgeons v. Paychex

632 F.3d 31 (1st Cir. 2011)

FACTS

Paychex provided direct deposit payroll services for Ophthalmic Surgeons (OSL). Carleen Connor handled payroll for OSL and was its office manager. For a period of six years, Connor provided Paychex with false information about her salary status and thereby had Paychex pay her $233,159 more than her annual salary of $33,280. Paychex sent to OSL reports confirming all payments made. These reports were sent to Connor's attention and her supervisor saw none of them. OSL discovered the unauthorized payments when another employee took over Connor's duties. OSL sued Paychex for the excess money paid to Connor, arguing that Paychex was liable because Connor had no authority to order the excess payments.

ISSUE

Did Connor have authority to order the payments?

DECISION

Yes. It is undisputed that Connor was in fact authorized to handle payroll contracts and was the designated payroll contact assigned to communicate with Paychex. Connor's actual authority, however, did not extend to embezzling funds by authorizing the issuance of paychecks in amounts in excess of her salary as this is not what OSL, the principal, instructed her to do. The question remains, however, as to whether Connor was cloaked with apparent authority such that Paychex could have reasonably relied upon her authority to issue additional paychecks in her name. Apparent authority can only be created through words or conduct of the principal, communicated to a third party such that a third party can reasonably rely on the appearance and belief that the agent possesses authority to enter into a transaction. We find that by placing Connor in a position where it appeared that she had authority to order additional checks and by acquiescing to Connor's acts through its failure to examine the payroll reports, OSL created apparent authority in Connor such that Paychex reasonably relied on her authority to issue the additional paychecks.

Ratification

Nature of Ratification

LO2

One may become liable through **ratification** for an unauthorized act that was done by an agent. Ratification may occur with respect to either an act of an agent who has exceeded the authority given or an act by someone who has not been appointed an agent at all. For example, suppose Alex is a buyer for Polly's furniture store, Scandinavian Imports. While in Norway, Alex finds a classic MG sports car for sale. Although his authority is limited to buying furniture, he contracts to buy it as agent for Polly, who is a collector of antique cars. She, not Alex, is liable on the contract if she ratifies it by instructing the seller to ship the car.

Any act that the principal could have authorized at the time the act was done may be ratified. Generally, the effect of ratification is the same as if the act had been authorized in the first place.

Concept Summary: Agency Authority

Category		Definition	Test	Contractual Liability*
Actual	Express	Special authority (oral or written)	The explicit agency agreement between the principal and the agent	Principal is liable to the third party.
	Implied	Supplemental authority reasonably necessary to accomplish the agency objectives	The justifiable belief of the agent	Principal is liable to the third party.
Apparent		Appearance of authority in the agent created by the principal	The justifiable belief of the third party dealing with the agent	Principal is liable to the third party, but the agent is liable to the principal.

* Liability is based on a fully disclosed agency. Fully disclosed, partially disclosed, and undisclosed agencies are discussed later in this chapter.

Ratification is basically a question of the **intent** of the principal. However, the principal need not express that intent; it may be implied by his acts or failure to act. Often ratification is inferred by a court from the fact that the principal accepted the benefits of an unauthorized contract. It may also be inferred from the principal's failure to repudiate an unauthorized contract after becoming aware of it.

Requirements for Ratification

For ratification to be effective, the agent or purported agent must have *acted on behalf of the principal.* (This requires that the principal has been disclosed to the third person.) The principal must have had **capacity** to do the act both at the time it was done in the principal's name by the agent and when ratification occurs. Thus, there can be no ratification of an act done in the name of a corporation that was not in existence when the act was done. Only the **entire act** of the agent can be ratified; the principal may not ratify what is beneficial and deny what is burdensome. Ratification of a contract must be done before cancellation by the third person. Before ratification, the third person may usually withdraw from an unauthorized transaction. A requirement that frequently causes disputes is that the principal must have had *knowledge of all material facts* at the time of ratification. It is not necessary, however, that the principal fully understand the legal significance of those facts.

Effect of Ratification

Ratification releases the agent from liability to both the principal and the third person for having exceeded his or her authority. It also gives the agent the same right to compensation that he or she would have had if there had been prior authorization. Simultaneously the principal is entitled to the full benefit of the contract. Likewise, the principal is bound in the same manner and to the same extent as if the agent had been fully authorized from the beginning.

North American Specialty Insurance v. Employers' Reinsurance

857 So. 2d 606 (La. Ct. App. 2003)

FACTS

T. Reid Methvin was an agent for North American Specialty Insurance Company (NAS), which was engaged in the business of underwriting performance or construction bonds. During the course of the agency relationship, Methvin issued numerous unauthorized performance bonds. After learning about the unauthorized bonds, NAS accepted and retained payment of the premiums on all of the unauthorized bonds issued by Methvin. Thereafter, 12 of the unauthorized bonds resulted in defaults, causing significant losses when NAS was forced to pay claims on them. NAS now argues that Methvin, not it, is legally responsible to pay the claims on the defaulted bonds because Methvin acted without authority.

ISSUE

Is NAS legally liable to the pay the claims on the defaulted bonds?

DECISION

Yes. Tacit ratification results when a person, with knowledge of an obligation incurred on his behalf by another, accepts the benefit of that obligation. Further, when a principal (such as NAS) ratifies the unauthorized acts of its agent, the ratification discharges the agent from personal liability. The acceptance and retention of the premiums for all of the unauthorized bonds, including the bonds that did not result in losses from defaults, clearly evidences an acceptance of a benefit, and, therefore, NAS's actions constitute a tacit ratification of the terms and obligations of the unauthorized bonds. NAS accepted the premiums in the same manner and in the same amount as if they had originally approved and authorized the bonds. NAS was willing to knowingly accept the full benefit of the premiums; therefore, NAS must be willing to accept the full liability from the risk that some of the bonds would result in losses.

Concept Summary: Ratification

When Necessary	Requirements	When Occurs	Effect
1. Agent exceeds authority 2. Nonagent acts as an agent	1. Agent or nonagent acts on behalf of principal 2. Principal had capacity to do act: a. At time it was done, *and* b. At time of ratification 3. Must ratify the entire act 4. Must ratify before third party cancels 5. Principal must have knowledge of all material facts	Principal demonstrates intent to ratify: 1. Express 2. Implied: a. Acceptance of benefits of act b. Failure to repudiate after discovering act	Same as if the act was originally authorized: 1. Agent or nonagent released from liability 2. Principal is bound to the contract with the third party: a. Gains full benefits b. Assumes all liabilities

Related Contractual Liability Issues

Principal's Liability for the Agent's Representations

The principal is bound by representations that the agent is expressly authorized to make. Likewise, the principal also is liable for representations that are reasonably necessary for the agent to make in order to accomplish the purpose of the agency since they would be impliedly authorized. Finally, the principal is bound by representations that are customary in the kind of business being transacted by the agent. The agent has apparent authority to make such statements. If the representation is a usual one, the principal is bound even though she has told the agent not to make such a statement. This is not true, of course, if the third person knows that the agent has exceeded his actual authority. So if the principal wishes to avoid such potential liability, she must be certain to inform third persons of any restrictions on the agent's actual authority. (Remember, of course, that the agent will be required to indemnify the principal for any losses the principal suffers as a result of the agents' exceeding her actual authority.)

A person who is induced to enter a contract by the misrepresentation of an agent has the same remedies as if he had contracted with any person who made a misrepresentation. As was discussed in Chapter 14, the remedy of rescission is available when a misrepresentation occurs. If the misrepresentation is considered to be a warranty or guaranty, the principal is liable for damages when the product or service is not as represented. Misrepresentations by an agent made with the intent to deceive will also make the agent liable to the third person. (Of course, the third person is entitled to only a single recovery.)

Exculpatory Clauses

To give notice of lack of authority in the agent, sellers often use an **exculpatory clause** in the printed offer forms they furnish their salespeople. The form has a provision that says, in effect, "It is understood and agreed that salespersons have no authority to make any representation other than those printed herein and that none has been made in connection with this sale." However, many courts permit a third person to rescind a contract when the person has relied on a misrepresentation by the agent even though the contract contains an exculpatory clause.

The use of printed offer forms is itself a device sellers use to control the contracts their sales agents make. This is done by arranging the transaction so that the salesperson merely solicits an order that is, by its terms, "subject to approval of the home office." There is no contract, then, until the seller has received the written offer and decided to accept it. The printed form makes it clear that the salesperson is only taking an order (offer). It also usually contains an exculpatory clause limiting the salesperson's authority.

Principal's Liability for Notice and Payments to the Agent

Effect of Notice

Known as the imputation doctrine, notice to the agent is notice to the principal if it relates to the business of the agency. This is because the agent has a duty to inform the principal of knowledge the agent gains in the course of his or her responsibilities. However, if the information does not relate to the scope of the agent's responsibilities and authority, the principal is bound only by the information that is actually passed on by the agent. For example, Gomez has a standing order to purchase fresh fish for his restaurant from Lee, a fish supplier. Gomez tells a janitor at Lee's office that he is revoking the order. This notice is not binding on Lee if the janitor fails to pass the message on.

Payments to the Agent

Payment to the agent of a debt owed to the principal discharges the debt if the agent has authority to receive such payments. This is true even if the agent steals the money. An agent who makes over-the-counter sales is viewed as having apparent authority to collect for the goods. The same is true of a selling agent who is given possession of the goods for delivery. However, these agents do not usually have apparent authority to collect on account for goods sold at an earlier time. Other salespersons generally have no authority to collect unless it is expressly or impliedly given to them. An agent who has negotiated a loan or sold property and has been permitted by the principal to keep the negotiable instrument payable to the principal has apparent authority to receive payment on that instrument.

Effect of Conflicts of Interest

Sometimes an agent does not tell the principal things learned while acting within the scope of the agency because it is to the agent's advantage not to do so. Likewise, the agent may withhold payments received on behalf of the agency. When this is the case, the principal will not be bound if the agent colludes with the third person to withhold knowledge or money from the principal or if the third person should otherwise be aware that the agent is likely to withhold such information or money. In the next case, the court refuses to apply the imputation doctrine. Why?

NCP Litigation Trust v. KPMG LLP

901 A.2d 871 (N.J. Sup. Ct. 2006)

FACTS

John Mortell and Thomas Wraback, two officers of Physician Computer Network (PCN), intentionally misrepresented details concerning the corporation's financial status to KPMG LLP (KPMG)—PCN's independent auditing firm. That firm in turn failed to detect those misrepresentations for several years. After subsequent audits revealed the officers' fraud, the corporation was forced to acknowledge previously unreported losses of tens of millions of dollars and to declare bankruptcy. A litigation trust (NCP Litigation Trust), acting as the corporation's successor-in-interest and representing the corporation's shareholders, filed suit against the auditor for negligently conducting the audit. KPMG defended on the basis of the imputation doctrine. KPMG asserted that the fraud was imputable to the litigation trust, as the corporation's successor, and that the litigation trust cannot sue the auditor unless the auditor intentionally and materially participated in the fraud.

ISSUE

Does the imputation doctrine bar the litigation trust from recovering against the auditor in an action for negligence?

DECISION

No. The imputation doctrine is derived from the agency rule which holds that a principal is deemed to know facts that are known to its agent. Under the doctrine, a third party may invoke imputation as a defense against a principal seeking to enforce an agreement when the principal's agent fraudulently induced the third party to enter into that agreement. Courts have found that it is unfair to allow a principal to enforce an agreement in such a situation However, the rationale for imputation in a simple principal–agent relationship begins to break down in the context of a corporate audit where the allocation of risk and liability among principals, agents, and third parties becomes more complicated. The imputation defense exists to protect innocent third parties from being sued by corporations whose agents have engaged in malfeasant behavior against those third parties. This matter does not present the typical circumstance for which the imputation defense was designed because PCN's agents did not directly defraud an innocent third party. They defrauded the corporation and its creditors instead. KPMG is not a victim of the fraud in need of protection.

Principal's Liability for Acts of Subagents

Agent's Authority to Appoint Subagents

A **subagent** is an agent of the agent. When a corporation is made an agent, of necessity the principal is served by subagents. Such authority is implied. (This is because a corporation can act only through agents.) Other agents may be given express authority to hire subagents to do some or all of the work of the agent. Such authority may also be either implied or apparent. If the agent is found to have such authority, both the principal and the agent are bound to a third party by acts of the subagent. Between the agent and the principal, however, it is the agent who is ultimately liable for the acts of the subagent. (It is possible for the agent to limit this liability to the principal through the use of an exculpatory clause.)

Some agents are given authority to employ agents for the principal rather than subagents. For example, a sales manager for a corporation would probably have authority to hire sales agents for the corporation. Such agents are not subagents; they are agents of the corporation. The sales manager would not be bound by their acts unless their failings were due, in part, to his negligence in their selection or supervision.

Agents May Have Employees

Agents may delegate to employees acts for the principal that involve no judgment or discretion. These are called **ministerial acts.** The principal is normally not bound by acts of employees of agents unless these employees are also subagents whose appointment by the agent has been authorized. This is a fairly confusing area of the law. But basically the principal will be liable for the acts of an agent's employees only if he would have been liable if the agent had performed the act herself.

Contract Liability of the Agent

Introduction

Generally, the agent is representing the principal when making contracts, and all three parties (the agent, the principal, and the third party) intend that the agreement bind only the principal and the third party. As a result, the agent usually will not be liable for the agreement. There are, however, some special situations in which the agent may become personally liable for the contract with the third person. These basic circumstances arise when there are

LO3

1. Unauthorized actions by the agent.
2. Nonexistent or incompetent principals.
3. Agreements by the agent to assume liability.
4. An undisclosed principal.
5. A partially disclosed principal.

Unauthorized Actions

A person who represents that he or she is making a contract on behalf of a principal but who has no authority to do so does not bind the principal. Therefore, the agent is liable to the third person for damages suffered if the principal refuses to perform the contract. The same is true whenever agents exceed their authority—express, implied, or apparent.

Liability is imposed on an agent who has exceeded his authority on the basis of an **implied warranty of authority.** The agent is treated as if he had guaranteed to the third party that he had authority to make the contract. Suppose that you are employed as a sales agent for Acme Machine Tool Company and guarantee that a machine that you sell to a customer will eliminate the need for three employees. If you have no express authority from Acme to make such a guaranty (and such a guaranty is not common in the machine tool industry), then you, not Acme, will be liable to the customer if the machine fails to replace the employees.

The intent, knowledge, and good faith of the agent are immaterial in deciding whether the implied warranty of authority applies. If the agent exceeds his or her authority, liability results—unless the principal ratifies the act. Knowledge on the part of the third person that the agent is not authorized to make the guaranty also relieves the agent of liability.

Nonexistent or Incompetent Principal

A person who acts as an agent for a principal that is not in existence at the time of the act is personally liable on the contract. Therefore, if an agent acts for a corporation that is not yet formed or for an entity that has no legal existence, such as an unincorporated association, the agent is liable.

Assume that a community jogging club makes arrangements to hold a marathon run. One of its members makes contracts for renting certain equipment for the group. If the club is not incorporated, he is an agent for a nonexistent principal. If the contracts are not performed by the club, he will be personally liable for them.

The same is true if the principal has been judged insane or is a minor. The law imposes an implied warranty by the agent that the principal has the capacity to be bound. However, if the third person is aware of the lack of capacity of the principal, the agent is protected.

Concept Summary: Implied Warranty of Authority

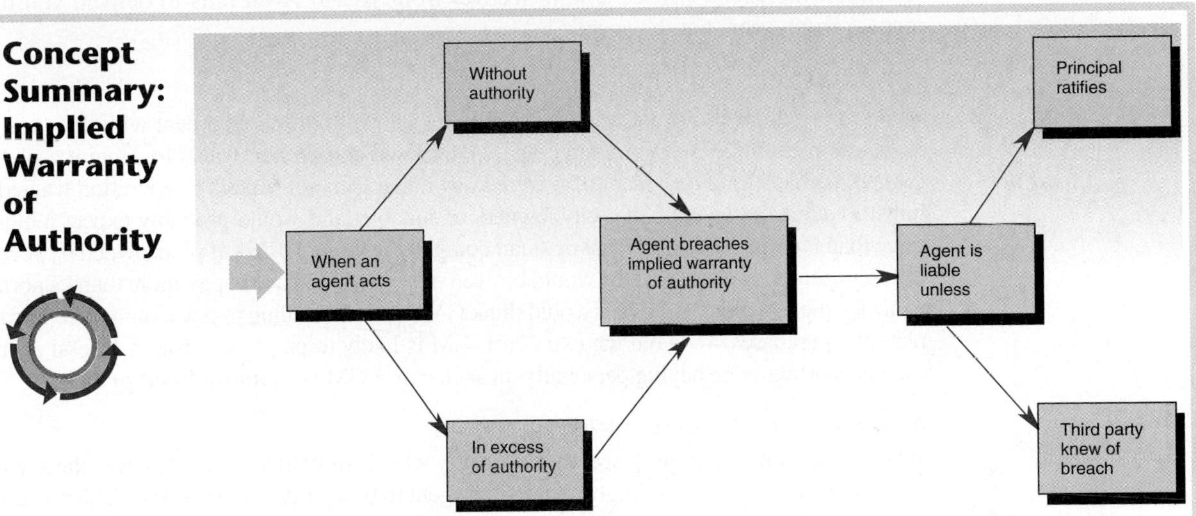

Agreements by the Agent to Assume Liability

Of course, an agent may make a contract in her own name while being employed as an agent. An agent may also become a party to a contract along with the principal, thus assuming joint liability. Or an agent may guaranty a contract made for the principal, in which case the agent becomes liable as a surety—that is, liable if the principal defaults.

To avoid liability because of confusion as to whether or not an agent is acting for herself or for the principal, the agent should sign all documents carefully. If she intends to act for a principal, the agent should

1. Fully disclose the identity of the principal.
2. Clearly indicate her capacity as an agent.

Disclosed Principal

Usually, a person who is dealing with an agent is aware of the fact and knows for whom the agent is acting. If a salesperson comes to your door and announces that "Avon is calling," you know that the person is an agent for a principal—Avon Products. In such a case, Avon Products is a **disclosed principal.**

Rights and Liabilities of Agent

When the principal is disclosed, all parties intend the contract to be between the principal and the third party. In ordering from the Avon agent, both you and the agent intend that you contract with Avon, not the agent. Therefore, the agent is not a party to the contract. If the agent has acted within his or her authority, the agent has no liability on the contract.

Generally, agents for disclosed principals cannot bring suit on contracts they make for principals. There are a few exceptions, however. For example, only the agent can bring an action on a negotiable instrument payable to her unless it is endorsed to the principal. Also, by custom an auctioneer is permitted to sue a buyer for breach of contract.

Rights and Liabilities of Principal

Since the principal rather than the agent is the intended party to the contract, the principal may enforce it. Likewise, the principal rather than the agent is liable on the contract. Suppose that goods you have ordered from the Avon agent are shipped and you fail to pay. Avon, not the agent, will be able to recover from you. If Avon fails to deliver, you may recover from Avon, not the agent.

Undisclosed Principal

Sometimes principals do not want their identities known to those who deal with their agents. A common example is when a large and well-known corporation wants to acquire a plot of ground, perhaps for a new plant. If it were known that General Motors Corporation wanted to buy 160 acres on the edge of a city, owners of suitable land would probably expect a higher price than if some local individual or small company were interested. If plots owned by several different people are desired, GM would be even more likely to have to pay more than its normal value for the last plot. The owner would think GM would be willing to pay a high price to complete the purchases. To avoid the extra cost, GM is likely to purchase through several agents, each purporting to be buying personally. In such cases, GM is an **undisclosed principal.**

Rights and Liabilities of Agent

When the principal is undisclosed, the third party who deals with the agent believes the agent is acting personally and accordingly expects the agent to be a party to the contract. Therefore, the agent is held liable on contracts entered into on behalf of an undisclosed principal. The agent is also permitted to sue on such a contract as a party to it. Of course, whenever an agent is found liable on a debt that he or she rightfully incurred on behalf of an undisclosed principal, the agent may in turn recover from the principal. This right of indemnification protects the agent in all instances except when the principal is unable to reimburse the agent due to insolvency.

Rights and Liabilities of Principal

Since the contract was made for his benefit, an undisclosed principal is permitted to enforce it. Further, if the third person learns of the principal's identity, she may elect to sue the principal instead of the agent. The third person cannot, of course, recover damages from both the principal and the agent. (If the third person elects to recover from the agent, the principal is then required to indemnify the agent.)

Ethics in Action

One reason a principal remains undisclosed is because the third party might demand a larger payment for the goods or services if she knew she was dealing with the principal. Yet contract law principles suggest that a party has a duty to disclose all material facts to his contracting partner. Is it ethical to contract through an undisclosed agency when it is clear that the third party would behave differently if she knew of this fact?

Partially Disclosed Principal

A principal is **partially disclosed** when the third person knows he is dealing with an agent but does not know the identity of the principal. This is likely to occur when an agent signs a contract or negotiable instrument, indicating her status as an agent, but forgetting to identify her principal.

Treadwell v. J.D. Construction

938 A.2d 794 (Me. Sup. Jud. Ct. 2007)

FACTS

Jesse Derr formed a corporation to conduct his construction business. Although the actual corporate name was JCDER, Inc., Derr regularly referred to the corporation as J.D. Construction Company. In fact, when Derr entered into a contract to build a house for Leah and William Treadwell, he signed the agreement: "*J.D. Construction Co., Inc. By: Jesse Derr.*" The name "JCDER" did not appear on the document and the Treadwells were unaware of its existence at the time of contracting. The Treadwells sued Derr after he abandoned the worksite without completing the house. Derr argues that he is not personally liable on the claim because he was acting as an agent for the corporation when he signed the contract.

ISSUE

Is Derr personally liable on the contract?

DECISION

Yes. In order for an agent to avoid personal liability for a contract negotiated in a principal's behalf, he must disclose not only that he is an agent but also the identity of the principal. Derr's use of the assumed trade name—J.D. Construction Company—was not sufficient to disclose his agency relationship with JCDER, Inc. The corporation was therefore an unidentified or partially disclosed principal. Derr is personally liable for performance of the contract entered into as an agent for the nonexistent J.D. Construction Company.

Concept Summary: Contractual Liability of Principals and Agents

Circumstance	Principal's Liability	Agent's Liability
Nonexistent or incompetent principal	Cannot be liable since lacks capacity or does not exist	Liable to third party
Unauthorized action	Not liable to third party unless act is ratified	Liable to third party unless act is ratified
Actual authority	Liable to third party	Not liable to third party unless undisclosed or partially disclosed agency (principal would then have to indemnify agent)
Apparent authority	Liable to third party	Not liable to third party but liable to principal for exceeding actual authority
Undisclosed or partially disclosed (actual authority)	May be liable if third party discovers identity (otherwise must indemnify agent)	May be liable if third party does not pursue principal (may then recover from principal)
Agent agrees to shared liability	Jointly liable with agent to third party (must indemnify agent in surety situations)	Jointly liable with principal to third party (may be indemnified by principal in surety situations)

The rights and duties of the parties when the principal is partially disclosed basically are the same as when the principal is undisclosed. If the principal is unknown, the third person must rely on the credit and trustworthiness of the agent. Therefore, the agent is held liable on the contract.

Concept Summary: Disclosed, Undisclosed, and Partially Disclosed Agency*

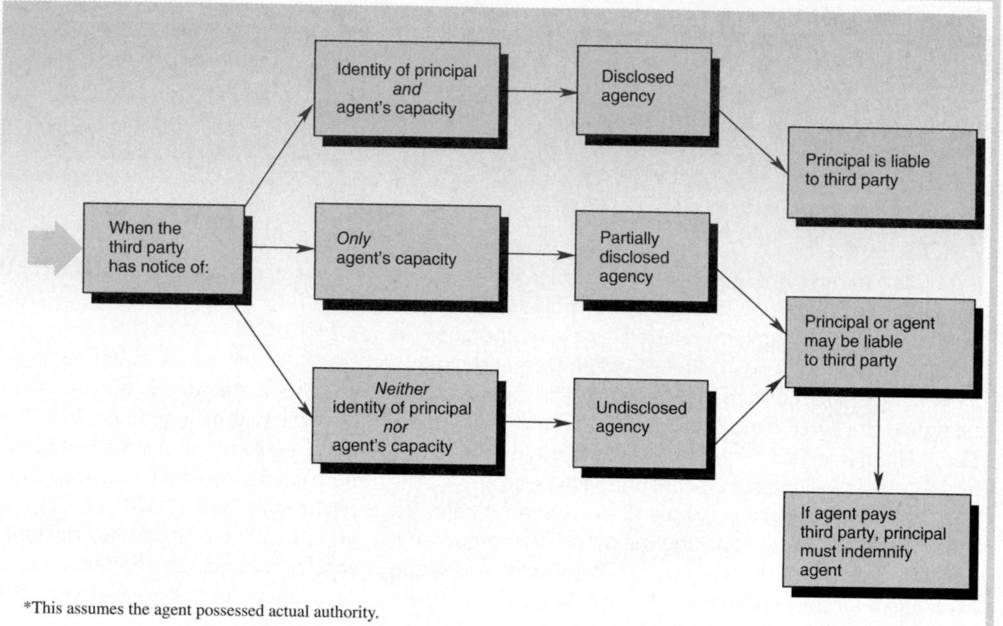

*This assumes the agent possessed actual authority.

Liability for Torts and Crimes

LO4

When an agent commits a tort or crime while working for the principal, the agent is personally liable for the consequences of his actions. This is true even when the agent is acting at the direction of the principal. An agent has no duty to comply with orders that are wrongful because his duty to society is greater than the duty to the principal.

The principal may also be liable for the torts and crimes committed by his agent. Of course, a third person who is injured through the conduct of an agent can get only one recovery. Thus, the injured person is more likely to sue the principal since there is a greater likelihood that the principal will have liability insurance.

Unfortunately, where and when the principal is liable is not always clear. This section discusses the two predominant theories courts have used to impose liability on principals for the injuries caused by their agents: respondeat superior and direct liability.

Respondeat Superior

Principals often are liable for the torts of their agents under the doctrine of ***respondeat superior,*** which means "*let the master answer.*" (A principal's liability under *respondeat superior* often is called *vicarious liability.*) This theory of liability makes the principal responsible without regard to whether the principal was actually at fault. As long as the agent was acting within the scope of the agency when the tort occurred, the principal is liable. Several factors are considered in deciding if the tort occurred within the scope of the agency:

1. Was the act committed within the time and space limits of the agency?
2. Was the action leading to the injury incidental to, or of the same general nature as, the responsibilities the agent is authorized to perform?
3. Was the agent motivated, at least in part, to benefit the principal when the injury occurred?

Roberts v. Danner

501 Fed. Appx. 759 (10th Cir. 2012)

FACTS

Danner was an employee of H-40 Drilling. One afternoon, after completing his shift at the drilling site, Danner drove his personal vehicle to a doctor's appointment for treatment for a spider bite. The bite had occurred outside of work several weeks before. While Danner was driving his vehicle around an obstacle on a private public road leased by H-40 Drilling, he struck and injured Roberts. Roberts sued Danner for negligence and H-40 Drilling under a theory of *respondeat superior.*

ISSUE

Is H-40 liable for the negligence of Danner under *respondeat superior?*

DECISION

No. Generally a master is not liable for the acts of his servant under the doctrine of *respondeat superior* unless the servant is acting within the scope of his employment at the time of the accident. When an employee is going to or coming from work the employee is not considered to be within the scope of employment. Many courts do recognize an exception to the "going and coming rule," where in the course of coming to or going home from work, the employee renders a service for the employer by the employer's consent, either express or implied. However, that did not occur here. Finally, our opinion is not altered by the fact that the accident occurred on a private road leased by Danner's employer. Danner was not rendering any service for H-40 Drilling when the accident occurred; instead, he was on his way home from work, intending to stop on the way for a personal doctor's appointment.

Direct Liability

Under **direct liability** the principal basically is liable because of its own tort. This may be because the principal personally directed conduct that caused the injury. It frequently occurs when the principal is *negligent in the hiring and/or the supervision of the agent.* Principals who fail to conduct thorough background checks or are remiss in supervising their agent's behavior are susceptible to direct liability when their agents commit torts or crimes.

TGM Ashley Lakes v. Jennings

590 S.E.2d 807 (Ga. Ct. App. 2003)

FACTS

Danielle Jennings was found strangled to death in her apartment. Approximately six months earlier, the apartment complex, owned by TGM, had hired Calvin Oliver, a convicted felon and recidivist, as a maintenance worker and gave him full access to all the residents' keys. On the day of the murder, Oliver entered Jennings's apartment while she was at work and killed her when she came home at lunchtime.

(continued)

TGM Ashley Lakes v. Jennings *(concluded)*

Beverly Glover, the leasing manager, had recommended Oliver for employment as a maintenance worker. Although Oliver told Glover that he had been in trouble with the law and had been in jail, Glover did not check into his criminal history or disclose that information to her supervisors. In fact, Oliver had spent most of his adult life in prison or on parole. He had felony convictions for rape, armed robbery, robbery, robbery by force, larceny, credit card theft, and at least three residential burglaries. Oliver was also the subject of an outstanding arrest warrant for a "failure to appear" in a burglary case involving the theft of personal checks. Between the time that TGM hired Oliver and the murder, residents of Ashley Lakes reported 10 or more unforced entries and burglaries of their apartments. Glover admitted knowing about the unforced entries.

ISSUE

Is TGM legally liable for the death of Jennings?

DECISION

Yes. TGM is directly liable under a theory of negligent hiring. TGM never attempted to determine whether Oliver had any prior criminal convictions. Also, contrary to company policy, TGM failed to obtain three letters of reference for character and work experience. Despite having actual knowledge about the criminal activity, management still did not undertake criminal background checks of Oliver or anyone else, and it continued to allow employees unfettered access to keys. Management also failed to alert residents about the criminal activity or the ongoing breaches in security in the apartment complex. With regard to negligent hiring, the manager who recommended Oliver for employment as a maintenance worker knew that Oliver had been in trouble with the law, including time spent in jail. This simple fact raises a duty to have further inquired into Oliver's past criminal record prior to hiring him.

Criminal Liability

When a principal instructs her agent to commit a crime, the agent is under no legal obligation to do so. In fact, an agent who commits a criminal act under instruction from her principal is guilty of that crime. Originally, it was extremely difficult to convict a principal for the crimes committed by her agent. This was because the commission of a crime normally fell outside of the scope of employment unless the agent received specific orders to violate the law. Today, however, revised criminal codes have made it much easier to impose criminal liability on principals. As with the tort cases, the courts look to see if the agent's criminal behavior occurred within the scope of employment.

Questions and Problem Cases

1. John Decina contracted with H.A. Smith Lumber & Hardware to buy materials for Decina Corporation. When John Decina completed the credit application with Smith Lumber, he wrote the type of ownership as "corporation" and listed himself as "president" but wrote the "name of Business/Individual" as "John Decina." He also provided his own builder's license number, not the builder's license number of Decina Corporaton. Further, he provided his personal Social Security number instead of a corporate tax identification number. Indeed, Decina Corporation was not written anywhere on the application. When Decina Corporation failed to pay for the materials, Smith Lumber sued John Decina personally. Is John Decina personally liable on the contract with Smith Lumber? Explain.
2. CSX Transportion is in the business of selling out-of-service railcars and parts. Albert Arillotta, of Interstate Demolition and Environmental Corporation (IDEC), sent an e-mail to Len Whitehead Jr. of CSX expressing interest in buying "rail cars as scrap." Arillotta represented himself to be "from interstate demolition and recovery express." The e-mail address from which Arillotta sent this inquiry was albert@recoveryexpress.com. Recovery Express shares offices with IDEC in Boston. CSX prepared and forwarded sales order forms that confirmed a sale to IDEC. Arrillotta then went to CSX's rail yard, disssembled railcars, and transported them away. After delivery, CSX sent invoices for the

scrap railcars totaling $115,757.36 addressed to IDEC at its Boston office (shared with Recovery). After a check from Arillotta to CSX purporting to pay the invoices bounced, Whitehead called Nancy Marto of Recovery. Because IDEC had gone out of business, CSX sued Recovery for the purchase price of the railcars. Specifically, CSX asserts that Arillotta represented that he was authorized to act on behalf of Recovery Express. CSX based this belief on the e-mail's domain name—recoveryexpress.com—and representations made by Arillotta in the email. CSX argues that at no time prior to delivery of the rail cars did anyone from Recovery inform Whitehead that Arillotta was not authorized to transact busing on behalf of Recovery. In response, Recovery claims that Arillotta never worked for it. Is recovery liable on the contract under a theory of apparent authority?

3. Harry Tighe opened an investment account with an investment firm, Legg Mason Wood Walker, Inc. Tighe's authorization was required for all investments on his account. One month after opening the account, Tighe discovered that L. Reed Huppman, his Legg Mason broker, had made an unauthorized purchase of units in a limited partnership for more than $220,000. When Huppman came to Tighe's home to explain the situation, he convinced Tighe that he should hold onto the limited partnership units because they were not readily marketable. In reality, they probably were marketable. Despite this unauthorized purchase, Tighe did not close out his Legg Mason account and continued to buy securities through Huppman for over two years. During this time, he received over $52,000 in distributions from the limited partnership units, which were deposited in his Legg Mason account. Tighe finally complained to a Legg Mason compliance officer about the deal and, ultimately, he sued the investment firm for damages. Legg Mason argued that it was not liable because, by his subsequent behavior, Tighe ratified the unauthorized purchase. Did Tighe ratify the unauthorized purchase by his agent?

4. *Video Case:* See "In the Cards." Jack runs a card shop. Linda, who knows little or nothing about baseball or baseball cards, agreed to run the shop for Jack while he went out for dinner. Jack told Linda she could sell any card for the price marked on the card. Then, he pointed to a case containing the more expensive cards and said that he might negotiate the price on those cards if customers would wait until he returned. Shortly, after Jack left, Linda sold a small boy an Ernie Banks rookie card for $12. The card bore a price sticker that stated: "1200." The boy apparently was unaware of the card's true value and did not try to negotiate its price. Did Linda have authority to sell the card for $12? Does Jack have any basis for suing her for his losses if the boy is able to keep the card?

5. Lisa M. visited the hospital for an ultrasound examination. After conducting the ordered examination, the technician left the ultrasound room for about 10 minutes to develop the photographic results. On his return, he asked Lisa if she wanted to know the sex of the baby, and she said she did. He told her, falsely, that he would need to scan "much further down," and that it would be uncomfortable. With her cooperation, the technician inserted the ultrasound-generating wand in her vagina. After a while he put down the wand and fondled her with his fingers. While fondling her, the technician explained that he needed to excite her to get a good view of the baby. After discussing the examination with her regular obstetrician, Lisa discovered that the technician's actions were improper. She sued the technician and the hospital. Is the hospital vicariously liable under the theory of *respondeat superior?*

6. Scott Busch invited his ex-girlfriend, Carolyn Freeman (who was 19 at the time), and her friends, Anne Huffman and Ricci Kowalski, to his Simpson College dorm room for a party. Busch's roommate, Gene Hildreth and another friend, John Hatfield, also attended the party. All three women accepted Busch's invitation with the expectation that there

would be alcohol served at the party. When Freeman became visibly intoxicated, Busch carried her to his bedroom to lie down. Eventually the others left to attend a fraternity party, leaving Freeman and Busch alone in Busch's bedroom. At some point later, Busch had a conversation with the on-duty resident assistant (R.A.), Brian Huggins. Busch informed Huggins that Freeman was his visitor; that she had consumed alcohol; and that after consuming it, she had passed out. Huggins told Busch—who knew Busch because both served as Simpson College security officers—to monitor Freeman's condition and, if the condition worsened, to report back to him. Later that evening, Busch and Freeman had sexual intercourse. After this sexual encounter, the others returned from the fraternity party to Busch's dorm room. When Hatfield was getting ready to leave, Busch called him into the bedroom. Busch directed Hatfield's attention to a then-unconscious Freeman. He then permitted Hatfield and Hildreth to fondle her breasts. Freeman sued Busch, Hildreth, and Hatfield for sexual battery. Is the college liable in negligence?

7. *Video Case:* See "Martin Manufacturing." Mr. Martin, the president of Martin Manufacturing, was talking with Arnold, a new traveling salesman, about Arnold's first week on the road. Arnold told Martin he hit one of Martin's customers in the customer's store, causing the customer some physical harm. The blow came after Arnold and the customer got into an argument, during which the customer ordered Arnold out of his store. In striking the customer, Arnold was motivated, at least in part, by a feeling that no Martin employee should have to endure such disrespect. Shortly after this, Martin also learned from Arnold that Arnold had gotten into an accident while driving the company van. The accident came after Arnold negligently ran a stop sign while thinking about the fight. The driver of the other car was seriously injured in the accident. On the assumption that Arnold is an employee, is Martin liable to the customer for any battery Arnold committed? Is Martin liable to the victim in the accident?
8. Carl Brown spoke to an insurance agent about obtaining automobile liability insurance for a Chevrolet Cavalier for which his stepson, who lived with Brown, would be the primary driver. Brown needed to obtain a new insurance policy for the car because the insurance company which had insured the stepson planned to cancel the stepson's insurance due to his poor driving record. (His license had been suspended more than once.) Brown informed the insurance agent that the stepson had accumulated more than one speeding ticket in the previous five years. The agent told Brown that the insurance on the stepson alone would cost more than $1,000 per year. However, in order to save Brown money, the agent filled out an application for insurance which misrepresented that Brown's wife was the only other person in Brown's household over the age of 12 and that no operator of the Cavalier had any moving violations or had had his or her license suspended within the previous five years. The policy contained a provision in which the applicant certified that all statements in the application were true and correct. Brown signed the application without reading it. Kemper Insurance issued Brown an automobile liability policy for the Cavalier based on the false application. It is not disputed that the insurer would not have issued the policy had it known that the stepson was the primary driver of the car. Later, the stepson was involved in an automobile accident that resulted in a fatality. Kemper denied coverage under Brown's automobile liability policy based upon the fraudulent application and sought to rescind the policy. Brown insists that, because he had disclosed all material information to the insurance agent, he cannot be charged with the agent's fraud in obtaining insurance from Kemper and the policy cannot be rescinded. Should the knowledge of the agent be imputed to Kemper?

Chapter 25

Employment Laws

LO

Learning Objectives

After you have studied this chapter, you should be able to:

1. Explain the main health and safety laws and what they cover.
2. Describe the wage and pension laws and tell which are federal and which are state laws.
3. Define an unfair labor practice and give examples from the employer and employee perspective.
4. Explain the coverage of the Equal Pay Act.
5. Tell what groups are protected by Title VII and what the two main theories are under which suit can be brought.
6. Discuss who is covered by the Age Discrimination in Employment Law.
7. Describe what must be shown to bring a claim for discrimination under the American with Disabilities Act.
8. Explain the concept of employment at will and how it interacts with whistleblowing.

Luedtke worked on oil drilling rigs on Alaska's North Slope. His employer required employees to take a drug test during their next week of "R&R" after their names appeared on a list. Luedtke refused to take the test, and he was fired.

- Can employees be forced to take drug tests to keep their jobs?
- Would Luedtke's job protection rights be different if he worked for the government?
- If Luedtke was wrongfully fired, what recourse does he have against his employer?

Introduction

If you operate a business that employs even one person outside your own family, you must comply with a myriad of statutes. These statutes impose duties on employers that supplement and greatly increase the duties imposed by the common law of agency. Many of the statutes require you to keep records and often to make reports to both state and federal agencies. In addition, recent changes in the common law doctrine of employment at will may impose new duties on you as an employer. This chapter will briefly discuss some of the most important of these statutes, as well as recent developments in the common law relating to employment.

Historical Background

There have long been statutes to govern the employment relationship. The objective of the early statutes in both England and the United States was to *control and restrict workers.* For example, the earliest statutes on wages set maximums rather than minimums. A statute of Edward VI in 1549 prohibited joint actions such as strikes or the formation of unions by workers.

The Industrial Revolution changed the nature and conditions of work. As more power machinery was used and the size of mining, manufacturing, and processing activities grew, accidents and industrial disease killed and disabled many workers. Women and children as well as men were drawn off the farms to work in factories. Hours were long—often 14 hours a day, six days a week.

Despite the fact that the workplace had become much more dangerous, both tort and contract law were interpreted in a manner that made it virtually impossible for workers to recover for workplace injuries, or to keep their jobs if they complained. Several states passed statutes whose aim was to protect workers. Many also passed laws setting 10 hours as the maximum workday for women and prohibiting the employment of young children in mining and manufacturing. However, these laws were often declared unconstitutional because they were interpreted as interfering with freedom of contract as guaranteed by the Due Process Clause of the Fourteenth Amendment of the U.S. Constitution.

The 20th century has seen a change in these conditions brought about by state and federal laws. Today, as discussed in Chapter 4, the Constitution is interpreted to put few limits on the power of both state and federal governments to regulate business. The regulation of the employment relationship itself is an important part of such power. These laws recognize the importance of the employment relationship to most individuals, the power that the employer has over the worker, and the abuses of that power that often occurred.

Health and Safety Legislation

LO1

Workers' Compensation

In the 19th century, it was very hard for an employee who was injured on the job to recover damages from the employer. This was true although the common law and some state statutes imposed a duty on the employer to furnish a reasonably safe workplace. It was difficult to prove that the employer had been negligent. Even if negligence could be proved, the common law defenses of *contributory negligence* and *assumption of risk* (discussed in Chapter 7) by the employee usually barred recovery. In addition, the employer could claim the *fellow-servant rule* as a defense. This rule declared that if the injury was the result of negligence by another worker, the employer had no liability.

In the period between 1917 and 1925, most states enacted workers' compensation laws. These put *liability* for injuries occurring within the scope of employment on the employer *without regard to fault.* The laws represent a compromise between the employer's and employee's interests. The employee gives up the right to sue the employer in exchange for the high probability of recovering without the cost of a lawsuit. The employer gives up the right to use the traditional negligence defenses in exchange for limited payments to the employee. Punitive damages and emotional damages such as pain and suffering cannot be recovered.

The statutes require the employer to furnish the employee with medical treatment and a fixed level of income during disability. Scheduled amounts are awarded for death or loss of limb. Generally, they also include some rehabilitation services. Disability income payments tend to be low. Although many statutes specify a rate of two-thirds of wages, they also establish a maximum that, because of inflation, has become quite low. The payments are funded through employer contributions to a state compensation fund, through insurance purchased by employers, or through self-insurance by large employers. Workers' compensation is administered by a state agency.

Not everyone is covered by workers' compensation. Employers with three or fewer employees are frequently exempted. Employees in certain types of employment, such as farming, charitable organizations, and household service, are also often excluded. Anyone not covered can sue the employer in tort. In addition, many states cover only certain occupational diseases. There is no federal law requiring injury compensation that applies to employers generally. Railroads and mining are covered by such federal legislation, however. Because of rather substantial differences in coverage and benefits under various state workers' compensation statutes, mandatory federal standards have often been proposed to Congress.

Employees can recover only for *work-related injuries.* This means that they must **arise out of employment** or be related to the type of employment involved. Thus, a secretary whose husband comes to her office and shoots her during work would not be able to recover under workers' compensation because her injury was not related to her work. The injuries must also happen **in the course of employment.** Generally, injuries occurring on the way to and from the job are not within the course of employment. Disputes as to the employer's liability are initially heard by an administrative board.

OSHA

Workers' compensation laws were designed to compensate for workplace injuries, not primarily to make the workplace safer. Most employers insure their risks under these statutes, and premiums vary according to the safety of the industry and the individual employer. Despite this fact and the efforts to promote safety in the workplace by insurance companies and some employers, many employers tolerated unsafe practices by workers, and workplaces were often hazardous.

The first federal safety statute that applied to all types of businesses was the Occupational Safety and Health Act of 1970. It applies to all businesses that affect interstate commerce, even those with only one employee. It seeks to protect the safety and health of employees through duties imposed on the employer and through enforcement by the Occupational Safety and Health Administration (OSHA).

The act imposes a *general duty* on covered employers to *prevent workplace hazards* that may cause death or serious physical harm. In addition, employers are required to report on-the-job fatalities and injuries that require hospitalization to the secretary of labor within

48 hours. Employers with more than 10 employees are required to keep a log of all work-related deaths, injuries, and illnesses.

The act also delegates to the secretary of labor authority to establish detailed *health and safety standards* that must be complied with by employers. Under this authority, the secretary has set maximum levels of exposure for certain hazardous substances such as asbestos and lead. Another regulation requires that manufacturing workers be informed of hazardous chemicals in the workplace. Regulations also protect workers from retaliation if they refuse to do work that they reasonably believe might cause their death or serious injury and if they reasonably believe no less drastic alternative is available.

The Occupational Safety and Health Administration, a division of the Department of Labor, enforces the act. Its inspectors may enter the workplace at any reasonable time and without advance notice. However, if an employer objects to the inspection, a search warrant must be obtained. Inspectors usually check workplaces after fatalities have occurred, often in response to complaints of workers, and occasionally on just a random basis. Violations of the act may result in citations, fines, and even criminal penalties for willful violations that result in death.

The statute permits states to develop and enforce their own health and safety programs. Such programs must provide protection to employees at least as great as that established by OSHA. Many states have approved programs.

Family and Medical Leave Act

The Family and Medical Leave Act (FMLA), passed in 1993, is designed to provide job security to employees with serious health conditions as well as to provide reasonable leave periods for family-related health issues. Another important goal is to make the workplace more accommodating to women and families.

Employers with 50 or more employees are required to give covered employees up to 12 *unpaid* workweeks of leave per year to deal with the care of themselves, a child, a spouse, or a parent with a serious health condition. Leave is also granted for the birth or adoption of a child. In most instances, the employee's job is protected during the leave, and benefits are continued. In order to be eligible for the leave, an employee must have worked at least 1,250 hours during the previous 12 months. Table 25.1 contains additional details.

In 2008, Congress revised the FMLA with respect to military families. It now allows employees to take up to 12 weeks of leave because of a "qualifying exigency" that arises out of the employee's spouse, son, daughter, parent, or next of kin being on active duty, on the temporary disability retired list, or being notified of an impending call to active duty.

Lewis v. School District #70

523 F.3d 730 (7th Cir. 2008)

FACTS

Lewis worked as a bookkeeper for the School District without a problem until 2004. During that year, both her parents became terminally ill and she tried to care for them at home. Her father died in May, and her mother came home from the hospital a week later. Lewis's boss, the district superintendent, gave her permission to take time off to care for them and to work from home when she could. She missed 72.5 days of work, and other employees had to alter their schedules to cover for her. During a school board meeting to discuss salaries, her boss said the office didn't function smoothly without her being there and suggested a smaller raise for her. It

(continued)

was suggested they start looking for a new bookkeeper, but instead he wrote her a letter saying she should resume her regular schedule at the beginning of the school year. However, she missed 6 of 21 days in September and 7 of 20 in October. At the October board meeting, her boss said there were problems in the office including a late tax payment and a problem with a credit check. Instead of firing her for absenteeism, they gave her intermittent FMLA leave, during which time she could set her own schedule but had to perform all her bookkeeping duties. Despite all the problems, the district never sought part-time help. In November, there were still some problems, and a board member suggested she be fired and expressed disdain for the FMLA. In March, the superintendent recommended she be replaced, and the board approved. She was given a choice to resign with paid insurance to the end of the school year or be permanently demoted to teacher's aide but paid her current salary until the end of the year. The letter said, "It was determined that you miss too much work to meet the essential functions of your present assignment." Lewis sued under the FMLA.

ISSUE

Did the School District violate the FMLA?

DECISION

Yes. Under the FMLA, an employer cannot discriminate against an employee for taking FMLA leave. In order to sue successfully, the plaintiff must only show that discrimination on the basis of her protected conduct was a motivating factor in the district's decision. The most prominent direct evidence of discrimination was the letter with the statement about her missing too much work. Circumstantial evidence showed they were aware of their FMLA obligations but that they decided not to inform her of her rights and put her on FMLA leave, but instead to build a case against her on the ground of incompetence. Additionally, there was evidence the board viewed the FMLA with disdain and they did nothing to help make up for her absence. Not only was she demoted permanently, but the board did not follow its own procedures. There is sufficient evidence to support her suit.

Health Insurance

The President and Congress have recently turned their attention to extending the availability of health insurance to all Americans. A limited step in this direction was Public Law 99-272, shown in Table 25.1, which continues the availability of health care insurance at the employer's group rate to certain terminated employees and their families for up to 36 months. A 2008 law also requires employers and health insurers to put their mental health and substance abuse coverage on par with physical health coverage.

In 2010, Congress passed and the President signed the Affordable Care Act, designed to extend insurance to almost all U.S. residents. However, at the time of this writing, the rules and regulations have not been finalized. Some provisions are in place, though. Young adults up to age 26 can stay on their parents' insurance plans, and people cannot be

TABLE 25.1 Health and Safety Regulation and Compensation

Workers' Compensation (state legislation)			
Compensates employee for work-related injury if injury arises: 1. Out of employment 2. In the course of employment	Compensable injuries include: 1. Accidental injuries 2. Occupational diseases (most) 3. Emotional illness (much) 4. Stress-related injury or illness (much)	Benefits include: 1. Medical expenses 2. Percentage of income 3. Death benefits 4. Rehabilitation 5. Scheduled payment for loss of bodily part	Special issue—in some states employee is allowed to sue for additional compensation if: 1. The employer recklessly or intentionally caused injury, or 2. The employer was acting in another capacity (such as manufacturer of employee-injuring product)

(continued)

TABLE 25.1 Health and Safety Regulation and Compensation *(concluded)*

Occupational Safety and Health Act (federal legislation) (many states have an equivalent act)			
Employer duties: 1. Provide workplace free from hazards likely to cause serious injury or death 2. Comply with agency rules and regulations 3. Keep records and make them available to employees and agency 4. Notify and instruct employees regarding hazardous chemicals in the workplace	Employee rights: 1. Can refuse to work if reasonably fears for safety 2. Can initiate safety complaints with agency	Agency duties: 1. Set health and safety standards 2. Investigate complaints and inspect for compliance 3. Bring enforcement actions and levy fines and penalties	Special issue—cutbacks and lack of enforcement in 1980s led to increases in injuries and criminal prosecutions
Family and Medical Leave Act (federal legislation)			
Protects job and benefits while employee is on unpaid leave for up to 12 weeks	Protections include: 1. Employee's same or similar job upon return 2. Group life insurance 3. Health insurance 4. Disability insurance 5. Vacation 6. Educational benefits 7. Pensions	Protected reasons for leave include: 1. Serious health condition of employee 2. Serious health condition of child, spouse, or parent 3. Birth or adoption of a child 4. Special rules for relatives of those in military	1. *Serious health condition* is any physical or mental illness, injury, or condition that involves a. Inpatient care (e.g., hospital, hospice) b. Continuing treatment of a health care provider 2. Employee can be required to use accumulated vacation, personal, or family leave time as part of 12-week period
Public Law 99-272 (federal legislation)			
Continues health insurance coverage under group rates for terminated employee and/or family	People covered include: 1. Terminated or reduced hours employee (unless terminated for gross misconduct) 2. Divorced or separated spouse of employee 3. Spouse of deceased, terminated, or Medicare-eligible employee 4. Dependent child of deceased, terminated, divorced, separated, or Medicare-eligible employee	Coverage is: 1. Same coverage as that provided employees under group plan 2. At 102 percent of cost 3. Up to 18 months for terminated or reduced hours employee (and spouse/family); up to 36 months for other causes	Coverage ceases when: 1. No group plan available for employees 2. Coverage is obtained under another plan 3. Person becomes eligible for Medicare 4. Person fails to pay premium
Mental Health Parity and Addiction Equity Act (federal legislation)			
Gives equal treatment for mental and physical insurance coverage	Coverage applies to: 1. Group health insurance plans 2. Plans that cover mental health or substance use disorders 3. Employers with 50 or more employees	Benefits for mental and substance use disorders must be treated the same as medical and surgical benefits in terms of cost and access to care	

excluded from coverage because they have a preexisting condition. Many preventative services such as mammograms are covered, and insurers are required to spend most of what they collect in premiums on actual care or quality improvement efforts. Lifetime limits on medical expenses are removed. Implementation of parts of the law have been delayed.

Wages and Pensions

LO2

Fair Labor Standards Act

In 1938, Congress passed the Fair Labor Standards Act (FLSA), which requires covered employers to pay their employees a minimum hourly wage and to pay time and a half for hours worked in excess of 40 in one week. Generally, employers are covered if they are engaged in interstate commerce or if their annual gross sales exceed $500,000 and their business affects interstate commerce. In 2007 Congress increased the minimum wage for the first time in many years. It is now $7.25 per hour.

Certain employees who are usually higher paid are exempt from the FLSA. They include executive, administrative, and professional employees and outside salespeople. To be exempt as an executive, one's primary duty must be to manage a business or a recognized subdivision. Such an employee must be involved in hiring and firing decisions. An administrative employee must have special expertise. Examples would be a credit or personnel manager. For exemption as a professional employee, one must be in a recognized profession or an occupation requiring special intellectual instruction. Examples would be lawyers, engineers, and actuaries (in an insurance company).

Time worked includes the time an employee is "suffered or permitted" to work. Therefore, employers may be liable for pay even when an employee works voluntarily, perhaps to increase his or her knowledge. Under the act, employees must be paid for time "on call." They must also be paid for short rest periods when they cannot use the time effectively for their own purposes. Employers are required to keep records that include the time worked by covered employees. Either the Department of Labor, which administers the act under its Wage and Hour Division, or an aggrieved employee can bring suit for violations. The employer must pay twice any amount wrongfully withheld from the employee.

The FLSA also prohibits *oppressive child labor*. Generally, this means employment of children under the age of 14 and the employment of older children in hazardous jobs.

Glatt v. Fox Searchlight Pictures, Inc.

(S.D.N.Y. 2013)

FACTS

Glatt and other interns sued Fox Searchlight Pictures (Fox) under the FLSA and state laws alleging that it violated the laws by classifying them as unpaid interns instead of paid employees as they worked on five pictures including Black Swan and 500 Days of Summer.

ISSUE

Were the students employees covered by the FLSA?

DECISION

Yes. Generally, the FLSA should be interpreted to have the widest possible impact in the national economy. The question of whether one is an employee is determined by looking at whether the alleged employer: (1) had the power to hire and fire; (2) supervised and controlled the work schedule or conditions of employment; (3) determined the rate and method of payment; and (4) maintained employment

(continued)

records. Also to be considered are whether the alleged employer's premises and equipment were used for the work and the extent to which the person performed a discrete line-job. The power to hire and fire focuses on the power, not whether it exercised it. This Fox had. It also had functional control over the interns. Additionally, it closely supervised the work. For example, it required daily call sheets and wrap reports, and weekly schedule and expense reports.

The plaintiffs do not fall under the trainee exception, which should be narrowly construed. The FLSA was not intended to penalize employers for providing, free of charge, the same kind of instruction as training that would be given in an educational environment. The internship must be for the benefit of the interns, who do not displace regular employees but work under close supervision of existing staff. The employer should derive no immediate advantage from the intern. The interns here received no formal training or acquired any new skills, other than things such as how the coffee machine and copier worked. The company, however, did benefit from their skills. Under the totality of circumstances, the plaintiffs worked as paid employees work, performing low-level tasks not requiring specialized training. They should be deemed paid employees.

State Wage Statutes

States also have minimum wage and overtime statutes. These statutes have become less important as coverage under the FLSA has increased. Some statutes specify how soon wages must be paid to the employee after they are earned. For example, a California statute requires the employer to pay off a discharged employee immediately. It also provides that in most types of employment, employees must be paid every two weeks and within seven days following the last day of the pay period.

Most states also have statutes dealing with the garnishment of wages. **Garnishment** is a court order that makes money or property held by a debtor (the *garnishee*) subject to the claim of a creditor. The statutes usually limit the amount of wages subject to garnishment. For example, Illinois limits attachment to 15 percent of gross wages. It also prohibits the firing of employees because their wages have become subject to garnishment.

Employment Retirement Income Security Act

Almost half the civilian workforce is covered by pension plans. Before the passage of the Employment Retirement Income Security Act (ERISA) in 1974, abuses and injustices under these plans were common. The act is designed to prevent problems such as underfunding, dishonest or careless management of funds, and the loss of benefits by long-service employees who change employers, who are fired, or whose employers go out of business. The act does not require employers to establish pension plans or to meet specific benefit levels. It primarily regulates the management and vesting of established plans. Pension funds **vest** when the employee's legal right to them cannot be taken away.

The act covers both employer and union-sponsored pension plans. Under the act, existing and new plans must comply with certain standards, which are listed in Table 25.2. The act also established the Pension Benefit Guaranty Corporation to provide insurance for plans whose total assets are insufficient to pay promised benefits. This might occur because of termination of the employer's business or certain other causes. The corporation is funded by a small premium for each covered employee, paid by the pension plan. Recently, the premiums were raised because of the bankruptcies of several large employers whose plans were not fully funded.

The language describing the coverage of ERISA is broad. There has been much litigation regarding ERISA's impact on nonpension benefits such as health insurance. Generally, the act has been interpreted to limit employer discretion and state regulation regarding such benefits.

TABLE 25.2 **Wage and Retirement Income Regulation**

Fair Labor Standards Act (FLSA) (federal legislation) (every state has its own wage and hour laws; most regulate garnishment)			
Regulates wages and hours: 1. Establishes minimum wage for covered employees 2. Minimum overtime rate of 1.5% of regular wages 3. Regulates employment of minors	Some covered times: 1. When on call 2. Brief rest periods 3. Required briefings 4. Staying to fill out reports 5. Incidental, integral preparatory activity	Employees not covered: 1. Executives, administrators, and professionals 2. Outside salespeople 3. Many agricultural workers 4. Self-employed and unpaid family workers 5. Members of armed forces	Some employers not covered: 1. Employers with less than $500,000 annual sales affecting interstate commerce 2. Railroads and carriers 3. Some fishery and forestry businesses
Employment Retirement Income Security Act (ERISA) (federal legislation)			
Regulates pension plans voluntarily provided by employer	Participation and vesting rules: 1. Participation in the plan must begin within one year of employment (unless immediate full vesting) 2. Voting rights must follow one of three plans implemented by the 1986 ERISA amendments	Employer must: 1. Manage the fund as a fiduciary and the managers must fulfill fiduciary duties 2. Provide required information about the plan to employees and the secretary of labor 3. Keep records 4. Provide sufficient funding for employees' credited service	The Pension Benefit Guaranty Corporation, created by the act and funded by employer contributions, insures pension fund participants against loss of pension funds.
Unemployment Compensation (state legislation under federal supervision)			
Provides replacement income through experience-based tax on employers	Eligible recipients—unemployed due to lack of suitable employment who: 1. Are making reasonable effort to find suitable employment 2. Were not discharged for misconduct or did not voluntarily quit without good cause	Covered termination examples: 1. Termination due to incompetence generally covered 2. Quit to follow transferred spouse 3. Quit due to harassment	
Social Security (FICA) (mainly financed by the Federal Insurance Contributions Act)			
Provides old-age, survivors', and disability benefits, and Medicare	A flat percentage tax is imposed on all income below a certain base figure; the employer is required to pay a matching amount.		

The Department of Labor and the Internal Revenue Service share in enforcing the act. Violations are subject to criminal and civil penalties. In addition, plan participants and beneficiaries may enforce their rights under the act.

The **Pension Protection Act of 2006** (PPA) was passed to reform the rules for funding defined benefit pension plans. It is designed to get more employees saving for retirement. Among other things, the law provides for automatic enrollment of employees in 401(k) plans, provides for employee contributions from 3 to 6 percent, requires matching contributions of at least 100 percent of the first 1 percent and 50 percent of the next 5 percent, and vesting in a maximum of two years.

Collective Bargaining and Union Activities

The first recorded organized action by workers in America was a strike for a $6-per-week wage by printers in Philadelphia in 1786. Workers in certain trades, including shoemakers, weavers, and tailors, organized unions in the early years of the 19th century to seek higher wages and shorter hours. Employers were able to get some of these workers prosecuted for conspiracy; the courts held that such activities were criminal because they restrained trade.

Although later they were unable to get criminal actions brought against union activity, most employers remained strongly opposed to unions. One device they developed was the "yellow-dog contract," which required a worker taking a job to promise not to join a union. Courts were often quick to enjoin a strike if the employer could show that there might be violence or that other persons' interests would be hurt. In addition, the employment at will doctrine allowed employers to fire pro-union employees, and blacklisting of such employees was common. Finally, periodic economic depressions sapped the growth and power of unions.

In 1932, when union membership and influence had been hurt severely by the Great Depression, Congress passed the Norris-LaGuardia Act to help unions offset some of the advantage held by employers. The act prohibited the federal courts from issuing injunctions against lawful strikes, picketing, and certain other activities, and it prohibited the enforcement of yellow-dog contracts. It did not give workers the right to organize and bargain collectively, though.

LO3

The National Labor Relations Act

The right of workers to organize and bargain collectively was expressly recognized in the National Labor Relations Act (Wagner Act) in 1935. The act also prohibited certain actions by employers that were thought to deter union organizing and bargaining. These were declared to be unfair labor practices. It established the National Labor Relations Board (NLRB) to administer the act. The NLRB's major functions are to conduct elections for employees to decide whether to be represented by a union and to hear charges of unfair labor practices.

An election is held after a petition is filed with the NLRB by a group of employees, a labor union, or an employer. Sometimes more than one union is on the ballot. The board determines what group of employees will be allowed to vote. This becomes the **bargaining unit.** A board of representatives supervises the election. If a union receives a majority of the votes of the employees who vote, the board certifies it as the exclusive bargaining representative for the unit. It then represents all employees in the unit whether or not they voted for or belong to the union.

The Labor–Management Relations Act

Union membership and power grew rapidly as World War II approached. After the war (1947), Congress amended the Wagner Act by the Taft-Hartley Act, presently known as the

TABLE 25.3 Examples of Unfair Labor Practices under the LMRA

Employer	Union
1. Interfering with the right of employees to form or join a labor union or to engage in concerted activities for their mutual aid or protection.	1. Coercing an employee to join a union and coercing an employer in the selection of representatives for collective bargaining.
Employer	**Union**
2. Establishing or dominating a labor union. 3. Discriminating against employees in hiring or any other terms of employment because of their union membership. 4. Discriminating against employees who have filed charges with the NLRB. 5. Refusing to bargain collectively with a union that represents the employees.	2. Coercing an employer to discriminate against an employee who is not a union member, except for failure to pay union dues under a union shop agreement. 3. Refusing to bargain collectively with the employer. 4. Picketing or conducting a secondary boycott or strike (that is, against someone other than the employer with whom the union has a dispute) for an illegal purpose. 5. Setting excessive initiation fees under a union shop agreement. 6. Forcing an employer to pay for work not performed (featherbedding). 7. Picketing to require an employer to recognize or bargain with a union that has not been certified as the bargaining agent.

Labor–Management Relations Act (LMRA). It was passed to limit what was seen to be the excessive power of unions. The coverage of the act is very broad. For NLRB jurisdiction, out-of-state purchases or sales of goods and services need equal only $50,000. However, federal, state, and local government employees, as well as agricultural laborers and household employees, are excluded.

Under the act, certain union and employer practices are declared to be unfair labor practices. Examples of unfair labor practices are listed in Table 25.3. The act also prohibits an employer and union from agreeing that the employer will refrain from dealing in the products of another employer who is considered to be unfair to the union. Such contracts are called *hot-cargo agreements.* Recently, there has been much litigation regarding whether it is an unfair labor practice for an employer to avoid its union contract by closing a plant, moving work to a nonunion site, or declaring bankruptcy. Generally, such actions have been allowed as long as they are not motivated by antiunion animus, and the employer has bargained with (although it does not have to come to agreement with) the union.

Karl Knauz Motors, Inc. and Robert Becker

358 NLRB No. 164 (Nat'l Labor Relations Board 2012)

FACTS

Karl Knauz Motors, a BMW dealer, had a policy in its employee handbook that required courtesy, stating that no one should be disrespectful or use profanity or any other language that injures the image or reputation of the dealership. Becker, a Knauz salesman, was fired after he posted several photos and comments on Facebook regarding incidents that happened at work. One involved an incident when a salesperson allowed the 13-year-old son of a customer to drive a Land Rover. The boy ran over his

(continued)

parent's foot, over a wall, and then into a pond. Becker posted a picture of the Rover in the pond and a caption criticizing the co-worker's actions. Another criticized a sales event. Becker filed a charge with the National Labor Relations Board, claiming he was fired for engaging in protected concerted activity. He alleged his posts were an effort to improve working conditions.

ISSUE

Did Becker engage in protected activity under the NLRA?

DECISION

Partially. The courtesy policy is unlawful because it could chill reasonable employees' right to exercise rights under the act. For example, if they objected to their working conditions and sought support of others in improving them, they might be in danger of violating the policy. It is fine to encourage polite and friendly behavior. But the policy's language is too broad. Becker's embarrassing posts involving the Land Rover were not protected concerted activity because they were posted solely by him without any discussion or connection to any employee's terms or conditions of employment. However, the comments and photo about the marketing campaign were protected concerted activity under the NLRA.

The NLRB processes unfair practice charges brought against unions and employers. If the board finds that the employer or union has committed an unfair labor practice, it orders the offending party to "cease and desist," or it may order affirmative action to remedy the harm caused by the violation. Suppose Jacob was discharged because he was trying to get co-workers to join a union. The employer would be ordered to reinstate him with back pay. An employer who has committed an unfair practice by making threats or promises before an election might be required to mail an NLRB notice to the employees, and a new election might be directed.

The LMRA further provides for an 80-day "cooling-off" period in strikes that the president finds likely to harm national safety or health. During this period, employees must return to work or continue working. A Federal Mediation and Conciliation Service provides skilled people to help unions and employers in their bargaining so as to prevent strikes or lockouts. A *lockout* occurs when the employer discontinues operations during a labor dispute.

The Labor–Management Reporting and Disclosure Act

The Labor–Management Reporting and Disclosure Act (Landrum-Griffin Act) was passed in 1959 as a further check on the unions. Congressional hearings during the 1950s uncovered much corruption and many undemocratic procedures within the unions. The act was designed to promote honesty and democracy in running the union's internal affairs. It requires a union to have a constitution and bylaws, and it sets forth a "bill of rights" for union members. It also requires certain reports to the secretary of labor. These reports must disclose a great deal about the financial situation of the union and its internal procedures.

Union membership, and therefore union power, have dramatically decreased in the past decades. Membership has fallen from a high of 39 percent of the private workforce in 1955 to around 10 percent today. This decline is due to a variety of reasons including loss of traditionally unionized jobs in the manufacturing sector, court recognition of worker rights such as job security outside the union setting, the passage of worker protection legislation by Congress and the states, and union abuse of power and participation in criminal activities.

Discrimination in Employment

LO4

The Equal Pay Act of 1963

The Equal Pay Act, passed as an amendment to the FLSA, prohibits sex discrimination in pay. It requires covered employers to pay employees of both sexes equally for jobs that require equal skill, effort, and responsibility, and that are performed under similar working conditions. The result is to raise the lower pay rate. Different rates of pay are permitted under seniority and merit systems as well as under piecework or other incentive systems. In addition, different rates are allowed for "any factor other than sex." Included within this catchall category would be differences based on factors such as shift differentials or bonuses paid because the job is part of a training program. The act is administered by the Equal Employment Opportunity Commission (EEOC). The employers covered are the same as those covered by the Wage and Hour Act.

Yant v. United States

588 F.3d 1369 (U.S. App. 2009)

FACTS

Yant and other nurse practitioners (NPs) worked for the U.S. Department of Veterans Affairs' (VA) Tennessee Valley Healthcare System. The VA paid the NPs in the Tennessee system, roughly 80 percent of whom were women, less money than it paid physician assistants (PAs), about 60 percent of whom-were men. The VA hires NPs and PAs to fill the same positions, and NPs and PAs have the same job descriptions. Moreover, NPs are required to have a master's degree, unlike PAs, and are licensed through their states. Yant and her co-workers claimed they get less pay and benefits for performing jobs of equal skill, effort, and responsibility under similar working conditions, which they say violates the Equal Pay Act.

ISSUE

Does the pay difference constitute gender discrimination?

DECISION

No. Paying different rates to two very similar jobs can be discriminatory, if the difference in pay was based on gender at some point. For instance, if women are more apt to take day shift jobs than men, it's discriminatory to pay the night shift more to attract available male workers, even if women later join the night shift. However, the nurse practitioners fail to show that the pay differential is either historically or presently based on sex. Through 1991, NPs and PAs were paid on the same national scale. After that, nurse practitioners' pay varied from region to region, while PAs remained on a national scale. The result is that, in some parts of the country, NPs make more than PAs, and male PAs have sued under the Equal Pay Act. The pay differential in this case reflects the effect of two scales, one national and one regional, and not any sex discrimination.

In 2009, Congress passed the Lilly Ledbetter Act, which said that each illegal pay differential payment renewed a cause of action until the discrimination was reasonably discovered. Thus, the action would not be time-barred until that discovery. Also, see the decision in the *Lewis* case on the next page.

LO5

Title VII, the Civil Rights Act of 1964

The major piece of legislation outlawing discrimination in employment is Title VII of the Civil Rights Act of 1964 (as amended in 1972). It prohibits discrimination on the basis of race, color, religion, sex, or national origin. Covered employers cannot use any of these human differences to make distinctions for purposes of hiring, firing, promoting, or fixing pay rates or other terms and conditions of employment including "fringe benefits" such as pensions and medical insurance. The act applies to employers engaged in an industry affecting interstate commerce that have at least 15 employees, to unions, and to employment agencies. It also applies to state and local government positions.

Discrimination is not defined in the act. It has gained meaning through interpretation by the EEOC, the agency that administers the act, and the courts. They have interpreted the act to include not only **intentional discrimination** (e.g., refusing to hire women) but also acts that have **discriminatory impact.** An example would be a neutral rule requiring police officers to be at least 5 feet 7 inches tall and weigh 140 pounds. Even though this rule is applied equally to all, it keeps a larger number of women and certain ethnic minorities from qualifying for the job than it does white males. If it can be shown that these requirements were not necessary to perform the job, the employer is in violation of Title VII when it uses them. Most such height and weight requirements have been struck down under this interpretation, as have many other employment screening devices and tests. Disparate impact is involved in the *Lewis* case.

Lewis v. Chicago

130 S.Ct. 2191 (2010)

FACTS

In 1995, Lewis and other African-Americans took a written test to be Chicago firefighters. Chicago then announced that it would randomly draw candidates for the positions from a list of "well qualified" applicants who scored at least 89 out of 100 points on the test. Those scoring 65 to 88 were deemed "qualified" and were notified they would be on the eligibility list but it was unlikely they would be selected. They repeated this process numerous times. In 1997, several African-Americans who were qualified but not chosen filed suit alleging that Chicago's practice had a disproportionate adverse impact on them in violation of Title VII. The city sought to block the suit, alleging the claimants did not meet the 300-day limitation period after the policy was adopted. After holding that the city's ongoing reliance on the 1995 test constituted a continuing violation, the trial court found that Chicago should hire 132 randomly selected members of the class and award back pay to the remaining class members. The court of appeals found the suit to be untimely and reversed the lower court.

ISSUE

Was there a series of discriminatory acts that would allow the suit to proceed?

DECISION

Yes. Title VII of the Civil Rights Act of 1964 prohibits employers from discriminating on the basis of race (among other factors). As originally enacted, the statute did not prohibit employment practices that had a disparate impact. It did protect against a variety of actions including classifying applicants in a way that would deprive an individual of employment opportunities. In 1971, in *Griggs v. Duke Power Company,* we interpreted that provision to include practices that are fair in form but discriminatory in practice. Plaintiff need not prove intent to discriminate in these types of cases. Congress codified this two decades later in the Civil Rights Act of 1991. Defendant's process is such a practice. If the suit was filed within the 300-day limit, then plaintiffs have a claim. The city argues that the 300 days began to run the first time that the applicants/plaintiffs were not picked and therefore the suit is barred. The original selection process did give rise to a claim, but it does not follow that it stopped there. Congress allows claims to be brought whether or not the employer has used the same process in the past. The subsequent acts were discriminatory.

The act has more recently been interpreted to encompass **sexual harassment** as a form of prohibited discrimination. The first kind of sexual harassment to be prohibited, *quid pro quo* harassment, involves some express or implied connection between the employee's submission to sexually oriented behavior and job benefits. For example, the refusal by Sondra's supervisor to promote her unless she has sexual relations with him would be quid pro quo harassment. The other kind of sexual harassment is a *sexually harassing environment.* If a company institutes and effectively enforces a sexual harassment policy, it may not be liable in a harassing environment case.

Sexual harassment has been recognized in many countries outside the United States. A successful sexual harassment case was litigated in Japan in 1992. Several other countries, including Canada, Australia, the United Kingdom, and France, have sexual harassment laws. As more women enter the workforce worldwide, more litigation in this area can be expected.

Discrimination based on religion, sex, or national origin is permitted where one of these characteristics is a bona fide occupational qualification (BFOQ). A Christian church would not have to consider a Muslim as an applicant for choir director. A health club could limit its employment of attendants in its men's locker room to men. The courts have given a very narrow interpretation to this exception, however. Discrimination based on stereotypes (e.g., that women are less aggressive) or the preferences of co-workers or customers is not permitted. No BFOQ exception is permitted with respect to discrimination based on race or color.

Affirmative action has also been upheld by the courts. The term refers to plans for increasing the proportion of minorities or women in an employer's workforce or in higher-level positions. The aim is to encourage an employer to apply greater effort in finding and promoting qualified minority and female candidates. A typical plan might involve hiring of one minority member for each white worker until a certain percentage of the workforce is composed of minorities. Generally, such plans must be temporary (until the goal is reached), must not unduly restrict the job opportunities of those not included in the plan, and must not involve the hiring or promotion of unqualified workers.

Such plans have resulted in gains in many fields and industries. However, these gains can be eroded when layoffs and reductions in the workforce occur. Since the first to be let go are traditionally those with least seniority, and since women and minorities are a large percentage of those most recently hired under such plans, their number in the workforce is drastically reduced. Bona fide seniority systems are specifically protected under Title VII, however; thus, applying affirmative action to seniority plans is particularly troublesome. In general, the Supreme Court has been more reluctant to allow protective actions in layoffs than it has in hiring.

Ethics in Action

Affirmative action, unless court ordered, is entirely voluntary. Does an employer have an ethical duty to help overcome the effects of societal discrimination by voluntarily implementing a program? What are the ethical implications of giving preference to a person simply because of that person's membership in a racial, ethnic, or gender group?

The EEOC can initiate action in response to complaints of discrimination by applicants or employees, or it can act on its own. It first attempts conciliation of discrimination charges. If attempts at settlement fail, the EEOC or the individual alleging discrimination may bring an action in the federal courts to require steps to correct discrimination that is found to exist. This may involve payment of lost wages and benefits to those discriminated against, "affirmative action" hiring or promotion plans, or other remedial measures such as reinstatement in the job.

A trend among employers is to have employees sign mandatory arbitration agreements as a condition of getting or keeping a job. These agreements keep employees from suing about any workplace dispute, including discrimination claims. The EEOC, which strongly supports ADR (alternative dispute resolution), objects to mandatory binding arbitration as a condition of employment because it denies employees the right to bring independent discrimination claims. The Supreme Court, however, has strongly supported such agreements.

Most states also have fair employment laws and enforcement schemes. In those states, employees must first file charges with the state agency. If no settlement results at this level, then the employee can file with the EEOC.

The Civil Rights Act of 1991

In the late 1980s the Supreme Court decided several cases in a manner that reduced the ability of employees to successfully bring discrimination claims. Congress reacted to the Court's decisions by passing the Civil Rights Act of 1991. The act, in effect, overturned the Court's decisions and restored the law to the way it had been. In addition, the act extended Title VII coverage to U.S. citizens working for U.S. companies overseas and established that an employment decision based partly on discriminatory motives and partially on legitimate reasons is still illegal discrimination. Remedies for people harmed by discrimination were also expanded. The act allows claimants to sue for damages, including punitive damages, in cases of intentional discrimination and provides for jury trials in such cases. The total amount of damages is limited by the size of the employer.

LO6

Age Discrimination in Employment Act

The Age Discrimination in Employment Act (ADEA) prohibits employers of 20 or more people from refusing to hire, paying less to, discharging, or otherwise discriminating against employees because of their age. Employment agencies are also covered by the act, as are labor unions, which are prohibited from excluding from their membership or otherwise discriminating against persons because of age. The protection given is to persons 40 years old and older. A BFOQ exemption is provided. For example, a drama company would be able to limit its casting for a teenager's part to young people. Like the Equal Pay Act and Title VII, the statute is enforced by the EEOC.

Retirement of employees less than 70 years old under a mandatory pension plan was made illegal by the 1978 amendments. There is an exception for executives and others receiving very high pension benefits. Earlier retirement for inability to do the work is permitted. Lawsuits under the ADEA are rising as more people enter the protected age group and reach retirement age.

LO7

Americans with Disabilities Act

The enactment of the Americans with Disabilities Act of 1990 (ADA) extended comprehensive federal coverage against discrimination on the basis of disability. The previous federal law, the Rehabilitation Act of 1973, applied only to employers with federal contracts. Most of the provisions of the ADA are very similar to those of the Rehabilitation Act.

The ADA protects a *qualified individual with a disability* from discrimination on the basis of that disability. A disability is defined as (1) a physical or mental impairment that substantially limits one or more of a person's major life activities, (2) a record of such an impairment, or (3) being regarded as having such an impairment. People with AIDS or AIDS-related conditions are specifically covered; people currently abusing drugs or alcohol are not. Mental disease is covered, but certain sex-related traits such as bisexuality and transvestism are not.

In 2008, Congress amended the ADA with the passage of the Americans with Disability Amendments Act (ADAA). It did so to overturn decisions of the Supreme Court that severely limited the coverage of the ADA. The ADAA makes clear that the ADA should be interpreted in favor of broad coverage. The ADAA specifies that the determination of whether an impairment limits a major life activity must be made without regard to whether people use tools like glasses, hearing aids, prosthetic limbs, or medication to help overcome their condition, unless the employer can show it meets the business necessity test and is job related.

A qualified individual is one who can perform the essential functions of a job with or without *reasonable accommodation* for his or her disability. Reasonable accommodation

Mauerhan v. Wagner Corporation

469 F.3d 1180 10th Cir. 2011)

FACTS

Mauerhan worked as a sales representative for Wagner from 1994 to 2005. In 2004 he voluntarily entered into an outpatient drug rehabilitation program, of which Wagner was aware. In 2005 Wagner asked him to take a drug test, which he admitted he would fail, and he was fired for being in violation of Wagner's drug policy. He then entered a one-month inpatient program, and the day after he completed that, he asked for his job back. He was told he could return but that he would not receive the same pay or accounts as before. He declined this offer, and later sued for discrimination under the ADA.

ISSUE

Was Mauerhan protected under the Americans with Disabilities Act?

DECISION

No. The ADA prevents employers from discriminating against a qualified individual on the basis of disability. The status of being an alcoholic or illegal drug user may merit ADA protection, but an employee is not protected if he or she is currently using. The ADA creates a "safe harbor" for those who are not using and who have either successfully completed a drug rehabilitation program, are participating in such a program, or are erroneously regarded as using drugs. Mauerhan had only been drug free for one month when he reapplied. There is no bright time line for when an individual is no longer "currently" using drugs. Instead, we adopt the rule that an individual is currently using drugs if the drug use was sufficiently recent to justify the employer's belief that usage remained an ongoing problem. Mere participation in a program is not enough. Certainly, the longer a person abstains, the more likely she or he will qualify for ADA protection. The focus should be on whether substance abuse prohibited the employee from performing essential job duties. Factors to be considered include the severity of the employee's addiction and the relapse rate for whatever drugs were used, the level of responsibility entrusted to the employee, and the competency required. When Mauerhan completed the in-patient program, his prognosis was "guarded." An addiction specialist testified that approximately three months was necessary for someone like Mauerhan to reach the threshold of significant improvement. Under these facts, he is not protected under the ADA.

involves a determination of what the employer can do to enable the disabled person to perform the job without undue hardship to the employer. In determining undue hardship the courts consider several factors such as the cost of the accommodation in relation to the size of the employer, the employer's income, how many people would be helped, and whether it would be a one-time expense. Accommodation would include making the facility readily accessible, restructuring jobs, and providing adaptive equipment such as amplification devices and electronic readers.

The ADA is administered by the EEOC. The Civil Rights Act of 1991 allows the disabled who suffer intentional discrimination to sue for damages, including punitive damages. Most states also have statutes protecting disabled persons from discrimination in employment.

Genetic Information Nondiscrimination Act

The Genetic Information Nondiscrimination Act (GINA), enacted in 2008, generally prohibits employers, unions, and employment agencies from collecting genetic information of employees or applicants or from requiring genetic tests. Under the GINA, genetic information includes family medical history. If such information is obtained, the employer, agency, or union cannot discriminate on the basis of that information. It must keep the information private and may only disclose it under very limited circumstances.

Similar to other discrimination laws, the GINA is administered by the EEOC. The procedures, remedies, and enforcement provisions are similar to those under Title VII. Two-thirds of states also have genetic protection laws, and the GINA does not preempt state laws that are more protective.

LO8 Employment at Will

The **employment-at-will** doctrine has been in existence for over 100 years. This doctrine allows employers to fire an employee who was not hired for a specific term (at-will employees) for any reason—good or bad. It is based on the laissez-faire values of the 19th century, for it leaves both the employer and employee with maximum freedom. The employee is free to quit at any time, and the employer can adjust its workforce as it sees fit. It also puts the risks of an uncertain economy on the employee and has led to many abuses. While the employment-at-will doctrine had been eroded in the past 50 years by statutes such as Title VII, the NLRA, and the ADEA, the majority of employees were still unprotected against arbitrary and unfair firing.

Over the past several years, courts have been creating exceptions to the employment-at-will doctrine in an attempt to curb some of these abuses. They have used three different theories to do so: (1) the firing is against public policy, (2) the firing is in violation of implied terms of the employment contract, and (3) the firing violates an implied covenant of good faith and fair dealing. Over 40 states recognize at least one of these exceptions. However, application is far from uniform.

Under the public policy exception, firing someone for exercising a statutorily recognized duty, right, or privilege such as filing a workers' compensation claim, serving jury duty, or refusing to commit perjury for the employer would be a wrongful discharge.

Additionally, employees who report employer wrongdoing to appropriate agencies and personnel are protected under the theory of wrongful discharge in violation of public policy. This activity is called *whistleblowing.* Employees often place themselves at great personal risk to disclose information about improper government or industry actions that are harmful to public health, the environment, the economy, or others. In response, legislators at both the state and federal levels have enacted laws to encourage and protect whistleblowers.

In implied contract cases, the courts find promises of job security and fair dealing made to employees in personnel manuals, handbooks, job interviews, and so on. Such actions as having a disciplinary procedure, a probationary period, or calling a job a career position have been sufficient for the court to infer the contract promises. In the third kind of case, which has been recognized by few courts, the employee argues that the firing is unlawful because it was done in bad faith. Generally, these cases involve terminations made on bases that have nothing to do with job performance but involve improper ulterior motives.

Employee Privacy

In addition to the erosion of employment at will, employee rights are being expanded by a growing recognition of an employee's right to privacy. Congress gave protection to this right through passage of the Employee Polygraph Protection Act, and the courts have done so through drug-testing decisions.

Lie Detector Tests

Increasing liability of employers for employee actions and rising employee theft were two of the reasons that polygraph examination of employees and applicants had risen to over 2 million per year. Because of invasive questions asked before and during such tests, and because the polygraph records answers whether or not the individual responded verbally, the tests can be very invasive of privacy. In addition, most workers had no meaningful way to refuse to take them or control over use of the results. In response to these problems, Congress passed the Employee Polygraph Protection Act in 1988.

The act prohibits private employers from using mechanical lie detector tests to screen applicants. It also prohibits employers from using these tests on employees unless the employer is engaged in an investigation of economic losses due to theft, embezzlement, industrial espionage, or similar causes. Even in this instance, the employer cannot use the test unless it can show that the employee had access to the material under investigation and some reasonable ground to believe the employee was involved. The act allows manufacturers and distributors of controlled substances and security service firms wider use of these tests.

Many states also have laws prohibiting or regulating the use of lie detector tests. Most establish minimum qualifications for those who administer the tests. If the state law is stricter than the federal law, it is not preempted.

Drug Testing

Privacy is at the center of challenges to the employer's right to test for drug use. By their nature such tests invade privacy: The tests can reveal such private facts as whether a person is pregnant, and they can reveal off-duty usage that had no impact on job performance. Most court cases so far have involved public employees or applicants who are protected by a constitutional right to privacy under the Fourth Amendment's search and seizure provisions. Use of drug tests in this context has generally been held to be violative of the right to privacy unless the employer can show a reasonable basis for suspecting that the individual employee was using drugs or that drug use in a particular job could threaten public safety or interest.

Private employees can challenge drug testing under tort theories such as invasion of privacy or infliction of emotional distress (discussed in Chapter 6), or as a wrongful firing under one of the theories eroding employment at will. So far, however, such challenges have met with limited success. For example, in the Luedtke case in the chapter opening, the court found that the employer's firing of Luedtke for refusing to take the drug test was not a breach of the implied covenant of good faith and fair dealing in his employment contract. The court recognized a right to privacy, but in highly dangerous jobs such as Luedtke held, his privacy interests were secondary to the employer's concern that Luedtke not be impaired by off-the-job drug use.

Some states have responded to the lack of protection for private employees by passing laws that extend to these employees protections similar to those constitutionally granted to public employees. They also regulate how a statutorily permitted test must be administered. A few states have taken the opposite approach and have passed laws making it easier for private employers to conduct drug tests. In addition, federal law requires drug testing of certain employees, such as those occupying safety-sensitive or security-related jobs in the transportation industry.

Other Privacy Concerns

Modern technology has given employers a variety of means to monitor employees' reliability and work performance. Congress and state legislatures are considering and enacting legislation regulating an employer's use of phone, computer, or video and other electronic monitoring because of its invasive and overreaching potential. There is also increasing litigation regarding employer searches of areas such as desks, lockers, offices, briefcases, and other things that an employee might reasonably believe are private. In such cases the courts weigh the employer's need to do the search against the intrusiveness on the employee's reasonable expectation of privacy. The *Ontario* case that follows involves the Fourth Amendment right to privacy, as discussed in the previous section.

Ontario v. Quon

177 L. Ed. 2d 216 (U.S. S.Ct. 2010)

FACTS

The city of Ontario provided police officer Quon with an alphanumeric pager that was capable of sending and receiving text messages. The contract with the pager carrier limited the number of characters each pager could send or receive. When Quon and other officers exceeded that limit several months in a row, the police chief sought to determine if the department needed to up the limit by determining whether the texts were mainly business related or personal. After looking at transcripts of Quon's messages, it was discovered that many were not work related, and some were sexually explicit. Quon was disciplined as a result. Quon and people who had exchanged text messages with him sued for invasion of privacy and violation of the Stored Communications Act.

ISSUE

Did the police department violate Quon's Fourth Amendment right to privacy by reviewing his messages?

DECISION

No. The Fourth Amendment guarantees a person's right to privacy, dignity, and security against arbitrary and invasive governmental acts. When an act is challenged under this guarantee, it must be shown to be reasonable under all the circumstances. Even if it is assumed that Quon had a reasonable expectation of privacy, in the messages he was sending and receiving on the city-provided equipment, the city did not necessarily violate the Fourth Amendment when it reviewed the messages. The search was reasonable at its inception and reasonably related to the objectives of the search. Also, it was not excessively intrusive in scope. The city had a justifiable interest in determining whether the character limit was sufficient to meet the city's needs. The scope was reasonable because reviewing the transcripts was an efficient and expedient way to determine this. The written policy of the department stating that e-mail on work computers was subject to search, plus a superior officer's oral warning that pager text messages would be similarly treated, in addition to Quon's status as a police officer should have alerted him that his actions might come under scrutiny. The city's conduct was reasonable under the circumstances.

Personnel and medical records are another area of privacy concern to employees. Congress recently enacted the Health Insurance Portability and Accountability Act (HIPAA) to help maintain the privacy and security of health information. Employers who obtain identifiable information from health plans they administer are regulated regarding what information they share and with whom it can be shared. The Department of Health and Human Services adopted final regulations, and compliance with those regulations is now required. Many states allow both public and private employees access to their personnel files, and some limit third-party access to those files.

Employee privacy is an area of growing concern to both employees and employers. It is likely to continue to be the subject of litigation, legislation, and expansion.

Questions and Problem Cases

1. Explain the duty an employer owes under OSHA.
2. What conditions are covered by the FMLA, and what relationships trigger the protection?
3. Explain the three main exceptions to the employment-at-will doctrine.
4. Who is protected under the Age Discrimination in Employment Act?
5. Mankins, who had worked at the paper for 16 years, was vice president of his union and was assistant chairman or substitute steward on his shift. He complained to his supervisor that a co-worker was spending too much time talking to the supervisor and was neglecting his duties. Months later, the supervisor had a meeting with the pressmen and told them their work the night before was not good and they needed to improve their teamwork. Mankins, who is black, as are most of the pressmen, told the supervisor, who is white, that he did not treat people equally, that he was a racist, and

that the paper was a racist place to work. An hour later he was called to the supervisor's office where he was told his behavior was unacceptable and he would be suspended if it continued. On exiting, he again called the supervisor and paper racist. He was suspended and told to go home. He then called the supervisor a "bastard" and a "redneck son of a bitch." He then was fired for insubordination. He claimed he was engaged in protected activity because he was protecting management's treatment of employees. Should he be protected under the NLRA? Why?

6. General Dynamics and the United Auto Workers entered into a new contract that eliminated full health benefits for retirees under the age of 50. Before that, General Dynamics had to provide full health insurance for all retired employees who had 30 years of seniority. A class of employees aged 40–49 sued, arguing that the ADA prohibited a loss of benefits based solely on age. Are they correct? Explain.
7. Akers, a licensed practical nurse (LPN) who worked for Southwood, a long-term care and rehabilitation facility, was assigned to care for 140 patients by herself. She wrote a letter to the assistant director explaining she could not care for them safely and she refused to violate the patient care laws. She was fired almost immediately. Was Akers's firing a wrongful discharge in violation of public policy? Why?
8. Hoban worked for Texas Tech as a First Responder Coordinator. She was responsible for training and quality assurance for those responding to nonmedical emergencies, establishing medical protocols for and assisting in maintaining medical accreditation of the fire department, and designing and implementing continuing education programs, among other duties. A male colleague held three positions during Hoban's employment: Education Director, Advanced Cardiac Life Support Coordinator, and Basic Life Support Regional Coordinator. These positions involved program coordination, instruction/training, and overseeing course schedules. He received almost $14,000 more in pay than Hoban. Hoban sued for discrimination under the Equal Pay Act. Will she succeed? Why?
9. Faragher worked as an ocean lifeguard in Boca Raton, Florida. She alleged that two of her immediate supervisors subjected her and other female lifeguards to uninvited and offensive touching, lewd remarks, and offensive comments about women. The lifeguards and supervisors were stationed at the city beach and worked out of a small one-story building. There was a clear chain of command, and the lifeguards had no significant contact with higher city officials. The city had a sexual harassment policy, but it failed to disseminate the policy among employees of the lifeguard section, and many of the supervisors and lifeguards were unaware of it. Faragher did not complain to higher management about the two supervisors. Although she spoke of their behavior to a third supervisor, Gordon, she did not regard these as formal complaints to a supervisor but as conversations with a person she held in high esteem. Because he did not feel it was his place to do so, Gordon did not report the complaints to his own supervisor or to any city official. Two months before Faragher resigned, a former female lifeguard complained to the city's personnel director about the supervisors' conduct; following an investigation, they were reprimanded. Faragher sued for sexual harassment after she resigned. Is the city liable for the sexually hostile work environment created by the supervisors? Why or why not?
10. A paralegal worked for a lawyer who was under investigation for alleged misdeeds by the Disciplinary Board of the Supreme Court of Pennsylavania. The paralegal revealed that the lawyer had written and backdated a letter in order to deceive the board into thinking he had communicated with his client earlier, thereby hoping to avoid the disciplinary complaint. The paralegal was fired after the lawyer learned of her revelation. Was the firing a wrongful discharge in violation of public policy?

Part 5

Business Organizations

Chapter

26

Which Form of Business Organization?

Learning Objectives

After you have studied this chapter, you should be able to:

1. Identify the various factors that should be considered when deciding which form of business organization to use.
2. Examine a list of business facts and objectives and explain which form of business organization is best suited for the particular situation.
3. Describe the basic attributes of a limited liability company.
4. Describe the basic attributes of a limited liability partnership.
5. Explain the advantages and disadvantages of doing business as a franchisee.

George, Kim, and Martha have decided to open a Polynesian restaurant that specializes in Oriental food and tropical drinks. George has no personal savings; however, he has a bartender's license as well as seven years of experience as an assistant manager at a large restaurant. Kim recently inherited a large sum of money and is interested in investing some of it in a business opportunity. However, as a full-time medical student, Kim has neither the time nor the desire to operate the business. Martha has personal savings of almost $20,000 and is willing to invest some of it in the restaurant. However, she also wants to set some money aside for her son's future college expenses. She plans on working full-time with George as co-manager of the restaurant. George, Kim, and Martha are now trying to decide which form of business organization they should select for the restaurant.

- Which form of business will be easiest for them to organize?
- Which will provide the greatest protection for Kim's and Martha's uncommitted savings?

(continued)

- Which form will provide the greatest relief from tax liability?
- Which form will be best suited for raising necessary operating capital if Kim's and Martha's contributions should prove inadequate?
- What are the potential risks and advantages of becoming a franchisee in a national restaurant chain?

Consider these issues as you read through this chapter.

Introduction

The legal form of a business can have great bearing on the successful operation and resulting profitability of the business venture. Accordingly, it is important to have a general understanding of the fundamental features of each of the basic types of business organization. This chapter will offer a general examination of

1. Sole proprietorships
2. Partnerships (both general and limited)
3. Corporations (publicly held and close)
4. Limited liability companies
5. Limited liability partnerships
6. Franchising

Sole Proprietorship

A **sole proprietorship** is a business operated by a person as his own personal property. The enterprise is merely an extension of the individual owner. Agents and employees may be hired, but the owner has all the responsibility; all the profits and losses are the owner's. For example, one might conduct a computer service business as an individual proprietorship. It would be very much like buying a house as an investment and renting it out. The person operating the business need not use his or her own name as the name of the business; it may be operated under an assumed or trade name, such as the Data Experts Company. Such a trade name would have to be registered with the proper state or local official, however. Employees of the business are the personal employees of the owner. The salaries and wages paid to employees of the business and other business expenses are deductible in determining taxable income.

Partnerships

General Partnership

A **partnership** is a voluntary association designed to carry on a business for profit. However, no express agreement to create a general partnership is necessary. All that is required is that the parties intend to have the relationship the law defines as a partnership. In a **general partnership,** each partner is an owner and has a right to share in the profits of the business. Unless it is otherwise agreed, a partner is not considered an employee and is not entitled to wages for the services he or she renders to the partnership. As with a sole proprietorship, each partner is personally liable for any losses suffered by the partnership business, even if the losses exceed the individual partner's contributions to the enterprise.

Limited Partnership

The **limited partnership,** a variation of the ordinary or general partnership, was designed to combine the informalities of the partnership with the capital-raising advantages of the corporation. It permits investors (the limited partners) who do not engage in management to share in the profits of the business without becoming personally liable for its debts.

Many states now offer a popular variation to the limited partnership. This organization, called a **limited liability limited partnership** (LLLP), has all of the attributes of a limited partnership except that it offers limited liability to both its limited and general partners. In all other ways, the two organizations are the same. General partnerships, limited partnerships, and LLLPs are discussed more fully in Chapter 27.

Corporations

A **corporation** is treated as an entity separate and distinct from its owners. Incorporating makes it is easier to hold property over long periods of time since corporate existence is not generally threatened by the death, bankruptcy, or retirement of an individual owner. A corporation can acquire, hold, and convey property in its own name. It can also sue and be sued in

Concept Summary: The Basic Forms of Business Organization

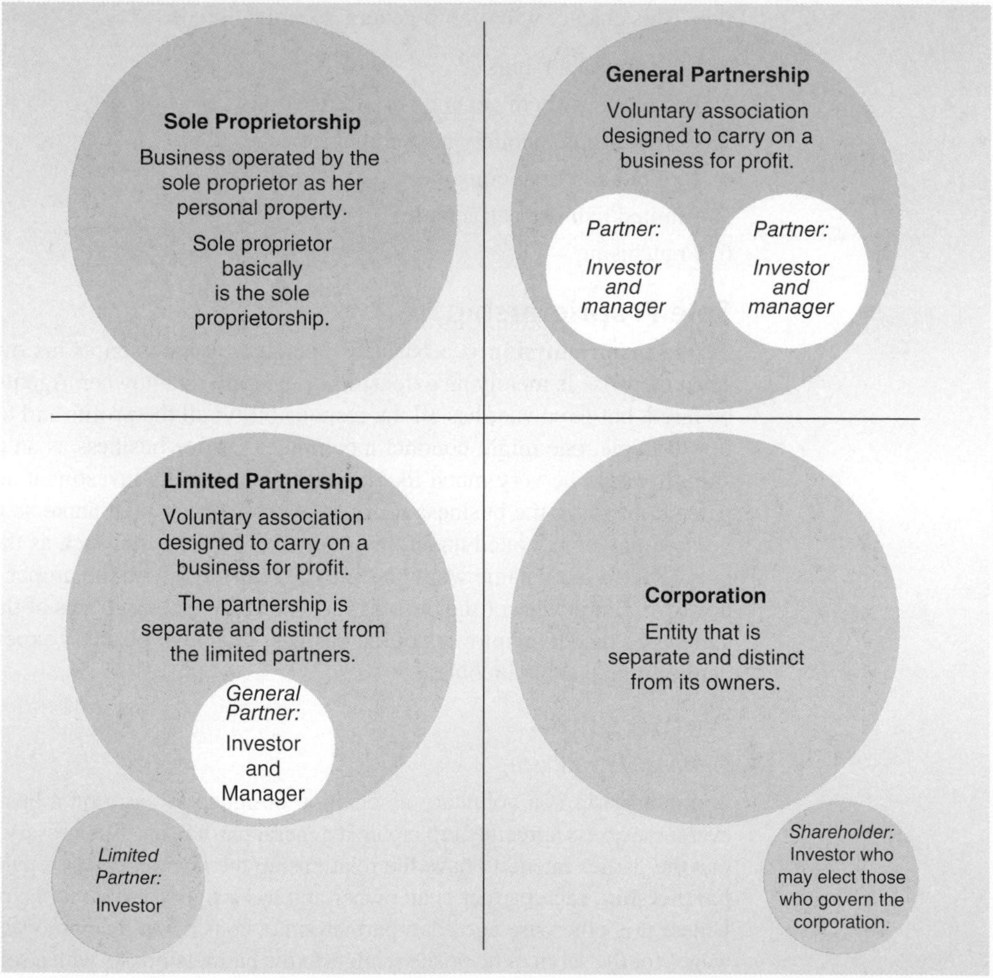
Sole Proprietorship
Business operated by the sole proprietor as her personal property.
Sole proprietor basically is the sole proprietorship.
General Partnership
Voluntary association designed to carry on a business for profit.
Partner: Investor and manager
Partner: Investor and manager
Limited Partnership
Voluntary association designed to carry on a business for profit.
The partnership is separate and distinct from the limited partners.
General Partner: Investor and Manager
Limited Partner: Investor
Corporation
Entity that is separate and distinct from its owners.
Shareholder: Investor who may elect those who govern the corporation.

its own name. The principal reason to incorporate a business today, however, is the limited liability of its shareholders. Ordinarily, the owners (shareholders) of a corporation are not personally liable for its debts; their loss is limited to their investment.

Corporations often are divided into publicly held and close corporations. The stock of the **close corporation** is held by a family or small group of people who know one another.

A **publicly held** corporation sells shares to people who may have little interest in it except as investors.

One's status as a shareholder gives one certain ownership rights in the corporate business, although this does not include an automatic right to be an employee. However, in numerous instances, the employees of a publicly held corporation will become shareholders, and the shareholders in a close corporation will serve as employees.

Factors to Consider in Choosing Forms of Business Organization

LO1

Each type of business structure possesses certain advantages and disadvantages that must be considered in deciding which form of business organization to select. Some of these important attributes are

1. Limited liability
2. Taxation
3. Formalities
4. Financing
5. Management
6. Life of the business
7. Liquidity of investment

Limited Liability

Safety is a prime consideration for most investors, particularly when they are not major participants in the enterprise. Limited partners who do not participate in management and shareholders in a corporation may lose their investment if the business fails. However, they have no further liability to creditors of the business or to victims of torts that are attributable to the business. In contrast, partners in a general partnership not only may lose their investment but also may be required to pay partnership debts from personal assets. Sole proprietors have the same risk of unlimited personal liability.

In many instances, shareholders in a small corporation may be induced to voluntarily waive their limited liability. Credit to such corporations, especially new ones without strong earnings records, may be granted only if the debt is guaranteed by one or more of the shareholders. Lending banks often require shareholders to cosign corporate notes. Suppliers may require shareholders to guarantee accounts. These acts are seldom demanded of limited partners because the general partners are liable. This exception to limited liability seldom occurs outside of the contractual context. For example, a victim of the negligence of an employee in driving the corporation's delivery truck cannot get the wealthiest shareholder to agree to assume liability after an accident. Therefore, from a risk standpoint, a shareholder or limited partner is better off than a general partner.

Concept Summary: Liability Features of the Traditional Forms of Business Organization

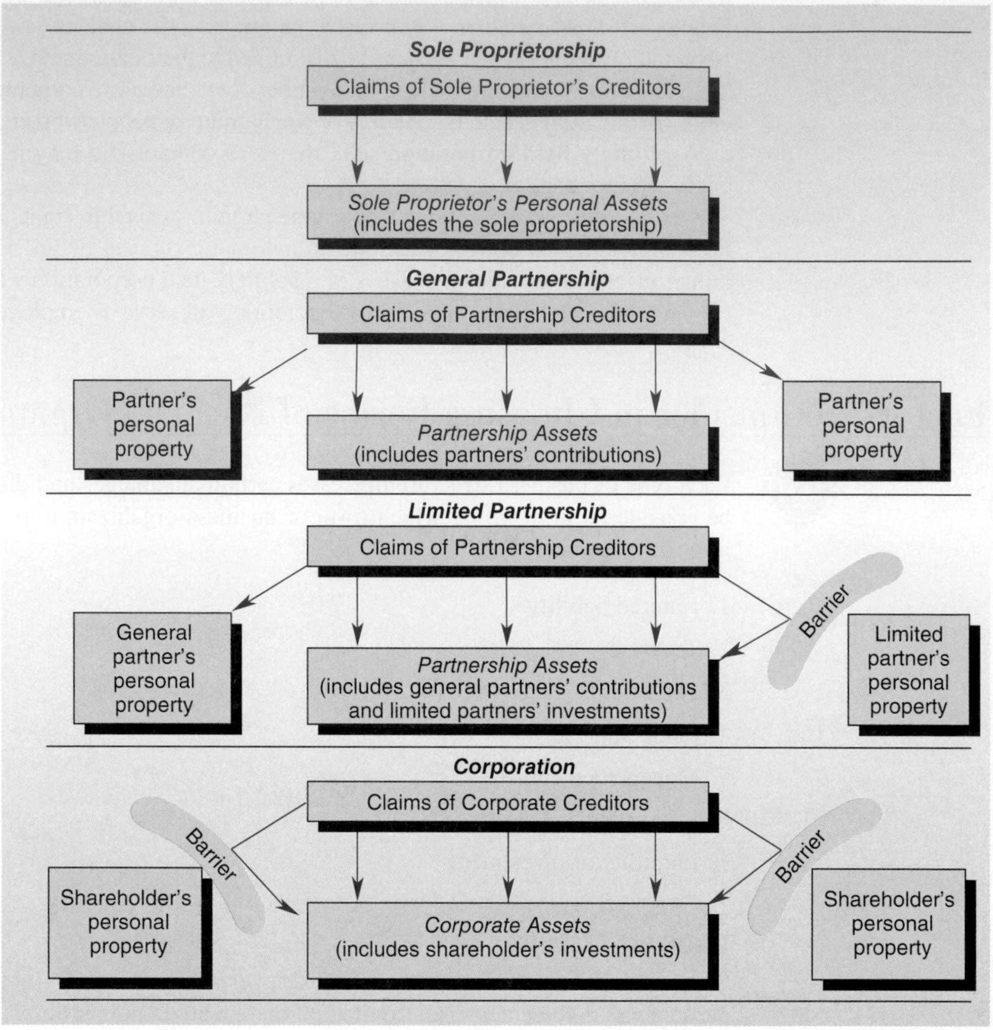

Sometimes courts strip corporate shareholders of their limited liability to prevent unfair results. This concept, known as "piercing the corporate veil," is more thoroughly discussed in Chapter 28. Consider the following case, where the court decides against piercing the veil.

North American Steel Connection v. Watson Metal Products

2013 U.S. App. LEXIS 5311 (3d Cir. 2013)

FACTS

North American Steel Connection (NASCO) formed a joint venture with Watson Metal Products Corporation. The purpose of the joint venture, called Worldwide Construction Projects (WCP), was to market and sell steel products. NASCO discovered that Watson had impermissibly intermingled WCP funds with its own separate corporate funds, and had then used those funds to pay its own corporate

(continued)

North American Steel Connection v. Watson Metal Products *(concluded)*

debts. When Watson was unable to repay the money, NASCO sued Gary Ostermueller, who was Watson's president and majority shareholder. NASCO argued that the court should pierce the corporate veil and hold Ostermueller personally liable for the corporate debt. NASCO argued that Ostermueller and the corporation lacked separate personalities. In support of this claim, it cited a personal loan that Ostermueller obtained to help satisfy Watson's corporate debt. According to NASCO, "Ostermueller's willingness to combine personal and corporate assets is an indication that he saw no difference between the two," and provides evidence that his and Watson's separate identities had "blurred."

ISSUE

Should the court hold Ostermueller personally liable for the corporate debt?

DECISION

No. In order for a court to pierce the corporate veil and hold a shareholder personally liable for a corporation's liabilities, two conditions must be met: first, there must be such unity of interest and ownership that the separate personalities of the corporation and the individual no longer exist and, second, adherence to the fiction of separate corporate existence would sanction a fraud or promote injustice. Even if we were to agree that Ostermueller's personal loan constituted a "blurring" of his and Watson's identities, that fact is insufficient to justify piercing the corporate veil. NASCO has not provided any evidence that Ostermueller dominated Watson to such a degree that the corporation had no will or existence of its own. It does not allege that Watson was using the corporation as an alter ego for his personal operations. In fact, taking out a personal loan for the benefit of the corporation is the opposite of siphoning of funds of the corporation by the dominant stockholder, which is the type of evidence typically used to justify disregarding the corporate form. Because there is no evidence that Watson's corporate form was a sham, we can find no basis for piercing the corporate veil.

Ethics in Action

In the previous case, how can Ostermueller defend not paying the corporate debt? After all, he was the majority shareholder of Watson.

Refer to the case that opened this chapter. There, Kim and Martha both were concerned about minimizing the risk of losing more than their investments in the restaurant business. Kim, not desiring to become actively involved in the operation of the restaurant, may prefer to organize the business as a limited partnership. Martha, on the other hand, wishes to actively manage while simultaneously safeguarding her personal savings. She may favor the corporate form of organization.

Taxation

The wealth-increasing potential of an investment in a business is greatly affected by the income tax laws. These laws change from time to time; however, the basic principles tend to remain constant. Changes in rates of taxation may shift the tax advantage between the partnership and corporate forms in certain circumstances. Since earnings projections for a business are also uncertain, the possibility of tax rate changes seldom affects the final choice of the form of organization.

The basic difference is between taxation as a partnership and taxation as a corporation. A corporation is a taxable entity. It pays income taxes on its own income, and its shareholders generally must pay income taxes on dividends from the corporation although they are paid out of income already taxed to the corporation. On the other hand, a partnership is not treated as a taxable entity. Income (or loss) is passed through pro rata to the partners and taxed to them. Likewise, a sole proprietorship is not a taxable entity.

S Corporations

S corporations, or Subchapter S corporations, represent an important variation that should be considered by certain closely held corporations. They are taxed very much like a partnership in that no corporate tax is paid. Instead, shareholders directly report their share of the corporation's losses or earnings on their individual tax returns. This can provide an important advantage over ordinary corporations. Several requirements (only a few of which will be mentioned here) must be maintained or the Subchapter S corporation loses its tax status:

1. There can be no more than 100 shareholders.
2. The shareholders must all be individuals or estates.
3. Shareholders must consent in writing to having the corporation taxed as a partnership.

Advantages of Corporate Taxation

When the maximum corporate tax rate was less than the maximum individual tax rate, the corporate form was desirable despite the threat of a double tax. If corporate profits were reinvested in expansion of the business rather than paid out in dividends, the corporation could serve as a tax shelter. The shareholder's interest in the retained earnings was not taxed until the stock was sold or the corporation was dissolved. Then the shareholder was taxed at a capital gains rate, which was lower than the ordinary income rate applied to dividends. However, in 1988, for the first time in history, the maximum corporate tax exceeded the maximum individual rate. This strengthened the threat of double taxation and discouraged the use of the corporate form of business.

Still, there are tax strategies that can minimize such disadvantages. When the corporation is involved in a business that has wide swings in income from year to year, it can reduce the tax burden experienced by shareholders by keeping the dividend rate constant. Partners and sole proprietors, on the other hand, will be individually taxed on their share of the income during the year in which it was earned.

The corporation tax burden can be lessened if the shareholders are active in the operation of the business. Shareholder-employees may be paid salaries that, although taxable as income to the shareholders, are deductible expenses for the corporation. Also, fringe benefits, such as pension plans or health insurance, can be provided to shareholder-employees if furnished to other employees. The cost can be deducted by the corporation, and there is no immediate taxation to the employees of the value to them of the plans. In contrast, partners are not treated as employees. Their benefits, as well as their drawings or salary, are viewed as distributions of partnership profits.

A tax advantage of corporations may be realized when the business is sold. A tax-free transaction is possible when the shares of a corporation are exchanged for shares of another corporation. The shareholders of the acquired corporation then become shareholders of the acquiring corporation without being required to pay a capital gains tax at that time. On the other hand, a sale of the business of a sole proprietorship or a partnership is usually a taxable transaction. If the sale is for an amount greater than the net book value of the business, an immediate capital gains tax will be due.

Advantages of Sole Proprietorship and Partnership Taxation

If losses are anticipated in the early years of a business and the owners have other income, the sole proprietorship and partnership forms will save taxes during that period. The owners can reduce their tax liability on their other income by the amount of the partnership losses.

Partnerships and individual proprietorships are not required to pay corporate franchise taxes. Usually, taxes on their operations (other than income taxes) are set at a lower level than those on corporations. Also, they do not need to pay privilege taxes to do intrastate business in another state.

Formalities

An individual proprietorship or a general partnership can be formed without the formalities required of a corporation or a limited partnership; no filing with a government official is necessary. The same is true at termination. Cancellation of the certificate is necessary for limited partnerships and corporations.

Less is also required when proprietorships and partnerships operate in other states. A corporation must be qualified if it wants to do interstate business in any state except the state in which it is incorporated. For example, if a corporation wanted to operate a retail shop in another state, it would have to file its articles of incorporation in the new state, appoint a local representative to accept legal papers for the corporation, and pay annual privilege or franchise taxes as well as pay for the privilege of qualification. None of this is required of an individual proprietorship or a general partnership.

Financing

For larger businesses, the corporate form makes financing easier. The wide variety of equity and debt securities available allows flexibility. Limited liability and the tendency of investors to relate corporate securities to familiar "blue chip" companies make them appear safer. For small corporations, the continuity factor may make it easier for the business to borrow money from a bank. If the principal shareholders put up their stock as collateral, the loan may be more acceptable. This would give the lender a chance to take control of the management or to sell the corporation as a going business rather than be forced to liquidate if the loan becomes uncollectible.

Management

The corporation can be very flexible in management arrangements. Day-to-day operating management can be given to one or more officers, while the board of directors retains general policy control. Shareholders who are not directors have a very limited voice in corporate decision making; however, they seldom risk liability by participating in management.

Limited partners, on the other hand, generally cannot participate in management at all without the danger of losing limited liability. General partners usually are free to take an active role in management, although they can delegate routine management decisions to one or more partners. Nevertheless, all general partners are likely to have apparent authority to bind the partnership. Because partners seldom give up their right to participate in management, business decisions may be delayed by time-consuming consultation, and deadlocks may occur.

The close corporation is no freer of serious problems than a partnership when owners cannot agree on management. Since it is more traditional in the corporate form to assign everyday management to a chief executive officer, conflicts and disputes may arise less often under that form.

Of course, the sole proprietorship provides the greatest ease of management. There, the proprietor is free, within the limits of the law, to unilaterally determine the destiny of the organization.

Ethics in Action

Suppose that you are the majority shareholder in a close corporation. Rather than generously distributing dividends to all of the shareholders, the corporation, under your direction, hires you as a well-paid management consultant. Is this ethical?

Freeze-Outs in Close Corporations

A minority shareholder in a close corporation has little power and, thus, may be "frozen out" (left out of important opportunities) by the majority regarding such issues as a reduction or elimination of dividends as well as a loss of employment. Traditionally, minority shareholders have had an uphill battle fighting such a freeze-out in court. Even if no attempt at freeze-out is made, without power to terminate the corporation (as is readily available in a partnership), the minority shareholder is at best "locked in" to the investment.

McCann v. McCann, Jr.

275 P.3d 824 (Ida. Sup.Ct. 2012)

FACTS

Ron McCann and his brother, Bill, originally each owned 36.7 percent of the shares of a close corporation. The remaining shares belonged first to their father, William and, upon his death, to his wife, Gertrude McCann. (Upon her death, they were transferred to Bill.) Immediately after William's death, Bill's corporate salary increased from $48,000 to $160,000 per year. At the same time, Ron was removed from the board of directors and was no longer permitted to work for the corporation. During this same time, Gertrude was receiving a sizable consultant fee even though she was not doing any consulting. Over a 20-year period, Ron received only three dividend payments amounting to about $25,000 in total. Ron now argues that the majority directors breached their fiduciary duty owed to him as a minority shareholder and were engaging in a freeze-out.

ISSUE

Has Ron sufficiently plead facts to justify a claim for a corporate freeze-out?

DECISION

Yes. Because of the predicament in which minority shareholders in a close corporation are placed by a freeze-out situation, courts have analyzed alleged oppressive conduct by those in control in terms of fiduciary duties owed by the majority shareholders to the minority. Ron's allegations resemble that list of activities commonly found in freeze-out cases: (1) not paying dividends despite sufficient cash flow; (2) not providing corporate employment to Ron; (3) not providing board membership to Ron; (4) authorizing phony transactions to Gertrude to avoid any benefit to Ron; (5) frustrating the intent of the founder of the corporation to provide an actual financial benefit to Ron; and (6) making management decisions that allow all of the cash flow to be obtained solely for the benefit of Bill and Gertrude at the expense of Ron.

Life of the Business

Legally, a corporation is not affected by the death or insolvency of a shareholder. Of course, if the knowledge or skill of the deceased was the principal reason for the corporation's success, the corporation may not remain profitable very long. A great advantage of the corporation in providing continuity is the ease of transferring ownership of the shares. Ownership of a family or other close corporation can be shifted gradually by gift or sale of shares to those who will succeed the present managers. This may minimize the tax consequences at death that would otherwise result from selling the business. Those who will not participate as employees can be given a claim to income through dividends. Two or more classes of stock can be established to separate the major share of ownership from control.

Generally, it is easier to preserve goodwill in a corporation as owners change than it is in a partnership or sole proprietorship. This results from the continuity of the corporation, which may be very important in a business that serves the public.

The business of a partnership may be continued when a partner dies, becomes insolvent, or wishes to retire. Nevertheless, the law treats the partnership as dissolved. Special agreements to keep the business operating must be made in advance of these events, or it may be difficult to attain agreement to form a new partnership. A partner can terminate an ordinary partnership at will. However, termination in violation of the partnership agreement may subject the terminating partner to liability for damages.

The success of an individual proprietorship usually depends on its owner. Therefore, successful continuation of the business by a widow, widower, son, or daughter is less likely than in a partnership.

Liquidity of Investment

The ease of selling one's investment in a publicly held corporation is one of the major advantages of the corporate form. Theoretically, the minority shareholders in a close corporation can also sell their shares. However, unless at least a seat on the board of directors can be obtained through cumulative voting, there may be little that is attractive to a potential buyer. Shareholders of the corporation have little incentive to buy out the minority interest because of the freeze-out potential discussed earlier. Shareholders in close corporations are often restricted in the sale of their stock. This may also make the investment less marketable and therefore less liquid.

General partners can sell their partnership interests but the purchaser does not become a partner unless he or she is accepted unanimously by the other general partners into what is essentially a new partnership. The partner who wants to sell out before the end of the agreed-on term of the partnership is in a weak bargaining position. Unless the partnership agreement changes the generally prevailing rules, such a partner is not entitled to force the partnership business to be liquidated. Nor is the departing partner entitled to share in the goodwill value of the business if the other partners exercise their right to continue it.

Limited partnership interests can be sold without such adverse effects; however, there seldom is a public market, such as a stock exchange, where they can be sold. Publicly offered partnership interests generally are designed to serve as tax shelters for the original purchasers during the early years of ownership and are generally unattractive to investors during their later years.

Making the Choice

LO2

Rarely do all of these factors point toward the choice of one form of business organization. For instance, in the case that opened this chapter, Kim may have favored either the corporate or the limited partnership form in order to shelter her private savings from business debts. However, under the corporate form, she faces the problem of double taxation when dividends are declared. George and Martha could lessen this problem for themselves by steering corporate earnings toward salaries and fringe benefits rather than toward dividend payments. George and Martha also could draw salaries and benefits under the limited partnership form. Kim, on the other hand, could not. And, as a passive investor, she could be taxed immediately on her share of any undistributed partnership earnings. Accordingly, each factor needs to be analyzed separately and then all the advantages and disadvantages need to be weighed together.

It is possible that a single factor such as limited liability will be so important as to outweigh other factors. However, if the business involves little risk or the owners have few other assets, this factor should be given little weight. In our restaurant case, Kim and Martha will want to give great weight to the limited liability factor. A restaurant, particularly one selling alcoholic beverages, would continually be faced with the risk of large personal injury suits.

Likewise, in starting a small business, financing a corporation will be no easier than financing a partnership or an individual proprietorship. If several years of substantial losses are expected and the owners have other income that can be offset by the losses, being taxed as a partnership may be the primary factor. The partnership can be changed to a corporation later, when profits are assured. At that time, pension plans and other employee fringe benefits and reinvestment of profits in the business will probably result in minimizing taxes through the corporate form.

It is wise to consult a public accountant and a lawyer who have had experience with businesses faced with these choices and who are familiar with the latest IRS rules. Certainly this should be done before forming a corporation if the business is beyond minimal size or capitalization. There are likely to be adverse tax consequences from liquidating a corporation or selling its assets to another form of business.

Limited Liability Companies

LO3

All 50 states have statutes that permit businesses to operate **limited liability companies** (LLCs). These statutes grant LLCs the taxation benefits of partnerships and the limited liability advantages of corporations. Unlike limited partnerships, all of the investors are able to share in management and, unlike S corporations, there are no restrictions on the number of members an LLC can have.

Creation

LLCs are similar to corporations and limited partnerships in that they require the filing of articles of organization with the secretary of state. The name of an LLC must include the words "limited liability company" or some other clear indication of its limited liability feature so the public is made aware of this fact. Some states require LLCs to file annual reports with the secretary of state.

Legal Status

Like a corporation, an LLC is a separate entity with a legal existence apart from its individual owners. It may sue or be sued in its own name and it can buy, hold, or sell property. Similarly, it may enter into contracts and incur liabilities in its own name.

Because of the LLC's separate legal identity, it generally is liable for its own obligations. In short, the members have limited liability. This means they risk no more than their investment in the LLC. However, as with corporations, courts will pierce the veil between the LLC and its members if an LLC is created with the intent to defraud its creditors. In those instances, the members will be personally liable on LLC debts.

Operation

Like corporations, LLCs are separate and distinct from their members. Thus, one member generally has no personal liability for the wrongful acts of other members. Many states permit professionals (doctors, lawyers, accountants, etc.) to organize as an LLC. This is an appealing option since one member is not personally liable for the malpractice of other members. However, professionals in a professional LLC do have unlimited liability for their own malpractice.

Individuals, partnerships, corporations, and even other LLCs can become LLC members. All that is required is that the member make the agreed-upon capital contributions. Members then share in the management of the entity in proportion to their capital contributions. Often they will appoint managers to carry out the actual operation of the business.

Because the members of an LLC often share management power, they frequently have considerable implied and apparent authority to bind the LLC to transactions in the ordinary course of business. If they have management authority, they also are fiduciaries of the LLC. As such, they must manage the business in the best interest of the LLC.

Katris v. Carroll

842 N.E.2d 221 (Ill. App. Ct. 2005)

FACTS

Doherty wrote a software program called "Viper" for Szlendak. Subsequently, Katris and Hamburg, both Ernst & Company employees, expressed interest in Viper. They joined Szlendak and Doherty in forming an LLC, Viper Execution Systems, to exploit the capabilities of the software. Each member held a 25 percent interest, and as a condition of the operating agreement, Szlendak and Doherty assigned their rights, interest, and title to Viper to the LLC. The operating agreement provided that the "business and affairs of the LLC shall be managed by its managers" and that the members agreed to elect Katris and Hamburg as the "sole managers" of the LLC. Ernst later hired Doherty to help the company adapt a software program ultimately called Worldwide Options Web (WWOW). Katris then complained that WWOW was functionally similar to Viper. He sued Doherty for breach of his fiduciary duties to Katris and to the LLC, asserting that Doherty usurped a corporate opportunity of the LLC by working in secret to develop competing software for Ernst.

ISSUE

Is Doherty liable for breach of his fiduciary duties to Katris and the LLC?

DECISION

No. Nonmanaging members of an LLC owe no duties to the company or to the other members solely by reason of being a member. Doherty would only owe fiduciary duties if he exercised some or all of the authority of a manager. The undisputed facts of this case show that Doherty was a member of a manager-managed LLC and exercised no managerial authority pursuant to the LLC's operating agreement. Accordingly, Doherty owed no fiduciary duties to Katris or the LLC.

Transferability

State statutes generally permit LLCs to restrict their members' ability to transfer their interests in the LLC. Transferees usually have no right to become a member and share in the management of the LLC unless the other members consent. A transferee who does not become a member is entitled only to the transferring member's share of the profits.

When a member withdraws from the LLC, she is entitled to receive either the value of her interest or a return of her capital investment. However, a distribution of assets to a departing member will occur only if the LLC's assets would exceed its liabilities after the distribution.

Dissolution

States frequently require limited liability companies to have a stated duration (generally no more than 30 years). Further, the LLC must be set up so that it can be easily dissolved. Otherwise it will not qualify for the single tax treatment available to partnerships under the federal tax laws. Thus, dissolution generally is caused by the death, retirement, bankruptcy, or dissolution of any member. However, the mere act of dissolution does not necessarily terminate the LLC's business. The remaining members may avoid liquidation by unanimously agreeing to continue the business operations.

In re Garrison-Ashburn, LC

253 B.R. 700 (Bankr. Ct. E.D. Va. 2000)

FACTS

Garrison-Woods, LC, is a Virginia limited liability company. Cralle Z. Comer and Stephen H. Chapman are the principals of the company; each owns a 50 percent membership interest. Comer was the LLC's operating manager and Chapman was the assistant operating manager. After Chapman filed a voluntary petition in bankruptcy, Comer attempted to sell a parcel of land owed by Garrison-Woods. Chapman claims that Garrison-Woods cannot sell its parcel without his consent. In particular, he argues that the Operating Agreement requires all deeds and sales contracts be executed by two officers of the company—the operating manager and the assistant operating manager. Since he refuses to sign the contract or the deed, Chapman argues the sale cannot be consummated.

ISSUE

Does Comer have authority to sell the property without Chapman's consent?

DECISION

Yes. Chapman fails to consider the effect of the filing of his voluntary petition in bankruptcy on his rights in the limited liability company. State law provides that a member is "dissociated" from a limited liability company upon the occurrence of certain events, one of which is filing a petition in bankruptcy. The effect on a member of becoming dissociated from a limited liability company is to divest the member of all rights to participate in the management or operation of the company. The only rights remaining are the dissociated member's rights to share in profits and losses. Thus, when Chapman filed his voluntary petition, he ceased to be a member and had no further voice or vote in the management of Garrison-Woods. Comer, as the sole remaining member, has the unilateral power to remove Chapman as assistant operating manager at any time and elect a new assistant operating manager. Comer could elect himself the new assistant operating manager. The operating agreement provides that any two or more offices may be held by the same person. Accordingly, Chapman cannot prevent Garrison-Woods from executing the sales contract for the parcel of land.

Limited Liability Partnerships

LO4

Facing growing numbers of costly lawsuits, the major accounting firms sought a new kind of business structure to shield partners' personal assets from malpractice claims. The states responded by permitting the formation of **limited liability partnerships** (LLPs). In recent years, many law firms have begun joining the accounting profession in making the switch from general partnerships and professional corporations to limited liability partnerships.

Creating an LLP

LLPs are relatively easy to organize around an existing partnership. The partners need merely file an LLP form with the state and then maintain an adequate amount of professional liability insurance. After this is done, the personal assets of partners not involved in wrongdoing by other members of the firm will be sheltered from malpractice claims against the firm. Partners who are directly involved in the litigation (those who actually committed the malpractice) still have unlimited personal liability.

Managing the LLP

As with general partnerships, all of the partners in an LLP have equal say in its management. Of course, this can be altered by agreement. New partners cannot join the LLP without the unanimous consent of the current partners. Thus, anyone who buys the interest of an LLP partner is not a partner unless the other partners unanimously agree.

LLP Taxation

LLPs are taxed as general partnerships. The LLP pays no income taxes. Instead, each partner reports her share of the LLP's profits and losses on her personal tax return.

Franchising

The Nature of Franchising

LO5

Franchising has become one of the most common ways of conducting business in the United States. Automobiles, gasoline, and certain home appliances like refrigerators and washing machines have long been sold through franchise arrangements. The great growth of franchising, however, has come in the last quarter century. It has become the most common arrangement in providing certain services. This is particularly true in the fast-food industry (e.g., McDonald's Corporation) and motels (Holiday Inns), but franchises are also used in many other fields. A few examples include Century 21 real estate brokerage firms, Culligan water softeners, H&R Block, Inc., tax-preparing services, and Muzak sound systems.

The franchising relationship is contractual. The franchisor has developed a product or service or a particular pattern of marketing it, and the franchisee becomes an outlet in what appears to be a regional or national (or even international) chain. The franchisor may conduct its business as a sole proprietorship, partnership, or corporation and so may the franchisee. Typically, the franchisor is a corporation, and often the franchisee forms a corporation to own and operate the franchised business.

Advantages of Franchising

Franchising may combine the advantages of a small business managed by its owner with the resources, especially marketing impact, available only to large firms. The franchisee may be interested mainly in securing the privilege of selling a highly advertised product. Usually, one of the most important advantages of a franchise to the franchisee is the right to use a trademark owned by the franchisor that is well known and/or highly advertised. In addition, many franchisors have developed a standardized and tested method of conducting the business, whether it is producing hamburgers, operating an employment service, or replacing automobile mufflers.

From the franchisee's standpoint, especially if he or she has had little or no experience in the business being franchised, the most important services of the franchisor are likely to be advertising, training in the business, and advice after the business is under way. Some franchisors also assist with financing. They may build and equip the place of business and lease it to the franchisee—a so-called **turnkey operation.**

Concept Summary: Factors to Consider in Selecting the Form of Business Organization

	Sole Proprietorship	General Partnership	Limited Liability Partnership	Limited Partnership	Limited Liability Limited Partnership	S Corporation	Corporation	Limited Liability Company
Liability	Unlimited	Unlimited	Unlimited for general obligations; limited for other partners' malpractice	Unlimited for general partners; limited for limited partners	Limited for all partners (both general and limited)	Limited	Limited	Limited
Taxation	Single tax	Single tax	Single tax	Single tax	Single tax	Single tax	Double tax	Single tax
Formalities	None	None	Comply with statute	Comply with statute; requires at least one limited and one general partner	Comply with statute; requires at least one limited and one general partner	Create corporation with no more than 75 shareholders; make an election with the IRS	Comply with statute	Comply with statute
Financing	Poor	Poor	Poor to average	Average to strong	Average to strong	Poor to average	Strong	Average to strong
Management	Right to manage	Right to manage	Right to manage	General partners may manage; limited partners may *not* manage	General partners may manage; limited partners may *not* manage	Shareholders may *not* manage unless elected to board	Shareholders may *not* manage unless elected to board	Right to manage
Life of Business	Ends on death or termination by sole proprietor	Dissolves on death or retirement of partner (business *may* continue)	Dissolves on death or retirement of partner (business *may* continue)	Dissolves on death or retirement of general partner (business *may* continue)	Dissolves on death or retirement of general partner (business *may* continue)	Perpetual	Perpetual	Fixed term. Dissolves on death or retirement of member (business *may* continue)
Liquidity of Investment	Poor to average	Poor	Poor	Poor to average	Poor to average	Average (transfer may be restricted)	High	Poor to average

One of the major advantages of franchising for the franchisor is the possibility of rapid expansion by using the financial resources of the franchisees. Through franchising, the franchisor can gain considerable control over the distribution of its products or services without owning the retail outlets. By carefully controlling the number and location of outlets, the franchisor can reduce competition among them and perhaps encourage them not to carry competitive products. This may make the franchise organization's competition against similar products (or services) more effective by encouraging bigger investments and more aggressive marketing by franchisees. Efforts may also be made to influence prices charged by the franchisee. Where the franchisee prepares a product such as food, or offers a service, the franchisor usually maintains a high degree of control over operations to standardize quality.

Franchisee Complaints

Although many franchisees have been very successful, some have quickly lost their life savings. Of course, there are risks in any business; not all of McDonald's franchises have been profitable. However, some franchisors have grossly misrepresented the opportunities for success of their franchisees and the assistance that the franchisor will actually provide.

Most franchise contracts are typical "contracts of adhesion" (see Chapter 14). Some contain terms that may bring hardship to franchisees that are acting in good faith and performing reasonably well under the contract. Termination clauses frequently give broad discretion to the franchisor. The term of the contract may be short—only a year for the typical service station contract—with no assurance of the right to renew or to transfer a going business to another person. Some contracts even prohibit franchisees from joining franchisee associations.

Boulanger v. Dunkin' Donuts

815 N.E.2d 572 (Mass. Sup. Jud. Ct. 2004)

FACTS

After working as an employee for a Dunkin' Donuts franchise for over 25 years, Craig Boulanger purchased his own Dunkin' Donuts franchise. The franchise agreement contained a covenant not to compete that restricted Boulanger from owning or working for a competing business within five miles of any Dunkin' Donuts establishment for two years after the expiration or termination of the agreement. Shortly after Boulanger sold his Dunkin' Donuts franchise, he contacted the corporate offices of Honey Dew Donuts and had an opportunity either to be an employee of Honey Dew or to own a franchise. However, Dunkin' Donuts refused Boulanger's request to waive the covenant not to compete.

ISSUE

Is the covenant not to compete enforceable?

DECISION

Yes. Boulanger, as a franchisee, was an independent contractor. Dunkin' Donuts maintained an advisory relationship with him. Boulanger had to pay to obtain his franchise. Moreover, he entered into his agreement and its attending covenants with his eyes wide open. He was represented by counsel. In addition to the obvious right to use Dunkin' Donuts' confidential information and trademarks and to receive profits from his franchise, Boulanger received other consideration. For example, he received long-term contracts of association with Dunkin' Donuts and protection from competition from former Dunkin' Donuts franchisees under the terms of the very covenant not to compete he now challenges. He voluntarily terminated the franchise agreements, profiting by $72,000. We conclude that the franchise agreement's covenant not to compete is reasonable.

Ethics in Action

Suppose that a franchisor now can make more money by owning its own retail outlets than by marketing its product through independent franchisees. However, language in its franchise agreements prohibits it from unilaterally terminating the franchisees. Could it ethically open franchisor-owned outlets in the territories presently served by the independently owned franchisees and sell to the public at prices lower than the wholesale prices available to the franchisees?

Franchisor Problems

In an attempt to control distribution to maximize its profits and perhaps those of its franchisees, the franchisor runs the risk of violating federal and state antitrust laws. Attempts to require franchisees to buy products, equipment, and supplies exclusively from the franchisor may violate the prohibition in the Clayton Act against tie-in sales. Attempts to require adherence to prices set by the franchisor and prohibitions against sales to customers outside an assigned sales territory may violate the Sherman Act. (These risks can be better understood after studying Chapter 45.)

Franchise contracts usually declare that the franchisee is an independent contractor and is not an agent or employee of the franchisor. However, in an effort to maintain the quality of the product or service offered by the franchisee, and thus the value of its trademark, the franchisor often exerts considerable control over many aspects of the franchisee's operations. This control has been sufficient in many cases to cause courts to hold that the franchisee is not an independent contractor. Thus, the franchisor becomes liable for torts committed by the franchisee's employees, as discussed in Chapter 24. Although insurance can cover this risk in most cases, lawsuits against the franchisor can be damaging to reputation as well as time-consuming for the franchisor's executives.

Government Regulation

Many inexperienced people have been ruined financially by believing extravagant claims of the wealth-building potential of franchises. Others have suffered unfair terminations, causing them large losses. As a result, both the federal and state governments now generally regulate the franchise relationship.

Federal Legislation

At the federal level, legislation has been passed specifically to protect automobile and service station franchisees. These laws aim to protect dealers from coercive practices, including abrupt terminations and unfair competition by their franchisors. The Federal Trade Commission has issued rules designed to give prospective franchisees more information. These rules require franchisors to explain the termination, cancellation, and renewal provisions of the franchise contract. Franchisors must disclose the number of franchisees terminated in the past year and the reasons for termination. All restrictions on franchisees must be included in the agreement. Finally, all representations made to prospective franchisees must have a "reasonable basis." Violations are subject to a \$10,000-per-day civil penalty, and the FTC can sue on behalf of injured franchisees.

State Legislation

Numerous states have enacted comprehensive laws governing the franchisee–franchisor business relationship. Several others have implemented legislation with general application to these business arrangements. These vary widely in their provisions. Often, they prohibit certain contract provisions and franchisor practices thought to be unfair to franchisees. Usually, they seek to prevent deceptive advertising of franchise opportunities and to limit the franchisor's power to terminate franchises. Others govern how close to an existing franchisee a new outlet can be.

Currently, automobile manufacturers, led by Tesla Motors, are challenging state franchising laws that prohibit automobile dealers from selling directly to consumers. (Chinese automakers also are considering direct sales to consumers.) In particular, the dealer associations are fighting against online sales. Some states require manufacturers to use only independent dealerships while others prohibit company-owned dealerships if the manufacturers also have independent franchises. Dealer groups, most of whom have strong alliances with state legislatures, strongly oppose these measures on the grounds that they threaten consumer welfare. See "Tesla Clashes with Car Dealers," *The Wall Street Journal*, June 18, 2013, p. B1.

Franchising in Foreign Countries

During the past 20 years, more than 400 U.S. franchisors have opened over 31,000 outlets around the world. While most of this expansion has occurred across the border into Canada, many opportunities also are being found in Western Europe and East Asia. During the next several years, we should expect to see a flurry of American franchising efforts in Mexico.

Differences in language, culture, business practices, and laws from one country to the next will raise new problems for franchisors in establishing and operating these overseas networks. More than ever franchisors will need to carefully investigate the target market, looking for signs of political and economic instability. They must be familiar with each legal system since many countries impose stringent limitations on franchise agreements in order to protect local franchisees.

Questions and Problem Cases

1. LaMontagne Builders, Inc. (LBI) entered into a construction agreement with the Bowman Green Development Corporation (BGDC). R. Scott Brooks was an officer of BGDC. Brooks, acting on behalf of BGDC, applied for a bank loan to develop the subdivision that was encompassed by the construction agreement. In his application, Brooks submitted a package of written materials including financial statements and a description of the project. The description of the project stated that the infrastructure had already been built. In reality, at the time of the loan application, no money had been paid for the construction of the infrastructure, and there was no mention in any of the materials submitted by Brooks to the bank of any money owed to LBI. The financial statement represented over $1 million in assets and a total liability of $687,000 in the form of a note payable to Great Oaks Family Holdings, LP (Great Oaks), an entity controlled by Brooks and his father. LBI billed Brooks for $315,459, which represented the entire contract price for the roadwork. A dispute arose between LBI and Brooks regarding the payment of the bill, and as a result, LBI halted work on the site. When LBI continued to demand payment from Brooks, Brooks stated that he was seeking financing for the project that would enable him to pay LBI. Brooks agreed to pay LBI's bill out of the proceeds of the loan. The bank, however, was never made aware of this agreement. Rather, the loan officer at the bank believed that all work performed by LBI on the site had been paid for by Great Oaks because of

the representations made by Brooks both prior to and at the closing on the loan. The subdivision property was then transferred to BGDC, which then completed the loan transaction with the bank. The purpose of the transfer was to allow BGDC to borrow the $840,000 from the bank. The proceeds of the loan to BGDC were to be used to repay Brooks and his father for money they claimed to have put into the development of the subdivision project as investors. In connection with the loan, Brooks, on behalf of BGDC, executed a promissory note to the bank and granted the bank a mortgage on the subdivision. At the closing, Brooks again represented that all improvements were paid for by executing mechanic's lien affidavits. Brooks also signed, on behalf of BGDC and Great Oaks, the financial statements originally submitted to the bank, which did not indicate that there was any debt to LBI. Brooks added the notation, "I represent no material change." After the closing, Brooks failed to honor his agreement and did not pay LBI. Instead, all of the loan proceeds went to Brooks individually or to his father or members of the Brooks family, either directly or through Great Oaks. Brooks made subsequent promises to pay LBI if certain work was performed; LBI performed the work, but still was not paid. LBI ultimately sued Brooks personally for the amount owed it under the construction agreement. Brooks defended on the basis that he had no personal liability because it was a corporate debt incurred by BGDC. Should the court hold Brooks personally liable for the corporate debt? Explain.

2. Raymond Brooks owned a 19 percent interest in H&B, a closely held corporation. Leroy Hill, Raymond's brother-in-law, owned the remaining interest. In 1993, Leroy persuaded Raymond to sell his shares in the corporation for $1.2 million ($62,987 per share). One year later, Raymond died and his widow, Dorothy, was appointed executrix of his estate. She filed a lawsuit against Leroy (her brother), asserting that he had breached his fiduciary duties as an officer and majority shareholder of H & B by using the assets of the corporation to benefit his own personal interests. This included having corporate employees perform personal services for himself and borrowing the corporate airplane for purposes unrelated to the business. Dorothy alleged that Leroy did these things as part of a scheme to devalue the corporation's stock so he could purchase it from Raymond at a deflated price. She claimed that Leroy knew that the value of the stock was far in excess of $62,987 per share and that he misrepresented its actual value to Raymond when he made the offer to buy Raymond's holdings. Specifically, Dorothy filed a complaint against Leroy for minority shareholder "oppression." Is Leroy liable for minority shareholder oppression? Explain.
3. Greater Kansas City Roofing (GKC) had been operated as a sole proprietorship owned by Judy Clarke and managed by her husband, Charlie Clarke. Because of numerous violations of the labor laws, the National Labor Relations Board (NLRB) ordered the business to pay a total of $133,742.47. Tina Clarke, Charlie's sister, began loaning money to GKC to help it out of its financial difficulties. Finally, when the business was unable to pay Tina the more than $38,000 it owed her, she decided to set up a new corporation and run the business herself. Tina Clarke became the sole shareholder, officer, and director of The New Greater Kansas City Roofing Corporation (New GKC). She was unaware at the time this corporation was formed that GKC had committed labor law violations and that the NLRB had an outstanding judgment against the business. New GKC basically took over the assets of its predecessor and retained many of its former customers. New GKC's staff consisted almost exclusively of the former employees of GKC, including Charlie Clarke, who was employed to manage the corporate business. Tina failed to adhere to corporate formalities in her dealings with New GKC. She used a trade name associated with the corporation, as well as its address and telephone number, to establish a credit card collection account

and to open a checking account for her escort service, Affaire d'Amour. There is no evidence New GKC had bylaws, accounts, stock, or corporate records, or held meetings. When the NLRB attempted to collect its outstanding judgment against GKC, it alleged that New GKC was the alter ego of GKC and that its corporate veil should be pierced so that Tina Clarke could be held personally liable on the claim. Should the court pierce the veil and find Tina Clarke liable on the corporate debt?

4. *Video Case:* See "The Reunion." When friends reunite at a wedding, they reveal their plans for business ventures. Al and Amy, an unmarried couple, propose opening a Thai restaurant. Al is a dentist and Amy is director of public relations for a publishing company. Amy will quit her job eventually to manage the restaurant. They will hire a chef whose restaurant is about to close. Carl is a successful real estate agent who wants to open his own real estate firm. Bob has tried several business ventures, but all have failed, including a venture to manufacture ski racks for motorcycles. Dave and Donna, a newly married couple, plan to quit their jobs, move to Wyoming, and open a software development business. They want the business to have few investors. They have lined up potential clients who will finance their initial efforts in return for software customization. What business forms should each of these individuals use for their business ventures? What additional questions do you want to ask to help you determine the best business forms for their ventures?

5. James Coduti was a minority shareholder in the Hudson Tool & Die Corporation (Hudson). Werner Hellwig, the majority shareholder in Hudson, had been feuding with Coduti for some time. Coduti brought suit against Hellwig for refusing to authorize bonuses or dividends while Hudson was amassing large cash reserves. At the time of the suit, Hudson had certificates of deposit of approximately $775,000. Coduti argued that reserves of between $350,000 and $400,000 were sufficient for a business of this type. Hellwig claimed the accumulations were necessary to protect against dislocations if a major account was lost, to cover replacement costs for equipment, and to permit plant expansion. Should the court compel Hudson to declare a dividend?

6. Herb Jones started making tooled leather belts as a hobby. Later, he learned how to cast bronze belt buckles. He had little trouble selling them to friends. He was taking some art classes while seeking a degree in business at the local college. His belts, which he sold on weekends at craft shows, paid his tuition and provided spending money. Now he has been able to get a few men's clothing stores to stock his belts on a consignment basis. Demand has increased beyond his ability to fill it. As he completes his program at the college, he decides he would like to get into the business of making and selling belts and other leather goods. He learns of the availability of a small shop location in a popular shopping mall. A friend, Bill Williams, who has another year to go at the college, is willing to help him in his spare time. Suburban Bank and Trust Company is willing to lend Herb $8,000, the amount he thinks he needs to pay rent for one year, to buy a stock of leather and brass from which to make the belts, and to pay Bill to work weekends for three months. The loan is conditional on Herb's father cosigning the note. Herb's Uncle Joe, who works for a large corporation, suggests that Herb should incorporate the business. Do you agree?

7. Assume that Herb's business in the preceding problem case has been operating for a year and has made a profit. Herb has expanded by purchasing other leather products to sell. All of the profit has been reinvested in the business. Herb has, however, paid off $2,000 of the loan to the bank. The bank is willing to renew the loan and even to increase it to $10,000 if Herb's father cosigns again. Bill Williams would like to join the firm full time but has no money or credit

to contribute. Herb and Bill think that if they had a salesman to visit men's clothing shops and perhaps other retailers, they could increase their sales substantially. A mutual friend, George Robbins, has had sales experience and would be willing to join the business. He could invest $10,000. The workshop in the back of the shop is already too small. Herb would like to rent a loft or other low-rent space for belt production where there would be no interruptions and enough space for several workers. Herb would also like to have Bill supervise this operation. Herb estimates that minimum capital of $40,000 is necessary. What he owns in equipment, supplies, and inventory is worth $10,000 at cost, and he believes that the value of his going business is at least $10,000 in addition. His father is willing to invest $5,000 but wants no further liability. Uncle Joe is also willing to invest $5,000 on the same basis. What form of business organization is appropriate? How should it be capitalized?

8. Richard Mueller, the president, chief executive officer, and director of Swing-N-Slide Corporation (SNS), joined with several officers of the corporation to form Greengrass Management, a limited liability company. Mueller and those officers were the sole members of the LLC. They formed the entity solely for the purpose of serving as one of two general partners in Greengrass Holdings (Holdings), a partnership that was created to make a public tender offer to buy 60 percent of SNS's common shares from the SNS shareholders. Robert Barbieri, a shareholder in SNS, sued Mueller, the other members of the LLC, and the LLC, claiming that they had breached their fiduciary duty to the SNS shareholders because they had a conflict of interest during the tender offer negotiations. The LLC moved to dismiss the claim against it on the grounds that it owed no fiduciary duty to the SNS shareholders. Does the LLC owe a fiduciary duty to the SNS shareholders?

Chapter 27

Partnerships

Learning Objectives

After you have studied this chapter, you should be able to:

1. Clearly explain how a general partnership is created.
2. Explain the rights and duties of partners in a general partnership.
3. Identify the various ways in which general partnerships terminate.
4. Explain the dissolution, winding up, and continuation processes.
5. Identify how assets are distributed when termination occurs.
6. Clearly describe the similarities and differences between limited partnerships and general partnerships.

Digges persuaded Levin and Wharton to join him in forming a law partnership. They enthusiastically agreed because Digges came from a long line of prominent Maryland attorneys dating back to the 17th century. Levin and Wharton devoted most of their time to trial work and left all of the money matters to Digges. According to Wharton, "[I]f you don't trust your partner, you ought not to be partners." Digges later pled guilty to stealing over $1 million from a client, Dresser Industries, by padding and falsifying invoices during a 3½-year period. He then stole the proceeds from the law firm and used the money to restore his mansion. Neither Levin nor Wharton was accused of any wrongdoing. However, since Digges was

(continued)

found to be acting within the scope of the partnership, both Levin and Wharton, as partners, were held individually liable for the money that Digges stole from Dresser.[1]

- What is the fundamental nature of the partnership form of business organization and how does it arise?
- What are the rights and responsibilities of partners?
- How do courts determine the contractual authority of partners?
- When is one partner individually liable for the torts and crimes committed by another partner?

Introduction

While the concept of partnerships is an ancient one, today the common law of partnerships has been largely supplanted by statutory law. Each state has its own partnership statute. However, most states have modeled their legislation after the Revised Uniform Partnership Act (RUPA). This model partnership act, an attempt to codify partnership law into a single document, has now replaced the Uniform Partnership Act (UPA) as the dominant source of partnership rules. Accordingly, the RUPA provides the framework for this chapter.

This chapter examines the partnership form of business organization. It demonstrates the ease with which partnerships may be created and explores the basic structure of this type of business. This includes a discussion of the authority generally vested in partners as well as a distinction between the rights of partnership creditors and those belonging to creditors of the individual partners. After a survey of the rights and duties of partners, there is a discussion of the procedures involved in terminating a partnership. The chapter closes with a brief examination of the legal aspects of limited partnership.

Creation of a Partnership

LO1

Most people are surprised to discover that there are amazingly few legal formalities involved in creating a partnership. In fact, a court may find two persons to be partners even though neither had the specific intent to create a partnership. This is so because no express agreement is necessary to create a partnership. All that is required is that the parties intended to have the relationship that the law defines as a partnership. The RUPA simply describes a partnership as "an association of two or more persons to carry on as co-owners of a business for profit."

An Association of Two or More Persons

A partnership is a voluntary and consensual association involving two or more persons. Nobody can be forced to become a partner, although one can engage unwittingly in

[1]"A Well-Born Lawyer Falls from Eminence," *The Wall Street Journal,* December 27, 1989, p. B4; "Prominent Maryland Lawyer," *The Wall Street Journal,* January 15, 1990, p. B5.

behavior that gives rise to the creation of a partnership. The RUPA is extremely liberal in that it permits individuals, partnerships, and corporations to qualify as persons that can form a partnership.

Carrying on a Business for Profit

The RUPA definition of a partnership applies only to instances in which two or more persons carry on a business for profit. However, any trade, occupation, or profession is treated as a business in determining the existence of a partnership. The key element in this definition is the fact that the objective must be to make a **profit.** People who are involved in a nonprofit association are not partners.

Concept Summary: Establishing the Existence of a Partnership

Definition	Key Elements
1. Association of two or more persons	• May be natural or artificial (corporate) persons. • Must be at least two partners.
2. Carrying on a business	• Objective must be to make a profit.
3. As co-owners	• Must have a community of interest. This is evidenced by: a. Sharing losses. b. Sharing profits. c. Sharing management.

Co-ownership

For there to be a partnership there must be **co-ownership,** which means ownership of the business as such. It does not require that the property used in the business be owned by the partnership or in equal shares by the partners. In fact, the property and capital used in the business of a partnership can be supplied entirely by a single partner or the property may be leased from others and the working capital borrowed.

Disputes on the Existence of a Partnership

Disputes often arise over whether or not a partnership has been created. When this occurs, courts generally look at all of the facts, paying particular attention to whether there appears to be a community of interest. Perhaps the two most important factors in determining whether such co-ownership exists are the **sharing of profits** and the **sharing of management** of the business. The RUPA states that, unless other evidence clearly disproves that individuals are partners, the sharing of profits is presumptive evidence that they are. However, the RUPA then lists certain factors that can overcome this presumption. For instance, if one receives a share of profits in payment of a debt, wages, or rent or for the sale of the goodwill of a business, no presumption of partnership exists.

While the sharing of management provides some evidence that a partnership exists, participation in management alone does not create a partnership. For instance, sometimes creditors are given substantial control over business operations, but they are not necessarily partners. In the case of creditors, a court may refuse to find the existence of a partnership even though the creditor shares in profits as well as management. Further, many businesses hire people to manage their businesses, but without a sharing of profits, the manager is unlikely to be treated as a partner by the courts.

Purported Partnerships

You can be liable as a partner without being a partner. If you go with a friend to a bank to borrow money and tell the banker that you and the friend are partners in a business, the banker can hold you liable as a partner. The same result would occur if the friend stated that you were his partner and you failed to correct the statement. However, if the friend went alone to the bank and told the banker you were his partner, you would not be liable.

As with the concept of *estoppel,* the person who seeks to hold another liable as a partner must prove that she relied on the holding out of consent. The reliance must be justifiable and must result in loss to the person who sold goods or otherwise relied on the credit of the person held out as a partner. If reliance is justifiable, the defendant is estopped from claiming that there was, in fact, no partnership.

Articles of Partnership

Although generally not required, it is highly desirable to have written articles of partnership. (Partnership agreements may need to be in writing when they create an interest in real property or have a term in excess of one year.) A written contract tends to minimize misunderstanding and disagreement. The process of preparing such an agreement is likely to cause the parties to provide for contingencies they might not otherwise consider. This is especially true if a lawyer is called on who is experienced in drafting partnership agreements.

It should be noted that lawsuits raising the question of whether or not there is a partnership usually arise where arrangements among the partners have been casual. Disputes are more likely when there are no written articles of partnership.

Articles of partnership usually state how profits and losses are to be shared. They should provide a means for continuing the business on the death or disability of a partner. Other matters usually included in articles of partnership are the name of the firm, the business to be carried on, the term for which the partnership is to exist, salary and drawing accounts, the authority of the partners to bind the firm, and provisions for withdrawal of partners.

Joint Ventures

Many courts distinguish a **joint venture** from a partnership. The elements of a joint venture are (1) an express or implied agreement to carry on an enterprise; (2) a manifestation of intent by the parties to be associated as joint venturers; (3) a joint interest as reflected in the contribution of property, finances, effort, skill, or knowledge by each party to the joint venture; (4) a measure of proprietorship of joint control of the enterprise; and (5) a provision for the sharing of profits or losses.

The major distinction between a joint venture and partnership is that a joint venture relates to a single enterprise or transaction, and a partnership relates to a continuing business. Both require a meeting of the minds and contract formation. However, some courts hold that the requirement for joint ventures is less formal and may be implied entirely by conduct. Further, they state that, with joint ventures, any agreement that does exist need not cover as many terms as are necessary for a partnership. For instance, an agreement to jointly buy, develop, and resell one particular plot of land may be considered a joint venture. On the other hand, an agreement to jointly buy, develop, and resell land on a long-term basis may well be construed as a partnership.

For the purposes of this chapter, the distinction between a partnership and a joint venture is not very important. This is so because courts generally apply partnership law to joint ventures. Perhaps the only significant difference is that joint venturers sometimes are held to have less implied and apparent authority than partners. This is because of the more limited scope of the joint venture enterprise.

McGregor v. Crumley

775 N.W.2d 91 (S.Dak. Sup. Ct. 2009)

FACTS

Clint and Paige (a married couple) lived on a dairy farm, which Clint managed on a day-to-day basis. Paige, hired hands, and Paige's mother and father also worked with the cattle. By telephone, Clint ordered a herd of dairy cows from McGregor. When McGregor delivered the cows, Paige handed McGregor a check for payment. While at Clint's farm, McGregor observed Paige, Paige's mother and father, and two farm hands working with the dairy cows and on the farm. McGregor and Clint then engaged in a series of telephone calls concerning the purchase of between 20 and 30 more dairy cows. The calls were exclusively between McGregor and Clint. After that sale, the bill of lading prepared by McGregor's bookkeeper listed the purchasers as Clint and Paige. Clint contacted McGregor a few days later to complain about the condition of several of the cows. McGregor sent a cattle truck to Clint's dairy farm and 8 of the original 25 dairy cows were loaded and returned for credit against the bill. The second bill listed both Clint and Paige as the purchasers. When the bill for the cattle was not paid, McGregor attempted to discuss the matter with Paige but was unable to get her do so. McGregor testified that Clint became angry after finding out that McGregor had attempted to discuss the bill with Paige, stressing that he ran the dairy business. When the bill remained unpaid, McGregor sued both Clint and Paige, claiming that Paige was a partner in the dairy operation and was therefore jointly and severally liable.

ISSUE

Should the court find that Paige is a partner in the dairy farm?

DECISION

No. A partnership is formed when two or more persons carry on as co-owners a business for profit whether or not the persons intend to form a partnership. In this case, no evidence was presented at trial to show that Paige shared in the title to the dairy farm. There was also no evidence presented that she shared in the gross returns generated by the dairy operation, or that she had a common right in the cattle. There was no evidence presented that Paige shared in the profits of the business, that there were any profits to share, or that she was compensated as an employee for her labor on the dairy farm. McGregor did not explore the type of business entity used by Clint at the time of the cattle sale. McGregor assumed that because the husband and wife worked on the dairy farm together they were engaged in a partnership. However, the burden to show Clint and Paige were operating the dairy farm as a partnership was with McGregor in order to obtain a judgment against Paige for which she would be jointly and severably liable. The billing statements do not provide conclusive evidence. There is no evidence to suggest that McGregor's decision to invoice Clint and Paige for the cattle was anything more than an assumption on his part that the couple operated the dairy farm as a partnership.

Management and Authority of Partners

Voice in Management

Each partner normally has an equal voice in managing the business. A vote of the majority prevails if there are more than two partners. This may be changed by agreement, however. One or a group of partners may, by agreement of the partners, be granted authority to make the day-to-day operating decisions of the business. These might include making usual contracts for goods and services and hiring and firing employees.

LO2

Unanimous agreement is required to act contrary to the partnership agreement or to act outside of the ordinary course of the partnership business. Assume you are a member of a retail partnership. You decide that it would be a good investment to buy a nearby residence for rental purposes. Approval of all the partners is necessary. Likewise, unanimity would be required for an agreement to guarantee the debt of another, such as that of a partner, if contracts of surety or indemnity fall outside the scope of the partnership's usual business. Such approval would also be required to authorize a sale of the store's entire inventory or the building in which the business is conducted.

When a certain action is proposed and there is an even split among the partners, the action cannot be taken. If it is an important matter and the deadlock continues, it may be impossible to continue the business. In such a case, any partner may petition a court for dissolution of the partnership.

Authority

Authority to act for a partnership may be of three types: express, implied, and apparent. These concepts have the same meaning as under agency law, and the tests for implied and apparent authority are the same. Both implied and apparent authority are influenced by customs and usages of the particular partnership and those of similar businesses in the area.

Express Authority

A partner has express authority to do whatever he or she is authorized to do by the articles of partnership. In addition, express authority stems from any other agreement of the partners.

Implied Authority

The RUPA gives every partner implied authority to bind the partnership on contracts that are usually appropriate to that business. For example, if your partnership runs a women's ready-to-wear clothing store, any partner has the authority to buy dresses for resale. However, this implied authority may be abolished or limited by agreement of the partners.

Apparent Authority

When the agency authority of a partner is abolished or limited by agreement, the partner may still have apparent authority. Suppose, in a clothing store, that you and your partners, Roger and Jane, have agreed that all merchandise buying will be done by Jane. Suppose further, as is likely, that it is customary for all partners in this type of business to give merchandise orders. A manufacturer takes and fills an order given by Roger. If the manufacturer is unaware of the restriction, the partnership and, ultimately, you are bound. (Apparent authority is discussed in Chapter 24.)

QAD Investors v. Kelly

776 A.2d 1244 (Me. Sup. Jud. Ct. 2001)

FACTS

Laurence Kelly entered into a partnership with Stephen MacKenzie to purchase a parking lot. While Kelly and MacKenzie were searching for investors, MacKenzie approached Russell Glidden, the principal of QAD Investors, and provided him with a copy of Kelly's personal financial statement. Kelly, MacKenzie, and Glidden met together repeatedly thereafter. At the meetings, MacKenzie's referred to Kelly as a partner

(continued)

in the project. Glidden had committed QAD to providing $20,000 to the venture. MacKenzie gave Glidden a written receipt stating that the money would be paid back pursuant to a note that Glidden would hold. The note had lines for the signatures of Kelly and MacKenzie, but only MacKenzie's line contained a witnessed signature; Kelly's line was blank. Later, when the partnership defaulted on the loan, QAD sued Kelly for payment. QAD argued that, at a minimum, MacKenzie had apparent authority to act for Kelly as a partner.

ISSUE

Did MacKenzie have apparent authority to bind Kelly on the note?

DECISION

Yes. Kelly's conduct would lead a reasonable third party to believe that MacKenzie was acting as the agent of the partnership and with the requisite authority. Kelly attended meetings with Glidden and MacKenzie during which they discussed the possibility of obtaining money from Glidden for the partnership. MacKenzie gave Kelly's personal financial statement to Glidden before negotiating with him. These facts adequately support the legal conclusion that MacKenzie was at least apparently authorized to bind the partnership.

Ratification

Generally, the partnership will not be liable for contracts created by a partner acting outside the scope of her authority. An exception to this rule arises when the other partners ratify the unauthorized action. (Ratification was discussed previously in Chapter 24.) It occurs when the partners, either expressly or implicitly, demonstrate the intent to accept the action of the partner who was lacking actual or apparent authority. Any act that the partnership could have authorized at the time it was done may be ratified. Ratification releases the partner from liability for having exceeded her authority and binds the partnership to the contract as if it had been authorized all along.

Property of Partnerships

What Is Partnership Property?

Disputes often arise among both partners and creditors over what property actually belongs to the partnership and what property belongs to individual partners. Partnership property includes all property that originally was contributed to the partnership as well as anything purchased then or later for the partnership. In addition, any property acquired with partnership funds is partnership property unless a contrary intent is clearly shown. The fact that property is used in the business does not make it partnership property; however, assets that appear on the account books of the partnership are presumed to be partnership property. Payment by the partnership of taxes or insurance on property is presumptive but not conclusive evidence that the property is owned by the partnership. The same is true if improvements are made on the property by the partnership.

The RUPA provides several rules for determining if property belongs to the partnership. It holds that property belongs to the partnership if it was transferred (1) to the partnership in its name, (2) to any partner acting as a partner by a transfer document that specifically names the partnership, or (3) to any partner by a transfer document indicating the partner's status as a partner or otherwise indicating that a partnership exists.

Ownership and Possession

A partner's ownership of partnership property is called a partnership interest. Partners have no separate interest in partnership property. They have no right to sell, mortgage, or devise to an heir any individual item of the firm's property.

A partner has a right to take possession of the firm's property for partnership purposes but not for personal use. For example, if you are a partner, you have no right to use the firm's automobile for your vacation. Permission of a majority of the partners would be required. You may, however, without special permission, drive the car to the bank to deposit the firm's receipts.

Concept Summary: Partnership Property

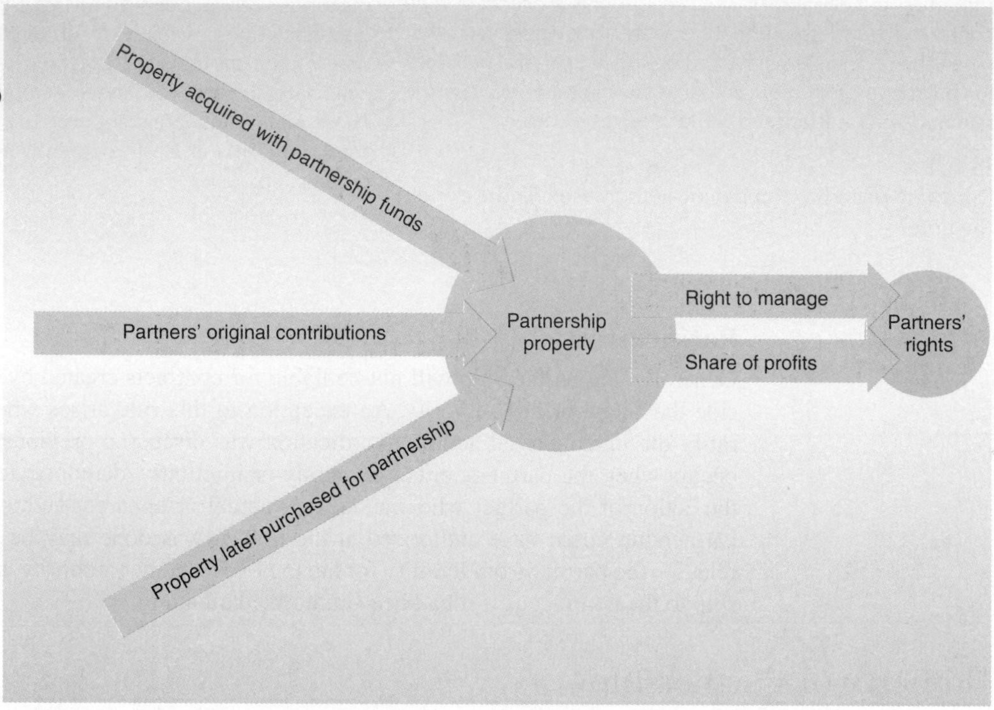

Creditors of Partners

A creditor of a partner may not attach any of the property owned by the partnership; however, a partner may assign her partnership interest to a creditor or to anyone else. This entitles the assignee to receive that partner's share of the profits. It does not give the assignee a right to any information about partnership affairs or a right to look at its books.

A creditor who gets a judgment against a partner may obtain from the court a **charging order** against the partner's interest in the firm. The court may appoint a receiver to look after the creditor's interests. If profits are insufficient to pay off the creditor, the court may order that the partner's interest be sold. The purchaser may dissolve the partnership if it is to exist for an indefinite time. If it is for a term of years that has not expired, the partnership will continue as originally agreed. The purchaser will not be a partner, nor can she exercise any of the partner's rights except to receive that share of the profits. The partnership or any partner may purchase the debtor's partnership interest by paying the debt.

Partners' Rights and Duties

Right to Compensation

LO2

A partner is not ordinarily entitled to salary or wages. The compensation is presumed to be the partner's share of profits. This is true even if one partner spends much more time than another on partnership business. The same principle applies to rent to a partner for use of the partner's property and to interest on a capital contribution. An exception is made by the RUPA when a partner dies. Then any surviving partner is entitled to reasonable compensation for winding up partnership affairs.

Concept Summary: Rights of Creditors

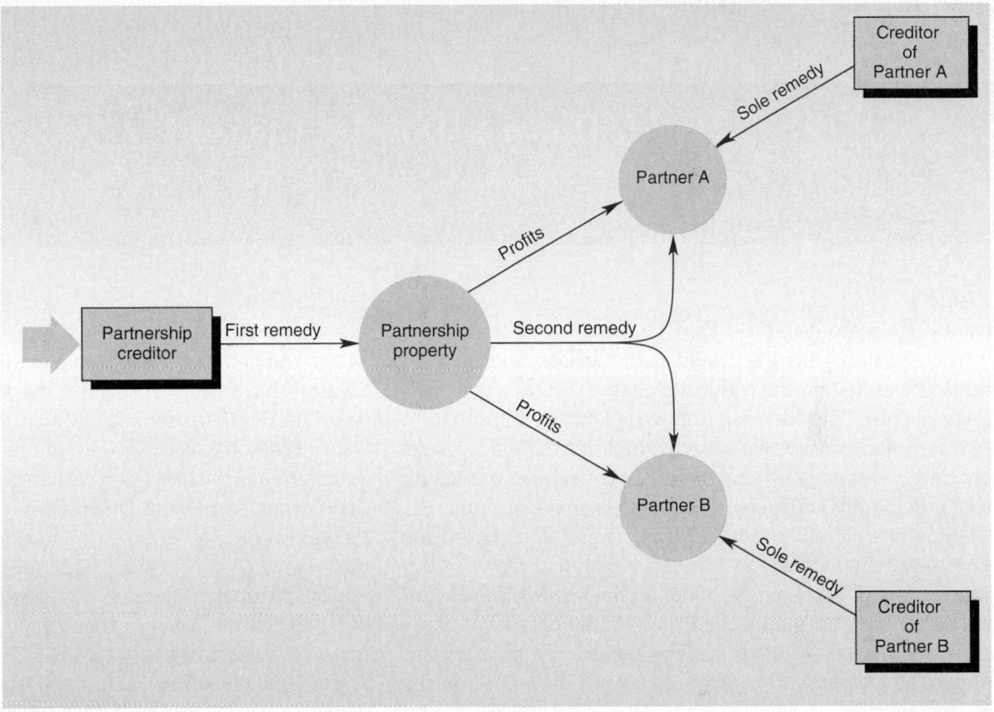

Of course, the partners may agree that one or more of them is to be paid salary, rent, interest, or wages in addition to sharing in profits. Often, drawing accounts for all partners are agreed on, or perhaps regular monthly payments are made. These are then deducted from the partner's share of profits when year-end settlements are made. In the absence of a contrary agreement, profits are shared equally even if capital contributions are unequal. The sharing of losses is the same as the sharing of profits unless there is a different agreement.

Ethics in Action

The relative ease with which a partnership may be formed often results in creation of this form of business organization without any real planning by the partners. Consequently, a partner who contributes considerably more time and money to the business than the other partners often is shocked to discover that, in the absence of agreement, she is not entitled to a salary or a greater share of the profits. Is it ethical for the other partners to oppose compensation for such a partner merely because of the failure to draft a more comprehensive agreement?

Duty of Loyalty and Good Faith

Partners not only must be honest but also must not permit self-interest to come before duty to the partnership. Partners may buy from or sell to the partnership. However, if they do, they must make full disclosure of any facts relevant to the deal that are not known to the other partners. Partners may not make secret profits from their position as members of a partnership.

Dowd & Dowd v. Gleason

816 N.E.2d 754 (Ill. Ct. App. 2004)

FACTS

Nancy J. Gleason and Douglas G. Shreffler were partners in the law firm Dowd & Dowd, Ltd. Gleason and Shreffler began investigating the possibility of establishing a new, separate law firm. They decided to take preliminary steps to form that firm and, within two months, had located office space, ordered furniture and equipment, and initiated a banking relationship with Harris Bank. One month later, on December 31, Gleason and Shreffler resigned from Dowd and started the GMS law firm. During her 13 years working at Dowd, Gleason was the primary person handling the firm's Allstate Insurance Company account. Lynn Crim was the head of Allstate's claims department and spoke with Gleason on a daily basis. Immediately after GMS was created, Crim gave Gleason the charge of moving Allstate's cases that currently were with Dowd to Gleason's new firm. Dowd filed suit against Gleason for soliciting Allstate's business before resigning from the firm.

ISSUE

Did Gleason breach a fiduciary duty owed to Dowd & Dowd?

DECISION

Yes. Leslie Henkels, a former legal assistant/paralegal at Dowd, testified that she was told in mid-December by Nancy Gleason that GMS had secured the Allstate business for the new firm. Further, Henkels testified that, on December 31, Nancy Gleason called her and told her that she was faxing a letter (announcing Allstate's switch to GMS) to be put on the desks of the partners at Dowd. Henkels recalled that the letter was on Allstate letterhead and signed by an Allstate official. Nancy Gleason called back shortly thereafter and told Henkels to retrieve the faxes and destroy them, on the advice of "their counsel." Nancy then called a third time indicating that she was on her way to Mike Dowd's house to resign. The time between the first call and the third call was approximately 30 to 45 minutes. While partners who are planning to leave a firm may take preliminary, logical steps of obtaining office space and supplies, they may not solicit clients for their new venture. Such conduct thoroughly undermines the loyalty owed to partners.

In the absence of a contrary understanding, each partner owes a duty to devote full time and his or her best efforts to the affairs of the partnership. A partner must not engage in activities that are in competition with or otherwise likely to injure the partnership. For example, suppose you join with a friend in forming a real estate brokerage partnership. If your partner accepts commissions for arranging sales of property not listed with the firm, the partnership is entitled to those commissions. A partner is also liable to the partnership for the value of partnership property that he or she uses for individual purposes.

Duty of Care in Partnership Business

Partners have a duty to exercise reasonable care and skill in transacting business for the partnership. A further duty is not to exceed the authority granted to them by the partnership. Partners are liable for their negligence while acting for the partnership but not for honest errors of judgment.

Duty to Inform

Partners owe a duty to pass on to the other partners all information coming to them that may be important to the operation of the partnership. This is because a notice by a third person to any partner is treated as having been given to the partnership. This rule stems from the agency relationship arising among partners. It is presumed that an agent will disclose to the principals all matters that it is his or her duty to disclose to them. Outsiders dealing with the agent are entitled to rely on this presumption, whether or not the agent in fact communicates the knowledge to the principals. Of course, this is not true if the third person has been told that all notices must be given to a certain partner.

Duty to Account

Partners have a duty to account for any expenditure of partnership funds they make. They must also account for the sale or other disposal of partnership property. The same is true for any benefit or profit coming to them as partners. They also have a right to be reimbursed by the partnership for expenses on its behalf.

The duty of keeping the account books is usually assigned to one partner. He then has a duty to keep them accurately. If the records do not properly show the application of the funds coming to the firm, the partner will be liable.

Enforcement of Partnership Rights and Liabilities

Liability on Contracts

Partnerships were not considered legal entities at common law. They could not sue or be sued in the firm name; rather, all partners had to be joined as plaintiffs or defendants. This requirement of joinder (naming and serving all parties as defendants or naming all as plaintiffs) made it hard for creditors to sue on partnership contracts. Today, under the RUPA, the firm is primarily liable if a contract is made by a partner or other agent who has express, implied, or apparent authority. If the partnership does not pay off the liability, then the partners become **jointly liable.** When liability is joint, all of those liable must be sued in the same suit at common law. However, at common law any partner is liable for the entire debt if the other partners are dead, beyond the jurisdiction of the court, or judgment proof (without property that can be seized for debt).

The RUPA permits suits against a partnership in the name under which it commonly does business. The partnership may also sue in its own name. This eliminates the common law requirement to get personal service on (to deliver the summons to) each partner. It permits a plaintiff who is suing on a partnership contract to get a judgment if one or more of the partners are served.

Liability for Torts

The doctrine of *respondeat superior* imposes liability on the partnership for torts committed by any partner or employee of the firm while engaged in partnership business. The principles of agency law (see Chapter 24) apply in determining whether a tort is committed within the scope and during the course of the partnership business. The liability of the partners for partnership torts is *joint and several.* This permits the injured person to sue any partner individually or all of them together.

In the case that opened this chapter, Dresser Industries could sue the law firm or any of the attorneys individually for Digges's overbilling since it occurred within the scope of the partnership. Thus, Wharton and Levin could be liable even though they were accused of no wrongdoing. After being found liable, however, Wharton or Levin could seek indemnification from the partnership.

A partner who commits a tort against another partner is, of course, liable for the resulting injury. Therefore, Wharton and Levin will have an action for an accounting against Digges in order to recover the money that he stole from the partnership.

Liability for Crimes

A partnership may commit a crime by the manner in which it carries on its business. Examples of such crimes would include violating antitrust laws, failing to obtain a necessary business license, or discharging a prohibited pollutant. The firm is liable for the resulting fines. The individual partners are liable if the firm has inadequate assets.

The other partners are not subject to imprisonment for a crime committed by a partner. This is true even if the crime was committed by the wrongdoing partner while acting for the partnership. Some direct participation or encouragement would be necessary for imprisonment.

Death of the Partnership

LO3

The next four sections examine the death of the partnership. They require the understanding of four important terms. Dissociation refers to any change in the relationships among partners, such as one of their deaths. Dissolution describes the beginning of the process of settling all of the partnership affairs. Winding up describes the orderly liquidation of partnership assets and their distribution among those with claims against the partnership. Finally, termination refers to the end of the partnership's existence. Limited partnerships and general partnerships treat dissociation, dissolution, winding up, and termination in the same manner.

Dissociation

The RUPA defines a **dissociation** as a change in the relation of the partners caused by any partner ceasing to be associated with the carrying on of the business. It may be triggered by a partner's death, retirement, or expulsion. It is the starting point for the partnership's dissolution, winding up (if a winding up occurs), and termination. As a general rule, each partner has the power to dissociate from the partnership at any time. However, the partner does not always have the right to do so. If the partner dissociates without the right (in violation of the partnership agreement), his action is wrongful.

The RUPA has the goal of avoiding unnecessary dissolutions of partnerships. As such it contains a significant change from prior partnership law. It dramatically changes the law governing partnership breakups and dissolution. This entirely new concept, "dissociation," is used in lieu of the UPA term "dissolution" to denote the change in the relationship caused by a partner's ceasing to be associated in the carrying on of the business. Under the RUPA, unlike the UPA, the dissociation of a partner does not necessarily cause a dissolution and winding up of the business of the partnership. The following discussion explains the practical difference between wrongful and nonwrongful dissociations.

Nonwrongful Dissociation

A partnership established for a certain period of time dissolves at the end of that period. A partnership that is formed for a certain objective, such as to subdivide a certain plot of ground and then to develop and sell residential lots, dissolves when that objective is reached. Of course, the partners can at any time unanimously agree to dissolve a partnership. They can do this although they earlier agreed on some specific time or the attainment of some objective not yet reached. Where no period of time or specific undertaking is agreed on, the partnership is a **partnership at will.** Such a partnership may be dissolved at any time by any partner. All that is necessary is for a partner to notify the other partners.

Concept Summary: Dissociation of the Partnership

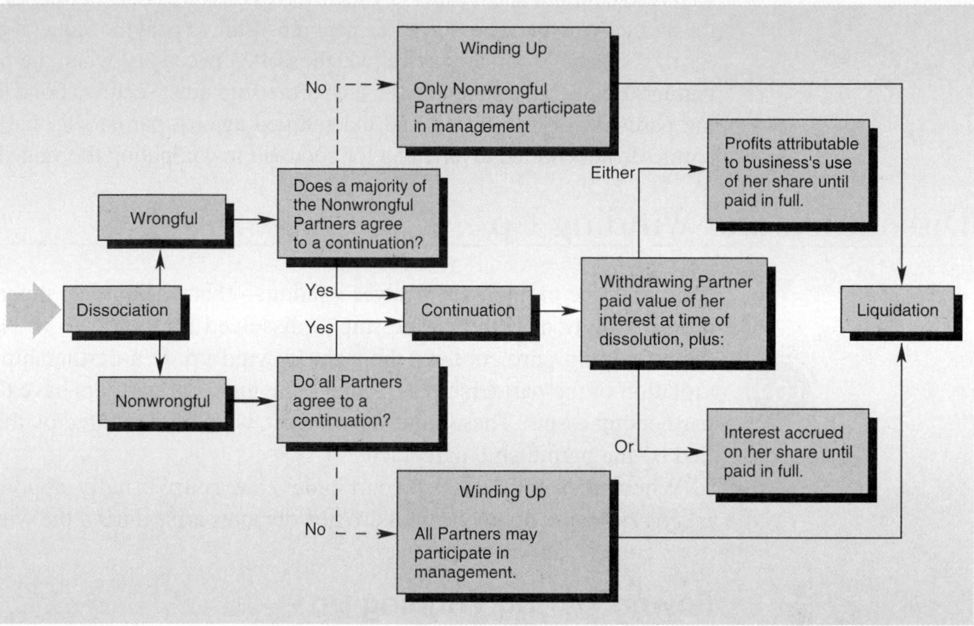

E-Commerce

If you are interested in more fully investigating the partnership rules embodied in the RUPA, you may visit the website for the National Conference of Commissioners on Uniform State Laws at www.nccul.org. At that site you can find the complete text and comments of the RUPA.

In the partnership agreement, the partners also may provide for expelling a partner. If so, and if the agreed-on procedure is followed, a partner may be forced out without violation of the agreement. Such a provision eliminates the right the expelled partner would otherwise have to insist on liquidation.

Each nonwrongful partner (including the partner demanding the dissociation) may demand that the business of the partnership be dissolved and wound up. Thus, the partnership business cannot be continued in the absence of the unanimous approval of all of the nonwrongful partners. Furthermore, nonwrongful partners have the right to participate fully in the winding up process.

Wrongful Dissociation

A partner has the *power* to dissociate a partnership even though she does not have the *right.* However, if a partner exercises the power to dissolve when she does not possess the right, she has caused a wrongful dissociation. Refusal by partners to carry out their obligations under a partnership agreement also may constitute a wrongful dissociation. So, if a partner fails to pay his partnership contribution or refuses to furnish the services agreed on, he may be treated as a wrongfully dissociating partner.

A partner who wrongfully dissociates loses the right to demand a dissolution and winding up. In addition, the wrongful partner forfeits the right to participate in the winding-up process should any nonwrongful partner decide on one. The innocent partners are given the right by the

RUPA to continue the business by themselves or with a new partner or partners. If this is done, the partner who breaches the agreement must still be paid the value of his interest less damages for the breach. As an alternative, which is often necessary when the partnership or remaining partners do not have enough cash, the partnership must secure a bond to ensure that the departing partner will be paid off and indemnified against partnership liabilities. The wrongdoing partner is not entitled to anything for goodwill in computing the value of his partnership share.

Dissolution and Winding Up

LO4

Normally, the partners themselves wind up—that is, liquidate the assets of the business—after dissolution. If the partnership is dissolved by the death or bankruptcy of a partner, the remaining partners have the right to wind up. If a partnership has been dissolved in violation of the partnership agreement, the innocent partners have the right to liquidate the partnership assets. These rights to wind up, which are granted by the RUPA, may be modified by the partnership agreement.

Where dissolution is by court order, the court usually appoints a representative as *receiver* to wind up the business. When disputes arise during the winding up, a partner may ask a court to appoint a receiver.

Powers during Winding Up

The purpose of the winding up is to liquidate the assets at their highest value and bring the affairs of the partnership promptly to an end. This may involve completing partnership contracts. For example, in a partnership involved in the construction business, it may be desirable to finish contracts for constructing large buildings that may take two or three years to complete. In order to finish these jobs, the winding-up partners would have authority to enter into new contracts with subcontractors, with material suppliers, and with workers. As a result, it may be necessary that the winding-up partners borrow money on behalf of the partnership in order to complete these contracts.

It is possible, however, that the partners may desire to assign such long-term contracts to other contractors. In most cases, they would be authorized to make such assignments. Of course, the winding-up partners have no authority to enter contracts for new business. They would be liable to the partnership for any loss suffered on such contracts.

Duties of Partners during Winding Up

Partners continue to have fiduciary duties to their copartners during winding up. A partner who is entitled to participate in the winding up cannot be excluded, nor can a partner claim specific partnership property without the agreement of the others.

Long v. Lopez

115 S.W.3d 221 (Tex. Ct. App. 2003)

FACTS

Wayne A. Long, Sergio Lopez, and Don Bannister entered into a partnership agreement in which they formed Wood Relo (the partnership). The three partners agreed to share equally one-third of the profits and losses of the partnership. Further, all three partners were authorized to sign checks on Wood Relo's bank account. Long entered into an office equipment lease with IKON Capital Corporation

(continued)

(IKON) on behalf of the partnership. Ultimately, Wood Relo was unable to continue its business. Long then negotiated a settlement with IKON for a total of $9,000. IKON had been claiming over $16,000. An agreed judgment was entered in conjunction with the settlement agreement providing that if Long did not pay the settlement, Wood Relo and Long would owe IKON $12,000. Long then sent Lopez and Bannister a letter advising them that they were jointly and severally liable for the $9,000 that extinguished the partnership's debt to IKON, plus attorney's fees. When Lopez refused to pay anything, Long brought suit against him.

ISSUE

Is Long liable for one-third of debt and attorneys' fees?

DECISION

Yes. Long entered into the settlement agreement with IKON to save the partnership a substantial amount of money. The inability of the partnership to continue its business was an event requiring the partners to wind up the affairs of the partnership. Long entered into the settlement with IKON when the partnership was in its final stages and the partners were going their separate ways. Accordingly, he was authorized by the RUPA to settle the IKON lawsuit on behalf of the partnership. If a partner reasonably incurs a liability in excess of the amount he agreed to contribute in properly conducting the business of the partnership or for preserving the partnership's business or property, he is entitled to be repaid by the partnership for that excess amount. All partners are liable jointly and severally for all debts and obligations of the partnership.

Compensation for Winding Up

Under the RUPA, the partners who wind up a partnership business are entitled to be paid for that work. They also may receive their share of the profits.

Continuation

The general rule is that there is no right to continue a partnership beyond the originally agreed-on term. If a partnership is established for a term of 10 years, none of the partners has a right to continue the business beyond that time except with the unanimous agreement of all. Further, in a partnership at will, the remaining partners have no right to continue the business when one of the partners chooses to have it liquidated. Accordingly, in order to preserve the value of the goodwill developed by the business, the partnership agreement often will include language modifying the right to insist on liquidation.

Continuation without Winding Up

Some courts take the view that there is an automatic dissolution of the partnership on the withdrawal or death of a partner. However, many partnership agreements declare that there will be no dissolution at such an event even if a new partner or partners enter into the partnership. This usually is beneficial to all concerned because it preserves the value of the going business. Whether or not there has been a technical dissolution, courts enforce partnership agreements that provide for a continuation of the business. There is then no winding up or termination.

Partners may agree at any time that the interest of one partner shall be purchased by the partnership or by one or more of the other partners. They also may agree to take in an additional partner. Or they may agree to permit a partner to sell his or her interest to another and to accept that person as a substitute partner. These agreements are called **buyout agreements.** Normally, they include provisions seeking to protect the financial interests of the partners who are leaving (and those who are entering) the partnership. Usually, life insurance is bought to fund the purchase of the interests of partners who die.

Liability for Prior Obligations

The continuing partnership becomes liable for the debts incurred by the original partnership. A withdrawing partner or the representative of a deceased partner remains liable for those debts if the continuing partnership does not or cannot pay them.

Usually, the continuing partners agree to relieve the withdrawing partners of liability on the debts of the old partnership. However, such agreements are not binding on creditors unless they have joined in a *novation*. This involves an agreement by the creditor with both the withdrawing partners (or representatives of deceased partners) and the continuing partners. The continuing partners agree to assume the obligation, and the creditor agrees to hold only them liable and to release the withdrawing partners or their representatives.

A novation is sometimes inferred by courts from the conduct of the creditor of the original partnership. Acceptance of a check or other negotiable instrument from a continuing partner has been held to be a novation if it is in full settlement of the claim and the creditor had knowledge of the change of membership. This would not apply to a partial payment.

The RUPA declares that a new partner has no liability for partnership debts that arose before he became a partner. However, this rule can be changed by agreement. Accordingly, many partnership agreements require new partners to assume liability for all partnership obligations as a condition of joining the partnership.

Liability for New Obligations

Former partners may be held liable for the new obligations of a continuing partnership when the new or continuing partners have apparent authority to bind the former partner. Such authority is likely to arise when creditors of the old partnership have not been notified of the departure of the former partner and rely on his continued presence in the partnership when extending new credit. Accordingly, withdrawing partners should protect themselves by notifying the world of their departure through actual and constructive notice.

Concept Summary: Liability to Creditors

	Prior Obligations	New Obligations
Continuing Partners	Liable	Liable
Withdrawing Partners	Liable (unless released by a novation)	Not liable (if they have given notice of withdrawal)
New Partners	Liable only to extent of contribution unless they agree to greater liability	Liable

Distribution of Assets

Order of Distribution

LO5

The final act of winding up a dissolved partnership is the distribution of assets. There is no problem if the partnership has been profitable; all creditors and partners will be paid in full. Where there have been losses, however, the distribution rules are extremely important. Under the RUPA, distribution is simple. All partnership creditors (including partners who have made loans to the partnership) are paid first. (Under the RUPA, all outside creditors are paid in full before partners who loaned money are given anything.) Then, if there still are assets remaining, the proceeds from their sale are distributed pro rata among the partners based on the net amounts in their capital accounts. Each partner's capital account is composed of his share of profits from the sale of the assets as well as the amount of his capital contributions.

When the net amount of a partner's capital account is negative, he is required by law to contribute to the partnership the amount of the deficiency. When all partners' capital accounts are negative, some of the partnership creditors will remain unpaid. In that case, the creditors may proceed against any or all of the individual partners. The partners who pay may then recover from other partners for their share of the debt.

Warnick v. Warnick

76 P.3d 316 (Wyo. Sup. Ct. 2003)

FACTS

Wilbur, Dee, and Randall Warnick formed Warnick Ranches general partnership to purchase and operate a ranch. The partnership agreement recited that the initial capital contributions of the partners totaled $60,000, paid 36 percent by Wilbur, 30 percent by Dee, and 34 percent by Randall. Their agreement further stated that additional contributions, or withdrawals, may be made to or from the capital of the partnership by unanimous agreement of all three partners. Over the years, Wilbur and Dee contributed additional funds to the ranch. However, because Randall needed cash, the partners also received cash distributions from time to time. Wilbur, however, left in the partnership account two $12,000 cash distributions that were otherwise payable to him. Ultimately, the net cash contributions of the partners, considering the initial contributions, payments to or on behalf of the partnership, draws not taken, and distributions from the partnership were as follows: Wilbur $170,112.60 (51 percent); Dee $138,834.63 (41 percent); and Randall $25,406.28 (8 percent). When Randall asked for a buyout of his share of the partnership, he claimed that he was entitled to the amount of his cash contributions plus 34 percent of the partnership's assets.

ISSUE

Has Randall correctly calculated his share of the partnership assets?

DECISION

No. RUPA states that a dissociated partner's interest in the partnership shall be purchased by the partnership for a buyout price. The buyout price is equal to the amount that would have been distributable to the dissociating partner if, on the date of the dissociation, the partnership's assets had been sold. However, partnership assets must first be applied to discharge partnership liabilities to creditors, including partners who are creditors. In calculating Randall's buyout price, it is necessary to first calculate the amount that the partnership owes to each partner for advances to the partnership, with interest accrued from the date of each advance. Next, there is the matter of two $12,000 draws, or "guaranteed payments," that Wilbur was entitled to, but were actually left in the partnership account and he did not receive. At the time he became entitled to the "guaranteed payment," the $12,000 was Wilbur's personal money and his leaving it with the partnership was the functional equivalent of another advance to the partnership. Upon remand, therefore, in calculating the buyout price for Dee and Randall's share, it is necessary to first calculate the amount the partnership owes Wilbur for the two $12,000 draws he left with the partnership, with interest from the date he was entitled to the payments.

Termination

The winding up process is complete when the partnership assets are entirely distributed and the claims of the partnership creditors are satisfied. Only after completion of this liquidation process is the partnership terminated.

Limited Partnerships

The purpose of the limited partnership form of business organization is to permit some partnership investors to have limited liability. The limited partner gives up the right to participate in the management of the partnership business in return for limited liability. Like a corporate shareholder, the limited partner may lose his investment but no more.

Characteristics

LO6

Limited partnerships have one or more general partners and one or more limited partners. Normally, limited partners have no obligation for the debts of the partnership. Management of the business of the partnership is in the hands of the general partner or partners. Because limited liability is a privilege given by the state, limited partnerships can be created only under a state statute. All states have such statutes.

Business Form: Certificate of a Limited Partnership

Limited Partnership Certificate

I. The name of the Limited Partnership is Sunset Acres Estates, Limited Partnership.

II. The business of the Limited Partnership shall be the development and operation of a mobile home park in Monroe County, Indiana.

III. The location of the principal place of business of the Limited Partnership shall be 400 North Walnut Street, Bloomington, IN 47401, or wherever the General Partner may from time to time designate.

IV. The name and address of each Partner are as follows:

A. The name of the General Partner is Bloomington Realty, Inc., 400 North Walnut Street, Bloomington, IN 47401.

B. The names and residences of the Limited Partners are:
George E. Ash, 4210 Saratoga Avenue, Bloomington, IN 47401
Helen V. Brown, 4203 E. 3rd Street, Bloomington, IN 47401
Alice A. Jones, 468 Elm Street, Bloomington, IN 47401
Roger S. Smith, 1807 E. 2nd Street, Bloomington, IN 47401

V. The Limited Partnership shall continue until dissolved by any one of the following events:

A. The mutual consent of all Partners,

B. The sale of the Partnership business,

C. The adjudication that the General Partner is bankrupt or the filing of a voluntary petition of bankruptcy or an admission by the General Partner that it is unable to pay its debts.

D. Or in any event, at midnight, December 31, 2013.

VI. The initial capital contribution of the General Partner is $20,000, the agreed value of its services in acquiring the tract to be developed by the Partnership. The initial contribution of each of the Limited Partners is $50,000 in cash.

VII. Each Limited Partner agrees to contribute an additional $30,000 on or before May 1, 2008, and an additional $20,000 on or before May 1, 2009. In addition, each Limited Partner agrees to make an additional capital contribution not to exceed $20,000 on or before May 1, 2010, if in the sole discretion of the General Partner additional capital is needed for the proper development, maintenance, or sale of the property.

VIII. The capital contribution of the Partners shall be repaid upon dissolution and winding up of the Partnership.

(*continued*)

Business Form: Certificate of a Limited Partnership *(concluded)*

IX. The net profits and net losses of the Partnership for any calendar year shall be allocated among the Partners in the same proportion as their capital contributions. However, the profit, if any, from the sale of the property shall be divided equally among the General Partner and the Limited Partners. If any Limited Partner has failed to make any of the capital contributions called for in Articles VI or VII, his share shall be proportionately reduced and reallocated to the other Partners.

X. A Limited Partner or his legal representative may assign his partnership interest at any time and substitute the assignee as a Limited Partner upon notification to the General Partner and all Limited Partners, with a copy of the assignment furnished to the General Partner.

XI. Additional Limited Partners may be added upon the approval of the General Partner and a majority of the then existing Limited Partners.

XII. No Limited Partner shall have priority over any other Limited Partner as to the return of his capital contributions.

IN WITNESS WHEREOF, the Partners have executed this Certificate this 5th day of January, 2008.

LIMITED PARTNERS:

George E. Ash

Helen V. Brown

Alice A. Jones

Roger S. Smith

GENERAL PARTNER:

Bloomington Realty, Inc.

by President

Formalities

The statutory formalities must be complied with to form a limited partnership. A certificate must be filed with the secretary of state or the county recorder. The certificate must describe the nature of the business, its location, and the term of its existence. It must also give the names and addresses of all partners and their capital contributions, listing separately the limited and general partners. A description and a statement of the agreed value of contributions in property other than cash must be included. Certain other information must be provided, such as whether the partnership may admit additional partners and whether limited partners may assign their interests to others. The certificate should also include a statement of the events permitting a partner to withdraw from the limited partnership. Note that the withdrawal of a limited partner does not automatically dissolve the limited partnership.

Rights and Liabilities

Partnership law applies to limited partnerships except to the extent changed by the applicable limited partnership statutes. One fundamental difference from general partnership principles, however, is that limited partners are not fiduciaries. The rights and liabilities of general partners are essentially the same as those of partners in an ordinary partnership. However, without the approval of all the limited partners, the general partners cannot admit other general partners, and they may not add other limited partners unless this right is given in the certificate.

In the Matter of Harwood

637 F.3d 615 (5th Cir. 2011)

FACTS

Harwood was a 50 percent shareholder of B & W Finance Corporation. He served as the president, chief operating officer, and a director of the corporation. B & W owned a 51 percent partnership interest in, and was the sole general partner of, FNFS—a limited partnership. Harwood managed the day-to-day business affairs of the corporation, which had exclusive management authority over the limited partnership. It later was discovered that Harwood was drawing funds from the limited partnership for his personal use, including unsecured loans which he never repaid. When Harwood filed for bankruptcy, the limited partners argued that his debt to FNFS was nondischargeable because he violated the fiduciary duty he owed the limited partners. Harwood conceded that, as an officer and director of B & W, he owed a fiduciary duty to the corporation. Nor did he dispute that, as a general partner of FNFS, the corporation owed a fiduciary duty to the limited partners. However, he contended that he owed no fiduciary duty to the limited partners because he was not a partner of FNFS.

ISSUE

Did Harwood owe a fiduciary duty to the limited partners?

DECISION

Yes. The corporate board of directors basically rubber-stamped his activities regarding the limited partnership. In addition, he exercised virtually all executive power over the limited partnership's operations on a daily basis. No one with daily involvement in FNFS's affairs could challenge Harwood's authority or decision making. The corporate board's entrustment in Harwood of the management of the partnership's affairs and the partners' investments, when combined with the practically complete control that Harwood actually exercised over the partnership's management, compels a conclusion that Harwood stood in a fiduciary capacity to the limited partners.

Liabilities When Formalities Are Absent

Formerly, if the limited partnership failed to file the proper certificate, it would be treated as a general partnership. This resulted in all of the partners, limited and general alike, being personally liable on all partnership debts, Now, however, those who erroneously believe they are limited partners may escape liability under certain conditions. In some states those intended to be limited partners must renounce any interest in the profits of the firm on discovering the error. In others, they must cause a proper certificate to be filed or withdraw from participation in future distributions of profits. However, the limited partners are liable as general partners to any person who extended credit to the partnership before the proper filing of the certificate and who was under the good faith belief that the limited partners were general partners.

Control by Limited Partners

A limited partner who takes part in the control of the business becomes liable to partnership creditors like a general partner. There have been few cases, but it appears that *control* means participation in day-to-day management decisions. If a limited partner is acting substantially like a general partner, she has the liability of a general partner to all creditors of the limited partnership. If she takes part in control of the business but does not act substantially like a general partner, she is liable only to those persons who deal with the limited partnership with actual knowledge of her participation in control.

Dissolution of a Limited Partnership

As with an ordinary partnership, a limited partnership may be dissolved and its business wound up. However, not all events that would have dissolved a general partnership will have the same effect on a limited partnership. This is so because the limited partners are not involved in the actual management of the partnership business. Accordingly, the personality of the limited partners will not always be vital to the existence of the limited partnership.

The death or bankruptcy of a limited partner does not result in dissolution; neither does the addition or substitution of a limited partner. However, the limited partnership certificate must be canceled when all limited partners have died or withdrawn. The retirement, death, or insanity of a general partner usually dissolves a limited partnership. But dissolution can be avoided if the right to continue is granted in the certificate or if all other general and limited partners agree.

Limited Liability Limited Partnership

Some individuals, when forming their business organization, select a variation of a limited partnership, known as a **limited liability limited partnership** (LLLP). Basically, this is a limited partnership except that limited liability is extended to both limited and general partners. However, a general partner does have unlimited liability for any tort or crime she commits. Formation of the LLLP is simple—the partners merely need to indicate the intention of creating an LLLP in their limited partnership certificate, which is then filed with the secretary of state where the business is located.

With the exception of giving limited liability to the general partners, the rules governing LLLPs are identical to those covering limited partnerships. This includes the management responsibilities and the rights and duties of both types of partners. Further, as with limited partnerships, general partners in defectively formed LLLPs may still have limited liability if there was at least substantial compliance with the formation requirements. A growing number of states now offer the LLLP option and, where they do, most limited partnerships are converting to the LLLP form.

Questions and Problem Cases

1. For 12 years, Thomas Wang was the manager and part owner of a hotel in Aurora, Illinois. His sister-in-law, Irene, was aware that Thomas was interested in acquiring another hotel and wired $1,000,000 to Thomas to use for that purpose. Thomas was told that $750,000 of this amount was provided by Irene's sister, Kuei-Ying Chen. Thomas had decided the North Aurora Inn would be a good property to purchase. Its sale price was approximately $1,750,000. Thomas and his wife, Susanna, discussed the purchase with Kuei. In this conversation, Susanna informed Kuei that she would contribute $1,000,000 of her own money so they could then afford to buy the property and have an additional $250,000 for renovations and working capital. Ownership of the hotel and profits therefrom were to be shared proportionately to the promised contributions, 50 percent for Susanna, 37.5 percent for Kuei, and 12.5 percent for Irene. Thomas was to manage the hotel without compensation until the business became profitable. It also was agreed that title to the property would be in all three sisters' names. The hotel was purchased for the $1,750,000 price. However, Susanna did not contribute any cash. It was purchased with $900,000 of Kuei's and Irene's money, with the other $850,000 being financed by a mortgage provided by the seller. The title to the hotel was only in the name of Susanna and Thomas. They formed North Aurora Inn, Inc., a corporation which was owned by Susanna and Thomas only, to manage the hotel. All subsequent losses generated by the business were reported only on Thomas's and Susanna's tax returns. All lease payments that North Aurora Inn, Inc. paid to the hotel were kept by Thomas and Susanna. When Kuei questioned Thomas about the deed, he told her that it had not yet been recorded, even though it actually had been recorded one month earlier. The following August, a document was signed by the three sisters that listed each of their contributions. During the next two years,

Thomas borrowed $940,000 from Kuei. She thought the money was for personal loans to Thomas, when in reality he was using the money for hotel renovations and to make mortgage payments. He later began repaying these loans with funds from the business. When Kuei finally discovered what was occurring, she sued Susanna for breach of her fiduciary duties as a partner. Has Susanna violated her partnership duties to Kuei? Explain.

2. Jerry Gregg engaged in business as a railroad consultant. S.R. Investors, Ltd. (SRI) was formed in 1983 purportedly as a limited partnership to own and operate the Sierra Railroad. Gregg entered into a consulting agreement with SRI, pursuant to which he was to provide services to Sierra. After SRI terminated the relationship, Gregg claimed that he had not been paid for his services. He sued Russell J. Barron and Richard Cohn, claiming they were personally liable on the debt. While Barron and Cohn both invested in SRI as limited partners, Gregg argued that Illinois law does not allow limited partnerships to operate a railroad. Specifically, the state law provides: "*a limited partnership may carry on any business that a partnership without limited partners may carry on except . . . the operation of railroads.*" According to Gregg, because SRI could not be formed properly as a limited partnership, all the "limited partners," including Barron and Cohn, must be construed to be general partners. As general partners, Gregg alleges they are liable for all debts of the partnership. Barron and Cohn assert that they cannot be held liable as general partners because once they learned of Gregg's argument that SRI could not be formed as a limited partnership, they timely withdrew from the partnership pursuant to state law. Did Barron and Cohn lose their limited liability? Explain.

3. Dean Wilkerson and Walter Helms created a corporation, DWA, that operated a furniture factory. They then formed the H&W Partnership for the purpose of buying DWA's facility and leasing it back to the corporation. After purchasing several leather shipments from United States Leather, DWA fell behind in its payments. Wilkerson then met with U.S. Leather officials and gave them a promissory note for the $438,000 balance on DWA's account. He signed the note on behalf of DWA. However, a few days before the first payment was due, Wilkerson requested an extension of time. U.S. Leather agreed to the extension on the condition that H&W was included as a maker of the note. Wilkerson consented and signed the note on behalf of DWA and H&W. When DWA went out of business without ever making a payment, U.S. Leather sued H&W on the note. The partnership argued that it was not liable on the note because Wilkerson did not have authority to bind it. Did Wilkerson have authority to bind H&W on the note?

4. *Video Case:* See "The Partnership." Art, Ben, and Diedre are partners of Alphabet Builders, a partnership in the construction business. They meet at a restaurant with a prospective new partner, Don, who says he will decide whether to enter the partnership after discussing the matter with his wife. During the meeting, they are approached by John, with whom the partnership has been attempting to do business. Art introduces Don to John, stating, "We're celebrating Don's joining Alphabet Builders." Don and John shake hands, and John says, "Congratulations! Alphabet Builders has a very good reputation. In fact, I'm about to become one of your new clients. I signed the contract this morning." Don says nothing in response to John's statement. Subsequently, Don decides not to join Alphabet Builders. Nonetheless, when Alphabet Builders breaches its contract with John, John sues Don on the contract. Is Don liable to John?

5. *Video Case:* See "The Partnership." Art is a partner of Alphabet Builders, a partnership in the construction business. The three partners of Alphabet Builders have agreed

that the partnership may not borrow money unless all the partners approve the borrowing. In the name of the partnership, but without the consent of his partners, Art borrows money from a bank. Art tells the bank that the partnership will use the money for general purposes. Art endorses the loan check in the name of the partnership but deposits the money in his personal account. Art uses the money to purchase commodities futures. Art loses the money on the futures and is unable to repay the loan. The bank sues Alphabet Builders and its partners. Are Alphabet Builders and its partners liable to the bank on the loan? Does Art have any liability to the other two partners?

6. *Video Case:* See "The Partnership." Art retires from Alphabet Builders, a partnership with Ben and Diedre. Zack agrees to replace Art in the partnership. Zack signs an agreement with Art in which Zack assumes Art's liability for all partnership obligations. After Art leaves the partnership, Alphabet Builders falls behind in payments to its creditors, including the following: (a) the bank from which Art obtained a loan in the name of the partnership prior to his leaving the partnership. Art pocketed the money and used it for personal investments. Art did not disclose the loan to his partners or to Zack; (b) the creditor who leases office equipment to Alphabet Builders. The lease agreement predates the time Art left the partnership; and (c) subcontractors owed money on contracts entered into after Art left and Zack entered the partnership. What is Art's liability on these obligations? What liability does Zack have? What other facts might you need to help answer these questions?
7. Schymanski and Conventz entered into an oral partnership agreement for the purpose of building and operating a fishing lodge. The partnership was on a 50–50 basis, with each to contribute equal shares of cash and equal shares of personal services according to their respective expertise. Conventz was to supervise the construction of the lodge and to handle the advertising in Alaska. Schymanski was to conduct a promotional campaign in Germany. After numerous delays and disagreements, Conventz expressed his desire to terminate the partnership. He claimed that he was entitled to compensation for his architectural efforts. Schymanski denied that there was ever an agreement for such compensation. In the absence of an agreement, is Conventz entitled to compensation for the architectural efforts?
8. Parham-Woodman Medical Associates, a general partnership, entered into a loan agreement with Citizens Bank to fund construction of a medical office for the partnership. Ante and King were the partners at the time the loan was extended. As contemplated by the loan agreement, the bank made advances to the partnership from time to time. Nada and Joseph Tas later became partners as well. After their admission to the partnership, the bank made several more advances. After the building was completed, the partnership defaulted on the loan and Ante and King went into bankruptcy, thereby extinguishing their personal liability. The bank then sued Nada and Joseph, claiming they were personally liable for over $500,000 in advances made after their admission into the partnership. Are Nada and Joseph personally liable for those advances?

Chapter 28

Formation and Termination of Corporations

Learning Objectives

After you have studied this chapter, you should be able to:

1. Explain the legal liability of both promoters and corporations for preincorporation contracts.
2. Identify the basic steps in the incorporation process and explain legal rules when there has been a defective incorporation.
3. Recognize when a court will pierce the corporate veil and hold shareholders personally liable for corporate obligations.
4. Identify the special problems accompanying close corporations and explain how to protect against those risks.
5. Describe the various ways in which a corporation may be terminated.

Jane Vosseller decided to operate a retail establishment. She intended to organize the business as a corporation that would be named Pottery Warehouse, Inc. On February 28, she executed a lease with Company Stores Corporation for rental of store premises for a five-year term. She signed the lease, "THE POTTERY WAREHOUSE, INC., a corporation to be formed under the laws of the State of Tennessee. By Jane M. Vosseller, Its President." Pottery Warehouse was not incorporated until

(continued)

March 29. Later, when the corporation breached the terms of the lease, Company Stores attempted to hold Vosseller personally liable on the lease.[1]

- What is a corporate promoter? When is she liable for preincorporation contracts? How can this potential liability be reduced?
- What is a defectively formed corporation? When are people personally liable for the debts of defectively formed corporations?
- How much capitalization and what level of formalities must be met before a corporation will be treated as an entity separate and apart from its owners? When will a court "pierce the veil" and make shareholders personally liable on corporate obligations?

Introduction

Corporations are extremely important in today's society. The growth of the modern corporation has been largely responsible for the dynamic economic development attained by this country over the last century. Through corporations, people are able to invest money in a business enterprise without worrying about unlimited liability or management responsibilities. Thus, corporation law gives business the capability to raise the capital necessary to achieve the economies of scale vital to economic efficiency.

If you plan to form a new business, you may very well decide that it should be a corporation. After all, not all corporations are huge economic entities; most of them are small businesses. Further, today it is very easy to form a corporation.

This chapter will look at the basic issues that arise in the incorporation process. Specifically, it will examine

1. The nature of a corporation.
2. The preincorporation process.
3. The actual incorporation.
4. Liability for defective incorporation.
5. When courts will pierce the corporate veil.
6. Close corporations.
7. The termination process.

Nature of a Corporation

The Principal Characteristics of the Corporation

The concept of a corporation developed in early law. One advantage of the corporate form of business is that it makes it easier to hold property for long periods of time. This

[1]*Company Stores Development Corporation v. The Pottery Warehouse, Inc.*, 733 S.W.2d 886 (Ct. App. Tenn. 1987).

is because the corporation is treated as an intangible being with a life separate from the lives of its owners.

Other powers also came to be associated with the corporate form of organization early on. Because of its separate identity, the corporation can hold and convey property in its own name. Further, it can sue and be sued in its own name. Finally, a corporation possesses the right to make bylaws to govern the relations among its members.

Types of Corporations

Today, three principal types of corporations are commonly recognized.

Governmental Corporations

The **governmental corporation** is often called a **municipal corporation.** Examples are a city, a school corporation, and a sewage district. Such governmental corporations usually, although not always, have the power to tax. They frequently operate much like business corporations except that they do not seek to make a profit. Examples are the Tennessee Valley Authority and the Federal Home Loan Bank.

Nonprofit Corporations

Nonprofit corporations are similar to nontaxing governmental corporations. They differ, however, in that they are formed and operated by private persons. Examples include hospitals, clubs, and some very large businesses such as Blue Cross-Blue Shield Association. Their founders and members are not permitted to make a profit from the operation of the corporation, although the officers and employees are paid salaries. Each of the states has a special statute under which nonprofit corporations are to be formed and operated.

For-Profit Corporations

For-profit corporations are by far the most common of the various types. The aim of such corporations is usually to make a profit that may be distributed to the shareholders as dividends. Sometimes, however, most or all of the profits are reinvested in the corporation in order to make the business grow. Then, at a later time, shareholders may sell their stock or the entire business may be sold. In this way, the shareholders receive their profits while paying only the lower capital gains tax rather than an income tax on the retained profits.

Concept Summary: Types of Corporations

Government Corporation		• Examples: city, school corporation • Generally don't seek profit • Often have power to tax
Nonprofit Corporation		• Examples: hospital, club • Not permitted to make profit • Members may draw salaries • Incorporated under special statute
For-Profit Corporation	Publicly Held	• Public investors • Profits generally distributed as dividends • Formed under general incorporation statutes
	Close	• Small group of investors • Earnings often reinvested • Greater management flexibility is permitted

For-profit corporations are often divided into publicly held and close corporations. The stock of a **close corporation** is generally held by a small group of people who know one another. Usually some or all of them intend to be active in management. An example is a family-owned and -operated retail shop. The close corporation can be contrasted with the **publicly held corporation,** which sells shares to people who often have little interest in it except as investors. General Motors Corporation is a good example. Of course, most publicly held corporations are much smaller than GM. However, most of the largest corporations are publicly held. In a large corporation with stock owned by many scattered shareholders, ownership of less than 10 percent of the shares may be enough to control the enterprise.

From here on we shall discuss only the for-profit corporation. However, many of the legal principles and rules are the same for all types of corporations. Therefore, some of the cases may involve nonprofit corporations.

Regulation of Corporations

The Model Business Corporation Act (MBCA), prepared by the Corporation, Banking, and Business Law Section of the American Bar Association, was drafted as a model statute for adoption by the legislatures of the various states. The MBCA has been amended many times and was completely revised in 1984. While the old MBCA is still the basis for the statutes of the majority of the states, most of the provisions of the revised MBCA do represent the rule of the majority of the courts in the United States. Accordingly, this book will concentrate on the revised MBCA, although the old MBCA provisions will be noted when they deviate greatly from the revised model statute.

The Preincorporation Process

Promoters

LO1

Promoters are people who bring a corporation into being. Thus, promotion is a vital activity in a free enterprise system. The promoter is the person who has the idea for a business. She finds people who are willing to finance it—to buy shares of stock and/or to lend money and credit. Contracts must be made for building or leasing space, buying or renting equipment, hiring employees, buying supplies and advertising, and whatever else is required for the early operation of the business. Most state incorporation statutes permit reserving a name for a proposed corporation. This is also done by the promoter. She must arrange for the filing of the legal papers to incorporate the business, and she will usually guide the corporation through the early months or years before the new company is a "going concern."

While the promoter may start with an idea and build a corporate business around it, this is not always the case. In many instances, the promoter will take a sole proprietorship or partnership and convert it into the corporate form. And, of course, rather than always having a single promoter, frequently the corporation will be created through the vision and efforts of a group of promoters.

Legal Liability of Promoters

Liability to the Corporation

The relation of promoters to the corporation, to its shareholders, and to those with whom they contract is unique. Promoters are not agents of the corporation prior to its incorporation because the corporation (the principal) is not yet in existence. Promoters are not agents of the persons who are interested in the venture because the promoters were not appointed by them and are not under their control.

Nevertheless, promoters owe a fiduciary duty to the corporation and to the persons interested in it. This includes the duties of full disclosure, good faith, and absolute honesty to the corporation and to the original shareholders. Thus, it would be a breach of duty to use money received on stock subscriptions to pay the expenses of forming the corporation unless this intent were disclosed.

A promoter often takes an option on property or makes an outright purchase on behalf of the corporation. If he or she misrepresents the price paid or to be paid, the corporation may recover the secret profit made by the promoter. However, if the promoter makes a full disclosure of the expected profit to an independent board of directors, the corporation cannot recover. Of course, if the board of directors is under the control of the promoter, the corporation could rescind the contract or recover damages for breach of the fiduciary duty.

Liability to Third Parties

Promoters are generally held liable on contracts they make on behalf of corporations that are not yet formed. If the corporation is never formed, or if it fails to adopt the promoter's preincorporation agreement, the promoter is liable. This is based on agency law: An agent who makes a contract for a nonexistent principal is personally liable for it. If there is more than one promoter, they are all liable under a joint enterprise theory. Promoters sometimes attempt to escape this potential liability by having the third party agree, when the preincorporation contract is made, that the promoter is not to be liable. The disadvantage of this strategy, however, is that neither the promoter nor the corporation can force the third party to perform such a contract. This results from the rule for bilateral contracts that if one party is not bound, neither is the other because such contracts lack *mutuality.*

After the corporation comes into existence, it may agree to assume liability for the promoter's preincorporation contracts. Such an agreement between the promoter and the corporation, in and of itself, is not sufficient to relieve the promoter from all liability on the contracts. This is so because the third party contracted directly with the promoter. The promoter is released from liability on the preincorporation contracts only if the corporation, the promoter, and the third party all agree that the corporation will be substituted for the promoter. This agreement is called a *novation.*

In the case that opened this chapter, Vosseller acted as a promoter in negotiating the preincorporation contract for The Pottery Warehouse. However, the court held that she was not personally liable on the contract. This is so because many courts find against personal liability when a contract is made in the name and solely on the credit of the proposed corporation and the other contracting party knows that the corporation does not yet exist.

Liability of the Corporation

Liability to the Promoter

As a general rule, corporations are not required to compensate promoters for the services they render during the preincorporation period. However, there is nothing illegal or wrong if promoters are paid for their services. Profit to the promoters is illegal only if it is not disclosed. After formation of the corporation, it may agree to pay the promoters not only for their expenses but also for their services. Frequently, promoters are issued shares of the stock of the new corporation for their services. In the past, many states had not permitted promotional services to be used as consideration for shares in the new corporation. However, the current trend in law, as evidenced by the revised MBCA, is to permit the corporation to issue shares in return for the promoters' preincorporation services.

Liability to Third Parties

When the corporation comes into existence, it is not automatically liable on the contracts made by the promoter. As indicated above, the corporation cannot be liable as principal since it was not in existence. The same fact prevents the corporation from ratifying the promoter's contracts; ratification requires capacity to contract at the time the contract was made.

Nevertheless, all American courts, except those of Massachusetts, have held corporations liable if, after incorporation, the *board acts to adopt the contract* (adoption is similar to ratification in its effect). Mere acceptance of the benefits of the contract is generally sufficient to bind the corporation. Massachusetts, however, requires that the parties expressly create a novation before the corporation can be held liable for the preincorporation contracts.

The next case examines a corporation's right to enforce a preincorporation contract against the party with whom the promoter dealt. Note how generous the court was in determining if the corporation had ratified, assumed, or adopted the contract.

SmithStearn Yachts v. Gyrographic Communications

2006 Conn. Super. LEXIS (Super. Ct. 2006)

FACTS

Leathem Stearn, claiming to act on behalf of a limited liability company, contracted with Gyrographic Communications. The agreement called for Gyrographic to provide advertising and marketing services for the limited liability company's yachting business. In reality, the limited liability company never came into existence. Instead, a corporation, SmithStearn Yachts, Inc., was created. Later, the corporation sued Gyrographic, asserting that the company failed to provide its services in a timely and workmanlike manner. Gyrographic moved to dismiss the lawsuit on the grounds that SmithStearn Yachts had no standing to bring the claim because the contract was with the limited liability company and not the corporation. SmithStearn responded that Leathem Stearn acted as a promoter for the corporation and that the corporation assumed and ratified the contract after its creation.

ISSUE

Did the corporation have standing because it ratified the preincorporation contract?

DECISION

Yes. A corporation may after its organization become liable on preliminary contracts made by its promoters by expressly adopting such contracts or by receiving the benefits from them. Although the corporation was formed after the execution of the agreement, it received the benefit of the services pursuant to the agreement. It also made payments to Gyrographic. Furthermore, ratification, adoption, or acceptance of a preincorporation contract by a promoter need not be expressed, but may be implied from acts or acquiescence on the part of the corporation or its authorized agents. SmithStearn implicitly ratified the agreement when it brought this action. By suing under the agreement, the corporation is also assuming the liabilities under it, thereby enforcing and adopting the agreement.

Ethics in Action

When might a corporation refuse to adopt a preincorporation contract? Is it right for a corporation to refuse to adopt a contract entered into on its behalf by a corporate promoter?

Incorporation

The Right to Incorporate

All business corporations derive their existence from the state in which they are incorporated. The earliest business corporations in the American colonies obtained charters from the King of England, since the colonies were governed by the English monarch. The Constitutional Convention of 1797 considered giving this power to the federal government; however, no such power was included in the Constitution. Therefore, this power was left to the states. To form a corporation, the promoters had to find a legislator who was willing to introduce a bill. The legislature then decided whether to grant a charter.

Early legislators feared the growth of corporate power. Charters, therefore, tended to be for short periods of time. For example, a charter might have to be renewed after 10 years. The powers granted and the amount of capital involved were generally rather limited. Most of the earliest corporations were formed to supply public facilities such as bridges, toll roads, and waterworks. A few, however, were mining and manufacturing businesses.

As commercial and industrial development progressed in the United States, legislators were impressed by the resultant benefits brought to the people and, accordingly, they wanted to encourage corporations. At this time, there was also an expanding belief in greater freedom and equality for all people. These factors resulted in the passage of **general incorporation laws,** which made incorporation a right instead of a legislative privilege. Under these statutes, all that is necessary to form a corporation is to prepare **articles of incorporation** that comply with the state's incorporation statute. If they do, a state official—usually the secretary of state—has a duty to issue a certificate of incorporation.

Deciding Where to Incorporate

Frequently, the corporation will be incorporated in the state where most of its business will be conducted. However, if the enterprise is conducting its affairs in interstate commerce, the promoters may decide to incorporate in a state other than the state in which the principal offices are located. Many large corporations shop around for the state that will offer the most benefits to the enterprise.

Concept Summary: Deciding Where to Incorporate

Expenses	Restrictions on Internal Governance
Incorporation fees	Incorporation statute
Annual fees	Judicial decisions
Taxes	General regulations

Two fundamental considerations frequently arise when the promoters are trying to decide where to incorporate. First, the business may be incorporated in a state where the incorporation fees, taxes, annual fees, and other charges tend to be lower. Second, the promoters may decide to incorporate in a state where the corporation statute and judicial decisions grant management considerable freedom from shareholder interference in the operation of corporate affairs. Traditionally, Delaware and, more recently, Ohio, have been attractive states for incorporation.

Steps in Incorporation

The following steps governing the incorporation process are included in the MBCA:

LO2

1. Preparation of the articles of incorporation.
2. Signing and authenticating the articles by one or more of the incorporators.
3. Filing the articles with the secretary of state and paying all required fees.
4. Issuance of the certificate of incorporation by the secretary of state.
5. Holding an initial organizational meeting.

Different states may vary slightly in exactly what they require in order to incorporate; however, the above requirements are included in the corporation laws of most states. Further, many states require that a minimum of $1,000 be contributed to the business before it can receive a certificate of incorporation. Some states have an additional requirement directing that a copy of the articles of incorporation be filed in the county where the corporation has its principal place of business.

Concept Summary: Liability on Preincorporation Contracts

	Before Incorporation	After Incorporation, before Adoption	After Incorporation, after Adoption
Promoter Contracts with Third Party	Promoter: liable to third party	Promoter: liable to third party	Promoter: liable until novation
Third Party Unaware That Contract Is for Corporation	Corporation: no liability	Corporation: no liability	Corporation: liable to third party
	Third party: liable to promoter	Third party: liable to promoter	Third party: liable to corporation after novation
Promoter Contracts with Third Party	Promoter: no liability	Promoter: no liability	Promoter: no liability
	Corporation: no liability	Corporation: no liability	Corporation: liable to third party
Third Party Agrees to Hold Only the Corporation Liable	Third party: no liability	Third party: no liability	Third party: liable to corporation
Promoter Contracts with Third Party for Benefit of Corporation without Disclaiming Liability	Promoter: liable to third party	Promoter: liable to third party	Promoter: no liability
	Corporation: no liability	Corporation: no liability	Corporation: liable to third party
	Third party: liable to promoter	Third party: liable to promoter	Third party: liable to corporation

Business Form: Articles of Incorporation of Universal Enterprises, Inc.

Article I. The name of the corporation is Universal Enterprises, Inc.

Article II. The purpose of the Corporation is to engage in any lawful activity for which corporations may be organized under the Domestic Corporations for Profit Act of Indiana.

Article III. The term of existence of the Corporation shall be perpetual.

Article IV. The post office address of the principal office of the Corporation is 205 North College Avenue, Bloomington, IN 47401. The name of its Resident Agent is Charles Smith, 205 North College Avenue, Bloomington, IN 47401.

Article V. The total number of authorized shares shall be 1,000 common shares, each with a par value of $100.

Article VI. The shares may be issued in one (1) or more classes. Each class shall have such relative rights, preferences, and limitations, and shall bear such designations, as shall be determined by resolution of the Board of Directors prior to the issuance of any shares of such classes.

Article VII.

(a) Each share shall be entitled to one (1) vote on all matters.

(b) Cumulative voting shall not be permitted on any matter.

Article VIII. The Corporation will not commence business until at least $1,000 has been received for the issuance of shares.

Article IX.

(a) The initial Board of Directors of the Corporation shall be composed of three members. The number of Directors may from time to time be fixed by the Bylaws of the Corporation at any number not less than three (3). In the absence of a Bylaw, the number shall be three (3).

(b) Directors need not be shareholders of the Corporation.

Article X. The initial Board of Directors of the Corporation and their post office addresses are as follows:

Alvin B. Cortwright, 1234 Saratoga Drive, Bloomington, IN 47401
Douglas E. Fenske, 567 East 9th Street, Bloomington, IN 47401
Gordon H. Inskeep, 8910 East 10th Street, Bloomington, IN 47401

Article XI. The name and post office address of the Incorporator is: P. D. Quick, 1112 North Walnut Street, Bloomington, IN 47401.

Article XII. Provisions for the conduct of the affairs of the Corporation shall be contained in the Bylaws. The Bylaws may be amended from time to time by the affirmative vote of the majority of the Board of Directors.

IN WITNESS WHEREOF, the undersigned, being the Incorporator designated in Article XI, has executed these Articles of Incorporation and certifies to the truth of the facts above stated, this 12th day of November, 2008.

P. D. Quick

P. D. QUICK

Contents of the Articles of Incorporation

The articles of incorporation serve the same function as a charter. They are rather like a constitution in that they are the basic document of the corporation and a major source of its powers. The articles will generally be prepared for the corporation by a lawyer because most states have statutes that prescribe the general form of the document; however, these requirements may vary from state to state.

Mandatory Contents

The MBCA lists the following matters that *must* be included in the articles of incorporation:

1. The name of the corporation, which must not be deceptively similar to that of any other corporation registered earlier. (It must contain the word *corporation, incorporated, company,* or *limited,* or an abbreviation.)
2. The number of shares of capital stock that the corporation shall have authority to issue.
3. The address of the initial registered office of the corporation and the name of its registered agent.
4. The name and address of each incorporator.

Optional Contents

Under the MBCA, the following matters *may* be included in the articles:

1. The duration of the corporation, which may be, and usually is, perpetual.
2. The purpose of the corporation. Frequently, this is stated very broadly, such as to "engage in any lawful activity."
3. The par value of the shares of the corporation.
4. The number and names of the initial board of directors.
5. Any additional provisions that are not inconsistent with the state's corporation law. These may include dividend rights and quorum requirements, as well as procedures for the election and removal of directors.

Who May Be Incorporators?

Some states require that at least three natural persons who are adults serve as the incorporator. The MBCA relaxes this rule by permitting a single person, a partnership, an unincorporated association, or even another corporation to act as an incorporator. The incorporator does not incur any special liabilities as a result of her status. She really has no function beyond lending her name and signature to the incorporation process.

The Certificate of Incorporation

The secretary of state reviews the articles of incorporation in order to ensure that they comply with the requirements of the state's incorporation statute. If they do, the secretary of state issues a certificate of incorporation, which certifies that the corporation is in existence.

Organization Meeting

After approval of the articles of incorporation, the MBCA requires that an organization meeting be conducted by the board of directors. In some states, this first meeting is to be held by the incorporators rather than by the directors. The MBCA specifies that bylaws shall be adopted and officers elected at the organization meeting. Usually a corporate seal is adopted, the form of stock certificates is approved, stock subscriptions are accepted, and issuance of stock is authorized. Other business may include adoption of the promoter's contracts, authorization of payment of or reimbursement for expenses of incorporation, and determination of the salaries of officers.

Corporate Seal

Generally, a corporation will adopt a seal. In many states, the corporation must authenticate all real estate documents (deeds and mortgages) by affixing the seal to them. The seal is usually kept by the corporate secretary.

Bylaws

The function of bylaws is to establish rules for the conduct of the internal affairs of the corporation. The bylaws usually supplement the articles of incorporation by more precisely defining rights and responsibilities of the parties. (If the articles of incorporation are analogous to a constitution, the bylaws are analogous to statutes.)

The bylaws usually set out the duties and authority of the officers and the conduct of meetings. This would include the time and place of the annual shareholders' meeting and how special meetings of shareholders are to be called. They may establish the quorum necessary for the meetings and how elections to the board of directors shall be conducted. They also provide for the organization of directors into committees, if desired, and for the frequency and conduct of board meetings. The bylaws usually set up the procedures for the transfer of shares, for the keeping of stock records, and for declaring and paying dividends.

Occasionally, particularly in close corporations, some of these matters are included in the articles. However, some managerial freedom is lost if too many detailed issues are included in the articles rather than in the bylaws. This is because amendment of the articles of incorporation can be expensive and requires a filing with the secretary of state. Amendments to bylaws, however, usually can be made by the directors at any time without special formalities.

To be valid, bylaws must be consistent with state law and the articles of incorporation. Directors, officers, and shareholders of the corporation are bound by bylaws that are properly adopted. Others, including corporate employees, are not bound by them unless they have notice or knowledge of them.

The MBCA gives the directors the power to adopt the initial bylaws. Some statutes give this power to the incorporators or the initial shareholders. The MBCA and most statutes give the power of amendment and repeal to the directors; however, shareholders have an inherent right to make bylaws. Thus, if they choose to do so, the shareholders may amend or repeal the bylaws adopted by the directors.

The *Ultra Vires* Doctrine

A corporation obtains its legal powers from the state in which it is incorporated. These powers come from the corporation statute, the court decisions of that state, and the articles of incorporation. Simultaneously, there are limitations imposed on the powers of the corporation and its management. Such constraints generally arise in statutes, the articles of incorporation, and the bylaws.

For many years, courts took the view that acts done by corporations that were beyond the authority given them by either the state of incorporation or their articles were void and of no effect. A transaction that was beyond the corporation's powers was said to be ***ultra vires.*** The state (through the attorney general), a shareholder, or the corporation itself, could prevent the enforcement of an *ultra vires* contract. This view was often used by the corporation to avoid a contract that later looked unattractive because of a change of conditions; unfairness to the other party to the contract was often the result.

Courts have not all agreed in handling these cases. Most of them have refused to enforce wholly executory contracts but have let stand contracts that had been performed by both parties. Contracts that had been partially executed were the most difficult for the courts. The majority of courts have held that such a contract is enforceable if one of the parties has received a benefit.

The MBCA has eliminated the use of *ultra vires* as a defense to the enforcement of a contract. However, it permits a shareholder to seek a court injunction to stop a corporation from carrying out a proposed action beyond its powers. It also permits the corporation itself, a shareholder, or a receiver in a bankruptcy to bring a suit for damages to the corporation against the officers and/or directors who entered into an *ultra vires* contract. The state's attorney general is also permitted to enjoin the corporation from entering into unauthorized transactions.

Keene v. Brookhaven Academy

28 So.2d 1285 (Miss. Sup. Ct. 2010)

FACTS

Brookhaven Academy is a for-profit corporation. It is a general-purpose corporation. One of the enumerated corporate purposes for the Academy in its articles of incorporation is for the organization and operation of schools. It has many others, including "To have and to exercise all powers conferred by the laws of the State of Mississippi upon corporations," and to act in matters concerning the sale, lease, acquisition, and disposal of real and personal property. Keene, an Academy shareholder, sued the corporation after it set up and transferred the use of assets to a nonprofit, educational foundation. Keene argued that the court should block the transfer of assets because the transfer was outside of the Academy's corporate powers.

ISSUE

Was the transfer of assets an *ultra vires* act?

DECISION

No. The term "ultra vires" has been used to refer to acts that the corporation's charter does not authorize. However, the Academy is a general-purpose corporation. This is clear from the broad grant of authority in its articles of incorporation. Therefore, Keene's contention that the corporation's transfer of assets to the educational foundation was *ultra vires* in nature is without merit. It clearly was within the confines of the power conferred on the Academy.

Defective Incorporation

LO2

Many times, corporate promoters and others will claim to be acting for a corporation before all of the incorporation requirements have been met. When such misrepresentations arise, it is important to determine the liability of parties involved in the defectively formed corporation. Several approaches are currently being used to resolve these situations.

Modern Approaches

Liability under the Old MBCA

A majority of the states follow the "old MBCA." It holds that the *issuance of the certificate of incorporation* is conclusive proof of incorporation in all challenges to the corporate status except a *quo warranto* action brought by the secretary of state. (A *quo warranto* action is a suit brought by the state attempting to force the business to stop acting as a corporation.)

Under the old MBCA approach, all persons who assume to act as a corporation when the certificate of incorporation has not been issued are jointly and severally liable for the business debts. It is not altogether clear whether this personal liability would attach to all shareholders or only to those people involved in managing the business.

Liability under the Revised MBCA

The *filing* of the articles of incorporation, evidenced by the return of the copy stamped by the secretary of state, is conclusive proof of incorporation under the revised MBCA. As with the old MBCA, however, this presumption may be overcome in a *quo warranto* proceeding brought by the state.

The revised MBCA somewhat clarifies exactly who will be jointly and severally liable for the business debts after the defective incorporation. Such liability would be imposed only on promoters, managers, and shareholders who both (1) participated in management and policy decisions and (2) knew of the defective incorporation. All others would be released from any liability in excess of their initial investment.

Shareholders and others who take no active part in a defectively formed corporation are frequently able to avoid personal liability. Similarly, those who mistakenly believe that the corporation is in existence have no personal liability.

Historical Approaches

The MBCA approaches to defective incorporation brought greater clarity than existed under the traditional approaches to the problem. Historically, a defective incorporation might lead to personal liability on the part of promoters, managers, and shareholders, as well as rescission of contracts made on behalf of the defectively formed business. In deciding what consequences should arise, the courts often made their determination based on the intent of the parties and their amount of compliance with the incorporation statute. The consequences that attended the failure to properly incorporate depended on whether the business was described as a *de jure* corporation, a *de facto* corporation, or a corporation by estoppel.

Concept Summary: Liability for Defective Incorporation

	Old MBCA	Revised MBCA	*De Jure*	*De Facto*	Corporation by Estoppel
Time When Incorporation Occurs	Issuance of certificate of incorporation	Return of "stamped" articles of incorporation	Substantial compliance with all mandatory provisions	Honest attempt to comply with mandatory provisions	Reliance on representation of incorporation
Liability for Defective Attempt to Incorporate	All who assume to act as a corporation	All who: 1. Participate in management *and* 2. Knew of defect	Generally, nobody (a few states permit a *quo warranto* action)	May be *quo warranto* action	Active managers (tort liability on everyone)

De Jure Corporation

In a *de jure* corporation, the promoters substantially complied with all *mandatory* provisions. (Mandatory provisions are those that the corporation statute says "must" be done in order to protect the public interest. Other provisions are merely directory and their omission will not destroy the enterprise's corporate identity.) In these instances, the business was treated as a corporation in all instances except a *quo warranto* proceeding.

De Facto Corporation

A *de facto* corporation existed when there was an honest attempt to comply with the mandatory provisions of the corporate statute, yet the attempt still failed in some material respect (e.g., the business failed to hold an organizational meeting). The *de facto* corporation could not be challenged by a third party, and the corporation itself was not permitted to deny its corporate existence.

Corporation by Estoppel

Sometimes people hold themselves out as representing a corporation when no real attempt to incorporate has been made. In these instances, the courts would not let either of the parties to the contracts avoid them due to the misrepresentation of the corporation status. This is so because the promoter pretending to represent a corporation should not be able to benefit from his misrepresentation and the other party suffers no undue harm since he intended to contract with a business possessing only limited liability.

Hildreth v. Tidewater Equipment Co.

838 A.2d 1204 (Md. Ct. App. 2003)

FACTS

John Hildreth was the sole shareholder, director, and officer of a New Jersey corporation known as HCE, Inc. (HCE-NJ). The corporation engaged in the construction business as a subcontractor on various commercial construction projects. It began doing business in Maryland. Although Hildreth had formed a number of other corporations in Maryland, he did not register HCE-NJ in the state as was required by Maryland law. When HCE-NJ began to do business in Maryland, there was already existing a Maryland corporation by the name of HCE, Inc. (HCE-Md). It was properly incorporated in the state and had no connection with Hildreth or HCE-NJ. Ultimately, the Maryland corporation's president learned of Hildreth's existence and threatened legal action if Hildreth did not stop using the HCE name immediately. Such use did not stop. Instead, Hildreth registered HCE-NJ with the Maryland Department of Assessments and Taxation. By this time, HCE-NJ stopped making payments on a crane it had been leasing from Tidewater Equipment Company. That company then claimed Hildreth was personally liable. Tidewater argued that Hildreth knew that there was a Maryland corporation known as HCE, Inc., and that he had no right to do business in Maryland under that name, especially since Tidewater did not know there was another HCE, Inc., or that the company operated by Hildreth was a New Jersey corporation.

ISSUE

Is Hildreth personally liable on the lease agreement?

DECISION

No. HCE-NJ was a *de jure* corporation. Hildreth correctly notes that officers and directors of a foreign *de jure* corporation are not personally liable for corporate debts solely because the corporation fails to qualify to do business in a state. This is particularly true because Tidewater cannot deny the existence of HCE-NJ when that corporation was a *de jure* corporation and Tidewater knew that it was dealing with a corporation. HCE-NJ was a valid, subsisting corporation which, until it suffered a reversal of fortunes, had substantial assets and business prospects. Although the conclusion is certainly warranted that Hildreth deliberately permitted HCE-NJ to operate in Maryland without benefit of registration and with knowledge of the existence of HCE-Md, there is no evidence that conduct in any way influenced Tidewater to enter into the contractual arrangement from which this debt arose. Tidewater knew that it was dealing with a corporation and, in fact, had visited HCE-NJ's offices several times.

E-Commerce Tidewater believed that Hildreth should be personally liable on HCE-NJ's contract, in part, because HCE-NJ, a New Jersey corporation, failed to register to do business in Maryland. Some corporations employ online consultants to assist them in registering to do business. One such company can be found at www.usregisteredagents.com.

Piercing the Corporate Veil

Effect

LO3 Normally, shareholders in corporations are not personally liable for the debts of the corporation. This limited liability probably is the principal reason that people incorporate a business today. Through incorporation, the owners' loss is limited to the extent of their investment in the corporation. However, in some instances, a creditor may be able to persuade a court to disregard this separateness between shareholder and corporation. If so, it is said that the court has pierced the corporate veil. This is done by the court in order to give the creditor a judgment against one or more of the shareholders. The shareholders held personally liable on the debt usually are only those who are active in the management of the business.

Common Situations

There are several situations in which a court may pierce the veil. One is when the corporation is given so few assets by its promoters that it could not be expected to pay its debts. Starting a corporation "on a shoestring" (called **undercapitalization**) is not in itself unlawful. However, it may amount to fraud if the objective seems to be to operate a risky business while avoiding the foreseeable claims of creditors.

A number of cases have held shareholders personally liable where they mixed their personal dealings and corporate transactions as if all were personal. The corporation is then viewed as the **alter ego** of the shareholder-manager. The likelihood of the court's piercing

Kertesz v. Korn

698 F.3d 89 (2d Cir. 2012)

FACTS

Emery Kertesz sought indemnification from his employer, General Video Corporation (GVC), for legal fees he incurred while successfully defending himself in a lawsuit brought by GVC against him in his role as a corporate officer. In this case, Kertesz asserts that Justin Korn, the majority shareholder of GVC, is personally liable for GVC's payments on an alter-ego, veil-piercing theory. In his defense, Korn argues that Kertesz cannot maintain that he is entitled to corporate indemnification and at the same time seek to challenge the very existence of the corporate structure he claims legally entitles him to officer/director indemnification.

ISSUE

May Kertesz use a veil-piercing strategy while attempting to protect his rights as a corporate officer?

DECISION

Yes. Specifically, Korn is claiming that, by trying to pierce the veil, Kertesz is asking the court to disregard the corporate form, while claiming the rights of a corporate officer. An action to pierce the corporate veil does not deny a corporation's legal existence. Rather, such an action charges that the corporation's owners used the corporation as a mere instrumentality or alter ego and disregarded corporate formalities. Where a corporation's owners abuse the corporation's legally limited liability to effect injustice, the corporation may be considered as an agency, adjunct, or instrumentality of its owner, and a court may exercise its equitable power to disregard the legal privilege of the corporate form to reach the owner's assets. The alter-ego claim thus turns on the facts of the owner's operation of the corporation and its relationship to the alleged victim. But if successful, the claim does not affect the corporation's legal structure or existence as against all persons. It is therefore not inconsistent for a party both to seek indemnification from a corporation as its officer and also to seek recovery from the personal assets of a corporation corporate owner who abused the corporation's legal form for his own gain. Of course, an officer who seeks indemnification may face *factual* obstacles on the road to an alter-ego claim. In contrast to an innocent outsider, a corporate officer is more likely to have inside knowledge of the corporation's activities. It may be more difficult for a majority shareholder to deceive a fellow insider, which in turn may make it more difficult for an insider to prove the overall injustice or unfairness necessary to pursue an alter-ego claim.

the veil is greater if there is undercapitalization coupled with the absence of strict adherence to corporate formalities such as holding shareholders' and directors' meetings.

Similar principles are followed by courts in dealing with suits against corporations that operate a part of their business through a subsidiary corporation. (A subsidiary corporation is one in which a majority of stock is owned by a parent corporation.) If the subsidiary is given a few assets and most decisions are made by the parent, the parent corporation may be held liable for the subsidiary's debts.

Requirements

The traditional judicial rule is that the court will pierce the veil when two requirements are met.

1. There must be *domination* of the corporation by one or more of its shareholders.
2. The domination must result in an *improper* purpose.

Ethics in Action

Suppose that Smith incorporates his restaurant and is the sole shareholder of the corporation. While he has purchased the normal insurance coverage for a restaurant of this size and type, the policy is not large enough to satisfy the claims of his many injured customers after the ceiling collapses, causing substantial personal injury when the restaurant was particularly crowded. Is it ethical for Smith to oppose the efforts of the injured patrons to reach his personal assets when the corporate assets prove insufficient?

Concept Summary: Piercing the Corporate Veil

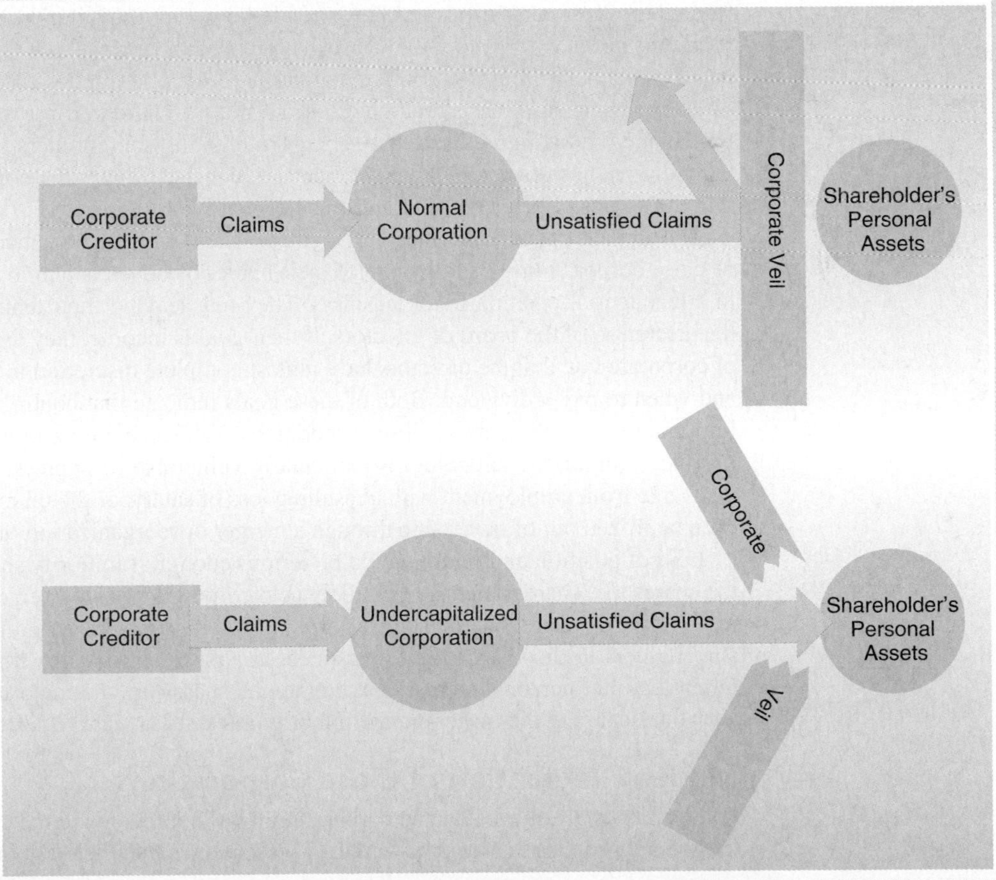

The improper purpose most frequently arises when the corporation defrauds its creditors by not having sufficient assets available to meet expected claims.

Close Corporations

Most incorporated businesses are close corporations. In fact, most of the firms listed among the Fortune 500 began as close corporations. Generally, businesses do not start out as publicly traded corporations. Instead, they are originally organized as close corporations and go public only after several years.

While there is no uniform definition for a close corporation, most such entities do share certain characteristics. Four traits are common:

LO4

1. The shareholders are few in number.
2. Shareholders usually live in the same geographic area and know one another and their skills.
3. All or most of the shareholders are active in the business.
4. There is no established market for the stock.

Unsuitability of Traditional Corporation Law

Those establishing businesses usually form corporations rather than partnerships. They seek limited liability, certain tax consequences, and perhaps other perceived or actual advantages for shareholders. However, because relationships between shareholders are frequently close and informal, they often believe that they should be able to work their problems out in any manner they wish, as can usually be done in a partnership. One of the basic principles of corporation law is that majority rule applies to both shareholder and director action. Another is that the directors, not the shareholders, are given the authority to manage the business. Also, the general rule is that shareholders are free to dispose of their shares by sale or gift. This is, of course, consistent with the common law principles that the owner of property is free to transfer it at will.

The application of these rules is often inconsistent with the objectives of the shareholders of close corporations. Usually, one of their main objectives is employment for themselves in a managerial position in the business. They fear leaving their tenure in that position to the discretion of the board of directors. If their goal is income, they are faced with the rules of corporate law that the directors have almost complete discretion in determining whether and when to pay a dividend. Both of these goals indicate that control of the corporation is important to shareholders in close corporations. Yet, since corporation law calls for majority rule, a minority shareholder is particularly vulnerable to oppression. This may involve discharge from employment with a resulting loss of salary, or the minority shareholder may even be frozen out of ownership through a merger or reorganization of the corporation.

Loss of position and salary would be serious enough if minority shareholders could sell the shares like shareholders in a publicly held corporation. However, due to the vulnerability of minority shareholders in close corporations, it is usually very difficult for dissatisfied shareholders to dispose of their investment at a price consistent with its economic value. Often the only persons interested in buying the shares are the majority shareholders—the very ones causing the owners of the minority interests to want to sell.

Modern Regulation of Close Corporations

Today, most states have enacted corporation laws that recognize the close corporation and the special problems associated with it. These statutes may be classified into three types:

1. A special section or chapter in the general incorporation statute that deals exclusively with close corporations.
2. Scattered provisions throughout the general corporation act that permit close corporations to voluntarily adopt less rigid organizational and operational arrangements.
3. Statutes that do not specifically mention close corporations but permit corporations to adopt in their articles or bylaws provisions that are particularly attractive to close corporations.

In general, all three types of statutes give legal recognition to some or all of the devices developed by lawyers to ensure private ownership and to protect minority shareholders.

Transferability of Shares

Close corporation shares are seldom intended to be sold to the public at large. Usually, the shareholders in such corporations desire not only to choose their original business associates but future owners as well. Likewise, few people are interested in buying into a small business dominated by strangers. These similarities between the close corporation and a partnership create compelling reasons for the shareholders of close corporations to demand special rules governing the transferability of shares.

There are several basic types of transfer restrictions. Under the **right of first refusal,** either the corporation or its shareholders are given the right to buy shares offered for sale to an outsider willing to purchase them. This device is generally employed to maintain the balance of power in a close corporation. However, it is also useful in preventing unwanted persons from buying into the corporation. One way of dealing with the problem of guaranteeing that a shareholder receives the value of her investment upon death or retirement is through a **buy-and-sell agreement.** The shareholder or her estate is required to sell and the corporation is obligated to purchase the shares at an agreed-upon price. A way of keeping unwanted persons out of the corporation is through a **consent restraint.** With this arrangement, a would-be seller must gain the permission of the corporation's board of directors or shareholders for any sale of shares other than to the corporation or pro rata to present shareholders. Consider the following case examining the enforceability of transfer restrictions in a close corporation.

F.B.I. Farms v. Moore

798 N.E.2d 440 (Ind. Sup. Ct. 2003)

FACTS

F.B.I. Farms, Inc., was formed by Ivan and Thelma Burger, their children, Linda and Freddy, and the children's spouses. Each of the three couples transferred a farm and related machinery to the corporation in exchange for common stock. At the time, Birchell Moore was married to Linda. The board of directors of F.B.I. adopted the following restrictions on the transfer of shares: (1) F.B.I. and its present shareholders held a right of first refusal to purchase at book value and (2) if F.B.I. or its shareholders did not exercise their right of first refusal, any "blood member" of the family could purchase at book value. When Linda's marriage to Moore was dissolved, she was awarded all of the F.B.I. shares and Moore was awarded a monetary judgment in the amount of $155,889.80, secured by a lien on Linda's shares. Ultimately, a sheriff's sale was held and Moore purchased all of Linda's shares for $290,450.67. Moore now claims that the transfer restrictions are not enforceable because they are unreasonable.

(continued)

ISSUE

Should the court invalidate the transfer restrictions because they are unreasonable?

DECISION

No. For a party to be bound by share transfer restrictions, that party must have notice of the restrictions. Here, the restrictions on transfer of F.B.I. shares were not "noted conspicuously" on the certificates, but there is no doubt that Moore, the buyer at the sheriff's sale, had notice of the restrictions. He was therefore bound by them. Because of the right of first refusal in F.B.I., before Linda could transfer her shares, she was obliged to offer them to F.B.I. and the other shareholders. Moore was on notice of that requirement. But the corporation and its shareholders were aware of the sheriff's sale and did nothing to assert the right of first refusal. As a result, the sale to Moore proceeded as if the shares had been offered and the corporation refused the opportunity. We also find the "blood-member" restriction to be enforceable as protecting a viable interest. These are family farmers in corporate form. Although we agree with Moore that he could purchase the shares at the sale, it is also the case that he purchased the shares with knowledge of the restrictions. To be sure, the effect of such a restriction may be to make the shares unmarketable to any buyer. If Moore had wanted the shares free of this restriction, he should have negotiated for that at the outset of the arrangement.

Governance Issues

Minority shareholders in close corporations are particularly vulnerable. The very nature of the close corporation greatly reduces the marketability of their shares, eliminating the option of selling out if things get too unbearable. For this reason, minority shareholders frequently fear leaving corporate decisions to a majority vote. They could be outvoted on a matter they believe to be crucial to their interests. This may apply to basic decisions that must be made by shareholders, such as amendment of the articles of incorporation. It may also be true of matters that are decided by the directors, such as employment and salary decisions as well as dividend policy.

Judicial Protection of Minority Shareholders

Courts have begun to recognize a fiduciary duty in corporate officers and majority shareholders to treat minority shareholders fairly. This has resulted in a greater willingness on the part of the judiciary to intervene to protect minority shareholders in intracorporate conflicts. Such intervention has occurred even in the absence of statutory authority for it.

Circumstances in which many courts will act without specific statutory authority include the following:

1. The officers or majority shareholders have been guilty of fraud, have oppressed minority shareholders, or have grossly mismanaged the business.
2. A deadlock among shareholders has resulted in a failure to hold corporate meetings, or one or more shareholders have taken control to the exclusion of other shareholders.
3. The business cannot be carried on profitably because of deadlock or dissension.

Courts have even turned to partnership law to determine the rights and duties of shareholders to one another in a close corporation. This has occurred when the parties themselves have acted as if they viewed their relationship as one between partners rather than investors in a corporation.

Corporations in a Global Environment

Businesses engaging in international commerce frequently will choose the corporate form for carrying out their global operations. A corporation domiciled in another country but doing business in the United States is called an **alien corporation.** Most of the rules governing foreign corporations apply equally to alien corporations. U.S. corporations doing business in other countries will frequently be protected against discriminatory treatment by *bilateral investment treaties* that are in force between the United States and many of its trading partners.

In many circumstances, a U.S. investor will choose to incorporate its business in the country where it is conducting its overseas operations. It may establish such a subsidiary in order to avoid exposing its domestic assets to foreign tax laws and potential product liability suits. Further, many nations will require that foreign investors maintain no more than a minority interest in certain sensitive sectors of their economy (i.e., telecommunications, natural resources, or transportation). In those instances, the U.S. investor may become a minority shareholder in an incorporated joint venture in which a foreign company holds the controlling interest.

Termination of the Corporation

Dissolution by Agreement

LO5

Since the corporation is an entity created by the state, it must have the state's consent to dissolve. If the articles of incorporation provide for a limited rather than an indefinite life, the corporation automatically terminates at the end of the designated time. This is so rare that the MBCA does not even make clear whether any statement must be filed with the secretary of state after such automatic dissolution.

Incorporation statutes establish procedures for other situations in which termination is voluntary. The MBCA provides for dissolution by a majority of the incorporators if the corporation has not begun business or issued any shares. The corporation may also be dissolved by written consent of all shareholders. The MBCA authorizes the board of directors to propose dissolution and hold a shareholders' meeting. Dissolution results if a majority of the shareholders entitled to vote do so in favor of the proposal. Corporations with more than one class of shareholders sometimes provide for voting on dissolution and other matters by class. In such a case, the majority of each class must vote in favor of dissolution.

A corporation that merges into another is dissolved. If two corporations consolidated into a new corporation, both of the old ones are dissolved.

Involuntary Dissolution

A corporation may be dissolved by a judgment of a court. Under the MBCA, the attorney general of the state may file an action for dissolution. Grounds for dissolution include failure to pay the annual franchise tax and failure to file the corporation's annual report with the secretary of state. Failure to appoint or maintain a registered agent in the state is also grounds for dissolution.

A shareholder may ask a court to dissolve a corporation. The MBCA allows this where the directors are in conflict, their deadlock cannot be broken by the shareholders, and the corporation faces ruin as a result. If directors are acting illegally or are being very unfair to shareholders, a court may dissolve the corporation. Misapplication or waste of corporate assets is also a basis for dissolution. Finally, a creditor may be able to convince a court to dissolve a corporation if it is insolvent and cannot pay its debts.

Concept Summary: Involuntary Dissolution

Petition Filed By	Justification for Involuntary Dissolution
Attorney General	1. Failure to pay franchise tax. 2. Failure to pay corporation's annual fee. 3. Failure to appoint or maintain a registered agent in the state.
Shareholder	1. Directors are in conflict *and* deadlock cannot be broken by shareholders *and* corporation faces ruin. 2. Directors are acting illegally or unfairly. 3. Misapplication or waste of corporate assets.
Creditor	Corporation is insolvent *and* not paying its debts.

Questions and Problem Cases

1. George C. Richert appointed Colman Borowsky, a real estate broker with Crye-Leike Realtors, as his sole and exclusive real estate broker to aid him in the leasing and/or acquisition of industrial property. Richert agreed that, if he entered into any lease or purchase agreement within 24 months after the period of the agreement, Richert would recognize and provide for Borowsky as the broker in the transaction. At the time they executed the agreement, the parties understood that Richert would be forming a new corporation that would actually acquire the property. Because the corporation was not yet in existence, Richert signed the agreement in his individual capacity. Richert then formed WDM, Inc., and became its president and chief executive officer. Soon thereafter, Richert, on behalf of WDM, executed a lease agreement for a different piece of property with Memphis Zane May Associates. Contrary to the original agreement between Crye-Leike and Richert, neither Borowsky nor Crye-Leike received a commission despite the fact that they had been searching for suitable property for WDM. Richert, using WDM letterhead and signing as president of WDM, then terminated his agreement with Crye-Leike and Borowsky by mail. When it learned of the lease transaction, Crye-Leike sued WDM for breach of contract. WDM argued that it was not liable on the contract because it neither adopted nor ratified the contract between Richert and Crye-Leike. Is WDM liable on the preincorporation contract?
2. Stufft Farms, Inc., was a corporation that owned and operated a family farm. Esther Stufft owned 17,077 of the corporation's shares and Carmen Stufft owned 17,018 shares, while Carol Stufft Larsen, Dorene Stufft Badgett, and David Stufft each owned 20 shares. To ensure that the corporation remained in the hands of the family, the corporate bylaws included a right of first refusal restriction. This provision stated: *"No shareholder shall have the right or power to pledge, sell or otherwise dispose of, except by will, any share or shares of this company without first offering the said share or shares to the company and shareholders at the then book value."* On February 24, Neil Johnson offered to buy all of Stufft Farms's shares. However, the offer was contingent upon all the shareholders selling their shares to Johnson. All the shareholders, except David Stufft, agreed to accept Johnson's offer. On March 9, David attempted to invoke the right of first refusal to buy the other shareholders' shares at book value. They refused his demand to sell their shares to him at book value, but instead, on March 10, offered to sell them to him at the same price Johnson offered. David rejected that offer. Finally, on March 27, the board of directors voted to dissolve the corporation and sell all of its assets to Johnson. David sued to void the sale on the

grounds that this sale violated his rights under the right of first refusal. Has there been a violation of David's right of first refusal?

3. Cook Construction, a general contractor, entered into a subcontract providing that Bryant Construction was to perform certain portions of work on a highway project for Cook. The two corporations signed the contract on October 19, 1984. Later, after Bryant had completed its work, Cook refused to pay the prices that Cook had quoted. Bryant filed suit. In preparing to defend the suit, Cook discovered that on January 27, 1984, the chairman of the Mississippi State Tax Commission had suspended Bryant's corporate charter for failure to file annual reports and pay franchise taxes. Cook argued that the actual effect of the suspension was that Bryant was deprived of its power and capacity to act and, therefore, the contract was unenforceable because it was *ultra vires.* Was the subcontract unenforceable because it was an *ultra vires* act?
4. Monogram, Inc., wished to buy a company that produced and sold smoke detectors. Accordingly, Monogram formed Monotronics, Inc., for the sole purpose of buying and operating the business. Monogram contributed $1.8 million cash to Monotronics and held 100 percent of its stock. After several profitable months, Monotronics's sales began to fall until its total assets dwindled to $10,000. Monotronics finally ceased doing business altogether, although it owed its largest creditor, Edwards Company, $352,000. Edwards Company attempted to hold Monogram liable for Monotronic's debts. Should the court pierce the corporate veil and hold Monogram liable on the Monotronics contractual obligations?
5. Joseph Bitter and two brothers, Joseph Smith and Steve Smith, became good friends. As a result of their friendship, they decided to go into the tavern business together. The parties bought an existing tavern and took title in the name of their corporation, Gomer's, Inc. Soon, the brothers began feuding with Bitter and, because of their combined two-thirds interest, assumed virtual control of the business. In response, Bitter claimed that he and the brothers (the promoters), not the corporation, held title to the real estate. He claimed that Gomer's, Inc., could not own the building because the corporation was not yet in existence when the contract was made. Do the promoters, rather than the corporation, own the building?
6. Jacobson, as promoter for A.L.W., Inc., contracted with Stern, an architect, to draw plans for a new hotel and casino to be built on the north shore of Lake Tahoe. It was to be known as King's Castle. About 19 months after King's Castle opened, A.L.W., Inc., filed for bankruptcy. At that time, only $120,000 of the $250,000 fee for Stern's services had been paid by A.L.W., Inc. Stern brought suit against Jacobson, as promoter, for the balance due. Was Jacobson liable to Stern for the amount unpaid for his services?
7. Cusack was an officer and director of Quality Steel, Inc., a closely held corporation. Basically, Cusack had complete control over the corporation, making every important decision, controlling its day-to-day operations, and exercising unlimited access to its funds. Later, the corporation and Cusack were indicted for violating two occupational health and safety standards at a construction project. Cusack was specifically charged with violating a federal statute that provided that "[a]ny employer who willfully violates any standards . . . shall . . . be punished by a fine of not more than $10,000." Cusack defended on the basis that he was not an employer. He claimed that the corporation was the employer. Was Cusack the employer?
8. Leonard N. Perle was the owner of one-half of the stock in Protameen Chemicals, Inc. Emanuel Balsamides owned the other one-half interest. These two men built up

a successful chemical business by utilizing Perle's technical talents and administrative skills and Balsamides sales acumen and knowledge of the market. Each had two sons who eventually came into the business. Balsamides's sons worked in the field and earned substantial salaries and commissions. Perle's sons started learning the administrative areas, intending eventually to be salesmen, with Perle attempting to see that their remuneration matched that of the Balsamides sons. During their final years together, Perle engaged in numerous instances of wrongful conduct that ultimately deadlocked the corporation. All of these actions were allegedly done in an effort to embarrass Balsamides with his customers. Should Perle be required to sell his stock to Balsamides? Explain.

Chapter 29

Management of the Corporate Business

Learning Objectives

After you have studied this chapter, you should be able to:

1. Explain the duty of due care and diligence imposed on directors and officers.
2. Describe the business judgment rule and explain how it is modified in the takeover context.
3. Examine a fact situation and explain whether a director or officer has engaged in self-dealing.
4. Examine a fact situation and determine whether a director or officer has usurped a corporate opportunity.
5. Explain the test for determining when a corporation is liable for the torts or crimes of its employees.
6. Explain the test for determining when officers or directors are liable for tortious or criminal behavior.

John R. Park was the chief executive officer of Acme Markets, Inc., a national retail chain with over 36,000 employees, 874 retail outlets, and 16 warehouses. The Food and Drug Administration (FDA) notified Park of certain unsanitary conditions at Acme's Baltimore warehouse. After receiving the complaint, Park conferred with Acme's vice president for legal affairs, who assured him that the Baltimore division vice president was investigating and would be taking corrective action. Two months later, a subsequent FDA inspection of the warehouse found improved sanitary conditions; however, there was still evidence of rodent infestation. The FDA filed criminal charges against both Acme and Park, citing evidence of an

(continued)

earlier letter informing Park of similar problems in the company's Philadelphia warehouse. Acme pleaded guilty to the charges but Park refused to do so. The United States Supreme Court upheld Park's criminal conviction and the resulting fine of $250.[1]

- What are the responsibilities that directors and officers owe to their corporations?
- When are officers and directors liable for the torts and crimes committed by the corporation?
- What protections are available to officers and directors when they are charged with torts or crimes?

Introduction

The shareholders are the owners of the corporation. They can affect the way the business is run through their power to elect directors and to amend the articles of incorporation. They do not, however, have the power to make management decisions. All statutes of incorporation give that power to the directors. The directors, in turn, usually delegate the making of at least the day-to-day operating decisions to the officers.

If the shareholders are dissatisfied with those decisions, they can replace the directors, who in turn will probably replace the officers. The shareholders generally have no right to instruct the directors or the officers on the operating decisions they should make. Shareholders must approve certain extraordinary corporate transactions such as a merger, a sale or lease of substantially all the assets of the corporation, or the dissolution of the corporation. However, the Model Business Corporation Act (MBCA) requires that the proposal for these actions come from the board of directors.

As this discussion should make clear, the board of directors and officers of a publicly held corporation have broad management authority. However, their managerial discretion is not unlimited. There are limits placed on this power beyond the voting rights of the shareholders. Basically, the directors and officers must act in a manner consistent with the powers and objectives of the corporation and with the state and federal laws that govern corporate activities.

The Board of Directors

Powers and Duties

Most state incorporation statutes declare that "the business of the corporation shall be managed by a board of directors." Of course, in a large corporation, especially where a number of the directors have full-time jobs elsewhere, this is impossible. The directors tend to ratify management decisions made by the top executives rather than to take the initiative in making the decisions. Recognizing this, the MBCA now says: "All

[1] *United States v. Park,* 421 U.S. 658 (U.S. Sup. Ct. 1975).

corporate powers shall be exercised by or under the authority of, and the business and affairs of a corporation shall be managed under the direction of, a board of directors."

Kirschner v. K&L Gates

46 A.2d 737 (Pa. Super. Ct. 2012)

FACTS

Greg Podlucky founded Le-Nature's, a Delaware corporation. During a routine audit, Le-Nature's chief financial officers expressed concerns about the accuracy of the corporation's sales figures. The next day all three submitted resignation letters, explaining that they suspected Podlucky of engaging in improper conduct with Le-Nature's suppliers. The auditor recommended that Le-Nature hire a competent legal counsel to conduct a thorough investigation of the allegations. Accordingly, Le-Nature's board of directors appointed a special committee of three independent directors to conduct the investigation. The special committee retained the services of a law firm, K&L Gates, to lead the inquiry. In its retention letter, the law firm stressed that it was "engaged to act as counsel for the special committee and for no other individual or entity, including the Company." Upon completion of its inquiry, and before issuing any report to the special committee, the law firm sent a message to Podlucky, announcing that it had found no evidence of fraud or malfeasance. In reality, K&L Gates had failed to uncover a massive fraud being perpetrated by Podlucky and, as a result, he continued to "loot" the company. When the fraud was finally uncovered, the corporation, which was forced into bankruptcy, sued the law firm for malpractice. K&L Gates petitioned the court to dismiss the claim, asserting that since it was retained only by the special committee, it did not owe a duty to the corporation or its shareholders.

ISSUE

Did the law firm owe a duty to the corporation?

DECISION

Yes. Notwithstanding the retention letter issued by the law firm, an implied attorney-client relationship between K&L Gates and the corporation exists. Le-Nature is a Delaware corporation and Delaware law provides that the board of directors has the ultimate responsibility for managing the business and affairs of a corporation. In discharging this function, the directors owe fiduciary duties of care and loyalty to the corporation and its shareholders. The corporation, acting through its board and its special committee, sought the law firm's legal advice and assistance in investigating the allegations of fraud and in preparing its findings. The special committee was vested with the power and authority of the board and, accordingly, acted on behalf of the board. Although the retention letter stated that the special committee alone was the law firm's client, the investigator's draft report was sent first to Podlucky, who was not a member of the special committee. Further, the cover letter of the final report was directed to the board of the directors. We therefore find the existence of an attorney-client relationship between the law firm and the corporation.

General Powers of the Board

Certain corporate actions can be taken by the board of directors acting alone. Statutes of the states vary on this. The MBCA permits the board to take the following actions by itself: declaring a dividend; establishing the price for the sale of shares of stock; electing and removing officers; filling vacancies on the board of directors; and selling, leasing, and mortgaging assets of the corporation outside the normal course of its business.

Actions Requiring Board Initiative

Some corporate actions can be taken only through **board initiative.** The initiative process requires that the board of directors propose the matter to the shareholders, who then must approve the action. Board initiative is generally required for any fundamental changes in the corporation, for example, amendment of the articles of incorporation, merger of the corporation, sale of all or substantially all of the corporation's assets, and voluntary dissolution of the corporation.

Online Communications

During the year 2000, the Delaware General Corporation Law was amended to enable Delaware corporations to make use of the Internet. The amendments eliminated language from the corporation statutes that blocked the use of modern communications technology. Thus, directors can now legally communicate official business by e-mail since electronic communications are permitted for corporate business. Specifically, the term "electronic communications" includes forms of communication that do not involve the physical transmission of paper if the communication creates a record that can be retained, retrieved, or reviewed by the recipient and can be reproduced in paper form.

While the statute does not allow board meetings to take place electronically, it does permit director resignations to be transmitted electronically. Further, director actions taken by unanimous consent may be taken by electronic transmission.

Powers and Rights of a Director as an Individual

Directors are not agents for the corporation by virtue of that office. They have power to act for the corporation only as a part of the board, not as individuals. Of course, a director can become an agent if she is also serving as an employee of the corporation.

A director has the right to inspect the corporate books and records. This right is necessary to carrying out the director's duty of overseeing the management. However, the right to inspect can be denied where it can be shown that the director has an interest that conflicts with that of the corporation. If such an adverse interest arises, it would probably be a sound reason for removal of the director.

Election of Directors

Number of Directors

Some states require corporations to have a minimum of three directors. The MBCA requires only one, recognizing that it would be superfluous to have more than one director when a single individual or another corporation owns all the stock. The MBCA allows the number of directors to be fixed in either the articles or the bylaws. If it is fixed in the bylaws, the directors can easily vary the number as conditions change. It is not necessary to go to the trouble and expense of amending the articles when a director dies or resigns and the directors are not ready to nominate a successor.

Qualifications

A few state statutes require directors to be shareholders. Some require that a certain percentage of the directors be citizens of the state of incorporation or of the United States. Qualifications for directors can be set out in the articles, if desired.

Nomination

Directors are elected by the shareholders at their annual meeting. Usually, they are nominated by the current directors, although nominations can be made from the floor during the shareholders' meeting. However, candidates nominated from the floor are seldom elected in large corporations that solicit proxies, as will be discussed in Chapter 30.

Term of Office

Directors normally hold office only until the next annual meeting, or until a successor has been elected and qualified. The MBCA permits corporations to provide for staggered terms in their articles. A corporation that has a board of nine or more members may establish either two or three nearly equal classes of directors. Then only one class of directors is elected at each annual meeting unless there are vacancies. Staggered terms are said to ensure that experienced directors remain on the board; however, they are usually adopted to make a corporate takeover more difficult.

Vacancies

Vacancies on the board can be filled only by a vote of the shareholders unless the state statute, the articles, or the bylaws give this power to the board itself. The MBCA permits a majority of the remaining directors, even though less than a quorum, to elect directors to serve out unexpired terms. It also permits the board to increase the size of the board and then to elect a director to the vacancy created. Such a director may serve only until the next shareholders' meeting.

Removal of Directors

A director may not be removed without cause unless this is permitted by statute or by articles or bylaws adopted prior to the director's election. The MBCA permits shareholders to remove directors with or without cause. A director who has failed to or is unable to attend and participate in directors' meetings or who has acted contrary to the interests of the corporation can be removed for cause. Shareholders can remove a director for cause at any time even though the power of removal has been given by the articles or bylaws to the directors. Before being removed for cause, a director must be given notice and a hearing.

Directors' Meetings

Frequency

Boards of directors usually schedule regular meetings. Today, boards of large corporations typically meet monthly; however, some corporations have regular meetings only quarterly. Small corporations, in which most of the directors are active in the business, may have only one formal meeting each year. The directors' other meetings are informal, with no minutes kept.

Concept Summary: Removal of Directors

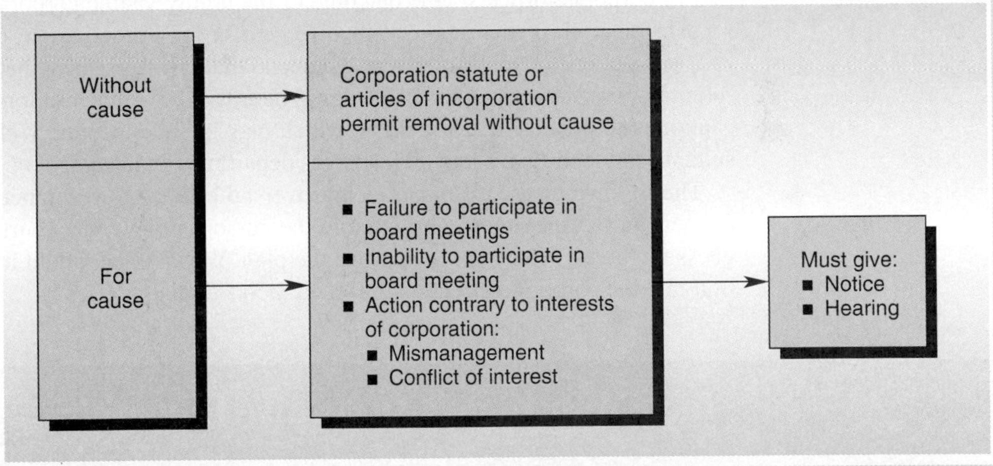

Notice

Reasonable notice must be given for special meetings. If all of the directors attend a meeting, this cures any defect in or failure to give notice. However, a director who has not received a proper notice may attend solely to complain of the notice. In this case, he or she would not be held to have been in attendance. Directors may also cure a defect in the notice by waiving notice. The corporate secretary usually prepares and gets such waivers signed if notice is late or otherwise defective. Under common law, a waiver of notice has to be signed by all of the directors either before or during the meeting. The MBCA permits the waiver to be signed after the meeting.

Formality

Under common law, directors could act only when properly convened as a board and could not vote by proxy. This rule was based on belief in the value of mutual counsel and collective judgment. Today, the MBCA permits directors to act without a meeting if all of the directors consent in writing to the action taken. It also permits a director to attend a meeting through the use of a telephone hookup. The only requirement is that the directors be able to hear one another simultaneously.

Quorum

Each director has only one vote, regardless of his or her shareholdings. Actions taken by a board are ineffective unless a quorum is present. Normally, a quorum is a majority of the number of directors fixed by the articles or bylaws. The articles or bylaws may set the quorum at a higher figure. If there is a quorum present, the vote of a majority of the directors is the act of the board.

Compensation of Directors

Under the common law, directors had no power to fix their own salaries and were not entitled to compensation for their ordinary duties as directors. The MBCA permits directors to fix their compensation unless this is prohibited by the articles of incorporation. Outside directors (those who are not employees of the corporation) are paid rather modest fees even in the largest corporations. However, directors' fees have been rising rapidly in recent years as the duties and liabilities of directors have become greater.

In recent years, attention has turned to the oversight role of directors in the compensation of corporate officers. One outcome of the highly visible corporate scandals has been a push for more proactive board involvement in the executive pay-setting process. This has been but one manifestation of the demand that directors spend more time in the boardroom, both in supporting and challenging their CEOs. Compensation committees are now cautioned to practice real oversight, which may include meeting with compensation consultants and their firm's human resources department independent of top management.

The following case examines a controversial hiring and severance package issued to a former Walt Disney president. Despite the cursory review, the court declined to second-guess the board's decision to approve the plan. Why? What would it take for the court to find that the corporate directors breached their fiduciary duties?

In re Walt Disney Derivative Litigation

906 A.2d 27 (Del. Sup. Ct. 2006)

FACTS

Michael Eisner, the chief executive officer (CEO) of the Walt Disney Company, had been Ovitz's close friend for over 25 years. Eisner decided to hire Ovitz despite internal memos questioning both the hiring decision and the lucrative compensation terms. However, none of these documents were submitted to the board before hiring Ovitz. In fact, no discussions or presentations were made until the actual

(continued)

In re Walt Disney Derivative Litigation *(concluded)*

meeting where the compensation committee was asked to OK the agreement. The compensation committee met for just under an hour. Immediately thereafter, the committee adopted a resolution of approval.

ISSUE

Were the board's actions protected under the business judgment rule?

DECISION

Yes. Boards of directors may appoint committees and delegate to them a broad range of responsibilities, which may include setting executive compensation. The overall thrust of this claim is that the compensation committee approved provisions that could potentially result in an enormous payout, without informing themselves of what the full magnitude of that payout could be. It does appear that the compensation committee members were informed that the payout to Ovitz could exceed $100 million if he was terminated without cause after one year. If measured in terms of the documentation that would have been generated if "best practices" had been followed, the actions of compensation committee leave much to be desired. However, we still are convinced that the compensation committee had adequately informed itself of the potential magnitude of the entire severance package. For these reasons, we hold that the compensation committee members did not breach their fiduciary duty of care in approving this hiring package.

Ethics in Action

The Sarbanes-Oxley Act is a response to recent revelations of executives of publicly traded corporations securing loans from corporate bank accounts to fund extravagant lifestyles. One provision in this legislation generally prohibits publicly traded corporations from making loans to their directors and executive officers. What are your thoughts about this legislation? Is it wrong to ban all such loans? Should the law have gone farther and banned loans to any corporate employee?

Officers of the Corporation

Powers

The MBCA provides that a corporation shall have a president, one or more vice presidents (as stated in the bylaws), a secretary, and a treasurer. Any two or more offices may be held by the same person except the offices of president and secretary. This permits dual signatures on corporate documents. Many corporations have established the office of chairman of the board; the chairman of the board may be the chief executive of the corporation. Occasionally, this is only a part-time position.

President or Chairman

The power of the officers to bind the corporation on contracts they make on its behalf is the same as that of any agent. In addition to their express authority, they have implied and apparent authority. Certain officers may also have ***ex officio*** authority—that is, authority by virtue of their offices. This, however, is more restricted than is generally believed. The president or chairman of the board has no power to bind the corporation solely because of his position. However, if he is also the chief executive, then broad authority is implied to make contracts and do other acts appropriate to the ordinary business of the firm. A corporate officer is liable to the corporation for resulting losses if he acts beyond his authority.

Vice President

A vice president has no authority by virtue of that office. However, if the title indicates that the person is the principal officer of some area of the business, she has considerable implied authority. For example, the vice president of marketing has implied authority to do those acts normally done by a manager of sales.

Corporate Secretary

The corporate secretary (called *clerk* in some states) keeps the minutes of meetings of the shareholders and directors and other general corporate records such as stockholder records. The office gives the secretary no authority to bind the corporation on contracts. However, there is a presumption that a document to which the secretary has affixed the corporate seal has been properly authorized.

Treasurer

The treasurer has charge of the funds of the corporation. He or she has power to pay out corporate funds for proper purposes and is the person who receives payments to the corporation. The treasurer binds the corporation on receipts, checks, and endorsements. However, the treasurer does not have authority by virtue of the office alone to borrow money or issue negotiable instruments.

Duties of Directors and Officers

Unlike directors, the corporate officers are agents of the corporation. However, the directors share with the officers the same fiduciary duties that an agent owes the principal. The recent trend has been to raise the standard of conduct required of directors and officers. This has been done through the SEC and the federal securities laws it administers. It has also been done by courts in interpreting the common law.

The fiduciary duties that officers and directors owe the corporation include:

1. The duty to act within one's authority and within the powers of the corporation.
2. The duty to act diligently and with due care in conducting the affairs of the corporation.
3. The duty to act with loyalty and good faith for the benefit of the corporation.

Duty to Act within Authority

Directors and officers must act within the authority given to them and to the corporation by statute, the articles, and the bylaws. Directors or officers may be liable to the corporation if it is damaged by an act exceeding their authority or if they act outside of the scope of the corporation's authority. However, if they enter an *ultra vires* transaction, justifiably believing it to be within the scope of the corporation's business, they are not held liable. (*Ultra vires* transactions were discussed in Chapter 28.)

Ratification

Like any principal, a corporation may ratify an unauthorized act by its officers or other agents. This may be done through a resolution of the board of directors or of the shareholders. It may also be implied from acceptance of benefits from the unauthorized act. Ratification, when it occurs, releases the officer or director from liability to the corporation and binds the corporation as if the act originally had been authorized.

Duty of Due Care and Diligence

Prudent Person Standard

LO1

Directors and officers may be liable to the corporation for failure to act with due care and diligence. The MBCA requires that a director or officer discharge his duties with "such care as an ordinarily prudent person in a like position would use under similar circumstances." Thus, officers and directors are not liable to the corporation if they act with the *common sense, practical wisdom,* and *informed judgment* that could be expected of an ordinarily prudent person. Of course, the greater the actual qualifications of the individual, the greater the level of the duty that would be expected.

There are three dimensions to this prudent person standard. An officer or director will be found to have discharged her duty of care if she acts:

1. In good faith.
2. As would an ordinarily prudent person under like circumstances.
3. Under the reasonable belief that she is acting in the best interests of the corporation.

The duty of care requires that directors and officers make a reasonable investigation before making any corporate decisions. These standards, however, take into consideration the complexities of many corporate decisions and understand that it would be impossible for any manager to personally investigate every facet of every business decision. As a result, the MBCA standard permits directors and officers to rely on the opinions, reports, and statements of persons who reasonably appear to be competent and reliable.

Business Judgment Rule

Directors are not liable for mere errors of judgment when they act with care and good faith. This is the **business judgment rule.** The rule precludes the courts from substituting their business judgment for that of the corporation's managers. In short, it protects officers and directors from personal liability for honest mistakes in judgment.

In order to obtain the protection of the business judgment rule, the directors must meet three requirements in arriving at their decision:

1. An informed decision
2. No conflict of interest
3. Rational basis

First, they must make an informed decision. As stated above, they may rely on information collected and presented by other persons. Second, the decision makers must be free from conflicts of interest. Any self-dealing on the part of the directors in the course of making the decision would deprive them of the shelter provided by the business judgment rule. Third, the board of directors must have a rational basis for believing that the decision is in the best interests of the corporation. Generally, this means that the decision must not be "manifestly unreasonable." (Many courts hold that the directors' decision is not rational if their actions amount to "gross negligence.")

If the business decision violates any of these requirements, the officers or directors are stripped of the protection provided by the business judgment rule. Courts would then feel freer to substitute their judgment for that of the corporate decision makers. Further, if the court found the decision to be unwise, the officers or directors would be liable unless they could prove that the transaction at issue was intrinsically fair to the corporation.

The Business Judgment Rule in the Takeover Context

The newspapers often report the legal and economic controversies surrounding attempts by outsiders to acquire control of publicly held corporations. Generally, the outsiders make a tender offer (offer to purchase shares at prices above market price) for the controlling shares of the target corporation. (Tender offers will be discussed in Chapter 30.) The corporation's current management will often oppose such offers and may employ various defenses to defeat the tender offer. Successful defenses frequently trigger complaints from shareholders that the directors fought the tender offer solely to preserve their corporate positions.

Ethics in Action

The inside directors' financial interests may be directly assaulted by a takeover attempt from outsiders. Outside directors do not have such an apparent conflict of interest in evaluating the merits of a tender offer. Should the board ever fight a takeover when less than a majority of the outside directors are opposed to the offer?

Generally, directors are protected from liability for such opposition under the business judgment rule. However, recent judicial decisions have taken note of the greater risk of a conflict of interest in the tender offer context. Accordingly, there seems to be a preliminary burden that the directors must meet before they are accorded the business judgment rule defense when they oppose takeover attempts. First, the directors must demonstrate that they had reasonable grounds for believing that a danger to the corporation existed. And second, they must establish that their defensive measures were reasonable in relation to the threat to the corporate interest.

Gantler v. Stephens

965 A.2d 695 (Del. Sup. Ct. 2009)

FACTS

Shareholders of First Niles, Inc., sued certain officers of the corporation. The shareholders claimed that the officers violated their fiduciary duties by rejecting a valuable opportunity to sell the company and, instead, reclassified the corporate shares to benefit themselves. First Niles received three bids. First Niles did not pursue negotiations with one potential buyer after it indicated that it would not retain the First Niles board. A second buyer also indicated that it would terminate all incumbent board members. It then pulled out of the negotiations after First Niles failed to provide it with the due diligence materials it had requested. Then, even after the third potential buyer revised and improved its offer, the First Niles' board rejected it without any discussion or deliberation. Instead, the directors developed a plan to reclassify the corporation's shares. It gained shareholder approval of this plan after stating in proxy materials that "after careful deliberations," the board determined that offer to purchase as not in the bests of interests of the corporation or its shareholders.

ISSUE

Is this decision protected by the business judgment rule?

DECISION

No. Our analysis of whether the directors' actions merit the business judgment presumption is two pronged. First, did the board reach its decision in the good faith pursuit of a legitimate corporate interest? Second, did the board do so advisedly? For the board's decision here to be entitled to the business judgment presumption, both questions must be answered affirmatively. The defendants in this case did not pass the first step. They were conflicted when they distributed the reclassification proxy to the shareholders. Their failure to respond to the first bidder and their failure to provide due diligence materials to the second bidder both came in the face of revelations by those bidders that the officers and directors would not be retained if their bids were successful.

Deal Protection Devices

Corporation statutes generally provide that the board's management decision to enter into and recommend a merger transaction can become final only when ownership action is taken by a vote of the stockholders. This provides for a balance of power between boards and stockholders which makes merger transactions a shared enterprise and ownership decision. Consequently, a board of directors' decision to adopt defensive devices to protect a merger agreement may implicate the stockholders' right to effectively vote contrary to the initial recommendation of the board in favor of the transaction.

It is well established that conflicts of interest arise when a board of directors acts to prevent stockholders from effectively exercising their right to vote contrary to the will of the board. The appearance of such conflict may be present whenever a board adopts defensive devices to protect a merger agreement. The stockholders' ability to effectively reject a merger agreement is likely to bear an inversely proportionate relationship to the structural and economic devices that the board has approved to protect the transaction.

Defensive devices adopted by the board to protect the original merger transaction must withstand judicial scrutiny under an enhanced standard of review. There are several key features to this enhanced judicial scrutiny test. The first feature is a judicial determination regarding the adequacy of the decision-making process employed by the directors, including the information on which the directors based their decision. The second feature is a judicial examination of the reasonableness of the directors' action in light of the circumstances then existing. Further, the directors have the burden of proving that they were adequately informed and acted reasonably.

Legislative Responses to Increased Director Liability

At one time, the business judgment rule appeared to automatically shelter directors from liability for their decisions as long as they avoided self-dealing. And yet, even then, corporations were having difficulty attracting and retaining outside directors. In the wake of cases increasing directors' liability, insurance premiums for directors' policies have skyrocketed, precipitating what many states have perceived to be a real director liability crisis.

State legislatures across the country have responded by enacting legislation designed to limit directors' liability for breach of the duty of care. From this flurry of legislative activity, three fundamental types of statutory limitations have appeared. The most popular (pioneered by Delaware and adopted by over 30 states) are **charter option statutes.** This amendment to the state corporation law authorizes any corporation to adopt a specific amendment to its articles of incorporation that removes breach of duty as a cause of action for monetary damages against directors. Under this approach, both the board of directors and the shareholders would have to approve the limitation on director liability. Even then, officers and directors would still be liable for intentional misconduct, failure to act in good faith, self-interest, knowing violations, and breach of the duty of loyalty.

A second type of amendment to the state corporation law provides that directors will have no liability for breach of the duty of care in the absence of willful misconduct or recklessness. The state of Ohio has such a statute with an added provision—it presumes that a director acted in good faith unless it can be demonstrated by clear and convincing evidence that he did not. These types of statutes (in force in at least five states) are called **self-executing statutes** because they are automatically effective. No board or shareholder action is necessary to trigger their applicability.

A final type of limitation was adopted by the state of Virginia. It is a **cap on monetary damages statute.** Specifically, the law holds that the maximum liability that may be imposed on directors is the greater of $100,000 or the amount of cash compensation that the director received from the corporation during the previous 12 months. This approach shares certain aspects of the previous two types. It is self-executing in that the cap automatically applies in the absence of board and shareholder action. However, it has a charter option quality in that the board and shareholders of a corporation may amend the corporate charter to reduce the cap (they may not increase it).

Duty of Loyalty and Good Faith

Directors and officers must act in the best interests of the corporation. They breach their duty if they try to profit personally at the expense of the corporation.

Concept Summary: Legislative Limitations on Director Liability

Charter option statute	State corporation law permits corporation: ■ To remove breach of duty as cause of action for damages ■ Decision must be approved by board and shareholders
Self-executing statute	State corporation law: ■ Eliminates director liability except for willful misconduct or recklessness ■ No board or shareholder approval necessary
Cap on money damages statute	State corporation law: ■ Places ceiling on director liability for breach of duty ■ Board and shareholders may act to lower the ceiling

Self-Dealing

LO3

Directors and officers are not prohibited from entering into transactions with the corporation. At one time, courts held that such deals were voidable by the corporation, but today the majority of courts hold them voidable only if unfair to the corporation. However, before a director (or another business organization in which she has a major interest) enters a contract with the corporation, the director should make a *full disclosure* of her interest. This requires that the director or officer disclose all material facts of the transaction, including her interest in it.

After full disclosure, the disinterested members of the board or the shareholders themselves must approve the transaction. However, such approval does not automatically relieve the self-dealing director or officer from liability to the corporation. Under the MBCA, the initial burden of proving the fairness of the transaction lies with the self-dealing director or officer. After proper approval by the board of directors or shareholders, the burden of establishing unfairness merely shifts to the corporation.

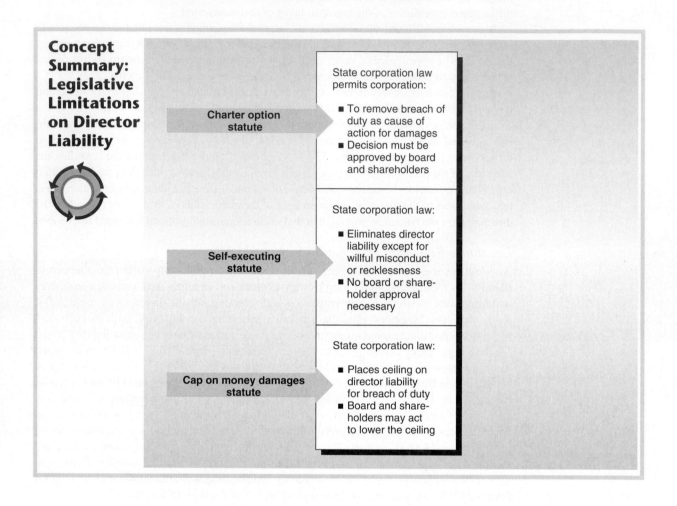

Usurping Corporate Opportunities

LO4

Directors and officers may not usurp a corporate opportunity. Such usurpation occurs when a business opportunity comes to them in their official capacities and the opportunity is within the corporation's normal scope of business. For example, directors may not buy the right to sell a product that would fit into the corporation's line of goods. If the corporation is financially unable to pursue the opportunity, a director or officer may take it.

Three elements must be met before directors or officers may be found to have usurped a corporate opportunity:

1. The opportunity must have come to them in their corporate capacity.
2. The opportunity must be related to the corporate business.
3. The corporation must have been able to take advantage of the opportunity.

Even when these three requirements are met, the director may still avoid liability if she can show that the corporation waived its rights to the opportunity. Thus, if the director offered the opportunity to the corporation with full disclosure of all material terms and a disinterested majority of the board rejected the transaction, the director may take it. In some instances, a court may find an implied waiver if the corporation knew of the opportunity and failed to act on it in a timely manner.

Telxon Corporation v. Meyerson

802 A.2d 257 (Del. Sup. Ct. 2002)

FACTS

Robert Meyerson was a member of the Telxon board of directors. Telxon develops and markets portable handheld computers for retailers and wholesalers in various industries. When the company began experiencing operational problems, Telxon entered into a consulting agreement with Meyerson's wholly owned company, Accipiter Corporation. The consulting agreement provided that Accipiter's work product, created pursuant to the contract, would become the property of Telxon, and Accipiter could not render similar consulting services to any direct competitors of Telxon. Soon thereafter, Meyerson formed Teletransaction for the purpose of developing a product known as "pen based computers" (PBCs). When shareholders sued Meyerson for usurping a corporate opportunity, he claimed that Telxon's CEO had considered and rejected the opportunity for Telxon to develop PBCs.

ISSUE

Should the court dismiss the corporate opportunity-based challenge to the sale?

DECISION

No. While presentation of a purported corporate opportunity to a board of directors, and the board's refusal thereof, creates a safe harbor for an interested director, that safe harbor does not extend to an opportunity presented only to the corporation's CEO. Rejection of a corporate opportunity by the CEO is not a valid substitute for consideration by the full board of directors. We do not know the basis of the CEO's decision not to develop PBCs. In fact, if Meyerson was the CEO's source of information, the decision cannot be considered an informed one.

Freeze-Outs, Oppression, and Bad Faith

There have been many lawsuits in which minority shareholders complain that they have been unfairly treated by the directors. Usually, these involve close corporations. The suits may claim a freeze-out. This occurs when the corporation is merged with a newly formed corporation under terms by which the minority shareholders receive cash or other securities for their shares, rather than receiving stock in the new corporation. Sometimes they claim oppression of minority shareholders. This frequently occurs when the majority shareholders refuse to pay dividends even though the corporation is able to do so. Others allege that the corporation will not hire minority shareholders while unreasonably high salaries have been paid to controlling shareholders and their friends. Still others involve purchases by or sales of assets to controlling shareholders where the price is said to be unfair. Usually, minority shareholders win such suits only where the acts of directors have clearly been in bad faith or have clearly abused the discretion given the directors under the business judgment rule.

Trading on Inside Information

When directors and officers buy or sell the corporation's stock, they may be in violation of their fiduciary duties. Any disclosure of the confidential information they have acquired through their position with the corporation might have a profound effect on the value of the corporation's securities. Yet current judicial trends point toward a greater and greater duty to disclose all material information to the buyers and sellers of stock. As a result, the federal securities laws prohibit **insiders,** those with confidential material information concerning the corporation, from buying or selling its stock. Insider trading, as well as the other duties imposed on directors and officers by the securities laws, will be discussed in greater detail in Chapter 31.

Directors' Right to Dissent

A director who assents to the actions of the board of directors may be held liable if the board has failed to abide by its duties to the corporation. Any director who attends a board meeting is held to have assented to the board's actions unless he specifically dissents. Under the MBCA, a director will not have dissented unless he refuses to vote for the proposed course of action and makes this dissent clear to the other board members by having it appear in the minutes or by giving a written notice of dissent to the chairman or secretary immediately following the meeting.

Ethics in Action

A dissenting director will be held liable for the actions of the board unless she formally registers her dissent. What are the practical problems that a director faces in complying with this process?

Liability for Torts and Crimes

LO5

Corporate Liability

Tort Liability

A corporation is liable for all torts committed by its employees while acting in the course of and within the scope of their employment. This may be true even when the corporation has instructed the employee to avoid the act. This rule is a simple application of the agency concept of *respondeat superior* (discussed in Chapter 24).

In recent years there has been a growing controversy over whether multinational corporations should be held liable when they aid or abet foreign governments who commit atrocities against people. A federal statute, the Alien Tort Statute, grants U.S. courts jurisdiction to hear cases when: (1) an alien sues (2) for a tort (3) committed in violation of the law of nations. In the next case, the court determines that a corporation may be found liable under this statute.

Sarei v. Rio Tinto

671 F.3d 736 (9th Cir. 2011)

FACTS

This is an Alien Tort Statute (ATS) case arising out of the operations of the Rio Tinto mining group on the island of Bougainville in Papua New Guinea (PNG) and the uprising against Rio Tinto that resulted in the use of military force and many deaths. Although the alleged torts all occurred outside of the United States, Rio Tinto has substantial operations in this country. The plaintiffs are current or former residents of the island of Bougainville. The ATS provides that U.S. federal courts have original jurisdiction of any civil action by an alien for a tort committed in violation of the law of nations or a treaty of the United States. When the plaintiffs sued Rio Tinto for genocide under the ATS, Rio Tinto argued that the statute does not apply to corporations.

ISSUE

Does the Alien Tort Statute apply to corporate defendants?

DECISION

Yes. We conclude that no principle of domestic or international law supports the conclusion that the norms enforceable through the ATS—such as the prohibition by international law of genocide—apply only to natural persons and not to corporations, leaving corporations immune from suit and free to retain profits earned through such acts. The ATS contains no such language and has no such legislative history to suggest that corporate liability was excluded and that only liability of natural persons was intended. We next address the scope of liability for private actors, including corporate liability with respect to those claims we conclude can allege a violation of a sufficiently established international norm. While corporations are recognized legal entities, even amorphous groups may be guilty of genocide. Given that an amorphous group, a state, and a private individual may all violate the international norm prohibiting genocide, corporations likewise can commit genocide under international law because the prohibition is universal.

Soon after the *Sarei* decision, the U.S. Supreme Court severely limited the reach of the Alien Tort Statute. See *Kiobel v. Royal Dutch Petroleum,* 133 S.Ct. 1659 (2013). The Court held that U.S. courts generally will not have jurisdiction over violations that occur outside of the United States. Still, it left open the possibility that corporations, like Rio Tinto, could be sued in the United States if the claims touch and concern this country with sufficient force.

Ethics in Action

Doing what seems right does not always lead to a happy ending. After McKesson HBOC publicly disclosed that its auditors had discovered improperly recorded revenues, the Justice Department and SEC began an investigation. The corporation conducted an extensive internal review and turned its findings over to the U.S. Attorney and SEC on the condition that, unless they decided to prosecute, the government agencies would preserve the confidentiality of the materials. After both entities terminated their investigations without prosecuting, several civil suits were filed against McKesson. Those plaintiffs demanded access to the materials in the corporation's internal review. The court, despite McKesson's claim of confidentiality, ruled that the documents must be turned over to the plaintiffs because the corporation effectively waived its attorney-client and attorney work product privileges by voluntarily submitting the documents to the government. *McKesson HBOC v. Superior Court,* 9 Cal. Rptr. 3d 812 (Cal. Ct. App. 2004). Both of these privileges are more fully discussed in Chapter 1.

Crimes

Many criminal statutes are clearly intended to apply to corporations. Examples include the securities acts, the antitrust laws, and the numerous laws regulating the employment relationship. The traditional view was that a corporation could not be guilty of a crime involving intent. However, today, courts are especially likely to find criminal liability when a crime is committed, requested, or authorized by the board of directors, an officer, or a high-level manager.

Liability of Officers and Directors

LO6

Torts

Modern courts are much more willing to find negligence on the part of corporate directors and officers. Accordingly, where corporate activities cause injury or economic damage to others, the officer in charge, or even the directors, may be held liable. An officer or director may be held liable for the torts of employees of the corporation if she authorizes or participates in the commission of the tort.

Concept Summary: Liability for Torts and Crimes

If:	Employee commits a crime or tort	**While:**	Acting in scope of employment	**Then:**	Corporation is liable
When:	Corporate officer		Knew of employee's crime or tort and could have prevented it	**Then:**	Officer may be liable

Crimes

The criminal liability of officers has leaped to the attention of business leaders as state courts have upheld state criminal prosecutions against corporate officials for workplace injuries. Similarly, officers and directors both have been held personally liable under federal statutes imposing liability for hazardous waste cleanup costs. Directors and officers traditionally could be found guilty of crimes if they requested, authorized, or assisted in the commission of a crime by an employee. Now, they may be held criminally liable for failing in their supervisory duties.

Specifically, an officer can be found criminally liable for the illegal behavior of a subordinate when the officer (1) knew of or should have known of the illegal conduct and (2) failed to take reasonable measures to prevent it. Thus, in the case that opened this chapter, Park, the chief executive officer of Acme, was found guilty for failing to see to it that the rodent infestation was removed. The Supreme Court held that he was not justified in relying on the employees to whom he had delegated the task since they had previously failed to adequately resolve the matter.

The Sarbanes-Oxley Act requires CEOs and CFOs of publicly traded corporations to certify that, to their knowledge, all financial information in quarterly and annual reports is not false or misleading. If they certify false or misleading information, they are subject to fines of $5 million and up to 20 years' imprisonment. Further, they must disgorge any bonus, incentive-based or equity-based compensation, and profit from the sale of corporate securities received during a period in which the company was forced to restate a financial statement due to material noncompliance with any financial reporting requirement. This reimbursement provision applies to CEOs and CFOs even when the wrongdoing was attributable to another officer or employee.

Section 1103 of the Sarbanes-Oxley Act gives the SEC authority to ensure that assets of an issuer of securities which have been fraudulently obtained are not dissipated during the investigation and litigation of securities fraud cases. Specifically, Section 1103 provides that whenever, during the course of a lawful investigation of an issuer of publicly traded securities, it appears that the issuer will make "extraordinary payments" to directors, officers, partners, controlling persons, employees, or agents, the SEC may petition a federal district court for an order requiring the issuer to escrow those payments in an interest-bearing account. The following case examines the definition of "extraordinary payments" within the context of Section 1103.

SEC v. Gemstar-TV Guide International

401 F.3d 1031 (9th Cir. 2005) (en banc)

FACTS

After learning that its earnings had been overstated by some $40 million, Gemstar announced plans to restructure its management and corporate governance. As part of the restructuring plans, Gemstar provided termination agreements to its chief executive officer. and chief financial officer. The Restructuring Payments provided them with more than five times their base salary as well as large shares of stock and stock options. The SEC, ultimately, charged both with fraudulently inflating Gemstar's revenue reports by $223 million. Pursuant to Section 1103 of the Sarbanes-Oxley Act, the SEC informed Gemstar that the Restructuring Payments were to be placed in escrow during the course of its action against them.

ISSUE

Were the Restructuring Payments "extraordinary payments"?

DECISION

Yes. There can be little dispute that the Restructuring Payments are not being made in a normal and usual course of business, but rather are for an exceptional purpose or a special occasion. A nexus between the suspected wrongdoing and the payment itself may demonstrate that the payment is extraordinary, although such a connection is not required. Evidence of the company's deviation from an industry standard—or the practice of similarly situated businesses—also might reveal whether a payment is extraordinary. Courts need to look in context at (1) the circumstances of the payment, (2) the purpose of the payment, and (3) the size of the payment. If we use as a measure what ordinarily goes on in the process of the issuer's business, these facts are clearly unusual and extraordinary. This scenario is not business as usual.

Indemnification

The cost of defending and/or settling a suit or criminal charge brought against a director, officer, or employee may be very high. To encourage people to become officers and directors, corporations often indemnify them for such expenses. Today, however, all of the states place some limitations on the ability of corporations to indemnify officers and directors in order to strengthen the deterrence element of tort and criminal law.

In all instances, indemnification is *mandatory* if the officer or director prevails on the merits of the suit against him. When that occurs, the corporation must reimburse him for all of his costs and expenses. In cases in which the officer or director is found guilty, he still may be indemnified under **voluntary indemnification** if he acted in a manner that he believed not to be opposed to the corporation's best interests and had no reasonable cause to believe his conduct was unlawful. Such optional indemnification will occur if a majority of disinterested directors, an independent legal counsel, or the shareholders decide it to be appropriate. Many times, directors and corporations will have agreed in advance that indemnification should be mandatory under such circumstances. Such agreements are permissible and provide greater certainty and security for officers and directors. In the case that opened this chapter, it is extremely likely that Park would be indemnified by Acme corporation.

Concept Summary: Indemnification of Officers and Directors

Mandatory	Director or officer prevails on the merits Director or officer guilty but in good faith with preexisting indemnification agreement
Permissible	Director or officer guilty but: ■ In good faith ■ Believed acting in corporate interest ■ Unaware action illegal ■ Disinterested board, legal counsel, or shareholders agree to indemnify
Impermissible	Director or officer guilty and: ■ Liable to corporation or ■ In bad faith or ■ Violated federal securities laws

Concept Summary: Duties of Officers and Directors

Act within Authority	Unauthorized actions may be ratified by disinterested board.
Due Care and Diligence	Due care met by prudent person standard. Informed, disinterested, and rational decisions sheltered by business judgment rule.
Loyalty and Good Faith	Avoid self-dealing or usurping corporate opportunities unless they are fair to corporation.

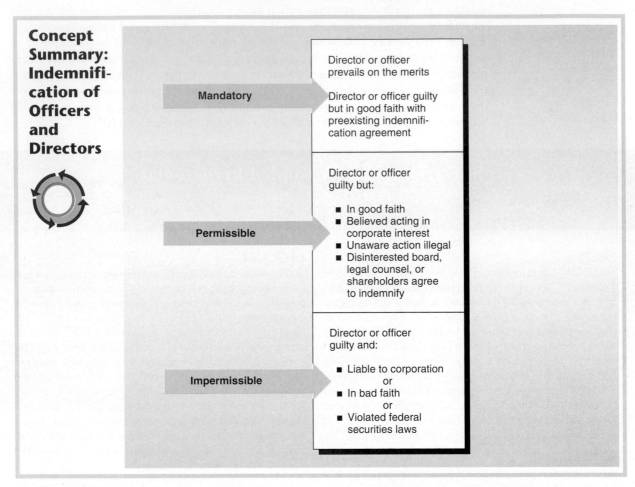

An officer or director who has acted in bad faith or who is found liable to the corporation may not be indemnified under any circumstances. Further, the SEC will oppose on public policy grounds indemnification of damages sustained as a result of violations of the federal securities laws.

Questions and Problem Cases

1. Southern Management Corporation (SMC) fired Mukhtak Taha after some personality conflicts with his supervisor, Debra Wylie-Forth. Soon thereafter, Michael McGovern, a maintenance supervisor, notified Wylie-Forth that several items were missing from a locked area. Two employees informed Wylie-Forth that they previously had witnessed Taha behaving suspiciously in the area. While investigating the incidents, the police interviewed McGovern, Wylie-Forth, and the two other employees. Based on these interviews, the police subsequently arrested and charged Taha with burglary. However, the charges were dropped when Taha produced alibi evidence that placed him out of town during the dates in question. Taha first sued Wylie-Forth and McGovern for malicious prosecution. When that lawsuit failed, he brought the same suit against SMC. The corporation argued that it cannot be liable if its employees were not liable. Can the corporation be held liable for the tort if its employees are not liable as well? Explain.
2. Barnet Stepak was a shareholder in Southern Company, a corporation whose subsidiaries provide electricity to consumers in the southern United States. Stepak demanded that Southern's board of directors bring suit to recover damages from two groups of current and former directors and officers for various illegal activities they committed in connection with their duties at the corporation. The board of directors investigated Stepak's charges. However, it entrusted the investigation to the law firm of Troutman Sanders, which had previously represented the suspected officers and directors in criminal investigations carried out by the Justice Department, the IRS, and the SEC. After various presentations dominated by Troutman Sanders's attorneys, the outside directors of the board voted unanimously to reject Stepak's demand. When Stepak claimed that the board had wrongfully refused his demand, the board argued that its decision was protected by the business judgment rule. Was the board's decision protected by the business judgment rule? Explain.
3. The corporate bylaws of Liquid Audio provide for a staggered board of directors that is divided into three classes. By only having one class of directors up for election in any given year, insurgents are unable to obtain control of the company in under two years. MM, a group of shareholders, announced its intention to nominate its own candidates for the two seats on Liquid Audio's board of directors that were up for election at the next annual meeting. MM also informed the board of its intention to amend the bylaws and increase the size of the board from five to nine. MM intended to nominate four individuals to fill the four newly created directorships. If MM's two directors were elected and its four proposed directors were also placed on the board, MM would control a majority of the board. In response, Liquid Audio amended the bylaws to increase the size of the board to seven members and immediately appointed two individuals to fill the newly created directorships. MM sued, challenging the board's appointment of the two additional directors. Should the court invalidate Liquid Audio's expansion of the board of directors? Explain.
4. Evertson and others formed a Wyoming corporation to engage in oil well servicing. Evertson served as the corporation's vice president. The funds obtained for the corporation's initial capitalization were insufficient to purchase all the equipment that it needed to function fully. Therefore, Evertson formed and was the only shareholder of

another corporation (Rental) that would purchase the equipment that the Wyoming corporation lacked. Evertson enjoyed substantial profits from leasing equipment to the Wyoming corporation. The Wyoming corporation alleged that in forming Rental, Evertson wrongfully appropriated for himself an opportunity that properly belonged to it. Should Evertson be liable for having usurped a corporate opportunity?

5. After the board of directors of NCS Healthcare agreed to the terms of a merger with Genesis Health Ventures (Genesis), the board withdrew its recommendation in favor of the Genesis merger. Instead, it recommended that the stockholders reject the Genesis transaction after deciding that a competing proposal from Omnicare offered the NCS stockholders an amount of cash equal to more than twice the then current market value of the shares to be received in the Genesis merger. However, the merger agreement between Genesis and NCS required that the Genesis agreement be placed before the corporation's stockholders for a vote, even if the NCS board of directors no longer recommended it. At the insistence of Genesis, the NCS board also agreed to omit any effective fiduciary out clause from the merger agreement. In connection with the Genesis merger agreement, two stockholders of NCS, who held a majority of the voting power, agreed unconditionally to vote all of their shares in favor of the Genesis merger. Thus, the combined terms of the voting agreements and merger agreement guaranteed that the transaction proposed by Genesis would obtain NCS stockholder's approval. After the merger with Genesis, a group of NCS shareholders sought to invalidate it on the ground that the directors of NCS violated their fiduciary duty of care. Did the NCS directors violate their fiduciary duty? Explain.
6. Loft, Inc., manufactured and sold candies, syrups, and beverages. It also operated 115 retail candy and soda fountain stores. Loft sold Coca-Cola at all of its stores, purchasing its 30,000-gallon annual requirement of the syrup and mixing it with carbonated water at its various soda fountains. In May 1931, Charles Guth, the president and general manager of Loft, became dissatisfied with the price of Coca-Cola syrup and suggested to Loft's vice president that Loft buy its syrup from National Pepsi-Cola Company. Soon thereafter, Guth bought Pepsi's secret formula and trademark for only $10,000. He organized a new corporation, Pepsi-Cola Company, of which he and his family owned a majority interest. From 1931 to 1935, without the knowledge or approval of Loft's board of directors, Guth used Loft's working capital, its credit, its plant and equipment, and its key personnel to produce Pepsi-Cola syrup. In addition, by dominating Loft's board of directors, Guth made Loft the chief customer of Pepsi-Cola. By 1935, the value of Pepsi-Cola's business was several million dollars. Loft brought suit, charging Guth with usurping a corporate opportunity and demanded that Guth give his Pepsi-Cola shares to Loft. Did Guth usurp a corporate opportunity?
7. During an inspection of Smokey's Steakhouse, a restaurant and bar, police officers arrested two 20-year-old women for being in the bar while underage. Neither woman had been asked for proof of age by any Smokey's employee and both had been served alcoholic beverages. Smokey's Steakhouse was charged with commission of a criminal act for allowing a person under the age of 21 to remain on premises where alcoholic beverages were being sold. Smokey's contended that, as a corporate defendant, it could not be liable for the crime because its bartender was acting outside of the scope of her employment in serving the women. Specifically, it asserted that one of the women was the bartender's underage sister and that the bartender intentionally violated Smokey's company policy against serving underage patrons. Is Smokey's criminally liable in spite of its employee's violation of company policy?

8. McLean, a former vice president of International Harvester's international division, was charged with violation of the Foreign Corrupt Practices Act (FCPA). Harvester pleaded guilty and admitted that the government had adequate evidence that two of its employees had aided and abetted violations of the FCPA. McLean believed that Harvester's plea negotiations and guilty plea implicated him in the bribery scheme, making him a scapegoat. At the trial, all of the substantive counts against him were dismissed because of a rule providing that an employee could not be convicted of violating the FCPA unless his employer was also convicted. (This rule was later repealed by the 1988 amendments to the FCPA.) McLean was then tried and acquitted of conspiring to violate the FCPA. He requested indemnification of $158,000 in legal fees and expenses incurred in defending himself. Harvester claimed that McLean waived any right to indemnification because he refused the services of the attorney that Harvester offered him. Must Harvester indemnify McLean for his legal fees?

Chapter 30

Financing the Corporation and the Role of the Shareholders

Learning Objectives

After you have studied this chapter, you should be able to:

1. Describe the various sources of corporate financing.
2. Explain with particularity the various rights of shareholders (including proxy voting, shareholder proposals, and rights of inspection).
3. Identify the various types of dividends, as well as the legal limits on dividends.
4. Clearly describe the difference between traditional lawsuits and derivative lawsuits, including the restrictions placed on derivative actions.

Holmes A. Court had a reputation for taking over a corporation, extracting quick profits, and leaving the company and its remaining shareholders staggering. Accordingly, Asarco's board of directors was alarmed to discover that Court was buying up the company's common stock. In preparation for a full-fledged assault, the board fashioned a formidable takeover defense. It unanimously approved the issuance of a new preferred stock series to be distributed as a dividend. The voting rights of this new stock were such that if Court acquired 20 percent of the

(continued)

common and 20 percent of the Series C Preferred, he would have only 4.1 percent of the total vote although he owned one-fifth of the stock.[1]

- Will a court uphold the board's defensive tactics?
- What is common stock? How does it differ from preferred stock?
- What are the rights and obligations of the holders of various types of stock?

Financing the Corporation

Sources of Corporate Financing

LO1

One of the major reasons that promoters select the corporate form of business is the variety of funding sources available to businesses that incorporate. The initial funds and property may come directly from the promoters or it may come from many diverse types of investors. An important source of financing is the sale of corporate securities in the form of shares, debentures, bonds, and long-term notes.

Other sources of funding are also prevalent. Short-term bank loans may provide at least part of the operating capital of the corporation. (Frequently, the promoters and major shareholders will be required to cosign these notes.) Often, this short-term funding will come in the form of accounts receivable financing and inventory financing. Of course, once the corporation is operating profitably, retained earnings may generate an important source of funds.

The remainder of the discussion of corporate funding in this chapter will be confined to the two types of corporate securities. The first type, **equity securities,** arises through the sale of ownership interests in the business in the form of shares of corporate stock. The second, **debt securities,** is typified by bonds and other obligations of the enterprise.

Equity Securities

A corporation must issue some common stock. It may also, if authorized by its articles, issue preferred stock. Both kinds of stock are equity securities. Certificates are issued to represent the shares of stock but they are not the stock; they are merely evidence of ownership.

Common Stock

If a corporation has only one class of stock, it is **common stock.** If there is more than one class, the common shareholders usually bear the major risks of the business and will benefit most from success. They receive what is left over after the preferences of other classes have been satisfied. This is usually true both for income available for dividends and for net assets on liquidation. Common stock usually carries voting rights. There may be more than one class of common stock, however, such as Class A and Class B. One class may have no right to vote.

[1] *Asarco, Inc. v. Court,* 611 F. Supp. 468 (D. N.J. 1985).

Preferred Stock

Any stock that has a preference over another class of stock is call **preferred stock.** Usually, preferred shareholders have a preference as to dividends and the distribution of assets when the corporation is dissolved. (The dividend rights of various types of preferred stock will be discussed more fully later in this chapter.)

The rights of preferred shareholders may vary from corporation to corporation. In some instances, preferred stock may be made convertible into common stock. And sometimes preferred stockholders will be given voting rights. However, the right to vote is usually granted only in the event that dividends due are not paid. In the case that opened this chapter, the defensive tactics of the Asarco board of directors were not permitted by the court. They were prohibited because the corporation had no power to issue preferred stock that would result in differing voting rights within the same class.

Preferred stock can be **redeemed**—that is, paid off and canceled by the corporation—if the articles permit. Under the Model Business Corporation Act (MBCA), the redemption price must be stated in the articles. Redemption permits the corporation to buy back the shares even if the holders do not wish to sell. It is very common for a corporation to issue preferred shares subject to redemption at the option of the corporation. Although it is not as common, a corporation may also have a redeemable class of common shares. Redemption will not be permitted, however, if the cost would make the corporation insolvent.

Consideration for Shares

Shares of stock are generally issued in exchange for money, property, or services already performed for the corporation. The board of directors is entrusted with the authority to decide what is the proper amount and form of consideration for the shares. Corporation statutes, however, will frequently place some limitations on the discretion of the board of directors in order to protect the rights of creditors and other shareholders.

Presently, most states follow the old MBCA approach, which requires that shares be issued only for money, tangible or intangible property, and services already performed for the corporation. Most of these states do not permit the promoter's preincorporation services to be proper consideration for shares because the services were not technically rendered to the corporation. (The corporation was not in existence at the time of these services.) Likewise, these states do not consider promissory notes or pledges of future services to be acceptable forms of consideration for shares in the corporation. This is so because such promises may overstate the value of the corporation since they may never be performed.

The revised MBCA permits promises of future services and promissory notes to be exchanged for shares since they do have value to a corporation. (Of course, because of the risk of nonperformance, the value may not be as great as the value of services that have already been rendered to the corporation.) Further, the new MBCA allows the corporation to issue shares to the promoters in exchange for their preincorporation efforts because the corporation has benefited from such services. (Without these services, the corporation would probably not exist.)

Value of Shares

Sometimes, a value is assigned to the shares in the articles of incorporation. This arbitrary amount is referred to as **par value.** If the stock has no par value, the board of directors may assign a **stated value** when the shares are issued.

Stated Capital

Par value and stated value reflect the minimum amount of consideration for which the shares can be issued. This is so because the stated capital of the corporation is determined by multiplying the number of outstanding shares times the par or stated value of each share. If the shares were issued for less than the par or stated value, the stated capital of the corporation would exaggerate the actual value of the corporation. As a result, the board of directors as well as the purchasers of shares are liable to the corporation when shares have been issued for less than the par or the stated value.

Capital Surplus

Many times, the shares are actually worth more than the par or the stated value. In these instances, the directors have a duty to the corporation to receive the *fair value* of the stock. In order to avoid liability to the corporation, the directors must exercise good faith and the care of ordinary prudent directors in determining the amount of consideration that is to be collected for the shares. When the shares sell for more than their par or stated value, the excess amount is referred to as *capital surplus.* While the MBCA has abandoned the use of the terms *stated value* and *capital surplus,* most states still use the concepts.

Options, Warrants, and Rights

The MBCA expressly permits directors to issue options to purchase shares of the corporation. These may be given in connection with the sale of other securities, or they may be issued to employees as an incentive to increase profitability in order to maximize the market value of the corporation's stock. Shareholder approval is required under the MBCA for employee and director stock option plans.

Concept Summary: Stated Capital and Capital Surplus

$$\text{Stated capital} = (\text{Par value}) \times \begin{pmatrix}\text{Number of shares}\\ \text{outstanding}\end{pmatrix}$$

$$\text{Capital surplus} = \begin{pmatrix}\text{Amount received}\\ \text{per share}\end{pmatrix} - \text{Par value}\Big) \times \begin{pmatrix}\text{Number of shares}\\ \text{outstanding}\end{pmatrix}$$

Options represented by certificates are known as *warrants.* They are sometimes part of a package of securities sold as a unit; for example, they may be given along with notes, bonds, or even shares. The term *rights* is usually applied to short-term and often nonnegotiable options. Rights are used to give present security holders a right to subscribe to some proportional quantity of the same or a different security of the corporation. Often they are given in connection with a preemptive right requirement.

Treasury Stock

A corporation may purchase its securities from any willing seller. It does not need specific authority to do so in its articles. However, the MBCA permits such purchases only out of unrestricted earned surplus. Earned surplus arises when a corporation retains all or part of its operating profit rather than paying it out in dividends. Capital surplus may be used only on a two-thirds vote of shareholders. Capital surplus can come from several sources. One is sales of shares above par value. Repurchased shares become treasury shares. They cannot be voted in elections, and they can be resold without regard to par value or original issue price.

The MBCA recommends abolishing the concept of treasury shares. Under this approach, repurchased shares are restored to unissued status. They may then be reissued unless the articles of incorporation require cancellation.

Debt Securities

Corporations have the power to borrow money necessary for their operations by issuing debt securities. This power is inherent; it need not appear in the articles of incorporation. Unlike equity securities, debt securities do not transfer an ownership interest in the corporation.

Concept Summary: Sources of Financing the Corporation

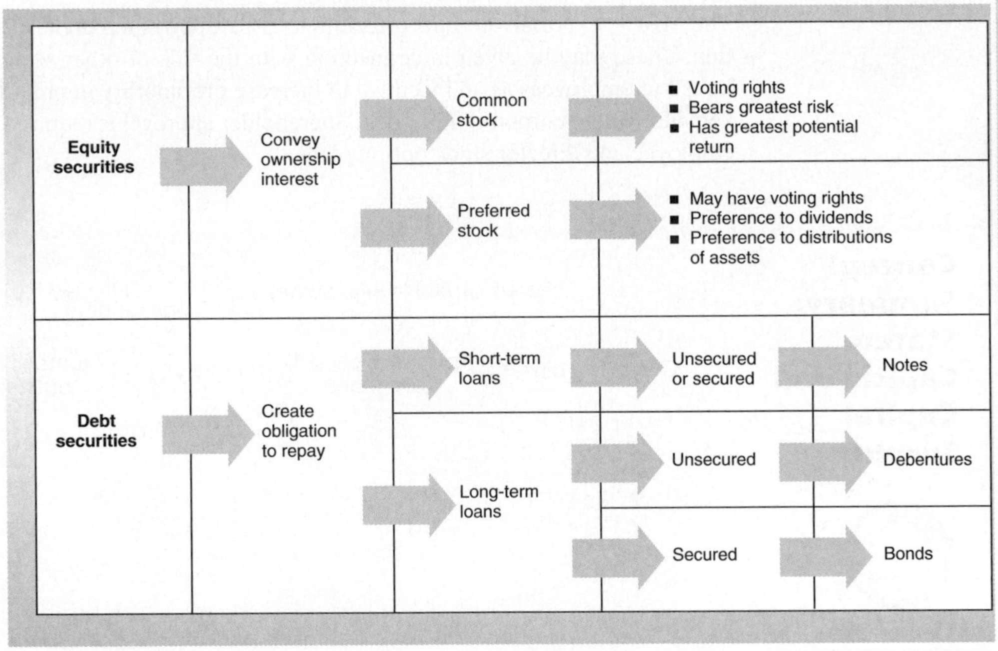

They create a debtor–creditor relationship. Accordingly, the corporation/debtor is obligated to pay a periodic interest charge as well as the balance of the debt on the maturity date. Debt securities arise in the form of notes, debentures, or bonds.

Notes

Short-term debt instruments are called **notes.** They seldom have terms in excess of five years. Notes may be either secured or unsecured. When they are secured, the creditor may force the sale of the collateral if the debt is not paid according to the terms of the agreement.

Debentures

Long-term unsecured debt instruments are called **debentures.** They may have a term of 30 years or more. Frequently, debentures will have an indenture. An **indenture** is a contract protecting the rights of the debenture holders. It will define what acts constitute default by the corporation as well as stipulate the rights of the holder on default. In many instances, it will place restrictions on the corporation's right to issue other debt securities in order to prevent the corporation from overextending itself.

Bonds

Long-term, secured debt securities are called **bonds.** They generally have indentures and therefore differ from debentures only because they are secured. The security may be real property such as a building or personal property such as machinery, raw materials, or even accounts due from customers. Bondholders, as well as holders of secured notes, have priority as to the assets securing the debt. Therefore, they are more likely than unsecured noteholders and debenture holders to receive greater portions of their claims should the corporation be forced to liquidate.

Levco Alternative Fund Ltd. v. The Reader's Digest Association

803 A.2d 428 (Del. Sup. Ct. 2002)

FACTS

The Reader's Digest Association (RDA) formulated a recapitalization plan that called for it (a) to purchase all the shares of its Class B voting stock at a premium ratio of 1.24 to 1 with the newly issued common stock at one vote per share and (b) to recapitalize each share of the Class A nonvoting stock into one share of the new voting common stock. A group of Class A nonvoting shareholders opposed implementation of the recapitalization plan. Specifically, they argued that the Special Committee established to evaluate the fairness of the transaction breached its fiduciary duty to consider the separate interests of the Class A shareholders.

ISSUE

Should the court issue a preliminary injunction against implementation of the recapitalization plan?

DECISION

Yes. The independent committee who negotiated the recapitalization never sought, nor did its financial advisor ever tender, an opinion as to whether the transaction was fair to the Class A shareholders. The financial advisor directed its fairness opinion to the interests of RDA as a corporate entity. Given the obvious conflicting interests of the shareholder classes, the conceded absence of an evaluation of the fairness of the recapitalization on the Class A shareholders is significant.

Becoming a Shareholder

If you are not already the owner of shares of stock in a corporation, you may wish to become one. No large investment is necessary. Many shares sell for less than $10 per share, but those of companies with good financial prospects usually sell for more. Although you will find in this chapter that shareholders have a number of rights, most shareholders are interested in only one—the right to share in the profits of the corporation.

Functions of Shareholders

Although owners of the corporation, shareholders have few functions, and in most publicly held corporations they exercise little influence. Normally, their principal function is the election of the directors. In large corporations, the proxy system of voting and the tendency of most shareholders to follow the recommendations of management usually result in the election of persons nominated by management.

Shareholders are also required to approve unusual or extraordinary corporate transactions such as a merger, sale of substantially all corporate assets, or a voluntary dissolution. In addition, their favorable vote is necessary to amend the corporate articles. Some states require shareholder approval for other matters as well. For example, the MBCA requires shareholder approval of stock option plans for corporate officers and other managers. It also requires approval of loans to officers by the corporation. These functions are performed at shareholders' meetings. The meetings may be either the regular annual meeting or special meetings.

Means of Acquiring Stock

One can become a shareholder by several means. One is by subscribing to shares in a new corporation being formed. Another is by subscribing to shares that are being issued by an existing corporation. A more common method is to buy newly issued shares that have been underwritten by an investment banker and sold through a stockbroker. (An underwriter of a stock issue agrees to market it to investors and usually guarantees to sell the entire issue at an agreed-on price.) The most common way of becoming a shareholder is by buying previously issued shares from a former owner, either directly or through a broker.

Subscriptions to buy stock in a corporation that is not yet in existence are usually treated as offers until incorporation is completed. The MBCA makes such subscriptions irrevocable for six months. Generally, corporate acceptance of preincorporation subscriptions occurs by action of the board of directors after incorporation. It is at this time (the time of acceptance) that the subscriber becomes a shareholder. (Some state statutes provide that the acceptance automatically occurs at the time of the issuance of the certificate of incorporation.)

A subscription for unissued shares in an existing corporation is usually treated as an offer. A contract is formed, and the subscriber becomes a shareholder when the corporation accepts the offer. The making of the subscription contract is called **issuing stock.** The stock certificate cannot, under the MBCA, be issued until the shares are fully paid for.

Shareholders' Meetings

Annual Meeting

All of the state laws except Delaware's require corporations formed in the state to have an annual meeting. A Delaware corporation can use a mail ballot instead of holding a meeting. The main purpose of the annual meeting is the election of directors. Many larger corporations ask the shareholders to approve the selection of public auditors. There may be other proposals by management for shareholder approval, such as an executive stock option or profit-sharing plan or an amendment to the articles of incorporation. There may also be resolutions proposed by shareholders to be voted on. It is customary for the chief executive and perhaps other officers to give brief reports on the corporation's operations during the past year and its prospects for the current year. Shareholders may ask questions of the top officers, usually during a question period scheduled to follow the officer reports.

Special Meetings

Special meetings of shareholders are quite rare in most corporations. One is called when shareholder approval of a corporate action is necessary between annual meetings. The most common purpose is probably to get approval of a proposal by the directors to merge with another corporation.

The MBCA provides that a special meeting may be called by the president, the board of directors, or the holders of one-tenth or more of the shares entitled to vote at the meeting. Under the MBCA, the bylaws may provide that other officers or persons (such as the chairman of the board) may call a special meeting of shareholders.

Notice of Meetings

The MBCA requires **notice** of all shareholders' meetings to be given not less than 10 or more than 50 days before the meeting. The notice must give the place, day, and hour of the meeting. For special meetings, the purpose of the meeting must be given. If an extraordinary corporate transaction such as a merger is to be voted on, notice of the proposal must be given to *all* shareholders, even if there are shareholders who own a class of stock not usually entitled to vote. The shareholders entitled to notice are those "of record." They are the people whose names appear on the stock-transfer book of the corporation.

If the required notice is not given, actions taken at a meeting are of no effect. However, shareholders who did not get proper notice may **waive** notice. As in the case of directors' meetings (discussed in the previous chapter), attendance at the meeting is an automatic waiver. However, there is no waiver if the shareholder attends only to object to the holding of the meeting. Waiver is effective only if all shareholders who did not get proper notice either attend or waive in writing.

Remote Participation

Amendments to Delaware's corporation laws now permit directors to allow shareholders who are not physically present at a meeting to participate by remote communication. In fact, the directors may dispense with a physical location entirely and conduct the entire meeting by modern communications technology. Four requirements must be met if a shareholder meeting is to be conducted remotely: (1) the corporation must have implemented some reasonable means for ensuring that those persons participating are indeed shareholders, (2) those participating shareholders and proxy holders must be afforded a

Accipiter Life Sciences Fund v. Helfer

905 A.2d 115 (Del. Ch. Ct. 2006)

FACTS

LifePoint announced its annual stockholders' meeting in a press release devoted mainly to financial results. Accipiter, a substantial stockholder, failed to realize that, under the corporation's advance notice bylaw, it had 10 days from the date of that public announcement to nominate a slate of directors to the board. It discovered its mistake two months later, when its belated attempts to nominate candidates were rebuffed for tardiness.

ISSUE

Should the court set aside the election?

DECISION

No. Clearly, the annual meeting announcement would have been completely unmistakable had LifePoint specifically included it in the caption of the press release or had it issued a separate press release to that effect. Even a separate subheading in the press release alerting readers to the additional topic would have considerably improved the quality of LifePoint's disclosure. However, LifePoint's concededly troubling way of announcing its annual meeting does not reach the standard required for equitable relief. LifePoint's actions did not make Accipiter's challenge extremely difficult or impossible.

reasonable opportunity to both participate and vote, (3) some means must be provided so that participants have the opportunity to read or hear the ongoing proceedings, and (4) the corporation must keep a record of any remote votes or other actions taken at the meeting.

The rules governing remote participation by shareholders do not have to meet the same retention, retrieval, review, and reproduction requirements imposed on directors' actions. Thus, while a directors' action by remote transmission would not be valid unless it could be reproduced in paper form (see Chapter 29), shareholder meetings may now be conducted by conference call.

For many years, corporations were required to maintain and make available a list of all shareholders during the 10 days prior to a shareholder meeting. The new amendments to Delaware law now permit the corporation either to maintain the list at its principal place of business or to post it on an electronic network. For meetings that are conducted entirely by remote communications, the list is to be made available throughout the meeting on an accessible electronic network.

Shareholders Entitled to Vote

Sources of the Right to Vote

LO2

If you are a shareholder, your right to vote at a shareholders' meeting depends on the incorporation statute and the articles and bylaws of the corporation. If you own common stock and have it listed in your name, you probably have a right to vote.

Determining Who May Vote

The person who has legal title to the stock is the one usually entitled to vote. Directors of publicly held corporations usually establish a record date prior to each shareholders' meeting. Those who are shareholders of record on that date are allowed to vote. Those who are owners of shares held in the name of another, such as a stockbroker, may obtain a proxy from the record holder. SEC rules require brokers to mail proxy material to customers for whom they hold shares.

Nonvoting Stock

Owners of a nonvoting class of stock have a right to vote only under certain circumstances. The MBCA gives holders of such stock the right to vote on extraordinary corporate transactions, which are discussed later in this chapter. Neither a corporation nor its subsidiary may vote treasury shares. Unissued stock, of course, carries no vote.

Proxy Voting

As a shareholder, you may appoint another person, known as a *proxy,* to vote for you. The MBCA requires a written document appointing the proxy as an agent to vote for you. This document is also, rather confusingly, called a **proxy.** Some states permit an oral proxy. A proxy may generally be revoked at any time; it is automatically revoked if you later give another proxy on the same shares of stock.

Modern corporation statutes permit creation of irrevocable proxies. These statutes usually specifically define when a proxy may be irrevocable. The MBCA allows a proxy to be irrevocable if it so states and if it is "coupled with an interest." A proxy will be coupled with an interest when, among other things, the proxy holder is a party to a shareholder voting agreement or has agreed to purchase the shares under a "buy-and-sell agreement."

Solicitation of Proxies

As indicated above, usually in publicly held corporations only a small proportion of the shares are owned by persons who attend shareholders' meetings. Management then solicits proxies. It asks the shareholders who do not expect to attend to appoint, as their proxy, one or more of the directors or some other person friendly to management. Most shareholders sign and return their proxies.

Regulation of Proxies

The SEC has power under the 1934 Act to make rules about proxy statements. The proxy statement must give certain information. For example, if directors are to be elected, information must be given about any employment contract and pension or stock option benefits and any material transaction between a nominee and the corporation. An annual statement must be mailed with or before the proxy statement for an annual meeting.

The proxy document, under SEC rules, must permit shareholders a choice of voting for or withholding their vote from all of the management slate of directors. They may also exempt one or more directors from their favorable vote. They must also be permitted to abstain or vote for or against any resolutions that have been proposed.

Finally, SEC rules require corporations subject to them to furnish a shareholder list to any shareholder who desires to solicit proxies. As an alternative, the corporation may mail the proxy material for the soliciting shareholder. (The regulation of proxies will be discussed in greater detail in Chapter 31.)

Expenses

The corporation pays for the preparation and mailing of a proxy statement on behalf of management. If someone else or a group wants to nominate directors, that group must bear the expense of soliciting proxies. A proxy battle tends to be very expensive, and relatively few challengers

American Federation v. American International Group

462 F.3d 121 (2d Cir. 2006)

FACTS

AFSCME holds 26,965 shares of voting common stock of American International Group (AIG or Company), a multinational corporation operating in the insurance and financial services sectors. AFSCME submitted to AIG for inclusion in the Company's proxy statement a shareholder proposal that, if adopted by a majority of AIG shareholders at the Company's annual meeting, would amend the AIG bylaws to require the Company, under certain circumstances, to publish the names of shareholder-nominated candidates for director positions together with any candidates nominated by AIG's board of directors (Proposal). AIG excluded the Proposal from the Company's proxy statement.

ISSUE

Should the court require the shareholder proposal to be included in the proxy materials?

DECISION

Yes. If a shareholder seeking to submit a proposal meets certain eligibility and procedural requirements, a corporation generally is required to include the proposal in its proxy statement. However, there is an exception to this requirement for a shareholder proposal that "relates to an election" for membership on the company's board of directors. A shareholder proposal that seeks to amend the corporate bylaws to establish a procedure by which shareholder-nominated candidates may be included on the corporate ballot does not relate to an election within the meaning of the applicable rule. Therefore, it cannot be excluded from corporate proxy materials.

win. If they do, they are entitled to be reimbursed by the corporation for their expenses because it is assumed from their shareholder support that the corporation has benefited.

Effect

Shareholders usually follow the recommendation of management in their voting or merely sign the proxy without voting. The proxy also usually gives management authority to vote the shares on any other matter coming before the meeting. The effect, of course, is to determine the outcome of the meeting before it is held. An argument made for or against a resolution at the meeting can affect only the votes of those present. A resolution made from the floor has no chance of passing unless the management votes its proxies in favor of it. Through the proxy system, management is able to control the corporation without owning many shares itself.

Shareholder Proposals and Right to Speak

Sources of Shareholder Rights

LO2

Shareholders have the right both to ask questions and to propose resolutions at shareholders' meetings. The first right is that of an owner to be informed about his or her investment. The second is the right of an owner to participate in establishing the framework within which the directors exercise their powers of management. It is related to the shareholders' rights to make bylaws.

Shareholder Resolutions

In recent years, shareholder activists have submitted resolutions at the annual meetings of quite a number of the largest corporations. They generally fall into two types. One type aims to protect or enhance the interests of small shareholders. Proposals to amend the corporate articles to permit cumulative voting for directors (discussed in the next section), to put ceilings on the salaries of top executives, and to limit corporate gifts to charitable and educational organizations are of this type. The other type had its beginnings about 1970. Proposals of this type are usually offered by groups that have goals of social or political change or that oppose certain corporate activities. A few shares may be purchased solely to permit making the proposal. Other such groups, particularly church groups, may have owned quite a few shares as an investment for some time.

Concept Summary: Shareholder Rights

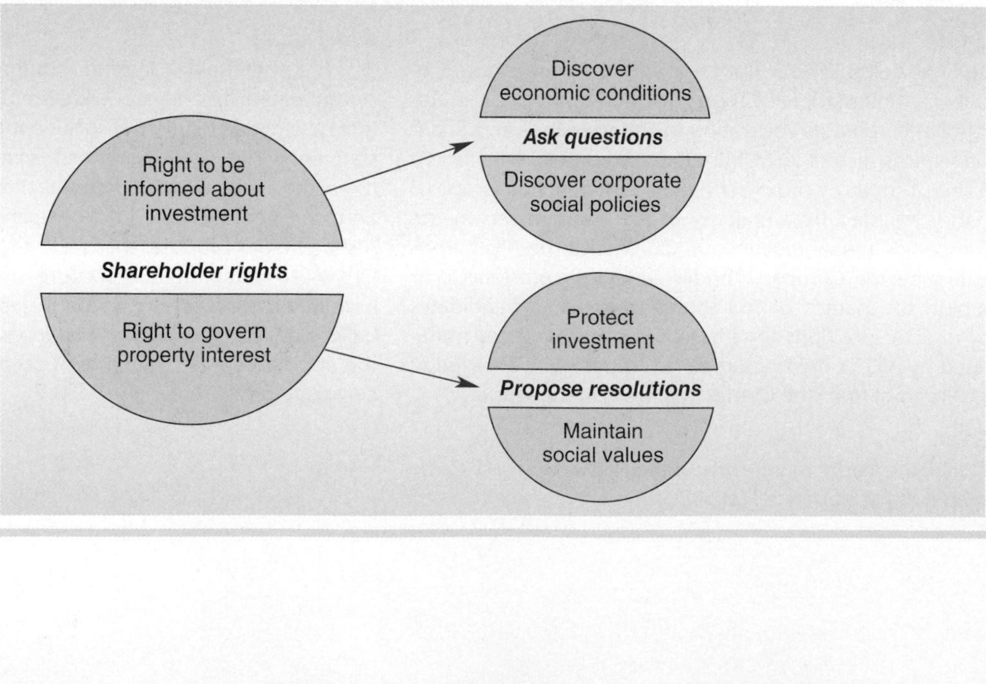

Some resolutions seeking a change in corporate policy asked the directors of corporations to withdraw from South Africa until apartheid ended. Some have merely asked the corporation to publicize certain information withheld as confidential, such as statistics on minority employment.

Ethics in Action

Do shareholders have a moral responsibility to monitor the activities of the corporations in which they hold stock? Do they have a responsibility to urge those corporations to behave in a socially responsible manner?

Cumulative Voting

Most corporations elect directors on the basis that each share is entitled to one vote for each director. Many corporations, however, permit shareholders to cumulate their votes. By using all their votes to support one director, a group of minority shareholders may be able to elect a director of their choice. If they spread their votes among all nominees, on the other hand, they would not be able to elect any.

A number of states require businesses incorporated in them to permit shareholders to cumulate their votes for directors. Few large publicly held corporations are incorporated in these states. The purpose of **cumulative voting** is to give minority shareholders an opportunity to be represented on the board. Opponents say that this is likely to be divisive and to cause friction among board members that will damage the firm.

The formula for determining the number of shares, *X*, required to elect one director under cumulative voting is

$$X = \frac{S}{D + 1} + 1$$

where *S* is the number of shares voting and *D* is the total number of directors to be elected. Clearly, the fewer directors to be elected, the greater is the percentage of shares required to elect one director. Dividing directors into three classes, one class to be elected each year, makes it more difficult for minority shareholders to attain representation on the board.

Rights of Inspection and Preemptive Right

The Shareholder's Right to Inspect

LO2

The MBCA requires a corporation to send its latest financial statements to any shareholder on request. It also requires the corporation to permit a shareholder, on written request, to examine in person, or through an agent such as a lawyer or an accountant, its "relevant books and records of account, minutes, and record of shareholders." The shareholder or agent may make extracts from these records.

Proper Purpose

The shareholder must have a proper purpose for examining the records. To learn business secrets or to gain a competitive advantage is not a proper purpose. To determine the value of one's shares or to identify fellow shareholders in order to communicate with them concerning corporate affairs is a proper purpose. It is a proper purpose to make a copy of the shareholder list in order to wage a proxy contest to unseat present management.

Ethics in Action

Is it ethical for a businessperson to purchase shares of stock in a competing company in order to gain access to its books and records?

Denials

The MBCA gives shareholders an absolute right to inspect the shareholder list. In order to discourage the denial of proper demands to inspect, the MBCA makes a corporate official who denies a proper demand liable for a penalty of 10 percent of the value of the shares of the demanding shareholder. Many state statutes have no such penalty provision and, as a result, denials are common.

Preemptive Rights

A number of states require corporations domiciled there to give their current shareholders an option to purchase their proportionate share of any new issue of stock.

Barasch v. Williams Real Estate

2013 N.Y. App. Div. LEXIS 1564 (N.Y. App. Div. 2013)

FACTS

Candace Barasch was a shareholder and corporate director of Williams Real Estate Co. Barasch objected when the corporation sold a 65 percent interest in the company to a third-party investor. After the sale, Barasch sought to compel the corporation to pay the fair value of her shares. At that time, she discovered an e-mail between the corporation's in-house counsel and its outside counsel—Moses & Singer—that described Barasch as "hostile" to the transaction and warned that her attorneys could use provisions of the shareholder agreement to her benefit. When Barasch petitioned the court for discovery of communications between the corporation and Moses & Singer, the company demanded return of the e-mail which it claimed was inadvertently forwarded to her. It asserted that the communications between it and its law firm were privileged. Barasch claimed that as a corporate director, she had an absolute right to inspect corporate books and records, including attorney–client communications.

ISSUE

Does Barasch have a legal right to examine the communications between the corporation and its attorneys?

DECISION

No. This case involves a party who is both a corporate director and a shareholder, suing in her capacity as a shareholder and seeking to invade the corporation's attorney–client privileged communications about her. These communications took place at a time when she was adverse to the corporation and attempting to advance her own interests as a shareholder. Thus, her request must be denied. Our courts have long held that a director of a corporation should not be allowed to use her corporate position to waive the privilege that attaches to the corporation in a litigation relating to her own rights or in which she is asserting claims that are or may be adverse to the corporation. To find otherwise would thwart the purpose of the attorney–client privilege, which is to encourage full and frank communication between attorneys and their clients.

This enables the shareholder to maintain the same relative interest in the corporation as before. Granting such a preemptive right creates difficult problems in large corporations that have several classes of stock. Generally, courts do not apply preemptive rights to treasury shares, shares issued in connection with a merger or consolidation, or shares issued in exchange for property or past services. Further, most of the states provide that there is no preemptive right unless the articles of incorporation create such a right.

Dividends

Directors' Discretion to Pay Dividends

Shareholders have a right to share in the net income of the corporation; however, the declaration of dividends is subject to the business judgment of the board of directors. They may not pile up unneeded cash in the treasury or pay it out in unreasonably high salaries to management. However, the burden of proof is on the shareholder to show that the directors have abused their discretion.

Types of Dividends

Cash and Property Dividends

Dividends are usually paid in cash. However, in some instances the corporation may distribute corporate assets other than cash. These property dividends may take the form of shares of stock that the corporation owns in another corporation or any other noncash asset of the corporation.

Stock Dividends

Distributions of shares in the corporation itself are called **stock dividends.** They are usually paid when management wants to retain all or an unusually high proportion of earnings for reinvestment. A large stock dividend may have as its main purpose a reduction in the market price per share to encourage greater investor interest in the stock. Stock dividends payable in the same class of shares do not change a shareholders' stake in the corporation. The proportion of shares owned remains the same; the shareholder just has a higher number of shares.

Legal Limits on Dividends

LO3

Incorporation statutes all put limits on the dividends a corporation may pay. The MBCA permits paying dividends only out of retained earnings. It also prohibits the payment of a dividend that would make the corporation insolvent. A business is *insolvent* when it cannot pay its debts as they become due.

Stock Splits

A **stock split** is not a dividend; it merely changes the par value or stated value of the shares and the number outstanding, not the retained earnings account. A stock split increases the number of shares outstanding; a reverse stock split reduces the number of shares outstanding. The reason for either action is to adjust the price of the stock to one that the management of the corporation believes is more appropriate. Brokers' commissions tend to be lower on 100-share lots. If the stock price is high, this may discourage investors from buying it. If it is too low, it may appear to be less than a sound investment.

If the articles of incorporation have not previously authorized a share split, it cannot be made until they are amended to permit it. Therefore, there must be a favorable vote of shareholders. Only the vote of the directors is necessary for a stock dividend unless additional shares must be authorized. An amendment of the articles of incorporation is required to increase the number of authorized shares.

Dividends on Preferred Stock

The contract with preferred shareholders usually gives them a preference in dividends over common shareholders. This preference means that common shareholders cannot receive any dividends until preferred shareholders have been fully paid. Dividends on **cumulative preferred** stock, if not paid in any year, will be payable later when funds are available. Dividends on **noncumulative preferred** stock need not be paid later if they are not earned and paid in the year due. Sometimes, **participating preferred** stock is issued. Holders of such stock get their usual dividend. Then, after the common shareholders receive a prescribed "normal" dividend, the preferred shareholders participate with the common shareholders in income available for dividends. Of course, if there are no funds available for dividends, none will be paid to either class. If the preference is **cumulative to the extent earned,** the preferred shareholder has a right, before common shareholders receive any dividends, to be paid all dividends that were not declared when earned in prior fiscal years.

Concept Summary: Dividends on Preferred Stock

Noncumulative	Has preference to dividends actually paid in year earned
Cumulative	Receives omitted dividends from previous years before others are paid
Cumulative to the extent earned	Has right to all dividends, not declared but previously earned, before others are paid
Participating	Receives usual preference plus right to share income left after common shares paid normal dividend

Effect of Dividend Declaration

Once the directors have voted to pay a lawful dividend, it becomes a debt of the corporation. It may treat as the shareholders the persons registered as such on its records; therefore, directors usually set a record date. If a sale of the stock is made on a stock exchange, the purchaser is entitled to the dividend unless the sale occurs on or after the *ex dividend date,* which is two business days before the record date for the dividend.

Shareholder Rights in Extraordinary Corporate Transactions

Amendment of Articles

Any amendment to the articles of incorporation must be approved by the shareholders. The MBCA requires approval by a majority of the shares entitled to vote but permits the articles of incorporation to impose a higher requirement. If the amendment would affect the rights of a class of shares, then shareholders of that class have a right to vote as a class even though those shareholders normally have no vote. For example, if the proposal is to eliminate a provision for cumulative dividends on a class of preferred stock, a majority of the shares of that class must approve.

Other Extraordinary Transactions

Under the MBCA, approval of all classes of shares is required for a merger or consolidation. A *merger* occurs when one corporation is absorbed into another existing corporation. A *consolidation* occurs when two or more corporations become part of a new corporation. A sale of most of the corporation's assets or a voluntary dissolution of the corporation also requires the favorable vote of the shareholders.

Appraisal Rights

The statutes in many states give appraisal rights to shareholders who vote against certain transactions. Suppose you vote against a proposal to merge your corporation with another but the majority supports the merger. If you have an appraisal right, you may demand that the corporation pay you the fair value of your shares.

Actions Covered

Under the MBCA, the **right of appraisal** applies in cases of mergers or a sale of most of the corporate assets. It would also apply to amendments to the articles of incorporation that would materially affect liquidation, dividend, redemption, preemptive, or voting rights. Some state statutes permit an appraisal right when there is a consolidation.

Procedures

The MBCA and most state statutes limit the right of appraisal to shareholders who have a right to vote. Further, shareholders can exercise the right only if they did not vote in favor of the transaction triggering the right of appraisal. (Some state laws require that they have actually voted against the action.) Next, most statutes insist that the dissenting shareholders notify the corporation of their intent to exercise the right before the actual vote has taken place. If these steps are met, the corporation will instruct them where they may demand payment. Finally, they must actually demand payment. If the shareholders and the corporation cannot agree on the value of the shares, they may ask a court to determine ("appraise") their value.

Exclusions

Most state statutes deny the right of appraisal to shares that are traded on a recognized securities exchange. This exclusion is grounded on the belief that the securities market is the best determinant of the value of the shares. No such exclusions are recommended by the MBCA.

Lawsuits by Shareholders

Individual Actions

Shareholders may sue the corporation for a breach of their shareholder contract, the basis for the relationship between the corporation and the shareholder. The contract is a product of the corporate articles and bylaws and any board of directors resolution applicable to the particular stock issue, as well as the corporation statute. It is not a document signed by the shareholder and the corporation. Suppose you are a shareholder and other shareholders of the same class are paid a dividend but you are not. You as an individual could sue the

LO4

corporation to get the same dividend on your shares because you have not received a benefit to which you are entitled as a shareholder.

Class Actions

When a number of people have a right or claim against the same defendant growing out of essentially the same set of facts, a class action may be brought by any one of them. For example, if the corporation did not pay a preferred dividend that was due, you could bring a suit demanding that the dividend be paid. If you win, the corporation would have to pay the dividend to all of the preferred shareholders of the class. You would then be able to recover from the corporation your expenses in bringing suit. If you lose, there would be no reimbursement.

Derivative Actions

Shareholders are not usually able to sue to enforce a right of the corporation. Suppose an officer of the corporation has breached his duty by setting up a business to compete with the corporation and has made $1 million at the expense of the corporation. A shareholder could not sue him to recover the proportionate share of that loss. This is so because the corporation is a legal entity separate from the shareholders.

However, under certain conditions, a shareholder is permitted to sue as a representative of the corporation. There are two basic requirements: first, the shareholder must have owned shares at the time of the wrong; and second, the shareholder must urge the directors and, if appropriate, the other shareholders to direct that such a suit be brought by the corporation. A shareholder is permitted to bring suit only if the directors refuse or have a conflict of interest that is likely to keep them from suing. If the shareholder wins, the damages normally go to the corporation, not to the shareholder directly. However, as in the case of a successful class action, the shareholder will be reimbursed for her expenses in bringing the suit.

Pirelli Armstrong Tire Corporation v. Raines

534 F.3d 779 (C.C. Cir. 2008)

FACTS

A governmental review of Fannie Mae's books uncovered deficiencies in accounting policies, internal controls, and financial reporting. Ultimately, the corporation was compelled by the Securities Exchange Commission (SEC) to draft a $9 billion earnings restatement. Six days later, two Fannie Mae officers (CEO Franklin D. Raines and CFO Timothy Howard) resigned. The corporate board did not fire Raines or Howard for cause, and as a result, they were able to leave the company with $31 billion in severance benefits. Several corporate shareholders filed a derivative lawsuit against the corporation's directors, claiming that the board should have terminated Raines and Howard for cause.

ISSUE

Are the shareholders excused from asking the board to have the corporation pursue the claim?

DECISION

No. To prevail on this claim, the shareholders have to present particularized facts sufficient to raise (1) a reason to doubt that the action was taken honestly and in good faith or (2) a reason to doubt that the board was adequately informed in making the decision. There is no showing here that the process was flawed or that the directors acted without adequate information or deliberation. In fact, the termination decision was made in a series of board meetings held over several days. While the grounds might have existed to dismiss Raines and Howard for cause, there also existed business reasons that could support the board's decision not to do so. For example, the board may have decided that it did not wish to spend enormous time and resources litigating the matter.

Special Litigation Committees

When shareholders file a derivative lawsuit, corporations may establish a **special litigation committee** (SLC) to determine if the claim should be pursued, settled, or otherwise terminated. They provide an opportunity for a corporation to control a derivative claim in circumstances when a majority of its directors cannot impartially consider a demand. However, if the SLC recommends that a derivative suit be terminated, the court requires that the SLC persuade it that (1) its members were independent, (2) they acted in good faith, and (3) they had reasonable bases for their recommendations. If the SLC meets that burden, the court is free to follow the SLC recommendation or it may, at its discretion, undertake its own examination of whether the suit should proceed.

In examining whether the SLC has met its burden to demonstrate that there is no material dispute of fact regarding its independence, the court keeps in mind the function of special litigation committees. They are the primary means by which corporate defendants may obtain a dismissal of a derivative suit if they conclude that the plaintiffs have not met their pleading burden. In simple terms, these tests permit a corporation to terminate a derivative suit if its board consists of directors who can impartially consider a demand. Consider the following case where the derivative suit is permitted to continue because the SLC members failed to demonstrate their independence.

Lerner v. Immelt

2013 U.S. App. LEXIS (2d Cir. 2013)

FACTS

Lerner alleges that the management and board of directors of General Electric violated their duties of loyalty and care. Specifically, she claims they had engaged in risky corporate transactions and disguised the risks with misstatements about the corporation's financial condition. The corporation's board of directors refused her demand that the corporation sue the offenders. General Electric allowed only outside (nonmanagement) directors to vote on her demand. However, Lerner complained that the outside directors lacked independence because of the social and professional relationships they had with the inside directors. She also asserts that the board violated its duty of care by referring her demand to the board's audit committee for investigation instead of forming a special litigation committee.

ISSUE

Should the court permit Lerner to bring a derivative action?

DECISION

No. First, simply alleging social and professional relationships is not in and of itself sufficient to cast doubt upon an outside director's independence. She has made no factual allegations with any specificity that would support a plausible inference that the outside directors were self-interested with respect to consideration of her demand. Second, we reject her argument that the audit committee was not the appropriate body to investigate her complaint. This is because she fails to allege with particularity any facts demonstrating that the members of the audit committee were conflicted. Absent plausible allegations showing that the directors are not disinterested, the board is not required to refer a shareholder demand to a special litigation committee.

Shareholder Liability

Liability on Shares

If a person buys stock that was fully paid for when issued, he normally has no further liability to the corporation or its creditors. The same is true of subsequent buyers of the stock regardless of the price paid. However, a shareholder who did not pay the full subscription price for newly issued shares is liable for the balance due. This would include "watered stock" situations where property exchanged for shares is overvalued.

The shareholder is also liable if the consideration given for the shares is not lawful payment under the incorporation statute. Remember, most states follow the rule that permits property or services actually performed to be exchanged for stock but does not permit the exchange of a promissory note or the promise of future services. Those states adopting the revised MBCA do permit promissory notes and promises of future services as consideration for shares.

Concept Summary: Shareholder Derivative Suit

1. Shareholder sues as a representative of the corporation.
2. To enforce a right of the corporation.
3. Shareholder owned shares at time the right accrued.
4. Shareholder first urged the board to enforce the right *unless* the request would be futile because the board was:
   a. Acting in bad faith
   b. Acting fraudulently
   c. Self-dealing
5. Damages to the corporation, but:
   a. If successful, shareholder recovers expenses.
   b. If unsuccessful, shareholder pays own expenses.

Liability for Illegal Dividends

A dividend that was paid illegally may be recovered from a shareholder who received it knowing it was illegal. If the corporation was insolvent at the time, the shareholder is liable even if he was unaware of the illegality.

Transfer and Redemption of Shares

Restrictions

A shareholder has a right to sell or give away her shares unless there is a valid restriction. Under SEC rules, selling may be restricted because the shares were part of a private offering. In close corporations, the original shareholders may not want to have to deal with strangers. An agreement by all of them to require any shareholder who desires to sell to give the corporation or the other shareholders a first right to purchase the shares would be upheld by courts. Notice of a restriction on the right of sale must be conspicuously placed on the stock certificate to be effective against a purchaser who is unaware of it.

Transfer Procedure

To transfer the stock, the owner endorses the assignment form usually printed on the back of the stock certificate. An assignment may also be made by a separate document called a *stock power*. Banks usually use such assignment forms when stock is put up as collateral. If no transferee is named, the certificate and the shares it represents are transferable by mere delivery. Sending such a certificate through the mails would be risky.

Questions and Problem Cases

1. Frank D. Seinfeld brought suit to compel Verizon Communications to produce, for his inspection, its books and records related to the compensation of Verizon's three highest corporate officers. Seinfeld, a Verizon shareholder, claimed that their executive compensation, individually and collectively, was excessive and wasteful. Seinfeld alleges that the three executives were all performing in the same job and were paid amounts, including stock options, above the compensation provided for in their employment contracts. However, he also acknowledged he had no factual support for his claim that mismanagement had taken place. Verizon asserted that Seinfeld should not be permitted to inspect the corporate books and records because Delaware law required Seinfeld to present some evidence that established a credible basis from which a court could infer there were legitimate issues of possible waste, mismanagement, or wrongdoing that warranted further investigation. Seinfeld argued, in response, that such a burden erects an insurmountable barrier for the minority shareholder of a public company. Should Seinfeld be permitted to inspect the corporate books and records? Explain.
2. John R. Dyer owns approximately 6 percent of the stock in the Indium Corporation. All of the remaining outstanding shares are owned by the corporation's chief executive officer and chair of its board of directors. Suspecting that the corporation was improperly retaining income otherwise payable to him, Dyer sought to inspect its books and records. He was provided the minutes of its shareholders and board of directors meetings, but otherwise rebuffed in his requests for records. Instead, the chief executive officer offered to purchase Dyer's shares. Dyer sued, demanding inspection of the records that his accountant deemed necessary in order to determine the value of his shares. Should Dyer be given a right to inspect the corporate records? Explain.
3. Paul Lohnes was issued a stock warrant to purchase 8,541 shares of Level 3 Communications' common stock. Both the exercise price and the expiration date were formalized in the warrant document. The warrant also contained a two-paragraph antidilution provision which described events that would automatically adjust the number of shares to which Lohnes would be entitled upon exercise of the warrant. There were five separate contingencies: capital reorganization, reclassification of common stock, merger, consolidation, and sale of all (or substantially all) the capital stock or assets. The warrant did not explicitly provide for an adjustment of shares in the event of a stock split. After Level 3 authorized a two-for-one stock split, Lohnes attempted to purchase 17,082 shares (twice the number of shares specified in the warrant). Lohnes argued that he was entitled to the additional shares based on the warrant's antidilution provision because he believed the stock split could be equated with a capital reorganization and/or a reclassification. Should Lohnes be permitted to purchase the additional shares of Level 3's common stock? Explain.
4. Patrick Tooley and Kevin Lewis are former minority stockholders of Donaldson, Lufkin & Jenrette, Inc. (DLJ), a Delaware corporation engaged in investment banking. DLJ was acquired by Credit Suisse Group. Before that acquisition, AXA Financial, Inc., which owned 71 percent of DLJ stock, controlled DLJ. Pursuant to a stockholder agreement between AXA and Credit Suisse, AXA agreed to exchange with Credit Suisse its DLJ stockholdings for a mix of stock and cash. The tender offer was to expire 20 days after its commencement. However, by agreement between DLJ and Credit Suisse, the merger was postponed. Tooley and Lewis (the plaintiffs) challenged the extension that resulted in a 22-day delay. They contended that this delay was not properly authorized and harmed minority stockholders while improperly benefiting AXA. They claim damages representing the time value of money lost through the delay. DLJ argued that the plaintiffs had no standing to sue. Specifically, DLJ claimed

that the claims were claims of the corporation being asserted derivatively. This meant that the plaintiffs lost their standing to bring this action when they tendered their shares in connection with the merger. Are the plaintiffs asserting a derivative claim? Explain.

5. Shareholders of Oracle Corporation alleged that four members of the corporation's board of directors engaged in insider trading. Oracle formed a special litigation committee (SLC) in order to investigate the derivative action and to determine whether the corporation should press the claims raised by the shareholders, settle the case, or terminate it. The SLC was granted full authority to decide these matters without the need for approval by the other members of the Oracle board. The two SLC members—both of whom are professors at Stanford University—were being asked to investigate fellow Oracle directors who have important ties to Stanford. Of the directors accused of insider trading, one was a Stanford professor who taught one of the SLC members, one was a Stanford alumnus who directed millions of dollars to Stanford, and one was Oracle's CEO (who has made millions of dollars in donations to Stanford through a personal foundation and large donations indirectly through Oracle, and who was considering making donations of his $100 million house and $170 million for a scholarship program at around the same time period the SLC members were added to the Oracle board). After an extensive investigation, the SLC moved to terminate the derivative lawsuit against the directors. Did the SLC members lacked independence? Explain.

6. Avatex is a corporation that has outstanding both common and preferred stock. It created and incorporated Xetava Corporation as its wholly owned subsidiary and the following day announced its intention to merge with and into Xetava. Under the terms of the proposed merger, Xetava is to be the surviving corporation. Once the transaction is consummated, Xetava will immediately change its name to Avatex Corporation. The proposed merger will cause a conversion of the preferred stock of Avatex into common stock of Xetava. The merger will effectively eliminate Avatex's certificate of incorporation, which includes the certificate of designation creating the Avatex preferred stock and setting forth its rights and preferences. The terms of the merger do not call for a class vote of these preferred stockholders. The preferred stockholders filed suit to enjoin the proposed merger, arguing that the transaction required the consent of two-thirds of the holders of the preferred stock. Under the terms of the Avatex certificate of incorporation, preferred stockholders have no right vote except on "*any amendment, alteration or repeal of the certificate of incorporation, whether by merger, consolidation or otherwise, that materially and adversely affects the rights of the preferred stockholders.*" The text of the terms governing the voting rights of the preferred stockholders required that such an alteration or repeal of the certificate required "*the consent of the holders of at least two-thirds of the shares*" of the preferred stock. Did this corporate action require the consent of two-thirds of the preferred stockholders? Explain.

7. Community Hotel Corporation had paid no dividend on its preferred stock for 24 years. The arrearage totaled $645,000, or about $149 per share. Community Hotel wanted to be able to obtain additional capital. In order to do this, it incorporated a subsidiary corporation, Newport Hotel Corporation. It then proposed merging with the subsidiary under a plan that would eliminate the arrearage. It proposed converting each preferred share into five shares of common stock in Newport. Under Rhode Island's corporation statute, the merger could be accomplished if two-thirds of each class of stockholders voted in favor of it. To amend the articles,

on the other hand, required a unanimous vote of each class. Bove and some other preferred shareholders sought to enjoin the merger. Can Community Hotel eliminate the arrearage on the preferred stock through a merger with a subsidiary approved by less than all shareholders?

8. MacAndrews & Forbes Group (MAF) and Technicolor agreed that MAF would acquire Technicolor in a two-step acquisition. The first step was an all-cash tender offer of $23 per share for all of Technicolor's outstanding shares. If not all of Technicolor's shareholders tendered their shares to MAF, the second step was a merger of MAF and Technicolor, by which all remaining Technicolor shareholders would receive $23 per share and Technicolor would merge with MAF. After MAF had acquired 82 percent of Technicolor's shares under the first step of the acquisition, as the controlling shareholder, MAF began looking for buyers for Technicolor's less profitable divisions. After Technicolor's shareholders approved the second step, a Technicolor shareholder dissented from the merger and sought to have the court appraise its shares under its statutory dissenters' rights. Specifically, the dissenter argued that the court should value Technicolor with regard to the strategies that had been conceived and implemented by MAF as of the merger date. Technicolor argued that the court should consider the value of the shares only as Technicolor existed prior to the discussion of the two-step acquisition (with its less profitable divisions included). Should the appraisal of the Technicolor shares include the value added by the merger plan? Explain.

Chapter 31

Securities Regulation

Learning Objectives

After you have studied this chapter, you should be able to:

1. Clearly describe the fundamental differences between the Securities Act of 1933 and the Securities Exchange Act of 1934.
2. Explain the registration requirements under the 1933 Act.
3. Examine a fact situation and determine whether behavior has violated Section 11 of the 1933 Act.
4. Describe the short-swing trading rules imposed by the 1934 Act.
5. Clearly identify and apply the elements of the liability provisions in Section 10(b) and Rule 10b-5.
6. Explain the theories of insider trading liability.
7. Identify when there is a violation of the Foreign Corrupt Practices Act after reading a factual situation.

Robert Willis was a psychiatrist. During a therapy session, one of his patients explained that she was upset because her husband, the chief executive officer of Shearson Loeb Rhodes, was seeking to become BankAmerica's chief executive officer. On the basis of this information, Willis bought BankAmerica stock and made a profit of $27,475. As a result, Dr. Willis was charged with securities fraud for trading on inside information.[1]

- What is a security?
- What liabilities do the federal securities acts impose on those who deal in securities?
- What is insider trading? What limits are placed on those who obtain inside information?

[1] "Insider Trading Rule Extends to Therapy," *The Wall Street Journal,* May 17, 1990, p. B10.

Introduction

The federal securities laws have two purposes. First, they provide investors with more information to help them make buying and selling decisions. Second, they prohibit some of the unfair, deceptive, and manipulative practices that caused substantial losses to the less informed and less powerful investors during the stock market debacle at the end of the 1920s.

Overview of the Federal Legislation

LO1

The Securities Act of 1933

The Securities Act of 1933 (1933 Act) is concerned primarily with **public distributions** of securities. It regulates the sale of securities while they are passing from the hands of the issuer into the hands of the public investors. Issuers selling securities publicly must make necessary disclosures at the time the issuer sells the securities to the public. The 1933 Act is chiefly a **one-time disclosure** statute, although some of its liability provisions purport to cover all fraudulent sales of securities.

LO1

Securities Exchange Act of 1934

By contrast, the mandatory disclosure provision of the Securities Exchange Act of 1934 (1934 Act) requires **periodic disclosures** from issuers of securities. An *issuer with publicly traded equity securities* must report annually and quarterly to its shareholders. Any other material information about the issuer must be disclosed as it is obtained by the issuer, unless the issuer has a valid business purpose for withholding disclosure.

Securities and Exchange Commission

The Securities and Exchange Commission (SEC) was created by the 1934 Act. Its responsibility is to administer the 1933 and 1934 Acts and five other securities statutes. Like other federal administrative agencies, the SEC has legislative, executive, and judicial functions. Its legislative branch promulgates rules and regulations, its executive branch brings enforcement actions against alleged violators of the statutes and their rules and regulations, and its judicial branch decides whether a person has violated the securities statutes.

What Is a Security?

If a transaction involves no security, the securities regulations do not apply. Thus, it is important to understand the precise definition of a **security.** The 1933 Act broadly defines the term *security* as

> any note, stock, . . . bond, debenture, evidence of indebtedness, certificate of interest of participation in any profit-sharing agreement, . . . preorganization certificate or subscription, . . . investment contract, voting trust certificate, . . . fractional undivided interest in oil, gas, or mineral rights, . . . or, in general, any interest or instrument commonly known as a "security."

The 1934 Act definition is similar except that it excludes notes and drafts that mature not more than nine months from the date of issuance. Many state statutes are equally broad in their interpretation of what constitutes a security.

Concept Summary: Disclosure: 1933 Act versus 1934 Act

1933 Act	1934 Act
One-time disclosure	Periodic disclosure
Occurs when new securities are issued	Occurs throughout the life of the securities
• File registration statement with SEC • Make prospectus available to buyers	• File 10-K annually • File 10-Q quarterly • File 8-K monthly (when special events occur)

Investment Contracts

Sales of limited partnerships, Scotch whisky receipts, live animals with contracts to care for them, restaurant properties and citrus groves with management contracts, and franchises have all been held to be securities. They are all examples of an **investment contract,** a device that is specifically included in the definition of a security. The term *investment contract* is broadly defined by the courts as an *investment of money* in a *common enterprise* with an *expectation of profits from the efforts of others.* The fact that there is no certificate or that what is being offered for sale is labeled tangible property is immaterial.

SEC v. Charles Edwards

124 S.Ct. 892 (U.S. Sup. Ct. 2004)

FACTS

ETS Payphones sold pay phones to the public via independent distributors. The pay phones were offered packaged with a site lease, a five-year leaseback and management agreement, and a buyback agreement. Under the leaseback and management agreement, purchasers received $82 per month, a 14 percent annual return. Purchasers were not involved in the day-to-day operation of the pay phones they owned. ETS selected the site for the phone, installed the equipment, arranged for connection and long-distance service, collected coin revenues, and maintained and repaired the phones. Under the buyback agreement, ETS promised to refund the full purchase price of the package at the end of the lease or within 180 days of a purchaser's request. In its marketing materials and on its website, ETS trumpeted the "incomparable pay phone" as "an exciting business opportunity." The pay phones did not generate enough revenue for ETS to make the payments required by the leaseback agreements, so the company depended on funds from new investors to meet its obligations.

ISSUE

Could these sale-and-leaseback arrangements be considered to be investment contracts that required registration under the federal securities laws?

DECISION

Yes. The term *security* encompasses virtually any instrument that might be sold as an investment. It includes "any note, stock, treasury stock, security future, bond, debenture, investment contract, or any instrument commonly known as a security." The test for whether a particular scheme is an investment contract looks to whether the scheme

(continued)

involves an investment of money in a common enterprise with profits to come solely from the efforts of others. There is no reason to distinguish between promises of fixed returns and promises of variable returns for purposes of the test. In both cases, the investing public is attracted by representations of investment income, as purchasers were in this case by ETS's invitation to "watch the profits add up." Moreover, investments pitched as low-risk (such as those offering a "guaranteed" fixed return) are particularly attractive to individuals more vulnerable to investment fraud, including older and less sophisticated investors. We hold that an investment scheme promising a fixed rate of return can be an "investment contract" and thus a "security" subject to the federal securities laws.

The Securities Act of 1933

The 1933 Act has two principal regulatory components: (1) registration provisions and (2) antifraud provisions. The registration requirements of the 1933 Act are designed to give investors the information they need to make intelligent decisions about whether to purchase securities. The issuer of the securities is required to file a registration statement with the Securities and Exchange Commission and to make a prospectus available to prospective purchasers. The various antifraud provisions in the 1933 Act impose liability on sellers of securities for mistaking or omitting facts of material significance to investors.

E-Commerce

SG Ltd. operated a website offering online users the opportunity to purchase shares of 11 different "virtual companies" listed on the website's "virtual stock exchange." SG placed no upper limit on the amount of funds that an investor could squirrel away in its virtual offerings. It advised potential purchasers to pay particular attention to shares in a "privileged company" and boasted that investing in those shares was a "game without any risk." According to SG's representations, capital inflow from new participants provided liquidity for existing participants who might choose to sell their virtual shareholdings. As a backstop, SG pledged to create a special reserve fund designed to maintain the price of the privileged company's shares. At least 800 U.S participants, paying real cash, purchased virtual shares in the virtual companies listed on SG's virtual stock exchange. In one year alone, more than $7 million in participants' funds was deposited in an SG bank account. However, soon thereafter, SG stopped responding to participant requests for a return of funds, yet continued to solicit new participants through its website. When the SEC filed a civil action alleging that SG's operations constituted a fraudulent scheme in violation of the registration and antifraud provision of the federal securities laws, SG argued that the securities rules did not apply to its operations because its virtual shares were games and not securities. The court, in *SEC v. SG Ltd.,* 265 F.3d 42 (1st Cir. 2001), disagreed, holding that the opportunity to invest in the privileged company constituted an invitation to enter into an investment contract within the reach of the federal securities laws.

Registration Requirements of the 1933 Act

LO2

The 1933 Act requires the issuer of securities to register the securities with the SEC prior to their offer or sale to the public. Historical and current data about the issuer and its business (including certified financial statements), full details about the securities to be offered, and the use of the proceeds of the issuance, among other information, must be included in a **registration statement** prepared by the issuer of the securities. The issuer must file the registration statement with the SEC.

The registration statement becomes effective after it has been reviewed by the SEC. The SEC review involves only the completeness of the registration statement and whether it contains **per se fraudulent** statements. Examples of per se fraudulent statements are those that tout the securities ("these are the best securities you can buy") and forecasts that are not reasonably based (a new company promising a 35 percent annual return on investment on its common stock).

Most of the information in the registration statement must be included in the **prospectus,** which is the basic selling document of a 1933 Act registered offering. It must be furnished to every purchaser of the registered security prior to or concurrently with the delivery of the security to the purchaser. The function of the prospectus is to allow an investor to make his investment decision based on all relevant data concerning the issuer, not merely the favorable information that the issuer would be inclined to disclose voluntarily.

The 1933 Act restricts the issuer's ability to communicate with prospective purchasers of the securities. It includes basic rules regarding the timing, manner, and content of offers and sales.

E-Commerce

During 1992, the SEC's new computerized system for corporate filings became operational. Known as **EDGAR,** the Electronic Data Gathering, Analysis, and Retrieval system permits corporations to download their SEC-required reports on their quarterly and annual finances and other matters directly into a government computer. While EDGAR does not save the SEC or corporate filers much money, it provides tremendous savings for the public because reports going into the SEC electronically now are retrievable electronically. This provides access within hours or minutes rather than days. The SEC's Internet homepage (www.sec.gov) provides access to the EDGAR database.

Exemptions from the Registration Requirements

Complying with the registration requirements of the 1933 Act is a burdensome and time-consuming process. It is also expensive. An issuer's first public offering may consume six months and cost in excess of $1 million. It is understandable why some issuers prefer to avoid registration when they sell securities. Fortunately for them, there are several exemptions from registration available for issuers. However, every student must learn the most important rule of the 1933 Act: *Every transaction in securities must be registered with the SEC or be exempt from registration.*

There are two types of exemptions from the registration requirements of the 1933 Act: securities exemptions and transaction exemptions. **Exempt securities** never need to be registered, regardless of who sells the securities, how they are sold, or to whom they are sold. Securities sold in **exempt transactions** are exempt from the registration requirements for those particular transactions only. Each transaction stands by itself. A security sale may be exempt today because it is sold pursuant to a transaction exemption, yet tomorrow it may have to be registered when the security is offered or sold again in a transaction for which there is no exemption.

Concept Summary: Periods in the Life of a New Security

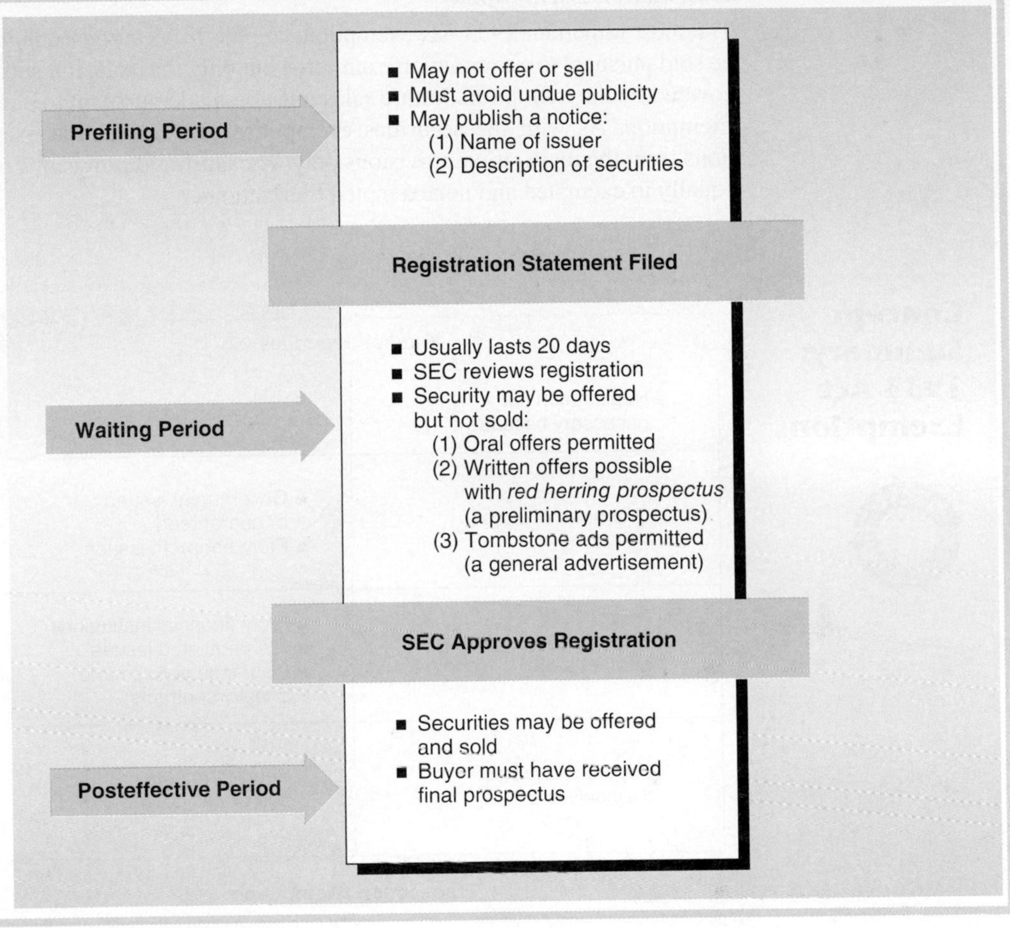
Prefiling Period
■ May not offer or sell
■ Must avoid undue publicity
■ May publish a notice:
(1) Name of issuer
(2) Description of securities
Registration Statement Filed
Waiting Period
■ Usually lasts 20 days
■ SEC reviews registration
■ Security may be offered but not sold:
(1) Oral offers permitted
(2) Written offers possible with *red herring prospectus* (a preliminary prospectus)
(3) Tombstone ads permitted (a general advertisement)
SEC Approves Registration
Posteffective Period
■ Securities may be offered and sold
■ Buyer must have received final prospectus

Exempt Securities

Some securities are exempted from the registration provisions of the 1933 Act either because (1) the character of the issuer makes registration unnecessary, (2) the issuance of such securities is subject to regulation under another statutory scheme, or (3) the purchasers of the securities can adequately protect themselves. The following are the most important securities exemptions:

1. Government-issued or -guaranteed securities:
2. Short-term notes and drafts.
3. Securities of nonprofit issuers.
4. Financial institution securities.
5. ICC-regulated issuers.
6. Insurance policies and annuity contracts.

Although these securities are exempt from the registration provisions of the 1933 Act, they are *not* exempt from the antifraud provisions of the act. Therefore, any fraud committed in the course of selling these securities can be attacked by the SEC and by those persons who were defrauded.

Transaction Exemptions

The most important 1933 Act exemptions are the *transaction exemptions.* A security may be sold pursuant to a transaction exemption but only that sale, not subsequent sales, will be covered by the exemption. Future sales must be made pursuant to a registration or another exemption. As with the securities exemptions, the transaction exemptions are exemptions from the registration provisions only. The antifraud provisions of the 1933 Act apply equally to exempted and nonexempted transactions.

Concept Summary: 1933 Act Exemptions

Exempt Securities

Registration not necessary because of:	
Character of issuer	■ Government issued or guaranteed ■ From nonprofit issues
Securities regulated under another statutory scheme	■ From financial institutions ■ ICC-regulated issues ■ Insurance policies and annuity contracts
Buyers can protect themselves	Short-term notes and drafts

Transaction Exemptions

Exemptions for issuers	■ Private offering ■ Intrastate offering ■ Small offering
Exemption for nonissuers	Transactions by any person other than an issuer, underwriter, or dealer

The most important transaction exemptions are those available for **issuers.** They are the private offering, the intrastate offering, and the small offering. There also are several exemptions that allow **nonissuers**—average investors, usually—to offer and sell the securities they own, yet avoid the need to have the issuer register the securities. One provision exempts "transactions by any person other than an issuer, underwriter, or dealer." This exemption is used by most investors when they sell securities. For example, if you buy General Motors Corporation common shares on the New York Stock Exchange, you may freely resell them without a registration. You are not an issuer

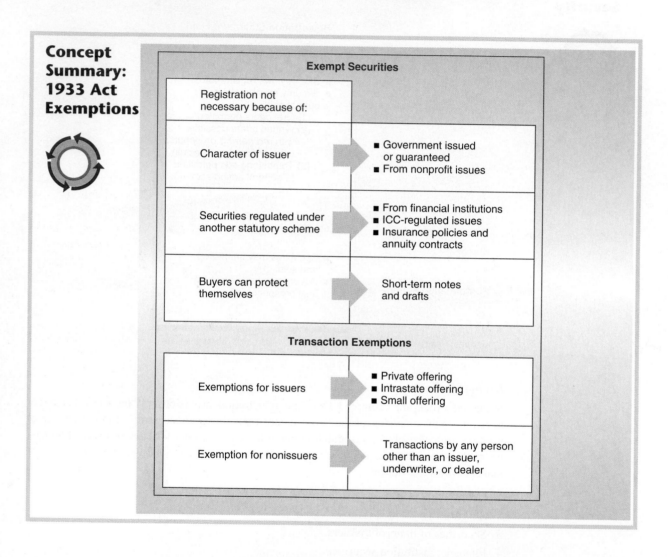

(GM is); you are not an underwriter (because you are not helping GM distribute the shares to the public); and you are not a dealer (because you are not in the business of selling securities).

Antifraud Provisions of the 1933 Act

To accomplish its objective of preventing fraud and unfair, deceptive, or manipulative practices and providing remedies to the victims of such practices, Congress included a number of liability provisions in the Securities Act of 1933. Violations of the act may subject the defendant to both civil and criminal actions.

Liability for Improper Offers and Sales

Section 12(1) of the 1933 Act imposes liability on any person who has violated the timing, manner, and content restrictions on offers and sales of new issues. The purchaser's remedy is rescission or damages. These violations occur when a person offers or sells unregistered and nonexempt securities in violation of the 1933 Act.

Liability for Defective Registration Statements

LO3

Section 11 of the 1933 Act provides civil liabilities for damages resulting to an investor who finds, after purchasing the security, that the registration statement for the security contained an untrue statement or omitted a material fact. Potentially liable for such misleading or false information in the registration statement are all of its signers, all directors (whether or not they signed), all "experts" who gave consent to be named in the registration statement as having prepared or certified part of it (such as auditors, lawyers, geologists, or engineers), and the underwriters of the distribution of the security. The purchaser's remedy under Section 11 is for damages caused by the misstatement or omission.

Section 11 was a radical liability section when it was enacted and remains so today. It is radical for three reasons. First, reliance is not usually required. The purchaser need not show that she relied on the misstatement or omission in the registration statement. In fact, the purchaser need not have even read the registration statement or seen it. Second, privity is not required. A purchaser need not prove that she purchased the securities from the defendant. All she need prove is that the defendant is in one of three classes of persons liable under Section 11. Third, the purchaser need not prove that the defendant negligently or intentionally misstated or omitted a material fact. Instead, the defendant has the burden of proving that she exercised **due diligence.** (The only other defense available to a defendant is to prove that the purchaser knew of the misstatement or omission when she purchased the security.) See Chapter 32 for further discussion of Section 11.

Other Liability Provisions

Section 12(2) prohibits misstatements or omissions of material fact made in a prospectus or in an oral communication related to the prospectus or an initial offering (except government-issued or -guaranteed securities). Its reach is significant because mere *negligence,* rather than *scienter,* is enough to trigger liability under Section 12(2). (Scienter is the intent to deceive, manipulate, or defraud the purchaser.)

Section 12(2) has a *privity* requirement; this means that the purchaser may sue only those persons from whom she purchased the security. Further, she must show that she *relied* on the misstatement or omission and that she did not know of the untruth or omission. The defendant may escape liability by proving that he did not know and could not reasonably have known of the untruth or omission. The purchaser's remedy is rescission or damages, as it is under Section 12(1). Recoveries are available to purchasers of initial distributions, not to those trading in the secondary market.

Concept Summary: Section 11 of the 1933 Act

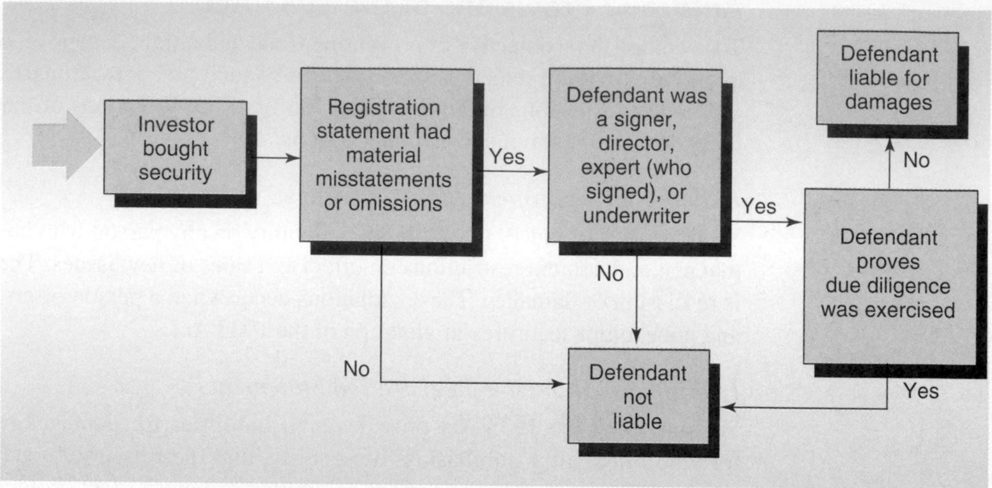

Section 17(a) broadly prohibits the use of any device or artifice to defraud and the use of any untrue or misleading statement in connection with the offer or sale of any security. Two of the subsections of Section 17(a) require that the defendant merely act negligently, while the third subsection requires proof of scienter. The Supreme Court has not decided whether a buyer has a private right of action for damages under Section 17(a), and the courts of appeals are split on the issue.

Securities Exchange Act of 1934

The Securities Exchange Act of 1934 is chiefly concerned with disclosing material information to investors. Unlike the 1933 Act, which is primarily a one-time disclosure statute, the 1934 Act requires *periodic disclosure* by issuers with publicly held equity securities. In addition, the 1934 Act regulates insiders' transactions in securities, proxy solicitations, tender offers, brokers and dealers, and securities exchanges. Finally, the 1934 Act has several sections prohibiting fraud and manipulation in securities transactions.

Registration of Securities under the 1934 Act

Two types of securities must be registered under the 1934 Act. First, an issuer must register a class of equity securities with at least 500 shareholders if the issuers' total assets exceed $10 million. The securities must be traded in interstate commerce. Second, an issuer must register any security traded on a national security exchange, such as common shares traded on the American Stock Exchange. The information required in the 1934 Act registration statement is similar to that required under the 1933 Act.

Periodic Reports

To maintain a steady flow of material information to investors, the 1934 Act requires that those issuers required to register under the 1934 Act, as well as any issuer who has made a registered offering under the 1933 Act, file periodic reports with the SEC. These issuers must regularly file several types of reports; however, the most important are the annual and quarterly reports.

The 10-K annual report must include audited financial statements for the fiscal year plus current information about the conduct of the business, its management, and the status of its securities. In effect, the 10-K report is intended to update the information required in the 1934 registration statement.

The quarterly report, the 10-Q, requires only a summarized, unaudited operating statement and unaudited figures on capitalization and shareholders' equity. An 8-K monthly report is required within 15 days of the end of any month in which any specified event occurs, such as a change in the amount of securities, a default under the terms of an issue of securities, acquisition or disposition of assets, a change in control of the corporation, or any materially important event.

Ethics in Action

The blatant financial irregularities of Enron, Global Crossing, and WorldCom and dozens of other companies cost investors billions of dollars. In response, the Sarbanes-Oxley Act made sweeping changes to the responsibilities owed by executives and auditors of publicly traded corporations. For example, it now requires that the 10-Ks and 10-Qs filed with the SEC disclose material off-balance-sheet transactions. Further, it prohibits auditors from performing most types of consulting services for the corporations they oversee in order to increase auditor independence from management. This measure is reinforced by requiring that auditors be hired and supervised by an audit committee composed of members who are independent of the CEO and other corporate executives. And, as was noted in Chapter 29, CEOs and CFOs must disgorge personal profits made in the 12-month period before any restatement of corporate earnings. Finally, the SEC may freeze payments made to officers and directors during a lawful investigation and may bar "unfit" persons from serving as directors or officers of publicly traded corporations.

Sarbanes-Oxley is also concerned about the conflicts of interest faced by securities analysts at investment firms when issuing stock recommendations and research reports. Legislators worried that full-service investment firms might discourage securities analysts from giving poor recommendations for corporations' stocks out of the fear that the corporations might retaliate by awarding their investment banking business to other investment firms. Accordingly, the legislation directs the SEC to adopt or have the national securities exchanges and NASD adopt rules to address such conflicts. Even before passage of Sarbanes-Oxley, the NASD and NYSE promulgated rules banning favorable research for pay and restricting submission of reports to issuers prior to their publication.

Section 906 of the Sarbanes-Oxley Act

Under Section 906 of the Sarbanes-Oxley Act of 2002, chief executive officers and chief financial officers of companies that issue publicly traded stocks are required to certify by written statements the accuracy of the company's periodic financial reports required under the Securities Exchange Act of 1934. Specifically, the statute requires that each periodic report containing financial statements filed by an issuer with the SEC be accompanied by a written statement by the chief executive officer and chief financial officer (or equivalent thereof) of the issuer. That statement must certify that the periodic report containing the financial statements fully complies with the requirements of the 1934 Act and that the information *fairly presents, in all material respects,* the financial condition and results of operations of the issuer.

A federal district court (*United States v. Scrushy,* 2004 U.S. Dist. LEXIS 23820 (N.D. Ala. 2004)) has clarified, in a step-by-step manner, the requirements for compliance with Section 906. Subsection (a) requires a CEO to make a written statement to accompany the company's periodic financial report. Subsection (b) defines the content of the statement, requiring the CEO certify that the report complies with the applicable law *and* fairly presents, in all material respects, the financial condition and results of operations of the issuer. Subsection (c) provides the criminal penalties for violating the statute and describes the conduct required for conviction. In the penalty provision the CEO must *willfully*—that is volitionally, intentionally, and not by accident—make a written statement certifying the truth and accuracy of the periodic financial report describing the financial condition and results of operations of the issuer. This section further requires that, to be convicted of violating this subsection, the CEO must have *knowledge* that the periodic report he or she is willfully certifying does not meet the statute's requirements of fair representation of the company's financial condition and operations in all material respects. Thus, to be convicted, the CEO must *willfully certify* the accuracy of the periodic financial report *while knowing* it does not fairly state, in all material respects, the financial condition of the company. By these terms, the statute gives fair warning and defines the scienter required to be proven for conviction.

Section 906 provides harsh criminal penalties for violation of the reporting requirements. For instance, whoever *willfully certifies* any statement *knowing* that the periodic report accompanying the statement does not comport with all the statutory requirements can be fined up to $5 million and/or imprisoned for as long as 20 years.

Short-Swing Trading by Insiders

LO4

Section 16(b) of the 1934 Act requires that insiders individually file a statement disclosing their holdings of any class of equity securities of the issuer. An **insider** is an officer of a corporation with equity securities registered under the act, a director of such a corporation, or an owner of 10 percent or more of a class of equity securities registered under the 1934 Act. In addition, these insiders must report any transaction in such securities within 10 days following the end of the month in which the transaction occurs. Purchases and sales made six months before and six months after one becomes an officer, director, or 10 percent holder must also be reported.

Under the 1934 Act, any profit made by an insider is recoverable by the issuer if the profit resulted from the purchase and sale (or the sale and purchase) within less than a six-month period of any class of the issuer's equity securities. This regulation of **short-swing profits** is designed to stop speculative insider trading on the basis of information that "may have been obtained by such owner, director, or officer by reason of his relationship to the issuer." The application of the provision is without regard to intent or actual use of insider information.

SEC Rule 16b-3(d) exempts from the coverage of Section 16(b) transactions between an issuer and a director that are approved by the board of directors of the issuer. In creating the Rule 16b-3(d) exemption, the SEC asserted that when the issuer, rather than the trading markets, is on the other side of an officer or director's transaction in the issuer's equity securities, any profit obtained is not at the expense of uninformed shareholders and other market participants of the type contemplated by the statute.

Gibbons v. Malone

703 F.3d 595 (2d Cir. 2013)

FACTS

Over a 14-day period, John Malone, a director and large shareholder of Discovery Communications, engaged in 9 sales of Discovery's "Series C" stock (totaling 953,506 shares) and 10 purchases of Discovery's "Series A" stock (totaling 632,700 shares). Malone allegedly realized over $300,000 in profit as a result of these transactions. Discovery's Series A stock and Series C stock are different equity securities, are separately registered, and are traded separately on the NASDAQ stock exchange under the ticker symbols DISCA

(continued)

and DISCK, respectively. The principal difference between the two securities is that Series A stock comes with voting rights—one vote per share—whereas Series C stock does not confer any voting rights. Series A stock and Series C stock are not convertible into each other. A shareholder lawsuit was filed against Malone, asserting that he must disgorge his earnings because they are illegal short-swing profits.

ISSUE

Does the short-swing profit rule apply when a corporate insider sells shares of one type of stock from his company and purchases shares of a different type of stock issued by the same company?

DECISION

No. Section 16(b) prohibits a corporate insider from realizing any profit "from any purchase and sale, or any sale and purchase, of any equity security" issued by the insider's company within any period of less than six months. If the conversion can be paired with another sale or purchase, and the paired transactions occur within a six-month period, the paired transactions are the type of insider activity that Section 16(b) was designed to prevent. However, transactions of securities that cannot be "paired" are not within the scope of Section 16(b). The statute's use of the singular term "*any equity security*" supports an inference that transactions involving *different* equity securities cannot be paired under Section 16(b). Though we do not decide the issue here, we note that Section 16(b) could apply to transactions where the securities at issue are not meaningfully distinguishable. Discovery's Series A stock and Series C stock, however, are readily distinguishable. Most importantly, Series A shares confer voting rights, whereas Series C shares do not. The two securities, therefore, are distinct not merely in name but also in substance. An insider could easily prefer one security over the other for reasons not related to short-swing profits. We hold that an insider's purchase and sale of shares of different types of stock in the same company does not trigger liability under Section 16(b), where those securities are separately traded, nonconvertible, and come with different voting rights.

Liability Provisions of the 1934 Act

Congress included several liability provisions in the 1934 Act. These provisions provide remedies to victims of fraudulent, deceptive, or manipulative practices.

Manipulation of a Security's Price

Section 9 specifically prohibits a number of deceptive practices that may be used to cause security prices to rise or fall by fraudulently stimulating market activity. This violation may occur when a person simultaneously buys and sells the same stock in order to stimulate substantial trading activity and thereby affect the price of the security. This type of illegal practice is called a **wash sale.**

Liability for False Statements in Filed Documents

Section 18 is the 1934 Act counterpart to Section 11 of the 1933 Act. Section 18 imposes liability on any person responsible for a false or misleading statement of material fact in any document filed with the SEC. (Filed documents include the 10-K, 10-Q, and proxy statements.) Any person who relies on a false or misleading statement may sue for damages. As with Section 11, the purchaser need not prove that the defendant was negligent or acted with scienter (bad motive). However, the defendant has a defense that he acted in good faith and had no knowledge that the statement was false or misleading. This defense is easier to meet than the Section 11 due diligence defense, requiring only that the defendant prove that he did not act with scienter. Partly for this reason, Section 18 is rarely used.

Section 10(b) and Rule 10b-5

LO5

The most important liability section in the 1934 Act is Section 10(b). Section 10(b) is an extremely broad provision prohibiting the use of any manipulative or deceptive device in

Morrison v. National Australia Bank

130 S.Ct. 2869 (U.S. Sup. Ct. 2010)

FACTS

National Australia Bank is the largest bank in Australia; however, none of its shares are traded on any stock exchange in the United States. The bank bought a mortgage servicing company headquartered in Florida and touted its success in annual reports and public statements. Soon thereafter, the bank announced that it was writing down the value of the mortgage servicing company assets and its shares slumped. Three Australian shareholders had purchased the bank's shares before the write-downs. They sued the bank in a U.S. federal court under §10(b), alleging that it had had been manipulating its financial models in order to cause the mortgage-servicing rates to appear more valuable than they really were. The bank petitioned the court to dismiss the lawsuit, arguing that §10(b) does not apply extraterritorially.

ISSUE

Does §10(b) have extraterritorial application?

DECISION

No. In deciding this case, we must begin with a presumption that domestic statutes do not have extraterritorial effect unless the statutory language clearly says they do. The relevant statutory language makes clear that §10(b) does not punish deceptive conduct, but only deceptive conduct "in connection with the purchase or sale of any security registered on a national securities exchange or any security not so registered." The transaction test we adopt here looks to see if the purchase or sale is made in the United States or involves a security listed on a U.S. stock exchange. Accordingly, this lawsuit must be dismissed.

contravention of any rules the SEC may prescribe as "necessary or appropriate in the public interest or for the protection of investors." Rule 10b-5 was adopted by the SEC under Section 10(b). Securities need not be registered under the 1933 Act or the 1934 Act for Rule 10b-5 to apply. The rule applies to transactions executed on a securities exchange as well as face-to-face transactions.

The most important elements of a Rule 10b-5 violation are a misstatement or omission of material fact, scienter, and reliance. In addition, private persons suing under the rule must be purchasers or sellers. Finally, the wrongful action must be accomplished by the mails, an instrumentality of interstate commerce (use of a telephone within one state has been held to meet this requirement), or a national securities exchange.

Misstatement or Omission

The essence of fraud, deception, and manipulation is falsity or nondisclosure when there is a duty to speak. Rule 10b-5 imposes liability on persons who **misstate material facts.** For example, if a manager of an unprofitable business induces shareholders to sell their stock to him by representing that the business will fail, although he knows that the business has become potentially profitable, he violates Rule 10b-5.

In addition, a person is liable if he **omits material facts** when he has a duty to disclose. For a person to be liable for an omission, there must be duty of trust or confidence breached either by a nondisclosure or by the selective disclosure of confidential information. For example, a securities broker is liable to his customer for not disclosing that he owns the shares he recommends to the customer. As an agent of the customer, he owes a fiduciary duty to his customer to disclose his conflict of interest. In addition, a person is liable for omitting to tell all the material facts after he has chosen to disclose some of the facts. His selective disclosure created the duty to disclose all the material facts.

Ethics in Action

In recent years, both health concerns and the entry of discount brands in the marketplace have led to a decline in the sales of premium brands of cigarettes, such as Philip Morris's Marlboro line. In order to sustain or increase its profit levels, Philip Morris historically responded to decreasing demand for Marlboro by raising Marlboro's price, as well as the price for discount brands, in order to make the discount brands seem less attractive. However, one year, without advance warning to investors, Philip Morris reversed its traditional strategy by substantially cutting Marlboro prices in the face of declining demand. That move reduced its earnings by $2 billion that year and caused its stock to fall almost 25 percent. Investors claimed that the company violated Rule 10b-5 by failing to disclose to the market that a new strategy was necessary because Marlboro sales were declining at such a rate that raising prices would not compensate for the loss of sales. A federal court of appeals, in *San Leandro Emergency Medical Group v. Philip Morris,* 75 F.3d 801 (2d Cir. 1996), disagreed, holding that the company had no duty to disclose its new marketing plan. The law did not impose such a duty on Philip Morris. However, did the company have an ethical duty to its investors that exceeded the requirements of the law?

Materiality

The misstated or omitted fact must be **material.** In essence, material information is any information that is likely to have an impact on the price of a security in the market. Such matters as proposed mergers, tender offers for the corporation's stock, plans to introduce an important new product, or indications of an abrupt change in the expectations of the company are examples of what would be considered material facts.

Scienter

For fraud, deception, or manipulation to exist, the defendant must have acted with **scienter.** Mere negligence is not enough under Rule 10b-5. **Scienter** is an intent to deceive, manipulate, or defraud. Recklessness ("the pretense of knowledge where knowledge there is none") may constitute scienter.

As a check against abusive litigation by private parties alleging violations of Section 10(b), Congress enacted the Private Securities Litigation Reform Act (PSLRA). While conceding that private actions to enforce the securities laws are an important supplement to criminal prosecutions and enforcement actions brought by the SEC, this legislation simultaneously recognizes that frivolous litigation can impose substantial costs on companies and individuals whose conduct conforms to the law. In part, the PSLRA imposes heightened pleading requirements when a private securities complaint alleges that a defendant made false or misleading statements. As this relates to the scienter element of a Section 10(b) action, it means that the plaintiff must state with particularity facts giving rise to a "strong inference" that the defendant acted with scienter.

The U.S. Supreme Court (*Tellabs v. Makor Issues & Rights,* 127 S. Ct. 2499 (2007)) provides the following guidance for determining whether the "strong inference" test has been met. First, the inquiry is whether all of the facts alleged, taken collectively, give rise to a strong inference of scienter, not whether any individual allegation, scrutinized in isolation, meets that standard. Second, in determining whether the pleaded facts give rise to a "strong" inference of scienter, the court must take into account plausible opposing inferences. The strength of an inference cannot be decided in a vacuum. The inquiry is inherently comparative: How likely is it that one conclusion, as compared to others, follows from the underlying facts? A complaint will survive only if a reasonable person would

Matrixx Initiatives V. Siracusano

131 S.Ct. 1309 (U.S. Sup. Ct. 2011)

FACTS

Zicam Cold Remedy accounts for approximately 70 percent of Matrixx Initiatives' sales. For a period of several years, Matrixx had received customer complaints that its cold remedy was causing a loss of smell in some users. When the press publicly reported the existence of such complaints, Matrixx issued a press release assuring the public that the company believes the reports to be unfounded. In a Form 8-K filing with the SEC, Matrixx reported that it had convened a two-day meeting of physicians and scientists, which concluded there is insufficient evidence to determine if the product affects a person's ability to smell. An investor claimed that Matrixx violated §10(b) of the Securities Exchange and SEC Rule 10b-5 by making untrue statements of fact and failing to disclose material facts necessary to make the statements not misleading. Matrixx contends that the complaint does not adequately allege that Matrixx made a material representation or omission or that it acted with scienter because the complaint does not allege that Matrixx knew of a statistically significant number of adverse events requiring disclosure.

ISSUE

Has the plaintiff stated a viable claim under §10(b) of the Securities Exchange and Rule 10b-5?

DECISION

Yes. To prevail on his claim a plaintiff must show that a false statement was misleading as to a material fact. This materiality requirement is satisfied when there is a substantial likelihood that the disclosure of the omitted fact would have been viewed by the reasonable investor as having significantly altered the "total mix" of information made available. Here, the investor's complaint has adequately pleaded materiality because this is not a case about a handful of anecdotal reports. The information provided to Matrixx revealed a plausible causal relationship between its cold remedy and the possible loss of smell. The complaint also must show that Matrixx acted with scienter. Recklessness satisfies the scienter requirement. These allegations give rise to a cogent and compelling inference that Matrixx elected not to disclose the reports of adverse events not because it believed they were meaningless but because it understood their likely effect on the market. A reasonable person would deem the inference that Matrixx acted with deliberate recklessness (or even intent) at least as compelling as any opposing inference one could draw from the facts alleged.

deem the inference of scienter cogent and at least as compelling as any opposing inference one could draw from the facts alleged.

Purchaser or Seller

In order to seek damages under Rule 10b-5, the private plaintiff must be an actual *purchaser or seller* of securities. Thus, a person who was deterred from purchasing a security because of false statements cannot recover his lost profits because he was not an actual purchaser.

Reliance

Private plaintiffs using Rule 10b-5 must prove that they relied on the misstatement of material fact. However, **reliance** is not usually required in *omission* cases; the investor need merely prove that the omitted fact was material. The reliance element also might be met where material misrepresentations were available to the public. Under this *fraud-on-the-market* theory the investor's reliance on the integrity of the market was found to justify a presumption of reliance on the misrepresentation.

Statute of Limitations

For many years, fraud claims under Section 10(b) and Rule 10b-5 were governed by statutes of limitations established under the various state laws. (A statute of limitation establishes the period of time within which a lawsuit will be permitted to be brought.) The policy of borrowing from state law was quite controversial because of the multistate nature of most securities violations and the lack of uniformity from state to state. Accordingly, the

U.S. Supreme Court established a uniform federal statute of limitations that requires that litigation be commenced within one year after discovery of the facts constituting the violation and no more than three years after the violation has occurred.

Conduct Covered by Rule 10b-5

Numerous activities are prohibited by Rule 10b-5. However, while one can easily see that actual fraud and price manipulation are covered by the rule, two other areas are less obvious: the corporation's continuous disclosure obligation and insider trading.

Continuous Disclosure of Material Information

The purpose of the securities acts is to ensure that investors have the information to make intelligent investment decisions at all times. The periodic reporting requirements of the 1934 Act are designed to accomplish this result. If important developments arise between the disclosure dates of reports, however, investors will not have all the information they need to make intelligent decisions unless the corporation discloses immediately the material information. Rule 10b-5 may be read to require a corporation to immediately and accurately disclose material information unless it has a valid business purpose for withholding disclosure.

Trading on Inside Information

Many interesting Rule 10b-5 cases involve the failure to disclose nonpublic, corporate information known to an insider. Some of these cases involve face-to-face transactions between an insider and another shareholder. For example, a corporation's president acquires at a low price all of the corporation's outstanding shares. His failure to tell the sellers about contracts that would increase the value of the shares violates Rule 10b-5. In other cases, the buyer and seller have not met face-to-face. Instead, the transaction has been executed on a stock exchange. The trading on an exchange by a person in possession of confidential corporate information has been held to violate Rule 10b-5, even though the buyer and seller never met.

The essential rule is that a person with inside information must either disclose the information before trading or refrain from trading. Thus, it is a violation of Rule 10b-5 to buy or sell either on an exchange or in a direct transaction when one is privy to material information that is not generally available to the investing public. This applies to almost anyone, not just to those who are usually viewed as insiders, such as directors, officers, and owners of a major interest in the company. It includes secretaries, such employees as researchers or geologists, and their supervisors. It also includes outside consultants, lawyers, engineers, financial and public relations advisors, and others who are given "inside" information for special purposes, such as news reporters and personnel of government agencies. Furthermore, **tippees** (those who are given or acquire the information without the need to know), such as stockbrokers or financial analysts and even relatives or friends of those with access to the inside information, are forbidden to trade on the information.

In the case that opened this chapter, Dr. Willis received the information that his patient's husband was seeking to become BankAmerica's chief executive officer in a confidential setting. Thus, according to the court, Willis should have known that the information was to remain secret. As a result, he was found guilty of trading on inside information. For violation of the insider trading rules, the SEC may seek a civil penalty of three times the profit gained or loss avoided. This treble penalty is paid to the Treasury of the United States. Since Dr. Willis made a $27,475 profit, under the treble damages provisions, he must pay the Treasury Department $82,425. He could also be punished by criminal fines of up to $1 million and a 10-year prison term. Unlike the rest of Section 10(b) and Rule 10b-5, the statute of limitations for insider trading permits lawsuits to be instituted up to five years after the violations occurred.

Theories of Insider Trading Liability

LO6

Under the *classical theory* of insider trading liability, Section 10(b) and Rule 10b-5 are violated when a corporate insider trades in the securities of his corporation on the basis of material, nonpublic information. Trading on such information qualifies as a "deceptive device" under Section 10(b) because a relationship of trust and confidence exists between the shareholders of a corporation and those insiders who have obtained confidential information by reason of their position with that corporation. The relationship creates a duty to abstain from trading to prevent a corporate insider from taking unfair advantage of uniformed stockholders. The classical theory applies not only to officers, directors, and other permanent insiders of a corporation, but also to attorneys, accountants, consultants, and others who temporarily become fiduciaries of a corporation.

The *misappropriation theory* holds that a person violates Section 10(b) and Rule 10b-5 when he misappropriates confidential information for securities trading purposes, in breach of a duty owed to the individual from whom he learned of the information. Under this theory, a person's undisclosed, self-serving use of another's information to purchase or sell securities, in breach of a duty of loyalty and confidentiality, defrauds the individual who provided the information.

The classical theory targets a corporate insider's breach of duty to shareholders with whom the insider transacts; the misappropriation theory outlaws trading on the basis of nonpublic information by a corporate outsider in breach of a duty, not to a trading party, but to the source of the information. The misappropriation is thus designed to protect the integrity of the securities markets against abuses by individuals outside a corporation who have access to confidential information that will affect the corporation's security price when revealed, but who owe no fiduciary or other duty to that corporation's shareholders. The next case provides an example of the misappropriation theory.

SEC v. Rocklage

470 F.3d 1 (1st Cir. 2006)

FACTS

The SEC alleged that Patricia B. Rocklage intentionally used deceptive means to obtain from her husband highly negative and nonpublic information about his publicly traded company in order to tip her brother who owned company stock, which then led to trading of the stock by her brother and another. Mrs. Rocklage initially concealed from her husband her prior agreement with her brother to tip him if she learned significant negative information about the company. After Mrs. Rocklage acquired the information, and shortly before she actually tipped her brother, however, she told her husband that she was going to give her brother the information. Her husband asked her not to do so, but she did so anyway. Her brother sold his stock in the company on the next day the market opened and he passed the information on to a friend who did the same. The SEC filed a complaint alleging a violation of Section 10(b) and Rule 10b-5 under the misappropriation theory. In defense, Mrs. Rocklage's argued that her pre-tip disclosure to her husband, telling him that she intended to tip off her brother, completely negated any liability under the misappropriation theory.

ISSUE

May the SEC proceed with this action under the misappropriation theory?

DECISION

Yes. Mrs. Rocklage's view is that a pre-tip disclosure to the source of an intention to trade or tip completely eliminates any deception involved in the transaction. However, it would be unreasonable to expect Mr. Rocklage to have risked marital discord by taking action against his wife; once she made clear she would tell her brother despite her husband's wishes, his interest may have shifted to protecting her against liability. It makes little sense to assume that disclosure of an intention to tip using deceptively acquired information would necessarily negate the original deception.

Ethics in Action

Suppose that you overhear a lunchtime conversation between the presidents of two corporations in which they are discussing an upcoming yet still unannounced takeover. Is it ethical for you to purchase shares of the target company's stock based on this information without disclosing the reason for your decision to the sellers?

Safe Harbor Legislation

At the end of 1995, Congress passed new legislation designed to curb lawsuits against companies whose stock performance fails to live up to expectations. Specifically, the law discourages the filing of lawsuits by requiring that plaintiffs plead specific facts that corporate insiders knew they were committing fraud when they made statements projecting a company's future performance.

Perhaps most important, the new law also erects a **safe harbor** for companies that make optimistic forecasts about future earnings or new products. As long as companies warn the public about factors that might undermine their forecasts, they will be immune from liability if the predictions prove false. Unfortunately, the legislation is vague about how specific the warning must be and fails to define exactly what types of factors must be identified in the cautionary statements. It remains to be seen how the courts will resolve these ambiguities.

Concept Summary: Provisions of the 1934 Act

Disclosure	Registration of securities Periodic reports by issuers Holdings and transactions reports by insiders
Proxies	Regulation of proxy statements and proxy contests
Antifraud	Fraudulently stimulating market activity False statements in filed documents Manipulative or deceptive devices Continuous disclosure Insider trading
Tender Offers	Reporting and procedural requirements

Tender Offer Regulation

History

Until the early 1960s, the predominant procedure by which one corporation acquired another was the merger, a transaction requiring the cooperation of the acquired corporation's management. Since the 1960s, the tender offer has become an often-used acquisition device. A **tender offer** is a public offer by a bidder to purchase a target company's equity securities directly from its shareholders at a specified price for a fixed period of time. The offering price is usually well above the market price of the shares. Such offers often are made even though there is opposition from the target company's management. These are called **hostile tender offers.**

The Williams Act

In 1968, the Williams Act amendments to the 1934 Act were passed to provide investors with more information to make tender offer decisions. The aim of the amendments is to give the bidder (usually a corporation) and the target company equal opportunities to present their cases to the shareholders. Strict reporting and procedural requirements are established for both parties. The Williams Act applies only when the target company's equity securities are registered under the 1934 Act.

A bidder making a tender offer must file a tender offer statement with the SEC before the offer is made. The information in this statement includes the terms of the offer (for example, the price), the background of the bidder, and the purpose of the tender offer (including whether the bidder intends to control the subject company). An SEC rule requires the bidder to keep the tender offer open for at least 20 business days and prohibits any purchase of shares during that time. The purpose of this rule is to give shareholders adequate time to make informed decisions to tender their shares. If the bidder increases the offering price during the term of the tender offer, all shareholders must be paid the higher price even if they tendered their shares at a lower price. If more shares are tendered than the bidder offered to buy, the bidder must prorate purchases among all the shares tendered. This proration rule is designed to foster careful shareholder decisions about whether to sell shares.

State Regulation of Tender Offers

Most of the states have enacted statutes regulating tender offers. Generally, such legislation has been enacted to protect local corporations from hostile takeovers, requiring long periods of advance notice to the target company and long minimum offering periods. Despite early questions concerning the constitutionality of such legislation, the Supreme Court has made clear that a properly worded statute will be permitted.

State Securities Legislation

Purpose and History

State securities laws are frequently referred to as **blue-sky laws,** since the early statutes were designed to protect investors from promoters and security salespersons who offered stock in companies organized to pursue visionary schemes. All of the states have such legislation, and all provide penalties for fraudulent sales and permit the issuance of injunctions to protect investors from additional or anticipated fraudulent acts. Most statutes grant broad power to investigate fraud to some state official—usually the attorney general or his appointee as securities administrator. All statutes provide criminal penalties for selling fraudulent securities and conducting fraudulent transactions.

Broker–Dealer Registration

Most of the state securities statutes regulate professional sellers of securities, notably securities brokers and dealers. These statutes register securities brokers and require proof of the financial responsibility of dealers. Dealers must disclose pertinent facts about the securities they are selling and avoid sales of fraudulent securities.

Uniform Securities Act

In August 1985, the National Conference of Commissioners on Uniform State Laws adopted a new Uniform Securities Act. The new act replaced the Uniform Securities Act of 1956. Both acts contain antifraud provisions, require the registration of securities, and demand broker–dealer registration.

Both Uniform Securities Acts permit an issuer to register its securities by coordination. Instead of filing a registration statement under the 1933 Act and a different one as required by state law, registration by coordination allows the issuer to file the 1933 Act registration statement with the state securities administrator. Registration by coordination decreases the issuer's expense of complying with state law when making an interstate offering of its securities.

Foreign Corrupt Practices Act

LO7

In an attempt to prevent bribery and other questionable payments, the United States enacted the Foreign Corrupt Practices Act (FCPA). The FCPA makes it a crime for any American firm to offer, promise, or make payments or gifts of anything of value to foreign government officials. It also establishes recordkeeping and internal controls requirements for any corporation (foreign or domestic) whose shares are publicly traded in the United States.

The Payments Prohibition

The antibribery prohibition makes it unlawful for any U.S. individual or firm to offer, promise, or make payments or gifts of anything of value to foreign government officials for the purpose of obtaining business. Payments are prohibited if the person making the payment knows or should know that some or all of it will be used for the purpose of influencing a governmental decision. An offer or promise to make a prohibited payment is a violation, even if the offer is not accepted or the promise is not otherwise carried out.

Permissible Payments

The FCPA allows a company to pay governmental officials to secure *routine governmental action*. These **grease payments** are not illegal if the recipient has no discretion in carrying out a governmental function. For instance, suppose a U.S. corporation applies for an import license in China and makes a payment to the government official responsible for issuing licenses. If the official grants licenses to every applicant and the payment merely accelerates the processing time, the FCPA is not violated. On the other hand, if only a few applicants are granted licenses and the payment is made to ensure that the U.S. company obtains an import license, the payment is illegal.

Payments to foreign governmental officials also are permitted by the FCPA when they are legal under the published laws of the country where the payments were made. However, this is an extremely narrow exception because, even in those countries where bribery is rampant, there generally are written statutes prohibiting it. Finally, a U.S. company also may reimburse foreign officials for the costs they incur in connection with visits to promotions, product demonstrations, and tours of business facilities. Thus, if a company invites a foreign governmental official to the United States to inspect the company's assembly operations, it lawfully could cover the costs of her travel and lodging.

Finally, the FCPA only deals with payments to foreign governmental officials. Thus, payments of kickbacks to foreign businesses and their corporate officials are not prohibited by the FCPA (although they may violate other laws or ethical responsibilities), unless the U.S. firm has knowledge that the payments will be passed on to government officials or other illegal recipients.

Usa v. Lindsey

783 F.Supp.2d 1108 (C.D. Cal. 2011)

FACTS

The government charged Keith E. Lindsey, Steve K. Lee, and Lindsey Manufacturing Company with violations of the Foreign Corrupt Practices Act (FCPA), alleging that they paid bribes to high-ranking employees of an electric utility company wholly owned by the Mexican government. The defendants moved to dismiss the charges, arguing that an officer or employee of a state-owned corporation cannot be a foreign official under the FCPA.

ISSUE

Can an officer or employee of a state-owned corporation be a foreign official for purposes of FCPA liability?

DECISION

Yes. The FCPA makes it unlawful for any American company or person acting on behalf of such company to provide money or other benefits to any foreign official in order to obtain or retain business. The FCPA defines a "foreign official" as "any officer or employee of a foreign government or any department, agency, or instrumentality thereof, or of a public international organization, or any person acting in an official capacity for or on behalf of any such government or department, agency or instrumentality, or for or on behalf of any such public international organization." We deny the motion to dismiss because a state-owned corporation may be an instrumentality of a foreign government within the meaning of the FCPA and officers of such a state-owned corporation may therefore be "foreign officials" within the meaning of the FCPA. It is not difficult to point to various characteristics of government agencies and departments that might fall within the definition of "instrumentality." The nonexclusive list includes: (1) The entity provides a service to the citizens—indeed, in many cases to all the inhabitants—of the jurisdiction. (2) The key officers and directors of the entity are, or are appointed by, government officials. (3) The entity is financed, at least in large measure, through governmental appropriations or through revenues obtained as a result of government-mandated taxes, licenses, fees or royalties, such as entrance fees to a national park. (4) The entity is vested with and exercises exclusive or controlling power to administer its designated functions. (5) The entity is widely perceived and understood to be performing official (i.e., governmental) functions. (Ultimately, the court threw out this conviction after concluding that the prosecutorial team had engaged in misconduct. *United States v. Lindsey,* C.D. Cal. No. CR 10-01031-AHM, 12, 1, 11.)

RecordKeeping and Internal Controls

The FCPA also imposes recordkeeping and internal controls requirements on any corporation whose shares are publicly traded in the United States. The purpose of the controls is to prevent unauthorized payments and transactions as well as unauthorized access to corporate assets. This provision requires corporations to keep records that accurately reflect all of their transactions. It also requires the establishment and maintenance of a system of internal accounting controls. The system must provide reasonable assurances that unauthorized transactions are not taking place.

Each corporation must maintain its records in a fashion that will permit it to prepare financial statements that conform to generally accepted accounting principles. Further, at reasonable intervals, management must compare the records with the actual assets available to make certain they are accurate. It they are not, it must find out why.

Liability for Actions of Foreign Agents

A U.S. firm is liable for bribes made by its foreign agents when it *had knowledge* of the illicit payments. This requirement is met if the company was aware of the bribery or was aware of the high probability that such behavior was occurring. Thus, a company cannot consciously ignore the activities of its foreign agents. Instead, it should exercise a reasonable amount of diligence to ensure compliance with the FCPA's antibribery provisions.

Ensuring Compliance

Global traders often have little choice but to use foreign agents in their overseas operations. Sometimes the costs of staffing a foreign office with U.S. employees are too great. In other instances, customer preferences or governmental rules demand the appointment of a local agent. Whatever the reason, whenever a U.S. company retains foreign agents to solicit business abroad, it should establish an **FCPA compliance program.**

At its most basic level, the company should have a procedure for conducting a **background check** of each potential agent. This should include an investigation of the agent's overall reputation for honest dealings. Further, since payments to government officials generally are prohibited, it is important to determine the relationship between the agent and the foreign government.

Company officials must be on the lookout for **red flags** that warn of the likelihood of illicit payments. For example, bribery seems to be much more widespread in some countries than in others. Thus, companies should exercise extreme caution when retaining agents in nations where bribery is rampant. Further, some industries tend to be more prone to corrupt practices than others. The defense, oil, and construction industries have well-known reputations for illicit payments. When an agent requests that payments be made in cash or that the money be delivered to a third country, company officials should be suspicious. Likewise, when the agent requests an extremely high commission, there is a probability that bribes are being made.

To discourage the likelihood of corrupt payments, a company should conduct regular audits of the expenditures of its agents. It might also request that agents sign agreements verifying that they will not make illegal payments. When a U.S. parent corporation holds a majority interest in a subsidiary, the FCPA requires it to maintain accounting records and internal audit controls. If the parent owns less than a majority interest in the foreign corporation, it still is required to make a good faith effort to encourage the company to comply with the recordkeeping and internal auditing rules.

ETHICS IN ACTION

Suppose you are competing with several companies for a contract to supply goods to a foreign government and your overseas agent informs you that you will not land the deal unless you bribe certain key governmental officials. You are fairly certain that your competitors have bribed officials in the past and are likely to do so again. Your agent also is confident that any illegal payments he makes are unlikely to be discovered by the government. Should you pay the bribe? How do you decide?

Questions and Problem Cases

1. Gustafson, McLean, and Butler (collectively Gustafson) were the sole shareholders of Alloyd, Inc. Gustafson decided to sell Alloyd and engaged KPMG Peat Marwick to find a buyer. In response to information distributed by KPMG, Wind Point agreed to buy substantially all of the issued and outstanding stock of the corporation. In preparation for negotiating the contract with Gustafson, Wind Point undertook an extensive analysis of the company, relying in part on a formal business review prepared by KPMG. After the sale, a year-end audit of Alloyd revealed that Alloyd's actual earnings were lower than the estimates relied upon by the parties. Wind Point claimed that the contract of sale was a prospectus, so that any misstatements contained in the agreement gave rise to liability under Section 12(2) of the 1933 Act. Is the contract of sale a prospectus that creates Section 12(2) liability? Explain.

2. For many years the FDA inspected Abbott Laboratories and found deficiencies in manufacturing quality control. Abbott never made sufficient changes to satisfy the FDA's concerns. The FDA sent Abbott another letter demanding compliance with all regulatory requirements and threatening severe consequences. Despite publication of this warning in the financial periodicals, Abbott's stock prices remained firm. By early September 1999, the FDA began insisting on substantial penalties plus changes in Abbott's methods of doing business. On September 29, after the markets had closed, Abbott issued a press release describing the FDA's position, asserting that Abbott was in substantial compliance with federal regulations and revealing that the parties were engaged in settlement talks. Abbott's stock fell more than 6 percent the next business day. On November 2, a court entered a consent decree requiring Abbott to remove 125 diagnostic products from the market until it had improved its quality control and to pay a $100 million civil fine. Did Abbott have a duty to disclose all information relating to the FDA investigation as soon as it was available to the corporation? Explain.
3. Life Partners, Inc., facilitates the sale of life insurance policies from AIDS victims to investors at discount. The investors then recover the face value of the policy after the policyholder's death. Meanwhile, the terminally ill sellers secure much-needed income in the final years of life when employment is unlikely and medical bills are often staggering. This process is known as "viatical settlements." For acceptance into the standard Life Partners program, an insured must meet the following criteria: (1) be diagnosed with "Full Blown AIDS," (2) have a life expectancy of 24 months or less as determined by Life Partners' "independent reviewing physician," and (3) be certified as mentally competent. Life Partners also represents that a policy qualifies for purchase only if it is issued by an insurance company rated "A−" or higher by a national rating service. In addition, the policy must be in good standing. The policies are assigned to Life Partners, not to investors. After the insured's death, the benefits are also paid directly to Life Partners, which then pays the investors. Investors have no direct contractual rights against the insurance companies that issue the policies. Whether they receive a return on their investment or even recover their principal depends upon Life Partners' ability to honor its contractual obligations to them. The SEC claims that Life Partners sold unregistered securities and made untrue and misleading statements in violation of the federal securities laws. Life Partners argues that the viatical settlements are not securities within the scope of the securities laws. Are the viatical settlements investment contracts that qualify as securities?
4. A group of Tellabs shareholders accused the corporation's CEO, Richard Notebaert, of engaging in a scheme to deceive the investing public about the true value of Tellabs's stock. Their complaint stated that Tellabs and Notebaert had engaged in securities fraud in violation of Section 10(b) of the Securities Exchange Act of 1934. Specifically, they claimed that Notebaert knowingly misled the public in four ways. First, he made statements indicating that demand for Tellabs's flagship networking device was continuing to grow, when in fact demand for that product was waning. Second, Notebaert made statements indicating that Tellabs's next-generation networking device was available for delivery and that demand for that product was strong and growing, when in truth the product was not ready for delivery and demand was weak. Third, he falsely represented Tellabs's financial results for the fourth quarter. Fourth, Notebaert made a series of overstated revenue projections, when demand for Tellabs's products was drying up and production was behind schedule. Based on Notebaert's sunny assessments, the shareholders contend, market analysts recommended that investors buy Tellabs's stock. Explain the analysis a court would use to determine if this complaint met the scienter requirement.

5. Washington Mutual (WAMU) is a publicly traded financial services company that serves individuals and small businesses, offering consumer banking, mortgage lending, commercial banking, and other services. Defendants Kerry Killinger, Thomas Casey, and Deanna Oppenheimer all served as officers of WAMU, with Killinger serving as the chairman of WAMU's board of directors, president, and CEO, Casey serving as executive vice president and CFO, and Oppenheimer serving as president of WAMU's consumer group. Thus, they held key officer positions at relevant times. South Ferry, a WAMU shareholder, alleges violations of Section 10(b) and Rule 10b-5 by Killinger, Casey, and Oppenheimer. The complaint relates to several related aspects of WAMU's mortgage lending business. That business involves originating home loans, buying and selling home loans in the secondary markets, servicing mortgages, and providing mortgage-insurance products. South Ferry claims that the individual defendants made materially false or misleading statements concerning WAMU's ability to manage risk. In addition, it asserts that the individual defendants repeatedly assured investors that WAMU would thrive in an environment where interest rates were increasing, and that the individual defendants assured investors that WAMU had fully integrated the information systems that are central to WAMU's ability to maintain and update their various hedges in a timely fashion during periods of interest rate volatility. The three defendants moved to dismiss the securities fraud action, arguing that it would be improper to infer that they had knowledge of WAMU's core operations based entirely on their management positions. In short, they asserted that the scienter requirement was not met. Has the scienter requirement been met? Explain.
6. Stuart Carson, Hong "Rose" Carson, Paul Cosgrove, and David Edmonds were charged with offering bribes to officials of foreign, state-owned companies for the purpose of obtaining or retaining business for their employer, Controlled Components Inc. (CCI). CCI is in the business of manufacturing control valves for use in the nuclear, oil and gas, and power generation industries worldwide. CCI's customers include state-owned companies in China (China National Offshore Oil Corporation, China Petroleum Materials and Equipment Corporation, Dongfang Electric Corporation, Guohua Electric Power, Jiangsu Nuclear Power Corporation, and PetroChina), Korea (Korea Hydro and Nuclear Power), Malaysia (Petronas), and United Arab Emirates (National Petroleum Construction Company). The government alleges that $4.9 million in bribes or "corrupt payments" were made to officers and employees of CCI's foreign, state-owned customers over a four-year period. The defendants contend that employees of state-owned companies can never be "foreign officials" under the Foreign Corrupt Practices Act (FCPA). Should the charges be dismissed because employees of state-owned companies can never be foreign officials within the context of the FCPA? Explain.
7. Escott and other investors brought suit to recover the loss of their investment in debentures issued by BarChris Construction Corporation. BarChris became bankrupt when the owners of bowling alleys built by the corporation failed to make their payments. The defendants were those who had signed the registration statement filed with the SEC. In its prospectus for the debentures, BarChris overstated sales and earnings and its current assets. It also understated its liabilities on some sales contracts and failed to disclose that a large part of the proceeds from the sale of the debentures would be used to pay off the old debts. It also failed to disclose that it was in the business of operating bowling alleys. (It had begun operating some of the alleys when the owners defaulted on their payments to the corporation.) Some of the defendants were unaware of the misleading statements and omissions. Auslander was an outside director who had just joined the board before the debentures were registered and had not read the

registration statement. Trilling, a junior officer who was controller, also claimed that he had been unaware of the false and misleading statements. Another defendant was Peat, Marwick, Mitchell & Co., the public accounting firm that had prepared an audit for the corporation. Were those who had signed the registration statement liable because of the misleading statements and omissions even if they were unaware of them?

8. R. Foster Winans was coauthor of a *Wall Street Journal* investment advice column ("Heard on the Street") that, because of its perceived quality and integrity, had an impact on the market prices of the stocks it discussed. Winans was familiar with the *Journal*'s rule that the column's contents were the *Journal*'s confidential information prior to publication. In spite of this, he gave advance information to Felis, a stockbroker, as to the timing and contents of the column. Felis bought and sold stocks based on the column's probable impact on the market and shared the profits with Winans. The court did not find that the content of any of the columns was altered to further the profits of this stock-trading scheme. Both were convicted of violating Section 10(b) and Rule 10b-5. (They also were found guilty of violating the federal mail and wire fraud statutes.) Should the insider trading convictions be upheld?

Chapter 32

Legal Liability of Accountants

Learning Objectives

After you have studied this chapter, you should be able to:

1. Compare and contrast each of the current approaches used to determine an accountant's liability to both clients and third parties.
2. Examine a fact situation and explain whether there has been a violation of Section 11 of the 1933 Act.
3. Examine a fact situation and explain whether there has been a violation of Section 10(b) and Rule 10b-5 of the 1934 Act.
4. Explain when an accountant's working papers are protected against discovery in a judicial proceeding.

Steve Noles relied on his trusted accountant, James Checksfield, to keep him out of trouble with the IRS. That was a serious mistake. Checksfield ended up being a controlled informant for the government. Checksfield revealed evidence that Noles skimmed untaxed income from his restaurant; Noles was indicted on six counts of income tax evasion and faced up to 24 years in prison and $900,000 in fines. During the time Checksfield was gathering evidence for the IRS, he received more than $20,000 in accounting fees from Noles. According to Mr. Noles, "Jim Checksfield often sat in my living room with my wife and two children. We treated

(continued)

him like family. I trusted him. Why, I even gave him power of attorney to represent me before the Internal Revenue Service!"[1]

- Did Checksfield breach a duty owed to Noles for which he could be liable in contract or tort?
- What are the ethical implications of accountants voluntarily disclosing the improprieties of their clients to the government?
- To what extent does an accountant–client privilege protect people like Noles?

Introduction

Bases for Liability

There are numerous legal theories under which an accountant might be found liable. Many of the previous chapters in this book have offered fairly detailed discussions of these causes of action. However, the main basis of liability for accountants is the *duty to exercise ordinary skill and care.* Breach of this duty may lead to an action grounded in the tort of negligence (see Chapter 7). Closely related are the suits stemming from the agency relationship (see Chapters 23 and 24) between the accountant and the client. Because this relationship is contractual in nature, breach of the duty might also trigger an action in breach of contract (see Chapter 18). Sometimes, the violation by the accountant is fraudulent (see Chapter 14) and perhaps even criminal (see Chapter 5). Further, many suits brought against accountants in recent years have been based on violations of the provisions of the federal securities laws (see Chapter 31). Finally, many times the accountant involved in the action will be a partner in a public accounting firm. If so, the law of partnership (see Chapter 27) will be involved, probably resulting in liability for all of the partners in the firm. (If the accountant is an employee and not a partner, the firm may still be liable under the doctrine of *respondeat superior* (see Chapter 24).)

The liability of the accountant can be both civil and criminal. (In Chapter 31 we examined how violations of the federal securities laws could subject the defendant to both civil and criminal remedies.) Further, when an accountant violates a duty, he may be called before a judicial body, an administrative body, or both. In addition, the accountant's liability may be to a client, a third person, or both. These and other issues will be discussed in this chapter.

GAAP and GAAS

Organizations representing the public accounting profession have developed and issued guidelines for conducting accounting work. Generally accepted accounting principles (GAAP) apply to the way business transactions should be recorded. Generally accepted auditing standards (GAAS) give directions to accountants in auditing the books of an enterprise. Accountants are rarely held liable if they have followed these

[1] "Accountant's Sideline as an IRS Informant Brings Grief to Client," *The Wall Street Journal,* February 22, 1990, p. A1.

standards, but failure to comply may constitute negligence. However, compliance with the standards is not always a sufficient defense. In a few cases, courts have refused to recognize this defense where they believed the accountants' work was misleading. This is particularly true in securities cases. There courts insist that financial statements, taken as a whole, fairly present the financial condition of the company and the results of its operations.

Common Law Liability to Clients

LO1

A business may have several reasons for employing an outside accountant to review its books. Often a formal audit is demanded by a creditor or prospective creditor. However, assurance that the internal bookkeeping of the business is accurate and that periodic financial statements are reliable are almost certain to be among the major reasons for the employment.

Contractual Liability

Like anyone, accountants have a duty to perform their contractual obligations. If an accountant agrees to complete an engagement by a certain time and fails to do so, there will be liability for whatever damages result. For example, suppose an accounting firm agrees to complete an audit by February 15 because it has been informed of a deadline set by a prospective lender to the client. If the audit report is not finished until March and the lender has no more funds available at that time, the accountant would be liable for the client's resulting loss. The fact that the accounting firm had other deadlines would not be a defense. Of course, the firm would not be liable if it could be shown that the delay was due to the client's having obstructed performance of the audit. This might occur if the client refused to give the firm access to needed records.

Ordinarily, an accountant may not delegate her responsibilities without the consent of the client. This is because the contract is a personal one, based on the skill, training, and personality of the accountant. The **no delegation rule** frequently becomes an issue at tax return time when demand for the accountant's services becomes overwhelming and there is a temptation to take on more work than can possibly be accomplished in a timely manner. (Again, as in the late audit report example, an accountant who files a late return cannot defend on the ground that she had too much work to perform.)

Tort Liability

Negligence

Even when there is no express agreement, the law imposes a duty of care on public accountants engaged to provide services to a client. The law implies that the public accountants have promised to exercise the skill, knowledge, and care generally used by accountants. Failure to comply with these standards might lead to an action against the accountant grounded in *negligence* if, as a result, the client suffers damages. For certified public accountants, a court would look to the higher standards that certification implies. These standards would include following GAAP and GAAS. Further, an accountant's failure to follow the instructions of her firm in performing the job is also likely to be treated by a court as negligence. (These standards would be applicable whether the suit is brought in contract or tort.)

The failure of an accountant to discover fraud by the client's employees or others is not in itself proof of negligence by the accountant. The investigative techniques used by accountants will not always uncover the fraud of a skillful and careful crook. However, accountants cannot overlook questionable entries or omissions in the accounts and supporting records of the client. For example, if the application of GAAS should raise the suspicions of a careful person trained as an accountant, an auditor who fails to follow through with appropriate inquiries and tests is negligent. (If the purpose of an audit is to look for suspected irregularities, more would be expected of an accountant.)

The individual circumstances will determine what action the accountant is required to take when he discovers irregularities. Certainly, it is necessary to notify an appropriate person in management if an accountant has a basis for suspicion of fraud. Notifying a person thought to be a participant in the suspected fraud would never be appropriate.

The traditional defenses of *contributory negligence* and *comparative negligence* may apply in a negligence action against an accountant. (See Chapter 7 for discussion of these defenses.) However, many courts hesitate to allow the client's contributory negligence to excuse the accountant's negligence because of the accountant's superior skills. The defense is more likely to succeed in an instance in which the client failed to follow the accountant's advice or in which the client already was aware of the irregularities before the accountant failed to discover them.

Intentional Misrepresentation

The intentional misrepresentation of material facts or the intentional failure to disclose such information to a client may result in the accountant being found liable for fraud. In Chapter 31, and later in this chapter we describe such behavior as acting with scienter—the knowledge of an untruth or the reckless disregard for the truth. Suppose that an accountant represents that he completed an audit of the client when in reality he merely accepted the accuracy of the client's books without investigation. A careful audit would have discovered that an employee of the client was regularly embezzling funds from the client. The accountant may be liable in fraud for any losses suffered by the client from the time when the audit should have discovered the embezzlement.

Generally, in a negligence or contract action, the client is limited to recovering compensatory damages. That is, the damage award is limited to the amount that will replace the actual loss caused by the accountant's wrong. If the accountant is found liable in fraud, however, the client may be able to recover punitive damages as well. (Under a punitive damage award, the client will receive an amount in excess of his actual loss. This award is designed to punish the accountant for her fraudulent conduct.)

Common Law Liability to Third Persons

Creditors, shareholders, and other investors often rely on financial statements that have been prepared or certified by public accountants. Sometimes firms engage an accountant to do an audit solely because this has been requested by a prospective or present creditor. Historically, LO1 third-party suits against accountants were generally barred by the **privity doctrine.** (This doctrine limited recovery to those with a direct contractual relationship to the accountant.)

Contract

At common law, recovery by a creditor was possible on the theory that the creditor was a third-party beneficiary of the contract employing the accountant. (See Chapter 17 for a discussion of such contracts.) This required showing that the accountant was aware that the audit was ordered to satisfy the demand of a creditor or prospective creditor. Then, the exception extended only to that person or firm. In the absence of these special circumstances, contract law has not been widely used by third persons (nonclients) suffering damages as a result of an accountant's breach.

Negligence

Many courts carried the privity doctrine over to negligence suits against an accountant by third persons who may have relied on her work. Thus, these nonclients—creditors, shareholders, and other investors of the accountant's client—were prevented from recovering damages caused by her negligence. In effect, this meant that accountants did not owe a duty of care and skill to nonclients.

Current Approaches to Third-Party Negligence Actions

Many courts today have refused to apply the privity doctrine to third-party negligence suits against accountants. Currently, there are five major judicial approaches for handling such suits. They are

1. The *Ultramares* approach.
2. The Near Privity approach.
3. The Restatement approach.
4. The Reasonably Foreseeable Users approach.
5. The Balancing approach.

The Ultramares *Approach*

The rationale for the application of the privity doctrine in suits against accountants stems from the landmark case of *Ultramares v. Touche.*[2] In *Ultramares,* the auditor had not been told that Ultramares Corporation was to receive 1 of the 32 signed copies of the certified balance sheet. Yet the auditors were clearly negligent in making their audit. They had accepted without question as accounts receivable $700,000 in fictitious sales, although these and other entries should have aroused their suspicions. Judge Cardozo refused to hold the accounting firm liable, and his rationale has been much quoted. He said: "If liability for negligence exists, a thoughtless slip or blunder, the failure to detect a theft or forgery beneath the cover of deceptive entries, may expose accountants to a liability in an indeterminate amount for an indeterminate time to an indeterminate class."

The Near Privity Approach

In contrast to the strict privity rule of *Ultramares,* several courts have adopted a near privity approach. It grew out of a case in which a seller employed a weigher to certify the weight of beans and to provide a copy of the certification to the buyer. Judge Cardozo, the author of *Ultramares,* held for the buyer in a suit against the weigher for inaccurately certifying the weight of the beans. Drawing from this opinion, several recent courts have held that accountants may be liable in negligence to third parties when three prerequisites are satisfied: (1) The accountants must have been aware that the financial reports were to be used for a particular purpose. (2) The accountant must have known the identity of the third parties and that they would rely on the reports. (3) There must have been some conduct on the part of the accountant linking her to the third party that evidences the accountant's understanding of the third party's reliance.

Bernard Madoff, a greatly respected New York money manager, was convicted in 2009 of orchestrating a $65 billion Ponzi scheme. After Madoff was sentenced to 150 years in prison, the thousands of investors bilked by his massive fraud scrambled to recover their missing money. The next case is an example of one such attempt by investors arguing that an auditor who failed to detect Madoff's ruse must compensate them for their losses.

[2] 174 N.E. 441 (N.Y. Ct. App. 1931).

Delollis v. Friedberg, Smith & Co.

2013 U.S. Dist. LEXIS 43222 (D.C. Conn. 2013)

FACTS

Beacon Associates had a substantial portion of its assets (73 percent) invested with Bernard Madoff. Empire Funds invested tens of millions of dollars in Beacon. Throughout this time period, Friedberg, Smith & Co., an accounting firm, was responsible for performing annual audits of Beacon's financial statements and each year would issue its auditor's report of Beacon. None of Friedberg, Smith's audit reports disclosed any concerns regarding the reported value of Beacon assets invested with Madoff or regarding the reported value of the Empire Funds' capital accounts with Beacon. After Madoff's Ponzi scheme became public, it was discovered that more than $330 million in assets that Madoff claimed to have purchased with Beacon funds did not exist. Empire Funds sued the accounting firm, arguing that the accounting firm's negligence in auditing Beacon's financial statements caused Empire Funds to suffer losses when it relied on those audit reports to decide whether to invest in Beacon. Specifically, Empire Funds asserts that Friedberg, Smith's audits failed to give any indication that the assets invested with Madoff might be nonexistent or that the reported value of those investments could be inaccurate or fictitious.

ISSUE

Should the auditor be found liable for Empire Funds' losses?

DECISION

No. Friedberg, Smith has not contracted with Empire Funds, thus we must determine whether the parties here have a relationship that approaches "near privity." Friedberg, Smith was aware that the audit reports would be used and relied upon to make and hold investments in Beacon, satisfying the first prong of the near privity test. Friedberg, Smith also was aware that the Empire Funds, specifically, would rely on the reports, satisfying the "known party" prong of the test. The third prong is met as well. This requires that there be some "linking conduct" between the auditor and nonclient establishing the auditors' understanding of the nonclient's reliance. The accounting firm specifically addressed the audit reports to the Empire Funds and provided them to the Empire Funds. Despite the fact that Friedberg, Smith owed a duty of care to Empire Funds, there is no showing that this duty was violated. We reject the argument that auditors owe a duty to nonclients to conduct what amounts to an audit of the accounts of entities in which their clients have invested, or to do more than rely on the third-party confirmations from those entities, when engaged in auditing their client's financial statements. Friedberg, Smith's only role was to audit Beacon's financial statements.

The Restatement Approach

A third theory of liability is set forth in the Restatement (Second) of Torts. Under this theory, the accountant is liable only to those third parties who are "specifically foreseeable." This standard imposes greater liability on accountants than does the *Ultramares* rule. However, the Restatement requires that the accountant be aware of the third parties and also know of the possibility that the third parties will rely on the financial statements. Thus, this approach does not protect the typical investor who was unknown to the accountant and her client when the financial statements were prepared. Of the state courts that have abandoned the *Ultramares* approach, the majority have chosen to replace it with the Restatement approach.

The Reasonably Foreseeable Users Approach

This theory exposes a negligent accountant to greater liability than do the *Ultramares* and Restatement approaches. Under this approach, the accountant could be liable to unknown but reasonably foreseeable users if three conditions are met. First, the user must have received the financial statements from the accountant's client for a proper business purpose. Second, the third person must have reasonably relied on the accuracy of those financial statements. And third, the damages suffered by the third party must be a foreseeable result of the accountant's negligence.

The Balancing Approach

Some courts have identified the need for a more flexible and equitable standard for resolving third-party negligence suits against accountants. They believe that the determination of whether a defendant will be held liable to a third person not in privity is a matter of policy and involves the balancing of various factors. Accordingly, they have devised a six-factor balancing test that examines (1) the extent to which the transaction was intended to affect the plaintiff, (2) the foreseeability of harm to the plaintiff, (3) the degree of certainty that the plaintiff suffered injury, (4) the closeness of the connection between the defendant's conduct and the injury suffered, (5) the moral blame attached to the defendant's conduct, and (6) the policy of preventing future harm.

Concept Summary: Third-Party Negligence Suits

Ultramares	Third party cannot recover unless in privity
Near Privity	Third party cannot recover unless accountant knew purpose of reports, identity of user, and that reliance would occur
Restatement	Third party may recover when accountant knew audited material would be used
Foreseeable Users	Third party may recover if member of class of persons who would foreseeably use audited material
Balancing	Third party may recover if determinative factors make such liability desirable

Fraud

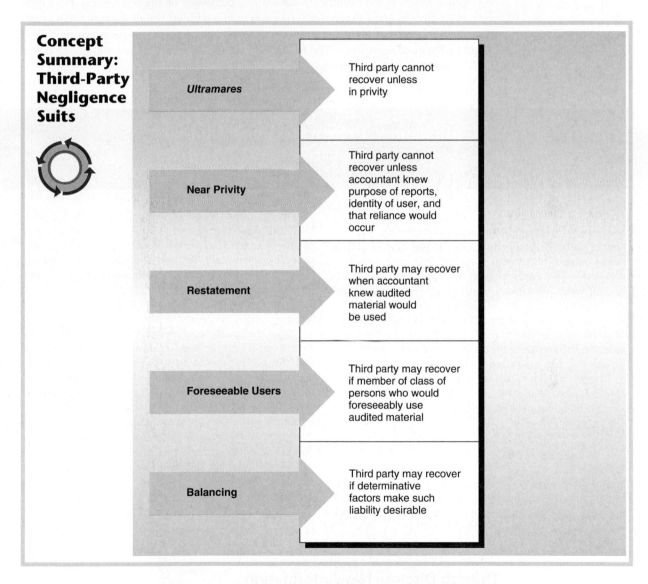

Because of its reprehensible nature, most courts have extended an accountant's liability for fraudulent conduct to all foreseeable users of her work product who suffered damages that were proximately caused by the accountant's fraud. Thus, third persons have a much greater likelihood of success in suits against an accountant if they can prove that in making the misstatement or omission in a report, the accountant committed fraud. To prove fraud it must be shown that the accountant acted with a special type of intent, called **scienter.** An accountant acts with scienter when he knows of the falsity of a statement or when making the statement, he recklessly disregards the truth.

Thus, the scienter standard of fraud would be met if an accountant, rather than examining the current figures in a client's books (perhaps because he was overwhelmed with other clients' work as well), relies on the previous year's figures. It would also include recognizing obvious evidence of embezzlement yet failing to notify a client of its existence.

Courts throughout the country are not entirely consistent on the precise test that a third party must meet in order to recover for an accountant's fraud. Yet all seem to be in agreement that the third party's path to recovery is easier once fraud has been proven than it would be for mere negligence. The following case presents another lawsuit arising out of the Bernard Madoff Ponzi scheme.

Stephenson v. PricewaterhouseCoopers

482 Fed. Appx. 618 (2d Cir. 2012)

FACTS

Stephenson invested $60 million in Greenwich Sentry, a limited partnership operating as a "feeder fund" into Bernard L. Madoff Investment Securities, LLC, which was later revealed to be a Ponzi scheme. For three years, PricewaterhouseCoopers (PwC) was Greenwich Sentry's auditor and issued Greenwich Sentry unqualified audit reports attesting to the accuracy of Greenwich Sentry's financial statements. After learning of the Madoff Ponzi scheme, Stephenson attempted to withdraw the entirety of his Greenwich Sentry investment, but it was gone. Alleging that PwC had failed to comply with generally accepted auditing standards in conducting its audits of Greenwich Security, Stephenson filed a lawsuit against PwC for fraud.

ISSUE

Should the court dismiss the fraud claim against PwC?

DECISION

Yes. The elements of fraud are: (1) defendant made a representation as to a material fact; (2) such representation was false; (3) defendant intended to deceive plaintiff (scienter); (4) plaintiff believed and justifiably relied upon the statement and was induced by it to engage in a certain course of conduct; and (5) as a result of such reliance, plaintiff sustained pecuniary loss. To meet the scienter requirement, plaintiffs must plead a factual basis which gives rise to a "strong inference" of fraudulent intent. Recklessness is sufficient to create such an inference if the reckless conduct is highly unreasonable and represents an extreme departure from the standards of ordinary care to the extent that the danger was either known to the auditor or so obvious that the auditor should have been aware of it. This has been found to occur in instances wheres auditors failed to review or check information that they had a duty to monitor, or ignored obvious signs of fraud. However, allegations of generally accepting accounting principles violations or accounting irregularities, standing alone, are insufficient to create a fraud claim absent evidence of a corresponding fraudulent intent. In this case, Stephenson has failed to show the existence of red flags of which PwC was aware and failed to investigate.

Duty to Disclose New Information

It has been held that the duty of care of accountants extends beyond their actions during the audit itself. In one case, an accounting firm learned through further work for a client that figures in financial statements that it had certified a short time earlier were false and misleading. The court held that the accountants had a duty to disclose the unreliability of the earlier report to anyone who they knew was relying on it. Liability for failure to comply with this duty may be based on either negligence or fraud.

Ethics in Action

How far should an accountant's liability to disclose the unreliability of earlier reports extend? Should the accountant contact all persons who might possibly be using the inaccurate statements although they were not foreseen users at the time the audit was performed?

Statutory Liability of Accountants

Federal Securities Acts

In Chapter 31, we discussed the federal and state securities laws and the various causes of action that arise when they are violated. Generally, violations of the statutes give the injured person a right to sue in negligence or fraud. Because of the privity rules, third persons (nonclients) frequently sue under these laws. And, as we will discuss, both the 1933 Act and the 1934 Act contain criminal penalties.

Civil Actions under the 1933 Act

LO2

Section 11(a) of the Securities Act of 1933 explicitly imposes liability on accountants for *misstatements or omissions of material facts* in the information they furnish for *registration statements* required by the 1933 Act. It also applies to lawyers and other "experts" such as engineers and consulting geologists. If this information is misleading, these experts are liable unless they can prove that they exercised due diligence. In other words, an accountant is liable for a defective registration statement unless she can prove that she made a reasonable investigation and reasonably believed that the certified financial statements were accurate. This lack of negligence can usually be proved by demonstrating that the accountant was in compliance with GAAS and GAAP.

The accountant is liable to any purchaser of securities issued pursuant to a defective registration statement. Reliance is not essential. Thus, the purchaser can recover even if he had not read the registration statement containing the material misstatements or omissions. As a general rule, the accountant is liable for the purchaser's entire loss. Of course, if the accountant can demonstrate that the purchaser was aware of the misstatements or omissions in the registration statement before buying the securities, the purchaser could not recover. Further, recovery would be denied if the losses were the result of a general downturn in the price of the securities that was totally unrelated to the accountant's negligence.

As noted above, reliance normally is not an essential element in a Section 11 case. Instead, courts generally presume that an investor relied on the defective registration statement. However, as the next case makes clear, there are situations where a Section 11 claim will be dismissed if there is no possibility of reliance.

The accountant's duty is to have a reasonable belief in the accuracy of the figures at the time the registration statement becomes effective. Frequently, the effective date is several months after the audit has been completed. Therefore, the accountant has a continuing duty to review the audited statements until the effective date. If there is any material change in conditions following the audit, the figures must be reexamined and corrected before the registration becomes effective.

APA Excelsior III L.P. v. Premiere Technologies

476 F.3d 1261 (11th Cir. 2007)

FACTS

The plaintiffs are investment funds and individuals who held approximately 30 percent of the stock of Xpedite Systems. When Premiere Technologies expressed an interest in acquiring Xpedite in a stock-for-stock merger and acquisition, Xpedite began its due diligence investigation of Premiere. More than two months later, Premiere's registration statement for the Xpedite merger became effective. The plaintiffs filed a claim under Section 11 of the 1933 Act, alleging numerous material defects in the registration statement. Premiere argued that, since the plaintiffs made their investment commitment before the issuance of the registration statement, they could not recover under Section 11 since reliance on the registration statement was impossible.

ISSUE

Should the Section 11 claim be dismissed because reliance was not possible?

DECISION

Yes. The plaintiffs had made their investment commitment before the filing of the registration statement and, therefore, reliance on the registration statement would have been impossible. Section 11 creates a presumption that any person acquiring a security was legally harmed by the defective registration statement. However, if reliance were irrelevant to the analysis, as the plaintiffs suggest, no presumption would be required at all. To say that reliance is "presumed" is simply not the same thing as saying that reliance is "irrelevant."

Section 11 has a statute of limitations that limits the period of time for which an accountant might be held liable for a defective registration statement. The purchaser must sue the accountant within one year after the time the misstatement or omission was or should have been discovered. However, a suit may not be brought more than three years after the securities were offered to the public.

Concept Summary: Accountant's Liability to Third Persons

Legal Theory	Summary of Accountant's Liability
	Common Law Liability
Contract	Liable for breach of contract to third-party beneficiary only if accountant was aware that the audit was ordered for the third party's benefit.
Negligence	Liability is generally barred by the privity doctrine unless the accountant should have foreseen that the third party would rely on the audit.
Fraud	Liable to anyone injured by an intentional misstatement or an intentional omission.
	Statutory Liability
1933 Act Section 11(a)	Liable to any purchaser of a security when there is a misstatement or omission of a material fact in the registration statement. Purchaser need not prove reliance. Burden is on accountant to prove he exercised due diligence.
1934 Act Rule 10b-5	Liable for misstatement or omission of a material fact in connection with the purchase or sale of a security. Plaintiff must prove accountant acted with scienter.
1934 Act Section 18(a)	Liable for damages resulting from any false or misleading information in any report filed with the SEC. Plaintiff must prove reliance.

Other provisions of the 1933 Act and the Securities and Exchange Act have also been used against accountants. These sections are designed to protect investors. Therefore, there are no privity requirements that bar common law suits in many states. (See Chapter 31 for a detailed discussion of these provisions.)

Civil Liability under the 1934 Act

Section 10(b) and Rule 10b-5, discussed in Chapter 31, have been the basis of most of the suits by investors against accountants. Rule 10b-5 prohibits any person from making a *misstatement or omission of a material fact* in connection with the purchase or sale of any security. One element of this action is that the purchaser or seller must *rely* on the misstatement or omission. However, in recent years, the courts have greatly eroded this notion of reliance and allowed plaintiffs to recover even though they had not read the report containing the omissions.

LO3

The popularity of Rule 10b-5 among plaintiffs is somewhat diminished by the requirement that something more than negligence must be shown to make a defendant liable for damages. That something more was scienter. This means that there must have been an intentional or at least knowing misrepresentation before the accountant can be found liable under Rule 10b-5. And, as we noted above, a reckless disregard of facts known to the accountant that would cast doubt on the information she provides would probably also be sufficient for liability. Requiring scienter has greatly reduced the number of successful suits against accountants.

The 1934 Act has several other provisions under which an accountant might be held liable. Section 18(a) (discussed in Chapter 31) imposes liability on accountants who furnish false or misleading information in any report or document filed with the SEC. While privity is not a defense in a Section 18 action, it is still not widely used because it contains a stringent *reliance* requirement. The purchaser or seller must have actually read the false information. This is a major hurdle since investors seldom read many of the documents filed with the SEC.

Finally, accountants may be liable for assisting others in violating the securities laws. It is illegal to encourage or participate in the publication of misleading information. Even if the information were prepared by others, the accountant may be found liable for *aiding and abetting*. In 1994 the Supreme Court stripped the SEC of authority to pursue accountants who aided or abetted corporate fraud. However, at the end of 1995, Congress enacted legislation restoring this power to the SEC and federal prosecutors. Thus, the SEC may file disciplinary cases against accountants or lawyers who aid and abet others who commit fraud. The new legislation specifically requires accounting firms to report any illegal activities uncovered during an audit.

At the same time, the new legislation shields accountants from the joint-and-several-liability system that plagued them for many years. Under joint and several liability, an accounting firm could be held liable for the full amount of a judgment if the defendant corporation became insolvent. The new regulatory scheme limits the accounting firm's liability to the proportion of the fraud for which the accountants were responsible, plus a 50 percent premium when the main defendant is insolvent.

Criminal Liability

Both the 1933 and 1934 Securities Acts have criminal provisions. Although the criminal provisions do not specifically mention accountants, they may be and have been used against them. A willful (intentional) misrepresentation, including an omission, in a registration statement is made a criminal act under the 1933 Act. The 1934 Act makes it a crime to willfully make a false or misleading statement in reports that are required to be filed under the act. A willful violation of Rule 10b-5 is also a crime.

Arthur Andersen v. United States

544 U.S. 696 (U.S. Sup. Ct. 2005)

FACTS

Arthur Andersen audited Enron's publicly filed financial statements and provided internal audit and consulting services to it. As Enron's financial performance worsened, a senior accountant at the company warned the new CEO that Enron could "implode in a wave of accounting scandals." After the SEC opened an informal investigation of Enron, Michael Odom, one of Arthur Andersen's partners with supervisory authority over the accounting firm's Enron engagement team, urged everyone to comply with the firm's document retention policy. He added: "If it's destroyed in the course of the normal policy and litigation is filed the next day, that's great. We've followed our own policy, and whatever there was that might have been of interest to somebody is gone and irretrievable." In the days that followed, the engagement team repeatedly reminded everyone to ensure that people were following the document policy. These reminders were followed by the substantial destruction of paper and electronic documents. Arthur Andersen was indicted for violating a federal statute which makes it a crime to "knowingly . . . or corruptly persuade another person with intent to cause" that person to "withhold" documents from an "official proceeding." Arthur Andersen was convicted after the jury was instructed that the statute was violated even if Arthur Andersen honestly believed that its conduct was lawful and that it merely intended to impede the government's fact-finding efforts.

ISSUE

Should Arthur Andersen's conviction be overturned because of the jury instructions?

DECISION

Yes. It is, of course, not wrongful for a manager to instruct his employees to comply with a valid document retention policy under ordinary circumstances. Only persons conscious of wrongdoing can be said to "knowingly . . . corruptly persuade." And limiting criminality to persuaders, conscious of their wrongdoing, sensibly allows this statute to reach only those with the level of culpability we usually require before imposing criminal liability.

State Securities Acts

Each of the 50 states has a securities statute that contains liability provisions. In addition, some of the states have provisions that specifically impose criminal penalties on accountants for willful falsification of financial statements and other reports. In the past, few actions have been brought against accountants under these statutes. However, this may well change as plaintiffs begin to recognize the difficulty in proving the scienter requirement of Rule 10b-5 and some of the other federal provisions.

Liability for Tax Work

Accountants may be held liable for negligence in preparing tax returns and giving tax advice. For example, an accountant may be required to reimburse a client for a penalty imposed for late filing if the delay is caused by the accountant. An accountant who erroneously tells a client that a transaction is nontaxable may be liable for the extra costs incurred because of the bad advice. This is also true of losses suffered by a client who has participated in a tax shelter scheme on the erroneous advice of an accountant.

Administrative Proceedings

An accountant who violates the federal securities acts may be subjected to an administrative hearing conducted by the SEC. Under this procedure, an administrative law judge will first hear the case and make a determination. The SEC commissioners will then issue a final order. Through this procedure, the SEC possesses the authority to temporarily or permanently bar an accountant from practicing before it. The final order of the SEC may be appealed to a federal court of appeals.

Knappe v. United States

713 F.3d 1164 (9th Cir. 2013)

FACTS

Peter Knappe asked his accountant to apply for an extension of the deadline to file the estate-tax return from the Internal Revenue Service (IRS). The accountant told Knappe that the deadline had been extended one year, when in fact it had been extended only six months. Acting on the bad advice, Knappe filed the tax return several months late, and the IRS assessed significant penalties against the estate. Knappe requested an abatement of the penalty. The Internal Revenue Code excuses late-filing executors from penalties if the failure to file was "due to reasonable cause and not due to willful neglect."

ISSUE

Should the taxpayer be excused from the late penalty?

DECISION

No. To establish reasonable cause, a taxpayer must prove that he exercised ordinary business care and prudence and was nevertheless unable to file the return within the prescribed time. Cases addressing reasonable cause for late filing of tax returns fall into two general categories. In the first category are cases involving taxpayers who delegate the task of filing a return to an expert agent, only to have the agent file the return late or not at all. The Supreme Court has held that such reliance is not reasonable cause for delay because Congress has placed the burden of prompt filing on the taxpayer. In the second category are cases where an accountant *advises* a taxpayer on a matter of tax law, such as whether a liability exists. In those cases, it is reasonable for the taxpayer to rely on that advice. Most taxpayers are not competent to discern error in the substantive advice of an accountant. To require the taxpayer to challenge the accountant, to seek a "second opinion," or to try to monitor the accountant on the provisions of the Code itself would nullify the very purpose of seeking the advice of a presumed expert in the first place. Such reliance is clearly an exercise of ordinary business care and prudence. The question of whether a return is due is a matter of substantive tax law, and a taxpayer acts with ordinary business care and prudence when he relies on an expert's answer to that question. When there is no question that a return must be filed, the taxpayer has a personal, nondelegable duty to file the tax return when due. This case is more like the first category than the second because of the distinction between substantive and nonsubstantive tax advice. For that reason, Knappe did not exercise ordinary business care and prudence when he relied unquestioningly on his accountant's advice about the extended deadline, and he unreasonably abdicated his duty to ascertain the filing deadline and comply with it.

Professional Conduct

Most states also have licensing boards that regulate the ethical conduct of the accounting profession. These state agencies may suspend or revoke the accountant's license to practice in that state if she commits illegal or unethical acts. Historically, the state licensing boards regulated accountants' right to advertise their services to the public. However, strict regulation of advertising in the accounting profession now is a thing of the past.

Sarbanes-Oxley Act of 2002

The Sarbanes-Oxley Act of 2002 is a major piece of legislation bundling together a large number of diverse and independent statutes, all designed to improve the quality of and transparency in financial reporting and auditing of public companies. Its registration and reporting provisions apply to U.S. and foreign companies listed on U.S. securities exchanges. The act increases criminal penalties for securities fraud and other violations and provides for the promulgation of codes of ethics and various other means for holding public companies to higher reporting standards.

Title I of the act established the Public Company Accounting Oversight Board to oversee the audit of public companies that are subject to the securities laws. The goal of this oversight was to protect the interests of investors and further the public interest in the preparation of informative, accurate, and independent audit reports. The five members of the Board are appointed by the Securities and Exchange Commission (SEC) after consultation with the Chairman of the Board of Governors of the Federal Reserve and the Secretary of the Treasury. The Board, subject to the oversight of the SEC, has authority to register public accounting firms, establish auditing and ethics standards, conduct inspections and investigations of registered firms, impose sanctions, and establish its own budget.

Section 106 of the act deals expressly with foreign accounting firms, requiring them to register with the Board if they audit public companies but carving out exceptions tailored to difficulties inherent in U.S. regulation of overseas professionals. This reflects Congress's recognition that the application of domestic U.S. regulatory statutes to persons abroad presents problems in addition to those of purely domestic application, and of the need to address those problems specifically.

Qualified Opinions and Disclaimers

Normally, after performing an independent audit, the accountant **certifies** the financial statements by issuing an **opinion letter.** This letter states whether the audit was performed in conformity with GAAS and, if the financial statements accurately reflect the client's financial condition in compliance with GAAP, the accountant issues an **unqualified opinion** (meaning that in her opinion there has been compliance with GAAS and GAAP).

Qualified Opinion

In some instances, the accountant will issue a **qualified opinion.** For example, there may be litigation pending against the client. The uncertainty over how the litigation will be decided may cast a cloud of doubt over the financial picture of the client. The accountant will be relieved from any responsibility for major changes in the client's financial position due to an unfavorable verdict if he clearly stated his qualification in an opinion letter.

Ethics in Action

The Sarbanes-Oxley Act created the Public Company Accounting Oversight Board (PCAOB) to oversee the audits of publicly traded companies. Public accounting firms must register with the PCAOB and follow the rules it promulgates concerning auditing, quality control, ethics, and independence standards. The board may periodically inspect the accounting firms and report its findings. Sarbanes-Oxley also prohibits most kinds of consulting arrangements that audit firms might otherwise have with the publicly traded companies they audit. However, the PCAOB may, on a case-by-case basis, exempt certain services performed by audit firms for their corporate clients. Further, audit firms may provide certain nonaudit services, like tax work, if the audit client's audit committee approves the arrangement in advance. Finally, Sarbanes-Oxley requires that the audit partner-in-charge for an audit client be rotated at a minimum of every five years. What will be the result of these regulatory reforms? Will they get to the root of the problems that have plagued the corporate world and shattered investor confidence? One immediate outcome seems to be a sharp increase in audit fees. *The Wall Street Journal* has estimated that audit fees may now rise by as much as 25 percent.

Disclaimer

An accountant may have conducted such a limited audit that she does not feel able to offer an opinion as to the accuracy of the client's financial statements. In this situation, she may **disclaim** any opinion. However, she would still be liable for any irregularities that her limited audit should have revealed. She may avoid liability for these irregularities by discovering them and issuing an **adverse opinion.** Merely issuing an **unaudited** statement does not create a disclaimer as to the financial statement's accuracy. The fact that they were unaudited only lowers the level of inquiry for which the accountant will be responsible.

Protection of Accountants' Papers

Working Papers

LO4

The working papers that an accountant prepares in making an audit belong to the accountant, not the client. This is so because the accountant may need to justify his work before the IRS or a court. Working papers include many different kinds of notes. Among the items included might be plans for the audit, results of testing to determine the reliability of accounts, notes as to the handling of unusual matters, and comments about the client's internal controls and accounting policies. Although these papers do not belong to the client, the accountant must get the client's permission before they can be transferred to another accountant. Also, the client has a right of access to the working papers for any reasonable purpose. This would include use of the papers by an attorney defending the client in a tax case.

Accountant–Client Privilege

Communications between lawyers and their clients are treated by the courts as privileged. That is, under most circumstances they are protected from discovery procedures in a lawsuit. Generally, lawyers cannot be required to tell what their clients have said to them, nor can they be required to produce their working papers as exhibits in court or during discovery proceedings before trial. However, no such privilege has been generally recognized in the case of accountants.

Many states have statutes that grant protection to accountants' working papers and also to conversations, letters, and memorandums between accountants and their clients. However, federal courts do not always recognize such state statutes. For example, a privilege of confidentiality has not, in the past, been recognized in federal tax cases. An accountant may be forced by a subpoena to make available to the IRS working papers involving a client who is being investigated. The accountant may also be forced to testify about the client's records and about conversations that the accountant had with the client. The same is true in SEC investigations.

In 1998, a federal statue extended the attorney–client privilege to "a federally authorized tax practitioner." That term encompasses a nonlawyer who is nevertheless authorized to practice before the Internal Revenue Service. The new privilege protects communications between a taxpayer and this federally authorized tax practitioner to the extent the communication would be considered a privileged communication if it were between a taxpayer and an attorney. It does not protect work product. Further, nothing in the statute suggests that these nonlawyers are entitled to privilege when they are doing other than lawyers' work.

Work Product Privilege

The work product privilege provides a broad privilege against compelled disclosure of an attorney's work product. As originally articulated, this privilege was designed to permit an attorney to assemble information, sift what she considers to be the relevant from the irrelevant facts, prepare her legal theories, and plan her strategy without undue interference. Today the privilege has been extended to a broader class of professionals. It now protects from discovery any documents and tangible things prepared in anticipation of litigation by or for a party.

The party asserting the work product privilege bears the burden of establishing that the documents he seeks to protect were prepared in anticipation of litigation. The next case explores the privilege in the context of information provided to the Sarbanes-Oxley Oversight Board.

Bennett v. Sprint Nextel Corporation

2012 U.S. Dist. LEXIS 145902 (W.D. Mo. 2012)

FACTS

A lawsuit asserting securities fraud was filed against Sprint in the wake of its merger with Nextel. KPMG had performed accounting work for Sprint in connection with the merger. As a part of the Sarbanes-Oxley Act (SOX) of 2002, the Public Company Accounting Oversight Board (Board) is empowered to register public accounting firms, establish auditing and ethical standards, conduct inspections and investigations of registered firms, and impose sanctions. The Board inspected KPMG and the inquiry encompassed KPMG's pre-merger audit of Sprint. The plaintiffs in the securities fraud action against Sprint then sought to compel KPMG to produce its entire set of work papers reflecting contemporaneous evidence of KPMG's audits and reviews of Sprint's financial statements. KPMG withheld the production of numerous documents prepared for the Board's investigation, asserting that they contained privileged information.

ISSUE

Should KPMG be required to produce documents prepared for the Board's investigation?

DECISION

No. The privilege provision in SOX protects those who are under investigation by the Board from being required to divulge their responses to that investigation. Notably, however, the privilege does not extend to documents from the underlying transaction or work that is the subject of the investigation as such documents are not prepared for the Board. When those underlying documents are given to the Board, the fact they were delivered is privileged, but the documents themselves are not. The SOX privilege extends to both materials "prepared for" and "received by" the Board. Thus, the privilege not only protects the Board, but also those who are under investigation from being required to reveal their responses to the Board's inquiries. The privilege created by the statute covers two categories of information: (1) all documents and information prepared or received by or specifically for the Board; and (2) deliberations of the Board and its employees and agents. Internal KPMG communications that discuss confidential questions or comments made by the Board or reflect KPMG's development of responses to Board inquiries are protected. Because the final version of the Board comments and KPMG responses to those comments are all privileged, then it also holds that any internal KPMG communications that reveal those comments, or the work to develop the responses to the comments, are also privileged. All of these communications are specifically for the Board because absent the inspection, these documents and communications would not exist.

Ethics in Action

An accountant may be forced by subpoena to reveal the contents of working papers to the IRS. Is it ethical for the accountant to voluntarily reveal this information in the absence of a subpoena when he discovers that his client has engaged in tax fraud? Should the accountant voluntarily reveal such findings to other persons who might be injured by the client's fraudulent content?

Questions and Problem Cases

1. Anicom entered into an asset purchase agreement (Agreement) to acquire the wire and cable distribution assets of Tricontinental Industries in exchange for cash and Anicom stock. During this time, PricewaterhouseCoopers (PwC) rendered accounting, audit, and various types of consulting services to Anicom. During the Tricontinental negotiations, Anicom engaged in improper accounting procedures to enable it to report that it had met sales and revenue goals. The procedures included the use of fictitious sales orders for goods that were not ordered. PwC became aware of these practices when it was asked to investigate Anicom's billing practices at one of its branches. PwC reported to Anicom's chief financial officer that improper billing had occurred and that, in the absence of controls, the practice might arise at other branches as well. However, no mention of these irregularities was made in PwC's later audits and financial statements. Indeed, PwC certified that Anicom's financial statements were accurate, complete, and in conformity with generally accepted accounting procedures (GAAP) and that its audits were performed according to generally accepted accounting standards (GAAS). Soon thereafter, Anicom filed for bankruptcy. Tricontinental Industries sued PwC for negligent misrepresentation. May Tricontinental recover from PwC for negligence? Explain.
2. Richard Frederick is both a lawyer and an accountant. He both provides legal representation to, and prepares the tax returns of, Randolph and Karin Lenz and their company, KCS Industries. The IRS is investigating the Lenzes and their company. As a part of this investigation, it has issued summonses directing Frederick to hand over hundreds of documents that may be germane to the investigation. Frederick has balked at handing over all of the documents, claiming that some were protected by either the attorney–client privilege or the lawyer's work-product privilege (or both). Most of the documents in issue were created in connection with Frederick's preparation of the Lenzes' tax returns. They are drafts of the returns (including schedules), worksheets containing the financial data and computations required to fill in the returns, and correspondence relating to the returns. The IRS argues that these documents are not privileged because they are the kinds of documents that accountants and other preparers generate incident to preparing their clients' returns, or that the taxpayers themselves generate if they prepare their own returns. Frederick claims that, because he is simultaneously acting as the Lenzes' attorney, all of the requested documents are protected from discovery. Does the fact that Frederick is the Lenzes' attorney automatically render the documents privileged?
3. Max Mitchell, a certified public accountant, went to First Florida Bank for the purpose of negotiating a loan on behalf of his client, C. M. Systems. After informing the bank vice president that he was a CPA, Mitchell gave the vice president audited financial statements of C. M. Systems for the two previous years, assuring the bank that he was thoroughly familiar with his client's financial condition. In reliance on these statements the bank granted the loan. When C. M. Systems failed to repay the loan, the bank discovered that Mitchell had overstated his client's assets, understated his client's liabilities, and overstated his client's net income. Is Mitchell liable to the bank in negligence under the *Restatement* approach?
4. *Video Case:* See "Cafeteria Conversation." Steve has authority to write checks on the account of his employer, a public company under the Securities Exchange Act of 1934. Because Steve is a compulsive gambler and substance abuser, he needs a constant supply of cash to finance his habits. Steve regularly issues checks payable to actual suppliers who are not currently owed money. He then steals the checks, signs the names of the payees, and cashes the checks. Because Steve is also in charge of

reconciling his employer's bank statements, his embezzlement scheme is not discovered by the employer's independent auditor during a routine audit. Is the independent auditor liable to the employer for its losses resulting from Steve's embezzlement?

5. Oregon Steel Mills (OSM) retained Coopers & Lybrand, LLP, for many years to provide accounting and auditing services. Due to its negligence, Coopers wrongly advised OSM that a transaction should be reported as a $12.3 million gain on OSM's financial statements and reports. When Coopers audited its financial statements for that year, it gave its opinion that OSM's consolidated financial statements fairly represented its financial position in accordance with generally accepted accounting principles. Shortly before OSM was planning to make a public offering of its stock and debt, Coopers advised OSM that the earlier transaction might have been reported incorrectly. Because of the time required to restate the financial statements and change other documents related to the planned offering, OSM's public offering was delayed by several months. Is Coopers liable for the difference between what OSM actually received and what it could have received if the stock offering had not been delayed by Coopers' negligence? Explain.
6. Gulf Resources & Chemical Corporation retained Peat Marwick to audit its financial statements. The completed auditor's report was included in Gulf's annual report, which became publicly available the following February. One year before that date, D. S. Kennedy & Company had reported to the SEC that it had acquired over two million shares of Gulf common stock and that it intended to acquire a controlling interest in Gulf. Peat Marwick was aware of this SEC filing. In fact, Gulf's management discussed with Peat Marwick the potential for purchasing Kennedy's shares. Thus, Peat Marwick was aware of Kennedy's interest in acquiring a controlling interest in Gulf and that Gulf intended to treat Kennedy as a hostile takeover threat. In March, Kennedy entered into discussions with Gulf concerning the possible purchase of a large block of Gulf shares, and during the course of those discussions, Gulf provided Kennedy with a copy of its annual report. Thereafter, Kennedy purchased almost four million shares of Gulf and gained operating control of the corporation. Peat Marwick first learned of this transaction a few days prior to the July closing. Gulf filed for bankruptcy protection two years later, rendering Kennedy's investment worthless. Kennedy then filed a civil complaint against Peat Marwick as a result of its alleged reliance on the auditors' report. Kennedy claimed the report materially misrepresented the financial condition of Gulf. Did Peat Marwick owe a legal duty to Kennedy? Explain.
7. Giant Stores Corporation hired Touche Ross & Co. to audit its financial statements. It was later discovered that Giant had manipulated its books by falsely recording assets that it did not own and omitting substantial amounts of accounts payable so that the financial information that Touche had certified was incorrect. The Rosenblums, allegedly relying on the correctness of the audits, acquired Giant stock in conjunction with the sale of their business to Giant. That stock subsequently proved to be worthless after the financial statements were found to be false. The Rosenblums claimed that Touche negligently conducted the audits and that Touche's negligence proximately caused their loss. If the court uses the reasonably foreseeable users approach, could Touche be liable to the Rosenblums in spite of the lack of privity?
8. Arnold Chait founded Ambassador Insurance and served as the company's president and chief executive officer. Under state law, Ambassador was required to file an annual financial statement with the state Insurance Department. There was no requirement that these statements be audited. However, Ambassador also was required to file annual financial statements with the SEC and these statements had to be audited.

To audit the annual SEC statements, Ambassador retained PricewaterhouseCoopers (PwC). Although PwC did not audit the annual statements that Ambassador filed with the state Insurance Department, those statements incorporated PwC's loss reserves calculations from the audited annual SEC statements. Ultimately, when Ambassador suffered a financial collapse, its receiver—the State Insurance Commissioner—sued PwC. Specifically, the commissioner claimed that as a result of its audit of Ambassador, PwC either knew or should have known that Ambassador was only marginally solvent and should not have continued writing new insurance policies. He further alleged that if PwC had issued the adverse audit opinion that it should have, the regulators could have acted to protect Ambassador and its policyholders, claimants, and creditors. PwC defended on the grounds that Chait's mismanagement of company should be imputed to Ambassador, thus relieving PwC of auditor liability. Should PwC be relieved from liability because of Chait's mismanagement? Explain.

Part 6

Property

Chapter 33

Personal Property and Bailments

Learning Objectives

After you have studied this chapter, you should be able to:

1. Understand the concept of ownership of property as a bundle of rights that the law recognizes.
2. Differentiate personal property from real property.
3. List the primary ways to acquire ownership of personal property.
4. Explain how the rights of finders of abandoned, lost, and mislaid property differ.
5. List and discuss the elements that are necessary for making a valid gift of property.
6. List the three essential elements of a bailment.
7. List and compare the three different types of bailments.
8. Explain the basic duties of the bailee and the bailor of personal property.
9. Discuss the special rules applicable for bailments to common carriers and hotelkeepers.

Claudio is a skilled craftsman employed by Goldcasters Jewelry to make handcrafted jewelry. Working after his normal working hours and using materials he paid for himself, Claudio crafts a fine ring by skillfully weaving together strands of gold wire. He presents the ring to his fiancée, Cheryl, as an engagement ring in anticipation of their forthcoming marriage. While visiting the restroom in a steak and ribs restaurant, Cheryl removes the ring so she can wash some barbeque sauce from her hands. In her haste to get back to her table, she leaves the ring on the washstand when she exits the restroom. Sandra, a part-time janitor for the

(continued)

restaurant, finds the ring and slips it into her purse. When Cheryl realizes she is missing the ring and returns to the restroom to look for it, neither the ring nor Sandra is still there. Later that evening Sandra sells the ring to her cousin, Gloria, who gives her $200 for it. Several days later, Cheryl breaks her engagement to Claudio, telling him that she no longer loves him. Claudio asks Cheryl to return the ring, indicating that he intended for her to have it only if their engagement led to marriage.

This situation raises a number of questions concerning rights and interest in personal property that will be discussed in this chapter. They include:

- Who was the owner of the ring at the time Claudio created it, Goldcasters or Claudio?
- Did Claudio make an effective gift of the ring to Cheryl? Or was it a conditional gift that he could revoke when Cheryl decided to call off the marriage?
- What was Sandra's responsibility when she found the ring? Between Sandra and the restaurant, who had the better right to the ring?
- Did Cheryl have the right to recover the ring from Sandra?
- Did Gloria become the owner of the ring when she paid the $200 to Sandra?
- Does Cheryl have the right to recover the ring from Gloria if she finds that Gloria has it?

Nature and Classification

Property

LO1

The concept of property has special importance to the organization of society. The essential nature of a particular society is often reflected in the way it views property, including the degree to which property ownership is concentrated in the state, the extent to which the state permits individual ownership of property, and the rules that govern such ownership. History is replete with wars and revolutions that arose out of conflicting claims to, or views concerning, property. And significant documents in our own Anglo-American legal tradition, such as the Magna Carta and the Constitution, deal explicitly with property rights.

The word **property** has a variety of meanings. It may refer to an object such as a building, or it may refer to legal rights connected with an object such as are found in the lease of a building, giving the tenant the right to occupy and use the building. However, the word *property* can also refer to legal rights that have economic value but are not connected with an object. A patent is an example of this kind of property.

When we talk about **ownership** of property, we are talking about a *bundle of legal rights* recognized and enforced by society. For example, ownership of a building includes the exclusive right to use, enjoy, sell, mortgage, or rent the building. If someone else tries to use the property without your consent, you can use the courts and legal procedures to eject the person. Ownership of a patent includes the rights to sell it, to license others to use it, or to produce the patented article personally.

In the United States, private ownership of property is of considerable importance and is protected by the Fifth Amendment to the Constitution, which provides that no person shall be deprived by the state of "life, liberty, or property, without due process of law." We recognize and encourage the rights of individuals to acquire, enjoy, and use property. These rights, however, are not unlimited. For example, a person cannot use the property in an unreasonable manner to the injury of others. Also, the state has the "police power" to impose reasonable regulations on the use of property, to tax it, and to take it for public use by paying compensation for it to the owner.

Real and Personal Property

LO2

Property can be divided into different classes based on its characteristics. The same piece of property may fall into more than one class. The most important classification is that of real property and personal property. **Real property** is the earth's crust and all things firmly attached to it. **Personal property** includes all other objects and rights that can be owned.

Real property can be turned into personal property if it is detached from the earth. Similarly, personal property can be attached to the earth and become real property. For example, marble in the ground is real property. When the marble is quarried, it becomes personal property, but if it is used in constructing a building, it becomes real property again. Perennial vegetation, such as trees, shrubs, and grass, that does not have to be seeded every year is usually treated as part of the real property. When trees and shrubs are severed from the land, they become personal property. Crops that must be planted each year, such as corn, oats, and potatoes, are usually treated as personal property. However, if the real property on which they are growing is sold, the new owner of the real property also becomes the owner of the crops.

When personal property is attached to, or used in connection with, real property in such a way as to be treated as part of the real property, it is known as a **fixture.** The law concerning fixtures is discussed in Chapter 34.

Tangible and Intangible Property

Tangible property has a physical existence; land, buildings, and furniture are examples. Property that has no physical existence is called **intangible property;** patent rights, easements, and bonds are examples of intangible property.

The distinction between tangible and intangible property is important primarily for tax and estate-planning purposes. Generally, tangible property is subject to tax in the state in which it is located, whereas intangible property is usually taxable in the state where its owner lives.

Public and Private Property

Property is also classified as public or private based on the ownership of the property. If the property is owned by the government or a government unit, it is classified as **public property;** if the property is owned by an individual, group of individuals, a corporation, or some other business organization, it is **private property.**

Acquiring Ownership of Personal Property

Production or Purchase

LO3

The most common ways of obtaining ownership of property are by producing it or by purchasing it. A person owns the property he makes unless the person has agreed to do the work for someone else. In that case, the employer is the owner of the product of the work. For example, a person who creates a painting, knits a sweater, or develops a computer program is the owner unless she was hired by someone to do the painting, knit the sweater, or develop the program.

The scenario set out at the start of this chapter posits that Claudio, a skilled craftsman employed by Goldcasters to make handcrafted jewelry, works after his normal working hours and uses materials he paid for himself to make a gold ring. Who should be considered to be the owner of the ring at the time Claudio created it, Claudio or Goldcasters? What are the critical factors that lead you to this conclusion?

Another major way of acquiring property is by purchase. The law of sale of goods was discussed in Chapters 19–22.

Possession of Unowned Property

In very early times, the most common way of obtaining ownership of personal property was simply by taking possession of unowned property. For example, the first person to take possession of a wild animal became its owner. Today, one can still acquire ownership of personal property by possessing it if the property is unowned. The two major examples of unowned property that can be acquired by possession are wildlife and abandoned property. Thus, a person with a fishing license fishing in a public lake who catches a fish, a hunter with a hunting license who shoots a deer in a state forest, or a person with a shellfish permit who recovers clams or mussels would become the owner of the fish, deer, clams, or mussels, provided they were taken in accord with the provisions of the license. The ownership of the property on which the wild animal is taken is a factor in the ownership of a captured wild animal. For example, a trespasser on private property normally would not have a better right to a fish caught in a private lake than the owner of the lake, who would be considered its owner.

LO4

Rights of Finders of Lost, Mislaid, and Abandoned Property

The old saying "finders keepers, losers weepers" is not a reliable way of predicting the legal rights of those who find personal property that originally belonged or still belongs to another.

The rights of the finder will be determined by whether the property he finds is classified as abandoned, lost, or mislaid.

1. **Abandoned property.** Property is considered to be abandoned if the owner intentionally placed the property out of his possession with the intent to relinquish ownership of it. For example, Kristin takes her television set to the city dump and leaves it there. The finder of abandoned property who takes possession of it with the intention of claiming ownership becomes the owner of the property. This means he acquires better rights to the property than anyone else in the world including the original owner. For example, if Todd finds the TV set, puts it in his car, and takes it home, Todd becomes the owner of the TV set.

Additional issues are presented when abandoned property is found on property owned by another person. First, when abandoned property is embedded in the soil, it belongs to the owner of the soil. Second, when the owner of the land where the property is found (whether on or embedded in the soil) has constructive possession of the property such that the property is not "lost" or abandoned, it belongs to the owner of the land.

2. **Lost property.** Property is considered to be lost if the owner did not intend to part with possession of the property. For example, if Barbara's iPhone fell out of her handbag while she was walking down the street, it would be considered lost property. The person

who finds lost property does not acquire ownership of it, but he acquires better rights to the lost property than anyone other than the true owner. For example, suppose Laura finds Barbara's iPhone in the grass where it fell. Leslie then steals the iPhone from Laura's house. Barbara is still the owner of the iPhone. She has the right to have it returned to her if she discovers where it is or if Laura knows that it belongs to Barbara. As the finder of lost property, Laura has a better right to the iPhone than anyone else except its true owner (Barbara). This means that she would have the right to require Leslie to return it to her if she finds out that Leslie has it.

If the finder of lost property knows who the owner of it is and refuses to return it, the finder is guilty of conversion and must pay the owner the fair value of the property.

A finder who sells the property that he has found can pass to the purchaser only those rights that he has; he cannot pass any better title to the property than he himself has. Thus, the true owner could recover the property from the purchaser.

3. **Mislaid property.** Property is considered mislaid if the owner placed the property somewhere and accidentally left it there, not intending to relinquish ownership of the property. For example, Sam places his backpack on a coatrack at Campus Bookstore while shopping for textbooks. Forgetting the backpack, Sam leaves the store and goes home. The backpack would be considered to be mislaid rather than lost because Sam intentionally and voluntarily placed it on the coatrack. The consequences of property's being classified as mislaid are that the finder acquires no rights to the property. Rather, the person in possession of the real property on which the personal property was mislaid has the right to hold the property for the true owner. For example, if Sarah found Sam's backpack in Campus Bookstore, Campus Bookstore would have the right to hold the mislaid property for Sam. Sarah would acquire neither possession nor ownership of the backpack.

The rationale for this rule is that it increases the chances that the property will be returned to its real owner. A person who knowingly put it down but forgot to pick it up might well remember later where the property had been left and return for it.

Some states have a statute, known as an **estray statute,** that allows finders of property to clear their title to the property after taking steps to see whether the true owner can be located. The statutes generally provide that the person must give public notice of the fact that the property has been found, perhaps by putting an ad in a local newspaper. All states have **statutes of limitations** that require the true owner of property to claim it or bring a legal action to recover possession of it within a certain number of years. A person who keeps possession of lost or unclaimed property for longer than that period of time will become its owner.

In the case that follows, *Corliss v. Wenner and Anderson,* the court awarded found property to the owner of the land on which it was found.

Corliss v. Wenner and Anderson

2001 Ida. App. LEXIS 79 (Ct. App. Idaho 2001)

FACTS

In the fall of 1996, Jann Wenner hired Anderson Asphalt Paving to construct a driveway on his ranch. Larry Anderson, the owner of Anderson Asphalt Paving, and his employee, Gregory Corliss, were excavating soil for the driveway when they unearthed a glass jar containing paper-wrapped rolls of gold coins. Anderson and Corliss collected, cleaned, and inventoried the gold pieces dating from 1857 to 1914.

(continued)

The 96 coins weighed about 4 pounds. Initially, Anderson and Corliss agreed to split the coins between themselves, with Anderson retaining possession of all the coins. Subsequently, Anderson and Corliss argued over ownership of the coins, and Anderson fired Corliss. Anderson later gave possession of the coins to Wenner in exchange for indemnification on any claim Corliss might have against him regarding the coins.

Corliss sued Anderson and Wenner for possession of some or all of the coins. Corliss contended that the coins should be considered "treasure trove" and awarded to him pursuant to the "finders-keepers" rule of treasure trove. Wenner, defending both himself and Anderson, contended that he had the better right to possession of the gold coins. The trial court held Idaho did not recognize "treasure trove" and that the coins, having been carefully concealed for safekeeping, fit within the legal classification of mislaid-property, to which the right of possession goes to the landowner. Alternatively, the court ruled that the coins, like the topsoil being excavated, were a part of the property owned by Wenner and that Anderson and Corliss were merely Wenner's employees. Corliss appealed.

ISSUE

Does the finder of the buried gold coins have a better right to the coins than the owner of the property on which they were found?

DECISION

No. The court of appeals affirmed the district court's decision. The court noted that at common law, all found property is generally categorized in one of five ways: (1) abandoned property—that the owner had discarded or voluntarily forsaken with the intention of terminating his ownership but without vesting ownership in any other person; (2) lost property—that property the owner has involuntarily and unintentionally parted with through neglect, carelessness, or inadvertence, and of which he does not know the whereabouts; (3) mislaid property—that the owner has intentionally set down in a place where he can resort to it and then forgets where he put it; (4) treasure trove—a category reserved exclusively for gold or silver in coin, plate, bullion, and sometimes its paper money equivalents, found concealed in the earth or in a house or other private place, normally under circumstances indicating the treasure has been concealed for so long as to indicate that the owner is probably dead or unknown; and (5) embedded property—that personal property which has become a part of the natural earth, such as pottery, the sunken wreck of a steamship, or a rotted-away sack of gold-bearing quartz rock buried or partially buried in the ground.

Here, the coins had been wrapped in paper and buried in a glass jar, evidencing a desire to keep them safe and clearly not lost or abandoned. The court then declined to adopt the rule of treasure trove, finding it out of harmony with modern notions of fair play. It noted the rule invited trespassers to roam over the property of others with metal detecting devices and to claim whatever was found to be theirs; it found this notion to be repugnant to the normal common law's treatment of trespassers. Accordingly, the court held that the owner of land has constructive possession of all personal property secreted in, on, or under his land and that the landowner is entitled to possession to the exclusion of all but the true owner absent a contract between the landowner and finder.

In the scenario set out at the start of this chapter, Cheryl visits the restroom in a steak and ribs restaurant in order to wash some barbeque sauce from her hands. She removes her engagement ring and places it on the washstand, but in her haste to get back to her table, she leaves the ring on the washstand when she exits the washroom. Sandra, a part-time janitor for the restaurant, finds the ring, slips it in her purse, and later sells the ring to her cousin, Gloria, for $200. When Cheryl returns to the restroom to look for the ring, neither the ring nor Sandra is still there.

At the time Sandra discovers the ring, should it be considered abandoned, lost, or mislaid property? What factors lead you to this conclusion? What should Sandra do with the ring at that point? Between Sandra and the owner of the restaurant, who has the better claim to the ring? Between the restaurant owner, Sandra, and Cheryl, who has the best claim to it? Why? If Cheryl discovers that Gloria has the ring, does she have the right to recover it from her? Explain.

Concept Summary: Rights of Finders of Personal Property

Character of Property	Description	Rights of Finder	Rights of Original Owner
Lost	Owner unintentionally parted with possession.	Rights superior to everyone except the owner.	Retains ownership; has the right to the return of the property.
Mislaid	Owner intentionally put property in a place but unintentionally left it there.	None; person in possession of real property on which mislaid property was found holds it for the owner, and has rights superior to everyone except owner.	Retains ownership; has the right to the return of the property.
Abandoned	Owner intentionally placed property out of his possession with intent to relinquish ownership of it.	Finder who takes possession with intent to claim ownership acquires ownership of property.	None.

Ethics in Action

"FINDERS-KEEPERS": IT MAY BE LEGAL, BUT IS IT ETHICAL?

You're walking along the beach, and you find a toilet kit washed ashore. It contains some sodden cosmetics and a few dollars in change, but no identification. What should you do? The ordinarily ethical person probably tosses the potions and keeps the cash, persuaded by three arguments: Whatever drifts ashore falls under the heading of "finders-keepers," whatever has no identification is difficult to return, and whatever has trivial value would cost more to advertise for the proper owner than it's worth.

The next day on the same beach you find a dinghy with a small outboard motor attached, but no name or registration number. What should you do? While the "finders-keepers" and anonymity tests still hold, the triviality test does not: The dinghy clearly has significant value. The ordinarily ethical person probably, at the very least, contacts nearby harbormasters to see if anyone is missing a boat, leaving a phone number in case the owner calls.

The third day, astonishingly, you find 40 shipping containers that have washed off the deck of a vessel grounded on a sandbar in plain view a mile offshore. One contains a dozen brand-new BMW motorcycles, each worth more than $20,000. What should you do?

This third case is not hypothetical. The ship was the *Napoli,* a 62,000-ton cargo ship. On January 19, 2007, she encountered a terrific storm and was abandoned by her crew off the coast of Devon, England. As she was being towed to a nearby port, she began to list and was deliberately grounded. When the containers came loose, scores of people came from miles around, swarmed across Branscombe Beach under the eyes of helpless police, opened the containers, and made off with everything of value, including the motorcycles.

Why? They apparently saw this opportunity as somewhere between winning a lottery and finding money in a hollow tree. "It's great, isn't it?" one man told the *Guardian* newspaper, "a cross between a bomb site and a car boot [trunk] sale." Another said it was like finding "Aladdin's cave." In their view, the stuff was there for the taking, and they were in the right place at the right time.

(continued)

Ethics in Action *(concluded)*

To call these people "looters" gives the wrong impression. These weren't professional second-story men, cat burglars, or back-alley thugs. By all accounts, they were ordinary people. Two questions, then: Were their actions legal, and were they ethical?

What they did clearly fails the triviality test. As for anonymity, there's no doubt about the source of their loot, and no difficulty tracing its ownership. The "finders-keepers" test, however, is more complex. In fact, the police were legitimately flummoxed. English law allows salvagers to take whatever marine wreckage they find, as long as they fill out a form and take it to the Maritime and Coastguard Agency within 28 days. That entitles them to a reward if the property is claimed—and to legal ownership if, after a year, it is not. So the police felt they could do little more than hand out forms. By day's end, some of the items began showing up for sale on eBay, brazenly described as coming from the *Napoli,* suggesting that even the pretense of legality had been breached by some of these collectors.

What's being tested here, then, is not simply the law but the ethics underlying the law. Given the circumstances, would we expect a reasonably ethical person to remove objects clearly belonging to someone else, or would we want them to help restore lost property to its owners? Surely the latter. Cynics, of course, will yawp that if you don't take it, others will—a line of reasoning so thin that it also would permit you to slaughter your obnoxious neighbor if you thought others were also upset with him. Cynics also will argue that the shipper's insurance will recompense the owner for anything removed—an argument that, along with driving up insurance costs for everyone else, fails to account for one woman's loss of a collection of letters and pictures, personal and irreplaceable, that disappeared from Branscombe Beach as she was moving her home to South Africa.

So suppose we grant that, except for those who fenced their wares on eBay, the rest intended to behave legally by filing proper forms. Even so, does that made them ethical?

Source: Excerpted from the January 29, 2007, issue of *Ethics Newsline* (www.glopalethics.org/newsline), a publication of the Institute for Global Ethics.

Gifts

Title to personal property can be obtained by **gift.** A gift is a voluntary transfer of property to the **donee** (the person who receives a gift), for which the **donor** (the person who gives the gift) gets no consideration in return. To have a valid gift, all three of the following elements are necessary:

LO5

1. The donor must *intend* to make a gift.
2. The donor must make *delivery* of the gift.
3. The donee must *accept* the gift.

The most critical requirement is delivery. The person who makes the gift must actually give up possession and control of the property to either the *donee* or a third person to hold it for the donee. Delivery is important because it makes clear to the donor that she is voluntarily giving up ownership without getting something in exchange. A promise to make a gift is usually not enforceable; the person must actually part with the property. In some cases, the delivery may be symbolic. For example, handing over the key to a strongbox can be symbolic delivery of the property in the strongbox.

There are two kinds of gifts: gifts *inter vivos* and gifts *causa mortis.* A gift *inter vivos* is a gift between two living persons; a gift *causa mortis* is a gift made in contemplation of death. For example, Uncle Ernie is about to undergo a serious heart operation. Ernie gives his watch to his nephew Ted and tells Ted he wants him to have it if he does not survive the operation. A gift *causa mortis* is a conditional gift. It is not effective if (1) the donor recovers from the peril or sickness under fear of which the gift was made, (2) the donor revokes or withdraws the gift before he dies, or (3) the donee dies before the donor. If one of these events takes place, ownership of the property goes back to the donor. In the case that follows, *Kenyon v. Abel,* the court concluded that where the alleged donor had not intended to make a gift of a painting, there was not an effective transfer of title to a painting by gift.

Kenyon v. Abel

36 P.3d 1161 (Sup. Ct. Wyo. 2001)

FACTS

Rick Kenyon purchased a painting by a noted Western artist, Bill Gollings, valued at between $8,000 and $15,000, for $25 at a Salvation Army thrift store. Claude Abel filed suit against Kenyon seeking the return of the painting, which had belonged to his late aunt. Abel claimed that the Salvation Army mistakenly took the painting from his aunt's house when the box in which it was packed was mixed with items being donated to the thrift store.

Abel's aunt, Billie Taylor, was a friend of the artist, whose works were known for their accurate portrayal of the Old West. Sometime before his death in 1932, Gollings gave a painting to Taylor depicting a Native American on a white horse in the foreground with several other Native Americans on horses in the background traveling through a traditional western prairie landscape. The painting remained in Taylor's possession at her home in Sheridan, Wyoming, until her death on August 31, 1999.

After Taylor's death, Abel traveled from his home in Idaho to Sheridan for the funeral and to settle the estate. Abel was the sole heir of Taylor's estate, so he inherited all of her personal belongings, including the Gollings painting. Abel and his wife sorted through Taylor's belongings, selecting various items they would keep for themselves. Abel and his wife, with the help of a local moving company, packed those items into boxes marked for delivery to their home in Idaho.

Items not being retained by Abel either were packed for donation to the Salvation Army or, if they had sufficient value, were taken by an antiques dealer for auction. The scene at the house was one of some confusion as Abel tried to vacate the residence as quickly as possible while attempting to make sure all of the items went to their designated destinations. The painting was packed by Abel's wife in a box marked for delivery to Idaho. However, in the confusion and unbeknownst to Abel, the box containing the Gollings painting was inadvertently picked up with the donated items by the Salvation Army. It was priced at $25 in its thrift store and sold to Kenyon.

After returning to Idaho, Abel discovered that the box containing the painting was not among those delivered by the moving company. He also learned that the painting had gone to the Salvation Army and had been sold to Kenyon. When Kenyon refused to acknowledge he had the painting, Abel brought suit seeking its return. Kenyon claimed that he was a good faith purchaser of the painting that had been given to the Salvation Army. The trial court concluded that, among other reasons, Abel was entitled to possession of the painting under the common law doctrines of gift and conversion. Kenyon appealed the decision.

ISSUE

Was Abel entitled to have the painting returned to him on the grounds that not having made a gift of the painting, he was still the owner, and that its sale by the Salvation Army was a conversion of his property?

DECISION

Yes. Abel is entitled to recover the painting from Kenyon. A valid gift consists of three elements: (1) a present intention to make an immediate gift, (2) actual or constructive delivery of the gift that divests the donor of dominion and control, and (3) acceptance of the gift by the donee. The pivotal element in this case is the first one. The trial court correctly concluded that Abel did not have any intent to donate the painting to the Salvation Army; therefore, it was correct in ruling that the transfer of the painting to the Salvation Army did not constitute a valid gift.

Conversion occurs when a person treats another's property as their own, denying to the true owner the benefits and rights of ownership. As the heir to his aunt's estate, Abel had legal title to the painting, he possessed the painting at the time it was removed from his aunt's residence, and the Salvation Army exercised dominion over the property in a manner that deprived Abel of the right to enjoy and use the painting—i.e., the Salvation Army sold the painting. As a converter of Abel's property, the Salvation Army had no title whatsoever (their title is void), and they therefore had no title they could pass on to Kenyon.

Conditional Gifts

Sometimes a gift is made on condition that the donee comply with certain restrictions or perform certain actions. A conditional gift is not a completed gift, and it may be revoked by the donor before the donee complies with the conditions. However, if the donee has partially complied with the conditions, the donor cannot withdraw the gift without giving the donee an opportunity to comply fully.

Gifts in contemplation of marriage, such as engagement rings, have given rise to much litigation. Generally, gifts of this kind were considered to have been made on an implied condition that they are to be returned if the donee breaks the engagement without legal justification or if it is broken by mutual consent. If the engagement was unjustifiably broken by the donor, the traditional rule generally bars the donor from recovering gifts made in contemplation of marriage. This traditional approach is illustrated in *Clippard v. Pfefferkorn,* which follows. However, it should be noted that an increasing number of courts have rejected the traditional approach and its focus on fault. Among the reasons cited by the courts for dropping an inquiry into whose fault it is that the marriage is not going forward are that it avoids an inquiry into what are often complex circumstances and also the need to consider whether a person had sound reasons that justified the action. They cite a concern that this kind of inquiry would invite bitter and unpleasant accusations against a person they almost made their spouse—and inevitably invite acrimony and encourage persons to present their ex-fiancés in the worst possible light. Finally, the courts note that a no-fault approach is consistent with the movement away from the notion of fault in divorce statutes. Some states have enacted legislation prescribing the rules applicable to the return of engagement presents.

In the scenario set out at the beginning of this chapter, Claudio gave the ring to Cheryl as an engagement ring in anticipation of their forthcoming marriage. Later, Cheryl breaks off the engagement, telling Claudio that she no longer loves him. Claudio then asks Cheryl to return the ring to him.

What argument would Claudio make to support his claim that he has the legal right to have the ring returned to him? What argument might Cheryl make to support her contention that she should have the legal right to retain the ring? If Claudio and Cheryl lived in Missouri, where the *Clippard v. Pfefferkorn* case was decided, would Claudio be entitled to recover the ring from Cheryl? Why or why not? Would it make a difference if they lived in a state that used a no-fault approach concerning gifts given in anticipation of marriage?

Clippard v. Pfefferkorn

168 S.W.3d. 616 (Ct. App. Mo. 2005)

FACTS

Chad Clippard and Jamie Pfefferkorn dated for four or five months in late 2002. On December 23, Chad proposed marriage to Jamie and presented her with a 2.02-carat diamond engagement ring valued at approximately $13,500. Jamie accepted the proposal and the ring. Several days later, they exchanged Christmas gifts.

During the weeks following Christmas 2002, the couple experienced difficulties in their relationship. On February 8, 2003, Chad terminated the engagement. He attributed the decision not to go forward with marriage to a belief that Jamie was not the "right" person and to the influence of his brother, sisters, and parents. There were times during the engagement when it was "off" and Jamie returned the ring

(continued)

to Chad, but when the parties renewed the engagement he gave it back to her. When the couple finally broke up, Chad asked Jamie to return the ring, but she refused.

In July 2003, Chad filed a petition in court seeking a court order to have Jamie return the ring or, in the alternative, to pay damages in the amount of $13,500, the approximate value of the ring. Jamie took the position that the ring was a Christmas gift. Chad denied that it was a Christmas gift. He claimed that it was a gift in contemplation of marriage and thus a conditional gift that had to be returned upon the termination of the engagement.

ISSUE

Is Jamie entitled to retain the ring?

DECISION

Yes. At the outset the court rejected Jamie's claim that the ring was a completed *inter vivos* gift that could not be revoked once delivery had been made to the donee. The court found that the ring was a gift given in contemplation of marriage and made on the implied condition that the gift will become absolute when the marriage takes place. When the marriage does not, or will not, take place, Missouri courts use a fault-based approach to determine which party is entitled to the property. Chad would have been entitled to the ring if the engagement had been broken by Jamie for no fault of Chad. The reverse also applies—as donee of the conditional gift, Jamie was entitled to retain the ring because the engagement was terminated by Chad for no fault of Jamie. Here the engagement was terminated because Chad believed Jamie was not the right person for him and because of pressure from his family. The court went on to note that Jamie was also entitled to retain the ring because Chad, by terminating the engagement, breached his promise to marry Jamie.

Uniform Gifts to Minors Act

The Uniform Gifts to Minors Act, which has been adopted in one form or another in every state, provides a fairly simple and flexible method for making gifts of money and securities to minors. Under it, an adult can make a gift of money to a minor by depositing the money with a broker or a bank in an account in the donor's name, or with another adult or a bank with trust powers, as custodian for the minor under the Uniform Gifts to Minors Act. Similarly, a gift of registered securities can be made by registering the securities in the name of another adult, a bank trustee, or a broker as custodian for the minor. A gift of unregistered securities can be made by delivering the securities to another adult or a bank trustee along with a statement that the adult, trustee, or broker is to hold the securities as custodian and then obtaining a written acknowledgment from the custodian. The custodian is given fairly broad discretion to use the gift for the minor's benefit but may not use it for the custodian's benefit. If the donor fully complies with the Uniform Act, the gift is considered to be irrevocable.

Will or Inheritance

Ownership of personal property can also be transferred on the death of the former owner. The property may pass under the terms of a will if the will was validly executed. If there is no valid will, the property is transferred to the heirs of the owner according to state laws. Transfer of property at the death of the owner will be discussed in Chapter 36, "Estates and Trusts."

Confusion

Title to personal property can be obtained by **confusion.** Confusion is the intermixing of goods belonging to different owners in such a way that the goods cannot later be separated. For example, suppose wheat belonging to several different people is mixed in a grain elevator. If the mixing was by agreement or if it resulted from an accident without negligence on anyone's part, then each person owns his proportionate share of the entire quantity of wheat.

However, a different result would be reached if the wheat was wrongfully or negligently mixed together. Suppose a thief steals a truckload of Grade 1 wheat worth $8.50 a bushel that belongs to a farmer. The thief dumps the wheat into a storage bin that contains a lower-grade wheat worth $4.50 a bushel. Once mixed, the wheat cannot be separated into the two grades, so it is worth only $4.50 a bushel. The farmer has first claim against the entire mixture to recover the value of his wheat that was mixed in. The thief, or any other person whose intentional or negligent act results in confusion of goods, must bear any loss caused by the confusion.

Accession

Title to personal property can also be obtained by **accession.** Accession means increasing the value of property by adding materials and/or labor. As a general rule, the owner of the original property becomes the owner of the improvements. For example, Harry takes his automobile to a shop that replaces the engine with a larger engine and puts in a new four-speed transmission. Harry is still the owner of the automobile as well as the owner of the parts added by the auto shop.

Problems can arise if materials are added or work is done on personal property without the consent of the owner. If property is stolen from one person and improved by the thief, the original owner can get it back and does not have to reimburse the thief for the work or materials in improving it. For example, a thief steals Ralph's used car, puts a new engine in it, replaces the tires, and repairs the muffler. Ralph is entitled to get his car back from the thief and does not have to pay him for the engine, tires, or muffler.

The result is more difficult to predict, however, if property is mistakenly improved in good faith by someone who believes that he is its owner. Then two innocent parties—the original owner and the person who improved the property—are involved. Usually the person who improved the property in good faith is entitled to recover the cost of the improvement made to it. Alternatively, the improver can keep the property and pay the original owner the value of the property as of the time that he obtained it. Whether the original owner has the right to recover the property after paying for the improvements depends on several factors. First, what is the relative increase in value? Second, has the form or identity of the property been changed? Third, can the improvements be separated from the original property? This is illustrated in the case that follows, *Ballard v. Wetzel.*

Ballard v. Wetzel

1997 WL 650878 (Ct. App. Tenn. 1997)

FACTS

Faith Ballard's Corvette was substantially damaged in an accident and was being stored in her garage. Her son, Tyrone Ballard, told her that he would take the vehicle and have it restored. Instead, he sold it to Lambert Auto Parts. Johnny Wetzel purchased the Corvette "hull" for $900 from Lambert, whose regular business is selling parts. Wetzel obtained a receipt documenting the purchase of the parts. He also checked the VIN numbers through the county clerk's office to make sure the parts were not stolen. Wetzel spent approximately $5,000 and 100 hours of labor restoring the vehicle. When completed, the restoration had a market value of $7,950.

(continued)

Ballard v. Wetzel *(concluded)*

George Martin, an employee of Lambert, testified that he purchased only a "hull" of a car—rather than a whole vehicle—from Tyrone Ballard. Martin also testified that he usually received a title when he bought a "whole" vehicle but had not received one in this case, because he had purchased only part of one. Under Tennessee law, a certificate of title is not required to pass ownership of a motor vehicle, but any owner dismantling a registered vehicle is to send the certificate of title back to the state.

Faith Ballard brought suit against Wetzel to recover possession of the Corvette. Wetzel contended that he was a good faith purchaser for value and had become the owner of the restored auto hull by accession.

ISSUE

Did Wetzel become the owner of the Corvette by accession?

DECISION

Yes. The sale of the vehicle by Tyrone constituted theft and normally a buyer from a thief gets only the title which the thief has, which is a void title. However, the courts have held that title may pass to an innocent purchaser where there is a great disparity in the value between the original article and the new product resulting from the purchaser's labor and/or materials. Here, Wetzel acquired title to the Corvette by accession because his labor significantly increased the value of the vehicle.

Nature of Bailments

LO6

Elements of a Bailment

A **bailment** is the delivery of personal property by one person (the **bailor**) to another person (the **bailee**) who accepts it and is under an express or implied agreement to return it to the bailor or to someone designated by the bailor. These are essential elements:

1. The bailor must own or have the right to possess the item of property.
2. The bailor must deliver exclusive possession and control of the property, but not title, to the bailee.
3. The bailee must knowingly accept the property with the understanding that he owes a duty to return the property as directed by the bailor.

Creation of a Bailment

A bailment is created by an express or implied contract. Whether the elements of a bailment have been fulfilled is determined by examining all the facts and circumstances of a particular situation. A critical requirement in the creation of a bailment is whether the person to whom the property was delivered *intended to assume possession and control over the property.* Suppose you go into a restaurant and hang your hat and coat on an unattended rack. It is unlikely that this created a bailment because the restaurant owner never assumed control over the hat and coat. However, if there is a checkroom and you check your hat and coat with the attendant, a bailment will arise.

If you park your car in a parking lot, keep the keys, and can drive the car out yourself whenever you wish, a bailment has not been created. The courts treat this situation as a lease of space. Suppose you take your car to a parking garage where an attendant gives you a claim check and then parks the car. In this case, there is a bailment of your car since the parking garage has accepted delivery and possession of your car. However, a distinction is made between the car and some packages locked in the trunk. If the parking garage was not aware of the packages, it would probably not be a bailee of them as it did not knowingly accept possession of them.

Custody

A distinction is made between delivering **possession** of goods and merely giving **custody** of goods. If a shopkeeper entrusts goods to a clerk in the store, the shopkeeper is considered to have given the clerk custody of the goods but to have retained possession of them. Because the shopkeeper has retained legal possession, there has not been a bailment of goods to the clerk.

Types of Bailments

Bailments are commonly divided into three different categories:

1. Bailments for the sole benefit of the bailor.
2. Bailments for the sole benefit of the bailee.
3. Bailments for mutual benefit.

The type of bailment can be important in determining the liability of the bailee for loss of or damages to the property. However, some courts no longer rely on these distinctions for this purpose.

Bailments for Benefit of Bailor

A bailment for the sole benefit of the bailor is one in which the bailee renders some service but does not receive a benefit in return. For example, you allow your neighbor to park her car in your garage while she is on vacation and she does not pay you anything for the privilege. Your neighbor (bailor) has received a benefit from you (bailee), but you have not received a benefit in return.

LO7

Bailments for Benefit of Bailee

A bailment for the sole benefit of the bailee is one in which the owner of the goods allows someone else to use them free of charge. For example, you loan your lawn mower to your neighbor so he can cut his grass.

Mutual Benefit Bailments

If both the bailee and the bailor receive benefits from the bailment, it is a mutual benefit bailment. For example, you rent a U-Haul trailer from a store. You, the bailee, benefit by being able to use the trailer while the store benefits from your payment of the rental charge. Similarly, if you store some furniture at a commercial warehouse, it is a mutual benefit bailment. You get the benefit of having your goods cared for while the storage company benefits from the storage charge you pay. On some occasions, the benefit to the bailee is less tangible. Suppose you check your coat at an attended coatroom at a restaurant. Even if no charge is made for the service, it is likely to be treated as a mutual bailment because the restaurant is benefiting from your patronage.

Rights and Duties

LO8

Duties of the Bailee

The bailee has two basic duties: (1) to take reasonable care of the property that has been entrusted to him and (2) to return the property at the termination of the bailment.

Bailee's Duty of Care

The bailee is responsible for using **reasonable care** to protect the property during the time he has possession of it. If the bailee does not exercise reasonable care and the property is lost or damaged, the bailee is liable for negligence. Thus, the bailee would have to reimburse the bailor for the amount of loss or damage. If the property is lost or damaged without the fault or negligence of the bailee, the bailee is not liable to the bailor.

Whether the bailee in a particular case exercised reasonable care depends in part on who is benefiting from the bailment. If it is a mutual benefit bailment, then the bailee must use ordinary care, which is the same kind of care a reasonable person would use to protect his own property in that situation. If the bailee is a professional that holds itself out as a professional bailee—such as a warehouse—it must use the degree of care a person in that profession would use. This is likely to be more care than the ordinary person would use. In addition, there is usually a duty on a professional bailee to explain any loss or damage to property, that is, to show it was not negligent. If it cannot do so, it will be liable to the bailor.

If the bailment is solely for the benefit of the bailor, then the bailee may be held to a somewhat lower degree of care. If the bailee is doing you a favor, it is not reasonable to expect him to be as careful as when you are paying a bailee for keeping your goods. Usually, the bailee in this situation is liable only for gross negligence. On the other hand, if the bailment is for the sole benefit of the bailee, it is reasonable to expect that the bailee will use a higher degree of care. If you loan your sailboat to your neighbor, you probably expect her to be even more careful with it than you would be. In this situation, a bailee is liable for even slight negligence.

Who benefits from a bailment is one consideration in determining what is reasonable care. Other factors include the nature and value of the property, how easily it can be damaged or stolen, whether the bailment was paid for or free, and the experience of the bailee. Using reasonable care includes using the property only as was agreed between the parties. For example, you loan your lawn mower to your neighbor to cut his lawn. However, if he uses it to cut the weeds on a trash-filled vacant lot and the mower is damaged, he would be liable because he was exceeding the agreed purpose for the bailment—that is, to cut his lawn.

Bailee's Duty to Return the Property

One of the essential elements for a bailment is the duty of the bailee to return the property at the termination of the bailment. The bailee must return the goods in an undamaged condition to the bailor or to someone designated by the bailor. If the goods have been damaged or lost, there is a rebuttable presumption of negligence on the part of the bailee. To overcome the presumption, the bailee has the burden of showing that the accident, damage, or loss resulted from some cause consistent with the exercise of the relevant level of due care on his part.

In the case that follows, *Gyamfoah v. EG&G Dynatrend,* a warehouse that was unable to return goods that had been entrusted to it for safekeeping or to account for their disappearance was held liable to the bailor for the value of the goods.

Gyamfoah v. EG&G Dynatrend (now EG&G Technical Services)

51 UCC Rep. 2d 805 (E.D. Penn. 2003)

FACTS

On May 7, 1999, Yaa Gyamfoah, a citizen of Ghana, arrived at JFK International Airport with two suitcases containing a number of watches she had purchased in Hong Kong. The suitcases were seized by the United States Customs because they suspected the watches were counterfeit. Gyamfoah was given a receipt for 3,520 watches. The watches were transported to a warehouse operated by EG&G Dynatrend (EG&G), now known as EG&G Technical Services, under contract with the U.S. Department of Treasury to provide seized management services for all agencies of the department. The warehouse accepted and signed for the watches on June 2, 1999.

On October 13, U.S. Customs advised Gyamfoah's agent that the non-violative (ones that were not counterfeit) portion of the seizure (2,940 watches) would be released upon payment of $1,470. On November 18, a Customs agent,

(continued)

Gyamfoah v. EG&G Dynatrend (now EG&G Technical Services) *(concluded)*

observed by EG&G's warehouse supervisor, separated the watches into a group of 580 "violative" watches, which were placed in a carton, and 2,940 "non-violative" watches, which were placed back in the suitcases. The carton and the suitcases were then returned to the custody of EG&G. When the Customs agent returned on November 24 to again, under the observation of the warehouse supervisor, examine the watches, there were only 1,002 watches in the carton and suitcases; some 2,518 were missing.

Gyamfoah subsequently brought suit against the United States and EG&G. The claim against the United States was dismissed and the case went to trial on the claim against EG&G. At the trial, EG&G was able to show that it had taken reasonable precautions against loss by having the watches shrink-wrapped to a pallet and stored in a secured area on a high shelf that required a forklift to be reached. Moreover, the area in which it was stored was armed and only EG&G employees were allowed to enter. However, it was unable to explain what happened to the missing watches.

ISSUE

Is EG&G liable for the missing watches whose disappearance it could not explain?

DECISION

Yes. The court noted that under the common law of bailment, the bailor must first present a *prima facie* case of conversion by proving: (1) delivery of the bailed goods to the bailee; (2) demand for return of the bailed goods from the bailor; and (3) failure of the bailee to return the bailed goods. Once the bailee has proved these points, the burden shifts to the bailee to show how the bailed goods were lost. If the bailee cannot prove how the bailed goods were lost, the bailee is liable for conversion. Here, EG&G was unable to rebut the presumption of negligence that arises from its failure to produce the watches or explain their disappearance.

In most instances, the bailee must return the identical property that was bailed. If you loan your 1999 Jeep to your friend, you expect to have that particular car returned to you. In some cases, the bailor does not expect the identical goods back. For example, if a farmer stores 1,500 bushels of wheat at a local grain elevator, that farmer expects to get back 1,500 bushels of similar wheat when the bailment is terminated, but not the identical wheat that he deposited.

The bailee is also liable to the bailor if she misdelivers the bailed property at the termination of the bailment. The property must be returned to the bailor or to someone specified by the bailor.

Limitations on Liability

Bailees may try to limit or relieve themselves of liability for the bailed property. Common examples include the signs near checkrooms, "Not responsible for loss or damage to checked property," and **disclaimers** on claim checks, "Goods left at owner's risk." Any attempt by the bailee to be relieved of liability for intentional wrongful acts is against public policy and will not be enforced.

A bailee's ability to be relieved of liability for negligence is also limited. The courts look to see whether the disclaimer or limitation of liability was *communicated* to the bailor. Did the attendant point out the sign near the checkroom to the person when the coat was checked? Did the parking lot attendant call the person's attention to the disclaimer on the back of the claim check? If not, the court may hold that the disclaimer was not communicated to the bailee and did not become part of the bailment contract. Even if the bailee was aware of the disclaimer, it still may not be enforced on the ground that it is contrary to public policy.

Courts do not look with favor on efforts by a person to be relieved of liability for negligence. We expect people to use reasonable care and to be liable if they do not and someone or something is injured as a result. If the disclaimer was offered on a take-it-or-leave-it basis and was not the subject of arm's-length bargaining, it is not likely to be enforced. A bailee may be able to limit liability to a certain amount. Ideally, the bailee will give the bailor a chance to declare a higher value and to pay an additional charge to be protected up to the declared value of the goods. Common carriers such as railroads and trucking companies often take this approach.

In the case that follows, *Weissman v. City of New York*, the court refused to enforce an exculpatory clause to protect the city against its negligence in storing a kayak at a marina owned and operated by the city.

Weissman v. City of New York

(860 N.Y.S.2d 393 (City of N.Y., Civil Court 2009))

FACTS

In 2005, Ken Weissman rented storage space at the West 79th Street Boat Basin which is owned and operated by the City of New York Parks & Recreation Department. The written agreement contained an exculpatory clause which stated:

> I understand that the city of New York Parks & Recreation department will not be responsible for any damages incurred to my vessel while at the dinghy dock or while in the facility at the 79th Street Boat Basin, and that I store my vessel at my own risk.

The policy and practice at the facility was that users would store their vessels in an enclosed cagelike structure which had storage bins. Each user had a key to the storage area and had unrestricted access. Within the cage, users could further secure their vessels to the bin with their own devices such as chain and lock.

In 2007, Weissman had two brand new kayaks stolen from the caged area. The lock to the caged area was intact but his kayaks and locks were missing. Weissman reported this theft to the police, staff, and management. He indicated to the Boat Basin that he was no longer going to use the facility because of the theft. The manger of the facility spoke to him and urged him to continue to use the facility because they were changing their practice and policy by adding more security measures. Only West 79th Street boat Basin employees would have keys to the caged storage area. Users no longer had unrestricted access and would have to get an employee to escort them, open the lock, and admit them to the storage area. Security cameras were going to be installed.

The Boat Basin posted a notice with the new changes which said:

> Attention Kayak Owners
>
> Please see marina staff to gain access to kayak storage area. We have had a security issue and have temporarily changed the locks. We will be adding security cameras to the area shortly. We apologize for any inconvenience in the meantime.

Based on the assurances by the manager that the security would be better, Weissman purchased two used kayaks and again stored them in the caged area. He and the others no longer had keys to the area and had to be admitted and escorted by an employee to access the vessels in the storage area. On or about July 23, 2007, a week after the first two kayaks were stolen, one of Weissman's replacement kayaks, which cost $1,400, was missing from the storage area. He filed a notice of claim and then brought suit against the City of New York, seeking the value of the missing kayak and a refund of the unused portion of the storage fee. The city contended that the exculpatory clause in the initial contract protected it against any liability for negligence on its part.

ISSUE

Did the exculpatory clause protect the city from any liability for damages attributable to its negligence?

DECISION

The general rule is that a marina is not liable for negligence for loss of a vessel not due to the condition of the docking facility. The privilege of keeping a vessel in a marina without an agreement to keep daily or continuous guard over the vessel or without the marina taking over or assuming custody of the vessel does not constitute a bailment. This was initially the situation under the original arrangement between Weissman and the Boat Basin. Weissman had exclusive custody of his vessels and unrestricted access because he had a key to the storage area. He had the privilege of storing his kayaks there but Boat Basin was not an insurer.

However, the arrangement between the parties changed when Boat Basin took custody of the kayaks by retaining

(continued)

Weissman v. City of New York *(concluded)*

the key and controlling access to the kayaks, notifying users that this was the new temporary policy, promising better security, and urging Weissman to keep his kayaks there because of the new security measures. Under these facts, a bailment was established.

A bailment gives rise to the duty of exercising ordinary care in keeping and safeguarding property. In the instant case, Weissman made out a prima facie case of breach of that duty by establishing that Boat Basin had exclusive possession of the kayak under lock and key and that the kayak was now missing. It then became the obligation of the Boat Basin to come forward with evidence to rebut the presumption of negligence. Here, Boat Basin did not come forward with any evidence and argued that it had no duty of care. However, when Boat Basin took exclusive possession of Weissman's kayak and urged him to continue using the facility because of its improved security, it created the duty of ordinary care in safeguarding the property.

Boat Basin argued that it cannot be held liable for negligence because of the exculpatory clause in the original 2005 contract which Weissman conceded was subsequently renewed by his yearly payments. Although exculpatory clauses are enforceable, they are strictly construed against the party seeking exemption from liability. Unless the intention of the parties to insulate one of them from liability for its own negligence is expressed in unequivocal terms, the clause will not operate to have such an effect.

The exculpatory clause in this case is vague and does not suggest an intent to shield Boat Basin from its own negligence in carrying out its duty to care for Weissman's kayak. This makes perfect sense because the city did not initially have any duty to safeguard Weissman's vessel. There was no bailment. Weissman had the key to the storage cage and retained custody and control of his kayak. He stored the vessel at his own risk and the Boat Basin would not be responsible for any damages. This was the intent of the exculpatory clause.

However, the relationship changed when Boat Basin took it upon itself to secure and take control of Weissman's vessel. Boat Basin had the only key and assured Weissman that his kayaks would be safer under Boat Basin's custody because of the heightened security. The initial contract could not have been meant to cover this new arrangement. The court held that under the facts of this case, a bailment was created and Boat Basin was negligent by breaching its duty of care. The exculpatory clause in the original contract was too vague to shield Boat Basin from liability for its own negligence. The court granted Judgment in favor of Weissman for $1,400, the value of the missing kayak.

Right to Compensation

Whether a bailee is paid for keeping property or must pay for the right to use it depends on the bailment contract or the understanding of the parties. If the bailment is a favor, then the bailee is not entitled to compensation even though the bailment is for the benefit of the bailor. If the bailment is the rental of property, then the bailee must pay the agreed-on rental rate. If the bailment is for the storage or repair of property, then the bailee is entitled to the contract price for the storage or repair services. If no price is agreed on, the bailee gets the reasonable value of the services provided.

In many instances, the bailee will have a **lien** on the bailed property for the reasonable value of the services. Suppose you take a chair to an upholsterer to have it recovered. This is a mutual benefit bailment. When the chair has been recovered, the upholsterer has the right to keep it until you pay the agreed price or—if no price was set—the reasonable value of the work. (Artisan's liens are discussed in Chapter 42.)

Bailor's Liability for Defects in the Bailed Property

When personal property is rented or loaned, the bailor makes an **implied warranty** that there are no hidden defects in the property that make it unsafe for use. If the bailment is for the sole benefit of the bailee, then the bailor is liable for injuries that result from defects in the bailed property only if the bailor knew about the defects and did not tell the bailee. For example, Paul loans his car, which has bad brakes, to Sally. If Paul does not tell Sally about the bad brakes and if Sally is injured in an accident because the brakes fail, Paul is liable for Sally's injuries.

If the bailment is a mutual benefit bailment, then the bailor has a larger obligation. The bailor must use reasonable care in inspecting the property and seeing that it is safe for the purpose for which it is rented. The bailor is liable for injuries suffered by the bailee because of defects that the bailor either knew about or should have discovered by reasonable inspection. For example, Frank's Rent-All rents trailers. Suppose Frank's does not inspect the trailers after they come back from being rented. A wheel has come loose on a trailer that Frank's rents to Harold. If the wheel comes off while Harold is using the trailer and the goods Harold is carrying in the trailer are damaged, Frank's is liable to Harold.

In addition, product liability doctrines that apply a higher standard of legal responsibility have been applied to bailors who are commercial lessors of personal property. This includes express and implied warranties of quality under either Article 2 or Article 2A of the UCC. Thus, if goods are rented to someone (mutual benefit bailment) for her personal use, there may be an *implied warranty* that the goods are fit for the purpose for which they are rented. Liability does not depend on whether the bailor knew about or should have discovered the defect. The only question is whether the property was fit for the purpose for which it was rented.

Some courts have also imposed **strict liability** on lessors/bailors of goods that turn out to be more dangerous than the lessee/bailee would have expected. This liability is imposed regardless of whether the lessor was negligent or at fault. Implied warranties and strict liability were discussed in detail in Chapter 20.

Concept Summary: Duties of Bailees and Bailors

Type of Bailment	Duties of Bailee	Duties of Bailor
Sole benefit of bailee	1. Must use great care; liable for even slight negligence. 2. Must use goods consistent with bailment agreement. 3. Must return goods to bailor or dispose of them at his direction. 4. May have duty to compensate.	1. Must notify the bailee of any known defects.
Mutual benefit	1. Must use reasonable care; liable for ordinary negligence. 2. Must use goods consistent with bailment agreement. 3. Must return goods to bailor or dispose of them at his direction. 4. May have duty to pay reasonable compensation.	1. Must notify the bailee of all known defects and any hidden defects that are known or could be discovered on reasonable inspection. 2. Commercial lessors may be subject to warranties of quality and/or strict liability in tort. 3. May have duty to compensate bailee.
Sole benefit of bailor	1. Must use at least slight care; liable for gross negligence. 2. Must use goods consistent with bailment agreement. 3. Must return goods to bailor or dispose of them at his direction.	1. Must notify bailee of all known defects and any hidden defects that are known or could be discovered on reasonable inspection. 2. May have duty to compensate bailee.

Special Bailment Situations

Common Carriers

LO9

Bailees who are **common carriers** are held to a higher level of responsibility than bailees who are private carriers. Common carriers are persons who are licensed by government agencies to carry the property of anyone who requests the service. The rates and terms under which a common carrier will carry property are normally subject to the approval of these government agencies. **Private contract** carriers are persons who carry goods only for persons selected by the carrier.

Both common carriers and private contract carriers are bailees. However, the law makes the common carrier the **absolute insurer** of the goods it carries. The common carrier is responsible for any loss or damage to goods entrusted to it. The common carrier can avoid responsibility only if it can show that the loss or damage was caused by (1) an act of God, (2) an act of a public enemy, (3) an act or order of the government, (4) an act of the person who shipped the goods, or (5) the nature of the goods themselves.

The common carrier is liable if goods entrusted to it are stolen by some unknown person but not if the goods are destroyed when a tornado hits its warehouse. If the shipper improperly packages or crates the goods and this results in their being damaged, then the carrier is not liable. Similarly, if perishable goods are not in suitable condition to be shipped and deteriorate in the course of shipment, the carrier is not liable so long as it uses reasonable care in handling them. Common carriers are usually permitted to limit their liability to a stated value unless the bailor declares a higher value for the property and pays an additional fee.

E-Commerce

ONLINE TRACKING OF BAILMENTS

To lower package loss and increase consumer confidence, many large shipping companies such as UPS and FedEx provide an online tracking system. The tracking system is used by companies to identify and trace all packages as they move through the company's system to their destination. Often a package is assigned a tracking code or number that the customer, using an online mapping system, can use to locate the package. If a package is feared to be lost, Internet access to the tracking system allows customers immediate confirmation of its location in route, or place and time of delivery. The confidence that Internet tracking systems give consumers increases the possibility that they will become repeat customers. Furthermore, the tracking system reveals the company's internal systems of operation to the consumer. This transparency of operation creates a forcing function that encourages companies to be certain that their shipping system is in smooth working order. Also, companies can view the tracking system to determine what shipping routes their competitors are using. Finally, the online tracking system saves a company money by lowering the cost of paying for representatives to deal with customer inquiries.

Hotelkeepers

Hotelkeepers are engaged in the business of offering lodging and/or food to transient persons. They hold themselves out to serve the public and are obligated to do so. Like the common carrier, the hotelkeeper is held to a higher standard of care than the ordinary bailee.

The hotelkeeper is not a bailee in the strict sense of the word. The guest does not usually surrender the exclusive possession of her property to the hotelkeeper. However, the hotelkeeper is treated as the virtual insurer of the guest's property. The hotelkeeper is not liable for loss of or damage to property if he can show that it was caused by (1) an act of God, (2) an act of a public enemy, (3) an act of government authority, (4) the fault of a member of the guest's party, or (5) the nature of the goods.

Most states have passed laws that limit the hotelkeeper's liability. Commonly, they require the hotel owner to post a notice advising guests that any valuables should be checked into the hotel vault. The hotelkeeper's liability is then limited for valuables that are not so checked.

Safe-Deposit Boxes

If you rent a safe-deposit box at a local bank and place some property in the box, the box and the property are in manual possession of the bank. However, it takes both your key and the key held by the bank to open the box, and in most cases the bank does not know the nature, amount, or value of the goods in your box. Although a few courts have held the rental of a safe-deposit box to be a lease, not a bailment, most courts have found that the renter of the box is a bailor and the bank a bailee. As such, the bank is not an insurer of the contents of the box. However, it is obligated to use due care and to come forward and explain loss or damage to the property entrusted to it.

Involuntary Bailments

Suppose you own a cottage near a lake. After a violent storm, you find a sailboat washed up on your beach. You may be considered the **involuntary bailee** or **constructive bailee** of the sailboat. This relationship may arise when you find yourself in possession of property that belongs to someone else without having agreed to accept possession.

The duties of the involuntary bailee are not well defined. The bailee does not have the right to destroy the property or to use it. If the true owner shows up, the property must be returned to the owner. Under some circumstances, the involuntary bailee may be under an obligation to assume control of the property and/or to take some minimal steps to ascertain who the owner is.

Questions and Problem Cases

1. Leonard Charrier was an amateur archeologist. After researching colonial maps and records, he concluded that the Trudeau Plantation near Angola, Louisiana, was the possible site of an ancient village of the Tunica Indians. Charrier obtained the permission of the caretaker of the Trudeau Plantation to survey the property with a metal detector for possible burial locations. At the time, he mistakenly believed that the caretaker was the Plantation's owner. He located and, over the next three years, excavated approximately 150 burial sites containing beads, European ceramics, stoneware, and glass bottles; iron kettles, vessels, and skillets; knives, muskets, gunflints, balls, and shots; crucifixes, rings, and bracelets; and native pottery. He began discussions with Harvard University to sell the collection to its Peabody Museum. While the university inventoried, cataloged, and displayed the items pursuant to a lease agreement, it was unwilling to go through with a sale unless Charrier could establish title to the artifacts. He then brought suit against the owners of the Trudeau Plantation seeking a declaratory judgment that he was the owner of the artifacts. The state of Louisiana intervened in the litigation to assert the rights of the lawful heirs of the artifacts. Charrier argued

that the Indians abandoned the artifacts when they moved from the Trudeau Plantation in 1764. He contended that they were unowned property until he found them and reduced them to his possession. He compared them to wild game and fish, which are unowned until someone takes possession of them. Were the artifacts abandoned property of which Charrier could become the owner by taking possession?

2. Alex Franks was staying at a Comfort Inn in Searcy, Arkansas, while working on a highway project. He checked into the hotel on Monday, September 10. Two days later, after he had checked out and returned to his room to retrieve some laundry, he discovered $14,200 in plain view in a drawer of the dresser in the room. It was wrapped tightly with masking tape, like a brick, with some of the money showing. Franks notified the hotel manager, who in turn notified the police. The police determined that there were two bundles of money separated by denominations and then bundled together. The bundle contained 46 one-hundred dollar bills and 480 twenty-dollar bills. The officer who took custody of the money testified that the money appeared to be intentionally and meticulously wrapped because all the bills faced in the same direction. Franks brought suit against the city of Searcy claiming the money. The city joined the owners of the hotel as third-party defendants and then withdrew any claim on its part to the money. Should the court hold that the money is abandoned, lost, or mislaid? Between Franks and the owner of the hotel, who has the best right to it? Why?

3. Hunter Taylor lived with Hattie Smith. Taylor rented a safe-deposit box at the Crown Center Bank in the name of Hattie Smith and gave her both keys to the box. Smith signed a card that authorized and directed the bank to allow Hunter Taylor to enter "my box" at any time. On several occasions, Taylor borrowed the keys to the box without explanation and then returned them to Smith. Smith claimed that Taylor told her he had put money in the box for her. Smith did not see Taylor put any money in the box, and none was put in the day the box was rented. Taylor was murdered, and at the time of the murder he had both of the keys to the box in his possession. Smith had the box opened by the bank, and $8,000 was found in it. The administrator of Taylor's estate claimed the money was for the estate. Smith claimed that the money was a gift to her. Had Taylor made a valid gift of money to Smith?

4. Charles Miller and Nicolette Chiaia met each other through work in 2007 and began a relationship. In October 2008 Miller moved into Chiaia's home where she lived with her minor children from a prior marriage. Miller had also been married and was recently divorced. The parties living arrangement was predicated on a mutual belief that they would become engaged and would marry. In early November 2008, the parties took a trip to Italy during which Miller proposed and presented Chiaia with a ring. She accepted the proposal and the ring. Subsequently she asked Miller where he had purchased the ring, was disappointed with the answer, and gave it back to him. When they got back from Italy, Miller took the ring back to the seller and received a full refund of the amount he had paid, $5,000. Chiaia suggested the style of a different ring she would like and Miller purchased one like it from a jeweler for $12,000. Miller then "reproposed" and presented Chiaia with the second ring.

   Over the next few months, Miller, who was self-employed, had business difficulties that caused friction between the parties and the relationship soured. In February 2009, Miller moved out of Chiaia's house and the parties never reconciled. Miller asked for the ring back but Chiaia refused. Miller then brought a lawsuit, seeking return of the ring. Chiaia contended that there had been a completed gift and that she owned the ring. Miller claimed that it was a conditional gift given at the time of the engagement and in contemplation of marriage. Is Miller entitled to recover the ring from Chiaia?

5. R. B. Bewley and his family drove to Kansas City to attend a week-long church convention. When they arrived at the hotel where they had reservations, they were unable to park their car and unload their luggage because of a long line of cars. They then drove to a nearby parking lot where they took a ticket, causing the gate arm to open, and drove in 15 or 20 feet. A parking attendant told them that the lot was full, that they should leave the keys with him, and that he would park the car. They told the attendant that they had reservations at a nearby hotel and that after they checked in they would come back for their luggage. Subsequently, someone broke into the Bewley's car and stole their personal property from the car and its trunk. Was the parking lot a bailee of the property?

6. On September 2, Deborah Jones signed a storage rental agreement with Econo-Self Storage owned by Ernie Hanna. Jones needed to store her personal belongings and furniture because of the flooding of her apartment. The self-storage agreement was written as a lease and designated the parties as landlord and tenant. The warehouse space leased by Jones was 10 feet by 10 feet, on a monthly term of $45. The agreement provided in part: "All property kept, stored, or maintained within the premises by Tenant shall be at Tenant's sole risk."

   On May 2, Jones learned that the lock to her storage unit had been cut and virtually all of her possessions were stolen. The circumstances of the theft were not known. The storage units, 180 in all, were protected by a 6-foot fence and a locked gate. The tenants placed their own locks on the units. No security dogs or watchmen were provided. Access could be made to the units between 6am and 9pm daily. No inventory was made of the goods by the facility owner, and the goods were never placed in his hands and he did not know what was stored. Jones brought suit to recover damages for the loss of her property. Was Econo-Self Storage the bailee of Jones's goods?

7. On March 27, 2001, Felice Jasphy brought three fur coats to Illana Osinsky's establishment trading as Cedar Lane Furs in Teaneck, New Jersey, for storage and cleaning. The three coats included a ranch mink coat, a Shearling, and a blush mink. In addition to storage of the three coats, Jasphy also sought cleaning of the ranch mink. In 1997, the ranch mink had been appraised for $11,500, the Shearling for $3,500, and the blush mink for $3,995.

   Jasphy signed a written agreement, labeled "fur storage sales receipt," that included Jasphy's name and address, and the price of the storage and cleaning. On the back of the receipt, the following preprinted provision limiting Cedar Lane Furs' liability read:

   > This receipt is a storage contract, articles listed are accepted for storage until December 31, of dated year, subject to the terms and conditions hereof, in accepting this receipt, the depositor agrees to be bound by all its terms and conditions and acknowledges that this receipt is the entire agreement with the furrier, which cannot be changed except by endorsement herein signed by the furrier. If no value is specified, or if no separate insurance covering the garment is declared at the time of issuance of this receipt, insurance in the amount of $1.00 will be placed on the garment.

   Immediately above the location on the receipt for a customer's signature, the following was printed: "I understand and agree that Cedar Lane Furs' liability for loss or damage from any cause whatsoever, including their own negligence or that of employees and others, is limited to the declared valuation."

   Jasphy did not state the value of the coats or declare whether she had separate insurance coverage when the receipt was issued. There is no identifiable room provided on the receipt to specify such information. The limitation of the furrier's liability was not brought to Jasphy's attention, nor was she asked to furnish the value of her coats for storage.

The following day, March 28, 2001, a fire swept through Cedar Lane Furs, causing Jasphy's furs to be completely destroyed. A hot iron, which Cedar Lane Furs employees apparently forgot to unplug overnight, caused the fire. Jasphy subsequently learned that her furs had not been place in the fur vault before the fire and were destroyed in the fire. Jasphy filed a claim form with Cedar Lane Furs' insurance company but never received any reimbursement. She then brought suit against Osinsky and Cedar Lane Furs. They contended that their liability was limited by the contract provision to $1 per garment. Should the court enforce the contractual provision limiting the furrier's liability to $1 per garment?

8. Marie Wallinga was staying at the Commodore Hotel. She had her son take her two diamond rings to the hotel clerk for safekeeping. The rings were shown to the clerk and then placed in a "safe-deposit envelope," which was sealed. The son received a depositor's check stub, which had a number corresponding to the number on the envelope. He also signed his name on the safe-deposit envelope. Both the stub and his signature were necessary to get the envelope back. The envelopes were kept in a safe located in the hotel's front office, which was four to five feet behind the reception desk. The safe was used to keep cash for use in the hotel as well as the valuables of guests. The safe was equipped with a combination lock but for many years it had never been locked. A clerk was always on duty at the reception desk. One morning, at 3:30 AM, the hotel was robbed by two armed men, and Wallinga's rings were taken. She sued the hotel for the value of the rings. The hotel claimed that the robbery relieved it of liability for them. Was the hotelkeeper liable for the theft of property left with it for safekeeping?

Chapter 34

Real Property

Learning Objectives

After you have studied this chapter, you should be able to:

1. Define the term *fixture* and list the factors that are considered in determining whether an item of personal property has become a fixture.
2. List and describe the various kinds of interests that can be created in real property.
3. List and discuss the seven types of co-ownership of real property recognized in the United States.
4. Identify and explain the different methods of obtaining title to real property.
5. Discuss the steps in the sale and purchase of real property.
6. Explain the difference between a *quitclaim deed* and a *warranty deed.*
7. Identify and discuss the three major constraints that society places on owners of real property.

As a businessperson, investor, or consumer, you are likely to acquire an interest in real property at some time during your life. Suppose that you decide to acquire a cottage on Lake Michigan to use as a summer vacation home for your family and to rent out at times when you are not planning on occupying it. You engage a real estate broker who indicates she has listings of such property for sale, and she takes you to visit one possibility. As you arrive at the property, you see that an old ship's anchor has been embedded in concrete near the road and a mailbox welded to it. As you look over the cottage, you note that old hurricane lanterns have been wired to serve as light fixtures both outside the entrances as well as in the interior, and artifacts taken from ships have been attached to the walls. The property has a dock that extends into the lake; while you are looking out at the lake, someone arrives in a motorboat, ties it up at the dock, and then walks across the property to an adjacent cottage. As you and the agent retire to the local village to discuss over

(continued)

a cup of coffee your making an offer on the property, your eye is drawn to the headline in the local paper that someone left in the booth where you are sitting. It indicates that the mayor is proposing that the village exercise the right of eminent domain to acquire some "substandard" cottages along the lake and resell the property to a developer interested in putting up an "upscale" condo that would produce greater tax revenues for the village.

This hypothetical situation raises a number of questions that we will consider in this chapter. These include:

1. When is personal property, such as the lanterns, the ship artifacts, and the anchor, treated as part of the real property?
2. What kinds of interests can be acquired in real property? For example, what rights might the neighbor who uses the dock and walks across the property to get to his own property have—and what rights would you have if you bought the property?
3. What are the various steps and aspects involved in purchasing real property? For example, when is a broker entitled to a commission on the sale of property?
4. What are the controls that society places on a person's ability to use his property, and under what circumstances can the government take private property?

Scope of Real Property

Real property includes not only land but also things firmly attached to or embedded in land. Buildings and other permanent structures are thus considered real property. Unlike readily movable personal property, real property is immovable or attached to something immovable. Distinguishing between real and personal property is important because rules of law governing real property transactions such as sale, taxation, and inheritance are frequently different from those applied to personal property transactions.

Fixtures

LO1

An item of personal property may, however, be attached to or used in conjunction with real property in such a way that it ceases being personal property and instead becomes part of the real property. This type of property is called a **fixture.**

Fixtures belong to the owner of the real property. One who provides or attaches fixtures to real property without a request to that effect from the owner of the real property is normally not entitled to compensation from the owner. A conveyance (transfer of ownership) of real property also transfers the fixtures associated with that property, even if the fixtures are not specifically mentioned.

People commonly install items of personal property on the real property they own or rent. Disputes may arise regarding rights to such property. Suppose that Jacobsen buys an elaborate ceiling fan and installs it in his home. When he sells the house to Orr, may Jacobsen remove the ceiling fan, or is it part of the home Orr has bought? Suppose that

Luther, a commercial tenant, installs showcases and tracklights in the store she leases from Nelson. May Luther remove the showcases and the lights when her lease expires, or do the items now belong to Nelson? If the parties' contracts are silent on these matters, courts will resolve the cases by applying the *law of fixtures.* As later discussion will reveal, Jacobsen probably cannot remove the ceiling fan because it is likely to be considered part of the real property purchased by Orr. Luther, on the other hand, may be entitled to remove the showcases and the lights under the special rules governing trade fixtures.

Factors Indicating Whether an Item Is a Fixture

There is no mechanical formula for determining whether an item has become a fixture. As the *Chevron USA* case, which follows shortly, reveals, courts tend to consider these factors:

1. *Attachment.* One factor helping to indicate whether an item is a fixture is the degree to which the item is **attached** or **annexed** to real property. If firmly attached to real property so that it cannot be removed without damaging the property, the item is likely to be considered a fixture. An item of personal property that may be removed with little or no injury to the property is less likely to be considered a fixture.

Actual physical attachment to real property is not necessary, however. A close physical connection between an item of personal property and certain real property may enable a court to conclude that the item is **constructively annexed.** For example, heavy machinery or remote control devices for automatic garage doors may be considered fixtures even though they are not physically attached to real property.

2. *Adaptation.* Another factor to be considered is **adaptation**—the degree to which the item's use is necessary or beneficial to the use of the real property. Adaptation is a particularly relevant factor when the item is not physically attached to the real property or is only slightly attached. When an item would be of little value except for use with certain real property, the item is likely to be considered a fixture even if it is unattached or could easily be removed. For example, keys and custom-sized window screens and storm windows have been held to be fixtures.

3. *Intent.* The third factor to be considered is the **intent** of the person who installed the item. Intent is judged not by what that person subjectively intended, but by what the circumstances indicate he intended. To a great extent, intent is indicated by the annexation and adaptation factors. An owner of real property who improves it by attaching items of personal property presumably intended those items to become part of the real estate. If the owner does not want an attached item to be considered a fixture, he must specifically reserve the right to keep the item. For instance, if a seller of a house wants to keep an antique chandelier that has been installed in the house, she should either replace the chandelier before the house is shown to prospective purchasers or specify in the contract of sale that the chandelier will be excluded from the sale.

In the following case, *Chevron U.S.A., Inc. v. Sheikhpour*, the court held that underground fuel tanks on property used as a gas station were fixtures and not personal property that could be removed by the owner when he sold the real property.

Express Agreement

If the parties to an express agreement have clearly stated their intent about whether a particular item is to be considered a fixture, a court will generally enforce that agreement. For example, the buyer and seller of a house might agree to permit the seller to remove a fence or shrubbery that would otherwise be considered a fixture.

Chevron U.S.A., Inc. v. Sheikhpour

2011 U.S. Dist. LEXIS 19566 (U.S.D.C., C.D. Cal. 2011)

FACTS

In July 2007, Chevron sued to enforce a contract that it had made with Sheikhpour that entitled Chevron to buy and remodel Sheikhpour's Manhattan Beach gas station. The parties entered into a settlement agreement that required Sheikhpour to complete certain reconstruction obligations by October 31, 2009. When he failed to complete the reconstruction by the deadline, Chevron obtained an order enforcing the settlement agreement and ordering Sheikhpour to convey the station to Chevron. Chevron's efforts to possess the property were met with additional objections from Sheikhpour.

In December 2010, Sheikhpour requested continuing access to the property for 14 days to remove his "personal property," including "equipment, supplies, materials, security fence, etc." The parties then executed a release and indemnification agreement, which authorized Sheikhpoiur to access the property during a two-week period for the sole purpose of removing the personal property. Several days after the agreement was signed, Sheikhpour informed Chevron that he intended to dig up and remove the fuel storage tanks. The tanks, which were valued at about $120,000, sat in a tank pit area and were covered by gravel.

Both parties filed motions with the court seeking an order resolving the question whether Sheikhpour was entitled to remove the fuel storage tanks.

ISSUE

Were the fuel storage tanks personal property that could be removed by Sheikpour?

DECISION

No. The court began by noting that the release and indemnification agreement, which authorized the removal of Sheikhpour's "personal property," was the only viable source of Sheikhpour's putative right to remove the tanks. Nothing in the express contractual language, the prior dealing between the parties, or the ordinary understanding of the term *personal property* gives rise to the conclusion that the parties understood personal property under the agreement to include the underground fuel storage tanks in its definitional scope.

This conclusion is also consonant with California law regarding fixtures. In determining whether an item is a fixture, California courts consider three factors: (1) physical annexation; (20 adaptions to sue with the property; and (3) intention to annex to realty. As to the first factor, California courts consider heavy machinery physically annexed to property even where the machinery is attached only by gravity. Thus, here the first factor is satisfied because the fuel tanks are heavy machinery that can be annexed to property, even if attached only by gravity. In fact, the tanks here were not only annexed to the property by gravity due to their large size—they were actually buried under gravel.

Second, the court concluded that the second factor, adaption to use of the property, was satisfied. The fuel tanks were specifically adapted to the use of the gas station because they were inserted into the ground and covered with gravel. The third element of intent, regarded as a crucial and overwhelming factor in the analysis, was also met. Given that the fuel storage tanks were highly necessary to the gas station and could serve almost other use than gasoline storage, it was reasonable to infer that Sheikhpour intended the tanks to become annexed to the property.

Therefore, as all three elements were satisfied, the court concluded that the fuel tanks were fixtures, not personal property, under California law.

Trade Fixtures

An exception to the usual fixture rules is recognized when a tenant attaches personal property to leased premises for the purpose of carrying on her trade or business. Such fixtures, called **trade fixtures,** remain the tenant's personal property and may normally be removed at the termination of the lease. This trade fixtures exception encourages commerce and industry. It recognizes that the commercial tenant who affixed the item of personal property did not intend a permanent improvement of the leased premises.

The tenant's right to remove trade fixtures is subject to two limitations. First, the tenant cannot remove the fixtures if doing so would cause substantial damage to the landlord's realty. Second, the tenant must remove the fixtures by the end of the lease if the lease is for a definite period. If the lease is for an indefinite period, the tenant usually has a reasonable time after the expiration of the lease to remove the fixtures. Trade fixtures not removed within the appropriate time become the landlord's property.

Leases may contain terms expressly addressing the parties' rights in any fixtures. A lease might give the tenant the right to attach items or make other improvements, and to remove them later. The reverse may also be true. The lease could state that any improvements made or fixtures attached will become the landlord's property at the termination of the lease. Courts generally enforce parties' agreements on fixture ownership.

Security Interests in Fixtures

Special rules apply to personal property subject to a lien or security interest at the time it is attached to real property. Assume, for example, that a person buys a dishwasher on a time-payment plan from an appliance store and has it installed in his kitchen. To protect itself, the appliance store takes a security interest in the dishwasher and perfects that interest by filing a financing statement in the appropriate real estate records office within the period of time specified by the Uniform Commercial Code. The appliance store then is able to remove the dishwasher if the buyer defaults on his payments. The store could be liable, however, to third parties such as prior real estate mortgagees for any damage removal of the dishwasher caused to the real estate. The rules governing security interest in personal property that will become fixtures are explained more fully in Chapter 43.

Concept Summary: Fixtures

Concept
A *fixture* is an item of personal property attached to or used in conjunction with real property in such a way that it is treated as being part of the real property.

Significance
A *conveyance* of the real property will also convey the fixtures on that property.

Factors Considered in Determining Whether Property Is a Fixture

1. Attachment: Is the item physically attached or closely connected to the real property?
2. Adaptation: How necessary or beneficial is the item to the use of the real property?
3. Intent: Did the person who installed the item manifest intent for the property to become part of the real property?

Express Agreement
Express agreements clearly stating intent about whether property is a fixture are generally enforceable.

Trade Fixtures (Tenants' Fixtures)
Definition of *trade fixtures:* personal property attached to leased real property by a tenant for the purpose of carrying on his trade or business.

Trade fixtures can be removed and retained by the tenant at the termination of the lease except when one or more of the following apply:

1. Removal would cause substantial damage to the landlord's real property.
2. Tenant fails to remove the fixtures by the end of the lease (or within a reasonable time, if the lease is for an indefinite period of time).
3. An express agreement between the landlord and tenant provides otherwise.

Rights and Interests in Real Property

LO2

When we think of ownership of real property, we normally think of somebody owning all the rights in a particular piece of land. However, a variety of different interests can be created in a particular piece of land, and it is possible to divide those interests among a number of people. The interests include leases, licenses, easements, life estates, and mineral or timber rights.

Fee Simple

The **fee simple** is the basic land ownership interest in the United States. A person who owns real property in fee simple has the right to the entire property for an unlimited period of time and the unconditional power to dispose of it either during his lifetime or on his death. If the person does not make a will, the land will automatically pass to the person's heirs on his death. A person who owns land in fee simple may grant many rights to others without giving up the ownership of his fee simple interest.

For example, Arnold, who has a fee simple interest in land, may give Bob a mortgage on the land, grant Cindy an easement or right-of-way across the land, and lease the land to a farmer for a period of time. Arnold has granted rights to Bob, Cindy, and the farmer, but Bob still owns the land in fee simple. When the rights of Bob, Cindy, and the farmer terminate, they pass back to Arnold and again become part of his bundle of ownership rights.

Life Estate

A **life estate** is a property interest that gives a person the right to use property only for his own lifetime or for a time that is measured by the lifetime of somebody else. A person who has a life estate in a piece of real property has the right to use the property but does not have the right to commit acts that will result in permanent injury to the property.

Leasehold

A **lease** gives the tenant the right to occupy and use a particular piece of property. This right may be for a fixed period of time such as a month or year. If no time period is specified, then it is known as a **tenancy at will.** Under a tenancy at will, either the landlord or the tenant can terminate the leasehold after giving notice to the other person of her intention to do so. The law of landlord and tenant will be discussed in Chapter 35.

Easement

A person may have the right to use or enjoy the land of another person but not to actually occupy it on a long-term basis; this is known as an **easement.** An easement can be either an affirmative or a negative easement. An **affirmative easement** is the right to make certain uses of the land of another. The right to drive across another person's property to reach your property, to run a sewer line across it, or to drill for oil and gas on the land of another person is an affirmative easement.

A **negative easement** is the right to have someone who owns an adjoining piece of property refrain from making certain uses of his or her land. The right to have your neighbor refrain from erecting a building on his property that would cut off light and air from your building is a negative easement.

Easements may be acquired in a number of ways. They may be bought or sold, or they may be held back when the owner of a piece of property sells other rights to the property. Sometimes an easement is implied even though the parties did not specifically grant or purchase it. For example, Arthur owns 80 acres of land fronting on a dirt road and bounded on the other three sides by a limited-access highway. If Arthur sells the back 40 acres to Byron, Byron will get an easement by **necessity** across Arthur's remaining property because that would be the only way he could get to his property.

An easement can also be created by **adverse possession** (prescription). Obtaining a property interest by adverse possession is discussed later in this chapter. As an example, if someone without your permission openly uses a shortcut across a corner of your property for the statutory period of time, that person will obtain an easement. She will have a continuing right to engage in that activity. The true owner of the property must assert his rights during that period and stop the other person or end up losing an interest in his property.

Because an easement is a type of interest in land, it is within the coverage of the statute of frauds. An express agreement granting or reserving an easement must be in writing to be enforceable. Under the statutes of most states, the grant of an easement must be executed with the same formalities as are observed in executing the grant of a fee simple interest in real property. However, easements not granted expressly, such as easements by prior use, necessity, or prescription or adverse possession are enforceable even though they are not in writing.

The *Michigan Department of Natural Resources v. Carmody-Lahti Real Estate, Inc.* case, which follows, involves a situation where an easement for a limited purpose was granted by agreement and later considered "abandoned" when the property was being used for a purpose other than the limited use allowed by the easement.

Michigan Department of Natural Resources v. Carmody-Lahti Real Estate, Inc.

699 N.W.2d 272 (Sup. Ct. Mich. 2005)

FACTS

In 1873, the Quincy Mining Company conveyed an interest in real property located in Houghton County, Michigan, to the Mineral Range Railroad Company. The parties labeled the interest, consisting of a strip of land 100 feet in width across the described tract of land, a "right-of-way" for the railroad of Mineral Mining. Quincy Mining reserved the right to all ore and minerals on the strip of land as well as the right to mine the minerals from underneath the surface in such a manner as not to interfere with the construction or operation of the railroad.

Quincy Mining subsequently transferred its remaining interest in the Houghton County property to the Armstrong-Thielman Lumber Company, which in turn sold its interest to Carmody-Lahti Real Estate, Inc. Mineral Range later conveyed its right-of-way to the Soo Line Railroad, which until the early 1980s continued to utilize the right-of-way for railroad purposes.

In the Transportation Act of 1920, Congress required, among other things, that railroad companies obtain the permission of the Interstate Commerce Commission (ICC) before abandoning any extant rail line; although the requirement remained, the procedure was changed in subsequent legislation adopted in 1976 and 1980. In September 1982, the Soo Line sought federal permission to abandon the railway. The ICC granted the request in a written order on September 29, 1982, which required the Soo Line to keep the line intact for 120 days to permit any state or local agency or other interested party an opportunity to negotiate the acquisition for public use of all or any portion of the right-of-way—and subsequently to afford any public agency or private organization wishing to acquire it for public use the right of first refusal for its acquisition.

In 1988, the Soo Line conveyed the right-of-way to the Michigan Department of Natural Resources (MDNR). By that time the railroad tracks had largely been removed. The MDNR used the right-of-way as a snowmobile and recreation trail until 1997 when Carmody-Lahti Real Estate installed a fence that blocked a portion of the right-of-way.

The MDNR then filed suit, seeking an order to enjoin Carmody-Lahti Real Estate from blocking the right-of-way with its fence. The MDNR argued that it had an unlimited right to use the right-of-way for any purpose because the 1873 deed conveyed to Mineral Range Railroad, its predecessor in interest, a fee simple estate. Carmody-Lahti Real Estate argued in response that the deed had conveyed only an easement limited to railroad

(continued)

purposes. Because the MDNR had exceeded the scope of the easement, it has thereby extinguished the right-of-way.

ISSUE

Was the right-of-way an easement that was subsequently abandoned?

DECISION

Yes. Where a grant of a property interest is not of the land itself, but is merely for the use or of the right-of-way, the conveyance is an easement only. Typically, the owner of property subject to an easement may continue to use the property. Railroad easements, however, are essentially different from other easements. A railroad easement granted by a landowner cannot be used by the landowner for any reason, even if the use does not interfere with the use by the easement holder. For this reason, it is common for grantors of railroad rights-of-way to include language in deeds to delineate their continuing use rights in the portion of their fee estate burdened by a railroad easement.

The Michigan Supreme Court has consistently held that deeds conveying a right-of-way transferred an easement unless the deed unmistakably expresses the grantor's intent to convey a fee simple. As a limited property interest, an easement is a right to use the land burdened by the easement rather than the right to occupy the land. Accordingly, an easement is generally confined to a specific purpose. An easement holder abandons a railroad right-of-way when non-use is accompanied by acts on the part of the owner of either the property or the easement which manifest an intention to abandon, and which destroy the object for which the easement was created or the means of its enjoyment. Non-use is not enough by itself to constitute abandonment, but must be accompanied by some act showing a clear intent to abandon.

Here, the 1873 deed conveyed an easement limited to railroad uses and the Soo Line abandoned that easement for state property law purposes when it sought, obtained, and acted upon the ICC's permission to abandon the railway in 1982. Consequently, the Soo Line did not have a valid property interest in the Houghton County right-of-way to convey to the MDNR in 1988. Carmody-Lahti Real Estate has an unencumbered fee simple interest in the right-of-way and, as any property owner in Michigan may do with its property, may limit its use as it sees fit.

Profits

A **profit** is a right to enter another person's land and remove some product or part of the land. Timber, gravel, minerals, and oil are among the products and parts frequently made the subject of profits. Generally governed by the same rules applicable to easements, profits are sometimes called *easements with a profit.*

License

A **license** is usually a temporary right to use another person's land for a limited and specific purpose. A license is similar in some ways to an easement; however, it is not considered to be an interest in land and usually does not have to be in writing to be enforceable. It may be created orally. A common example of a license is obtaining permission to hunt or fish on another person's land.

Private Restrictions

Within certain limits, a person who sells real estate may obtain the agreement of the buyer to certain restrictions on the subsequent use of the land. Similarly, the owner of real estate may, by agreement or by a declaration in trust, impose restrictions on the use that will be made of that property.

For example, Frank owns two adjacent lots. He sells one to Rose but gets Rose to promise not to operate any business involving the sale of liquor on the property. This commitment is included in the deed Frank gives to Rose along with a statement that the property is to revert to Frank if the commitment is broken. Similarly, suppose that a developer sells lots in a subdivision and puts a restriction in each deed concerning the minimum size and cost of houses that can be built on the property. He might also restrict the types of design. Alternatively, the restrictions may be put in the plat for the subdivision that is filed in the local land records office.

The validity and enforceability of such private restrictions on the use of real property depend on the *purpose, nature, and scope* of the restriction. If a restraint is so great that it effectively prevents the sale or transfer of the property to anyone else, it is not enforceable. If a restriction is reasonable and its purpose is not against public policy, it is enforceable. For example, a restriction that prohibits future sale of the property to a non-Caucasian is not enforceable. However, restrictions that relate to the minimum size of lots, maintenance of the area as a residential community, or the cost, size, and design of buildings are frequently enforceable.

These restrictions are usually enforceable by the parties to the agreement or by persons who are intended to benefit by them. If the restriction is contained in a subdivision plat in the form of a general building scheme, other property owners in the subdivision may be able to enforce it. Restrictions can be waived; the right to enforce them can be lost by abandonment; or they can end by their own terms. If a restriction is invalid, waived, abandoned, or lost due to dramatically changed circumstances, the basic deed remains valid but the deed is treated as if the restriction had been stricken from it.

The case that follows, *Honeycutt v. Brookings,* illustrates the enforcement of a restriction.

Honeycutt v. Brookings

996 So. 2d 553 (Ct. App. La. 2008)

FACTS

Dr. Virginia Brookings, a veterinarian, owned a home in Lawler Gardens Subdivision in Blanchard, Louisiana. The subdivision is a semi-rural setting, with large lots, some of which include several acres of land. Dr. Brookings raises and shows dogs, mainly miniature Doberman pinchers and Japanese Chins. Since 1999 she has housed approximately 10 dogs at her residence (and at times as many as 20), with the dogs eating and sleeping inside the residence but having extended periods of unattended recreational time outside in the backyard.

In 2003, Dr. Brookings built two outside kennels—fenced areas surrounded by a small chain link fence—for the dogs. They were built immediately adjacent to the neighboring property. In November 2006, Dr. Brookings began constructing a 900-square-foot outbuilding/kennel in her backyard with seven dog runs connected to it. The runs were indoor/outdoor with guillotine-style dog doors connecting each outdoor run to the indoor unit. Unless the dog doors were closed, the dogs could run freely inside or outside. Each run can house two dogs; the facility can house 14 dogs. The structure was built on a slab and was fully plumbed, heated, and cooled. Once completed, all of her dogs were housed in the facility. The dogs had the free run of the outside and inside areas during the day but generally were confined inside in the evening.

Lawler Gardens Subdivision contained 14 lots and a number of protective covenants were in place, having been adopted on September 10, 1992. Among the restrictions were the following:

1. LAND USE AND BUILDING TYPE. No lot shall be used except for *residential* purposes. No building shall be erected, altered, placed, or permitted to remain on any lot other than detached single-family dwellings not to exceed three stories in height. . . .

11. NUISANCES. No noxious or offensive activities shall be carried on upon any lot, nor shall anything be done thereon which may be or may become an annoyance or nuisance to the neighborhood.

12. TEMPORARY STRUCTURES. No structure of a temporary character, trailer, basement, tent, shack, garage, barn, or other outbuilding shall be used on any lot at any time as a residence, either temporarily or permanently.

16. LIVESTOCK AND POULTRY. No animals, livestock, or poultry of any kind shall be raised, bred, or kept on

(continued)

Honeycutt v. Brookings *(concluded)*

> any lot, except dogs, cats, or other household pets may be kept, provided they are not kept, bred, or maintained for commercial purposes. No more than two (2) outside dogs per family will be permitted.

As the building of the kennel facility began, several neighbors objected. Once it was completed, they complained that they could hear the dogs barking and that when they were out in their yard at night, the dogs would come out into the runs and bark incessantly. They hired an attorney who sent a letter to Dr. Brookings, advising her that the activity was in violation of the protective covenants of the subdivision. When no response was forthcoming after a second letter was sent, the neighbors filed a lawsuit seeking an injunction.

ISSUE

Should Dr. Brookings be enjoined from keeping her dogs in the outdoor kennels on the grounds that it violates the subdivision's restrictive covenants?

DECISION

Yes. The court found that the dog-related activity was not a nuisance or actionably annoying or offensive until the dogs became outdoor dogs and began living full time in the kennel facility that allowed them to go outside at will. The court did not order the demolition of the outbuilding but did order the outdoor runs to be dismantled and that the dogs had to be kept in the residence. Two dogs that had to be the same two dogs could be kept as "outdoor dogs."

Concept Summary: Interests in Real Property

Possessory Interests	Description
Fee simple	The basic and highest form of land ownership. Owner has the absolute power to possess and use the property (subject to government regulation and private restrictions), the right to dispose of it during his lifetime or on his death, and the ability to grant many subsidiary interests to others without giving up his basic ownership.
Life estate	The right to possess and use property for a time measured by the person's lifetime or that of another person.
Leasehold (see Chapter 35)	The right to possession for a time specified by contract or by law as in tenancies for years, periodic tenancies, and tenancies at will.

Nonpossessory Interests	Description
Easement	The right to make certain uses of another person's property or the right to prevent another person from making certain uses of his own property.
Private restrictions	A restraint imposed by contract on the subsequent use of land, which may be enforceable against subsequent owners depending on the purpose, nature, and scope of the restriction.
License	*Not* an interest in land but a temporary right to use another's land for a limited and specific purpose.

Co-ownership of Real Property

LO3

Co-ownership of real property exists when two or more persons share the same ownership interest in certain property. The co-owners do not have separate rights to any portion of the real property; each has a share in the whole property. Seven types of co-ownership are recognized in the United States.

Tenancy in Common

Persons who own property under a **tenancy in common** have undivided interests in the property and equal rights to possess it. When property is transferred to two or more persons without specification of their co-ownership form, it is presumed that they acquire the property as tenants in common. The respective ownership interests of tenants in common may be, but need not be, equal. One tenant, for example, could have a two-thirds ownership interest in the property with the other tenant having a one-third interest.

Each tenant in common has the right to possess and use the property. Individual tenants, however, cannot exclude the other tenants in common from also possessing and using the property. If the property is rented or otherwise produces income, each tenant is entitled to share in the income in proportion to her ownership share. Similarly, each tenant must pay her proportionate share of property taxes and necessary repair costs. If a tenant in sole possession of the property receives no rents or profits from the property, she is not required to pay rent to her co-tenant unless her possession is adverse to or inconsistent with her co-tenant's property interests.

A tenant in common may dispose of his interest in the property during life and at death. Similarly, his interest is subject to his creditors' claims. When a tenant dies, his interest passes to his heirs or, if he has made a will, to the person or persons specified in the will. Suppose Peterson and Sievers own Blackacre as tenants in common. Sievers dies, having executed a valid will in which he leaves his Blackacre interest to Johanns. In this situation, Peterson and Johanns become tenants in common.

Tenants in common may sever the co-tenancy by agreeing to divide the property or, if they are unable to agree, by petitioning a court for *partition.* The court will physically divide the property if that is feasible, so that each tenant receives her proportionate share. If physical division is not feasible, the court will order that the property be sold and that the proceeds be appropriately divided.

Joint Tenancy

A **joint tenancy** is created when equal interests in real property are conveyed to two or more persons by means of a document clearly specifying that they are to own the property as joint tenants. The rights of use, possession, contribution, and partition are the same for a joint tenancy as for a tenancy in common. The joint tenancy's distinguishing feature is that it gives the owners the **right of survivorship,** which means that upon the death of a joint tenant, the deceased tenant's interest automatically passes to the surviving joint tenant(s). The right of survivorship makes it easy for a person to transfer property at death without the need for a will. For example, Devaney and Osborne purchase Redacre and take title as joint tenants. At Devaney's death, his Redacre interest will pass to Osborne even if Devaney did not have a will setting forth such an intent. Moreover, even if Devaney had a will that purported to leave his Redacre interest to someone other than Osborne, the will's Redacre provision would be ineffective.

A joint tenant may mortgage, sell, or give away his interest in the property during his lifetime. If one of the joint tenants does sell or convey his interest to someone else, the joint tenancy is broken as to the share sold. The new person comes into the joint ownership as a tenant in common rather than as part of a joint tenancy. The rights of use, possession, contribution, and partition of joint tenants are the same as those of tenants in common.

Tenancy by the Entirety

Approximately half of the states permit married couples to own real property under a **tenancy by the entirety.** This tenancy is essentially a joint tenancy with the added requirement that the owners be married. As does the joint tenancy, the tenancy by the entirety features the right of survivorship. Neither spouse can transfer the property by will if the other is still living. Upon the death of the husband or wife, the property passes automatically to the surviving spouse.

A tenancy by the entirety cannot be severed by the act of only one of the parties. Neither spouse can transfer the property unless the other also signs the deed. Thus, a creditor of one tenant cannot claim an interest in that person's share of property held in tenancy by the entirety. Divorce, however, severs a tenancy by the entirety and transforms it into a tenancy in common. The Concept Summary that follows compares the features of tenancy in common, joint tenancy, and tenancy by the entirety.

Concept Summary: Tenancy in Common, Joint Tenancy, and Tenancy by the Entirety

	Tenancy in Common	Joint Tenancy	Tenancy by the Entirety
Equal possession and use?	Yes	Yes	Yes
Share income?	Yes	Yes	Presumably
Contribution requirement?	Generally	Generally	Generally
Free conveyance of interest?	Yes; transferee becomes tenant in common	Yes, but joint tenancy is severed on conveyance and reverts to tenancy in common	Both must agree; divorce severs tenancy
Effect of death?	Interest transferable at death by will or inheritance	Right of survivorship; surviving joint tenant takes decedent's share	Right of survivorship; surviving spouse takes decedent's share

Community Property

A number of western and southern states recognize the **community property** system of co-ownership of property by married couples. This type of co-ownership assumes that marriage is a partnership in which each spouse contributes to the family's property base. Property acquired during the marriage through a spouse's industry or efforts is classified as *community* property. Each spouse has an equal interest in such property regardless of who produced or earned the property. Because each spouse has an equal share in community property, neither can convey community property without the other's joining in the transaction. Various community property states permit the parties to dispose of their interests in community property at death. The details of each state's community property system vary, depending on the specific provisions of that state's statutes.

Not all property owned by a married person is community property, however. Property a spouse owned before marriage or acquired during marriage by gift or inheritance is *separate* property. Neither spouse owns a legal interest in the other's separate property. Property exchanged for separate property also remains separately owned.

Tenancy in Partnership

When a partnership takes title to property in the partnership's name, the co-ownership form is called **tenancy in partnership.** Co-ownership of property in the partnership form of organization is discussed in Chapter 27.

Condominimum Ownership

Condominiums have become very common in the United States in recent years, even in locations outside urban and resort areas. Under condominium ownership, a purchaser takes title to her individual unit and becomes a tenant in common with other unit owners in shared facilities such as hallways, elevators, swimming pools, and parking areas. The condominium owner pays property taxes on her individual unit and makes a monthly payment for the maintenance of the common areas. She may generally mortgage or sell her unit without the other unit owners' approval. For federal income tax purposes, the condominium owner is treated as if she owned a single-family home and is thus allowed to deduct her property taxes and mortgage interest expenses.

Cooperative Ownership

In a cooperative, a building is owned by a corporation or group of persons. One who wants to buy an apartment in the building purchases stock in the corporation and holds his apartment under a long-term, renewable lease called a *proprietary lease.* Frequently, the cooperative owner must obtain the other owners' approval to sell or sublease his unit.

Acquisition of Real Property

LO4

Among the different methods of obtaining title to real property are

1. Purchase
2. Gift
3. Will or inheritance
4. Tax sale
5. Adverse possession

Original title to land in the United States was acquired either from the federal government or from a country that held the land prior to its acquisition by the United States. The land in the 13 original colonies had been granted by the king of England either to the colonies or to certain individuals. The land in the Northwest Territory was ceded by the states to the federal government, which in turn issued grants or patents of land. Original ownership of much of the land in Florida and in the Southwest came by grants from the rulers of Spain.

Acquisition by Purchase

The right to sell one's property is a basic ownership right. In fact, any restriction on the right of an owner to sell his property is usually considered to be against public policy and is not enforced. Most people who own real property acquired title by buying it from someone else. Each state sets the requirements for transferring a piece of real property located in that state. The various elements of selling and buying real property, including broker agreements, contracts to buy real estate, and deeds, will be covered in the next section of this chapter.

Acquisition by Gift

Ownership of real property may be acquired by *gift.* For such a gift to be valid, the donor must *deliver* a properly executed deed to the property to the donee or to some third person to hold it for the donee. It is not necessary that the donee or the third person take possession of the property. The essential element of the gift is the delivery of the deed. Suppose a man makes out a deed to the family farm and leaves it in a safe-deposit box for delivery to his son when he dies. The attempted gift will not be valid because there was no delivery of the gift during the donor's lifetime.

Acquisition by Will or Inheritance

The owner of real property generally has the right to dispose of that property by **will.** The requirements for making a valid will are discussed in Chapter 36. If the owner of real property dies without making a valid will, the property will go to his heirs as determined under the laws of the state in which the real property is located.

Acquisition by Tax Sale

If the taxes assessed on real property are not paid, they become a lien on the property. This lien has priority over all other claims of other persons to the land. If the taxes remain unpaid for a period of time, the government sells the land at a tax sale, and the purchaser at the tax sale acquires title to the property. However, in some states the original owner has the option for a limited time (perhaps a year) to buy it from the purchaser at the tax sale for her cost plus interest.

Acquisition by Adverse Possession

Each state has a statute of limitations that provides an owner of land only a fixed number of years to bring a lawsuit to regain possession of his land from someone who is trespassing on it. This time period generally varies between 5 and 20 years, depending on the state. Thus, if someone moves onto your land and acts as if he is the owner, you must take steps to have that person ejected from your land. If you do not do so during the statutory period, you will lose your right to do so. The person who stayed in possession of your property for the statutory period will be treated as the owner. He will have acquired title to it by *adverse possession* or *prescription.*

To acquire title by adverse possession, a person must possess land in a manner that puts the true owner on notice that he has a cause of action against that person. There must be actual occupancy that is hostile to the real owner's title, with an open claim to title (i.e., not with the owner's permission) continuously for the statutory period. In some states, the person in possession of land who is claiming the right to be there must also pay the taxes. It is not necessary that the same person occupy the land for the statutory period; however, the possession must be continuous for the necessary time.

Adverse possession can take place in some fairly common situations. For example, Buzz Miller and Claire Alton own adjoining lots on which they have built houses. In 1978 Alton builds a fence to separate the two lots; however, she erects it about four feet onto Miller's land. She also builds a driveway that extends into the four-foot strip even though Miller did not give her permission to do so. He does not take steps to have the fence moved to its rightful position on the line between their lots. For 10 years Alton acts as if she owns the four-foot strip. Then she sells her lot to Edgar Gray, who also uses it and acts as if he is the owner. If the statute of limitations in that state is 20 years, in 1998 Gray will be the owner of the four-foot strip by adverse possession. The case that follows, *Vezey v. Green,* involves the acquisition of ownership of a parcel of land by adverse possession.

Vezey v. Green

35 P.3d 14 (Sup. Ct. Alaska 2001)

FACTS

In 1982 Angela Green's grandmother, Billie Harrild, offered Green a piece of the family's land near Shaw Creek. Billie was declining in health and wanted her granddaughter to have a home near the Harrild's home. Green selected a parcel of land on a bluff across Shaw Creek from her grandparents' house. The alleged gift was not recorded and Billie and Elden Harrild, the grandparents, and John Harrild, a cousin, remained the owners of record. During the 10 years following Green's entrance on the property, all three recognized the property as belonging to Green, and neighbors testified that Billie consistently referred to the land as Green's property. Elden and Billie Harrild died in the winter of 1995–1996.

Between 1982 and 1992, Green gradually built a house and cultivated the grounds on the bluff. She worked on the property over the summers and worked as a nurse in California the rest of the year. In 1982 she planned the site of the house and cleared trees on the lot. In the summer of 1983 and 1984 she lived in a camper on the property, cleared more vegetation and excavated the foundation of the house-to-be. In the following years, she completed the construction of the house, planted trees, and built a coop for turkeys and chickens. In 1986, while working in Fairbanks, Alaska, she visited the house during the entire year. She posted "No trespassing" signs and built benches in some areas away from the house. She put up a chain across the road entering the property, but did not fence the entire area. In 1990, the house was damaged by vandalism, and Green repaired the damage when she returned to Alaska in the spring.

Green arranged with her grandparents that for the remainder of their lives they could extract and sell small quantities of rock from the property, but she strongly opposed the use of rock extraction equipment on the property. One year the grandparents executed a contract allowing an extraction company, Earthmovers, to excavate rock from the family property, including the portion occupied by Green on the bluff. Earthmovers excavated a trench on the bluff one day when Green was not at home. When she returned and found workers and equipment on the property, she told them they were not allowed to excavate there, allowed them to finish the task at hand, and ordered the workers and the equipment off the property.

In 1988 Allen Vezey became interested in Shaw Creek area properties and approached the Harrilds about purchasing their land. In 1994, while Vezey was still in negotiations with the Harrilds, Green called Vezey and told him that the land on the bluff belonged to her. In the winter of 1994–1995 Vezey bought Elden Harrild's one-third interest in a property that included the bluff. After Vezey bought the property, Green brought suit against him and others, asserting that she owned the property.

ISSUE

Did Green acquire title to the property on the bluff by adverse possession?

DECISION

Yes. The court held that Green could claim title to the property by adverse possession if she showed by clear and convincing evidence that she possessed the property for 10 consecutive years. To do so she had to show that for the statutory period her use of the land was continuous, open and notorious, exclusive, and hostile to the true owner. The court noted that continuity, notoriety, and exclusivity of use are not susceptible to fixed standards, but rather depend on the character of the land in question.

Here, the court found that the evidence supported the conclusion that Green possessed the property at least from early summer of 1983 to the same season in 1993 in fulfillment of the statutory 10-year-period requirement. To meet the continuity requirement, Green had to show that she used the property as an average owner of similar property would use it. Because there was testimony that "it'd take a fool to live up there on the bluff property in the cold winter months," Green had used the property as an average owner would do so because of its unsuitability for habitation in the winter months. Similarly, allowing her relatives to remove some of the rock from the property was consistent with what an average owner of similar property might do, as was her ordering trespassers off the property. The notoriety requirement was met because all of the record owners of the bluff property were aware of her presence on the property. The determinative questions concerning hostile use are whether Green acted toward the property as if she owned it and whether she simply was occupying it with permission. Here Green's continued presence was not dependant on the consent of the Harrilds and her ordering of Earthmovers off the property was clearly hostile to their interests. The fact that she claimed the land was a gift (although ineffective as a transfer by gift) strengthened her claim to be owner of the property in her own right. Thus, Green met the requirements for establishing title through adverse possession.

Author's Note: After a subsequent appeal and remand, the Alaska Supreme Court held that the property acquired by adverse possession was limited to an area near the cabin and did not include any claim to the public road on the property.

Transfer by Sale

LO5

Steps in a Sale

These are major steps normally involved in the sale and purchase of real property:

1. Contracting with a real estate broker to sell the property or to locate suitable property for sale.
2. Negotiating and signing a contract to sell the property.
3. Arranging for the financing of the purchase and the satisfaction of other contingencies such as a survey or an acquisition of title insurance.
4. Closing the sale, at which time the purchase price is usually paid and the deed is signed and delivered.
5. Recording of the deed.

Real Estate Brokers

Although engaging a real estate broker is not a legal requirement for the sale of real property, it is common for one who wishes to sell his property to "list" the property with a broker. A listing contract empowers the broker to act as the seller's agent in procuring a ready, willing, and able buyer and in managing details of the property transfer. A number of states' statutes of frauds require listing contracts to be evidenced by a writing and signed by the party to be charged.

Real estate brokers are regulated by state and federal law. They owe *fiduciary duties* (duties of trust and confidence) to their clients. Chapter 23 contains additional information regarding the duties imposed on such agents.

Types of Listing Contracts

Listing contracts specify such matters as the listing period's duration, the terms on which the seller will sell, and the amount and terms of the broker's commission. There are different types of listing contracts:

1. *Open listing.* Under an open listing contract, the broker receives a *nonexclusive* right to sell the property. This means that the seller and third parties (e.g., other brokers) also are entitled to find a buyer for the property. The broker operating under an open listing is entitled to a commission only if he was the first to find a ready, willing, and able buyer.

2. *Exclusive agency listing.* Under an exclusive agency listing, the broker earns a commission if he *or any other agent* finds a ready, willing, and able buyer during the period of time specified in the contract. Thus, the broker operating under such a listing would have the right to a commission even if another broker actually procured the buyer. Under the exclusive agency listing, however, the seller has the right to sell the property himself without being obligated to pay the broker a commission.

3. *Exclusive right to sell.* An exclusive right to sell contract provides the broker the exclusive right to sell the property for a specified period of time and entitles her to a commission no matter who procured the buyer. Under this type of listing, a seller must pay the broker her commission even if it was the seller or some third party who found the buyer during the duration of the listing contract.

Contract for Sale

The principles regarding contract formation, performance, assignment, and remedies that you learned in earlier chapters are applicable to contracts for the sale of real estate. The agreement

ETHICS IN ACTION

In a January 30, 2008, article, *The Wall Street Journal* reported that in the wake of the collapse of the real estate market in Florida, the Related Group, a closely held luxury developer with 6,500 condo units valued at $3.7 billion, was suing real estate brokers to recover the 3 percent commissions they had been paid (amounting to between $15,000 to $90,000) for each of 24 condominiums in a 389-unit project when buyers walked away from their contracts to purchase units and the deals did not close. The developer had paid the commission at the time the buyers entered into the contracts instead of waiting until the buildings were complete and the buyers actually went forward with the transaction. The developer claimed it followed this practice in order to entice brokers to bring in prospective buyers. The brokers contend that they should not have to repay commissions where the poor market was caused by overbuilding on the part of the developers. Under these circumstances, is it ethical for the developer to seek repayment of the commissions? What is the ethical thing for the brokers to do?

between the seller and the buyer to purchase real property should be in writing to be enforceable under the statute of frauds. The agreement commonly spells out such things as the purchase price, the type of deed the purchaser will get, and what items of personal property such as appliances and carpets are included. It may also make the "closing" of the sale contingent on the buyer's ability to obtain financing at a specified rate of interest and the seller's procurement of a survey, title insurance, and termite insurance. Because they are within the statute of frauds, real estate sales contracts must be evidenced by a suitable writing signed by the party to be charged in order to be enforceable.

Financing the Purchase

Various arrangements for financing the purchase of real property, such as mortgages, land contracts, and deeds of trust, are discussed in Chapter 42.

Federal Disclosure Laws

Congress has enacted several statutes designed to protect purchasers of real estate. The federal Real Estate Settlement Procedures Act (RESPA) requires that a buyer receive advance disclosure of the settlement costs that will be incurred in settlement. RESPA also requires that a record be kept of the actual settlement charges in all real estate transactions involving federally related loans such as Veterans Administration and Federal Housing Administration loans. The required settlement/disclosure statement itemizes each settlement cost charged to the buyer and each charged to the seller. These settlement charges commonly include (1) real estate broker's commissions, (2) loan origination fees, (3) loan discount points, (4) appraisal fees, (5) credit report fees, (6) lender's inspection fees, (7) insurance premiums, (8) settlement closing/escrow fees, (9) prepaid interest and taxes, (10) title search fees, (11) notary's and/or attorney's fees, (12) survey fees, (13) title insurance premiums, and (14) transfer and recording fees.

Among the purposes of the settlement statement are to give the buyer notice of the cash needed at settlement and an opportunity to engage in "comparison shopping" of settlement terms so that the buyer can arrange the most favorable terms.

RESPA prohibits a number of practices, including kickbacks or payments for referral of business to title companies. It also prohibits any requirement by the seller that title insurance be purchased from any particular company.

In response to fraud and misrepresentations made by some sellers of land, particularly retirement and vacation properties, Congress enacted the Interstate Land Sales Full

Disclosure Act. The act generally applies to developers who subdivide property into 50 or more lots and who use interstate means such as the mails and the telephone to sell the property. The act requires that a "property report" be prepared disclosing certain kinds of information about the property and the developer's plans regarding it. The report is filed with the U.S. Department of Housing and Urban Development and must be made available to prospective buyers. Developers who violate the law are subject to civil and criminal penalties.

Fair Housing Act

The Fair Housing Act, enacted by Congress in 1968 and substantially revised in 1988, is designed to prevent discrimination in the housing market. Its provisions apply to real estate brokers, sellers (other than those selling their own single-family dwellings without the use of a broker), lenders, lessors, and appraisers.

Originally, the act prohibited discrimination on the basis of race, color, religion, sex, and national origin. The 1988 amendments added handicap and "familial status" to the list. The familial status category was intended to prevent discrimination in the housing market against pregnant women and families with children. "Adult" or "senior citizen" communities restricting residents' age do not violate the Fair Housing Act even though they do exclude families with children so long as the housing meets the requirements of the act's "housing for older persons" exemption.

The act prohibits discrimination on the above-listed bases in a wide range of matters relating to the sale or rental of housing. These matters include refusals to sell or rent, representations that housing is not available for sale or rental when in fact it is, and discriminatory actions regarding the provision of services and facilities involved in sale or rental. The act also prohibits discrimination in connection with brokerage services, appraisals, and financing of dwellings.

A violation of the Fair Housing Act can result in a civil action brought either by the government or the aggrieved individual. If the aggrieved individual brings suit and prevails, the court may issue injunctions, award actual and punitive damages, assess attorneys' fees and costs, and grant other appropriate relief.

Transfer by Deed

Each state has enacted statutes that set out the formalities for transferring land located within its borders. As a general rule, the transfer of land is accomplished by the execution and delivery of a **deed.** A deed is an instrument in writing whereby the owner of an interest in real property (the **grantor**) conveys to another (the **grantee**) some right, title, or interest in that property. Two types of deeds, the quitclaim deed and the warranty deed, are in general use in the United States.

LO6

Quitclaim Deeds

When the grantor conveys by a **quitclaim deed,** she conveys to the grantee whatever title she has at the time she executes the deed. However, in a quitclaim deed the grantor does not claim to have good title or, in fact, any title. If the title proves to be defective or if the grantor has no title, the grantee has no right to sue the grantor under the quitclaim deed. Quitclaim deeds are frequently used to cure a technical defect in the chain of title to property. In such a case, the grantor may not be claiming any right, title, or interest in the property.

Warranty Deeds

A **warranty deed** contains covenants of warranty; that is, the grantor, in addition to conveying title to the property, guarantees to make good any defects in the title he has conveyed (see Figure 34.1). A warranty deed may be a deed of general warranty or of special warranty. In a **general warranty deed** the grantor warrants against all defects in the title and all encumbrances (such as liens and easements). In a **special warranty deed,** the grantor warrants against only those defects in the title or those encumbrances that arose after he acquired the property. If the property conveyed is mortgaged or subject to some other encumbrance such as an easement or a long-term lease, it is a common practice to give a special warranty deed that contains a provision excepting those specific encumbrances from the warranty.

Form and Execution of Deed

Some states have enacted statutes setting out the form of deed that may be used in these states. However, a deed may be valid even though it does not follow the statutory form. The statutory requirements of the different states for the execution of deeds are not uniform, but they do follow a similar pattern. As a general rule, a deed states the name of the grantee, contains a recitation of consideration and a description of the property conveyed, and is signed by the grantor. In most states the deed, to be eligible for recording, must be acknowledged by the grantor before a notary public or other officer authorized to take an **acknowledgment.**

No technical words or conveyance is necessary. Any language is sufficient that indicates with reasonable certainty an intent to transfer the ownership of the property. The phrases "give, grant, bargain, and sell" and "convey and warrant" are in common use. A consideration is recited in a deed for historical reasons. The consideration recited is not necessarily the purchase price of the real property. It is sometimes stated to be "one dollar and other valuable consideration."

The property conveyed must be described in such a manner that it can be identified. In urban areas, descriptions are as a general rule given by lot, block, and plat (see Figure 34.1). In rural areas, the land, if it has been surveyed by the government, is usually described by reference to the government survey; otherwise, it is described by metes and bounds, which is a surveyor's description using distances and angles measured in the survey.

A deed must be delivered to be valid. Suppose a woman executes a deed to her home and puts it in her safe-deposit box together with a note directing that the deed be delivered to her son after her death. The deed is not effective to pass title after the woman's death. A deed, to be valid, must be delivered in the lifetime of the grantor.

Recording Deeds

The delivery of a valid deed conveys title from a grantor to a grantee. Nevertheless, in order to prevent his interest from being defeated by third parties who may claim an interest in the same property, the grantee should immediately **record** the deed. When a deed is recorded, it is deposited and indexed in a systematic way in a public office, where it operates to give notice of the grantee's interest to the rest of the world.

Each state has a recording statute that establishes a system for the recording of all transactions that affect the ownership of real property. The statutes are not uniform in their provisions. In general, they provide for the recording of all deeds, mortgages, and other such documents and declare that an unrecorded transfer is void as against an innocent purchaser or mortgagee for value.

Methods of Assuring Title

One of the things that a person must be concerned about in buying real property is whether the seller of the property has *good title* to it. In buying property, a buyer is really buying the seller's ownership interests. Because the buyer does not want to pay a large sum of

FIGURE 34.1
A Warranty Deed

Warranty Deed

THIS DEED, made in the City of Washington, District of Columbia on the 8th day of September, two thousand and eleven

BETWEEN William S. Clark, an unmarried man, party of the first part, and Samuel D. Butler, party of the second part.

WITNESSETH, that the party of the first part, in consideration of Eighty-seven Thousand Five Hundred Dollars ($87,500.00) lawful money of the United States, paid by the party of the second part, does hereby grant and release unto the party of the second part, his heirs and assigns forever.

ALL that certain plot, piece or parcel of land located in the District of Columbia and known and described as Lot numbered Thirty-nine (39) in William D. Green's subdivision of part of Lot numbered Twenty-two (22) in Square numbered Twelve Hundred Nineteen (1219), as per plat recorded in the Office of the Surveyor for the District of Columbia in Liber 30 at folio 32, together with the buildings and improvements thereon and all the estate and rights of the party of the first part in and to said property.

TO HAVE AND TO HOLD THE premises herein granted unto the party of the second part, his heirs and assigns forever.

And the party of the first part covenants as follows:

FIRST—That the party of the first part is seized of the said premises in fee simple, and has good right to convey the same.

SECOND—That the party of the second part shall quietly enjoy the said premises.

THIRD—That the premises are free of encumbrances.

FOURTH—That the party of the first part will execute or procure and further necessary assurances of the title to said premises.

FIFTH—That the party of the first part will forever warrant the title to said premises.

IN WITNESS WHEREOF, the party of the first part has set his hand and seal the day and year above written.

In presence of:

Millicent A. Fenton — William S. Clark (SEAL)

ACKNOWLEDGEMENT OF DEED

District of Columbia, ss:

I, an officer authorized to take acknowledgements according to the laws of the District of Columbia, duly qualified and acting, HEREBY CERTIFY that William S. Clark to me personally known, this day personally appeared and acknowledged before me that he executed the foregoing Deed, and I further certify that I know the said person making said acknowledgement to be the individual described in and who executed the said Deed.

Kathryn R. Cole
Notary Public

money for something that turns out to be worthless, it is important for him to obtain some assurance that the seller has good title to the property. This is commonly done in one of three ways.

In some states, it is customary for the seller to give the buyer an **abstract of title** certified to the date of closing. The abstract is a history of the passage of title of the real property according to the records but is not a guarantee of title. The buyer, for his or her own protection, should have the abstract examined by a competent attorney who will give an opinion as to the title held by the grantor. The opinion will state whether or not the grantor has a **merchantable title** to the property. A merchantable title is one that is readily salable and not subject to objection because of defects in it. If the title is defective, the nature of the defects will be stated in the title opinion.

In many states, the buyer obtains protection against defects in the title by acquiring **title insurance.** This insurance is designed to reimburse the buyer for loss if the title turns out to be defective. When the purchase of the property is being financed by a third party, the lender often requires that a policy of title insurance be obtained for the lender's protection.

Several states have adopted the **Torrens system.** Under this system, the person who owns the land in fee simple obtains a certificate of title. When the real property is sold, the grantor delivers a deed and certificate of title to the grantee. The grantee then delivers the deed and certificate of title to the designated government official and receives a new certificate of title. All liens and encumbrances against the property are noted on the certificate of title, and the purchaser is assured that the title is good except as to the liens and encumbrances noted on it. However, it should be noted that some claims or encumbrances, such as adverse possession or easements by prescription, do not appear on the records. They must be discovered by making an *inspection* of the property. In some states, certain encumbrances, such as liens for taxes, short-term leases, and highway rights, are good against the purchaser even though they do not appear on the certificate.

Seller's Responsibilities Regarding the Quality of Residential Property

Buyers of real estate normally consider it important that any structures on the property be in good condition. This factor becomes especially significant if the buyer intends to use the property for residential purposes. The rule of *caveat emptor* (let the buyer beware) traditionally applied to the sale of real property unless the seller committed misrepresentation or fraud or made express warranties about the property's condition. In addition, sellers had no duty to disclose hidden defects in the property. In recent years, however, the legal environment for sellers—especially real estate professionals such as developers and builder-vendors of residential property—has changed substantially. This section examines two important sources of liability for sellers of real property.

Implied Warranty of Habitability

Historically, sellers of residential property were not regarded as making any **implied warranty** that the property was habitable or suitable for the buyer's use. The law's attitude toward the buyer–seller relationship in residential property sales began to shift, however, as product liability law underwent rapid change in the late 1960s. Courts began to see that the same policies favoring the creation of implied warranties in the sale of goods applied with equal force to the sale of residential real estate. Both goods and housing are frequently mass-produced. The disparity of knowledge and bargaining power often existing between a buyer of goods and a professional seller is also likely to exist between a buyer of a house and a builder-vendor (one who builds and sells houses). Moreover, many defects in houses are not readily discoverable during a buyer's inspection. This creates the possibility of serious loss, because the purchase of a home is often the largest single investment a person ever makes.

For these reasons, courts in most states now hold that builders, builder-vendors, and developers make an implied warranty of habitability when they build or sell real property for residential purposes. An ordinary owner who sells her house—in other words, a seller who was neither the builder nor the developer of the residential property—does not make an implied warranty of habitability.

The implied warranty of habitability amounts to a guarantee that the house is free of latent (hidden) defects that would render it unsafe or unsuitable for human habitation. A breach of this warranty subjects the defendant to liability for damages, measured by either the cost of repairs or the loss in value of the house.

A related issue that has led to considerable litigation is whether the implied warranty of habitability extends to subsequent purchasers of the house. For example, PDQ Development Co. builds a house and sells it to Johnson, who later sells the house to McClure. May McClure successfully sue PDQ for breach of warranty if a serious defect renders the house uninhabitable? Although some courts have rejected implied warranty actions brought by subsequent purchasers, many courts today hold that an implied warranty made by a builder-vendor or developer would extend to a subsequent purchaser. Naturally, the extension of the warranty to subsequent purchasers greatly increases the legal vulnerability of builders and developers. This is illustrated in the *Speight v. Walters Development Company, Ltd.*, case that follows.

Speight v. Walters Development Company.

744 N.W.2d 108 (Sup. Ct. Iowa 2008)

FACTS

In 1995, Walters Development Company, Ltd., custom built a home for the original buyers, named Roche. The Roches sold the house to people named Rogers, who in turn sold it to Robert and Beverly Speight on August 1, 2000. Sometime after purchasing the home, the Speights noticed waster damage and mold. A building inspector determined that the damage was the result of a defectively constructed roof and defective rain gutters. There was no evidence that any of the earlier owners had any actual or imputed knowledge of these defects.

The Speights filed suit against Walters on May 23, 2005, alleging a breach of implied warranty of workmanlike construction and general negligence in the construction of the home. Walters contended that the Speights, as remote purchasers not in privity with it, could not pursue a claim for breach of an implied warranty of workmanlike construction. It also contended that the claim was barred by the five-year statute of limitation in Iowa for such actions, which it asserted began to run when the house was originally sold.

ISSUE

Can a subsequent purchaser bring an action to recover damages on a claim of implied warranty of workmanlike construction?

DECISION

Yes. The court noted that some jurisdictions do not permit subsequent purchasers to recover for breach of the implied warranty of workmanlike construction. The reasons given for this position include: (1) the implied warranty arises out of a contract to which the subsequent purchaser was not a party; (2) because the subsequent purchaser was not in privity of contract with the builder, there was no reliance by the subsequent purchaser on any representations made by the builder; and (3) the reasons for eliminating the privity requirement in product liability cases do not exist in the sale of real estate. However, the court adopted the view of other jurisdictions that do permit such suits by subsequent purchasers. It noted that the purpose of the warranty of workmanlike construction is to ensure that innocent homebuyers are protected from latent defects, and this principle is equally applicable to subsequent purchasers who are in no better position to discover those defects than the original purchaser.

The court held that Iowa should follow the modern trend allowing subsequent purchasers to recover. The same policy considerations that lead the courts to recede from the doctrine of *caveat emptor* in the sale of new homes apply here. Latent defects are by definition undiscoverable by a reasonable inspection and the subsequent purchaser is in no better position to discover those defects than the original purchaser. It would be inequitable to allow an original purchaser to recover while simultaneously prohibiting a subsequent purchaser from recovering for latent defects in homes that are of the same age.

The court also held that the statute of limitations would begin to run from the time at which the injured party has actual or imputed knowledge of the facts that would support a cause of action. In this case, the Speights could not have had such knowledge more than five years before they initiated this lawsuit.

May the implied warranty of habitability be *disclaimed* or *limited* in the contract of sale? It appears at least possible to disclaim or limit the warranty through a contract provision, subject to limitations imposed by the unconscionability doctrine, public policy concerns, and contract interpretation principles. Courts construe attempted disclaimers very strictly against the builder-vendor or developer and often reject disclaimers that are not specific regarding rights supposedly waived by the purchaser.

Duty to Disclose Hidden Defects

Traditionally, contract law provided that a seller had no duty to disclose to the buyer defects in the property being sold, even if the seller knew about the defects and the buyer could not reasonably find out about them on his own. The seller's failure to volunteer information, therefore, could not constitute misrepresentation or fraud. This traditional rule of nondisclosure was another expression of the prevailing *caveat emptor* notion. Although the nondisclosure rule was subject to certain exceptions, the exceptions seldom applied. Thus, there was no duty to disclose in most sales of real property.

Today, courts in many jurisdictions have substantially eroded the traditional nondisclosure rule and have placed a duty on the seller to disclose any known defect that materially affects the property's value and is not reasonably observable by the buyer. The seller's failure to disclose such defects effectively amounts to an assertion that the defects do not exist—an assertion on which a judicial finding of misrepresentation or fraud may be based.

Public Controls on the Use of Land

LO7 Societal Restraints

Although the owner of an interest in real property may generally make such use of her property as she desires, the owner does not have an unlimited right to do so. Society places a number of restraints on the owner of real property: (1) the owner cannot use the property in such a way as to unduly injure others; (2) through the use of the "police power," government units have the right to impose reasonable regulations on the use of property; and (3) the government has the right to take the property through the power of **eminent domain.**

Nuisance Law

One's enjoyment of her own land depends to a great extent on the uses her neighbors make of their land. When the uses of neighboring landowners conflict, the aggrieved party sometimes institutes litigation to resolve the conflict. A property use that unreasonably interferes with another person's ability to use or enjoy her own property may lead to an action for **nuisance** against the landowner or possessor engaged in the objectionable use.

The term *nuisance* has no set legal definition. It is often regarded, however, as encompassing any property-related use or activity that unreasonably interferes with the rights of others. Property uses potentially constituting nuisances include uses that are inappropriate to the neighborhood (such as using a vacant lot in a residential neighborhood as a garbage dump), bothersome to neighbors (such as keeping a pack of barking dogs in one's backyard), dangerous to others (such as storing large quantities of gasoline in 50-gallon drums in one's garage), or of questionable morality (such as operating a house of prostitution or a drug den).

To amount to a nuisance, a use need not be illegal. The fact that relevant zoning laws allow a given use does not mean that the use cannot be a nuisance. The fact that a use was in existence before complaining neighbors acquired their property does not mean that the use may not be considered a nuisance, although it does lessen the likelihood that the use would be held to be a nuisance.

The test for determining the presence or absence of a nuisance is highly dependent on the facts in the individual case. Nuisance actions involve a balancing of the various interests and rights involved. For example, the courts may weigh the social utility of the objectionable conduct and the burden of stopping it against the degree to which the conduct is infringing on the rights of other property owners.

Nuisances may be private or public. To bring a *private nuisance* action, the plaintiff must be a landowner or occupier whose enjoyment of his own land is substantially lessened by the alleged nuisance. The remedies for private nuisance include damages and injunctive relief designed to stop the offending use.

A *public nuisance* occurs when a nuisance harms members of the public, who need not be injured in their use of property. For example, if a power plant creates noise and emissions posing a health hazard to pedestrians and workers in nearby buildings, a public nuisance may exist even though the nature of the harm involves no loss of enjoyment of property. Public nuisances involve a broader class of affected parties than do private nuisances. The action to abate a public nuisance must usually be brought by the government. Remedies generally include injunctive relief and civil penalties that resemble fines. This is illustrated in the case that follows, *United States v. Wade*. Private parties may sue for abatement of public nuisances or for damages caused by public nuisances only when they suffer unique harm different from that experienced by the general public.

United States v. Wade

992 F.Supp. 6 (D. D. C. 1997)

FACTS

Beginning in early 1994, the Washington D.C. Metropolitan Police Department received reports that individuals were selling drugs in front of a brick row house at 647 G Street, S.E. From April 1995 through January 1997, the police received 42 complaints about the alleged drug-trafficking activity. The local citizen's association took their complaints about the recurring drug transactions to their D.C. councilman and to the United States Attorney for the District of Columbia.

In October 1994, the police began an undercover investigation of the alleged narcotic trafficking inside and in front of 647 G Street. According to police reports written in conjunction with the investigation, the distribution of the drugs usually took place in front of the house, with the distributor coming out of the house with a small quantity of drugs to sell either to pedestrians or to individuals who were driving by the house. Upon making the sale, the distributor would take the money into the house and would retrieve additional drugs for sale. Over the course of the two-year investigation, the police made purchases from seven different individuals on ten different occasions; they also confiscated drugs from the house on three occasions.

On December 19, 1996, a grand jury indicted seven individuals, including Charles, Eugene, James, and Love Wade, for narcotics and other violations. Charles and Eugene pled guilty to a number of the charges, including keeping a disorderly house. The court entered an order requiring abatement of the nuisance of keeping a disorderly house. The order directed the United States Marshal (1) to effectively close the house and to keep it closed for a period of a year, (2) to remove all fixtures, furniture, and movable property used in conducting the nuisance; (3) to give the residents the opportunity to take all personal items and property that are not contraband, paraphernalia, or plainly used in conducting the nuisance of unlawfully selling crack cocaine base; and (4) to provide public notice that anyone who breaks and enters the house shall be punished for contempt of court, including by fine or imprisonment.

The Wades—and a number of other residents/owners of the house—objected to the abatement order and sought to have it vacated. This group included Dorothy, Shelton, Angel, and Jean Wade, all related by blood or marriage to Rosie B. Wade, the last titled owner of the house at 647 G Street, who died intestate (see Chapter 36, "Estates and Trusts") in 1994. They contended that abatement of the nuisance of a "disorderly house" was inappropriate in this case: (1) it should be limited to situations where the property was being used for lewdness or prostitution; (2) the nuisance had been effectively abated because all of the alleged offend-

(continued)

ers were either sentenced, awaiting trial, or no longer at, or near, 647 G Street; and (3) the nondefendant owners were without guilty knowledge that any drug-trafficking activity was taking place on the premises. At the hearing, Charles and Eugene expressed great concern about where their mother, father, and sister, who was retarded, would relocate.

ISSUE

Should the house be closed as a public nuisance?

DECISION

Yes. The concept of a public nuisance in the form of a "disorderly house" includes a variety of different kinds of establishments, including bawdy houses, gambling houses, unlicensed taverns, and places where stolen goods are received. The common element is that the premises are used to commit illegal acts and either disturb the public peace or corrupt the morals of the community. Here, the multiplicity of public complaints along with statements from nearby residents that they were fearful of venturing outside because of the drug traffic amply demonstrates that the activity at the house constitutes a public nuisance. The owners had sufficient grounds to be aware of the illegal activity taking place on the premises. And the argument that the nuisance had been abated was dismissed by the court because some of those indicted in connection with activity near the house were not currently in the custody of the law.

Other Property Condition–Related Obligations of Real Property Owners and Possessors

In recent years, the law has increasingly required real property owners and possessors to take steps to further the safety of persons on the property and to make the property more accessible to disabled individuals. This section discusses two legal developments along these lines: the trend toward expansion of *premises liability* and the inclusion of property-related provisions in the Americans with Disabilities Act.

Expansion of Premises Liability

Premises liability is the name sometimes used for negligence cases in which property owners or possessors (such as business operators leasing commercial real estate) are held liable to persons injured while on the property. As explained in Chapter 7, property owners and possessors face liability when their *failures to exercise reasonable care* to keep their property reasonably safe result in injuries to persons lawfully on the property. The traditional premises liability case was one in which a property owner's or possessor's negligence led to the existence of a potentially hazardous condition on the property (e.g., a dangerously slick floor or similar physical condition at a business premises), and a person justifiably on the premises (e.g., a business customer) sustained personal injury upon encountering that unexpected condition (e.g., by slipping and falling).

Security Precautions against Foreseeable Criminal Acts Recent years have witnessed a judicial inclination to expand premises liability to cover other situations in addition to the traditional scenario. A key component of this expansion has been many courts' willingness to reconsider the once-customary holding that a property owner or possessor had no legal obligation to implement security measures to protect persons on the property from the wrongful acts of third parties lacking any connection with the owner or possessor. Today, courts frequently hold that a property owner's or possessor's duty to exercise reasonable care includes the obligation to take reasonable security precautions designed to protect persons lawfully on the premises from foreseeable wrongful (including criminal) acts by third parties.

This expansion has caused hotel, apartment building, and convenience store owners and operators to be among the defendants held liable—sometimes in very large damage amounts—to guests, tenants, and customers on whom violent third-party attackers inflicted severe physical injuries. In such cases, the property owners' or possessors' negligent failures to take security precautions restricting such wrongdoers' access to the premises served as at least a *substantial factor* leading to the plaintiffs' injuries. The security lapses amounting to a lack of reasonable care in a particular case may have been, for instance, failures to install deadbolt locks, provide adequate locking devices on sliding glass doors, maintain sufficient lighting, or employ security guards.

Determining Foreseeability The security precautions component of the reasonable care duty is triggered only when criminal activity on the premises is foreseeable. It therefore becomes important to determine whether the foreseeability standard has been met. In making this determination, courts look at such factors as whether previous crimes had occurred on or near the subject property (and if so, the nature and frequency of those crimes), whether the property owner or possessor knew or should have known of those prior occurrences, and whether the property was located in a high-crime area. The fact-specific nature of the foreseeability and reasonable care determinations makes the outcome of a given premises liability case difficult to predict in advance. Nevertheless, there is no doubt that the current premises liability climate gives property owners and possessors more reason than ever before to be concerned about security measures.

Americans with Disabilities Act In 1990, Congress enacted the broad-ranging Americans with Disabilities Act (ADA). This statute was designed to eliminate long-standing patterns of discrimination against disabled persons in matters such as employment, access to public services, and access to business establishments and similar facilities open to the public. The ADA's Title III focuses on places of public accommodation. It imposes on certain property owners and possessors the obligation to take reasonable steps to make their property accessible to disabled persons (individuals with a physical or mental impairment that substantially limits one or more major life activities).

Places of Public Accommodation Title III of the ADA classifies numerous businesses and nonbusiness enterprises as places of public accommodation. These include hotels, restaurants, bars, theaters, concert halls, auditoriums, stadiums, shopping centers, stores at which goods are sold or rented, service-oriented businesses (running the gamut from gas stations to law firm offices), museums, parks, schools, social services establishments (day care centers, senior citizen centers, homeless shelters, etc.), places of recreation, and various other enterprises, facilities, and establishments. Private clubs and religious organizations, however, are not treated as places of public accommodation for purposes of the statute.

Modifications of Property Under the ADA, the owner or operator of a place of public accommodation cannot exclude disabled persons from the premises or otherwise discriminate against them in terms of their ability to enjoy the public accommodation. Avoiding such exclusion or other discrimination may require alteration of the business or nonbusiness enterprise's practices, policies, and procedures.

Prohibited discrimination may also include the "failure to remove architectural barriers and communication barriers that are structural in nature," if removal is "readily achievable." When the removal of such a barrier is not readily achievable, the property owner or possessor nonetheless engages in prohibited discrimination if he, she, or it does not adopt "alternative methods" to ensure access to the premises and what it has to offer.

New Construction Newly constructed buildings on property used as a place of public accommodation must contain physical features making the buildings *readily accessible* to disabled persons. The same is true of additions built on to previous structures.

Remedies A person subjected to disability-based discrimination in any of the respects discussed above may bring a civil suit for injunctive relief. An injunction issued by a court must include "an order to alter facilities" to make the facilities "readily accessible to and usable to individuals with disabilities to the extent required" by the ADA. The court has discretion to award attorney's fees to the prevailing party. The U.S. Attorney General also has the legal authority to institute a civil action alleging a violation of Title III of the ADA. In such a case, the court may choose to grant injunctive and other appropriate equitable relief, award compensatory damages to aggrieved persons (when the Attorney General so requests), and assess civil penalties (up to $50,000 for a first violation and up to $100,000 for any subsequent violation) "to vindicate the public interest." When determining the amount of any such penalty, the court is to give consideration to any good faith effort by the property owner or possessor to comply with the law. The court must also consider whether the owner or possessor could reasonably have anticipated the need to accommodate disabled persons.

Zoning Ordinances

State legislatures commonly delegate to counties, cities, towns, and other local governments the **police power** to impose reasonable regulations designed to promote the public health, safety, morals, and general welfare of the community. **Zoning ordinances** are an exercise of such a power to regulate. Generally, zoning ordinances divide a city or town into a number of districts, specify or limit the use to which property in those districts can be put, and restrict improvements on and use of the land.

Such restrictions and controls may be of four basic types:

1. *Control of use.* The activity on the land may be regulated or limited, for example, to single- or multifamily dwellings, commercial establishments, light industry, or heavy industry.
2. *Control of height and bulk.* The regulation may control the height of buildings; the setback from front, side, and rear lot lines; and the portion of a lot that can be covered by a building.
3. *Control of population density.* The regulation may provide how much living space must be provided for each person and may specify the maximum number of persons who can be housed in a given area.
4. *Control of aesthetics.* These regulations are commonly used to control billboards but may also be used to enforce similarity and dissimilarity of buildings as well as to preserve historic areas.

When a zoning ordinance is passed, it has only a prospective effect, so existing uses and buildings are permitted to continue. However, the ordinance may provide for the gradual phasing out of such uses and buildings that do not conform to the general zoning plan. If a property owner later wants to use the property in a way other than that permitted by the zoning ordinance, the owner must try to have the ordinance amended. To do this, the owner must show that the proposed changes are in accordance with the overall plan or must try to obtain a **variance** on the ground that the ordinance creates an undue hardship by depriving him of the opportunity to make a reasonable use of the land. Such attempts to obtain amendments or variances often conflict with the interests of nearby property owners who have a vested interest in the zoning status quo. These conflicts sometimes produce heated battles before the zoning authorities.

A disgruntled property owner might also attack the constitutionality of a zoning ordinance. Zoning ordinances have produced a great deal of litigation in recent years as cities and towns have used their zoning power as a means of social control. For example, a city might create a special zone for adult bookstores or other uses that are considered moral threats to the community. This has given rise to challenges that such ordinances unconstitutionally restrict freedom of speech.

Another type of litigation has involved ordinances designed to restrict single-family residential zones to living units of traditional families related by blood or marriage or to no more than two unrelated adults. Many cities and towns have attempted to "zone out" such other living groups as groups of unrelated students, communes, religious cults, and group homes by specifically defining the word *family* in a way that excludes these groups. In the case of *Belle Terre v. Boraas,*[1] the Supreme Court upheld such an ordinance as applied to a group of unrelated students. It subsequently held, however, that an ordinance that defined "family" in such a way as to prohibit a grandmother from living with her grandsons was an unconstitutional intrusion on personal freedom regarding marriage and family life. In some cases, restrictive definitions of the term *family* have been held unconstitutional under state constitutions. In others, such definitions have been narrowly construed by the courts.

Subdivision Ordinances

Many local governments also have ordinances that deal with proposed subdivisions. The ordinances often require that the developer meet certain requirements as to lot size, street and sidewalk layout, and sewers and water. The ordinances commonly require city approval of the proposed development before it can be started. In some cases the developer may be required to dedicate land to the city for streets, parks, and schools. The purpose of such ordinances is to protect the would-be purchasers in the subdivision as well as the city population as a whole by ensuring that minimum standards are met by the developer.

Some urban planners believe that it is undesirable to segregate totally the living, working, shopping, and entertainment areas, as is commonly done with a zoning scheme. They argue that a more livable environment is one that combines these uses so as to ensure the vitality of an area for the vast part of each day. In response to this philosophy, cities and counties are allowing "planned unit developments" and "new towns" that mix such uses so long as the plans are submitted to the authorities and approved pursuant to general guidelines established for such developments.

People are also becoming more aware of the shortcomings of making land-use decisions on a piecemeal basis at the local level. Airports, major shopping centers, highways, and new towns require a regional, rather than local, planning focus. Moreover, sensitive ecological areas such as marshes can be readily destroyed if encroached on in a piecemeal manner. Accordingly, a number of states and the federal government have passed, or are considering, legislation to put some land-use planning on a regional or a statewide basis.

Eminent Domain

The Fifth Amendment to the Constitution provides that private property shall not be taken for public use without "just compensation." Implicit in this provision is the principle that the government has the power to take property for public use if it pays "just compensation" to the owner of the property. This power, called the power of **eminent domain,** makes it possible for the government to acquire private property for highways, water control projects, municipal and civic centers, public housing, urban renewal, and other public uses. Governmental units may delegate their eminent domain power to private corporations such as railroads and utility companies.

Although the eminent domain power is a useful tool of efficient government, there are problems inherent in its use. Determining when the power can be properly exercised presents an initial problem. When the governmental unit itself uses the property taken, as would

[1] 416 U.S. 1 (U.S. Sup. Ct. 1974).

be the case with property acquired for construction of a municipal building or a public highway, the exercise of the power is proper. The use of eminent domain is controversial, however, when the government acquires the property and transfers it to a private developer. In the *Kelo* case, which follows shortly, the U.S. Supreme Court grappled with this issue.

Determining *just compensation* in a given case poses another frequently encountered eminent domain problem. The property owner is entitled to receive the "fair market value" of his property. Critics assert, however, that this measure of compensation falls short of adequately compensating the owner for her loss, because *fair market value* does not cover such matters as the lost goodwill of a business or one's emotional attachment to his home.

A third problem sometimes encountered is determining when there has been a "taking" that triggers the government's just compensation obligation. The answer is easy when the government institutes a formal legal action to exercise the eminent domain power (often called an action to *condemn* property). In some instances, however, the government causes or permits a serious physical invasion of a landowner's property without having instituted formal condemnation proceedings. For example, the government's dam-building project results in persistent flooding of a private party's land. Courts have recognized the right of property owners in such cases to institute litigation seeking compensation from the governmental unit whose actions effectively amounted to a physical taking of their land. In these so-called **inverse condemnation** cases, the property owner sends the message that "you have taken my land; now pay for it."

Kelo v. City of New London

125 S. Ct. 2655 (U.S. Sup. Ct. 2005)

FACTS

The City of New London, Connecticut, had experienced decades of economic decline. In 1990, a state agency designated the city a "distressed municipality." In 1996, the federal government closed a U.S. naval facility in the Fort Trumbull area of the city that had employed over 1,500 people. In 1998, the city's unemployment rate was nearly double that of the rest of the state, and its population of just under 24,000 residents was at its lowest since 1920. These conditions prompted state and local officials to target New London, and particularly its Fort Trumbull area, for economic revitalization.

To this end, the New London Development corporation (NLDC), a private nonprofit entity established some years earlier to assist the city in planning economic development, was reactivated. In January 1998, the state authorized a $5.35 million bond issue to support the NLDC's planning activities. In February, the pharmaceutical company Pfizer Inc. announced that it would build a $300 million research facility on a site immediately adjacent to Fort Trumbull; local planners hoped that Pfizer would draw new business to the area, thereby serving as a catalyst to the area's rejuvenation. In May, the city council authorized the NLDC to formally submit its plan to the relevant state agencies for review. Upon obtaining state-level approval, the NLDC finalized an integrated development plan focused on 90 acres of the Fort Trumbull area, which comprises approximately 115 privately owned properties, as well as the 32 acres formerly occupied by the naval facility.

The development plan called for the creation of restaurants, shops, a marina for both recreational and commercial uses, a pedestrian "riverwalk," 80 new residences, a new U.S. Coast Guard Museum, research and development office space, and parking. The NLDC intended the development plan to capitalize on the arrival of the Pfizer facility and the new commerce it was expected to attract. In addition to creating jobs, generating tax revenue, and helping to build momentum for the revitalization of downtown New London, the plan was also designed to make the city more attractive and to create leisure and recreational opportunities on the waterfront and in the park. The city council approved the plan in January 2000, and designated the NLDC as its development agent in charge of implementation. The city council also authorized the NLDC to purchase

(continued)

property or to acquire property by exercising eminent domain in the city's name.

The NLDC successfully negotiated the purchase of most of the real estate in the 90-acre area, but its negotiation with nine property owners, including Susette Kelo, Wilhelmina Dery, and Charles Dery, failed. As a result, in November 2000, the NLDC commenced condemnation proceedings. Kelo had lived in the Fort Trumbull area since 1997. She had made extensive improvements to her house, which she "prizes for its water view." Wilhelmina Dery was born in her Fort Trumbull house in 1918 and had lived there her entire life. Her husband, Charles, had lived in the house since they married some 60 years ago. The nine property owners owned 15 properties in Fort Trumbull. There was no allegation that any of the properties were blighted or otherwise in poor condition; rather, they were condemned only because they happened to be located in the development area.

In December 2000, the nine property owners brought an action against the City of New London claiming, among other things, that the taking of their properties would violate the "public use" restriction in the Fifth Amendment.

ISSUE

Does the condemnation action by the City of New London violate the property owners' Fifth Amendment right that authorized the taking of private property for "public use" by the payment of just compensation?

DECISION

No. The court began by noting two polar propositions. First, that it had long been accepted that the government could not take the property of one person for the sole purpose of transferring it to another person, even though the property owner is paid full compensation for the taking. Second, that it is equally clear that the government may transfer property from one private party to another if future "use by the public" is the purpose of the taking, the condemnation of land for a railroad with common-carrier duties being an example. Over time, the concept of "public use" has evolved as an inquiry as to whether the taking has a "public purpose." In reviewing challenges to takings, the courts eschew rigid formulations in favor of affording legislatures broad discretion as to what public needs justify the use of the taking power.

Those who govern the city were not confronted with the need to remove the blight in the Fort Trumbull areas, but their determination that the area was sufficiently distressed to justify a program of economic rejuvenation is entitled to deference from the court. The city has carefully formulated an economic development plan that it believes will provide appreciable benefits to the community including—but not limited to—new jobs and increased tax revenue. As with other exercises in urban planning and development, the city is endeavoring to coordinate a variety of commercial, residential, and recreational uses of land, with the hope that they will form a whole greater than the sum of its parts. To effectuate this plan, the city has invoked a state statute that specifically authorizes the use of eminent domain to promote economic development. Given the comprehensive nature of the plan, the thorough deliberation that preceded its adoption, and the limited scope of judicial review, it is appropriate for the court to resolve the challenges of the individual owners, not on a piecemeal basis, but rather in light of the entire plan. Because that plan unquestionably serves a public purpose, the takings challenged in this case satisfy the public purpose requirement of the Fifth Amendment to the Constitution.

In affirming the city's authority to take these properties, the court did not minimize the hardships that condemnations may entail, notwithstanding the payment of just compensation. States are not precluded from placing further restrictions on its exercise of the takings power. Indeed, many states already impose "public use" requirements that are stricter than the federal baseline. Some of these requirements have been established as a matter of state constitutional law, whereas others are expressed in state eminent domain statutes that carefully limit the grounds on which takings may be exercised. The necessity and wisdom of using eminent domain to promote economic development are certainly matters of legitimate public debate. However, the authority of the Supreme Court extends only to determining whether the city's proposed condemnations are for a "public purpose" within the meaning of the Fifth Amendment to the Federal Constitution.

Questions and Problem Cases

1. Yancy rented a building to Roberts, who operated a restaurant on the first floor and converted the second floor into apartments. The lease contained a provision permitting Roberts to remove from the second floor any fixture he furnished provided that such removal did not injure the real estate. Shortly before the lease was to expire, Roberts began to remove property from the building to move it to a new building. He removed booths, stools, sinks, dishwashers, refrigerators, and other items of equipment used in his

restaurant business. He also took various lighting fixtures, paneling, and sheetrock from the walls, and canopies and false ceilings from over the booths. The lighting fixtures were replacements for ones on the premises when Roberts took possession. The paneling was nailed to wooden strips nailed to sheetrock and in turn the wooden walls. The false ceilings were made of 2-by-4s nailed to the walls and covered by paneling and Celotex. On the second floor, Roberts was preparing to take plumbing fixtures, hot-water heaters, shower stalls, commodes, lighting fixtures, the heating system, and other items that he had installed. Yancy filed a lawsuit against Roberts seeking to obtain damages for injuries caused to the property and to enjoin him from removing "permanent improvements, fixtures, and attachments from the property." Which of these items of property was Roberts entitled to take, and which did he have to leave when he vacated the property?

2. William D. Robinson left a will in which he gave his real estate as follows: "I give all of my real estate to my wife, Lela S. Robinson, and at her death it goes to Frank M. Robinson, and at his death to his two boys, David Robinson and Richard Robinson." Does Lela have a *fee simple* interest in the property or a *life estate?*

3. Sewell and Reilly owned adjoining lots. They entered into a written agreement whereby each agreed to allow the other to use the south 10 feet of his lot for alley purposes "for so long as the alley" over the other party's lot remained open. Did this agreement create an easement or a license?

4. Mains Farm is a platted subdivision. A declaration of restrictive covenants for the subdivision was recorded in 1962. Worthington purchased a residential lot in Mains Farm in 1987. At that time a house already existed on the property. Before purchasing, Worthington obtained and read a copy of the restrictive covenants, which stated, in pertinent part, that all lots in Mains Farm "shall be designated as 'Residential Lots' and shall be used for single family residential purposes only."

   Worthington later began occupying the residence with four adults who paid her for 24-hour protective supervision and care. The four adults, who were not related to Worthington, were unable to do their own housekeeping, prepare their own meals, or attend to their personal hygiene. In providing this supervision and care on a for-profit basis, Worthington complied with the licensing and inspection requirements established by Washington law governing such enterprises.

   When her intended use of the property became known, other property owners objected. Despite that knowledge, she applied for a building permit to add a fifth bedroom to the house. She was advised that her intended facility did not comply with applicable zoning. Worthington later obtained the permit by stating that only her family would be living with her. In her words: "I told them what they wanted to hear."

   The Mains Farm Homeowners Association (Association), which consisted of owners of property in the subdivision, filed suit against Worthington and asked the court to enjoin her from using her property as an adult care business. The Association asserted that Worthington's use violated the restrictive covenants.

   Should Worthington's use of her property as an adult care business be enjoined as a violation of restrictive covenant?

5. On February 7, C. L. Hollaway, a real estate broker, obtained an open listing to sell Forshee's residence. The property was listed for sale at $55,000, and Hollaway was to receive a 6 percent commission if he sold it. On May 17, Elaine Sparks, a real estate agent who worked for Hollaway, showed the Forshee property to Mr. and Mrs. Corris Bell. She told the Bells where Forshee lived. She also offered to help the Bells find financing but was told that they were obtaining financing themselves. On May 23, Sparks learned that the Forshee property had been sold to the Bells. Hollaway then

brought a lawsuit against Forshee to recover a commission. Was Hollaway entitled to a commission on the grounds that his sales agent had been the effective procuring cause of the sale?

6. William and Alice Carter purchased two lots in a subdivision called Payson Ranchos in Payson, Arizona. Each lot in the subdivision had a restriction in the deed that prohibited the use of house trailers on the lots except for a period of up to 90 days during the time that a house was being constructed on the lot. The Carters moved a trailer onto one of their lots. They removed the tongue and wheels and set the trailer up on concrete blocks. They also connected it to a septic tank and attached power and water lines. A number of Carters' neighbors brought a lawsuit to require them to remove the trailer because it was in violation of the deed restriction. The Carters claimed that the restriction did not apply because their home was no longer a trailer. They also claimed that other neighbors were violating other deed restrictions concerning the erection of fences, so they should not be able to enforce the trailer restriction against the Carters. Could the restriction against trailers be used to force the Carters to remove their trailer?
7. The Schlemeyers purchased a frame apartment house and discovered shortly after the purchase that there was substantial termite infestation. They undertook some of the steps suggested by a specialist in pest control but did not take all the measures he indicated would be necessary to ensure success. Six years later, the Schlemeyers sold the apartment house to Fred Obde but did not advise him of the termite condition. When Obde later discovered the termite infestation, he brought a lawsuit for damages against the Schlemeyers, contending that they had fraudulently concealed the infestation from him when they had been under a duty to disclose it. Can Obde recover?
8. Hartford Penn-Cann Service, Inc., operated a gas station, restaurant, and truck wash directly across the highway from a gas station and truck stop operated under the name "Hartford 65." It brought suit against the operators of Hartford 65, contending that dust from their property was blowing onto the Penn-Cann Service property to the detriment of its business and to the health of its employees. Dust from Hartford 65 frequently blew onto Penn-Cann Service's property and prevented some of its employees from wearing contact lenses and one had to wear a dust mask; its machinery, including its gas pumps, had to be replaced more frequently; the windows in its restaurant could not be opened; dust collected on packages of food in the restaurant and the packages had to be wiped off before they could be opened; and business at its truck wash fell off. Should the owners of Hartford 65 be enjoined from operating a gas station or truck stop on the grounds such use constitutes a nuisance?
9. The state of Oregon enacted a comprehensive land use management program in 1973 that required all Oregon cities to adopt new comprehensive land use plans that were consistent with statewide planning goals. The city of Tigard, a community of some 30,000 residences on the southwest edge of Portland, developed a comprehensive plan and codified it as its Community Development Code (CDC). The CDC required property owners in the area zoned as the Central Business District to comply with a 15 percent open space requirement, limiting total site coverage including all structures and paved parking to 85 percent of the parcel. It also required that any new development facilitate a plan for a pedestrian/bicycle pathway by dedicating land for that purpose wherever required in the plan. The city also adopted a master drainage plan that suggested a series of improvements to the Fanno Creek Basin.

   Florence Dolan owned a plumbing and electric supply store located on Main Street in the central business district of Tigard. The 1.67-acre property was adjacent to Fanno

Creek and a portion of it was in the 100-year floodplain and unusable for commercial development. Dolan applied to the city for a permit to redevelop the site, proposing to nearly double the size of her store and pave a 39-space parking lot.

The City Planning Commission granted the permit application, subject to conditions imposed by the city's CDC. The commission required Dolan to dedicate the portion of her property lying within the 100-year floodplain for improvement of a storm drainage system along Fanno Creek and to dedicate an additional strip of land adjacent to the floodplain as a pedestrian/bicycle pathway. The dedication required by the condition encompassed approximately 7,000 square feet, or roughly 10 percent, of the property. Dolan requested variances from the CDC standards, as permitted in case of undue or unnecessary hardship, but the request was denied. The commission found that customers and employees of the store could utilize the pathway, that it would offset some of the traffic demand the store created on nearby streets, and that the increased storm water runoff from the parking lot would add to the public need to manage the stream channel and floodplain for drainage purposes.

Dolan appealed to the Land Use Board of Appeals on the ground that the city's dedication requirements were not related to the proposed development, and therefore, those requirements constituted an uncompensated taking of her property under the Fifth Amendment. The board denied the appeal, finding a "reasonable relationship" between alleviating the impacts of the proposed development and the required dedications. The Oregon Court of Appeals and its Supreme Court affirmed, and Dolan appealed to the United States Supreme Court. Did the condition placed by the city of Tigard constitute an unconstitutional taking of Dolan's property for public purposes without payment of just compensation?

Chapter 35

Landlord and Tenant

Learning Objectives

After you have studied this chapter, you should be able to:

1. Recognize that the legal principles applicable to landlord–tenant relationships are drawn from property law, contract law, and the law of negligence and that they incorporate the common law as well as legislative enactments.
2. Describe and differentiate the four main types of tenancies.
3. Understand the importance of a carefully drafted lease that makes clear the parties' rights and obligations and complies with any applicable provisions of state law, including the statute of frauds.
4. List and discuss the primary rights, duties, and liabilities of the landlord.
5. List and discuss the primary rights, duties, and liabilities of the tenant.
6. Describe the different ways that a lease may be terminated and identify the legal principles that apply to each method of termination.

Frank Johnson and Sonia Miller, along with several other friends, were looking to rent a house near campus for the following school year. In June, they orally agreed with a landlord on a one-year lease to begin the following August 15 with a monthly rent of $1,250 and provided a $1,500 security deposit. When they arrived at school in August, the current tenants were still in possession and did not move out until September 1, leaving the house a mess. The landlord told Frank and Sonia to move in and that he would clean it up later; however, he never did so despite repeated requests. They complained to the city housing department, which conducted an inspection and found numerous violations of the city's housing code. The city gave the landlord 15 days to make the necessary repairs. Before any of the repairs were made, a friend who was visiting was injured when she fell through some rotten floorboards on the porch. At the end of September, Frank, Sonia, and the other tenants moved out, but the landlord refused to return their security deposit.

(continued)

Among the legal issues raised by this scenario are:

- Did the oral agreement create an enforceable lease?
- Were the tenants' rights violated when they were unable to take possession on August 15?
- Does the landlord have any liability to the injured friend?
- Are the tenants entitled to cancel the lease on the grounds the house is not habitable and obtain the return of their security deposit?

Leases and Tenancies

Landlord–Tenant Relationship

Landlord–tenant law has undergone dramatic change, owing in large part to the changing nature of the relationship between landlords and tenants. In England and in early America, farms were the most common subject of leases. The tenant sought to lease land on which to grow crops or graze cattle. Accordingly, traditional landlord–tenant law viewed the lease as primarily a conveyance of land and paid relatively little attention to its contractual aspects.

In today's society, however, the landlord–tenant relationship is typified by the lease of property for residential or commercial purposes. The tenant occupies only a small portion of the total property. He bargains primarily for the use of structures on the land rather than for the land itself. He is likely to have signed a landlord-provided form lease, the terms of which he may have had little or no opportunity to negotiate. In areas with a shortage of affordable housing, a residential tenant's ability to bargain for favorable lease provisions is further hampered. Because the typical landlord–tenant relationship can no longer be characterized fairly as one in which the parties have equal knowledge and bargaining power, it is not always realistic to presume that tenants are capable of negotiating to protect their own interests.

LO1

Although it was initially slow to recognize the changing nature of the landlord–tenant relationship, the law places greater emphasis than it once did on the contract components of the relationship. As a result, modern contract doctrines such as unconscionability, constructive conditions, the duty to mitigate damages, and implied warranties are commonly applied to leases. Such doctrines may operate to compensate for tenants' lack of bargaining power. In addition, state legislatures and city councils have enacted statutes and ordinances that regulate leased property and the landlord–tenant relationship.

This chapter's discussion of landlord–tenant law focuses on the nature of leasehold interests, the traditional rights and duties of landlords and tenants, and statutory and judicial developments affecting those rights and duties.

Nature of Leases

A **lease** is a contract by which an owner of property, the **landlord** (also called the *lessor*), conveys to the **tenant** (also called the *lessee*) the exclusive right to possess property for a period of time. The property interest conveyed to the tenant is called a **leasehold estate.**

LO2

Types of Tenancies

The duration of the tenant's possessory right depends upon the type of **tenancy** established by or resulting from the lease. There are four main types of tenancies.

1. *Tenancy for a term.* In a **tenancy for a term** (also called a *tenancy for years*), the landlord and tenant have agreed on a specific duration of the lease and have fixed the date on which the tenancy will terminate. For example, if Amber, a college student, leases an apartment for the academic year ending May 25, 2015, a tenancy for a term will have been created. The tenant's right to possess the property ends on the date agreed upon without any further notice unless the lease contains a provision permitting extension.

2. *Periodic tenancy.* A **periodic tenancy** is created when the parties agree that rent will be paid in regular successive intervals until notice to terminate is given but do not agree on a specific lease duration. If the tenant pays rent monthly, the tenancy is from month to month; if the tenant pays yearly, as is sometimes done under agricultural leases, the tenancy is from year to year. (Periodic tenancies therefore are sometimes called *tenancies from month to month* or *tenancies from year to year.*) To terminate a periodic tenancy, either party must give advance notice to the other. The precise amount of notice required is often defined by state statutes. For example, to terminate a tenancy from month to month, most states require that the notice be given at least one month in advance.

3. *Tenancy at will.* A **tenancy at will** occurs when property is leased for an indefinite period of time and either party may choose to conclude the tenancy at any time. Generally, tenancies at will involve situations in which the tenant either does not pay rent or does not pay it at regular intervals. For example, Kim allows her friend Eric to live in the apartment over her garage. Although this tenancy's name indicates that it is terminable "at [the] will" of either party, most states require that the landlord give reasonable advance notice to the tenant before exercising the right to terminate the tenancy.

4. *Tenancy at sufferance.* A **tenancy at sufferance** occurs when a tenant remains in possession of the property (holds over) after a lease has expired. In this situation, the landlord has two options: (1) treating the holdover tenant as a trespasser and bringing an action to eject him and (2) continuing to treat him as a tenant and collecting rent from him. Until the landlord makes her election, the tenant is a tenant at sufferance. Suppose that Frank has leased an apartment for one year from Jim. At the end of the year, Frank holds over and does not move out. Frank is a tenant at sufferance. Jim may have him ejected or may continue treating him as a tenant. If Jim elects the latter alternative, a new tenancy is created. The new tenancy with be either a tenancy for a term or a periodic tenancy, depending on the facts of the case and any presumptions established by state law. Thus, a tenant who holds over for even a few days runs the risk of creating a new tenancy he might not want.

Concept Summary: Types of Tenancies

Type of Lease	Characteristics	Termination
Tenancy for a Term	Landlord and tenant agree on a specific duration of the lease and fix the date on which the tenancy will end.	Ends automatically on the date agreed upon; no additional notice necessary.

(continued)

Concept Summary: Types of Tenancies *(concluded)*

Periodic Tenancy	Landlord and tenant agree that tenant will pay rent at regular, successive intervals (e.g., month to month).	Either party may terminate by giving the amount of advance notice required by state law.
Tenancy at Will	Landlord and tenant agree that tenant may possess property for an indefinite amount of time, with no agreement to pay rent at regular, successive intervals.	May be terminated "at will" by either party, but state law requires advance notice.
Tenancy at Sufferance	Tenant remains in possession after the termination of one of the leaseholds described above until landlord has brought ejectment action against tenant or collected rent from him.	Landlord has a choice of: 1. Treating tenant as a trespasser and bringing ejectment action against him, or 2. Accepting rent from tenant, thus creating a new leasehold.

Execution of a Lease

As transfers of interests in land, leases may be covered by the statute of frauds. In most states, a lease for a term of more than one year from the date it is made is unenforceable unless it is evidenced by a suitable writing signed by the party to be charged. A few states, however, require leases to be evidenced by a writing only when they are for a term of more than three years.

The vignette at the start of this chapter poses a situation with an oral lease entered into in June that will run for a year beginning on August 15. This lease would not be enforceable in a state where the statute of frauds requires a lease for more than a year from the date it is made to be in writing. However, it would be enforceable in a state where an oral lease for a period of less than three years is allowed.

LO3

Good business practice demands that leases be carefully drafted to make clear the parties' respective rights and obligations. Care in drafting leases is especially important in cases of long-term and commercial leases. Lease provisions normally cover such essential matters as the term of the lease, the rent to be paid, the uses the tenant may make of the property, the circumstances under which the landlord may enter the property, the parties' respective obligations regarding the condition of the property, and the responsibility (as between landlord and tenant) for making repairs. In addition, leases often contain provisions allowing a possible extension of the term of the lease and purporting to limit the parties' rights to assign the lease or sublet the property. State or local law often regulates lease terms. For example, the Uniform Residential Landlord and Tenant Act (URLTA) has been enacted in a substantial minority of states. The URLTA prohibits the inclusion of certain lease provisions, such as a clause by which the tenant supposedly agrees to pay the landlord's attorneys' fees in an action to enforce the lease. In states that have not enacted the URLTA, lease terms are likely to be regulated at least to a moderate degree by some combination of state statutes, common law principles, and local housing codes.

Schultz v. Wurdlow

1995 Ohio App. LEXIS 333 (Ct. App. Ohio 1995)

FACTS

Emily Schultz and Kerri Minnich submitted a "Rental Application and Agreement" to rent an apartment owned and managed by Earl Wurdlow. Both Schultz and Minnich were students at Ohio State University and wished to rent the apartment only during the school year (September through June). Schultz had rented the same apartment during the preceding school year.

Wurdlow informed both women that it would be necessary to have their parents complete and sign a "Parent Agreement," which was basically identical to the lease documents. Although it was his policy not to permit residents to move in before providing him with a signed copy of the parental agreement, he permitted Schultz to move in because her mother promised to sign and return the form to him. Minnich provided him a copy of the form; however, it included her signature rather than those of her parents. Both women moved into the apartment.

After realizing that neither of the women's respective parents were willing to complete the agreement, Wurdlow gave them 30 days' notice to move out of the apartment. Both did so but requested that Wurdlow return the $410 security deposit they had paid on signing the rental agreement. Wurdlow refused to return it. He did not assert that there was any rent past due or damage to the apartment; however, he did claim that they were responsible for rerental expenses and loss of rent revenue. Schultz and Minnich then filed an action in small claims court to recover the security deposit.

ISSUE

Was a tenancy at will created where there was no valid written lease but the party took possession of the premises?

DECISION

Yes. Under the statute of frauds in Ohio, a lease, whether for a short term or for a long term, must be in writing. Where, as here, there is an agreement purporting to be a lease that has a defect and the tenant enters into possession and pays rent, a tenancy at will is created. The tenancy is subject to all other terms of the purported lease except duration. Duration is determined by the period covered by the expected rent payment. Because rent was paid here on a monthly basis, a month-to-month tenancy resulted. Therefore, either party had the right to terminate the lease with one month's notice. Wurdlow gave such notice. When the women moved out of the apartment, Wurdlow would be permitted to deduct any past due rent or any damages that he sustained as a result of the tenants' noncompliance with the housing code or the rental agreement. Wurdlow here was not claiming any past due rent or damages. His only claim was for rerental expenses and loss of rent revenue; however, these are not recoverable under a properly terminated month-to-month tenancy, and the tenants were entitled to the return of their full security deposit.

Rights, Duties, and Liabilities of the Landlord

LO4

Landlord's Rights

The landlord is entitled to the *agreed rent* for the term of the lease. Upon expiration of the lease, the landlord has the right to the *return of the premises in as good a condition as when leased* except for normal wear and tear and any destruction by an act of God.

Security Deposits

Landlords commonly require tenants to make security deposits or advance payments of rent. Such deposits operate to protect the landlord's right to receive rent as well as her right to reversion of the property in good condition. Many cities and states have enacted statutes or ordinances designed to prevent landlord abuse of security deposits. These laws typically limit the amount a landlord may demand and require that the security deposit be refundable, except for portions withheld by the landlord because of the tenant's nonpayment of rent or tenant-caused property damage beyond ordinary wear and tear. Some statutes or ordinances also require the landlord to place the funds in interest-bearing accounts when the lease is for more than a minimal period of time. As a general rule, these laws require landlords to provide tenants a written accounting regarding their security deposits and any portions being withheld. Such an accounting normally must be provided within a specified period of time (30 days, for example) after the termination of the lease. The landlord's failure to comply with statutes and ordinances regarding security deposits may cause the landlord to experience adverse consequences that vary state by state.

Landlord's Duties

Fair Housing Act

As explained in Chapter 34, the Fair Housing Act prohibits housing discrimination on the basis of race, color, sex, religion, national origin, handicap, and familial status. The Fair Housing Act prohibits discriminatory practices in various transactions affecting housing, including the rental of dwellings. The act does provide an exemption for certain persons who own and rent single-family houses. To qualify for this exemption, owners must not use a real estate broker or an illegal advertisement and cannot own more than three such houses at one time. It also exempts owners who rent rooms or units in dwellings in which they themselves reside if those dwellings house no more than four families.

Included within the act's prohibited instances of discrimination against a protected person are refusals to rent property to such a person; discrimination against him or her in the terms, conditions, or privileges of rental; publication of any advertisement or statement indicating any preference, limitation, or discrimination operating to the disadvantage of a protected person; and representations that a dwelling is not available for rental to such a person when, in fact, it is available.

The act also makes it a discriminatory practice for a landlord to refuse to permit a tenant with a handicap to make—at his own expense—reasonable modifications to leased property. The landlord may, however, make this permission conditional on the tenant's agreement to restore the property to its previous condition upon termination of the lease, reasonable wear and tear excepted. In addition, landlords are prohibited from refusing to make reasonable accommodations in rules, policies, practices, or services if such accommodations are necessary to afford a handicapped tenant equal opportunity to use and enjoy the leased premises. When constructing certain types of multifamily housing for first occupancy, property owners and developers risk violating the act if they fail to make the housing accessible to persons with handicaps.

Because of a perceived increase in the frequency with which landlords refused to rent to families with children, the act prohibits landlords from excluding families with children. If, however, the dwelling falls within the act's "housing for older persons" exception, this prohibition does not apply.

Implied Warranty of Possession

Landlords have certain obligations that are imposed by law whenever property is leased. One of these obligations stems from the landlord's **implied warranty of possession.** This warranty guarantees the tenant's right to possess the property for the term of the lease. Suppose that Pat rents an apartment from Julia for a term to begin on September 1, 2014, and to end on August 31, 2015. When Pat attempts to move in on September 1, 2014, she finds that Sam, the previous tenant, is still in possession of the property. In this case, Julia has breached the implied warranty of possession.

Implied Warranty of Quiet Enjoyment

By leasing property, the landlord also makes an **implied warranty of quiet enjoyment** (or *covenant of quiet enjoyment*). This covenant guarantees that the tenant's possession will not be interfered with as a result of the landlord's act or omission. In the absence of a contrary provision in the lease or an emergency that threatens the property, the landlord may not enter the leased property during the term of the lease. If he does, he will be liable for trespass. In some cases, courts have held that the covenant of quiet enjoyment was violated when the landlord failed to stop third parties, such as trespassers or other tenants who make excessive noise, from interfering with the tenant's enjoyment of the leased premises.

Landlord's Responsibility for Condition of Leased Property

The common law historically held that landlords made no implied warranties regarding the *condition* or quality of leased premises. As an adjunct to the landlord's right to receive the leased property in good condition at the termination of the lease, the common law imposed on the *tenant* the duty to make repairs. Even when the lease contained a landlord's express warranty or express promise to make repairs, a tenant was not entitled to withhold rent if the landlord failed to carry out his obligations. This was because a fundamental contract performance principle—that a party is not obligated to perform if the other party fails to perform—was considered inapplicable to leases. However, changing views of the landlord–tenant relationship have resulted in dramatically increased legal responsibility on the part of landlords for the condition of leased residential property.

Implied Warranty of Habitability

The legal principle that landlords made no implied warranty regarding the condition of leased property arose during an era when tenants used land primarily for agricultural purposes. Buildings existing on the property were frequently of secondary importance. They also tended to be simple structures lacking modern conveniences such as plumbing and wiring. These buildings were fairly easily inspected and repaired by the tenant, who was generally more self-sufficient than today's typical tenant. In view of the relative simplicity of the structures, landlord and tenant were considered to have equal knowledge of the property's condition upon commencement of the lease. Thus, a rule requiring the tenant to make repairs seemed reasonable.

The position of modern residential tenants differs greatly from that of an earlier era's agricultural tenants. The modern residential tenant bargains not for the use of the ground itself but for the use of a building (or portion thereof) as a dwelling. The structures on land today are complex, frequently involving systems (such as plumbing and electrical systems) to which the tenant does not have physical access. Besides decreasing the likelihood of perceiving defects during inspection, this complexity compounds the difficulty of making repairs—something at which today's tenant already tends to be less adept than his grandparents were. Moreover, placing a duty of tenants to negotiate for express warranties and duties to repair is no longer feasible. Residential leases are now routinely executed on standard forms provided by landlords.

For these reasons, statutes or judicial decisions in most states now impose an **implied warranty of habitability** on many landlords who lease residential property. According to the vast majority of cases, this warranty is applicable to *residential* property, not to property leased for commercial uses. The implied warranty of habitability's content in lease settings is basically the same as in the sale of real estate: The property must be safe and suitable for human habitation. In lease settings, however, the landlord not only must deliver a habitable dwelling at the beginning of the lease but must also *maintain* the property in a habitable condition during the term of the lease. Various statutes and judicial decisions provide that the warranty includes an obligation that the leased property comply with any applicable housing codes.

In the scenario set out at the start of this chapter, the tenants who arrived on the date when the lease is to begin and find that the property is not in a suitable condition for habitation, including violations of the city's housing code, would be entitled to cancel the lease and obtain the return of their security deposit on the grounds the implied warranty of habitability had been violated.

Remedies for Breach of Implied Warranty of Habitability

From a tenant's point of view, the implied warranty of habitability is superior to "constructive eviction" (discussed below) because a tenant does not have to vacate the leased premises in order to seek a remedy for breach of the warranty. The particular remedies for breach of the implied warranty of habitability differ from state to state. Some of the remedies a tenant may pursue include these.

1. *Action for damages.* The breach of the implied warranty of habitability violates the lease and renders the landlord liable for damages. The damages generally are measured by the diminished value of the leasehold. The landlord's breach of the implied warranty of habitability may also be asserted by the tenant as a counterclaim and defense in the landlord's action for eviction and/or nonpayment of rent.

2. *Termination of lease.* In extreme cases, the landlord's breach of the implied warranty of habitability may justify the tenant's termination of the lease. For this remedy to be appropriate, the landlord's breach must have been substantial enough to constitute a material breach.

3. *Rent abatement.* Some states permit rent abatement, a remedy under which the tenant withholds part of the rent for the period during which the landlord was in breach of the implied warranty of habitability. Where authorized by law, this approach allows the tenant to pay a reduced rent that reflects the *actual* value of the leasehold in its defective condition. There are different ways of computing this value. State law determines the amount by which the rent will be reduced.

4. *Repair-and-deduct.* A number of states have statutes that permit the tenant to have defects repaired and to deduct the repair costs from her rent. The repairs authorized in these statutes are usually limited to essential services such as electricity and plumbing. They also require that the tenant give the landlord notice of the defect and an adequate opportunity to make the repairs himself.

Constructive Eviction

The doctrine of **constructive eviction** may aid a tenant when property becomes unsuitable for the purposes for which it was leased because of the landlord's act or omission, such as the breach of a duty to repair or the convenant of quiet enjoyment. Under this doctrine, which applies to both residential and commercial property, the tenant may terminate the lease because she has effectively been evicted as a result of the poor condition or the objectionable circumstances there. Constructive eviction gives a tenant the right to vacate the property without further rent obligation if she does so *promptly* after giving the landlord reasonable notice and an opportunity to correct the problem. Because constructive eviction requires the tenant to vacate the leased premises, it is an unattractive option for tenants who cannot afford to move or do not have a suitable alternative place to live.

The principle of constructive eviction is illustrated in *Welsch v. Groat.*

Welsch v. Groat

2005 Conn. Super. LEXIS 1359 (Super. Ct. Conn. 2005) aff'd 897 A.2d 710 (Conn. App. Ct. 2006)

FACTS

On June 1, 2003, James Welsch, as owner, entered into to a written agreement with Michael Groat, as tenant, for a one-year lease of a single-family residence located in Old Saybrook, Connecticut, at a monthly rent of $1,500 due on the first day of each month. At the execution of the lease Groat paid the June rental of $1,500 and a security deposit of $3,000. He made an additional payment of $1,500 for a total of $6,000 but ended up occupying the premises for only three months.

When Groat began occupancy along with his children, he discovered leaks and water damage in the basement of the premises. In early July, Groat advised Welsch that, in addition to water damage and the presence of mold and mildew, the premises contained many other deficiencies. Groat had intended to use a basement room as a bedroom for his children, but the water damage made such use impossible.

In response to Groat's notification of the poor condition of the premises, Welsch's attorney referred Groat to section 12 of the lease he had signed which stated he had inspected the premises and accepted them as he found them.

By letter dated August 1, 2003, Groat outlined the defects in the premises including gutters clogged, spilling over; driveway severely cracked and crumbling; side storm door falling apart, missing screen; front storm door pump broken, missing screen; faucet leaks from stem when on; oven temperature gauge off; sink drain does not work; tub drain does not work; cold water handle is stripped; water ends up on basement floor; small bedroom closet door does not clear carpet; large bedroom entry door does not close; basement is constantly wet; there are puddles when it rains and a constant wet slime along the east wall; the paneling and trim are badly rotted, obviously a long-term problem; paint is peeling from concrete walls; latex floor is bubbling and peeling from wetness; only one basement window is operational; there are significant mold and mildew issues with the entire basement, especially the finished living area.

Groat moved out in August. On October 11, 2003, Welsch brought an action against Groat for breach of the lease. Groat filed a counterclaim claiming, among other things, constructive eviction.

ISSUE

Did the conditions at the house and the landlord's failure to make the necessary repairs in a timely fashion constitute a breach of the lease and justify termination of the lease on the grounds of constructive eviction?

DECISION

Yes. The court found that Welsch did not remedy the conditions with the urgency and intensity warranted by the scope and nature of the needed repairs, particularly the water damage and mold and mildew formation. The failure to adequately and timely make the repairs rendered the premises uninhabitable and constituted a constructive eviction of Groat and a breach of the lease by Welsch. The court awarded the following damages to Groat because of Welsch's breach of the lease: $1,500 overpayment of rent; $1,000 moving expenses; and $300 damage to clothing, for a total of $2,800 along with the costs of the suit. Groat also was awarded judgment on Welsch's suit against him for breach of the lease.

Housing Codes

Many cities and states have enacted housing codes that impose duties on a property owner with respect to the condition of leased property. Typical of these provisions is Section 400.3 of the District of Columbia Municipal Regulations, which provides: "No person shall rent or offer to rent any habitation or the furnishing thereof unless such habitation and its furnishings are in a clean, safe, and sanitary condition, in repair and free from rodents or vermin." Such codes also commonly call for the provision and maintenance of necessary services such as heat, water, and electricity, as well as suitable bathroom and kitchen facilities. Housing codes also tend to require that specified minimum space-per-tenant standards be met, that windows, doors, floors, and screens be kept in repair, that the property be painted and free of lead paint, that keys and locks meet certain specifications, and that the landlord issue written receipts for rent payments. A landlord's failure to comply with an applicable housing code may result in a fine or in liability for injuries resulting from the property's disrepair. The noncompliance may also result in the landlord's losing part or all of his claim to the agreed-upon rent. Some housing codes establish that tenants have the right to withhold rent until necessary repairs have been made and the right to move out in cases of particularly egregious violations of housing code requirements.

Americans with Disabilities Act

Landlords leasing property constituting a *place of public accommodation* (primarily commercial property as opposed to private residential property) must pay heed to Title III of the Americans with Disabilities Act. Under Title III, owners and possessors of real property that is a place of public accommodation may be expected to make reasonable accommodations, including physical modifications of the property, in order to allow disabled persons to have access to the property. Chapter 34 contains a detailed discussion of Title III's provisions.

Landlord's Tort Liability

Traditional No-Liability Rule

There are two major effects of the traditional rule that a landlord had no legal responsibility for the condition of the leased property. The first effect—that the uninhabitability of the premises traditionally did not give a tenant the right to withhold rent, assert a defense to nonpayment, or terminate a lease—has already been discussed. The second effect was that landlords normally could not be held liable in tort for injuries suffered by tenants on leased property. This state of affairs stemmed from the notion that the tenant had the ability and responsibility to inspect the property for defects before leasing it. By leasing the property, the tenant was presumed to take it as it was, with any existing defects. As to any defects that might arise during the term of the lease, the landlord's tort immunity was seen as justified by his lack of control over the leased property once he had surrendered it to the tenant.

Traditional Exceptions to No-Liability Rule

Even before the current era's pro-tenant legal developments, however, courts created exceptions to the no-liability rule. In the following situations, landlords have traditionally owed the tenant (or an appropriate third party) a duty, the breach of which could constitute a tort:

1. *Duty to maintain common areas.* Landlords have a duty to use reasonable care to *maintain the common areas* (such as stairways, parking lots, and elevators) over which they retain control. If a tenant or a tenant's guest sustains injury as a result of the landlord's negligent maintenance of a common area, the landlord is liable.

2. *Duty to disclose hidden defects.* Landlords have a duty to disclose hidden defects about which they know if the defects are not reasonably discoverable by the tenant. The landlord is liable if a tenant or appropriate third party suffers injury because of a hidden danger that was known to the landlord but went undisclosed.

3. *Duty to use reasonable care in performing repairs.* If a landlord repairs leased property, he must *exercise reasonable care in making the repairs.* The landlord may be liable for the consequences stemming from negligently performed repairs, even if he was not obligated to perform them.

4. *Duty to maintain property leased for admission to the public.* The landlord has a duty to suitably maintain property that is leased for *admission to the public.* A theater would be an example.

5. *Duty to maintain furnished dwellings.* The landlord who rents a *fully furnished dwelling* for a short time impliedly warrants that the premises are safe and habitable.

Except for the above circumstances, the landlord traditionally was not liable for injuries suffered by the tenant on leased property. Note that none of these exceptions would apply to one of the most common injury scenarios—when the tenant was injured by a defect in her own apartment and the defect resulted from the landlord's failure to repair rather than from negligently performed repairs.

Current Trends in Landlord's Tort Liability

Today, the traditional rule of landlord tort immunity has largely been abolished. The proliferation of housing codes and the development of the implied warranty of habitability have persuaded a majority of courts to impose on landlords the duty to use *reasonable care* in their maintenance of the leased property. As discussed earlier, a landlord's duty to keep the property in repair may be based on an express clause in the lease, the implied warranty of habitability, or provisions of a housing code or statute. The landlord now may be liable if injury results from her negligent failure to carry out her duty to make repairs. As a general rule, a landlord will not be liable unless she had *notice* of the defect and a reasonable opportunity to make repairs.

Applying these principles to the vignette at the beginning of this chapter, a landlord who was on notice of a significant defect in property he had leased, namely rotten floorboards in a porch, and who failed to make repairs in a timely fashion probably would be liable for injuries sustained by an invitee of the tenants.

The duty of care landlords owe tenants has been held to include the duty to take reasonable steps to protect tenants from substantial risks of harm created by other tenants. Courts have held landlords liable for tenants' injuries resulting from dangerous conditions (such as vicious animals) maintained by other tenants when the landlord knew or had reason to know of the danger.

It is not unusual for landlords to attempt to insulate themselves from negligence liability to tenants by including an *exculpatory clause* in the standard form of leases they expect tenants to sign. An exculpatory clause purports to relieve the landlord from legal responsibility that the landlord could otherwise face (on negligence or other grounds) in certain instances of premises-related injuries suffered by tenants. A number of state legislatures and courts have frowned upon exculpatory clauses when they are included in leases of residential property. There has been an increasing judicial tendency to limit the effect of exculpatory clauses or declare them unenforceable on public policy grounds when they appear in residential leases.

In the case that follows, *Brooks v. Lewin Realty III, Inc.*, the court held that a landlord could be liable for injuries to a child that were caused by the landlord's failure to comply with the city's housing code.

Brooks v. Lewin Realty III, Inc.

835 A.2d 616 (Ct. App. Md. 2003)

FACTS

In August 1988, Shirley Parker rented a house in Baltimore City. Fresh paint was applied to the interior of the house at the beginning of the tenancy. Sharon Parker, Shirley's daughter, moved into the house shortly after her mother rented it. On December 6, 1989, Sharon gave birth to Sean, who then also lived there. Early in 1991, when Sean was slightly more than a year old, Lewin Realty purchased the house at an auction. Before the purchase, one of the owners of Lewin Realty walked through the house accompanied by Sharon as he

(continued)

inspected it. At the time of the walk-through there was peeling, chipping, and flaking paint present in numerous areas of the interior of the house, including in Sean's bedroom. After Lewin Realty purchased the house, it entered into a new lease with Shirley but did not paint its interior at that time.

In February 1992, Sean was diagnosed with an elevated blood lead level. In May 1992 the house was inspected and found to contain 56 areas of peeling, chipping, and flaking lead paint, and the Baltimore City Health Department (BCHD) issued a lead paint violation notice to Lewin Realty.

Section 702(a) of the Baltimore City Housing Code requires that a dwelling be kept in "good repair" and "safe condition" and prohibits a landlord from leasing a dwelling that violates the housing code. The housing code further provides that maintaining a dwelling in good repair and safe condition includes keeping all interior walls, ceilings, woodwork, doors, and windows clean and free of any flaking, loose, or peeling paint. It also mandates the removal of loose and peeling paint from interior surfaces and requires that any new paint be free of lead. The housing code also grants the landlord the right of access to rental dwellings at reasonable times for the purpose of making inspections and such repairs as are necessary to comply with the Code.

Sharon Parker brought a lawsuit on behalf of her son, alleging negligence among other things. The negligence claim was founded on several grounds, including (*a*) Lewin Realty's violation of the Baltimore City Housing Code; (*b*) Sean's exposure to an unreasonable risk of harm from the lead-based paint while Lewin Realty knew that its dangerous properties were not known to Sean and not discoverable in the exercise of reasonable care; (*c*) Lewin Realty's failure to exercise reasonable care in properly maintaining the walls, doors, and ceilings after Lewin Realty had actual and constructive knowledge of the flaking paint condition; and (*d*) Lewin Realty's failure to exercise reasonable care to inspect the dwelling's paint when a reasonable inspection would have revealed the flaking paint condition.

One of the questions in the litigation was whether the tenants were required to show that the landlord had notice of the violation in order to establish a prima facie case of negligence. Lewin Realty argued that because the tenant had control over the property and neither the common law nor any statute expressly required inspections during the tenancy, the court should not impose such a duty. Lewin Realty further argued it should not be held liable unless it had actual knowledge of the violation and that landlords who do not perform periodic inspections should not be charged with knowledge of what such inspections would reveal.

ISSUE

Should Lewin Realty be liable for the tenant's injuries only if it had actual knowledge of the violation of the housing code?

DECISION

No. Initially, the court noted that under the common law and in the absence of a statute, a landlord ordinarily has no duty to keep rental premises in repair or to inspect the rental premises. However, there are exceptions to this general rule. Where there is an applicable statutory scheme designed to protect a class of persons such as the plaintiff in this case, the well-settled rule in Maryland is that the defendant's duty is prescribed by the statute or ordinance and the violation of the statute or ordinance is itself evidence of negligence. Accordingly, the tenants were not required to show that the landlord had actual notice of the violation of the law (the lead-based paint that was flaking or peeling from the walls of the leased dwelling). The city council sought to protect children from lead paint poisoning by putting landlords on notice of conditions which could enhance the risk of such injuries. The landlord's duty is not limited to a one-time duty at the inception of the lease; rather, the landlord must take whatever measures are necessary during the pendency of the lease to ensure the dwelling's continued compliance with the Code. To facilitate the continuous maintenance of leased premises, the Code explicitly grants to the landlord a right of entry to ensure that the landlord can make such inspections and such repairs as are necessary to comply with the Code.

DISSENT

Under the common law and the prior decisions of this court, a plaintiff seeking to hold a landlord liable for common law negligence for injuries resulting from flaking, loose, or peeling paint had to establish that the landlord had notice of the problem. Here, the majority holds that by enacting the Baltimore City Housing Code, the city council intended to abolish the element of notice. The majority also reads into the Code an ongoing, affirmative duty by landlords to inspect periodically each of their housing units for loose or flaking paint as long as they retain ownership of the premises. I disagree with the majority's conclusion that the ordinance does away with the traditional common law notice requirement by the landlord as a precursor to liability for negligence.

The majority essentially imposes strict liability upon landlords and makes landlords the insurers of its tenants for injuries sustained by a minor plaintiff due to exposure to lead-based paint. This new rule also means that plaintiff-tenants will no longer be required to notify landlords of hazards in their dwelling home, hazards that they, not the landlord, are in the best position to identify. The common law notice requirement exists to deal with this unfairness.

Ethics in Action

WHAT IS THE ETHICAL THING TO DO?

Suppose you own an older house that in the past was painted with lead-based paint. You rent it to a family with three young children. A state statute forbids painting new property with lead-based paint, but it does not forbid renting older property previously painted with lead-based paint. Should you disclose the lead-based paint to your tenants? What legal liability might you incur if you do not do so?

Landlord's Liability for Injuries Resulting from Others' Criminal Conduct

Another aspect of the trend toward increasing landlords' legal accountability is that many courts have imposed on landlords the duty to take reasonable steps to protect tenants and others on their property from foreseeable criminal conduct. Although landlords are not insurers of the safety of persons on their property, a number of courts have found them liable for injuries sustained by individuals who have been criminally attacked on the landlord's property if the attack was facilitated by the landlord's failure to comply with housing codes or maintain reasonable security. This liability has been imposed on residential and commercial landlords (such as shopping mall owners). Some courts have held that the implied warranty of habitability includes the obligation to provide reasonable security. In most states that have imposed this type of liability, however, principles of negligence or negligence per se furnish the controlling rationale. The law of negligence is covered in detail in Chapter 7.

In the case that follows, *Tan v. Arnel Management Company*, a California court applied negligence principles in holding that a landlord violated its duty of care to a tenant who was rendered a quadriplegic when shot in the course of an attempted carjacking on a common area of an apartment complex.

Tan v. Arnel Management Company

88 Cal.Rptr.3d 754 (Cal. Ct. App. 2009)

FACTS

Arnel Management Company manages the Pheasant Ridge Apartments, a 620 unit, multibuilding apartment complex with over 1,000 residents situated on 20.59 acres in Rowland Heights, California. The entrance road bisects the property. The beginning of the entrance road has a grassy median and is bordered on both sides by tennis courts. A little farther up the road lie two open parking lots. One is a visitor lot, located on one side of the entrance road, and the other is the parking lot for the leasing office, located on the other side of the road. Just before the two parking lots, in the middle of the entrance road, sits a "guard shack." Continuing past the two parking lots to the back of the property, the entrance road fans out into a circle by which vehicles can turn left or right through two security gates. The apartments are located beyond the security gates. The gates are remote-control operated. Most of the property's parking spaces lie behind these gates by the apartments.

Yu Fang Tan, his wife Chun Kuei Chang, and their son moved into Pheasant Ridge in July 2002 and received one assigned parking space. Tenants could pay an additional fee for a garage, but Tan and his family chose not to rent one. At the time they leased the apartment, they learned that if they had a second car, they could park it in unassigned parking spaces throughout the complex, or in one of the two lots for visitors and the leasing office, as long as the car was removed from the leasing office lot before 7:00 AM.

At around 11:30 PM on December 28, 2002, Tan arrived home and drove around the property looking for an open parking space because his wife had parked the family's

(continued)

other car in their assigned space. Unable to locate an available space, Tan parked in the leasing office parking lot outside the gated area.

As Tan was parking his car, an unidentified man approached him and asked for help. When Tan opened his window, the man pointed a gun at Tan and told him to get out of the car because the man wanted it. Tan responded, "Okay. Let me park my car first." But the car rolled a little, at which point the assailant shot plaintiff in the neck. The incident rendered Tan a quadriplegic.

Tan and his wife brought suit against Arnel Management alleging, among other things, negligence and loss of consortium. Arnel Management sought and obtained a pre-trial hearing to ascertain whether Tan's proposed evidence of prior similar criminal conduct was sufficiently similar to make the assault on Tan foreseeable.

Tan's expert, a UCLA sociology professor, looked at police reports, complaints to the police, property management reports, and records of Pheasant Ridge's security services. After excluding from his analysis those prior incidents involving attacks by acquaintances, he found 10 incidents he viewed as being "particularly significant warning signs," of which three involved "prior violent incidents." All of the incidents involved a sudden attack without warning late at night by a stranger who was on the ungated portion of the premises. Tan also presented nearly 80 examples of thefts from garages or cars or thefts of cars occurring on the Pheasant Ridge property, but the trial court excluded the evidence because the incidents did not involve robberies or violent attacks on people.

In response to a question from the court as to what additional security measures Tan was contending fell within the apartment manager's duty to have in place in order to prevent the harm he sustained, Tan's counsel indicated they wanted gates installed on the entrance roadway before the leasing office and visitor parking lots, rather than at the back of the entrance road. The purpose would be to effectively deter escape and to reduce the probability of a carjack occurring. He also indicated that Tan was not asking that any measure be undertaken that would require ongoing surveillance or monitoring or necessitate the expenditure of funds. The expert presented evidence that when gates were installed in crime areas, the rate of violence went down as potential offenders want to anticipate an easy escape. Moreover, gates deter strangers who must explain their presence on the property.

The trial court ruled that Tan had failed to demonstrate that enclosing the entire complex, moving the gates, and installing some system or a guard that would let invited guests enter the complex at night, as Tan proposed, would be any less burdensome than providing full-time security guards at night. Therefore, the court observed that in order to impose a duty on the apartment manager, Tan would have to demonstrate a high degree of foreseeability of the crime committed against Tan based upon prior similar incidents of violent crime at Pheasant Ridge. However, the court ruled that none of the prior incidents referenced by Tan's expert involved a prior attempted carjacking, or of an attempted murder, or of anyone being shot, or shot at. Therefore, the trial court held that Arnel Management had no duty to take the additional security measures proposed by Tan to enhance the security in the common areas, including the leasing office parking lot where the crime occurred. Tan appealed.

ISSUE

Did the landlord owe Tan a duty to take additional security measures to prevent the kind of third-party criminal act that took place?

DECISION

To succeed in a negligence action, a plaintiff must show that: (1) the defendant owed the plaintiff a legal duty, (2) the defendant breached the duty, and (3) the breach proximately or legally caused (4) the plaintiff's damages or injuries. The California Supreme Court has clearly articulated the scope of a landowner's duty to provide protection from foreseeable third-party criminal acts. It is determined in part by balancing the foreseeability of the harm against the burden of the duty to be imposed. In cases where the burden of preventing future harm is great, a high degree of foreseeability may be required. On the other hand, in cases where there are strong policy reasons for preventing the harm, or the harm can be prevented by simple means, a lesser degree of foreseeability may be required. Duty in such circumstances is determined by a balancing of foreseeability of the criminal acts against the burdensomeness, vagueness, and efficacy of the proposed security measures. The higher the burden to be imposed on the landowner, the higher the degree of foreseeability is required.

First, the court must determine the specific measures the defendant should have taken to prevent the harm. This frames the issue for the court's determination by defining the scope of the duty under consideration. Second, the court must analyze how financially and socially burdensome these proposed measures would be to a landlord, which measures could range from minimally burdensome to significantly burdensome under the facts of the case. Third, the court must identify the nature of the third-party conduct that the plaintiff claims could have been prevented had the landlord taken the proposed measures and assess how foreseeable (on a continuum from a mere possibility to a reasonable probability) it was that this conduct would occur. Once the burden and foreseeability have been independently assessed, they can be compared in determining

Tan v. Arnel Management Company *(concluded)*

the scope of the duty the court imposes on a given defendant. The more certain the likelihood of harm, the higher the burden a court will impose on a landlord; the less foreseeable the harm, the lower the burden a court will impose on a landlord.

As to the first step of the analysis, i.e., the specific security measures that Tan proposed defendants should have taken, the record shows that Tan requested minimal changes. Professor Katz recommended (1) moving the existing security gates from the back of the access road, or (2) installing very similar gates before the visitor and leasing office parking lots. Any gate could remain open during the day to allow business in the leasing office. Plaintiffs clearly stated they were *not* asking for the hiring of a guard or for any form of ongoing surveillance or monitoring. Furthermore, existing fencing extends around almost the entire perimeter of the property, only a "very minor" extension over a "very small area" would be necessary to close the fencing gap.

The second issue requires the court to analyze how financially and socially onerous the proposed measures would be to the landlord. The evidence adduced at the hearing was that the cost to defendants to install the two security gates barricading the two roads at the back of the property was about $13,500. And Tan suggested using the same gates for the front of the property. Although Tan presented no evidence about the cost of extending the fence, notably, Professor Katz testified that would necessitate only a "minor extension" because the property is already almost completely surrounded by walls *and could even involve merely mounding dirt.* As Tan observed, their proposed security measures involved a one-time expenditure and did not require ongoing surveillance of any kind, or the expenditure of significant funds. These proposed security measures are not onerous.

Turning to the heart of the case, the third element of foreseeability, Tan demonstrated three prior incidents of sudden, unprovoked, increasingly violent assaults on people in *ungated parking* areas on the Pheasant Ridge premises by a stranger in the middle of the night, causing great bodily injury. Thus, Tan presented substantial evidence of prior similar incidents or other indications of a reasonably foreseeable risk of violent criminal assaults on the property so as to impose on defendants a duty to provide the comparatively minimal security measures plaintiffs described.

The trial court required a heightened showing of foreseeability necessitating nearly identical prior crimes, in part, because the court perceived the proposed security to be onerous. However, the actual measures sought were not especially burdensome under the facts of this case. Thus, the court's ruling is erroneous that where none of these incidents involved guns, shootings, attempted carjacking, or attempted murder, the incidents were not sufficiently similar to meet the heightened standard of foreseeability. Perfect identity of prior crimes to the attack on plaintiff is not necessary. Because Tan only asked for relatively minimal security measures—ones already taken by defendants in another portion of the property—the degree of foreseeability here is not especially high. As a matter of law, therefore, the three prior incidents cited are sufficiently similar to make the assault on plaintiff foreseeable and to place a duty of care on defendants.

Concept Summary: Rights, Duties, and Liabilities of Landlords

Rights

1. To receive the agreed-on rent for the term of the lease.
2. To the return of the property at the expiration of the lease in as good a condition as it was when leased, except for normal wear and tear and any destruction by the weather or an act of God.

Duties

1. To assure the tenant the right to possess the property for the term of the lease (implied warranty of possession).
2. To guarantee that the tenant's possession will not be interfered with as a result of any act or omission on the landlord's part.
3. To provide and maintain, in the case of residential property, a habitable dwelling (implied warranty of habitability).
4. To conform to any relevant housing codes or regulations that apply to the leasing of property, including provisions that concern the condition of property, duty to repair, handling of security deposits, control of rents, and eviction of tenants.

(continued)

Concept Summary: Rights, Duties, and Liabilities of Landlords *(concluded)*

5. To maintain common areas, to disclose hidden defects that they know about if the defects are not reasonably discoverable by tenants, and to use reasonable care in making repairs.
6. To use reasonable care to protect tenants and others on their property from foreseeable criminal conduct.
7. To comply with the terms of the lease agreement.

Liabilities

1. To persons, including the tenant, who suffer personal injury or property damage as a result of the landlord's failure to perform a duty that proximately results in a foreseeable injury.
2. To the tenant for failure to perform duties required by law or by the lease agreement.
3. To government agencies for failure to comply with applicable codes, regulations, or laws.

Rights, Duties, and Liabilities of the Tenant

Rights of the Tenant

LO5

The tenant has the right to *exclusive possession* and *quiet enjoyment* of the property during the term of the lease. The landlord is not entitled to enter the leased property without the tenant's consent unless an emergency threatens the property or the landlord is acting under an express lease provision giving her the right to enter. The tenant may use the leased premises for any lawful purpose that is reasonable and appropriate unless the purpose for which it may be used is expressly limited in the lease. Furthermore, the tenant has both the right to receive leased residential property in a habitable condition at the beginning of the lease and the right to have the property maintained in a habitable condition for the duration of the lease.

Duty to Pay Rent

The tenant, of course, has the duty to pay rent in the agreed amount and at the agreed times. If two or more persons are co-tenants, their liability under the lease is *joint and several.* This means that each co-tenant has complete responsibility—not just partial responsibility—for performing the tenants' duties under the lease. For example, Allan and Bob rent an apartment from Cyndi, with both Allan and Bob signing a one-year lease. If Allan moves out after three months, Cyndi may hold Bob responsible for the entire rent, not just half of it. Naturally, Bob remains liable on the lease—as well as to Allan under any rent-sharing agreement the two of them had—but Cyndi is free to proceed against Bob solely if she so chooses.

Duty Not to Commit Waste

The tenant also has the duty not to commit **waste** on the property. This means that the tenant is responsible for the routine care and upkeep of the property and that he has the duty not to commit any act that would harm the property. In the past, fulfillment of this duty required that the tenant perform necessary repairs. Today, the duty to make repairs has generally been shifted to the landlord by court ruling, statute, or lease provision. The tenant now has no duty to make major repairs unless the relevant damage was caused by his own negligence. When damage exists through no fault of the tenant and the tenant therefore is not obligated to make the actual repairs, the tenant nonetheless has the duty to take reasonable interim steps to prevent further damage from the elements. This duty would include, but not necessarily be limited to, informing the landlord of the problem. The duty would be triggered, for instance, when a window breaks or the roof leaks.

Assignment and Subleasing

As with rights and duties under most other types of contracts, the rights and duties under a lease may generally be assigned and delegated to third parties. **Assignment** occurs when the landlord or the tenant transfers all of her remaining rights under the lease to another person. For example, a landlord may sell an apartment building and assign the relevant leases to the buyer, who will then become the new landlord. A tenant may assign the remainder of his lease to someone else, who then acquires whatever rights the original tenant had under the lease (including, of course, the right to exclusive possession of the leased premises).

Subleasing occurs when the tenant transfers to another person some, but not all, of his remaining right to possess the property. The relationship of tenant to sublessee then becomes one of landlord and tenant. For example, Donald, a college student whose 18-month lease on an apartment is to terminate on December 31, 2012, sublets his apartment to Wendy for the summer months of 2012. This is a sublease rather than an assignment, because Donald has not transferred all of his remaining rights under the lease.

The significance of the assignment–sublease distinction is that an assignee acquires rights and duties under the lease between the landlord and the original tenant, but a sublessee does not. An assignee steps into the shoes of the original tenant and acquires any rights she had under the lease. For example, if the lease contained an option to renew, the assignee would have the right to exercise this option. The assignee, of course, becomes personally liable to the landlord for the payment of rent.

Under both an assignment and a sublease, the original tenant remains liable to the landlord for the commitments made in the lease. If the assignee or sublessee fails to pay rent, for example, the tenant has the legal obligation to pay it. The next Concept Summary compares the characteristics of assignments and subleases.

Lease Provisions Limiting Assignment

Leases commonly contain limitations on assignment and subleasing. This is true especially with commercial leases. Such provisions typically require the landlord's consent to any assignment or sublease or purport to prohibit such a transfer of the tenant's interests. Provisions requiring the landlord's consent are upheld by the courts, although some courts hold that the landlord cannot withhold consent unreasonably. Total prohibitions against

Concept Summary: Comparison of Assignment and Sublease

	Assignment	Sublease
Does the tenant transfer to the third party *all* his remaining rights under the lease?	Yes	No
Does the tenant remain liable on the lease?	Yes	Yes
Does the third party (assignee or sublessee) acquire rights and duties under the tenant's lease with the landlord?	Yes	No

assignment may be enforced as well, but they are disfavored in the law. Courts usually construe them narrowly, resolving ambiguities against the landlord.

Tenant's Liability for Injuries to Third Persons

The tenant is normally liable to persons who suffer harm while on the portion of the property over which the tenant has control *if the injuries resulted from the tenant's negligence.*

Concept Summary: Rights, Duties, and Liabilities of Tenants

Rights

1. To the exclusive possession of the property for the term of the lease.
2. To the quiet enjoyment of the property so that his possession is not interfered with as a result of any act or omission on the landlord's part.
3. To be able to assign his interest in the leased property, consistent with any reasonable limitations in the lease agreement.

Duties

1. To pay the rent in the amount and at the times agreed on.
2. To use the property consistent with the agreed-on purpose of the lease and in conformance with any applicable housing and zoning codes or regulations.
3. To return the property at the termination of the lease in the same condition as it was when leased, except for normal wear and tear and any destruction caused by the weather or an act of God.
4. Not to commit waste on the property and to take reasonable steps to protect it from further damage from the elements when there is an accident or act of God.
5. To use reasonable care in his maintenance and use of the property so as to avoid foreseeable injuries to other persons or property.
6. To comply with the terms of the lease agreement.

Liabilities

1. To persons who suffer foreseeable physical injury or property damage as a proximate result of the tenant's failure to exercise due care on the property over which the tenant has control.
2. To the landlord for failure to comply with the duties imposed by the lease or by law.
3. To government agencies for failure to comply with applicable codes, regulations, and laws.

Termination of the Leasehold

LO6

A leasehold terminates typically because the lease term has expired. Sometimes, however, the lease is terminated early because of a party's material breach of the lease or because of mutual agreement.

Eviction

If a tenant breaches the lease (most commonly, by nonpayment of rent), the landlord may take action to **evict** the tenant. State statutes usually establish a relatively speedy **eviction** procedure. The landlord who desires to evict a tenant must be careful to comply with any applicable state or city regulations governing evictions. These regulations usually forbid self-help measures on the landlord's part, such as forcible entry to change locks. They may also prohibit the landlord from evicting a tenant under circumstances in which the eviction is deemed to be in retaliation for a tenant's complaints to a government agency about the condition of the premises.

At common law, a landlord had a lien on the tenant's personal property. The landlord therefore could remove and hold such property as security for the rent obligation. This lien has been abolished in many states. Where the lien still exists, it is subject to constitutional limitations requiring that the tenant be given notice of the lien, as well as an opportunity to defend and protect his belongings before they can be sold to satisfy the rent obligation.

Agreement to Surrender

A lease may terminate prematurely by mutual agreement between landlord and tenant to **surrender** the lease (i.e., return the property to the landlord prior to the end of the lease). A valid surrender discharges the tenant from further liability under the lease.

Abandonment

Abandonment occurs when the tenant unjustifiably and permanently vacates the leased premises before the end of the lease term and defaults in the payment of rent. If a tenant abandons the leased property, he is making an offer to surrender the leasehold. As shown in the Concept

Concept Summary: Termination of a Leasehold by Abandonment

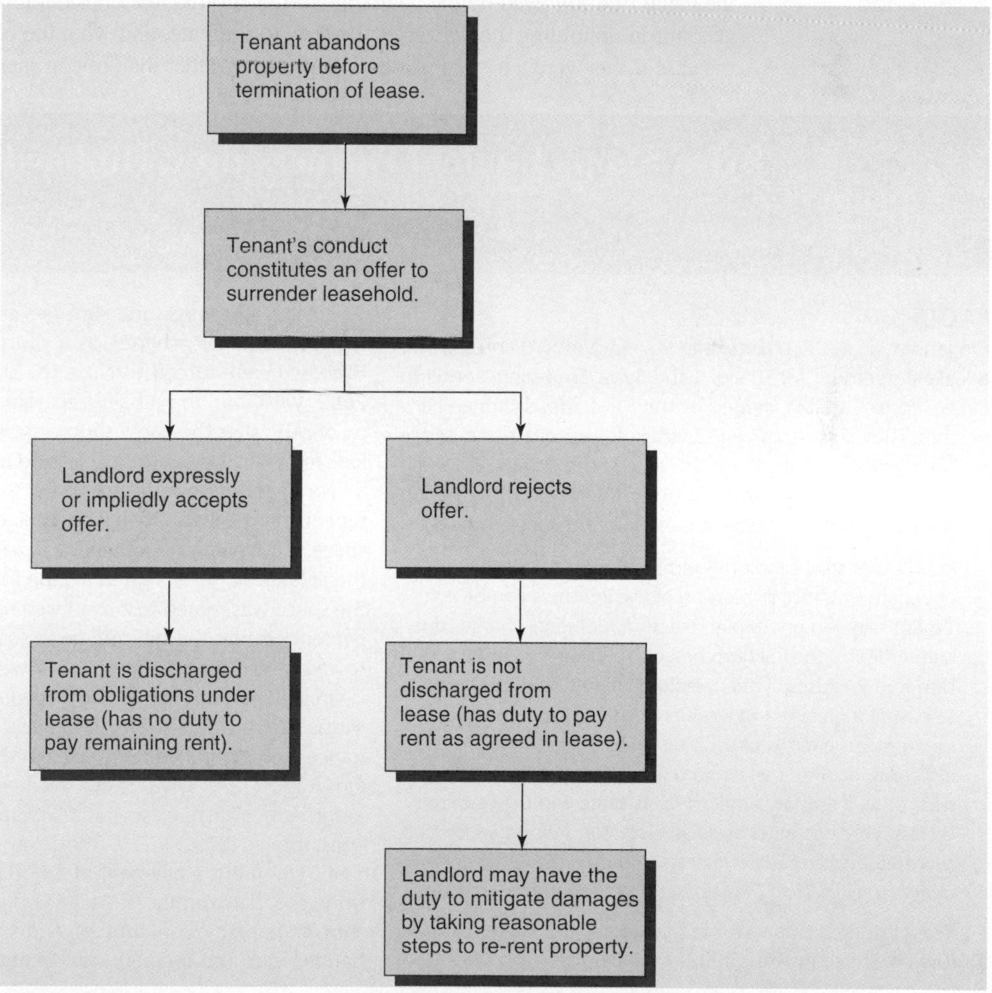
Tenant abandons property before termination of lease.
Tenant's conduct constitutes an offer to surrender leasehold.
Landlord expressly or impliedly accepts offer.
Landlord rejects offer.
Tenant is discharged from obligations under lease (has no duty to pay remaining rent).
Tenant is not discharged from lease (has duty to pay rent as agreed in lease).
Landlord may have the duty to mitigate damages by taking reasonable steps to re-rent property.

Summary, the landlord must make a decision at this point. If the landlord's conduct shows acceptance of the tenant's offer of surrender, the tenant is relieved of the obligation to pay rent for the remaining period of the lease. If the landlord does not accept the surrender, she may sue the tenant for the rent due until such time as she rents the property to someone else, or, if she cannot find a new tenant, for the rent due for the remainder of the term.

Under common law, the landlord had no obligation to mitigate (decrease) the damages caused by the abandonment by attempting to rent the leased property to a new tenant. In fact, taking possession of the property for the purpose of trying to rent it to someone else was a risky move for the landlord—her retaking of possession might be construed as acceptance of the surrender. Some states still adhere to the rule that the nonbreaching landlord has no duty to mitigate damages. Many states, however, now place the duty on the landlord to attempt to mitigate damages by making a reasonable effort to rerent the property. These states also hold that the landlord's retaking of possession for the purpose of rerenting does not constitute a waiver of his right to pursue an action to collect unpaid rent.

In the case that follows, *Sylva Shops Limited Partnership v. Hibbard,* the court was presented with a situation in which a commercial tenant signed a lease that included a clause relieving the landlord of any duty to mitigate damages by attempting to release the property when the tenant went out of business and left the property before the end of the lease. As you read the case, note the usual rule followed by the courts in North Carolina, the considerations the court took into account in upholding the waiver of the duty to mitigate, and what the court implies would be the case if this were a lease of residential property rather than of commercial property.

Sylva Shops Limited Partnership v. Hibbard

623 S.E.2d 785 (Ct. App. N.C. 2005)

FACTS

On January 2, 2002, Loanne and Stanley Hibbard entered into a lease agreement for space at the Sylva Shopping Center in Sylva, North Carolina, owned by the Sylva Shops Limited Partnership. They signed a five-year lease for an out-parcel space that had good visibility from the road. An out-parcel space is normally more expensive than other locations in the rest of the shopping center. The lease contained the following clause:

> In no event shall Landlord's termination of this Lease and/or Tenant's right to possession of the Premises abrogate Tenant's agreement to pay rent and additional charges due hereunder for the full term hereof. Following re-entry of the Demised Premises by the Landlord, Tenant shall continue to pay all such rent and additional charges as same become due under the terms of this Lease, together with all other expenses incurred by Landlord in regaining possession until such time, if any, as Landlord relets same and the Demised Premises are occupied by such successor, *it being understood that Landlord shall have no obligations to mitigate Tenant's damages by reletting the Demised Premises* (emphasis added).

The Hibbards opened their business, the Bagel Bin and Sandwich Shop, in April 2002. Initially, the shop was quite successful, but when the summer came and the local college students left, there was a sharp decline in sales. The Hibbards were forced to close the shop on September 30, 2002, with four and a half years remaining on their lease.

Shortly after the bagel shop closed, Sylva Shops began to look for a new tenant using a leasing agent. The agent placed a "For Lease" sign in the window, sent mailings to national tenants, and called other local businesses about leasing the space. It ultimately negotiated with a Mexican restaurant, but the restaurant never signed a lease for the space. Eventually, the space was rented to a sandwich restaurant. The Hibbards contended that the difficulty in releasing the space was due to an unwillingness to agree to a lower rent.

In January 2003, Sylva Shops filed a complaint against the Hibbards for unpaid rent, late fees, common area maintenance fees, insurance, and taxes in the amount of $14,170. On August 27, Sylva Shops filed a motion for summary judgment, attaching an affidavit indicating that its damages totaled $35,511.70 (rent, fees, and interest equaled $44,515.40 but a payment of $9,003.70 had been received from the bankruptcy court in connection with the bagel shop's Chapter 7 bankruptcy). A jury found that Sylva Shops had failed to use ordinary care to mitigate the effects of the

(continued)

Hibbards' breach of contract and the judge award judgment against the Hibbards in the amount of $13,110. Sylva Shops appealed, contending that the lease clause relieved it of any duty to mitigate damages upon the default by the Hibbards. The Hibbards contended that the clause violated the public policy of the state and should be declared invalid.

ISSUE

Should the clause relieving the landlord of any duty to mitigate damages on the default by the tenant be declared invalid as contrary to public policy?

DECISION

No. The existence of a common law duty of care does not absolutely preclude parties from agreeing in a contract to relieve a party of that duty. While contracts exempting persons from liability for negligence are not favored by the law, the majority rule, to which North Carolina adheres, is that subject to certain limitations, a person may effectively bargain against liability for harm caused by his ordinary negligence in the performance of a legal duty arising out of a contractual relationship. Such a clause is enforced unless it violates a statute, is gained through inequality of bargaining power, or is contrary to a substantial public interest.

The court noted that here there was no claim that the clause was obtained through an inequality of bargaining power. The lease represented an arm's-length commercial transaction in which both parties used brokers or advisors to assist them in getting the best possible bargain.

The court held that the clause does not violate the public policy of the state nor is it contrary to some substantial public interest. The lease is a private contract between businesses relating to a bagel shop and does not create the risk of injury to the public or the rights of third parties. This is not a residential lease, which would present an entirely different situation. Other states do not impose any duty to mitigate in the case of commercial real estate transactions. Negotiations in commercial transactions generally involve relatively equal bargaining power to the availability of other space and the fact that either party is compelled to make a deal. Each lessee has to determine whether the lease offered is acceptable in business terms. Through negotiations, the parties to a commercial lease often include specific provisions for almost every contingency that could arise from their agreement and exact from each other concessions in order to obtain the desired provisions. Ultimately, if the rent is too high, or the provisions unacceptable to the lease, a prospective commercial tenant can always look for another location.

Questions and Problem Cases

1. On August 2, Dan Maltbie and John Burke, students at Indiana University, entered into a one-year written lease with Breezewood Management Company for the rental of an apartment in an older house in Bloomington, Indiana. When they moved in, they discovered numerous defects: rotting porch floorboards, broken and loose windows, an inoperable front door lock, leaks in the plumbing, a back door that would not close, a missing bathroom door, inadequate water pressure, falling plaster, exposed wiring, and a malfunctioning toilet. Later they discovered a leaking roof, cockroach infestation, the absence of heat and hot water, more leaks in the plumbing, and pigeons in the attic. The city of Bloomington had a minimum housing code in effect at that time. Code enforcement officers inspected the apartment and found over 50 violations, 11 of which were "life safety" violations, defined as conditions that might be severely "hazardous to the health of the occupant." These conditions remained largely uncorrected after notice by the code officers and further complaints by Maltbie and Burke. On May 3 of the following year, Maltbie vacated the apartment, notified Breezewood, and refused to pay any further rent. Breezewood agreed to let Burke remain and pay half the rate of the originally agreed-upon rent. Breezewood then filed suit against Maltbie and Burke for the balance due under the original rental contract plus a number of additional charges. Maltbie and Burke each filed counterclaims against Breezewood, claiming damages and abatement of the rent for breach of the implied warranty of habitability. Was there an implied warranty of habitability in the lease of the property that was breached?
2. Mary Ajayi and Wemi Alakija were tenants in an apartment complex managed for the landlord by Lloyd Management. Neighboring tenants complained on various occasions

to Lloyd about repeated disturbances that continued late into the night and included yelling and loud noises coming from the apartment shared by Ajayi and Alakija. The sound of running could also be heard during those disturbances. Neighbors whose apartment walls adjoined those of the Ajayi–Alakija apartment also complained that items were knocked off their walls as a result of banging and jarring coming from that apartment. Do Lloyd and the landlord have any obligation to take responsive action? If so, why? What course(s) of action might they pursue?

3. Linda Schiernbeck rented a house from Clark and Rosa Davis. Approximately one month after she moved in, Schiernbeck noticed a discolored area on one of the walls. There was a screw in the middle of this area. Schiernbeck determined that a smoke detector had been attached to the wall, but no smoke detector was present during the time she lived there. Schiernbeck later contended that she had notified the Davises about the missing smoke detector, but the Davises denied this. About 15 months after Schiernbeck's occupancy began, a fire broke out in the house. Schiernbeck and her daughter were severely injured. Contending that the Davises should have installed a smoke detector, Schiernbeck sued them for negligence and breach of contract. Did the Davises owe Schiernbeck a duty to install a smoke detector?
4. A tenant rented an apartment from the landlord pursuant to a lease that required her to surrender the premises in "as good a state and condition as reasonable use and wear and tear will permit" and to make a refundable security deposit. After the lease was executed, the landlord notified the tenants in the building that no tenant was to shampoo the wall-to-wall carpet on surrender of the lease because the landlord had retained a professional carpet cleaner to do it. The cost of the carpet cleaner's services was to be automatically deducted from the security deposit. When the tenant left the building, a portion of her security deposit was withheld to cover carpet cleaning and she sued for a refund of the full deposit. Is the tenant entitled to a refund?
5. On February 14, Don Weingarden entered into a written rental agreement with Eagle Ridge Condominiums for an apartment in Maumee, Ohio. Weingarden paid $150 as a security deposit with a monthly rental rate of $750 payable on the first of each month; the month of March was rent free. The parties also agreed that the landlord would replace the bedroom door, repair the electrical outlet in the bedroom, and replace the boards in the basement.

   Weingarden took possession on March 1. On March 23, he notified the apartment manager in writing that the basement of the apartment would leak when snow melted and also after a rain. The leak would saturate the carpeting in the basement and render the basement useless. When wet, the carpet would become mildewed and odorous. Weingarden also indicated that the stairway in the unit was not in compliance with the Ohio Basic Building Code and that he had fallen as a result and, further, that the door in the bedroom had not been repaired and/or replaced and that the frame on the master bedroom door was cracked. Weingarden indicated that as a result he would vacate the premises on or before July 1.

   The landlord attempted to remedy the basement leak by applying cement to the interior basement walls; however, the basement continued to leak and soak the carpet. On April 1, the landlord replied to Weingarden that it would not release him from his obligations under the lease agreement. On June 16, Weingarden surrendered his keys to the apartment and indicated in writing that his deposit should be forwarded to the address in Michigan that was on the application he had submitted for the lease.

   The landlord did not return any security deposit to Weingarden and did not send any itemization of disbursements to him. The landlord spent the security deposit on a water bill of $27.11 and for the cost of carpet cleaning, with the balance being applied to unpaid rent pursuant to the terms of the lease.

Weingarden brought suit against the landlord to recover the balance of his security deposit and damages of $250 per month for the diminution of value of the rental unit because of the inability to utilize the basement which constituted one-third of the apartment. The landlord counterclaimed for the unpaid rent due for the balance of the lease term. One of the issues in the case was whether the conditions in the basement amounted to a constructive eviction of Weingarden. Did the wet conditions in the basement substantially affect the habitability of the apartment and amount to a constructive eviction of the tenant?

6. De Ette Junker leased an apartment from F. L. Cappaert in the Pecan Ridge Apartment Complex, which consisted of six buildings, each with 12 apartments. Junker's apartment was upstairs, and she and the tenants in two other apartments used a common stairway for access to their apartments. Junker slipped on the stairway and was injured. She sued Cappaert for damages on the grounds that he had been negligent in maintaining the stairway. Junker's lease contained an exculpatory clause in which Cappaert disclaimed any liability for injury due to his negligence. Did the exculpatory clause immunize the landlord against damages caused by his own negligence in maintaining a common area in leased residential property?
7. Donna Marie Morgan resided in an apartment building owned by the 253 East Delaware Condominium Association and managed by Joseph Moss Realty. One evening at about 8:30 PM Morgan walked from her class at Loyola University's downtown campus to the building, where she entered the lobby, checked her mail, and entered the elevator in the lobby. As she had first entered the building, she had observed a man talking to the doorman. The man followed her into the elevator. When it arrived at the 10th floor, he poked a gun into her back, forced her off the elevator, and robbed her and beat her with the gun, causing severe injuries. Morgan brought a lawsuit against the Association and Moss alleging that they were negligent for failing to protect her from the criminal acts of the unknown third party because they undertook to provide security and performed it in a negligent fashion. Morgan testified that when she first rented the apartment she was told the neighborhood was safe and the building had security, including a 24-hour doorman. The doorman testified that the man had responded to an inquiry as to whether he could help him by replying, "Unit 13G." The doorman had then called the tenant in Unit 13G, told him his guest was here, and was told by the tenant to "let him up." The tenant had earlier told the doorman he was expecting guests. In these circumstances did the Association and Moss have a legal duty to protect Morgan from the criminal act of the third party?
8. Kridel entered into a lease with Sommer, owner of the Pierre Apartments, to lease apartment 6-L for two years. Kridel, who was to be married in June, planned to move into the apartment in May. His parents and future parents-in-law had agreed to assume responsibility for the rent because Kridel was a full-time student who had no funds of his own. Shortly before Kridel was to have moved in, his engagement was broken. He wrote Sommer a letter explaining his situation and stating that he could not take the apartment. Sommer did not answer the letter. When another party inquired about rental apartment 6-L, the person in charge told her that the apartment was already rented to Kridel. Sommer did not enter the apartment or show it to anyone until he rented apartment 6-L to someone else when there were approximately eight months left on Kridel's lease. He sued Kridel for the full rent for the period of approximately 16 months before the new tenant's lease took effect. Kridel argued that Sommer should not be able to collect rent for the first 16 months of the lease because he did not take reasonable steps to rerent the apartment. Was Sommer entitled to collect the rent he sought?

Chapter 36

Estates and Trusts

Learning Objectives

After you have studied this chapter, you should be able to:

1. List and explain the basic requirements for making a valid will.
2. Describe the differences between a nuncupative will and a holographic will.
3. Identify and explain the legal tools (advance directives) available for planning for possible future disability.
4. Explain what is meant by dying *intestate* and explain how a person's property is distributed at his death if he dies *intestate.*
5. Identify the major steps in the process of administering an estate and explain the responsibilities of the personal representative of the estate.
6. Explain the nature of a trust and list some of the reasons for creating trusts.
7. Explain the powers and responsibilities of a trustee.

George, an elderly widower, has no children of his own but enjoys a very close relationship with his two stepdaughters, his late wife's children by her first marriage. George's only living blood relative is his brother, from whom he has been estranged for many years. George has a substantial amount of property—his home, two cars, stocks and bonds, rental property, bank accounts, and a valuable collection of baseball cards. Though retired, George is an active volunteer for, and supporter of, several community charities and organizations. Presently, George does not have a will, but he is considering writing one.

- What will happen to George's property upon his death if he does not have a will at that time?
- What are the requirements for executing a valid will?
- What can cause a will to be invalid?
- After George's death, how would his estate be probated?
- If George decided to create a trust to benefit his stepdaughters, what is required to create a trust, and what are the duties of a trustee?

Introduction

One of the basic features of the ownership of property is the right to dispose of the property during life and at death. You have already learned about the ways in which property is transferred during the owner's life. The owner's death is another major event for the transfer of property. Most people want to be able to choose who will get their property when they die. There are a variety of ways in which a person may control the ultimate disposition of his property. He may take title to the property in a form of joint ownership that gives his co-owner a right of survivorship. He may create a trust and transfer property to it to be used for the benefit of a spouse, child, elderly parent, or other beneficiary. He may execute a will in which he directs that his real and personal property be distributed to persons named in the will. If, however, a person makes no provision for the disposition of his property at his death, his property will be distributed to his heirs as defined by state law. This chapter focuses on the transfer of property at death and on the use of trusts for the transfer and management of property, both during life and at death.

Each state has its own statutes and common law regulating the distribution of property upon death. Legal requirements and procedures may vary from state to state, but many general principles can be stated. The **Uniform Probate Code** (UPC) is a comprehensive, uniform law that has been enacted in 19 states. It is intended to update and unify state law concerning the disposition and administration of property at death. Several relevant UPC provisions will be discussed in this chapter.

Estate Planning

A person's estate is all of the property owned by that person. **Estate planning** is the popular name for the complicated process of planning for the transfer of a person's estate in later life and at death. Estate planning also concerns planning for the possibility of prolonged illness or disability. An attorney who is creating an estate plan will take an inventory of the client's assets, learn the client's objectives, and draft the instruments necessary to carry out the plan. This plan is normally guided by the desire to reduce the amount of tax liability and to provide for the orderly disposition of the estate.

Wills

Right of Disposition by Will

The right to control the disposition of property at death has not always existed. In the English feudal system, the king owned all land. The lords and knights had only the right to use land for their lifetime. A landholder's rights in land terminated on his death, and no rights descended to his heirs. In 1215, the king granted the nobility the right to pass their interest in the land they held to their heirs. Later that right was extended to all property owners. In the United States, each state has enacted statutes that establish the requirements for a valid will, including the formalities that must be met to pass property by will.

Nature of a Will

LO1

A **will** is a document that is executed with specific legal formalities by a person and contains her instructions about the way her property will be disposed of at her death. A man who makes a will is known as a **testator** and a woman who makes one is a **testatrix.**

A will can dispose only of property belonging to the testator at the time of his death. Furthermore, wills do not control property that goes to others through other planning devices (such as life insurance policies) or by operation of law (such as by right of survivorship). For example, property held in joint tenancy or tenancy by the entirety is not controlled by a will because the property passes automatically to the surviving co-tenant by right of survivorship. In addition, life insurance proceeds are usually controlled by the insured's designation of beneficiaries, not by any provision of a will.

Common Legal Terminology Used in Wills

Some legal terms commonly used in wills include the following:

1. *Bequest.* A **bequest** (also called **legacy**) is a gift of personal property or money. For example, a will might provide for a bequest of a family heirloom to the testator's daughter. Since a will can direct only property that is owned by the testator at the time of his death, a specific bequest of property that the testator has disposed of before his death is ineffective. This is called **ademption.** For example, Samuel's will states that Warren is to receive Samuel's collection of antique guns. If the guns are destroyed before Samuel's death, however, the bequest is ineffective because of ademption.

2. *Devise.* A **devise** is a gift of real property. For example, the testator might devise her family farm to her grandchild.

3. *Residuary.* A **residuary** is the balance of the estate that is left after specific devises and bequests are made by the will. After providing for the disposition of specific personal and real property, a testator might provide that the residuary of his estate is to go to his spouse or be divided among his descendants.

4. *Issue.* A person's **issue** are her lineal descendants (children, grandchildren, great-grandchildren, and so forth). This category of persons includes adopted children.

5. *Per capita.* This term and the next one, *per stirpes,* are used to describe the way in which a group of persons are to share a gift. **Per capita** means that each of that group of persons will share equally. For example, Grandfather dies, leaving a will that provides that the residuary of his estate is to go to his issue or descendants *per capita.* Grandfather had two children, Mary and Bill. Mary has two children, John and James. Bill has one child, Margaret. Mary and Bill die before Grandfather (in legal terms, *predecease* him), but all three of Grandfather's grandchildren are living at the time of his death. In this case, John, James, and Margaret would each take one-third of the residuary of Grandfather's estate.

6. *Per stirpes.* When a gift is given to the testator's issue or descendants **per stirpes** (also called **by right of representation**), each surviving descendant divides the share that her parent would have taken if the parent had survived. In the preceding example, if Grandfather's will had stated that the residuary of his estate was to go to his issue or descendants *per stirpes,* Margaret would take one-half and John and James would take one-quarter each (that is, they would divide the share that would have gone to their mother).

Testamentary Capacity

The legal capacity to make a valid will is called **testamentary capacity.** To have testamentary capacity, a person must be *of sound mind* and *of legal age,* which is 18 in most states. A person does not have to be in perfect mental health to have testamentary capacity. Because people often delay executing wills until they are weak and in ill health, the standard for mental capacity to make a will is fairly low. To be of "sound mind," a person need only be sufficiently rational to be capable of understanding the nature and character of her property, of realizing that she is making a will, and of knowing the persons who would normally be the beneficiaries of her affection. A person could move in and out of periods of lucidity and still have testamentary capacity if she executed her will during a lucid period.

Lack of testamentary capacity is a common ground upon which wills are challenged by persons who were excluded from a will. *Fraud* and *undue influence* are also common grounds for challenging the validity of a will. In assessing a claim of undue influence, the court looks to see whether a bequest appears to be made on the basis of natural affection or of some improper influence. The actions of fiduciaries such as attorneys are scrutinized carefully, particularly for improper influence. This is especially true if the fiduciaries are not related to the deceased person, were made beneficiaries, and had a critical role in preparing the will.

Execution of a Will

Unless a will is executed with the formalities required by state law, it is *void.* The courts are strict in interpreting statutes concerning the execution of wills. If a will is declared void, the property of the deceased person will be distributed according to the provisions of state laws that will be discussed later.

The formalities required for a valid will differ from state to state. For that reason, an individual should consult the laws of his state before making a will. If he should move to another state after having executed a will, he should consult a lawyer in his new state to determine whether a new will needs to be executed. All states require that a will be *in writing.* State law also requires that a formal will be *witnessed,* generally by two or three *disinterested* witnesses (persons who do not stand to inherit any property under the will), and that it be *signed* by the testator or by someone else at the testator's direction. Most states also require that the testator *publish* the will—that is, declare or indicate at the time of signing that the instrument is his will. Another formality required by most states is that the testator sign the will in the presence and the sight of the witnesses and that the witnesses sign in the presence and the sight of each other. As a general rule, an **attestation clause,** which states the formalities that have been followed in the execution of the will, is written following the testator's signature. These detailed formalities are designed to prevent fraud.

Commonly, a will must be in writing, signed by the testator (or in the testator's name by some other individual in the testator's conscious presence and by the testator's direction), and signed by at least two individuals, each of whom signed within a reasonable time after she witnessed either the signing of the will or the testator's acknowledgment of that signature or will. Also, any individual who is generally competent to be a witness usually may witness a will. See Figure 36.1 for an example of a will.

In some situations, a lawyer might arrange to have the execution of a will *videotaped* to provide evidence relating to the testator's capacity and the use of proper formalities. (Note that the will is executed in the normal way; the videotape merely records the execution of the will.) Some state probate codes specifically provide that videotapes of the executions of wills are admissible into evidence.

Joint and Mutual Wills

In some circumstances, two or more people—a married couple, for example—decide together on a plan for the disposition of their property at death. To carry out this plan, they may execute a **joint will** (a single instrument that constitutes the will of both or all of the testators and is executed by both or all) or they may execute **mutual wills** (joint or separate, individual wills that reflect the common plan of distribution).

FIGURE 36.1
Example of a Will

LAST WILL AND TESTAMENT
OF
WILLIAM R. FOLGER

I, WILLIAM R. FOLGER, of McLean, County of Fairfax, Commonwealth of Virginia, being of sound and disposing mind and memory, do make this to be my Last Will and Testament, hereby revoking all former wills and codicils made by me.

FIRST. I direct that the expenses of my funeral and burial, including a grave site, gravestone, and perpetual care, be paid out of my estate in such amount as my Executrix may deem proper and without regard to any limitation in the applicable law as to the amount of such expenses and without necessity of prior Court approval.

SECOND. I direct that all estate, inheritance, succession, and other death taxes and duties occasioned by my death, whether incurred with respect to property passing by this Will or otherwise, shall be paid by my Executrix out of the principal of my residuary estate with no right of reimbursement from any recipient of any such property.

THIRD. I further direct my Executrix to pay all of my legal obligations and debts (exclusive of any debt or debts secured by a deed of trust or mortgage on real estate, not due at the time of my death or becoming due during the period of administration of my estate). In determining what are my obligations and debts, I direct my Executrix to avail herself of every defense that would have been available to me.

FOURTH. I hereby confirm my intention that the beneficial interest in all property, real or personal, tangible or intangible (including joint checking or savings accounts in any bank or savings and loan association), which is registered or held, at the time of my death, jointly in the names of myself and any other person (including tenancy by the entireties, but excluding any tenancy in common), shall pass by right of survivorship or operation of law and outside of the terms of this Will to such other person, if he or she survives me. To the extent that my intention may be defeated by any rule of law, I give, devise, and bequeath all such jointly held property to such other person or persons who shall survive me.

FIFTH. I give my tangible personal property, including furniture, clothing, automobiles and their equipment, and articles of personal or household use or ornament, but not including money, securities, or the like, to my wife Kristin A. Folger, if she survives by thirty (30) days, and if she does not so survive me, I give the same absolutely to my issue who so survive me, such issue to take *per stirpes.*

I express the hope that my wife or my issue will dispose of my tangible personal property according to my wishes, however my wishes may be known to her or to them, but I expressly declare that I do not intend to create any trust in law or in equity with respect to my tangible personal property.

SIXTH. I give the sum of $10,500 to St. Christopher's Church, McLean, Virginia, for its unrestricted use.

SEVENTH. I give, bequeath, and devise all the rest and residue of my estate, of whatsoever nature and wheresoever situated, to my wife Kristin A. Folger, if she survives me by more than thirty (30) days. If she does not so survive me, I give the same absolutely to my issue who so survive me, such issue to take *per stirpes.*

EIGHTH. I nominate, constitute, and appoint my wife Kristin A. Folger, to be the Executrix of this my Last Will and Testament. My Executrix shall have full power in her discretion to do any and all things necessary for the complete administration of my estate, including the power to sell at public or private sale, and without order of court, any real or personal property belonging to my estate, and to compound, compromise, or otherwise to settle or adjust any and all claims, charges, debts, and demands whatsoever against or in favor of my estate, as fully as I could do if living.

(continued)

FIGURE 36.1 *(concluded)*

NINTH. I direct that no bond or other security be required of my Personal Representative appointed hereunder in any jurisdiction, any provision of law to the contrary notwithstanding.

IN WITNESS WHEREOF, I have set my hand and seal to this Last Will and Testament, typewritten upon two (2) pages, each one of which has been signed by me this 15th day of August, 2014, at McLean, Virginia.

William R. Folger

William R. Folger

The foregoing instrument consisting of two (2) typewritten pages was signed, published, and declared by the testator to be his Last Will and Testament in the presence of us, who, at his request, in his presence, and in the presence of each other, have subscribed our names as witnesses this 15th day of August, 2014.

Carole K. Carson of McLean, Virginia

Robert A. Carson of McLean, Virginia

Sandra A. Somers of Falls Church, Virginia

Underlying a joint or mutual will is an agreement on a common plan. This common plan often includes an express or implied contract (a contract to make a will or not to revoke the will). One issue that sometimes arises is whether a testator who has made a joint or mutual will can later change the will. Whether joint and mutual wills are revocable depends on the language of the will, on state law, and on the timing of the revocation. For example, a testator who made a joint will with his spouse may be able to revoke his will during the life of his spouse because the spouse still has a chance to change her own will, but he may be unable to revoke or change the will after the death of his spouse. The Uniform Probate Code (UPC), which has been adopted by a number of states, provides that the mere fact that a joint or mutual will has been executed does *not* create the presumption of a contract not to revoke the will or wills.

LO2

Informal Wills

Some states recognize certain types of wills that are not executed with these formalities. These are:

1. *Nuncupative wills.* A **nuncupative** will is an oral will. Such wills are recognized as valid in some states but only under limited circumstances and to a limited extent. In a number of states, for example, nuncupative wills are valid only when made by soldiers in military service and sailors at sea, and even then they will be effective only to dispose of personal property that was in the actual possession of the person at the time the oral will was made. Other states place low dollar limits on the amount of property that can be passed by a nuncupative will.

2. *Holographic wills.* **Holographic wills** are wills that are written and signed in the testator's handwriting. The fact that holographic wills are not properly witnessed makes them suspect. They are recognized in about half of the states and by Section 2–502(b) of the UPC, even though they are not executed with the formalities usually required of valid wills. For a

holographic will to be valid in the states that recognize them, it must evidence testamentary intent and must actually be *handwritten* by the testator. A typed holographic will would be invalid. Some states require that the holographic will be *entirely* handwritten, other states require only that the signature and material portions of the will be handwritten by the testator, and some also require that the will be dated.

In the case that follows, *Estate of Abshire,* the court concluded that the handwritten document offered for probate met the requirements for a valid holographic will. You might compare the facts in this case with those in problem case 3 at the end of the chapter where the court reached a different conclusion. What are the key differences in the facts that led to that different result?

Estate of Abshire

2011 Tex. App. LEXIS 66676 (Ct. App. Texas 2011)

FACTS

On January 6, 2001, Marjorie Abshire drafted, in her own handwriting, a holographic will. On January 17, 2001, she added a holographic codicil on the same page. In their entirety, the will and codicil state:

> 611 Haley Lane
> Fort Worth, T 76132
> January 9, 2001
>
> To: Ernestine C. Nichols
> 3820 Westerly
> Fort Worth, Texas 76116
>
> "Holographic Will of Marjorie B. Abshire"
>
> I would like to make you administrator of my estate to serve as independent Executor without bond or other form of security.
>
> As of this date, January 9, 2001, there are no claims for any debt against me; house, car and other purchases are free from debt. The only things I owe are current utilities and telephone accounts that are drafted from my bank account.*1/17/01
>
> I would like to make Page Nichols Nickell as alternative Executor with same powers and rights as Ernestine C. Nichols in case she does not survive me or is incapacitated to act in my behalf.
>
> This will is revoking all others which have been destroyed.
>
> Marjorie B. Abshire
>
> *Just as a rough guide as to the distribution of my estate, I would like Ernestine C. Nichols to have half of my funds, one-fourth to Margaret C. Dennis, and one-fourth to Travis Avenue Baptist Church which will not include annuities I have designated to other charities.

Marjorie passed away on August 30, 2007. Abshire was Nichols's maternal first cousin (their mothers were sisters) and a member of Travis Avenue Baptist Church.

On October 22, 2007, the trial court entered an order admitting the will and codicil to probate and appointing Page Nickell, named as successor independent executor in the will, as independent executor. The document admitted to probate as the will and codicil were found among Abshire's financial papers in an envelope labeled, "Holographic Will of Marjorie Abshire." Also in the envelope were three handwritten notes about making a will, three lists of assets, and newspaper clippings relating to preparation of wills.

In March 2009, Nickell filed an action for a declaratory judgment to construe the will and identified 28 interested parties. Seven of those interested persons, who were related to Abshire on her paternal side (and who would stand to share in the estate if the codicil was invalidated and, instead, the estate was distributed under the intestacy[1] laws' objected. They contended that while the will was valid, the codicil was invalid because it contained precatory language and did not purport to distribute any portion of Abshire's estate.

The trial court held: (1) that the purported codicil dated January 17, 2001, was unambiguous as a matter of law; (2) the sentence that began "Just as a rough guide as to distribution of my estate" was precatory; (3) the word funds in that same sentence does not include real property; and (4) the purported codicil did not make an effective disposition of property so that Abshire died intestate

(continued)

[1] The concept of intestacy is discussed later in this chapter on pages 694–96

with regard to the disposition of her property. Ernestine Nichols and Travis Avenue Baptist Church appealed.

ISSUE

Was the document signed by Abshire a valid holographic will that was effective to control the disposition of her property following her death?

DECISION

Yes. The court of appeals stated that in considering whether words were precatory or mandatory, it was necessary to look to the decedent's intent as evidenced by the context of the will and surrounding circumstances. The court then determined that the codicil was not precatory and that it expressed Abshire's intent to dispose of her property, rather than leave the distribution of her funds to the discretion of others. Because "funds" could reasonably be construed in light of the will and codicil to include both real and personal property, the court adopted that construction to avoid intestacy.

Limitations on Disposition by Will

A person who takes property by will takes it subject to all outstanding claims against the property. For example, if real property is subject to a mortgage or other lien, the beneficiary who takes the real property gets it subject to the mortgage or lien. In addition, the rights of the testator's creditors are superior to the rights of beneficiaries under her will. Thus, if the testator was insolvent (her debts exceeded her assets), persons named as beneficiaries do not receive any property by virtue of the will.

Under the laws of most states, the surviving spouse of the testator has statutory rights in property owned solely by the testator that cannot be defeated by a contrary will provision. This means that a husband cannot effectively disinherit his wife and vice versa. Even if the will provides for the surviving spouse, he can elect to take the share of the decedent's estate that would be provided by state law rather than the amount specified in the will. In some states, personal property, such as furniture, passes automatically to the surviving spouse.

At common law, a widow had the right to a life estate in one-third of the lands owned by her husband during their marriage. This was known as a widow's **dower** right. A similar right for a widower was known as **curtesy.** A number of states have changed the right by statute to give a surviving spouse a one-third interest in fee simple in the real and personal property owned by the deceased spouse at the time of her death. (Naturally, a testator can leave her spouse more than this if she desires.) Under the Uniform Probate Code Section 2–201, the surviving spouse's elective share varies depending on the length of the surviving spouse's marriage to the testator—the elective share increases with the length of marriage.

As a general rule, a surviving spouse is given the right to use the family home for a stated period as well as a portion of the deceased spouse's estate. In community property states, each spouse has a one-half interest in community property that cannot be defeated by a contrary will provision. (Note that the surviving spouse will obtain *full* ownership of any property owned by the testator and the surviving spouse as joint tenants or tenants by the entirety.)

Children of the testator who were born or adopted after the will was executed are called **pretermitted** children. There is a presumption that the testator intended to provide for such a child unless there is evidence to the contrary. State law gives pretermitted children the right to a share of the testator's estate. For example, under Section 2–302 of the UPC, a pretermitted child has the right to receive the share he would have received under the state intestacy statute unless it appears that the omission of this child was intentional, the testator gave substantially all of her estate to the child's other parent, or the testator provided for the child outside of the will.

Revocation of Wills

One important feature of a will is that it is *revocable* until the moment of the testator's death. For this reason, a will confers *no present interest* in the testator's property. A person is free to revoke a prior will and, if she wishes, to make a new will. Wills can be revoked in a variety of ways. Physical destruction and mutilation done with intent to revoke a will constitute revocation, as do other acts such as crossing out the will or creating a writing that expressly cancels the will.

In addition, a will is revoked if the testator later executes a valid will that expressly revokes the earlier will. A later will that does not *expressly* revoke an earlier will operates to revoke only those portions of the earlier will that are inconsistent with the later will. Under the UPC, a later will that does not expressly revoke a prior will operates to revoke it by inconsistency if the testator intended the subsequent will to *replace* rather than *supplement* the prior will [2–507(b)]. Furthermore, the UPC presumes that the testator intended the subsequent will to replace rather than supplement the prior will if the subsequent one makes a complete disposition of his estate, but it presumes that the testator intended merely to supplement and not replace the prior will if the subsequent will disposes of only part of his estate [2–507(c), (d)]. In some states, a will is presumed to have been revoked if it cannot be located after the testator's death, although this presumption can be rebutted with contrary evidence.

Wills can also be revoked by operation of law without any act on the part of the testator signifying revocation. State statutes provide that certain changes in relationships operate as revocations of a will. In some states, marriage will operate to revoke a will that was made when the testator was single. Similarly, a divorce may revoke provisions in a will made during marriage that leave property to the divorced spouse. Under the laws of some states, the birth of a child after the execution of a will may operate as a partial revocation of the will.

Concept Summary: Wills

Type of Will	Requirements
Formal Will	1. Must be in writing. 2. Must be witnessed by two or three disinterested witnesses. 3. Must be signed by the testator or at his direction. 4. May have to be published or declared by the testator to be his will. 5. Must be signed by testator in the presence and sight of witnesses. 6. Witnesses must sign in the presence and sight of the testator and each other.

Type of Will	Requirements
Holographic Will	1. Must be entirely written and signed in the testator's handwriting. 2. Must evidence testamentary intent. 3. Not permitted in all states.
Noncupative Will	1. Oral will made before witnesses and valid only to transfer personal property and not real property. 2. Not permitted in all states; some limit it to soldiers or sailors or place low dollar limits on property it can govern.

Codicils

A **codicil** is an amendment of a will. If a person wants to change a provision of a will without making an entirely new will, she may amend the will by executing a codicil. One may *not* amend a will by merely striking out objectionable provisions and inserting new provisions. The same formalities are required for the creation of a valid codicil as for the creation of a valid will.

Advance Directives: Planning for Disability

LO3

Advances in medical technology now permit a person to be kept alive by artificial means even in many cases in which there is no hope of the person being able to function without life support. Many people are opposed to their lives being prolonged with no chance of recovery. In response to these concerns, almost all states have enacted statutes permitting individuals to state their choices about the medical procedures that should be administered or withheld if they should become incapacitated in the future and cannot recover. Collectively, these devices are called **advance directives.** An advance directive is a written document (such as a *living will* or *durable power of attorney*) that directs others how future health care decisions should be made in the event that the individual becomes incapacitated.

Living Wills

Living wills are documents in which a person states in advance her intention to forgo or obtain certain life-prolonging medical procedures. Almost all states have enacted statutes recognizing living wills. These statutes also establish the elements and formalities required to create a valid living will and describe the legal effect of living wills. Currently, the law concerning living wills is primarily a matter of state law and differs from state to state. Living wills are usually included with a patient's medical records. Many states require physicians and other health care providers to follow the provisions of a valid living will. Because living wills are created by statute, it is important that all terms and conditions of one's state statute be followed. Figure 36.2 shows an example of a living will form for the state of Indiana.

The case that follows, *Pettis v. Smith,* illustrates how a person who carefully thinks through how she wants to be cared for if she is incapacitated and follows the process set out by the state legislature can have her preferences respected when she later is, in fact, incapacitated.

Durable Power of Attorney

Another technique of planning for the eventuality that one may be unable to make decisions for oneself is to execute a document that gives another person the legal authority to act on one's behalf in the case of mental or physical incapacity. This document is called a durable **power of attorney.**

A *power of attorney* is an express statement in which one person (the **principal**) gives another person (the **attorney in fact**) the authority to do an act or series of acts on his behalf. For example, Andrew enters into a contract to sell his house to Willis, but he must be out of state on the date of the real estate closing. He gives Paulsen a power of attorney to attend the closing and execute the deed on his behalf. Ordinary powers of attorney terminate upon the principal's incapacity. By contract, the *durable power of attorney* is not affected if the principal becomes incompetent.

A durable power of attorney permits a person to give someone else extremely broad powers to make decisions and enter transactions such as those involving real and personal

FIGURE 36.2
Living Will

LIVING WILL DECLARATION*

Declaration made this ______ day of ______ (month, year). I, ______, being at least eighteen (18) years of age and of sound mind, willfully and voluntarily make known my desires that my dying shall not be artificially prolonged under the circumstances set forth below, and I declare:

If at any time my attending physician certifies in writing that: (1) I have an incurable injury, disease, or illness; (2) my death will occur within a short time; and (3) the use of life prolonging procedures would serve only to artificially prolong the dying process, I direct that such procedures be withheld or withdrawn, and that I be permitted to die naturally with only the performance or provision of any medical procedure or medication necessary to provide me with comfort care or to alleviate pain, and, if I have so indicated below, the provision of artificially supplied nutrition and hydration. (Indicate your choice by initially or making your mark before signing this declaration):

______ I wish to receive artificially supplied nutrition and hydration, even if the effort to sustain life is futile or excessively burdensome to me.

______ I do not wish to receive artificially supplied nutrition and hydration, if the effort to sustain life is futile or excessively burdensome to me.

______ I intentionally make no decision concerning artificially supplied nutrition and hydration, leaving the decision to my health care representative appointed under IC 16-36-1-7 or my attorney in fact with health care powers under IC 30-5-5.

In absence of my ability to give directions regarding the use of life prolonging procedures, it is my intention that this declaration be honored by my family and physician as the final expression of my legal right to refuse medical or surgical treatment and accept the consequences of the refusal.

I understand the full import of this declaration.

Signed: ______________________
City, County, and State of Residence

The declarant has been personally known to me, and I believe (him/her) to be of sound mind. I did not sign the declarant's signature above for or at the direction of the declarant. I am not a parent, spouse, or child of the declarant. I am not entitled to any part of the declarant's estate or directly financially responsible for the declarant's medical care. I am competent and at least eighteen (18) years of age.

Witness: ________________ Date: ________________
Witness: ________________ Date: ________________

*From Ind. Code 16-36-4-10 (1999).

Pettis v. Smith

880 So.2d 145 (Ct. App. La. 2004)

FACTS

Doris Smith (referred to in the case as "Mrs. Doris"), is an 89-year-old resident of Chatham, Louisiana. An active, outgoing, and religious person, she suffered a debilitating stroke in March 2004. Although she survived, she no longer has any significant brain function. In the opinion of her treating physician, she suffers from global aphasia, meaning she can neither understand nor speak, and any further improvement in her condition would require a "miracle." Another physician assessed her condition her condition as a "vegetative state," with no chance of improvement.

Mrs. Doris is unable to feed herself or eat and receives nourishment through a gastric feeding tube. Both doctors indicate that she could be kept alive for a year or two, or even longer; however, if the tube were withdrawn, she would live only a "few days, to a week." While in the care

(continued)

facility, Glenwood Regional Medical Center, she had developed bedsores and was receiving antibiotics for a urinary tract infection but did not require a ventilator.

On May 26, 2004, after consideration of their mother's condition, her son, Steve Smith, and one of her daughters, Diana Smith Braddock, indicated to Glenwood, by completing a form, that the hospital should stop providing Mrs. Doris nutrition through the gastric feeding tube. They advised her treating physician that Mrs. Doris had executed living wills in 2001. The doctors signed the form, attesting that Mrs. Doris would die whether or not life-sustaining procedures were utilized, and that the application of such procedures would serve only to prolong artificially the dying process.

Another daughter, Oris Smith Pettis, opposed the withdrawal of nutrition and filed a petition for an injunction with the district court. The district court issued a temporary restraining order preventing Glenwood from withdrawing "any life-sustaining procedure" from Mrs. Doris. Subsequently, after holding a hearing, the court upheld the living will declaration signed by Mrs. Doris and denied the requested injunction.

On March 24, 2001, Mrs. Doris had executed three essentially identical documents entitled "Power of Mandatary to Make Health Care Decisions." They were executed in the presence of Steve and Diane, their spouses, and two other individuals who served as witnesses. There were two substantive sections. In the first, captioned "Power of mandatary to make health care decision on behalf of principal," Mrs. Doris appointed Oris Pettis, Dianna Braddock, and Steve Smith as her mandataries to make health care decisions. The documents did not specify whose judgment would have priority in case of a disagreement. However, the declarations specifically prohibited her daughters and son from making decisions about life-sustaining procedures as authorized by Louisiana law.

The second section, captioned "Declaration of living will for terminal illness," declares:

> I willfully and voluntarily make known my desire that my dying should not be artificially prolonged under the circumstances set forth below and do hereby declare:
>
> If at any time I should be diagnosed as having incurable injury, disease, or illness certified to be a terminal and irreversible condition by two physicians who have examined me, one of whom shall be my attending physician, and the physicians have determined that my death will occur whether or not life-sustaining procedures are utilized and where the application of life-sustaining procedures would serve only to prolong artificially the dying process; I direct that such procedures shall be withheld or withdrawn and that I be permitted to die naturally with only the administration of medication or the performance of any medical procedure deemed necessary to provide me with comfort care.
>
> In the absence of my ability to give directions regarding the use of such life-sustaining procedures, it is my intention that this declaration shall be honored by my family and physician(s) as the final expression of my legal right to refuse medical or surgical treatment and accept the consequences of such refusal. I understand the full import of this declaration and appointment of my Attorney in Fact and I am emotionally and mentally competent to make this declaration.

The declaration tracked almost verbatim the language in the form provided by the Louisiana legislature. Several witnesses testified that Mrs. Doris on a number of occasions had indicated she did not want to be kept artificially alive if she was terminally ill beyond recovery—and one witness stated that she had specifically mentioned ventilators and feeding tubes as examples of the therapies she did not wish to have continued.

ISSUE

Should the court uphold the directions in the living will executed by Mrs. Doris and allow the feeding tube to be withdrawn?

DECISION

Yes. The court concluded that the living will was validly executed, having been witnessed by two disinterested witnesses, and should be given effect. The court noted that the case was not about the aspirations that loving children have for their mother, but rather about Mrs. Doris's right to make her own decisions about health matters. When it enacted its living will statute, the Louisiana legislature determined that all persons have the fundamental right to control the decisions relating to their own medical care, including the right to have life-sustaining procedures withheld or withdrawn in instances where such persons are diagnosed as having a terminal and irreversible condition. The court also rejected the claim of Oris Pettis that the nutrition constituted "comfort care" and that Mrs. Doris had not given informed consent "that the execution of the living will could condemn her to death by starving or dehydration."

property, bank accounts, and health care and to specify that those powers will not terminate upon incapacity. The durable power of attorney is an extremely important planning device. For example, a durable power of attorney executed by an elderly parent to an adult child at a time in which the parent is competent would permit the child to take care of matters such as investments, property, bank accounts, and hospital admission. Without the durable power of attorney, the child would be forced to apply to a court for a guardianship, which is a more expensive and often less efficient manner in which to handle personal and business affairs.

Durable Power of Attorney for Health Care

The majority of states have enacted statutes specifically providing for **durable powers of attorney for health care** (sometimes called **health care representatives**). This is a type of durable power of attorney in which the principal specifically gives the attorney in fact the authority to make certain health care decisions for her if the principal should become incompetent. Depending on state law and the instructions given by the principal to the attorney in fact, this could include decisions such as consenting or withholding consent to surgery, admitting the principal to a nursing home, and possibly withdrawing or prolonging life support. Note that the durable power of attorney becomes relevant only in the event that the principal becomes incompetent. So long as the principal is competent, she retains the ability to make her own health care decisions. This power of attorney is also revocable at the will of the principal. The precise requirements for creation of the durable power of attorney differ from state to state, but all states require a written and signed document executed with specified formalities, such as witnessing by disinterested witnesses.

Federal Law and Advance Directives

A federal statute, the Patient Self-Determination Act, requires health care providers to take active steps to educate people about the opportunity to make advance decisions about medical care and the prolonging of life and to record the choices that they make. This statute, which became effective in 1992, requires health care providers, such as hospitals, nursing homes, hospices, and home health agencies, to provide written information to adults receiving medical care about their rights concerning the ability to accept or refuse medical or surgical treatment, the health care provider's policies concerning those rights, and their right to formulate advance directives. The act also requires the provider to document in the patient's medical record whether the patient has executed an advance directive, and it forbids discrimination against the patient based on the individual's choice regarding an advance directive. In addition, the provider is required to ensure compliance with the requirements of state law concerning advance directives and to educate its staff and the community on issues concerning advance directives.

Intestacy

LO4

If a person dies without having made a will, or if he makes a will that is declared invalid, he is said to have died **intestate.** When that occurs, his property will be distributed to the persons designated as the intestate's heirs under the appropriate state's **intestacy** or **intestate succession** statute. The intestate's real property will be distributed according to the intestacy statute of the state in which the property is located. His personal property will be distributed according to the intestacy statute of the state in which he was domiciled at the time of his death. A **domicile** is a person's permanent home. A person can have only one domicile at a time. Determinations of a person's domicile turn on facts that tend to show that person's intent to make a specific state his permanent home.

Characteristics of Intestacy Statutes

The provisions of intestacy statutes are not uniform. Their purpose, however, is to distribute property in a way that reflects the *presumed intent* of the deceased—that is, to distribute it to the persons most closely related to her. In general, such statutes first provide for the distribution of most or all of a person's estate to her surviving spouse, children, or grandchildren. If no such survivors exist, typically, the statutes provide for the distribution of the estate to parents, siblings, or nieces and nephews. If no relatives at this level are living, the property may be distributed to surviving grandparents, uncles, aunts, or cousins. Generally, persons with the same degree of relationship to the deceased person take equal shares. If the deceased had no surviving relatives, the property **escheats** (goes) to the state. The Concept Summary that follows shows an example of a distribution scheme under an intestacy statute.

In the scenario presented at the outset of the chapter, an elderly widower has no children of his own but is close to his stepdaughters, who were the product of his now-deceased wife's first marriage, and is estranged from his only surviving brother. According to the distribution scheme set out in the Concept Summary, how would the widower's estate be distributed if he should die today without having executed a valid will?

Special Rules

Under the intestacy statutes, a person must have a relationship to the deceased person through blood or marriage in order to inherit any part of his property. State law includes adopted children within the definition of "children" and treats adopted children in the same way as it treats biological children. (An adopted child would inherit from her adoptive parents, not from her biological parents.) Half-brothers and half-sisters are usually treated in the same way as brothers and sisters related by whole blood. An illegitimate child may inherit from his mother, but as a general rule, illegitimate children do not inherit from their fathers unless their paternity has been either acknowledged or established in a legal proceeding.

Concept Summary: Example of a Distribution Scheme under an Intestacy Statute

Person Dying Intestate Is Survived By	Result
1. Spouse* and child or issue of a deceased child	Spouse ½, Child ½
2. Spouse and parent(s) but no issue	Spouse ¾, Parent ¼
3. Spouse but no parent or issue	All of the estate to spouse
4. Issue but no spouse	Estate is divided among issue
5. Parent(s), brothers, sisters, and/or issue of deceased brothers and sisters but no spouse or issue	Estate is divided among parent(s), brothers, sisters, and issue of deceased brothers and sisters
6. Issue of brothers and sisters but no spouse, issue, parents, brothers, and sisters	Estate is divided among issue of deceased brothers and sisters
7. Grandparents, but no spouse, issue, parents, brothers, sisters, or issue of deceased brothers and sisters	All of the estate goes to grandparents
8. None of the above	Estate goes to the state

* Note, however, that second and subsequent spouses who had no children by the decedent may be assigned a smaller share.

A person must be alive at the time the decedent dies to claim a share of the decedent's estate. An exception may be made for pretermitted children or other descendants who are born *after* the decedent's death. If a person who is entitled to a share of the decedent's estate survives the decedent but dies before receiving her share, her share in the decedent's estate becomes part of her own estate.

In the case that follows, *Estate of Jennie Nicole Gonzalez,* the court held that a father who was deemed to have abandoned his daughter was not entitled to take a share of her estate.

Estate of Jennie Nicole Gonzalez

768 N.Y.S.2d 276 (Surrogates Ct., Bronx County, N.Y. 2003)

FACTS

Jennie Nicole Gonzalez died tragically on September 11, 2001, in the World Trade Center attacks, a week short of her 28th birthday. Following her death, her father filed a petition seeking to be appointed administrator of Jennie's estate. Jennie's brother and sister opposed the father's petition, and also filed their own petition seeking to be appointed to administer her estate as well as a petition for a judgment declaring that their father was disqualified from taking a distributive share in Jennie's estate because he abandoned her.

Jennie's parents were never married and it appeared that they were unable to maintain a home for their three children. Jennie's mother died in February 2001. The father moved to Florida with his mother when Jennie was seven years old, leaving both of his daughters in the care of their maternal grandmother and great-grandmother and his son with foster parents. He provided virtually nothing for any of the children by way of support while they were minors. He claimed that he left the children with others because he knew they would be better off with them, and that he provided no support for Jennie and her sister because he was not asked to do so and because he believed that both of them received public assistance. He also said that the people who raised Jennie and her sister would have been brokenhearted if he had attempted to move them to Florida. The father conceded that there were times when he was employed and that he purchased real property with an inheritance he received from his father.

The father testified that he saw Jennie occasionally when he came to New York and on Jennie's last trip to Florida when they had a meal together for which Jennie paid. The father also said they spoke by phone twice a year—in calls Jennie initiated. The father admitted that when he was in New York, he never taught Jennie anything, never took her to the park, never attended her birthday parties, and never bought her a birthday present.

The father was not aware until after her death that Jennie had worked in the World Trade Center for a year. However on learning of her death, he received a total of $53,000 from Jennie's employer and from the Red Cross as her next of kin. Jennie's employer also paid for his transportation to New York City, hotel accommodations, and meals.

New York law provides that:

> No distributive share in the estate of a decedent child shall be allowed to a parent who has failed or refused to provide for, or has abandoned such child while such child is under the age of twenty-one years, whether or not such child dies before having attained the age of twenty-one years, unless the parental relationship and duties are subsequently resumed and continue until the death of the child. . . .

ISSUE

Should the father be disqualified from sharing in Jennie's estate on the alternative grounds that either he failed or refused to provide for her or that he had abandoned her?

DECISION

Yes. Here the father evinced an intent to forgo his parental rights as manifested by his failure to visit with her or to communicate with her when she was a child. The alleged long-distance love and very occasional visits with Jennie do not constitute the natural and legal obligations of training, care, and guidance owed by a parent to a child. This is a father who was quite content to absent himself from Jennie's life and to allow others to take the responsibility of raising and caring for her. Parents have a duty to support their minor children in accordance with their means. The father never offered support to either daughter and made no claim that he had ever given Jennie or her grandmother any cash payments. The fact that he had a sporadic employment record does not excuse a failure to provide any support during periods when he was employed or when he received an inheritance from his father. Accordingly, the court concluded that as a matter of law, the father had abandoned and failed to support Jennie during her minority and had not resumed his parental responsibilities at the time of her death. Consequently, he was not entitled to a distributive share of her estate or to share in any wrongful death recovery.

Simultaneous Death

A statute known as the Uniform Simultaneous Death Act provides that where two persons who would inherit from each other (such as husband and wife) die under circumstances that make it difficult or impossible to determine who died first, each person's property is to be distributed as though he or she survived. This means, for example, that the husband's property will go to his relatives and the wife's property to her relatives.

Administration of Estates

LO5

When a person dies, an orderly procedure is needed to collect his **estate**—his property—settle his debts, and distribute any remaining property to those who will inherit it under his will or by intestate succession. This process occurs under the supervision of a probate court and is known as the **administration process** or the **probate** process. Summary (simple) procedures are sometimes available where the estate is relatively small—for example, where it has assets of less than $7,500.

The Probate Estate

The probate process operates only on the decedent's property that is considered to be part of her **probate estate.** The probate estate is that property belonging to the decedent at the time of her death other than property held in joint ownership with right of survivorship, proceeds of insurance policies payable to a trust or a third party, property held in a revocable trust during the decedent's lifetime in which a third party is the beneficiary, or retirement benefits, such as pensions, payable to a third party. Assets that pass by operation of law and assets that are transferred by other devices such as trusts or life insurance policies do not pass through probate.

Note that the decedent's probate estate and his *taxable estate* for purposes of federal estate tax are two different concepts. The taxable estate includes all property owned or controlled by the decedent at the time of his death. For example, if a person purchased a $1 million life insurance policy made payable to his spouse or children, the policy would be included in his taxable estate but not in his probate estate.

Determining the Existence of a Will

The first step in the probate process is to determine whether the deceased left a will. This may require a search of the deceased person's personal papers and safe-deposit box. If a will is found, it must be *proved* to be admitted to probate. This involves the testimony of the persons who witnessed the will if they are still alive. If the witnesses are no longer alive, the signatures of the witnesses and the testator will have to be established in some other way. In some states, a will may be proved by an affidavit (declaration under oath) sworn to and signed by the testator and the witnesses at the time the will was executed. This is called a **self-proving affidavit.** If a will is located and proved, it will be admitted to probate and govern many of the decisions that must be made in the administration of the estate.

Selecting a Personal Representative

Another early step in the administration of an estate is the selection of a personal representative to administer the estate. If the deceased left a will, it is likely that she designated her personal representative in the will. The personal representative under a will is also known as the **executor.** Almost anyone could serve as an executor. The testator may have chosen, for example, her spouse, a grown child, a close friend, an attorney, or the trust department of a bank.

If the decedent died intestate, or if the personal representative named in a will is unable to serve, the probate court will name a personal representative to administer the estate. In the case of an intestate estate, the personal representative is called an **administrator.** A preference is usually accorded to a surviving spouse, child, or other close relative. If no relative is available and qualified to serve, a creditor, bank, or other person may be appointed by the court.

Most states require that the personal representative *post a bond* in an amount in excess of the estimated value of the estate to ensure that his duties will be properly and faithfully performed. A person making a will often directs that her executor may serve without posting a bond, and this exemption may be accepted by the court.

Responsibilities of the Personal Representative

The personal representative has a number of important tasks in the administration of the estate. She must see that an inventory is taken of the estate's assets and that the assets are appraised. Notice must then be given to creditors or potential claimants against the estate so that they can file and prove their claims within a specified time, normally five months. As a general rule, the surviving spouse of the deceased person is entitled to be paid an allowance during the time the estate is being settled. This allowance has priority over other debts of the estate. The personal representative must see that any properly payable funeral or burial expenses are paid and that the creditors' claims are satisfied. The case below, *Probate Proceedings, Will of Doris Duke, Deceased,* illustrates the consequences of a failure by the personal representatives to meet their responsibilities.

Probate Proceedings, Will of Doris Duke, Deceased

632 N.Y.S.2d 532 (Sup. Ct., App. Div., N.Y. 1995)

FACTS

Doris Duke died leaving a will in which she designated her butler, Bernard Lafferty, as executor. He was authorized to appoint a corporate co-executor, and he appointed the United States Trust Company of New York as co-executor. As a personal assistant to Duke, Lafferty had a mother–son relationship with her and assisted her with her personal affairs, the operation of her various properties, and the supervision of over 100 employees. The property and department managers reported to Lafferty, who had a salary of $100,000 a year. Under the terms of the will, Lafferty was to receive a trust income of $500,000 a year for life and a commission of $5 million for his services as executor. The bulk of Duke's $1.2 billion estate was bequeathed primarily to charity.

Lafferty continued to live in the Duke properties, living as if they were his own, and paid himself a generous salary and lavish benefits. This was authorized only by Lafferty and the United States Trust Company as co-executor. Lafferty routinely commingled his personal assets with the estate assets. He also was hospitalized on a number of occasions after he went on drunken binges. The United States Trust Company granted Lafferty unsecured loans totaling $825,000 to pay for his "personal needs"—more luxuries.

The Surrogate's Court, New York County, summarily removed Lafferty and the United States Trust Company as co-executors and appointed temporary administrators for the estate. Lafferty and his co-executor appealed their removal.

ISSUE

Should the co-executors designated in the will be removed for failing to properly carry out their fiduciary responsibilities?

DECISION

Yes. Lafferty wasted estate assets by collecting a salary and living in the estate as if it were his own. There is no justification for these emoluments because he was also entitled to lucrative commissions as executor. The commingling of assets is a serious breach of fiduciary duty and the fact they could be repaid is no defense. Moreover, the surrogate was not obligated to expose the estate to the risk that Lafferty's drunkenness might affect his performance. Finally, the corporate co-executor created a conflict of interest when it granted Lafferty unsecured loans. This gave it a financial stake in Lafferty's continued service as executor so that he could repay the loans out of his commissions. It was also improper for United States Trust Company to acquiesce in Lafferty's misconduct.

DISSENT

The testator has the right to determine who is most suitable among those legally qualified to manage his affairs and execute his will and his solemn selection should not be lightly disregarded. The residual charitable beneficiaries are not objecting to Lafferty's continued service and, at this point, it is not clear that injury to the estate has been occasioned or threatened by the alleged excesses of Lafferty or the conduct of the corporate fiduciary.

Both the federal and state governments impose estate or inheritance taxes on estates of a certain size. The personal representative is responsible for filing estate tax returns. The federal tax is a tax on the deceased's estate, with provisions for deducting items such as debts, expenses of administration, and charitable gifts. In addition, an amount equal to the amount left to the surviving spouse may be deducted from the gross estate before the tax is computed. State inheritance taxes are imposed on the person who receives a gift or statutory share from an estate. It is common, however, for wills to provide that the estate will pay all taxes, including inheritance taxes, so that the beneficiaries will not have to do so. The personal representative must also make provisions for filing an income tax return and for paying any income tax due for the partial year prior to the decedent's death.

When the debts, expenses, and taxes have been taken care of, the remaining assets of the estate are distributed to the decedent's heirs (if there was no will) or to the beneficiaries of the decedent's will. Special rules apply when the estate is too small to satisfy all of the bequests made in a will or when some or all of the designated beneficiaries are no longer living.

When the personal representative has completed all of these duties, the probate court will close the estate and discharge the personal representative.

Trusts

LO6

Nature of a Trust

A **trust** is a legal relationship in which a person who has legal rights to property has the duty to hold it for the use or benefit of another person. The person benefited by a trust is considered to have "equitable title" to the property because it is being maintained for his benefit. This means that he is regarded as the real owner even though the trustee has the legal title in his or her name. A trust may be created in a number of different ways:

1. The owner of the property may declare that he is holding certain property in trust. For example, a mother might state that she is holding 100 shares of General Motors Corporation stock in trust for her daughter.
2. The owner of property may transfer property to another person with the expressed intent that that person is not to have the use of it but rather is to hold it for the benefit of either the original owner-donor or a third person. For example, Arthur transfers certain stock to First Trust Bank, with instructions to pay the income to Arthur's daughter during her lifetime, and after her death to distribute the stock to her children.
3. A trust may be created by operation of law. For example, where a lawyer who represents a client injured in an automobile accident receives a settlement payment from an insurance company, the lawyer holds the settlement as trustee for her client.

Most commonly, however, trusts are created through *express instruments* whereby an owner of property transfers title to the property to a trustee who is to hold, manage, and invest the property for the benefit of either the original owner or a third person.

Trust Terminology

A person who creates a trust is known as **settlor** or **trustor.** The person who holds the property for the benefit of another person is called the **trustee.** The person for whose benefit the property is held in trust is the **beneficiary.** A single person may occupy more than one of these positions; however, if there is only one beneficiary, he cannot be the sole trustee. The property held in trust is called the **corpus** or **res.** A distinction is made between the property in trust, which is the principal, and the income that is produced by the principal.

A trust that is established and effective during the settlor's lifetime is known as an **inter vivos trust.** A trust can also be established in a person's will. Such trusts take effect only at the death of the settlor. They are called **testamentary trusts.**

Concept Summary: Trust

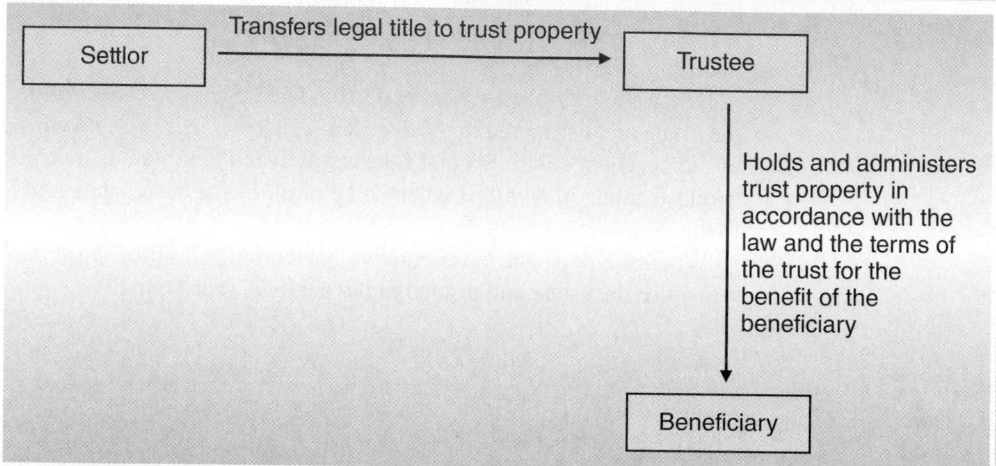

Why People Create Trusts

Barbara owns a portfolio of valuable stock. Her husband has predeceased her. She has two children and an elderly father for whom she would like to provide. Why might it be advantageous to Barbara to transfer the stock to a trust for the benefit of the members of her family?

First, there may be income tax or estate tax advantages in doing so, depending on the type of trust she establishes and the provisions of that trust. For example, she can establish an irrevocable trust for her children and remove the property transferred to her trust from her estate so that it is not taxable at her death. In addition, the trust property can be used for the benefit of others and may even pass to others after the settlor's death without the necessity of having a will. Many people prefer to pass their property by trust rather than by will because trusts afford more privacy: unlike a probated will, they do not become an item of public record. Trusts also afford greater opportunity for postgift management than do outright gifts and bequests. If Barbara wants her children to enjoy the income of the trust property during their young adulthood without distributing unfettered ownership of the property to them before she considers them able to manage it properly, she can accomplish this through a trust provision. A trust can prevent the property from being squandered or spent too quickly. Trusts can be set up so that a beneficiary's interest cannot be reached by his creditors in many situations. Such trusts, called **spendthrift trusts,** will be discussed later.

Placing property in trust can operate to increase the amount of property held for the beneficiaries if the trustee makes good investment decisions. Another important consideration is that a trust can be used to provide for the needs of disabled beneficiaries who are not capable of managing funds.

Creation of Express Trusts

There are five basic requirements for the creation of a valid express trust, although special and somewhat less restrictive rules govern the establishment of charitable trusts. The requirements for forming an express trust follow.

1. *Capacity.* The settlor must have had the **legal capacity** to convey the property to the trust. This means that the settlor must have had the capacity needed to make a valid contract if the trust is an *inter vivos* trust or the capacity to make a will if the trust is a testamentary trust. For example, a trust would fail under this requirement if at the time the trust was created, the settlor had not attained the age required by state law for the creation of valid wills and contracts (age 18 in most states).

2. *Intent and formalities.* The settlor must *intend* to create a trust at the present time. To impose enforceable duties on the trustee, the settlor must meet certain formalities. Under the laws of most states, for example, the trustee must accept the trust by signing the trust instrument. In the case of a trust of land, the trust must be in writing so as to meet the statute of frauds. If the trust is a testamentary trust, it must satisfy the formal requirements for wills.

3. *Conveyance of specific property.* The settlor must convey *specific property* to the trust. The property conveyed must be property that the settlor has the *right to convey.*

4. *Proper purpose.* The trust must be created for a *proper purpose.* It cannot be created for a reason that is contrary to public policy, such as the commission of a crime.

5. *Identity of the beneficiaries.* The *beneficiaries* of the trust must be described clearly enough so that their identities can be ascertained. Sometimes, beneficiaries may be members of a specific class, such as "my children."

Charitable Trusts

A distinction is made between private trusts and trusts created for charitable purposes. In a private trust, property is devoted to the benefit of specific persons, whereas in a charitable trust, property is devoted to a charitable organization or to some other purposes beneficial to society. While some of the rules governing private and charitable trusts are the same, a number of these rules are different. For example, when a private trust is created, the beneficiary must be known at the time or ascertainable within a certain time (established by a legal rule known as the **rule against perpetuities**). However, a charitable trust is valid even though no definitely ascertainable beneficiary is named and even though it is to continue for an indefinite or unlimited period.

Doctrine of Cy Pres

A doctrine known as **cy pres** is applicable to charitable trusts when property is given in trust to be applied to a particular charitable purpose that becomes impossible, impracticable, or illegal to carry out. Under the doctrine of *cy pres,* the trust will not fail if the settlor indicated a general intention to devote the property to charitable purposes. If the settlor has not specifically provided for a substitute beneficiary, the court will direct the application of the property to some charitable purpose that falls within the settlor's general charitable intention.

Totten Trusts

A **Totten trust** is a deposit of money in a bank or other financial institution in the name of the depositor *as trustee* for a named beneficiary. For example, Bliss deposits money in

First Bank in trust for his daughter, Bessie. The Totten trust creates a revocable living trust. At Bliss's death, if he has not revoked this trust, the money in the account will belong to Bessie.

Powers and Duties of the Trustee

In most express trusts, the settlor names a specific person to act as trustee. If the settlor does not name a trustee, the court will appoint one. Similarly, a court will replace a trustee who resigns, is incompetent, or refuses to act.

The trust codes of most states contain provisions giving trustees broad management powers over trust property. These provisions can be limited or expanded by express provisions in the trust instrument. The trustee must use a *reasonable degree of skill, judgment, and care* in the exercise of her duties unless she holds herself out as having a greater degree of skill, in which case she will be held to a higher standard. Section 7–302 of the Uniform Probate Code provides that the trustee is held to the standard of a prudent person dealing with the property of another, and if she has special skills or is named trustee based on a representation of special skills, she is required to use those special skills. She *may not commingle* the property she holds in trust with her own property or with that of another trust.

A trustee owes a *duty of loyalty* (fiduciary duty) to the beneficiaries. This means that he must administer the trust for the benefit of the beneficiaries and avoid any conflict of interest between his personal interests and the interest of the trust. For example, a trustee cannot do business with the trust that he administers without express permission in the trust agreement. He must not prefer one beneficiary's interests to another's and he must account to the beneficiaries for all transactions. Unless the trust agreement provides otherwise, the trustee must make the trust productive. He may not delegate the performance of discretionary duties (such as the duty to select investments) to another, but he may delegate the performance of ministerial duties (such as the preparation of statements of account).

A trust may give the trustee discretion as to the amount of principal or income paid to a beneficiary. In such a case, the beneficiary cannot require the trustee to exercise her discretion in the manner desired by the beneficiary.

Allocating between Principal and Income

One of the duties of the trustee is to distribute the principal and income of the trust in accordance with the terms of the trust instrument. Suppose Wheeler's will created a testamentary trust providing that his wife was to receive the income from the trust for life, and at her death, the trust property was to be distributed to his children. During the duration of the trust, the trust earns profits, such as interest or rents, and has expenses, such as taxes or repairs. How should the trustee allocate these items as between Wheeler's surviving spouse, who is an **income beneficiary,** and his children, who are **remaindermen?**

The terms of the trust and state law bind the trustee in making this determination. As a general rule, ordinary profits received from the investment of trust property are allocated to income. For example, interest on trust property or rents earned from leasing real property held in trust would be allocated to income. Ordinary expenses such as insurance premiums, the cost of ordinary maintenance and repairs of trust property, and property taxes would be chargeable to income. The principal of the trust includes the trust property itself and any extraordinary receipts, such as proceeds or gains derived from the sale of trust property. Extraordinary expenses—for example, the cost of long-term permanent improvements to real property or expenses relating to the sale of property—would ordinarily be charged against principal.

Liability of Trustee

A trustee who breaches any of the duties of a trustee or whose conduct falls below the standard of care applicable to trustees may incur personal liability. For example, if the trustee invests unwisely and imprudently, the trustee may be personally liable to reimburse the trust estate for the shortfall. The language of the trust affects the trustee's liability and the level of care owed by the trustee. A settlor might, for example, include language lowering the trustee's duty of care or relieving the trustee of some liability that she might otherwise incur.

The trustee can also have liability to third persons who are injured by the operation of the trust. Because a trust is not in itself a legal entity that can be sued, a third party who has a claim (such as a tort claim or a claim for breach of contract) must file his claim against the trustee of the trust. The trustee's actual personal liability to a third party depends on the language of the trust and of any contracts she might enter on behalf of the trust as well as the extent to which the injury complained of by the third party was a result of the personal fault or omission of the trustee.

Spendthrift Trusts

Generally, the beneficiary of a trust may voluntarily assign his rights to the principal or income of the trust to another person. In addition, any distributions to the beneficiary are subject to the claims of his creditors. Sometimes, however, trusts contain provisions known as **spendthrift clauses,** which restrict the voluntary or involuntary transfer of a beneficiary's interest. Such clauses are generally enforced, and they preclude assignees or creditors from compelling a trustee to recognize their claims to the trust. The enforceability of such clauses is subject to four exceptions, however:

1. A person cannot put his own property beyond the claims of his own creditors. Thus, a spendthrift clause is not effective in a trust when the settlor makes himself a beneficiary.
2. Divorced spouses and minor children of the beneficiary can compel payment for alimony and child support.
3. Creditors of the beneficiary who have furnished necessaries can compel payment.
4. Once the trustee distributes property to a beneficiary, it can be subject to valid claims of others.

Termination and Modification of a Trust

Normally, a settlor cannot revoke or modify a trust unless she reserves the power to do so at the time she establishes the trust. However, a trust may be modified or terminated with the consent of the settlor and all of the beneficiaries. When the settlor is dead or otherwise unable to consent, a trust can be modified or terminated by consent of all the persons with a beneficial interest but only when this would not frustrate a material purpose of the trust. Because trusts are under the supervisory jurisdiction of a court, the court can permit a deviation from the terms of a trust when unanticipated changes in circumstances threaten accomplishment of the settlor's purpose.

Implied and Constructive Trusts

Under exceptional circumstances in which the creation of a trust is necessary to effectuate a settlor's intent or avoid unjust enrichment, the law *implies* or imposes a trust even though no express trust exists or an express trust exists but has failed. One trust of this type is a **resulting trust,** which arises when there has been an incomplete disposition of trust property. For example, if Hess transferred property to Wickes as trustee to provide for the needs of Hess's grandfather and the grandfather died before the trust funds were exhausted, Wickes will be deemed to hold the property in a resulting trust for Hess or Hess's heirs. Similarly, if Hess had transferred the property to Wickes as trustee and the trust had failed because Hess did not meet one of the requirements of a valid trust, Wickes would not be permitted to keep the trust property as his own. A resulting trust would be implied.

A **constructive trust** is a trust created by operation of law to avoid fraud, injustice, or unjust enrichment. This type of trust imposes on the constructive trustee a duty to convey property she holds to another person on the grounds that the constructive trustee would be unjustly enriched if she were allowed to retain it. For example, when a person procures the transfer of property by means of fraud or duress, she becomes a constructive trustee and is under an obligation to return the property to its original owner. The case that follows, *Pagliai v. del Re,* illustrates a situation in which a constructive trust was imposed.

Pagliai v. del Re

2001 U.S. Dist. LEXIS 2195 (S.D.N.Y. 2001)

FACTS

In 1952, Dr. Bruno Pagliai acquired a 15th century painting by Master Cima Da Conegliano ("Cima"). On his death in 1983, the painting passed to his son. At his request, his sister, Francesca, took the painting to Sotheby's in New York to have it appraised. Subsequently, the painting was stored at Marisa del Re Gallery, apparently pursuant to a consignment agreement with the brother. The brother later died, and ownership of the painting passed to Francesca, his sole heir, by intestate succession.

In April 1996 del Re gave the painting to James Goodman of Goodman Galleries, who was arbitrating a dispute between Marisa del Re Gallery (MDRG) and International Art Investors (IAI) concerning money MDRG owed for art work. The arbitration agreement signed by MDRG stated that it would post collateral with Goodman to secure the amount which Goodman determined due to IAI, which collateral was to be "free of all liens, encumbrances and claims of third parties." Del Re gave Goodman her verbal assurance that the painting was free and clear of encumbrances, but Goodman did not ask for and del Re did not provide to him any record or proof of ownership of the painting.

On April 19, 1996, Goodman issued an arbitration award in which he found that MDRG owed IAI $413,650. Del Re failed to pay the award within the time stipulated and confirmed by letter that she would allow James Goodman Gallery to sell the collateral she put up against the award. She valued the Cima painting at $80,000. In November 1996, Goodman consigned the painting to Christie's for auction. The consignment agreement included a warrant by Goodman that he had the right and title to consign the painting for sale and that it was free and clear of liens, claims, and encumbrances of others. Christie's subsequently checked the Art Loss Register to see if the painting had been registered as lost or stolen—and it had not. On January 31, 1997, Christie's sold the painting at auction painting, which it had valued in its catalogue as worth between $50,000 and $80,000, at auction to a purchaser from Tokyo for $65,000. The proceeds of the sale, less Christie's commission, were applied to the award owed by MDRG to IAI.

In January 1997, Pagliai spoke with del Re to ask for the return of the painting. She had forgotten about it after her brother's death and remembered its existence only at this time. Del Re indicated that she would get back to Pagliai, but she never did. In 1999 Pagliai filed suit against del Re seeking, among other things, a declaration of a constructive trust.

ISSUE

Should the court declare del Re to be the trustee of a constructive trust in favor of Pagliai for the value of the painting?

DECISION

Yes. The court noted that a constructive trust is an equitable remedy designed to prevent unjust enrichment. Commonly there are four elements of a constructive trust: (1) a confidential or fiduciary relationship, (2) a promise, (3) a transfer in reliance, and (4) unjust enrichment. However, the elements are only guideposts for what is an equitable remedy, and the lack of a fiduciary relationship does not defeat the imposition

(continued)

of a constructive trust. Here, Pagliai has established the existence of a constructive trust. The painting was left in del Re's custody on her implicit representation that it would be safe to do so. Using the painting to satisfy her debt against IAI allowed del Re to reap the benefits of property which did not belong to her. Accordingly, the court imposed a constructive trust on the amount of debt which del Re satisfied by using the painting.

Author's Note: Pagliai's claims in her lawsuit included a claim of conversion. However, to the extent her claim was based on the fact del Re had used the painting as collateral in connection with the IAI dispute, it was barred by New York's three-year statute of limitations for conversion. To the extent the claim was based on a bailment of "indefinite" duration, the court held that while Pagliai had a "reasonable time" to make a demand for return of the bailed property, the delay of 14 years in making the demand was unreasonable. This left "constructive trust" as her most viable basis for recovery against del Re.

Questions and Problem Cases

1. For 36 years, Ward Duchett lived in Washington, DC, with his sister Mary in her home. On numerous occasions, Mary had promised Ward she would leave him her real estate if he remained single and continued to live with her. At age 60, Mary became seriously ill and was put in a hospital. Three weeks later, her sister Maude, who was a nurse in Philadelphia, came to Washington and took Mary home even though her doctors advised against it and she did not ask to be taken home. Maude took complete charge of Mary, repeatedly prevented other relatives, including Ward, from seeing Mary, and told them she was doing it on doctor's orders. That statement was false. Mary was in a very weak physical condition, sometimes could recognize people only by their voices, and could not sit up or carry on a conversation. Mary secretly arranged for a lawyer to come and prepare a will, which was quickly executed. It left everything to Maude in "consideration for her kindness, untiring devotion, and personal service to me during my illness when no other relative offered or came to do for me, and without hope of reward." The will was witnessed by the lawyer and by a cousin who was very close to Maude. Mary died the next day. There was no evidence that Mary had previously felt any ill will toward any of her relatives. Ward moved to set the will aside. Should the will be set aside?
2. Roy and Icie Johnson established two revocable *inter vivos* trusts in 1966. The trusts provided that upon Roy and Icie's deaths, income from the trusts was to be paid in equal shares to their two sons, James and Robert, for life. Upon the death of the survivor of the sons, the trust was to be "*divided equally between all of my grandchildren, per stirpes.*" James had two daughters, Barbara and Elizabeth. Robert had four children, David, Rosalyn, Catherine, and Elizabeth. James and Robert disclaimed their interest in the trust in 1979, and a dispute arose about how the trust should be distributed to the grandchildren. The trustee filed an action seeking instructions on how the trusts should be distributed. What should the court hold?
3. Mildred Rowell died on August 6, 1989. She was 65 years old and a widow, and she possessed a 10th-grade education. She was survived by seven children. On December 21, 1989, one of the children, Evelyn Hollingsworth, filed a Petition for Letters of Administration, alleging that her mother had left no will and asking that she be named administratrix of her mother's estate, which she subsequently was.

On February 6, 1990, another daughter, Kathey Amyotte, filed a Petition for Probate of Will. She alleged that her mother had left a holographic will, handwritten on two sides of one sheet of paper. The will began, "I Mildred Rowell of Route 2 Box 210 Vossburg Miss 39366 of Clark County Mississippi, being of sound and disposing mind and memory, do hereby make, ordain, publish and declare this instrument to be my last will and testament. . . ." The purported will left most of the property either to her two sons or to Kathey's son (Mildred's grandson). It was not signed at the end of the document.

At a hearing, Paul Rowell testified that his mother had given him a blue plastic folder approximately two years before her death and asked him to keep it for her. A few days after she died, Paul examined the folder and found the holographic will, which appeared to be fairly accurate as to Mildred Rowell's possessions. Mildred's sons and Kathey testified that they were familiar with their mother's handwriting and that the will had been written by her. The other sisters sought to dismiss the Petition on the grounds that the will had not been subscribed as required by statute.

The Mississippi Code sets forth the following requirements for execution of wills: "Who may execute, Every person eighteen (18) years of age or older, being of sound and disposing mind, shall have power, by last will and testament, or codicil in writing, to devise the estate . . . and personal estate of any description whatever, provided such last will and testament, or codicil, be signed by the testator or testatrix, or by some other person in his or her presence and by his or her express direction. Moreover, if not wholly written and subscribed by himself or herself, it shall be attested by two or more credible witnesses in the presence of the testator or testatrix." Was the document handwritten by Mildred Rowell a valid holographic will?

4. Fickes, a resident of Washington, died in December 1943, leaving a will dated November 19, 1940. The will provided for the creation of a trust upon his death. The will also provided that upon the death of Fickes's last surviving child, one-half of the trust property was to be distributed to Renssalaer Polytechnic Institute and the other half of the trust property distributed "in equal portions" between Fickes's "grandchildren then living." At the time of death of Fickes's last surviving child, there were four biological grandchildren living. In addition, there were four adopted grandchildren living. Two of them, grandsons, had been adopted by Fickes's son while Fickes was still living. The other two, granddaughters, were adopted by Fickes's son in 1962 and 1965, long after Fickes's death. Were the granddaughters entitled to share in the trust distribution?
5. When Peter Kaufman died, his son William reluctantly qualified to become the administrator of his father's estate. William was a farmer with relatively little schooling or experience in financial matters. He agreed to serve as administrator only on the understanding that he could hire an attorney who would do most of the work. William Kaufman retained W. L. Doolan as the attorney and put the management of the estate entirely in his hands. Doolan was a highly respected lawyer with a good reputation. Over a period of five years, Doolan systematically embezzled money from the estate. When the embezzlement was discovered, Doolan was insolvent and unable to repay the money. While Kaufman checked with Doolan about once a week, he never demanded an accounting from him. A new administrator was appointed for the estate, and he sued William Kaufman to hold him liable for the amount of the embezzlement. Was the administrator of an estate liable where an agent he appointed embezzled money entrusted to him that belonged to the estate?

6. Maggie Gaines, an elderly and infirm woman, maintained certain savings deposits and certificates in the Jefferson Federal Savings and Loan Association. During her lifetime, she had the name of her son, Billy Gaines, placed on the accounts along with her own. Her purpose in doing this was not to make a gift to Billy but to enable him to handle the funds for her support and benefit in the event she became incapacitated. Because of her deteriorating physical condition, she had to leave her residence and be cared for in Billy's home. She stayed there about two years before being moved to a nursing home for about four months immediately preceding her death.

   During the time Maggie was living with Billy, he took control of and disposed of all of the funds which were formerly on deposit at Jefferson Federal together with Maggie's Social Security checks. Billy invested some of the funds in his own personal newspaper business and used some of the funds for Maggie's support and maintenance.

   On Maggie's death, her estate claimed that a constructive trust arose between Billy and Maggie whereby he was obligated to reasonably use the funds for Maggie's benefit and to account for the balance. Did the placing of the son's name on the mother's account under these circumstances create a constructive trust?

Chapter 37

Insurance

Learning Objectives

After you have studied this chapter, you should be able to:

1. Look at a fact situation involving an insurance policy that contains a coinsurance clause and/or pro rata clause and determine how much recovery an insured person will receive when he suffers a loss.
2. Explain the liability of an insurer under a liability insurance contract.
3. Describe the rules governing health insurance contracts.
4. Examine a fact situation and identify and resolve the contract issues governing insurer liability.
5. Compare and contrast the insurable interest rules for life insurance and property insurance.

Benjamin Born purchased an insurance policy from Medico Life Insurance Company. As a part of the application process, Benjamin gave a complete health history and was asked specific questions about preexisting medical conditions. Adeline Born, his wife, answered all of the questions, stating that Benjamin had no preexisting medical problems and was in good health. After the policy was issued, Medico discovered that Benjamin had a history of heart disease, degenerative arthritis, and urinary system disorders. When Medico rescinded the policy and refunded the premiums, Born refused to cash the premium refund and claimed he was still insured.[1]

- What are the contractual rules governing the creation of the insurance relationship?
- How do courts determine the liability of insurers?
- When and how may insurers cancel insurance policies?

[1] *Born v. Medico Life Insurance Co.*, 428 N.W.2d 585 (Ct. App. Minn. 1988).

Introduction

Generally, property owners must bear the risk of loss to their own property. However, throughout this book, you have seen situations in which a person might be held liable for the risk of damage or loss to the property of another. Chapters 6 and 7 are filled with examples of persons who negligently or intentionally damaged another's property and were held liable for the resulting losses. And Chapter 19 discusses instances when buyers of goods could be liable for losses involving property they do not technically own. The purpose of insurance contracts, as this chapter will discuss, is to allow people to shift to another a risk of loss that they would ordinarily have to bear.

Terminology

In essence, the insurance relationship is a contract that may involve more than two persons. The **insurer** (usually a corporation), in exchange for the payment of consideration (called a **premium**), agrees to pay for losses caused by specific events (perils). The **beneficiary** is the person to whom the insurance proceeds are payable. The **insured** is the person whose life is covered by a life insurance policy or the person who acquires insurance on property in which she possesses an insurable interest. (Insurable interests will be discussed later in this chapter.) In most instances, the insured is also the **owner** of the policy (the person who can exercise the contractual rights set out in the insurance contract); however, this is not always the case.

A distinction is made between valid insurance contracts and wagering contracts. A *wagering contract* creates a new risk that did not previously exist and is illegal as contrary to public policy. *Insurance contracts,* on the other hand, transfer existing risks. This chapter will discuss four major types of insurance contracts: life insurance, fire insurance, liability insurance, and health insurance.

Life Insurance Contracts

In life insurance contracts, the insurer is bound to pay a certain sum when a certain event (the death of the insured) occurs. Only the time that the event occurs is uncertain. The insurance contract is a **valued policy;** that is, the insurer is required to pay a fixed amount (referred to as the **face value** of the policy). The rate of the premiums to be paid depends on the face value of the policy. (The higher the face value, the higher will be the premiums that must be paid.) There are two basic kinds of insurance: whole life and term life.

Whole Life Insurance

A policy for **whole life** insurance, also called *ordinary* or *straight life* insurance, normally binds the insurer to pay the face value of the policy on the death of the insured. The insured must pay the specified premium for the duration of his or her life. In addition to its risk-shifting character, a whole life insurance policy has an important savings feature. As premiums are paid on the policy, it develops a *cash surrender value* that the insured can recover if the policy is terminated. In the same way, a whole life policy develops a loan value. This increases with the age of the policy and enables the insured to borrow money from the insurer at relatively low interest rates.

Term Life Insurance

A **term life** insurance contract obligates the insurer to pay only the face amount of the policy if the insured dies within a specified period of time—the term of the policy. The insured is obligated to pay premiums for the term of the policy. Term contracts, unlike whole life contracts, do not build up any cash surrender value or loan value. Many term contracts have a *guaranteed renewability* feature that allows the insured to renew the policy for additional terms up to a stated age without proving insurability (good health). However, the premium rate for additional terms is likely to be higher than that for the original term. Many term contracts also contain a *guaranteed convertibility* feature that allows the insured to convert the policy to a whole life policy.

Property Insurance Contracts

Property insurance contracts are **indemnity** contracts. The insurer is obligated to reimburse the insured for any actual losses that the insured suffered due to damage to the insured property. The loss must occur during the period of time that the policy is in force. The amount that the insured may recover is generally limited to the extent of the loss sustained as long as it does not exceed the amount of coverage that the insured purchased.

Types of Losses Covered

Insurers generally do not provide coverage for losses to property resulting from any and all types of causes. Instead, they usually specify certain *covered perils* or list various *excluded perils.*

Covered Perils

Property insurance contracts generally provide coverage for a broad range of perils. Losses resulting from fire, lightning, hail, wind, vandalism, aircraft or automobile crashes, and overflows from burst pipes often are included in the lists of covered perils.

Fire insurance contracts are an extremely common type of property insurance contract. These policies generally cover losses only from *hostile* fires—those that burn where no fire is intended to be (fires caused by lightning, outside sources, or electrical shorts, or fires that escape from places where they are intended to be, like a *friendly* fire in a fireplace that spreads). Fire insurance policies generally cover more than direct damage caused by the fire. They also cover indirect damage caused by smoke and heat, and the damage caused by the efforts of firefighters to put out the fire.

Excluded Perils

Flood-related damage to property is a common excluded peril. Earthquake damage and harm caused by acts of war or nuclear contamination are also typical exclusions. Losses resulting from the deliberate acts of an insured that were intended to damage the property are also likely to be excluded.

Nationwide Insurance v. Central Laborers' Pension Fund

704 F.3d 522 (7th Cir. 2013)

FACTS

While employed as an accountant at an accounting firm, Jeanne Hentz had a compact disc belonging to the firm stolen from her personal vehicle which was parked at her house. The compact disc contained confidential information belonging to over 30,000 of her employer's clients. Hentz had a duty to safeguard the confidential information on the disc as a condition of her employment. Those clients and her employer sued

(continued)

Nationwide Insurance v. Central Laborers' Pension Fund *(concluded)*

Hentz for credit monitoring and insurance expenses incurred to mitigate potential misuse of the stolen information. Hentz asked Nationwide Insurance, which had written her homeowner's insurance policy, to indemnify her for the damages she may have to pay. The insurer refused, stating that Hentz's claim was not covered because the policy does not cover "'property damage' arising out of or in connection with a 'business' conducted from an 'insured location' or engaged in by an 'insured', whether or not the 'business' is owned or operated by an 'insured' or employs an 'insured'."

ISSUE

Is the loss of the disc covered by the liability provision in her insurance policy?

DECISION

No. Because the handling and care of confidential information is vital to Hentz's work as an accountant, the compact disc containing such information is a necessary element of her ordinary employment activities. The policy's business exclusion precludes coverage in this case. The accounting firm is a "business" which employs Hentz, and she had a duty to safeguard the confidential information on the compact disc because she was an accountant employed by the firm. Therefore, the policy's business exclusion applies.

Additional Coverages

Property owners may be able to purchase a specialized policy (such as flood insurance) to make up for gaps in a standard insurance contract. Further, many standard policies permit an insured to obtain broader coverage by paying additional premiums. This is common for people who wish to secure coverage for earthquake damages.

Personal Property Insurance

Up to this point, the discussion of property insurance has focused on policies providing protection for *real* property. However, *personal* property also may be insured. **Homeowners' policies** often insure both the insured's dwelling and the personal property located on or inside the real property. In fact, many homeowners' policies cover personal property that was temporarily removed from the dwelling at the time it was damaged.

Automobile insurance policies are in part personal property insurance contracts because they provide coverage under their *comprehensive and collision* sections for car damages resulting from fire, wind, hail, vandalism, and collisions with animals or trees. (*Note:* Automobile insurance also is a type of liability insurance contract.) There are other types of property insurance as well. For instance, farmers may buy crop insurance to protect against the risk that crops will be damaged by wind or flooding.

State Farm Mutual Automobile Insurance Company v. Kastner

77 P.3d 1256 (Colo. Sup. Ct. 2003)

FACTS

As Christina Kastner was leaving a shopping mall, a man forced her to get into the passenger seat of her car. He took Kastner to a wooded park and sexually assaulted her in her car. In the park, she opened the passenger door to attempt escape, but was held in by her automatic seatbelts. Kastner later sought coverage from her automobile insurer, State Farm Mutual Automobile Insurance Company (State Farm), for her personal injuries. The personal injury portion of her automobile policy provided that State Farm would pay "for bodily injury to an insured, caused by an accident resulting from the use or operation of a motor vehicle."

(continued)

State Farm Mutual Automobile Insurance Company v. Kastner *(concluded)*

ISSUE

Are Kastner's personal injuries covered by her automobile insurance policy?

DECISION

No. Kastner must show that at the time of the accident, the vehicle was being used in a manner contemplated by the policy in question. The most we can say about the assailant's use of the car was that it served as the site of the sexual assault and that the assailant employed the car's furnishings to help complete the assault inside the car. These uses are not foreseeably identifiable with the inherent purpose of a motor vehicle.

Concept Summary: Insurance Recovery for a Total Loss

Face Value of Policy	Fair Market Value at Time of Loss	Valued Policy Recovery	Open Policy Recovery
$100,000	$84,000	$100,000	$84,000
$100,000	$130,000	$100,000	$100,000

Types of Policies

Valued Policies

Some property insurance contracts are called **valued policies.** If property covered by a valued policy is totally destroyed, the insured can recover the face amount of the policy regardless of the fair market value of the building. For example, Smith bought a home with a fair market value of $100,000 in 1994 and purchased a valued policy with a face value of $100,000 to insure the house against the risk of fire. In the next few years, because of deterioration in the surrounding neighborhood, the home's fair market value decreased. In 1999, when the home had a fair market value of only $84,000, it was totally destroyed by fire. Despite the reduced fair market value, Smith is entitled to $100,000 (the face value of the policy).

Open Policies

Most property insurance policies are **open policies.** These allow the insured to recover the fair market value of the property at the time it was destroyed, up to the limits stated in the policy. Thus, in the example presented in the previous paragraph, Smith would be entitled to only $84,000 when the home was destroyed in 1999.

Suppose, instead, that Smith's home had increased in value so that at the time of the fire, its fair market value was $130,000. In this case, it does not matter what type of policy Smith had. Under both the valued and open policies, his recovery would be limited to the face value of the policy—$100,000.

Special Terms

The insurance contract may contain special terms relating to the insured's rights on destruction of the property. It is common for some policies to give the insurer the option of replacing or restoring the damaged property instead of paying its fair market value.

Coinsurance Clause

Some fire insurance policies contain a coinsurance clause that can operate to limit the insured's right to recovery. The coinsurance provision requires the insured to insure the property to a specified percentage of its fair market value in order to fully recover the value of partial losses. Generally, most policies require that the insured purchase insurance equal to at least 80 percent of the fair market value.

LO1

For example, ABC Manufacturing Company has a fire insurance policy on its warehouse with Friendly Mutual Insurance Group. The policy has an 80 percent coinsurance clause. The warehouse had a fair market value of $100,000. (Therefore, ABC was supposed to carry at least $80,000 of insurance on the building.) However, ABC purchased a policy with a face value of only $60,000. A fire partially destroyed the building, causing $40,000 worth of damage to the structure. Because of the coinsurance clause, ABC will recover only $30,000 from Friendly. This figure was arrived at by taking the amount of insurance carried ($60,000) divided by the amount of insurance required ($80,000) times the loss ($40,000).

Concept Summary: Coinsurance Clause

Fair Market Value at Time of Loss	Face Value of Policy	Amount of Insurance Required	Actual Loss	Recovery
$100,000	$60,000	$80,000	$40,000	$30,000
$100,000	$60,000	$80,000	$100,000	$60,000

The coinsurance formula for recovery for partial losses is stated as follows:

$$\frac{\text{Amount of insurance carried}}{\text{Coninsurance percent} \times \text{Fair market value}} \times \text{Loss} = \text{Recovery}$$

Remember that the coinsurance formula applies only to "partial" losses of property. If the warehouse had been totally destroyed by the fire, ABC could have recovered $60,000 (the face value of the policy). The formula would not have been applicable. If it had been used, it would have indicated that Friendly owed ABC $75,000. Yet this would have been more than the face amount of the policy. This is not possible; whether the loss is total or partial, the insured can never recover more than the face value of the policy.

Pro Rata Clause

With the limited exception of the valued policy discussed above, the insured can never recover more than the amount of the actual loss. To allow otherwise would encourage unscrupulous people to intentionally destroy their property. Accordingly, when the insured has purchased insurance policies from more than one insurer, the loss will be apportioned among the insurance companies. The amount for which any particular insurer is liable is calculated by determining the total amount of the insurer's policy in proportion to the total amount of insurance covering the property.

LO1

For example, Andrew purchased two insurance policies to cover his home against the risk of fire. His policy from Farmers Mutual had a face value of $50,000 while the coverage by States Insurance was for $100,000. The home was partially destroyed by fire, with the losses amounting to $30,000. Farmers Mutual is responsible for $10,000, while States Insurance is liable for the remaining $20,000.

The formula for determining each insurer's liability is stated as follows:

$$\frac{\text{Amount of insurer's policy}}{\text{Total coverage by all insurers}} \times \text{Loss} = \text{Liability of insurer}$$

Thus, Farmers' liability was calculated as follows:

$$\frac{\$50{,}000 \text{ (Farmers' policy)}}{\$150{,}000 \text{ (Total of both policies)}} \times \$30{,}000 \text{ (Loss)} = \$10{,}000$$

The liability of States Insurance could be similarly calculated by substituting $100,000 (States' policy) for the $50,000 (Farmers' policy) in the numerator of the equation. This formula may be used for both partial and total losses. However, note again that each company's liability is limited by the face value of the policy. Thus, Farmers could never be liable for more than $50,000 and States' liability is limited to a maximum of $100,000.

Pro rata clauses do not apply to life insurance contracts. In a life insurance case, the beneficiary would recover the face value of all of the policies.

Concept Summary: Pro Rata Insurance

Policy A	Policy B	Total Insurance (Policy A plus Policy B)	Actual Loss	Liability of Insurer A	Liability of Insurer B
$50,000	$100,000	$150,000	$30,000	$10,000	$20,000

Liability Insurance Contracts

LO2

Under liability insurance policies the insurer agrees to pay the sums for which the insured becomes legally obligated to pay to another person. There are various types of liabilities that insurers are willing to assume. They range from personal liability policies to business liability contracts to workers' compensation policies. Some insurance contracts, such as automobile policies, combine the liability features with property insurance coverage. Typical homeowners' policies also combine these features.

Liability Coverage

While the terms of the various liability insurance contracts may vary, they frequently share certain coverage terms. For instance, most liability policies provide coverage against the insured's liability for negligence but not for liability resulting from the insured's deliberately wrongful acts (intentional torts and crimes). Like property insurance agreements, the liability insurance policies tend to define their particular coverages by listing either covered or excluded liabilities.

Personal Liability Policies

Personal liability insurance contracts, including the liability provisions in homeowners' policies, often restrict their coverage to bodily injury and property damages suffered by third persons as a result of an *occurrence* for which the insured is legally liable. They generally define "occurrence" as some type of accident that causes bodily injury or property damage.

Business Liability Policies

Business liability insurance contracts often provide broader coverage than personal liability policies. While their coverage is limited to injuries resulting from the "conduct of business," they frequently cover claims arising from the insured's intentional tort liability springing from defamation or invasion of privacy lawsuits. They may also include liability for a third person's economic losses as well as their claims for bodily injury or property damage. **Malpractice insurance** is similar to business liability coverage in that it provides protection for professionals whose negligent professional conduct causes injuries to third persons.

One special type of business liability policy is designed to protect corporate directors and officers from personal liability. These insurance contracts are called *Director and Officer (D&O) liability policies.*

Insurer's Obligations

The actual insurance contract defines the duties that each insurer assumes. However, there are several general duties common to liability insurance policies. These include a duty to defend and the duty to pay the sums owed by the insured.

Duty to Defend

Each liability insurance provider has a **duty to defend** the insured when a third party files a legal claim against the insured that falls within the coverage terms of the policy. Of course, this duty generally does not arise unless the insured notifies the insurance company of the claims against her. Such notification triggers the insurer's duty to furnish an attorney to represent the insured in any resulting litigation.

Duty to Pay

When the third party's legal claims fall within the liability coverage provisions of the insurance policy, the insurance company has a **duty to pay** the sums owed by the insured. This includes any compensatory damages as well as any court costs assessed against the insured. Of course, this liability is subject to any policy limits contained in the insurance contract. Thus, if the liability policy was for $500,000, the insurer would not be required to pay claims against the insured in excess of that amount. Those additional amounts would be the responsibility of the insured.

Insurance companies need not wait until litigation has been concluded to satisfy their duty to pay. Most policies permit the insurer to seek voluntary settlements of liability claims against the insured. These settlements involve payment of a negotiated amount of money to the third person in exchange for the third person's giving up his legal claim against the insured.

ISBA Mutual Insurance v. Frank M. Greenfield

980 N.E.2d 1120 (Ill. App. Ct. 2012)

FACTS

An attorney, Frank M. Greenfield, made a mistake in drafting a client's will that resulted in the beneficiaries of a trust established by his client receiving less money than they otherwise would have received. Upon the death of the client, Greenfield discovered the error and sent a letter to all of the trust's beneficiaries in which he admitted to making the error. The beneficiaries sued Greenfield and his law firm. Greenfield had a professional liability insurance policy through Illinois State Bar Association Mutual Insurance Company (ISBA Mutual) but did not inform ISBA Mutual prior to sending the letter to the beneficiaries. ISBA Mutual claims that, by failing to inform it of the letter prior to sending it, Greenfield violated a provision of his insurance policy and, consequently, ISBA Mutual had no duty to defend Greenfield in the subsequent legal malpractice action. The professional liability insurance policy contains a provision entitled "Voluntary Payments," which provides: *"The INSURED, except at its own cost, will not admit any liability, assume any obligation, incur any expense, make any payment, or settle any CLAIM, without the COMPANY'S prior written consent."* Greenfield argued that he had an ethical duty to inform the beneficiaries of his mistake.

ISSUE

May the insurance company deny coverage to Greenfield?

DECISION

No. Greenfield had a duty to disclose his mistake to the beneficiaries. However, ISBA Mutual claims that Greenfield went beyond his ethical obligation, since he was not obliged to admit to the elements of a legal-malpractice action, as his letter did—certainly not before contacting his liability insurer to notify it of a possible claim for which the insurer might be responsible and seek its advice in handling that delicate situation. We do not find ISBA Mutual's argument persuasive. ISBA Mutual claims that it would not have interfered with Greenfield's discharge of his professional duties but argues that it would certainly have played a role in his disclosure of his error and its consequences, even if only by advising Greenfield in how to fulfill his ethical obligations in a way that would not compromise his defense to a malpractice case. However, we are uncomfortable with the idea of an insurance company advising an attorney of his ethical obligation to his clients, especially since, as in the case at bar, the insurance company may advise the attorney to disclose less information than the attorney would otherwise choose to disclose. Accordingly, we find that a provision such as the one at issue here is against public policy.

Health Insurance Contracts

Rising costs of hospitalization, medical treatment, and medication have directed widespread attention to the need for insurance protection against financially crippling costs of illness or injury. This section examines the basic features of health insurance contracts.

LO3

Coverage

Health insurance contracts provide coverage for medical expenses resulting from a wide range of illnesses and injuries suffered by the insured or members of her immediate family. As with the previously discussed insurance contracts, health insurance policies generally specify a list of covered illnesses and injuries and also include a range of excluded illnesses or injuries. Preexisting health conditions (those that befell the insured or her family before the effective date of the policy) normally were excluded from coverage. However, this was changed by the primary portions of the new federal health care legislation.

Group Policies

Most people receive their insurance coverage from *group policies* that are provided by employers or other organizations. Participation in group policies tends to enable people to significantly reduce the cost of the premiums they must pay for health insurance. However, these policies frequently result in an insurance crisis for the insured when his employment or other type of group membership ends. He may then be required to pay significantly higher costs for a new insurance policy or, in many cases, may find that a new insurer will not cover extended illnesses that arose while he was covered by the group policy.

Many states have enacted legislation creating *portable health insurance.* Such statutes generally try to guarantee some level of health insurance coverage to people who change or lose their jobs. They do this by limiting the waiting periods before new coverage takes effect or by requiring insurance companies to provide coverage to people who have left a job.

Further, under federal law, businesses that provide group health insurance plans must offer self-paid, continued group coverage to qualified employees for at least 18 months after termination of employment. The Consolidated Omnibus Budget Reconciliation Act (COBRA) was enacted as a legislative response to the growing number of Americans without health insurance and the reluctance of hospitals to treat the uninsured. By offering the opportunity to obtain continuation of coverage, COBRA provides an alternative to prohibitively expensive individual health care insurance policies for those people who, because of certain events such as divorce or the loss of a job, are at risk of losing their employment-related group health insurance.

Payment Obligations

Health insurance policies generally require the insured to pay up to a certain amount each year before the insurer's payment obligation begins. This specific amount, which varies from policy to policy, is known as the **deductible.** After the insured has paid the deductible amount, the insurer must pay all of the remaining medical expenses incurred during that year.

Some policies establish a payment obligation that is a percentage of the medical expenses. While this amount may vary, health insurance contracts often require the insurer to pay 80 percent of the expenses. For long-term hospitalization or extended illnesses, the policies also may obligate the insurer to pay a designated percentage of expenses up to a certain amount. The insurer then pays all expenses that exceed that amount.

More and more insurers place a cap on the amount they will pay for certain medical treatments or procedures. These companies will not pay amounts in excess of that amount. Many insurers will not pay for experimental medical treatments.

Health insurers may make their payments in either of two ways. They may pay the insured if she already has paid the health care provider. In other instances, the health care provider bills the insurer directly and seeks payment from the insured for amounts not covered by the insurer.

Affordable Health Care

As health care costs skyrocket, the number of people without health insurance (perhaps over 40 million Americans) is reaching crisis proportions. Even those people fortunate to have insurance are finding that limits in their coverage often require that they pay growing percentages of the overall medical bill. The most affordable health care policies generally are group policies that often are available in the employment setting. Of course, this alternative generally is out of the reach of the unemployed or of those who have part-time jobs. Further, even the cost of group policies has been rising.

To address this problem, Congress enacted the Patient Protection and Affordable Care Act. This controversial legislation has been battling its way through the courts since its enactment in 2010. The most controversial of its many provisions requires that every person have a health care policy. A penalty will be imposed on those who do not comply.

The Affordable Care Act addresses another common health care problem as well. Refer back to the chapter opener as well as to the *Kutlenios* case in the next section of the chapter. In both cases, an individual withheld information about prior medical conditions in his health insurance application. This is a common problem as insurance companies are reluctant to issue insurance to people with prior health problems. The new health care law denies insurers the right to refuse health care coverage on the basis of preexisting medical conditions. In addition, it extends to adult children the right to coverage under their parents' policies until they reach the age of 26 years. It also prohibits insurers from capping the benefit amount an insured may receive over her lifetime.

Insurance Policies as Contracts

The insurance relationship is basically contractual in nature. As a result, insurance policies must satisfy all of the elements required for a binding contract.

Offer and Acceptance

LO4

The standard practice in insurance is to have the potential insured make an offer to enter an insurance contract by completing an application provided by the insurer's agent and submitting it and the premium to the insurer. The insurer may then either accept or reject this offer. What constitutes acceptance depends on the kind of insurance requested and the language of the application. It is very important to know the precise time when an acceptance occurs. Any losses suffered prior to this point must be borne by the insured, not the insurer.

Applications for life insurance often provide that acceptance does not occur until the insurer delivers the policy to the insured. Most courts hold that delivery occurs when the insurer has executed and mailed the policy. A few courts, to avoid hardship, have held that delivery occurred when the policy was executed, even though it was still in the insurer's hands. If the application calls for the policy to be delivered to an agent of the insured, delivery to the agent constitutes acceptance, unless the agent has discretionary power to not deliver the policy. Some recent decisions have abandoned the purely contractual approach to insurance contracts in an attempt to seek "fair" results.

In property insurance contracts, the application may be worded so that insurance coverage begins when the insured signs the application. This can provide temporary coverage until the insurer either accepts or rejects the policy. The same result may also be achieved by the use of a **binder,** an agreement for temporary insurance pending the insurer's decision to accept or reject the risk. Acceptance in property insurance contracts generally occurs when the insurer (or agent, if authorized to do so) indicates to the insured an intent to accept the application.

A common problem that occurs in insurance law is the effect of the insurer's delay in acting on the application. If the applicant suffers a loss after applying but before the insured formally accepts, who must bear the loss? As a general rule, the insurer's delay does not constitute acceptance. Some states, however, have held that an insurer's retention of the premium for an unreasonable time constitutes an acceptance. Others have allowed tort suits against insurers for negligent delay in acting on an application. The theory of these cases is that insurance companies have a public duty to insure qualified applicants and that an unreasonable delay prevents applicants from obtaining insurance protection from some other source. A few states have also enacted statutes holding that insurers are bound to the insurance contract unless they have rejected the application within a specified period of time.

Concept Summary: Creation of an Insurance Contract

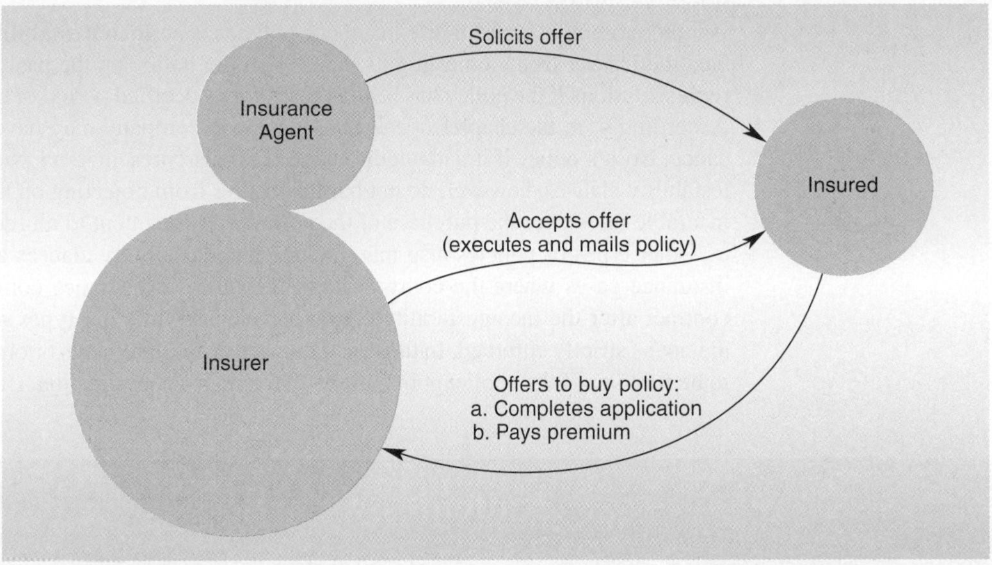

Ethics in Action

Suppose that an insurance company places a 60-day waiting period on its policies in order to permit its underwriting department to determine whether the applicant is insurable. Would it be ethical for the company to delay coverage for the full 60 days in order to make sure that nothing happened to the applicant during that time even though the medical investigation is completed in much less time?

Misrepresentation

Applicants for insurance have a duty to reveal fully to insurers all the material facts about the nature of the risk so that the insurer can make an intelligent decision about whether to accept the risk. Misrepresentation of material facts or failure to disclose such facts generally has the same effect in insurance cases that it does in other contracts cases; it makes the contract voidable at the election of the insurer. Thus, in the case that opened this chapter, Medico Life Insurance had the right to cancel Born's policy because of his fraudulent statements about his medical history. There are, however, two common provisions in life insurance policies that help to offset the potentially harsh effects that could otherwise result from strictly applying the general rule.

Misstatement of Age Clause

It is common for life insurance policies to contain a **misstatement of age clause.** Such clauses allow the insurer, in cases in which the insured has misstated his or her age, to adjust the benefits payable on the insured's death to reflect the amount of protection that the insured's premiums would have purchased for a person of the insured's true age. For example, Bob buys a $50,000 life insurance policy from Friendly Mutual Insurance and states his age as 35. When Bob dies, Friendly Mutual finds out that Bob was in fact 40 when he took out the policy. Since premium rates increase with the insured's age at the time the policy is taken out, Bob's premiums would have bought only $40,000 in coverage at the correct rate. Bob's estate is therefore entitled to only $40,000.

Incontestability Clause

Another common clause in life insurance policies is an **incontestability clause.** This clause bars the insurer from contesting its liability on the policy on the basis of the insured's misrepresentations if the policy has been in force for a specified period of time (often two years). Accordingly, in the chapter opener, the insurance company may have forfeited its right to cancel Born's policy if it had not discovered his misrepresentations within two years. Incontestability clauses, however, do not bar the insurer from objecting on the basis of absence of insurable interest or the purchase of the policy with the intent to murder the insured.

Other types of policies also may include incontestability clauses as well. Unlike in life insurance cases where the courts make it difficult for insurance companies to rescind the contract after the incontestability period has elapsed, in other types of policies the clauses are not as strictly enforced. In those situations, the misstatements or omissions are less likely to be forgiven if the applicant intentionally falsifies the application. Consider this next case.

Kutlenios v. Correa

475 Fed. Appx. 550 (6th Cir. 2012)

FACTS

Kutlenios applied for disability income insurance from Unum and attested on the application that his answers to the questions on the application were true and complete. On both the written application and during a telephone history review with the insurance company, Kutlenios answered no when asked if he had ever been diagnosed with arthritis or seen any medical practitioner not listed on the application. The policy contained an incontestability clause that prevented Unum from denying Kutlenios benefits because of a misstatement or omission on the application two years after the policy's effective date, unless the misstatements or omissions were fraudulent. Two years and three weeks after the policy's effective date, Kutlenios filed a claim for disability benefits. He was suffering from a type of arthritis that causes vertebrae in the spine to fuse together. At that time, the insurance company discovered that Kutlenios had seen a doctor for that condition nearly one year before he applied for this insurance policy.

ISSUE

May the insurance rescind the policy?

DECISION

Yes. An insured is charged with knowledge of the information in an insurance application. Kutlenios omitted the fact on his application that he was suffering from, and had been treated for, this condition before he applied for the disability policy. When specifically asked about such a condition, he falsely answered no. Unum stated it would not have issued a policy to Kutlenios if it had known about his prior condition. Thus, Unum suffered an injury when it relied on Kutlenios's intentionally misstated medical history. Since it is clear that Kutlenios falsely answered questions to obtain his disability policy, the policy is rescinded notwithstanding its incontestability clause.

Warranties

It is important to distinguish between warranties and representations that the insured makes to induce an insurer to enter an insurance contract. Warranties are express terms in an insurance policy that are intended to operate as conditions on which insurer liability is based. Breach of such a condition by the insured terminates the insurer's duty to perform under the policy. Traditionally, this has been true whether or not the breach was material to the insurer's risk. Thus, a fire insurance policy requiring that the property owner maintain a working sprinkler system might be voided if such a system was never installed. In view of the potential harshness of this rule, some states have passed statutes providing that all statements made by applicants for life insurance are to be treated as representations, not as warranties. Also, some courts have refused to allow insurers to escape liability on the ground of breach of warranty unless such breach was material.

Capacity

Generally speaking, both parties to a contract must have the capacity to contract for the agreement to be enforceable. Therefore, an insurance policy taken out by a minor would be voidable at the election of the minor. Many states, however, have made the insurance contracts of minors enforceable against them by statute. Note that an insurance contract taken out on the life of a minor (the insured) by an adult (the owner) is not voidable. It is only when the minor is the owner of the policy that this rule of capacity comes into effect.

Form and Content

Most states require that life insurance contracts be in writing. Property insurance contracts may not be required to be in writing but wisdom dictates that the parties reduce their agreement to written form.

The insurance business is highly regulated. This is due partly to the importance of the interests protected by insurance and partly to the states' recognition of the difference in bargaining power that often exists between insurers and their insureds. Many states, in an attempt to remedy this imbalance, require the inclusion of certain standard clauses in insurance policies. Some states also regulate things such as the size and style of the print used in insurance policies.

Interpreting Insurance Contracts

Modern courts realize that many people who buy insurance do not have the training to fully understand the technical language contained in many policies. As a result, such courts interpret provisions in insurance contracts as they would be understood by an average person. Any ambiguities in insurance contracts are generally interpreted against the insurer that drafted the contract.

Terra Nova Insurance v. Fray-Witzer

449 Mass. 406 (Mass. Sup. J.Ct. 2007)

FACTS

Metropolitan Antiques is an auctioneer services company that used facsimile telemarketing as a strategy to expand its business. Approximately 360,000 facsimile advertisements were sent to Massachusetts numbers. After Metropolitan was sued for violating the Telephone Consumer Protection Act (TCPA), the company asked its insurance carrier, Terra Nova, to intervene. Metropolitan's commercial general liability policy from Terra Nova provided coverage for "oral or written publication of material that violates a person's right of privacy."

ISSUE

Is Metropolitan's liability for sending unsolicited faxes covered by the insurance policy?

DECISION

Yes. An insurance policy should be interpreted according to its plain and ordinary meaning. However, when the meaning of a phrase is ambiguous, the ambiguity is resolved in favor of the insured and in line with an insured's objectively reasonable expectations. In this case, the mass transmission of facsimile advertisements constitutes a communication of the material to the public, and we therefore hold that Metropolitan's facsimile advertising campaign satisfied the first phrase of the policy definition of "oral or written publication of material." On its face, the use of the phrase "right of privacy" does not evince a plain meaning. It is fair to say that even the most sophisticated and informed insurance consumer would be confused as to the boundaries of advertising injury coverage here. We thus hold the term "right of privacy" to be ambiguous. Accordingly, the violations of recipients' right of privacy constitute covered injuries under the insurer's policy.

Third Parties and Insurance Contracts

As a general rule, contracts are assignable only when the assignment will not materially alter the promisor's burden of performance. Applying this rule to life insurance policies leads to the conclusion that a life insurance contract should be assignable because assignment will not increase the risk of the insurer since the identity of the insured will remain unchanged. If, however, the named beneficiary of the policy has been irrevocably designated because no right to change beneficiaries has been reserved in the policy, the policy may not be assigned without the beneficiary's consent. It is also common for the policy's terms to limit assignability. Many policies require notice to the insurer of any assignment. Failure to comply with such requirements renders an attempted assignment void.

An important element of the risk in property insurance policies is the character of the insured. Therefore, such policies are generally nonassignable. Those who purchase property from the insured get no interest in any policy the insured owned covering the purchased property. After a loss has occurred, however, the insured can assign the right to receive benefits under the policy, since no change in the insurer's risk is involved.

Insurable Interest

In order for an insurance contract not to be considered an illegal wagering contract, the person who purchases the policy (the owner) must have an **insurable interest** in the life or property being insured. A person who will suffer a financial loss from the destruction of the insured property or the death of the insured person has the required insurable interest. If no insurable interest is present, the policy is void.

Mayo v. Hartfield Life Insurance Co.

354 F.3d 400 (5th Cir. 2004)

FACTS

Walmart established a trust to serve as the legal holder of life insurance policies insuring the lives of its employees and naming itself as beneficiary. Walmart's policies insured the lives of all employees with service time sufficient for enrollment in the Walmart Associates' Health and Welfare Plan, unless those employees elected not to participate in a special death benefit program that Walmart introduced in conjunction with the program. Walmart's program was intended to be "mortality neutral," such that the death benefits paid to Walmart upon employees' deaths would fund employee benefit plans and death expenses. Douglas Sims was a Walmart employee until his death and was insured under a policy. After his estate discovered the existence of this policy, it sought to recover the policy benefits. Specifically, it contended that Walmart violated the Texas insurable interest doctrine because the company lacked a sufficient financial interest in the lives of its rank-and-file employees.

ISSUE

Did Walmart have an insurable interest in the life of Sims?

DECISION

No. Courts have recognized three categories of individuals having an adequate insurable interest: (1) close relatives, (2) creditors, and (3) those having an expectation of financial gain from the insured's continued life. The employment relationship alone does not give an employer an insurable interest. Although Walmart possesses an expectation of financial gain from the continued lives of its employees by virtue of the costs associated with the death of an employee, this is not persuasive because these are costs that are associated with the loss of *any* employee.

Insurable Interest in Life Insurance

LO5

In life insurance contracts, the required insurable interest must exist *at the time* the policy was issued. It need not exist at the time of the insured's death. Those who have a legitimate interest in the continuation of the insured's life have the required insurable interest.

In addition to the insured, the insured's spouse, parents, children, and any other persons who are dependents of the insured have an insurable interest in the insured's life. The insured's business associates, such as partners, employer, and fellow shareholders in a closely held corporation, may also have the required insurable interest. Likewise, the insured's creditors have an insurable interest to the extent of the debt owed them by the insured.

Insurable Interest in Property Insurance

LO5

Those who have an insurable interest in property must have that interest *at the time the loss occurs*. This means that, in addition to the legal owner of the insured property, any other person who has an interest in the insured property when the loss occurs has the required insurable interest. So life tenants, lessees, secured creditors (mortgagees or lienholders), and those holding future interests in the insured property all have the required insurable interest.

The extent of a person's insurable interest in property is limited to the value of his or her interest in the property. For example, Fidelity Savings & Loan extended Marcia a $65,000 loan on her home and retained a mortgage interest in the house as security. In order to protect this investment, it obtained a $65,000 insurance policy on the property. Several years later, the house was completely destroyed by fire. At the time of the fire, the balance due on the loan was $43,000. Accordingly, $43,000 is all that Fidelity can recover under the insurance policy. That amount is the full extent of its insurable interest.

Ethics in Action

How would you feel about your employer's taking out an insurance policy on your life? Is it ethical for companies to profit from the death of their employees?

Notice and Proof of Loss

A person who seeks to recover benefits under an insurance policy must notify the insurer that a loss covered by the policy has occurred and must furnish proof of loss. In life insurance contracts, the beneficiary is usually required to complete and return a proof-of-death form and may be required to furnish a certified copy of the insured's death certificate. Property insurance policies ordinarily require the insured to furnish a sworn statement of loss.

Time Limits

It is common for insurance policies to specify that notice and proof of loss must be given within a specified time. The policy may state that compliance with these requirements is a condition of the insured's recovery and that failure to comply terminates the insurer's obligation. Some policies, however, merely provide that failure to comply suspends the insurer's duty to pay until proper compliance is made. Some courts require the insurer to prove it has been injured by the insured's failure to give notice before they allow the insurer to avoid liability on the ground of tardy notice.

Right of Subrogation

The insurer may be able to exercise a right of **subrogation** if it is required to pay for the loss of property under an insurance contract. Under the right of subrogation, the insurer obtains all of the insured's rights to pursue legal remedies against anyone who may have negligently or intentionally damaged the property. For example, Ellen purchased a fire insurance policy on her home from Countywide Insurance Company. The house was completely destroyed in a fire that was caused when David threw a firecracker in the garage while Ellen was away at work. After Countywide pays Ellen the face amount of her policy, it may sue David for that amount under its right of subrogation.

A general release of the third party from liability by the insured will release the insurer from liability to the insured. Thus, in the previous example, suppose that David persuaded Ellen to sign an agreement releasing him from any liability for the fire. Because this interferes with Countywide's right of subrogation, Countywide may not have to pay Ellen for the loss. A partial release between David and Ellen will relieve Countywide of liability to Ellen to the extent of her release. (The right of subrogation is not available in life insurance contracts.)

Concept Summary: Insurable Interest

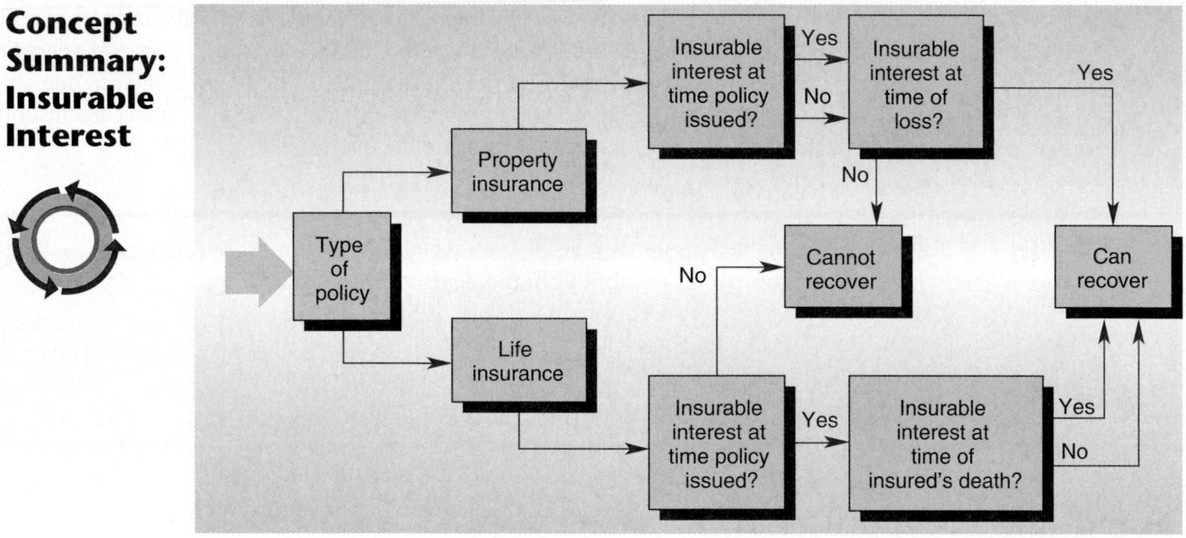

Cancellation and Lapse

Cancellation of an insurance policy occurs when a party that has the power to terminate the policy (extinguish all rights under the policy) has exercised that power. *Lapse* occurs when the policy is permitted to expire by failure to renew it after its term has run or by some default on the part of the insured.

Cancellation

Ordinarily, the insurer cannot cancel a life insurance contract. Allowing insurers to do so would be unfair to insureds since insurers would be tempted to terminate old or seriously ill insureds to avoid paying benefits. The insured can cancel a life insurance policy by surrendering the policy to the insurer. The insured who surrenders a whole life policy is generally allowed under the policy provisions to recover the accumulated cash surrender value of the policy or to purchase a paid-up or extended insurance policy. A paid-up policy provides the insured with a fully paid policy in the amount that his or her cash surrender value will purchase at his or her age. An extended policy is a term policy with the same face value as the insured's original policy; the length of the term is determined by the cash surrender value of the original policy. Generally, either party may cancel a property insurance contract after giving notice to the other party. The amount and form of the notice required may be specified in the policy or regulated by state statute. Insurers that cancel must return the unearned portion of any premiums paid by the insured. Insureds who terminate are entitled to a return of the premium on a short-rate basis, which means that the insurer may compute the premiums owed for the time the policy was in effect at a slightly higher rate than the rate that would apply to the full term of the policy.

Property insurance policies frequently contain clauses that terminate the insurer's liability if the insured does anything that materially increases the insurer's risk. They may also specifically list certain kinds of behavior that will cause termination. Common examples of such behavior are keeping flammable or explosive material and allowing the premises to remain vacant for a stated period of time.

Lapse

Insurance policies that are written for a stated period of time lapse at the expiration of the policy term. The insured's failure to pay premiums also causes a policy to lapse. The insured who allows a whole life insurance policy to lapse generally has the same rights to cash surrender value, paid-up, or extended term insurance as the insured who surrenders a policy.

Many states have passed statutes that give the insured who fails to pay a life insurance premium a grace period, usually 30 or 31 days after the date the premium was due, to pay the overdue premium and prevent policy lapse. In addition, some life insurance contracts contain a reinstatement clause that allows an insured to reinstate a lapsed policy that has not been surrendered for its cash surrender value by requesting reinstatement within a specified period after default. To secure reinstatement, the insured must pay all past-due premiums and a stated amount of interest and furnish proof of insurability (good health).

Questions and Problem Cases

1. At the time of the terrorist attack on the World Trade Center on September 11, 2001, over 20 individual insurance companies had signed binders that obligated them to provide property damage insurance, but they had not issued formal insurance policies. The insurer argues that at the time it, issued its binder it agreed to be bound on the basis of a specific form of insurance that contained a definition of *occurrence* under which the terrorist attack on the World Trade Center is unambiguously a single occurrence. Accordingly, the insurer seeks to limit its liability to one single payment in the face amount of the policy. (If the two plane crashes are construed as two occurrences, the insurer may be obligated to pay in excess of the face value of the policy since it would be liable for each occurrence.) Does the definition of occurrence contained in the binder govern these contracts? Explain.
2. Robert Zimmerman was the president and sole shareholder of Airport & Airline Taxi-Cab Corporation. He and a female employee became involved in a sexual relationship. Although the relationship had ended, Zimmerman attempted to rekindle it. Unsuccessful, he found it difficult to see the employee on a daily basis because of

his romantic feelings. He asked her to explore other job options, despite the fact that he admitted that he was satisfied with her work. The employee begged Zimmerman for her job, prompting an outburst from Zimmerman that included sexual innuendoes. She finally resigned her employment and sued Zimmerman, claiming sexual harassment in the workplace. When Zimmerman was sued, he tendered his defense to Safeco Insurance Company under his homeowner's insurance policy. Safeco declined to accept the tender, asserting that liability for sexual harassment was not covered under the policy because it was a loss that fell within the business pursuits exclusion to coverage. The policy listed as an exclusion to liability coverage any damages "arising out of business pursuits of any insured." However, the policy also had an exception to the exclusion for "activities which are ordinarily incident to non-business pursuits." Is Zimmerman's sexual harassment liability covered by his homeowner's insurance policy?

3. Anthony Howell was diagnosed as suffering from chronic granulocytic leukemia and told that, barring a successful bone marrow transplant, he had only a short time to live. Several months later, Howell and his ex-wife, Katherine Nyonteh, applied to Peoples Security Life Insurance for an insurance policy on Howell's life. In answering the health insurance questions on the application, both of them fraudulently concealed Howell's terminal leukemic condition. As a result, the policy was issued in Howell's name. (Ownership was later transferred to Nyonteh.) The policy contained an incontestability clause which became effective after two years. After the policy had been in effect for more than two years, Nyonteh was late in paying her insurance premiums and the policy lapsed. She later applied for reinstatement. In the reinstatement application, both Nyonteh and Howell again concealed Howell's medical condition. The reinstatement contract also contained a two-year incontestability period. Before this incontestability period had run, Howell died. Is Nyonteh entitled to life insurance benefits?
4. When Jose Morales applied for a life insurance policy from Amex, he lied on the application form and denied having the AIDS virus. As a part of the application process, Amex required him to have a medical examination. Instead, an impostor claiming to be Morales gave blood and urine samples. Amex issued Morales a life insurance policy containing a two-year incontestability clause. Two and one-half years later, Morales died of AIDS-related causes. The company then conducted an investigation and denied the claim for the policy proceeds. The beneficiary of the policy argued that any fraud perpetrated by Morales was now excused by the policy's incontestability clause. Does the incontestability clause make the insurer liable on the policy? Explain.
5. Joseph Alberici entered into an agreement to purchase a theater property for a price of $210,000. The named purchaser on the purchase agreement was "Joseph Alberici or his nominee." A down payment of $21,000 was made by withdrawing funds from a savings account owned jointly by Joseph and his wife, Theresa. After signing the agreement to purchase the theater, Alberici purchased property insurance on the property in the name of himself and Theresa. Prior to the closing of the sale, the theater was seriously damaged by fire. Because Joseph was suspected of arson in connection with the fire and ultimately convicted of submitting false fire loss claims, his insurance claims were denied. Theresa's insurance claims also were denied because the insurer argued she did not have an insurable interest in the property. Did Theresa have an insurable interest in the property?
6. Property Owners Insurance (POI) was the insurer and Thomas Cope was the insured under a business liability insurance contract for Cope's roofing business. The policy

excluded coverage except in instances of liability "with respect to the conduct of the business" owned by Cope. While the policy was in force, Cope traveled to Montana with Urbanski, a person with whom Cope did significant business. While on this trip, Cope snowmobiled with a group of persons that included Gregory Johnson, who died in a snowmobiling accident. When Johnson's estate brought a wrongful death suit against Cope, POI argued that it had no obligations under the business liability insurance contract because the accident did not occur with respect to Cope's business. Should the court give POI a summary judgment because, as a matter of law, the insurance company has no liability for this claim?

7. Wheeler's church was damaged by smoke and soot when two gas heating units in the church overheated, causing flames to leap out of the top of the units. The church's insurer refused to pay for the damage, claiming that the fire that caused it was a "friendly" one not covered by the church's fire insurance policy. Is the church entitled to payment?
8. Robert Lea instructed Dick Guffey, an insurance agent, to secure property insurance coverage for his apartment buildings. Using the standard insurance industry form, Guffey prepared an application and submitted it to Independent Fire Insurance Company. The company's underwriter mailed Guffey a quote. Her quotation letter stated: "If you would like to have this policy issued, please forward written confirmation." In a telephone conversation, Guffey told the underwriter that the premiums were too high. She then orally provided Guffey with a revised quotation which Guffey said he would discuss with Lea. There was no further contact between Guffey and the underwriter until two months later when Guffey submitted, on behalf of Lea, a claim for fire damage to one of Lea's apartment buildings. Was the property insured by Independent?

Part 7

Commercial Paper

Chapter 38

Negotiable Instruments

Learning Objectives

After you have studied this chapter, you should be able to:

1. Explain the advantages of commercial paper that can qualify as a negotiable instrument.
2. Identify the different types of negotiable instruments and the key features of each type of instrument.
3. List and discuss the formal requirements that commercial paper must have to qualify as a negotiable instrument.
4. Apply the Code's rules that are applicable when the terms of an instrument conflict or are ambiguous.

Chances are that you are using a variety of negotiable instruments in your everyday life, perhaps without realizing the special qualities that have led to their widespread use in commerce and the rules that govern them. If you have a job, your employer probably pays you by check, and you likely have a checking account that you use to make purchases and pay your bills. If you have accumulated some savings, you may have invested them in a certificate of deposit at a bank. And, if you have borrowed money, you very likely were asked to sign a promissory note acknowledging the debt and committing to repay it on specified terms.

In this chapter, you will learn about:

- The special qualities and benefits of negotiable instruments.
- The basic types of commercial paper.
- The formal requirements that must be met for instruments, such as checks, notes, and certificates of deposit, to qualify as negotiable instruments.
- What happens when you receive a check in which there is a conflict between the amount set forth in figures and the one written out in words.

Introduction

As commerce and trade developed, people moved beyond exclusive reliance on barter to the use of money and then to the use of substitutes for money. The term **commercial paper** encompasses substitutes in common use today such as checks, promissory notes, and certificates of deposit.

History discloses that every civilization that engaged to an appreciable extent in commerce used some form of commercial paper. Probably the oldest commercial paper used in the carrying on of trade is the promissory note. Archaeologists found a promissory note made payable to bearer that dated from about 2100 BC. The merchants of Europe used commercial paper, which under the "law merchant" was negotiable in the 13th and 14th centuries. Commercial paper does not appear to have been used in England until about 1600 AD.

This chapter and the three following chapters outline and discuss the body of law that governs commercial paper. Of particular interest are those kinds of commercial paper having the attribute of *negotiability*—that is, they generally can be transferred from party to party and accepted as a substitute for money. This chapter discusses the nature and benefits of negotiable instruments and then outlines the requirements an instrument must meet to qualify as a negotiable instrument. Subsequent chapters discuss transfer and negotiation of instruments, the rights and liabilities of parties to negotiable instruments, and the special rules applicable to checks.

Over the past three decades, many new mechanisms have emerged for transferring money electronically without the need for paper money or the use of paper-based negotiable instruments such as checks. Financial institutions, merchants, and providers of service encourage customers to use these mechanisms to expedite the payment of money in a more cost-effective manner, to the benefit of all parties involved in financial transactions.

The electronic funds transfer systems (EFTs) utilized by consumers include (1) automatic teller machines; (2) point-of-sale terminals that allow customers to use their EFT cards, such as debit cards and prepaid, as they would checks to transfer money from their checking account to the merchant; (3) preauthorized payments using the Automated Clearing House System (ACH), such as automatic deposits of paychecks and government benefits or payments of mortgage, credit card, and utility bills; and (4) telephone transfers between accounts or authorization to pay specific bills; (5) Internet payments, including payments processed directly by the account holder's bank or through intermediaries such as PayPal; and (6) mobile payments applications (apps), including payments processed directly by the account holder's bank or through intermediaries such as PayPal or Square, and "remote deposit capture" offered by depositary institutions, including USAA. Remote deposit capture customers send images of checks payable to their order to their banks using special applications on smart phones. And, for large businesses, wire transfers of funds are commonly used to move large sums of money around the country or around the world.

As these mechanisms have emerged and are increasingly supplanting traditional methods for transferring money, they have required new legal constructs to deal with the issues and problems that do not fit well within existing legal regimes such as Articles 3 (Negotiable Instruments) and 4 (Bank Deposits and Collections) of the Uniform Commercial Code. These mechanisms for transferring money, many of which you may frequently use, will be discussed in detail in Chapter 41 ("Checks and Electronic Fund Transfers").

But first, we need to discuss the legal regime applicable to **paper-based negotiable instruments.**

Nature of Negotiable Instruments

When a person buys a television set and gives the merchant a check drawn on his checking account, that person uses a form of negotiable commercial paper. Similarly, a person who goes to a bank or a credit union to borrow money might sign a promissory note agreeing to pay the money back in 90 days. Again, the bank and borrower use a form of negotiable commercial paper.

Commercial paper is basically a *contract for the payment of money.* It may serve as a substitute for money payable immediately, such as a check, or it can be used as a means of extending credit. When a television set is bought by giving the merchant a check, the check is a substitute for money. If a credit union loans a borrower money now in exchange for the borrower's promise to repay it later, the promissory note signed by the borrower is a means of extending credit.

Uniform Commercial Code

The law of commercial paper is covered in Article 3 (Negotiable Instruments) and Article 4 (Bank Deposits and Collections) of the Uniform Commercial Code. Other negotiable documents, such as investment securities and documents of title, are treated in other articles of the Code. The original Code Articles 3 and 4, adopted initially in the 1960s, generally followed the basic, centuries-old rules governing the use of commercial paper, but at the same time they adopted modern terminology and coordinated, clarified, and simplified the law. However, business practices continued to evolve, and new technological developments have changed the way that banks process checks. Accordingly, in 1990 a Revised Article 3, along with related amendments to Articles 1 and 4, were developed and have now been adopted by all the states except New York.

Negotiable Instruments

The two basic types of negotiable instruments are *promises to pay money* and *orders to pay money.* Promissory notes and certificates of deposit issued by banks are promises to pay someone money. Checks and drafts are orders to another person to pay money to a third person. A check, which is a type of draft, is an order directed to a certain kind of person, namely, a bank, to pay money from a person's account to a third person.

Negotiability

LO1

Negotiable instruments are a special kind of commercial paper that can pass readily through our financial system and are accepted in place of money. This gives negotiable instruments many advantages.

For example, Searle, the owner of a clothing store in New York, contracts with Amado, a swimsuit manufacturer in Los Angeles, for $10,000 worth of swimsuits. If negotiable instruments did not exist, Searle would have to send or carry $10,000 across the country, which would be both inconvenient and risky. If someone stole the money along the way, Searle would lose the $10,000 unless he could locate the thief. By using a check in which Searle orders his bank to pay $10,000 from his account to Amado, or to someone designated by Amado, Searle makes the payment in a far more convenient manner. He sends only a single piece of paper to Amado. If the check is properly prepared and sent, sending the check is less risky than sending money. Even if someone steals the check along the way, Searle's bank may not pay it to anyone but Amado or someone authorized by Amado. And because the check gives Amado the right either to collect the $10,000 or to transfer the right to collect it to someone else, the check is a practical substitute for cash to Amado as well as Searle.

In this chapter and in the three following chapters, we discuss the requirements necessary for a contract for the payment of money to qualify as a negotiable instrument. We also explain the features that distinguish a negotiable instrument from a simple contract and that led to the widespread use of negotiable instruments as a substitute for money.

Kinds of Negotiable Instruments

LO2

Promissory Notes

The promissory note is the simplest form of commercial paper; it is simply a promise to pay money. A **promissory note** is a two-party instrument in which one person (known as the **maker**) makes an unconditional promise in writing to pay another person (the payee), a person specified by that person, or the bearer of the instrument, a fixed amount of money, with or without interest, either on demand or at a specified, future time (3–104).[1]

The promissory note, shown in Figures 38.1 and 38.2, is a credit instrument; it is used in a wide variety of transactions in which credit is extended. For example, if a person purchases an automobile using money borrowed from a bank, the bank has the person sign a promissory note for the unpaid balance of the purchase price. Similarly, if a person borrows money to purchase a house, the lender who makes the loan and takes a mortgage on the house has the person sign a promissory note for the amount due on the loan. The note probably states that it is secured by a mortgage. The terms of payment on the note should correspond with the terms of the sales contract for the purchase of the house.

Certificates of Deposit

The certificate of deposit given by a bank or a savings and loan association when a deposit of money is made is a type of note, namely, a note of a bank. A **certificate of deposit** is an instrument containing (1) an acknowledgment by a bank that it has received a deposit of money and (2) a promise by the bank to repay the sum of money (3–104[j]).

Many banks no longer issue certificates of deposit (CDs) in paper form. Rather, the bank maintains an electronic deposit and provides the customer with a statement indicating the amount of principal held on a CD basis and the terms of the CD, such as the maturity and interest rate. In these instances, the certificate of deposit is not in negotiable instrument form.

FIGURE 38.1 **A Promissory Note**

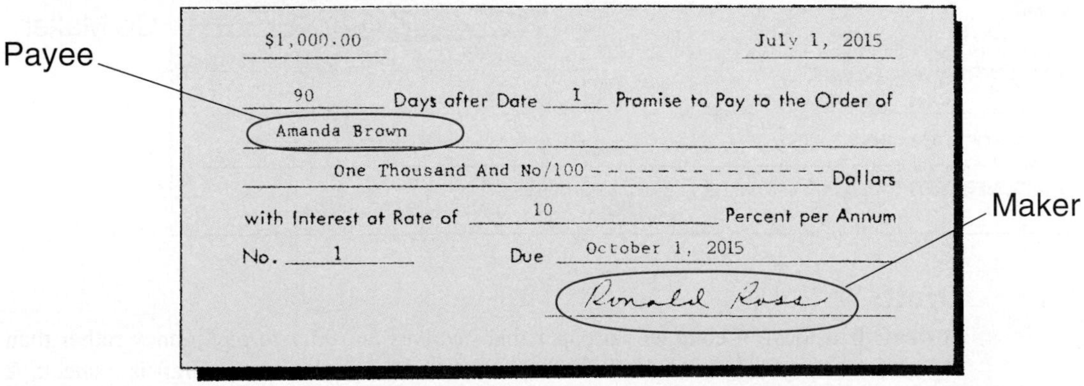

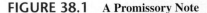

[1] The numbers in parentheses refer to the sections of the 1990 Revised Article 3 (and the conforming amendments to Articles 1 and 4) of the Uniform Commercial Code.

FIGURE 38.2 A Promissory Note (Consumer Loan Note)

The National BANK OF WASHINGTON

CONSUMER LOAN NOTE

#

Date November 21, , 20 15

The words I and me mean all borrowers who signed this note. The word bank means The National Bank of Washington.

Promise to Pay

30 ~~months from today, I promise~~ to pay to ~~the order of~~ The National Bank of Washington Seventy-Eight Hundred Seventy Five and no/100 ------------------ dollars ($ 7,875.00).

Payee

Responsibility

Although this note may be signed below by more than one person. I understand that we are each as individuals responsible for paying back the full amount.

Breakdown of Loan

This is what I will pay:

Amount of loan	1.$ 6,800.00
Credit Life Insurance (optional)	2.$ 100.00
Other (describe)	3.$ -0-
Amount Financed (Add 1 and 2 and 3)	4.$ 6,900
FINANCE CHARGE	5.$ 975.00
Total of Payments (Add 4 and 5)	$ 7,875.00
ANNUAL PERCENTAGE RATE	10.5 %

Repayment

This is how I will repay:

I will repay the amount of this note in 30 equal uninterrupted monthly installments of $ 262.50 each on the 1st day of each month starting on the 1st day of December , 20 12 and ending on May 1, , 20 16 .

Prepayment

I have the right to prepay the whole outstanding amount of this note at any time. If I do, or if this loan is refinanced—that is, replaced by a new note—you will refund the unearned finance charge, figured by the rule of 78—a commonly used formula for figuring rebates on installment loans.

Late Charge

Any installment not paid within ten days of its due date shall be subject to a late charge of 5% of the payment, not to exceed $5.00 for any such late installment.

Security

To protect The National Bank of Washington, I give what is known as a security interest in my auto and/or other: (Describe) Honda Accord

Serial #115117-12-11974 .

See the security agreement.

Credit Life Insurance

Credit life insurance is not required to obtain this loan. The bank need not provide it and I do not need to buy it unless I sign immediately below. The cost of credit life insurance is $ 100.00 for the term of the loan.

Signed: A. J. Smith

Date: November 21, 2012

Default

If for any reason I fail to make any payment on time. I shall be in default. The bank can then demand immediate payment of the entire remaining unpaid balance of this loan, without giving anyone further notice. If I have not paid the full amount of the loan when the final payment is due, the bank will charge me interest on the unpaid balance at six percent (6%) per year.

Right of Offset

If this loan becomes past due, the bank will have the right to pay this loan from any deposit or security I have at this bank without telling me ahead of time. Even if the bank gives me an extension of time to pay this loan, I still must repay the entire loan.

Collection Fees

If this note is placed with an attorney for collection, then I agree to pay an attorney's fee of fifteen percent (15%) of the unpaid balance. This fee will be added to the unpaid balance of the loan.

Co-borrowers

If I am signing this note as a co-borrower. I agree to be equally responsible with the borrower for this loan. The bank does not have to notify me that this note has not been paid. The bank can change the terms of payment and release any security without notifying or releasing me from responsibility for this loan.

Copy Received

I received a completely filled in copy of this note. If I have signed for Credit Life Insurance. I received a copy of the Credit Life Insurance certificate.

Borrower: A. J. Smith — Maker

A. J. Smith

3412 Brookdale, S. W. Washington D.C.

Address

Co-borrower: Andrea H. Smith — Co-Maker

Andrea H. Smith

3412 Brookdale, S. W., Washington D. C.

Address

Co-borrower: ________

Address

CONSUMER CREDIT HOTLINE: If you have any questions, please call us immediately at (202) 624-3450.

1-Bank's copy 2-File copy 3-Customer's copy

Drafts

A **draft** is a form of commercial paper that involves an *order* to pay money rather than a promise to pay money (3–104[e]). The most common example of a draft is a check. A draft has three parties to it: one person (known as the **drawer**) orders a second person (the **drawee**) to pay a certain sum of money to a third person (the **payee**), to a person specified by that person, or to bearer. (See Figure 38.3.)

FIGURE 38.3
A Draft

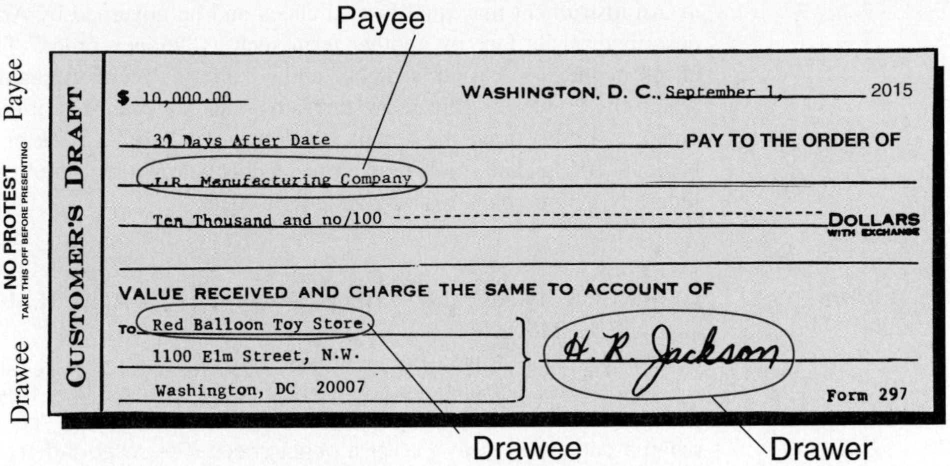

As a consumer, you are most likely to encounter drafts when your insurance company pays a claim—you'll see that often it is denoted as a "DRAFT" and indicates that it is payable through a particular bank. This notation means that the bank will pay the draft to you only after it has checked with the insurance company (the drawer) and the insurance company authorizes the bank to pay the instrument.

Drafts other than checks are used in a variety of commercial transactions. For example, automobile dealers selling to each other or selling cars at auctions commonly use drafts, as do sellers and buyers of livestock.

Checks

A **check** is a *draft payable on demand* and drawn on a bank (i.e., a bank is the drawee or person to whom the order to pay is addressed). Checks are the most widely used form of commercial paper. The issuer of a check orders the bank at which she maintains an account to pay a specified person, or someone designated by that person, a fixed amount of money from the account. For example, Elizabeth Brown has a checking account at the National Bank of Washington. She goes to Home Depot and agrees to buy a washing machine priced at $459.95. If she writes a check to pay for it, she is the drawer of the check, the National Bank of Washington is the drawee, and Home Depot is the payee. By writing the check, Elizabeth is ordering her bank to pay $459.95 from her account to Home Depot or Home Depot's order, that is, to whomever Home Depot asks the bank to pay the money. (See Figure 38.4.)

FIGURE 38.4 **A Check**

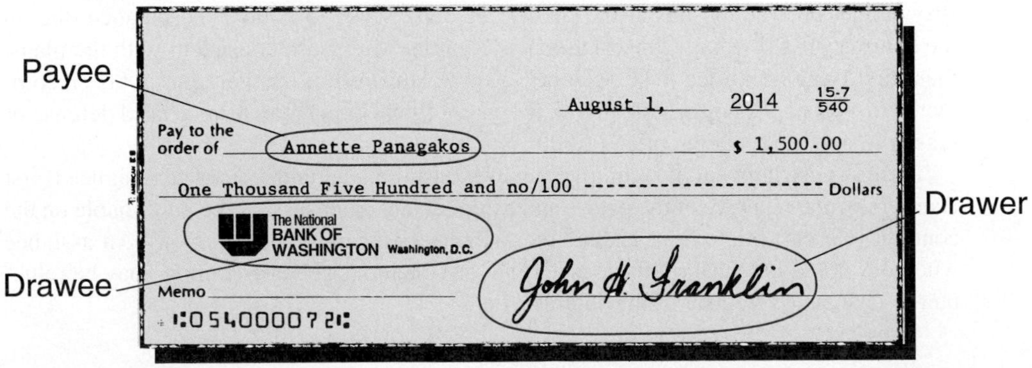

An instrument may qualify as a check and be governed by Article 3 even though it is described on its face by another term such as "money order." The Code definition of a check includes a "cashier's check" and a "teller's check." A **cashier's check** is a draft on which the drawer or drawee are the same bank (or branches of the same bank); a **teller's check** is a draft drawn by a bank (as drawer) on another bank or payable at or through a bank (3–104 [g] and [h]). For example, a check drawn by a credit union on its account at a federally insured bank would be a teller's check.

E-Commerce

CYBERLAW IN ACTION: CHECK CONVERSION AND REMOTELY CREATED CHECKS

In addition to electronic fund transfers consumers initiate through ATMs and point-of-sale readers, retailers increasingly transform paper checks they take from customers and process them electronically. This process, which is known as "check conversion," starts when a consumer gives a seller a paper check. The seller gathers information from the check including the buyer's bank account number, the routing number that identifies the buyer's bank, and the serial number of the check. The seller hands the paper check back to the buyer and completes the payment transaction by adding the amount of the purchase to an electronic file. Check conversion saves the seller time and money it otherwise would spend collecting the paper through the buyer's bank manually.

In addition, consumers often pay using "telephone checks" (also called "remotely created checks") by giving the same pieces of information from a paper check to a seller over the phone. The seller uses the information to create a paper check, which it can deposit in the ordinary manner, or to create an electronic file of information that it can send to its depositary bank. The legal rules concerning check conversion and remotely created checks are discussed in Chapter 41, "Checks and Electronic Fund Transfers."

Benefits of Negotiable Instruments

Rights of an Assignee of a Contract

As we noted in Chapter 17, "Third Parties' Contract Rights," the assignee of a contract can obtain no greater rights than the assignor had at the time of the assignment. For example, Browning Construction Company agrees to build an in-ground swimming pool pursuant to plans provided by Geraldo Garcia. At the time the contract is signed by the two parties on March 1, Garcia makes a down payment of $5,000 and agrees to pay the balance of $20,000 when Browning Construction completes the pool. If on April 1, Browning Construction assigns its rights under the contract to First Bank—including the right to collect the money from Garcia—then First Bank will obtain whatever rights Browning Construction has at the time First Bank seeks to collect the balance due on the contract. If Browning Construction has completed its work consistent with the plans, then First Bank is entitled to be paid the $20,000. However, if the work has not been completed or was not done consistent with the plans, then Garcia may have a valid defense or reason to avoid paying the full $20,000.

Taking an assignment of a contract involves assuming certain risks. The assignee (First Bank) may not be aware of the nature and extent of any defenses that the party liable on the contract (Garcia) might have against the assignor (Browning Construction). An assignee who does not know what rights he is getting, or which risks he is assuming, may be reluctant to take an assignment of the contract.

Rights of a Holder of a Negotiable Instrument

The object of a negotiable instrument is to have it accepted readily as a substitute for money. In order to accept it readily, a person must be able to take it free of many of the risks assumed by the assignee of a regular contract. Under the law of negotiable instruments, this is possible if two conditions are met: (1) the contract for the payment of money must meet the formal requirements to qualify as a negotiable instrument and (2) the person who acquires the instrument must qualify as a holder in due course. Basically, a *holder in due course* is a person who has good title to the instrument, paid value for it, acquired it in good faith, and had no notice of certain claims or defenses against payment. In addition, the instrument cannot bear facial irregularities (evidence of forgery or alteration or questions concerning its authenticity).

The next section of this chapter discusses the formal requirements for a negotiable instrument. Chapter 39, "Negotiation and Holder in Due Course," outlines the requirements that a person must meet to qualify as a holder in due course.

A holder in due course of a negotiable instrument takes the instrument free of all defenses and claims to the instrument except those that concern its validity. For example, a holder in due course of a note given in payment for goods may enforce the obligation in spite of the buyer's claim that the seller breached a warranty. However, if the maker of a note wrote it under duress, such as a threat of force, or was a minor, then even a holder in due course is subject to the defenses of duress or infancy to the extent other law (1) would nullify the obligation for duress or (2) would permit infancy as a defense to a simple contract. The person who holds the note could not obtain the payment from the maker but would have to recover from the person from whom he got the note.

The Federal Trade Commission (FTC) has adopted a regulation that alters the rights of a holder in due course in consumer purchase transactions. This regulation allows a consumer who gives a negotiable instrument to use additional defenses (breach of warranty or fraudulent inducement) against payment of the instrument against even a holder in due course. Similarly, some states have enacted the Uniform Consumer Credit Code (UCCC), which produces a similar result. Chapter 39 discusses the rights of a holder in due course, as well as the FTC rule.

Formal Requirements for Negotiability

Basic Requirements

LO3

An instrument such as a check or a note must meet certain formal requirements to be a negotiable instrument. If the instrument does not meet these requirements, it is nonnegotiable; that is, it is treated as a simple contract, not as a negotiable instrument. A primary purpose for these formal requirements is to ensure the willingness of prospective purchasers of the instrument, particularly financial institutions such as banks, to accept it as a substitute for money.

For an instrument to be negotiable, it must

1. Be in writing.
2. Be signed by the issuer (the *issuer* of a promissory note is the *maker,* the person who is promising to pay; similarly, the *issuer* of a check is the *drawer,* the person giving an order or instruction to pay).

3. Contain an unconditional promise or order to pay a fixed amount of money, with or without interest or other charges described in the promise or order.
4. Be payable to order or to bearer.
5. Be payable on demand or at a definite time.
6. Not state any other undertaking or instruction by the person promising or ordering to do any act in addition to the payment of money; however, it may contain (*a*) an undertaking or promise relative to collateral to secure payment, (*b*) an authorization for confession of judgment, or (*c*) a waiver of benefit of any law intended for the advantage or protection of an obligor (3–103; 3–104).

Importance of Form

Whether or not an instrument satisfies these formal requirements is important only for the purpose of determining whether an instrument is negotiable or nonnegotiable. Negotiability should not be confused with validity or collectibility. If an instrument is negotiable, the law of negotiable instruments in the Code controls in determining the rights and liabilities of the parties to the instrument. If an instrument is nonnegotiable, the general rules of contract law control. The purpose of determining negotiability is to ascertain whether a possessor of the instrument can become a holder in due course.

An instrument that meets all of the formal requirements is a negotiable instrument even though it is void, voidable, unenforceable, or uncollectible for other reasons. Negotiability is a matter of form and nothing else. Suppose a person gives an instrument in payment of a gambling debt in a state that has a statute declaring that any instrument or promise given in payment of a gambling debt is void. The instrument is a negotiable instrument if it is negotiable in form even though it is absolutely void. Also, an instrument that is negotiable in form is a negotiable instrument even though it is issued by a minor. The instrument is voidable at the option of the minor if state law makes infancy a defense to a simple contract, but it is negotiable.

In Writing

To be negotiable, an instrument must be in writing. An instrument that is handwritten, typed, or printed is considered to be in writing (1–201[46]). The writing does not have to be on any particular material; all that is required is that the instrument be in writing. A person could create a negotiable instrument in pencil on a piece of wrapping paper. It would be poor business practice to do so, but the instrument would meet the statutory requirement that it be in writing.

Signed

To qualify as a negotiable instrument, an instrument in the form of a note must be signed by the person undertaking to pay (the maker) and an instrument in the form of a draft must be signed by the person giving the instruction to pay (the drawer) (3–103). An instrument has been signed if the maker or drawer has put a name or other symbol on it with the intention of validating it (3–401[b]). Normally, the maker or drawer signs an instrument by writing his name on it; however, this is not required. A person or company may authorize an agent to sign instruments for it. A typed or rubber-stamped signature is sufficient if it was put on the instrument to validate it. A person who cannot write her name might make an *X* and have it witnessed by someone else.

E-Commerce

CYBERLAW IN ACTION: E-PAYMENTS COMPARED TO "NEGOTIABLE INSTRUMENTS"

Article 3 has numerous requirements for the appearance and content of promises to pay (notes) and orders to pay (drafts/checks) if they are to qualify as negotiable instruments and be readily transferable. Two of these requirements contemplate paper-based transactions—the requirement that promises to pay and orders to pay be "in writing" (see 3–103) and be "signed" (see 3–104). For this reason, at present, it would be difficult to "electrify" negotiable instruments successfully.

In contrast, e-payments—more commonly substitutes for traditional "check" payments—are neither in writing nor "signed" by affixing a signature in ink to a sheet of paper. Instead, the transaction is documented electronically—such as by sending an e-mail message or fax to a bank to direct them to pay a third-party seller of goods or services (such as the seller of an online information product).

The buyer and seller using e-payments have many of the same concerns as buyers and sellers using traditional payment methods: They want to be certain that they are dealing with each other honestly and that it will not be easier for the seller to double-charge the buyer's account or to get away with taking payment but not delivering the goods or services that the buyer seeks from the transaction; and they want to guard against unscrupulous persons hacking into their records and stealing from either the buyer or the seller.

Different laws apply to different means of making payments. Payments made with a credit card and payments made with a debit or ATM card or through check conversion are subject to federal laws. Payments made with paper checks not converted into electronic files are subject to state laws and a different federal law than applies to purely electronic transmission of payment information. Consumers increasingly need to understand what laws apply to the payments they make and how they work so that they can take full advantage of the consumer protections those laws afford them.

Unconditional Promise or Order

Requirement of a Promise or Order

If an instrument is promissory in nature, such as a note or a certificate of deposit, it must contain an unconditional promise to pay or it cannot be negotiable. Merely acknowledging a debt is not sufficient (3–103[9]). For example, the statement "I owe you $100" does not constitute a promise to pay. An IOU in this form is not a negotiable instrument.

If an instrument is an order to pay, such as a check or a draft, it must contain an unconditional order. A simple request to pay as a favor is not sufficient; however, a politely phrased demand, such as "please pay," can meet the requirement. Checks commonly use the language "Pay to the order of." This satisfies the requirement that the check contain an order to pay. The order is the word "pay," not the word "order." The word "order" has another function—that of making the instrument payable "to order or to bearer."

Promise or Order Must Be Unconditional

An instrument is not negotiable unless the promise or order is unconditional. For example, a note that provides, "I promise to pay to the order of Karl Adams $1,000 if he replaces the roof on my garage," is not negotiable because it is payable on a condition.

To be negotiable, an instrument must be written so that a person can tell from reading the instrument alone what the obligations of the parties are. If a note contains the statement "Payment is subject to the terms of a mortgage dated November 20, 2009," it is not negotiable. To determine the rights of the parties on the note, one would have to examine another document—the mortgage.

However, a reference to another document for a statement of rights with respect to collateral, prepayment, or acceleration does not destroy the negotiability of a note (3–106[b]). For example, a note could contain the statement "This note is secured by a mortgage dated August 30, 2009," without affecting its negotiability. In this case, the mortgage does not affect rights and duties of the parties to the note. It would not be necessary to examine the mortgage document to determine the rights of the parties to the note; the parties need only examine the note.

The negotiability of an instrument is not affected by a statement of the consideration for which the instrument was given or by a statement of the transaction that gave rise to the instrument. For example, a negotiable instrument may state that it was given in payment of last month's rent or that it was given in payment of the purchase price of goods. The statement does not affect the negotiability of the instrument.

In the case that follows, *Jackson v. Luellen Farms,* the court concluded that a reference in a note that incorporated the terms of a mortgage did not qualify as a negotiable instrument.

A check may reference the account to be debited without making the check conditional and thus nonnegotiable. For example, a check could contain the notation "payroll account" or "petty cash."

Revised Article 3 also addresses the negotiability of traveler's checks that commonly require, as a condition to payment, a countersignature of a person whose specimen signature appears on the draft. Under the revision, the condition does not prevent the instrument from meeting the "unconditional promise or order" requirement (3–106[c]). However, if the person whose specimen signature appears on the instrument fails to countersign it, the failure to sign becomes a defense to the obligation of the issuer to pay. This concept will be discussed in the following chapter.

Jackson v. Luellen Farms

64 UCC Rep.2d 639 (Ct. App. Ind. 2007)

FACTS

John Jackson was the owner and president of Hartford Packing Company, a business that purchased tomatoes from farmers and produced canned tomato products. Luellen Farms grew tomatoes and sold then to Hartford for more than 30 years. Frequently, Hartford would not pay for the tomatoes on delivery but would wait until after the first of the following year to pay. On several occasion Luellen extended loans to Hartford, which Hartford had repaid in full.

As of October 1, 1999, Hartford owed Luellen $224,656.78 for tomatoes delivered by Luellen in 1998 and 1999. On that date, the president of Luellen presented a Note in the amount of $225,000 to Jackson to memorialize the amount owed by Hartford to Luellen. The Note read as follows:

> $225,000 Moreland, Ind., Oct. 1, 1999
>
> [Left blank] Days after date we or either of us promise to pay to order of Luellen Farms, Inc.
>
> Two Hundred twenty-five Thousand Dollars
>
> And Attorney's Fees. Value Received * * * with seven percent interest from date until paid. The drawers and endorsers waive presentment for payment, protest and notice of protest and non-payment of this note. This note

(continued)

> is in renewal of a note or balance due thereon dated [left blank] and described in a certain mortgage recorded in Chattel Mortgage Record No. [left blank] of the mortgage records of Henry County, Indiana, and not in payment of such original note, the original note being filed with said mortgage and not delivered. Payment of this renewal note shall entitle the maker to the delivery and cancellation of said original note. All covenants and agreements in said mortgage shall apply to this renewal note and this renewal note shall be taken and considered only as an extension of time for the payment of said debt secured by said mortgage or the proportionate part thereof and not in release or discharge of said original debt and in no sense a novation thereof, and this covenant shall be binding upon subsequent purchasers of the property pledged in said mortgage with covenant to assume and pay the same.
>
> Negotiable and payable at Farmers State Bank of Mooreland, Indiana.

Jackson signed the Note "Hartford Packing Company, Inc." with "John K. Jackson" underneath. Hartford made several payments on the Note, ultimately repaying Luellen $55,000. In November 1999, Hartford went out of business, owing creditors somewhere between $2.5 and $3 million and unable to repay the remaining balance on the Note.

Luellen then brought suit against both Hartford and Jackson to recover on the Note. One of the issues in the litigation was whether the note was a negotiable instrument.

ISSUE

Can an instrument that includes the language indicating that all covenants and agreements in another document, a mortgage, are deemed to apply to the note in question qualify as a negotiable instrument?

DECISION

No. Initially, the court noted that the fact a note refers to a mortgage does not strip it of negotiability. However, here the reference to the mortgage went further than merely indicating the mortgage's statement of rights with respect to collateral tied to the note and indicated that all agreements and covenants in the mortgage applied to the note. The rationale behind negotiable instruments requires that the holder of a negotiable instrument should not be required to examine another document to determine rights with respect to payment. Accordingly, the note here does not qualify as a negotiable instrument.

Fixed Amount of Money

Fixed Amount

The promise or order in an instrument must be to pay a fixed amount of money, with or without interest or other charges described in the promise or order. The requirement of a "fixed amount" applies only to principal, and the amount of any interest payable is that described in the instrument. If a variable rate of interest is prescribed, the amount of interest is calculated by reference to the formula or index referenced in the instrument. If the description of interest in the instrument does not allow the amount of interest to be ascertained, then interest is payable at the judgment rate in effect at the place of payment at the time interest first accrues (3–112). The judgment rate is the rate of interest courts impose on losing parties until they pay the winning parties.

Payable in Money

The amount specified in the instrument must be payable in money. "Money" is a medium of exchange authorized or adopted by a domestic or foreign government and includes a monetary unit of account established by an intergovernmental organization or by agreement between two or more nations (1–201[24]). Unless the instrument otherwise provides, an instrument that states the amount payable in foreign money may be paid in the foreign money or in an equivalent dollar amount (3–107). If the person obligated to pay off an instrument can do something other than pay money, the instrument is not negotiable. For example, if a note reads, "I promise to pay to the order of Sarah Smith, at my option, $40 or five bushels of apples, John Jones," the note is not negotiable.

Payable on Demand or at a Definite Time

To be negotiable, the promise or order must be payable either on demand or at a specified time in the future. The reason for this requirement is so that the time when the instrument is payable can be determined with some certainty. An instrument that is payable on the happening of some uncertain event is not negotiable. Thus, a note payable "when my son graduates from college" is not negotiable, even though the son does graduate subsequently.

Payable on Demand

A promise or order is "payable on demand" if (1) it states that it is payable on "demand" or "sight" (or otherwise at the will of the holder of the instrument) or (2) it does not state any time for payment (3–108[a]). For example, if the maker forgets to state when a note is payable, it is payable immediately at the request of the holder of the note.

An instrument may be antedated or postdated, and normally an instrument payable on demand is not payable before the date of the instrument (3–113[a]). However, revised Article 3 makes an important exception for checks; a payor bank (a bank that is the drawee of a draft) may pay a postdated check before the stated date *unless* the drawer has notified the bank of postdating pursuant to a procedure set out in the Code (3–113[a]; 4–401[c]). The procedure is similar to that required when a drawer wants the drawee bank to "stop payment" on a check (see Chapter 41).

Payable at a Definite Time

A promise or order is "payable at a definite time" if it is payable at a fixed date or dates or at a time or times readily ascertainable at the time the promise or order is issued (3–108[b]). Thus, a note dated March 25, 2014, might be made payable at a fixed time after a stated date, such as "30 days after date."

Under the Code, an instrument that names a fixed date or time for payment—without losing its negotiable character—also may contain a clause permitting the time for payment to be accelerated at the option of the maker. Similarly, an instrument may allow an extension of time at the option of the holder or allow a maker or acceptor to extend payment to a further definite time. Or the due date of a note might be triggered by the happening of an event, such as the filing of a petition in bankruptcy against the maker. The Code permits these clauses so long as one can determine the time for payment with certainty (3–108).

If an instrument is undated, its "date" is the date it is issued by the maker or drawer (3–113[b]).

Payable to Order or Bearer

For an instrument (other than a check) to be negotiable, it must be "payable to order or to bearer." A note that provides "I promise to pay to the order of Sarah Smith" or "I promise to pay to Sarah Smith or bearer" is negotiable. However, one that provides "I promise to pay to Sarah Smith" is not. The words "to the order of " or "to bearer" show that the drawer of a draft, or the maker of a note, intends to issue a negotiable instrument. The drawer or maker is not restricting payment of the instrument to just Sarah Smith but is willing to pay someone else designated by Sarah Smith. This is the essence of negotiability.

In the original version of Article 3, an order in the form of a check also had to be "payable to order or bearer" to qualify as a negotiable instrument. However, the drafters of Revised Article 3 created an exception for instruments that otherwise meet the requirements for a negotiable instrument as well as the definition of a check (3–104[c]). Under the revised article, a check that reads "Pay John Doe" could qualify as a negotiable instrument. As a result the Code treats checks, which are payment instruments, as negotiable instruments whether or not they contain the words "to the order of."

The drafters explained that most checks are preprinted with these words but that occasionally the drawer may strike out the words before issuing the check and that a few check forms have been in use that do not contain these words. In these instances, the drafters preferred not to limit the rights of holders of such checks who may pay money or give credit for a check without being aware that it is not in the conventional form for a negotiable instrument.

The most common forms of a promise or order being payable to bearer use the words "payable to bearer," "payable to the order of bearer," "payable to cash," or "payable to the order of cash" (3–109[a]). A promise or order is considered to be payable "to order" if it is payable (1) to the order of an identified person or (2) to an identified person or that person's order (3–109[b]). Examples would include: "Pay to the order of Sandy Smith" and "Pay to Sandy Smith or order." A check sent with the payee line blank is payable to bearer. However, it also is considered an incomplete instrument, the rules concerning which will be discussed in the following two chapters.

In the case that follows, *Scott v. Zimmerman*, the court held that an otherwise complete promissory note with the payee line blank was a valid note and payable to the bearer.

Scott v. Zimmerman

74 UCC Rep.2d 283 (Ct. App. Mich. 2011)

FACTS

Sheri Zimmerman executed a "Promissory Note" dated March 20, 2007. The total amount on the note was $46,378 with a principal amount of $40,000 and $6,378 in interest. The promissory note stated as follows:

> FOR VALUE RECEIVED, the undersigned here by jointly and severally promises to pay to the order of ________
>
> ____,
>
> the sum of *forty six thousand three hundred seventy eight ($46,378.00),* together with interest thereon at a rate of *six percent (6%)* per annum on the unpaid balance. Said sum shall be paid in the manner following: *See attached schedule.*

The promissory note further stated that any payments under it had to be made to such address as may be designated by "any holder."* It was signed by Zimmerman alone as "Borrower" and it appeared that she had signed in her individual capacity because she did not sign in any other capacity. No other borrowers signed the note and it was not witnessed or notarized. Attached to the promissory note was a loan amortization schedule showing a total of 60 payments (12 payments a year for five years) totaling $46,378 ($40,000 principal and $6,378 interest).

Robert Scott and Sheri Zimmerman, who had known each other for a long time, decided to go into a new business venture called Aggressive Suspensions involving the fabrication of race car components. Scott, a skilled welder and fabricator of race cars, was to do the fabrication and Zimmerman was going to take care of the books. Scott borrowed $40,000 from his mother, issued two checks totaling $40,000 that went into the business venture, and received the note from Zimmerman who considered herself the 75 percent owner of the business.

* The holder of an instrument is generally one in possession of an instrument that is either payable to that person or payable to "bearer," will be covered in Chapter 39.

(continued)

On January 29, 2009, Scott filed suit against Zimmerman for breach of contract and unjust enrichment, alleging that he had never received any payment from her, despite multiple requests to her for payment. One of the issues in the case was whether the promissory note was a valid note.

ISSUE

Did the absence of a named payee invalidate the note?

DECISION

No. The court noted that a promise or order on an instrument is payable to the bearer if it does not state a payee. The court found further evidence that the language of the promissory note itself signifies that it can properly be read as a bearer instrument in that it provided "all payments hereunder shall be made to such address as may from time to time be designated by any holder thereof."

[Author's note: In this case, Zimmerman also argued that the promissory note was defective on its face because it was not certain as to the sum to be paid or the time of payment. The court noted that while there were no actual dates listed in the amortization schedule, but rather a defined period of five years for repayment, the UCC provides that a promise or order is payable at a definite time if it is payable on elapse of a definite period of time after acceptance. When the note was given to Scott who accepted it, the promissory note became payable five years after that date, making both the sum to be paid and the time of repayment sufficiently certain to meet the requirements for a valid promissory note.]

The original payee of a check or a note can transfer the right to receive payment to someone else. By making the instrument payable "to the order of" or "to bearer," the drawer or maker is giving the payee the chance to negotiate the instrument to another person and to cut off certain defenses that the drawer or maker may have against payment of the instrument.

A check that is payable to the order of a specific person is known as "order paper." Order paper can be negotiated or transferred only by indorsement. A check payable "to bearer" or "to cash" is known as "bearer paper"; it can be negotiated or transferred without indorsement (3–201[b]). The rules governing negotiation of instruments will be detailed in the next chapter.

An instrument can be made payable to two or more payees. For example, a check could be drawn payable "to the order of John Jones and Henry Smith." Then, both Jones and Smith have to be involved in negotiating it or enforcing its payment. An instrument can also be made payable to alternative persons, for example, "to the order of Susan Clark or Betsy Brown." In this case, either Clark or Brown could negotiate it or enforce its payment (3–110[d]).

Concept Summary: Requirements for Negotiability

Requirement	Basic Rules
Must Be in Writing	1. The instrument may be handwritten, typed, or printed.
Must Be Signed by the Maker or Drawer	1. Person issuing the instrument must sign with intent of validating his or her obligation. 2. Person issuing may affix the signature in a variety of ways—for example, by word, mark, or rubber stamp. 3. Agent or authorized representative may supply the "signature."
Must Contain a Promise or Order to Pay	1. Promise must be more than acknowledgment of a debt. 2. Order requirement is met if the drawer issues an instruction to "pay."

(continued)

Concept Summary: Requirements for Negotiability *(concluded)*

Promise or Order Must Be Unconditional	1. Entire obligation must be found in the instrument itself and not in another document or documents. 2. Payment cannot be conditioned on the occurrence of an event.
Must Call for Payment of a Fixed Amount of Money	1. Must be able to ascertain the principal from the face of the instrument. 2. May contain a clause providing for payment of interest or other charges such as collection or attorney's fees.
Must Be Payable in Money	1. Obligation must be payable in a medium of exchange authorized or adopted by a government or by an international organization or agreement between two or more nations. 2. Maker or drawer cannot have the option to pay in something other than money.
Must Be Payable on Demand or at a Definite Time	1. Requirement is met if instrument says it is payable on demand or if no time for payment is stated (then it is payable on demand). 2. Requirement is met if it is payable on a stated date or at a fixed time after a stated date. 3. Instrument may contain an acceleration clause or a clause allowing maker or holder to extend the payment date.
Generally Must Be Payable to Bearer or to Order	1. Bearer requirement is met if instrument is payable "to bearer" or "to cash." 2. Order requirement is met if instrument is payable "to the order of" a specified person or persons. 3. Exception from requirement is made for instruments meeting both the definition of a check and all the other requirements for a negotiable instrument.
May Not State Any Other Undertaking or Instruction by the Person Promising or Ordering Payment to Do Any Act in Addition to the Payment of Money	However, it may contain (*a*) an undertaking or power to give, maintain, or protect collateral to secure payment, (*b*) an authorization or power to the holder to confess judgment or realize on or dispose of collateral, or (*c*) a waiver of the benefit of any law intended for the advantage or protection of an obligor on the instrument.

Special Terms

Additional Terms

Generally, if an instrument is to qualify as a negotiable instrument, the person promising or ordering payment may not state undertakings or instructions in addition to the payment of money (3–104[a][3]). However, the instrument may include clauses concerning (1) giving, maintaining, or protecting collateral to secure payment, (2) an authorization to confess judgment or to realize on or dispose of collateral, and (3) waiving the benefit of any law intended for the protection or benefit of any person obligated on the instrument.

Thus, a term authorizing the confession of judgment on an instrument when it is due does not affect the negotiability of the instrument. A "confession of judgment" clause authorizes the creditor to go into court if the debtor defaults and, with the debtor's acquiescence, to have a judgment entered against the debtor. However, some states prohibit confessions of judgment.

Banks and other businesses often use forms of commercial paper that meet their particular needs. These forms may include certain other terms that do not affect the negotiability of an instrument. For example, a note may designate a place of payment without affecting the instrument's negotiability. Where the instrument does not specify a place of payment, the Code sets out rules for ascertaining where payment is to be made (3–111).

LO4

Ambiguous Terms

Occasionally, a person may write or receive a check on which the amount written in figures differs from the amount written in words. Or a note may have conflicting terms or an ambiguous term. Where a conflict or an ambiguous term exists, there are general rules of interpretation that are applied to resolve the conflict or ambiguity: Typewritten terms prevail over printed terms, handwritten terms prevail over printed and typewritten terms, and where words and numbers conflict, the words control the numbers (3–114).

Questions and Problem Cases

1. Is the following instrument a note, a check, or a draft? Why? If it is not a check, how would you have to change it to make it a check?

To: Arthur Adams	January 1, 2012
TEN DAYS AFTER DATE PAY TO THE ORDER OF: Bernie Brown	
THE SUM OF: One thousand and no/100 DOLLARS	
	SIGNED: Carl Clark

2. Frank agrees to build a garage for Sarah for $25,000. Sarah offers to sign either a contract showing her obligation to pay Frank $25,000 or a negotiable promissory note for $25,000 payable to the order of Frank. Would you advise Frank to ask for the contract or the promissory note? Explain.
3. A handwritten note provided as follows:

   I Robert Harrison owe Peter Jacob $25,000 (twenty-five thousand dollars) as of 3/27/98 for the following:

   1) $15,000 for Caterpillar loader.

   2) $5,000 for a loan.

   3) $5,000 for a tag-a-long trailer.

   Would this instrument qualify as a negotiable instrument?
4. Jerome Bruha maintained a revolving line of credit with the Sherman County Bank. On December 6, 2008, Bruha signed a promissory note on which the bank was listed as the payee whereby he promised to pay "the principal amount of Seventy-five Thousand & 00/100 ($75,000) or so much as may be outstanding, together with interest on the unpaid outstanding balance of each advance." The note also contained a variable interest rate on an index maintained by the bank. The note stated that it "evidenced a revolving line of credit." Does the promissory note with a varying principal qualify as a "negotiable instrument"?

5. Darryl Young presented five photocopied checks to the Lynnwood Check-X-Change on five different days between June 13 and June 21. Lynnwood cashed the first four checks presented. The fifth check, which was presented on a Saturday, was drawn on a different account from the first four checks and was payable on the following Monday. Lynnwood's practice was to cash checks on Saturday that are dated the following Monday. Young was convicted of five counts of forgery. On appeal, Young argued that the postdated check was not a legal instrument for purposes of the forgery statute. The crime of forgery requires an instrument that, if genuine, may have legal effect or be the foundation of legal liability. Young argued that the postdated check did not meet this requirement "because the time for payment had not arrived and thus the check could not have created any legal liability on the part of any person at that time." If a check is postdated, can it qualify as a negotiable instrument and create legal liability?
6. Holliday made out a promissory note to Anderson, leaving the date of payment of the note blank. Anderson filled in the words "on demand" in the blank without Holliday's knowledge. Does this alter the rights or obligations of the parties?
7. Galatia Community State Bank honored a check it took for collection for $5,550, which was the amount imprinted by a check-writing machine in the center underlined section of the check commonly used for stating the amount in words. The imprint looked like this:

RegistereD
No. 497345** **5550 DOL'S 00 CTS

   The impression made by the check-writing machine could be felt on the front and back of the check, and "**5550 DOL'S 00 CTS" was imprinted in red ink. In the box on the right-hand side of the check commonly used for numbers, "6,550.00" appeared in handwriting. The check was in partial payment of the purchase price of two engines that Eugene Kindy was buying from the payee on the check, Tony Hicks. Kindy postdated the check by a month and deliberately placed two different amounts on the check because he thought the bank would check with him before paying it. Kindy wanted to be sure that the engines had been delivered to Canada before he paid the $6,550 balance of the purchase price.

   After the check was deposited in the Galatia Bank and Hicks was given $5,550, an employee of the bank altered the "6" by hand to read "5." Because Kindy had stopped payment on the check, the drawee bank refused to pay it to Galatia Bank. Galatia Bank then brought suit against Kindy as the drawer of the check. One of the issues in the lawsuit was how the check should be construed. The trial court found that the rules on construction provided in the Code were not helpful because they were contradictory. Does the amount in figures imprinted by the check-writing machine ($5,550) control over the amount written by hand in figures ($6,550)?

Chapter 39

Negotiation and Holder in Due Course

Learning Objectives

After you have studied this chapter, you should be able to:

1. Explain how negotiable instruments are transferred from one person to another.
2. Describe how *order* paper and *bearer* paper are negotiated.
3. Distinguish among blank, special, restrictive, and qualified indorsements.
4. Explain the importance of being a holder in due course of a negotiable instrument.
5. Identify and apply the requirements for becoming a holder in due course.
6. Define *holder.*
7. Distinguish real defenses from personal defenses.
8. Explain how the Federal Trade Commission has changed the holder in due course rule as it applies to consumer credit transactions.

Rachel Allen purchases a used Honda from Friendly Fred's Used Cars, paying $1,500 down and signing a promissory note in which she promises to pay $2,000 to Fred or to his order 12 months from the date of the note with interest at 8.5 percent. Fred assures Rachel that the car is in good condition and has never been involved in an accident. Fred indorses (signs) his name on the back of the promissory note and discounts (assigns) the note to Factors, Inc. Subsequently, Rachel discovers that, contrary to Fred's assurance, the Honda had in fact been involved in an accident that caused a front-end alignment problem. When Factors notifies her of the assignment to it of the note and asks for payment on the due date, Rachel wants to assert a defense of failure of consideration or breach of contract (warranty) against full payment of the note.

(continued)

Among the legal issues raised in this scenario are:

- When Fred transferred the promissory note to Factors after signing his name to the back of it, what rights did Factors obtain?
- Will Rachel be able to assert a defense of failure of consideration or breach of contract against full payment of the note to Factors?
- If the promissory note contained the clause required by the Federal Trade Commission in consumer notes or installment sales contracts, would it change Rachel's rights?

Introduction

The preceding chapter discussed the nature and benefits of negotiable instruments. It also outlined the requirements an instrument must meet to qualify as a negotiable instrument and thus possess the qualities that allow it to be accepted as a substitute for money.

This chapter focuses on negotiation—the process by which rights to a negotiable instrument pass from one person to another. Commonly, this involves an indorsement and transfer of the instrument. This chapter also develops the requirements that a transferee of a negotiable instrument must meet to qualify as a holder in due course and thus attain special rights under negotiable instruments law. These rights, which put a holder in due course in an enhanced position compared to an assignee of a contract, are discussed in some detail.

Negotiation

Nature of Negotiation

LO1

Under Revised Article 3, **negotiation** is the transfer of possession (whether voluntary or involuntary) of a negotiable instrument by a person (other than the issuer) to another person who becomes its *holder* (3–201). A person is a **holder** if she is in possession of an instrument (1) that is payable to bearer or (2) that is made payable to an identified person and she is that identified person (1–201[20]).[1]

For example, when an employer gives an employee, Susan Adams, a paycheck payable "to the order of Susan Adams," she is the holder of the check because she is in possession of an instrument payable to an identified person (Susan Adams) and she is that person. When she indorses (writes her name on) the back of the check and exchanges it for cash and merchandise at Ace Grocery, she has negotiated the check to the grocery store and the store is now the holder because it is in possession by transfer of a check that now is payable to bearer. Similarly, if Susan Adams indorsed the check "Pay to the Order of Ace Grocery, Susan Adams" and transferred it to the grocery store, it would be a holder through the negotiation of the check to it. The grocery store would be in

[1] The numbers in parentheses refer to sections of the Uniform Commercial Code.

possession of an instrument payable to an identified person (Ace Grocery) and would be the person identified on the check.

In certain circumstances, Revised Article 3 allows a person to become a holder by negotiation even though the transfer of possession is involuntary. For example, if a negotiable instrument is payable to bearer and is stolen by Tom Thief or found by Fred Finder, Thief or Finder becomes the holder when he obtains possession. The involuntary transfer of possession of a bearer instrument results in a negotiation to Thief or Finder.

LO2 Formal Requirements for Negotiation

The formal requirements for negotiation are very simple. If an instrument is payable to the order of a specific payee, it is called **order paper** and it can be negotiated by transfer of possession of the instrument after indorsement by the person specified (3–201[b]).

For example, if Rachel's father gives her a check payable "to the order of Rachel Stern," then Rachel can negotiate the check by indorsing her name on the back of the check and giving it to the person to whom she wants to transfer it. Note that the check is order paper, not because the word *order* appears on the check but rather because it named a specific payee, Rachel Stern.

If an instrument is payable to bearer or to cash, it is called **bearer paper** and negotiating it is even simpler. An instrument payable to bearer may be negotiated by transfer of possession alone (3–201[b]). Thus, if someone gives you a check that is made payable "to the order of cash," you can negotiate it simply by giving it to the person to whom you wish to transfer it. No indorsement is necessary to negotiate an instrument payable to bearer. However, the person who takes the instrument may ask for an indorsement for her protection. By indorsing the check, you agree to be liable for its payment to that person if it is not paid by the drawee bank when it is presented for payment. This liability will be discussed in Chapter 40, "Liability of Parties."

Nature of Indorsement

An indorsement is made by adding the signature of the holder of the instrument to the instrument, usually on the back of it, either alone or with other words. **Indorsement** is defined to mean "a signature (other than that of a maker, drawer, or acceptor) that alone or accompanied by other words is made on an instrument for purpose of (i) negotiating the instrument, (ii) restricting payment of the instrument, or (iii) incurring indorser's liability on the instrument" (3–204[a]). The negotiation and restriction-of-payment aspects of indorsements will be discussed later in this chapter; indorser's liability will be covered in the next chapter.

The signature constituting an indorsement can be put there either by the holder or by someone who is authorized to sign on behalf of the holder. For example, a check payable to "H&H Meat Market" might be indorsed "H&H Meat Market by Jane Frank, President," if Jane is authorized to do this on behalf of the market.

Wrong or Misspelled Name

When indorsing an instrument, the holder should spell his name in the same way as it appears on the instrument. If the holder's name is misspelled or wrong, then legally the indorsement can be made either in his name or in the name that is on the instrument. However, any person who pays the instrument or otherwise gives value for it may require the indorser to sign both names (3–204[d]).

Suppose Joan Ash is issued a check payable to the order of "Joanne Ashe." She may indorse the check as "Joan Ash" or "Joanne Ashe." However, if she takes the check to a bank to cash, the bank may require her to sign both "Joanne Ashe" and "Joan Ash."

Checks Deposited without Indorsement

Occasionally when a customer deposits a check to her account with a bank she may forget to indorse the check; also, it is common practice for depositary banks to receive unindorsed checks under what are known as "lockbox" arrangements with customers who receive a high volume of checks. Normally, a check payable to the order of an identified person would require the indorsement of that person in order for a negotiation to the depositary bank to take place and for it to become a holder. Under the original Article 3, the depositary bank (a bank that takes an item for collection), in most cases, had the right to supply the customer's indorsement. Instead of actually signing the customer's name to the check as the indorsement, the bank might just stamp on it that it was deposited by the customer or credited to her account. Banks did not have the right to put the customer's indorsement on a check that the customer had deposited if the check specifically required the payee's signature. Insurance and government checks commonly require the payee's signature.

The revision to Article 3 and the conforming amendments to Articles 1 and 4 take a different approach to the situation in which a check is deposited in a depositary bank without indorsement. The depositary bank becomes a holder of an item delivered to it for collection, whether or not it is indorsed by the customer, if the customer at the time of delivery qualified as a holder (4–205). Concomitantly, the depositary bank warrants to other collecting banks, the payor bank (drawee), and the drawer that it paid the amount of the item to the customer or deposited the amount to the customer's account.

Transfer of Order Instrument

Except for the special provisions concerning depositary banks, if an order instrument is transferred without indorsement, the instrument has not been negotiated and the transferee cannot qualify as a holder. For example, Sue Brown gives a check payable "to the order of Susan Brown" to a drugstore in payment for some cosmetics. Until Sue indorses the check, she has not negotiated it and the druggist could not qualify as a holder of the check.

Transfer of an instrument, whether or not the transfer is a negotiation, vests in the transferee any right of the transferor to enforce the instrument. However, the transferee cannot obtain the rights of a holder in due course (discussed later in this chapter) if he is engaged in any fraud or illegality affecting the instrument. Unless otherwise agreed, if an instrument is transferred for value but without a required indorsement, the transferee has the right to the unqualified indorsement of the transferor; however, the "negotiation" takes place only when the transferor applies her indorsement (3–230[c]).

Indorsements

Effects of an Indorsement

There are three functions of an indorsement. First, an indorsement is necessary in order for the negotiation of an instrument that is payable to the order of a specified person to occur. Thus, if a check is payable "to the order of James Lee," James must indorse the check before it can be negotiated. Second, the form of the indorsement that the indorser uses also affects future attempts to negotiate the instrument. For example, if James indorses it "Pay to the order of Sarah Hill," Sarah must indorse it before it can be negotiated further.

Third, an indorsement generally makes a person liable on the instrument. By indorsing an instrument, a person incurs an obligation to pay the instrument if the person primarily liable on it (for example, the maker of a note) does not pay it. We discuss the contractual liability of indorsers in Chapter 40. In this chapter, we discuss the effect of an indorsement on further negotiation of an instrument.

LO3

Kinds of Indorsements

There are three basic kinds of indorsements: (1) special, (2) blank, and (3) restrictive. In addition, an indorsement may be "qualified."

Special Indorsement

A **special indorsement** contains the signature of the indorser along with the words indicating to whom, or to whose order, the instrument is payable. For example, if a check is drawn "Pay to the Order of Marcia Morse" and Marcia indorses it "Pay to the Order of Sam Smith, Marcia Morse" or "Pay to Sam Smith, Marcia Morse," it has been indorsed with a special indorsement. An instrument that is indorsed with a special indorsement remains "order paper." It can be negotiated only with the indorsement of the person specified (3–205[a]). In this example, Sam Smith must indorse the check before he can negotiate it to someone else.

Blank Indorsement

If an indorser merely signs his name and does not specify to whom the instrument is payable, he has indorsed the instrument in **blank.** For example, if a check drawn "Pay to the Order of Natalie Owens" is indorsed "Natalie Owens" by Natalie, Natalie has indorsed it in blank. An instrument indorsed in blank is payable to the bearer (person in possession of it) and from that act is "bearer paper." As such, the bearer negotiates it by transfer alone and no further indorsement is necessary for negotiation (3–205[b]).

If Natalie indorsed the check in blank and gave it to Kevin Foley, Kevin would have the right to convert the blank indorsement into a special indorsement (3–205[c]). He could do this by writing the words "Pay to the Order of Kevin Foley" above Natalie's indorsement. Then the check would have to be indorsed by Kevin before it could be negotiated further.

If Kevin took the check indorsed in blank to a bank and presented it for payment or for collection, the bank normally would ask him to indorse the check. It does this not because it needs his indorsement for the check to be negotiated to it; the check indorsed in blank can be negotiated merely by delivering it to the bank cashier. Rather, the bank asks for his indorsement because it wants to make him liable on the check if it is not paid when the bank sends it to the drawee bank for payment. Chapter 40, "Liabilities of Parties," discusses the liability of indorsers.

Restrictive Indorsement

A **restrictive indorsement** is one that specifies the purpose of the indorsement or specifies the use to be made of the instrument. The more common restrictive indorsements are these:

1. Indorsements for deposit. For example, "For Deposit Only" or "For Deposit to My Account at First National Bank."

2. Indorsements for collection, which are commonly put on by banks involved in the collection process. For example, "Pay any bank, banker, or trust company" or "For collection only."
3. Indorsements indicating that the indorsement is for the benefit of someone other than the person to whom it is payable. For example, "Pay to Arthur Attorney in trust for Mark Minor."

Generally, the person who takes an instrument with a restrictive indorsement must pay or apply any money or other value he gives for the instrument consistently with the indorsement. In the case of a check indorsed "for deposit" or "for collection," any person other than a bank who purchases the check is considered to have **converted** the check unless (1) the indorser received the amount paid for it or (2) the bank applied the amount of the check consistently with the indorsement (e.g., deposited it to the indorser's account). Similarly, a depositary bank or payor bank (the drawee bank) that takes an instrument for deposit or for immediate payment over the counter that has been indorsed "for deposit" or "for collection" will be liable for conversion unless the indorser received the amount paid for the instrument or the proceeds or the bank applied the amount consistently with the indorsement (3–206[c]).[2]

By way of illustration, assume that Robert Franks has indorsed his paycheck "For Deposit to My Account No. 4068933 at Bank One." While on his way to the bank he loses the check, and Fred Finder finds it. If Finder tries to cash the check at a check-cashing service, the service must ensure that any value it gives for the check either is deposited to Franks's account at Bank One or is received by Franks. If it gives the money to Finder, it will be liable to Franks for converting his check. This principle is illustrated in the following case, *Lehigh Presbytery v. Merchants Bancorp,* which involves a bank that failed to apply value given for checks consistently with restrictive indorsements on the checks.

[2] Otherwise a payor bank as well as an intermediary bank may disregard the indorsement and is not liable if the proceeds of the instrument are not received by the indorser or applied consistently with the indorsement (3–206[c][4]).

Lehigh Presbytery v. Merchants Bancorp

17 UCC Rep.2d 163 (Super. Ct. Pa. 1991)

FACTS

Mary Ann Hunsberger was hired by the Lehigh Presbytery as a secretary/bookkeeper. In this capacity, she was responsible for opening the Presbytery's mail, affixing rubber-stamp indorsements to checks received by the Presbytery, and depositing the checks into the Presbytery's account at Merchants Bancorp, Inc. Over a period of more than five years, Ms. Hunsberger deposited into her own account 153 of these checks. Each check was indorsed: "For Deposit Only to The Credit of Presbytery of Lehigh, Ernest Hutcheson, Treas." The bank credited the checks to Ms. Hunsberger's account, despite the rubber-stamp restrictive indorsement, because it relied solely on the account number handwritten on the deposit slips submitted by Ms. Hunsberger with the checks at the time of deposit. Ms. Hunsberger obtained the deposit slips in the lobby of the bank, wrote the proper account title, "Lehigh Presbytery," but inserted her own account number rather than the account number of her employer. When the diversionary scheme was discovered, Lehigh Presbytery filed suit against the bank to recover the funds credited to Ms. Hunsberger's account.

ISSUE

Was the bank legally bound to follow the restrictive indorsements on the 153 checks deposited instead to the personal account of Ms. Hunsberger?

(continued)

DECISION

Yes. First, the court noted that the indorsement stamped on each check was a restrictive indorsement within the meaning of the UCC because it included the words "for deposit" signifying a purpose of deposit or collection and it stated the instrument was to be deposited for the benefit or use of the indorser. Next, the court observed that under the UCC, a transferee of an instrument containing a restrictive indorsement must pay or apply any value given by it consistently with the indorsement. Accordingly, the UCC requires application of the value of the checks consistent with the indorsement—that is, for deposit to Lehigh Presbytery's account. Thus, the bank is liable to its customer for crediting checks bearing the restrictive indorsement to the personal account of Ms. Hunsberger.

AUTHOR'S NOTE

Although this case was decided under the original version of Article 3, the same result would be expected under Revised Article 3.

Some indorsements indicate payment to the indorsee as an agent, trustee, or fiduciary. A person who takes an instrument containing such an indorsement from the indorsee may pay the proceeds to the indorsee without regard to whether the indorsee violates a fiduciary duty to the indorser *unless* he is on *notice* of any breach of fiduciary duty that the indorser may be committing (3–206[d]). A person would have such notice if he took the instrument in any transaction that benefited the indorsee personally (3–307). Suppose a person takes a check indorsed to "Arthur Attorney in trust for Mark Minor." The money given for the check should be put in Mark Minor's trust account. A person would not be justified in taking the check in exchange for a television set that he knew Attorney was acquiring for his own—rather than Minor's—use.

There are two other kinds of indorsements that the original Article 3 treated as restrictive indorsements, but that the Revised Article 3 no longer considers restrictive indorsements:

1. Indorsements purporting to prohibit further negotiation. For example, "Pay to Carl Clark Only."
2. Conditional indorsements, which indicate that they are effective only if the payee satisfies a certain condition. For example, "Pay to Bernard Builder Only if He Completes Construction on My House by November 1, 2009."

Under Revised Article 3, any indorsement that purports to limit payment to a particular person or to prohibit further transfer or negotiation of the instrument is not effective to prevent further transfer or negotiation (3–206[a]). Thus, if a note is indorsed "Pay to Carl Clark Only" and given to Clark, he may negotiate the note to subsequent holders who may ignore the restriction on the indorsement.

Indorsements that state a condition to the right of the indorsee to receive payment do not affect the right of the indorsee to enforce the instrument. Any person who pays the instrument or takes it for value or for collection may disregard the condition. Moreover, the rights and liabilities of the person are not affected by whether the condition has been fulfilled (3–206[b]).

Qualified Indorsement

A **qualified indorsement** is one by which the indorser disclaims her liability to make the instrument good if the maker or drawer defaults on it. Words such as "Without Recourse" are used to qualify an indorsement. They can be used with either a blank indorsement or a special indorsement and thus make it a qualified blank indorsement or a qualified special indorsement. The use of a qualified indorsement does not change the negotiable nature of the instrument. Its effect is to eliminate the contractual liability of the indorser. The next chapter, "Liability of Parties," will discuss this liability in detail.

Rescission of Indorsement

Negotiation is effective to transfer an instrument even if the negotiation is (1) made by a minor, a corporation exceeding its powers, or any other person without contractual capacity; (2) obtained by fraud, duress, or mistake of any kind; (3) made in breach of duty; or (4) part of an illegal transaction. A negotiation made under the preceding circumstances is subject to *rescission* before the instrument has been negotiated to a transferee who can qualify as a holder in due course (3–202). The situation in such instances is analogous to a sale of goods where the sale has been induced by fraud or misrepresentation. In such a case, the seller may rescind the sale and recover the goods, provided that the seller acts before the goods are resold to a bona fide purchaser for value.

Concept Summary: Indorsements

(Assume a check is payable "To the Order of Mark Smith.")

Type	Example	Consequences
Blank	Mark Smith	1. Satisfies the indorsement requirement for the negotiation of order paper. 2. The instrument becomes bearer paper and can be negotiated by delivery alone. 3. The indorser becomes obligated on the instrument. (See Chapter 40, "Liability of Parties.")
Special	Pay to the Order of Joan Brown, Mark Smith	1. Satisfies the indorsement requirement for the negotiation of order paper. 2. The instrument remains order paper and Joan Brown's indorsement is required for further negotiation. 3. The indorser becomes obligated on the instrument. (See Chapter 40.)
Restrictive	For deposit only to my account in First American Bank Mark Smith	1. Satisfies the indorsement requirement for the negotiation of order paper. 2. The person who pays value for the instrument is obligated to pay it consistent with the indorsement (i.e., to pay it into Mark Smith's account at First American Bank). 3. The indorser becomes obligated on the instrument. (See Chapter 40.)
Qualified	Mark Smith (without recourse)	1. Satisfies the indorsement requirement for negotiation of order paper. 2. Eliminates the indorser's obligation. (See Chapter 40.)

Holder in Due Course

LO4

A person who qualifies as a holder in due course of a negotiable instrument gets special rights. Normally, the transferee of an instrument—like the assignee of a contract—receives only those rights in the instrument that are held by the person from whom he received the instrument. But a holder in due course can obtain better rights. A holder in due course takes a negotiable instrument free of all **personal defenses, claims to the instrument,** and **claims in recoupment** either of the person obligated on the instrument or of a third party. A holder in due course does not take the instrument free of the **real defenses,** which go to the validity of the instrument or of claims that develop after he becomes a holder. We develop the differences between personal and real defenses in more detail later in this chapter and explain claims to the instrument and claims in recoupment. The following example illustrates the advantage that a holder in due course of a negotiable instrument may have.

Assume that Carl Carpenter contracts with Helen Homeowner to build her a garage for $25,500, payable on October 1 when he expects to complete the garage. Assume further that Carpenter assigns his rights to the $25,500 to First National Bank in order to obtain money for materials. If the bank tries to collect the money from Homeowner on October 1 but Carpenter has not finished building the garage, then Homeowner may assert the fact that the garage is not complete as a defense to paying the bank. As assignee of a simple contract, the bank has only those rights that its assignor, Carpenter, has and is subject to all claims and defenses that Homeowner has against Carpenter.

Now assume that instead of simply signing a contract with Homeowner, Carpenter had Homeowner give him a negotiable promissory note in the amount of $25,500 payable to the order of Carpenter on October 1 and that Carpenter then negotiated the note to the bank. If the bank is able to qualify as a holder in due course, it may collect the $25,500 from Homeowner on October 1 even though she might have a personal defense against payment of the note because Carpenter has not completed the work on the garage. Homeowner cannot assert that personal defense against a holder in due course. She would have to pay the note to the bank and then independently seek to recover from Carpenter for breach of their agreement. The bank's improved position is due to its status as a holder in due course of a negotiable instrument. If the instrument in question were not negotiable, or if the bank could not qualify as a holder in due course, then it would be in the same position as the assignee of a simple contract and would be subject to Homeowner's personal defense.

We turn now to a discussion of the requirements that must be met for the possessor of a negotiable instrument to qualify as a holder in due course.

LO5

General Requirements

In order to become a **holder in due course,** a person who takes a negotiable instrument must be a *holder,* and take the instrument:

1. For *value.*
2. In *good faith.*
3. *Without notice* that it is *overdue* or has been *dishonored* or that there is any uncured default with respect to payment of another instrument issued as part of the same series.
4. *Without notice that the instrument contains an unauthorized signature or has been altered.*

5. *Without notice of any claim of a property or possessory interest in it.*
6. *Without notice* that any party has any *defense against it* or claim *in recoupment to it* (3–302[a][2]).

In addition, Revised Article 3 requires "that the instrument when issued or negotiated to the holder does not bear such *apparent evidence of forgery or alteration* or is not otherwise so *irregular* or *incomplete* as to call into question its authenticity" (3–302[a][1]).

If a person who takes a negotiable instrument does not meet these requirements, he is not a holder in due course. Then the person is in the same position as an assignee of a contract.

LO6

Holder

To be a **holder** of a negotiable instrument, a person must have possession of an instrument that is either payable to "bearer" or that is payable to him. For example, if Teresa Gonzales is given a check by her grandmother that is made payable "to the order of Teresa Gonzales," Teresa is a holder of the check because it is made out to her. If Teresa indorses the check "Pay to the order of Ames Hardware, Teresa Gonzales" and gives it to Ames Hardware in payment for some merchandise, then Ames Hardware is the holder of the check. Ames Hardware is a holder because it is in possession of a check that is indorsed to its order. If Ames Hardware indorses the check "Ames Hardware" and deposits it in its account at First National Bank, the bank becomes the holder. The bank is in possession of an instrument that is indorsed in blank and thus is payable to bearer.

It is important that all indorsements on the instrument at the time it is payable to the order of someone are *authorized indorsements.* With limited exceptions (discussed later), a forged indorsement is not an effective indorsement and prevents a person from becoming a holder.

To be a holder, a person must have a complete chain of authorized indorsements. Suppose the Internal Revenue Service mails to Robert Washington an income tax refund check payable to him. Tom Turner steals the check from Washington's mailbox, signs (indorses) "Robert Washington" on the back of the check, and cashes it at a shoe store. The shoe store is not a holder of the check because its transferor, Turner, was not a holder and because it needs Washington's signature to have a good chain of authorized indorsements. Robert Washington has to indorse the check in order for there to be a valid chain of indorsements. Turner's signature is not effective for this purpose because Washington did not authorize him to sign Washington's name to the check (1–201[20]; 3–403[a]; 3–416[a][2]).

The case that follows, *Golden Years Nursing Home v. Gabbard,* illustrates that a party in possession of a check indorsed in blank is a holder of the instrument.

Golden Years Nursing Home v. Gabbard

682 N.E.2d 682 731 (Ct. App. Ohio 1996)

FACTS

From 1972 until 1991, Nancy Gabbard, the office manager for the Golden Years Nursing Home, received at the nursing home Social Security checks drawn on the United States Treasury and made payable either to individual patients or to "Golden Years Nursing Home for [an individual patient]." From 1986 until 1991, Gabbard engaged in an embezzling scheme whereby she would have certain

(continued)

Golden Years Nursing Home v. Gabbard *(concluded)*

patients indorse their own checks in blank—each patient would sign his own name on the back of the check placing no restrictions on the manner in which the check could subsequently be negotiated. Gabbard would then cash the checks and either keep the cash or deposit the funds into her personal bank account.

In 1992, after Gabbard's scheme was discovered, Golden Years brought suit against Gabbard and against the Star Bank Corporation where the checks had been cashed. The patients had in other documents assigned their interests in the checks to Golden Years, and the claim against the bank alleged that it had converted Golden Years' property by cashing checks with forged indorsements. One of the issues in the lawsuit was whether the checks had been properly negotiated to Star Bank.

ISSUE

Did Star Bank become a holder of the checks that had been indorsed in blank by the payees?

DECISION

Yes. Negotiability is determined by what is on the face of the instrument, and any separate agreement with the patients does not affect the negotiability of these checks. Negotiation is the transfer of an instrument in such form that the transferee becomes a holder. If an instrument is payable to order, it is negotiated by delivery with any necessary indorsement. However, once a payee indorses a check in blank, it becomes bearer paper and can be negotiated by delivery alone. Thus, in this case, Gabbard became a holder of the checks when the checks, indorsed in blank by the patient–payees, were delivered to her. When Star Bank accepted the checks that were indorsed with the genuine signatures of the payees, the checks bore no indication that they had been assigned to Golden Years. Star Bank cashed the checks in good faith without notice of any defenses and thus became a holder in due course. This analysis does not change even if Gabbard presented the checks to the payees for their indorsement with the intent to embezzle the funds eventually.

E-Commerce

In Chapter 19, we noted that the Uniform Electronic Transactions Act adopted by many states along with the federal Electronic Signatures in Global and National Commerce Act (the "E-Sign Act") covered many kinds of commercial transactions and authorized the use of electronic signatures and messages indicating approval where the state law requires a "signed writing." However, both UETA and the E-Sign Act explicitly exclude items governed by Article 3—Negotiable Instruments of the Uniform Commercial Code. Thus, one cannot scan a promissory note into an electronic note and have the electronic version qualify as a negotiable instrument.

As a result, investors who believed they had acquired bundles of mortgages and accompanying notes in the form of securitized investment vehicles in recent years have encountered problems trying to enforce the notes when the borrowers defaulted because the courts have refused to recognize serial electronic assignments of the notes where there is no clear chain of ownership of a given note. For example, in *In re Wilhelm* (U.S.B.C., D. Idaho 2009), the court rejected the efforts of the assignees of mortgage obligations to enforce the obligations as holders. The court noted that to be a "holder," one must both possess the note and the note must be payable to the person in possession of the note or to bearer. In this instance, none of the notes were payable to the assignee seeking to enforce them and none of the notes had been indorsed, either in blank or specifically to the assignee.

Value

To qualify as a holder in due course of a negotiable instrument, a person must give **value** for it. Value is not identical to simple consideration. Under the provisions of the Revised Article 3, a holder takes for value if (1) the agreed-upon promise of performance has been performed—for example, if the instrument was given in exchange for a promise to deliver a refrigerator and the refrigerator has been delivered; (2) he acquires a security interest in, or a lien on, the instrument; (3) he takes the instrument in payment of, or as security for, an antecedent claim; (4) he gives a negotiable instrument for it; or (5) he makes an irrevocable commitment to a third person (3–303). Thus, a person who receives a check as a gift or merely makes an executory promise in return for a check has not given value for it and cannot qualify as a holder in due course.

A bank or any person who discounts an instrument in the *regular course of trade* has given value for it. In this context the discount essentially is a means for increasing the return or the rate of interest on the instrument. Likewise, if a loan is made and an instrument is pledged as security for the repayment of the loan, the secured party has given value for the instrument to the amount of the loan. If Axe, who owes Bell a past-due debt, indorses and delivers to Bell, in payment of the debt or as security for its repayment, an instrument issued to Axe, Bell has given value for the instrument. If a bank allows a customer to draw against a check deposited for collection, it has given value to the extent of the credit drawn against it.

If the promise of performance that is the consideration for an instrument has been partially performed, the holder may assert rights as a holder in due course of the instrument only to the fraction of the amount payable under the instrument equal to the partial performance divided by the value of the promised performance (3–302[d]). For example, Arthur Wells agrees to purchase a note payable to the order of Helda Parks. The note is for the sum of $5,000. Wells pays Parks $1,000 on the negotiation of the note to him and agrees to pay the balance of $4,000 in 10 days. Initially, Wells is a holder in due course for one-fifth of the amount of the note. If he later pays the $4,000 due, he may become a holder in due course for the full amount.

Good Faith

To qualify as a holder in due course of a negotiable instrument, a person must take it in **good faith,** which means that the person obtained it honestly and in the observance of reasonable commercial standards of fair dealing (3–103[a][4]). If a person obtains a check by trickery or with knowledge that it has been stolen, the person has not obtained the check in good faith and cannot be a holder in due course. A person who pays too little for an instrument, perhaps because she suspects that something may be wrong with the way it was obtained, may have trouble meeting the good faith test. Suppose a finance company works closely with a door-to-door sales company that engages in shoddy practices. If the finance company buys the consumers' notes from the sales company, it will not be able to meet the good faith test and qualify as a holder in due course of the notes.

Ethics in Action

If you are in the business of buying commercial paper—such as consumer notes—from businesses such as home improvement companies, how much of an ethical obligation, if any, do you have to look into the sales practices and performance records of the companies to whom the consumers have made the notes payable?

Overdue or Dishonored

In order to qualify as a holder in due course, a person must take a negotiable instrument before he has notice that it either is **overdue** or has been **dishonored.** The reason for this is that one should perform obligations when they are due. If a negotiable instrument is not paid when it is due, the Code considers the person taking it to be on notice that there may be defenses to the payment of it.

Overdue Instruments

If a negotiable instrument is payable on demand, it is overdue (1) the day after demand for payment has been made in a proper manner and form, (2) 90 days after its date if it is a check, and (3) if it is an instrument other than a check, when it has been outstanding for an unreasonably long period of time in light of the nature of the instrument and trade practice (3–304[a]). Thus, a check becomes stale after 90 days and, for other kinds of instruments, one must consider trade practices and the facts of the particular case. In a farming community, the normal period for loans to farmers may be six months. A demand note might be outstanding for six or seven months before it is considered overdue. On the other hand, a demand note issued in an industrial city where the normal period of such loans is 30 to 60 days would be considered overdue in a much shorter period of time.

If a negotiable instrument due on a certain date is not paid by that date, normally it is overdue at the beginning of the next day after the due date. For example, if a promissory note dated January 1 is payable "30 days after date," it is due on January 31. If it is not paid by January 31, it is overdue beginning on February 1.

As to instruments payable at a definite time, Revised Article 3 sets out four rules: (1) if the principal is not payable in installments and the due date has not been accelerated, the instrument is overdue on the day after the due date; (2) if the principal is due in installments and a due date has not been accelerated, the instrument is overdue upon default for nonpayment of an installment and remains overdue until the default is cured; (3) if a due date for principal has been accelerated, the instrument is overdue on the day after the accelerated due date; and (4) unless the due date of principal has been accelerated, an instrument does not become overdue if there is a default in payment of interest but no default in payment of principal (3–304[b]).

Dishonored Instruments

To be a holder in due course, a person must take not only a negotiable instrument before he has notice that it is overdue but also before it has been dishonored. A negotiable instrument has been *dishonored* when the holder has presented it for payment (or acceptance) and payment (or acceptance) has been refused.

For example, Susan writes a check on her account at First National Bank that is payable "to the order of Sven Sorensen." Sven takes the check to First National Bank to cash it but the bank refuses to pay it because Susan has insufficient funds in her account to cover it. The check has been dishonored. If Sven then takes Susan's check to Harry's Hardware and uses it to pay for some paint, Harry's cannot be a holder in due course of the check if it is on notice that the check has been dishonored. Harry's would have such notice if First National had stamped the check "Payment Refused NSF" (not sufficient funds).

Similarly, suppose Carol Carson signs a 30-day note payable to Ace Appliance for $500 and gives it to Ace as payment for a stereo set. When Ace asks Carol for payment, she refuses to pay because the stereo does not work properly. If Ace negotiates the note to First National Bank, First National cannot be a holder in due course if it knows about Carol's refusal to pay.

Notice of Unauthorized Signature or Alteration

A holder who has notice that an instrument contains an unauthorized signature or has been altered cannot qualify as a holder in due course of the instrument. For example,

Frank makes out a check in the amount of $5.00 payable to George Grocer and gives it to his daughter, Jane, to take to the grocery store to purchase some groceries. The groceries Jane purchases cost $20.00 and Jane changes the check to read $25.00, giving it to Grocer in exchange for the groceries and $5.00 in cash. Grocer cannot qualify as a holder in due course if he sees Jane make the alteration to the check or otherwise is on notice of it.

Notice of Claims

If a person taking a negotiable instrument is *on notice of an adverse claim* to the instrument by someone else (for example, that she is the rightful owner of the instrument) or that someone is seeking to rescind a prior negotiation of the instrument, the current holder cannot qualify as a holder in due course. For example, a U.S. Treasury check is payable to Susan Samuels. Samuels loses the check and it is found by Robert Burns. Burns takes the check to a hardware store, signs "Susan Samuels" on the back of the check in the view of a clerk, and seeks to use it in payment of merchandise. The hardware store cannot be a holder in due course because it is on notice of a potential claim to the instrument by Susan Samuels.

Notice of Breach of Fiduciary Duty

One situation in which the Code considers a person to be on notice of a claim is if she is taking a negotiable instrument from a fiduciary, such as a trustee. If a negotiable instrument is payable to a person as a trustee or an attorney for someone, then any attempt by that person to negotiate it for his own behalf or for his use (or benefit) or to deposit it in an account other than that of the fiduciary puts the person on notice that the beneficiary of the trust may have a claim (3–307).

For example, a check is drawn "Pay to the order of Arthur Adams, Trustee for Mary Minor." Adams takes the check to Credit Union, indorses his name to it, and uses it to pay off the balance on a loan Adams had from Credit Union. Credit Union cannot be a holder in due course because it should know that the negotiation of the check is in violation of the fiduciary duty Adams owes to Mary Minor. Credit Union should know this because Adams is negotiating the check for his own benefit, not Mary's.

Notice of Defenses and Claims in Recoupment

To qualify as a holder in due course, a person also must acquire a negotiable instrument without notice that any party to it has any **defenses** or **claims in recoupment.** Potential defenses include infancy, duress, fraud, and failure of consideration. Thus, if a person knows that a signature on the instrument was obtained by fraud, misrepresentation, or duress, the person cannot be a holder in due course.

A *claim in recoupment* is a claim of the person obligated on the instrument against the original payee of the instrument. The claim must arise from the transaction that gave rise to the instrument. An example of a claim in recoupment would be as follows: Buyer purchases a used automobile from Dealer for $8,000, giving Dealer a note for $8,000 payable in one year. Because the automobile is not as warranted, Buyer has a breach of warranty claim that could be asserted against Dealer as a counterclaim or "claim in recoupment" to offset the amount owing on the note.

Irregular and Incomplete Instruments

A person cannot be a holder in due course of a negotiable instrument if, when she takes it, it is irregular or some important or **material term** is blank. If the negotiable instrument contains a facial irregularity, such as an obvious alteration in the amount, then it is considered to be **irregular paper.** If you take an irregular instrument, you are considered to be on notice of any possible defenses to it. For example, Kevin writes a check for "one dollar" payable to Karen. Karen inserts the word "hundred" in the amount, changes the figure "\$1" to "\$100," and gives the check to a druggist in exchange for a purchase of goods. If the alterations in the amount should be obvious to the druggist, perhaps because there are erasures, different handwritings, or different inks, then the druggist cannot be a holder in due course. She would have taken irregular paper and would be on notice that there might be defenses to it. These defenses include Kevin's defense that he is liable for only \$1 because that is the amount for which he made the check.

Similarly, if someone receives a check that has been signed but the space where the amount of the check is to be written is blank, then the person cannot be a holder in due course of that check. The fact that a material term is blank means that the instrument is **incomplete** and should put the person on notice that the drawer may have a defense to payment of it. To be material, the omitted term must be one that affects the legal obligation of the parties to the negotiable instrument. Material terms include the amount of the instrument and the name of the payee. If a negotiable instrument is completed after the obligor signed it, but before a person acquires it, the person can qualify as a holder in due course if she had no knowledge about the completion.

In the case that follows, *Firststar Bank, N.A. v. First Service Title Agency,* the court concluded that a bank could not qualify as a holder in due course of several instruments because it took them with obvious irregularities that called their authenticity into question.

Firststar Bank, N.A. v. First Service Title Agency

54 UCC Rep.2d 701 (Ct. App. Ohio 2004)

FACTS

On January 22, 2002, as a result of a real estate transaction, First Service Title Agency issued three checks drawn on its account with Key Bank. The first check was for \$850 and was payable to the order of "Richard G. Knostman, Atty. and Mark F. Foster, Atty. and Resa Kermani & Badri Kermani." The second check was for \$36,295.80 and was made payable to "JD Properties and Resa Kermani & Badri Kermani." The third check was for \$4,010 and payable to "Knab Mortgage."

First Service Title subsequently learned that the underlying real estate transaction had been fraudulent. Consequently, on January 23, 2002, it put stop payment orders on all three checks and refunded the monies it had received in the transaction. First Service Title notified the parties and the payees of the stop payment orders.

On the same day that First Service Title Agency placed the stop payment orders on the checks, Randall Davis, who had various accounts at Firststar Bank, presented all three checks to Firststar Bank. Firststar Bank paid the checks to Davis even though Davis was not a party to any of the checks, the checks contained multiple indorsements that appeared to be in the same handwriting, and they all were marked "for deposit only."

Key Bank subsequently returned the checks to Firststar Bank with the notation "Payment stopped." Firststar Bank then filed suit against First Services Title Agency and Davis. One of the issues in the suit against First Services Title Agency was whether Firststar Bank was a holder in due course of the three checks.

ISSUE

Is Firststar Bank a holder in due course of the three checks that it paid to Davis and now wants to obtain payment on from the drawer, First Services Title Agency?

DECISION

No. The court concluded that Firststar Bank could not qualify as a holder in due course because it had notice of the irregularities on the faces of the three checks. The checks in question bore evidence of forgery and were so irregular on their face as to call into question their authenticity and to give notice to a reasonably prudent person exercising

(continued)

Firststar Bank, N.A. v. First Service Title Agency *(concluded)*

ordinary care of defects in the checks. In order to qualify as a holder in due course, a holder must take it (1) for value, (2) in good faith, and (3) without notice of any claims or defenses otherwise available to the person obligated on the instrument or of any various defects in the instrument. A person has notice of an irregularity when from all the facts and circumstances known to the person at the time in question, the person has reason to know that it exists. Moreover, when an instrument is negotiated to the holder it cannot bear evidence of forgery or alteration that is so apparent, or cannot otherwise be so irregular or incomplete, as to call into account its authenticity.

Concept Summary: Requirements for a Holder in Due Course

Requirement	Rule
1. Must be a *holder.*	A holder is a person in possession of an instrument payable to bearer or payable to him.
2. Must take for *value.*	A holder has given value: a. To the extent the agreed-on consideration has been paid or performed. b. To the extent a security interest or lien has been obtained. c. By payment of—or granting security for—an antecedent claim. d. By giving a negotiable instrument for it. e. By making an irrevocable commitment to a third person.
3. Must take in *good faith.*	Good faith means honesty in fact and the observance of reasonable commercial standards of fair dealing.
4. Must take *without notice* that the instrument is *overdue.*	An instrument payable on demand is overdue the day after demand for payment has been duly made. A check is overdue 90 days after its date. If it is an instrument other than a check and payable on demand, when it has been outstanding for an unreasonably long period of time in light of the nature of the instrument and trade practice, it is overdue. If it is an instrument due on a certain date, then it is overdue at the beginning of the next day after the due date.
5. Must take *without knowledge that the instrument has been dishonored.*	An instrument has been dishonored when the holder has presented it for payment (or acceptance) and payment (or acceptance) has been refused.
6. Must take *without notice* of any *uncured default* with respect to payment of another instrument issued as part of the same series.	If there is a series of notes, holder must take without notice that there is an uncured default as to any other notes in the series.

(continued)

Concept Summary: Requirements for a Holder in Due Course *(concluded)*

7. Must take *without notice* that the instrument contains an *unauthorized signature* or has been *altered.*	Notice of unauthorized signature or alteration—change in a material term—prevents holder from obtaining holder in due course (HDC) status.
8. Must take *without notice* of any *claim of a property or possessory interest* in it.	Claims of property or possessory interest include: a. Claim by someone that she is the rightful owner of the instrument. b. Person seeking to rescind a prior negotiation of the instrument. c. Claim by a beneficiary that a fiduciary negotiated the instrument for his own benefit.
9. Must take *without notice* that any party has a *defense* against it.	Defenses include real defenses that go to the validity of the instrument and personal defenses that commonly are defenses to a simple contract.
10. Must take *without notice* of a *claim in recoupment* to it.	A claim in recoupment is a claim of the obligor on the instrument against the original payee that arises from the transaction that gave rise to the instrument.
11. The instrument must not bear *apparent evidence of forgery or alteration* or be *irregular or incomplete.*	The instrument must not contain obvious reasons to question its authenticity.

Shelter Rule

The transferee of an instrument—whether or not the transfer is a negotiation—obtains those rights that the transferor had, including (1) the transferor's right to enforce the instrument and (2) any right as a holder in due course (3–230[b]). This means that any person who can trace his title to an instrument back to a holder in due course receives rights similar to a holder in due course even if he cannot meet the requirements himself. This is known as the **shelter rule** in Article 3.

For example, Archer makes a note payable to Bryant. Bryant negotiates the note to Carlyle, who qualifies as a holder in due course. Carlyle then negotiates the note to Darby, who cannot qualify as a holder in due course because she knows the note is overdue. Because Darby can trace her title back to a holder in due course (Carlyle), Darby has rights as a holder in due course when she seeks payment of the note from Archer.

There is, however, a limitation on the shelter rule. A transferee who has himself been a party to any fraud or illegality affecting the instrument cannot improve his position by taking, directly or indirectly, from a later holder in due course (3–230[b]). For example, Archer, through fraudulent representations, induced Bryant to execute a negotiable note payable to Archer and then negotiated the instrument to Carlyle, who took it as a holder in due course. If Archer thereafter took the note for value from Carlyle, Archer could not acquire Carlyle's rights as a holder in due course. Archer was a party to the fraud that induced the note, and, accordingly, cannot improve his position by negotiating the instrument and then reacquiring it.

Rights of a Holder in Due Course

Claims and Defenses Generally

Revised Article 3 establishes four categories of claims and defenses:

1. Real defenses—which go to the validity of the instrument.
2. Personal defenses—which generally arise out of the transaction that gave rise to the instrument.
3. Claims to an instrument—which generally concern property or possessory rights in an instrument or its proceeds.
4. Claims in recoupment—which also arise out of the transaction that gave rise to the instrument.

LO4

Importance of Being a Holder in Due Course

In the preceding chapter, we pointed out that one advantage of negotiable instruments over other kinds of contract is that they are accepted as substitutes for money. People are willing to accept them as substitutes for money because, generally, they can take them free of claims or defenses to payment between the original parties to the instrument. On the other hand, a person who takes an assignment of a simple contract gets only the same rights as the person had who assigned the contract.

There are two qualifications to the ability of a person who acquired a negotiable instrument to be free of claims or defenses between the original parties. First, the person in possession of a negotiable instrument must be a *person entitled to enforce the instrument* as well as a *holder in due course* (or must be a holder who has the rights of a holder in due course through the shelter rule). If the person is neither, then she is subject to all claims or defenses to payment that any party to it has. Second, the only claims or defenses that the holder in due course has to worry about are so-called real defenses—those that affect the validity of the instrument—or claims that arose after she became a holder. For example, if the maker or drawer did not have legal capacity because she was a minor, the maker or drawer has a real defense. The holder in due course does not have to worry about other defenses and claims that do not go to the validity of the instrument—the so-called personal defenses.

LO7

Real Defenses

There are some claims and defenses to payment of an instrument that go to the validity of the instrument. These claims and defenses are known as **real defenses.** They can be used as reasons against payment of a negotiable instrument to any holder, including a holder in due course (or a person who has the rights of a holder in due course). Real defenses include:

1. Minority or infancy that under state law makes the instrument void or voidable; for example, if Mark Miller, age 17, signs a promissory note as maker, he can use his lack of capacity to contract as a defense against paying it even to a holder in due course.
2. Incapacity that under state law makes the instrument void; for example, if a person has been declared mentally incompetent by a court, then the person has a real defense if state law declares all contracts entered into by the person after the adjudication of incompetency to be void.

3. Duress that voids or nullifies the obligation of a party liable to pay the instrument; for example, if Harold points a gun at his grandmother and forces her to execute a promissory note, the grandmother can use duress as a defense against paying it even to a holder in due course.
4. Illegality that under state law renders the obligation void; for example, in some states, checks and notes given in payment of gambling debts are void.
5. Fraud in the essence (or fraud in the *factum*). This occurs when a person signs a negotiable instrument without knowing or having a reasonable opportunity to know that it is a negotiable instrument or without knowing its essential terms. For example, Amy Jones is an illiterate person who lives alone. She signs a document that is actually a promissory note, but she is told that it is a grant of permission for a television set to be left in her house on a trial basis. Amy has a real defense against payment of the note even to a holder in due course. Fraud in the essence is distinguished from fraud in the inducement, discussed below, which is only a personal defense.
6. Discharge in bankruptcy; for example, if the maker of a promissory note has had the debt discharged in a bankruptcy proceeding, she no longer is liable on it and has a real defense against payment (3–305[a][1]).

Real defenses can be asserted even against a holder in due course of a negotiable instrument because it is more desirable to protect people who have signed negotiable instruments in these situations than it is to protect persons who have taken negotiable instruments in the ordinary course of business.

In addition to the real defenses discussed above, there are several other reasons that a person otherwise liable to pay an instrument would have a defense against payment that would be effective, even against a holder in due course. They include:

1. *Forgery.* For example, if a maker's signature has been put on the instrument without his authorization and without his negligence, the maker has a defense against payment of the note.
2. *Alteration of the completed instrument.* This is a partial defense against a holder in due course (or a person having the rights of a holder in due course), and a complete defense against a non-holder in due course. A holder in due course can enforce an altered instrument against the maker or drawer according to its original tenor.
3. *Discharge.* If a person takes an instrument with knowledge that the obligation of any party obligated on the instrument has been discharged, the person takes subject to the discharge even if the person is a holder in due course.

In the case which follows, *E & G Food Corp. v. Cumberland Farms,* the court held that a defense of forgery could be asserted against even a holder in due course of four checks.

E & G Food Corp. v. Cumberland Farms

75 UCC Rep.2d 571 (App. Div., Dist. Ct. Mass. 2011)

FACTS

In December 2008, Cumberland Farms issued four payroll checks to four of its employees. Each check was drawn on its account at Bank of America. Each bore the Cumberland Farms name as well as an eight-digit check number, the employee's name, and an authorized stamp of the signature of the company's CEO. The checks were subsequently negotiated.

In February 2009, unidentified individuals presented four checks to E & G Food Corporation, which is in the business of cashing checks for its customers for a fee. The checks,

E & G Food Corp. v. Cumberland Farms *(concluded)*

totaling $2,809.70, were very similar to the four payroll checks issued by Cumberland Farms in December. They bore the same check numbers. But the names of the payees on the checks were different, and the named payees were not employed by Cumberland Farms. It had given Bank of America a list of its employees so that the bank could verify that every employee payroll check presented for payment listed the proper employee. E & G did not contact Bank of America to verify the authenticity of the checks.

Each payroll check issued by Cumberland Farms in December and each of the checks presented to E & G in February also bore a notation stating that the check "contains ultraviolet fibers, chemical reactive paper, void pantograph, microprint signature line, and an artificial watermark on the back." Prior to cashing the checks, E & G's employees examined them, and scanned each check under a machine to detect alterations, but found nothing improper. At the same time those employees were unfamiliar with some of the enumerated security features of Cumberland Farms' actual payroll checks. Moreover, they did not have all of the equipment needed to verify that the checks presented had all of the listed safety features.

In addition, each of Cumberland Farms' actual payroll checks bore a three-digit number on the payee line. This number reflected the last three digits of the check number printed in the upper right corner of the check. The three-digit numbers on the four checks E & G received in February 2009, however, did not match the last three digits of the respective check numbers of the actual payroll checks. Despite these questionable circumstances, E & G cashed all four checks, only to be notified later by Bank of America that the checks would not be honored. Cumberland Farms refused E & G's subsequent demand that it make payment of the checks.

E & G then brought suit against Cumberland Farms, asserting that it was a holder in due course and that Cumberland Farms was obligated to make good on the checks. The trial court determined that the checks presented to E & G in February were counterfeits, that is, forged images of the true payroll checks previously issued to Cumberland Farms' employees. The checks had not been signed by any authorized representative or employee of Cumberland Farms; neither had they been produced from any misappropriated blank checks previously in its possession. Nonetheless, the trial court found Cumberland Farms legally responsible for E & G's loss based on E & G's status as a holder in due course. Cumberland Farms appealed, arguing that it had a defense to payment that could be asserted against even a holder in due course.

ISSUE

Was E & G entitled to enforce the checks against Cumberland Farms?

DECISION

No. The court noted that Massachusetts law provides that the right to enforce the obligation of a party to pay an instrument is subject to a defense based on "illegality of the transaction which, under other law, nullifies the obligation of the obligor." Even the right of a holder in due course to enforce an obligation is subject to this defense. When a negotiable instrument is claimed to be a forgery, until such time as its status as a genuine instrument is established, even a holder in due course takes subject to a forgery. Here, the creation of the checks and their presentment by the third-party actors constituted criminal acts. Thus, the right of E & G to enforce the checks as a holder in due course was subject to the defense of illegality—and Cumberland Farms is not liable on the checks.

Ethics in Action

ASSERTING THE DEFENSE OF ILLEGALITY AGAINST PAYMENT OF A GAMBLING DEBT

Assume that in the course of a vacation you drop by the casino in the hotel where you are staying. You decide to play a few hands of blackjack. After winning your first few hands, you then go on a sustained losing streak. Believing your luck is about to change, you keep going until you have lost $10,000, much more than you intended or could readily afford. At the end of the evening, you write the casino a check. Later, in the hotel bar, you tell your sad tale to a fellow drinker who is a local lawyer and who informs you that a state law makes gambling obligations void. Would it be ethical for you to stop payment on the check and then assert the defense of illegality against the holder of the check?

Personal Defenses

Personal defenses are legal reasons for avoiding or reducing liability of a person who is liable on a negotiable instrument. Generally, personal defenses arise out of the transaction in which the negotiable instrument was issued and are based on negotiable instruments law or contract law. A holder in due course of a negotiable instrument (or one who can claim the rights of one) is not subject to any personal defenses or claims that may exist between the original parties to the instrument. Personal defenses include

1. *Lack or failure of consideration.* For example, a promissory note for $100 was given to someone without intent to make a gift and without receiving anything in return (3–303[b]).
2. *Breach of contract, including breach of warranty.* For example, a check was given in payment for repairs to an automobile but the repair work was defective.
3. *Fraud in the inducement of any underlying contract.* For example, an art dealer sells a lithograph to Cheryl, telling her that it is a Picasso, and takes Cheryl's check for $500 in payment. The art dealer knows that the lithograph is not a genuine Picasso but a forgery. Cheryl has been induced to make the purchase and to give her check by the art dealer's fraudulent representation. Because of this fraud, Cheryl has a personal defense against having to honor her check to the art dealer.
4. *Incapacity to the extent that state law makes the obligation voidable, as opposed to void.* For example, where state law makes voidable the contract of a person who is of limited mental capacity but who has not been adjudicated incompetent, the person has a personal defense to payment.
5. *Illegality that makes a contract voidable, as opposed to void.* For example, when the payee of a check given for certain professional services was required to have a license from the state but did not have one.
6. *Duress, to the extent it is not so severe as to make the obligation void but rather only voidable.* For example, if the instrument was signed under a threat to prosecute the maker's son if it was not signed, the maker might have a personal defense.
7. *Unauthorized completion or material alteration of the instrument.* For example, the instrument was completed in an unauthorized manner, or a material alteration was made to it after it left the maker's or drawer's possession.
8. *Nonissuance of the instrument, conditional issuance, and issuance for a special purpose.* For example, that the person in possession of the instrument obtained it by theft or by finding it rather than through an intentional delivery of the instrument to him (3–105[b]).
9. *Failure to countersign a traveler's check* (3–106[c]).
10. *Modification of the obligation by a separate agreement* (3–117).
11. *Payment that violates a restrictive indorsement* (3–206[f]).
12. *Breach of warranty when a draft is accepted* (discussed in the following chapter) (3–417[b]).

The following example illustrates the limited extent to which a maker or drawer can use personal defenses as a reason for not paying a negotiable instrument he signed. Suppose Tucker Trucking bought a used truck from Honest Harry's and gave Harry a 60-day promissory note for $32,750 in payment for the truck. Honest Harry's "guaranteed" the truck to be in "good working condition," but in fact the truck had a cracked engine block. If Harry tries to collect the $32,750 from Tucker Trucking, Tucker Trucking could claim breach of warranty as a reason for not paying Harry the full $32,750 because Harry is not a holder in due course. However, if Harry negotiated the note to First National Bank and the bank was a holder in due course, the situation would be changed. If the bank tried to collect the $32,750 from Tucker Trucking, Tucker Trucking would have to pay the bank. Tucker Trucking's defense or claim of breach of warranty cannot be used as a reason for not paying a holder in due course. It is a personal defense. Tucker Trucking must pay the bank the $32,750 and then pursue its breach of warranty claim against Harry.

The rule that a holder in due course takes a negotiable instrument free of any personal defenses or claims to it has been modified to some extent, particularly in relation to certain instruments given by consumers. These modifications will be discussed in the next section of this chapter.

In the case that follows, *General Credit Corp. v. New York Linen Co., Inc.* the court held that a holder in due course of a check was not subject to the personal defense of failure of consideration that the drawer of the check had against the payee of the check.

General Credit Corp. v. New York Linen Co.

46 UCC Rep.2d 1055 (New York Civ. Ct., Kings County 2002)

FACTS

On February 25, 2001, New York Linen Co., a party rental company, agreed to purchase approximately 550 chairs from Elite Products, a company owned by Meir Schmeltzer. A deposit was given for the chairs and upon their delivery, a final check dated February 27, 2001, was issued for $13,300. After a final count of the chairs was made, New York Linen discovered that the delivery was not complete. New York Linen then contacted its bank and asked that the bank stop payment of the check. A second check, dated February 28, 2001, for $11,275, was drafted and delivered to New York Linen the next day. This check reflected the adjusted amount due for the chairs that had actually been delivered.

Unbeknownst to New York Linen, the original check for $13,300 was sold by Meir Schmeltzer to General Credit Corp., a company in the business of purchasing instruments from payees in exchange for immediate cash. When New York Linen's bank refused to pay the check to General Credit because of the stop payment order that had been placed on it, General Credit Corp. brought suit against New York Linen to collect on the check.

ISSUE

Was General Credit a holder in due course of the check and thus entitled to collect it from New York Linen despite the fact that New York Linen had a defense it could assert against Elite Products/Meir Schmeltzer?

DECISION

Yes. The court held that General Credit was a holder in due course of the check and thus under the UCC took the check free of all defenses New York Linen had that related to the purchase of the chairs. General Credit was a holder in due course of the first check because it took it for value, in good faith, and without notice of any defect or defense. At the time General Credit acquired the check it had no knowledge that a second check was to be issued or that the first check had been—or would be—dishonored. By tradition, the defenses from which a holder in due course takes free are called "personal defenses" and they include failure or lack of consideration, which is New York Linen's defense in this case. Elite's failure to deliver the agreed-upon number of chairs in not a defense available to New York Linen against the claim brought by General Credit on the check.

Claims to the Instrument

For purposes of Revised Article 3, the term **claims** to an instrument can include

1. A claim to ownership of the instrument by one who asserts that he is the owner and was wrongfully deprived of possession.
2. A claim of a lien on the instrument.
3. A claim for rescission of an indorsement.

A holder in due course takes free of claims that arose before she became a holder but is subject to those arising when or after she becomes a holder in due course. For example, if a holder impairs the collateral given for an obligation, she may be creating a defense for an obligor.

Claims in Recoupment

A *claim in recoupment* is not actually a defense to an instrument but an *offset* to *liability*. For example, Ann Adams purchases a new automobile from Dealership, giving it a note for the balance of the purchase price beyond her down payment. After accepting delivery, she discovers a breach of warranty that the dealer fails to remedy. If Dealer has sold the note to a bank that subsequently seeks payment on the note from Adams, she has a claim in recoupment for breach of warranty. If the bank is a holder in due course, the claim in recoupment cannot be asserted against it. However, if the bank is not a holder in due course, then Adams can assert the claim in recoupment to reduce the amount owing on the instrument at the time the action is brought against her on the note. Her claim could serve only to reduce the amount owing, not as a basis for a net recovery from the bank. However, if Dealer was the person bringing an action to collect the note, Adams could assert the breach of warranty claim as a counterclaim and potentially might recover from Dealer any difference between the claim and the damages due for breach of warranty.

The obligor (person obligated to pay the instrument) may assert a claim up to the amount of the instrument if the holder is the original payee but cannot assert claims in recoupment against a holder in due course. In addition, the obligor may assert a claim against a transferee who does not qualify as a holder in due course but only up to the amount owing on the instrument at the time it brought the claim in recoupment.

Concept Summary: Claims and Defenses against Payment of Negotiable Instruments

Claim or Defense	Examples
Real Defense Valid against all holders, including holders in due course and holders who have the rights of holders in due course.	1. Minority that under state law makes the contract void or voidable. 2. Other lack of capacity that makes the contract void. 3. Duress that makes the contract void. 4. Illegality that makes the contract void. 5. Fraud in the essence (fraud in the *factum*). 6. Discharge in bankruptcy.
Personal Defense Valid against plain holders of instruments—but not against holders in due course or holders who have the rights of in-due-course holders through the shelter rule.	1. Lack or failure of consideration. 2. Breach of contract (including breach of warranty). 3. Fraud in the inducement. 4. Lack of capacity that makes the contract voidable (except minority). 5. Illegality that makes the contract voidable. 6. Duress that makes the contract voidable. 7. Unauthorized completion of an incomplete instrument, or material alteration of the instrument. 8. Nonissuance of the instrument.

(continued)

Concept Summary: Claims and Defenses against Payment of Negotiable Instruments *(concluded)*

	9. Failure to countersign a traveler's check.
	10. Modification of the obligation by a separate agreement.
	11. Payment that violates a restrictive indorsement.
	12. Breach of warranty when a draft is accepted.
Claim to an Instrument	1. Claim of ownership by someone who claims to be the owner and that he was wrongfully deprived of possession.
	2. Claim of a lien on the instrument.
	3. Claim for rescission of an indorsement.
Claims in Recoupment	1. Breach of warranty in the sale of goods for which the instrument was issued.

Changes in the Holder in Due Course Rule for Consumer Credit Transactions

Consumer Disadvantages

The rule that a holder in due course of a negotiable instrument is not subject to personal defenses between the original parties to it makes negotiable instruments a readily accepted substitute for money. This rule can also result in serious disadvantages to consumers. Consumers sometimes buy goods or services on credit and give the seller a negotiable instrument such as a promissory note. They often do this without knowing the consequences of their signing a negotiable instrument. If the goods or services are defective or not delivered, the consumer would like to withhold payment of the note until the seller corrects the problem or makes the delivery. Where the note is still held by the seller, the consumer can do this because any defenses of breach of warranty or nonperformance can be asserted against the seller.

However, the seller may have negotiated the note at a discount to a third party such as a bank. If the bank qualifies as a holder in due course, the consumer must pay the note in full to the bank. The consumer's personal defenses are not valid against a holder in due course. The consumer must pay the holder in due course and then try to get her money back from the seller. This may be difficult if the seller cannot be found or will not accept responsibility. The consumer would be in a much stronger position if she could just withhold payment, even against the bank, until the goods or services are delivered or the performance is corrected.

State Legislation

Some state legislatures and courts have limited the holder in due course doctrine, particularly as it affects consumers. State legislatures limiting the doctrine, typically, amended state laws dealing with consumer transactions. For example, some state laws prohibit a seller from taking a negotiable instrument other than a check from a consumer in payment for consumer goods and services. Other state laws require promissory notes given by consumers in payment for goods and services to carry the words *consumer paper;* these state laws treat instruments with the legend "consumer paper" as nonnegotiable. Thus, the rights of a consumer who has signed a negotiable instrument vary from state to state.

LO8

Federal Trade Commission Rules

The Federal Trade Commission (FTC) has promulgated a regulation designed to protect consumers against operation of the holder in due course rule. The FTC rule applies to persons who sell to consumers on credit and have the consumer sign a note or an installment sale contract or arrange third party financing of the purchase. The seller must ensure that the note or the contract contains the following clause:

> NOTICE: ANY HOLDER OF THIS CONSUMER CREDIT CONTRACT IS SUBJECT TO ALL CLAIMS AND DEFENSES WHICH THE DEBTOR COULD ASSERT AGAINST THE SELLER OF THE GOODS OR SERVICES OBTAINED PURSUANT HERETO OR WITH THE PROCEEDS HEREOF. RECOVERY HEREUNDER BY THE DEBTOR SHALL NOT EXCEED AMOUNTS PAID BY THE DEBTOR HEREUNDER.[3]

The effect of the notice is to make a potential holder of the note or contract subject to all claims and defenses of the consumer. This is illustrated in the case below of *Music Acceptance Corp. v. Lofing.* If the note or contract does not contain the clause required by the FTC Rule, the consumer does not gain any rights that he would not otherwise have under state law, and the subsequent holder may qualify as a holder in due course. However, the FTC does have the right to seek a fine of as much as $10,000 against the seller who failed to include the notice.

In the hypothetical case set out at the start of this chapter, Rachel buys a used car and gives the seller a negotiable promissory note in which she promises to pay the balance in 12 months. The seller then negotiates the promissory note to a third party. When Rachel discovers that, contrary to the seller's assurances, the car had previously been involved in an accident, Rachel would like to assert a defense of failure of consideration or breach of contract (warranty) against payment. Normally, if the person to whom the note was assigned can qualify as a holder in due course, then the maker of a note will not be able to able to assert those particular defenses against payment because they are considered to be "personal defenses" and a holder in due course of an instrument takes the instrument free of such defenses against payment. However, the introductory hypothetical goes on to pose the question of whether it would make a difference if the promissory note contained the clause required by the Federal Trade Commission in consumer notes. You are now in a position to know that it would make a difference in Rachel's rights and that she would be able to assert such defenses against payment of the note to the current holder, even if he could qualify as holder in due course.

[3] Revised Section 3–106(d) covers this clause.

Music Acceptance Corp. v. Lofing

39 Cal. Rptr. 159 (Ct. App. Cal. 1995)

FACTS

Dan Lofing purchased a Steinway grand piano from Sherman Clay & Co., Steinway & Sons' Sacramento dealer, and received financing through Sherman Clay's finance company, Music Acceptance Corporation (MAC). The consumer note for $19,650.94 prepared by MAC and signed by Lofing included the following in bold-faced type:

NOTICE

ANY HOLDER OF THIS CONSUMER CREDIT CONTRACT IS SUBJECT TO ALL CLAIMS AND DEFENSES WHICH THE DEBTOR COULD ASSERT AGAINST THE SELLER OF THE GOODS OR SERVICES OBTAINED PURSUANT HERETO OR WITH THE PROCEEDS HEREOF. RECOVERY

(continued)

HEREUNDER SHALL NOT EXCEED AMOUNTS PAID BY THE DEBTOR HEREUNDER.

Lofing received a warranty from Steinway which provided the company "will promptly repair or replace without charge any part of this piano which is found to have a defect in material or workmanship within five years" from the date of sale.

Lofing became disenchanted with the piano after experiencing a variety of problems with it. There was a significant deterioration in the action and tonal quality of the piano which the Sherman Clay piano technician was unable to remedy despite lengthy and repeated efforts. A Steinway representative who was called in to inspect the piano concluded that it was in "terrible condition" and expressed surprise that it had ever left the factory. He concluded that the piano would have to be completely rebuilt at the factory.

Because the piano was impossible to play and was ruining his technique, Lofing stopped making payments on the piano. To mitigate his damages, Lofing sold the piano for $7,000 and purchased a Kawai piano from another dealer. He brought suit against Sherman Clay, Steinway, and MAC for, among other things, breach of warranty. One of the issues in the litigation was whether the notice in the note allowed him to assert the breach of warranty as a grounds for not continuing to pay off the note to MAC.

ISSUE

When a promissory note contains the notice required by the FTC, can the maker assert proposed breach of warranty in the underlying transaction against the holder of the note?

DECISION

Yes. The FTC rule was adopted because the FTC believed that it was an unfair practice for a seller to employ procedures in the course of arranging the financing of a consumer sale which separated the buyer's duty to pay for goods or services from the seller's reciprocal duty to perform as promised. Here, the clear breach of warranty on the part of Sherman Clay and Steinway relieves Lofing of his duty to continue to pay the consumer note to MAC.

Concept Summary: The Transfer of Commercial Paper

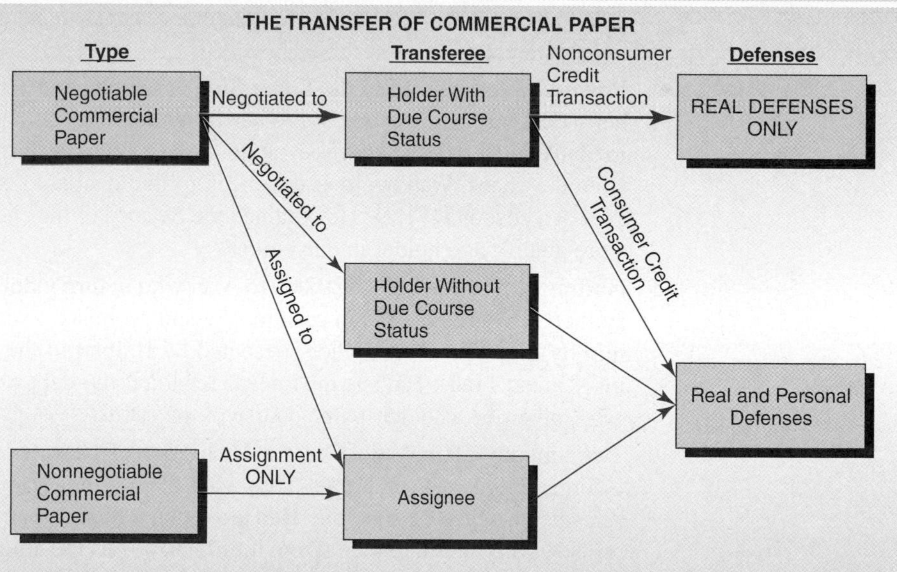

Source: Janell Kurtz and Wayne Wells, "Charting the Ways through the Transfer of Commercial Paper," *Journal of Legal Studies Education* 13 (1995), p. 191.

Questions and Problem Cases

1. Christina Cidon, individually and as president of Spectrum Settlement Group, Inc., maintained bank accounts at the Bay Shore branch of NSBC Bank USA (NSBC). Cidoni appeared at a real estate closing for the purchase and sale of residential property as an independent title closer. At the closing, a check drawn on the Fleet Bank Boston account of Laura Hamel, the attorney handling the closing, and payable to "ABN Amro Mortgage" was issued in the amount of $207,530.14. The check was intended to satisfy the existing mortgage of the sellers of the residential property. One of Spectrum's responsibilities was to see that the check was delivered to a representative of ABN Amro Mortgage. Instead, Cidoni indorsed the check on the back "for deposit" and deposited it into Spectrum's account at NSBC. Was the check negotiated to the bank?
2. A bank cashed the checks of its customer, Dental Supply, Inc., presented to the bank by an employee of Dental Supply named Wilson. The checks were indorsed in blank with a rubber stamp of Dental Supply, Inc. Wilson had been stealing the checks by taking cash rather than depositing them to Dental Supply, Inc.'s account. What could Dental Supply have done to avoid this situation?
3. Reliable Janitorial Service, Inc., maintained a bank account with AmSouth Bank. Rosa Pennington was employed by Reliable as a bookkeeper/office manager. She deposited checks made payable to Reliable but did not have authority to write checks on Reliable's account. Beginning in January 1985, Pennington obtained counter deposit slips from AmSouth. She wrote on the deposit slips that the depositor was "Reliable Janitorial Services, Inc.," but in the space for the account number, Pennington wrote the account number for her own personal account with AmSouth. She stamped the checks that were made payable to "Reliable Janitorial Services, Inc.," with the indorsement "For Deposit Only, Reliable Carpet Cleaning, Inc." Over an 11-month period, Pennington was able to deposit 169 checks so indorsed. AmSouth credited the deposits to Pennington, not Reliable. Pennington spent all the funds that she diverted to her account. When Reliable discovered the fraud, it brought suit against AmSouth for conversion and sought to have its account credited with the improperly paid checks. Was AmSouth Bank liable to Reliable for the value of the restrictively indorsed checks that it paid inconsistently with the indorsement?
4. Reggie Bluiett worked at the Silver Slipper Gambling Hall and Saloon. She received her weekly paycheck made out to her from the Silver Slipper. She indorsed the check in blank and left it on her dresser at home. Fred Watkins broke into Bluiett's house and stole the check. Watkins took the check to the local auto store, where he bought two tires at a cost of $171.21. He obtained the balance of the check in cash. Could the auto store qualify as a holder in due course?
5. Horton wrote a check for $20,000 to Axe, who in turn indorsed it to Halbert. In return, Halbert advanced $8,000 in cash to Axe and promised to cancel a $12,000 debt owed him by Axe. The check, when presented by Halbert to the bank, was not paid due to insufficient funds. Halbert thus never regarded the debt as canceled. To what extent can Halbert be a holder in due course of the check?
6. Two smooth-talking salesmen for Rich Plan of New Orleans called on Leona and George Henne at their home. They sold the Hennes a home food plan. One of the salesmen suggested that the Hennes sign a blank promissory note. The Hennes refused. The salesman then wrote in ink "$100" as the amount and "4" as the number of installments in which the note was to be paid, and the Hennes signed the note. Several days later, the Hennes received a payment book from Nationwide Acceptance. The payment book showed that a total of $843.37 was due, payable in 36 monthly installments. Rich Plan had erased the "$100" and "4" on the note and typed in the

figures "$843.37" and "36." The erasures were cleverly done but were visible to the naked eye. Rich Plan then negotiated the Hennes' note to Nationwide Acceptance. The Hennes refused to pay the note. Nationwide claimed that it was a holder in due course and was entitled to receive payment. Was Nationwide Acceptance a holder in due course?

7. A representative of Gracious Living, Inc., called on the Hutchinsons and identified himself as a "demonstrator" of water-softening equipment. After explaining the cost of the equipment, he told the Hutchinsons that Gracious Living would install it for a four-month trial. In return, the Hutchinsons were to give him a list of their friends and neighbors and permit a demonstration in their house. They were to receive a bonus if sales were made to any of their friends and neighbors. The Hutchinsons claimed that the man "asked them to sign a form that he could show to his boss to prove he had made the demonstration and also as a bond to cover the unit while it was on the Hutchinson's property." They signed the form. Later, the Hutchinsons received a payment book from the Reading Trust Company. They then realized that they had been tricked into signing a contract and a note. Hutchinson was a high school graduate, and his wife had completed her junior year in high school. Both could read and write the English language. Reading Trust had obtained the note from Gracious Living. It had no notice of Gracious Living's business practice and was a holder in due course. The Hutchinsons refused to pay the note, and Reading Trust sued them to collect on it. Did the Hutchinsons have a real defense that they could use against the Reading Trust Company even though it was a holder in due course?

9. Panlick, the owner of an apartment building, entered into a written contract with Bucci, a paving contractor, whereby Bucci was to install asphalt paving on the parking lot of the building. When Bucci finished the job, Panlick gave Bucci a check for $6,500 and a promissory note for $7,593 with interest at 10 percent due six months from its date. When the note came due, Panlick refused to pay it. Bucci brought suit to collect the note, and Panlick claimed that there had been a failure of consideration because the asphalt was defectively installed. Can Panlick assert this defense against Bucci.

10. Pedro and Paula de la Fuente were visited by a representative of Aluminum Industries, Inc., who was seeking to sell them aluminum siding for their home. They agreed to purchase the siding and signed a number of documents, including a retail installment contract and a promissory note for $9,137.24. The contract granted Aluminum Industries, Inc., a first lien on the de la Fuentes' residence; this was in violation of the Texas Civil Code, which prohibited such provisions. The promissory note contained a notice in bold type as required by the Federal Trade Commission. It read in part:

    NOTICE: ANY HOLDER OF THIS CONSUMER CREDIT CONTRACT IS SUBJECT TO ALL CLAIMS AND DEFENSES WHICH THE DEBTOR COULD ASSERT AGAINST THE SELLER OF GOODS OR SERVICES OBTAINED PURSUANT HERETO WITH THE PROCEEDS THEREOF.

    Aluminum Industries assigned the promissory note and first lien to Home Savings Association. Aluminum Industries subsequently went out of business. Home Savings brought suit against the de la Fuentes to collect the balance due on the note. Home Savings contended that it was a holder in due course and that the de la Fuentes could not assert any defense against it that they had against Aluminum Industries. Can an assignee of a consumer promissory note that includes the notice required by the FTC qualify as a holder in due course?

Chapter 40

Liability of Parties

LO

Learning Objectives

After you have studied this chapter, you should be able to:

1. Recall the obligations of makers, drawees or acceptors, drawers, indorsers, and accommodation parties.
2. Explain the difference between primary and secondary liability on a negotiable instrument.
3. Explain when a person's signature on a negotiable instrument makes the person contractually liable on it.
4. Explain what is meant by *presentment* of a note or of a check or draft.
5. List the six warranties made by persons who transfer negotiable instruments to someone else.
6. List the four warranties made by persons who present negotiable instruments for payment or acceptance.
7. Discuss the three exceptions to the normal liability rules: negligence, the impostor rule, and the fictitious payee rule.
8. Explain how the liability of a party to pay an instrument is normally discharged.

When you sign a promissory note, you expect that you will be liable for paying the note on the day it is due. Similarly, when you sign a check and mail it off to pay a bill, you expect that it will be paid by your bank out of your checking account and that if there are not sufficient funds in the account to cover it, you will have to make it good out of other funds you have. The liability of the maker of a note and of the drawer of a check is commonly understood.

However, there are other ways a person can become liable on a negotiable instrument. Moreover, some of the usual liability rules are modified when a party is negligent in issuing or paying a negotiable instrument—or otherwise contributes to a potential loss.

(continued)

The issues that will be discussed in this chapter include:

- Suppose you indorse a check that is payable to your order and "cash" it at a check cashing service. What liability have you assumed by indorsing and transferring the check?
- Suppose you make out a check in such a way that someone is able to raise (change) the amount of the check from $1 to $1,000 and then obtain payment of the check from the drawee bank. Will your bank be entitled to charge your account for $1,000 or can you limit the charge to $1, the original amount of the check?
- Suppose one of your employees who has responsibility for writing checks makes some of them payable to people you normally do business with and then keeps the checks, indorses the checks in the name of the named payee, and obtains payment of the checks for her own purposes. Are you entitled to have your account re-credited for the amount of the checks on the grounds they were paid over a forged indorsement?

Introduction

Thus far in Part 7, "Commercial Paper," the focus has been on the nature of, and requirements for, negotiable instruments, as well as the rights that an owner of an instrument can obtain and how to obtain them. Another important aspect to negotiable instruments concerns how a person becomes liable on a negotiable instrument and the nature of the liability incurred.

Liability in General

Liability on negotiable instruments flows from signatures on the instruments as well as actions taken concerning them. It can arise from the fact that a person has signed a negotiable instrument or has authorized someone else to sign it. The liability depends on the capacity in which the person signs the instrument. Liability also arises from (1) transfer or presentment of an instrument, (2) negligence relating to the issuance, alteration, or indorsement of the instrument, (3) improper payment, or (4) conversion.

Contractual Liability

When a person signs a negotiable instrument, whether as maker, drawer, or indorser, or in some other capacity, she generally becomes contractually liable on the instrument. As mentioned above, this contractual liability depends on the capacity in which the person signed the instrument. The terms of the contract of the parties to a negotiable instrument are not set out in the text of the instrument. Rather, Article 3 of the Uniform Commercial Code supplies the terms, which are as much a part of the instrument as if they were part of its text.

LO1 Primary and Secondary Liability

A party to a negotiable instrument may be either primarily liable or secondarily liable for payment of it. A person who is *primarily liable* has agreed to pay the negotiable instrument. For example, the maker of a promissory note is the person who is primarily liable on the note. A person who is *secondarily liable* is like a guarantor on a contract; Article 3 requires a secondary party to pay the negotiable instrument only if a person who is primarily liable defaults on that obligation. Chapter 42, "Introduction to Security," discusses guarantors.

Obligation of a Maker

LO2

The **maker** of a promissory note is primarily liable for payment of it. The maker promises unconditionally to pay a fixed amount of money and is responsible for making good on that promise. The obligation of the maker is to pay the negotiable instrument according to its terms at the time he issues it or, if it is not issued, then according to its terms at the time it first came into possession of a holder (3–412).[1] If the material terms of the note are not complete when the maker signs it, then the maker's obligation is to pay the note as it is completed, provided that the terms filled in are as authorized. If the instrument is incomplete when the maker signs it and it is completed in an unauthorized manner, then the maker's liability will depend on whether the person seeking to enforce the instrument can qualify as a holder in due course.

The case that follows, *American Federal Bank, FSB v. Parker,* illustrates a situation in which the maker of a note was negligent in signing a blank note and was required to pay the amount fraudulently filled in by a wrongdoer.

The obligation of the maker is owed to (1) a **person entitled to enforce the instrument** or (2) any indorser who paid the instrument pursuant to her indorser's liability (discussed below). A *person entitled to enforce an instrument* includes (1) the holder of the instrument, (2) a nonholder in possession of the instrument who has the rights of a holder, and (3) a person not in possession of the instrument who has the right to enforce the instrument under Section 3–309, which deals with lost, destroyed, or stolen instruments.

[1] The numbers in parentheses refer to sections of the Uniform Commercial Code.

American Federal Bank, FSB v. Parker

392 S.E.2d 798 (Ct. App. S.C. 1990)

FACTS

Thomas Kirkman was involved in the horse business and was a friend of John Roundtree, a loan officer for American Federal Bank. Kirkman and Roundtree conceived a business arrangement in which Kirkman would locate buyers for horses and the buyers could seek financing from American Federal. Roundtree gave Kirkman blank promissory notes and security agreements from American Federal. Kirkman was to locate the potential purchaser, take care of the paperwork, and bring the documents to the bank for approval of the purchaser's loan.

Kirkman entered into a purchase agreement with Gene Parker, a horse dealer, to copurchase for $35,000 a horse named Wills Hightime, which Kirkman represented he owned. Parker signed the American Federal promissory note in blank and executed in blank a security agreement that authorized the bank to disburse the funds to the seller of the collateral. Kirkman told Parker he would cosign the note and fill in the details of the transaction with the bank. While Kirkman did not cosign the note, he did complete it for $85,000 as opposed to $35,000. Kirkman took the note with Parker's signature to Roundtree at American Federal and received

(continued)

two checks from the bank payable to him in the amounts of $35,000 and $50,000. Kirkman took the $35,000 and gave it to the real owner of the horse. Parker then received the horse.

Parker began making payments to the bank and called upon Kirkman to assist in making the payments pursuant to their agreement. However, Kirkman skipped town, taking the additional $50,000 with him. Parker repaid the $35,000 but refused to pay any more. He argued that he agreed to borrow only $35,000 and the other $50,000 was unauthorized by him.

ISSUE

Was Parker's liability on the note limited to the $35,000 he had authorized Kirkman to fill in?

DECISION

No. Parker was liable to American Federal for the full $85,000. Parker executed a promissory note in blank. Under the UCC the maker of a note agrees to pay the instrument according to its tenor at the time of engagement or according to the rules governing incomplete instruments. If the completion of an instrument is unauthorized, then it is considered to be an alteration. However, a subsequent holder in due course may enforce an incomplete instrument as completed. The Official Comments to the Code indicate that where blanks are filled in or an incomplete instrument is otherwise completed, the loss is placed upon the party who left the instrument incomplete and the holder in due course is permitted to enforce it according to its completed form. Accordingly, American Federal, as a holder in due course, can enforce the note for $85,000.

Revised Article 3 provides that the **drawer of a cashier's check** has the same obligation as the maker or issuer of a note. Thus, it treats a draft drawn on a bank drawer the same as a note for purposes of the issuer's liability rather than treating the issuer as a drawer of a draft (3–412).

Obligation of a Drawee or an Acceptor

The **acceptor** of a draft is obligated to pay the draft according to the terms at the time of its acceptance. **Acceptance** is the drawee's signed engagement to honor the draft as presented—and is commonly indicated by the signature of the acceptor on the instrument itself. The acceptor's obligation extends to (1) a person entitled to enforce the draft, (2) the drawer, and (3) an indorser who paid the instrument pursuant to her indorser's liability (3–413).

If the certification of a check or other acceptance of a draft states the amount certified or accepted, the obligation of the acceptor is that amount. If the certification or acceptance does not state an amount, or if the amount of the instrument is subsequently raised, and then the instrument is negotiated to a holder in due course, the obligation of the acceptor is the amount of the instrument at the time a holder in due course takes it (3–413[b]).

At the time a check or other draft issues, no party is primarily liable on it. Usually, the drawee bank pays a check when it is presented for payment and no person becomes primarily liable. However, the drawer or a holder of the check may ask the drawee bank to *accept* or *certify* the check. The drawee bank certifies the check by signing its name to the check and, with that act, accepts liability as acceptor. The drawee bank debits, or takes the money out of, the drawer's account and holds the money to pay the check. If the drawee bank certifies the check, it becomes primarily or absolutely liable for paying the check as it reads at the time of its acceptance (3–413).

Similarly, when a trade draft is presented for acceptance or payment, no party is liable on it. If the named drawee accepts it, perhaps by writing his name on the face of it, then he accepts the obligations set forth in the instrument.

A drawee has no liability on a check or other draft unless it certifies or accepts the check or draft—that is, agrees to be liable on it. However, a drawee bank that refuses to pay a check when it is presented for payment may be liable to the drawer for wrongfully refusing payment, assuming the drawer had sufficient funds in his checking account to cover it. The next chapter discusses this liability of a drawee bank.

Obligation of a Drawer

The **drawer**'s obligation is that if the drawee dishonors an unaccepted check (or draft), the drawer will pay the check (or draft) according to its terms at the time he issued it. If the draft was not complete when issued but was completed as authorized, then the obligation is to pay it as completed. If any completion is not authorized, then the obligation will depend on whether the person seeking to enforce the instrument can qualify as a holder in due course. A person entitled to enforce the draft or an indorser who paid the draft pursuant to his indorser's liability may enforce the drawer's obligation (3–414[b]).

For example, Janis draws a check on her account at First National Bank payable to the order of Collbert. If First National does not pay the check when Collbert presents it for payment, then Janis is liable to Collbert on the basis of her drawer's obligation.

If a draft is accepted by a bank—for example, if the drawee bank certifies a check—the drawer is discharged of her drawer's obligation. If someone other than a bank accepts a draft, then the obligation of the drawer to pay the draft, if the draft is dishonored, is the same as an indorser (discussed next) (3–414[c] and [d]).

Obligation of an Indorser

A person who indorses a negotiable instrument usually is secondarily liable. Unless the indorser qualifies or otherwise disclaims liability, the **indorser**'s obligation on dishonor of the instrument is to pay the amount due on the instrument according to its terms as of the time he indorsed it or if he indorsed it when incomplete, then according to its terms when completed, provided that it is completed as authorized. The indorser owes the obligation to a person entitled to enforce the instrument or to any subsequent indorser who had to pay it (3–415).

In the opening vignette, the question is posed as to your liability if you indorse a check that is payable to your order and then cash it at a check cashing service. If that check is not paid when it is presented to the drawee bank for payment, then you would be liable for repaying the amount of the check to the check cashing service. It would then be up to you to locate—and try to recover from—the person from whom you took the check.

The indorser can avoid this liability only by qualifying the indorsement, such as writing "without recourse," on the instrument when he indorses it (3–415[b]).

Ethics in Action

Suppose you have taken a promissory note for $1,000 as payment for some carpentry work you did for a friend. You have some reason to believe that the maker is having some financial difficulty and may not be able to pay the note when it is due. You discuss the possible sale of the note to an elderly neighbor as an investment and she agrees to buy it. Would it be ethical for you to indorse the note with a qualified indorsement ("without recourse")?

Indorsers are liable to each other in the chronological order in which they indorse, from the last indorser back to the first. For example, Mark Maker gives a promissory note to

Paul Payee. Payee indorses it and negotiates it to Fred First, who indorses it and negotiates it to Shirley Second. If Maker does not pay the note when Second takes it to him for payment, then Second can require First to pay it to her. First is secondarily liable on the basis of his indorsement. First, in turn, can require Payee to pay him because Payee also became secondarily liable when he indorsed it. Then, Payee is left to try to collect the note from Maker. Second also could have skipped over First and proceeded directly against Payee on his indorsement. First has no liability to Payee, however, because First indorsed after Payee indorsed the note.

If a bank accepted a draft (for example, by certifying a check) after an indorsement is made, the acceptance discharges the liability of the indorser (3–415[d]). If notice of dishonor is required and proper notice is not given to the indorser, she is discharged of liability (3–415[c]). And, where no one presents a check or gives it to a depositary bank for collection within 30 days after the date of an indorsement, the indorser's liability is discharged (3–415[e]).

E-Commerce

CYBERLAW IN ACTION

With the advent of high resolution scanners, sophisticated desktop publishing programs, and laser printers that print in color, forgery of negotiable instruments has become increasingly easier and more common with significant financial risks for those who may unwittingly accept such instruments in payment for goods and services and/or pass them along to others.

The April 26, 2005, edition of *The New York Times* carried a story headlined "A Common Currency for Online Fraud: Forgers of U.S. Postal Money Orders Grow in Numbers and Skill." The story begins:

> Fake checks have been the stock in trade of online fraud artists for years. Now authorities are noting a surge in schemes involving sophisticated counterfeiting of a different form of payment: United States postal money orders. And the fleecing of victims often begins in an e-mail inbox.

After noting a very significant increase in counterfeit postal money orders that have been intercepted by federal law enforcement officials, the article details how the scams, often involving international forgers, work. Historically, postal money orders have been considered very difficult to forge, and sellers of goods view them as the same as cash and preferable to personal checks. In the recent scams, online buyers send money orders in payment for goods which are then shipped. By the time the seller becomes aware that the postal money order was counterfeit, the buyer has the goods and the seller has no way of getting the money or the goods back from the erstwhile buyer. Sometimes the purchases are of expensive items like computers. In another variant of the scam, the buyer sends a postal money order for much more than the cost of the item—and requests that the seller send the item and remit cash for the difference between the cost of the item and the amount of the money order. Thus the "buyer" gains both cash and merchandise in exchange for a worthless piece of paper.

In addition to the scrutiny from law enforcement officials that may come from being in possession of counterfeit postal money orders, or from trying to pass—or actually passing—them on to others, the person who takes and passes along a counterfeit order may well incur some of the liability discussed in this chapter. For example, Ralph has taken a postal money order in payment for a computer he sold and then shipped to a purchaser in Nigeria. When he deposits the postal money order in his account at his bank—or takes it to the post office to seek payment of it—he will be asked to indorse his name on the back of the order. You may recall from Chapter 38, "Negotiable Instruments," that money orders are commonly in a form that meets the requirements for being a negotiable instrument.

(continued)

E-Commerce (concluded)

When the bank—or the post office—discovers that the postal money order given to them by Ralph is a forgery, they will go back against him to recoup the money they credited to his account or paid to him. They can do so on the basis of his contractual liability as an indorser. By indorsing the instrument, he obligated himself to make the instrument good if it was dishonored. Ralph, in turn, is left with what may be a fairly worthless right to recoup the money from the person in Nigeria who sent him the counterfeit instrument.

A similar problem has been occurring with counterfeit cashier's checks. Many of the original victims of this version of this scam are lawyers. Potential new clients contact the lawyer target by e-mail, requesting assistance with the collection of a debt or judgment, or representation in a real estate transaction. The lawyer then receives a cashier's check from the client or from the client's counterparty, which the lawyer normally deposits into a deposit account. The client asks for the proceeds of the check to be wired to a foreign bank account quickly, often before the deposit can travel to the putative drawee bank and almost always before the drawee's notice of dishonor reaches the depositary bank. The bank then debits the deposit from the lawyer's account and pursues the lawyer for reimbursement of the funds wired to the foreign account. These counterfeit cashier's checks can be for large-dollar amounts and often result in litigation between the depositor and depositary bank, or the depositary bank and the drawee bank.

As bank and other officials are alerted to counterfeiting of particular kinds of negotiable instruments, we can expect that the scam artists will change their targets or increase the sophistication of their forgeries so as to more readily pass without detection. Legitimate negotiable instruments offer lots of advantages to those who use them. But in a world where things may not be what they appear to be, it can be important to your financial well-being to know the person you are taking an instrument from and be confident that if it turns out that there is something wrong with it, you will be able to recoup what you paid or gave for it.

Obligation of an Accommodation Party

An **accommodation party** is a person who signs a negotiable instrument for the purpose of lending her credit to another party to the instrument but is not a direct beneficiary of the value given for the instrument. For example, a bank might be reluctant to lend money to—and take a note from—Payee because of his shaky financial condition. However, the bank may be willing to lend money to Payee if he signs the note and has a relative or a friend also sign the note as an accommodation maker.

The obligation of an accommodation party depends on the capacity in which the party signs the instrument (3–419). If Payee has his brother Sam sign a note as an accommodation maker, then Sam has the same contractual liability as a maker. Sam is primarily liable on the note. The bank may ask Sam to pay the note before asking Payee to pay. However, if Sam pays the note to the bank, he has the right to recover his payment from Payee, the person on whose behalf he signed.

Similarly, if a person signs a check as an accommodation indorser, his contractual liability is that of an indorser. If the accommodation indorser has to make good on that liability, he can collect in turn from the person on whose behalf he signed.

Signing an Instrument

LO3

No person is contractually liable on a negotiable instrument unless she or her authorized agent has signed it and the signature is binding on the represented person. A signature can be any name, word, or mark used in place of a written signature (3–401). As discussed earlier, the capacity in which a person signs an instrument determines his liability on the instrument.

Signature of an Authorized Agent

An authorized agent can sign a negotiable instrument. If Sandra Smith authorized her attorney to sign checks as her agent, then she is liable on any checks properly signed by the attorney as her agent. All negotiable instruments signed by corporations have to be signed by an agent of the corporation who is authorized to sign negotiable instruments.

If a person purporting to act as a representative signs an instrument by signing either the name of the represented person or the name of the signer, that signature binds the represented person to the same extent she would be bound if the signature were on a simple contract. If the represented person has authorized the signature of the representative, it is the "authorized signature of the represented person," and the represented person is liable on the instrument, whether or not identified in the instrument. This brings the Code in line with the general principle of agency law that binds an undisclosed principal on a simple contract. For example, if Principal authorizes Agent to borrow money on Principal's behalf, and Agent signs her name to a note without disclosing that the signature was on behalf of Principal, Agent is liable on the note. In addition, if the person entitled to enforce the note can show that Principal authorized Agent to sign on his behalf, then Principal is liable on the note as well.

When a representative signs an authorized signature to an instrument, then the representative is not bound provided the signature shows "unambiguously" that the signature was made on behalf of the represented person who is named in the instrument (3–402[b][1]). For example, if a note is signed "XYZ, Inc., by Flanigan, Treasurer," Flanigan is not liable on the instrument in his own right but XYZ, Inc., is liable.

If an authorized representative signs his name as the representative of a drawer of a check without noting his representative status, but the check is payable from an account of the represented person who is identified on the check, the signer is not liable on the check as long as his signature was authorized (3–402[c]). The rationale for this provision is that because most checks today identify the person on whose account the check is drawn, no one is deceived into thinking that the person signing the check is meant to be personally liable. This principle is illustrated in the *Marion T, LLC v. Northwest Metals Processors, Inc.,* case that follows. The case also indicates that the criminal law takes a different view of this issue.

Marion T, LLC v. Northwest Metals Processors

67 UCC Rep.2d 379 (U.S.D.C. N.D. Ind. 2008)

FACTS

Marion T, LLC, contracted with Northwest Metals Processors to remove and salvage equipment and materials at Marion's facility located in Marion, Indiana. The company became in arrears on the payments it was to make on the salvaging contract, resulting in Troy Reed, the sole shareholder, board member, and officer of Northwest Metals, issuing two checks drawn on the company's account at Sky Bank and payable to Marion. Reed also issued a third check drawn on the account of Buckeye Industrial Sales & Service, Inc., a company in which again he was the sole shareholder. The checks were returned to Marion by the bank where it had deposited them marked "NOT SUFFICIENT FUNDS." In each instance, Reed knew there were insufficient funds to satisfy the amount of the check.

The checks were pre-printed Sky Bank checks showing in the upper left corner the name of the corporation account holder (i.e., Northwest or Buckeye), and each listed the respective corporation's account number. Reed was authorized to sign checks for both Northwest Metals and

(continued)

Buckeye, and each check was signed simply "Troy Reed," without any notation or indication of his agency status.

Reed then became the subject of a criminal proceeding brought by the state of Indiana for check deception. Marion also brought a civil suit against the two companies and Reed. Among other things, Marion contended that Reed should be personally liable for the dishonored checks.

ISSUE

Is Reed personally liable on the dishonored checks where he signed his name to the company checks as an authorized signatory, but without indicating his representative capacity?

DECISION

No. The court held that under the Indiana version of the Code, where a representative who signs his name as drawer of a check without indication of the representative status and the check is payable from an account of the represented person who is identified on the check (i.e., Northwest Metals or Buckeye), the signer is not liable on the check if the signature is an authorized signature of the represented person.

The court noted that a different rule prevails under the criminal law where a person who obtains money or property with fraudulent intent by means of a check which he draws or makes in a representative capacity can be held criminally liable. If he draws the check as the representative of a corporation, he is nonetheless the drawer within the contemplation of the statute making it a crime to do so. There is no doctrine of agency in the criminal law which will permit an officer to shield himself from criminal responsibility for his own act on the ground it was the act of the corporation and not his own act.

Except for the check situation noted above, a representative is personally liable to a holder in due course that took the instrument without notice that the representative was not intended to be liable if (1) the form of the signature does not show unambiguously that the signature was made in a representative capacity or (2) the instrument does not identify the represented person. As to persons other than a holder in due course without notice of the representative nature of the signature, the representative is liable *unless* she can prove that the original parties did not intend her to be liable on the instrument (3–402[b][2]).

Thus, if an agent or a representative signs a negotiable instrument on behalf of someone else, the agent should indicate clearly that he is signing as the representative of someone else. For example, Kim Darby, the president of Swimwear, Inc., is authorized to sign negotiable instruments for the company. If Swimwear borrows money from the bank and the bank asks her to sign a 90-day promissory note, Darby should sign it either "Swimwear, Inc., by Kim Darby, President" or "Kim Darby, President, for Swimwear, Inc." If Kim Darby signed the promissory note merely "Kim Darby," she could be personally liable on the note. Similarly, if Clara Carson authorizes Arthur Anderson, an attorney, to sign checks for her, Anderson either should make sure that the checks identify Clara Carson as the account involved or should sign them "Clara Carson by Arthur Anderson, Agent." Otherwise, he risks being personally liable on them.

Unauthorized Signature

If someone signs a person's name to a negotiable instrument without that person's authorization or approval, the signature does not bind the person whose name appears. However, the signature is effective as the signature of the unauthorized signer in favor of any person who in good faith pays the instrument or takes it for value (3–403[a]). For example, if Tom Thorne steals Ben Brown's checkbook and signs Brown's name to a check, Brown is not liable on the check because Brown had not authorized Thorne to sign Brown's name. However, Thorne can be liable on the check, because he did sign it, even though he did not sign it in his own name. Thorne's forgery of Brown's signature operates as Thorne's signature. Thus, if Thorne cashed the check at the bank, Thorne would be liable to the bank to make it good or if he negotiated it to a store for value, he would be liable to the store to make it good.

Even though a signature is not "authorized" when it is put on an instrument initially, it can be ratified later by the person represented (3–403[a]). It also should be noted that if more than one person must sign to constitute the authorized signature of an organization, the signature of the organization is unauthorized if one of the required signatures is lacking (3–403[b]). Corporate and other accounts sometimes require multiple signatures as a matter of maintaining sound financial control.

Concept Summary: Contract Liability Based on Signature on a Negotiable Instrument

Concept	Contractual Liability
Primary and Secondary Liability	Every party (other than an indorser who qualifies his/her indorsement) who *signs a negotiable instrument* is either primarily or secondarily liable for payment of the instrument when it comes due. 1. *Primary liability*—Makers and acceptors (a drawee that promises to pay the instrument when it is presented for payment at a later time) are primarily liable. 2. *Secondary liability*—Drawers and indorsers are secondarily liable. Parties who are secondarily liable on an instrument promise to pay the instrument only if the following events occur: a. The instrument is properly presented for payment. b. The instrument is dishonored. c. Timely notice of the dishonor is given to the party who is secondarily liable.
Accommodation Parties	An accommodation party is one who signs an instrument for the purpose of lending his credit to another party to the instrument but is not a direct beneficiary of the value given for the instrument. The obligation of the accommodation party depends on the capacity in which the party signs the instrument. Thus, an accommodation maker has the same obligation as a maker and is primarily liable while an accommodation indorser is secondarily liable on the instrument.
Signature by Agent	An authorized agent can sign an instrument on behalf of the principal and create liability for the principal on the instrument. 1. If the represented person authorized the signature, then the represented person is liable on the instrument whether or not identified in the instrument. 2. If the agent signs an authorized signature to an instrument, the agent is not personally bound on the instrument provided the signature shows unambiguously that the signature was made on behalf of the represented person. 3. If the agent does not identify the represented party in the instrument, then the agent is liable as well unless the instrument is a check drawn on an account for which the agent is an authorized signature.

(continued)

Concept Summary: Contract Liability Based on Signature on a Negotiable Instrument *(concluded)*		
	Unauthorized Signature	An unauthorized signature operates as the signature of the unauthorized signer in favor of a person who in good faith pays the instrument or takes it for value—but it is wholly inoperative as the signature of the person whose name is signed unless: 1. The person whose name is signed ratifies (affirms) the signature. 2. The person whose signature is signed is precluded from denying it.

Contractual Liability in Operation

To bring the contractual liability of the various parties to a negotiable instrument into play, it generally is necessary that the instrument be *presented for payment.* In addition, to hold the parties that are secondarily liable on the instrument to their contractual liability, it generally is necessary that the instrument be *presented for payment* and *dishonored.*

Presentment of a Note

LO4

The maker of a note is primarily liable to pay it when it is due. Normally, the holder takes the note to the maker at the time it is due and asks the maker to pay it. Sometimes the note may provide for payment to be made at a bank, or the maker sends the payment to the holder at the due date. The party to whom the holder presents the instrument, without dishonoring the instrument, may (1) require the exhibition of the instrument, (2) ask for reasonable identification of the person making presentment, (3) ask for evidence of his authority to make it if he is making it for another person, (4) return the instrument for lack of any necessary indorsement, (5) ask that a receipt be signed for any payment made, and (6) require surrender of the instrument if full payment is made (3–501).

Dishonor of a note occurs if the maker does not pay the amount due when (1) it is presented in the case of (a) a demand note or (b) a note payable at or through a bank on a definite date that is presented on or after that date or (2) if it is not paid on the date payable in the case of a note payable on a definite date but not payable at or through a bank (3–502). If the maker or payer dishonors the note, the holder can seek payment from any persons who indorsed the note before the holder took it. The basis for going after the indorsers is that they are secondarily liable. To hold the indorsers to their contractual obligation, the holder must give them notice of the dishonor. The notice can be either written or oral (3–503).

For example, Susan Strong borrows $1,000 from Jack Jones and gives him a promissory note for $1,000 at 9 percent annual interest payable in 90 days. Jones indorses the note "Pay to the order of Ralph Smith" and negotiates the note to Ralph Smith. At the end of 90 days, Smith takes the note to Strong and presents it for payment. If Strong pays Smith the $1,000 and accrued interest, she can have Smith mark it "paid" and give it back to her. If Strong does not pay the note to Smith when he presents it for payment, then she has dishonored the note. Smith should give notice of the dishonor to Jones and advise him that he intends to hold Jones secondarily liable on his indorsement. Smith may collect payment of the note from Jones. Jones, after making the note good to Smith, can try to collect the note from Strong on the ground that she defaulted on the contract she made as maker of the note. Of course, Smith also could sue Strong on the basis of Strong's maker's obligation.

Presentment of a Check or a Draft

The holder should present a check or draft to the drawee. The presentment can be either for payment or for acceptance (certification) of the check or draft. Under Revised Article 3, the presentment may be made by any commercially reasonable means, including a written, oral, or electronic communication (3–501). No one is primarily obligated on a check or draft, and the drawee is not obligated on a check or draft unless it accepts (certifies) it (3–408). An acceptance of a draft is the drawee's signed commitment to honor the draft as presented. The acceptance must be written on the draft, and it may consist of the drawee's signature alone (3–409).

A drawer who writes a check issues an order to the drawee to pay a certain amount out of the drawer's account to the payee (or to someone authorized by the payee). This order is not an assignment of the funds in the drawer's account (3–408). The drawee bank does not have an obligation to the payee to pay the check unless it certifies the check. However, the drawee bank usually does have a separate contractual obligation (apart from Article 3) to the drawer to pay any properly payable checks for which funds are available in the drawer's account.

For example, Janet Payne has $1,000 in a checking account at First National Bank and writes a check for $500 drawn on First National and payable to Ralph Smith. The writing of the check is the issuance of an order by Payne to First National to pay $500 from her account to Smith or to whomever Smith requests it to be paid. First National owes no obligation to Smith to pay the $500 unless it has certified the check. However, if Smith presents the check for payment and First National refuses to pay it even though there are sufficient funds in Payne's account, then First National is liable to Payne for breaching its contractual obligation to her to pay items properly payable from existing funds in her account. Chapter 41, "Checks and Electronic Fund Transfers," discusses the liability of a bank for wrongful dishonor of checks in more detail.

If the drawee bank does not pay or certify a check when it is properly presented for payment or acceptance (certification), the drawee bank has dishonored the check (3–502). Similarly, if a draft is not paid on the date it is due (or accepted by the drawee on the due date for acceptance), it has been dishonored. The holder of the draft or check then can proceed against either the drawer or any indorsers on their secondary liability. To do so, the holder must give them notice of the dishonor (3–503). Notice of dishonor, like presentment, can be by any commercially reasonable means, including oral, written, or electronic communication. Under certain circumstances set out in Section 3–504, presentment or notice of dishonor may be excused.

Suppose Matthews draws a check for $1,000 on her account at a bank payable to the order of Williams. Williams indorses the check "Pay to the order of Clark, Williams" and negotiates it to Clark. When Clark takes the check to the bank, it refuses to pay the check because there are insufficient funds in Matthews's account to cover the check. The check has been presented and dishonored. Clark has two options: He can proceed against Williams on Williams's secondary liability as an indorser (because by putting an unqualified indorsement on the check, Williams is obligated to make the check good if it was not honored by the drawee). Or he can proceed against Matthews on Matthews's obligation as drawer because in drawing the check, Matthews must pay any person entitled to enforce the check if it is dishonored and he is given notice. Because Clark dealt with Williams, Clark is probably more likely to return the check to Williams for payment. Williams then has to go against Matthews on Matthews's liability as drawer.

Time of Presentment

If an instrument is payable at a definite time, the holder should present it for payment on the due date. In the case of a demand instrument, the nature of the instrument, trade or bank usage, and the facts of the particular case determine a reasonable time for presentment for acceptance or payment. In a farming community, for example, a reasonable time to present a promissory note that is payable on demand may be six months or within a short time after the crops are ready for sale because the holder commonly expects payment from the proceeds of the crops.

Warranty Liability

Whether or not a person signs a negotiable instrument, a person who transfers such an instrument or presents it for payment or acceptance may incur liability on the basis of certain implied warranties. These warranties are (1) **transfer warranties,** which persons who transfer negotiable instruments make to their transferees, and (2) **presentment warranties,** which persons who present negotiable instruments for payment or acceptance (certification) make to payers and drawees.

Transfer Warranties

LO5

A person who transfers a negotiable instrument to someone else and for consideration makes five warranties to his immediate transferee. If the transfer is by indorsement, the transferor makes these warranties to all subsequent transferees. The six *transfer warranties* are these:

1. The warrantor is a person entitled to enforce the instrument. (In essence, the transferor warrants that there are no unauthorized or missing indorsements that prevent the transferor from making the transferee a person entitled to enforce the instrument.)
2. All signatures on the instrument are authentic or authorized.
3. The instrument has not been altered.
4. The instrument is not subject to a defense or a claim in recoupment that any party can assert against the warrantor.
5. The warrantor has no knowledge of any insolvency proceedings commenced with respect to the maker or acceptor or, in the case of an unaccepted draft, the drawer (3–416[a]). (Note that this is not a warranty against difficulty in collection or insolvency—the warranty stops with the warrantor's knowledge.)

In 2003, a sixth transfer warranty was added to the uniform version of Article 3 to deal with unauthorized or repetitive "remotely created checks." These are sometimes called *telephone checks* because the person on whose account the check will be drawn is not present to sign it and provides information to the payee over the telephone. The payee then "creates" a paper check or an ACH file including the information the account owner provided about the account. These checks have been the vehicles for certain consumer frauds, including telemarketing frauds, but they also serve a valuable function for consumers who need to pay creditors on time. The new transfer warranty provides: "(6) with respect to a remotely created consumer item, that the person on whose account the item is drawn authorized the issuance of the item in the amount for which the item is drawn." As of the time this book went to press, this warranty had been adopted by about half of the states.

Revised Article 3 provides that in the event of a breach of a transfer warranty, a beneficiary of the transfer warranties who took the instrument in good faith may recover from the warrantor an amount equal to the loss suffered as a result of the breach. However, the damages recoverable may not be more than the amount of the instrument plus expenses and loss of interest incurred as a result of the breach (3–416[b]).

Transferors of instruments other than checks may disclaim the transfer warranties. Unless the warrantor receives notice of a claim for breach of warranty within 30 days after the claimant has reason to know of the breach and the identity of the warrantor, the delay in giving notice of the claim may discharge the warrantor's liability to the extent of any loss the warrantor suffers from the delay, such as the opportunity to proceed against the transferor (3–416[c]).

Although contractual liability often furnishes a sufficient basis for suing a transferor when the party primarily obligated does not pay, warranties are still important. First, they apply even when the transferor did not indorse. Second, unlike contractual liability, they do not depend on presentment, dishonor, and notice but may be utilized before presentment has been made or after the time for giving notice has expired. Third, a holder may find it easier to return the instrument to a transferor on the ground of breach of warranty than to prove her status as a holder in due course against a maker or drawer.

In the case which follows, *Bank One, N.A. v. Streeter,* a customer who deposited a check on which the payee's name had been altered and that did not contain a valid indorsement of the original payee breached the transfer warranties that (1) he was entitled to enforce the instrument and (2) that it had not been altered.

Bank One, N.A. v. Streeter

58 UCC Rep.2d 1 (U.S.D.C. N.D. Ind. 2005)

FACTS

On August 20, 2003, Dennis Streeter deposited a check drawn by Economy Gas Company in the amount of $117,469.80 into his Bank One account. On August 22, 2003, Streeter deposited a check drawn by Newspaper Services of America in the amount of $137,374.08 into his Bank One account. Also, on August 22, 2003, Streeter deposited a money order issued by Kroger in the amount of $100,447.05 into his Bank One account. Bank One credited Streeter's account for the three checks. At this time, Bank One did not believe that the checks had been altered. However, after the deposits were made, Bank One received notice from the banks on which the three checks had been drawn that the checks had been altered.

When Economy Gas Company originally issued its check, the payee was "B.P. Products." The name of the payee was altered to "Dennis Streeter." This alteration was made without Economy Gas's knowledge or consent. When Newspaper Services of America originally issued its check, the payee was "N.Y. Times Co." The payee was changed to "Dennis Streeter," and the alteration was made without the knowledge or consent of Newspaper Services of America. When Kroger issued its money order, the initial payee was "SlimFast Foods Co." The payee was altered to "Dennis Streeter," and made without Kroger's knowledge.

Bank One brought suit against Streeter to recover the funds it had credited to his account. The bank asserted that the transfer warranties as set forth in Indiana's Uniform Commercial Code dictate that Streeter is liable to Bank One for its damages stemming from the altered checks. In response, Streeter argued that he had not breached any warranty because he was the person entitled to enforce the instruments and that there was no evidence that the checks were altered by him or that he had any knowledge of any alterations.

ISSUE

Is Streeter liable to Bank One on the grounds that he breached the transfer warranties that (1) he was a person entitled to enforce the instrument and (2) the instrument had not been altered?

DECISION

Yes. The court began by noting that the Indiana Code states that "a person who transfers an instrument for consideration warrants to the transferee . . . that: (1) the warrantor is a person entitled to enforce the instrument . . . (3) the instrument has not been altered. . . . " The evidence showed that Streeter made these transfer warranties to Bank One when he transferred the Economy Gas check, the Newspaper Services check, and the Kroger money order to Bank One for consideration. The court noted that an alteration is defined as "an unauthorized change in an instrument that purports to modify in any respect the obligation of a party." In this case, where the names of the payees on each of the checks were changed without the knowledge or authority of the drawer, this constituted an alteration. There is no requirement in the Uniform Commercial Code that the party transferring the instrument either a) to have altered it or b) to have knowledge of the alteration in order for the transfer warranty to be breached. Accordingly, on these facts, Streeter breached the warranty of no material alteration when he transferred the instruments with the names of the payees altered.

Bank One was also correct in contending that Streeter was not entitled to enforce the checks because he was not the proper payee of the instruments. Without the indorsements of the original intended payees, the bank could not get good title to the check. Similarly, without the indorsements of those payees, Streeter was not entitled to enforce the checks, and Streeter breached the warranty that he was entitled to enforce the instruments.

Concept Summary: Transfer Warranties

The six transfer warranties made by a person who transfers a negotiable instrument to someone else for consideration are

1. The warrantor is entitled to enforce the instrument.
2. All signatures on the instrument are authentic or authorized.
3. The instrument has not been altered.
4. The instrument is not subject to a defense or a claim in recoupment that any party can assert against the warrantor.
5. The warrantor has no knowledge of any insolvency proceedings commenced with respect to the maker or acceptor or, in the case of an unaccepted draft, the drawer.
6. With respect to a remotely created consumer item, that the person on whose account the item is drawn authorized the issuance of the item in the amount for which the item is drawn.

Who	What Warranties	To Whom
Nonindorsing Transferor	Makes all six transfer warranties	To his immediate transferor only
Indorsing Transferor	Makes all six transfer warranties	To all subsequent transferors

Presentment Warranties

LO6

Persons who present negotiable instruments for payment or drafts for acceptance also make warranties, but their warranties differ from those transferors make. If an unaccepted draft (such as a check) is presented to the drawee for payment or acceptance and the drawee pays or accepts the draft, then the person obtaining payment or acceptance warrants to the drawee making payment or accepting the draft in good faith that

1. The warrantor is, or was, at the time the warrantor transferred the draft, a person entitled to enforce the draft or authorized to obtain payment or acceptance of the draft on behalf of a person entitled to enforce the draft.
2. The draft has not been altered.
3. The warrantor has no knowledge that the signature of the drawer of the draft has not been authorized (3–417[a]).

In 2003, a fourth presentment warranty was added to the uniform version of Article 3 to deal with unauthorized or repetitive remotely created checks (telephone checks). The new presentment warranty provides: "(4) with respect to any remotely-created consumer item, that the person on whose account the item is drawn authorized the issuance of the item in the amount for which the item is drawn."

These warranties are also made by any prior transferor of the instrument at the time the person transfers the instrument; the warranties run to the drawee who makes payment or accepts the draft in good faith. Such a drawee would include a drawee bank paying a check presented to it for payment directly or through the bank collection process.

The effect of the third presentment warranty is to leave with the drawee the risk that the drawer's signature is unauthorized, unless the person presenting the draft for payment, or a prior transferor, had knowledge of any lack of authorization.

A drawee who makes payment may recover as damages for any breach of a presentment warranty an amount equal to the amount paid by the drawee less the amount the drawee received or is entitled to receive from the drawer because of the payment. In addition, the drawee is entitled to compensation for expenses and loss of interest resulting from the breach (3–417[b]). The drawee's right to recover damages for breach of warranty is not affected by any failure on the part of the drawee to exercise ordinary care in making payment.

If a drawee asserts a claim for breach of a presentment warranty based on an unauthorized indorsement of the draft or an alteration of the draft, the warrantor may defend by showing that the indorsement is effective under the *impostor* or *fictitious payee* rules (discussed later in this chapter) or that the drawer's negligence precludes him from asserting against the drawee the unauthorized indorsement or alteration (also discussed below) (3–417[d]).

If (1) a *dishonored draft* is presented for payment to the drawer or an indorser or (2) any other instrument (such as a note) is presented for payment to a party obligated to pay the instrument and the presenter receives payment, the presenter makes the following presentment warranty (3–417[d]):

> The person obtaining payment is a person entitled to enforce the instrument or authorized to obtain payment on behalf of a person entitled to enforce the instrument.

On breach of this warranty the person making the payment may recover from the warrantor an amount equal to the amount paid plus expenses and loss of interest resulting from the breach.

With respect to checks, the party presenting the check for payment cannot disclaim the presentment warranties (3–417[e]).

Unless the payor or drawee provides notice of a claim for breach of a presentment warranty to the warrantor within 30 days after the claimant has reason to know of the breach and the identity of the warrantor, the warrantor is discharged to the extent of any loss caused by the delay in giving notice of the claim of breach.

Concept Summary: Presentment Warranties

If an unaccepted draft (such as a check) is presented for payment or acceptance and the drawee pays or accepts the draft, then the person obtaining payment or acceptance warrants to the drawee:

1. The warrantor is a person entitled to enforce payment or authorized to obtain payment or acceptance on behalf of a person entitled to enforce the draft.
2. The draft has not been altered.
3. The warrantor has no knowledge that the signature of the drawer of the draft has not been authorized.
4. With respect to any remotely created consumer item, that the person on whose account the item is drawn authorized the issuance of the item in the amount for which the item is drawn.

If (*a*) a dishonored draft is presented for payment to the drawer or indorser or (*b*) any other instrument (such as a note) is presented for payment to a party obligated to pay the instrument and the presenter receives payment, the presenter (as well as a prior transferor of the instrument) makes the following warranty to the person making payment in good faith: The person obtaining payment is a person entitled to enforce the instrument or authorized to obtain payment on behalf of a person entitled to enforce the instrument.

Payment or Acceptance by Mistake

A long-standing general rule of negotiable instruments law is that payment or acceptance is final in favor of a holder in due course or payee who changes his position in reliance on the payment or acceptance. Revised Article 3 retains this concept by making payment final in favor of a person who took the instrument in good faith and for value. However, payment is not final—and may be recovered—from a person who does not meet these criteria where the drawee acted on the mistaken belief that (1) payment of a draft or check has not been stopped, (2) the signature of the purported drawer of the draft was authorized, and (3) the balance in the drawer's account with the drawee represented available funds (3–418[a]).

As a result, this means that if the drawee bank mistakenly paid a check over a stop-payment order, paid a check with a forged or unauthorized drawer's signature on it, or paid despite the lack of sufficient funds in the drawer's account to cover the check, the bank cannot recover if it paid the check to a presenter who had taken the instrument in good faith and for value. In that case, the drawee bank would have to pursue someone else, such as the forger or unauthorized signer, or the drawer in the case of insufficient funds. On the other hand, if the presenter had not taken in good faith or for value, the bank could, in these enumerated instances, recover from the presenter the payment it made by mistake.

Operation of Warranties

Following are three scenarios that show how the transfer and presentment warranties shift the liability back to a wrongdoer or to the person who dealt immediately with a wrongdoer and thus was in the best position to avert the wrongdoing.

Scenario 1

Arthur makes a promissory note for $200 payable to the order of Betts. Carlson steals the note from Betts, indorses Betts's name on the back, and gives it to Davidson in exchange for a television set. Davidson negotiates the note for value to Earle, who presents the note to Arthur for payment. Assume that Arthur refuses to pay the note because Betts has advised him that it has been stolen and that he is the person entitled to enforce the instrument. Earle then can proceed to recover the face amount of the note from Davidson on the grounds that as a transferor, Davidson has warranted that he is a person entitled to enforce the note and that all signatures were authentic. Davidson, in turn, can proceed against Carlson on the same basis—if he can find Carlson. If he cannot, then Davidson must bear the loss caused by Carlson's wrongdoing. Davidson was in the best position to ascertain whether Carlson was the owner of the note and whether the indorsement of Betts was genuine. Of course, even though Arthur does not have to pay the note to Earle, Arthur remains liable for his underlying obligation to Betts.

Scenario 2

Anderson draws a check for $10 on her checking account at First Bank payable to the order of Brown. Brown cleverly raises the check amount to $110, indorses it, and negotiates it to Carroll. Carroll then presents the check for payment to First Bank, which pays her $110 and charges Anderson's account for $110. Anderson then asks the bank to recredit her account for the altered check, and it does so. The bank can proceed against Carroll for breach of the presentment warranty that the instrument had not been altered, which she made to the bank when she presented the check for payment. Carroll in turn can proceed against Brown for breach of her transfer warranty that the check had not been altered—if she can find her. Unless she was negligent in drawing the check, Article 3 limits Anderson's liability to $10 because her obligation is to pay the amount in the instrument at the time she issued it.

Scenario 3

Bates steals Albers's checkbook and forges Albers's signature to a check for $100 payable to "cash," which he uses to buy $100 worth of groceries from a grocer. The grocer presents the check to Albers's bank. The bank pays the amount of the check to the grocer and charges Albers's account. Albers then demands that the bank recredit his account. The bank can recover against the grocer only if the grocer knew that Albers's signature had been forged. Otherwise, the bank must look for Bates. The bank had the responsibility to recognize the true signature of its drawer, Albers, and not to pay the check that contained an unauthorized signature. The bank may be able to resist recrediting Albers's account if it can show he was negligent. The next section of this chapter discusses negligence.

Other Liability Rules

LO7

Normally, a bank may not charge against (debit from) the drawer's account a check that has a forged payee's indorsement. Similarly, a maker does not have to pay a note to the person who currently possesses the note if the payee's signature has been forged. If a check or note has been altered—for example, by raising the amount—the drawer or maker usually is liable for the instrument only in the amount for which he originally issued it. However, there are a number of exceptions to these usual rules. These exceptions, as well as liability based on conversion of an instrument, are discussed below.

Negligence

A person can be so negligent in writing or signing a negotiable instrument that he in effect invites an alteration or an unauthorized signature on it. If a person has been negligent, Article 3 precludes her from using the alteration or lack of authorization as a reason for not paying a person who in good faith pays the instrument or takes it for value (3–406). For example, Mary Maker makes out a note for $10 in such a way that someone could alter it to read $10,000. Someone alters the note and negotiates it to Katherine Smith, who can qualify as a holder in due course. Smith can collect $10,000 from Maker. Maker's negligence precludes her from claiming alteration as a defense to paying it. Maker then has to find the person who "raised" her note and try to collect the $9,990 from him.

Where the person asserting the preclusion failed to exercise ordinary care in taking or paying the instrument and that failure substantially contributed to the loss, Article 3 allocates the loss between the two parties based on their comparative negligence (3–406[b]). Thus, if a drawer was so negligent in drafting a check that he made it possible for the check to be altered and the bank that paid the check, in the exercise of ordinary care, should have noticed the alteration, then any loss occasioned by the fact that the person who made the alteration could not be found would be split between the drawer and the bank based on their comparative fault.

Impostor Rule

Article 3 establishes special rules for negotiable instruments made payable to impostors and fictitious persons. An impostor is a person who poses as someone else and convinces a drawer to make a check payable to the person being impersonated—or to an organization the person purports to be authorized to represent. When this happens, the Code makes any indorsement "substantially similar" to that of the named payee effective (3–404[a]). Where the impostor has impersonated a person authorized to act for a payee, such as claiming to be Jack Jones, the president of Jones Enterprises, the impostor has the power to negotiate a check to Jones Enterprises.

An example of a situation involving the impostor rule would be the following: Arthur steals Paulsen's automobile and finds the certificate of title in the automobile. Then, representing himself as Paulsen, he sells the automobile to Berger Used Car Company. The car dealership draws its check payable to Paulsen for the agreed purchase price of the automobile and delivers the check to Arthur. Any person can negotiate the check by indorsing it in the name of Paulsen.

The rationale for the impostor rule is to put the responsibility for determining the true identity of the payee on the drawer or maker of a negotiable instrument. The drawer is in a better position to do this than is some later holder of the check who may be entirely innocent. The impostor rule allows that later holder to have good title to the check by making the payee's signature valid although it is not the signature of the person with whom the drawer or maker thought he was dealing. It forces the drawer or maker to find the wrongdoer who tricked him into signing the negotiable instrument or to bear the loss himself.

Fictitious Payee Rule

A fictitious payee commonly arises in the following situation: A dishonest employee draws a check payable to someone who does not exist—or to a real person who does business with the employer but to whom the dishonest employee does not intend to send the check. If the employee has the authority to do so, he may sign the check himself. If he does not have such authority, he gives the check to his employer for signature and represents that the employer owes money to the person named as the payee of the check. The dishonest employee then takes the check, indorses it in the name of the payee, presents it for payment, and pockets the money. The employee may be in a position to cover up the wrongdoing by intercepting the canceled checks or juggling the company's books.

The Code allows any indorsement in the name of the fictitious payee to be effective as the payee's indorsement in favor of any person that pays the instrument in good faith or takes it for value or for collection (3–404[b] and [c]). For example, Anderson, an accountant in charge of accounts payable at Moore Corporation, prepares a false invoice naming Parks, Inc., a supplier of Moore Corporation, as having supplied Moore Corporation with goods, and draws a check payable to Parks, Inc., for the amount of the invoice. Anderson then presents the check to Temple, treasurer of Moore Corporation, together with other checks with invoices attached. Temple signs all of these checks and returns them to Anderson for mailing. Anderson then withdraws the check payable to Parks, Inc. Anyone, including Anderson, can negotiate the check by indorsing it in the name of Parks, Inc.

The rationale for the fictitious payee rule is similar to that for the impostor rule. If someone has a dishonest employee or agent who is responsible for the forgery of some checks, the employer of the wrongdoer should bear the immediate loss of those checks rather than some other innocent party. In turn, the employer must locate the unfaithful employee or agent and try to recover from him.

Comparative Negligence Rule Regarding Impostors and Fictitious Payees

Revised Article 3 also establishes a comparative negligence rule if (1) the person, in a situation covered by the impostor or fictitious payee rule, pays the instrument or takes it for value or collection without exercising ordinary care in paying or taking the instrument and (2) that failure substantially contributes to the loss resulting from payment of the instrument. In these instances, the person bearing the loss may recover an allocable share of the loss from the person who did not exercise ordinary care (3–404[d]).

In the case that follows, *Victory Clothing Co., Inc. v. Wachovia Bank, N.A.,* the court applied comparative negligence principles to split the loss between a company whose employee forged checks and a depositary bank which allowed the forger to deposit the checks to her own personal account in violation of its own rules. As you read the case and note the reasons the court gave for assigning 30 percent of the risk to the employer, you might ask yourself whether the answer would be different today when many banks no longer return copies of canceled checks—or even photocopies of them—regularly to the customer. You might also ask what steps you would take to prevent something like this—an employee forging checks on the company's account without your being aware—from happening.

Victory Clothing Co., Inc. v. Wachovia Bank, N.A.

59 UCC Rep.2d 376 (Ct. Common Pleas Penn. 2006)

FACTS

Victory Clothing Company maintained a corporate checking account at Hudson Bank. Jeannette Lunny was employed by Victory as its office manager and bookkeeper for approximately 24 years until she resigned in May 2003. From August 2001 through May 2003, Lunny deposited approximately two hundred (200) checks drawn on Victory's corporate account totaling $188,273 into her personal checking account at Wachovia Bank.

Lunny's scheme involved double forgeries. She prepared checks in the company's computer system and made them payable to known vendors of Victory (e.g., Adidas) to whom no money was actually owed. The checks were for dollar amounts that were consistent with the legitimate checks to those vendors. She would then forge the signature of Victory's owner, Mark Rosenfeld, as drawer on the front of the check, and then forge the indorsement of the intended payee (Victory's various vendors) on the reverse of the check. After forging the indorsement of the payee, Lunny either indorsed the check with her name followed by her account number, or referenced her account number following the forged indorsement. She then deposited the checks into her personal account at Wachovia Bank.

At the time of the fraud by Lunny, Wachovia's policies and regulations regarding the acceptance of checks for deposit provided that "checks payable to a non-personal payee can be deposited ONLY into a non-personal account with the same name."

Rosenfeld reviewed the bank statements from Hudson Bank on a monthly basis. However, among other observable irregularities, he failed to detect that Lunny had forged his signature on approximately 200 checks. Nor did he have a procedure to match checks to invoices.

Victory brought suit against Wachovia pursuant to the Pennsylvania Commercial Code claiming that Wachovia should be liable to it for the entire amount of the losses it sustained by virtue of Lunny's forgery scheme. Victory contended that Wachovia had failed to exercise ordinary care in taking the instruments that were payable to various businesses and allowing them to be deposited into Lunny's personal accounts. They asserted that this was commercially unreasonable, contrary to Wachovia's own internal rules and regulations, and exhibited a lack of ordinary care, substantially contributing to the loss resulting from the fraud. Under Section 3–405 of the Code, in such circumstances, the person bearing the loss can recover from the person failing to exercise ordinary care to the extent the failure to exercise ordinary care contributed to the loss.

Wachovia, in turn, argued that because Lunny made the fraudulent checks payable to actual vendors of Victory with the intention that the vendors not get paid, Victory's action against it should be barred by the fictitious payee rule set out in Section 3–404. Because Section 3–404 contains a comparative negligence provision, the court also needed to decide whether it should be applied in this case.

ISSUE

Should comparative negligence principles be applied to determine the relative liability of the employer of a dishonest employee/embezzler and a bank which took the forged checks for deposit to the account of the forger?

DECISION

Yes. The court held that comparative negligence principles should be applied in this case to establish the relative liability of the employer and the depositary bank. Although the case involves a "double" forgery because both the drawer's and the payee's signatures were forged, the court treated it as essentially a "fictitious payee" case. Normally, in this situation the depositary bank is protected because any signature in the name of the named payee on a fictitious payee check is deemed to be an effective signature for purposes of making the person in possession of it a "holder." However, as set out in Section 3–404, the fictitious payee rule contains a comparative negligence provision. It provides that if the person taking the instrument fails to exercise ordinary care, the person bearing the loss may recover from the person failing to exercise ordinary care to the extent the failure to exercise ordinary care contributed to the loss.

The court found that in this instance Wachovia Bank was 70 percent liable for Victory's loss because it violated its own rules in repeatedly depositing corporate checks into the employee/embezzler's personal account. It found that Victory was 30 percent liable because it was negligent in its supervision of the employee and for not discovering the fraud for almost two years. Although Rosenfeld, Victory's owner, received copies of the canceled checks on a monthly basis from the drawee, Hudson Bank, he was negligent in neither recognizing his own forged signature on the front of the checks nor spotting his bookkeeper's name and/or account number on the back of the check.

Fraudulent Indorsements by Employees

Revised Article 3 specifically addresses employer responsibility for fraudulent indorsements by employees and adopts the principle that the risk of loss for such indorsements by employees who are entrusted with responsibilities for instruments (primarily checks) should fall on the employer rather than on the bank that takes the check or pays it (3–405). As to any person who in good faith pays an instrument or takes it for value, a fraudulent indorsement by a responsible employee is effective as the indorsement of the payee if it is made in the name of the payee or in a substantially similar name (3–405[b]). If the person taking or paying the instrument failed to exercise ordinary care and that failure substantially contributed to loss resulting from the fraud, the comparative negligence doctrine guides the allocation of the loss.

A fraudulent indorsement includes a forged indorsement purporting to be that of the employer on an instrument payable to the employer; it also includes a forged indorsement purporting to be that of the payee of an instrument on which the employer is drawer or maker (3–405[a][2]). "Responsibility" with respect to instruments means the authority (1) to sign or indorse instruments on behalf of the employer, (2) to process instruments received by the employer, (3) to prepare or process instruments for issue in the name of the employer, (4) to control the disposition of instruments to be issued in the name of the employer, or (5) to otherwise act with respect to instruments in a responsible capacity. "Responsibility" does not cover those who simply have access to instruments as they are stored, transported, or that are in incoming or outgoing mail (3–405[a][3]).

Conversion

Conversion of an instrument is an unauthorized assumption and exercise of ownership over it. A negotiable instrument can be converted in a number of ways. For example, it might be presented for payment or acceptance, and the person to whom it is presented might refuse to pay or accept and refuse to return it. An instrument also is converted if a person pays an instrument to a person not entitled to payment, for example, if it contains a forged indorsement.

Revised Article 3 modifies and expands the previous treatment of conversion and provides that the law applicable to conversion of personal property applies to instruments. It also specifically provides that conversion occurs if (1) an instrument lacks an indorsement necessary for negotiation and (2) it is (*a*) purchased, (*b*) taken for collection, or (*c*) paid by a drawee to a person not entitled to payment. An action for conversion may be brought by (1) the maker, drawer, or acceptor of the instrument or (2) a payee or an indorsee who did not receive delivery of the instrument either directly or through delivery to an agent or copayee (3–420).

Thus, if a bank pays a check that contains a forged indorsement, the bank has converted the check by wrongfully paying it. The bank then becomes liable for the face amount of the check to the person whose indorsement was forged (3–420). For example, Arthur Able draws a check for $50 on his account at First Bank, payable to the order of Bernard Barker. Carol Collins steals the check, forges Barker's indorsement on it, and cashes it at First Bank. First Bank has converted Barker's property because it had no right to pay the check without Barker's valid indorsement. First Bank must pay Barker $50, and then it can try to locate Collins to get the $50 back from her. In the case that follows, *Jones v. Wells Fargo* Bank, N.A., a bank, was held liable for conversion for paying an instrument to an entity not entitled to enforce it.

Jones v. Wells Fargo Bank, N.A.

76 UCC Rep.2d 529 (5th Cir. 2012)

FACTS

In September 2006, Adley Abdulwahab ("Wahab") opened a business cash management account on behalf of W Financial Group, L.L.C. with Wells Fargo Bank, N.A. Wahab, along with Michael K. Wallens and Michael K. Wallens, Jr., was an authorized signer on the account.

On January 29, 2007, Wahab withdrew $1,701,250 from W Financial's account at Wells Fargo Post Oak Branch in Houston. Wahab used the funds to buy a cashier's check payable to Lubna Lateef, Misba Lateef, Shahed Lateef, and Zahed Lateef (the "Lateefs"). Later that same day, Wahab returned to a different Wells Fargo Branch in Spring, Texas. Wahab deposited the check into the Wells Fargo account of a separate entity, CA Houston Investment Center, L.L.C. Wahab was CA Houston's managing member and the only authorized signer on its account. The Lateefs never received or indorsed the cashier's check. Rather, Wells Fargo stamped the following on the back of the check: "CREDITED TO THE ACCOUNT OF WITHIN NAMED PAYEE LACK OF ENDORSEMENT GUARANTEED WELLS FARGO BANK, N.A." The account number for CA Houston was handwritten below the stamp.

In March 2008, the Securities and Exchange Commission ("SEC") brought an enforcement action against W Financial, alleging that it had engaged in the fraudulent sale of securities. The United States District Court for the Northern District of Texas, where that action was filed, entered an order appointing Vernon T. Jones as receiver for W Financial for the purpose of recovering the company's assets for the benefit of its investors. Pursuant to his responsibilities as receiver, Jones filed an action against Wells Fargo, asserting conversion and breach of contract based on the January 29, 2007, transaction.

ISSUE

Is Wells Fargo liable for conversion for making payment on the cashier's check to a person not entitled to enforce the instrument or receive payment?

DECISION

Yes. Under the UCC, a bank may be liable for conversion of a cashier's check if it makes or obtains payment with respect to the instrument for a person not entitled to enforce the instrument or receive payment. Wells Fargo paid the check to CA Houston by depositing the money into CA Houston's account. But CA Houston was not a party entitled to enforce the instrument: (1) It was not the holder of the instrument; (2) it was not a nonholder in possession with the rights of a holder; and (3) it was not a person not in possession of the instrument who is entitled to enforce it. In this instance, there never was a transfer of rights in the instrument from W Financial to CA Houston, so the payment to it by Wells Fargo constituted a conversion.

In addition, Wells Fargo is liable for conversion because it deposited the check into CA Houston's account without the necessary indorsement. Wells Fargo accepted and processed the check even though it had not been indorsed by the Lateefs. The UCC places the burden on the first bank in the collection chain to ensure an indorsement's authenticity, and the bank's payment of an instrument on a missing indorsement constitutes a conversion.

Discharge of Negotiable Instruments

Discharge of Liability

LO8

The obligation of a party to pay an instrument is discharged (1) if he meets the requirements set out in Revised Article 3 or (2) by any act or agreement that would discharge an obligation to pay money on a simple contract. Discharge of an obligation is not effective against a person who has the rights of a holder in due course of the instrument and took the instrument without notice of the discharge (3–601).

The most common ways that an obligor on an instrument is discharged from her liability are

1. Payment of the instrument.
2. Cancellation of the instrument.
3. Alteration of the instrument.

4. Modification of the principal's obligation that causes loss to a surety or impairs the collateral.
5. Unexcused delay in presentment or notice of dishonor with respect to a check (discussed earlier in this chapter).
6. Acceptance of a draft but varying the terms from the draft as presented (this entitled the holder to treat the draft as dishonored and the drawee, in turn, to cancel the acceptance) (3–410).

In addition, as noted earlier in the chapter, a drawer is discharged of liability of a draft that is accepted by a bank (e.g., if a check is certified by a bank) because at that point the holder is looking to the bank to make the instrument good.

Discharge by Payment

Generally, payment in full discharges liability on an instrument to the extent payable by or on behalf of a party obligated to pay the instrument to a person entitled to enforce the instrument. To the extent of payment, the obligation of a party to pay the instrument is discharged even though payment is made with knowledge of a claim to the instrument by some other person. However, the obligation is not discharged if (1) there is a claim enforceable against the person making payment and payment is made with knowledge of the fact that payment is prohibited by an injunction or similar legal process or (2) in the case of an instrument other than a cashier's, certified, or teller's check, the person making the payment had accepted from the person making the claim indemnity against loss for refusing to make payment to the person entitled to enforce payment. It also is not discharged if he knows that the instrument is a stolen instrument and pays someone who he knows is in wrongful possession of the instrument (3–602).

Also, if the holder has indorsed a negotiable instrument restrictively indorsed, the person who pays must comply with the restrictive indorsement to be discharged (3–603[1][b]). For example, Arthur makes a note of $1,000 payable to the order of Bryan. Bryan indorses the note "Pay to the order of my account no. 16154 at First Bank, Bryan." Bryan then gives the note to his employee, Clark, to take to the bank. Clark takes the note to Arthur, who pays Clark the $1,000. Clark then runs off with the money. Arthur is not discharged of his primary liability on the note because he did not make his payment consistent with the restrictive indorsement. To be discharged, Arthur has to pay the $1,000 into Bryan's account at First Bank.

Discharge by Cancellation

A person entitled to enforce a negotiable instrument may discharge the liability of the parties to the instrument by canceling or renouncing it. If the holder mutilates or destroys a negotiable instrument with the intent that it no longer evidences an obligation to pay money, the holder has canceled the obligation (3–604). For example, a grandfather lends $5,000 to his grandson for college expenses. The grandson gives his grandfather a promissory note for $5,000. If the grandfather later tears up the note with the intent that the grandson no longer owes him $5,000, the grandfather has canceled the note.

An accidental destruction or mutilation of a negotiable instrument is not a cancellation and does not discharge the parties to it. If an instrument is lost, mutilated accidentally, or destroyed, the person entitled to enforce it still can enforce the instrument. In such a case, the person must prove that the instrument existed and that she was its holder when it was lost, mutilated, or destroyed.

Altered Instruments; Discharge by Alteration

A person paying a fraudulently altered instrument or taking it for value, in good faith and without notice of the alteration, may enforce the instrument (1) according to its original terms or (2) in the case of an incomplete instrument later completed in an unauthorized manner, according to its terms as completed (3–407[c]). An alteration occurs if there is (1) an unauthorized change that modifies the obligation of a party to the instrument or (2) an unauthorized addition of words or numbers or other change to an incomplete instrument that changes the obligation of any party (3–407[a]). A change that does not affect the obligation of one of the parties, such as dotting an *i* or correcting the grammar, is not considered to be an alteration.

Two examples illustrate the situations in which Revised Article 3 allows fraudulently altered instruments to be enforced. First, assume the amount due on a note is fraudulently raised from $10 to $10,000; the contract of the maker has been changed. The maker promised to pay $10, but after the change has been made, he would be promising to pay much more. If the note is negotiated to a person who can qualify as a holder in due course who was without notice of the alteration, that person can enforce the note against the maker.

Second, assume Swanson draws a check payable to Frank's Nursery, leaving the amount blank. He gives it to his gardener with instructions to purchase some fertilizer at Frank's and to fill in the purchase price of the fertilizer when it is known. The gardener fills in the check for $100 and gives it to Frank's in exchange for the fertilizer ($7.25) and the difference in cash ($92.75). The gardener then leaves town with the cash. If Frank's had no knowledge of the unauthorized completion, it could enforce the check for $100 against Swanson.

In any other case, a fraudulent alteration **discharges** any party whose obligation is affected by the alteration *unless* the party (1) assents or (2) is precluded from asserting the alteration (e.g., because of the party's contributory negligence). Assume that Anderson signs a promissory note for $100 payable to Bond. Bond indorses the note "Pay to the order of Connolly, Bond" and negotiates it to Connolly. Connolly changes the $100 to read $100,000. Connolly's unauthorized change is fraudulent. As a result, Anderson is discharged from her primary liability as maker of the note and Bond is discharged from her secondary liability as indorser. Neither of them has to pay Connolly. The obligations of both Anderson and Bond were changed because the amount for which they are liable was altered.

No other alteration—that is, one that is not fraudulent—discharges any party, and a holder may enforce the instrument according to its *original* terms (3–407[b]). Thus, there would be no discharge if a blank is filled in in the honest belief that it is authorized or if a change is made, without any fraudulent intent, to give the maker on a note the benefit of a lower interest rate.

Discharge of Indorsers and Accommodation Parties

If a person entitled to enforce an instrument agrees, with or without consideration, to a material modification of the obligation of a party to the instrument, including an extension of the due date, then any accommodation party or indorser who has a right of recourse against the person whose obligation is modified is discharged *to the extent the modification causes a loss to the indorser or accommodation party.* Similarly, if collateral secures the obligation of a party to an instrument and a person entitled to enforce the instrument impairs the value of the collateral, the obligation of the indorser or accommodation party having the right of recourse against the obligor is discharged to the extent of the impairment. These discharges are not effective unless the person agreeing to the modification or causing the impairment knows of the accommodation or has notice of it. Also, no discharge occurs if the obligor assented to the event or conduct, or if the obligor has waived the discharge (3–605).

For example, Frank goes to credit union to borrow $4,000 to purchase a used automobile. The credit union has Frank sign a promissory note and takes a security interest in the automobile (i.e., takes it as collateral for the loan). It also asks Frank's brother Bob to sign the note as an accommodation maker. Subsequently, Frank tells the credit union he wants to sell the automobile and it releases its security interest. Because release of the collateral adversely affects Bob's obligation as accommodation maker, he is discharged from his obligation as accommodation maker in the amount of the value of the automobile.

Questions and Problem Cases

1. Terance Fitzgerald drew a check for $4,000 payable to New Look Auto Trim and Upholstery and delivered it to Yuvonne Goss and Benii Arrazza, the owners of New Look. Goss and Arrazza each indorsed the check in blank and deposited it in Goss's personal account at the Cincinnati Central Credit Union. When the credit union presented the check to Fitzgerald's bank, the check was dishonored for insufficient funds. The credit union then demanded that Goss and Arrazza honor the check. Are Goss and Arrazza obligated to make the check good to the credit union?
2. Formica Construction Company was the general contractor in the renovation of a restaurant owned by Mossi Inn, Inc. Mossi is a closely held corporation whose sole officers and shareholders are the parents of Daniel Mills. Mills is an employee of Mossi, manages the restaurant, and served as the authorized agent of the company in dealing with Formica Construction. At the time the construction load for the renovation was being converted into a mortgage on the property, the loan proceeds were insufficient to cover $37,000 Formica was owed for extras on the project. Mills signed a negotiable promissory note payable to the order of Formica in which he promised to pay the $37,000, but did not indicate he was signing in a representative capacity on behalf of Mossi. When a portion of the note remained unpaid, Formica brought suit against Mills seeking payment of the balance. Mills claimed that he was only an employee of Mossi and had signed only as a representative. On these facts, is Mills personally liable for payment of the note?
3. Maryellen Peterson was a part-time employee of Textiles Specialties & Chemicals doing business as CS Industries. Peterson signed a check in the amount of $13,789.80 on the account of CS Industries and payable to Holtrachem, Inc. The check was imprinted with name of CS Industries. However, Peterson signed only her name and did not indicate she was signing in her representative capacity on behalf of CS Industries. The drawee bank returned the check to Holtrachem due to insufficient funds in CS Industries' account. Holtrachem filed suit against Peterson, seeking to hold her liable in her personal capacity as the drawer of the check. Is an individual who signs a check drawn on a corporate account without indicating she is signing in representative capacity personally liable on the instrument?
4. In November 2005, Michele Fehl, an administrative assistant recently hired by AFT Trucking, stole eight company checks from the company's offices. She made out the checks to herself in various amounts. Fehl was not authorized to sign checks on behalf of the company. Over the next three weeks, Fehl presented the checks at Money Stop, a check cashing service, which gave her cash for the checks. Subsequently, the checks were dishonored by AFT Trucking. They fired Fehl, who was arrested and criminally prosecuted. Money Shop brought suit against AFT Trucking to recover the funds it

had disbursed. AFT Trucking asserted that Money Store's only recourse was against Fehl, the person who had signed the checks. Is Money Store entitled to recover from AFT Trucking?

5. A check was drawn on First National Bank and made payable to Howard. It came into the possession of Carson, who forged Howard's indorsement and cashed it at Merchant's Bank. Merchant's Bank then indorsed it and collected payment from First National. Assuming that Carson is nowhere to be found, who bears the loss caused by Carson's forgery?
6. Mrs. Gordon Neely hired Louise Bradshaw as the bookkeeper for a Midas Muffler shop they owned and operated as a corporation, J. Gordon Neely Enterprises, Inc. (Neely). Bradshaw's duties included preparing company checks for Mrs. Neely's signature and reconciling the checking account when the company received a bank statement and canceled checks each month. Bradshaw prepared several checks payable to herself and containing a large space to the left of the amount written on the designated line. When Mrs. Neely signed the checks, she was aware of the large gaps. Subsequently, Bradshaw altered the checks by adding a digit or two to the left of the original amount and then cashed them at American National Bank, the drawee bank. Several months later, Neely's hired a new accountant, who discovered the altered checks. Neely brought suit against American National Bank to have its account recredited for the altered checks, claiming American was liable for paying out on altered instruments. The bank contended that Neely's negligence substantially contributed to alterations of the instruments and thus Neely was precluded from asserting the alteration against the bank. Between Neely and American National Bank, who should bear the loss caused by Bradshaw's fraud?
7. Clarice Rich was employed by the New York City Board of Education as a clerk. It was her duty to prepare requisitions for checks to be issued by the board, to prepare the checks, to have them signed by authorized personnel, and to send the checks to the recipients. In some instances, however, she retained them. Also, on a number of occasions she prepared duplicate requisitions and checks, which, when signed, she likewise retained. She then forged the indorsement of the named payees on the checks she had retained and cashed the checks at Chemical Bank, where the Board of Education maintained its account. After the board discovered the forgeries, it demanded that Chemical Bank credit its account for the amount of the forged checks. Is Chemical Bank required to credit the board's account as requested?
8. Stockton's housekeeper stole some of his checks, forged his name as drawer, and cashed them at Gristedes Supermarket, where Stockton maintained check-cashing privileges. The checks were presented to Stockton's bank and honored by it. Over the course of 18 months, the scheme netted the housekeeper in excess of $147,000 on approximately 285 forged checks. Stockton brought suit against Gristedes Supermarket for conversion, seeking to recover the value of the checks it had accepted and for which it had obtained payment from the drawee bank. Was Gristedes Supermarket liable to Stockton for conversion for accepting and obtaining payment of the stolen and forged checks?

Chapter 41

Checks and Electronic Fund Transfers

Learning Objectives

After you have studied this chapter, you should be able to:

1. Recall that the basic duty of a bank is to pay any properly drawn and payable check if there are sufficient funds in the customer's account.
2. Discuss the rules pertaining to postdated checks.
3. Explain what is meant by a stop payment order and discuss the bank's duties and potential liabilities when it is given such an order.
4. Distinguish *certified checks* from *cashier's checks.*
5. Discuss the bank's obligations to its customer when it is presented with forged or altered checks.
6. Explain the customer's duty to report forgeries and alterations and the consequences for the customer if he does not do so in a timely manner.
7. Discuss the implications of Check 21 from the perspective of the customer of a bank.
8. Discuss the major features of the Electronic Funds Transfer Act as they relate to the rights, liabilities, and responsibilities of participants in electronic fund transfer systems.

Susan Williams opened a checking account at the First National Bank. She made an initial deposit of $1,800, signed a signature card that indicated to the bank that she was the authorized signator on the account, and was given a supply of blank checks. She also received an ATM/debit card that, when used along with an assigned PIN (personal identification number), allowed her to make deposits to her account, take cash from it, and make purchases from merchants, with the

(continued)

funds transferred electronically from her account to the merchant's. Each month the bank sent her a statement reflecting the activity in the account during the previous month along with the canceled checks. Several months after she opened the account, the bank erroneously refused to pay a check she had written to a clothing store even though she had sufficient funds in her account. As a result, the store filed a complaint with the local prosecutor indicating she had written a "bad check." On one occasion, Susan called the bank to stop payment on a check she had written to cover repairs to her automobile because while driving the car home, she discovered the requested repair had not been made. However, the bank paid the check later that day despite the stop-payment order she had given the bank. Another time, Susan's wallet fell out of her purse while she was shopping at a mall. She received a call the next morning indicating the wallet had been found and she retrieved it at that time. However, when she received her next monthly statement from the bank, she discovered that someone had apparently used her ATM card to withdraw $200 from her account on the day her wallet had been lost. Susan's experience raises a number of legal issues that will be covered in this chapter:

- What rights does Susan have against the bank for refusing to pay the check to the clothing store despite the fact she had sufficient funds on deposit to cover it?
- What rights does Susan have against the bank for failing to honor the stop-payment order she placed on the check she had written to the repair stop?
- What rights does Susan have against the bank because of the unauthorized use of her ATM card? What must she do to preserve those rights?

The Drawer–Drawee Relationship

There are two sources that govern the relationship between the depositor and the drawee bank: the deposit agreement and Articles 3 and 4 of the Code. Article 4, which governs Bank Deposits and Collections, allows the depositor and drawee bank (which Article 4 calls the "payor bank") to vary Article 4's provisions with a few important exceptions. The deposit agreement cannot disclaim the bank's responsibility for its own lack of good faith or failure to exercise ordinary care or limit the measure of damages for the lack or failure; however, the parties may determine by agreement the standards by which to measure the bank's responsibility so long as the standards are not manifestly unreasonable (4–103).[1]

The deposit agreement establishes many important relationships between the depositor and drawee/payor bank. The first of these is their relationship as creditor and debtor, respectively, so that when a person deposits money in an account at the bank, the bank no longer considers him the owner of the money. Instead, he is a creditor of the bank to the extent of his deposits and the bank becomes his debtor. Also, when the depositor deposits a check to a checking account, the bank becomes his agent for collection of the check. The bank as the person's agent owes a duty to him to follow his reasonable instructions

[1] The numbers in parentheses refer to sections of the Uniform Commercial Code.

concerning payment of checks and other items from his account and a duty of ordinary care in collecting checks and other items deposited to the account.

Bank's Duty to Pay

LO1

When a bank receives a properly drawn and payable check on a person's account and there are sufficient funds to cover the check, the bank is under a duty to pay it. If the person has sufficient funds in the account and the bank refuses to pay, or dishonors, the check, the bank is liable for the actual damages proximately caused by its wrongful dishonor as well as consequential damages (4–402). Actual damages may include charges imposed by retailers for returned checks, as well as damages for arrest or prosecution to the customer. Consequential damages include injury to the depositor's credit rating that results from the dishonor.

For example, Donald Dodson writes a check for $3,500 to Ames Auto Sales in payment for a used car. At the time that Ames Auto presents the check for payment at Dodson's bank, First National Bank, Dodson has $3,800 in his account. However, a teller mistakenly refuses to pay the check and stamps it NSF (not sufficient funds). Ames Auto then goes to the local prosecutor and signs a complaint against Dodson for writing a bad check. As a result, Dodson is arrested. Dodson can recover from First National the damages that he sustained because the bank wrongfully dishonored his check, including the damages involved in his arrest, such as his attorney's fees.

Bank's Right to Charge to Customer's Account

The drawee bank has the right to charge any properly payable check to the account of the customer, or drawer. The bank has this right even though payment of the check creates an overdraft in the account (4–401). If an account is overdrawn, the customer owes the bank the amount of the overdraft and the bank may take that amount out of the next deposit that the customer makes or from another account that the depositor maintains with the bank. Alternatively, the bank might seek to collect the amount directly from the customer. If there is more than one customer who can draw from an account, only that customer—or those customers—who sign the item or who benefit from the proceeds of an overdraft are liable for the overdraft.

Stale Checks

The bank does not owe a duty to its customer to pay any checks out of the account that are more than six months old. Such checks are called *stale checks.* However, the bank acting in good faith may pay a check that is more than six months old and charge it to the drawer-depositor's account (4–404).

Altered and Incomplete Items

If the bank in good faith pays a check drawn by the drawer-depositor that was subsequently altered, it may charge the customer's account with the amount of the check as originally drawn. Also, if an incomplete check of a customer gets into circulation, is completed, and is presented to the drawee bank for payment, and the bank pays the check, the bank can charge the amount as completed to the customer's account even though it knows that the check has been completed, unless it has notice that the completion was improper (4–401[d]). The respective rights, obligations, and liabilities of drawee banks and their drawer-customers concerning forged and altered checks are discussed in more detail later in this chapter.

Limitations on Bank's Right or Duty

Article 4 recognizes that the bank's right or duty to pay a check or to charge the depositor's account for the check (including exercising its right to set off an amount due to it by the depositor) may be terminated, suspended, or modified by the depositor's order to stop payment (which is discussed in the next section of this chapter). In addition, it may be stopped by events external to the relationship between the depositor and the bank. These external events include the filing of a bankruptcy petition by the depositor or by the depositor's creditors and the garnishment of the account by a creditor of the depositor. The bank must receive the stop-payment order from its depositor or the notice of the bankruptcy filing or garnishment before the bank has certified the check, paid it in cash, settled with another bank for the amount of the item without a right to revoke the settlement, completed the process necessary to its decision to pay the check, or otherwise become accountable for the amount of the check under Article 4 (4–403). These restrictions on the bank's right or duty to pay are discussed in later sections of this chapter.

Postdated Checks

LO2

Under original Articles 3 and 4, a postdated check was not properly payable by the drawee bank until the date on the check. The recent amendments to Article 4 change this. Under the revision, an otherwise properly payable postdated check that is presented for payment before the date on the check may be paid and charged to the customer's account *unless* the customer has given notice of it to the bank. The customer must give notice of the postdating in a way that described the check with reasonable certainty. It is effective for the same time periods as Article 4 provides for stop-payment orders (discussed below). The customer must give notice to the bank at such time and in such manner as to give the bank an opportunity to act upon it before the bank takes any action with respect to paying the check. If the bank charges the customer's account for a postdated check before the date stated in the notice given to the bank, the bank is liable for damages for any loss that results. Such damages might include those associated with the dishonor of subsequent items (3–113[a]; 4–401[c]).

There are a variety of reasons why a person might want to postdate a check. For example, a person might have a mortgage payment due on the first of the month at a bank located in another state. To make sure that the check arrives on time, the customer may send the payment by mail several days before the due date. However, if the person is depending on a deposit of her next monthly paycheck on the first of the month to cover the mortgage payment, she might postdate the check to the first of the following month. Under the original version of Articles 3 and 4, the bank could not properly pay the check until the first of the month. However, under the revisions it could be properly paid by the bank before that date if presented earlier. To avoid the risk that the bank would dishonor the check for insufficient funds if presented before the first, the customer should notify the drawee bank in a manner similar to that required for stop payment of checks.

Checks Not Properly Payable

While a bank has a duty to pay any check that is properly payable and to charge the customer's account, it may not do so if the check is not properly payable. In the case that follows, *Lor-Mar/Toto, Inc. v. 1st Constitution Bank,* the court held that five counterfeit checks were not properly payable and the bank had no right to charge them to the drawer's account.

Lor-Mar/Toto, Inc. v. 1st Constitution Bank

871 A.2d 871 (Super. Ct., App. Div. N.J. 2005)

FACTS

Lor-Mar/Toto, Inc., maintained a business checking account at the 1st Constitution Bank. The corporate banking resolution between Lor-Mar and the bank provided that checks drawn on the checking account could be honored upon one authorized signature of the four named officers stated in the resolution, including Loretta A. Van Middlesworth and Louis J. Toto, Jr., its president and vice president, respectively. On May 28, 1997, Lor-Mar notified the bank that the signatures of Van Middlesworth and Toto would be "stamped" on Lor-Mar's checks and provided the bank with samples of their stamped facsimile signatures. Thus, from May 1997 forward, the bank was authorized by Lor-Mar to honor checks bearing a stamped facsimile of either Van Middlesworth or Toto.

Beginning in June 2002 a series of five allegedly unauthorized checks totaling $24,350.00 were drawn against the Lor-Mar account. All five checks bore what appeared to be the stamped facsimile signature of Van Middlesworth as provided to the bank on May 28, 1997, and another signature which was illegible. However, the unauthorized checks were a different stock and color than Lor-Mar's regular checks, which were light yellow in color and the type routinely purchased from banks. On the front, under the preprinted check number they contained a numerical bank designation of "55-715/21201." The back of the authentic checks contained a repetitive pattern and the words "ORIGINAL DOCUMENT" with a security message stating: "IMPORTANT: The back of this document has been printed with a patented security process in order to deter check fraud. If you do not clearly see the words 'Original Document' and the Security Weave pattern, or the word VOID appears to the right of this message, do not cash." Sample checks provided by the company contained the facsimile signature of Toto and the actual signature of another corporate signatory, Maureen E. Zaleck.

In comparison, the challenged checks were computer-generated and laser printed on light blue paper and contained no bank designation number under the preprinted check number. Their purported security features were different from the legitimate checks; they contained the words "ORIGINAL DOCUMENT" in large letters once on the back with a boxed designation:

> THIS DOCUMENT INCLUDES THE FOLLOWING VALUGUARD SECURITY FEATURES; EXCEEDING FSA GUIDELINES:
>
> - INVISIBLE FLUORESCENT FIBERS
> - TWO SOLVENT STAINS
> - BROWNSTAIN
> - UV DULL
>
> ATTEMPTS TO COPY OR CHEMICALLY ALTER THIS DOCUMENT WILL ACTIVATE VALUGUARD SECURITY FEATURES.

Significantly, the unauthorized checks contained repeated duplicate numbers from legitimate checks that had already been issued by Lor-Mar. The five checks were debited to Lor-Mar's account from June 24 to July 1, 2002, and appeared on Lor-Mar's statements covering the periods May 31, 2002, through June 28, 2002, and June 28, 2002, through July 31, 2002. Upon receiving the statements Lor-Mar discovered and reported the unauthorized checks to the bank in July 2002. For each of the five checks, Toto executed an "Affidavit for Forged or Lost Check/Money Order" to the bank attesting that he never signed his name on the check or authorized any person to indorse his name, that the indorsement of his name that appears on the check is a forgery, and that he never received any of the funds the check represented.

Lor-Mar brought suit seeking to have its account recredited for the amount of the unauthorized checks.

ISSUE

Is Lor-Mar entitled to have its account recredited for the amount of the unauthorized checks on the grounds the checks were not properly payable from the account?

DECISION

Yes. The court held that when Lor-Mar reported the unauthorized counterfeit checks to the bank in a timely fashion, the bank was liable for improperly charging Lor-Mar's account. The checks were not properly payable within the meaning of the UCC where there was no evidence of negligence on the part of Lor-Mar that contributed to the forgeries. A check is "properly payable" only if it is authorized by the customer and in accordance with the agreement between the bank and its customer. Here, the court concluded that the signature on the bogus check had not been authorized and there was not a clear agreement to shift the loss of any check containing a facsimile signature to the customer, regardless of whether it had been authorized.

FIGURE 41.1 **Stop-Payment Order**

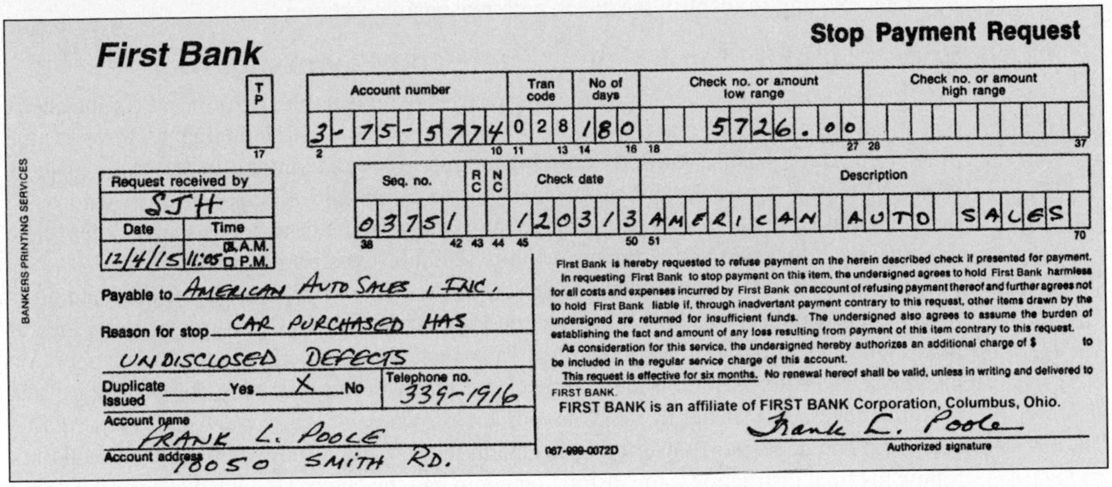

First Bank

Stop Payment Request

T P	Account number	Tran code	No of days	Check no. or amount low range	Check no. or amount high range
	3-75-5774	02	8/180	5726.00	

Seq. no.	RC	NC	Check date	Description
03751			1/20/3/13	AMERICAN AUTO SALES

Request received by SJH

Date 12/4/15 Time 11:05 A.M. / P.M.

Payable to AMERICAN AUTO SALES, INC.

Reason for stop CAR PURCHASED HAS UNDISCLOSED DEFECTS

Duplicate Issued ____ Yes X No

Telephone no. 339-1916

Account name FRANK L. POOLE

Account address 78050 SMITH RD.

First Bank is hereby requested to refuse payment on the herein described check if presented for payment. In requesting First Bank to stop payment on this item, the undersigned agrees to hold First Bank harmless for all costs and expenses incurred by First Bank on account of refusing payment thereof and further agrees not to hold First Bank liable if, through inadvertant payment contrary to this request, other items drawn by the undersigned are returned for insufficient funds. The undersigned also agrees to assume the burden of establishing the fact and amount of any loss resulting from payment of this item contrary to this request.

As consideration for this service, the undersigned hereby authorizes an additional charge of $ to be included in the regular service charge of this account.

This request is effective for six months. No renewal hereof shall be valid, unless in writing and delivered to FIRST BANK.

FIRST BANK is an affiliate of FIRST BANK Corporation, Columbus, Ohio.

Frank L. Poole
Authorized signature

067-999-0072D

BANKERS PRINTING SERVICES

Stop-Payment Order

LO3 A **stop-payment order** is a request made by a customer of a drawee bank instructing it not to pay or certify a specified check. As the drawer's agent in the payment of checks, the drawee bank must follow the reasonable orders of the customer/drawer about payments made on the drawer's behalf. Any person authorized to draw a check may stop payment of it. Thus, any person authorized to sign a check on the account may stop payment even if she did not sign the check in question (4–403[a]).

To be effective, a payor bank must receive a stop-payment order in time to give the bank a reasonable opportunity to act on the order. This means that the bank must receive the stop-payment order before it has paid or certified the check. In addition, the stop-payment order must come soon enough to give the bank time to instruct its tellers and other employees that they should not pay or certify the check (4–403[a]). The stop-payment order also must describe the check with "reasonable certainty" so as to provide the bank's employees the ability to recognize it as the check corresponding to the stop-payment order.

The customer may give an oral stop-payment order to the bank, but it is valid for only 14 days unless the customer confirms it in writing during that time. A written stop-payment order is valid for six months, and the customer can extend it for an additional six months by giving the bank instructions in writing to continue the order (4–403[b]). (See Figure 41.1.)

Sometimes the information given the bank by the customer concerning the check on which payment is to be stopped is incorrect. For example, there may be an error in the payee's name, the amount of the check, or the number of the check. The question then arises whether the customer has accorded the bank a reasonable opportunity to act on his request. A common issue is whether the stop-payment order must have the dollar amount correct to the penny. Banks usually take the position that the stop-payment order must be correct to the penny because they program and rely on computers to focus on the customer's account number and the amount of the check in question to avoid paying an item subject to a stop-payment order.

The amendments to Article 4 do not resolve this question. In the Official Comments, the drafters indicate that "in describing an item, the customer, in the absence of a contrary agreement, must meet the standard of what information allows the bank under the technology then existing to identify the check with reasonable certainty."

Bank's Liability for Payment after Stop-Payment Order

While a stop-payment order is in effect, the drawee bank is liable to the drawer of the check that it pays for any loss that the drawer suffers by reason of such payment. However, the drawer customer has the burden of establishing the fact and amount of the loss. To show a loss, the drawer must establish that the drawee bank paid a person against whom the drawer had a valid defense to payment. To the extent that the drawer has such a defense, he has suffered a loss due to the drawee's failure to honor the stop-payment order.

For example, Brown buys what is represented to be a new car from Foster Ford and gives Foster Ford his check for $25,280 drawn on First Bank. Brown then discovers that the car is in fact a used demonstrator model and calls First Bank, ordering it to stop payment on the check. If Foster Ford presents the check for payment the following day and First Bank pays the check despite the stop-payment order, Brown can require the bank to recredit his account. (The depositor-drawer bases his claim to recredit on the fact that the bank did not follow his final instruction—the instruction not to pay the check.) Brown had a valid defense of misrepresentation that he could have asserted against Foster Ford if it had sued him on the check. Foster Ford would have been required to sue on the check or on Brown's contractual obligation to pay for the car.

Assume, instead, that Foster Ford negotiated the check to Smith and that Smith qualified as a holder in due course. Then, if the bank paid the check to Smith over the stop-payment order, Brown would not be able to have his account recredited because Brown would not be able to show that he sustained any loss. If the bank had refused to pay the check, so that Smith came against Brown on his drawer's liability, Brown could not use his personal defense of misrepresentation of the prior use of the car as a reason for not paying Smith. Brown's only recourse would be to pursue Foster Ford on his misrepresentation claim.

The following case, *Seigel v. Merrill, Lynch, Pierce, Fenner & Smith, Inc.*, involves a situation in which the drawer was not entitled to have his account recredited for checks paid over his stop-payment order because the drawer was unable to demonstrate he suffered any loss because of the bank's failure to honor the stop-payment order.

Seigel v. Merrill, Lynch, Pierce, Fenner & Smith, Inc.

400 UCC Rep.2d 819 (Ct. App. D.C. 2000)

FACTS

Walter Seigel, a Maryland resident, traveled to Atlantic City, New Jersey, to gamble. While there, Seigel wrote a number of checks to various casinos, and, in exchange, received gambling chips with which to wager. The checks were drawn on Seigel's cash management account at Merrill, Lynch, Pierce, Fenner & Smith, which was established through its District of Columbia offices. There were sufficient funds in the account to cover all checks.

Seigel eventually gambled away all the chips he had received for the checks. Upon returning to Maryland, Seigel discussed the outstanding checks with Merrill Lynch, informing his broker of the gambling nature of the transactions and his desire to avoid realizing the apparent losses. Merrill Lynch informed Seigel that it was possible to escape paying the checks by placing a stop-payment order and liquidating his cash management account. He took the advice and instructed Merrill Lynch to close his account,

(continued)

liquidate the assets, and not to honor any checks drawn on the account. Merrill Lynch agreed and confirmed Seigel's instructions.

Many of the checks were subsequently dishonored. However, Merrill Lynch accidentally paid several of the checks totaling $143,000 despite the stop-payment order and account closure. Merrill Lynch then debited Seigel's margin account to cover the payments.

Seigel brought suit in the District of Columbia against Merrill Lynch for paying the checks over his stop-payment order. He argued that the District of Columbia Code precluded enforcement of the checks as void gambling debts or, in the alternative, that New Jersey law prohibited the enforcement of the check. Therefore, he contended, Merrill Lynch had no rights by way of subrogation as a defense to payment over the stop-payment order. Merrill Lynch denied the applicability of the D.C. statute or any New Jersey law and contended that it stood in the shoes of the casinos to whom valid and enforceable checks had been given.

ISSUE

Was Seigel entitled to have his account recredited for the checks paid by Merrill Lynch over his stop-payment order?

DECISION

No. While the depositor has the basic right to stop payment on any item drawn on his account, the depositor also has the burden of showing the fact and amount of any loss resulting from payment of an item contrary to a stop-payment order. In this instance, Seigel is unable to establish he suffered any loss. As the payee of dishonored checks, the casino would have a prima facie right to recover its amount from Seigel as drawer, and the burden would be on Seigel to establish any defense he might have on the instrument. Seigel's argument that the casinos would have no right to enforce the check under New Jersey law because he is a compulsive gambler is without merit. Nothing in New Jersey law prohibits the cashing and redemption of checks made by "compulsive gamblers." While D.C. law might preclude the enforcement of the checks as issued out of a gambling transaction and void, Seigel gains nothing by it because the checks could be enforced in New Jersey where the transaction occurred. Moreover, the court noted that the checks could also be enforced in Maryland where Seigel lives because Maryland courts will enforce gambling debts if legally incurred in a foreign jurisdiction. Accordingly, Seigel was unable to show he ultimately suffered any loss as a result of the payment of the checks by Merrill Lynch.

The bank may ask the customer to sign a form in which the bank tries to disclaim or limit its liability for the stop-payment order. As explained at the beginning of this chapter, the bank cannot disclaim its responsibility for its failure to act in good faith or to exercise ordinary care in paying a check over a stop-payment order (4–103).

If a bank pays a check after it has received a stop-payment order and has to reimburse its customer for the improperly paid check, it acquires all the rights of its customer against the person to whom it originally made payment, including rights arising from the transaction on which the check was based (4–407). In our example involving Brown and Foster Ford, assume that Brown was able to have his account recredited because First Bank had paid the check to Foster Ford over his stop-payment order. Then the bank would have any rights that Brown had against Foster Ford for the misrepresentation.

If a person stops payment on a check and the bank honors the stop-payment order, the person still may be liable to the holder of the check. Suppose Peters writes a check for $450 to Ace Auto Repair in payment for repairs to her automobile. While driving the car home, she concludes that the car was not repaired properly. She calls her bank and stops payment on the check. Ace Auto negotiated the check to Sam's Auto Parts, which took the check as a holder in due course. When Sam's takes the check to Peters's bank, the bank refuses to pay because of the stop-payment order. Sam's then comes after Peters on her drawer's liability. All Peters has is a personal defense against payment, which is not good against a holder in due course. So Peters must pay Sam's the $450 and pursue her claim separately against Ace. If Ace were still the holder of the check, however, the situation would be different. Peters could use her personal defense concerning the faulty work against Ace to reduce or possibly to cancel her obligation to pay the check.

Certified Check

LO4

Normally a drawee bank is not obligated to certify a check. When a drawee bank does certify a check, it substitutes its undertaking (promise) to pay the check for the drawer's undertaking and becomes obligated to pay the check. At the time the bank certifies a check, the bank usually debits the customer's account for the amount of the certified check and shifts the money to a special account at the bank. It also adds its signature to the check to show that it has accepted primary liability for paying it. The bank's signature is an essential part of the certification: The bank's signature must appear on the check (3–409). If the holder of a check chooses to have it certified, rather than seeking to have it paid at that time, the holder has made a conscious decision to look to the certifying bank for payment and no longer may rely on the drawer or the indorsers to pay it. See Figure 41.2 for an example of a certified check.

If the drawee bank certifies a check, then the drawer and any persons who previously indorsed the check are discharged of their liability on the check (3–414[c]; 3–415[d]).

Cashier's Check

A cashier's check differs from a certified check. A check on which a bank is both the drawer and the drawee is a *cashier's check.* The bank is primarily liable on a cashier's check. See Figure 41.3 for an example of a cashier's check. A teller's check is similar to a cashier's check in that it is a check on which one bank is the drawer and another bank is the drawee. An example of a teller's check is a check drawn by a credit union on its account at a bank.

Death or Incompetence of Customer

Under the general principles of agency law, the death or incompetence of the principal terminates the agent's authority to act for the principal. However, slightly different rules apply to the authority of a bank to pay checks out of the account of a deceased or incompetent person. The bank has the right to pay the checks of an incompetent person until it has notice that a court has determined that the person is incompetent. Once the bank learns

FIGURE 41.2 **Certified Check**

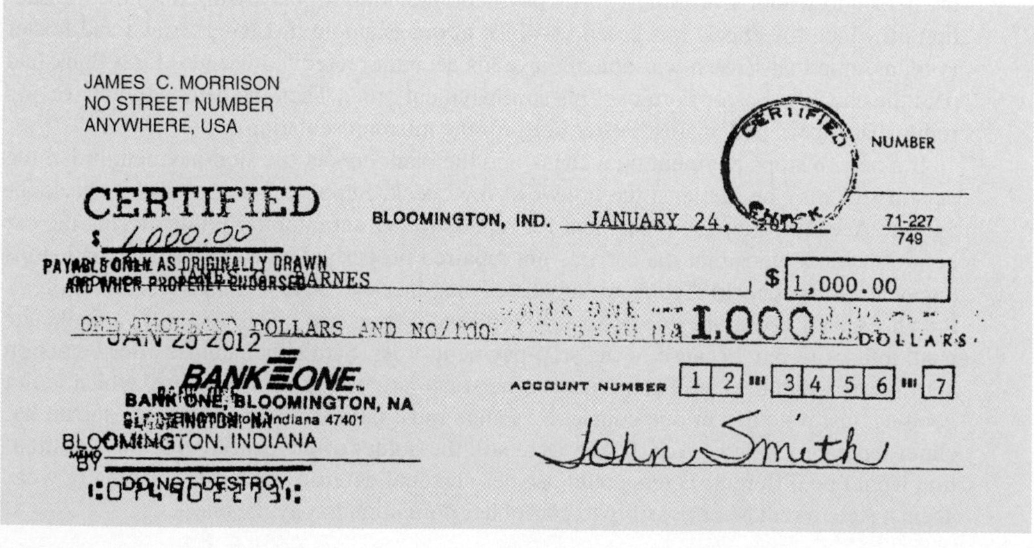

FIGURE 41.3 Cashier's Check

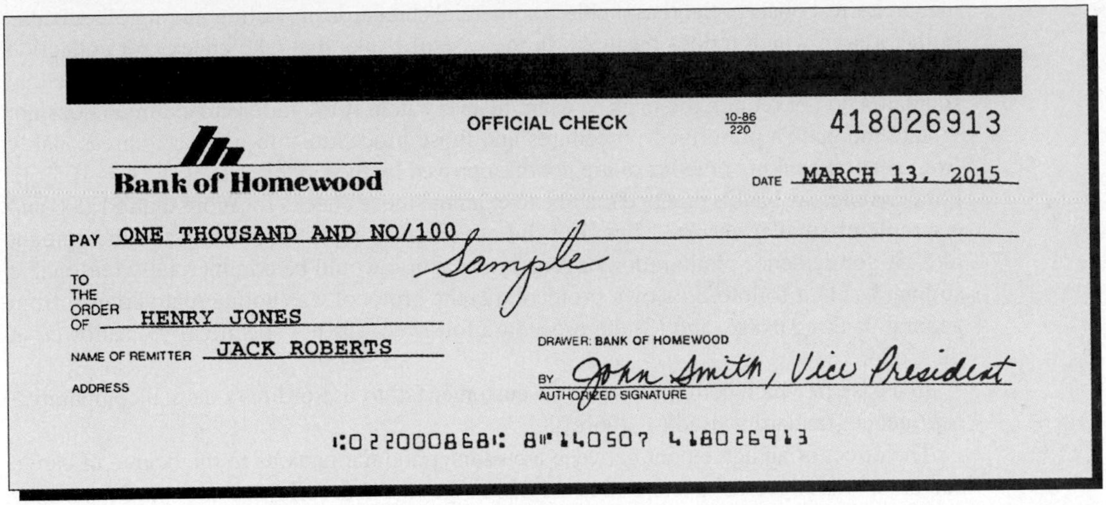

of this fact, it loses its authority to pay that person's checks—because the depositor is not competent to issue instructions to pay.

Similarly, a bank has the right to pay the checks of a deceased customer until it has notice of the customer's death. Even if a bank knows of a customer's death, for a period of 10 days after the customer's death, it can pay checks written by the customer prior to his death. However, the deceased person's heirs or other persons claiming an interest in the account can order the bank to stop payment (4–405).

Forged and Altered Checks

Bank's Right to Charge Account

LO5

A check that bears a forged signature of the drawer or payee generally is not properly payable from the customer's account because the bank is not following the instructions of the depositor precisely as he gave them. The bank is expected to be familiar with the authorized signature of its depositor. If it pays such a check, Article 4 will treat the transaction as one in which the bank paid out its own funds rather than the depositor's funds.

Similarly, a check that was altered after the drawer made it out—for example, by increasing the amount of the check—generally is not properly payable from the customer's account. However, as noted earlier, if the drawer is negligent and contributes to the forgery or alteration, he may be barred from claiming it as the reason that a particular check should not be charged to his account.

For example, Barton makes a check for $100 in a way that makes it possible for someone to easily alter it to read $1,100, and it is so altered. If the drawee bank pays the check to a holder in good faith, it can charge the $1,100 to Barton's account if Barton's negligence contributed to the alteration. Similarly, if a company uses a mechanical checkwriter to write checks, it must use reasonable care to see that unauthorized persons do not have access to blank checks and to the checkwriter.

If the alteration is obvious, the bank should note that fact and refuse to pay the check when it is presented for payment. Occasionally, the alteration is so skillful that the bank cannot detect it. In that case, the bank is allowed to charge to the account the amount for which the check originally was written.

The bank has a duty to exercise "ordinary care" in the processing of negotiable instruments; it must observe the reasonable commercial standards prevailing among other banks in the area in which it does business. In the case of banks that take checks for collection or payment using automated means, it is important to note that reasonable commercial standards do not require the bank to examine every item if the failure to examine does not violate the bank's prescribed procedures and those procedures do not vary unreasonably from general banking practice or are not disapproved by the Code (3–103[a][7]; 4–103[c]). For example, the bank's practice may be to examine those checks for more than $1,000 and a sample of smaller checks. Thus, if it did not examine a particular check in the amount of $250 for evidence of alteration or forgery, its action would be commercially reasonable so long as (1) it followed its own protocol, (2) the protocol was not a great variance from general banking usage, and (3) the procedure followed was not specifically disallowed in the Code.

In a case in which both a bank and its customer fail to use ordinary care, a comparative negligence standard is used (4–406[e]).

The effect of an agreement between a customer and the bank as to the degree of care a customer was expected to exercise is at issue in the case that follows, *Cincinnati Insurance Company v. Bank National Association.*

Cincinnati Insurance Company v. Wachovia Bank National Association

72 UCC Rep.2d 744 (U.S.D.C, D. Minn. 2010)

FACTS

Schultz Foods maintained a commercial checking account with Wachovia. Over the course of its relationship with Wachovia, Schultz Foods was the victim of check fraud on four separate occasions. Wachovia and Shultz Foods were able to amicably resolve the first three instances of check fraud. On those three occasions, Schultz Foods closed the compromised account and opened a new account, and Wachovia absorbed the fraud-related loss. The fourth occasion gave rise to this lawsuit.

In late 2005, Schultz issued a check in the amount of $153,856.46 to Amerada Hess Corporation. The check was stolen before it could be deposited by the intended recipient. In what is known as a "washing" scam, thieves removed the name of the original payee and substituted the name of Kenneth Payton—who was an unwitting accomplice of the thieves. Payton then endorsed the check and deposited it into his account at TCF. TCF presented the check to Wachovia, and Wachovia transferred $153,856.46 from Schultz's account at Wachovia to Payton's account at TCF. Following the instructions of the thieves, Payton then wired the money to a bank account in Singapore, and the thieves took the money and ran.

When the fraud came to light, Schultz Foods demanded that Wachovia re-credit its account, claiming that Wachovia must bear the loss because it processed the altered check in violation of Section 4-401(a) of the Uniform Commercial Code (UCC). Wachovia disagreed, citing the fact that Schultz Foods had declined to implement "Positive Pay," a check-fraud deterrence program that had been offered by Wachovia and that would have prevented the loss if Schultz had only implemented it. According to Wachovia, under the terms of the deposit agreement between Schultz Foods and Wachovia, the failure to implement Positive Pay made Schultz Foods liable for the loss. The deposit agreement provided:

> You agree that if you fail to implement any of these products or services, or you fail to follow these and other precautions reasonable for your particular circumstances, you will be precluded from asserting any claim against [Wachovia] for paying any unauthorized, altered, counterfeit or other fraudulent item that such product, service, or precaution was designed to detect or defer, and we will not be required to re-credit your account or otherwise have any liability for paying such items.

Unless a customer implements a program such as Positive Pay, a bank has little chance of identifying a forged or altered check, because the bank has no way of knowing whether a particular check was actually issued by a customer, whether a particular check was issued to the payee

(continued)

whose name appears on the check, or whether a particular check was issued in the account that appears on the check.

Positive Pay is a software program that enables a customer to transmit to its bank pertinent information about every check that the customer issues. For example, when a customer who uses Positive Pay issues check number 7394 to Acme, Inc. in the amount of $15,286.25, the customer's bank is promptly *informed* that the customer has issued check number 7394 to Acme, Inc., in the amount of $15,286.25. When a bearer then presents check number 7394 for payment, the bank's computer can compare the information on the check to the information that was transmitted by the customer. If the information does not match—if for example, the name of the payee on check number 7394 is Jane Smith instead of Acme, Inc.—the bank can contact the customer before clearing the check. Had Schultz Foods implemented Positive Pay, Wachovia would not have paid the Kenneth Payton check, and the loss would not have occurred.

Wachovia did pay the check, though, and thus $153,856.46 was deducted from the account of Schultz Foods. After Wachovia refused to re-credit the account, Schultz Foods filed a claim with its insurer, Cincinnati Insurance Company. Cincinnati paid the claim, and then filed a subrogation action against Wachovia.

ISSUE

Was Wachovia Bank required to re-credit Schultz Food's account for the check that was not properly payable from it?

DECISION

No. The court began by noting that UCC Section 4-401(a) provides that "[a] bank may charge against the account of a customer an item that is properly payable from that account. . . . An item is properly payable if it is authorized by the customer and in accordance with any agreement between the customer and the bank." Ordinarily, if a bank charges a customer's account for a check that is not properly payable—for example a check that has been forged and therefore has not been authorized by the customer—the bank will be liable to the customer for the loss. But this is merely a default rule. Section 4-103(a) permits banks and their customers to agree to a different rule, except that an agreement between a bank and a customer "cannot disclaim the responsibility of a bank for its lack of good faith or failure to exercise ordinary care."

Schultz Foods did not issue a check to Kenneth Payton. Wachovia conceded that the altered check, as it was presented to the teller at Payton's bank, was not authorized by Schultz Foods. Thus the check was not "properly payable" under Section 4-401(a), and absent an agreement to the contrary, Wachovia would be liable to Schultz Foods for charging the unauthorized check against the company's account.

The problem for Schultz Foods is that there was an agreement to the contrary—a deposit agreement signed by Schultz Foods when it opened its commercial checking account at Wachovia. After first describing the "precautions" that a customer could take on its own and then mentioning the "products and services" that Wachovia may offer, section 12 of the deposit agreement concluded with a conditional release of Wachovia's liability.

There is no dispute that Positive Pay *was* a "product or service" for purposes of section 12. There also is no dispute that Positive Pay was made available to Schultz Foods, and that Schultz Foods chose not to implement it. Finally, there is no dispute that Positive Pay was "designed to detect or deter" precisely the type of fraud that caused the $153,856.46 loss. On its face then, the release absolves Wachovia of any responsibility for that loss.

Customer's Duty to Report Forgeries and Alterations

LO6

A bank must send a monthly (or quarterly) statement listing the transactions in an account and commonly returns the canceled checks to the customer. Revised Article 3 recognizes the modern bank practice of truncating (or retaining) checks and permits the bank to supply only a statement showing the item number, amount, and date of payment (4–406[a]). When the bank does not return the paid items to the customer, the bank either must retain the items or maintain the capacity to furnish legible copies of the items for seven years after their receipt. The customer may request an item and the bank has a reasonable time to provide either the item or a legible copy of it (4–406[b]).

If the bank sends or makes available a statement of account or items, the customer must exercise reasonable promptness to examine the statement or items to determine whether payment was not authorized because of an alteration of any item or because a signature of the customer was not authorized. If, based on the statement or items provided, the customer discovers the unauthorized payment, the customer must notify the bank of the relevant facts promptly (4–406[c]).

Multiple Forgeries or Alterations

Revised Article 3 provides a special rule to govern the situation in which the same wrongdoer makes a series of unauthorized drawer's signatures or alterations. The customer generally cannot hold the bank responsible for paying, in good faith, any such checks after the statement of account or item that contained the first unauthorized customer's signature or an alteration was available to the customer for a reasonable period, not exceeding 30 calendar days. The rule holds (1) if the customer did not notify the bank of the unauthorized signature or alteration and (2) the bank proves it suffered a loss because of the customer's failure to examine his statement and notify the bank (4–406[d]). Unless the customer has notified the bank about the forgeries or alterations that he should have discovered by reviewing the statement or item, the customer generally bears responsibility for any subsequent forgeries or alterations by the same wrongdoer.

Suppose that Allen employs Farnum as an accountant and that over a period of three months, Farnum forges Allen's signature to 10 checks and cashes them. One of the forged checks is included in the checks returned to Allen at the end of the first month. Within 30 calendar days after the return of these checks, Farnum forges two more checks and cashes them. Allen does not examine the returned checks until three months after the checks that included the first forged check were returned to her. The bank would be responsible for the first forged check and for the two checks forged and cashed within the 30-day period after it sent the first statement and the canceled checks (unless the bank proves that it suffered a loss because of the customer's failure to examine the checks and notify it more promptly). It would not be liable for the seven forged checks cashed after the expiration of the 30-day period.

Regardless of which party may have been negligent, a customer must discover and report to the bank any unauthorized customer's signature or any alteration within one year from the time after the statement or items are made available to him. If the customer does not do so, he cannot require the bank to recredit his account for such items. Similarly, a customer has three years from the time his statement or item is made available to discover and report any unauthorized indorsements on the item. The customer's failure to discover and report these irregularities within the one- or three-year periods specified ends his right to have his account recredited for the amount of the checks (4–406[f]).

Concept Summary: Liability for Multiple Forgeries or Alterations of Checks or Drafts by the Same Person

Date First Statement Disclosing an Altered or Forged Check Is Available to Customer	Date 30 Days Later	Date Customer Gives Notice of Alteration or Forgery
Customer is not liable for forged/altered checks paid during this period unless bank suffers a loss from customer's unreasonable delay in notifying bank of forgery or alteration.	Customer is liable for forged or altered checks paid during this period unless customer gives bank notice of forgery or alteration within a reasonable time after date the first statement containing a forged or altered check was available to customer.	Customer is not liable for forged or altered checks paid during this period.

Check 21

LO7

The Check Clearing for the 21st Century Act, commonly known as Check 21, a federal law that is designed to enable banks to collect more checks electronically, became effective on October 28, 2004. As detailed in the previous section, for many years banks had to physically move checks from the bank where they are deposited to the drawee bank that pays them, a time-consuming, inefficient, and costly process. And, for many years, banks then returned the canceled checks to their customers along with their monthly account statement. In recent years, however, many banks have stopped providing canceled checks to their customers; you may have noticed this change in the way your own checking account has been handled by your bank. Instead, they provide images of the checks with multiple pictures of canceled checks appearing on pages of a paper or electronic bank statement. If the drawee bank keeps the original checks, this is called *check truncation*. (If the payee, such as a grocery store, keeps the original check, this is called *radical truncation*). Credit unions and an increasing number of commercial banks have been truncating checks for quite a while or have allowed their retailer customers to do so.

For many years, banks have had the capacity to capture information from the MICR lines of checks and to transmit that information electronically to collecting banks as well as the drawee bank if the later banks in the collection chain had electronic capabilities. But in order for the bank sending only the electronic image forward (as opposed to the paper check drawn by the drawer of the check) to do this, each bank had to have an "electronic presentment agreement" with the other banks in the collection chain. If one bank in the chain of collection or the drawee bank did not have electronic processing ability, then the use of electronic processing was ended. One bank could hold up the use of electronic innovations simply by refusing to take electronic items.

Check 21 authorizes banks to transform information they receive in electronic form back into a paper copy of the check. It grants to paper copies that meet specific standards and so qualify as "substitute checks" legal status that is the equivalent, as against all persons and for all purposes, of the paper check drawn by the drawer. As a result, if a bank with electronic capacity encountered a drawee bank that did not have electronic capacity, the first bank could use its electronic information file to create a "substitute check" (assuming it met the standards) and to present that substitute check for payment. Similarly, if all the banks in a check collection chain used electronic presentment processing, but the payee or drawer needed a paper copy of the check to prove it had paid an obligation, its bank could create and deliver a substitute check to the payee or drawer. In both cases, the resulting substitute check is legally the same as the original check if it accurately represents the information on the original check and includes the following statement: "This is a legal copy of your check. You can use it the same way you would use the original check." The substitute check must also have been handled by a bank.

Banks are not required to keep your original check for any specific period of time. Existing federal law requires that banks retain a legible copy of checks for seven years, but neither federal nor state law requires that the copies returned to customers with statements be legible. Check 21 does not add any new retention requirements. Under the new law, original checks are more likely to be destroyed. If you request your original check from your bank, your bank may provide you with the original check, a substitute check, or a paper or electronic copy of the check.

Articles 3 and 4 of the Uniform Commercial Code continue to provide protection against erroneous and unauthorized checks. In addition, Check 21 contains a number of new protections for customers. For example, Check 21 contains a special refund procedure, called "expedited recredit," for a customer who suffers a loss because of a "substitute check."

Because checks are now transmitted electronically from one bank to another, customers must make sure they have funds in their account to cover them and now no longer anticipate a "float" based on the time it would take the check to be physically transmitted back to the drawee bank. Consumer groups warn consumers to be aware that there is an increased risk that a check will bounce if funds are not in the account when the check is written. At the same time, customers may not get access to the funds from checks that they deposit to their account any sooner because Check 21 does not shorten the check hold times set out in the Federal Expedited Funds Availability Act.

Electronic Transfers

Over the past three decades, many new mechanisms have emerged for transferring money electronically without the need for paper money or the use of paper-based negotiable instruments such as checks. Financial institutions. merchants, and providers of service also have encouraged customers to use these mechanisms in order to expedite the movement of money in a more cost-effective manner to the benefit of all parties involved in financial transactions. The electronic funds transfer (EFT) systems utilized by consumers include (1) automated teller machines; (2) point-of-sale terminals, which allow consumers to use their EFT prepaid cards like checks to transfer money from their checking account to the merchant; (3) preauthorized payments, using the Automated Clearing House System (ACH) such as automatic deposit of paychecks and government benefits, or the payment of mortgage, credit-card, and utility bills; and (4) telephone transfers between accounts or authorization to pay specific bills. And for large business and financial institutions, wire transfers of funds are commonly used to move large sums of money very quickly across the country or around the world.

As these mechanisms have emerged and are increasingly supplanting the traditional methods for transferring money, they have required new legal constructs to deal with the issues and problems they present that do not fit well in existing legal regimes such as Articles 3 (Negotiable Instruments) and 4 (Bank Deposits and Collections) of the Uniform Commercial Code. The Electronic Funds Transfer Act (EFTA) now addresses many of the issues that arise out of consumer use of EFT systems while Article 4A (Funds Transfers) of the Uniform Commercial Code deals with the funds transfers that are outside of the overage of the EFTA.

E-Commerce

CYBERLAW IN ACTION: E-CHECKS

Chapter 38, "Negotiable Instruments," explains that the process known as "check conversion" is utilized by a number of large retailers. The process begins with the buyer giving the seller a paper check. The seller uses special equipment to gather information from the paper check; this information includes the buyer's bank account number, the bank routing number, and the serial number of the check. The retailer then names itself as the payee, codes in the amount of the purchase, and forwards it for collection through an automated clearing house (ACH) transaction instead of the collection route for paper checks.

The Federal Reserve Board decided that the Electronic Funds Transfer Act (EFTA) and Regulation E would govern "check conversion" transactions. The EFTA will govern even if the consumer gives a blank and unsigned check to the merchant. The act also governs if the merchant uses a paper check as a "source document" (source of critical account- and bank-related information) and then uses an electronic funds transfer rather than the ACH transfer mentioned above.

Electronic Fund Transfer Act

LO8

The consumer who used electronic funds transfer (EFT) systems in the early years often experienced problems in identifying and resolving mechanical errors resulting from malfunctioning EFT systems. In response to these problems, Congress passed the **Electronic Fund Transfer Act** in 1978 to provide "a basic framework, establishing the rights, liabilities, and responsibilities of participants in electronic funds transfer systems" and especially to provide "individual consumer rights."

The basic EFT systems are *automated teller machines; point-of-sale terminals,* which allow consumers to use their EFT cards, including payroll and prepaid gift or general purpose reloadable cards, checks at retail establishments; *preauthorized payments,* such as automatic paycheck deposits or mortgage or utility payments; and *telephone transfers* between accounts or payment of specific bills by phone.

Similar to the Truth in Lending Act and the Fair Credit Billing Act (FCBA), discussed in Chapter 46, "Consumer Protection Laws," the EFT Act requires disclosure of the terms and conditions of electronic fund transfers at the time the consumer contracts for the EFT service. Among the disclosures required are the following: the consumer's liability for unauthorized electronic funds transfers (those resulting from loss or theft), the nature of the EFT services under the consumer's account, any pertinent dollar or frequency limitations, any charges for the right to make EFTs, the consumer's right to stop payment of a preauthorized transfer, the financial institution's liability to the consumer for failure to make or stop payments, and the consumer's right to receive documentation of transfers both at the point or time of transfer and periodically. The act also requires 21 days' notice prior to the effective date of any change in the terms or conditions of the consumer's account that pertains to the required disclosures.

The EFT Act does differ from the Fair Credit Billing Act in a number of important respects. For example, under the EFT Act, the operators of EFT systems are given a maximum of 10 working days to investigate errors or provisionally recredit the consumer's account, whereas issuers of credit cards are given a maximum of 60 days under the FCBA. The consumer's liability if an EFT card is lost or stolen also differs from his liability if a credit card is lost or stolen.

The case that follows, *Kruser v. Bank of America NT & SA,* illustrates the application of the EFT Act's provisions that require a customer to provide timely notification of any unauthorized use of his card in order to limit his liability for the unauthorized use.

Kruser v. Bank of America NT & SA

281 Cal. Rptr. 463 (Ct. App. Cal. 1991)

FACTS

Lawrence and Georgene Kruser maintained a joint checking account with Bank of America, and the bank issued each of them a "Versatel" card and separate personal identification numbers that would allow access to funds in their account from automatic teller machines. The Krusers also received with their cards a "Disclosure Booklet" that provided to the Krusers a summary of consumer liability, the bank's business hours, and telephone number by which they could notify the bank in the event they believed an unauthorized transfer had been made.

The Krusers believed Mr. Kruser's card had been destroyed in September 1986. The December 1986 account statement mailed to the Krusers by the bank reflected a $20 unauthorized withdrawal of funds by someone using Mr. Kruser's card at an automatic teller machine. The Krusers reported this unauthorized transaction to the bank when they discovered it in August or September 1987.

(continued)

Mrs. Kruser underwent surgery in late 1986 or early 1987 and remained hospitalized for 11 days. She then spent a period of six or seven months recuperating at home. During this time she reviewed the statements the Krusers received from the bank.

In September 1987, the Krusers received bank statements for July and August 1987 that reflected 47 unauthorized withdrawals totaling $9,020 made from an automatic teller machine, again by someone using Mr. Kruser's card. They notified the bank of these withdrawals within a few days of receiving the statements. The bank refused to credit the Krusers' account with the amount of the unauthorized withdrawals.

ISSUE

Did the failure to notify the bank in a timely fashion of the first unauthorized use of the card relieve the bank of liability for the subsequent unauthorized transfers of funds?

DECISION

Yes. If the Krusers had notified the bank of the first unauthorized transfer of $20 in a timely fashion, the subsequent unauthorized transfers some seven months later could have been prevented. The bank would have simply canceled the card, and the subsequent transfers would not have been possible. Thus, under the Electronic Funds Transfer Act, this failure on the part of the Krusers relieved the bank of liability for the subsequent unauthorized transfers. The court also found that Mrs. Kruser's illness did not excuse the failure to notify where it was undisputed that she had in fact reviewed the statement showing the transfer.

Wire Transfers

While consumers increasingly are using various methods to transfer funds electronically, for some time electronic transfer has been an important part of the banking system and the business sector. The Federal Reserve operates a domestic wire transfer system known as "Fedwire" and the Clearing House Association, LLC, operates the New York Clearinghouse Payments System (CHIPS) inside the United States. International wire transfers also can be made through the CHIPS. The volume of payments over these two systems exceeds $1 trillion per day.

Electronic funds transfers between business and financial institutions—generally referred to as wholesale wire transfers—are governed by Article 4A (Funds Transfers) of the Uniform Commercial Code. Article 4A explicitly excludes consumer payments that are covered by the Electronic Funds Transfer Act (EFTA), which includes the payments made through automated clearing houses.

In the Prefatory Note to Article 4A, the Uniform Law Commission notes that the typical transfer covered by the Article is not a complex transaction and provide the following example which also illustrates the terminology used in wire transfers:

> X, a debtor, wants to pay an obligation owed to Y. Instead of delivering to Y a negotiable instrument such as a check or other writing such as a credit card slip that enables Y to obtain payment from a bank, X transmits an instruction to X's bank to credit a sum of money to the bank account of Y. In most cases X's bank and Y's bank are different banks. X's bank may carry out X's bank by instructing Y's bank to credit Y's account by the amount that X has requested. The instruction that X issues to its bank is a "payment order." X is the "sender" of the payment order and X's bank is the "receiving bank" with respect to X's order. Y is the "beneficiary" of X's order. When X's bank issues an instruction to Y's bank to carry out X's payment order, X's bank "executes" X's order. With respect to that order, X's bank is the sender, Y's bank is the receiving bank, and Y is the beneficiary. The entire series of transactions is known as the "funds transfer." With respect to the funds transfer, X is the

"originator," X's bank is the "originator's bank," Y is the "beneficiary" and Y's bank is the "beneficiary's bank." In more complex transactions there are one or more additional banks known as "intermediary banks" between X's bank and Y's bank.

Funds transfers have a number of advantages for those who utilize them—typically, sophisticated business or financial organizations. They allow significant sums of money to move at high speed so that transactions can be completed in a very short period of time and are an effective substitute for payments made by the delivery of paper instruments. And the cost of the transfers is very low compared to the amount of money being transferred. At the same time, the risk of loss if something goes wrong in the transaction can be very large. Among the possibilities: (1) the bank fails to execute the payment order of a customer; (2) a bank is late in executing a payment order; or (3) a bank makes an error in executing the payment order, either as to the amount to be paid or the identity or account numbers of the person to be paid or the identity of the beneficiary bank. A major policy issue in the drafting of Article 4A was the allocation of risk to the various parties in light of the price structure in the industry.

For example, if a receiving bank executes a payment order by paying more that the order calls for, or makes a duplicative payment, the bank is entitled to the amount of the payment order but is left to recover any excess or duplicative payment from the beneficiary under the law governing mistake and restitution. Where banks carry out a funds transfer but are late in executing it, the banks are obligated to pay interest to either the originator or the beneficiary of the funds transfer for the period of delay caused by the improper execution. For other types of improper execution or failure to execute payment orders, banks can be liable to the originator or sender for their expenses in the transaction along with incidental expenses and interest losses due to improper execution or failure to execute; however, consequential damages are recoverable only to the extent provided in an express written agreement of the receiving bank and are not otherwise recoverable.

Questions and Problem Cases

1. James Drumm and Debra Brading were dating and lived together on and off for several years. Drumm was providing financial support to Brading. Brading had written numerous checks on Drumm's checking account and had access to his corporate credit cards. However, she was not an authorized signator on either his checking or savings accounts. After one particularly ugly fight between the two on July 3, 2000, Brading went to the National City Bank and withdrew $314,000 from Drumm's individual savings account. She did so by approaching a teller, giving her Drumm's account number and electronic personal identification number (PIN), and providing the teller with a driver's license bearing the name Debra Brading along with a Racquet Club membership identifying her as Debra Drumm. She was also wearing a $20,000 diamond ring which appeared to be an engagement ring. On the basis of these facts, a teller allowed the transaction. Drumm brought suit against National City Bank for breach of contract for allowing an unauthorized transfer of funds from his account. Is National City Bank liable to Drumm?
2. Louise Kalbe drew a check in the amount of $7,260 payable to the "order of cash" on her account at the Pulaski State Bank. The check was lost or stolen, but Kalbe did not report this to the bank, nor did she attempt to stop payment on it. When the check was received by the Pulaski State Bank, Kalbe had only about $700 in her checking account. However, the bank paid the check, creating an overdraft in her account of $6,542.12. The bank then sued Kalbe to recover the amount of the overdraft. Kalbe asserted that

the check was not properly payable from her account. Was the bank legally entitled to pay a check that exceeded the balance in the drawer's account and to recover the overdraft from the drawer?

3. J. E. B. Stewart received a check in the amount of $185.48 in payment of a fee from a client. Stewart presented the check, properly indorsed, to the Citizen's & Southern Bank. The bank refused to cash the check even though there were sufficient funds in the drawer's account. Stewart then sued the bank for actual damages of $185.48 for its failure to cash a valid check drawn against a solvent account in the bank. Does Stewart have a good cause of action against the bank?

4. Dr. Sherrill purchased a Buick from Frank Morris Buick. He gave the auto dealer a check for $4,960.61 drawn on his account at First Alabama Bank. The check was dated "2/6/1976," was payable "to the order of Frank Morris Buick," and was not numbered. After buying the Buick, Sherrill became concerned about whether he had gotten valid title to it. The day after he gave the dealer the check, he called in an oral stop-payment order on it. He later confirmed the stop-payment order in writing. In the stop-payment order, Sherrill stated that the check was not numbered, was payable to "Walter Morris Buick," was dated "6/3/76," and was in the amount of $4,960.61. The bank paid the check when it was presented for payment. Sherrill then claimed that the bank should recredit his account for $4,960.61 because it paid the check over a valid stop-payment order. Did the stop-payment order describe the check accurately enough to constitute a valid stop-payment order?

5. Brenda Jones, who did business as Country Kitchen, purchased some cookware from an itinerant salesman, giving him a check in the amount of $200 for the purchase price. The salesman cashed the check at the First National Bank before noon on May 22, the day of the sale. Jones later became concerned about the lack of documentation from the salesman, thinking that the cookware might be stolen, and placed a stop-payment order with her bank, the State Bank of Conway Springs, at 3:30 that afternoon. State Bank refused to honor the check when it was presented for payment through banking channels. First National Bank, claiming to be a holder in due course, then brought suit against Jones to recover the $200 value of the check. Is the drawer of a check on which a stop-payment order was placed and honored by the bank liable to pay the check to a holder in due course?

6. In March 2008, Faux Themes Inc., a corporation in the construction business, opened a checking account with Chino National Bank. Brian Peters, the president of the company, and Marilyn Charlnoes, its treasurer, were authorized signers on the account. Until April 2009, the average monthly balance in the account ranged from $3,000 to $5,000 and the deposits in any one month never exceeded $10,000. In March 2009, Peters received an e-mail supposedly from Husaine Norman, a citizen of Malaysia. Norman said that certain third parties in the United States and Canada owed him money; however, they were insisting that "they cannot transfer the funds to any bank account outside the American continent due to their new company policy." He asked Peters to "assist me in receiving the funds and forward to me." He offered to pay Peters 12 percent of the money and Peters agreed after negotiating an increase of his fee to 15 percent.

   On April 30, 2009, Faux received a check for $178,000; Peters had Charlnoes deposit it. On May 8, 2009, the bank confirmed the check had cleared. Charlnoes then had the bank wire $80,000 to a bank in Hong Kong. Also on May 8, Faux received a second check for $373,988.90 which was deposited and on May 12 Charlnoes had the bank wire another $71,000 to the same bank in Hong Kong. On May 15, the bank confirmed that the second check had cleared, and Charlnoes had the bank wire $317,000 to a bank in China. On May 21, Faux received a third check for $257,000 which was deposited at the bank.

On May 22, 2009, the bank was notified that the name of the first check had been altered to change the name of the payee to Faux. On May 28, the bank was notified that the second and third checks had been similarly altered. Because all three checks were dishonored, the account was overdrawn in the amount of $458,782.60. When the bank got back the original checks, it found that they had been altered with an acid that was originally used by architects to remove ink from blueprints. They had no facial irregularities—no discoloration, smidges, misalignments or disturbances of the backgrounds or watermarks. The alterations were in fonts and type sizes that were consistent with the other printing on the check. Pursuant to bank policy concerning checks over $10,000, a bank officer had reviewed the checks for irregularities and to see whether the amounts were consistent with the customer—and had initialed the deposit slips to show the procedures had been followed. Before initialing, he also had determined that the amounts of the checks were consistent with deposits made to the accounts of related entities. This is consistent with industry practice nationally.

The bank sued Peters to recover the cost of the overdraft. Peters did not dispute that he was personally responsible for any overdrafts, but contended that the bank had not shown its lack of negligence in accepting the checks for deposit and therefore was not entitled to charge the items back to Faux's account. On these facts, was the bank entitled to charge the items back to Faux's account?

7. Rhona Graves opened checking and savings accounts at Riggs Bank. The customer agreement with Riggs included a provision that "your [account] statement is considered correct and we will not be liable for payments made and charged to your account . . . unless you notify us of an error, including unauthorized payment or other irregularity within (a) sixty (60) calendar days . . . of the mailing date of the earliest statement describing the charge or deposit to your account."

   Prior to June 2002, Graves won a substantial amount of money in the lottery and deposited the lump sum in her accounts at Riggs Bank. On June 8, she suffered a serious stroke and thereafter was unable to communicate. She was transferred to a nursing home where she died on November 9, 2002. Between May and her death in November, someone made 73 withdrawals from her account, 72 of which were at the $500 daily limit for withdrawals. Then 21 additional withdrawals were made during the 41 days after she died, including 19 at the $500 daily maximum. Thus, $46,547 was withdrawn from the account by this method, including $10,159.50 after her death. In addition, 128 checks were written, resulting in her account being debited $84,731,61. Six of the checks (totaling $62,000) were made out to her sister and another check was written to her sister's daughter. The signatures on the checks did not match the authorized signature on file with the bank. After her stroke, Graves did not have the capacity to review bank statements, and it does not appear she received any in the hospital.

   After her death, her son petitioned for letters of administration to handle her estate and received authority to open her safe-deposit box. After discovering that she had won the lottery, he sought to determine what had happened to the money, which at that point had essentially disappeared from her Riggs accounts. After asking Riggs for an investigation of the account and receiving only limited information, he filed suit on August 4, 2004, asking that her account be re-credited for the unauthorized ATM withdrawals and checks. Should Riggs be required to re-credit the account?

8. On August 16, Frederick Ognibene went to the ATM area at a Citibank branch and activated one of the machines with his Citibank card, pressed in his personal identification code, and withdrew $20. When he approached the machine, a person was using the customer service telephone located between two ATM machines and appeared to

be telling customer service that one of the machines was malfunctioning. As Ognibene was making his withdrawal the person said into the telephone, "I'll see if his card works in my machine." He then asked Ognibene if he could use his card to see if the other machine was working. Ognibene handed his card to him and saw him insert it into the adjoining machine at least two times while saying into the telephone, "Yes, it seems to be working."

When Ognibene received his Citibank statement, it showed that two withdrawals of $200 each from his account were made at 5:42 PM and 5:43 PM, respectively, August 16. His own $20 withdrawal was made at 5:41 PM. At the time, Ognibene was unaware that any withdrawals from his account were being made from the adjoining machine. Ognibene sought to have his account recredited for $400, claiming that the withdrawals had been unauthorized. Citibank had been aware for some time of a scam being perpetrated against its customers by persons who observed the customer inserting his personal identification number into an ATM and then obtaining access to the customer's ATM card in the same manner as Ognibene's card was obtained. After learning about the scam, Citibank posted signs in ATM areas containing a red circle approximately 2½ inches in diameter in which was written "Do Not Let Your Citicard Be Used For Any Transaction But Your Own." Was Citibank required under the Electronic Funds Transfer Act to recredit Ognibene's account on the grounds that the withdrawal of the $400 was unauthorized?

Part 8

Credit Transactions

Chapter 42

Introduction to Security

LO

Learning Objectives

After you have studied this chapter, you should be able to:

1. Explain the difference between unsecured credit and secured credit.
2. Recall the definition of a surety, relate how the principal and surety relationship is created, and explain the defenses that may be available to a surety as well as the duties that a creditor owes to a surety.
3. Describe common law liens and how they are created, and recall the rights that they provide to artisans and others who hold such a lien.
4. Compare and contrast mortgages, deeds of trust, and land contracts as mechanisms for holding a security interest in real property.
5. List the formalities necessary for the creation of a legally enforceable mortgage, and explain what is meant by "foreclosure" and the "right of redemption."
6. Describe mechanic's and materialman's liens, and explain how they are obtained and what rights they give the lienholder.

Eric Johnson decided to go into the commercial laundry and dry-cleaning business. He began by agreeing to buy the land, building, and equipment of a small dry cleaner. Johnson agreed to pay the owner $200,000 in cash and "to assume" a $50,000 existing mortgage on the property. He next entered into a contract with a local contractor to build, within five months, a large addition to the building for $150,000 with $40,000 payable with the signing of the contract and the balance to be paid in periodic installments as the construction progressed. Because Johnson had heard some horror stories from friends in the local Chamber of Commerce about contractors who walked away from jobs without completing them, he asked the contractor to post a security bond or provide a surety to assure the contract would be completed in a timely manner. Johnson also had some of the existing dry-cleaning equipment picked up for repair and refurbishment.

(continued)

When the work was completed, the repairman refused to redeliver it until Johnson paid in full for the work, claiming he had a lien on the equipment until he was paid.

Among the questions that will be addressed in this chapter are these:

- What legal rights and obligations accompany the "assumption" of a mortgage?
- Would Johnson risk losing any of his rights to recover against the surety if he granted the contractor additional time to complete the construction?
- If the contractor does not pay subcontractors or companies who provide construction material for the job, would they be able to assert a lien against the property until they are paid?
- Would the person who repaired and refurbished the dry-cleaning equipment still be able to assert a lien until Johnson paid for it? Would it make a difference if the repair work had been done on-site?

Credit

Nature of Credit

In the United States, a substantial portion of business transactions involve the extension of credit. The term *credit* has many meanings. In this chapter, **credit** will be used to mean a transaction in which money is loaned, goods are sold, or services are rendered in exchange for a promise to pay for them at some future date.

In some of these transactions, a creditor is willing to rely on the debtor's promise to pay at a later time; in others, the creditor wants some future assurance or security that the debtor will make good on his promise to pay. Various mechanisms are available to the creditor who wants to obtain security. These mechanisms include obtaining liens or security interests in personal or real property, sureties, and guarantors. Security interests in real property, sureties and guarantors, and common law liens on personal property will be covered in this chapter, and the Uniform Commercial Code rules concerning security interests in personal property will be covered in Chapter 43. Chapter 44 will deal with bankruptcy law, which may come into play when a debtor is unable to fulfill his obligation to pay his debts when they are due.

LO1

Unsecured Credit

Many common transactions are based on *unsecured credit.* For example, you may have a charge account at a department store or a MasterCard account. If you buy a sweater and charge it to your charge account or your MasterCard account, unsecured credit has been extended to you. You have received goods in return for your unsecured promise to pay for them later. Similarly, if you go to a dentist to have a cavity in a tooth filled and he sends you a bill payable by the end of the month, services have been rendered on the basis of unsecured credit. Consumers are not the only people who use unsecured credit. Many transactions between businesspeople utilize it. For example, a retailer buys merchandise or a manufacturer buys raw materials, promising to pay for the merchandise or materials within 30 days after receipt.

The unsecured credit transaction involves a maximum of risk to the creditor (the person who extends the credit). When goods are delivered, services rendered, or money loaned on unsecured credit, the creditor gives up all rights in the goods, services, or money. In return, the creditor gets a promise by the debtor to pay or to perform the requested act. If the debtor does not pay or keep the promise, the creditor's only course of action is to bring a lawsuit against the debtor and obtain a judgment. The creditor may then have the sheriff execute the judgment on any property owned by the debtor that is subject to execution. The creditor might also try to garnish the wages or other monies to which the debtor is entitled. However, the debtor might be **judgment proof;** that is, the debtor might not have any property subject to execution or might not have a steady job. Under these circumstances, execution or garnishment would be of little aid to the creditor in collecting the judgment.

A businessperson may obtain credit insurance to stabilize the credit risk of doing business on an unsecured credit basis. However, the costs to the business of the insurance or of the unsecured credit losses it sustains are passed on to the consumer. The consumer pays a higher price for goods or services purchased or a higher interest rate on any money borrowed from a business that has high credit losses.

Secured Credit

To minimize her credit risk, a creditor can contract for **security.** The creditor may require the debtor to convey to the creditor a **security interest** or lien on the debtor's property. Suppose you borrow $3,000 from a credit union. It might require that you put up your car as security for the loan. The creditor might also ask that some other person agree to be liable if the debtor defaults. For example, if a student who does not have a regular job goes to a bank to borrow money, the bank might ask that the student's father or mother cosign the note for the loan.

When the creditor has security for the credit he extends and the debtor defaults, the creditor can go against the security to collect the obligation. Assume that you borrow $20,000 from a bank to buy a new car and the bank takes a security interest (lien) on the car. If you fail to make your monthly payments, the bank has the right to repossess the car and have it sold so that it can recover its money. Similarly, if your father cosigned for the car loan and you default, the bank can sue your father to collect the balance due on the loan.

Suretyship

LO2

Sureties and Guarantors

A **surety** is a person who is liable for the payment of another person's debt or for the performance of another person's duty. The surety joins with the person who is primarily liable in promising to make the payment or to perform the duty. For example, Kathleen, who is 17 years old, buys a used car on credit from Harry's Used Cars. She signs a promissory note, agreeing to pay $200 a month on the note until the note is paid in full. Harry's has Kathleen's father cosign the note; thus, her father is a surety. Similarly, the City of Chicago hires the B&B Construction Company to build a new sewage treatment plant. The city will probably require B&B to have a surety agreement to be liable for B&B's performance of its contract. There are insurance companies that, for a fee, will agree to be a surety for a company like B&B on its contract. If the person who is primarily liable (the principal) defaults, the surety is liable to pay or perform. Then the surety is entitled to be reimbursed by the principal.

A **guarantor** does not join in making a promise; rather, a guarantor makes a separate promise and agrees to be liable on the happening of a certain event. For example, a father tells a merchant, "I will guarantee payment of my son Richard's debt to you if he does not pay it," or "In the event that Richard becomes bankrupt, I will guarantee payment of his debt to you." A guarantor's promise must be made in writing to be enforceable under the statute of frauds.

The rights and liabilities of the surety and the guarantor are substantially the same. No distinction will be made between them in this chapter except where the distinction is of basic importance.

Creation of Principal and Surety Relationship

The relationship of principal and surety, or that of principal and guarantor, is created by contract. The basic rules of contract law apply in determining the existence and nature of the relationship as well as the rights and duties of the parties.

Defenses of a Surety

Suppose that Jeff's father agrees to be a surety for Jeff on his purchase of a motorcycle on credit from a dealer. If the motorcycle was defectively made and Jeff refuses to make further payments on it, the dealer might try to collect the balance due from Jeff's father. As a surety, Jeff's father can use any defenses against the dealer that Jeff has if they go to the merits of the primary contract. Thus, if Jeff has a valid defense of breach of warranty against the dealer, his father can use it as a basis for not paying the dealer.

Other defenses that go to the merits include (1) lack or failure of consideration, (2) inducement of the contract by fraud or duress, and (3) breach of contract by the other party. The personal defenses of the principal cannot be used by the surety. These personal defenses include lack of capacity, such as minority or insanity, and bankruptcy. Thus, if Jeff is only 17 years old, the fact that he is a minor cannot be used by Jeff's father to defend against the dealer. This defense of Jeff's lack of capacity to contract does not go to the merits of the contract between Jeff and the dealer and cannot be used by Jeff's father.

A surety contracts to be responsible for the performance of the principal's obligation. If the principal and the creditor change that obligation by agreement, the surety is relieved of responsibility unless the surety agrees to the change. This is because the surety's obligation cannot be changed without his consent.

For example, Fred cosigns a note that his friend Kathy has given to Credit Union to secure a loan. Suppose the note was originally for $2,500 and payable in 12 months with interest at 11 percent a year. Credit Union and Kathy later agree that Kathy will have 24 months to repay the note but that the interest will be 13 percent per year. Unless Fred consents to this change, he is discharged from his responsibility as surety. The obligation he agreed to assume was altered by the changes in the repayment period and interest rate.

The most common kind of change affecting a surety is an extension of time to perform the contract. If the creditor merely allows the principal more time without the surety's consent, this does not relieve the surety of responsibility. The surety's consent is required only where there is an agreement between the creditor and the principal as to the extension of time. In addition, the courts usually make a distinction between accommodation sureties and compensated sure ties. An **accommodation surety** is a person who acts as a surety without compensation, such as a friend who cosigns a note as a favor. A **compensated surety** is a person, usually a professional such as a bonding company, who is paid for serving as a surety.

The courts are more protective of accommodation sureties than of compensated sureties. Accommodation sureties are relieved of liability unless they consent to the extension of time. Compensated sureties, on the other hand, must show that they will be harmed by an extension of time before they are relieved of responsibility because of an extension of time to which they have not consented.

Creditor's Duties to Surety

The creditor is required to disclose any material facts about the risk involved to the surety. If he does not do so, the surety is relieved of liability. For example, a bank (creditor) knows that an employee, Arthur, has been guilty of criminal conduct in the past. If the bank applies to a bonding company to obtain a bond on Arthur, the bank must disclose that information to the surety. Similarly, suppose the bank has an employee, Alice, covered by a bond and discovers that Alice is embezzling money. If the bank agrees to give Alice another chance but does not report her actions to the bonding company, the bonding company is relieved of responsibility for further wrongful acts by Alice.

If the principal posts security for the performance of an obligation, the creditor must not surrender that security without the consent of the surety. If the creditor does so, the surety is relieved of liability to the extent of the value surrendered. The *Camp* case illustrates this principle.

Camp v. First Financial Federal Savings and Loan Association

772 S.W.2d 602 (Sup. Ct. Ark. 1989)

FACTS

Rusty Jones, a used-car dealer, applied to First Financial Federal Savings and Loan Association for a $50,000 line of credit to purchase an inventory of used cars. First Financial refused to make the loan to Jones alone but agreed to do so if Worth Camp, an attorney and friend of Jones, would cosign the note. Camp agreed to cosign as an accommodation maker or surety. The expectation of the parties was that the loans cosigned by Camp would be repaid from the proceeds of the car inventory.

The original note for $25,000 was signed on August 2, 1984, and renewals were executed on January 25, 1985, September 11, 1985, and March 15, 1986, and the amount was eventually increased to $50,000. In August 1985, as Camp was considering whether to sign the September renewal note, he was advised by First Financial's loan officer that the interest on the loan had been paid. In fact, interest payments were four months delinquent. In addition, unknown to Camp, as the $50,000 credit limit was approached, First Financial began making side, or personal, loans to Jones totaling around $25,000, which were also payable out of the proceeds of the used-car inventory. Camp knew nothing of these loans and thought that Jones's used-car business was making payments only on the loans he had cosigned.

Jones defaulted on the $50,000 note cosigned by Camp, and First Financial brought suit against Camp on his obligation as surety on the note.

ISSUE

Was Camp relieved of his obligation as surety by First Financial's failure to disclose material facts to him?

DECISION

Yes. The court held that a surety has a defense against performance of his obligation if the creditor failed to disclose facts that materially increased the surety's risk. Here, the creditor was in possession of facts concerning the true state of Jones's payments and the secret side loans it had made. It knew that the surety, Camp, was not in possession of this information and that it was very relevant to Camp's assessment of the risk he would undertake as surety on the renewals of the note. First Financial's failure to communicate the information to Camp in a timely fashion gives him a defense to being required to perform his obligation as surety.

Subrogation and Contribution

If the surety has to perform or pay the principal's obligation, then the surety acquires all the rights that the creditor had against the principal. This is known as the surety's **right of subrogation.** The rights include the right to any collateral in the possession of the creditor, any judgment right the creditor had against the principal on the obligation, and the rights of a creditor in bankruptcy proceedings.

If the surety performs or pays the principal's obligation, she is entitled to recover her costs from the principal; this is known as the surety's **right to reimbursement.** For example, Amanda cosigns a promissory note for $250 at the credit union for her friend Anne. Anne defaults on the note, and the credit union collects $250 from Amanda on her suretyship obligation. Amanda then not only gets the credit union's rights against Anne but also the right to collect $250 from Anne.

Suppose several persons (Tom, Dick, and Harry) are cosureties of their friend Sam. When Sam defaults, Tom pays the whole obligation. Tom is entitled to collect one-third each from both Dick and Harry since he paid more than his prorated share. This is known as the cosurety's **right to contribution.** The relative shares of cosureties, as well as any limitations on their liability, are normally set out in the contract of suretyship.

Liens on Personal Property

Security Interests in Personal Property and Fixtures under the Uniform Commercial Code

Chapter 43 will discuss how a creditor can obtain a security interest in the personal property or fixtures of a debtor. It will also explain the rights of the creditor, the debtor, and other creditors of the debtors to the property. These security interests are covered by Article 9 of the Uniform Commercial Code, which sets out a comprehensive scheme for regulating security interests in personal property and fixtures. Article 9 does not deal with the liens that landlords, artisans, and materialmen are given by statute or with security interests in real estate. These security interests will be covered in this chapter.

LO3

Common Law Liens

Under the common—or judge-made—law, artisans, innkeepers, and common carriers (such as airlines and trucking companies) were entitled to liens to secure the reasonable value of the services they performed. An artisan such as a furniture upholsterer or an auto mechanic uses his labor and/or materials to improve personal property that belongs to someone else. The improvement becomes part of the property and belongs to the owner of the property. Therefore, the artisan who made the improvement is given a **lien** on the property until he is paid. For example, the upholsterer who recovers a sofa for you is entitled to a lien on the sofa.

The innkeeper and common carrier are in business to serve the public and are required by law to do so. Under the common law, the innkeeper was allowed to claim a lien on the guest's property brought to the hotel or inn to secure payment for the innkeeper's reasonable charges for food and lodging. Similarly, the common carrier, such as a trucking company, was allowed to claim a lien on the goods carried for the reasonable charges for the service. The justification for these liens was that because the innkeeper and common carrier were required by law to provide the service to anyone seeking it, they were entitled to the protection of a lien.

Statutory Liens

While common law liens are generally recognized today, many states have incorporated this concept in statutes. Some of the state statutes have created additional liens while others have modified the common law liens to some extent. The statutes commonly provide a procedure for foreclosing the lien. **Foreclosure** is the method by which a court authorizes the sale of the personal property subject to the lien so that the creditor can obtain the money to which he is entitled.

Characteristics of Liens

The common law lien and most of the statutory liens are known as **possessory liens.** They give the artisan or other lienholder the right to keep possession of the debtor's property until the reasonable charges for the service have been paid. For the lien to come into play, possession of the goods must have been entrusted to the artisan. Suppose you take a chair to an upholsterer to have it repaired. She can keep possession of it until you pay the reasonable value of the repair work. However, if the upholsterer comes to your home to make the repair, she would not have a lien on the chair because you did not give up possession of it.

The two essential elements of the lien are (1) *possession by the improver or provider of services* and (2) *a debt created by the improvement or provision of services concerning the goods.* If the artisan or other lienholder gives up the goods voluntarily, he loses the lien. For example, if you have a new engine put in your car and the mechanic gives the car back to you before you pay for the engine, the mechanic loses the lien on the car to secure your payment for the work and materials. However, if the debtor regains possession by fraud or other illegal act, the lien is not lost. Once the debt is paid, the lien is terminated, and the artisan or other lienholder no longer has the right to retain the goods. If the artisan keeps the goods after the debt has been paid, or keeps the goods without the right to a lien, he is liable for conversion or unlawful detention of goods.

In the case that follows below, *Swift, Inc. v. Sheffey*, the court had to decide whether an artisan was entitled to claim a lien on a truck that had been left with it for repair.

Foreclosure of Lien

The right of a lienholder to possess goods does not automatically give the lienholder the right to sell the property or to claim ownership if his charges are not paid. Commonly, there is a procedure provided by statute for selling the property once it has been held for a certain period of time. The lienholder is required to give notice to the debtor and to advertise the proposed sale by posting or publishing notices. If there is no statutory procedure, the lienholder must first bring a lawsuit against the debtor. After obtaining a judgment for his charges, the lienholder can have the sheriff seize the property and have it sold at a judicial sale.

Swift, Inc. v. Sheffey

2010 Iowa App. LEXIS 1384 (Ct. App. Iowa 2010)

FACTS

Michael Simons teamed up with other musicians to form The Swift, a gospel music group that traveled the country performing for young people at churches and conferences. They purchased a 2005 Ford E540 truck for $55,000 and spent between $14,000 and $15,000 customizing it with bunk beds and couches. While traveling through the Quad cities in Iowa on March 31, 2007, the group noticed the vehicle was having mechanical difficulties. The Swift stopped at Sergeant Peppers, a repair shop in Davenport, and received a referral to Sheffey, who reportedly worked on larger vehicles.

(continued)

When Sheffey inspected the vehicle, it began leaking water. Sheffey speculated that the problem was related to the water pump and took the vehicle to his shop to replace the pump. The Swift left the vehicle with Sheffey and traveled to its next show in Lakota. The following day, Sheffey called The Swift to inform the group he had discovered the radiator hose had blown off the water pump, that it was an easy fix, and that the vehicle would be ready when the group returned to Davenport. Sheffey clamped the radiator hose and replaced the serpentine belts.

As The Swift was making its return trip to Davenport, Sheffey phoned to report that his repair had not fixed the vehicle's problem. He told the group that there was something wrong with the vehicle, but he did not know what the problem was. The Swift returned to Nashville and told Sheffey to deliver word as soon as he knew what was wrong with the vehicle.

During the course of the next month, Simons called Sheffey to check on his progress in diagnosing and repairing the vehicle. In various conversations, Sheffey informed Simons that he was awaiting schematics from Ford, had removed the engine from the vehicle, and was awaiting the arrival of parts he had ordered. Simons claimed that Sheffey was unable to state what was wrong with the vehicle or what was needed to be done to repair it.

On April 30, 2007, Sheffey faxed Simons 24 pages of instructions on how to repair what he believed to be the problem. Sheffey claimed he sent the document at the group's behest in response to a question by one of the members as to what parts had been ordered. Sheffey also sent two invoices billing the group for repairs; the first was the bill for the initial repair of the radiator hose and the serpentine belts for $1,259.32 and the second was a bill for the work Sheffey had performed to that point in removing the vehicle's engine for $6,667.13, which included 45 hours worth of labor charges and $2,500 for parts. The parts were not itemized but Sheffey claimed the exact cost was more than $2,500, but that it had been rounded off.

The Swift contacted Reynolds Ford to reassemble the engine, but when a mechanic arrived at Sheffey's to retrieve the vehicle and engine, Sheffey said he needed payment for his services before he would relese the vehicle. On December 17, 2007, The Swift made a written demand for return of the vehicle and on July 15, 2008, they filed a petition in replevin, seeking against Sheffey the return of the vehicle and $21,658.16 for loss of the property. Sheffey took the position that it had a valid mechanic's lien on the vehicle that had to be satisfied before it had to release the vehicle.

Iowa Code section 577.1, provides that a person who

> Renders any material in the making, repairing, improving or enhancing the value of any inanimate person property with the assent of the owner, express or implied, shall have a **lien** thereon for the agreed or reasonable compensation for the service and material while such property is lawfully in the person's possession, which possession the person may retain until such compensation is paid. . . .

ISSUE

Does Sheffey have a valid mechanic's lien to secure compensation for the work it did removing the engine and obtaining parts to try to fix it?

DECISION

No. The court held that to show the existence of a valid artisan's lien, Sheffey was required to prove, first, the performance of a service in the making, repairing, improving, or enhancing the value of the vehicle, and second, that he performed the service with The Swift's assent.

The court found that the evidence showed substantial miscommunication between the parties concerning what was authorized and what was to be charged and was unable to find whether or not The Swift had authorized the repairs as conducted by Sheffey. Because the burden was on Sheffey to show by a preponderance of the evidence that the miscommunication amounted to The Swift's assent to dismantling the engine and it had not done so, Sheffey did not have a valid mechanic's lien, and The Swift were entitled to the immediate return of their vehicle.

Security Interests in Real Property

There are three basic contract devices for using real estate as security for an obligation: (1) the real estate mortgage, (2) the deed of trust, and (3) the land contract. In addition, the states have enacted statutes giving mechanics, such as carpenters and plumbers, and materialmen, such as lumberyards, a right to a lien on real property into which their labor or materials are incorporated. Some states give the right to a lien only to prime contractors, while other states also extend it to subcontractors.

LO4

Real Estate Mortgage

LO5

A **mortgage** is a security interest in real property or a deed to real property that is given by the owner (the **mortgagor**) as security for a debt owed to the creditor (the **mortgagee**). Because the real estate mortgage conveys an interest in real property, it must be executed with the same formality as a deed. Unless it is executed with the required formalities, it will not be eligible for recording in the local land records. Recordation of the mortgage does not affect its validity as between the mortgagor and the mortgagee. However, if it is not recorded, it will not be effective against subsequent purchasers of the property or creditors, including other mortgagees, who have no notice of the earlier mortgage. It is important to the mortgagee that the mortgage be recorded so that the world will be on notice of the mortgagee's interest in that property.

The owner (mortgagor) of property subject to a mortgage can sell the interest in the property without the consent of the mortgagee. However, the sale does not affect the mortgagee's interest in the property or claim against the mortgagor.

For example, Eric Smith owns a lot on a lake. Eric wants to build a cottage on the land, so he borrows $85,000 from First National Bank. Eric signs a note for $85,000 and gives the bank an $85,000 mortgage on the land and cottage as security for his repayment of the loan. Several years later, Eric sells his land and cottage to Melinda Mason. The mortgage he gave First National might make the unpaid balance due on the mortgage payable on sale. If it does not, Eric can sell the property with the mortgage on it. If Melinda defaults on the mortgage payments, the bank can foreclose on the mortgage. If, at the foreclosure sale, the property does not bring enough money to cover the costs, interest, and balance due on the mortgage, First National is entitled to a deficiency judgment against Eric. However, some courts are reluctant to give deficiency judgments where real property is used as security for a debt and some state laws specifically disallow them where personal residential property is involved. If, on foreclosure, the property sells for more than the debt, Melinda is entitled to the surplus.

A purchaser of mortgaged property can buy it "subject to the mortgage" or may "assume the mortgage." If she buys **subject to** the mortgage and there is a default and foreclosure, the purchaser is not personally liable for any deficiency. The property is liable for the mortgage debt and can be sold to satisfy it in case of default. If the buyer **assumes** the mortgage, then she becomes personally liable for the debt and for any deficiency on default and foreclosure.

The creditor (mortgagee) may assign his interest in the mortgaged property. To do this, the mortgagee must assign the mortgage as well as the debt for which the mortgage is security.

Foreclosure is the process by which any rights of the mortgagor or the current property owner are cut off. Foreclosure proceedings are regulated by statute in the state in which the property is located. The sale commonly takes place under the supervision of a court, but in a few states no court action is required. In the latter case, the mortgagee must give notice of the proposed sale to the mortgagor and advertise to the public, with the actual sale taking place by auction. If the property is sold at a foreclosure sale and not redeemed by the owner, then the proceeds of the sale are used to pay the foreclosure costs, the interest, and the debt. Any surplus from the sale is returned to the owner of the property. Commonly, the states provide a period of time (usually six months to a year) after default on the debt during which the owner or other person with an interest in the property can **redeem** it by paying off the mortgage.

A small number of states permit what is called **strict foreclosure.** The creditor keeps the property in satisfaction of the debt, and the owner's rights are cut off. This means that the creditor has no right to a deficiency and the debtor has no right to any surplus. Strict foreclosure is normally limited to situations in which the amount of the debt exceeds the value of the property.

Recent Developments Concerning Foreclosures

As the subprime lending crisis unfolded during 2007, the number of defaults and foreclosure actions on both subprime and conventional mortgages increased significantly, and the number of foreclosures remained high as this book went to press. In 2010, there were 3.8 million foreclosure filings in the United States, an increase of about 800,000 over the number filed the previous year. Historically, mortgage lenders were local banks that lent money to a homeowner who then paid the money back to the bank. If the loan was in difficulty, the borrower and local lender would work through the matter directly. Over time, local lenders began to resell or assign the loans they originated to others. And in recent years, the practice of bundling loans together as mortgage-backed securities became commonplace.

Securitization takes the role of the lender and breaks it down into different components. The loan is sold to a third party, the issuer, that bundles the loan into a security and then sells it to investors who are entitled to a share of the cash paid by the borrowers on their mortgages. Another party—the trustee—is created to represent the interests of the investor. And yet another party—the servicer—collects the payments, distributes them to the issuer, and deals with any delinquencies on the part of borrowers.

Thus, these arrangements involving bundles of hundreds or thousands of mortgages are much more complex than the simple assignment of a single mortgage, and concomitantly the paperwork involved is much more complicated—and the documentation sometimes incomplete when there is pressure to get deals done.

As some of the collateralized loans fell into default and the owners of the securities—often large banks—brought foreclosure actions, judges began to scrutinize the cases to make sure that the parties bringing the foreclosure actions actually were the legal holders of the mortgage obligation and to dismiss cases where that showing had not been made. The opinion that follows in *In re Foreclosure Cases* generated a lot of attention in the media and the financial and legal communities when it was issued in October 2007 to serve as a warning to would-be foreclosers that they needed to have their paperwork in order before they sought to put a homeowner out of his house.

In re Foreclosure Cases

2007 U.S. Dist. LEXIS 84011 (N.D. Ohio 2007)

BOYKO, U.S. DISTRICT JUDGE.

On October 10, 2007, this court issued an Order requiring Plaintiff-Lenders in a number of pending foreclosure cases to file a copy of the executed Assignment demonstrating Plaintiff was the holder and owner of the Note and Mortgage *as of the date the Complaint was filed,* or the Court would order a dismissal. After considering the submissions along with all the documents filed of record, the Court dismisses the captioned cases without prejudice.

To satisfy the requirements of Article III of the United States Constitution, the plaintiff must show he has personally suffered some actual injury as a result of the illegal conduct of the defendant. In each of the Complaints, the named Plaintiff alleges that it is the holder and owner of the Note and Mortgage. However, the attached Note and Mortgage identify the mortgagee and promisee as the original lending institution—one other than the named Plaintiff. Further the Preliminary Judicial Report attached as an exhibit to the complaint makes no reference to the named Plaintiff in the recorded chain of title/interest. The Court's Amended General Order requires Plaintiff to submit an affidavit along with the complaint, which identifies Plaintiff either as the original

(continued)

mortgage holder, or as an assignee, trustee, or successor-in-interest. Once again, the affidavits submitted in all these cases recite the averment that Plaintiff is the owner of the Note and Mortgage, without any mention of an assignment or trust or successor interest. Consequently, the very filings and submissions of the Plaintiff create a conflict. In every instance, then, Plaintiff has not satisfied its burden of demonstrating standing at the time of the filing of the Complaint.

Understandably, the Court requested clarification by requiring each Plaintiff to submit a copy of the Assignment of the Note and Mortgage, executed as of the date of the Foreclosure Complaint. In the above captioned cases, *none* of the Assignments show the named Plaintiff to be the owner of the rights, title, and interest under the Mortgage at issue as of the date of the Foreclosure Complaint. The Assignments, in every instance, express a present intent to convey all rights, title and interest in the Mortgage and the accompanying Note to the Plaintiff named in the Foreclosure Complaint upon receipt of sufficient consideration on the date the Assignment was signed and notarized. Those proferred documents belie Plaintiffs' assertion they own the Note and Mortgage by means of a purchase which predated the Complaint by days, months or years.

This Court is obligated to carefully scrutinize all filings and pleadings in foreclosure actions, since the unique nature of real property requires contracts and transactions concerning real property to be in writing. Ohio law holds that when a mortgage is assigned, moreover, the assignment is subject to the recording requirements. Thus, with regards to real property, before an entity assigned an interest in that property would be entitled to receive a distribution from the sale of the property, their interest therein must have been recorded in accordance with Ohio law.[1]

This Court acknowledges the right of banks, holding valid mortgages, to receive timely payments. And, if they do not receive timely payments, banks have the right to properly file actions on the defaulted notes—seeking foreclosure on the property securing the notes. Yet, this Court possesses the independent obligations to preserve the judicial integrity of the federal court and to jealously guard federal jurisdiction. Neither the fluidity of the secondary mortgage market, nor monetary or economic considerations of the parties, nor the convenience of the litigants, supersede those obligations.

Despite Plaintiffs' counsel's belief that "there appears to be some level of disagreement and/or misunderstanding amongst professionals, borrowers, attorneys and members of the judiciary," the Court does not require instruction and is not operating under any misapprehension.

Plaintiff's, "Judge, you just don't understand how things work," argument reveals a condescending mindset and quasi-monopolistic system where financial institutions have traditionally controlled, and still control, the foreclosure process. Typically, the homeowner who finds himself/herself in financial straits, fails to make the required mortgage payments and faces a foreclosure suit, is not interested in testing state or federal jurisdictional requirements, either *pre se* or through counsel. Their focus is either, "how do I save my home," or "if I have to give it up, I'll simply leave and find somewhere else to live."

In the meantime, the financial institutions or successors/assignees rush to foreclose, obtain a default judgment and then sit on the deed, avoiding responsibility for maintaining the property while reaping the financial benefits of interest running on a judgment. The financial institutions know the law charges the one with title (still the homeowner) with maintaining the property.

There is no doubt every decision made by a financial institution in the foreclosure process is driven by money. And the legal work which flows from winning the financial institution's favor is highly lucrative. There is nothing improper or wrong with financial institutions or law firms making a profit—to the contrary, they should be rewarded for sound business and legal practices. However, unchallenged by underfinanced opponents, the institutions worry less about jurisdictional requirements and more about maximizing returns. Unlike the focus of financial institutions, the federal courts must act as gatekeepers, assuring that only those who meet diversity and standing requirements are allowed to pass through. Counsel for the institutions are not without legal argument to support their position, but their arguments fall woefully short of justifying their premature filings, and utterly fail to satisfy their standing and jurisdictional burdens. The institutions seem to adopt the attitude that since they have been doing this for so long, unchallenged, this practice equates with legal compliance. Finally put to the test, their weak legal arguments compel the Court to stop them at the gate.

The Court will illustrate in simple terms its decision: "Fluidity of the market"—"X" dollars, "contractual arrangements between institutions and counsel"—"X" dollars, "purchasing mortgages in bulk and securitizing"—"X" dollars, "rush to file, slow to record after judgment"—"X" dollars, "the jurisdictional integrity of United States District Court"—"Priceless."

For all the foregoing reasons, the above-captioned Foreclosure Complaints are dismissed without prejudice.

[1] Astoundingly, counsel at oral argument stated that his client, the purchaser from the original mortgagee, acquired complete legal and equitable interest in land when money changed hands, even before the purchase agreement, let alone a proper assignment, made its way into his client's possession.

LO4

Deed of Trust

There are three parties to a **deed of trust:** (1) the owner of the property who borrows the money, (2) the trustee who holds legal title to the property put up as security, and (3) the lender who is the beneficiary of the trust. The purpose of the deed of trust is to make it easy for the security to be liquidated. However, most states treat the deed of trust like a mortgage in giving the borrower a relatively long period of time to redeem the property, thereby defeating this rationale for the arrangement.

In a deed of trust transaction, the borrower deeds to the trustee the property that is to be put up as security. The trust agreement usually gives the trustee the right to foreclose or sell the property if the borrower fails to make a required payment on the debt. Normally, the trustee does not sell the property until the lender notifies him that the borrower is in default and demands that the property be sold. The trustee then sells the property, usually at a public sale. The proceeds are applied to the costs of the foreclosure, interest, and debt. If there is a surplus, it is paid to the borrower. If there is a deficiency, the lender has to sue the borrower on the debt and recover judgment.

LO4

Land Contracts

The **land contract** is a device for securing the balance due the seller on the purchase price of real estate. The buyer agrees to pay the purchase price over a period of time. The seller agrees to convey title to the property to the buyer when the full price is paid. Usually, the buyer takes possession of the property, pays the taxes, insures the property, and assumes the other obligations of an owner. However, the seller keeps legal title and does not turn over the deed until the purchase price is paid. Purchases of farm property are commonly financed through the use of land contracts.

If the buyer defaults, the seller generally has the right to declare a forfeiture and take possession of the property. The buyer's rights to the property are cut off at that point. Most states give the buyer on a land contract a limited period of time to redeem his interest. Generally, the procedure for declaring a forfeiture and recovering property sold on a land contract is simpler and less time-consuming than foreclosure of a mortgage. However, as is illustrated in the case that follows, *Bennett v. Galindo,* some states protect purchasers against the severity of forfeiture and either provide a redemption period or require that a foreclosure procedure be used. In many states, the procedure to be followed in case of default on a land contract is specified by statute.

Bennett v. Galindo

1994 WL 613429 (D. Kan. 1994)

FACTS

Harold and Karen Galindo purchased a house from Carl Bennett and his wife, Lillian, pursuant to an installment land contract entitled "Conditional Sales Contract" and dated July 17, 1991. The contract included the following provisions: The $46,000 purchase price at a 9.5 percent fixed interest rate consisted of a down payment of $12,000 and 180 monthly installments of $355.04. The Galindos were to pay real estate taxes and insurance. They were given immediate possession of, but not legal title to, the premises. The title to the premises would not be conveyed to the Galindos until they paid the entire purchase price. The Galindos were entitled to remain in possession unless they defaulted under the contract. The contract defined "default" as failure to pay six monthly installments, real estate taxes, or insurance premiums. If the buyers defaulted under the

(continued)

contract, they forfeited all money previously paid to the Bennetts and were to surrender immediate possession of the premises to the Bennetts.

On December 17, 1993, counsel for the Bennetts mailed to the Galindos a written notice to cancel based upon the buyer's failure to pay monthly installments for April through June 1993, and September through December 1993, and $234.07 in real estate taxes owed for the last six months of 1993. Pursuant to the notice, the Galindos moved out of the property and turned over the property to the Bennetts' counsel.

On January 28, 1994, after consulting counsel concerning their rights, the Galindos filed an affidavit of equitable interest with the Register of Deeds of Crawford County, Kansas. They based their asserted equitable interest in the property upon the $19,451.34 in payments, including the down payment, that they made. A Kansas statute provides, in pertinent part:

> In the event a default occurs in the conditions of the mortgage or most senior lien foreclosed before 1/3 of the original indebtedness has been paid, the court shall order a redemption period of six months.

The Bennetts then brought suit in federal court alleging that the Galindos have no equitable interest in the property and asking the court to remove the cloud on their title. They argued that the Galindos' equitable redemption rights in the property lapsed, pursuant to the contract, prior to the surrender of the property.

ISSUE

Are the Galindos entitled to a six-month period to redeem the contract even though they defaulted on the contract by being in breach for more than six months?

DECISION

Yes. The $20,000 in payments made by the Galindos are substantial. Even though the installments were not always timely, forfeiture would be inequitable. The six-month equitable redemption period established by Kansas law is over and above any rights they had under the contract. Thus, the Galindos are entitled to have their equitable interest recognized and to have the six-month period provided by law to redeem the contract.

Ethics in Action

WHO WAS ETHICAL?

During the first half of the decade beginning in 2000, housing prices in many areas of the country escalated in price, creating a bubble in the housing market. At the same time, lenders began relaxing their standards for making loans to prospective homebuyers. In prior years, a purchaser would have to make a significant down payment on a house, putting up 10 or 20 percent of the purchase price. As banks and other mortgage originators increasingly sold the mortgages in packages to investors, they became less demanding about down payments and were willing to accept 5 percent or even nothing down. They also made loans that appeared very attractive to borrowers, with low interest rates and required monthly payments for the first few years of the loan—but then provided that both interest rates and monthly payments could escalate dramatically in a few years. Some borrowers entered into the loan agreements knowing they were a stretch but counting on prices continuing to rise, and they assumed they could always refinance into a more viable arrangement. Others experienced a change in their employment circumstances and no longer had the ability to make their payments. And others may not have understood the financial ramifications of what they had agreed to do or entered into the mortgage arrangements after making fraudulent statements about their financial circumstances and income. Do you find any of these actions to be unethical? Why?

LO6 Mechanic's and Materialman's Liens

Each state has a statute that permits persons who contract to furnish labor or materials to improve real estate to claim a lien on the property until they are paid. There are many differences among states as to exactly who can claim such a lien and the requirements that must be met to do so. In some states, the rights of all subcontractors and furnishers of materials are based on whatever rights the general contractor has and cannot exceed the amount of money due to the general contractor. In other states, subcontractors and materialmen such as lumberyards have the right to a direct lien for the full value of the work they did or the materials they furnished. The work and materials must be furnished for the improvement of a particular property or building. If they are sold generally without reference to a particular property, the provider of materials or labor is not entitled to a lien.

To obtain a lien, the person who furnishes labor or materials must comply strictly with the statutory requirements that cover the form, content, and time of notice of the lien. A mechanic's or materialman's lien is foreclosed in the same manner as a court foreclosure of a real estate mortgage. Under the provisions of some statutes, the right to a mechanic's lien can be waived by the supplier in the contract to make the improvement. Before the person who is having improvements made to his property makes final payment, he may require the contractor to sign an affidavit that all materialmen and subcontractors have been paid.

The case that follows, *Mutual Savings Association v. Res/Com Properties, LLC*, illustrates a situation where subcontractors were able to obtain a preferred position through compliance with a state lien statute.

Mutual Savings Association v. Res/Com Properties, LLC

79 P.3d 184 (Ct. App. Kansas 2003)

FACTS

In July 1999, George Kritos contracted with the Peridian Group to provide design and engineering services on a property known as the Whispering Meadows development in Eudora, Kansas. The work included boundary verification, topographical surveying, preparing preliminary and final site development plans, platting, storm water drainage studies, sanitary sewer design, street and storm sewer design, and water line design. The on-site work consisted of surveying, staking the boundary corners, staking of preliminary layouts for utilities and streets, plus horizontal and vertical control benchmark staking used for sewer, street, and storm water designs. Peridian's work began prior to May 22, 2000.

On May 22, 2000, Res/Com Properties, L.L.C., purchased the property from Kritos. That same day, Res/Com signed a promissory note and related mortgage in favor of Mutual Savings Association (Mutual). Mutual recorded its mortgage on May 24, 2000. Res/Com used the money it borrowed from Mutual to purchase the property from Kritos. Peridian then contracted with Res/Com to continue its design and engineering services.

On July 2, 2000, Modern Engineering Utilities Company, Inc. (Modern), began installing the sanitary sewers on the property under a subcontract with Heartland Building and Development Company, Res/Com's general contractor on the project. On July 19, Res/Com executed and delivered to Mutual a second mortgage to secure a further loan on the property; the mortgage was filed the following day, July 20, 2000. On August 30, LRM Industries, Inc. (LRM), entered into two contracts with Heartland to construct improvements on the property. LRM worked on the property from September through November 2000.

On October 26, 2000, Peridian filed its mechanic's lien. LRM filed its mechanic's lien on December 18, 2000, and Modern filed a lien on December 19, 2000. In March 2001, Mutual paid Peridian for its work, took an assignment of its lien, and filed a release of the lien. Res/Com subsequently defaulted on both of the notes it owed to Mutual. Mutual brought suit to foreclose its mortgages and one of the issues in the litigation was the relative priority of the mechanic's liens held by LRM and Modern. LRM and Modern argued that their liens were entitled to priority by "relating back" to Peridian's preliminary staking of the property and its off-site design and engineering work.

Kansas statute—K.S.A. Section 60–1101 entitled "Liens of contractors; priority"—states:

> Any person furnishing labor, equipment, material, or supplies used or consumed for the improvement of real property, under a contract or with the trustee, agent or spouse of the owner, shall have a lien upon the property for the labor, equipment, material or supplies furnished, and for the cost of transporting the same. The lien shall be preferred to all other liens or encumbrances which are

(continued)

Mutual Savings Association v. Res/Com Properties, LLC *(concluded)*

> subsequent to the furnishing of such labor, equipment, material or supplies at the site of the property subject to the lien. When two or more such contracts are entered into applicable to the same improvement, the liens of all claimants shall be similarly preferred to the date of the earliest unsatisfied lien of any of them.

K.S.A. 2002 Supp. 60–1103 entitled "Liens of subcontractors; procedure, recording and notice, owner's liability" states in part:

> (a) *Procedure.* Any supplier, subcontractor or other person furnishing labor, equipment, material or supplies, used or consumed at the site of the property subject to the lien, under an agreement with the contractor, subcontractor or owner contractor may obtain a lien for the amount due in the same manner and to the same extent as the original contractor.

ISSUE

Are the mechanic's liens, which relate to work done after mortgages on the property were filed, entitled to priority over those mortgages on the grounds that another mechanic's lien related to the same development was effective prior to the time the mortgages were filed?

DECISION

Yes. The purpose of the mechanic's lien law is to provide effective security to any persons furnishing labor, equipment, material, or supplies used or consumed for the improvement of real property under a contract with the owner. The theory underlying the granting of the lien against the property is that the property improved should be charged with the payment of the labor, equipment, material, or supplies. At the same time, a mechanic's lien is purely a creation of statute, and those claiming a mechanic's lien must bring themselves clearly within the provisions of the authorizing statute. Kansas law is clear that subcontractor's liens attach at the same time as the general work or construction. Here the engineering work by Peridian did not have to be visible before the work was lienable and it is irrelevant at what point in the construction process that work was used or consumed. The engineering firm's work was just as necessary in the project's development as was that of a contractor digging foundations. Accordingly, all the contractors' and subcontractors' liens were perfected as of the date the engineering firm started work, prior to Mutual's mortgage. The subcontractors' liens attached when they began work and had the same priority as the first unsatisfied lien, that of the engineering firm.

Concept Summary: Security Interests in Real Property

Type of Security Instrument	Parties	Features
Mortgage	1. Mortgagor (property owner/debtor) 2. Mortgagee (creditor)	1. Mortgagee holds a security interest (and in some states, title) in real property as security for a debt. 2. If mortgagor defaults on his obligation, mortgagee must *foreclose* on property to realize his security interest. 3. Mortgagor has a limited time after foreclosure to *redeem* his interest.
Deed of Trust	1. Owner/Debtor 2. Lendor/Creditor 3. Trustee	1. Trustee holds legal title to the real property put up as security. 2. If debt is satisfied, the trustee conveys property back to owner/debtor. 3. If debt is not paid as agreed, creditor notifies trustee to sell the property. 4. While intended to make foreclosure easier, most states treat it like a mortgage for purposes of foreclosure.

(continued)

Concept Summary: Security Interests in Real Property *(concluded)*

Type of Security Instrument	Parties	Features
Land Contract	1. Buyer 2. Seller	1. Seller agrees to convey title when full price is paid. 2. Buyer usually takes possession, pays property taxes and insurance, and maintains the property. 3. If buyer defaults, seller may declare a forfeiture and retake possession (most states) after buyer has limited time to redeem; some states require foreclosure.

Questions and Problem Cases

1. Bayer was the general contractor on a Massachusetts state highway contract. He hired Deschenes as a subcontractor to do certain excavation work. Deschenes was to start the job by November 24, 1988, and to complete it on or before March 1, 1989. Deschenes was required to furnish a bond of $91,000 to assure his faithful performance of the subcontract, and he purchased such a bond from Aetna Insurance Company. Deschenes began the work on December 1, 1988, and quit on June 22, 1989, after completing only about half of the work. Bayer had made numerous efforts to get Deschenes to do the work and then completed the job himself when Deschenes walked off the job. Bayer then brought a lawsuit against Aetna on the bond, and Aetna claimed that it was discharged by the extension of the time given to Deschenes. Should Bayer recover on the bond?
2. Mr. and Mrs. Marshall went to Beneficial Finance to borrow money but were deemed by Beneficial's office manager, Puckett, to be bad credit risks. The Marshalls stated that their friend Garren would be willing to cosign a note for them if necessary. Puckett advised Garren not to cosign because the Marshalls were bad credit risks. This did not dissuade Garren from cosigning a note for $480, but it prompted him to ask Beneficial to take a lien or security interest in Mr. Marshall's custom-built Harley-Davidson motorcycle, then worth over $1,000. Beneficial took and perfected a security interest in the motorcycle. Marshall defaulted on the first payment. Beneficial gave notice of the default to Garren and advised him that it was looking to him for payment. Garren then discovered that Beneficial and Marshall had reached an agreement whereby Marshall would sell his motorcycle for $700; he was to receive $345 immediately, which was to be applied to the loan, and he promised to pay the balance of the loan from his pocket. Marshall paid Beneficial $89.50 and left town without giving the proceeds of the sale to Beneficial. Because Beneficial was unable to get the proceeds from Marshall, it brought suit against Garren on his obligation as surety. When Beneficial released the security for the loan (the motorcycle) without Garren's consent, was Garren relieved of his obligation as surety for repayment of the loan?
3. Krista Babcock cosigned an automobile loan agreement that enabled her friend, Horne, to obtain a $5,000 loan to acquire an automobile from a third party. Horne defaulted on the loan after making a number of payments, and Babcock paid $2,000 to the lending institution to pay off the remaining balance on the loan. Babcock then brought suit against Horne to recover the $2,000. Is she entitled to recover the $2,000?

4. Philip and Edith Beh purchased some property from Alfred M. Gromer and his wife. Sometime earlier, the Gromers had borrowed money from City Mortgage. They had signed a note and had given City Mortgage a second deed of trust on the property. There was also a first deed of trust on the property at the time the Behs purchased it. In the contract of sale between the Behs and the Gromers, the Behs promised to "assume" the second deed of trust of approximately $5,000 at 6 percent interest. The Behs later defaulted on the first deed of trust on the property. Foreclosure was held on the first deed of trust but the proceeds of the sale left nothing for City Mortgage on its second deed of trust. City Mortgage then brought a lawsuit against the Behs to collect the balance due on the second trust. When the Behs "assumed" the second trust, did they become personally liable for it?
5. Pope agreed to sell certain land to Pelz and retained a mortgage on the property to secure payment of the purchase price. The mortgage contained a clause providing that if Pelz defaulted, Pope had the "right to enter upon the above-described premises and sell the same at public sale" to pay the purchase price, accounting to Pelz for any surplus. What type of foreclosure does this provision contemplate: (1) strict foreclosure, (2) judicial sale, or (3) private power of sale?
6. In October 1992, Verda Miller sold her 107-acre farm for $30,000 to Donald Kimball, who was acting on behalf of his own closely held corporation, American Wonderlands. Under the agreement, Miller retained title and Kimball was given possession pending full payment of all installments of the purchase price. The contract provided that Kimball was to pay all real estate taxes. If he did not pay them, Miller could discharge them and either add the amounts to the unpaid principal or demand immediate payment of the delinquencies plus interest. Miller also had the right to declare a forfeiture of the contract and regain possession if the terms of the agreement were not met. In 1995, Miller had to pay the real estate taxes on the property in the amount of $672.78. She demanded payment of this amount plus interest from Kimball. She also served a notice of forfeiture on him that he had 30 days to pay. Kimball paid the taxes but refused to pay interest of $10.48. Miller made continued demands on Kimball for two months, and then filed notice of forfeiture with the county recorder in August 1995. She also advised Kimball of this. Was Miller justified in declaring a forfeiture and taking back possession of the land?
7. Bowen-Rodgers Hardware Company was engaged in the business of furnishing materials for the construction of buildings. It delivered a quantity of materials to property owned by Ronald and Carol Collins. The materials were for the use of a contractor who was building a home for the Collinses as well as several other houses in the area. The hardware company was not paid for the materials by the contractor, and it sought to obtain a mechanic's lien against the Collinses' property. The Collinses claimed that even though the materials were delivered to their home, they were actually used to build other houses in the area. Was the Collinses' property subject to a mechanic's lien because payment had not been made for materials delivered to it?

Chapter 43

Security Interests in Personal Property

Learning Objectives

After you have studied this chapter, you should be able to:

1. Recognize and describe the different classes or types of collateral that can be used as collateral to secure a security interest under Article 9 of the Uniform Commercial Code.
2. List and explain the three requirements for creating a security interest in a debtor's property that will be enforceable against a debtor.
3. Explain why it is important that the creditor perfect his security interest and list the three main ways of perfecting a security interest.
4. Recall the general priority rules that the Code sets out for determining which of any conflicting security interests take precedence over other security interests or liens.
5. Explain what is meant by a purchase money security interest and discuss why the Code accords it preferential treatment.
6. Describe the steps a creditor can take when there is a default on the part of the debtor.

Emily Morales purchased a used Honda Civic from her local Honda dealer. She paid $500 down, and the dealer helped her arrange financing of the $4,500 balance through a local bank that placed a lien on the car to secure the loan. She fell behind in her payments when she was temporarily laid off from her job. Then the car was damaged by vandals one night while parked in the parking lot of the apartment complex where she rented an apartment. She took it to an automobile repair shop to have the damaged windshield and broken mirrors and headlamps replaced and portions of it repainted. When she went to pick it up, the repair shop

(continued)

refused to release it to her until she paid $950 cash for the repairs. Emily borrowed the money from her mother and was able to reclaim the car. However, several weeks later, she awoke one evening to see a flashing yellow light outside her apartment. She looked out the window and saw a tow truck was in the process of picking up her car by its rear end. She raced outside and confronted the driver as to what he was doing with her car. A loud shouting match ensued, during which the driver indicated he had been instructed by the bank to repossess the car because she was behind on her payments. Eventually, the truck driver got in his truck and drove away with the car towed behind, leaving Emily and a number of her neighbors, who had gathered to see what the commotion was about, cursing at the driver.

Among the issues posed by this hypothetical are these:

- What did the bank have to do to protect its interest in the Honda until Emily paid off the loan?
- If the bank had learned that the car was at the repair shop and sought to repossess it then, would the bank's lien or the repair shop's artisan's lien have the first priority?
- Was the bank within its rights in repossessing the car in the manner it did? If it was not, does Emily have any recourse?

Introduction

Article 9 of the Uniform Commercial Code

Today, a large portion of our economy involves the extension of credit. In many credit transactions, the creditor takes a security interest (or lien) in personal property belonging to the debtor in order to protect his investment. The law covering security interests in personal property is contained in Article 9 of the Uniform Commercial Code. Article 9, entitled Secured Transactions, applies to situations that consumers and businesspeople commonly face, such as the financing of an automobile, the purchase of a refrigerator on a time-payment plan, and the financing of business inventory.

If a creditor wants to obtain a security interest in the personal property of the debtor, he also wants to be sure that his interest will be superior to the claims of other creditors. To do so, the creditor must carefully comply with Article 9. Part 3 of this book, "Sales," pointed out that businesspersons sometimes leave out necessary terms in a contract or insert vague terms to be worked out later. Such looseness is a luxury that is not permitted when it comes to secured transactions. If a debtor gets into financial difficulties and cannot meet his obligations, it is important to the creditor that he carefully complied with Article 9. Even a minor noncompliance may result in the creditor's losing his preferred claim to the personal property of the debtor. A creditor who loses his secured interest will be only a general creditor of the debtor if the debtor is declared bankrupt. As a general creditor in bankruptcy proceedings, he may have little chance of recovering the money owed by the debtor because of the relatively low priority of such claims. This issue will be covered in detail in Chapter 44.

In 1998, the National Conference on Uniform State Laws adopted a Revised Article 9 that has now been adopted by all 50 states. Then in 2010 additional amendments to Article 9 were drafted to respond to filing issues and other matters that have arisen in practice following a decade of experience with the 1998 version. The 2010 amendments were designed to go into effect simultaneously on July 1, 2013. As of the time this book went to press, the amendments have been adopted by most, but not all, of the states. Because Article 9 has not been adopted in exactly the same form in every state, the law must be examined very carefully to determine the procedure in a particular state for obtaining a security interest and for ascertaining the rights of the creditors and debtors. However, the general concepts are the same in each state and will be the basis of our discussion in this chapter.

Security Interests

Basic to a discussion of secured transactions is the term **security interest.** A security interest is an interest in personal property or fixtures that a creditor obtains to secure payment or performance of an obligation (1–201[37]).[1] For example, when you borrow money from the bank to buy a new car, the bank takes a security interest in (puts a lien on) your car until the loan is repaid. If you default on the loan, the bank can repossess the car and have it sold and apply the sale price against the unpaid balance on the loan.

LO1

Types of Collateral

Goods—tangible items such as automobiles and business computers—are commonly used as collateral for loans. Article 9 of the Uniform Commercial Code also covers security interests in a much broader grouping of personal property. The Code breaks down personal property into a number of different classifications, which are important in determining how a creditor obtains an enforceable security interest in a particular kind of collateral.

The Code classifications include

1. *Instruments.* This includes checks, notes, drafts, and certificates of deposit (9–102[a][47]).
2. *Documents of title.* This includes bills of lading, dock warrants, dock receipts, and warehouse receipts (9–102[a][30]).
3. *Accounts.* This includes the rights to payment for goods sold or leased or for services rendered that are not evidenced by instruments or chattel paper but are carried on open accounts, including lottery winnings and health care–insurance receivables. Items in the "accounts" category include such rights to payment whether or not the rights have been earned by performance (9–102[a][2]).
4. *Chattel paper.* This includes written documents that evidence both an obligation to pay money and a security interest in specific goods (9–102[a][11]). A typical example of chattel paper is what is commonly known as a *conditional sales contract.* This is the type of contract that a consumer might sign when she buys a large appliance such as a refrigerator on a time-payment plan.
5. *General intangibles.* This is a catchall category that includes, among other things, patents, copyrights, software, and franchises (9–102[a][42]).
6. *Goods.* Goods (9–102[a][44]) are divided into several classes; the same item of collateral may fall into different classes at different times, depending on its use:
   a. *Consumer goods.* Goods used or bought primarily for personal, family, or household use, such as automobiles, furniture, and appliances (9–102[a][23]).
   b. *Equipment.* Goods other than inventory, farm products, or consumer goods (9–102[a][33]).

[1] The numbers in parentheses refer to the sections of the Uniform Commercial Code.

c. *Farm products.* Crops, livestock, or supplies used or produced in farming operations as long as they are still in the possession of a debtor who is engaged in farming (9–102[a][34]).

d. *Inventory.* Goods held for sale or lease or to be used under contracts of service, as well as raw materials, work in process, or materials used or consumed in a business (9–102[a][48]).

e. *Fixtures.* Goods that will be so affixed to real property that they are considered a part of the real property (9–102[a][41]).

7. *Investment property.* This includes securities such as stocks, bonds, and commodity contracts (9–102[a][49]).
8. *Deposit accounts.* This includes demand, time, savings, passbook, and similar accounts maintained with a bank (9–102[a][29]).

It is important to note that an item such as a stove could in different situations be classified as inventory, equipment, or consumer goods. In the hands of the manufacturer or an appliance store, the stove is *inventory.* If it is being used in a restaurant, it is *equipment.* In a home, it is classified as *consumer goods.*

Obtaining a Security Interest

The goal of a creditor is to obtain a security interest in identifiable personal property that will be good against (1) the debtor, (2) other creditors of the debtor, and (3) a person who might purchase the property from the debtor. In case the debtor defaults on the debt, the creditor wants to have a better right to claim the property than anyone else. Obtaining a security interest enforceable against third parties is a two-step process consisting of **attachment** and **perfection.**

Attachment of the Security Interest

LO2

Attachment

A security interest is not legally enforceable against a debtor until it is attached to a particular item or items of the debtor's property. The *attachment of the security interest* takes place in a legal sense rather than in a physical sense. There are three basic requirements for a security interest to be attached to the goods of a debtor (9–203). First, either there must be an *agreement* by the debtor granting the creditor a security interest in particular property (*collateral*) or the secured party must have possession of the property. Second, the creditor must give something of value to the debtor. The creditor must, for example, loan money or advance goods on credit to the debtor. Third, the debtor must have rights in the collateral or the owner of the collateral must agree to allow its use as collateral. Unless the debtor owes a *debt* to the creditor or an unfulfilled promise to perform, there can be no security interest. The purpose of obtaining the security interest is to secure a debt or performance.

The Security Agreement

The agreement in which a debtor grants a creditor a security interest in the debtor's property generally must be *in writing* and *signed by the debtor.* A written agreement is required in all cases except where the creditor has *possession* of the collateral (9–203). Suppose you borrow $50 from a friend and give him your wristwatch as security for the loan. The agreement whereby you put up your watch as collateral does not have to be in writing to be enforceable. Because the creditor (your friend) is in possession of the collateral, an oral agreement is sufficient.

The security agreement must *clearly describe the collateral* so that it can be readily identified. For example, the year, make, and serial number of an automobile should be listed. The security agreement usually goes on to spell out the terms of the arrangement between the creditor and the debtor. Also, it normally contains a promise by the debtor to pay certain amounts of money or to perform a duty in a certain way. It will specify what events will constitute a default, for example, nonpayment by the buyer. In addition, it may contain provisions that the creditor feels are necessary to protect his security interest; for example, the debtor may be required to keep the collateral insured and/or not to move it without the creditor's consent (see Figure 43.1).

In the case that follows, *In re Shirel,* the court found that the information contained in a credit application did not meet the requirements for a security agreement.

In re Shirel

251 B.R.175 (Bankr., W.D. Oklahoma 2000)

FACTS

Kevin Shirel applied for a credit card from Sight'N Sound Appliance Centers, Inc. The credit application, which constituted the agreement between the parties, was a barely legible, seven-page, single-spaced, small-print document. Shirel signed it on the first page. The form contained a statement that Sight'N Sound would have a "security interest" in all "merchandise" purchased with the credit card. This statement was located approximately four pages into the application.

Shirel's credit was approved, and he purchased a new refrigerator using the credit card. Several months later, Shirel filed a bankruptcy petition listing the remaining credit card debt as unsecured and the refrigerator as exempt from the claims of creditors. Subsequently, Sight'N Sound objected to the claim of exemption. It contended that Shirel had improperly listed the debt as unsecured and asserted that it held a secured interest in the refrigerator.

ISSUE

Did Sight'N Sound have a valid security interest in the refrigerator by virtue of its agreement with Shirel?

DECISION

No. The court began by noting that contracts of adhesion such as the one in this case—are interpreted most strongly against the party preparing the form. The court went on to hold that the security agreement was not enforceable against the debtor because it did not contain an adequate description of the collateral. The phrase "all merchandise" was too imprecise and not descriptive. The description does not have to be elaborate; a sufficient one must have listed "a refrigerator."

AUTHOR'S NOTE

Although this case was decided under the 1972 version of Article 9, the same result would be expected under Revised Article 9, which places more emphasis on the nature of the description.

Future Advances

A security agreement may cover extensions of credit to be made in the future (9–204[c]). Such later extensions of credit are known as **future advances.** A future advance is involved where a credit union agrees to give you a line of credit of $10,000 to buy and restore an antique car but initially gives you only $1,500 to buy the car. As you draw additional money against the line of credit, you have received a future advance. The security interest that the creditor obtained earlier also covers these later advances of money to you.

FIGURE 43.1 A Security Agreement

Account No. C-1005

December 1, 2014
Date

~~Mr. and Mrs.~~
~~Mrs.~~
BUYER Miss Cheryl Cole
ADDRESS 542 Oakdale
CITY Chicago, Il. TEL. NO. 828-0290
DELIVER TO: 542 Oakdale

SECURITY AGREEMENT
ACE APPLIANCE

THIS AGREEMENT, executed between Ace Appliance, as Secured Party ("Seller"), and Buyer named above, as Debtor ("Buyer"): Seller agrees to sell and Buyer agrees to purchase, subject to the terms, conditions, and agreements stated in this agreement, the goods described below (the "Collateral"), Seller reserving and Buyer granting a purchase money security interest in the Collateral to secure the payment of the balance owed (Item 7) and all other present and future obligations of Buyer to Seller.

DESCRIPTION OF COLLATERAL.

Quan.	Article	Unit Price		Total		TERMS	
1	Washer	425	–	425		(1) Cash Price	800.00
1	Dryer	375	–	375		(2) Down Payment	100.00
						Trade-in	
						Unpaid Principal	
						(3) Balance Owed	700.00
						(4) Finance Charge	100.00
						Time Balance	
						(5) Owed	800.00
						(6) Sales Tax	40.00
						(7) Balance Owed	840.00

Buyer agrees to pay Seller, without relief from valuation and appraisement laws, the balance owed (Item 7) of $840.00 in 11 successive weekly/monthly installments of $70.00 each and a final installment of $70.00, commencing on Jan. 1, 2015 and continuing thereafter on the same day of each week/month until paid, together with all delinquent charges, costs of repossession, collection, disposition, maintenance, and other like charges, allowed by law, and reasonable attorney's fees.

This sale is made subject to the terms, conditions, and agreements stated above and on the reverse side. Buyer represents that the correct name and address of Buyer is as stated above, and that all statements made by buyer as to financial condition and credit information are true.

Buyer acknowledges delivery by Seller to Buyer of a copy of this agreement.

Buyer warrants and represents that the Collateral will be kept at Buyer's address unless otherwise specified as follows: ______________________________;

and will be used or is purchased for use primarily for: (check one) family or household purposes ☒; business use ☐; farming operations ☐. The Collateral will not be affixed to real estate unless checked here ☐. If the Collateral is to be affixed to real estate, a description of the real estate is as follows: ______________________________

and the name of the record owner is ______________________________

FIGURE 43.1 *(concluded)*

IN WITNESS WHEREOF, the parties have executed this agreement on this 1st day of Dec., 2014.
BUYER'S SIGNATURE (Ace Appliance) Seller (as Secured party) Cheryl Cole (as debtor) By Frank Singer

TERMS, CONDITIONS, AND AGREEMENTS

1. The security interest of Seller shall extend to all replacements, proceeds (including tort claims and insurance), and accessories, and shall continue until full performance by Buyer of all conditions and obligations under this agreement.

2. Buyer shall maintain the Collateral in good repair, pay all taxes and other charges levied upon the Collateral when due, and shall defend the Collateral against any claims. Buyer shall not permit the Collateral to be removed from the place where kept without the prior written consent of Seller. Buyer shall give prompt written notice to Seller of any transfer, pledge, assignment, or any other process or action taken or pending, voluntary or involuntary, whereby a third party is to obtain or is attempting to obtain possession of or any interest in the Collateral. Seller shall have the right to inspect the Collateral at all reasonable times. At its option, but without obligation to Buyer and without relieving Buyer from any default, Seller may discharge any taxes, liens, or other encumbrances levied or placed upon the Collateral for which Buyer agrees to reimburse Seller upon demand.

3. If the Collateral is damaged or destroyed in any manner, the entire balance remaining unpaid under this agreement (the "Agreement Balance") shall immediately become due and payable and Buyer shall first apply any insurance or other receipts compensating for such loss to the Agreement Balance. Buyer shall fully insure the Collateral, for the benefit of both Seller and Buyer, against loss by fire, theft, and other casualties by comprehensive extended coverage insurance in an amount equal to the balance owed under this agreement.

4. Buyer shall pay all amounts payable when due at the store of Seller from which this sale is made or at Seller's principal office in Gary, Indiana, and upon default shall pay the maximum delinquent charges permitted by law. Upon prepayment of the Agreement Balance, Seller shall allow the minimum discount permitted by law.

5. Time is of the essence of this agreement. Buyer agrees that the following shall constitute an event of default under this Security Agreement: (*a*) the failure of Buyer to perform any condition or obligation contained in this agreement; (*b*) when any statement, representation, or warranty made by Buyer shall be found to have been untrue in any material respect when made; or (*c*) if Seller in good faith believes that the prospect of payment or performance is impaired. Upon a default, Seller, at its option and without notice or demand to Buyer, shall be entitled to declare the Agreement Balance immediately due and payable, take immediate possession of the Collateral and enter the premises at which the Collateral is located for such purpose or to render the Collateral unusable. Upon request, Buyer shall assemble and make the Collateral available to Seller at a place to be designated by Seller which is reasonably convenient to both parties. Upon repossession, Seller may retain or dispose of any or all of the Collateral in the manner prescribed by the Indiana Uniform Commercial Code and the proceeds of any such disposition shall be first applied in the following order; (*a*) to the reasonable expenses of retaking, holding, preparing for sale, selling, and the like; (*b*) to the reasonable attorney's fees and legal expenses incurred by Seller; and (*c*) to the satisfaction of the indebtedness secured by this security interest. Buyer convenants to release and hold harmless Seller from any and all claims arising out of the repossession of the Collateral. No waiver of any default or any failure or delay to exercise any right or remedy by Seller shall operate as a waiver of any other default, or of the same default in the future or as a waiver of any right or remedy with respect to the same or any other occurrence.

6. All rights and remedies of seller specified in this agreement are cumulative and are in addition to, and shall not exclude, any rights and remedies Seller may have by law.

7. Seller shall not be liable for any damages, including special or consequential damages, for failure to deliver the Collateral or for any delay in delivery of the Collateral to Buyer.

8. Buyer agrees that Seller may carry this agreement, together with any other agreements and accounts, with Buyer in one account upon its records and unless otherwise instructed in writing by Buyer, any payment of less than all amounts then due on all agreements and accounts shall be applied to any accrued delinquent charges, costs of collection and maintenance, and to the balances owing under all agreements or accounts in such order as Seller in its discretion shall determine.

9. Buyer authorizes Seller to execute and file financing statements signed only by Seller covering the Collateral described.

10. Any notice required by this agreement shall be deemed sufficient when mailed to Seller (state Seller's address), or to Buyer at the address at which the Collateral is kept.

11. Buyer shall have the benefit of manufacturers' warranties, if any; however, Seller makes no express warranties (except a warranty of title) and no implied warranties, including any warranty of MERCHANTABILITY or FITNESS. Buyer agrees that there are no promises or agreements between the parties not contained in this agreement. Any modification or rescission of this agreement shall be ineffective unless in writing and signed by both Seller and Buyer.

12. ANY HOLDER OF THIS CONSUMER CREDIT CONTRACT IS SUBJECT TO ALL CLAIMS AND DEFENSES WHICH THE DEBTOR COULD ASSERT AGAINST THE SELLER OF GOODS OR SERVICES OBTAINED WITH THE PROCEEDS HEREOF. RECOVERY HEREUNDER BY THE DEBTOR SHALL NOT EXCEED AMOUNTS PAID BY THE DEBTOR HEREUNDER.

By covering future advances in the security agreement, the creditor can use the collateral to protect his interest in repayment of the money advanced to the debtor at a later time. The creditor also saves transaction expense; the creditor does not need a new agreement for each future advance.

After-Acquired Property

A security agreement may also be drafted to grant a creditor a security interest in **after-acquired property** of the debtor, that is, property that the debtor does not currently own (or have rights in) but that he may acquire in the future. However, the security interest in the after-acquired property cannot attach to that property until the debtor obtains some property rights in the new property (9–204[a]). For example, Dan's Diner borrows $25,000 from the bank and gives it a security interest in all the restaurant equipment it currently has as well as all that it may "hereafter acquire." If, at the time, Dan's owns only a stove, then the bank has a security interest only in the stove. However, if a month later Dan's buys a refrigerator, the bank's security interest attaches to the refrigerator at the time Dan's acquires some rights to it.

Proceeds

The attachment of the security interest to the collateral automatically gives the secured party a security interest in the **proceeds** on the disposal of the collateral by the debtor (9–203[f]). The term *proceeds* is defined in (9–102[a][64]). Assume that Anne buys a television set from Ace Appliance on a time-payment plan. Ace Appliance has a security interest in the television set and in any money or other proceeds that Anne obtains if she sells the set to someone else.

Similarly, if a bank loans money to a dealer to enable him to finance an inventory of new automobiles and the bank takes a security interest in the inventory, then the bank has a security interest in the cash proceeds obtained by the dealer when the automobiles are sold to customers.

E-Commerce

REVISED ARTICLE 9 IS E-COMMERCE FRIENDLY

The revision to Article 9 that became effective in most states on July 1, 2001, is friendlier to e-commerce than the version it replaced. It no longer requires that the debtor "sign" a "security agreement" to create an enforceable interest in the collateral that supports the loan or performance obligation. Instead, it allows an "authenticated record"—one produced by the consumer online—to substitute for the signed "writing" of the earlier versions of Article 9 and the earlier state laws that Article 9 replaced. This is very advantageous for the buyer who wants to finance, for example, the purchase of an expensive computer or camera without using a credit card to pay for the purchase. The buyer will be able to complete the purchase transaction using an Internet seller of the type of merchandise desired and also finalize the secured transaction at the same time and using the same Internet-based system provided on the seller's website. If the seller is providing financing, in a "purchase-money" transaction, the seller can obtain an enforceable sales contract, an enforceable security agreement, and get the goods heading toward the consumer from the seller's warehouse without delay. The seller in many states also will be able to file an "authenticated record" in substitution for a paper "financing statement" and can complete the filing (and perhaps even pay the filing fee) using e-commerce applications.

Like the "click-through" method of forming a contract described in Chapter 8, click-through secured transactions give the buyer and seller the time- and money-saving advantages of other online transactions. They have similar risks to those present in the pure sales portion of the transaction—of unscrupulous persons trying to take advantage of either the buyer or seller, or both. But the speed and convenience are likely to outweigh the risks for many consumers and many sellers as well.

Perfecting the Security Interest

LO3

Perfection

A creditor protects her security interest in collateral against other creditors of the debtor and other third persons, including some buyers of the collateral, by **perfecting** the security interest. Attachment of a security interest to collateral provided by the debtor gives the creditor rights vis-à-vis the debtor. However, a creditor is also concerned about making sure she will have a better right to the collateral than any other creditor in the event that the debtor defaults. A creditor may also be concerned about protecting her interest in the collateral if the debtor sells it to someone else. The creditor gets this protection against other creditors or purchasers of the collateral by *perfecting* her security interest.

Under the Code, there are three main ways of perfecting a security interest:

1. By filing a *public notice* of the security interest.
2. By the creditor's taking *possession or control* of the collateral.
3. In certain kinds of transactions, by mere *attachment* of the security interest (automatic perfection).

Perfection by Public Filing

The most common way of perfecting a security interest is by filing a **financing statement** in the appropriate public office. The financing statement serves as constructive notice to the world that the creditor claims an interest in collateral that belongs to a certain named debtor. The financing statement usually consists of a multicopy form that is available from the secretary of state's office (see Figure 43.2). However, the security agreement can be filed as the financing statement if it contains the required information.

To be sufficient, the financing statement must meet three basic requirements and contain certain other information. The three basic requirements are that the financing statement must (1) provide the name of the debtor, (2) provide the name of the secured party, and (3) indicate the collateral covered by the financing statement. For certain kinds of collateral, such as fixtures, timber to be cut, or oil, gas, or other minerals, additional information concerning the property on which they are located must be set forth. Figure 43.2 illustrates the kind of other information that may be required.

As noted earlier in this chapter, the 2010 amendments to Article 9 that became effective in 2013 modify the earlier version of Article 9 to address problems that had arisen under it. Of most importance, the 2010 Amendments provide greater guidance as to the name of an individual debtor to be listed on a financing statement. The amendments offer two alternatives to each state:

1. Alternative A provides that, if the debtor holds a driver's license where the financing statement is filed, the debtor's name as it appears on the driver's license is the name required to be used on the financing statement. If the debtor does not have such a driver's license, either the debtor's actual name or the debtor's surname and first personal name may be used on the financing statement.
2. Alternative B provides that the debtor's driver's license name, the debtor's actual name, or the debtor's surname and first personal name may be used on the financing statement.

The amendments further improve the filing system for the filing of financing statements. More detailed guidance is provided for the debtor's name on a financing statement when the debtor is a corporation, a limited liability company, or limited partnership or when the collateral is held in a statutory or common law trust or in a decedent's estate.

In regard to collateral other than fixtures, most states require only central filing, usually in the office of the secretary of state. However, if you are a creditor taking a security interest, it is important to check the law in your state to determine where to file the financing statement (9–501).

A financing statement is effective for a period of five years from the date of filing, and it lapses then unless a continuation statement has been filed before that time. An exception is made for real estate mortgages that are effective as fixture filings—they are effective until the mortgage is released or terminates (9–515).

A **continuation statement** may be filed within six months before the five-year expiration date. The continuation statement must be signed by the secured party, identify the

FIGURE 43.2 A Financing Statement

UCC FINANCING STATEMENT
FOLLOW INSTRUCTIONS (front and back) CAREFULLY

A. NAME & PHONE OF CONTACT AT FILER [optional]

B. SEND ACKNOWLEDGMENT TO: (Name and Address)

THE ABOVE SPACE IS FOR FILING OFFICE USE ONLY

1. DEBTOR'S EXACT FULL LEGAL NAME - insert only one debtor name (1a or 1b) - do not abbreviate or combine names

1a. ORGANIZATION'S NAME				
OR 1b. INDIVIDUAL'S LAST NAME	FIRST NAME	MIDDLE NAME		SUFFIX
1c. MAILING ADDRESS	CITY	STATE	POSTAL CODE	COUNTRY
1d. TAX ID #: SSN OR EIN / ADD'L INFO RE ORGANIZATION DEBTOR / 1e. TYPE OF ORGANIZATION	1f. JURISDICTION OF ORGANIZATION	1g. ORGANIZATIONAL ID #, if any		NONE

2. ADDITIONAL DEBTOR'S EXACT FULL LEGAL NAME - insert only one debtor name (2a or 2b) - do not abbreviate or combine names

2a. ORGANIZATION'S NAME				
OR 2b. INDIVIDUAL'S LAST NAME	FIRST NAME	MIDDLE NAME		SUFFIX
2c. MAILING ADDRESS	CITY	STATE	POSTAL CODE	COUNTRY
2d. TAX ID #: SSN OR EIN / ADD'L INFO RE ORGANIZATION DEBTOR / 2e. TYPE OF ORGANIZATION	2f. JURISDICTION OF ORGANIZATION	2g. ORGANIZATIONAL ID #, if any		NONE

3. SECURED PARTY'S NAME (or NAME of TOTAL ASSIGNEE of ASSIGNOR S/P) - insert only one secured party name (3a or 3b)

3a. ORGANIZATION'S NAME				
OR 3b. INDIVIDUAL'S LAST NAME	FIRST NAME	MIDDLE NAME		SUFFIX
3c. MAILING ADDRESS	CITY	STATE	POSTAL CODE	COUNTRY

4. This FINANCING STATEMENT covers the following collateral:

5. ALTERNATIVE DESIGNATION [if applicable]: LESSEE/LESSOR CONSIGNEE/CONSIGNOR BAILEE/BAILOR SELLER/BUYER AG. LIEN NON-UCC FILING

6. This FINANCING STATEMENT is to be filed [for record] (or recorded) in the REAL ESTATE RECORDS. Attach Addendum [if applicable] 7. Check to REQUEST SEARCH REPORT(S) on Debtor(s) [ADDITIONAL FEE] [optional] All Debtors Debtor 1 Debtor 2

8. OPTIONAL FILER REFERENCE DATA

FILING OFFICE COPY — NATIONAL UCC FINANCING STATEMENT (FORM UCC1) (REV. 07/29/98)

(continued)

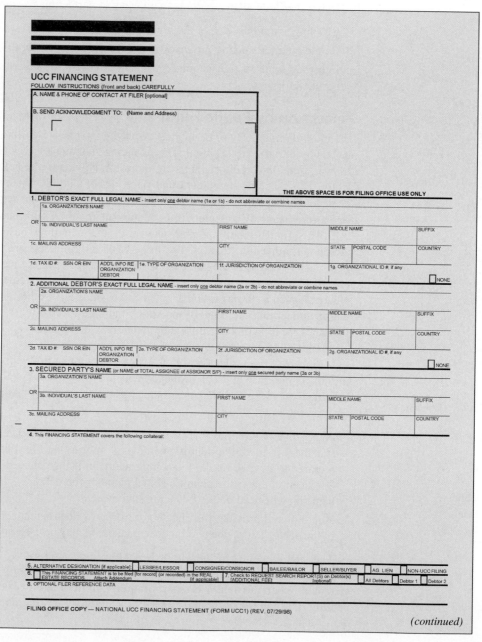

FIGURE 43.2 ***(concluded)***

UCC FINANCING STATEMENT ADDENDUM

FOLLOW INSTRUCTIONS (front and back) CAREFULLY

9. NAME OF FIRST DEBTOR (1a or 1b) ON RELATED FINANCING STATEMENT

9a. ORGANIZATION'S NAME

OR 9b. INDIVIDUAL'S LAST NAME | FIRST NAME | MIDDLE NAME, SUFFIX

10. MISCELLANEOUS:

THE ABOVE SPACE IS FOR FILING OFFICE USE ONLY

11. ADDITIONAL DEBTOR'S EXACT FULL LEGAL NAME - insert only one name (11a or 11b) - do not abbreviate or combine names

11a. ORGANIZATION'S NAME

OR 11b. INDIVIDUAL'S LAST NAME | FIRST NAME | MIDDLE NAME | SUFFIX

11c. MAILING ADDRESS | CITY | STATE | POSTAL CODE | COUNTRY

11d. TAX ID #: SSN OR EIN | ADD'L INFO RE ORGANIZATION DEBTOR | 11e. TYPE OF ORGANIZATION | 11f. JURISDICTION OF ORGANIZATION | 11g. ORGANIZATIONAL ID #, if any | ☐ NONE

12. ☐ ADDITIONAL SECURED PARTY'S or ☐ ASSIGNOR S/P'S NAME - insert only one name (12a or 12b)

12a. ORGANIZATION'S NAME

OR 12b. INDIVIDUAL'S LAST NAME | FIRST NAME | MIDDLE NAME | SUFFIX

12c. MAILING ADDRESS | CITY | STATE | POSTAL CODE | COUNTRY

13. This FINANCING STATEMENT covers ☐ timber to be cut or ☐ as-extracted collateral, or is filed as a ☐ fixture filing.

14. Description of real estate:

15. Name and address of a RECORD OWNER of above-described real estate (if Debtor does not have a record interest):

16. Additional collateral description:

17. Check only if applicable and check only one box.

Debtor is a ☐ Trust or ☐ Trustee acting with respect to property held in trust or ☐ Decedent's Estate

18. Check only if applicable and check only one box.

☐ Debtor is a TRANSMITTING UTILITY

☐ Filed in connection with a Manufactured-Home Transaction — effective 30 years

☐ Filed in connection with a Public-Finance Transaction — effective 30 years

FILING OFFICE COPY — NATIONAL UCC FINANCING STATEMENT ADDENDUM (FORM UCC1Ad) (REV. 07/29/98)

original statement by file number, and state that the original statement is still effective. Successive continuation statements may be filed (9–403[3]).

When a consumer debtor completely fulfills all debts and obligations secured by a financing statement, she is entitled to a **termination statement** signed by the secured party or an assignee of record (9–513).

Possession or Control by Secured Party as Public Notice

Public filing of a security interest is intended to put any interested members of the public on notice of the security interest. A potential creditor of the debtor or a potential buyer of the collateral can check the public records to see whether anyone else claims an interest in the debtor's property. The same objective can be reached if the debtor gives up *possession* of the collateral to the creditor or to a third person who holds the collateral for the creditor. If a debtor does not have possession of collateral he claims to own, then a potential creditor or debtor is on notice that someone else may claim an interest in it. Thus, change of possession of collateral from the debtor to the creditor/secured party, or his agent, perfects the security interest (9–313[a]).

For example, Sam borrows $150 from a pawnbroker and puts up his guitar as collateral for the loan. The pawnbroker's security interest in the guitar is perfected by virtue of his possession of the guitar.

Change of possession is not a common or convenient way for perfecting most security interests in consumer goods. It is more practicable for perfecting security interests in commercial collateral. In fact, it is the only way to perfect a security interest in money (9–312[b][3]).

Possession of collateral by the creditor is often the best way to perfect a security interest in chattel paper and negotiable documents of title. Possession is also a possible way of perfecting a security interest in inventory. This is sometimes achieved through a **field warehousing arrangement.** For example, a finance company makes a large loan to a peanut warehouse to enable it to buy peanuts from local farmers. The finance company takes a security interest in the inventory of peanuts. It sets up a field warehousing arrangement under which a representative of the finance company takes physical control over the peanuts. This representative might actually fence off the peanut storage area and control access to it. When the peanut warehouse wants to sell part of the inventory to a food processor, it must make a payment to the finance company. Then the finance company's representative will allow the peanut warehouse to take some of the peanuts out of the fenced-off area and deliver them to the processor. In this way the finance company controls the collateral in which it has a security interest until the loan is repaid.

Possession by the creditor is usually not a practicable way of perfecting a security interest in equipment or farm products. In the case of equipment, the debtor needs to use it in the business. For example, if a creditor kept possession of a stove that was sold on credit to a restaurant, it would defeat the purpose for which the restaurant was buying the stove, that is, to use it in its business.

Control

A secured party can provide a similar form of public notice by controlling the collateral (9–314). Control is the only perfection method if the collateral is a deposit account (9–312[b][1]). A secured party obtains control by one of three means: (1) the secured party is the bank with which the deposit account is maintained; (2) the debtor, secured party, and the bank have agreed that the bank will comply with the secured party's instructions regarding funds in the account; or (3) the secured party becomes the bank's customer for the deposit account.

Perfecting by Attachment: Automatic Perfection

A creditor who sells goods to a consumer on credit or who loans money to enable a consumer to buy goods can perfect a security interest merely by attaching the security interest to the goods (9–309). A creditor under these circumstances has what is called a **purchase money security interest** in consumer goods. For example, an appliance store sells a television set to Margaret Morse on a conditional sales contract (time-payment plan). The store does not have to file its purchase money security interest in the set. The security interest is considered perfected just by virtue of its attachment to the set in the hands of the consumer.

Consumer Goods

Perfection by attachment is not effective for three categories of consumer goods. First, if the consumer goods are motor vehicles for which the state issues certificates of title (9–303), and second, if the goods are to become fixtures, the creditor can get only limited protection through perfection by attachment; to protect himself against other claimants to the real estate, he must perfect by filing a financing statement with the real estate records. The special rules that cover motor vehicles and fixtures will be discussed later in this chapter.

The third situation is the sale by a consumer debtor to another consumer debtor if the secured party did not file a financing statement (9–320[b]). If the new buyer buys from the debtor (1) without knowledge of the security interest, (2) for value, and (3) primarily for the buyer's own personal, family, or household purposes, then the new buyer takes free of the security interest. However, if the secured party filed a financing statement for the collateral, then the new buyer does not take the collateral free of the security interest.

In the case that follows, *Meskell v. Bertone,* the bank that provided funds for the purchase of a boat obtained a purchase money security interest that was automatically perfected; however, because the bank did not file the security interest, when the original purchaser sold it to another consumer who intended to use it for household purposes and had no knowledge of the bank's purchase money security interest, the subsequent purchaser took it free of the bank's security interest.

One potential concern for a creditor is that the use of the collateral will change from that anticipated when the security interest was obtained. For example, a computer originally purchased to be used in the home is subsequently converted for use in a business. It is important that the creditor properly perfect the security interest initially so that it will not be adversely affected by a subsequent change in use and will continue to have the benefit of its initial perfection.

Meskell v. Bertone

55 UCC Rep.2d 179 (Super. Ct. Mass. 2004)

FACTS

On September 28, 2001, John Meskell borrowed $31,601.75 from Key Bank to finance his purchase of a 66-foot Chapparral boat. That same day, he executed a "Note, Security Agreement, and Disclosure Statement" in connection with the loan. The security agreement listed the boat as collateral for the loan. The terms of the note prohibited Meskell from transferring ownership or possession of the boat by sale, lease, or other means without first obtaining Key Bank's written permission. In addition, the note terms defined default as including breach of any significant term or condition. In the event of a default, Key Bank was entitled to repossess the boat and to require Meskell to repay the entire loan balance. The bank did not file a financing statement documenting its security interest.

In late 2002, Meskell advertised the boat for sale in the *Boston Globe.* Kimberly Friedman contacted Meskell in response to the advertisement and indicated that her husband, Dale Friedman of Sea Dog Yacht Sales, would be willing to procure a buyer for a commission of 10 percent of the purchase price. Meskell towed his boat to Sea Dog's yard where a "For Sale" sign was placed on it with an asking price of $49,000.

In the spring of 2003, John Bertone made an offer to purchase the boat for $44,000, which was accepted by Meskell. Bertone tendered a refundable deposit check payable to Sea Dog in the amount of $4,400 and signed a purchase and sales agreement that stated the obligation of the seller to deliver the yacht free and clear of any liens, mortgages, or applicable bills and agreed that the broker could deduct the applicable funds from the proceeds of the mortgage. Bertone tendered a check for $39,695, payable to the Sea Dog and other checks payable to the Commonwealth of Massachusetts to cover the boat sales tax, title, and registration. On July 12, 2003, Bertone took possession of the boat.

(continued)

Meskell v. Bertone *(concluded)*

On July 18, Meskell approved a final accounting that listed the sales price, Friedman's commission, the payoff of the amount owed to Key Bank, and the amount due to Meskell. Meskell received a check in the amount of $7,084.69 from Friedman. In August, Friedman absconded with the remaining sales proceeds without having satisfied the lien held by Key Bank; he was subsequently indicted for embezzlement.

Key Bank filed a complaint against Meskell and Bertone. The claim against Meskell was based on breach of contract and contended that as a result of the breach of the sales agreement by the sale to Bertone, the full amount owing on the note was due and payable. The bank asserted an equitable claim against Bertone, alleging that it was the rightful owner of the boat and seeking its repossession.

ISSUE

Was Key Bank entitled to repossess the boat from Bertone on the grounds that it had a perfected security interest in the boat?

DECISION

No. Initially, the court noted that where the bank provided the funds to purchase the boat, the bank obtained a purchase money security interest that was automatically perfected when (1) Meskell signed the security agreement describing the boat as collateral, (2) the bank gave Meskell value in the form of the loan, and (3) Meskell used the loan funds to obtain rights in the boat. The court noted that the bank's interest was enforceable between the parties, any purchasers of the collateral, and any creditors—but with one proviso for certain purchasers of consumer goods by buyers in good faith. That proviso came into play in this case. Because Bertone was buying the boat for his own household purposes, bought it in good faith, and had no knowledge of the bank's purchase money security interest, Bertone's ownership rights were superior to those of the bank. In this instance, the bank could have exercised the option of filing a financing statement to ensure that it would have priority in this kind of situation, but it had failed to do so.

Motor Vehicles

If state law requires a certificate of title for motor vehicles, then a creditor who takes a security interest in a vehicle must have the security interest noted on the title (9–311[a][2][3]). Suppose a credit union loans money to Carlos to buy a new car in a state that requires certificates of title for cars. The credit union cannot rely on attachment of its security interest in the car to perfect it; rather, it must have its security interest noted on the certificate of title.

This requirement protects the would-be buyer of the car or another creditor who might extend credit based on Carlos's ownership of the car. By checking the certificate of title to Carlos's car, a potential buyer or creditor would learn about the credit union's security interest in the car. If no security interest is noted on the certificate of title, the buyer can buy—or the creditor can extend credit—with confidence that there are no undisclosed security interests.

Fixtures

The Code also provides special rules for perfecting security interests in consumer goods that become fixtures by virtue of their attachment to or use with real property. A creditor with a security interest in consumer goods (including consumer goods that will become fixtures) obtains perfection merely by attachment of her security interest to a consumer good. However, as discussed in the "Priorities" section of this chapter, a creditor who relies on attachment for perfection will not prevail against other creditors *who hold an interest in the real estate* to which the consumer good is attached unless a special financing statement known as a *fixture filing* is filed with the real estate records to perfect the security interest (9–102; 9–334).

Concept Summary: Obtaining a Security Interest Enforceable against Third Parties

Step	Purpose	Necessary Action
Attachment of Security Interest	To secure a debt. The debtor gives the creditor rights in the debtor's property to secure the debt owed by the creditor to the debtor.	1. Agreement by the debtor giving the creditor a security interest in specific property (collateral) in which the debtor has a legal interest or when the debtor gives possession or control to the secured parties. Agreements can include after-acquired property. Proceeds of the collateral are automatically covered. 2. The creditor must give something of value to the debtor (e.g., money or goods). Future advances are value when actually given to the debtor, normally after the first advance.
Perfection	To obtain protection against other creditors of the debtor and against purchasers of the collateral from the debtor.	1. *Public filing.* Filing a financing statement with the appropriate state or local office to put the world on notice that the creditor claims an interest in specific collateral belonging to the debtor; or in the case of a motor vehicle, noting the security interest on the certificate of title; or 2. *Possession or control by creditor.* The creditor may take possession of the collateral or gain control, thus putting other creditors and potential purchasers on notice that the creditor has an interest in the collateral (this is not practical for all kinds of collateral); or 3. *Automatic perfection by attachment.* Limited perfection merely by attachment of the security interest is obtained where (a) a creditor sells consumer goods to a consumer on credit or (b) a creditor loans money to a consumer to enable him to buy consumer goods.

Priorities

Importance of Determining Priority

Because several creditors may claim a security interest in the same collateral of a debtor, the Code establishes a set of rules for determining which of the conflicting security interests has priority, that is, takes precedence over other security interests or liens. Determining which creditor has priority or the best claim takes on particular importance in bankruptcy cases. Unless a creditor has perfected a secured interest in collateral that fully protects the obligation owed to him, the creditor may realize only a few cents on each dollar he is owed by the bankrupt debtor.

LO4

General Priority Rules

The basic rule established by the Code is that when more than one security interest in the same collateral has been filed (or otherwise perfected), the first security interest to be filed (or perfected) has priority over any that is filed (or perfected) later (9–322[a][1]). If only one security interest has been perfected, for example, by filing, then that security interest has priority. However, if none of the conflicting security interests has been perfected, then the first security interest to be *attached* to the collateral has priority (9–322[a][3]).

Thus, if Bank A filed a financing statement covering a retailer's inventory on February 1, 2014, and Bank B filed a financing statement on March 1, 2014, covering that same inventory, Bank A would have priority over Bank B. This is true even though Bank B might have made its loan and attached its security interest to the inventory prior to the time that Bank A did so. However, if Bank A neglected to perfect its security interest by filing and Bank B did perfect, then Bank B would prevail, as it has the only perfected security interest in the inventory.

If both creditors neglected to perfect their security interest, then the first security interest that attached would have priority (9–322[a][3]). For example, if Loan Company Y has a security agreement covering a dealer's equipment dated June 1, 2014, and advances money to the dealer on that date, whereas Bank Z does not obtain a security agreement covering that equipment or advance money to the dealer until July 1, 2014, then Loan Company Y has priority over Bank Z. In connection with the last situation, it is important to note that unperfected secured creditors do not enjoy a preferred position in bankruptcy proceedings, thus giving additional importance to filing or otherwise perfecting a security interest.

LO5 Purchase Money Security Interests in Inventory

There are several very important exceptions to the general priority rules. First, a **perfected purchase money security interest in inventory** has priority over a conflicting security interest in the same inventory *if* all four of these requirements are met: (1) the purchase money security interest is perfected at the time the debtor receives possession of the inventory, (2) the purchase money secured party gives notification in writing to the prior secured creditor before the debtor receives the inventory, (3) the holder of the competing security interest received notification within five years before the debtor receives the inventory, and (4) the notification states that the person expects to acquire a purchase money security interest in inventory of the debtor and describes the inventory (9–324[b]).

Assume that Bank A takes and perfects a security interest in "all present and after-acquired inventory" of a debtor. Then the debtor acquires some additional inventory from a wholesaler, which retains a security interest in the inventory until the debtor pays for it. The wholesaler perfects this security interest. The wholesaler has a *purchase money security interest* in inventory goods and will have priority over the prior secured creditor (Bank A) if the wholesaler has perfected the security interest by the time the collateral reaches the debtor and if the wholesaler sends notice of its purchase money security interest to Bank A before the wholesaler ships the goods. Thus, to protect itself, the wholesaler must check the public records to see whether any of the debtor's creditors are claiming an interest in the debtor's inventory. When it discovers that some are claiming an interest, it should file its own security interest and give notice of that security interest to the existing creditors (9–324[b] and [c]).

Purchase Money Security Interests in Noninventory Collateral

The second exception to the general priority rule is that a *purchase money security interest in noninventory collateral* prevails over a prior perfected security interest if the purchase money security interest is perfected at the time the debtor takes possession or within 20 days afterward (9–324[a]). Assume that Bank B takes and perfects a security interest in all the present and after-acquired equipment belonging to a debtor. Then a supplier sells some equipment to the debtor, reserving a security interest in the equipment until it is paid for. If the supplier perfects the purchase money security interest by filing by the time the debtor obtains the collateral or within 20 days thereafter, it has priority over Bank B. This is because its purchase money security interest in noninventory collateral prevails over a prior perfected security interest that is perfected at the time the debtor takes possession or within 20 days afterward. This principle is illustrated in the case that follows, *In re McAllister.*

In re McAllister

267 B.R. 614 (U.S.B.C., N.D. Iowa 2001)

FACTS

In May 1985 Michael and Pamela McAllister executed a security agreement in favor of First Southeast Bank, granting it a security interest in all equipment owned and thereafter acquired. The bank filed a Financing Statement with the Iowa secretary of state on May 28, 1985, and filed proper continuation statements thereafter that kept the perfection current.

On January 16, 1998, the McAllisters and Ag Services of America entered into an Agricultural Security Agreement for the production of crops. In addition to granting Ag Services a security interest in the crops, the McAllisters also granted Ag Services a security interest in "All of Debtors' equipment and motorized vehicles, whether or not required to be licensed or registered, whether now owned or hereafter acquired, including, but not limited to, machinery and tools, together with all accessories, parts, accessions and repairs or hereafter attached and affixed thereto." The Ag Services security agreement with the McAllisters contained a future advances clause. Ag Services perfected its security interest by filing a Financing Statement on January 23, 1998.

Ag Services advanced funds to the McAllisters which enabled them to acquire an auger in November 1999 and a planter and trailer in January 2000. The current value of the auger is $2,500 and the value of the planter and trailer is $3,500. Subsequently, the McAllisters filed a petition in bankruptcy. One of the issues in the bankruptcy proceeding was whether Ag Services' lien on the auger, planter, and trailer was a perfected purchase money security interest that had priority over the earlier filed and perfected security interest of the bank.

ISSUE

Does Ag Services have a perfected purchase money security interest in the auger, planter, and trailer that has priority over the earlier filed and perfected security interest of the bank?

DECISION

Yes. Initially, the court noted that a security interest is perfected when it has attached and a financing statement has been filed. Where funds are delivered by a lender for the specific purpose of purchasing equipment that is described in a prior, perfected financing statement between the parties, that security interest is known as a purchase money security interest (PMSI) when and to the extent the funds are so used. As a general rule, when a conflict exists between creditors who perfected their security interests in the sale collateral by filing a financing statement, the first in time to file their security interest has priority. In this case both parties have perfected their security interests by filing financing statements, and normally the bank would have priority. However, the paramount exception to the first-to-file rule is the superpriority arising from a purchase money security interest. Under the UCC as enacted in Iowa, a purchase money security interest has priority if it has been perfected at the time the debtor receives possession of the collateral or within 20 days thereafter. Thus, the Ag Services security interest will have priority if there is a showing that future advances were used to acquire the after-acquired property, thus making it a purchase money security interest that, being perfected within the required time limits, would have superpriority.

Rationale for Protecting Purchase Money Security Interests

The preference given to purchase money security interests, provided that their holders comply with the statutory procedure in a timely manner, serves several purposes. First, it prevents a single creditor from closing off all other sources of credit to a particular debtor and thus possibly preventing the debtor from obtaining additional inventory or equipment needed to maintain its business. The preference also makes it possible for a supplier of inventory or equipment to have first claim on it until it is paid for, at which time it may become subject to the after-acquired property clause of another creditor's security agreement. By requiring that the first perfected creditor be given notice of a purchase money security interest at the time the new inventory comes into the debtor's inventory, the Code alerts the first creditor to the fact that some of the inventory in which it may be relying for security is subject to a prior secured interest until the debtor pays for the inventory in full.

Buyers in the Ordinary Course of Business

The third exception to the general priority rule is that a **buyer in the ordinary course of business** (other than a person buying farm product from a person engaged in farming operations) takes the purchase free from a security interest created by his seller even though the security interest is perfected and even though the buyer knows of its existence (9–320[a]). For example, a bank loans money to a dealership to finance the dealership's inventory of new automobiles and takes a security interest in the inventory, which it perfects by filing. Then the dealership sells an automobile out of inventory to a customer. The customer takes the automobile free of the bank's security interest even though the dealership may be in default on its loan agreement. As long as the customer is a buyer in the ordinary course of business, that is, buys from someone in the business of buying and selling automobiles, the customer is protected.

The reasons for this rule are that the bank really expects to be paid from the proceeds of the sale of the automobiles and that the rule is necessary to the smooth conduct of commerce. Customers would be very reluctant to buy goods if they could not be sure they were getting clear title to them from the merchants from whom they buy.

Artisan's and Mechanic's Liens

The Code also provides that certain liens that arise by operation of law (such as artisan's liens) have priority over even perfected security interests in collateral if the artisan or mechanic has possession of the goods, unless the lien is created by a statute that expressly provides otherwise (9–333). This keeps the Article 9 secured creditor from being unfairly enriched by the artisan's work on the collateral. Suppose First Bank has a perfected security interest in Mary's car. Mary takes the car to Frank's Garage to have it repaired. Under common law or statutory law, Frank may have a lien on the car to secure payment for his repair work. The lien permits him to keep the car until he receives payment for his work. If Mary defaults on her loan to the bank and refuses to pay Frank for the repairs, the car is sold to satisfy the liens. Frank is entitled to his share of the proceeds of the sale to pay his bill before the bank gets anything.

In the case that follows below, *In re Borden,* the court had to decide whether an artisan lost its priority claim to some farming equipment it had repaired when the owner of the equipment removed it from the artisan without permission and without paying for it.

In re Borden

361 B.R. 489 (U.S. Bankr. App. Panel 8th Cir. 2007)

FACTS

On June 25, 2002, Michael Borden and his wife granted the Genoa National Bank a blanket security interest on all of their personal property, including machinery and equipment then owned and thereafter acquired. The lender perfected its security interest by filing a UCC financing statement with the Nebraska Secretary of State on June 26, 2002.

On separate occasions in late 2004, Borden took a cornhead and a tractor to Bellamy's, Inc., for repairs. Bellamy's performed the repairs and in February 2005 sent the Bordens a bill in the amount of $3,811.46 for the work performed on the cornhead and in March 2005 sent a bill in the amount of $1,281.34 for the work performed on the tractor. Borden did not have the money to pay for the repairs and Bellamy's refused to release the tractor and

(continued)

cornhead to Borden without payment, so they remained in Bellamy's possession.

On April 1, Borden and his wife filed a voluntary petition for relief under Chapter 12 of the Bankruptcy Code. (Bankruptcy is discussed in Chapter 44.) On this date the tractor and cornhead were in Bellamy's possession. In June 2005, Borden took the tractor from Bellamy's lot without permission and used it in connection with his farming operation. Bellamy's discovered the tractor was missing and contacted Borden to inquire if he had it in his possession. Borden admitted he had taken the tractor, explained that he needed it for his farming operation, and agreed to return it to Bellamy's as soon as he was finished using it. The tractor broke down while he was using it, and he returned it to Bellamy's in the fall of 2005.

In September 2005, Borden took the cornhead from Bellamy's without permission. Bellamy's became aware that the cornhead was missing and contacted Borden. He admitted that he had taken the cornhead, explained that he needed it to harvest corn, and agreed to return it as soon as he completed harvesting the crop. Borden returned the cornhead to Bellamy's in November 2005.

In 2006, Genoa National Bank filed a motion with the bankruptcy court to determine the priority of the respective liens claimed by it and by Bellamy's. The central question was whether Bellamy lost its priority artisan's lien on the cornhead when it lost possession of the personal property through the action of the property owner.

ISSUE

Did Bellamy's lose its priority artisan's lien on the farming equipment that it had repaired when the owner of the equipment removed it without permission from Bellamy's possession and without paying for it?

DECISION

No. The court began by noting that Nebraska law provides a lien to any person who repairs a vehicle, machinery, or a farm implement while in such person's possession for the reasonable or agreed charges for the work done or materials furnished on or to such vehicle, machinery, or farm implement and authorizes the artisan to retain possession of the property until the charges are paid. Such a lien is referred to as an artisan's lien. Nebraska law also recognizes a possessory lien as an interest, other than a security interest or an agricultural lien, which secures payment or performance of an obligation for services or materials furnished with respect to goods by a person in the ordinary course of such person's business which is created by statute or rule in favor of the person and whose effectiveness depends on the person's possession of the goods. An artisan's lien falls within this definition of possessory lien under Nebraska law. A possessory lien on goods, such as an artisan's lien, has priority over a security interest in the goods unless the possessory lien is created by a statute that expressly provides otherwise. The artisan's lien statute does not provide otherwise; accordingly, an artisan's lien has priority over a previously perfected security interest in the same goods.

Possession is generally required for a possessory lien. If an artisan surrenders possession, the artisan no longer has a possessory lien with priority over preexisting security interests. Where the artisan loses possession involuntarily, the artisan does not necessarily lose the artisan's lien.

A lender who advances funds to acquire certain property or who loans money secured by existing property does so on the basis of the property at the time of the loan. The lender generally assumes the owner will maintain the property after the loan is made and often mandates such maintenance in the loan documentation. If the property later breaks or is in need of maintenance, the owner takes the property to an artisan for repair or maintenance. Such repair or maintenance enhances the value of the property, thus enhancing the value of the lender's collateral. The lender thus benefits from the repair.

Artisan's liens are designed to be equitable in nature and to protect the rights of artisans. If the artisan voluntarily surrenders possession, the artisan loses its lien. However, if the artisan loses possession through no action of his or her own, the artisan should not be punished. This is especially true where the lender benefitted from the repairs to its collateral and its interests in the equipment were in no way impaired when Borden took the equipment from Bellamy's nor when he later returned the equipment to Bellamy's. Accordingly, the court held that Bellamy's retained its priority artisan's claim to the equipment.

Liens on Consumer Goods Perfected by Attachment

A retailer of consumer goods who relies on attachment of a security interest to perfect its security interest prevails over other creditors of the debtor-buyer. However, the retailer does not prevail over someone who buys the collateral from the debtor if the buyer (1) has no knowledge of the security interest, (2) gives value for the goods, or (3) buys the goods for his personal, family, or household use (9–320[b]). The retailer does not have priority over such a **bona fide purchaser** unless it filed its security interest.

For example, an appliance store sells a television set to Arthur for $750 on a conditional sales contract, reserving a security interest in the set until Arthur has paid for it. The store does not file a financing statement but relies on attachment for perfection. Arthur later borrows money from a credit union and gives it a security interest in the television set. When Arthur defaults on his loans and the credit union tries to claim the set, the appliance store has a better claim to the set than does the credit union. The first to attach has priority if neither security interest is perfected (9–322[a][2]).

Now, suppose Arthur sells the television set for $500 to his neighbor Andrews. Andrews is not aware that Arthur still owes money on the set to the appliance store. Andrews buys it to use in her home. If Arthur defaults on his obligation to the store, it cannot recover the television set from Andrews. To be protected against such a purchaser from its debtor, the appliance store must file a financing statement rather than relying on attachment for perfection (9–320[b]).

Fixtures

A separate set of problems is raised when the collateral is goods that become fixtures by being so related to particular real estate that an interest in them arises under real estate law. Determining the priorities among a secured party with an interest in the fixtures, subsequent purchasers of the real estate, and those persons who have a secured interest such as a mortgage on the real property can involve both real estate law and the Code. The general rule is that the interest of an encumbrancer of real estate (such as a mortgagee) or the interest of the owner of real estate (other than the debtor) has priority over a security interest in fixtures (9–334[c]). However, a perfected security interest in fixtures has priority over the conflicting interest of an encumbrancer or owner of the real property if (1) the debtor has an interest of record in the real property or is in possession of it, (2) the security interest is a purchase money security interest, (3) the interest of the encumbrancer arose before the goods became fixtures, and (4) the fixtures' security interest is perfected by a "fixtures filing" either before the goods became fixtures or within 20 days after the goods became fixtures (9–334[d]).

For example, Restaurant Supply sells Arnie's Diner a new stove on a conditional sales contract, reserving a security interest until Arnie's pays for it. The stove is to be installed in a restaurant where Arnie's is in possession under a 10-year lease. Restaurant Supply can ensure that its purchase money security interest in the stove will have priority over a conflicting claim to the stove by the owner of the restaurant and anyone holding a mortgage on the restaurant if Restaurant Supply (1) enters into a security agreement with Arnie's prior to the time the stove is delivered to him and (2) perfects its security interest by fixture filing before the stove is hooked up by a plumber or within 20 days of that time.

Yeadon Fabric Domes, Inc. v. Maine Sports Complex, LLC

60 UCC Rep.2d 367 (Sup. Jud. Ct. Maine 2006)

FACTS

In 2001, the Maine Sports Complex entered into a series of business transactions to build a sports complex in Hampden, Maine. It purchased real estate and gave a mortgage to the seller, H. O. Bouchard, Inc. It engaged Kiser & Kiser Company to provide engineering services for construction of the complex and Harriman Brothers to provide groundwork for the sports complex. Subsequently, both Kiser and Harriman filed mechanic's liens on the property in 2002. Maine Sports Complex entered into a contract to purchase an inflatable fabric dome from Yeadon Fabric Domes, along with the materials and equipment to erect and operate the

(continued)

Yeadon Fabric Domes, Inc. v. Maine Sports Complex, LLC *(concluded)*

dome. It also obtained a loan from Bangor Savings Bank, giving the bank a mortgage.

Maine Sports Complex defaulted on its obligations to each of these entities, and litigation resulted as they attempted to realize on the security for their competing claims. Yeadon had filed a financing statement for the dome and equipment with the secretary of state on July 22, 2002. It brought an action seeking the right to enter the property and to recover the dome. The court dismissed the action after concluding that the dome was a fixture and not personal property. Subsequently, on February 27, 2004, Yeadon recorded a financing statement in the Penobscot County Registry of Deeds.

Yeadon filed a collection action against Maine Sports Complex, which was consolidated with other collection actions that had been filed by Harrison and Kiser to enforce their lien claims. The court found that Kiser began its work for Maine Sports Complex on December 3, 2001, and that Harriman began its work on December 7, 2001. The court put Yeadon last in the order of priority. Yeadon appealed, contending that its security interest should have priority.

ISSUE

Should Yeadon's security interest in the dome have priority over the two mechanic's liens?

DECISION

No. The Maine version of the UCC provides that a security interest in fixtures can be filed either with the registry of deeds in the county in which the real property is located or in the secretary of state's office. However, to constitute a "fixture filing," the filing must contain certain information as to the real property on which the fixture is to be located. In this instance, Yeadon perfected its security interest in the dome and equipment when it filed with the secretary of state in July 2002. This filing did not qualify as a fixture filing, but its February 27, 2004, filing with the registry of deeds did qualify as a fixture filing.

Under Maine's version of the UCC, the general rule is that a security interest in fixtures is subordinate to a conflicting interest of an encumbrancer or owner of the related real property other than the debtor (in the secured transaction). However, there are exceptions to the general rule. One of the exceptions is in Section 9–1334(4), which gives a perfected security interest in fixtures priority when (1) the debtor has an interest of record in, or is in possession of, the real property; (2) the security interest in fixtures is a purchase money security interest; (3) the encumbrancer's interest arose before the goods became fixtures; and (4) the security interest was perfected by a fixture filing before or within 20 days of the time the goods became fixtures. The court noted that while the date the dome became a fixture was not clear from the record in this case, it clearly had become a fixture before Yeadon filed its action in July 2003 to access the property and remove the dome. Because the fixture filing was not made until February 2004 and both of the competing liens were of record in 2002, Yeadon does not have priority over them because it had not filed its fixture filing within 20 days of the time the dome became a fixture.

The Code contains several other rules concerning the relative priority of a security interest in fixtures (see 9–334[e]–[h]). For example, the secured party whose interest in fixtures is perfected will have priority where (1) the fixtures are removable factory or office machines or readily removable replacements of domestic appliances that are consumer goods and (2) the security interest is perfected *prior* to the time the goods become fixtures. Suppose Harriet's dishwasher breaks and she contracts with an appliance store to buy a new one on a time-payment plan. The mortgage on Harriet's house provides that it covers the real property along with all kitchen appliances or their replacements. The appliance store's security interest will have priority on the dishwasher over the interest of the mortgage if the appliance store perfects its security interest prior to the time the new dishwasher is installed in Harriet's home (9–334[e][2]). Perfection in consumer goods can, of course, be obtained merely by attaching the security interest through the signing of a valid security agreement.

Note that a creditor holding a security interest in consumer goods that become fixtures who relies on attachment for perfection prevails over other creditors with an interest in the real property *only* where the consumer goods are "readily removable replacements for domestic appliances."

Suppose a hardware store takes a security interest in some storm windows. Because the storm windows are likely to become fixtures through their use with the homeowner's home, the hardware store cannot rely merely on attachment to protect its security interest. It should file a financing statement to protect that security interest against other creditors of the homeowner with an interest in his home. This rule helps protect a person interested in buying the real property or a person considering lending money based on the real property. By checking the real estate records, the potential buyer or creditor would learn of the hardware store's security interest in the storm windows.

Once a secured party has filed his security interest as a fixture filing, he has priority over purchasers or encumbrances whose interests are filed after that of the secured party (9–334[e][1]).

Concept Summary: Outcome of Priority Contests

Parties	Outcome of Contest
Secured Party vs. Debtor	Secured party has priority (9–201[a]; 9–203).
Secured Party vs. Secured Party (as to collateral other than fixtures)	1. *General rule for nonfixtures.* When more than one security interest in the collateral has been filed or otherwise perfected, the first security interest to be filed or perfected has priority over other security interests so long as there is no period after the filing or perfection when there is neither filing nor perfection (9–322[a]). In addition, a. a perfected security interest has priority over an unperfected security interest (9–322[a]). b. if neither conflicting security interest is perfected, then the first security interest to attach has priority over the later-attached security interest (9–322[a]). 2. *Purchase money security interest exceptions to the general rule.* Purchase money security interests are able to gain priority over other perfected security interests under some circumstances. a. *Inventory purchase.* A perfected purchase money security interest in inventory has priority over a conflicting interest in the same inventory if the purchase money security interest is perfected when the debtor receives possession of the inventory, the purchase money secured party notifies the holder of the conflicting security interest, the holder of the conflicting security interest receives the notification within five years before the debtor receives possession of the inventory, and the notification states that the sender has or expects to acquire a purchase money security interest in inventory of the debtor and describes the inventory (9–324[b]). b. *Livestock purchase money security interests.* (See 9–324[d].) c. *Collateral other than inventory and livestock.* A perfected purchase money security interest in goods other than inventory or livestock has priority over a conflicting security interest in the same goods if the purchase money security interest is perfected when the debtor receives possession of the collateral or within 20 days after the debtor receives possession of the goods (9–324[a]). 3. *Exceptions for possessory liens arising by operation of law.* Liens that arise under other state statutes—such as those that create liens in favor of artisans and mechanics—have priority over perfected security interests in the same collateral so long as the artisan has possession of the collateral unless the statute expressly provides that the lien does not have priority. To obtain priority, these liens must secure payment or performance of services or materials furnished by a person in the ordinary course of the person's business (9–333).

(continued)

Concept Summary: Outcome of Priority Contests *(concluded)*		
	Secured Creditor vs. Creditor with Interest in Real Property on Which Fixture Is Located	1. *General rule.* Except as expressly provided in 9–334(d)–(h), a security interest in fixtures is subordinate to a conflicting interest of an encumbrancer or owner of the related real property other than the debtor (9–334[c]). 2. *Exceptions to the general rule.* a. *Purchase money security interests.* A perfected security interest in fixtures has priority over a conflicting interest of an encumbrancer or owner of the real property if the debtor has an interest of record in or is in possession of real property, the security interest of the encumbrancer or owner arises before the goods become fixtures, and the security interest is perfected by fixture filing before the goods became fixtures or within 20 days afterward. b. *Interest in special classes of fixtures.* A perfected security interest in fixtures has priority over the encumbrancer or owner of record of real property if, before the goods become fixtures, (1) the security interest was perfected by any of the means permitted by the Code, (2) the fixtures are readily removable, and (3) the fixtures are one of the following types: factory or office machines, equipment that is not primarily used or leased for use in the operation of the real property, or replacements of domestic appliances such as washing machines or dishwashers that are consumer goods (9–324[e]).
	Buyers of Collateral from Debtor vs. Secured Creditor	1. *General rule.* A security interest in collateral continues despite the debtor's sale of the collateral to another person unless the secured party authorized the sale or disposition free of the security interest (9–315[a][1]). 2. *Exceptions for buyers.* There are several exceptions to the general rule. The two most common exceptions are these: a. *Buyers in the ordinary course of the seller's business of items in inventory.* Buyers in the ordinary course of the seller's business take free of security interests created by the seller in the favor of a secured party even if the security interest is perfected and the buyer knows of its existence. This rule applies to consumers, as well as commercial buyers of inventory (9–320[a], 1–202[9]). This rule does not cover buyers of farm products from a person engaged in farming operations. b. *Exceptions for buyers of consumer goods from other consumers.* Unless the secured party perfects by possession, a consumer who buys consumer goods from another consumer takes them free of a security interest even if perfected if the buyer buys without knowledge of the security interest, for value, primarily for personal, family, or household purposes, and before the secured party has filed a financing statement covering the goods (9–320[b]).

Default and Foreclosure

LO6

Default

The Code does not define what constitutes default. Usually the creditor and debtor state in their agreement what events constitute a default by the buyer, subject to the Code requirement that the parties act in "good faith" in doing so. If the debtor defaults, the secured creditor has several options: (1) forget the collateral and sue the debtor on his note or promise to pay, (2) repossess the collateral and use strict foreclosure (except in some consumer goods cases) to keep collateral in satisfaction of the remaining debt (9–620), or (3) repossess and foreclose on the collateral (9–609; 9–610) and then, depending on the circumstances, either sue for any deficiency or return the surplus to the debtor.

Right to Possession

The agreement between the creditor and the debtor may authorize the creditor to repossess the collateral in case of default. If the debtor does default, the creditor is entitled under the Code to possession of the collateral. If the creditor can obtain possession peaceably, he may do so (9–609[b][2]). If the collateral is in the possession of the debtor and cannot be obtained without disturbing the peace, then the creditor must take court action to repossess the collateral (9–609[b][1]). The considerations involved in determining whether there was a breach of the peace are illustrated in *Giles v. First Virginia Credit Services, Inc.*

Giles v. First Virginia Credit Services, Inc.

46 UCC Rep.2d 913 (Ct. App. N.C. 2002)

FACTS

On January 18, 1997, Joann Giles entered into an installment sale contract for the purchase of an automobile. The contract was assigned to First Virginia Credit Services, which obtained a senior perfected purchase money security interest in the automobile. The contract required Giles to make 60 regular monthly payments to First Virginia and stated that her failure to make any payment due under the contract within 10 days after its due date would be a default. The contract contained an additional provision agreed to by Giles that stated:

> If I am in default, you may consider all my remaining payments to be due and payable, without giving me notice. I agree that your rights of possession will be greater than mine. I will deliver the property to you at your request, or you may use lawful means to take it yourself without notice or other legal action. . . . If you excuse one default by me, that will not excuse later defaults.

During the early morning hours of June 27, 1999, Professional Auto Recovery, at the request of First Virginia, repossessed the locked automobile from Giles's front driveway. At the time she was in arrears for payments due on May 2 and June 2, 1999. Giles's neighbor testified that he was awakened about 4:00 AM by the running of a loud diesel truck engine on the road outside his house. When he went to the window to look, he saw a large rollback diesel truck with a little pickup truck on the bed behind it. He then saw a man jump out of the truck and run up the driveway to the Giles house. Then the car came flying out of the driveway and started screeching off down the street. About the same time, the rollback truck also took off at a high rate of speed making a loud diesel noise. The neighbor then called the Gileses and told them someone was stealing their car. Giles's husband came out of the house and hollered back and forth with the neighbor. Then the neighbor jumped in his truck and contacted the police. Eventually three police cars came to the scene, producing a great commotion in the neighborhood. The Gileses testified that neither of them saw the car being repossessed and were only awakened by the neighbor after it was gone. During the actual repossession there was no contact between Professional Auto Recovery and the Gileses or their neighbor.

Giles brought suit against First Virginia and Professional Auto Recovery for wrongful repossession of an automobile, alleging, among other things, that they had mailed a payment on the account just prior to the repossession which First Virginia had accepted and applied to their account after the repossession, and that the removal of the automobile constituted breach of the peace in violation of UCC Section 9–503.

ISSUE

Did the repossession under these circumstances constitute a breach of the peace in violation of the UCC?

DECISION

No. Initially, the court noted that the term "breach of the peace" had a somewhat broader meaning under the UCC than it had under the criminal law. The court stated

Giles v. First Virginia Credit Services, Inc. *(concluded)*

that under the UCC the focus is on the reasonableness of the time and manner of repossession. It applied a balancing test and identified five factors for consideration: (1) where the repossession took place, (2) the debtor's express or constructive consent, (3) the reaction of third parties, (4) the type of premises entered, and (5) the creditor's use of deception. Applying these factors to the facts in this situation, the court concluded that there had not been a breach of the peace. Professional Auto Recovery went on Giles's driveway in the early morning hours, when presumably no one would be outside, thus decreasing the possibility of confrontation. Professional Auto Recovery did not enter Giles's home or any enclosed area. Consent to repossession was expressly given in the contract signed by Joann Giles. Although the neighbor was awakened by the noise of Professional Auto Recovery's truck, the neighbor did not speak with their representatives or go outside until they had departed with the automobile. Neither of the Gileses were awakened by the truck and there was no confrontation with the repossessors who had gone by the time the Gileses went outside. Moreover, no deception in the removal of the automobile was alleged by the Gileses. The court also rejected the defense that the check curing the default was in the mail, finding that Giles was in fact in default at the time the automobile was repossessed.

Ethics in Action

WHAT IS THE ETHICAL THING TO DO?

Suppose you own an appliance business in a working-class neighborhood where most sales are made on credit. What considerations would you take into account in determining whether and when to foreclose or repossess items on which customers have fallen behind in making their payments? Should you be swayed by the personal circumstances of your debtors or look only to protecting your financial interests? For example, would you consider the value of the item to the debtor—is it a necessity for her life, such as a refrigerator, or a luxury? Would you consider the reason the person had fallen behind—that is, whether she had been ill or recently lost her job?

Sale of the Collateral

If the creditor has a security interest in consumer goods and the debtor has paid 60 percent or more of the purchase price or debt (and has not agreed in writing to a strict foreclosure), the creditor must sell the repossessed collateral. If less than 60 percent of the purchase price or debt has been paid or if the collateral is other than consumer goods, the creditor may propose to the debtor that the creditor keep the collateral in satisfaction of the debt. The debtor has 20 days to object in writing. If the consumer objects, the creditor must sell the collateral. Otherwise, the creditor may keep the collateral in satisfaction of the debt.

In disposing of the collateral, the creditor must try to produce the greatest benefit both to him and to the debtor. The method of disposal must be **commercially reasonable** (9–620, 9–627). If the creditor decides to sell the collateral at a public sale such as an auction, then the creditor must give the debtor notice of the time and place of the public sale. Similarly, if the creditor proposes to make a private resale of the collateral, notice must be given to the debtor. This gives the debtor a chance to object or to otherwise protect his or her interests (9–613).

Until the collateral is actually disposed of by the creditor, the buyer has the right to **redeem** it. This means that the buyer can pay off the debt and recover reasonable expenses and fees resulting from repossession and preparation for a disposition and recover the collateral from the creditor (9–623).

Distribution of Proceeds

The Code sets out the order in which any proceeds of sale of collateral by the creditor are to be distributed. First, any expenses of repossessing the collateral, storing it, and selling it, including reasonable attorney's fees, are paid (if the security agreement provides for them). Second, the proceeds are used to satisfy the debt being foreclosed. Third, any other junior security interests or liens are paid. Finally, if any proceeds remain, the debtor is entitled to them. If the proceeds are not sufficient to satisfy the debt, then the creditor is usually entitled to a **deficiency judgment.** This means that the debtor remains personally liable for any debt remaining after the sale of the collateral (9–615[d][2]).

For example, suppose that a loan company loans Chris $5,000 to purchase a used car and takes a security interest. After making several payments and reducing the debt to $4,800, Chris defaults. The loan company pays $150 to have the car repossessed and then has it sold at an auction, incurring a sales commission of 10 percent ($450) and attorney's fees of $250. The car sells for $4,500 at the auction. From the $4,500 proceeds, the repossession charges, sales commission, and attorney's fees totaling $850 are paid first. The remaining $3,650 is applied to the $4,800 debt, leaving a balance due of $1,150. Chris remains liable to the loan company for the $1,150, unless Chris challenges the amount of the deficiency claimed (9–626[a]).

Liability of Creditor

A creditor who holds a security interest in collateral must be careful to comply with the provisions of Article 9 of the Code. If a creditor acts improperly in repossessing collateral or in the foreclosure and sale of it, he is liable to the parties injured. Thus, a creditor can be liable to a debtor if he acts improperly in repossessing or selling collateral (9–625).

Questions and Problem Cases

1. Symons, a full-time insurance salesman, bought a set of drums and cymbals from Grinnel Brothers, Inc. A security agreement was executed between them but was never filed. Symons purchased the drums to supplement his income by playing with a band. He had done this before, and his income from his two jobs was about equal. He also played several other instruments. Symons became bankrupt, and the trustee tried to acquire the drums and cymbals as part of his bankruptcy estate. Grinnel's claimed that the drums and cymbals were consumer goods and thus it had a perfected security interest merely by attachment of the security interest. Were the drums and cymbals consumer goods?
2. Richard Silch purchased a camcorder at Sears, Roebuck & Co. by charging it to his Sears charge account. Printed on the face of the sales ticket made at that time was the following:

   > This credit purchase is subject to the terms of my Sears Charge Agreement which is incorporated herein by reference and identified by the above account number. I grant Sears a security interest or lien in this merchandise, unless prohibited by law, until paid in full.

   Silch's signature appeared immediately below that language on the sales ticket. The ticket also contained the brand name of the camcorder and a stock number.

Silch subsequently filed a Chapter 7 bankruptcy proceeding and was eventually discharged. Sears filed a petition to recover the camcorder from Silch, contending that it had a valid and enforceable security interest in the camcorder. Silch, in turn, contended that the sales ticket did not constitute a valid and enforceable security agreement. Does the sales ticket constitute a valid security agreement?

3. Nicolosi bought a diamond ring on credit from Rike-Kumber as an engagement present for his fiancée. He signed a purchase money security agreement giving Rike-Kumber a security interest in the ring until it was paid for. Rike-Kumber did not file a financial statement covering its security interest. Nicolosi filed for bankruptcy. The bankruptcy trustee claimed that the diamond ring was part of the bankruptcy estate because Rike-Kumber did not perfect its security interest. Rike-Kumber claimed that it had a perfected security interest in the ring. Did Rike-Kumber have to file a financing statement to perfect its security interest in the diamond ring?
4. Jacob Phillips and his wife, Charlene, jointly owned the Village Variety 5 & 10 Store in Bluefield, Virginia. In addition, Mrs. Phillips was a computer science teacher at the Wytheville Community College. On December 1, Mrs. Phillips entered into a retail installment sales contract with Holdren's, Inc., for the purchase of a Leading Edge computer and a Panasonic color printer. The contract, which was also a security agreement, provided for a total payment of $3,175.68, with monthly payments of $132.32 to begin on March 5. On the same day it was signed by Mrs. Phillips, Holdren's assigned the contract to Creditway of America. At the time of purchase, Mrs. Phillips advised Holdren's that she was purchasing the computer for professional use in her teaching assignments as well as for use in the variety store. One of the software programs purchased was a practical accounting program for business transactions. Mrs. Phillips also received a special discount price given by Holdren's to state instructors buying for their teaching use. She used the computer in the Village Variety 5 & 10 Store until it closed the following April. In June, the Phillipses filed a petition under Chapter 7 of the Bankruptcy Act. At the time, they owed $2,597.79 on the computer. No financing statement was ever filed. Creditway filed a motion in the bankruptcy proceeding, claiming that it had a valid lien on the computer and seeking to be permitted to repossess it. Does Creditway have a perfected security interest in the computer?
5. On November 18, Firestone and Company made a loan to Edmund Carroll, doing business as Kozy Kitchen. To secure the loan, a security agreement was executed, which listed the items of property included, and concluded as follows: "together with all property and articles now, and which may hereafter be, used or mixed with, added or attached to, and/or substituted for any of the described property." A financing statement that included all the items listed in the security agreement was filed with the town clerk on November 18 and with the secretary of state on November 22. On November 25, National Cash Register Company delivered a cash register to Carroll on a conditional sales contract. National Cash Register filed a financing statement on the cash register with the town clerk on December 20 and with the secretary of state on December 21. Carroll defaulted in his payments to both Firestone and National Cash Register. Firestone repossessed all of Carroll's fixtures and equipment covered by its security agreement, including the cash register, and then sold the cash register. National Cash Register claimed that it was the title owner of the cash register and brought suit against Firestone for conversion. Did Firestone or National Cash Register have the better right to the cash register?
6. Benson purchased a new Ford Thunderbird automobile. She traded in her old automobile and financed the balance of $4,326 through the Magnavox Employees Credit

Union, which took a security interest in the Thunderbird. Several months later, the Thunderbird was involved in two accidents and sustained major damage. It was taken to ACM for repairs, which took seven months and resulted in charges of $2,139.54. Benson was unable to pay the charges, and ACM claimed a garageman's lien. Does Magnavox Credit Union's lien or ACM's lien have priority?

7. Lester Ivy borrowed money from General Motors Acceptance Corp. (GMAC) to purchase a van, and GMAC acquired a security interest in the van. The security agreement contained a so-called insecurity clause that provided GMAC with the right to repossess the van immediately upon default; notice was not prerequisite to repossession. Ivy defaulted on his obligation on the loan, and GMAC hired American Lenders Service of Jackson to repossess Ivy's van. About 6:30 AM, Dax Freeman and Jonathan Baker of American Lenders Service drove to Ivy's home. They drove on Ivy's gravel driveway, which is about a quarter-mile long, past a chicken house and the van parked near Ivy's mobile home. They quietly attempted to start the van, but their attempt failed. They then hitched the van to their tow truck and towed it away.

   When Freeman and Baker reached the end of Ivy's driveway, Freeman stopped the tow truck and checked the van. At that point he saw someone running from the chicken house toward the mobile home. Ivy testified that prior to running toward the mobile home, he ran toward the tow truck "hollering and flagging for them to stop" but Freeman and Baker apparently did not see or hear Ivy at the time. Freeman jumped back into the tow truck and drove off Ivy's property and onto an adjacent road. Ivy decided to chase Freeman and Baker because he thought they were stealing his van. He jumped into a pickup truck, passed Freeman and Baker, and, according to them, pulled in front of the tow truck and slammed on his brakes. Freeman claimed he was forced to slam on his brakes but was unable to avoid a slight collision with the rear bumper of Ivy's truck. Ivy claimed he stopped well ahead of the tow truck, affording Freeman plenty of time to stop, but that he revved the engine and "rammed him." Ivy claimed that his head hit the rear window of the truck as a result of the collision and that he sustained a "severe vertical sprain." However, Ivy's medical bill totaled only $20 and he did not miss any work.

   When Ivy exited the truck, Freeman showed him some "official looking documents," advising him that he worked for American Lenders, and stated that they were repossessing his truck at GMAC's request. There was a dispute as to whether Ivy sought to have the sheriff called concerning the accident. Freeman allowed Ivy to retrieve some personal belongings from the van and gave Ivy a telephone number to call to get his van back; at that point, they all departed the scene.

   Seven months later, on October 20, Ivy filed a complaint against GMAC and American Lenders contending that the repossession of his van was invalid because there was a breach of the peace and he had been caused "personal injuries." Ivy sought actual and punitive damages. At the conclusion of a jury trial, the jury awarded Ivy $5,000 in actual damages and $100,000 in punitive damages. Was there a "breach of the peace" in the repossession of Ivy's van, entitling him to damages?

Chapter 44

Bankruptcy

Learning Objectives

After you have studied this chapter, you should be able to:

1. List and describe the major types of bankruptcy proceedings.
2. Compare the purpose, basic procedure, and advantages of each of those types of bankruptcy proceedings.
3. Explain the procedure by which Chapter 7 (liquidation) proceedings are begun and the roles the court and the bankruptcy trustee play in managing the bankruptcy process.
4. Understand what assets are included in the bankruptcy estate, the nature of the exemptions, and when the trustee can avoid prior transactions made by the debtor to reclaim assets for the bankruptcy estate.
5. Distinguish among claims, allowable claims, secured claims, and priority claims of creditors.
6. Describe the process by which the property in a debtor's estate is distributed to creditors and the debtor is granted a discharge in bankruptcy.
7. List the kinds of debts that are not dischargeable.

Bob and Sue Brown are a young couple with two small children. When they were students, they borrowed about $80,000 to finance their undergraduate educations, as well as an MBA for Bob and a teaching certificate for Sue. Within the past three years they stretched themselves further financially in the course of acquiring and furnishing their first home and starting their family. Recently, Bob was laid off from his job managing computer technology operations for a telecom company. Then, Sue was injured in an automobile accident and has been unable to continue substitute teaching. Bob's unemployment benefits are insufficient to provide for the ordinary family expenses, much less meet the heavy financial obligations the family has taken on. The bank has filed a notice of intent to foreclose

(continued)

the mortgage on their home and other creditors have sent letters threatening to repossess their car and furnishings. A friend has suggested that Bob and Sue consult with an attorney who specializes in bankruptcy matters who may be able to get them some relief from their creditors and gain a new start financially.

This situation raises a number of questions that will be addressed in this chapter:

- If the Browns file a petition in bankruptcy, what assets would they be able to retain as exempt from the claims of their creditors?
- Which of their debts could be discharged in a bankruptcy proceeding?
- What advantages and disadvantages would the Browns have if they filed under Chapter 7 (liquidation) as opposed to filing under Chapter 13 (consumer debt adjustment), which would require them to continue to make payments on their debts?

Introduction

When an individual, partnership, or corporation is unable to pay its debts to its creditors, a number of problems can arise. Some creditors may demand security for past debts or start court actions on their claims in an effort to protect themselves. Such actions may adversely affect other creditors by depriving them of their fair share of the debtor's assets. In addition, quick depletion of the debtor's assets may effectively prevent a debtor who needs additional time to pay off his debts from having an opportunity to do so.

At the same time, creditors need to be protected against actions to their detriment that a debtor who is in financial difficulty might be tempted to take. For example, the debtor might run off with his remaining assets or might use them to pay certain favored creditors, leaving nothing for the other creditors.

Finally, a means is needed by which a debtor can get a fresh start financially and not continue to be saddled with debts beyond his ability to pay. This chapter focuses on the laws and procedures that have been developed to deal with the competing interests that are present when a debtor is unable to pay his debts in a timely manner.

The Bankruptcy Code

The Bankruptcy Code is a federal law that provides an organized procedure under the supervision of a federal court for dealing with insolvent debtors. Debtors are considered insolvent if the sum of their debts exceeds the fair value of all their property. The power of Congress to enact bankruptcy legislation is provided in the Constitution. Through the years, there have been many amendments to the Bankruptcy Code. Congress completely revised it in 1978 and then passed significant amendments to it in 1984, 1986, and 1994. On April 20, 2005, President Bush signed the Bankruptcy Abuse, Prevention and Consumer Protection Act of 2005, the most substantial revision of the bankruptcy law since the 1978 Bankruptcy Code was adopted.

The Bankruptcy Code has several major purposes. One is to ensure that the debtor's property is fairly distributed to the creditors and that some of the creditors do not obtain unfair advantage over the others. At the same time, the Code is designed to protect all of the creditors against actions by the debtor that would unreasonably diminish the debtor's assets to which they are entitled. The Code also provides the honest debtor with a measure of protection against the demands for payment by creditors. Under some circumstances, the debtor is given additional time to pay the creditors free of pressures that the creditors might otherwise exert. If a debtor makes a full and honest accounting of his assets and liabilities and deals fairly with the creditors, the debtor may have most, if not all, of the debts discharged and thus have a fresh start.

At one time, bankruptcy carried a strong stigma for those debtors who became involved in it. Today, this is less true. It is still desirable that a person conduct his financial affairs in a responsible manner; however, there is a greater understanding that some events, such as accidents, natural disasters, illness, divorce, and severe economic dislocations, are often beyond the ability of individuals to control and may lead to financial difficulty and bankruptcy.

Bankruptcy Proceedings

LO1

The Bankruptcy Code covers several types of bankruptcy proceedings. In this chapter our focus will be on the following:

1. Straight bankruptcy (liquidation).
2. Reorganizations.
3. Consumer debt adjustment.

The Bankruptcy Code also contains provisions that cover municipal bankruptcies, but these will not be covered in this book.

LO2

Liquidations

A liquidation proceeding, traditionally called **straight bankruptcy,** is brought under Chapter 7 of the Bankruptcy Code. Individuals, as well as businesses, may file under Chapter 7. The debtor must disclose all property she owns (the bankruptcy estate) and surrender it to the **bankruptcy trustee.** The trustee separates out certain property that the debtor is permitted to keep and then administers, liquidates, and distributes the remainder of the bankrupt debtor's estate. There is a mechanism for determining the relative rights of the creditors for recovering any preferential payments made to creditors and for disallowing any preferential liens obtained by creditors. If the bankrupt person has been honest in her business transactions and in the bankruptcy proceeding, she is usually given a **discharge** (relieved) of her debts.

Reorganizations

Chapter 11 of the Bankruptcy Code provides a proceeding whereby a debtor who is engaged in business can work out a plan to try to solve financial problems under the supervision of a federal court. A reorganization plan is essentially a contract between a debtor and its creditors. The proceeding is intended for debtors, particularly businesses, whose financial problems may be solvable if they are given some time and guidance and if they are relieved of some pressure from creditors.

Family Farms and Fishing Operations

Historically, farmers have been accorded special attention in the Bankruptcy Code. Chapter 12 of the Bankruptcy Code provides a special proceeding whereby a debtor involved in a family farming operation or a family-owned commercial fishing operation can develop a plan to work out his financial difficulties. Generally, the debtor remains in possession of the farm or fishing operation and continues to operate it while the plan is developed and implemented.

Consumer Debt Adjustments

Chapter 13 of the Bankruptcy Code sets out a special procedure that enables individuals with regular income who are in financial difficulty to develop a plan under court supervision to satisfy their creditors. Chapter 13 permits compositions (reductions) of debts and/or extensions of time to pay debts out of the debtor's future earnings.

The Bankruptcy Courts

Bankruptcy cases and proceedings are filed in federal district courts. The district courts have the authority to refer the cases and proceedings to bankruptcy judges, who are considered to be units of the district court. If a dispute falls within what is known as a **core proceeding,** the bankruptcy judge can hear and determine the controversy. Core proceedings include a broad list of matters related to the administration of a bankruptcy estate. However, if a dispute is not a core proceeding but involves a state law claim, then the bankruptcy judge can only hear the case and prepare draft findings and conclusions for review by the district court judge. Certain kinds of proceedings that will have an effect on interstate commerce have to be heard by the district court judge if any party requests that this be done. Moreover, even the district courts are precluded from deciding certain state law claims that could not normally be brought in federal court, even if those claims are related to the bankruptcy matter.

Chapter 7: Liquidation Proceedings

LO2 LO3

Petitions

All bankruptcy proceedings, including liquidation proceedings, are begun by the filing of a petition. The petition may be either a voluntary petition filed by the debtor or an involuntary petition filed by a creditor or creditors of the debtor. A **voluntary petition** in bankruptcy may be filed by an individual, a partnership, or a corporation. However, municipal, railroad, insurance, and banking corporations and savings and loan associations are not permitted to file for liquidation proceedings. It is not necessary that a person who files a voluntary petition be **insolvent,** that is, his debts exceed the fair value of his assets. However, the person must be able to allege that he has debts. The primary purpose for filing a voluntary petition is to obtain a discharge from some or all of the debts.

The 2005 revisions establish a new "means test" for consumer debtors to be eligible for relief under Chapter 7. The purpose of the test is to ensure that individuals who will have income in the future that might be used to pay off at least a portion of their debts must pursue relief under Chapter 13 as opposed to pursuing relief and a discharge of liabilities through the liquidation provisions of Chapter 7. This means test is discussed in detail later in this chapter in the section entitled "Dismissal for Substantial Abuse."

Involuntary Petitions

An **involuntary petition** is a petition filed by creditors of a debtor. By filing it, the creditors seek to have the debtor declared bankrupt and his assets distributed to the creditors. Involuntary petitions may be filed against many kinds of debtors; however, involuntary petitions in straight bankruptcy cannot be filed against (1) farmers; (2) ranchers; (3) nonprofit organizations; (4) municipal, railroad, insurance, and banking corporations; (5) credit unions; and (6) savings and loan associations.

If a debtor has 12 or more creditors, an involuntary petition to declare him bankrupt must be signed by at least 3 creditors. If there are fewer than 12 creditors, an involuntary petition can be filed by a single creditor. The creditor or creditors must have valid aggregate claims against the debtor that exceed by $14,425 or more the value of any security they hold. To be forced into involuntary bankruptcy, the debtor must be unable to pay his debts as they become due—or have had a custodian for his property appointed within the previous four months.

If an involuntary petition is filed against a debtor who is engaged in business, the debtor may be permitted to continue to operate the business. However, an **interim trustee** may be appointed by the court if this is necessary to preserve the bankruptcy estate or to prevent loss of the estate. A creditor who suspects that a debtor may dismantle his business or dispose of its assets at less than fair value may apply to the court for protection.

Requirement for Credit Counseling and Debtor Education

Under the 2005 revisions, individuals are ineligible for relief under any chapter of the Bankruptcy Code unless within 180 days preceding their bankruptcy filing they received individual or group credit counseling from an approved nonprofit budget and credit counseling agency or receive an exemption from the requirement. The required briefing, which may take place by telephone or on the Internet, must "outline" the opportunities for credit counseling and assist the debtor in performing a budget analysis. The debtor is required to file a certificate from the credit counseling agency that describes the services that were provided to the debtor and also to file any debt repayment plan developed by the agency. Because individuals who have not received the required briefing are not eligible for relief under the Bankruptcy Code, it is difficult for a creditor to force an individual debtor into bankruptcy by filing an involuntary petition against the debtor.

Attorney Certification

The 2005 act increases the legal responsibilities for an attorney who signs a bankruptcy petition. The attorney's signature constitutes a certification that the attorney, after inquiry, has no knowledge that the information contained in the schedules filed by the debtor is incorrect. In addition, the attorney's signature on a petition, motion, or other written pleading constitutes a certification that the attorney, after inquiry, has determined that the pleading is well grounded in fact and is either warranted by existing law or is based on a good faith argument for extending existing law. In cases where the trustee files a motion to dismiss a case for substantial abuse, the court may order the debtor's attorney to reimburse the trustee for reasonable costs, including attorney's fees, for prosecuting the motion and may order that the attorney pay a civil penalty to the trustee or to the United States Trustee.

Automatic Stay Provisions

The filing of a bankruptcy petition operates as an **automatic stay** (holds in abeyance) of various forms of creditor action against a debtor or his property. These actions include (1) actions to begin or continue judicial proceedings against the debtor; (2) actions to obtain possession of the debtor's property; (3) actions to create, perfect, or enforce a lien against the debtor's property; and (4) actions to set off indebtedness owed to the debtor that arose before commencement of the bankruptcy proceeding. A court may give a creditor relief from the stay if the creditor can show that the stay does not give him "adequate protection" and jeopardizes his interest in certain property. The relief to the creditor might take the form of periodic cash payments or the granting of a replacement lien or an additional lien on property.

Concerned that debtors were taking advantage of the automatic stay provisions to the substantial detriment of some creditors, such as creditors whose claims were secured by an interest in a single real estate asset, in 1994 Congress provided specific relief from the automatic stay for such creditors. Debtors either must file a plan of reorganization that has a reasonable chance of being confirmed within a reasonable time or must be making monthly payments to each such secured creditor that are in an amount equal to interest at a current fair market rate on the value of the creditor's interest in the real estate.

The automatic stay provisions are not applicable to actions to establish paternity; to establish or modify orders for alimony, support, or maintenance; for the collection of alimony, maintenance, or support from property that is not the property of the bankruptcy estate; or to withhold, suspend, or restrict a driver's license or a professional, occupational, or recreational license.

In 2005, Congress added two additional exceptions from the automatic stay provisions for the benefit of landlords seeking to evict tenants. First, any eviction proceeding in which the landlord obtained a judgment of possession prior to the filing of the bankruptcy petition can be continued. Second, in cases where the landlord's claim for eviction is based on the use of illegal substances on the property or "endangerment" of the property, the eviction proceedings are exempt from the stay even if they are initiated after the bankruptcy proceeding was filed so long as the endangerment occurred within 30 days before the filing. Debtors are able to keep the stay in effect by filing certifications that certain nonbankruptcy laws allow the lease to remain in effect and that they have cured any defaults with 30 days of the bankruptcy filing.

Order of Relief

Once a bankruptcy petition has been filed, the first step is a court determination that relief should be ordered. If a voluntary petition was filed by the debtor or if the debtor does not contest an involuntary petition, this step is automatic. If the debtor contests an involuntary petition, then a trial is held on the question of whether the court should order relief. The court orders relief only if (1) the debtor is generally not paying his debts as they become due or (2) within four months of the filing of the petition, a custodian was appointed or took possession of the debtor's property. The court also appoints an interim trustee pending election of a trustee by the creditors.

Meeting of Creditors and Election of Trustee

The bankrupt person is required to file a list of his assets, liabilities, and creditors, and a statement of his financial affairs. The 2005 revisions impose a number of new production requirements on debtors. Individual debtors must file, along with their schedules of assets and liabilities:

- A certificate that they have received and/or read the notice from the Clerk of the Bankruptcy Court that they must receive credit counseling to be eligible for relief under the Bankruptcy Code.
- Copies of all payment advices and other evidence of payments they have received from any employer within 60 days before the filing of the petition.
- A statement of the amount of monthly net income, itemized to show how the amount is calculated.
- A statement showing any anticipated increase in income or expenditures over the 12-month period following the date of filing the petition.

Should an individual debtor in a voluntary Chapter 7 case or in a Chapter 13 case fail to file the required information within 45 days of the filing of the petition, the case is to be automatically dismissed. A court, upon finding that an extension is justified, can extend the time period to file for up to an additional 45 days.

Individual debtors must also provide copies of their most recent tax returns to the trustee and to creditors making a timely request; failure to do so can result in dismissal of the case. Debtors must also, at the request of the judge or a party in interest, file at the same time they file with the IRS copies of federal tax returns due while the bankruptcy case is pending and also file copies of tax return (including any amended returns) for tax years that ended within three years before the bankruptcy petition was filed.

Once the court receives the petition and the required schedules and certification, an appointed trustee calls a meeting of the creditors. At the meeting, the United States Trustee is required to examine the debtor to make sure he is aware of (1) the potential consequences of seeking a discharge in bankruptcy, including the effects on credit history, (2) the debtor's ability to file a petition under other chapters (such as 11, 12, or 13) of the Bankruptcy Code, (3) the effect of receiving a discharge of debts, and (4) the effect of reaffirming a debt (discussed later in this chapter).

The **trustee** takes over administration of the bankrupt's estate. The trustee represents the creditors in handling the estate. At the meeting, the creditors have a chance to ask the debtor questions about his assets, liabilities, and financial difficulties. The questions commonly focus on whether the debtor has concealed or improperly disposed of assets.

Duties of the Trustee

The trustee takes possession of the debtor's property and has it appraised. The debtor must also turn over his records to the trustee. For a time, the trustee may operate the debtor's business. The trustee also sets aside the items of property that a debtor is permitted to keep under state exemption statutes or under federal law.

The trustee examines the claims that have been filed by various creditors and objects to those that are improper in any way. The trustee separates the unsecured property from the secured and otherwise exempt property. The trustee also sells the bankrupt's nonexempt property as soon as it is possible and consistent with the best interest of the creditors.

The 2005 act places restrictions on the authority of the trustee to sell personally identifiable information about individuals to persons who are not affiliated with the debtor. Congress was concerned about situations where individuals had provided information to persons and entities on the understanding and with the commitment that the information would remain in confidence with the recipient. These data files are often a valuable asset of a debtor involved in bankruptcy proceedings, but Congress concluded that it was not reasonable to allow that information to be sold to a third party that was not in their contemplation when they provided the information to the debtor under a promise of confidentiality.

The trustee is required to keep an accurate account of all property and money that he receives and to promptly deposit moneys into the estate's account. The trustee files a final report with the court, with notice to all creditors who then may file objections to the report.

Health Care Businesses

The 2005 revisions reflect Congress's concern with what happens if a petition for bankruptcy is filed by a health care business and contains a number of provisions dealing with that possibility. First, the trustee is instructed to use his reasonable best efforts to transfer patients in a health care business that is in the process of being closed to an appropriate health care business that offers similar services and maintains a reasonable quality of care. Second, the actual, necessary costs of closing a health care business are considered administrative expenses entitled to priority. Third, the automatic stay provisions do not apply to actions by the secretary of health and human services to exclude the debtor from participating in Medicare and other federal health care programs. Finally, the act sets out requirements for the disposal of patient records when there are insufficient funds to continue to store them as required by law. The requirements include giving notice to the affected patients and specifying the manner of disposal for unclaimed records.

Liquidation of Financial Firms

The Bankruptcy Code contains special provisions for the liquidation of stockbrokers, commodity brokers, and clearing banks that are designed to protect the interests of customers of the entities who have assets on deposit with the bankrupt debtor. These responsibilities are overseen by the trustee.

The Bankruptcy Estate

LO4

The commencement of a Chapter 7 bankruptcy case by the filing of a voluntary or involuntary petition creates a bankruptcy estate. The estate is composed of all of the debtor's legal and equitable interests in property, including certain community property. Certain property is exempted (see the "Exemptions" section below). The estate also includes:

1. Profits, royalties, rents, and revenues, along with the proceeds from the debtor's estate, received during the Chapter 7 proceeding.
2. Property received by the debtor in any of the following ways within 180 days of the filing of the Chapter 7 petition: (*a*) by bequest or inheritance, (*b*) as a settlement with a divorced spouse or as a result of a divorce decree, or (*c*) as proceeds of a life insurance policy.
3. Property received by the bankruptcy trustee because (*a*) a creditor of the debtor received a voidable preferential transfer or (*b*) the debtor made a fraudulent transfer of her assets to another person. Preferential and fraudulent transfers are discussed later in this chapter.

Exemptions

Even in a liquidation proceeding, the debtor is generally not required to give up all of his property but rather is permitted to **exempt** certain items of property. Exemptions are only available to individual debtors—never to debtors who are corporations or other entities. Under the Bankruptcy Code, the debtor may choose to keep *either* certain items of property that are exempted by state law *or* certain items that are exempt under federal law—unless state law specifically forbids use of the federal exemption. However, any such property that has been concealed or fraudulently transferred by the debtor may not be retained.

The 2005 revisions specify that the state or local law governing the debtor's exemptions is the law of the place where the debtor was domiciled for 730 days before filing. If the debtor did not maintain a domicile in a single state for that period, then the law governing the exemptions is the law of the place of the debtor's domicile for the majority of the 180-day period that is between two and two and one-half years before the filing of the petition.

The debtor must elect to use either the set of exemptions provided by the state or the set provided by the federal bankruptcy law; she may not pick and choose between them. A husband and wife involved in bankruptcy proceedings must both elect either the federal or the state exemptions; where they cannot agree, the federal exemptions are deemed elected.

The **exemptions** permit the bankrupt person to retain a minimum amount of assets considered necessary to life and to his ability to continue to earn a living. They are part of the "fresh start" philosophy that is one of the purposes behind the Bankruptcy Code. The general effect of the federal exemptions is to make a minimum exemption available to debtors in all states. States that wish to be more generous to debtors can provide more liberal exemptions.

The specific items that are exempt under state statutes vary from state to state. Some states provide fairly liberal exemptions and are considered to be "debtor's havens." Items that are commonly made exempt from sale to pay debts owed to creditors include the family Bible, tools or books of the debtor's trade, life insurance policies, health aids (such as wheelchairs and hearing aids), personal and household goods and jewelry, furniture, and motor vehicles worth up to a certain amount. In the *In re Rogers* case that follows, a debtor sought to obtain an exemption under state law.

In re Rogers (Wallace v. Rogers)

513 F.3d 212 (5th Cir. 2008)

FACTS

On January 17, 1994, Sarah Rogers inherited a 72.5-acre tract of real property in Forney, Texas. Rogers was single at the time she inherited the property from her mother. Subsequently, Rogers married George Rogers and they purchased a 5.1-acre property in Rockwall, Texas, and built a residence on it which they claimed as their homestead.

In January 2004, Rogers separated from her husband, moved into a mobile home on the Forney property, and claimed it as her homestead. On April 6, Rogers and her husband divorced. Pursuant to the divorce decree, she gave up all right, title, and interest in the property in Rockwall, and no equity from that property was rolled into the property in Forney. The divorce decree awarded the Forney property to Rogers, reflecting the fact that it was her separate property, having inherited it from her mother before her marriage.

Prior to 2004, Rogers and her husband had borrowed money from Jack Wallace to embark on an ultimately unsuccessful business venture. Wallace sued to recover the unpaid balance on the loan, and on April 19, 2004, he obtained a judgment against both Rogers and her ex-husband for $316,180.95.

On September 28, 2005, Rogers filed for relief under Chapter 7 of the Bankruptcy Code. She elected state law exemptions and claimed her homestead exemption on the Forney property in the amount of $359,000.

Wallace objected to the claimed homestead exemption, arguing that the Bankruptcy Code capped the exemption at the federal statutory amount of $125,000 because the debtor acquired her homestead interest in the Forney property within the 1,215-day period preceding the filing of her bankruptcy petition.

ISSUE

Was Rogers's claim for a homestead exemption limited to $125,000 as having been acquired within 1,215 days of filing for bankruptcy?

DECISION

No. The court held that the limitation established by the federal Bankruptcy Code refers to economic interests acquired during the 1,215-day period preceding the bankruptcy petition. Here, Rogers's economic interest in the property was acquired in 1994 and no economic proceeds from a prior residence were invested in the property during the 1,215-day period. The fact that she established her homestead during the 1,215-day period on property which she had owned prior to that period does not cause the property to be subjected to the federal limitation.

The court noted that the concern of Congress when it enacted the provisions limiting homestead interests acquired within the 1,215-day period to $125,000 was to address the situation where a wealthy individual in a state like Texas or Florida that had an unlimited homestead exemption could invest millions in a huge house and land, file for bankruptcy, and protect virtually all they own from their creditors. Under the 2005 amendments to the Bankruptcy Code, the homestead exemption for such an investment made within two and one-half years before the filing of a bankruptcy petition is limited to $125,000. However, the limit does not apply to properties like Rogers acquired prior to that period and claimed as a homestead.

Limits on State Homestead Exemptions

Concerns that very generous homestead exemptions in a number of states were leading to abuses by debtors who transferred assets into large homes in those states and then filed for bankruptcy led Congress in 2005 to place some limits on state homestead exemptions. These limits include the following:

- The value of the debtor's homestead for purposes of a state homestead exemption is reduced to the extent that it reflects an increase in value on account of the disposition of nonexempt property by the debtor during the 10 years prior to the filing with the intent to hinder, delay, or defraud creditors.
- Any value in excess of $125,000—irrespective of the debtor's intent—that is added to the value of a homestead during the 1,215 days (about three years, four months)

preceding the bankruptcy filing may not be included in a state homestead exemption unless it was transferred from another homestead in the same state or the homestead is the principal residence of a family farmer.

- An absolute $125,000 homestead cap applies if either (*a*) the bankruptcy court determines that the debtor has been convicted of a felony demonstrating that the filing of the case was an abuse of the provisions of the Bankruptcy Code or (*b*) the debtor owes a debt arising from a violation of federal or state securities laws, fiduciary fraud, racketeering, or crimes or intentional torts that caused serious injury or death in the preceding five years. In certain cases, a discharge of a debtor under Chapters 7, 11, or 13 may be delayed where the debtor is subject to a proceeding that might lead to a limitation of a homestead exemption.

Federal Exemptions

Twelve categories of property are exempt under the federal exemption, which the debtor may elect in lieu of the state exemptions. The federal exemptions include:

1. The debtor's interest (not to exceed $22,975 in value) in real property or personal property that the debtor or a dependent of the debtor uses as a residence.
2. The debtor's interest (not to exceed $3,675 in value) in one motor vehicle.
3. The debtor's interest (not to exceed $550 in value for any particular item) up to a total of $12,250 in household furnishings, household goods, wearing apparel, appliances, books, animals, crops, or musical instruments that are held primarily for the personal, family, or household use of the debtor or a dependent of the debtor.
4. The debtor's aggregate interest (not to exceed $1,550 in value) in jewelry held primarily for the personal, family, or household use of the debtor or a dependent of the debtor.
5. $1,225 in value of any other property of the debtor's choosing, plus up to $11,500 of unused homestead exemption.
6. The debtor's aggregate interest (not to exceed $2,300 in value) in any implements, professional books, or tools of the trade.
7. Life insurance contracts.
8. Interest up to $12,250 in certain dividends or interest in certain life insurance policies.
9. Professionally prescribed health aids.
10. Social security, disability, alimony, and other benefits reasonably necessary for the support of the debtor or his dependents.
11. The debtor's right to receive certain insurance and liability payments.
12. Retirement funds that are in a fund or account that is exempt from taxation under the Internal Revenue Code. For certain retirement funds, the aggregate amount exempted is limited to $1 million. Also protected are some contributions to certain education and college savings accounts made more than a year prior to bankruptcy.

The term *value* means "fair market value as of the date of the filing of the petition." In determining the debtor's interest in property, the amount of any liens against the property must be deducted.

Ethics in Action

SHOULD THE HOMESTEAD EXEMPTION BE LIMITED?

As of June 2002, six states, including Florida and Texas, provide an unlimited household exemption that allows bankrupt debtors to shield unlimited amounts of equity in a residential estate. The unlimited exemption has come under increased scrutiny in recent years as a number of public figures as well as noted wrongdoers have taken advantage of the unlimited exemption to shield significant amounts of wealth from creditors. For example, a prominent actor who was declared bankrupt in 1996 was allowed to keep a $2.5 million estate located in Hobe Sound, Florida, and a corporate executive convicted of securities fraud kept his Tampa, Florida, mansion from the claims of his creditors in bankruptcy, including federal regulators seeking to collect civil fines. When the Enron and WorldCom corporate scandals broke in 2001 and 2002, the media called attention to a $15 million mansion under construction in Boca Raton, Florida, for the former CFO of WorldCom and to a $7 million penthouse owned by the former CEO of Enron as well as to the fact that the liberal exemption laws in Florida and Texas might be utilized by them to protect a significant amount of their wealth against claims from creditors and regulators.

As noted above, in the 2005 act, Congress took some steps to limit the ability of debtors to shift assets into an expensive home in a state with an unlimited household exemption shortly before filing for bankruptcy and also to limit the exemption for debtors convicted of violations of the federal securities laws. While the act was pending in the conference committee, a group of about 80 law professors who teach bankruptcy and commercial law wrote to the committee urging that it adopt a hard cap on the homestead exemption contained in the Senate version of the bill. They pointed out the fundamental unfairness created when residents of one state can protect in a supposedly "uniform" federal bankruptcy proceeding an asset worth millions while residents in other states face sharp limitations on what they can protect. As an example, they noted that a wealthy investor in Texas could keep an unencumbered home worth $10 million while a factory worker in Virginia puts at risk anything over $10,000 in equity.

The law professors described various ways that the formulation the conference committee had adopted could be gamed. They also asserted that the provisions to limit the homestead exemption for those who violate securities laws, who commit fraud while in a fiduciary capacity, or who commit certain felonies or intentional torts were too tightly drawn and would create a "playground of loopholes for wealthy individuals and clever lawyers." They noted, for example, that the provisions "would not cap the homestead exemption for someone who finds a dozen ways to bilk the elderly out of their money, someone who takes advantage of first-time home buyers, or someone who deceives people trying to set up college funds for their children."

Should Congress adopt a uniform cap on the homestead exemption?

Avoidance of Liens

The debtor is also permitted to **void** certain liens against exempt properties that **impair** his exemptions. The liens that can be avoided on this basis are judicial liens (other than judicial liens that secure debts to a spouse, former spouse, or child for alimony, maintenance, or support) or nonpossessory, non-purchase money security interests in (1) household furnishings, household goods, wearing apparel, appliances, books, animals, crops, musical instruments, and jewelry that are held primarily for the personal, family, or household use of the debtor or a dependent of the debtor; (2) implements, professional books, and tools of trade of the debtor or of a dependent of the debtor; and (3) professionally prescribed health aids for the debtor or a dependent of the debtor.

Under the 2005 revisions, the "household goods" as to which a nonpossessory purchase money security interest can be avoided have been limited. The new definition limits electronic equipment to one radio, one television, one VCR, and one computer with related equipment. Specifically excluded are works of art other than those created by the debtor or family member, jewelry worth more than $600 (except wedding rings), and motor vehicles (including lawn tractors, motorized vehicles such as ORVs [off-road vehicles], watercraft, and aircraft).

Redemptions

Debtors are also permitted to **redeem** exempt personal property from secured creditors by paying them the full allowed secured claim at the time the property is redeemed. Then the creditor is an unsecured creditor as to any remaining debt owed by the debtor. Under the 2005 revisions, the value of personal property securing a claim of an individual debtor in a Chapter 7 proceeding is based on the cost to the debtor of replacing the property—without deduction for costs of sale or marketing—and if the property was acquired for personal, family, or household purposes, the replacement cost will be the retail price for property of similar age and condition. The debtor is not permitted to retain collateral without redemption or reaffirmation of the debt (discussed later in this chapter) by just continuing to make the payments on the secured debt.

Preferential Payments

A major purpose of the Bankruptcy Code is to ensure equal treatment for all creditors of an insolvent debtor. The Code also seeks to prevent an insolvent debtor from distributing his assets to a few favored creditors to the detriment of the other creditors. Thus, the trustee has the right to recover for the benefit of the estate **preferential payments** above a certain threshold that are made by the bankrupt debtor. In the case of an individual debtor whose debts are primarily consumer debts, the trustee is not entitled to avoid preferences unless the aggregate value of the property is $600 or more. In the case of a corporate debtor, a transfer by a debtor of less than $5,000 in the aggregate is not subject to avoidance.

A **preferential payment** is a payment made by an insolvent debtor within 90 days of the filing of the bankruptcy petition that enables the creditor receiving the payment to obtain a greater percentage of a preexisting debt than other similar creditors of the debtor receive.[1]

For example, Fred has $1,000 in cash and no other assets. He owes $650 to his friend Bob, $1,500 to the credit union, and $2,000 to the finance company. If Fred pays $650 to Bob and then files for bankruptcy, he has made a preferential payment to Bob. Bob has obtained his debt paid in full, whereas only $350 is left to satisfy the $3,500 owed to the credit union and the finance company. They stand to recover only 10 cents on each dollar that Fred owes to them. The trustee has the right to get the $650 back from Bob.

If the favored creditor is an "insider"—a relative of an individual debtor or an officer, director, or related party of a company—then a preferential payment made up to one year prior to the filing of the petition can be recovered.

The 1994 amendments provided that the trustee may not recover as preferential payments any bona fide payments of debts to a spouse, former spouse, or child of the debtor for alimony, maintenance, or support pursuant to a separation agreement, divorce decree, or other court order.

[1] In the case of an individual debtor whose debts are primarily consumer debts, the trustee is not entitled to avoid preferences unless the aggregate value of the property is $600 or more.

Preferential Liens

Preferential liens are treated in a similar manner. A creditor might try to obtain an advantage over other creditors by obtaining a lien on the debtor's property to secure an existing debt. The creditor might seek to get the debtor's consent to a lien or to obtain the lien by legal process. Such liens are considered *preferential* and are invalid if they are obtained on property of an insolvent debtor within 90 days of the filing of a bankruptcy petition and the lien is to secure a preexisting debt. A preferential lien obtained by an insider within one year of the bankruptcy can be avoided.

The provisions of the Bankruptcy Code that negate preferential payments and liens do not prevent a debtor from engaging in current business transactions. For example, George, a grocer, is insolvent. George's purchase of new inventory such as produce and meat for cash would not be considered a preferential payment. George's assets have not been reduced; he simply has traded money for goods to be sold in his business. Similarly, George could buy a new display counter and give the seller a security interest in the counter until he has paid for it. This is not a preferential lien. The seller of the counter has not gained an unfair advantage over other creditors, and George's assets have not been reduced by the transaction. The unfair advantage comes where an existing creditor tries to take a lien or obtain a payment of more than his share. Then the creditor has obtained a preference and it will be disallowed.

The Code also permits payments of accounts in the ordinary course of business. Such payments are not considered preferential.

In the Ordinary Course of Business

The Bankruptcy Code provides several exceptions to the trustee's avoiding power that are designed to allow a debtor and his creditors to engage in ordinary business transactions. The exceptions include (1) transfers that are intended by the debtor and creditor to be a contemporaneous exchanges for new value or (2) the creation of a security interest in new property where new value was given by the secured party to enable the debtor to obtain the property and where the new value was in fact used by the debtor to obtain the property and the security interest was perfected within 20 days after the debtor took possession of the collateral.

The Bankruptcy Code also provides an exception for transfers made in payment incurred in the ordinary course of the business or financial affairs of the debtor or made according to ordinary business terms. Thus, for example, a consumer could pay her monthly utility bills in a timely fashion without the creditor/utility being vulnerable to having the transfer of funds avoided by the trustee. The purpose of this exception is to leave undisturbed normal financial relations, and it is consistent with the general policy of the preference section of the Code to discourage unusual action by either a debtor or her creditors when the debtor is moving toward bankruptcy.

Fraudulent Transfers

If a debtor transfers property or incurs an obligation with *intent to hinder, delay, or defraud creditors,* the transfer is **voidable** by the trustee. Similarly, transfers of property for less than reasonable value are voidable by the trustee. Suppose Kathleen is in financial difficulty. She "sells" her $5,000 car to her mother for $100 so that her creditors cannot claim it. Kathleen did not receive fair consideration for this transfer. It could be declared void by a trustee if it was made within a year before the filing of a bankruptcy petition against Kathleen. The provisions of law concerning fraudulent transfers are designed to prevent a debtor from concealing or disposing of his or her property in fraud of creditors. Such transfers may also subject the debtor to criminal penalties and prevent discharge of the debtor's unpaid liabilities.

In the case that follows, *Kingsville Dodge, LLC v. Almy, Trustee,* the trustee was able to avoid the transfer of funds to an insider through a consulting contract on the grounds that the transfers was fraudulent.

Kingsville Dodge, LLC v. Almy, Trustee

2007 U.S. Dist. LEXIS 5931 (U.S.D.C., D. Maryland 2007)

FACTS

Kingsville Motors was placed into involuntary bankruptcy by its creditors. Five months prior to the filing of the petition by the creditors, William Bell, the president and 100 percent shareholder of Kingsville Motors, and his wife Lucia Bell, who served on the company's board of directors, approved the sale of substantially all of the Kingsville Dodge's assets to an unrelated third party, Howard Castleman, operating as Kingsville Dodge, LLC, for $200,000. The sale of Kingsville Motors was part of a larger structured transaction in which Castleman also purchased three other adjacent parcels of land, which served as the dealership's customer and inventory parking. In addition, Castleman set aside $167,500 for Lucia Bell to serve as a consultant to Kingsville Dodge pursuant to an independent contractor agreement.

Monique Almy, who had been appointed to serve as the Chapter 7 Trustee for Kingsville Motors, brought an adversary proceeding against William and Lucia Bell, alleging that in their capacity as directors of Kingsville Motors, they fraudulently conveyed $167,500 to Lucia Bell under the guise of the consulting agreement when they approved the sale of the company's assets to Castleman and Kingsville Dodge, knowing that the company was insolvent. Almy also alleged that this was a breach of the Bells' fiduciary duties owed to Kingsville Motors' creditors.

The bankruptcy court found that the diversion of Kingsville Motors' assets vis-à-vis the consulting agreement constituted a fraudulent conveyance and held that the conveyance was voidable. The court ordered that all past and future monies owed under the contract were to be paid to the Kingsville Motors bankruptcy estate. The bankruptcy court's decision was appealed to the United States District Court.

ISSUE

Was the consulting contract a fraudulent conveyance that could be avoided in the bankruptcy proceeding?

DECISION

Yes. Section 548 of the Bankruptcy Code authorizes the trustee to avoid any transfer to or for the benefit of an insider under an employment contract that was made by the debtor within two years before the filing of the bankruptcy petition if the debtor voluntarily or involuntarily received less than a reasonable value in exchange for the transfer or obligation and was insolvent on the date the transfer was incurred or became insolvent as a result of the transfer or obligation.

Here, the consulting agreement with Lucia Bell added no value to the transaction with Castleman, who cared only about the dealership's total price. The Bells had set the offering price at $367,500 and had requested the consulting contract. Given the insider status of Lucia Bell, the bankruptcy court properly found that the consulting agreement was money diverted from the purchase price of Kingsville Motors which the court valued at $367,500 at the time of sale. Given the fact that Lucia Bell did little work and the large difference between the $200,000 received for the business compared to the market value, the purchase price did not constitute fair consideration or reasonably equivalent value. Thus the transfer of $167,500 to Lucia Bell was properly voided as fraudulent, and the monies should be recovered for the benefit of the bankruptcy estate.

LO5 Claims

If creditors wish to participate in the estate of a bankrupt debtor, they must file a **proof of claim** in the estate within a certain time (usually 90 days) after the first meeting of creditors. Only unsecured creditors are required to file proofs of claims; secured creditors do not have to do so. However, a secured creditor whose secured claim exceeds the value of the collateral is an unsecured creditor to the extent of the deficiency. A proof of claim must be filed to support the recovery of the deficiency.

Allowable Claims

The fact that a claim is provable does not ensure that a creditor can participate in the distribution of the assets of the bankruptcy estate. The claim must also be **allowed.** If the trustee has a valid defense to the claim, she can use the defense to disallow the claim or to reduce it. For example, if the claim is based on goods sold to the debtor and the seller breached a warranty, the trustee can assert the breach as a defense. All the defenses that would have been available to the bankrupt person are available to the trustee.

Secured Claims

The trustee must also determine whether a creditor has a lien or secured interest to secure an allowable claim. If the debtor's property is subject to a secured claim of a creditor, that creditor has the first claim to it. The property is available to satisfy claims of other creditors only to the extent that its value exceeds the amount of the debt secured.

Priority Claims

The Bankruptcy Code declares certain claims to have **priority** over other claims. The 10 classes of priority claims are as follows:

1. Domestic support obligations of the debtor, including claims for debts to a spouse, former spouse, or child for alimony to, maintenance for, or support of such spouse or child in connection with a separation agreement, divorce decree, or other court order (but not if assigned to someone else other than a governmental unit). Expenses of a trustee in administering assets that might otherwise be used to pay the support obligations have priority before the support obligations themselves. Also, support obligations owed directly to, or recoverable by, spouses and children have priority over support obligations that have been assigned to or are directly to a governmental unit.
2. Expenses and fees incurred in administering the bankruptcy estate.
3. Unsecured claims in involuntary cases that arise in the ordinary course of the debtor's business after the filing of the petition but before the appointment of a trustee or the order of relief.
4. Unsecured claims of up to $12,475 per individual (including vacation, severance, and sick pay) for employees' wages earned within 180 days before the petition was filed or the debtor's business ceased.
5. Contributions to employee benefit plans up to $12,475 per person (moreover, the claim for wages plus pension contributions is limited to $12,475 per person).
6. Unsecured claims up to $6,150 for (*a*) grain or the proceeds of grain against a debtor who owns or operates a grain storage facility or (*b*) by a U.S. fisherman against a debtor who operates a fish produce storage or processing facility and who has acquired fish or fish produce from the fisherman.
7. Claims of up to $2,775 each by individuals for deposits made in connection with the purchase, lease, or rental of property or the purchase of goods or services for personal use that were not delivered or provided.
8. Certain taxes owed to governmental units
9. Allowed unsecured claims based on a commitment by the debtor to a federal depository institution regulatory agency (such as the FDIC).
10. Allowed claims for liability for death or personal injury resulting from operation of a motor vehicle where the operator was unlawfully intoxicated from alcohol, drugs, or other substances.

Distribution of Debtor's Estate

LO6

The priority claims are paid *after* secured creditors realize on their collateral or security but *before* other unsecured claims are paid. Payments are made to the 10 priority classes in

Concept Summary: Distribution of Debtor's Estate (Chapter 7)

Secured creditors proceed directly against the collateral. If debt is fully satisfied, they have no further interest; if debt is only partially satisfied, they are treated as general creditors for the balance.

↓

Debtor's Estate Is Liquidated and Distributed

↓

Priority Creditors (10 classes)

1. Domestic support obligations of the debtor and expenses of administration of assets used to pay support obligations.
2. Costs and expenses of administration.
3. If involuntary proceeding, expenses incurred in the ordinary course of business after petition filed but before appointment of trustee.
4. Claims for wages, salaries, and commissions earned within 180 days of petition; limited to $12,475 per person.
5. Contributions to employee benefit plans arising out of services performed within 180 days of petition; limit of $12,475 (including claims for wages, salaries, and commissions) per person.
6. Unsecured claims (a) up to $6,150 for grain or the proceeds of grain against a debtor who owns or operates a grain storage facility or (b) by a United States fisherman against a debtor who operates a fish produce or processing facility and who has acquired fish or fish produce from the fisherman.
7. Claims of individuals, up to $2,775 per person, for deposits made on consumer goods or services that were not received.
8. Government claims for certain taxes.
9. Allowed unsecured claims based on a commitment by the debtor to a federal depository institution regulatory agency.
10. Allowed claims for liability for death or personal injury resulting from operation of a motor vehicle where the operator was intoxicated.

A. Distribution is made to 10 classes of priority claims in order.
B. Each class must be fully paid before next class receives anything.
C. If funds not sufficient to satisfy everyone in a class, then each member of the class receives the same proportion of claim.

↓

General Creditors

1. General unsecured creditors.
2. Secured creditors for the portion of their debt that was not satisfied by collateral.
3. Priority creditors for amounts beyond priority limits.

If funds are not sufficient to satisfy all general creditors, then each receives the same proportion of their claims.

↓

Debtor

Debtor receives any remaining funds.

order to the extent there are funds available. Each class must be paid before the next class is entitled to receive anything. To the extent there are insufficient funds to satisfy all the creditors within a class, each class member receives a pro rata share of his claim.

Unsecured creditors include (1) those creditors who had not taken any collateral to secure the debt owed to them, (2) secured creditors to the extent their debt was not satisfied by the collateral they held, and (3) priority claimholders to the extent their claims exceed the limits set for priority claims. Unsecured creditors, to the extent any funds are available for them, share in proportion to their claims; they frequently receive little or nothing on their claims. Secured claims, trustee's fees, and other priority claims often consume a large part or all of the bankruptcy estate.

Special rules are set out in the Bankruptcy Code for distribution of the property of a bankrupt stockbroker or commodities broker.

Discharge in Bankruptcy

LO7

Discharge

A bankrupt person who has not been guilty of certain dishonest acts and who has fulfilled his duties as a bankrupt is entitled to a **discharge** in bankruptcy. A discharge relieves the bankrupt person of further responsibility for those debts that are dischargeable and gives the person a fresh start. A corporation is not eligible for a discharge in liquidation bankruptcy proceedings. A bankrupt person may file a written waiver of her right to a discharge. An individual may not be granted a discharge if she has obtained one within the previous eight years.

Objections to Discharge

After the bankrupt has paid all the required fees, the court gives creditors and others a chance to file objections to the discharge of the bankrupt. Objections may be filed by the trustee, a creditor, or the U.S. attorney. If objections are filed, the court holds a hearing to listen to them. At the hearing the court must determine whether the bankrupt person has committed any act that would bar discharge. If the bankrupt has not committed such an act, the court grants the discharge. If she committed an act that is a bar to discharge, the discharge is denied. It is also denied if the bankrupt fails to appear at the hearing on objections or refused earlier to submit to the questioning of the creditors.

Acts That Bar Discharges

Discharges in bankruptcy are intended for honest debtors. Therefore, there are a number of acts that will bar a debtor from being discharged. These acts include (1) unjustified falsifying, concealing, or destroying of records; (2) making false statements, presenting false claims, or withholding recorded information relating to the debtor's property or financial affairs; (3) transferring, removing, or concealing property in order to hinder, delay, or defraud creditors; (4) failing to account satisfactorily for any loss or deficiency of assets; and (5) failing to obey court orders or to answer questions by the court.

Nondischargeable Debts

Certain debts are not affected by the discharge of a bankrupt debtor. The Bankruptcy Code provides that a discharge in bankruptcy releases a debtor from all provable debts except for those that:

1. Are due as a tax or fine to the United States or any state or local unit of government.
2. Result from liabilities for obtaining money by false pretenses or false representations.

3. Arise out of a debtor's purchase of more than $650 in luxury goods or services on credit from a single creditor within 90 days of filing a petition (presumed to be nondischargeable).
4. Are cash advances in excess of $925 obtained by use of a credit card or a revolving line of credit at a credit union and obtained within 70 days of filing a bankruptcy petition (presumed to be nondischargeable).
5. Were not scheduled in time for proof and allowance because the creditor holding the debt did not have notification of the proceeding even though the debtor was aware that he owed money to that creditor.
6. Were created by the debtor's larceny or embezzlement or by the debtor's fraud while acting in a fiduciary capacity.
7. Are for domestic support obligation, unless excepting them from discharge would impose an undue hardship on the debtor's dependents.
8. Are due for willful or malicious injury to a person or his property.
9. Are educational loans.
10. Are judgments arising out of a debtor's operation of a motor vehicle while legally intoxicated.
11. Are debts incurred to pay a tax to the United States that would not be dischargeable.
12. Are property settlements arising from divorce or separation proceedings that are not covered by the support provisions that are priority claims.

In the case that follows, *Krieger v. Educational Credit Management Corporation,* the court confirmed a bankruptcy court's discharge of student loans on the grounds that their repayment would constitute an undue hardship.

Krieger v. Educational Credit Management Corporation

_____ F.3d _____ (7th Cir. 2013)

FACTS

Susan Krieger was 53 years old and lived with her mother, age 75, in a rural community where few jobs were available. Between mother and daughter, they had only a few hundred dollars a month from various government programs to live on. She was too poor to move in search of better employment prospects elsewhere, and her car, which was more than a decade old, needed repairs. She had no Internet access, which with the lack of transportation, hampered her search for work.

Krieger had not held a job since 1986 when she left the workforce to raise a family. She had not earned more than $12,000 a year in her working career between 1978 and 1986. In 1999, Krieger received an associate of arts degree in business accounting from St. Charles Community College. In 2000, she enrolled in Webster University in Webster Groves, Missouri, where she earned a paralegal certificate and graduated with a bachelor of arts in legal studies. She had a high GPA and received significant recognition for her academic achievements. Over the next decade, she applied for about 200 jobs but was unsuccessful in obtaining any of them.

In obtaining her education, Krieger had accumulated $17,000 in student loans which through years of nonpayment had grown to $25,000. Faced with a situation with no job prospects, Krieger filed a petition in bankruptcy seeking a discharge, including discharge of the student loans which were her largest obligation. The Education Credit Management Corporation, which acts on behalf of some federal loan guarantors, asked the bankruptcy judge to exempt her student

(continued)

loans from the discharge, citing a provision of the bankruptcy code that excludes educational loans "unless exempting such debt from discharge would impose an undue hardship on the debtor."

The bankruptcy judge concluded that she had satisfied the standard for obtaining a discharge of her educational loans, noting her thorough effort to find a job and her good faith in using a substantial portion of a divorce settlement to pay off as much of the educational loan as she could. The district court judge reversed and held that educational debt could not be discharged. The judge thought Krieger should have searched harder for work, especially in later years (when, she conceded, her applications had tapered off in light of the failure of the many earlier applications). And, the judge thought that Krieger had failed the good-faith standard because she had not enrolled in a program that would have offered her a 25-year repayment schedule. Even if she could not make even one payment a year now, the judge thought that accepting a deferred payment schedule would have shown good faith by committing to pay some of the debt should she become employed in the future. Krieger appealed the decision to the United States Court of Appeals for the Seventh Circuit.

ISSUE

Was Krieger entitled to a discharge of her educational loans on the grounds that excepting it from discharge would constitute an undue hardship?

DECISION

Yes. The court upheld the decision of the bankruptcy court, holding that the finding of "undue hardship" was neither clearly erroneous, nor an abuse of discretion. The court began by noting that "undue hardship" requires a three-part showing (1) that the debtor cannot maintain, based on current income and expenses, a "minimal" standard of living for himself and his dependents if forced to repay the loans; (2) that additional circumstances exist indicating that this state of affairs is likely to persist for a significant portion of the repayment period of the student loans; and (3) that the debtor has made good faith efforts to repay the loans.

Noting that the district court judge had found that Krieger had paid as much as she could during the 11 years since receiving the educational loans, the court took issue with the judge's conclusion that good faith entailed a commitment to future efforts to repay. The court further noted that if this was so, then no educational loan could ever be discharged because it is always possible to pay in the future if prospects should improve. However, the statutory language states that a discharge is possible when payment could cause an "undue hardship."

The bankruptcy judge had found that Krieger's circumstances were likely to persist indefinitely. She lacked the resources to travel in search of employment opportunities elsewhere, she had applied for many jobs without success, and at 56, and not having held a job since 1986, did not possess the kind of background that employers were looking for. Returning to the first criteria, the court observed that even Educational Credit Management conceded that Krieger simply could not pay. She was essentially out of the money economy and living a rural, subsistence life. She did not have any assets or income and was not likely to acquire any. Therefore, the bankruptcy court's finding of undue hardship should be upheld.

CONCURRING OPINION

In his concurring opinion, one of the three judges on the appeals panel agreed that the decision of the appeals court was correct as a matter of law and then went on to offer additional views on how petitions in bankruptcy for discharge of educational loans should be handled. He was concerned that the Krieger case should be seen as an extreme exception and outlier, but that with many people struggling to make payments on their student loans, some might see the case and decision as an excuse to avoid their own student loan obligations. Acknowledging that with college tuition increasing, and job opportunities appearing to be contracting, hope should remain that an eventually improving economy will create more jobs. But even for those who perceive that their employment-seeking efforts are at a dead end, bankruptcy should not be the answer. Rather they should be required to enroll in the William D. Ford Income-Based Repayment Plan. Under that plan, a borrower's monthly payment is limited to 15 percent of discretionary income (defined as any income above 150 percent of the poverty line.) After 25 years under the IBR program, any remaining debt is forgiven. He indicated that while this might sound like an unattractive option it was better than erasing what should be an undischargeable debt given Ms. Krieger's age, good health, and education.

All of these nondischargeable debts are provable debts. The creditor who owns these debts can participate in the distribution of the bankrupt's estate. However, the creditor has an additional advantage: His right to recover the unpaid balance is not cut off by the bankrupt's discharge. All other allowed claims are dischargeable; that is, the right to recover them is cut off by the bankrupt's discharge.

Reaffirmation Agreements

Sometimes creditors put pressure on debtors to *reaffirm* (agree to pay) debts that have been discharged in bankruptcy. When the 1978 amendments to the Bankruptcy Code were under consideration, some individuals urged Congress to prohibit such agreements. They argued that reaffirmation agreements were inconsistent with the fresh-start philosophy of the Bankruptcy Code. Congress did not agree to a total prohibition, but it set up a rather elaborate procedure for a creditor to go through to get a debt reaffirmed. Essentially, the agreement must be made *before* the discharge is granted and must contain a clear and conspicuous statement that advises the debtor (1) that the agreement may be rescinded at any time prior to discharge or within 60 days after filing with the court and (2) that the reaffirmation is not required by the bankruptcy law and any other law or agreement. The agreement must be filed with the court accompanied by a statement from the debtor's attorney that (1) it represents a voluntary agreement by the debtor, (2) it does not impose an undue hardship on the debtor, and (3) the attorney fully apprised the debtor of the legal effect and consequences of the agreement and of any default under such an agreement. If the attorney refuses, the court must hold a hearing. Also, a debtor may voluntarily pay any dischargeable obligation without entering into a reaffirmation agreement.

Ethics in Action

One of the purposes of the bankruptcy laws is to give honest debtors a fresh start. However, should a debtor who has had some of his debts discharged in a Chapter 7 proceeding feel an ethical obligation to repay those debts even if he is no longer legally obligated to pay them?

Dismissal for Substantial Abuse

In 1984, Congress, concerned that too many individuals with an ability to pay their debts over time pursuant to a Chapter 13 plan were filing petitions to obtain Chapter 7 discharges of liability, authorized the Bankruptcy Courts to dismiss cases that they determined were a **substantial abuse** of the bankruptcy process.

Means Testing

In the 2005 act, Congress amended the Bankruptcy Code to provide for the dismissal of Chapter 7 cases—or with the debtor's consent their conversion to Chapter 13 cases—on a finding of **abuse** by an individual debtor with primarily consumer debts. The abuse can be established in two ways: (1) through an unrebutted finding of abuse based on a new means test that is included in the Code or (2) on general grounds of abuse, including bad faith, determined under the totality of the circumstances.

The means test is designed to determine the debtor's ability to repay general unsecured claims. It has three elements: (1) a definition of "current monthly income," which is the total income a debtor is presumed to have available; (2) a list of allowed deductions from the current monthly income for the purpose of supporting the debtor and his family and the repayment of higher-priority debts; and (3) defined "trigger points" at which the income remaining after the allowed deductions would trigger the presumption of abuse.

For example, if the debtor's current monthly income after the defined deductions is more than $195.41, the presumption of abuse arises irrespective of the amount of debt; and if the debtor has at least $117.08 per month of current monthly income after the allowed deductions (which would amount to $7,025 over five years), then abuse is presumed if the income would be sufficient to pay at least 25 percent of the debtor's unsecured debts over five years. To rebut the presumption, the debtor must show "special circumstances" that would decrease the income or increase expected expenses so as to bring the debtor's income below the trigger points. Debtors have to file a statement of their calculations under the means test as part of their schedule of income and expenditures.

As illustrated in the case below, *In re Mestemaker,* a court has some leeway in deciding whether or not a debtor's Chapter 7 proceeding represents a substantial abuse of the bankruptcy code and should be dismissed if the debtor does not convert it to a Chapter 13 proceeding.

In re Mestemaker

359 B.R. 849 (U.S.B.C., N.D. Ohio 2007)

FACTS

William and Shanna Mestemaker filed a Chapter 7 petition on December 22, 2007. At the time both were employed; one had been employed in the same position for more than six years. Their bankruptcy schedules showed unsecured nonpriority debt in the amount of $117,884.93, secured debt related to four vehicles in the amount of $17,954.93, and minimal, if any, nonexempt assets. The Debtors' Schedule I showed total monthly income after payroll taxes and deductions of $3,587.45, which did not include a $158.43 withheld monthly as a payroll deduction in payment of three 401(k) plan loans. Their Schedule J showed total monthly expenses in the amount of $3,288.00, leaving monthly net income of $299.45.

Because the petition was filed after the effective date of the 2005 amendments to the Bankruptcy Code, they were subject to its provisions, one of which provides that the bankruptcy court may dismiss a Chapter 7 proceeding filed by a debtor with primarily consumer debts or, with the debtor's consent, may convert the case to one under Chapter 13 if it finds that granting relief would be an abuse of the Code. A presumption of abuse arises if current monthly income is greater than the median family income of the applicable state for a family of the same (or fewer) number of individuals, and if such income, reduced by the amounts as determined under the act and multiplied by 60, is not less than the lesser of (1) 25 percent of the debtor's nonpriority secured claims in the case, or $6,000, whichever is greater, or (2) $10,000.

In this case, the information filed by the Debtors indicated that their income is above the median family income for a family of their size, but that the presumption of abuse does not arise because the expenses they are permitted are greater than the Debtors' current monthly income. Thus, they passed the "means" test. However, because the Debtors' schedules showed excess income over expenses ($299.45) that is available to pay a substantial portion of their unsecured nonpriority debt, the United States Trustee took the position that pursuing the Chapter 7 proceeding would be an abuse of the Bankruptcy Code. Accordingly, he moved to dismiss the Debtors' Chapter 7 case unless they converted the case to a Chapter 13 proceeding.

ISSUE

Should the Mestemakers' Chapter 7 case be dismissed on the grounds it is a substantial abuse of the bankruptcy process?

DECISION

Yes. The court held that it was not limited in making a finding of abuse to whether the debtors had tripped the abuse threshold in the Code. It concluded that, where the actual disposable income exceeded the threshold, that fact was a sufficient basis for it to conclude there would be abuse if the Debtors were allowed to continue under Chapter 7. In this case, the approximately $300 a month of excess disposable income amounted to about $3,600 a year and roughly $18,000 for the five-year period a Chapter 13 plan would cover. The $18,000 is well above the $10,000 figure in the statute.

Chapter 11: Reorganizations

LO2

Relief for Businesses

Sometimes creditors benefit more from a continuation of a bankrupt debtor's business than from a liquidation of the debtor's property. Chapter 11 of the Bankruptcy Code provides a proceeding whereby the debtor's financial affairs can be reorganized rather than liquidated under the supervision of the Bankruptcy Court. Chapter 11 proceedings are available to virtually all business enterprises, including individual proprietorships, partnerships, and corporations (except banks, savings and loan associations, insurance companies, commodities brokers, and stockbrokers).

Chapter 11 cases for individuals look much like the Chapter 13 cases, which are discussed later in this chapter, but the amount of debt is usually much larger and it commonly is predominately nonconsumer debt. The 2005 act created a special subclass of "small business debtors," debtors with less than $2,490,925 in debts, and provides special rules for them, including expedited decision making.

Petitions for reorganization proceedings can be filed voluntarily by the debtor or involuntarily by its creditors. Once a petition for a reorganization proceeding is filed and relief is ordered, the court usually appoints (1) a committee of creditors holding unsecured claims and (2) a committee of equity security holders (shareholders). Normally, the debtor becomes the "debtor in possession" and has the responsibility for running the debtor's business. It is also usually responsible for developing a plan for handling the various claims of creditors and the various interests of persons such as shareholders.

The reorganization plan is essentially a contract between a debtor and its creditors. This contract may involve recapitalizing a debtor corporation and/or giving creditors some equity or shares in the corporation in exchange for part or all of the debt owed to them. The plan must (1) divide the creditors into classes; (2) set forth how each creditor will be satisfied; (3) state which claims, or classes of claims, are impaired or adversely affected by the plan; and (4) provide the same treatment to each creditor in a particular class, unless the creditors in that class consent to a different treatment.

For example, when Kmart's Chapter 11 reorganization plan was accepted by its creditors and approved by the bankruptcy court in 2003, the plan called for its banks, which held secured claims, to receive about 40 cents on each dollar they were owed and for the holders of unsecured claims to receive new stock valued at 14.4 percent of their claim.

The Bankruptcy Code provides for an initial 120-day period after the petition is filed during which only the debtor can file a reorganization plan and a 180-day period within which only the debtor may solicit acceptances of the plan from creditors. The bankruptcy court, at its discretion, may extend these periods. The 2005 act limits the debtor's exclusive plan proposal period to 18 months and the exclusive solicitation period to 20 months. After the initial periods pass, the trustee and creditors are free to propose plans and seek acceptance of them by other creditors. In some cases, debtors develop what is known as a **prepackaged plan** whereby the debtor solicits acceptances of the plan prior to filing for bankruptcy. The 2005 act contains a number of provisions designed to facilitate the use of such plans.

A reorganization plan must be confirmed by the court before it becomes effective. Plans can be confirmed either through the voluntary agreement of creditors or, alternatively, through what is known as a "**cram down,**" whereby the court forces dissenting creditors whose claims would be impaired by a proposed plan to accept the plan when the court can find that it is fair and equitable to the class of creditors whose claims are impaired. If the plan is confirmed, the debtor is responsible for carrying it out. However, until a plan is confirmed, the bankruptcy court has no authority to distribute any portion of the bankruptcy assets to unsecured creditors.

In the case that follows, *In re Made In Detroit, Inc.*, the court rejected a reorganization plan proposed by a debtor and confirmed a plan proposed by a committee of creditors.

In re Made In Detroit, Inc.

299 B.R. 170 (U.S.B.C., E.D. Mich. 2003)

FACTS

In 1997, Made In Detroit, Inc., purchased approximately 410 acres of property for the purpose of development. The property is located on the Detroit River in Gibraltar and Trenton, Michigan, and is Made In Detroit's only significant asset. For the next five years, Made In Detroit attempted to develop the property. Due to problems obtaining permits, and because Made In Detroit was not generating income, it became delinquent to secured creditors. In 2002, the primary secured creditor, Standard Federal, commenced a foreclosure action against Made In Detroit. As a result, on October 23, 2002, Made In Detroit filed for bankruptcy protection under Chapter 11 of the Bankruptcy Code.

On July 15, 2003, Made In Detroit filed its Third Amended Combined Plan and Disclosure Statement (the Debtor's Plan). The Debtor's Plan provided that it would be funded with a $9 million loan from Kennedy Funding and that the Kennedy loan would be contingent on certain conditions precedent, including the payment of a nonrefundable $270,000 commitment fee and an appraisal of the property that indicated it would have a "quick sale" value of at least $15,000,000. The Kennedy commitment also provided a condition on its part, namely, that it intended to bring participants into the transaction and if it was unable to do so, it would be obligated only to refund the commitment fee less compensation for its time and expenses. The Debtor's Plan provided that once the $9 million loan was obtained, the secured creditors and administrative claimants would be paid in full, the unsecured creditors would receive an initial distribution of $750,000 (with the balance of the claims to be paid from the sale of lots), and equity shareholders would retain their interest.

The Official Committee of Unsecured Creditors (the "Committee") and the Wayne County Treasurer filed objections to confirmation of the Debtor's Plan. In addition, on July 9, 2003, the Committee filed its own plan of reorganization. The Committee's Plan provided that it would be financed by an "as is" immediate cash sale of the property to the Trust for Public Land for $4,000,000. Under the Plan the Trust for Public Land would pay the $4,800,000 to the Debtor's Estate to settle all claims with respect to the real property and would receive title to the property free of all liens, claims, and other encumbrances. Under the terms of the Committee's Plan, the secured creditors would be paid in full, the unsecured creditors would receive a pro rata payment (after payment of the administrative claims and higher classes of claims), and the equity shareholders would not receive any distribution nor would they retain any property interest.

Made In Detroit objected to the Committee's Plan and the Bankruptcy Court held a hearing on confirmation of both the Debtor's and the Committee's Plans. The Bankruptcy Code provided that to confirm a plan of reorganization, the court must find that the proposed plan, among other things, is feasible. A plan can be confirmed only if confirmation is not likely to be followed by the liquidation, or the need for further reorganization of the debtor or any successor to the debtor, unless such liquidation or reorganization is proposed in the plan. And plans submitted on a condition basis are not considered feasible. While success need not be guaranteed, the plan must be "doable" and based on more than "visionary promises."

ISSUE

Should the court confirm the Debtor's Plan for reorganization?

DECISION

No. The court denied the Debtor's Plan and approved the Committee's Plan. The court found that the Debtor's Plan was not realistic. It was not sufficiently concrete as to be feasible because it was contingent on exit funding from Kennedy, and there was no reasonable assurance that the Kennedy loan would ever close or that the property would be appraised at a value high enough to provide a $9 million loan. There was testimony that the property if sold "as is" would bring $4.2 million and the court found that the best evidence of the value was the Trust for Public Land's offer to buy the property for $4.8 million. A higher valuation of the property would have been dependent on the improvement of the property, for example, by getting approval to construct, and actually constructing, docks on the Detroit River. The court also considered the fact that if the Debtor's Plan was adopted, the conditions that might or might not take place would cause a delay until some unspecified time in the future. In the meantime, interest would be running on the secured loans at the rate of $20,000 per month and property taxes of $200,000 would be accruing annually.

Use of Chapter 11

During the 1980s, attempts by a number of corporations to seek refuge in Chapter 11 as a means of escaping problems they were facing received considerable public attention. Some of the most visible cases involved efforts to obtain some protection against massive product liability claims and judgments for breach of contract and to escape from collective bargaining agreements. Thus, for example, Johns-Manville Corporation filed under Chapter 11 because of the claims against it arising out of its production and sale of asbestos years earlier; A. H. Robbins Company was concerned about a surfeit of claims arising out of its sale of the Dalkon Shield, an intrauterine birth control device. And, in 1987, Texaco, Inc., faced with a $10.3 billion judgment in favor of Pennzoil in a breach of contract action, filed a petition for reorganization under Chapter 11. Companies such as LTV and Allegheny Industries sought changes in retirement and pension plans, and other companies such as Eastern Airlines sought refuge in Chapter 11 while embroiled in labor disputes.

In the 1990s, a number of companies that were the subject of highly leveraged buyouts (LBOs), including a number of retailers and numerous real estate developers, resorted to Chapter 11 to seek restructuring and relief from their creditors. Similarly, companies such as Pan Am and TWA that were hurt by the economic slowdown and the increase in fuel prices filed Chapter 11 petitions. In 2001, Enron and Kmart filed for reorganization under Chapter 11.

In recent years Chapter 11 has been the subject of significant criticism and calls for its revision. Critics point out that many of the Chapter 11 cases are permitted to drag on for years, thus depleting the assets of the debtor through payments to trustees and lawyers involved in administration and diminishing the assets available to creditors.

For example, *The Wall Street Journal* noted in a July 11, 2003, article, "The Chapter 11 restructuring of Enron, whose controversial collapse became a symbol of corporate malfeasance, has dragged on for 19 months, generating more than 11,000 court filings and nearly $500 million in professional fees." This took the case to the point where the company was about to file its proposed reorganization plan and seek acceptance from creditors and approval by the bankruptcy court.

In the 2005 act, Congress responded to some of those concerns by establishing tighter time frames and placing some limits or restrictions on the availability of extensions of time. Examples include the limitation on the time period in which the debtor has the exclusive right to develop a reorganization plan and special rules forcing debtors to make decisions as to whether to assume or reject unexpired leases of nonresidential property such as space in shopping centers and office buildings.

Collective Bargaining Agreements

Collective bargaining contracts pose special problems. Prior to the 1984 amendments, there was concern that some companies would use Chapter 11 reorganization as a vehicle for trying to avoid executed collective bargaining agreements. Congress then acted to try to prevent the misuse of bankruptcy proceedings for collective bargaining purposes.

The 1984 amendments adopt a rigorous multistep process that must be complied with in determining whether a labor contract can be rejected or modified as part of a reorganization. Among other things that must be done before a debtor or trustee can seek to avoid a collective bargaining agreement are the submission of a proposal to the employees' representative that details the "necessary" modifications to the collective bargaining agreement and assures that "all creditors, the debtor, and all affected parties are fairly treated." Then, before the bankruptcy court can authorize a rejection of the original collective bargaining agreement, it must review the proposal and find that (1) the employees' representative refused to accept it without good cause and (2) the balance of equities clearly favors the rejection of the original collective bargaining agreement.

Ethics in Action

Is it ethical for a company such as that is faced with significant liability for defective products it made and sold to seek the protection accorded by the bankruptcy laws? Similarly, is it ethical for a company that believes it is hampered by a labor contract under which it incurs higher labor costs than some of its competitors to try to use a Chapter 11 proceeding to get out of the labor contract?

Chapter 12: Family Farmers and Fishermen

Historically, farmers have been accorded special treatment in the Bankruptcy Code. In the 1978 act, as in earlier versions, farmers were exempted from involuntary proceedings. Thus, a small farmer who filed a voluntary Chapter 11 or Chapter 13 petition could not have the proceeding converted into a Chapter 7 liquidation over his objection as long as he complied with the Code's requirements in a timely fashion. Additional protection was also accorded through the provision allowing states to opt out of the federal exemption scheme and to provide their own exemptions. A number of states used this flexibility to provide generous exemptions for farmers so they would be able to keep their tools and implements.

Despite these provisions, the serious stress on the agriculture sector during the mid-1980s led Congress in 1986 to further amend the Bankruptcy Code by adding a new Chapter 12 targeted to the financial problems of the family farm. During the 1970s and 1980s, farmland prices appreciated and many farmers borrowed heavily to expand their productive capacity, creating a large debt load in the agricultural sector. When land values subsequently dropped and excess production in the world kept farm prices low, many farmers faced extreme financial difficulty. In the 2005 act, Chapter 12 proceedings were made available to family fishermen.

Chapter 12 is modeled after Chapter 13, which is discussed next. It is available only to family farmers and fishermen with regular income. To qualify, a farmer and spouse must not have less than 50 percent of their total noncontingent liquidated debts arising out of their farming operations. The aggregate debt must be less than $4,031,575 and at least 50 percent of an individual's or couple's income during the year preceding the filing of the petition must have come from the farming operation. A corporation can also qualify, provided that more than 50 percent of the stock or equity is held by one family or its relatives, they conduct the farming operation, and at least 80 percent of the assets are related to the farming operation.

In the case of a family fisherman, the debtor and spouse engaged in a commercial fishing operation are eligible for relief under Chapter 12 if their aggregate debts do not exceed $1,868,200 and not less than 80 percent of their aggregate noncontingent liquidated debts (excluding a debt for their principal residence) arise out of the commercial fishing operation.

A debtor is usually permitted to remain in possession to operate the farm or fishing operation. The debtor is required to file a plan within 90 days of the filing of a Chapter 12 petition—although the bankruptcy court has the discretion to extend the time. A hearing is held on the proposed plan, and it can be confirmed over the objection of creditors. The debtor may release to any secured party the collateral that secures the claim.

Unsecured creditors are required to receive at least liquidation value under the Chapter 12 plan. If an unsecured creditor or the trustee objects to the plan, the court may still confirm the plan despite the objection so long as it calls for full payment of the unsecured creditor's claim or it provides that the debtor's disposable income for the duration of the plan is applied to making payments on it. A debtor who fulfills his plan, or is excused from full performance because of subsequent hardship, is entitled to a discharge.

Chapter 13: Consumer Debt Adjustments

LO2

Relief for Individuals

Chapter 13 ("Adjustment of Debts for Individuals") of the Bankruptcy Code provides a way for individuals who do not want to be declared bankrupt to be given an opportunity to pay their debts in installments from future income under the protection of a federal court. Under Chapter 13, debtors have this opportunity free of problems such as garnishments and attachments of their property by creditors. Only individuals with regular incomes (including sole proprietors of businesses) who owe individually (or with their spouse) liquidated, unsecured debts of less than $383,175 and secured debts of less than $1,149,525 are eligible to file under Chapter 13.

Procedure

Chapter 13 proceedings are initiated by the voluntary petition of a debtor filed in the Bankruptcy Court. Creditors of the debtor may *not* file an involuntary petition for a Chapter 13 proceeding. Commonly, the debtor files at the same time a list of his creditors as well as his assets, liabilities, and executory contracts. The court then appoints a trustee.

Following the filing of the petition, the trustee calls a meeting of creditors, at which time proofs of claims are received and allowed or disallowed. The debtor is examined, and he submits a plan of payment. If the court is satisfied that it is proposed in good faith, meets the legal requirements, and is in the interest of the creditors, the court approves the plan.

If the debtor's income is above the state's median income for a family of the size of his family, then the plan must provide for payments over a period of five years unless all claims will be fully paid in a shorter period. In the case of a debtor whose income is less than the median income of the applicable state, the plan may not provide for payments over a period that is longer than three years, unless the court, for cause, approves a longer period, which in no case can be more than five years.

The plan must provide that all of the debtor's disposable income during the applicable period will be applied to make payments to unsecured creditors under the plan. Unsecured creditors must receive at least what they would receive under Chapter 7. All priority claims must be paid in full.

No plan may be approved if the trustee or an unsecured creditor objects unless the plan provides for the objecting creditor to be paid the present value of what he is owed *or* provides for the debtor to commit all of his projected disposable income for the applicable period to pay his creditors. A critical question that the trustee and other creditors commonly focus on is whether the plan appears to have been proposed in "good faith."

A Chapter 13 debtor must begin making the installment payment proposed in her plan within 30 days after the plan is filed. The interim payments must continue to be made until the plan is confirmed or denied. If the plan is denied, the money, less any administrative expenses, is returned to the debtor by the trustee. The interim payments give the trustee an opportunity to observe the debtor's performance and to be in a better position to make a recommendation as to whether the plan should be approved.

Once approved, a plan may be substantially modified on petition of a debtor or a creditor when there is a material change in the debtor's circumstances.

Suppose Curtis Brown has a monthly take-home pay of $1,000 and a few assets. He owes $1,500 to the credit union for the purchase of furniture, on which he is supposed to pay $75 per month. He owes $1,800 to the finance company on the purchase of a used car, which he is supposed to repay at $90 a month. He also has run up charges of $1,200 on his MasterCard account, primarily for emergency repairs to this car; he must repay this at $60 per month. His rent of $350 per month and food and other living expenses cost him another $425 per month.

Curtis was laid off from his job for a month and fell behind on his payments to his creditors. He then filed a Chapter 13 petition. In his plan he might, for example, offer to repay the credit union $50 a month, the finance company $60 a month, and MasterCard $40 a month, with the payments spread over three years rather than the shorter time for which they are currently scheduled.

Discharge

As soon as practicable after the completion by the debtor of all payments under the plan, the court is required to grant the debtor a discharge of all debts provided for by the plan, or specifically disallowed, except for the following:

- Debts covered by a waiver of discharge executed by the debtor and approved by the court.
- Debts that are for taxes required to be collected or paid and for which the debtor is liable.
- Certain debts that are not dischargeable under Chapter 7, such as those that result from liabilities for obtaining money by false pretenses or false representations (page 885–886).
- Debts for restitution or a criminal fine included in a sentence on the debtor's conviction of a crime.
- Restitution or damages awarded in a civil action against the debtor as a result of willful or malicious injury by the debtor that caused personal injury to an individual or the death of an individual.

A debtor who is subject to a judicial or administrative order, or by statute, to pay a domestic support obligation must, in addition to making the payments pursuant to his plan, certify that all amounts under the order or statute have been paid up to the date of the certification in order to be entitled to a discharge.

Repeat Bankruptcies

The 2005 act prohibits a court from granting a discharge of the debts provided for in the plan or disallowed if the debtor received a discharge in a case filed under Chapters 7, 11, or 12 of the Bankruptcy Code in the four-year period preceding the date of the order of relief under Chapter 13—or in a case filed under Chapter 13 during the two-year period preceding the date of the order of relief in the current case.

In the case that follows, *In re Lavilla,* the trustee objected to confirmation of a Chapter 13 plan by debtors who had received a discharge of their debts a little more than four months before they filed their Chapter 13 petition. The court required the debtors to establish their "good faith" in making the filing and to explain the circumstances that compelled them to seek another discharge of virtually all of their debts and obtain another "fresh start" at a time when they were not eligible for another Chapter 7 discharge.

In re Lavilla

425 B.R. 572 (U.S.B.C., E.D. Cal. 2010)

FACTS

In February 2005, Daniel and Molly Lavilla filed a petition for relief under Chapter 7, and they received a discharge in May 2005. In September 2009, four years and seven months after filing the earlier case, they again needed relief and filed another petition under Chapter 7. When they realized that they would not be eligible for another discharge in Chapter 7 until February 2013, they sought to convert the case to Chapter 13, where they would be eligible for a discharge if they were able to confirm and complete their Chapter 13 plan.

The working parents of two elementary-school-age children, the Lavillas were "below median income" debtors within the meaning of that term in the Bankruptcy Code. Daniel Lavilla earned $3,600 per month as a security officer and Molly earned $1,370 per month as an assistant librarian for the local school district. Together their net take home pay was $3,420 per month. The schedule they filed with their petition indicated that their household expenses, including an automobile payment of $392, were $3,452, leaving a negative monthly net income of $32.

Other schedules filed by the Lavillas showed that they owned no real property and rented their residence. Their personal property, including their automobile, was stated to be worth $16,500 and all of the assets were either encumbered or exempt.

Their scheduled unsecured debts totaled $18,524, which included debts for medical services, credit cards, "payday" loans, and various claims assigned to collection agencies. The Lavillas had no priority debts. Five unsecured claims had been filed in the matter totaling $11,068. The only secured debt in the schedules was for their automobile, a 2005 Ford Escape, which they valued at $10,000. There was nothing in the schedules that suggested the Lavillas had experienced any unusual hardship, medical emergency, or catastrophic loss.

The plan proposed by the Lavillas provided that they would make monthly payments to the Trustee in the amount of $417 for a term of 60 months. The plan payments would be applied to pay the Trustee's compensation, the secured automobile claim, and their attorney's fees in the amount of $2,100. The automobile claim would be paid in full at the rate of $324.50 per month with 5 percent interest. The plan called for a 4.8 percent distribution to the other unsecured creditors.

The Trustee objected to the plan. He noted that the Lavillas, who were not eligible for a Chapter 7 discharge, were proposing to make an insignificant distribution to their unsecured creditors in exchange for a Chapter 13 discharge. Based on that combination of circumstances, the Trustee argued that both the bankruptcy petition and the Chapter 13 plan failed to satisfy the good faith test.

ISSUE

In light of the objection raised by the Trustee, should the court confirm the plan submitted by the Lavillas?

DECISION

No. The court began by noting that it was not a *per se* violation of the good faith test for the Lavillas to pursue relief under Chapter 13 since they were outside the four-year period prescribed by the Bankruptcy Code for such a filing. However, given the Trustee's objection to the plan, it was incumbent on the Lavillas to persuade the court that they were proceeding in "good faith" and that, considering all the circumstances, they were in need of another "fresh start" which they could not get at this time under Chapter 7. The Lavillas have to explain the circumstances that compel them to seek another discharge of virtually all of their obligations at a time when they are not yet eligible for another Chapter 7 discharge.

Advantages of Chapter 13

A debtor may choose to file under Chapter 13 to try to avoid the stigma of a Chapter 7 bankruptcy or to try to retain more of his or her property than is exempt from bankruptcy under state law. Chapter 13 can provide some financial discipline to a debtor as well as an opportunity to get some protection from her financial creditors so long as payments are made as called for by the plan. The debtor's creditors stand to benefit by possibly being able to recover a higher percentage of the debt owed to them than they would get in straight bankruptcy proceedings.

Concept Summary: Comparison of Major Forms of Bankruptcy Proceedings

Purpose	Chapter 7 Liquidation	Chapter 11 Reorganization	Chapter 12 Adjustments of Debts	Chapter 13 Adjustments of Debts
Eligible Debtors	Individuals, partnerships, and corporations *except* municipal corporations, railroads, insurance companies, banks, and savings and loan associations. Farmers and ranchers are eligible only if they petition voluntarily.	Generally, same as Chapter 7 except a railroad may be a debtor, and a stockbroker and commodity broker may not be a debtor under Chapter 11.	Family farmer with regular income, at least 50 percent of which comes from farming, and less than $4,031,575 in debts, at least 50 percent of which is farm related. Family fishermen with regular income whose aggregate debts do not exceed $1,868,200 and at least 80 percent of which arose out of the fishing operation.	Individual with regular income with liquidated unsecured debts less than $383,175 and secured debts of less than $1,149,525.
Initiation of Proceeding	Petition by debtor (voluntary). Petition by creditors (involuntary).	Petition by debtor (voluntary). Petition by creditors (involuntary).	Petition by debtor.	Petition by debtor.
Basic Procedure	1. Appointment of trustee. 2. Debtor retains exempt property. 3. Nonexempt property is sold and proceeds distributed based on priority of claims. 4. Dischargeable debts of individuals are terminated.	1. Appointment of committees of creditors and equity security holders. 2. Debtor submits reorganization plan. 3. If plan is approved and implemented, debts are discharged.	1. Trustee is appointed but debtor usually remains in possession. 2. Debtor submits a plan in which unsecured creditors must receive at least liquidation value. 3. If plan is approved and fulfilled, debtor is entitled to a discharge.	1. Trustee is appointed but debtor usually remains in possession. 2. Debtor submits a plan in which unsecured creditors must receive at least liquidation value. 3. If plan is approved and fulfilled, debts covered by plan are discharged.

(continued)

Concept Summary: Comparison of Major Forms of Bankruptcy Proceedings *(concluded)*

Purpose	Chapter 7 Liquidation	Chapter 11 Reorganization	Chapter 12 Adjustments of Debts	Chapter 13 Adjustments of Debts
Advantages	After liquidation and distribution of assets, most or all debts may be discharged and debtor gets a fresh start.	Debtor remains in business and debts are liquidated through implementation of approved reorganization plan.	Debtor generally remains in possession and has opportunity to work out of financial difficulty over period of time (usually three years) through implementation of approval plan.	Debtor has opportunity to work out of financial difficulty over period of time (usually three to five years) through implementation of approved plan.

Questions and Problem Cases

1. Suppose you are the creditor of a debtor who is involved in straight bankruptcy (liquidation) proceedings. Would you be best off if your claim were *(a)* covered by a perfected security interest in collateral of the debtor, *(b)* based on a claim for wages, or *(c)* unsecured? Explain.
2. Suppose a friend of yours is insolvent and asks for your assistance in choosing between filing for straight bankruptcy (liquidation) under Chapter 7 and filing under Chapter 13. What would you tell your friend are the major differences between the two kinds of proceedings?
3. Gilbert and Kimberly Barnes filed a voluntary Chapter 7 petition in the U.S. Bankruptcy Court for the District of Maryland. Subsequently they moved to avoid a nonpurchase money lien held by ITT Financial Services on their exempt "household goods." Among the goods that the Barneses were claiming as "household goods" were a videocassette recorder (VCR), a 12-gauge pump shotgun, a 20-gauge shotgun, a 30-06 rifle, and a .22 pistol. ITT contended that the VCR and the firearms were not household goods that they could exempt. Under Maryland law, household goods are items of personal property necessary for the day-to-day existence of people in the context of their homes. Should the court consider the VCR and firearms to be "household goods"?
4. In 2008 Virgil Hurd was kicked out of his home by his ex-wife. At that time he moved into his horse trailer (the "Trailer") to keep warm. The Trailer is 20 feet long and 6 feet wide. Virgil gets electricity for the Trailer from a socket and water from a barrel with a pump. He receives his mail at the land where the Trailer is parked. Since January of 2010, Virgil spends approximately 70 percent of his time at his girlfriend's house. In addition to using the Trailer as a place to sleep, Virgil also uses it for transporting his horses and his girlfriend's horses. In April of 2010, he filed a voluntary petition for relief under Chapter 7 in the United States Bankruptcy Court for Western District of Missouri. In his schedule of exemptions, he listed the entire $3,000 value of the Trailer as exempt under a Missouri statute, which exempts any mobile home used as

Trailer as exempt under a Missouri statute, which exempts any mobile home used as the principal residence that does not exceed $5,000 in value. The term *mobile home* is not defined in that statute. The Chapter 7 trustee objects to Virgil's claim of a Missouri exemption in a horse trailer used as his living quarters. The trustee contends that the Trailer was not Virgil's principal residence during the 6 to 12 month period before filing his bankruptcy petition, and that the Trailer does not qualify as a mobile home under the Missouri statute. Should the Trailer be exempt from the bankruptcy estate?

5. William Kranich, Jr., was the sole shareholder in the DuVal Financial Corporation (DFC). On November 10, Kranich filed a voluntary petition for relief under Chapter 7; on the following January 6, DFC also filed a voluntary petition under Chapter 7. Prior to the commencement of the Chapter 7 proceedings, Kranich conveyed his personal residence in Clearwater, Florida, to DFC. The transfer was wholly without consideration. Shortly thereafter, DFC transferred the property to William Kranich III and June Elizabeth Kranich, Kranich's son and daughter, as tenants in common. This transfer was also without consideration. The bankruptcy trustee brought suit to recover the property from the son and daughter on the grounds that the transfer was fraudulent. Could the trustee recover the property on the grounds that its transfer, without consideration, was fraudulent?

6. Brian Scholz was involved in an automobile collision with a person insured by The Travelers Insurance Company. At the time, Scholz was cited for, and pled no contest to, a criminal charge of driving under the influence of alcohol arising out of the accident. Travelers paid its insured $4,303.68 and was subrogated to the rights of its insured against Scholz. Subsequently, Travelers filed a civil action against Scholz to recover the amount it paid, and a default judgment was entered against Scholz. Eleven months later, Scholz sought relief from the bankruptcy court by filing a voluntary petition under Chapter 7. One of the questions in the bankruptcy proceeding was whether the debt owing to Travelers was nondischargeable. Is the debt dischargeable?

7. Jonathon Gerhardt was a professional cellist who had obtained over $77,000 in government-insured student loans to finance his education at the University of Southern California, the Eastman School of Music, the University of Rochester, and the New England Conservatory of Music. He was 43 years old, healthy, and had no dependents. He subsequently defaulted on each loan owed to the United States government, having paid a total of only $755 on those loans. In 1999, Gerhardt filed for Chapter 7 bankruptcy and subsequently sought discharge of his student loans.

   At the time he filed for bankruptcy, Gerhardt was earning $1,680.47 per month as the principal cellist for the Louisiana Philharmonic Orchestra (LPO), including a small amount of supplemental income earned as a cello teacher for Tulane University. His monthly expenses, which included a health club membership and Internet access, averaged $1,829.39. During the LPO off-season, Gerhardt collected unemployment.

   Should the court discharge Gerhardt's student loans on the grounds that their repayment would constitute an undue hardship?

8. Doug Boyce works as a claims adjuster for GEICO. He makes $57,000 a year as a base salary plus several thousand more as a part of a discretionary annual profit-sharing agreement. In 2008 he earned $67,961 from GEICO. GEICO also provides Boyce with a vehicle for his work and personal use. In 2007, Boyce took out a $16,000 loan from his 401k to purchase a house. He lives in the home and rents out some of the rooms for an additional rental income of approximately $5,800 a year. In October of 2007, Boyce finalized his divorce and assumed responsibility

for $34,000 in student loans and $16,000 in credit card debt. By October of 2008 Boyce had added an additional $17,000 to his credit card debt. In March of 2008, Boyce purchased a Ford F350 with a $2,000 down payment and a monthly payment of $186. Boyce filed for bankruptcy protection under Chapter 7 on October 28, 2008. After filing for bankruptcy, Boyce surrendered his Ford F350 and borrowed $14,750 from his 401k to purchase a Dodge Ram truck. He later sold the truck and purchased a Chevrolet truck and borrowed another $6,000 from his 401k to purchase a recreational camper. At the time of filing, Boyce did not disclose the money he earned from the profit-sharing agreement or his rental income and his reported monthly income was short by $109. In addition, Boyce did not include the $34,000 student loan debt on his schedules. The United States Trustee commenced a contested proceeding against Boyce seeking dismissal of the Chapter 7 proceeding. Should the court dismiss Boyce's Chapter 7 bankruptcy filings or alternatively force him into Chapter 13?

9. Paul Kelly was a graduate student at the University of Nebraska and had been working on his Ph.D. since 1991. He expected to complete it in 1999. He was also working as a clerk in a liquor store approximately 32 hours per week and earning $5.85 per hour. His monthly expenses were $743, and his monthly take-home pay was $761. Kelly borrowed money through student loans to enable him to pay tuition, fees, books, and other school-related expenses and expected to continue to do so until he finished his Ph.D.

   On July 26, 1994, the U.S. District Court in Minnesota entered a judgement in the amount of $30,000 against Kelly and in favor of Capital Indemnity Corporation. The judgement was based on a misappropriation of funds by Kelly from a bank insured by Capitol. The court's order provided that the judgement was not dischargeable in bankruptcy.

   Kelly filed a Chapter 13 petition. In his Chapter 13 plan, Kelly proposed to pay a total of $7,080 by paying off $118 per month, $100 of which would come from student loans. In the proceeding, Kelly testified that, among other things, he was currently qualified to teach at the college or university level and could earn about $20,000 but preferred to work part-time as a clerk while he completed graduate school. Capitol objected to the proposed plan on the ground it was not proposed in good faith. Capitol contended that Kelly should not be allowed to languish in graduate school, remain underemployed, and obtain the benefit of Chapter 13 discharge. Capitol asserted that Kelly was attempting to discharge a debt that was nondischargeable under Chapter 7, proposed to make payments primarily from his student loans, and would be paying a dividend to unsecured creditors of only 8.5 percent. These factors, Capitol contended, demonstrated that the plan had not been proposed in good faith and that it should not be confirmed. Should confirmation of Kelly's plan be denied on the grounds it was not proposed in good faith?

Part 9

Government Regulation

Chapter 45

The Antitrust Laws

Learning Objectives

After you have studied this chapter, you should be able to:

1. Explain the standing and jurisdictional aspects of the Sherman Act.
2. Describe when joint action occurs and why it is important in a case involving Section 1 of the Sherman Act.
3. Examine a fact situation and apply the correct (per se, rule of reason, or abbreviated rule of reason) analysis from Section 1 of the Sherman Act.
4. Examine a fact situation and apply the correct analysis from Section 2 of the Sherman Act.
5. Compare and contrast the Clayton Act with the Sherman Act.
6. Examine a fact situation and apply the correct Robinson-Patman Act analysis.

For many years, athletic footwear manufacturers have been accused of routinely pressuring retailers to sell their shoes at suggested retail prices. This benefits manufacturers by ensuring their brand image will not be tarnished by price-cutting and assures retailers that rival stores will not steal customers by offering special discounts. Reebok was accused of prohibiting its retail dealers from selling shoes below designated price levels. In a consent decree with the government, Reebok, without admitting any guilt, agreed not to try to set or control retail prices and not to threaten retailers with suspension or termination if they do not follow suggested retail prices.

- What is price-fixing? Why is it unlawful?
- What procedure should the courts follow in determining whether Reebok violated the antitrust laws?
- How might Reebok lawfully control the retail price of its athletic footwear?

Introduction

The purpose of U.S. antitrust law is to encourage and protect competition. With the growth of national markets after the Civil War, the United States witnessed an important development on the economic scene: the growth of large industrial combines and trusts. Many of these huge business entities engaged in practices aimed at destroying their competitors. This behavior led to a public outcry for legislation designed to preserve competitive market structures and prevent the accumulation of great economic power in the hands of a few firms. Congress responded by passing the **Sherman Act** in 1890, and later supplemented it with the Clayton Act and the **Robinson-Patman Act.**

Antitrust in a Global Environment

The prime focus of U.S. antitrust enforcement is to protect American consumers from anticompetitive conduct. In an increasingly global environment this sometimes entails bringing antitrust actions against foreign defendants or prohibiting conduct that occurs outside of the actual territory of this country. The United States is not alone in its maintenance of domestic and international competition through the enforcement of antitrust laws. Most industrial nations have such legislation. International businesses must be more and more alert to the reach of these antitrust laws as they expand their operations around the world.

Procedural Aspects of the Sherman Act

Penalties

The Sherman Act makes contracts in restraint of trade and monopolization illegal. It provides criminal penalties of violations of its provisions (up to a $1 million fine and/or 10 years' imprisonment for individuals and up to a $100 million fine for corporate violators). It also gives the federal courts broad injunctive powers to remedy antitrust violations. The courts can order convicted defendants to divest themselves of the stock or assets of other companies or to divorce themselves from a functional level of their operations (e.g., they can order a manufacturer to sell a captive retail chain). In extreme cases, courts can order dissolution—force the defendant to liquidate its assets and go out of business.

Private individuals who have been injured by antitrust violations have strong incentives to sue under the civil provisions of the antitrust laws. A successful antitrust plaintiff may recover **treble damages** (three times its actual losses) plus court costs and attorney's fees. This can mean tremendous liability for antitrust defendants. Reebok, in the case that opened this chapter, agreed to a settlement without admitting any wrongdoing. Such an admission would have made the company extremely vulnerable to treble damage lawsuits by retailers claiming injury.

Legislation provides opportunities for corporate defendants to detreble the civil damage remedy by cooperating with federal investigations of cartel conduct. In exchange for detrebling civil damages, the defendant must pay full restitution to private plaintiffs and assist them in their actions against co-conspirators.

The Corporate Leniency Policy

Under the Antitrust Division's Corporate Leniency Policy, the U.S. government agrees not to charge a firm criminally for the activity being reported if (in the case of an applicant who comes forward after an investigation has begun) seven conditions are met: (1) the applicant is the first to report the illegal activity; (2) the government does not, at the time the applicant comes forward, have enough information to sustain a conviction; (3) the applicant, upon its discovery of the illegal activity being reported, took prompt and effective action to terminate its part in the activity; (4) the applicant's report is made with candor and completeness and provides full, continuing, and complete cooperation with the government's investigation; (5) the applicant confesses to illegal anticompetitive conduct as a corporation and not merely through individual confessions by corporate officers; (6) the applicant makes restitution where possible; and (7) the government determines that granting leniency to the applicant would not be unfair to others. The officers and directors of the corporation who assist with the investigation are considered for immunity from prosecution on the same basis as if they had come forward individually.

Standing

LO1

Private plaintiffs who seek to recover treble damages must first convince the court that they have *standing* to sue, that is, that they have suffered a direct injury as a result of the defendant's claimed antitrust violations. For instance, suppose all of the lumberyards in a city conspired to fix prices in order to ensure that lumber was not sold below some inflated figure. This is a clear violation of the antitrust laws. Builders who were forced to purchase lumber at the artificially high price would be directly injured and, accordingly, able to bring an antitrust suit. In all likelihood, however, the builders probably passed these increased costs on to home buyers in the form of higher prices for new homes. The buyers of these homes, although injured by the price-fixing, could not bring an antitrust case. They are **indirect purchasers** of the lumber and are therefore precluded from suing the lumberyards (their indirect sellers). They have no suit against the builders since it is not an antitrust violation to pass the increased costs on to the ultimate buyer.

Jurisdiction

Since the federal government's power to regulate business flows from the Commerce Clause of the U.S. Constitution, the federal antitrust laws apply only to behavior that substantially affects interstate commerce or international trade. Behavior that affects only *intrastate* (purely local) commerce is outside the scope of the federal antitrust laws and must be challenged under state antitrust statutes, some of which are not vigorously enforced.

LO1

In view of the fact that a large portion of business in the United States is conducted across state lines, it is often relatively easy to show the required impact on interstate commerce. Even behavior that takes place solely within the borders of one state can have an interstate impact in today's economy.

Extraterritorial Reach

Antitrust violations that occur within the territory of the United States (whether committed by U.S. or foreign persons) fall squarely within the jurisdictional reach of the U.S. antitrust laws. However, U.S. antitrust enforcement is not limited to conduct that occurs within U.S. borders. The Sherman Act has been interpreted to reach actions of foreign entities that have an anticompetitive effect in the United States as well as acts that limit American access to markets abroad.

Foreign Trade Antitrust Improvement Act

Seeking to clarify the confusion surrounding the extraterritorial reach of the antitrust laws, Congress enacted the Foreign Trade Antitrust Improvement Act. Specifically, this statute provides that the Sherman Act shall not apply to nonimport trade unless the conduct has a **direct, substantial, and reasonably foreseeable effect** on trade or commerce within the United States, on U.S. import trade, or on the activities of U.S. exporters.

Section 1 of the Sherman Act

Section 1 of the Sherman Act provides:

> Every contract, combination in the form of trust or otherwise, or conspiracy, in restraint of trade or commerce among the several states, or with foreign nations is declared to be illegal.

A *contract* is any agreement, express or implied, between two or more persons to restrain competition; a *combination* is a continuing partnership in restraint of trade; and a *conspiracy* occurs when two or more persons join together for the purpose of restraining trade.

Joint Action

LO2

From the language of the statute, it is apparent that the purpose of Section 1 is to attack joint action in restraint of trade. Accordingly, unilateral actions, even if they have an anticompetitive effect, do not violate Section 1. For instance, a wholesaler may "suggest" that a retail outlet sell an item at a certain price. As long as the two businesses did not *agree* that the goods would be sold at that price, Section 1 has not been violated. Further, a manufacturer may terminate a dealer who has failed to follow a "suggested marketing practice" (e.g., selling below the suggested resale price or failing to provide a service department) even though such a practice may tend to raise prices and lower competition. Such a unilateral refusal to deal is not joint action and therefore cannot be prohibited by Section 1.

Determining when a court will infer an agreement from the actions of the defendants is a constant problem for businesses. Some areas are fairly clear-cut. For example, it has long been held that a corporation cannot conspire with itself or with its employees. And the Supreme Court has ruled that a corporation could not conspire with a wholly owned subsidiary. Consignments have also been held to be unilateral action. A consignment agreement is one in which the owner of goods delivers them to another who is to act as the owner's agent in selling the goods. If a manufacturer delivers all goods to its dealers on a consignment basis, it can lawfully fix the price of those goods since the goods remain its property and are not the property of the dealers. (The dealer is the agent of the manufacturer and, like the employee situation above, cannot conspire with its principal/employer.) Courts appear more likely to infer joint action if the defendants are both competitors (as opposed to dealings between a supplier and a distributor) and/or if the dealings involve the discussion of price.

Valuepest.com v. Bayer

561 F.3d 282 (4th Cir. 2009)

FACTS

Bayer Corporation began distributing its termiticide through an agency agreement. Bayer would retain title to its termiticide until it was sold to a pest management professional (PMP). In addition, Bayer would set the retail prices, and the distributors would receive a fixed commission for each sale. A distributor filed a lawsuit against Bayer, alleging vertical price-fixing. Bayer asked the court to dismiss the lawsuit, arguing there is no violation of Section 1 of the Sherman Act when there is a genuine principal-agent relationship between the manufacturer and its distributors.

ISSUE

Should the court dismiss this antitrust lawsuit?

DECISION

Yes. Where a manufacturer sells its products through its genuine agents, there is no contract, combination, or conspiracy, and thus no basis for Section 1 antitrust liability exists. In this case, Bayer bore the risk of loss and retained title on the products while they were in the distributor's possession. In addition, Bayer used the agency sales as a method for legitimate business reasons. It wanted the termiticide to be seen as a premium product of high efficacy and thus wanted to retain control over how the product was presented to PMPs. Finally, there is no evidence that the agency agreements were the products of coercion. Because the agency relationships were genuine, there is no violation of Section 1.

The Theory of Interdependence

Courts are cautious in accepting inferences from circumstantial evidence in cases involving allegations of horizontal price-fixing among oligopolists. The theory of interdependence suggests that, in highly concentrated markets, any rational decision will take into account the anticipated reaction of the other firms.

Conscious Parallelism

According to the theory of interdependence, firms in a concentrated market may maintain their prices at *supracompetitive* levels, or even raise them to those levels, without engaging in any overt concerted action. Such *oligopolistic rationality* cannot only forestall price-cutting, it can also provide for price increases through, for example, price leadership. Despite the noncompetitive nature of such conduct, which is called **conscious parallelism,** it is not unlawful. This is because interdependent behavior is not an "agreement" within the term's meaning under the Sherman Act.

Plus Factors

In order to prevail on a claim of collusion based on inferences from consciously parallel behavior, plaintiffs must show that certain **plus factors** also exist. These plus factors tend to ensure the existence of an actual agreement, rather than unilateral, independent conduct of competitors. In short, the plus factors provide circumstantial evidence of an agreement. Courts have identified at least three plus factors: (1) evidence that the defendant had a motive to enter into a price-fixing conspiracy, (2) evidence that the defendant acted contrary to its interests, and (3) evidence implying a traditional conspiracy.

Evidence that the defendant had a motive to enter into a price-fixing conspiracy means evidence that the industry is conducive to oligopolistic price-fixing. In other words, it is evidence that the structure of the market was such as to make secret price-fixing feasible. Evidence that the defendant acted contrary to its interests means evidence of conduct that would be irrational assuming that the defendant operated in a competitive market. In a competitive industry, for example, a firm would cut its price with the hope of increasing its market share if its competitors were setting prices above marginal costs.

The first two plus factors are important to a court's analysis, but since they often merely restate interdependence, they must be supplemented by evidence implying a traditional conspiracy. That evidence may involve proof that the defendants got together and exchanged assurances of common action or otherwise adopted a common plan even though no meetings, conversations, or exchanged documents are shown.

Ethics in Action

An agreement between a manufacturer and a retailer fixing the retail price at which the manufacturer's products would be sold to the public would be illegal joint action. However, because of the express language in Section 1, a suggestion by the manufacturer (which was complied with by the retailer) would be perfectly legitimate since it would be unilateral action. Yet if the suggestion was strongly worded, the ultimate effect would be the same—the retailer would comply with the manufacturer's wishes. Is it ethical to circumvent Section 1 through such verbal gymnastics?

Section 1 Analysis

LO3

After a finding of joint action, the court must examine the nature of the alleged violation to determine its legal status. Such joint action will be treated as either a per se or a rule of reason violation. Per se activities are automatically illegal, while the legality of a rule of reason action can be determined only after examining the behavior's ultimate effect on competition.

Per Se Restraints

When faced with the difficult problem of deciding what kinds of joint action amounted to a restraint of trade, the courts concluded that some kinds of behavior always have a negative effect on competition that can never be excused or justified. These kinds of acts are classed as **per se** illegal; they are conclusively presumed to be illegal. While per se rules have been criticized as shortcuts that sometimes oversimplify economic realities, they do speed up lengthy trials and provide sure guidelines for business.

Price-Fixing

The essential characteristic of a free market is that the price of goods and services is determined by the play of forces in the marketplace. Attempts by competitors to interfere with the market and control prices are called **horizontal price-fixing** and are illegal per se under Section 1. Price-fixing may take the form of direct agreements among competitors about what price they will sell a product for or what price they will offer for a product. It may also be accomplished by agreements on the quantities to be produced, offered for sale, or bought. Whether done directly or indirectly, horizontal price-fixing is always illegal and can never be legally justified.

Attempts by manufacturers to control the resale price of their products are also within the scope of Section 1. This kind of behavior is called **vertical price-fixing** or *resale price maintenance.* As was discussed above, manufacturers can lawfully state a "suggested retail price" for their products, since this does not involve joint action. If the manufacturer gets the retailer to agree to follow the suggested price, however, such an agreement is joint action in restraint of trade and may be illegal per se under Section 1.

For almost 80 years, courts consistently found that all resale price maintenance was a per se violation of Section 1. However, this position began to erode when, in 1997, the U.S. Supreme Court distinguished between vertical, minimum price-fixing and vertical, maximum price-fixing. Specifically, the Court ruled that minimum price-fixing arrangements between suppliers and distributors were per se illegal, while vertical, maximum price-fixing should be examined under rule of reason analysis. Today, the distinction between vertical maximum and vertical minimum price-fixing no longer exists. In the case that follows, the Supreme Court, believing there to be procompetitive explanations for vertical, minimum price-fixing, held that all vertical price-fixing should be scrutinized under rule of reason analysis.

Leegin Creative Leather Products v. PSKS

551 U.S. 877 (U.S. Sup. Ct. 2007)

FACTS

In an attempt to distance itself from megastores, Leegin instituted a pricing and promotion policy in which it offered incentives to retailers who agreed to sell at Leegin's suggested prices. Kay's Kloset agreed to do so. When Leegin discovered that Kay's Kloset had been marking down Brighton's entire line by 20 percent, it requested that Kay's Kloset cease discounting. Its request refused, Leegin stopped selling to the store. PSKS sued, arguing that vertical minimum price-fixing agreements are per se illegal.

ISSUE

Should vertical price-fixing be examined under rule of reason analysis?

DECISION

Yes. The procompetitive justifications for vertical price restraints are similar to those for other vertical restraints. Minimum resale price maintenance can stimulate interbrand competition—the competition among manufacturers selling different brands of the same type of product—by reducing intrabrand competition—the competition among retailers selling the same brand. A single manufacturer's use of vertical price restraints tends to eliminate intrabrand price competition; this in turn encourages retailers to invest in tangible or intangible services or promotional efforts that aid the manufacturer's position as against rival manufacturers. Absent vertical price restraints, the retail services that enhance interbrand competition might be underprovided. This is because discounting retailers can free ride on retailers who furnish services and then capture some of the increased demand those services generate. For all of the foregoing reasons, we think the rule of reason is the appropriate standard to judge vertical price restraints.

Group Boycotts and Concerted Refusals to Deal

A single firm can lawfully refuse to deal with certain firms or agree to deal only on certain terms. However, any such agreement by two or more firms to boycott or terminate another is a per se violation of Section 1. Thus, if a distributor persuades a manufacturer to refuse to deal with a rival distributor, the two conspiring parties would have committed a per se violation of Section 1.

Division of Markets

Any agreement among competing firms to divide up the available market by assigning each other exclusive territories is a horizontal division of markets and is illegal per se. The idea is that each firm is given a monopoly in its assigned territory.

Rule of Reason Violations

LO3

Any behavior that has not been classified as a per se violation is judged under rule of reason analysis. A rule of reason trial involves a complex, often lengthy attempt by the court to balance the anticompetitive effects of the defendants' acts against any competitive justifications for their behavior. If the court concludes that the defendants' acts had a significant anticompetitive effect that was not offset by any positive impact on competition, their behavior is held illegal. Recent antitrust decisions indicate that the Supreme Court is moving away from per se rules in favor of rule of reason treatment for many kinds of economic activity. This trend is consistent with the Court's increased willingness to consider new economic theories seeking to justify behavior previously declared illegal per se.

Actually, the per se rules might be viewed merely as special applications of the rule of reason for certain types of restraints that experience shows will always or almost always fail the rule of reason. Rule of reason itself has been broken into two categories: full rule of reason analysis and abbreviated rule of reason analysis.

Full rule of reason analysis applies to a broader category of restraints in which the competitive reasonableness cannot be ascertained without a thorough examination of their pernicious and beneficial effects in the relevant product and geographic markets. Restraints of this type may ultimately be found anticompetitive and illegal, but, unlike per se restraints, they are not facially so. Their legality cannot be determined until after a court conducts a full market analysis.

Abbreviated rule of reason analysis is utilized for restraints that have an obvious adverse impact on competition; however, they do not deserve per se treatment because their overall reasonableness cannot be ascertained without a preliminary assessment of their procompetitive effects. This "quick look" form of rule of reason analysis skips the inquiry into anticompetitive effects because they are obvious from the general nature of the restraint. In these types of cases, the judicial analysis focuses solely on any procompetitive justifications offered in support of the activity.

Vertical Nonprice Restraints on Distribution

A manufacturer can lawfully, as a matter of business policy, "unilaterally" assign exclusive dealerships to its dealers or limit the number of dealerships it grants in any geographic area. (Since there is no joint action, there is no violation of Section 1.) However, manufacturers may run afoul of Section 1 if they require their dealers to "agree" to refrain from selling to customers outside their assigned territories or to unfranchised dealers inside their assigned territories. Such vertical, nonprice restraints are analyzed under the rule of reason.

Joint Ventures and Strategic Alliances

Joint ventures (or strategic alliances) are arrangements in which two or more entities collaborate with respect to research, development, production, marketing, or distribution. Because they generally involve cooperation between actual or potential competitors, joint ventures could possibly violate Section 1 of the Sherman Act. Recognizing the tremendous competitive advantages that the United States might gain from joint research and development and joint production, Congress enacted the National Cooperative Research and Production Act, which mandates that U.S. courts examine research and development joint ventures as well as joint production ventures under rule of reason analysis. Further, if the venture partners have complied with the act's notification requirements, they are liable for only actual (rather than treble) damages in any civil suits that successfully challenge the arrangement.

While marketing and distribution joint ventures do not fall within the statute act, the Department of Justice recommends that they also be scrutinized under rule of reason analysis. However, courts will not employ rule of reason analysis unless the joint arrangement truly constitutes some form of economic integration. If the cooperation actually is no more than a "sham" joint venture designed to restrict output or maintain prices, it will be treated as a per se violation of Section 1.

Texaco v. Dagher

547 U.S. 1 (U.S. Sup. Ct. 2006)

FACTS

Shell Oil and Texaco formed a joint venture, Equilon Enterprises, which combined Shell's and Texaco's downstream operations in the western United States. The Federal Trade Commission approved the formation of the joint venture. Shell and Texaco signed noncompetition agreements which prohibited them from competing with Equilon. Shell and Texaco also continued to operate as distinct corporations. The joint venture agreement required that Equilon sell Shell and Texaco brands at the same price in the same market areas.

(continued)

ISSUE

Is this pricing policy per se illegal?

DECISION

No. Price-fixing agreements between two or more competitors, otherwise known as horizontal price-fixing agreements, fall into the category of arrangements that are per se unlawful. This case does not present such an agreement, however, because Texaco and Shell Oil did not compete with one another in the relevant market—namely, the sale of gasoline to service stations in the western United States—but instead participated in that market jointly through their investments in Equilon. In other words, the pricing policy challenged here amounts to little more than price-setting by a single entity—albeit within the context of a joint venture—and not a pricing agreement between competing entities with respect to their competing products. As such, though Equilon's pricing policy may be price-fixing in a literal sense, it is not price-fixing in the antitrust sense.

Licensing Arrangements

A firm will frequently attempt to exploit the market by licensing its intellectual property (e.g., patents, copyrights, trade secrets, know-how) to manufacturers or distributors. These licenses give the licensee the right to use the licensor's technology (generally for a limited period of time) for certain purposes. They permit the licensor to combine its intellectual property with the manufacturing or distribution skills of the licensee in order to more efficiently exploit its special technology. However, licensing arrangements often raise antitrust issues because they generally involve restraints on the competitive activities of the licensor and/or licensee. (For example, an exclusive license means that no one other than the licensee can manufacture or sell the product in a designated territory.)

Concept Summary: Section 1 of the Sherman Act

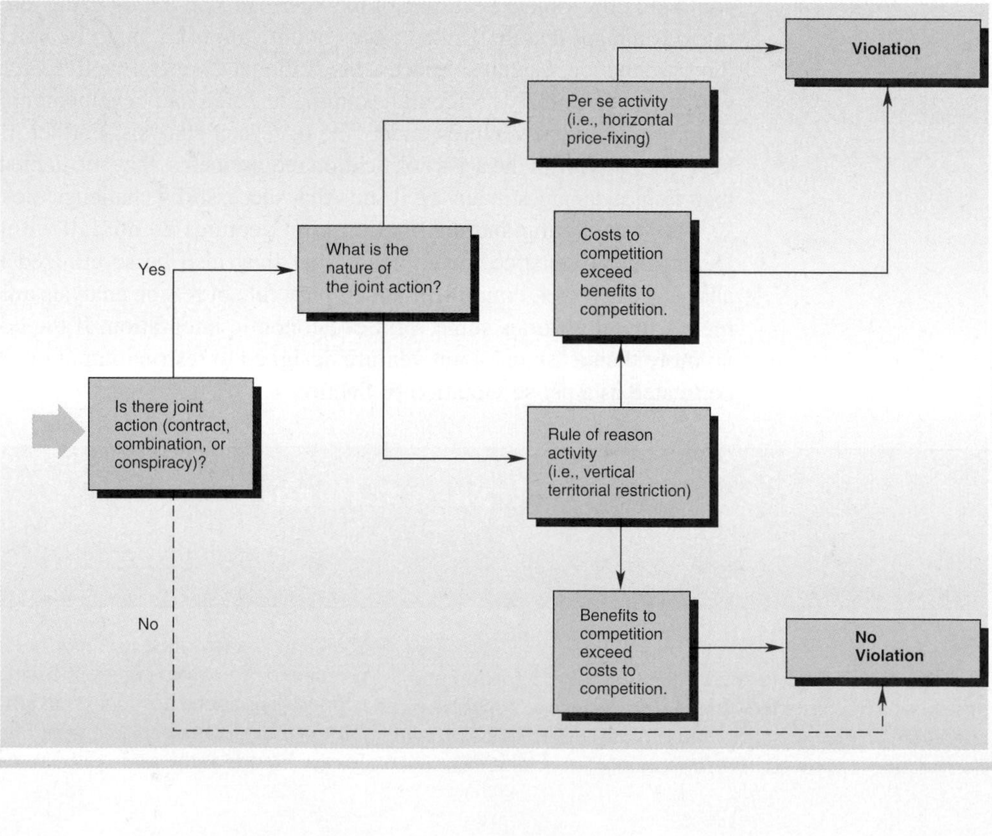

Is there joint action (contract, combination, or conspiracy)?
Yes
No
What is the nature of the joint action?
Per se activity (i.e., horizontal price-fixing)
Rule of reason activity (i.e., vertical territorial restriction)
Costs to competition exceed benefits to competition.
Benefits to competition exceed costs to competition.
Violation
No Violation

Despite their restrictive potential, licensing arrangements can maximize consumer welfare by ensuring that new technology reaches the marketplace in the quickest and most efficient manner. Further, by guaranteeing that new ideas realize their maximum return, they encourage the development of new technology. For these reasons, the Justice Department has recommended that licensing agreements undergo rule of reason analysis.

Reverse Settlement Marketing Agreements

In the normal patent licensing agreement, the patent holder contracts with others whereby they are able to produce the patented product in return for their making payments to the patent holder. However, in a **reverse payment settlement agreement,** the payment goes the other way. That is, a patent holder may offer payments to a producer of generic products if they promise not to challenge the validity of the patent holder's patent. Most reverse payment settlement agreements arise in the context of pharmaceutical drug regulation and, specifically, in the context of suits brought under statutory provisions allowing a generic drug manufacturer (seeking speedy marketing approval) to challenge the validity of a patent owned by an already-approved brand-name drug owner.

Courts have held that a reverse payment settlement agreement generally is immune from antitrust attack so long as its anticompetitive effects fall within the scope of the exclusionary potential of the patent. That is, if the time remaining on the patent was 10 years, a reverse payment settlement agreement would be immune from antitrust enforcement as long as it was not scheduled to last for more than those 10 years. In the next course, the U.S. Supreme Court challenges this presumption, holding that, under the proper circumstances, such a settlement might violate the antitrust laws.

Federal Trade Commission v. Actavis

2013 U.S. LEXIS 4545 (U.S. Sup.Ct. 2013)

FACTS

Solvay Pharmaceuticals claimed that it owned a valid patent for a brand-name drug called AndroGel. Two other pharmaceuticals, Actavis and Paddock, challenged the validity of Solvay's patent and sought FDA approval to market generic drugs modeled after AndroGel. (A third company agreed to join forces with Paddock and share patent litigation costs in return for a share of profits if Paddock obtained approval for its generic drug.) Although the FDC approved Actavis's generic product, all of the parties reached a settlement agreement. Under the terms of the settlement, Actavis agreed that it would not bring its generic product to market until 65 months before Solvay's patent expired (unless someone else marketed a generic sooner). Actavis also agreed to promote AndroGel to urologists. The other generic manufacturers made roughly similar promises. Solvay agreed to pay millions of dollars to each generic—$12 million in total to Paddock; $60 million in total to Par; and an estimated $19–$30 million annually, for nine years, to Actavis. The Federal Trade Commission sued, arguing that the agreement violated the antitrust laws by unlawfully agreeing "to share in Solvay's monopoly profits, abandon their patent challenges, and refrain from launching their low-cost generic products to compete with AndroGel for nine years". Sovay argues that such reverse payment settlements are immune from antitrust attack as long as their anticompetitive effects fall within the scope of the exclusionary potential of the patent.

ISSUE

Is the reverse payment settlement immune from antitrust enforcement?

DECISION

No. The likelihood of a reverse payment bringing about anticompetitive effects depends upon its size, its scale in relation to the payor's anticipated future litigation costs, its independence from other services for which it might represent payment, and the lack of any other convincing

(continued)

justification. Although parties may have reasons to prefer settlements that include reverse payments, the relevant antitrust question is: What are those reasons? If the basic reason is a desire to maintain and to share patent-generated monopoly profits, then, in the absence of some other justification, the antitrust laws are likely to forbid the arrangement. Thus, a reverse payment, where large and unjustified, can bring with it the risk of significant anticompetitive effects. One who makes such a payment may be unable to explain and to justify it under rule of reason analysis. Such a firm or individual may well possess market power derived from the patent. A court, by examining the size of the payment, may well be able to assess its likely anticompetitive effects along with its potential justifications without litigating the validity of the patent itself. Further, there may be ways to settle patent disputes without the use of reverse payments. In our view, these considerations, taken together, outweigh the policy in favor of settlements that is behind the former notion of automatic immunity.

Section 2 of the Sherman Act

When a firm acquires monopoly power—the power to fix prices or exclude competitors—in a particular market, the antitrust laws' objective of promoting competitive market structures has been defeated. Monopolists have the power to fix price unilaterally, since they have no effective competition. Section 2 of the Sherman Act was designed to attack monopolies. It provides:

> Every person who shall monopolize, or attempt to monopolize, or combine or conspire with any other person or persons to monopolize any part of trade or commerce among the several states, or with foreign nations shall be deemed guilty of a felony.

The first thing a student should note about the language of Section 2 is that it does not outlaw monopolies. It outlaws the act of "monopolizing." In order to show a violation of Section 2, the government or a private plaintiff must show not only that the defendant firm has monopoly power but also that there is an intent to monopolize on the defendant's part. Second, joint action is not necessary in order to violate Section 2; a single firm can be guilty of *monopolizing* or *attempting to monopolize.*

Intent to Monopolize

LO4

Courts look at how the defendant acquired monopoly power. If the defendant intentionally acquired monopoly power or attempted to maintain it after having acquired it, intent to monopolize has been shown. However, if the defendant acquires a dominant market position through superior products and service or other demonstrations of business acumen, the intent to monopolize will not be found.

So, the defendant must convince the court that its monopoly power simply happened and is not the result of a conscious attempt to acquire or maintain it. If the defendant has monopoly power because it "built a better mousetrap," made wise decisions when other competitors did not, or simply was the first entrant or only survivor in a market that can support only one firm of its kind (e.g., the only newspaper in a small town), no violation of Section 2 exists.

The intent to monopolize often occurs when a monopolist engages in predatory pricing. In a typical predatory-pricing scheme, the predator reduces the sale price of its product (its output) to below cost, hoping to drive competitors out of business. Then, with competition vanquished, the predator raises output prices to a supracompetitive level. For the scheme to make economic sense, the losses suffered from pricing goods below cost must be recouped (with interest) during the supracompetitive-pricing stage of the scheme. Thus, there are two prerequisites to recovery on claims of predatory pricing: (1) proof that the low prices were below an appropriate measure of its rival's costs and (2) a dangerous probability that the monopolist will later recoup its investment in below-cost prices.

Monopoly Power

LO4

Monopoly power exists when a firm controls a very high percentage share of the relevant market. The decided cases in this area indicate that a firm must have captured approximately 70 percent or more of the relevant market to have monopoly power. In order to determine the defendant's market share, the court in a Section 2 case must define the relevant market. This is a crucial part of the proceedings, since the more broadly the relevant market is drawn, the smaller the defendant's market share will be. There are two components to a relevant market determination: the geographic market and the product market.

Geographic Market

The relevant geographic market is determined by economic realities. Where do the sellers of the goods or services in question customarily compete? Transportation cost is often a critical factor that limits geographic market size. Thus, the relevant geographic market may be a small area for cement but the whole nation for transistors.

Concept Summary: Monopolization

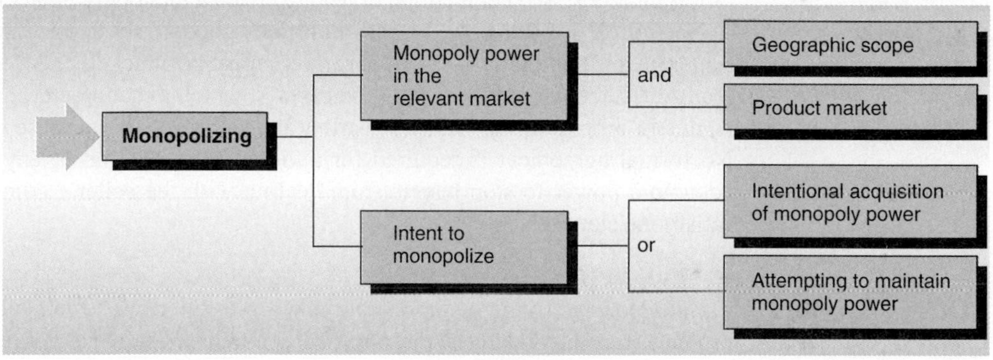

Product Market

The relevant product market is composed of those products that are "reasonably interchangeable by consumers for the same purposes" (the **functional interchangeability test**). The idea here is that a firm's power to fix price is limited by the availability of competing products that buyers find acceptable.

E-Commerce

In 2001, a federal court of appeals found that Microsoft had violated Section 2 of the Sherman Act for, among other things, using its monopoly power in the operating systems market to unseat Netscape Navigator as the preeminent Web browser. (See *United States v. Microsoft Corporation,* 253 F.3d 34 (D.C. Cir. 2001).) In deciding the case, the court observed that it had been six years since Microsoft engaged in the first anticompetitive conduct at issue and that six years seems like an eternity in the computer industry. Thus, in six years Microsoft was able to do a lot of damage. How does a monopolist ethically justify its anticompetitive behavior?

The Clayton Act

The Clayton Act was passed in 1914 to supplement the Sherman Act by attacking specific practices that monopolists had historically followed to gain monopoly power. The idea was to "nip monopolies in the bud" before a full-blown restraint of trade or monopoly power was achieved. The Clayton Act was intended to be "preventive" in nature, and in most cases only the **probability** of a significant anticompetitive effect must be shown to establish a violation.

LO5

Since the Clayton Act deals with probable harms to competition, there is no criminal liability for Clayton Act violations. Treble damages are available to private plaintiffs, however, and the Federal Trade Commission has the power to enforce the act through the use of cease and desist orders.

Section 3

Section 3 of the Clayton Act was basically designed to attack three kinds of anticompetitive behavior: tie-in (or tying) contracts, exclusive dealing contracts, and requirements contracts. Section 3 makes it illegal to lease or sell commodities or to fix a price for commodities on the condition or agreement that the buyer or lessee will not deal in the commodities of the competitors of the seller or lessor if doing so may "substantially lessen competition or tend to create a monopoly in any line of commerce."

Section 3 applies only to **commodities** (goods), so tie-in, exclusive dealing, and requirements contracts that involve services must be attacked under Section 1 of the Sherman Act. Section 3 does not apply to cases in which a manufacturer has entered true consignment arrangements with its distributors, since no sale or lease occurs in such cases. No formal agreement is required for a violation of Section 3; any use by the seller of economic power to stop buyers from dealing with the seller's competitors is enough to satisfy the statute.

Tie-In Contracts

Tie-in contracts (tying contracts) occur when a seller refuses to sell a product (the tying product) to a buyer unless the buyer also purchases another product (the tied product) from the seller. So, if Acme Seeds, Inc., refuses to sell its seeds (the tying product) to farmers unless they also agree to buy fertilizer (the tied product) from Acme, this is a tie-in contract; the sale of fertilizer is tied to the sale of seeds.

The economic harm from such contracts is that Acme's competitors in the sale of fertilizer are foreclosed from competing for sales to Acme's buyers, since Acme has used its power in the seed market to force its buyers to buy its fertilizer. There is no legitimate reason why Acme's buyers would ever want to enter tie-in contracts, and therefore the courts have treated such agreements harshly. Tie-in contracts are illegal under Section 3 if (1) the seller has monopoly power in the tie-in product or (2) the seller has foreclosed competitors from a substantial volume of commerce in the tied product. So, if Acme has monopoly power in its seeds or has managed to tie in a substantial dollar volume in fertilizer sales, its tie-in contracts violate Section 3.

Tie-in contracts may also violate Section 1 of the Sherman Act. For example, in the *Microsoft* case, the government also complained that Microsoft illegally tied its Internet Explorer Web browser (the tied product) to its Windows operating system (the tying product). However, in that case, the appellate court reversed the district court's conclusion that Microsoft's tying behavior was per se illegal. The appellate court believed that rule of reason analysis was more appropriate because per se analysis is reserved for those instances where courts have considerable experience with the business relationships. In *Microsoft,* on the other hand, the appellate court felt the case was providing the judiciary with its first up-close look at the technological integration of added functionality into software that serves as a platform for third-party applications. Ultimately, the Department of Justice decided to drop the tying claim.

Concept Summary: A Tie-In Case under Section 3 of the Clayton Act

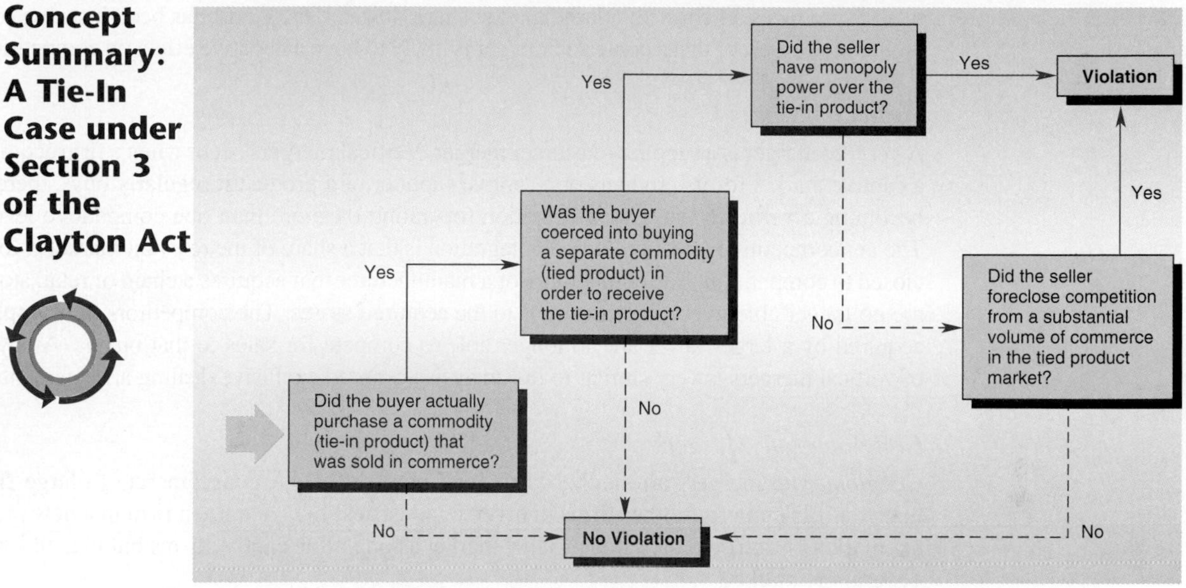

Exclusive Dealing and Requirements Contracts

An *exclusive dealing contract* is created when a buyer agrees to sell only the product lines of his seller. For example, a lawn and garden store agrees to sell only Brand A lawn mowers. A *requirements contract* is created when a buyer agrees to purchase all of its needs in a certain item from one seller, for example, a candy manufacturer that agrees to buy all the sugar it requires from one sugar refiner. The economic harm of such contracts is that the competitors of the seller are foreclosed from competing for sales to the buyer for the duration of the contract.

These contracts were initially treated like tie-in contracts, with the courts looking at the dollar amount of commerce foreclosed from competition to determine their legality. However, courts today recognize that, unlike tie-in contracts, exclusive dealing and requirements contracts can benefit both the buyer and the seller by reducing selling costs and assuring buyers of a supply of needed items. Therefore, in determining the legality of an exclusive dealing or requirements contract, courts today look at the percentage share of the relevant market foreclosed to competition by the contract.

Section 7

Section 7 of the Clayton Act was designed to provide a tool for attacking **mergers**—a term broadly used in this section to refer to the acquisition of one company by another. It prohibits any corporation engaged in commerce from acquiring all or part of the stock or assets of any other corporation engaged in commerce, except for investment purposes only, when the effect of the acquisition may be to "substantially lessen competition" or "tend to create a monopoly" in "any line of commerce in any section of the country."

The "line of commerce" and "section of the country" concepts in Section 7 are similar to the relevant product and geographic market concepts in Section 2 of the Sherman Act, but they may be more loosely applied due to the preventive nature of Section 7. Similarly, Section 7 invalidates mergers that involve a probable anticompetitive effect at the time of the merger.

Horizontal Mergers

A court seeking to determine the legality of a *horizontal* merger (between competitors) under Section 7 considers the market share of the resulting firm. In recent years, the Supreme Court has been less willing to presume that anticompetitive effects result whenever a horizontal merger produces a firm with a large market share. Instead, the Court has been insisting on a higher level of proof that a contested merger is likely to have a negative effect on competition.

Vertical Mergers

A *vertical* merger is a supplier–customer merger. Vertical mergers occur when a firm acquires a captive market for its products or a captive supplier of a product it regularly buys, thereby becoming a vertically integrated operation (operating on more than one competitive level). The anticompetitive effect of vertical integration is that a share of the relevant market is foreclosed to competition. The competitors of a manufacturer that acquires a chain of retail stores are no longer able to compete for sales to the acquired stores. The competitors of a supplier acquired by a larger buyer are no longer able to compete for sales to that buyer. (Analysis of vertical mergers is very similar to the analysis accorded exclusive dealing arrangements.)

Conglomerate Mergers

Conglomerate mergers are neither horizontal nor vertical. A conglomerate (a large firm that controls numerous other firms in diverse industries) may acquire a firm in a new product market or a firm in the same product market as one of its captive firms but in a different geographic market.

Concept Summary: Types of Mergers

Category	Description	Example
Horizontal	Between competitors	One automobile manufacturer merges with another automobile manufacturer.
Vertical	Between a supplier and its customer	An oil producer merges with an oil refiner.
Conglomerate	Between two largely unrelated businesses	A candy company merges with a greeting cards company.

Conglomerate mergers that create a potential for reciprocal dealing have been successfully challenged under Section 7. If a conglomerate purchases a firm that produces a product that another member of the conglomerate regularly buys, or buys a product that another member firm regularly sells, the potential for reciprocal buying is obvious. A conglomerate may also acquire a firm that produces products that the conglomerate's suppliers regularly purchase. Suppliers that are eager to continue selling to the conglomerate may therefore be induced to purchase their requirements from the acquired firm.

Sometimes a conglomerate merger can have an adverse effect on competition by eliminating a potential entrant in the product market. This would occur if a manufacturer of detergents merged with a producer of bleach. Arguably, the detergent manufacturer, since its product line is so closely related to bleach, imposes a competitive check on the bleach industry by the very fact that it might independently enter the market if bleach producers begin reaping monopoly profits.

Hart-Scott-Rodino Antitrust Improvements Act

Proposed mergers or acquisitions affecting U.S. commerce that exceed certain size thresholds must be reported to the Federal Trade Commission and the Department of Justice.

Then under the terms of the Hart-Scott-Rodino Antitrust Improvements Act, there is a prescribed waiting period before the transaction can be completed. This waiting period can be extended if the government requests additional information regarding the proposed deal.

The Robinson-Patman Act

Direct Price Discrimination

LO6

Section 2(a) of the Robinson-Patman Act prohibits discrimination in price between different purchasers of "commodities of like grade and quality" when the effect of the price discrimination may be to "substantially lessen competition or tend to create a monopoly" in any relevant market, or to "injure, destroy, or prevent competition with any person who either grants or knowingly receives the benefits of such discrimination, or with the customers of either of them." To violate Section 2(a), the discriminatory sales must occur roughly within the same period of time and involve goods of like grade and quality. Some substantial physical difference is necessary to justify a different price to competing buyers. So, a manufacturer that sells "house brand" products to a chain store for less than it sells its own brand name products to the chain's competitors has violated Section 2(a) if the only difference between the products is their label. The Robinson-Patman Act, like the Clayton Act, requires only that price discrimination have a probable anticompetitive effect.

Defenses to Direct Price Discrimination

A seller who can **cost justify** discriminatory prices by showing that the difference in price is solely the product of actual cost savings, such as lower transportation or production costs, has a defense under Section 2(a). Sellers can also lawfully discriminate in price when doing so reflects **changing conditions** in the marketplace that affect the marketability of goods, such as their deterioration or obsolescence. Finally, Section 2(b) allows sellers to **meet competition** in good faith by granting a discriminatory price to a customer who has been offered a lawful, lower price by one of the seller's competitors.

Water Craft Management v. Mercury Marine

457 F.3d 484 (5th Cir. 2006)

FACTS

Water Craft operated as a Mercury Marine retail dealership in Baton Rouge selling Mercury Marine outboard motors until it went out of business after two years of operation. Water Craft alleges that Mercury Marine discriminated in favor of Water Craft's largest competitor, Travis Boating Center, by offering Travis discounts on motors that far exceeded the discounts available to other Mercury retail dealerships in the Baton Rouge market. Mercury explains that it was forced to offer these lower prices to Travis in order to compete with the Outboard Marine Corporation (OMC)—one of Mercury's principal competitors. Before Mercury began selling motors to Travis, Mercury was rapidly losing market share to OMC in the Gulf Coast region. To offset this, Mercury approached Travis several times in an effort to sign them up but was rebuffed because their prices were not competitive with OMC's.

ISSUE

Does Mercury's price discrimination fall within the meeting competition defense?

DECISION

Yes. Mercury has shown the existence of facts which would lead a reasonable and prudent person to believe that the granting of a lower price would in fact meet the equally low price of a competitor. Travis repeatedly refused Mercury's advances and favorable price offerings until an agreement was finally reached. This refusal indicates that the final lower price was necessary to compete, not a predatory attempt to undermine competition.

Indirect Price Discrimination

In passing the Robinson-Patman Act, Congress recognized that sellers could indirectly discriminate among competing buyers by making discriminatory payments to them or by furnishing them with certain services that were not available to their competitors. Section 2(d) prohibits sellers from making discriminatory payments to competing customers for services (such as advertising or promotional activities) or facilities (such as shelf space furnished by the customers in connection with the marketing of the goods). Section 2(e) prohibits sellers from discriminating in the services they furnish to competing customers. Thus, a seller would violate this provision if he provided a favored customer with a display case or a demonstration kit.

Concept Summary: Price Discrimination

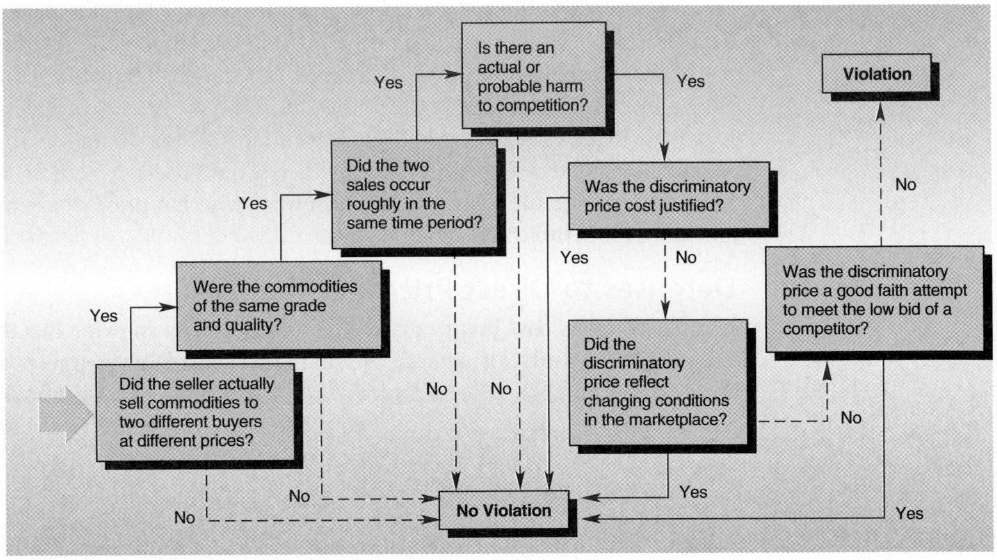

Sellers may lawfully provide such payments or services only if these are made available to competing customers on proportionately equal terms. This means notifying customers of the availability of such services and distributing them according to some rational basis, such as the quantity of goods the customer purchases. The seller must devise a flexible plan that enables various classes of buyers, large chains or small independents, to participate.

Ethics in Action

ETHICAL IMPLICATIONS

Is it ethical for a buyer to lie to her seller, claiming that she received a lower bid from one of the seller's competitors?

Limits on Antitrust

The Parker Doctrine

The Parker Doctrine, often referred to as the **state action exemption,** exempts many anticompetitive acts from the antitrust laws. This exemption embraces the actions of state officials under the authority of state law and the actions of private firms or individuals under the supervision of authorized state officials. Thus, many of the licensing schemes limiting entry into the various professions are permissible, notwithstanding their anticompetitive effects, because they are shielded from antitrust by the state action exemption.

The Noerr Doctrine

The Noerr Doctrine allows people and businesses to join together and lobby governmental officials for various ends even though the desired action may harm their competitors or otherwise limit competition. This exception was based on the right of petition recognized by the Constitution and the policy of ensuring that governmental officials have an adequate supply of information.

International Trade Limitations

Sovereign Immunity

When foreign governments are involved in commercial activities affecting U.S. competitors, our antitrust policy may be at odds with our foreign policy. Accordingly, the Foreign Sovereign Immunities Act of 1976 (FSIA) provides that the governmental actions of foreign sovereigns and their agents are exempt from antitrust liability. The commercial activities of foreign sovereigns, however, are not included within this **sovereign immunity** doctrine. Significant international controversy exists over the proper criteria for determining when a governmental activity is commercial.

Sovereign Compulsion

Closely related to sovereign immunity is the foreign **sovereign compulsion** defense. Under this doctrine, private parties may be excused from complying with our antitrust laws when their anticompetitive conduct has been directed or compelled by a foreign government. The defense is not available unless the foreign government has actually compelled, rather than merely permitted or encouraged, the anticompetitive activity. Further, it will not apply if the anticompetitive conduct has occurred primarily within the territory of the United States.

In re Vitamin C Antitrust Litigation

810 F.Supp.2d 522 (E.D. N.Y. 2011)

FACTS

Four Chinese manufacturers of vitamin C captured over 60 percent of the worldwide market for vitamin C. China's share of vitamin C imports to the United States rose to over 80 percent. It is not disputed that these four companies fixed prices and agreed on output restrictions. However, they argued that their cartel arrangement did not subject them to antitrust liability in the United States because their price-fixing activities were compelled by the Chinese government and, as such, fell within the sovereign compulsion doctrine. The four companies (defendants) are members of the Chamber of Commerce of Medicines and Health Products Importers and Exporters (the Chamber). Many of the price-fixing agreements

(continued)

at issue were reached at meetings of the Chamber and appear to have been, at the very least, facilitated by the Chamber.

ISSUE

Is the price-fixing behavior protected by the sovereign compulsion doctrine?

DECISION

No. The Chinese law relied upon by defendants did not compel their illegal conduct. During China's planned economy era, the control of foreign trade was centralized under the Ministry of Commerce (the highest authority in China authorized to regulate foreign trade) and all foreign trade was conducted through state-owned import and trade companies according to state trade plans. After some reforms in the mid-1980s led to aggressive forms of competition, the government imposed new administrative controls, which involved the establishment of the various China Chambers of Commerce for Import and Export including the chamber at issue here. The formation of the chambers was part of China's national policy requiring Chinese exporting companies to unite and act in unison in foreign trade. The authority to regulate import and export commerce was eventually transferred from the state-owned trading companies to these chambers. When the chambers were created, they were staffed with personnel transferred directly from the government. Reforms in the mid-1990s gave the ministry the power to punish enterprises for exporting goods at lower-than-normal prices. Potential punishments include a notice of criticism and monetary fines. The ministry could request the chambers to investigate alleged violations of the regulations. However, those regulations were formally repealed in 2010. As a result, there was no mechanism in place to punish companies that refused to participate in any price-fixing activities. Without compulsion there can be no sovereign compulsion defense.

Export Trading Company Act

As the U.S. trade balance worsened and its imports began to exceed its exports, the importance of facilitating exports was recognized. One response to this was the passage of the Export Trading Company Act of 1982. This act allows exporters whose goods or services will not be resold in the United States to apply to the Department of Commerce for a "certificate of review." If the Commerce Department finds that the exporter's activities will not unduly restrain trade or affect domestic prices or unfairly compete against other U.S. exporters, the Commerce Department, with the concurrence of the Justice Department, will issue the certificate.

The export trade certificate imparts a presumption of legality on the certified conduct of the export trading company and, even if an injured party can prove that a violation has occurred, it can receive only actual (rather than treble) damages. The Commerce Department may modify or revoke an export trade certificate if it determines that the trading company is no longer complying with the terms of the certificate.

Questions and Problem Cases

1. Dentsply International manufactures artificial teeth for use in dentures and other restorative appliances and sells them to dental products dealers. The dealers, in turn, supply the teeth and various other materials to dental laboratories, which fabricate dentures for sale to dentists. The relevant market is the sale of prefabricated artificial teeth in the United States. Because of advances in dental medicine, artificial tooth manufacturing is marked by a low- or no-growth potential. Dentsply has long dominated the industry consisting of 12–13 manufacturers and enjoys a 75 percent–80 percent market share on a revenue basis, 67 percent on a unit basis, and is about 15 times larger than its next closest competitor. For more than 15 years, Dentsply has operated

under a policy that discouraged its dealers from adding competitors' teeth to their lines of products. Dentsply adopted "Dealer Criterion 6." It provides that in order to effectively promote Dentsply-York products, authorized dealers "may not add further tooth lines to their product offering." Did the exclusivity policy imposed on the dealers violate Section 2 of the Sherman Act?

2. Empagran is a foreign corporation, domiciled overseas, that purchased vitamins abroad from F. Hoffman-Laroche and other vitamin producers that distribute and sell vitamins around the world. Empagran claims that F. Hoffman-Laroche and other vitamin companies, both foreign and domestic, engaged in an overarching worldwide conspiracy to raise, stabilize, and maintain the prices of vitamins by directly fixing prices as well as by allocating market share. It contends that this cartel operated on a global basis and affected virtually every market where the producers operated worldwide. Further, it asserts that this unlawful price-fixing conduct had adverse effects in the United States and in other nations that caused injury to Empagran in connection with its foreign purchases of vitamins. It seeks both injunctive relief and damages under Section 1 of the Sherman Act. F. Hoffman-Laroche and the other vitamin producers move to dismiss Empagran's lawsuit for lack of subject matter jurisdiction under the U.S. antitrust laws because the injuries Empagran seeks to redress were allegedly sustained in transactions that lack any direct connection to U.S. commerce. Should the court dismiss this lawsuit because it lacks subject matter jurisdiction? Explain.
3. Blaine was licensed to operate a Meineke discount muffler shop in Hartford, Connecticut. In the franchise agreement, Meineke agreed not to license or operate another muffler shop within a three-mile area of Blaine's franchise. This dispute arose when Blaine alleged that Meineke licensed other franchises within his territory. He also claimed that Meineke wrongfully refused his request to operate another Meineke franchise in another community. Blaine sued Meineke and the other franchisees, claiming that they violated his franchise agreement and ignored his request for a new franchise in furtherance of a combination or conspiracy to monopolize the Hartford area. Did Meineke violate Section 2 of the Sherman Act?
4. Roland, a substantial dealer in construction equipment, was for many years the area's exclusive distributor of International Harvester construction equipment. After buying Harvester's construction equipment division, Dresser signed a dealership agreement with Roland. The agreement was terminable at will by either party on 90 days' notice. It did not contain an exclusive dealing clause. Eight months later, Roland signed a similar agreement with Komatsu. Several months after discovering this fact, Dresser gave notice to Roland of its intention to terminate its dealership. Roland argued that Dresser's decision to terminate the dealership demonstrated the existence of an implied exclusive dealing contract in violation of Section 3 of the Clayton Act. Did Dresser and Roland have an illegal exclusive dealing contract?
5. For many years Spray-Rite Service Corporation, a wholesale distributor of agricultural chemicals, sold herbicides manufactured by Monsanto. Spray-Rite was a discount operation, buying in large quantities and selling at low margins. Monsanto then announced that it would appoint distributors on a yearly basis and renew distributorships according to whether the distributor could be expected "to exploit fully" the market in its geographic area of primary responsibility. After receiving numerous complaints from other distributors about Spray-Rite's pricing policies, Monsanto refused to renew Spray-Rite's distributorship on the grounds that Spray-Rite had failed to hire trained salesmen and to promote sales to dealers adequately. Spray-Rite filed suit against Monsanto, arguing that Monsanto had terminated Spray-Rite's distributorship

as a part of a conspiracy with the complaining distributors. Does the fact that Monsanto terminated Spray-Rite in response to complaints from its other distributors make the termination illegal?

6. Hoover Color Corporation alleges that Bayer Corporation, its supplier, discriminated in favor of Bayer's larger distributors of Bayferrox by implementing a volume-based incentive discount pricing system. Under this system, the price each distributor paid for Bayferrox depended on the total amount of the product it purchased. Bayer began its system of volume-based incentive discounts when it was building a large manufacturing plant which had high fixed costs. Bayer pursued its volume-based pricing strategy in order to obtain the bulk orders necessary to make the new plant profitable. Hoover sued Bayer for price discrimination. Is Bayer's price discrimination protected by the meeting competition defense? Explain.
7. Trident is a manufacturer of printheads and holds a patent over its printhead technology. Printer manufacturers use Trident's printhead technology to manufacture printers. Trident also manufactures ink for use with its patented printheads. Trident's standard form licensing agreement allowing printer manufacturers to use its patented product requires them to purchase their ink for Trident-based systems exclusively. Independent Ink manufactures ink usable in Trident's printheads. It brought suit under Section 1 of the Sherman Act, alleging that Trident was engaging in illegal tying arrangements. Trident argued that the lawsuit should be dismissed because it did not have market power in the printhead (tying product) market. Independent responded that, because the printhead was a patented product, the court should presume the existence of market power. Should the court presume the existence of market power in the tying product market when it is a patented product? Explain.
8. U-Haul rents its branded trucks, vans, and other moving equipment for both one-way and in-town moving. U-Haul conducts its rental business through a network of about 1,200 company-owned rental centers and about 14,500 independent dealers. U-Haul describes its relationship with the dealers as an agency. U-Haul agrees in the dealership contract to bear the risk of liability incurred by the dealers' U-Haul rental operations and to assume responsibility for loss due to theft, vandalism, or other damage to U-Haul equipment in their possession. U-Haul fixes flat rates for in-town rentals based on the size of the truck rented. Is U-Haul engaged in price fixing in violation of Section 1 of the Sherman Act? Explain.

Chapter 46

Consumer Protection Laws

Learning Objectives

After you have studied this chapter, you should be able to:

1. Explain the role of the Federal Trade Commission in protecting consumers.
2. Explain the rights protected under the Telemarketing Act.
3. Discuss the 2010 consumer protection laws passed in response to the financial crisis.
4. Describe the main consumer protections contained in the Truth in Lending and Fair Credit Reporting Acts.
5. Identify the several ways the Fair Debt Collection Practices Act helps consumers.
6. Discuss how consumers are protected by the Consumer Product Safety Commission.

Fischl applied to General Motors Acceptance Corporation (GMAC) for financing to buy a BMW. GMAC turned him down after receiving a report from a credit agency that erroneously listed his current job as past employment. The letter rejecting his application stated that his credit references were insufficient.

- Is Fischl entitled to a better explanation of why his credit application was rejected?
- Can Fischl get the erroneous information corrected?
- Can Fischl sue for any damages he suffered?

Introduction

For many years, consumers dealt with merchants and providers of services on the basis of *caveat emptor* (let the buyer beware). Buyers were expected to look out for and protect their own interests. In addition, much of the law concerning the sales of goods and the extension of credit was structured to protect business interests rather than consumer interests.

Beginning in the mid-1960s, at about the same time that the law of product liability was changing, many consumers recognized that these sales and credit laws put them at a disadvantage in trying to protect what they thought were their rights. Consumer groups lobbied Congress, state legislatures, and city halls to pass statutes or ordinances changing this body of law to make it more favorable to consumers.

Many everyday consumer problems are addressed by these laws. For example, have you, like Fischl, ever been denied credit without getting an adequate explanation from the creditor? Have you ever had a department store or charge card company credit your payment to the wrong account or refuse to correct an error in your bill? Have you ever been harassed by a debt collector for a bill you do not owe or one you have already paid? The laws covering these situations will be discussed in this chapter.

Federal Trade Commission Act

LO1

The Federal Trade Commission Act, which is the grandfather of "consumer protection" legislation, was passed in 1914. Under the act, the five-member Federal Trade Commission (FTC) has authority to decide whether specific marketing and sales practices are unfair or deceptive, and whether those practices may be harmful to competition among manufacturers, distributors, and sellers. After making such a decision, the FTC may order the company that is engaged in the unlawful conduct to cease and to take corrective action. It may also ask a federal court to award redress, such as giving refunds or damages to injured consumers. The FTC has the power to establish rules that govern conduct in certain industries. It also enforces most of the federal consumer protection laws and regulations that are discussed in this chapter, as well as many others. (See Table 46.1.) The increased use of the Internet has caused the FTC to exercise its power to regulate unfair and deceptive practices in cyberspace. The 2006 Undertaking Spam, Spyware and Fraud Enforcement with Enforcers Beyond Borders Act (US SAFE WEB ACT) amended the existing FTC Act to give the FTC the legal authority to assist overseas investigations to track down Internet scammers using devices such as spam and spyware.

FTC v. Accusearch, Inc.

570 F.3d 1187 (2009 U.S. App. LEXIS 14480)

FACTS

The Telecommunications Act of 1996 bans phone carriers from disclosing telephone records unless a customer agrees, with few exceptions. Accusearch ran Abika.com, a website that sold personal data ranging from "romantic preferences" to tax liens. From 2003 to 2006, the site sold phone records with details of incoming and outgoing calls, stopping when it learned a subcontractor may have gotten the information fradulently. Four months later, the Federal Trade Commission (FTC) asked a court to enjoin the sales and make Accusearch return its profits, saying the sales were unfair under the Federal Trade Commission Act (FTCA). Accusearch lost and appealed, arguing that the 1996 Telecommunications Act only applies to telephone carriers, not Internet publishers, and that the FTC has no authority to enforce the Telecomm Act.

ISSUE

Can the FTC act against an Internet company for violating the Telecommunications Act?

(continued)

DECISION

Yes. The FTCA gives the FTC authority to regulate "unfair or deceptive acts or practices in or affecting commerce," including asking a court for an injunction. Selling the private phone information led to phone harassment, forced people to change numbers or carriers, and is unfair. The fact that the FTC does not enforce the Telecomm Act and that Accusearch is not a phone company are irrelevant. The FTC did not sue under the Telecomm Act but under the FTCA, which allows the FTC to act broadly against unfair practices, including ones banned by other laws, and even unfair acts not specifically outlawed. The injunction stands.

The states are also active in taking measures to prevent consumer fraud. Prevention of identity theft is a particular focus. Approximately half the states have legislation giving consumers the right to "freeze" their credit reports. This prevents people from opening new lines of credit in the name on the frozen account. A few of the states with such legislation only allow freezing if the individual has been the victim of identity theft.

LO2 Telemarketing and Consumer Fraud and Abuse Prevention Act

Under the **Telemarketing and Consumer Fraud and Abuse Prevention Act** (Telemarketing Act), the FTC established the Telemarketing Sales Rules in 1995 to prevent deceptive and abusive telemarketing practices. The rules require that telemarketers disclose to customers the total cost of the goods or services offered, any material restrictions or conditions on the use or purchase of the goods or services, and the terms of any refund or exchange policies mentioned in the solicitation. These disclosures must be made before the customer pays for the goods or services. Other disclosures must be made if the solicitation pertains to a prize promotion. The FTC also prohibits prerecorded telemarketing sales calls unless the consumers has expressly agreed, in writing, to receive them.

In an effort to protect consumers from harassing solicitations, the rules prohibit telemarketers from engaging in abusive practices including causing the phone to ring or engaging in phone conversations repeatedly with the intent to harass, abuse, or annoy the person called, or calling a person who previously said that she does not want to get calls from the seller. Calls cannot be made after 9:00 PM or before 8:00 AM local time. In addition, the telemarketer must clearly disclose the seller, the sales purpose of the call, what is being sold, and the fact that no purchase or payment is necessary to win a prize or participate in a prize promotion.

In 2003, the FTC amended its rules in an effort to protect consumers from unwanted telemarketing calls by establishing a do-not-call registry. This prohibits a telemarketer or a seller from initiating an outbound call to a person whose telephone number is listed on the national registry. It also prohibits telemarketers and sellers from denying or interfering with a person's right to be placed on the registry. Finally, it prohibits a person from using the registry for purposes other than complying with the rules. Similarly, Congress gave the FTC oversight over the 2005 Fax Protection Act, which limits transmissions of unsolicited fax messages.

TABLE 46.1 Some of the Major Acts Enforced by the FTC

Regulation of Economic Competition
FTC Act Section 5 (including Sherman Act standards)—discussed in this chapter and in Chapter 45
Clayton Act—discussed in Chapter 45
Robinson-Patman Act—discussed in this chapter and Chapter 45
Hart-Scott-Rodino Antitrust Improvements Act of 1976—requires that certain companies planning mergers notify and provide information to the FTC and the Justice Department—discussed in Chapter 45
Magnuson-Moss Warranty Act—discussed in Chapter 20

(continued)

TABLE 46.1 ***(concluded)***

Consumer Protection Measures Discussed in This Chapter
FTC Act Section 5
Truth in Lending Act (including 1988 Fair Credit and Charge Card Disclosure Act and Home Equity Loan Consumer Protection Act)
Consumer Leasing Act
Fair Credit Billing Act
Fair Credit Reporting Act
Equal Credit Opportunity Act
Fair Debt Collection Practices Act
Telemarketing and Consumer Fraud and Abuse Prevention Act
FTC Holder in Due Course Rule
Other Measures
Export Trade Act—empowers FTC to supervise registration and operation of associations of U.S. exporters engaged in export trade
Fair Packaging and Labeling Act—regulates packaging and labeling of consumer products to ensure accurate quality and value comparisons
Flammable Fabrics Act—FTC has some enforcement powers under the act regulating the manufacture, sale, and importation of flammable fabrics
Fur Products Labeling Act—regulates labeling, other identification, and advertising of fur products
Hobby Protection Act—regulates certain imitations of political campaign materials and certain imitation coins and paper money
Lanham Act—empowers FTC to petition for the cancellation of certain trademarks
Smokeless Tobacco Act—empowers FTC to approve manufacturers' plans for rotation and display of statements on smokeless tobacco packages and ads
Textile Fiber Products Identification Act—regulates labeling and other identification of textile fiber products
Wool Products Labeling Act—regulates labeling and other identification of wool products

Source: *1993 United States Government Manual* and various statutes.

Consumer Credit Laws

Because of the widespread use of credit by consumers, the federal government and the states have enacted a series of statutes and regulations to govern credit transactions. These credit laws are designed to increase consumers' knowledge before they enter into credit transactions and to give consumers certain rights. The laws are also intended to ensure that consumers are treated fairly and without discrimination throughout the course of a credit transaction.

LO3

The Consumer Financial Protection Bureau and CARD Acts

In 2010 Congress created the Consumer Financial Protection Bureau (CFPB) as part of the Dodd-Frank Wall Street Reform and Consumer Protection Act. It is intended to regulate consumer financial services and products and take action to mandate clear, accurate disclosures of information that consumers can use to make wise choices regarding bank loans, credit cards, mortgages, and other financial products and services. Its oversight and enforcement authority overlaps with some agencies regarding financial transactions, most notably, the FTC. The CFPB and the FTC agreed to cooperate to prevent duplication of efforts and to provide consistency. The CFPB is part of the Federal Reserve but is designed to have a significant level of independence. Insurance companies, real estate brokers, car dealers, and lawyers are not regulated by the CFPB.

The CFPB has been active in the short time it has been in existence, particularly in regard to credit cards. For example, major credit card companies have agreed to pay millions in fines and return funds to customers relating to unlawful late fees, deceptive marketing of payment protection, and other add-on products. It has new rules about mortgages such as that lenders cannot give loans for more than 43 percent of a borrower's income, banning interest-only loans, and requiring lenders to verify and inspect borrowers' financial documents. The Bureau takes complaints (online, www.consumerfinance.gov, phone, fax, or mail) by category such as bank accounts, credit agencies, debt collectors, and credit cards. It uses those to focus on actions it will take. As the following case shows, under Dodd-Frank, state consumer protection laws, which can be more protective then federal laws, can still be enforced.

Cline v. Bank of America, NA

823 F. Supp. 2d 387 (S.D. W.V. 2011)

FACTS

Cline, a chiropractor, took out a loan from Bank of America (BOA) on which he defaulted. In attempting to collect, BOA made over 400 phone calls to Cline and his business, as well as his employees, who then learned details of his indebtedness. Cline sued under the West Virginia Consumer Credit and Protection Act (WVCCPA) that prohibits the use of a phone to "repeatedly or continuously or at unusual times or at times known to be inconvenient" to annoy or threaten a person in an effort to collect a debt. BOA claimed the suit was preempted by the federal law.

ISSUE

Is Cline's suit preempted by federal law?

DECISION

No. While federal statutes and regulations can nullify conflicting state or local actions, they do not necessarily do so. Dodd-Frank makes it clear that Congress did not intend to preempt state consumer protection laws. It states that a state consumer protection law is preempted only if it "prevents or significantly interferes with" the exercise by the national bank of its powers. There is no indication that the regulation impairs BOA's rights, increases its liability, or imposed new duties. The WVCCPA provisions are focused on protecting West Virginia residents from unfair and abusive collection practices. Basic contract laws or unfair and deceptive act or practices laws are not preempted. Generally applicable restrictions on annoying and abusive collection calls, disclosing indebtedness to others, or calling debtors represented by counsel in no way interfere with the purposes and objectives of the federal laws. Cline's WVCCPA suit is not preempted.

Before the creation of the Consumer Financial Protection Bureau, but also in response to the financial crisis, Congress enacted the **Credit Card Accountability and Disclosure Act (CARD)** to help consumers deal with credit card debt. Fees imposed on credit card holders had risen so high that in 2009, 47 percent of banks' revenue came from this source. In response to the new rules, which became effective in 2010, fees rose even higher as banks sought to protect that income before the new rules took effect.

Under the new rules, credit card companies must tell cardholders how long it will take to pay off their balance if they only make the minimum payment. Interest rate increases can only be applied to new purchases unless the cardholder has missed payments for more than 30 days. Card companies must give 45 days' notice before new rates can be applied. Cardholders cannot exceed their credit limit unless they have received notice and information about their options and have agreed in advance to pay a penalty fee for the privilege. An additional consumer protection is the regulation of the billing cycle to help avoid late fees. Double-cycle billing is banned, and statements must be mailed out 21 days before the payment due date. Card applicants under age 21 years must have a cosigner unless they can prove they can independently make payments. Under rules effective in August 2010, a penalty fee for late payments or other breaches of credit or debit cards cannot exceed $25 unless there are repeated violations. The fees also cannot exceed the minimum balance due. Banks are still free to do things such as raise rates on new cards and impose annual fees.

The 2010 laws are in addition to many decades of attempts to regulate transactions between consumers and the companies with which they deal. These prior laws, which are still in effect, are discussed below.

Another type of popular card, the gift card, has been the subject of recent regulation. Recipients now have five years to use the cards. A fee can only be assessed if the card has not been used within a year, no more than a monthly fee can be assessed, and the consumer must be notified of the fees.

LO4 Truth in Lending Act

In 1969, Congress gave consumers the right to be advised of all terms of their credit transactions (purchases on credit) at or before the time they sign the credit contract. The **Truth in Lending Act (TILA)** is intended to furnish the consumer with a better opportunity to shop for credit among merchants, finance companies, credit unions, and banks. Another purpose is to enable the consumer to understand all the charges made in connection with credit. The TILA requires that the interest rate be stated clearly in terms of an annual percentage rate. The contract or disclosure form must also show the dollar costs of credit as the finance charge. The term *finance charge* includes all costs related to the extension of credit. These costs may include loan fees and fees for credit reports. Charges for life, health, or accident insurance written in connection with the purchase on credit may also be part of the finance charge if the insurance is required for the extension of credit. The act does not fix or limit interest rates or other credit charges. However, state laws may set limits on the interest rates that can be charged in a credit transaction.

One of the act's most significant protections is the buyer's (debtor's) right to cancel the contract. The act provides a cancellation right, technically called a "right of rescission," for three business days after the purchase on credit or after such time as the creditor makes the required disclosure. The right is limited to cases in which the debtor's home is used as collateral but does not apply to first mortgages that finance the purchase or construction of a home. The creditor must give the purchaser written notice of the right to cancel. If the purchaser cancels, he also must give notice in writing. A typical example of the kind of transaction in which the debtor has the right to cancel is major home repair or remodeling on credit. Consumers who purchase a furnace or carpeting for their home have the same right if the lender takes a security interest or lien on the home. The cancellation right can be waived under certain circumstances.

Handy v. Anchor Mortgage Corp.

464 F.3d 760 (7th Cir. 2006)

FACTS

Handy had a 30-year variable mortgage on her home. In 2000 she then refinanced the mortgage with Anchor Mortgage Corporation (Anchor). Under that, she got a 15-year, fixed-rate $80,500 loan, of which $75,000 was used to pay off the old mortgage. At the closing Handy was given two different forms telling her she had the right to rescind the loan within three days. One was intended for use during refinancing when a new creditor was involved, the other for use during refinancing with the same creditor. Two years later Handy sought to rescind the loan because the notice violated the TILA.

ISSUE

Can the loan be rescinded?

DECISION

Yes. The TILA was adopted by Congress to ensure that consumers receive meaningful disclosures regarding the terms of their credit. It requires lenders to give consumers notice "clearly and conspicuously" of the right to rescind when the lender takes a security interest on the consumer's principal dwelling. Additionally, it must state how to rescind, the effects of rescission, the date the rescission period ends, and forms for rescission must be provided. The Fed created two different forms for different lending situations: one for new lenders and one for refinancing with the same lender. Giving the lender both forms was not "clearly and conspicuously" informing her of her rights. The sufficiency of the TILA disclosures is determined from the point of view of the ordinary consumer and is a matter to be determined by the court. The TILA does not easily forgive technical errors. It is plausible that the form did not provide a clear notice of what the right to rescind entails.

The act also requires disclosure of all credit terms in advertising if the advertiser mentions one or more of the credit terms. An advertisement that states "$10 down payment" or "12 percent interest" or "$99 per month" must also include all of the relevant terms. These include the annual percentage rate, the down payment, and the terms of repayment. This requirement helps the consumer put the advertised terms into perspective. The act also regulates advertising about *home equity loans* and the information that must be revealed on the application form for such a loan, the terms of the home equity loan, and the actions the creditor can take pursuant to it. For example, the creditor cannot unilaterally terminate the plan and require immediate payment.

The TILA contains many terms regulating credit card plans. One of the most important is the rule limiting a cardholder's liability for unauthorized use of a credit card to a maximum of $50. *Unauthorized use* is defined as use by a person who lacks express, implied, or apparent authority to use the card. Thus, charges on a stolen credit card that exceed $50 would generally not have to be paid by the cardholder. The $50 limit has also been extended to debit cards if the loss is reported within two days. However, the cost of a lost debit card or PIN number may increase to $500 after that time.

Despite TILA's goal of assuring meaningful disclosure of credit terms, many consumers were still not receiving accurate information about the potential costs of credit cards. In particular, Congress determined that consumers were being inundated with credit card solicitations that failed to disclose basic cost information because the TILA did not require issuers to provide such information until the consumer actually received the card. In response, Congress enacted the **Fair Credit and Charge Card Disclosure Act,** requiring more detailed and uniform disclosure by credit and charge card issuers, at the time of application or solicitation, of information relating to interest rates and other costs which may be incurred by consumers using the credit or charge card. Congress decided that early disclosure would enable consumers to shop around for the best cards.

The TILA requires a credit card provider to disclose certain information in direct-mail applications and solicitation, including annual percentage rates. The TILA requires that information, such as annual percentage rates, must be clearly and conspicuously disclosed in tabular format. This is commonly referred to as the "Schumer Box."

The biggest purchase most consumers make is a home. The financial crisis emphasized many of the problems in this market. Some important consumer protection rules were promulgated in 2010 that are designed to help consumers in this regard. Among other things, TILA regulations now bar mortgage brokers or loan officers from steering consumers to certain kinds of loans in order to increase their compensation. Another agency, the Department of Housing and Urban Development, enacted rules to make comparisons between lenders easier and more meaningful so consumers can get the best deal. When fees, points, and costs are factored in, the lowest interest rate is not always the best deal. The rules require a three-page, standard form, the Good Faith Estimate, be provided to the consumer within three days of receiving the loan application. It encourages consumers to shop around and informs them that they don't have to take the title insurance, which is typically the biggest fee, suggested by the lender. The form requires the lender to put all the fees and points together into an origination charge. While Good Faith forms have existed for a long time, there was no standardization, and comparisons were thus difficult. Another recent protection gives consumers the right to be notified if negative credit data may cause them to be charged higher interest rates or make larger down payments. This gives them a chance to correct erroneous or outdated reports.

Consumer Leasing Act

An amendment to the TILA, the **Consumer Leasing Act,** requires the creditor to disclose the aggregate costs of leasing consumer goods. It also requires that the lease agreement define the consumer's liability at the end of the lease. The act applies to leases of consumer goods if the leases are for more than four months and the total contractual obligation does not exceed \$25,000. Lessors who violate the act's requirements are subject to the same penalties as those prescribed under the TILA.

Fair Credit Billing Act

In 1974, Congress supplemented the Truth in Lending Act with the **Fair Credit Billing Act (FCBA).** The FCBA provides certain protections for users of credit cards. It prescribes the procedures to be followed both by the holder of the credit card and by the issuer of the card. If the credit card holder thinks that the card issuer has made an error on the statement, such as not crediting a payment or showing a charge that was not made by the customer, he has 60 days from the time the statement was mailed to report, in writing, the error. The card issuer then has 30 days to tell the cardholder that his report has been received. In no more than 90 days, or two billing cycles, the card issuer must either correct the account or, after investigating the bill, explain why it believes the original bill or statement was accurate.

The FCBA also limits the card issuer's freedom to report items the consumer disputes as late payments (delinquencies) to credit reporting agencies such as credit bureaus until the investigation is complete and the cardholder has had the opportunity to pay the charge. In such cases, the card issuer must inform the cardholder of the persons or companies to which the card issuer sends its report. The card issuer that fails to comply with the act forfeits the right to collect up to $50 from the cardholder. The act also permits the seller to offer discounts if the buyer pays cash for a purchase rather than using a credit card.

LO4

Fair Credit Reporting Act

The principal purpose of the **Fair Credit Reporting Act (FCRA)** is to ensure that information concerning a person's credit background supplied to her creditors is both up-to-date and accurate. It covers credit information supplied to potential creditors, insurers, or employers of that person. Accuracy has become even more important as employers increase their use of credit agency reports to screen applicants. A secondary goal of the act is to guard against disclosure of such confidential information to persons who request it for purposes other than those specified in the act. The act does not apply when an individual applies for commercial, rather than consumer, credit or insurance.

The FCRA offers special protection to persons who have been denied credit, insurance, or employment, such as Fischl, the consumer in the introductory case. A consumer who is denied credit by the person who received a credit report is entitled to disclosure of the name and address of the credit reporting agency (credit bureau) that made the report. The consumer may require the credit reporting agency (as the provider of the information) to reinvestigate information disputed by the consumer and to delete any inaccurate or obsolete information from the file. If the dispute is not resolved at that point (for example, if the consumer still questions the accuracy of the information), the consumer may file a brief statement of her version of the dispute for the credit file. The credit reporting agency is then required by the act to state that the consumer disputes the information when it gives out the information in the consumer's file. If inaccurate or unverifiable information is deleted from the consumer's file, the consumer may request the reporting agency to contact any person who had been given the deleted information. Recipients who obtained the credit report for *credit* or *insurance purposes* within six months prior to deletion must be advised of the deletion. If the request for credit information was for *employment purposes* and was made within two years of the deletion, then the requestor must be notified of the deletion of the inaccurate or unverifiable information.

Employers who obtain credit information about a job applicant must notify the applicant if he was not hired at least in part on the basis of a credit report. Several states have also enacted laws that require such disclosure as well as limit the kinds of information employers can obtain from applicants' credit reports.

The act offers several additional protections to consumers. First, a consumer has the right to have a consumer report withheld from anyone who under the law does not have a legitimate business need for the information. Second, the consumer can sue for damages for negligent violation of the act and for the collection of attorney's fees and court costs if the suit is successful. If the violation of the act is found to be willful, punitive damages may also be awarded. Third, the credit reporting agency may not report most adverse information more than seven years old. However, the fact that the consumer was declared bankrupt can be reported for 10 years after the bankruptcy. Fourth, the FCRA imposes a duty of disclosure on people who deny credit or increase its cost to the consumer because of information obtained from a person *other than a consumer reporting agency* if the consumer so requests.

Because of the increasing reliance of companies, employers, insurers, and others on credit reports, it is important for individuals to regularly check their credit information. This is especially true because of the growing problem of identity theft.

Wen Y. Chiang v. Verizon New England, Inc.

595 F.3d 26 (2010 U.S. App. LEXIS 2634)

FACTS

In 2006 and 2007, Wen Chiang sued his cell phone company, Verizon, over several billing disputes, later settled in state court. For several months, while Chiang refused to pay some disputed charges, Verizon reported to consumer credit agencies that his account was delinquent. Chiang notified the credit agencies of the disputes. When the agencies contacted Verizon to investigate, Verizon reaffirmed that his account was delinquent. Chiang sued Verizon in federal court, claiming the company violated the Fair Credit Reporting Act (FCRA) by failing to adequately investigate the disputes he brought with the consumer credit agencies.

ISSUE

Was Verizon wrong to report the disputed charges as unpaid and delinquent to the credit reporting agencies?

DECISION

No. A company may not give consumer credit reporting agencies inaccurate information and, under the FCRA, must investigate a consumer claim that provided "incomplete or inaccurate" information. Chiang provided no evidence that Verizon's reports were inaccurate, and when Verizon checked the disputes, it confirmed that he was refusing to pay for parts of his bills. While those charges were being disputed in court, those suits do not themselves show that the charges are inaccurate. Indeed, Verizon is "neither qualified nor obligated to resolve" the question about the charges' accuracy, which at this point "can only be resolved by a court of law." Chiang essentially argued that any investigation that did not agree with his initial disputes of the charges was inappropriate under FCRA. This argument is unreasonable, and he fails to show any FCRA violation.

In December 2003 the **Fair and Accurate Credit Transactions Act of 2003** was signed into law. The act amends the FCRA and makes the FCRA's preemption provisions permanent so that national rules for a number of key reporting functions are uniform. However, the act also imposes new obligations on banks, retailers, insurance companies, finance companies, and other credit reporting agencies. First, the act entitles every consumer to a copy of his or her credit report free of charge each year. A 2010 rule also requires online ads for free credit reports to disclose whether the consumer must buy credit monitoring or other products or services to get the report. Consumers can obtain a free report at AnnualCreditReport.com. Second, in an effort to stem identity theft, the act requires merchants to delete all but the last five digits of a credit card number on store receipts. Third, the act creates a national system of fraud detection so that identify theft can be tracked and dealt with earlier. And fourth, the act encourages lenders and credit agencies to take action before a victim even knows an identity crime has occurred.

Long v. Tommy Hilfiger U.S.A., Inc.

671 F.3d 371 (3d Cir. 2012)

FACTS

Long bought men's neckwear with his credit card at a Hilfiger store. Hilfiger gave him an electronically printed receipt that redacted all but the last four digits of his credit card number and displayed the month, but not the year, of his card's expiration date. Long sued Tommy Hilfiger U.S.A. (THU) under FACTA because it violated the law's prohibition against printing the expiration date. THU argued that printing just the month did not constitute the printing of an expiration date. Also, it argued that if it was a violation, it was not willful.

ISSUE

Did THU violate FACTA by printing the expiration month but not the year on the receipt?

(continued)

DECISION

Yes. Congress amended the Fair Credit Reporting Act by enacting FACTA. As part of an effort to prevent identity theft, FACTA prohibits merchants who accept credit or debit cards from printing certain data on receipts including the card's number except the last five digits, and the expiration date of the cards, on any receipt provided to the cardholder at the point of the sale. FACTA does not define "expiration date" but the most natural reading is that it refers to the data contained in the expiration date field on the face of the card. While FACTA allows a partial printing of the card's number, it was silent regarding a partial printing of the date. This indicates Congress chose not to allow partial printing of it. The remedies for violation are dependent on whether the violation was negligent or willful. If the former, the plaintiff can recover only actual damages, but if willful, the plaintiff can choose whether to recover actual damages or statutory damages of between $100 and $1,000. In addition, the court can award punitive damages for willful violations. THU's violation was not willful. It is not objectively unreasonable for THU to assume that printing a partial date would violate the act.

Further Protection of Borrower Privacy

Another key federal statute protecting consumers is the **Gramm-Leach-Bliley Act of 1999** (GLBA). While the FCRA and its amendments protect consumers from unfair or inaccurate credit reporting, the GLBA protects information sharing more generally. The statute sets forth basic privacy protections that must be provided by financial institutions and requires financial institutions to respect the privacy of their customers' nonpublic personal information. The GLBA applies to information sharing by both affiliate organizations and nonaffiliated third parties. With regard to affiliates, the GLBA requires that financial institutions disclose their policies and practices regarding the disclosure of customers' personal information. While the same requirement also applies to nonaffiliates, the GLBA further requires that financial institutions give consumers the right to "opt-out" (the ability to direct that information not be provided to nonaffiliates at all).

Equal Credit Opportunity Act

The **Equal Credit Opportunity Act (ECOA)** prohibits discrimination in credit transactions on grounds of sex, marital status, race, color, religion, national origin, and age. For example, the ECOA protects the 63-year-old applicant for a mortgage who plans to work 5 to 7 years longer and seeks a 15-year mortgage. The lender cannot turn down the application solely because of the applicant's age. The act also assists the widow or divorced woman who may not have a credit history in her own name as well as the young applicant so long as she is old enough to enter into a valid contract. The act applies to banks, finance companies, retail stores, credit card issuers (such as gasoline companies or Diners Club International), and other firms that regularly extend credit.

The protections afforded by the ECOA cover all phases of the credit transaction. The creditor may not do any of the following: discourage the application for credit, refuse to grant a separate account to a married woman if she is a credit applicant, or ask about the applicant's marital status if a separate account is requested. There are two exceptions to the prohibition against asking about marital status. The creditor may do so if security is required for the account or if state laws (such as community property laws) require otherwise.

The creditor must either accept or reject a credit application within 30 days. If the creditor denies a credit application, it must provide the specific reasons for that denial within a reasonable time or tell the consumer that he or she has the right to specific reasons. Such statements as "You didn't meet our minimum standards" or "You didn't receive enough points on our credit scoring system" do not comply with the ECOA.

The consumer is also entitled to have creditors report to credit reporting agencies in the names of both spouses the credit history of any account shared by a married couple. In other words, if Mrs. Ray Hughes shares an account in her husband's name, she may ask the credit agency to retroactively report that account in her name as well as her husband's. The credit experience concerning all accounts that both spouses may use and on which both are liable must be reported by creditors in both names. The ECOA also prohibits a creditor from using unfavorable information about an account that an applicant shared with a spouse or former spouse. To trigger this prohibition, the applicant must show that the bad credit rating does not accurately reflect his or her willingness or ability to pay.

The ECOA does not guarantee credit or unlimited credit to any person. Creditors may still set standards on which they will grant credit. They may not set standards that have the effect of denying credit to a protected class (such as women or the elderly), and they may not apply their standards on a discriminatory basis.

LO5

Fair Debt Collection Practices Act

Public concern about harassment by debt collectors, including late-night phone calls and threats of violence, led Congress in 1977 to pass the **Fair Debt Collection Practices Act (FDCPA).** Most states also have laws aimed at abuses by debt collectors. The federal act allows exemptions for states with similar laws as long as there are adequate provisions for enforcement. The federal act affects only the practices of debt collection agencies that collect consumer bills for creditors other than themselves. It does not cover retail stores, banks, or businesses that collect their own debts in their own name.

Actions prohibited in the FDCPA are listed in the Consumer Credit Laws Concept Summary later in this chapter. The act is enforced by the Federal Trade Commission. The consumer may sue for violations of the act; however, there are limits on the damages and penalties that the consumer may recover from the collection agency. The consumer may recover attorney's fees if she wins the suit. If a debt collector brings a suit that is found to be harassing, the winning consumer defendant may also collect attorney's fees.

Dunham v. Portfolio Recovery Associates, LLC

663 F.3d 997 (2011)

FACTS

Portfolio Recovery Associates (PRA) is a debt collection agency that purchases pools of commercial and noncommercial payment obligations that the lenders have been unable to collect. One of the debts it bought was that of a James Dunham. PRA sent a form notification letter to Dunham requesting payment. It also stated, "unless you notify this office within 30 days after receiving this notice that you dispute the validity of this debt . . . this office will assume [it] is valid." Dunham sent a letter disputing the validity and demanding validation of the payment obligation. PRA sent him the name, address, and the last four digits of the debtor's social security number, among other information. Dunham recognized that the four digits did not match his social security number. Dunham did not respond but several months later filed suit against PRA for violating the FDCPA because it failed to state that it verified information with the original creditor. PRA argued Dunham could not sue because he was not the intended recipient of its letter.

ISSUE

Was Dunham a consumer who could sue under the FDCPA?

DECISION

No. The purpose of the FDCPA is to eliminate abusive debt collection practices by debt collectors, and collectors are liable for failure to comply with any provisions of it. The act provides that if the debtor disputes the debt within 30 days, then the debt collector must cease collection

(continued)

until it gets verification of the debt. The act talks in terms of a "consumer" and defines it as any person obligated or allegedly obligated to pay any debt. PRA, in its letter, alleged that Dunham owed a payment and demanded payment. Even though mistaken, a mistaken allegation falls within the act's coverage. The FTC supports this reasoning. It has stated that a debt collector must verify a disputed debt because the section is intended to assist the consumer when a debt collector inadvertently contacts the wrong person. However, Dunham's suit must be dismissed because PRA complied with the terms of the act when it sent him the information about the Dunham who owed the debt. Verification is only intended to eliminate the problem of dunning the wrong person. The information sent allowed plaintiff to know he did not owe the debt.

FTC Holder in Due Course Rule

Consumers who have purchased defective goods or services on credit have frequently been frustrated when the seller assigns the right to payment (the debt) to a third party. The consumer may face demands for payment from the third party, while at the same time she finds that the seller is unwilling to correct the defects or has disappeared. In fact, the consumer might be obligated to pay the third party even though there is no likelihood that the defective performance will be remedied. This could happen if (1) the consumer signed a negotiable instrument that had been negotiated to a holder in due course (see Chapter 39) or (2) the consumer signed an installment sales contract containing a waiver of defenses clause whereby the consumer agreed to assert any defenses she had on the contract against the seller only and not against any assignee of the sales contract.

For example, Harold agrees to pay Ace Improvement $2,500 to put aluminum siding on his house. He signs a promissory note agreeing to pay the note in 24 monthly installments. Ace negotiates the note to a finance company and goes out of business after completing only part of the work on Harold's house. If the finance company can qualify as a holder in due course of the note, it may be able to enforce payment against Harold even though he will not get what he bargained for from Ace Improvement. This results from the basic principle of negotiable instruments law that a holder in due course takes the instrument free of personal defenses (e.g., misrepresentation, nondelivery, nonperformance, or breach of warranty) between the original parties to the instrument.

In 1975, the Federal Trade Commission took action to deal with such situations and adopted the **Holder in Due Course** rule. The rule is designed to preserve for consumers in most purchase money credit transactions the right to use claims and defenses against a holder in due course. It makes it an unfair trade practice for a seller, in the course of financing a consumer purchase or certain leases of goods or services, to use procedures to separate the consumer's duty to pay from the seller's duty to perform.

When the buyer executes a sales contract that includes a promissory note, or signs an installment sales contract that includes a waiver of defenses clause, the following statement (titled "Notice") must be included in bold type:

NOTICE

Any holder of this consumer credit contract is subject to all claims and defenses which the debtor could assert against the seller of goods or services obtained pursuant hereto or with the proceeds hereof. Recovery hereunder by the debtor shall not exceed amounts paid by the debtor hereunder.

If the seller arranges with a third-party lender for a direct loan to finance the buyer's purchase, the seller may not accept the proceeds of the loan unless the consumer credit contract between the buyer and the lender contains the following statement in bold type:

NOTICE

Any holder of this consumer credit contract is subject to all claims and defenses which the debtor could assert against the seller of goods or services obtained with the proceeds hereof. Recovery hereunder by the debtor shall not exceed amounts paid by the debtor hereunder.

The required statement provides that all defenses available to the purchaser against the seller of the merchandise are also available against the holder in due course. It does this *only* when the consumer's credit contract (promissory note or installment sales contract) contains the required provision. The provision is treated in the same manner as other written terms and conditions in the agreement. It must appear without qualification. A consumer credit contract that includes the required statement in conjunction with other clauses that limit or restrict its application does not satisfy the requirement that the contract "contain the notice."

The FTC rule does not eliminate any rights that the consumer may have as a matter of federal, state, or local law. It creates no new claims or defenses. For example, the rule does not create a warranty claim or defense where the product is sold "as is." The rule also does not alter statutes of limitations or other state-created limitations on the consumer's enforcement of claims and defenses. Finally, the claims or defenses relied on must relate to

Concept Summary: Consumer Credit Laws

Truth-in-Lending Act	Provides the consumer with important credit information (including credit advertising).	Requires: 1. The interest rate to be clearly stated as an annual percentage rate. 2. Disclosure of the *finance* charge (all costs of the credit). 3. The debtor be allowed to rescind for three business days when the home is used for collateral.
Fair Credit Reporting Act	Designed to ensure timely and accurate reporting about a person's credit background and to control disclosure in consumer credit situations.	Requires: 1. A person denied credit be allowed to challenge the information supplied. 2. The credit reporting agency to investigate information claimed wrong. 3. Correction of outdated or wrong information and notification of credit information recipients. 4. Information not be disclosed to those without a legitimate business need for it.
Consumer Leasing Act	Provides the consumer with important credit information involving leases of consumer goods for more than four months.	Requires: 1. Disclosure of aggregate cost of leasing goods. 2. Disclosure of consumer's liability at the end of the lease.

(continued)

Concept Summary: Consumer Credit Laws

Equal Credit Opportunity Act	Prohibits discrimination in credit transactions on the grounds of sex, marital status, race, color, religion, national origin, or age.	Requires: 1. Creditor to accept or reject application within 30 days. 2. If it is rejected, creditor must specify reasons. 3. Applicant cannot be asked about marital status when asking for a separate account, and a married woman cannot be refused a separate account on that basis. 4. Creditor not to discourage the application for credit.
Fair Debt Collection Practices Act	Prohibits debt collection agencies from using certain harassing techniques when collecting another's debt.	Actions prohibited: 1. Debt collectors may not contact a consumer at unusual or inconvenient times, or at all if the consumer is represented by an attorney. 2. Debt collectors may not contact a consumer where he or she works if the employer objects. 3. Debt collectors may not use harassing or intimidating tactics or abusive language against *any* person, including the debtor. 4. Debt collectors may not use false or misleading tactics, such as posing as lawyers or police officers. 5. Debt collectors may not contact third parties other than the consumer's attorney, the creditor, the attorney of the creditor, the attorney of the debt collector, or a consumer reporting agency if otherwise permitted by the law, about payment of a debt, unless authorized. 6. Debt collectors cannot communicate again with the consumer, after receiving the consumer's written refusal to pay the debt, except to inform the consumer of actions that the collector may take. 7. Debt collectors may not deposit a postdated check prior to the date on it.

(continued)

Concept Summary: Consumer Credit Laws *(concluded)*

Telemarketing and Consumer Fraud and Abuse Prevention Act	Prevents deceptive and abusive telemarketing practices.	Requires: 1. Disclosure of who is calling, what is being sold, the total cost, restrictions, and rules about prizes. Prohibits: 1. Calling between 9:00 PM and 8:00 AM. 2. Harassing or abusive calls.
Holder in Due Course Rule	Preserves the right of consumers to use claims and defenses against a holder in due course of their credit contract.	Requires: 1. Bold type notices in the consumer's credit contract and the lender's contract. 2. All defenses available to the purchaser against the seller can also be available against the holder in due course.

the sale transaction that is financed; for example, the consumer cannot sue on the grounds of the seller's negligent maintenance of business premises that caused the buyer to break her leg while waiting for warranty service. Failure to comply with the regulation exposes the seller to a possible fine of $10,000 per violation in a civil action brought by the FTC.

In many industrialized nations, the problem of deceptive advertising is addressed through self-regulation. Several countries have established governmental offices and agencies similar to the FTC. In 1984, the European Union (EU) enacted the Directive on Misleading Advertising, which requires that all EU nations have laws in place that address misleading advertising.

Consumer Product Safety Act

Background

LO6

The large number of injuries caused by defective consumer products led Congress to pass the **Consumer Product Safety Act (CPSA)** in 1972. In order to advance Congress's goal of promoting product safety, the act established the Consumer Product Safety Commission (CPSC), an independent regulatory agency composed of five presidentially appointed commissioners, each serving a seven-year term. The CPSC is the main federal agency concerned with product safety. Its authority is basically limited to *consumer products.* Not within the commission's domain, however, are certain products regulated by other agencies, including motor vehicles and equipment, firearms, aircraft, boats, drugs, cosmetics, and food products.

Standards

The CPSC is empowered to issue *product safety standards.* These may (1) involve the performance of consumer products or (2) require product warnings or instructions. A product safety standard should be issued only when the product in question presents an *unreasonable* risk of injury and the standard is *reasonably necessary* to prevent or reduce that risk. The commission may also issue rules *banning* certain "hazardous" products. Such rules are permissible when, in addition to presenting an unreasonable risk of injury, the product is so dangerous that no feasible product safety standard would protect the public from the risks it poses.

Remedies

In addition, the CPSC can bring suit in federal district court to eliminate the dangers presented by *imminently hazardous* consumer products. These are products that pose an immediate and unreasonable risk of death, serious illness, or severe personal injury. Finally, manufacturers, distributors, and retailers are required to notify the CPSC if they have reason to know that their products present a *substantial product hazard.* Such a hazard exists when the product creates a substantial risk of injury to the public, either because it violates a CPSC safety rule or for other reasons. In such cases, the commission may, among other things, order the private party to give notice of the problem to those affected by it, repair or replace the product, or submit its own corrective action plan.

The CPSA provides a host of other remedies and enforcement devices in addition to those already discussed. The commission and the U.S. attorney general may sue for *injunctive relief* or the *seizure* of products to enforce various provisions of the act. *Civil penalties* against those who knowingly violate various CPSA provisions and CPSC rules are also possible. *Criminal penalties* may be imposed on those who knowingly and willfully violate such provisions and rules after CPSC notification of their failure to comply. In addition, any *private party* may sue for an *injunction* to enforce any CPSC rule or order, after giving proper notice, if at the time of the suit the commission or the attorney general has not begun an action based on the alleged violation. Finally, those injured because of a knowing and willful violation of a CPSC rule or order may sue for *damages* if the amount in controversy exceeds $10,000.

Lemon Laws

Next to homes, vehicles are the most expensive purchase most consumers make. Unfortunately for many, vehicles often came with significant problems that the consumers were unable to get their dealers to fix. By 1981, complaints about auto dealers were first on the list of consumer complaints received by the FTC. While the UCC provided some remedies for the consumer, these often proved inadequate or difficult to pursue. In response, a majority of states have now passed **"lemon laws"** that are designed to provide more appropriate relief.

While the laws vary from state to state, they tend to have the same structure. If a car under warranty has a significant defect affecting the car's use or value, and the seller does not fix that defect in a specified number of times or the car is out of commission for a specified period of time, the consumer is entitled to a remedy. Remedies generally include return of the purchase price or a new car. For example, assume Jill's car has a defective seal that allows significant amounts of water to leak in when it rains. Jill has taken it back to the dealer four times; each time, she is assured that it is fixed but it still leaks. If the statute in Jill's state says that the dealer is allowed four attempts to fix the defect, Jill would now be entitled to pursue the remedies established by the statute. (See Figure 46.1.)

Most statutes require that disputes arising under them be arbitrated. The arbitration, which is usually binding on the manufacturer but not on the consumer, is handled by panels set up by the car companies. Because of the practice of "lemon laundering" (reselling cars that manufacturers have been forced to take back without telling the new owners about

FIGURE 46.1
Typical Lemon Law Coverage

Requires car manufacturers (and sometimes manufacturers of other goods) to: → Replace the product or refund purchase price if: → The defect is major and covered by a warranty, and a number of unsuccessful attempts were made to repair it; or sufficient "down time" was involved; or there is a failure to show the defect is curable.

the car's problem history), some states have expanded their statutes. Under these statutes, manufacturers are required to fully disclose to the subsequent buyer the car's problems and, in some cases, physically brand it as a lemon.

In addition to the lemon laws, other laws regulate consumer car transactions. For example, the Federal Trade Commission requires used car dealers to display a *Buyer's Guide* on each car that tells whether the car is covered by a warranty and, if it is, the type and duration of the warranty as well as the name of the person to contact if a problem arises. If the sale is conducted in Spanish, the guide must be in Spanish. For problems with new cars, the National Highway Traffic Safety Administration requires manufacturers to tell new-car buyers about a hotline they should call, in addition to their dealer, if they suspect their vehicle has a safety defect.

Computers are quickly gaining the status of a necessity in consumers' lives. Like cars, some may be lemons. Several states are now considering computer lemon laws that would set relatively short time periods in which the computer must be fixed and allow the manufacturer only two or three chances to fix it. If it is not fixed, the consumer must be given the choice of a new computer of equal or greater value, or a refund.

Questions and Problem Cases

1. What is the main purpose of the Consumer Financial Protection Bureau and how can it be contacted?
2. Explain the purpose of the Holder in Due Course rule.
3. What is a "lemon law"? How are disputes under these laws usually handled?
4. Zuccarini did business under a variety of names. He diverted consumers from their intended Internet site to his by using domain names that were misspellings of, or confusingly similar to, domain names of other parties. He also made it difficult to exit his website by causing pop-up windows, multiple copies of browser windows, or multiple copies of browser software to launch when the consumer used a "Close," "Exit," or "X" function. He was compensated by the advertisers displaying their ads on these pop-ups. The FTC argued that these tactics were unfair under the FTC Act because they used misleading practices. Is the FTC correct? Explain.
5. Roberts received a packet from Fleet Bank urging her to apply for its new Titanium Master Card. Among the enclosures was a flier and a letter that announced a 7.99% fixed APR. The letter twice touted that the rate was "Not an introductory rate" and that it "won't go up in just a few short months." The form Roberts filled out stated the same rate. The back of the form stated that the terms were subject to change. When Roberts got her card and cardholders agreement, it said the bank had "the right to change any of the terms . . . at any time." Fleet later sent Roberts a letter notifying her that it was increasing the rate to 10.5%. She sued, claiming Fleet violated the TILA. Is she correct? Why?

6. National Action, a debt collector, sent Chuway a letter identifying a credit card company as the creditor and stating that the "balance" owed was $367.42. The letter added that the credit card company "has assigned your delinquent account to our agency for collection. Please remit the balance listed above in the return envelope provided. To obtain your most current balance information, please call 1-800-916-9006. Our friendly and experienced representatives will be glad to assist you and answer any questions you may have." Did National violate the FDCPA's requirement to state the amount of the debt? Explain.
7. The Cannons bought a motor home manufactured by Newmar. It suffered from multiple defects: the engine malfunctioned, the driver's side windshield failed, it leaked fuel, and the power system failed. Each time the Cannons came back for repairs, Newmar ineffectively fixed the defects. Thus, the Cannons could no longer use the motor home. They filed a claim under the state's Lemon Law. Should they be successful? Explain.

Chapter 47

Environmental Regulation

Learning Objectives

After you have studied this chapter, you should be able to:

1. Explain when an environmental impact statement must be prepared and what it must contain.
2. List and briefly discuss the major provisions in the Clean Air Act.
3. Assess how governmental action to deal with greenhouse gas emission and global climate change may affect businesses.
4. List and briefly discuss the major provisions in the Clean Water Act.
5. Explain why Congress passed the Oil Pollution Act of 1990 and list its major provisions.
6. List and briefly discuss the purpose and major provisions of the Resource Conservation and Recovery Act.
7. Discuss the purpose of the Comprehensive Environmental Response, Compensation, and Liability Act ("Superfund").

The B-P Paper Company is planning to build a new papermaking facility on property it owns in the Atlanta, Georgia, area that borders on the Chattahoochee River. The facility will have an industrial boiler that burns wood wastes to generate process steam for plant operation and will emit sulfur oxides, nitrogen oxides, and particulate emissions to the air. The company plans to draw water from the river to use in the papermaking process and will return it to the river after some in-house treatment to remove some of the pollutants that have been added by the process. Significant quantities of sludge from the papermaking process will have to be disposed of, as will empty containers in which the chlorine used at the facility was delivered.

(continued)

- What major requirements will the facility have to meet to control its anticipated air emissions?
- What major requirements will the facility have to meet to control its discharge of wastewater to the Chattahoochee River?
- What major requirements will the company have to meet in dealing with the waste sludge and containers?

Introduction

Today's businessperson must be concerned with not only competing effectively against competitors but also complying with a myriad of regulatory requirements. For many businesses, particularly those that manufacture goods or that generate wastes, the environmental laws and regulations loom large in terms of the requirements and costs they impose. They can have a significant effect on the way businesses have to be conducted, as well as on their profitability. This area of the law has expanded dramatically over the last four decades, and environmental issues are a concern of people and governments around the world. This chapter briefly discusses the development of environmental law and outlines the major federal statutes that have been enacted to control pollution of air, water, and land.

Historical Perspective

Historically, people assumed that the air, water, and land around them would absorb their waste products. In recent times, however, it has become clear that nature's capacity to assimilate people's wastes is not infinite. Burgeoning population, economic growth, affluence, and the products of our industrial society pose risks to human health and the environment. Indeed, one of the challenges of our time is how to achieve "sustainable development"—that is, the level and kind of economic development that do not unreasonably trade off long-term sustainability for the sake of short-term benefits.

Concern about the environment is not a recent phenomenon. In medieval England, Parliament passed "smoke control" acts making it illegal to burn soft coal at certain times of the year. Where the owner or operator of a piece of property is using it in such a manner as to unreasonably interfere with another owner's (or the public's) health or enjoyment of his property, the courts have long entertained suits to abate the nuisance. Nuisance actions, which are discussed in Chapter 33, are frequently not ideal vehicles for dealing with widespread pollution problems. Rather than a hit-or-miss approach, a comprehensive across-the-board approach may be required.

Realizing this, the federal government, as well as many state and local governments, had passed laws to abate air and water pollution by the late 1950s and 1960s. As the 1970s began, concern over the quality and future of the environment produced new laws and fresh public demands for action. During the 1980s, these laws were refined, and in some cases, their coverage was extended. Today, environmental concerns continue to be in evidence around the globe, and many countries, both individually and collectively, continue to take steps to address those concerns. Accordingly, it is important that the businessperson be cognizant of the legal requirements and the public's environmental concerns in operating a business.

The Environmental Protection Agency

In 1970, the Environmental Protection Agency (EPA) was created to consolidate the federal government's environmental responsibilities. Over the decade of the 1970s, Congress passed comprehensive new legislation covering, among other things, air and water pollution, pesticides, ocean dumping, and waste disposal. Among the factors prompting these laws were protection of human health, aesthetics, economic costs of continued pollution, and protection of natural systems.

The initial efforts were aimed largely at pollution problems that could be seen, smelled, or tasted. As control requirements have been put in place, implemented by industry and government, and progress has been noted in the form of cleaner air and water, attention has focused increasingly on problems that are somewhat less visible but potentially more threatening—the problems posed by toxic substances. These problems have come into more prominence as scientific research has disclosed the risks posed by some substances, as the development of new technology has facilitated the detection of the suspect substances in ever more minute quantities, and increased monitoring and testing are carried out.

Other changes are evolving in the tools and approaches being used by the government to deal with environmental problems. Much of the initial effort to address such problems involved what is known as command and control regulation, an approach that is heavily prescriptive and relies on an intensive enforcement presence to ensure the regulations are followed. In the 1990s, however, the government looked to supplement—or to replace in part—the command and control system with the use of economic incentives and voluntary approaches to try to bring about the desired results.

Today, many of the laws and regulations in place are in serious need of being updated, to take account of changing circumstances and emerging issues. Between 1970 and 1990, most of the environmental regulatory scheme was enacted by Congress with strong bipartisan support with the aim of crafting solutions to known problems. However, in recent years the environment has become a much more politicized issue, with bipartisan consensus hard to come by, and with markedly different approaches being taken at EPA, depending on which party holds the presidency. The resulting gridlock, and swings in policy between administrations, can make it challenging for businesses to plan in an era of uncertainty.

LO1 The National Environmental Policy Act

The National Environmental Policy Act (NEPA) was signed into law on January 1, 1970. In addition to creating the Council of Environmental Quality in the Executive Office of the President, the act required that an **environmental impact statement** be prepared for every recommendation or report on legislation and for every *major federal action significantly affecting the quality of the environment.* The environmental impact statement must (1) describe the environmental impact of the proposed action, (2) discuss impacts that cannot be avoided, (3) discuss the alternatives to the proposed action, (4) indicate differences between short- and long-term impacts, and (5) detail any irreversible commitments of resources.

NEPA requires a federal agency to consider the environmental impact of a project before the project is undertaken. Other federal, state, and local agencies, as well as interested citizens, have an opportunity to comment on the environmental impact of the project before the agency can proceed. Where the process is not followed, citizens can and have gone to court to force compliance with NEPA. A number of states and local governments have passed their own environmental impact laws requiring NEPA-type statements for major public and private developments.

While the federal and state laws requiring the preparation of environmental impact statements appear directed at government actions, it is important to note that the government actions covered often include the granting of permits to private parties. Thus, businesspeople may readily find themselves involved in the preparation of an environmental impact statement—for example, in connection with a marina to be built in navigable waters or a resort development that will impact wetlands, both of which require permits from the U.S. Army Corps of Engineers. Similarly, a developer seeking a local zoning change so she can build a major commercial or residential development may find that she is asked to finance a study of the potential environmental impact of her proposed project.

Air Pollution

Background

LO2

Fuel combustion, industrial processes, and solid waste disposal are the major contributors to air pollution. People's initial concern with air pollution related to what they could see—visible or smoke pollution. In the 1880s, Chicago and Cincinnati enacted smoke control ordinances. As the technology became available to deal with smoke and particulate emissions, attention was given as well to other, less visible gases that could adversely affect human health and vegetation and that could lead to increased acidity of lakes, thus making them unsuitable for fish.

Clean Air Act

The Clear Air Act—enacted in 1970 and amended in 1977 and 1990—provides the basis for our present approach to air pollution control.

Ambient Air Control Standards

The Clean Air Act established a comprehensive approach for dealing with air pollution. The EPA is required to set **national ambient air quality standards** for the major pollutants that have an adverse impact on human health—that is, to set the amount of a given pollutant that can be present in the air around us. The ambient air quality standards are to be set at two levels: (1) **primary standards,** which are designed to protect the public's health from harm, and (2) **secondary standards,** which are designed to protect vegetation, materials, climate, visibility, and economic values. Pursuant to this statutory mandate, the EPA has set ambient air quality standards for carbon monoxide, nitrogen oxide, sulfur oxide, ozone, lead, and particulate matter.

Each state is required to develop—and to obtain EPA approval for—a **state implementation plan** for meeting the national ambient air quality standards. This necessitates an inventory of the various sources of air pollution and their contribution to the total air pollution in the air quality region. The major emitters of pollutants are then required to reduce their emissions to a level that ensures that overall air quality will meet the national standards.

For example, a factory may be required to limit its emissions of volatile organic compounds (a contributor to ozone or smog) to a certain amount per unit of production or hour of operation; similarly, a power plant might have its emissions of sulfur oxides and nitrogen oxides limited to so many pounds per Btu of energy produced. The states have the responsibility for deciding which activities must be regulated or curtailed so that emissions will not exceed the national standards.

Because by the late 1980s many of the nation's major urban areas were still not in compliance with the health-based standards for ozone and carbon monoxide, Congress in its 1990 amendments imposed an additional set of requirements on the areas that were not in compliance. Thus, citizens living in the areas and existing businesses, as well as prospective businesses seeking to locate in the designated areas, face increasingly stringent control measures designed to bring the areas into alignment with the national standards. These new requirements mean that businesses such as bakeries that are generally not thought of as major polluters of the air must further control their emissions and that paints and other products that contain solvents may have to be reformulated. In addition, businesses seeking to build new facilities, modify existing facilities, or increase production may have to "offset" any increased emissions by decreasing emissions or by buying pollution emission rights from others in the area.

Acid Rain Controls

Responding to the 1970 Clean Air Act, which sought to protect the air in areas near sources of air pollution, many electric-generating facilities built tall smokestacks so that emissions were dispersed over a broader area. Unwittingly, this contributed to long-range transport of some of the pollutants, which changed chemically en route and fell to earth many miles away in the form of acid rain, snow, fog, or dry deposition. For a number of years, a considerable debate ensued over acid rain, in particular as to whether it was a problem, what kind of damage it caused, whether anything should be done about it, and who should pay for the cost of limiting it.

The 1990 amendments addressed acid deposition by among other things placing a cap on the overall emissions of the contributors to it (the oxides of sulfur and nitrogen) and requiring electric utilities to reduce their emissions to specified levels in two steps by 2000. This requires most electric-generating facilities in the country to install large control devices known as *scrubbers,* to switch to lower-sulfur coal, or to install so-called clean coal technologies. The 1990 amendments also provided an innovative system whereby companies whose emissions are cleaner than required by law can sell their rights to emit more sulfur oxide to other companies that may be finding it more difficult to meet the standards. This emission trading scheme has worked well to achieve reductions in emissions in an economically efficient way.

Control of Air Toxics

The Clean Air Act also requires the EPA to regulate the emission of **toxic air pollutants.** Under this authority, the EPA set standards for asbestos, beryllium, mercury, vinyl chloride, benzene, and radionuclides. Unhappy with the slow pace of regulation of toxic air pollutants, Congress in 1990 specified a list of 189 chemicals for which the EPA is required to issue regulations requiring the installation of the *maximum available control technology.* The regulations are to be developed and the control technology installed by industry in phases. Thus, while many toxic emissions largely went unregulated, that situation has changed. In addition, a number of companies are voluntarily reducing their emissions of toxic chemicals to levels below those they are required to meet by law.

Ethics in Action

Suppose a manufacturing facility emits into the air a chemical that it has reason to believe is inadequately regulated by the EPA and that poses a significant threat to nearby residents even at levels lower than those permitted by the EPA. As manager of the facility, would you be satisfied to meet the EPA required level or would you install the additional controls you believe necessary to achieve a reasonably safe level?

New Source Controls

The act requires that **new stationary sources,** such as factories and power plants, install the **best available technology** for reducing air pollution. The EPA is required to establish the standards to be met by new stationary sources and has done so for the major types of stationary sources of air pollution. This means that a new facility covered by the regulations must install state-of-the-art control technology, even if it is locating in an area where the air quality is better than that required by law.

The act also requires that facilities that undergo major "modifications"—defined as physical changes that result in significant increases in emissions of air pollutants—must go through a preconstruction review, obtain a permit, and meet the same new source performance standards or emission limits that must be met by new facilities. The rationale for imposing these standards when a new facility is built or when an existing facility undergoes a major modification is that it is the easiest time to design and incorporate state-of-the-art environmental controls into the facility. Routine maintenance, repair, and replacement activities as well as increases in hours of production that are not accompanied by increases in emissions are excluded from the definition of modification. The preconstruction review process that is required—known as new source review, or NSR—is the subject of very contentious debate and various proposals to modify it. Industry is concerned that the process slows down its ability to make changes to increase efficiency, take advantage of new technologies, or gain a competitive edge, while environmentalists claim that some companies are increasing emissions and avoiding the installation of required controls on emissions.

In the case that follows, *United States v. Ohio Edison Company,* the court rejected a utility's argument that its work on its coal-fired electric generating units was "routine maintenance, repair, and replacement" and thus exempt from the preconstruction review and permitting requirements applicable to facilities that are "modified" resulting in a significant increase in their emissions.

United States v. Ohio Edison Company

276 F.Supp.2d 829 (S.D. Ohio 2003)

FACTS

The Sammis Plant is a coal-fired electric generating plant owned by the Ohio Edison Company and situated along the Ohio River in the Village of Stratton, Ohio. The plant consists of seven separate generating units, numbered 1 through 7. Units 1 through 4 were placed in service from 1959 to 1962, Unit 5 in 1967, Unit 6 in 1969, and Unit 7 in 1971.

Coal-fired power plants, such as the Sammis plant, generate electricity using three major components: the boiler, turbine, and generator. The boiler is a large building-like structure (150–200 feet high) in which coal is burned inside the furnace and the energy from the combustion process converts water to produce steam. The steam is then directed to the turbine where it is further converted to mechanical energy in the form of a spinning turbine shaft, which in turn drives the generator that produces electricity. The walls, roof, and floor of the boiler are comprised of tubes, as are the other major components of the boiler, which are made up of densely packed assemblies of tubes that incrementally raise the temperature of the steam before it leaves the boiler to generate electricity.

The Sammis units are fueled by pulverized coal (coal that has been ground to a powdery consistency) that is fed through pipes to burners where it is ignited and combusts within the furnace area of the boiler. In the combustion of coal, chemical energy, gas by-products, and particulate matter are released. The gases are known as flue gas. The flue gases produced from the combustion process form carbon dioxide, carbon monoxide, sulfur dioxide, and nitrogen oxides. The flue gases are discharged to the atmosphere. At the time the seven units were built, Ohio Edison installed electrostatic precipitators to collect fly ash coming out of the boilers. At the time of installations, the precipitators were state-of-the-art technology. Over time the tubing that is in contact with the flue gases, combusting coal, and water inside the tubing deteriorates and periodically must be replaced.

Fossil-fuel–fired generating stations have traditionally been built with an assumed nominal design and economic

(continued)

life of about 30 years. The implicit expectation was that these units would be replaced at the end of this period with new units that would meet load requirements and, through the use of technological improvements, produce power at lower cost, higher availability, and higher efficiency. For a number of reasons, these expectations have not been realized and many utility companies have undertaken so-called life extension projects which offer the prospect of retaining units in service for 50 to 60 years or longer.

In the 1980s and 1990s Ohio Edison developed a program and undertook 11 projects at Sammis with the purpose of extending the life of the seven units and making them more efficient. The projects went beyond the normal replacement of tubing and focused on other components that would require repair or replacement in the next 30 years. All of the projects involved replacement of major components that had never before been replaced on the particular units. The total cost of the projects was approximately $136.4 million. By replacing aging or deficient components, Ohio Edison intended and achieved a significant increase in the operation and output of the units. In turn, the amount of emission of sulfur dioxide, nitrogen oxides, and particulate matter also increased. The vast majority of the expenditures were treated for accounting purposes as capital, as opposed to maintenance, expenses. Most of the work was performed by outside contractors, as opposed to in-house maintenance crews.

Congress provided in the Clean Air Act that when there is a "modification" of a plant, the plant must undergo a preconstruction review by the EPA, obtain a preconstruction permit, and meet the same emission standards—known as "new source performance standards"—that must be met by newly constructed plants. The EPA, by regulations, has defined "modification" to include only activities which involve both a "physical change" to a unit and a resulting "significant increase in emissions." Excluded from the definition of modification are projects involving only "routine maintenance, repair, or replacement."

The United States and the states of Connecticut, New York, and New Jersey brought suit against Ohio Edison alleging that it had violated the Clean Air Act by not coming into compliance with the preconstruction review, permitting, and new source performance standards for fossil-fueled generating units at the time it carried out the life-extension projects. Ohio Edison argued that the projects were "routine maintenance, repair, and replacement" and did not require preconstruction review and a permit.

ISSUE

Did the projects performed by Ohio Edison on units at the Sammis Plant constitute "modifications" subjecting the plant to preconstruction review and permitting requirements, and more stringent pollution control standards, under the Clean Air Act?

DECISION

Yes. The court indicated that while the analysis required to distinguish between a modification sufficient to trigger compliance from routine maintenance, repair, and replacement is complex, the distinction is hardly subtle. Routine maintenance, repair, and replacement occurs regularly, involves no permanent improvements, is typically limited in expense, is usually performed in large plants by in-house employees, and is treated for accounting purposes as an expense. In contrast to routine maintenance, capital improvements, which generally involve more expense, are large in scope, often involve outside contractors, involve an increase of value in the unit, are usually not undertaken with regular frequency, and are treated for accounting purposes as capital expenditures on the balance sheet.

The 11 projects in issue in this case were extensive, involving an outlay of $136.4 million, the vast majority of which was treated for accounting purposes as capital, as opposed to maintenance, expenses. The work was largely done by outside contractors as opposed to in-house maintenance crews. The purpose of the projects was to increase the life and the reliability of the units. By replacing aging or deficient components, Ohio Edison intended and achieved a significant increase in the operation and output of the units. In turn, the amount of emission of sulfur dioxide, nitrogen oxides, and particulate matter also increased. The court then concluded that the 11 projects at issue in this case were major modifications sufficient to trigger application of the Clean Air Act's required preconstruction review and permitting requirements.

Permits

In the 1990 amendments to the Clean Air Act, Congress established a permit system whereby major sources of air pollution—particularly those subject to the NSPS, air toxics, nonattainment, and acid rain provisions of the act—as well as certain other sources, have to obtain permits that will specify the limits on emissions from the sources. The permits also contain monitoring and reporting requirements. Once a state permitting program is approved by EPA, the permits are issued by the state. A controversial issue in the permitting regulations is when a source has to seek a modification of the permit because of process or operational changes that might increase emissions. This can greatly complicate the timely execution of business plans.

Enforcement

The primary responsibility for enforcing the air quality standards lies with the states, but the federal government has the right to enforce the standards if the states fail to do so. The Clean Air Act also provides for suits by citizens to force the industry or the government to fully comply with the act's provisions.

Automobile Pollution

The Clean Air Act provides specifically for air pollution controls on transportation sources such as automobiles. The major pollutants from automobiles are carbon monoxide, hydrocarbons, and nitrogen oxides. Carbon monoxide is a colorless, odorless gas that can dull mental performance and even cause death when inhaled in large quantities. Hydrocarbons, in the form of unburned fuel, are part of a category of air pollutants known as volatile organic compounds (VOCs). VOCs combine with nitrogen oxides under the influence of sunlight to become ozone. We sometimes know it as *smog*.

The 1970 Clean Air Act required a reduction by 1975 of 90 percent in the amount of the carbon monoxide and hydrocarbons emitted by automobiles and by 1976 of 90 percent in the amount of the nitrogen oxides emitted. At the time, these requirements were "technology forcing"; that is, the manufacturers could not rely on already existing technology to meet the standards but had to develop new technology. Ultimately, most manufacturers had to go beyond simply making changes in engine design and utilize pollution control devices known as *catalytic converters*.

Subsequently, Congress addressed the question of setting even more stringent limits on automobile emissions while requiring that the new automobiles get better gas mileage. The 1990 amendments required further limitations on emissions from tailpipes, the development of so-called clean-fueled vehicles for use in cities with dirty air, and the availability of oxygenated fuels (which are cleaner burning) in specified areas of the country that are having difficulty meeting the air quality limits at least part of the year. These new requirements have had significant ramifications for the oil and automobile industries. In the case of the oil industry, it has had to "reformulate" some of the gasoline it sells.

Under the Clean Air Act, no manufacturer may sell vehicles subject to emission standards without prior certification from the EPA that the vehicles meet the required standards. The tests are performed on prototype vehicles, and if they pass, a certificate of conformity covering that type of engine and vehicle is issued. The EPA subsequently can test vehicles on the assembly line to make sure that the production vehicles are meeting the standards. The manufacturers are required to warrant that the vehicle, if properly maintained, will comply with the emission standards for its useful life. If the EPA discovers that vehicles in actual use exceed the emission standards, it may order the manufacturer to recall and repair the defective models; this is a power that the EPA has exercised on a number of occasions.

The act also provides for the regulation and registration of fuel additives such as lead. In the 1980s, lead was largely phased out of use as an octane enhancer in gasoline. As indicated previously, the 1990 amendments provide for the availability of alternative fuels based on ethanol and methanol.

Recently, EPA and the Department of Transportation have promulgated regulations requiring automobile and light-duty trucks sold after January 1, 2011, to meet restrictive fuel economy standards that will have the additional benefit of reducing emissions, including those of greenhouse gases. They have also proposed even more restrictive fuel economy standards for 2017–2025 model year vehicles.

International Air Problems

During the late 1970s and 1980s, concern developed that the release of chlorine-containing substances such as chlorofluorocarbons (CFCs) used in air conditioning, refrigeration, and certain foam products was depleting the stratospheric ozone layer. This could lead to more ultraviolet radiation reaching the earth and, in turn, more skin cancer. Subsequently, a number of nations, acting under the aegis of the United Nations, signed a treaty agreeing first to limit any increases in production of CFCs and ultimately to phase out their use. The 1990 amendments to the Clean Air Act implement the obligations of the United States under the treaty and provide for the phase-down and phaseout of a number of chlorofluorocarbons; accordingly, many businesses have developed or located substitutes for those chemicals that are henceforth available only in reduced quantities, if at all.

Other air pollution issues with international dimensions that may result in multinational control efforts are acid rain and global warming/climate change resulting, in part, from increased emissions of carbon dioxide to the atmosphere.

Climate Change

Currently, the issue of global warming/climate change is the focus of considerable debate, discussion, and some action by governments and private entities. The crux of the issue is whether human activity, primarily in the form of increased emissions of carbon dioxide to the atmosphere, is creating conditions that over time are resulting in the warming of the earth's atmosphere, a rise in sea level, an increase in number and severity of various weather events, and changes in the climate in many parts of the world. An international treaty known as the Kyoto Protocol was drafted with the intention of addressing this issue through collective international action. While it was signed by many nations, it has generated significant controversy in many countries, including the United States, and to date, it has not proved an effective mechanism for addressing global climate change.

LO3 The issue raises important concerns for many kinds of businesses, including insurance companies, producers and users of fossil fuels, and producers of products such as motor vehicles that emit carbon dioxide and may at some point be subjected to controls under either domestic or international regimes. The implications turn on the extent, nature, pace, and location of possible warming-induced changes, as well as on the reactions and the policy decisions of individuals, businesses, and governments to those changes. The issue also holds potential business opportunities for individuals and firms, and many are developing business plans to try to take advantage of the issue.

The next few years will likely see continued debate and discussion of global warming/climate change and the appropriate responses to it. As of 2013, the United States does not have a comprehensive legal regime in place to address environmental and energy-related aspects of the issue. In the absence of such a federal response, a number of organizations and state and local governments have sought to use litigation to force the federal government to take some steps using existing authority. The case that follows, *Massachusetts v. EPA,* illustrates such an effort, which ended with the Supreme Court, in a 5–4 vote, agreeing that the EPA had not provided sufficient legal justification to refuse to exercise the legal authority it had to regulate greenhouse gas emission from automobiles.

Massachusetts v. EPA

127 S. Ct. 1438 (2007)

FACTS

Section 202(a)(1) of the Clean Air Act provides:

> The [EPA] Administrator shall by regulation prescribe (and from time to time revise) in accordance with the provisions of this section, standards applicable to the emission of any air pollutant from any class or classes of new motor vehicles or new motor vehicle engines, which in his judgment cause, or contribute to, air pollution which may reasonably be anticipated to endanger public health or welfare. . . .

The act defines "air pollutant" to include "any air pollution agent or combination of such agents, including any physical, chemical, biological, radioactive . . . substance or matter which is emitted into or otherwise enters the ambient air." "Welfare" is also defined broadly: among other things, it includes "effects on . . . weather . . . and climate."

On October 20, 1999, a group of 19 private organizations filed a rule-making petition asking the EPA to regulate "greenhouse gas emissions from new motor vehicles under § 202 of the Clean Air Act." Petitioners maintained that 1998 was the "warmest year on record"; that carbon dioxide, methane, nitrous oxide, and hydrofluorocarbons are "heat-trapping greenhouse gases"; and that greenhouse gas emissions have significantly accelerated climate change. They also noted that in a 1995 report, the Intergovernmental Panel on Climate Change, a multinational scientific body organized under the auspices of the United Nations, warned that "carbon dioxide remains the most important contributor to [man-made] forcing of climate change." The petition further alleged that climate change will have serious adverse effects on human health and the environment. As to the EPA's statutory authority, the petition observed that the agency itself had already confirmed that it had the power to regulate carbon dioxide. In 1998, Jonathan Z. Cannon, then the EPA's General Counsel, prepared a legal opinion concluding that "CO emissions are within the scope of the EPA's authority to regulate," even as he recognized that the EPA had so far declined to exercise that authority. Cannon's successor, Gary S. Guzy, reiterated that opinion before a congressional committee just two weeks before the rule-making petition was filed.

Fifteen months after the petition's submission, the EPA requested public comment on "all the issues raised in [the] petition," adding a "particular" request for comments on "any scientific, technical, legal, economic or other aspect of these issues that may be relevant to EPA's consideration of this petition." The EPA received more than 50,000 comments over the next five months.

Before the close of the comment period, the White House sought "assistance in identifying the areas in the science of climate change where there are the greatest certainties and uncertainties" from the National Research Council, asking for a response "as soon as possible." The result was a 2001 report titled "Climate Change: An Analysis of Some Key Questions (NRC Report)," which, drawing heavily on the 1995 IPCC report, concluded that "[g]reenhouse gases are accumulating in Earth's atmosphere as a result of human activities, causing surface air temperatures and subsurface ocean temperatures to rise. Temperatures are, in fact, rising."

On September 8, 2003, the EPA entered an order denying the rule-making petition. The agency gave two reasons for its decision: (1) that contrary to the opinions of its former general counsels, the Clean Air Act does not authorize EPA to issue mandatory regulations to address global climate change; and (2) that even if the agency had the authority to set greenhouse gas emission standards, it would be unwise to do so at this time. Among the reasons given by the EPA for declining to regulate were: (1) that the administration preferred to rely on a number of voluntary actions to reduce greenhouse gasses which it believed constituted an effective response to the threat of global warming; (2) that regulating greenhouse gasses might impair the president's ability to negotiate with "key developing nations" to reduce emissions; and (3) that curtailing motor vehicle emission would reflect "an inefficient, piecemeal approach to address the climate change issue."

The petitioners, joined by a number of states and local governments, sought review of the EPA's order in the United States Court of Appeals for the District of Columbia Circuit. Although each of the three judges on the panel wrote a separate opinion, two judges agreed that the EPA Administrator properly exercised his discretion under Section *202(a)(1)* in denying the petition for rule-making. The court therefore denied the petition for review. The Supreme Court granted a petition for certiorari and agreed to hear the case.

ISSUE

Does the EPA have the authority to regulate the emission of greenhouse gas emissions from motor vehicles?

DECISION

The Court held that the EPA had the legal authority in Section 202 of the Clean Air Act to regulate the emission of greenhouse gasses from motor vehicles since they clearly were air pollutants within the meaning of the act. The Court went on to say that if the EPA found that the

(continued)

emission of greenhouse gasses from motor vehicles might reasonably be anticipated to endanger human health or welfare, it was required to regulate emission of the pollutants from motor vehicles. It concluded that under the clear terms of the Clean Air Act, the EPA could avoid further action only if it determined that greenhouse gasses do not contribute to climate change or if it provided some reasonable explanation as to why it cannot or will not exercise its discretion to determine whether they do. The Court found that the reasons offered by the EPA as to why it chose not to regulate were not factors contemplated by the statute.

Following the decision of the Supreme Court in *Massachusetts v. EPA,* the EPA undertook a number of actions. It issued a formal "endangerment finding" and, as noted earlier in this chapter, proceeded to promulgate, in conjunction with the Department of Transportation, new emission standards for future motor vehicles that addressed both fuel economy and emissions of carbon dioxide. It also required large emitters of greenhouse gasses to report their annual emissions and announced that major emitters will have to address greenhouse gasses in the permits they obtain under the Clean Air Act. Because this is an evolving area, you and your instructor will need to be alert for further legislative and regulatory developments in this area.

E-Commerce

ONLINE PERMITTING

The Clean Air Act, the Clean Water Act, and the Resource Conservation and Recovery Act, as well as a number of other federal and local environmental laws, require certain businesses to obtain permits and to periodically report their discharges and/or other information to administrative agencies by filing permits or monitoring reports. Now the EPA and most, if not all, states make permit applications and motoring report forms available online. In addition, some states make specific companys' reports, or permit files, available to the public on their websites. Online permit and report transactions can streamline the process of complying with environmental law and regulations. Also, businesses can quickly access information on their competition's compliance with environmental standards by viewing, or ordering, their competitor's monitoring reports and permits on the Internet. Such information might provide insight into what materials another company is using in its processes—or how product volume may be changing over time. Moreover, the online permitting and reporting systems make environmental regulations more transparent, which helps ensure that businesses and regulatory agencies remain accountable to the public. (See, for example, http://www.epa.gov/airmarkets/arp/permits/index.html, http://www.in.gov/idem/air/permits/Air-Permits-Online/index.html.)

Water Pollution

LO4

Background

History is replete with plagues and epidemics brought on by poor sanitation and polluted water. Indeed, preventing waterborne disease has, through time, been the major reason for combating water pollution. In the early 1970s, fishing and swimming were prohibited in many bodies of water, game fish could no longer survive in some waters where they had formerly thrived, and Lake Erie was becoming choked with algae and was considered to be dying. The nation recognized that water pollution could affect public health, recreation, commercial fishing, agriculture, water supplies, and aesthetics. During the 1970s, Congress enacted three major statutes to deal with protecting our water resources: the Clean Water Act; the Marine Protection, Research, and Sanctuaries Act; and the Safe Drinking Water Act.

Early Federal Legislation

Federal water pollution legislation dates back to the 19th century when Congress enacted the River and Harbor Act of 1886. The act provided that in order to deposit or discharge "refuse" into a navigable waterway, a discharge permit had to be obtained from the Army Corps of Engineers. Under some contemporary court decisions, even hot water discharged from nuclear power plants has been considered "refuse." The permit system established pursuant to the "Refuse Act" was replaced in 1972 by a more comprehensive permit system administered by the EPA.

Clean Water Act

The 1972 amendments to the Federal Water Pollution Control Act (FWPCA)—known as the *Clean Water Act*—were as comprehensive in the water pollution field as the 1970 Clean Air Act was in the air pollution field. They proclaimed two general goals for this country: (1) to achieve wherever possible by July 1, 1983, water clean enough for swimming and other recreational uses and clean enough for the protection and propagation of fish, shellfish, and wildlife, and (2) by 1985 to have no discharges of pollutants into the nation's waters. The goals reflected a national frustration with the lack of progress in dealing with water pollution and a commitment to end such pollution. The new law set out a series of specific actions that federal, state, and local governments and industry were to take by certain dates and provided strong enforcement provisions to back up the deadlines. In 1977, and again in 1987, Congress enacted some modifications to the 1972 act that adjusted some of the deadlines and otherwise fine-tuned the act.

Under the Clean Water Act, the states have the primary responsibility for preventing, reducing, and eliminating water pollution, but the states have to do this within a national framework, with the EPA empowered to move in if the states do not fulfill their responsibilities.

Discharge Permits

The keystone of the Clean Water Act is a prohibition against persons discharging pollutants from "point sources" into "waters of the United States" except in compliance with the requirements of the act; these requirements normally include obtaining a permit from the federal or state government for the discharge. Thus, anyone who discharges industrial wastewater (wastewater that contains pollutants other than only domestic sewage such as wastes from bathrooms) from a point source (such as a pipe or ditch) into a river must obtain a **National Pollution Discharge Elimination System (NPDES) permit** from the state where the discharge takes place or from the EPA. Similarly, anyone who discharges wastewater other than just domestic sewage to a publicly owned treatment works (POTW) must obtain what is known as an industrial discharge permit from the local sewage treatment plant where the discharge is being sent or from the state.

Typically, these permits (1) establish limits on the concentration and amount of various pollutants that can be discharged and (2) require the discharger to keep records, to install equipment to monitor the discharges, and report the monitoring results to the state environmental agency. All of the permits contain limits established by the EPA in the form of **nationally applicable, technology-based effluent limits.** In the case of the industrial discharge permits, the limitations are known as **pretreatment standards** because they normally require the discharger to provide some on-site treatment of the wastewater before it enters the sewer system. For industries that discharge directly into rivers, the technology-based limits established by the EPA can be tightened if necessary to ensure that the water quality standards established by the state for that body of water are met and that the designated uses are protected.

Water Quality Standards

The act continued and expanded the previously established system of setting **water quality standards** that define the uses of specific bodies of water such as recreational water supply, public water supply, propagation of fish and wildlife, and agricultural and industrial water supply. Then, the maximum daily loads of various kinds of pollutants are set so that the water will be suitable for the designated type of use. The final step is to establish limits on the dischargers' pollutants so that the standards should be met.

Enforcement

Dischargers are also required to keep records, install and maintain monitoring equipment, and sample their discharges. Penalties for violating the law range from a minimum of $2,500 for a first offense up to $50,000 per day and two years in prison for subsequent violations. In *United States v. Hopkins,* which follows, a corporate vice president was convicted and sentenced to prison for his role in knowingly violating the Clean Water Act.

United States v. Hopkins

53 F.3d 533 (2d Cir. 1995)

FACTS

Spirol International Corporation is a manufacturer of metal shims and fasteners and is located in northeastern Connecticut. Spirol's manufacturing operation involves a zinc-based plating process that generates substantial amounts of wastewater containing zinc and other toxic materials; this wastewater is discharged into the nearby Five Mile River. The U.S. Environmental Protection Agency (EPA) has delegated to the state of Connecticut's Department of Environmental Protection (DEP) the authority to administer the Clean Water Act provisions applicable to Spirol's discharges into the river. In 1987, Spirol entered into a consent order with DEP requiring Spirol to pay a $30,000 fine for past violations and to comply in the future with discharge limitations specified in the order. In February 1989, DEP issued a modified "wastewater discharge permit" imposing more restrictive limits on the quantity of zinc and other substances that Spirol was permitted to release into the river.

From 1987 through September 6, 1990, Robert Hopkins was Spirol's vice president for manufacturing. Hopkins signed the 1987 consent decree on behalf of Spirol and had the corporate responsibility for ensuring compliance with the order and the DEP permit. The DEP permit required Spirol each week to collect a sample of its wastewater and send it to an independent laboratory by Friday morning of that week. Spirol was required to report the laboratory results to DEP in a discharge monitoring report once a month. Under the DEP permit, the concentrations of zinc in Spirol's wastewater were not to exceed 2.0 milligrams per liter in any weekly sample nor to average more that 1.0 milligram per liter in any month.

During the period March 1989 to September 1990, Spirol began its weekly sampling process on Monday. A composite sample was taken and analyzed in house. If it contained less than 1.0 milligram of zinc, it was sent to the independent laboratory with a "chain of custody" record signed by Hopkins. However, if it exceeded 1.0 milligram of zinc, it was discarded and another sample taken and tested the following day. In 54 of the 78 weeks, the samples were sent to the laboratory later than Tuesday. If the

(continued)

Wednesday sample also failed the in-house test, Hopkins would sometimes order that it be discarded and another taken on Thursday, but more often he instructed his subordinates doing the testing to dilute the sample with tap water or to reduce the zinc concentration using an ordinary coffee filter. Any Friday sample that failed the in-house test was always diluted or filtered so that a good sample could be sent to the laboratory by the Friday deadline. In some samples sent to the laboratory there was more tap water than wastewater.

During this period Hopkins filed with DEP monthly discharge monitoring reports consolidating the weekly tests from the independent laboratory. The reports showed no zinc concentrations above 1.0 milligram per liter. On each report, Hopkins signed the following certification:

> I certify under penalty of law that this document and all attachments were prepared under my direction or supervision in accordance with a system designed to assure that qualified personnel properly gather and evaluate the information submitted. Based on my inquiry of the person or persons who administer the system, or those persons directly responsible for gathering the information, the information is, to the best of my knowledge and belief, true, accurate and complete. I am aware that there are significant penalties for submitting false information, including the possibility of fine and imprisonment for knowing violations.

Contrary to Hopkins's certifications, his subordinates testified that he had caused the samples to be tampered with about 40 percent of the time. On some 25–30 occasions when he had been told that a satisfactory sample had finally been obtained by means of dilution or filtration, Hopkins responded, "I know nothing, I hear nothing." Hopkins was told that the testing procedures were improper, yet he continued to sign the certifications and Spirol continued its discharges into the river.

In December 1993, Hopkins was charged in a three-count indictment alleging (1) that he had knowingly falsified or tampered with Spirol's discharge sampling methods, (2) that he had knowingly violated the conditions of the permit, and (3) that he had conspired to commit those offenses. Hopkins was convicted following a jury trial and sentenced to 21 months in prison, with two years' probation following that, and a $7,500 fine. Hopkins appealed, arguing that the government should have been required to prove that he intended to violate the law and that he had specific knowledge of the particular statutory, regulatory, or permit requirements imposed under the Clean Water Act. The government contended that it was enough to prove that he had acted voluntarily or intentionally to falsify, tamper with, or render inaccurate a monitoring method—or to violate the permit—and that he did not do so by mistake, accident, or other innocent reason.

ISSUE

Could Hopkins be convicted of a knowing violation where it was shown he had acted intentionally to falsify the monitoring information and to violate the permit?

DECISION

Yes. A knowing violation of the Clean Water Act can be established by the intentional doing of certain acts, even though the actor is not aware of the precise proscription set out in the law.

Any citizen or group of citizens whose interests are adversely affected has the right to bring a court action against anyone violating an effluent standard or limitation or an order issued by the EPA or a state. Citizens also have the right to take court action against the EPA if it fails to carry out mandatory provisions of the law.

Wetlands

Another aspect of the Clean Water Act that has the potential to affect businesses as well as individual property owners involves the provisions concerning wetlands. Generally, wetlands are transition zones between land and open water. Under Section 404 of the act, any dredging or filling activity in a wetland that is part of the navigable waters of the United States requires a permit before the activity can be commenced. The permit program is administered by the Army Corps of Engineers with involvement of the Environmental Protection Agency.

As can be seen in *Bersani v. U.S. Environmental Protection Agency,* the permit requirement can limit a landowner's use of his property where the fill activity is viewed as injurious to the values protected by the act.

Ocean Dumping

LO5

The Marine Protection, Research, and Sanctuaries Act of 1972 set up a **permit system** regulating the dumping of all types of materials into ocean waters. The EPA has the responsibility for designating disposal sites and for establishing the rules governing ocean disposal. The Ocean Dumping Ban Act of 1987 required that all ocean dumping

Bersani v. U.S. Environmental Protection Agency

674 F. Supp. 405 (N.D. N.Y. 1987)

FACTS

Pyramid Companies was an association of partnerships in the business of developing, constructing, and operating shopping centers; John Bersani was a principal in one of the partnerships. In 1983, Pyramid became interested in developing a shopping mall in the Attleboro, Massachusetts, area and focused its attention on an 82-acre site located on an interstate highway in South Attleboro known as "Sweeden's Swamp."

The project contemplated altering or filling some 32 acres of the 49.6 acres of wetlands on the property. At the same time, Pyramid planned to excavate 9 acres of uplands (nonwetlands) to create new wetlands and to alter some 13 acres of existing wetlands to enhance their value for fish and wildlife.

In 1984, Pyramid applied to the U.S. Army Corps of Engineers for a permit under Section 404 of the Clean Water Act to do the dredge and fill work in the wetlands. As part of its application, it was required to submit information on practicable alternative sites for its shopping mall. One site that subsequently was focused on by the Corps and the Environmental Protection Agency was about three miles north in North Attleboro. Pyramid relied on several factors in claiming that the site was not a practicable alternative to its proposed site; namely, the site lacked sufficient traffic volume and access from local roads, potential department store tenants had expressed doubts about the feasibility of the site, and previous attempts to develop the site had met with strong resistance from the surrounding community. However, subsequent to the time Pyramid examined the site, another major developer of shopping centers had taken an option to acquire the property.

The New England Division Engineer of the Corps recommended that the permit be denied because a practicable alternative with a less adverse effect on the environment existed. The Chief of Engineers directed that the permit be issued, noting that the alternative site was not available to Pyramid since it was owned by a competitor and that even if it was considered available, Pyramid had made a convincing case that the site would not fulfill its objectives for a successful project. The EPA then exercised its prerogative under the Clean Water Act to veto the permit on the grounds that filling Sweeden's Swamp to build the shopping mall would have an unacceptable adverse effect on the environment. In its view, another less environmentally damaging site had been available to Pyramid at the time it made its site selection and thus any adverse effects on Sweeden's Swamp were avoidable. Bersani and Pyramid then brought suit challenging the denial of its permit application.

ISSUE

Should Pyramid be permitted to drain and fill a wetland if another less environmentally damaging site was available for the construction of a shopping center?

DECISION

No. The court noted that a shopping center is not water dependent and does not need to be located with access or proximity to a wetland or other aquatic body. Accordingly, practicable alternatives are presumed to be available that do not require the filling of a wetland. In order to overcome the presumption, an applicant must prove that no such alternative exists. Here, it was reasonable for the EPA to find that there was an alternative site available in the area for the construction of a shopping center and thus to deny Pyramid a permit to fill a wetland to construct its proposed shopping center.

of municipal sludge and industrial wastes be terminated by the end of 1991. Thus, the remaining questions of ocean dumping concern the disposal of dredge spoils to keep harbors open.

Liability for Oil Spills

In March 1989, the supertanker *Exxon Valdez* ran aground on a reef in Alaska's scenic Prince William Sound spilling 11 million gallons of crude oil in an environmentally sensitive area. The accident occurred after the tanker's captain, who had a history of alcohol abuse and a high-blood alcohol level 11 hours after the spill, inexplicitly exited the bridge, leaving a tricky course correction to unlicensed subordinates. The massive spill and the subsequent efforts to deal with its consequences focused attention on the then-current legal mechanisms for dealing with such spills. At that time, the liability for oil spills in U.S. waters was governed by a patchwork maze of five federal laws, three international conventions, private international agreements, and numerous state laws. In general, those laws and agreements were designed to limit the liability of ship owners in case of a major spill. One of those laws—the Limitation of Liability Act of 1851—limited the liability to the value of a ship after an accident occurred. Some of the laws focused on where the oil came from (e.g., a ship or the Trans-Alaska Pipeline) while others focused on where the oil was spilled (e.g., in a port or on the Outer-Continental Shelf).

Exxon spent an estimated $2.1 billion in cleanup costs, pled guilty to criminal violations that resulted in fines, settled a civil action by the United States and Alaska for some $900 million, and paid another $303 million in voluntary payments to private parties. A number of civil actions against Exxon and the captain seeking recovery for economic losses sustained as a result of the spill were consolidated into a single-lawsuit that found its way to the U.S. Supreme Court in 2008, some 19 years after the spill occurred. The issue in that case, *Exxon Shipping Co. v. Baker,* which follows, is whether the recovery was barred by the Clean Water Act and whether the multibillion dollar punitive damage award against Exxon was excessive as a matter of federal maritime law.

Following the Exxon disaster, Congress enacted the Oil Pollution Act of 1990. Among other things, the act created a $1 billion trust fund, the Oil Spill Liability Trust Fund, funded by a five-cent-per-barrel tax on oil to pay for cleanup costs in excess of the liability limit in the act. The act provides for fines of $1,000 for every barrel spilled with the amount increasing to $3,000 per barrel if negligence can be shown. Those entities found responsible for oil spills are liable for the costs of cleanup and for economic damages, such as those to fisheries, up to $75 million. However, that cap does not apply if the loss was proximately caused by gross negligence or willful misconduct or violation of a federal regulation. Moreover, it is important to note that the federal law does not preempt state laws which may provide for additional liability for such accidents.

The explosion and fire that led to the sinking of the Deepwater Horizon drilling rig in April 2010 that resulted in a massive oil spill in the Gulf of Mexico, with widespread damage to the coastal estuaries, fishing grounds, and economies of the region. In the wake of that accident and the investigations into the causes, we have seen considerable litigation as well as changes in the laws and regulations concerning offshore oil drilling.

Exxon Shipping Co. v. Baker

128 S. Ct. 2605 (2008)

FACTS

On March 24, 1989, the supertanker *Exxon Valdez* grounded on Bligh Reef off the Alaskan coast, fracturing its hull and spilling millions of gallons of crude oil into Prince William Sound. The tanker was over 900 feet long and was being used by Exxon to carry crude oil from the end of the Trans-Alaska Pipeline in Valdez, Alaska, to the lower 48 states. On the night of the spill it was carrying 53 million gallons of crude oil, or over a million barrels. Its captain, Joseph Hazelwood, had recently completed a 28-day alcohol treatment program while employed by Exxon but had dropped out of a prescribed follow-up program. Witnesses testified that before the ship left port on the night of the disaster, the captain downed at least five double vodkas in waterfront bars of Valdez, an intake of about 15 ounces of 80-proof alcohol. Eleven hours after the tanker hit the reef, his blood alcohol level was .061, three times the legal limit for driving in most states.

A state-licensed pilot guided the ship through the Valdez Narrows, and then two hours into the voyage the captain took command. However, just as the ship was about to execute a very difficult maneuver near a reef, the captain inexplicably left the deck and went to his cabin to "do paperwork." He was the only person on board licensed to maneuver the boat in this part of Prince William Sound. With an unlicensed pilot at the helm, the ship ran aground and split open, resulting in a spill of 11 million gallons of crude oil.

In addition to seeking cleanup costs from Exxon, the United States charged the company with criminal violations of the Clean Water Act, the Refuse Act of 1899, the Migratory Bird Treaty Act, the Ports and Waterways Safety Act, and the Dangerous Cargo Act. The company pled guilty to violations of the Clean Water Act, the Refuse Act, and the Migratory Bird Treaty Act, and agreed to pay a $150 million fine, later reduced to $25 million plus restitution of $100 million. A civil action brought by the United States and Alaska for environmental harms ended with a consent decree for Exxon to pay $900 million toward restoring natural resources, and it paid another $303 million in voluntary settlements with fishermen, property owners, and other private parties.

A number of other civil cases were consolidated into one case where the plaintiffs seeking damages were divided into three classes: commercial fishermen, Native Americans, and landowners. At Exxon's request, the court also certified a mandatory class of all plaintiffs seeking punitive damages, whose number topped 32,000. For the purposes of the case, Exxon stipulated to its negligence in the *Valdez* disaster and its ensuing liability for compensatory damages. The trial court divided the trial into several phases: Phase I considered Exxon's and the captain's recklessness and thus their potential for punitive damages; Phase II set compensatory damages for commercial fishermen and Native Americans; and Phase III determined the amount of punitive damages for which Exxon and the captain were each liable.

In Phase I, the judge instructed the jury that a corporation is responsible for the reckless acts of those employees who are employed in a managerial capacity while acting in the scope of their employment. Exxon did not dispute that the captain was a managerial employee under the definition of managerial employee used by the judge, and the jury found both the captain and Exxon reckless and thus potentially liable for punitive damages. In Phase II, the jury awarded $287 million in compensatory damages to the commercial fishermen, and the Native Americans settled their compensatory claims. In Phase III, the court instructed the jurors that the purpose of punitive damages was not to provide compensatory relief but rather to punish and deter the defendants. The court charged the jury to consider the reprehensibility of the defendant's conduct, their financial condition, the magnitude of the harm, and weigh mitigating facts. The jury awarded $5,000 in punitive damages against Hazelwood and $5 billion against Exxon.

The Ninth Circuit upheld the Phase I jury instructions on corporate liability for acts of managerial agents and, after twice remanding the case for adjustments to the amount of punitive damages, adjusted the award to $2.5 billion. The U.S. Supreme Court agreed to review the case to consider: (1) whether maritime law allows corporate liability for punitive damages on the basis of acts of managerial agents; (2) whether the Clean Water Act forecloses the award of punitive damages in maritime spill cases; and (3) whether the punitive damages awarded against Exxon were excessive as a matter of maritime common law.

ISSUE

Should the award of punitive damages against Exxon be upheld?

DECISION

The Supreme Court was equally divided on the question of whether the ship owner could be held vicariously liable for punitive damages so that determination by the Ninth Circuit was upheld. The Court then concluded that the penalties for pollution under the Clean Water Act did not displace compensatory and punitive remedies for the consequences of such pollution, including the economic harm suffered by the individuals. However, the Court went on to hold that punitive damages in a maritime tort case were not warranted in any amount greater than the amount of the compensatory damages (i.e., a 1:1 ratio of compensatory-to-punitive damages), and thus the punitive damage award here was excessive. Accordingly, the Court vacated the lower court judgment upholding the punitive damage award against Exxon and sent the case back to the lower court to adjust the award.

Drinking Water

In 1974 Congress passed, and in 1986 and again in 1996 it amended, the Safe Drinking Water Act, which was designed to protect and enhance the quality of our drinking water. Under the act, the EPA sets **primary drinking water standards,** which provide minimum levels of quality for water to be used for human consumption. The standards must be met by "public water systems" and apply at the point the drinking water enters the water distribution system. A public water system is defined to include any supplier of water to the public that has 15 or more service connections or serves 25 people or more at least 660 days a year. Thus, the standards are applicable to private water suppliers as well as municipalities that provide water to their citizens and can be applied to a trailer park that has a well providing water to more than 15 trailers in the park.

The act also establishes a program governing the injection of wastes into wells. The primary responsibility for complying with the federally established standards lies with the states. Where the states fail to enforce the drinking water standards, the federal government has the right to enforce them.

Global Business Environment

International Voluntary Consensus Standards and Certification: ISO 14000 Environmental Management Standards

Today, national and international companies competing in a global economy face a daunting array of challenges, including complying with increasingly complex environmental regulations in those countries in which they operate or do business. Also, differing national standards can not only create nontariff trade barriers but also increase costs and the difficulty of doing business. Managers who want to be proactive in systematically improving the environmental performance of their organization can adopt and follow the ISO 14000 series of environmental management standards.

The ISO, located in Geneva, Switzerland, was founded in 1947 to promote the development of international manufacturing, trade, and communication standards. The ISO standards—which are international voluntary consensus standards—are developed with input from industry, government, and other interested parties. The standards have legal standing only if actually adopted by a country, but they have been utilized by many organizations on a voluntary basis. In addition to the performance enhancement that can be obtained by following the standards, in some instances certification of compliance with the standards can lead to competitive advantages and/or may be necessary to do certain types of business.

The most prominent of the ISO standards is the worldwide quality standard, ISO 9000. It provides organizations with a process for producing quality products through a systems approach that involves all phases of production. You may have encountered these standards in other business school classes. They have been adopted by many countries and utilized by many organizations—and more than 100,000 ISO 9000 certificates have been issued worldwide.

Development of the ISO 14000 series of standards began in 1993, and the initial set of standards was finalized in 1996. These include (1) ISO 14001 Environmental management systems—specification with guidance for use; (2) ISO 14004 Environmental management systems—general guidelines on principles, systems, and supporting techniques; (3) ISO 14010 Guidelines for environmental auditing—general principles; (4) ISO 14011 Guidelines for environmental auditing—audit procedures—Part 1: Auditing of environmental management programs; (5) ISO Guidelines for environmental auditing—qualification criteria for environmental auditors; (6) ISO 14024 Environmental labeling—guidance principles, practices, and criteria for multiple criteria-based practitioner programs (Type 1)—guide for certification procedures; (7) ISO 14040 Life cycle assessment—principles and guidelines; and (8) ISO Guide for the inclusion of environmental aspects in product standards.

Organizations can be certified that they comply with ISO 14001. Certification is a procedure by which a third party gives written assurance that a product, process, or service conforms to the specific requirements of the ISO standard. An organization that obtains ISO certification can claim that it has an environmental management system (EMS) meeting the ISO standards that has been implemented and is being consistently followed. This certification would be based on an audit of the EMS system by the third-party certifier. It should be noted that the certification goes to the nature of the management system employed by the organization—and does not give it a basis for claiming that its products or services are environmentally superior to those of other organizations. However, such certification can be either a matter of competitive advantage or of necessity as some companies will do business only with ISO-certified entities. In the United States, the American National Standards Institute (ANSI) is the organization responsible for certifying that an organization meets the requirements of ISO 14001.

Waste Disposal

Background

Historically, concern about the environment focused on air and water pollution as well as the protection of natural resources and wildlife. Relatively little attention was paid to the disposal of wastes on land. When the EPA was formed, much of the solid and hazardous waste generated was being disposed of in open dumps and landfills. While some of the waste we produce can be disposed of without presenting significant health or environmental problems, some industrial, agricultural, and mining wastes, and even some household wastes, are hazardous and can present serious problems. Unless wastes are properly disposed of, they can cause air, water, and land pollution as well as contamination of the underground aquifers from which much of our drinking water is drawn. Once aquifers have been contaminated, it can take them a very long time to cleanse themselves of pollutants.

In the 1970s, the discovery of abandoned dump sites such as Love Canal in New York and the "Valley of the Drums" in Kentucky heightened public concern about the disposal of toxic and hazardous wastes. Congress has enacted several laws regulating the generation and disposal of hazardous waste. The Resource Conservation and Recovery Act is aimed at the proper management and disposal of wastes that are being generated currently. The Comprehensive Environmental Response, Compensation, and Liability Act focuses on the cleanup of past disposal sites that threaten public health and the environment.

The Resource Conservation and Recovery Act

LO6

The Resource Conservation and Recovery Act (RCRA) was originally enacted in 1976 and significantly amended in 1984. It provides the federal government and the states with the authority to regulate facilities that *generate, treat, store, and dispose of hazardous waste.* Most of the wastes defined as *hazardous* are subject to a "cradle to the grave" tracking system and must be handled and disposed of in defined ways.

RCRA requires persons who generate, treat, store, or transport specified quantities of hazardous waste to notify the EPA of that fact, to obtain an ID number that must be placed on a manifest that accompanies all shipments, to meet certain standards, to follow specified procedures in the handling of the wastes, to keep records. Those who treat, store, or dispose of hazardous wastes must obtain permits. See Figure 47.1 for a sample of the form that must accompany all shipments of hazardous waste from point of generation until its final treatment or disposal.

FIGURE 47.1 Sample Uniform Hazardous Waste Manifest Form*

Please print or type. (Form designed for use on elite (12-pitch) typewriter.)

Form Approved. OMB No. 2050-0039

VOID

GENERATOR

UNIFORM HAZARDOUS WASTE MANIFEST	1. Generator ID Number	2. Page 1 of	3. Emergency Response Phone	4. Manifest Tracking Number

5. Generator's Name and Mailing Address — Generator's Site Address (if different than mailing address)

Generator's Phone:

6. Transporter 1 Company Name — U.S. EPA ID Number

7. Transporter 2 Company Name — U.S. EPA ID Number

8. Designated Facility Name and Site Address — U.S. EPA ID Number

Facility's Phone:

9a. HM	9b. U.S. DOT Description (including Proper Shipping Name, Hazard Class, ID Number, and Packing Group (if any))	10. Containers No.	10. Containers Type	11. Total Quantity	12. Unit Wt./Vol.	13. Waste Codes
	1.					
	2.					
	3.					
	4.					

14. Special Handling Instructions and Additional Information

15. GENERATOR'S/OFFEROR'S CERTIFICATION: I hereby declare that the contents of this consignment are fully and accurately described above by the proper shipping name, and are classified, packaged, marked and labeled/placarded, and are in all respects in proper condition for transport according to applicable international and national governmental regulations. If export shipment and I am the Primary Exporter, I certify that the contents of this consignment conform to the terms of the attached EPA Acknowledgement of Consent.
I certify that the waste minimization statement identified in 40 CFR 262.27(a) (if I am a large quantity generator) or (b) (if I am a small quantity generator) is true.

Generator's/Offeror's Printed/Typed Name — Signature — Month Day Year

INT'L

16. International Shipments ☐ Import to U.S. ☐ Export from U.S. Port of entry/exit: ______
Transporter signature (for exports only): Date leaving U.S.:

TRANSPORTER

17. Transporter Acknowledgment of Receipt of Materials

Transporter 1 Printed/Typed Name — Signature — Month Day Year

Transporter 2 Printed/Typed Name — Signature — Month Day Year

DESIGNATED FACILITY

18. Discrepancy

18a. Discrepancy Indication Space ☐ Quantity ☐ Type ☐ Residue ☐ Partial Rejection ☐ Full Rejection

Manifest Reference Number:

18b. Alternate Facility (or Generator) — U.S. EPA ID Number

Facility's Phone:

18c. Signature of Alternate Facility (or Generator) — Month Day Year

19. Hazardous Waste Report Management Method Codes (i.e., codes for hazardous waste treatment, disposal, and recycling systems)

1.	2.	3.	4.

20. Designated Facility Owner or Operator: Certification of receipt of hazardous materials covered by the manifest except as noted in Item 18a

Printed/Typed Name — Signature — Month Day Year

EPA Form 8700-22 (Rev. 3-05) Previous editions are obsolete.

DESIGNATED FACILITY TO DESTINATION STATE (IF REQUIRED)

In addition, operators of land disposal facilities must meet financial responsibility requirements and monitor groundwater quality. The EPA determines whether certain kinds of wastes should be banned entirely from land disposal unless treated first.

Underground Storage Tanks

In 1984, Congress directed that the EPA also regulate underground product storage tanks such as gasoline tanks to prevent and respond to leaks from them that might contaminate underground water. Subsequently, owners of tanks have had to upgrade or replace them with tanks that are corrosion resistant and have the capacity to be monitored for leaks.

State Responsibilities

The EPA sets minimum requirements for a state RCRA program and then delegates the responsibility for conducting the program to the states when they have the legal ability and interest to administer it. Until a state assumes partial or complete responsibility for an RCRA program, the federal government administers the program.

Enforcement

Failure to comply with the hazardous waste regulations promulgated under RCRA can subject the violator to civil and criminal penalties. In *United States v. Southern Union Co.* which follows, an employee of a company that disposed of hazardous waste without an RCRA permit was held criminally liable.

United States v. Southern Union Co.

643 F.Supp.2d 201 (U.S.D.C., C. R. I. 2009)

FACTS

Southern Union Company is a Delaware corporation, based in Texas and primarily engaged in the business of transporting and distributing natural gas. In 2000, Southern Union acquired several separate gas companies in Rhode Island and Massachusetts, consolidated those companies, and formed the New England Gas Company (NEGC). Through NEGC, Southern Union supplied natural gas to Rhode Island and parts of Southeastern Massachusetts. In connection with this business it owned a vacated, dilapidated, and frequently vandalized facility at the end of Tidewater Street in Pawtucket, Rhode Island. Located along the Seekonk River, the Tidewater facility consisted of several buildings and two unused natural gas storage tanks.

After forming NEG in June 2001, Southern Union started a mercury reclamation program at Tidewater known as the Mercury-Sealed Regulator Removal Program. Prior to the 1960s, many of the homes in the NEGC service area used gas meters that operated with mercury-sealed regulators, or MSRs. Recognizing that mercury is a dangerous substance, Southern Union began a program by which workers went to customers' homes and replaced MSRs with nonmercury regulators. The work crews would then transport the MSRs and any recovered liquid mercury to the Tidewater facility. There, it employed an environmental services company, International Environmental Trading Company, Inc. (IETC), to pour off the liquid mercury from inside the regulators into special containers that were shipped to a reclamation facility in Pennsylvania. The MSR housings were decontaminated through a rinsing process, and IETC also ensured that all mercury contaminated rags, protective clothing, and cleaning agents were properly disposed.

In November 2001, Southern Union stopped removing MSRs from customers' homes, but kept IETC at the Tidewater site to finish processing the remaining MSRs through the end of the year. In the spring of 2002, Southern Union again began removing MSRs from customers' homes; however, it did not recontract with IETC to ensure the proper reclamation of the liquid mercury. Instead, it stored the MSRs removed from customers' homes in one of the vacant buildings at the Tidewater facility. To prevent the spillage of liquid mercury into the environment, Southern Union

(continued)

double-bagged each MSR in heavy duty plastic bags and then piled those bags in plastic kiddie swimming pools. Liquid mercury that was spilt during the removal process was kept in assorted containers (i.e., paint cans, plastic jugs, glass bottles, etc.) and stored inside the building in a plywood cabinet secured by a hasp and padlock.

Southern Union accumulated MSRs and liquid mercury at the Tidewater facility over the course of 2002, 2003, and 2004. Despite drafting several requests for proposals to solicit bids from contractors to dispose of the liquid mercury, it did not restart the reclamation component to the MSR Removal Program.

Throughout this time period, the Tidewater facility (including the mercury storage building) was in a state of utter disrepair and Southern Union was aware of the shoddy security conditions. Although it periodically stationed a security guard at the facility, graffiti covered the building, the doors and windows were broken, the perimeter security fencing contained numerous gaps, and the site was subject to repeated break-ins and had become the periodic home to several homeless people.

In September 2004, three youths broke into the mercury storage building. Once inside, they removed several containers of waste liquid mercury and proceeded to spill the mercury throughout the building and the outside grounds. The vandals also brought some of the liquid mercury to a nearby residential apartment complex where they littered it in and around the parking lots and outdoor common areas.

The spilled liquid mercury lay undiscovered on the Tidewater property for approximately three weeks. On October 19, 2004, an employee discovered the spill and a cleanup was conducted. The ensuing investigation then led to the discovery of the second spill at the apartment complex.

The United States charged Southern Union in a three-count criminal indictment with, among other things, violating the Resource Conservation and Recovery Act (RCRA) by storing a hazardous waste (i.e. liquid mercury) without a permit. Southern Union took the position that the material was not a waste because it intended to recycle it. Following a jury trial, the jury rendered a verdict that the company was guilty of storing hazardous waste without the required permit. Southern Union appealed, seeking a new trial.

ISSUE

Should the court sustain the jury's finding that Southern Union stored a hazardous waste without the required storage permit?

DECISION

Yes. The court began by noting that Congress enacted RCRA to address the nation's problems with hazardous waste disposal. The intent behind RCRA is to facilitate the safe management of hazardous waste from the time it is generated to its ultimate disposal, to protect human health and the environment from the dangers of hazardous waste, and to encourage the conservation and recovery of natural resources.

A key feature of RCRA is that the Federal Government, namely the U.S. Environmental Protection Agency, may authorize states to enact their own hazardous waste management programs. Once authorized, a state's program effectively supplants the federal regulations and operates "in lieu of" the federal program as long as the state's regulations are "equivalent to" and "consistent with" the federal hazardous waste management regulations. In developing their own programs, states may add to the federally mandated requirements and may impose requirements that are "more stringent" than the federal counterpart, but not less. In effect, the federal regulatory scheme establishes a uniform baseline standard. The Federal Government retains authority to enforce an authorized state program and may criminally prosecute violations of state hazardous waste management regulations.

The court noted that a key question at trial was whether the liquid mercury was a waste (as claimed by the government) or a "commercial chemical product" (as claimed by Southern Union). At the heart of this dispute was what, if anything, Southern Union intended to do with the mercury (nothing said the government; recycle it, said Southern Union). Southern Union claimed the jury could not have found the mercury was a waste because the evidence "clearly" showed it could be poured and was at least 99 percent pure mercury. And, it argued, employee testimony, contemporaneous documents, and company actions all demonstrated an intent to recycle.

The court observed that evidence presented to the jury was such that reasonable minds could differ. As to whether the mercury was "pure," the government showed some degree of contamination and established that some degree of reprocessing would have been necessary to make this mercury truly a pure commercial grade.

The more important point was the Southern Union's intent. Here, the jury sided with the government as to what the evidence showed: that the company did not intend to recycle and stored the mercury at Tidewater in lieu of disposal. There was more than ample evidence to support the jury's conclusion; for example, the storage and security conditions at Tidewater, the employee testimony that items were stored at Tidewater "instead of" throwing them away, and numerous references in company documents to the mercury as "waste" and to Tidewater as a "disposal area."

Accordingly, the court denied Southern Union's motion for a new trial.

Solid Waste

Mining, commercial, and household activity generate a large volume of waste material that can present problems if it is not disposed of properly. As population density has increased, also increasing the total volume of waste, it has become more difficult to find places where the waste material can be disposed of on land or incinerated. RCRA authorized the EPA to set minimum standards for such disposal, but states and local government bear the primary responsibility for the siting and regulation of such activity.

As the cost and difficulty of disposing of wastes increase, attention is focused on reducing the amount of waste to be disposed of, on looking for opportunities to recycle some of the material in the waste stream, and on changing the characteristics of the material that must ultimately be disposed of so that it poses fewer environmental problems. One of the significant challenges faced by tomorrow's businessperson will be in designing products, packaging, and production processes so as to minimize the waste products that result.

A significant problem for both government and industry is the difficulty in trying to site new waste facilities. The NIMBY, or not-in-my-backyard, syndrome is pervasive as people almost universally desire to have the wastes from their everyday lives and from the economic activity in their community disposed of in someone else's neighborhood—any place but their own. As governments try to cope with the reality of finding places to dispose of wastes in an environmentally safe manner and at the same time cope with public opposition to siting new facilities, the temptation is strong to try to bar wastes from other areas from being disposed of in local facilities.

In the landmark case of *City of Philadelphia v. New Jersey,* the U.S. Supreme Court struck down an attempt by the state of New Jersey to prohibit the importation of most solid waste originating outside the state on the grounds that it violated the Commerce Clause of the United States Constitution. In recent years the Supreme Court has had the occasion to reiterate its holding in *City of Philadelphia v. New Jersey* in a series of new cases involving efforts by states to block or limit the flow of solid and hazardous waste from outside their state to disposal sites within the state.

Superfund

LO7

In 1980, Congress passed the Comprehensive Environmental Response, Compensation, and Liability Act (CERCLA), commonly known as "Superfund," to deal with the problem of *uncontrolled or abandoned hazardous waste sites.* In 1986, it strengthened and expanded the law. Under the Superfund law, the EPA is required to identify and assess the sites in the United States where hazardous wastes had been spilled, stored, or abandoned.

The EPA has now identified more than 30,000 such sites. The sites are ranked on the basis of the type, quantity, and toxicity of the wastes; the number of people potentially exposed to the wastes; the different ways (e.g., air or drinking water) in which they might be exposed; the risks to contamination of aquifers; and other factors. The sites with the highest ranking are placed on the National Priority List to receive priority federal and/or state attention for cleanup. These sites are subjected to a careful scientific and engineering study to determine the most appropriate cleanup plan. Once a site has been cleaned up, the state is responsible for managing it to prevent future environmental problems. The EPA also has the authority to quickly initiate actions at hazardous waste sites—whether or not the site is on the priority list—to address *imminent hazards* such as the risk of fire, explosion, or contamination of drinking water.

The cleanup activity was initially financed by a tax on chemicals and feedstocks, but Congress has suspended the imposition of the tax. However, the EPA has the authority to require that a site be cleaned up by those persons who were responsible for it, either as the owner or operator of the site, a transporter of wastes to the site, or the owner of wastes deposited at the site. Where the EPA expends money to clean up a site, it has the legal authority to recover its costs from those who were responsible for the problem. The courts have held that such persons are *jointly and severally* responsible for the cost of cleanup. The concept of joint liability is discussed in Chapter 7. The concept of joint and several liability is of concern to many businesspeople because this stringent and potentially very expensive liability can in some instances be imposed on a current owner who had nothing to do with the contamination, such as a subsequent purchaser of the property.

In the case that follows, *United States v. Domenic Lombardi Realty,* a subsequent purchaser was held liable for cleaning up a property that had been contaminated by the actions of its predecessor in title.

United States v. Domenic Lombardi Realty

290 F.Supp.2d 198 (D. R.I. 2003)

FACTS

During the early 1980s Armand Allen acquired 31 acres of property located off of Robin Hollow Road in West Greenwich, Rhode Island. Allen began construction of a home on the property, but never completed the structure. Allen, along with his wife, lived in a 60-foot trailer on the site. Although he never obtained the licenses required to operate a junkyard, Allen stored a number of junk cars and trucks in various states of disrepair on the property. The town of West Greenwich denied Allen's multiple applications for a junkyard license but never ordered him to clean up his property.

In the fall of 1986 Domenic Lombardi, an employee of Lombardi Realty, approached Allen regarding a "For Sale" sign that was posted at the site. Allen indicated that his price for the property was $135,000, but that he was willing to drop the price to $85,000 in order to make a quick sale. Lombardi later testified that while he was on the property, he noticed stripped down cars and trucks as well as other solid waste. Lombardi instructed his real estate agent, Ray Walsh, to make an offer on the property of $85,000, which Allen immediately accepted on December 11, 1986.

Lombardi testified that Allen informed him that at one time he stripped electrical transformers on the site to recover copper from them. He also had a witness who claimed he had taken a load of transformers to the site sometime between 1982 and 1986; this witness was a convicted felon with a history of lying in court. Moreover, this testimony was contradicted by Allen's wife that she never saw any transformers brought on site.

Walsh testified that in preparation for the purchase, he obtained a plat map from the city in order to estimate the future assessment of taxes that Lombardi would incur, but he did not perform any additional background investigation, such as an environmental assessment or a walk around the property, nor did he contact authorities concerning the prior use of the property.

After the purchase, Lombardi completed work on the partially constructed, single-family home. He also began renting out the trailer. The tenant testified that within a few months after she began renting the trailer, she saw transformers among the solid waste debris on the property. Other neighbors testified that they witnessed Lombardi Realty trucks dumping trash, including electrical transformers, on the site.

In November 1987, the Rhode Island Department of Environmental Management (RIDEM), believing that Lombardi Realty was permitting the property to be used for the disposal of solid waste without a permit, issued Lombardi Realty a notice of violation and ordered it to remove all solid waste that had been disposed of at the site. Subsequently, RIDEM discovered the presence at the site of oil that contained PCBs. RIDEM ordered Lombardi, among other things, to submit and implement a sampling plan, to contract for the removal of all hazardous wastes from the site, and to submit and implement a cleanup plan. Lombardi Realty did not comply with any of the orders until 1989 when it arranged for the excavation of some of the PCB-contaminated soil, which was put in uncovered piles on the site.

In 1991, John Lombardi became president of Lombardi Realty after Domenic was sent to prison for the arson of the trailer on the site. John Lombardi knew little about the seriousness of the contamination on the site prior to becoming president, never having been informed about it by his father. The information withheld included the fact that children were using the piles as ramps for their dirt bikes.

(continued)

United States v. Domenic Lombardi Realty *(concluded)*

In November 1994, the EPA became involved at the request of RIDEM. From February though July 1995, the EPA removed the contaminated soil from the site and replaced it with clean backfill. In total, the EPA excavated about 900 tons of soil. The EPA then initiated an action against Lombardi Realty to recover the $481,068 "response costs" incurred in removing the hazardous substances from the site. Lombardi asserted that it was an "innocent landowner" and that it should not be liable for the response costs.

ISSUE

Can Lombardi Realty avoid liability for the response costs incurred by the EPA in cleaning up the hazardous waste on the grounds that Lombardi Realty was an "innocent purchaser" of contaminated property?

DECISION

No. Initially the court noted that the Comprehensive Environmental Response, Compensation, and Liability Act (CERCLA) provides the EPA with a mechanism to compel parties associated with contaminated property to clean up, or pay for the cleanup, of the contaminated property. In order for the EPA to successfully pursue its CERCLA claim against Lombardi Realty, it must prove that (1) a release or threatened release of hazardous substances has occurred (2) at a facility (3) causing the EPA to incur response costs, and that Lombardi Realty is a responsible party as defined in the act (which includes the current owner or operator of the contaminated property). The EPA has established these elements, so unless Lombardi can take advantage of one of CERCLA's affirmative defenses, it will be liable for the cleanup costs incurred by the EPA.

The affirmative defense asserted here is the innocent landowner defense. Congress provided an affirmative defense for landowners who, innocently and in good faith, purchase property without knowledge that a predecessor in the chain of title had allowed hazardous substances to be disposed of on the property. The innocent landowner defense provides a statutory defense to liability where the release of hazardous substances was due to "an act or omission of a third party other than an employee or agent of the defendant, or other than one whose act or omission occurs in connection with a contractual relationship, existing directly or indirectly, with the defendant." In order to assert this defense, a party must demonstrate that (1) the contamination occurred prior to the defendant's purchase of the property; (2) the defendant had no reason to know that the property was contaminated; (3) the defendant took all appropriate inquiry into the previous ownership and uses of the property in accordance with generally accepted good commercial and customary standards and practices; and (4) once the contamination was discovered, the defendant took reasonable steps to stop any continuing release, prevent any future release, and prevent or limit exposure to any previously released hazardous substance.

Here, Lombardi was unable to establish that any contamination and subsequent release was caused solely by the act or omission of a third party. Moreover, it did not make any environmental assessment or other meaningful inquiry into the site's environmental state, including all appropriate inquiries into the prior use of the site. Lombardi also failed to establish that it had taken due care with respect to the PCB-contaminated soil as, among other things, it stored the excavated soil in an uncovered state.

Community Right to Know and Emergency Cleanup

As part of its 1986 amendments to Superfund, Congress enacted a series of requirements for emergency planning, notification of spills and accidents involving hazardous materials, disclosure by industry to the community of the presence of certain listed chemicals, and notification of the amounts of various chemicals being routinely released into the environment in the area of a facility. This legislation was in response to the accident at Bhopal, India, in 1984 and to several industrial accidents in the United States.

Firms subject to the requirements have to carefully plan how they will communicate with the surrounding community what chemicals are being regularly released and what precautions the facility has taken to protect the community from regular or accidental releases. Mindful of the difficulty of explaining to a community why large emissions of hazardous substances are taking place, a significant number of companies have undertaken to reduce those emissions below levels they are currently required to meet by law.

Concept Summary: Major Environmental Laws

Act	Focus
National Environmental Policy Act	Requires that federal agencies prepare an environmental impact statement in connection with every major federal action significantly affecting the environment.
Clean Air Act	Protects quality of ambient (outdoor) air through national ambient air quality standards, state implementation plans, control of hazardous air pollutants, new source performance standards, and controls on automobiles and fuels.
Clean Water Act	Protects and enhances quality of surface waters by setting water quality standards and limiting discharges by industry and municipalities to those waters through permit system; also regulates dredging and filling of wetlands.
Marine Protection, Research, and Sanctuaries Act	Regulates dumping of all types of material into ocean waters.
Safe Drinking Water Act	Protects and enhances quality of our drinking water. Also regulates disposal of wastes in wells.
Resource Conservation and Recovery Act (RCRA)	Establishes a cradle-to-the-grave regulatory system for handling and disposal of hazardous wastes; also deals with solid waste.
Comprehensive Environmental Response, Compensation, and Liability Act (CERCLA, commonly known as "Superfund")	Provides a program to deal with hazardous waste that was inadequately disposed of in the past; financed in part by tax on chemicals and feedstocks.

Ethics in Action

Suppose that a multinational chemical company with its primary manufacturing facilities in the United States plans to build a manufacturing facility in a developing country where there are few, if any, real state-imposed environmental regulations. Is it sufficient for the company to simply meet the environmental requirements of the host country? Is there any ethical obligation to do more—for example, to build the facility to meet the requirements it would have to meet in this country?

Questions and Problem Cases

1. In August 1986, Tzavah Urban Renewal Corporation purchased from the city of Newark a building formerly known as the Old Military Park Hotel. While the buyer was given an opportunity to inspect the building, it was not informed by the city that the building was permeated with asbestos-containing material. At the time of the purchase, the building was in great disrepair and had been uninhabited for many years. Its proposed renovation was to be a major urban renewal project. In June 1987, Tzavah contracted with Greer Industrial Corporation to "gut" the building. While the work was going on, an EPA inspector visited the site and concluded that the hotel was

contaminated with asbestos. He observed Greer employees throwing asbestos-laced objects out of the windows of the building and noted an uncovered refuse pile next to the hotel that contained asbestos. The workers were not wetting the debris before heaving it out the windows, and the refuse pile was also dry. As a result, asbestos dust was being released into the air. Although the hotel was located in a commercial district, there were private homes nearby. Renovation of buildings contaminated with asbestos is regulated under the Clean Air Act. The EPA regulations require building owners or operators to notify the EPA before commencing renovation or demolition and prescribe various procedures for storage and removal of the asbestos. Tzavah failed to provide the required notice or to comply with procedures required. After being notified by the EPA of the violation of the law, Tzavah stopped the demolition work, left the building unsecured, and left the waste piles dry and uncovered. The EPA tried informally to get Tzavah to complete the work in accordance with the asbestos regulations; when Tzavah did not take action, the EPA brought a lawsuit against Tzavah to do so. Should the court issue an injunction requiring Tzavah to abate the hazard posed by the dry asbestos remaining in the hotel?

2. In July, Vanguard Corporation began operating a metal furniture manufacturing plant in Brooklyn, New York. The plant is located in an area that has not attained the national ambient air quality standards for ozone. The plant is a major stationary source (i.e., has the potential to emit more than 100 tons a year) of volatile organic compounds that contribute to the formation of ozone in the atmosphere. The New York State implementation plan (SIP) requires that metal-coating facilities use paint that contains less than 3 pounds of organic solvent (minus water) per gallon at the time of coating. On August 24, the EPA notified Vanguard that it was not in compliance with the SIP provision concerning coatings and issued it a notice of violation. Vanguard sought to defend against the notice of violation on the grounds that it had used its best faith efforts to comply but that it was technologically and economically infeasible. It indicated that it wanted 18 more months to come into compliance. Should Vanguard be held to be in violation of the Clean Air Act?
3. Charles Hanson owned land abutting Keith Lake, a freshwater lake that was subject to some tidal flooding as a result of its connection with tidal waters. In order to minimize the detrimental effects from the tidal activities and consequent flooding, Hanson deposited a large quantity of dirt, rock, bricks, sheet metal, and other debris along the shoreline of his property. He did so without obtaining a permit from the U.S. Army Corps of Engineers under Section 404 of the Clean Water Act, which controls dumping and filling activities in navigable waters of the United States. Under the law, discharges of pollutants into navigable waters without a permit are forbidden. The term *pollutant* is defined to include "dredged spoil, solid waste, incinerator residue, sewage, garbage, sewage sludge, munitions, chemical wastes, biological materials, radioactive materials, heat, wrecked or discarded equipment, rock, sand, cellar dirt, and industrial, municipal and agricultural waste discharged into water." The EPA brought an enforcement action against Hanson claiming he had violated the Clean Water Act. Should the court find that Hanson violated the act?
4. Mall Properties, Inc., was an organization that for many years had sought to develop a shopping mall in the town of North Haven, Connecticut, a suburb of New Haven. Because the proposed development would require the filling of some wetlands, Mall Properties was required to obtain a permit from the Corps of Engineers pursuant to Section 404 of the Clean Water Act. The City of New Haven opposed development of the mall—and the granting of the permit—on the grounds it would jeopardize the fragile economy of New Haven. The Corps of Engineers found the net loss of wetlands

would be substantially compensated for by a proposed on-site wetland creation. Relying primarily on the socioeconomic concerns of the City of New Haven, the district engineer rejected the proposed permit. Mall Properties then brought suit against the Corps of Engineers, claiming that the decision was arbitrary and capricious. Should the district engineer have relied on socioeconomic factors unrelated to the project's environmental impacts in making a decision on the permit?

5. Johnson & Towers, Inc., is in the business of overhauling large motor vehicles. It uses degreasers and other industrial chemicals that contain chemicals classified as "hazardous wastes" under the Resource Conservation and Recovery Act (RCRA), such as methylene chloride and trichloroethylene. For some period of time, waste chemicals from cleaning operations were drained into a holding tank and, when the tank was full, pumped into a trench. The trench flowed from the plant property into Parker's Creek, a tributary of the Delaware River. Under RCRA, generators of such wastes must obtain a permit for disposal from the Environmental Protection Agency (EPA). The EPA had neither issued nor received an application for a permit for the Johnson & Towers operations. Over a three-day period, federal agents saw workers pump waste from the tank into the trench, and on the third day toxic chemicals flowed into the creek. The company and two of its employees, Jack Hopkins, a foreman, and Peter Angel, the service manager, were indicted for unlawfully disposing of hazardous wastes. The company pled guilty. The federal district court dismissed the criminal charges against the two individuals, holding that RCRA's criminal penalty provisions imposing fines and imprisonment did not apply to employees. The government appealed. Can employees of a corporation be held criminally liable if their actions on behalf of the corporation violate the federal hazardous waste law?
6. The Royal McBee Corporation manufactured typewriters at a factory in Springfield, Missouri. As a part of the manufacturing process, Royal McBee generated cyanide-based electroplating wastes, sludge from the bottom of electroplating tanks, and spent plating bath solution. As a part of their duties, Royal McBee employees dumped the wastes onto the surface of the soil on a vacant lot adjoining the factory. This took place between 1959 and 1962. Over time, the waste materials migrated outward and downward from the original dumping site, contaminating a large area. In 1970, the manufacturing facility and lot were sold to General Electric, which operated the plant but did not engage in any dumping of wastes on the vacant lot. In the mid-1980s, General Electric was required by the EPA and the state of Missouri, under the authority of the federal Superfund law, to clean up the contamination at the site. General Electric then brought a lawsuit against the successor corporation of Royal McBee's typewriter business, Litton Business Systems, to recover for the costs it incurred in cleaning up the site. Under the Superfund law, "any person who at the time of disposal of any hazardous substance owned or operated any facilities at which such hazardous substances were disposed of, shall be liable for any other necessary costs of response incurred by any other person" consistent with the Superfund law and regulations. Is General Electric entitled to recover its cleanup costs from Litton?

Appendixes

A. The Constitution of the United States of America
B. Glossary of Legal Terms and Definitions
C. Spanish–English Equivalents for Important Legal Terms

Appendix A

The Constitution of the United States of America

Preamble

We the People of the United States, in Order to form a more perfect Union, establish Justice, insure domestic Tranquility, provide for the common defense, promote the general Welfare, and secure the Blessings of Liberty to ourselves and our Posterity, do ordain and establish this Constitution for the United States of America.

Article I

Section 1

All legislative Powers herein granted shall be vested in a Congress of the United States, which shall consist of a Senate and House of Representatives.

Section 2

The House of Representatives shall be composed of Members chosen every second Year by the People of the several States, and the Electors in each State shall have the Qualifications requisite for Electors of the most numerous Branch of the State Legislature.

No Person shall be a Representative who shall not have attained to the age of twenty five Years, and been seven Years a Citizen of the United States, and who shall not, when elected, be an Inhabitant of that State in which he shall be chosen.

Representatives and direct Taxes shall be apportioned among the several States which may be included within this Union, according to their respective Numbers, which shall be determined by adding to the whole Number of free Persons, including those bound to Service for a Term of Years, and excluding Indians not taxed, three fifths of all other Persons.[1] The actual Enumeration shall be made within three Years after the first Meeting of the Congress of the United States, and within every subsequent Term of ten Years, in such

[1]Changed by the Fourteenth Amendment.

Manner as they shall by Law direct. The Number of Representatives shall not exceed one for every thirty Thousand, but each State shall have at Least one Representative, and until such enumeration shall be made, the State of New Hampshire shall be entitled to choose three, Massachusetts eight, Rhode-Island and Providence Plantations one, Connecticut five, New York six, New Jersey four, Pennsylvania eight, Delaware one, Maryland six, Virginia ten, North Carolina five, South Carolina five, and Georgia three.

When vacancies happen in the Representation from any State, the Executive Authority thereof shall issue Writs of Election to fill such Vacancies.

The House of Representatives shall choose their Speaker and other Officers; and shall have the sole Power of Impeachment.

Section 3

The Senate of the United States shall be composed of two Senators from each State, chosen by the Legislature thereof,[2] for six Years; and each Senator shall have one Vote.

Immediately after they shall be assembled in Consequence of the first Election, they shall be divided as equally as may be into three Classes. The Seats of the Senators of the first Class shall be vacated at the Expiration of the second Year, of the second Class at the Expiration of the fourth Year, and of the third Class at the Expiration of the sixth Year, so that one third may be chosen every second Year; and if Vacancies happen by Resignation, or otherwise, during the Recess of the Legislature of any State, the Executive thereof may make temporary Appointments until the next Meeting of the Legislature, which shall then fill such Vacancies.[3]

No Person shall be a Senator who shall not have attained to the Age of thirty Years, and been nine Years a Citizen of the United States, and who shall not, when elected, be an Inhabitant of that State for which he shall be chosen.

The Vice President of the United States shall be President of the Senate, but shall have no Vote, unless they be equally divided.

The Senate shall chuse their other Officers, and also a President pro tempore, in the Absence of the Vice President, or when he shall exercise the Office of President of the United States.

The Senate shall have the sole Power to try all Impeachments. When sitting for that Purpose, they shall be on Oath or Affirmation. When the President of the United States is tried, the Chief Justice shall preside: And no Person shall be convicted without the Concurrence of two thirds of the Members present.

Judgment in Cases of Impeachment shall not extend further than to removal from Office, and disqualification to hold and enjoy any Office of honor, Trust or Profit under the United States: but the Party convicted shall nevertheless be liable and subject to Indictment,Trial, Judgment and Punishment, according to Law.

Section 4

The Times, Places and Manner of holding Elections for Senators and Representatives, shall be prescribed in each State by the Legislature thereof; but the Congress may at any time by Law make or alter such Regulations, except as to the Places of chusing Senators.

The Congress shall assemble at least once in every Year, and such Meeting shall be on the first Monday in December, unless they shall by Law appoint a different Day.[4]

[2]Changed by the Seventeenth Amendment.

[3]Changed by the Seventeenth Amendment.

[4]Changed by the Twentieth Amendment.

Section 5

Each House shall be the Judge of the Elections, Returns and Qualifications of its own Members, and a Majority of each shall constitute a Quorum to do Business; but a smaller Number may adjourn from day to day, and may be authorized to compel the Attendance of absent Members, in such Manner, and under such Penalties as each House may provide.

Each House may determine the Rules of its Proceedings, punish its Members for disorderly Behaviour, and with the Concurrence of two thirds, expel a Member.

Each House shall keep a Journal of its Proceedings, and from time to time publish the same, excepting such Parts as may in their Judgment require Secrecy; and the Yeas and Nays of the Members of either House on any question shall, at the Desire of one fifth of those Present, be entered on the Journal.

Neither House, during the Session of Congress, shall, without the consent of the other, adjourn for more than three days, nor to any other Place than that in which the two Houses shall be sitting.

Section 6

The Senators and Representatives shall receive a Compensation for their Services, to be ascertained by Law, and paid out of the Treasury of the United States. They shall in all Cases, except Treason, Felony and Breach of the Peace, be privileged from Arrest during their Attendance at the Session of their respective Houses, and in going to and returning from the same; and for any Speech or Debate in either House, they shall not be questioned in any other Place.

No Senator or Representative shall, during the Time for which he was elected, be appointed to any civil Office under the Authority of the United States, which shall have been created, or the Emoluments whereof shall have been increased during such time; and no Person holding any Office under the United States, shall be a Member of either House during his Continuance in Office.

Section 7

All Bills for raising Revenue shall originate in the House of Representatives; but the Senate may propose or concur with Amendments as on other Bills.

Every Bill which shall have passed the House of Representatives and the Senate, shall, before it becomes a Law, be presented to the President of the United States; If he approves he shall sign it, but if not he shall return it, with his Objections to that House in which it shall have originated, who shall enter the Objections at large on their Journal, and proceed to reconsider it. If after such Reconsideration two thirds of that House shall agree to pass the Bill, it shall be sent, together with the Objections, to the other House, by which it shall likewise be reconsidered, and if approved by two thirds of that House, it shall become a Law. But in all such Cases the Votes of both Houses shall be determined by Yeas and Nays, and the Names of the Persons voting for and against the Bill shall be entered on the Journal of each House respectively. If any Bill shall not be returned by the President within ten Days (Sundays excepted) after it shall have been presented to him, the Same shall be a Law, in like Manner as if he had signed it, unless the Congress by their Adjournment prevent its Return, in which Case it shall not be a Law.

Every Order, Resolution, or Vote to which the concurrence of the Senate and House of Representatives may be necessary (except on a question of Adjournment) shall be presented to the President of the United States; and before the Same shall take Effect, shall be approved by him, or being disapproved by him, shall be repassed by two thirds of the

Senate and House of Representatives, according to the Rules and limitations prescribed in the Case of a Bill.

Section 8

Congress shall have Power To lay and collect Taxes, Duties, Imposts and Excises, to pay the Debts and provide for the common Defence and general Welfare of the United States; but all Duties, Imposts and Excises shall be uniform throughout the United States;

To borrow Money on the credit of the United States;

To regulate Commerce with foreign Nations, and among the several States, and with the Indian Tribes;

To establish an uniform Rule of Naturalization, and uniform Laws on the subject of Bankruptcies throughout the United States;

To coin Money, regulate the Value thereof, and of foreign Coin, and fix the Standard of Weights and Measures;

To provide for the Punishment of counterfeiting the Securities and current Coin of the United States;

To establish Post Offices and post Roads;

To promote the Progress of Science and useful Arts, by securing for limited Times to Authors and Inventors the exclusive Right to their respective Writings and Discoveries;

To constitute Tribunals inferior to the supreme Court;

To define and punish Piracies and Felonies committed on the high Seas, and Offences against the Law of Nations;

To declare War, grant Letters of Marque and Reprisal, and make Rules concerning Captures on Land and Water;

To raise and support Armies, but no Appropriation of Money to that Use shall be for a longer Term than two Years;

To provide and maintain a Navy;

To make Rules for the government and Regulation of the land and naval Forces;

To provide for calling forth the Militia to execute the Laws of the Union, suppress Insurrections and repel Invasions;

To provide for organizing, arming, and disciplining, the Militia, and for governing such Part of them as may be employed in the Service of the United States, reserving to the States respectively, the Appointment of the Officers, and the Authority of training the Militia according to the discipline prescribed by Congress;

To exercise exclusive Legislation in all Cases whatsoever, over such District (not exceeding ten Miles square) as may, by Cession of particular States, and the Acceptance of Congress, become the Seat of the Government of the United States, and to exercise like Authority over all Places purchased by the Consent of the Legislature of the State in which the Same shall be, for the Erection of Forts, Magazines, Arsenals, dock-Yards, and other needful Buildings;—And

To make all Laws which shall be necessary and proper for carrying into Execution the foregoing Powers, and all other Powers vested by this Constitution in the Government of the United States, or in any Department or Officer thereof.

Section 9

The Migration or Importation of such Persons as any of the States now existing shall think proper to admit, shall not be prohibited by the Congress prior to the Year one thousand eight hundred and eight, but a Tax or duty may be imposed on such Importation, not exceeding ten dollars for each Person.

The Privilege of the Writ of Habeas Corpus shall not be suspended, unless when in Cases of Rebellion or Invasion the public Safety may require it.

No Bill of Attainder or ex post facto Law shall be passed.

No Capitation, or other direct, Tax shall be laid, unless in Proportion to the Census of Enumeration herein before directed to be taken.[5]

No Tax or Duty shall be laid on Articles exported from any State.

No Preference shall be given by any Regulation of Commerce or Revenue to the Ports of one State over those of another, nor shall Vessels bound to, or from, one State, be obliged to enter, clear, or pay Duties in another.

No Money shall be drawn from the Treasury, but in Consequence of Appropriations made by Law; and a regular Statement and Account of the Receipts and Expenditures of all public Money shall be published from time to time.

No Title of Nobility shall be granted by the United States: And no Person holding any Office of Profit or Trust under them, shall, without the Consent of the Congress, accept of any present, Emolument, Office, or Title, of any kind whatever, from any King, Prince, or foreign State.

Section 10

No State shall enter into any Treaty, Alliance, or Confederation; grant Letters of Marque and Reprisal; coin Money; emit Bills of Credit; make any Thing but gold and silver coin a Tender in Payment of Debts; pass any Bill of Attainder, ex post facto Law, or Law impairing the Obligation of Contracts, or grant any Title of Nobility.

No State shall, without the consent of the Congress, lay any Imposts or Duties on Imports or Exports, except what may be absolutely necessary for executing its inspection Laws: and the net Produce of all Duties and Imposts, laid by any State on Imports or Exports, shall be for the Use of the Treasury of the United States; and all such Laws shall be subject to the Revision and Controul of the Congress.

No State shall, without the consent of Congress, lay any Duty of Tonnage, keep Troops, or Ships of War in time of Peace, enter into any Agreement or Compact with another State, or with a foreign Power, or engage in War, unless actually invaded, or in such imminent Danger as will not admit of delay.

Article II

Section 1

The executive Power shall be vested in a President of the United States of America. He shall hold his Office during the Term of four Years, and, together with the Vice President, chosen for the same Term, be elected, as follows.

Each state shall appoint, in such Manner as the Legislature thereof may direct, a Number of Electors, equal to the whole Number of Senators and Representatives to which the State may be entitled in Congress: but no Senator or Representative, or Person holding an Office of Trust or Profit under the United States, shall be appointed an Elector.

The Electors shall meet in their respective States, and vote by Ballot for two Persons, of whom one at least shall not be an inhabitant of the same State with themselves. And they shall make a List of all the Persons voted for, and of the Number of Votes for each; which List they shall sign and certify, and transmit sealed to the Seat of the Government of the

[5]Changed by the Sixteenth Amendment.

United States, directed to the President of the Senate. The President of the Senate shall, in the Presence of the Senate and House of Representatives, open all the Certificates, and the Votes shall then be counted. The Person having the greatest Number of Votes shall be the President, if such Number be a Majority of the whole Number of Electors appointed; and if there be more than one who have such Majority, and have an equal Number of Votes, then the House of Representatives shall immediately chuse by Ballot one of them for President; and if no Person have a Majority, then from the five highest on the List the said House shall in like Manner chuse the President. But in chusing the President, the Votes shall be taken by States, the Representation from each State having one Vote; A quorum for this purpose shall consist of a Member or Members from two thirds of the States, and a Majority of all the States shall be necessary to a Choice. In every Case, after the Choice of the President, the Person having the greatest Number of Votes of the Electors shall be the Vice President. But if there should remain two or more who have equal Votes, the Senate shall chuse from them by Ballot the Vice President.[6]

The Congress may determine the Time of chusing the Electors, and the Day on which they shall give their Votes; which Day shall be the same throughout the United States.

No Person except a natural born Citizen, or a Citizen of the United States, at the time of the Adoption of this Constitution, shall be eligible to the Office of President; neither shall any Person be eligible to that Office who shall not have attained to the Age of thirty five Years, and been fourteen Years a Resident within the United States.

In Case of the Removal of the President from Office, or of his Death, Resignation, or Inability to discharge the Powers and Duties of the said Office, the Same shall devolve on the Vice President, and the Congress may by Law provide for the Case of Removal, Death, Resignation or Inability, both of the President and Vice President, declaring what Officer shall then act as President, and such Officer shall act accordingly, until the Disability be removed, or a President shall be elected.[7]

The President shall, at stated Times, receive for his Services, a Compensation, which shall neither be encreased nor diminished during the Period for which he shall have been elected, and he shall not receive within that Period any other Emolument from the United States, or any of them.

Before he enters on the Execution of his Office, he shall take the following Oath or Affirmation:— "I do solemnly swear (or affirm) that I will faithfully execute the Office of President of the United States, and will to the best of my Ability, preserve, protect, and defend the Constitution of the United States."

Section 2

The President shall be Commander in Chief of the Army and Navy of the United States, and of the Militia of the several States, when called into the actual Service of the United States; he may require the Opinion, in writing, of the principal Officer in each of the executive Departments, upon any Subject relating to the Duties of their respective Offices, and he shall have Power to grant Reprieves and Pardons for Offences against the United States, except in Cases of Impeachment.

He shall have Power, by and with the Advice and Consent of the Senate, to make Treaties, provided two thirds of the Senators present concur; and he shall nominate, and by and with the Advice and Consent of the Senate, shall appoint Ambassadors, other public Ministers and Consuls, Judges of the supreme Court, and all other Officers of the United

[6]Changed by the Twelfth Amendment.

[7]Changed by the Twenty-fifth Amendment.

States, whose Appointments are not herein otherwise provided for, and which shall be established by Law; but the Congress may by Law vest the Appointment of such inferior Officers, as they think proper, in the President alone, in the Courts of Law, or in the Heads of Departments.

The President shall have Power to fill up all Vacancies that may happen during the Recess of the Senate, by granting Commissions which shall expire at the End of their next Session.

Section 3

He shall from time to time give to the Congress Information of the State of the Union, and recommend to their Consideration such Measures as he shall judge necessary and expedient; he may, on extraordinary Occasions, convene both Houses, or either of them, and in Case of Disagreement between them, with Respect to the Time of Adjournment, he may adjourn them to such Time as he shall think proper; he shall receive Ambassadors and other public Ministers; he shall take Care that the Laws be faithfully executed, and shall Commission all the Officers of the United States.

Section 4

The President, Vice President and all civil Officers of the United States, shall be removed from Office on Impeachment for, and Conviction of, Treason, Bribery, or other high Crimes and Misdemeanors.

Article III

Section 1

The judicial Power of the United States, shall be vested in one supreme Court, and in such inferior Courts as the Congress may from time to time ordain and establish. The Judges, both of the supreme and inferior Courts, shall hold their Offices during good Behaviour, and shall, at stated Times, receive for their Services, a Compensation, which shall not be diminished during their Continuance in Office.

Section 2

The judicial Power shall extend to all Cases, in Law and Equity, arising under this Constitution, the Laws of the United States, and Treaties made, or which shall be made, under their Authority;—to all Cases affecting Ambassadors, other public Ministers and Consuls;—to all Cases of admiralty and maritime Jurisdiction;—to Controversies to which the United States shall be a party;—to Controversies between two or more States;—between a State and Citizens of another State;[8] —between Citizens of different States;—between Citizens of the same State claiming Lands under Grants of different States, and between a State, or the Citizens thereof, and foreign States, Citizens or Subjects.

In all Cases affecting Ambassadors, other public Ministers and Consuls, and those in which a State shall be Party, the supreme Court shall have original Jurisdiction. In all the other Cases before mentioned, the supreme Court shall have appellate Jurisdiction, both as to Law and Fact, with such Exceptions, and under such Regulations as the Congress shall make.

[8]Changed by the Eleventh Amendment.

The Trial of all Crimes, except in Cases of Impeachment, shall be by Jury: and such Trial shall be held in the State where the said Crimes shall have been committed; but when not committed within any State, the Trial shall be at such Place or Places as the Congress may by Law have directed.

Section 3

Treason against the United States, shall consist only in levying War against them, or in adhering to their Enemies, giving them Aid and Comfort. No Person shall be convicted of Treason unless on the Testimony of two Witnesses to the same overt Act, or on Confession in open Court.

The Congress shall have Power to declare the Punishment of Treason, but no Attainder of Treason shall work Corruption of Blood, or Forfeiture except during the Life of the Person attained.

Article IV

Section 1

Full Faith and Credit shall be given in each State to the public Acts, Records, and judicial Proceedings of every other State. And the Congress may by general Laws prescribe the Manner in which such Acts, Records and Proceedings shall be proved, and the Effect thereof.

Section 2

The Citizens of each State shall be entitled to all Privileges and Immunities of Citizens in the several States.

A Person charged in any State with Treason, Felony, or other Crime, who shall flee from Justice, and be found in another State, shall on Demand of the executive Authority of the State from which he fled, be delivered up, to be removed to the State having Jurisdiction of the Crime.

No Person held to Service or Labour in one State, under the Laws thereof, escaping into another, shall, in consequence of any Law or Regulation therein, be discharged from such Service or Labour, but shall be delivered up on Claim of the Party to whom such Service or Labour may be due.[9]

Section 3

New States may be admitted by the Congress into this Union; but no new State shall be formed or erected within the Jurisdiction of any other State; nor any State be formed by the Junction of two or more States, or Parts of States, without the Consent of the Legislatures of the States concerned as well as of the Congress.

The Congress shall have Power to dispose of and make all needful Rules and Regulations respecting the Territory or other Property belonging to the United States; and nothing in this Constitution shall be so construed as to Prejudice any Claims of the United States, or of any particular State.

Section 4

The United States shall guarantee to every State in this Union a Republican Forum of Government, and shall protect each of them against Invasion; and on Application of

[9]Changed by the Thirteenth Amendment.

the Legislature, or of the Executive (when the Legislature cannot be convened) against domestic Violence.

Article V

The Congress, whenever two thirds of both Houses shall deem it necessary, shall propose Amendments to this Constitution, or, on the Application of the Legislatures of two thirds of the several States, shall call a Convention for proposing Amendments, which in either Case, shall be valid to all Intents and Purposes, as Part of this Constitution, when ratified by the legislatures of three fourths of the several States, or by Conventions in three fourths thereof, as the one or the other Mode of Ratification may be proposed by the Congress; Provided that no Amendment which may be made prior to the Year One thousand eight hundred and eight shall in any Manner affect the first and fourth Clauses in the Ninth Section of the first Article; and that no State, without its consent, shall be deprived of its equal Suffrage in the Senate.

Article VI

All Debts contracted and Engagements entered into, before the Adoption of this Constitution, shall be as valid against the United States under this constitution, as under the Confederation.

The Constitution, and the Laws of the United States which shall be made in Pursuance thereof; and all Treaties made, or which shall be made, under the Authority of the United States, shall be the supreme Law of the Land; and the Judges in every State shall be bound thereby, any Thing in the Constitution or Laws of any State to the Contrary notwithstanding.

The Senators and Representatives before mentioned, and the Members of the several State Legislatures, and all executive and judicial Officers, both of the United States and of the several States, shall be bound by Oath or Affirmation, to support this Constitution; but no religious Test shall ever be required as a Qualification to any Office or public Trust under the United States.

Article VII

The Ratification of the Conventions of nine States, shall be sufficient for the Establishment of this Constitution between the States so ratifying the Same.

Done in Convention by the Unanimous Consent of the States present the Seventeenth Day of September in the Year of our Lord one thousand seven hundred and eighty seven and of the Independence of the United States of America the Twelfth. In witness whereof We have hereunto subscribed our Names.

Amendments

[The first 10 amendments are known as the "Bill of Rights."]

Amendment 1 (Ratified 1791)

Congress shall make no law respecting an establishment of religion, or prohibiting the free exercise thereof; or abridging the freedom of speech, or of the press; or the right of the people peaceably to assemble, and to petition the Government for a redress of grievances.

Amendment 2 (Ratified 1791)

A well regulated Militia, being necessary to the security of a free State, the right of the people to keep and bear Arms, shall not be infringed.

Amendment 3 (Ratified 1791)

No Soldier shall, in time of peace be quartered in any house, without the consent of the Owner, nor in time of war, but in a manner to be prescribed by law.

Amendment 4 (Ratified 1791)

The right of the people to be secure in their persons, houses, papers, and effects, against unreasonable searches and seizures, shall not be violated, and no Warrants shall issue, but upon probable cause, supported by Oath or affirmation, and particularly describing the place to be searched, and the persons or things to be seized.

Amendment 5 (Ratified 1791)

No person shall be held to answer for a capital, or otherwise infamous crime, unless on a presentment or indictment of a Grand Jury, except in cases arising in the land or naval forces, or in the Militia, when in actual service in time of War or public danger; nor shall any person be subject for the same offence to be twice put in jeopardy of life or limb; nor shall be compelled in any criminal case to be a witness against himself, nor be deprived of life, liberty, or property, without due process of law; nor shall private property be taken for public use, without just compensation.

Amendment 6 (Ratified 1791)

In all criminal prosecutions, the accused shall enjoy the right to a speedy and public trial, by an impartial jury of the State and district wherein the crime shall have been committed, which district shall have been previously ascertained by law, and to be informed of the nature and cause of the accusation; to be confronted with the witnesses against him; to have compulsory process for obtaining Witnesses in his favor, and to have assistance of counsel for his defence.

Amendment 7 (Ratified 1791)

In Suits at common law, where the value in controversy shall exceed twenty dollars, the right of trial by jury shall be preserved, and no fact tried by a jury, shall be otherwise re-examined in any Court of the United States, than according to the rules of the common law.

Amendment 8 (Ratified 1791)

Excessive bail shall not be required, nor excessive fines imposed, nor cruel and unusual punishments inflicted.

Amendment 9 (Ratified 1791)

The enumeration in the Constitution, of certain rights, shall not be construed to deny or disparage others retained by the people.

Amendment 10 (Ratified 1791)

The powers not delegated to the United States by the Constitution, nor prohibited by it to the States, are reserved to the States respectively, or to the people.

Amendment 11 (Ratified 1795)

The Judicial power of the United States shall not be construed to extend to any suit in law or equity, commenced or prosecuted against one of the United States by Citizens of another State, or by Citizens or Subjects of any Foreign State.

Amendment 12 (Ratified 1804)

The Electors shall meet in their respective states, and vote by ballot for President and Vice-President, one of whom, at least, shall not be an inhabitant of the same state with themselves; they shall name in their ballots the person voted for as President, and in distinct ballots the person voted for as Vice-President, and they shall make distinct lists of all persons voted for as President, and of all persons voted for as Vice-President, and of the number of votes for each, which lists they shall sign and certify, and transmit sealed to the seat of the government of the United States, directed to the President of the Senate;—The President of the Senate shall, in the presence of the Senate and House of Representatives, open all the certificates and the votes shall then be counted;—The person having the greatest number of votes for President, shall be the President, if such number be a majority of the whole number of Electors appointed; and if no person have such majority, then from the persons having the highest numbers not exceeding three on the list of those voted for as President, the House of Representatives shall choose immediately, by ballot, the President. But in choosing the President, the votes shall be taken by states, the representation from each state having one vote; a quorum for this purpose shall consist of a member or members from two-thirds of the states, and a majority of all the states shall be necessary to a choice. And if the House of Representatives shall not choose a President whenever the right of choice shall devolve upon them, before the fourth day of March next following, then the Vice-President shall act as president, as in the case of the death or other constitutional disability of the President.[10]—The person having the greatest number of votes as Vice-President, shall be the Vice-President, if such number be a majority of the whole number of Electors appointed, and if no person have a majority, then from the two highest numbers on the list, the Senate shall choose the Vice-President; a quorum for the purpose shall consist of two-thirds of the whole number of Senators, and a majority of the whole number shall be necessary to a choice. But no person constitutionally ineligible to the office of President shall be eligible to that of Vice-President of the United States.

Amendent 13 (Ratified 1865)

Section 1

Neither slavery nor involuntary servitude, except as a punishment for crime whereof the party shall have been duly convicted, shall exist within the United States, or any place subject to their jurisdiction.

Section 2

Congress shall have power to enforce this article by appropriate legislation.

Amendment 14 (Ratified 1868)

Section 1

All persons born or naturalized in the United States, and subject to the jurisdiction thereof, are citizens of the United States and of the State wherein they reside. No State shall make

[10]Changed by the Twentieth Amendment.

or enforce any law which shall abridge the privileges or immunities of citizens of the United States; nor shall any State deprive any person of life, liberty, or property, without due process of law; nor deny to any person within its jurisdiction the equal protection of the laws.

Section 2

Representatives shall be apportioned among the several States according to their respective numbers, counting the whole number of persons in each State, excluding Indians not taxed. But when the right to vote at any election for the choice of electors for President and Vice President of the United States, Representatives in Congress, the Executive and Judicial officers of a State, or the members of the Legislature thereof, is denied to any of the male in-habitants of such State, being twenty-one[11] years of age, and citizens of the United States, or in any way abridged except for participation in rebellion, or other crime, the basis of representation therein shall be reduced in the proportion which the number of such male citizens shall bear to the whole number of male citizens twenty-one years of age in such State.

Section 3

No person shall be a Senator or Representative in Congress, or elector of President and Vice President, or hold any office, civil or military, under the United States, or under any State, who, having previously taken an oath, as a member of Congress, or as an officer of the United States, or as a member of any State legislature, or as an executive or judicial officer of any State, to support the Constitution of the United States, shall have engaged in insurrection or rebellion against the same, or given aid or comfort to the enemies thereof. But Congress may by a vote of two-thirds of each House, remove such disability.

Section 4

The validity of the public debt of the United States, authorized by law, including debts incurred for payment of pensions and bounties for services in suppressing insurrection or rebellion, shall not be questioned. But neither the United States nor any State shall assume or pay any debt or obligation incurred in aid of insurrection or rebellion against the United States, or any claim for the loss or emancipation of any slave; but all such debts, obligations and claims shall be held illegal and void.

Section 5

The Congress shall have power to enforce, by appropriate legislation, the provisions of this article.

Amendment 15 (Ratified 1870)

Section 1

The right of citizens of the United States to vote shall not be denied or abridged by the United States or by any State on account of race, color, or previous condition of servitude.

Section 2

The Congress shall have power to enforce this article by appropriate legislation.

[11]Changed by the Twenty-sixth Amendment.

Amendment 16 (Ratified 1913)

The Congress shall have power to lay and collect taxes on incomes, from whatever source derived, without apportionment among the several States, and without regard to any census or enumeration.

Amendment 17 (Ratified 1913)

The Senate of the United States shall be composed of two Senators from each State, elected by the people thereof, for six years; and each Senator shall have one vote. The electors in each State shall have the qualifications requisite for electors of the most numerous branch of the State legislatures.

When vacancies happen in the representation of any State in the Senate, the executive authority of such State shall issue writs of election to fill such vacancies: *Provided,* That the legislature of any State may empower the executive thereof to make temporary appointments until the people fill the vacancies by election as the legislature may direct.

This amendment shall not be so construed as to affect the election or term of any Senator chosen before it becomes valid as part of the Constitution.

Amendment 18 (Ratified 1919; Repealed 1933)

Section 1

After one year from the ratification of this article the manufacture, sale, or transportation of intoxicating liquors within, the importation thereof into, or the exportation thereof from the United States and all territory subject to the jurisdiction thereof for beverage purposes is hereby prohibited.

Section 2

The Congress and the several States shall have concurrent power to enforce this article by appropriate legislation.

Section 3

This article shall be inoperative unless it shall have been ratified as an amendment to the Constitution by the legislatures of the several States, as provided in the Constitution, within seven years from the date of the submission hereof to the States by the Congress.[12]

Amendment 19 (Ratified 1920)

The right of citizens of the United States to vote shall not be denied or abridged by the United States or by any State on account of sex.

Congress shall have power to enforce this article by appropriate legislation.

Amendment 20 (Ratified 1933)

Section 1

The terms of the President and Vice President shall end at noon on the 20th day of January, and the terms of Senators and Representatives at noon on the 3rd day of January, of the years in which such terms would have ended if this article had not been ratified; and the terms of their successors shall then begin.

[12]Repealed by the Twenty-first Amendment.

Section 2

The Congress shall assemble at least once in every year, and such meeting shall begin at noon on the 3rd day of January, unless they shall by law appoint a different day.

Section 3

If, at the time fixed for the beginning of the term of the President, the President elect shall have died, the Vice President elect shall become President. If a President shall not have been chosen before the time fixed for the beginning of his term, or if the President elect shall have failed to qualify, then the Vice President elect shall act as President until a President shall have qualified; and the Congress may by law provide for the case wherein neither a President elect nor a Vice President elect shall have qualified, declaring who shall then act as President, or the manner in which one who is to act shall be selected, and such person shall act accordingly until a President or Vice President shall have qualified.

Section 4

The Congress may by law provide for the case of the death of any of the persons from whom the House of Representatives may choose a President whenever the right of choice shall have devolved upon them, and for the case of the death of any of the persons from whom the Senate may choose a Vice President whenever the right of choice shall have devolved upon them.

Section 5

Sections 1 and 2 shall take effect on the 15th day of October following the ratification of this article.

Section 6

This article shall be inoperative unless it shall have been ratified as an amendment to the Constitution by the legislatures of three-fourths of the several States within seven years from the date of its submission.

Amendment 21 (Ratified 1933)

Section 1

The eighteenth article of amendment to the Constitution of the United States is hereby repealed.

Section 2

The transportation or importation into any State, Territory, or possession of the United States for delivery or use therein of intoxicating liquors, in violation of the laws thereof, is hereby prohibited.

Section 3

This article shall be inoperative unless it shall have been ratified as an amendment to the constitution by conventions in the several States, as provided in the Constitution, within seven years from the date of the submission hereof to the States by the Congress.

Amendment 22 (Ratified 1951)

Section 1

No person shall be elected to the office of the President more than twice, and no person who has held the office of President, or acted as President, for more than two years of a term to which some other person was elected President shall be elected to the office of the President more than once. But this Article shall not apply to any person holding the office of President when this Article was proposed by the Congress, and shall not prevent any person who may be holding the office of President, or acting as President, during the term within which this Article becomes operative from holding the office of President or acting as President during the remainder of such term.

Section 2

This Article shall be inoperative unless it shall have been ratified as an amendment to the Constitution by the legislatures of three-fourths of the several States within seven years from the date of its submission to the States by the Congress.

Amendment 23 (Ratified 1961)

Section 1

The District constituting the seat of Government of the United States shall appoint in such manner as the Congress may direct:

A number of electors of President and Vice President equal to the whole number of Senators and Representatives in Congress to which the District would be entitled if it were a State, but in no event more than the least populous State; they shall be in addition to those appointed by the States, but they shall be considered, for the purposes of the election of President and Vice President, to be electors appointed by a State; and they shall meet in the District and perform such duties as provided by the twelfth article of amendment.

Section 2

The Congress shall have power to enforce this article by appropriate legislation.

Amendment 24 (Ratified 1964)

Section 1

The right of citizens of the United States to vote in any primary or other election for President or Vice President, for electors for President or Vice President, or for Senator or Representative in Congress, shall not be denied or abridged by the United States or any State by reason of failure to pay any poll tax or other tax.

Section 2

The Congress shall have power to enforce this article by appropriate legislation.

Amendment 25 (Ratified 1967)

Section 1

In case of the removal of the President from office or of his death or resignation, the Vice President shall become President.

Section 2

Whenever there is a vacancy in the office of the Vice President, the President shall nominate a Vice President who shall take office upon confirmation by a majority vote of both Houses of Congress.

Section 3

Whenever the President transmits to the President pro tempore of the Senate and the Speaker of the House of Representatives his written declaration that he is unable to discharge the powers and duties of his office, and until he transmits to them a written declaration to the contrary, such powers and duties shall be discharged by the Vice President as Acting President.

Section 4

Whenever the Vice President and a majority of either the principal officers of the executive departments or of such other body as Congress may by law provide, transmit to the President pro tempore of the Senate and the Speaker of the House of Representatives their written declaration that the President is unable to discharge the powers and duties of his office, the Vice President shall immediately assume the powers and duties of the office as Acting President.

Thereafter, when the President transmits to the President pro tempore of the Senate and the Speaker of the House of Representatives his written declaration that no inability exists, he shall resume the powers and duties of his office unless the Vice President and a majority of either the principal officers of the executive department or of such other body as Congress may by law provide, transmit within four days to the President pro tempore of the Senate and the Speaker of the House of Representatives their written declaration that the President is unable to discharge the powers and duties of his office. Thereupon Congress shall decide the issue, assembling within forty-eight hours for that purpose if not in session. If the Congress, within twenty-one days after receipt of the latter written declaration, or, if Congress is not in session, within twenty-one days after Congress is required to assemble, determines by two-thirds vote of both Houses that the President is unable to discharge the powers and duties of his office, the Vice President shall continue to discharge the same as Acting President; otherwise, the President shall resume the powers and duties of his office.

Amendment 26 (Ratified 1971)

Section 1

The right of citizens of the United States, who are eighteen years of age or older, to vote shall not be denied or abridged by the United States or by any State on account of age.

Section 2

The Congress shall have power to enforce this article by appropriate legislation.

Amendment 27 (Ratified 1992)

No law, varying the compensation for the services of the Senators and Representatives, shall take effect, until an election of Representatives shall have intervened.

Appendix B

Glossary of Legal Terms and Definitions

abatement of nuisance Removal of a nuisance by court action.

ab initio From the beginning. A contract that is void ab initio is void from its inception.

absque injuria Without violation of a legal right.

abstract of title A summary of the conveyances, transfers, and other facts relied on as evidence of title, together with all such facts appearing of record that may impair its validity. It should contain a brief but complete history of the title.

abutting owners Those owners whose lands touch.

acceleration The shortening of the time for the performance of a contract or the payment of a note by the operation of some provision in the contract or note itself.

acceptance The actual or implied receipt and retention of that which is tendered or offered. The acceptance of an offer is the assent to an offer that is requisite to the formation of a contract. It is either express or evidenced by circumstances from which such assent may be implied.

accession In its legal meaning, it is generally used to signify the acquisition of property by its incorporation or union with other property.

accommodation paper A negotiable instrument signed without consideration by a party as acceptor, drawer, or indorser for the purpose of enabling the payee to obtain credit.

accord and satisfaction The adjustment of a disagreement as to what is due from one person to another, and the payment of the agreed amount.

account stated An account that has been rendered by one to another and that purports to state the true balance due, which balance is either expressly or impliedly admitted to be due by the debtor.

acknowledgment A form for authenticating instruments conveying property or otherwise conferring rights. It is a public declaration by the grantor that the act evidenced by the instrument is his act and deed. Also an admission or confirmation.

acquit To set free or judicially to discharge from an accusation; to release from a debt, duty, obligation, charge, or suspicion of guilt.

actionable Remedial by an action at law.

action ex contractu An action arising out of the breach of a contract.

action ex delicto An action arising out of the violation of a duty or obligation created by positive law independent of contract. An action in tort.

act of God An occurrence resulting exclusively from natural forces that could not have been prevented or whose effects could not have been avoided by care or foresight.

act of state An act done by the sovereign power of a country. It cannot be questioned by a court of law.

adjudge To give judgment; to decide; to sentence.

adjudicate To adjudge; to settle by judicial decree; to hear or try and determine, as a court.

ad litem During the pendency of the action or proceeding.

administrator A man appointed by a probate court to settle the estate of a deceased person. His duties are customarily defined by statute. If a woman is appointed, she is called the administratrix.

adverse possession Open and notorious possession of real property over a given length of time that denies ownership in any other claimant.

advisement When a court takes a case under advisement, it delays its decision until it has examined and considered the questions involved.

affidavit A statement or declaration reduced to writing and sworn or affirmed to before an officer who has authority to administer an oath or affirmation.

affirm To confirm a former judgment or order of a court. Also, to declare solemnly instead of making a sworn statement.

affirmative action Preferential hiring or promotion on the basis of minority status or gender.

after-acquired property Property of the debtor that is obtained after a security interest in the debtor's property has been created.

agent An agent is the substitute or representative of his principal and derives his authority from him.

aggrieved One whose legal rights have been invaded by the act of another is said to be aggrieved. Also, one whose pecuniary interest is directly affected by a judgment, or whose right of property may be divested thereby, is to be considered a party aggrieved.

alienation The voluntary act or acts by which one person transfers his or her own property to another.

alien corporation A corporation doing business in the United States while domiciled in another country.

aliquot Strictly, forming an exact proper divisor, but treated as meaning fractional when applied to trusts, and so on.

allegation A declaration, a formal averment or statement of a party to an action in a declaration or pleading of what the party intends to prove.

allege To make a statement of fact; to plead.

alternative dispute resolution (ADR) A general name applied to the many nonjudicial means of settling private disputes.

amortize In modern usage, the word means to provide for the payment of a debt by creating a sinking fund or paying in installments.

ancillary Auxiliary to. An ancillary receiver is a receiver who has been appointed in aid of, and in subordination to, the primary receiver.

answer The pleading of a defendant in which he or she may deny any or all the facts set out in the plaintiff's declaration or complaint.

anticipatory breach The doctrine of the law of contracts that when the promisor has repudiated the contract before the time of performance has arrived, the promisee may sue forthwith.

apparent authority When in absence of actual authority, a principal knowingly permits an agent to hold himself out as possessing authority to enter a contract on behalf of the principal.

appearance The first act of the defendant in court.

appellant A person who files an appeal.

appellate jurisdiction Jurisdiction to revise or correct the work of a subordinate court.

appellee A party against whom a cause is appealed from a lower court to a higher court, called the "respondent" in some jurisdictions.

applicant A petitioner; one who files a petition or application.

appurtenance An accessory; something that belongs to another thing; for example, buildings are appurtenant to the land and a bar would be appurtenant to a tavern.

arbitrate To submit some disputed matter to selected persons and to accept their decision or award as a substitute for the decision of a judicial tribunal.

argument The discussion by counsel for the respective parties of their contentions on the law and the facts of the case being tried in order to aid the jury in arriving at a correct and just conclusion.

articles of incorporation A document that must be filed with a secretary of state to create a corporation. Usually, it includes the basic rights and responsibilities of the corporation and the shareholders.

assent To give or express one's concurrence or approval of something done. Assent does not include consent.

assignable Capable of being lawfully assigned or transferred; transferable; negotiable. Also, capable of being specified or pointed out as an assignable error.

assignee A person to whom an assignment is made.

assignment A transfer or setting over of property or some right or interest therein, from one person to another. In its ordinary application, the word is limited to the transfer of choices in action; for example, the assignment of a contract.

assignor The maker of an assignment.

assumpsit An action at common law to recover damages for breach of contract.

assurance To provide confidence or to inform positively.

attachment Taking property into the legal custody of an officer by virtue of the directions contained in a writ of attachment. A seizure under a writ of a debtor's property.

attest To bear witness to; to affirm; to be true or genuine.

attorney-in-fact A person who is authorized by his principal, either for some particular purpose, or to do a particular act, not of a legal character.

authentication Such official attestation of a written instrument as will render it legally admissible in evidence.

authority Judicial or legislative precedent; delegated power; warrant.

averment A positive statement of fact made in a pleading.

avoidable Capable of being nullified or made void.

bad faith The term imports a person's actual intent to mislead or deceive another; an intent to take an unfair and unethical advantage of another.

bailee The person to whom a bailment is made.

bailment A delivery of personal property by one person to another in trust for a specific purpose, with a contract, express or implied, that the trust shall be faithfully executed and the property returned or duly accounted for when the special purpose is accomplished, or kept until the bailor reclaims it.

bailor The maker of a bailment; one who delivers personal property to another to be held in bailment.

bankruptcy The state of a person who is unable to pay his or her debts without respect to time; one whose liabilities exceeds his or her assets.

bar As a collective noun, it is used to include those persons who are admitted to practice law, members of the bar. The court itself. A plea or peremptory exception of a defendant sufficient to destroy the plaintiff's action.

barratry The habitual stirring up of quarrels and suits; a single act would not constitute the offense.

bearer The designation of the bearer as the payee of a negotiable instrument signifies that the instrument is payable to the person who seems to be the holder.

bench A court; the judges of a court; the seat on which the judges of a court are accustomed to sit while the court is in session.

beneficiary The person for whose benefit an insurance policy, trust, will, or contract is established but not the promisee. In the case of a contract, the beneficiary is called a third-party beneficiary. A donee beneficiary is one who is not a party to a contract but who receives the promised performance as a gift. A creditor beneficiary is one who is not a party to a contract but receives the performance in discharge of a debt owed by the promisee to him.

bequeath Commonly used to denote a testamentary gift of real estate; synonymous with "to devise."

bid To make an offer at an auction or at a judicial sale. As a noun, it means an offer.

bilateral contract A contract in which the promise of one of the parties forms the consideration for the promise of the other; a contract formed by an offer requiring a reciprocal promise.

bill of exchange An unconditional order in writing by one person to another, signed by the person giving it, requiring the person to whom it is addressed to pay on demand or at a fixed or determinable future time a sum certain in money to order or to bearer.

bill of lading A written acknowledgment of the receipt of goods to be transported to a designated place and delivery to a named person or to his or her order.

bill of sale A written agreement by which one person assigns or transfers interests or rights in personal property to another.

binder Also called a binding slip—brief memorandum or agreement issued by an issuer as a temporary policy for the convenience of all the parties, constituting a present insurance in the amount specified, to continue in force until the execution of a formal policy.

"blue sky" laws A popular name for statutes regulating the sale of securities and intended to protect investors against fraudulent and visionary schemes.

board initiative The board of directors' act of proposing a matter. This is required in any fundamental corporate change.

bona fide Good faith.

bond A promise under seal to pay money.

breaking bulk The division or separation of the contents of a package or container.

brief A statement of a party's case; usually an abridgement of either the plaintiff's or defendant's case prepared by his or her attorneys for use of counsel in a trial at law. Also, an abridgment of a reported case.

broker An agent who bargains or carries on negotiations in behalf of the principal as an intermediary between the latter and third persons in transacting business relative to the acquisition of contractual rights, or to the sale or purchase of property the custody of which is not intrusted to him or her for the purpose of discharging the agency.

bulk transfer The sale or transfer of a major part of the stock of goods of a merchant at one time and not in the ordinary course of business.

burden of proof The necessity or obligation of affirmatively proving the fact or facts in dispute on an issue raised in a suit in court.

buyer in ordinary course of business A person who, in good faith and without knowledge that the sale to him is in violation of a third party's ownership rights or security interest in the goods, buys in ordinary course from a person who is in the business of selling goods of that kind.

buyout The purchase of a corporation.

bylaw A rule or law of a corporation for its government. It includes all self-made regulations of a corporation affecting its business and members that do not operate on third persons, or in any way affect their rights.

call A notice of a meeting to be held by the stockholders or board of directors of a corporation. Also, a demand for payment. In securities trading, a negotiable option contract granting the bearer the right to buy a certain quantity of a particular security at the agreed price on or before the agreed date.

cancellation The act of crossing out a writing. The operation of destroying a written instrument.

capacity The ability to incur legal obligations and acquire legal rights.

caption The heading or title of a document.

carte blanche A signed blank instrument intended by the signer to be filled in and used by another person without restriction.

case law The law extracted from decided cases.

cashier's check A bill of exchange, drawn by a bank on itself, and accepted by the act of issuance.

cause of action A right to action at law arises from the existence of a primary right in the plaintiff, and an invasion of that right by some civil wrong on the part of the defendant; the facts that establish the existence of that right and that civil wrong constitute the cause of action.

caveat emptor Let the buyer beware. This maxim expresses the general idea that the buyer purchases at his peril, and that there are no warranties, either express or implied, made by the seller.

caveat venditor Let the seller beware. It is not accepted as a rule of law in the law of sales.

cease and desist order An administrative order prohibiting a party from doing something.

certification The return of a writ; a formal attestation of a matter of fact; the appropriate marking of a certified check.

certified check A check that has been "accepted" by the drawee bank and has been so marked or certified that it indicates such acceptance.

cestui que trust The person for whose benefit property is held in trust by a trustee.

champerty The purchase of an interest in a matter in dispute so as to take part in the litigation.

chancellor A judge of a court of chancery.

chancery Equity or a court of equity.

charge To charge a jury is to instruct the jury as to the essential law of the case. The first step in the prosecution of a crime is to formally accuse the offender or charge him with the crime.

charter An instrument or authority from the sovereign power bestowing the right or power to do business under the corporate form of organization. Also the organic law of a city or town, and representing a portion of the statute law of the state.

chattel An article of tangible property other than land.

chattel mortgage An instrument whereby the owner of chattels transfers the title to such property to another as security for the performance of an obligation subject to be defeated on the performance of the obligation. Under the UCC, called merely a security interest.

chattel real Interests in real estate less than a freehold, such as an estate for years.

check A written order on a bank or banker payable on demand to the person named or his order or bearer and drawn by virtue of credits due the drawer from the bank created by money deposited with the bank.

choice-of-law The law a court decides to use based on the agreement between parties or location of events or parties.

chose in action A personal right not reduced to possession but recoverable by a suit at law.

C.I.F. An abbreviation for cost, freight, and insurance, used in mercantile transactions, especially in import transactions.

citation A writ issued out of a court of competent jurisdiction, commanding the person therein named to appear on a day named to do something therein mentioned.

citation of authorities The reference to legal authorities such as reported cases or treatises to support propositions advanced.

civil action An action brought to enforce a civil right; in contrast to a criminal action.

class action An action brought on behalf of the plaintiff and others similarly situated.

close corporation A corporation in which directors and officers, rather than the shareholders, have the right to fill vacancies occurring in their ranks. Also used to refer to any corporation whose stock is not freely traded and whose shareholders are personally known to each other.

C.O.D. "cash on delivery" When goods are delivered to a carrier for a cash on delivery shipment, the carrier must not deliver without receiving payment of the amount due.

code A system of law; a systematic and complete body of law.

codicil Some addition to or qualification of one's last will and testament.

cognovit To acknowledge an action. A cognovit note is a promissory note that contains an acknowledgment clause.

collateral Property put up to secure the performance of a promise, so that if the promisor fails to perform as promised, the creditor may look to the property to make him whole.

collateral attack An attempt to impeach a decree, a judgment, or other official act in a proceeding that has not been instituted for the express purpose of correcting or annulling or modifying the decree, judgment, or official act.

collateral contract A contract in which one person agrees to pay the debt of another if the principal debtor fails to pay. See **guaranty.**

comaker A person who with another or others signs a negotiable instrument on its face and thereby becomes primarily liable for its payment.

commercial law The law that relates to the rights of property and persons engaged in trade or commerce.

commercial speech Truthful speech for the purpose of business (e.g., an advertisement) can be regulated if the government has a substantial interest and the regulation directly advances that interest in a manner no more extensive than necessary.

commission merchant A person who sells goods in his own name at his own store, and on commission, from sample. Also, one who buys and sells goods for a principal in his own name and without disclosing his principal.

commodity Goods that are traded.

common carrier One who undertakes, for hire or reward, to transport the goods of such of the public as choose to employ him.

compensatory damages See **damages.**

complaint A form of legal process that usually consists of a formal allegation or charge against a party, made or presented to the appropriate court or officer. The technical name of a bill in equity by which the complainant sets out his cause of action.

composition with creditors An agreement between creditors and their common debtor and between themselves whereby the creditors agree to accept the sum or security stipulated in full payment of their claims.

concurrent Running with, simultaneously with. The word is used in different senses. In contracts, concurrent conditions are conditions that must be performed simultaneously by the mutual acts required by each of the parties.

condemn To appropriate land for public use. To adjudge a person guilty; to pass sentence on a person convicted of a crime.

condition A provision or clause in a contract that operates to suspend or rescind the principal obligation. A qualification or restriction annexed to a conveyance of lands, whereby it is provided that in the case a particular event does or does not happen, or in case the grantor or grantees do or omit to do a particular act, an estate shall commence, be enlarged, or be defeated.

conditional acceptance An acceptance of a bill of exchange containing some qualification limiting or altering the acceptor's liability on the bill.

conditional sale The term is most frequently applied to a sale wherein the seller reserves the title to the goods, though the possession is delivered to the buyer, until the purchase price is paid in full.

condition precedent A condition that must happen before either party is bound by the principal obligation of a contract; for example, one agrees to purchase goods if they are delivered before a stated day. Delivery before the stated day is a condition precedent to one's obligation to purchase.

condition subsequent A condition that operates to relieve or discharge one from his obligation under a contract.

confession of judgment An entry of judgment on the admission or confession of the debtor without the formality, time, or expense involved in an ordinary proceeding.

conflict of interest Ethical implications in connection with public officials and fiduciaries and their relationship to matters of private interest or gain to them.

conservator (of an insane person) A person appointed by a court to take care of and oversee the person and estate of a mentally impaired or other incompetent person.

consideration In contract law, a basic requirement for an enforceable agreement under traditional contract principles, defined in this text as legal value, bargained for and given in exchange for an act or promise. In corporation law, cash or property contributed to a corporation in exchange for shares, or a promise to contribute such cash or property.

consignee A person to whom goods are consigned, shipped, or otherwise transmitted, either for sale or for safekeeping.

consignment A bailment for sale. The consignee does not undertake the absolute obligation to sell or pay for the goods.

consignor One who sends goods to another on consignment; a shipper or transmitter of goods.

construe To read a statute or document for the purpose of ascertaining its meaning and effect; but in doing so, the law must be regarded.

contempt Conduct in the presence of a legislative or judicial body tending to disturb its proceedings, or impair the respect due to its authority or a disobedience to the rules or orders of such a body that interferes with the due administration of law.

contra Otherwise; disagreeing with; contrary to.

contra bonos mores Contrary to good morals.

contract of adhesion A contract in which a stronger party is able to dictate terms to a weaker party, leaving the weaker party no practical choice but to adhere to the terms. If the stronger party has exploited its bargaining power to achieve unfair terms, the contract is against public policy.

contribution A payment made by each, or by any, of several having a common interest or liability of his share in the loss suffered, or in the money necessarily paid by one of the parties in behalf of the others.

conversion Any distinct act of dominion wrongfully exerted over another's personal property in denial of or inconsistent with his rights therein. A tort that is committed by a person who deals with chattels not belonging to him in a manner that is inconsistent with the ownership of the lawful owner.

conveyance In its common use, it refers to a written instrument transferring the title to land or some interest therein from one person to another. It is sometimes applied to the transfer of the property in personalty.

copartnership A partnership.

corporation An artificial being, invisible, intangible, and existing only in contemplation of law. It is exclusively the work of the law, and the best evidence of its existence is the grant of corporate powers by the commonwealth.

corporeal Possessing physical substance; tangible; perceptible to the senses.

counterclaim A claim that, if established, will defeat or in some way qualify a judgment to which the plaintiff is otherwise entitled.

counteroffer A cross-offer made by the offeree to the offeror.

course of dealing A sequence of previous conduct between the parties to a transaction that is fairly to be regarded as establishing a common basis for interpreting their contract.

convenant The word is used in its popular sense as synonymous to contract. In its specific sense, it ordinarily imparts an agreement reduced to writing, and executed by a sealing and delivery.

covenantor A person who makes a covenant.

coverture The condition of a married woman.

credible As applied to a witness, the word means competent.

cross-action Cross-complaint; an independent action brought by a defendant against the plaintiff.

culpable Blameworthy; denotes breach of legal duty but not criminal conduct.

cumulative voting A method of voting by which an elector entitled to vote for several candidates for the same office may cast more than one vote for the same candidate, distributing among the candidates as he chooses a number of votes equal to the number of candidates to be elected.

custody The bare control or care of a thing, as distinguished from the possession of it.

damages Indemnity to the person who suffers loss or harm from an injury; a sum recoverable as amends for a wrong. An adequate compensation for the loss suffered or the injury sustained.

compensatory Damages that will compensate a party for direct losses due to an injury suffered.

consequential Damages that are not produced without the concurrence of some other event attributable to the same origin or cause.

liquidated Damages made certain by the prior agreement of the parties.

nominal Damages that are recoverable where a legal right is to be vindicated against an invasion that has produced no actual present loss.

special Actual damages that would not necessarily but because of special circumstances do in fact flow from an injury.

date of issue As the term is applied to notes, bonds, etc., of a series, it usually means the arbitrary date fixed as the beginning of the term for which they run, without reference to the precise time when convenience or the state of the market may permit their sale or delivery.

D/B/A Doing business as; indicates the use of a trade name.

deal To engage in transactions of any kind, to do business with.

debenture A written acknowledgment of a debt; specifically, an instrument under seal for the repayment of money lent.

debtor A person who owes another anything, or who is under obligation, arising from express agreement, implication of law, or from the principles of natural justice, to render and pay a sum of money to another.

deceit A tort involving intentional misrepresentation or cheating by means of some device.

decision A decision is the judgment of a court, while the opinion represents merely the reasons for that judgment.

declaration The pleadings by which a plaintiff in an action at law sets out his cause of action. An admission or statement subsequently used as evidence in the trial of an action.

declaratory judgment One that expresses the opinion of a court on a question of law without ordering anything to be done.

decree An order or sentence of a court of equity determining some right or adjudicating some matter affecting the merits of the cause.

deed A writing, sealed and delivered by the parties; an instrument conveying real property.

deed of trust A three-party instrument used to create a security interest in real property in which the legal title to the real property is placed in one or more trustees to secure the repayment of a sum of money or the performance of other conditions.

de facto In fact, as distinguished from "de jure," by right.

defalcation The word includes both embezzlement and misappropriation and is a broader term than either.

default Fault; neglect; omission; the failure of a party to an action to appear when properly served with process; the failure to perform a duty or obligation; the failure of a person to pay money when due or when lawfully demanded.

defeasible (of title to property) Capable of being defeated. A title to property that is open to attack or that may be defeated by the performance of some act.

defend To oppose a claim or action; to plead in defense of an action; to contest an action suit or proceeding.

defendant A party sued in a personal action.

defendant in error Any of the parties in whose favor a judgment was rendered that the losing party seeks to have reversed or modified by writ of error and whom he names as adverse parties.

deficiency That part of a debt that a mortgage was made to secure, not realized by the liquidation of the mortgaged property. Something that is lacking.

defraud To deprive another of a right by deception or artifice. To cheat; to wrong another by fraud.

dehors Outside of; disconnected with; unrelated to.

de jure By right; complying with the law in all respects.

del credere agent An agent who guarantees his principal against the default of those with whom contracts are made.

deliver To surrender property to another person.

demand A claim; a legal obligation; a request to perform an alleged obligation; a written statement of a claim.

de minimis non curat lex The law is not concerned with trifles. The maxim has been applied to exclude the recovery of nominal damages where no unlawful intent or disturbance of a right of possession is shown, and where all possible damage is expressly disproved.

demurrage A compensation for the delay of a vessel beyond the time allowed for loading, unloading, or sailing. It is also applied to the compensation for the similar delay of a railroad car.

demurrer A motion to dismiss; an allegation in pleading to the effect that even if the facts alleged by the opposing party are true, they are insufficient to require an answer.

de novo, trial Anew; over again; a second time. A trial de novo is a new trial in which the entire case is retried in all its detail.

dependent covenants Covenants made by two parties to a deed or agreement such that the thing covenanted or promised to be done on each part enters into the whole consideration for the covenant or promise on the part of the other, or such covenants as are concurrent, and to be performed at the same time. Neither party to such a covenant can maintain an action against the other without averring and proving performance on his part.

deposition An affidavit; an oath; the written testimony of a witness given in the course of a judicial proceeding, either at law or in equity, in response to interrogatories either oral or written, and where an opportunity is given for cross-examination.

deputy A person subordinate to a public officer whose business and object is to perform the duties of the principal.

derivative action A suit by a shareholder to enforce a corporate cause of action.

descent Hereditary succession. It is the title whereby a person on the death of an ancestor acquires the ancestor's estate by right of representation as heir at law.

detinue A common law action, now seldom used, that lies where a party claims the specific recovery of goods and chattels unlawfully detained from him.

detriment A detriment is any act or forbearance by a promisee. A loss or harm suffered in person or property.

dictum The opinion of a judge that does not embody the resolution or determination of the court and is made without argument or full consideration of the point, and is not the professed deliberation of the judge herself.

directed verdict A verdict that the jury returns as directed by the court. The court may thus withdraw the case from the jury whenever there is no competent, relevant, and material evidence to support the issue.

discharge in bankruptcy An order or decree rendered by a court in bankruptcy proceedings, the effect of which is to satisfy all debts provable against the estate of the bankrupt as of the time when the bankruptcy proceedings were initiated.

discount A loan on an evidence of debt, where the compensation for the use of the money until the maturity of the debt is deducted from the principal and retained by the lender at the time of making the loan.

dismiss To order a cause, motion, or prosecution to be discontinued or quashed.

disparagement Action arising from negative false statements made about the quality of a company or product that causes lost business opportunities.

dissolution In partnership law, the change in the relation of the partners caused by any partner ceasing to be associated with the carrying on of the business.

diverse citizenship A term of frequent use in the interpretation of the federal constitutional provision for the jurisdiction of the federal courts that extends it to controversies between citizens of different states.

divided court A court is so described when there has been a division of opinion between its members on a matter that has been submitted to it for decision.

dividend A gain or profit. A fund that a corporation sets apart from its profits to be divided among its members.

domain The ownership of land; immediate or absolute ownership. The public lands of a state are frequently termed the public domain.

domicile A place where a person lives or has his home; in a strict legal sense, the place where he has his true, fixed, permanent home and principal establishment, and to which place he has, whenever he is absent, the intention of returning.

dominion (property) The rights of dominion or property are those rights that a person may acquire in and to such external things as are unconnected with his body.

donee A person to whom a gift is made.

donor A person who makes a gift.

dower The legal right or interest that his wife acquires by marriage in the real estate of her husband.

draft A written order drawn on one person by another, requesting him to pay money to a designated third person. A bill of exchange payable on demand.

drawee A person on whom a draft or bill of exchange is drawn by the drawer.

drawer The maker of a draft or bill of exchange.

due bill An acknowledgment of a debt in writing, not made payable to order.

due process A constitutional right that is either procedural (government must follow fair and consistent procedures) or substantive (the law itself must be fair).

dummy One posing or represented as acting for himself but in reality acting for another. A tool or "straw man" for the real parties in interest.

duress Overpowering of the will of a person by force or fear.

earnest Something given as part of the purchase price to bind the bargain.

easement The right that one person has to use the land of another for a specific purpose.

edict A command or prohibition promulgated by a sovereign and having the effect of law.

effects As used in wills, the word is held equivalent to personal property. It denotes property in a more extensive sense than goods and includes all kinds of personal property but will be held not to include real property, unless the context discloses an intention on the part of the testator to dispose of his realty by the use of the word.

e.g. An abbreviation for "exempli gratia," meaning for or by the way of example.

ejectment By statute in some states, it is an action to recover the immediate possession of real property. At common law, it was a purely possessory action, and as modified by statute, though based on title, it is still essentially a possessory action.

eleemosynary corporation A corporation created for a charitable purpose or for charitable purposes.

emancipate To release; to set free. Where parents expressly or impliedly, by their conduct, waive their right generally to the services of their minor child, the child is said to be emancipated and may sue on contracts made by him for his services.

embezzlement A statutory offense consisting of the fraudulent conversion of another's personal property by one to whom it has been intrusted, with the intention of depriving the owner thereof, the gist of the offense being usually the violation of relations of fiduciary character.

eminent domain A governmental power whereby the government can take or condemn private property for a public purpose on the payment of just compensation.

employment at will A rule stating that if an employment is not for a definite time period, either party may terminate the employment without liability at any time and for any reason.

en banc With all the judges of the court sitting.

encumbrance An encumbrance on land is a right in a third person in the land to the diminution of the value of the land, though consistent with the passing of the fee by the deed of conveyance.

endorsement See **indorsement.**

entry Recordation; noting in a record; going on land; taking actual possession of land.

environmental impact statement A document that the National Environmental Policy Act requires federal agencies to prepare in connection with any legislative proposals or proposed actions that will significantly affect the environment.

eo nominee By or in that name or designation.

equity A system of justice that developed in England separate from the common law courts. Few states in the United States still maintain separate equity courts, though most apply equity principles and procedures when remedies derived from the equity courts are sought. A broader meaning denotes fairness and justice.

error A mistake of law or fact; a mistake of the court in the trial of an action.

escheat The revision of land to the state in the event there is no person competent to inherit it.

estate Technically, the word refers only to an interest in land.

estate at will A lease of lands or tenements to be held at the will of the lessor. Such can be determined by either party.

estate for a term An estate less than a freehold that is in fact a contract for the possession of land or tenements for some determinate period.

estate for life An estate created by deed or grant conveying land or tenements to a person to hold for the term of his own life or for the life of any other person or for more lives than one.

estate in fee simple An absolute inheritance, clear of any conditions, limitations, or restrictions to particular heirs. It is the highest estate known to the law and necessarily implies absolute dominion over the land.

estate per autre vie An estate that is to endure for the life of another person than the grantee, or for the lives of more than one, in either of which cases the grantee is called the tenant for life.

estop To bar or stop.

estoppel That state of affairs that arises when one is forbidden by law from alleging or denying a fact because of his previous action or inaction.

et al. An abbreviation for the latin "et alius," meaning "and another." Also, for "et alii," meaning "and others."

et ux. An abbreviation for the latin "et uxor," meaning "and his wife."

eviction Originally, as applied to tenants, the word meant depriving the tenant of the possession of the demised premises, but technically, it is the disturbance of his possession, depriving him of the enjoyment of the premises demised or any portion thereof by title paramount or by entry and act of the landlord.

evidence That which makes clear or ascertains the truth of the fact or point in issue either on the one side or the other; those rules of law whereby we determine what testimony is to be admitted and what rejected in each case and what is the weight to be given to the testimony admitted.

exception An objection; a reservation; a contradiction.

ex contractu From or out of a contract.

exculpatory clause A clause in a contract or trust instrument that excuses a party from some duty.

ex delicto From or out of a wrongful act; tortious; tortiously.

executed When applied to written instruments, the word is sometimes used as synonymous with the word "signed" and means no more than that, but more frequently it imports that everything has been done to complete the transaction; that is, that the instrument has been signed, sealed, and delivered. An executed contract is one in which the object of the contract is performed.

execution A remedy in the form of a writ or process afforded by law for the enforcement of a judgment. The final consummation of a contract of sale, including only those acts that are necessary to the full completion of an instrument, such as the signature of the seller, the affixing of his seal, and its delivery to the buyer.

executor A person who is designated in a will as one who is to administer the estate of the testator.

executory Not yet executed; not yet fully performed, completed, fulfilled, or carried out; to be performed wholly or in part.

executrix Feminine of executor.

exemption A release from some burden, duty, or obligation; a grace; a favor; an immunity; taken out from under the general rule, not to be like others who are not exempt.

exhibit A copy of a written instrument on which a pleading is founded, annexed to the pleading and by reference made a part of it. Any paper or thing offered in evidence and marked for identification.

ex post facto laws Statutes that are unconstitutional because they punish people for acts that occurred before the law was passed.

expropriation A government's taking of a business's assets, such as a manufacturing facility, usually without just compensation.

face value The nominal or par value of an instrument as expressed on its face; in the case of a bond, this is the amount really due, including interest.

factor An agent who is employed to sell goods for a principal, usually in his own name, and who is given possession of the goods.

F.A.S. An abbreviation for the expression "free alongside steamer."

fee simple absolute Same as fee simple. See **estate in fee simple.**

felony As a general rule, all crimes punishable by death or by imprisonment in a state prison are felonies.

feme covert A married woman.

feme sole An unmarried woman.

fiction An assumption made by the law that something is true that is or may be false.

fiduciary One who holds goods in trust for another or one who holds a position of trust and confidence.

fieri facias "You cause to be made"—an ordinary writ of execution whereby the officer is commanded to levy and sell and to "make," if he can, the amount of the judgment creditors demand.

financing statement A document, usually a multicopy form, filed in a public office serving as constructive notice to the world that a creditor claims a security interest in collateral that belongs to a certain named debtor.

fixture A thing that was originally a personal chattel and that has been actually or constructively affixed to the soil itself or to some structure legally a part of the land.

F.O.B. An abbreviation of "free on board."

foreclosure To terminate the rights of the mortgagor/owner of property.

forum The state or county that will hear a given case.

forwarder A person who, having no interest in goods and no ownership or interest in the means of their carriage, undertakes, for hire, to forward them by a safe carrier to their destination.

franchise A special privilege conferred by government on individuals, and which does not belong to the citizens of a country generally, of common right. Also, a contractual relationship establishing a means of marketing goods or services giving certain elements of control to the supplier (franchiser) in return for the right of the franchisee to use the supplier's trade name or trademark, usually in a specific marketing area.

fungible goods Goods any unit of which is from its nature or by mercantile custom treated as the equivalent of any other unit.

futures Contracts for the sale and future delivery of stocks or commodities, wherein either party may waive delivery, and receive or pay, as the case may be, the difference in market price at the time set for delivery.

garnishee As a noun, the term signifies the person on whom a garnishment is served, usually a debtor of the defendant in the action. Used as a verb, the word means to institute garnishment proceedings; to cause a garnishment to be levied on the garnishee.

garnishment The term denotes a proceeding whereby property, money, or credits of a debtor in possession of another, the garnishee, are applied to the payment of the debts by means of process against the debtor and the garnishee. It is a statutory proceeding based on contract relations, and can only be resorted to where it is authorized by statute.

general issue A plea of the defendant amounting to a denial of every material allegation of fact in the plaintiff's complaint or declaration.

gift causa mortis A gift made in contemplation of the donor's death. It may be revoked if the donor does not die of the anticipated ailment or revokes the gift before dying.

gift inter vivos A gift given not in contemplation of the donor's death. They generally are not revocable after delivery has occurred.

going business An establishment that is still continuing to transact its ordinary business, though it may be insolvent.

good faith An honest intention to abstain from taking an unfair advantage of another.

grantee A person to whom a grant is made.

grantor A person who makes a grant.

gravamen Gist, essence; substance. The grievance complained of; the substantial cause of the action.

gray market goods Goods lawfully bearing trademarks or using patented or copyrighted material, but imported into a foreign market without the authorization of the owner of the trademark, patent, or copyright.

guarantor A person who promises to answer for the debt, default, or miscarriage of another.

guaranty An undertaking by one person to be answerable for the payment of some debt, or the due performance of some contract or duty by another person, who remains liable to pay or perform the same.

guardian A person (in some cases a corporation) to whom the law has entrusted the custody and control of the person, or estate, or both, of a minor, insane, or incompetent person.

habeas corpus Any of several common law writs having as their object to bring a party before the court or judge. The only issue it presents is whether the prisoner is restrained of his liberty by due process.

habendum The second part of a deed or conveyance following that part that names the grantee. It describes the estate conveyed and to what use. It is no longer essential and if included in a modern deed is a mere useless form.

hearing The supporting of one's contentions by argument and if need be by proof. It is an absolute right and if denied to a contestant, it would amount to the denial of one of his constitutional rights.

hedging A market transaction in which a party buys a certain quantity of a given commodity at the price current on the date of the purchase and sells an equal quantity of the same commodity for future delivery for the purpose of getting protection against loss due to fluctuation in the market.

heirs Those persons appointed by law to succeed to the real estate of a decedent, in case of intestacy. See also *intestate*.

hereditaments A larger and more comprehensive word than either "land" or "tenements," and meaning anything capable of being inherited, whether it be real, personal, or mixed property.

holder A person in possession of a document of title or an instrument payable or indorsed to him, his order, or to bearer.

holder in due course A holder who has taken a negotiable instrument under the following conditions: (1) that it is complete and regular on its face; (2) that he became the holder of it before it was overdue, and without notice that it had been previously dishonored, if such was the fact; (3) that he took it in good faith and for value; and (4) that at the time it was negotiated to him he had no notice of any infirmity in the instrument or defect in the title of the person negotiating it.

holding company A corporation whose purpose or function is to own or otherwise hold the shares of other corporations either for investment or control.

homestead In a legal sense, the word means the real estate occupied as a home and also the right to have it exempt from levy and forced sale. It is the land, not exceeding the prescribed amount, on which the dwelling house, or residence, or habitation, or abode of the owner thereof and his family resides, and includes the dwelling house as an indispensable part.

illusory Deceiving or intending to deceive, as by false appearances; fallacious. An illusory promise is a promise that appears to be binding but that in fact does not bind the promisor.

immunity A personal favor granted by law, contrary to the general rule.

impanel To place the names of the jurors on a panel; to make a list of the names of those persons who have been selected for jury duty; to go through the process of selecting a jury that is to try a cause.

implied warranty An implied warranty arises by operation of law and exists without any intention of the seller to create it. It is a conclusion or inference of law, pronounced by the court, on facts admitted or proved before the jury.

inalienable Incapable of being alienated, transferred, or conveyed; nontransferable.

in camera In the judge's chambers; in private.

incapacity In its legal meaning, it applies to one's legal disability, such as infancy, want of authority, or other personal incapacity to alter a legal relationship.

inception Initial stage. The word does not refer to a state of actual existence but to a condition of things or circumstances from which the thing may develop; as the beginning of work on a building.

inchoate Imperfect; incipient; not completely formed.

indemnify To hold harmless against loss or damage.

indemnity An obligation or duty resting on one person to make good any loss or damage another has incurred while acting at his request or for his benefit. By a contract of indemnity one may agree to saving another from a legal consequence of the conduct of one of the parties or of some other person.

indenture Indentures were deeds that originally were made in two parts, formed by cutting or tearing a single sheet across the middle in a jagged or indented line, so that the two parts might be subsequently matched; they were executed by both grantor and grantee. Later, the indenting of the deed was discontinued, yet the term came to be applied to all deeds that were executed by both parties.

independent contractor One who, exercising an independent employment, contracts to do a piece of work according to his or her own methods, and without being subject to the control of the employer except as to result. The legal effect is to insulate the employing party from liability for the misconduct of the independent contractor and his employees.

indictment An accusation founded on legal testimony of a direct and positive character, and the concurring judgment of at least 12 of the grand jurors that on the evidence presented to them the defendant is guilty.

indorsement Writing on the back of an instrument; the contract whereby the holder of a bill or note transfers to another person his right to such instrument and incurs the liabilities incident to the transfer.

infant See **minor.**

information A written accusation of crime brought by a public prosecuting officer to a court without the intervention of a grand jury.

injunction A restraining order issued by a court of equity; a prohibitory writ restraining a person from committing or doing an act, other than a criminal act, that appears to be against equity and conscience. There is also the mandatory injunction that commands an act to be done or undone and compels the performance of some affirmative act.

in pari delicto Equally at fault in tort or crime; in equal fault or guilt.

in personam Against the person.

in re In the matter; in the transaction.

in rem Against a thing and not against a person; concerning the condition or status of a thing.

inside information Confidential information possessed by a person due to his relationship with a business.

insolvency The word has two distinct meanings. It may be used to denote the insufficiency of the entire property and assets of an individual to pay his or her debts, which is its general meaning and its meaning as used in the Bankruptcy Code; but in a more restricted sense, it expresses the inability of a party to pay his debts as they become due in the regular course of his business, and it is so used when traders and merchants are said to be insolvent.

in statu quo In the existing state of things.

instrument In its broadest sense, the term includes formal or legal documents in writing, such as contracts, deeds, wills, bonds, leases, and mortgages. In the law of evidence, it has still a wider meaning and includes not merely documents but witnesses and things animate and inanimate that may be presented for inspection.

insurable interest Any interest in property the owner of which derives a benefit from the existence of the property or would suffer a loss from its destruction. It is not necessary, to constitute an insurable interest, that the interest is such that the event insured against would necessarily subject the insured to loss; it is sufficient that it might do so.

inter alia Among other things or matters.

interlocutory Something not final but deciding only some subsidiary matter raised while a lawsuit is pending.

interpleader An equitable remedy applicable where one fears injury from conflicting claims. Where a person does not know which of two or more persons claiming certain property held by him or her has a right to it, filing a bill of interpleader forces the claimants to litigate the title between themselves.

inter se Among themselves.

intervention A proceeding by which one not originally made a party to an action or suit is permitted, on his own application, to appear therein and join one of the original parties in maintaining his cause of action or defense, or to assert some cause of action against some or all of the parties to the proceeding as originally instituted.

intestate A person who has died without leaving a valid will disposing of his or her property and estate.

in toto In the whole, altogether, wholly.

in transitu On the journey. Goods are as a rule considered as in transitu while they are in the possession of a carrier, whether by land or water, until they arrive at the ultimate place of their destination and are delivered into the actual possession of the buyer, whether or not the carrier has been named or designated by the buyer.

ipso facto By the fact itself; by the very fact; by the act itself.

joint bank account A bank account of two persons so fixed that they shall be joint owners thereof during their mutual lives, and the survivor shall take the whole on the death of the other.

jointly Acting together or in concert or cooperating; holding in common or interdependently, not separately. Persons are "jointly bound" in a bond or note when both or all must be sued in one action for its enforcement, not either one at the election of the creditor.

jointly and severally Persons who find themselves "jointly and severally" in a bond or note may all be sued together for its enforcement, or the creditor may select any one or more as the object of his suit.

joint tenancy An estate held by two or more jointly, with an equal right in all to share in the enjoyments of the land during their lives. Four requisites must exist to constitute a joint tenancy: the tenants must have one and the same interest; the interest must accrue by one and the same conveyance; they must commence at one and the same time; and the property must be held by one and the same undivided possession. If any one of these four elements is lacking, the estate will not be one of joint tenancy. An incident of joint tenancy is the right of survivorship.

judgment The sentence of the law on the record; the application of the law to the facts and pleadings. The last word in the judicial controversy; the final consideration and determination of a court of competent jurisdiction on matters submitted to it in an action or proceeding.

judgment lien The statutory lien on the real property of a judgment debtor that is created by the judgment itself. At common law a judgment imposes no lien on the real property of the judgment debtor, and to subject the property of the debtor to the judgment it was necessary to take out a writ called an elegit.

judgment N.O.V. (judgment non obstante veredicto) Judgment notwithstanding the verdict. Under certain circumstances, the judge has the power to enter a judgment that is contrary to the verdict of the jury. Such a judgment is a judgment non obstante veredicto.

jurisdiction The right to adjudicate concerning the subject matter in a given case. The modern tendency is to make the word include not only the power to hear and determine but also the power to render the particular judgment in the particular case.

jury A body of lay persons, selected by lot, or by some other fair and impartial means, to ascertain, under the guidance of the judge, the truth in questions of fact arising either in civil litigation or a criminal process.

kite To secure the temporary use of money by issuing or negotiating worthless paper and then redeeming such paper with the proceeds of similar paper. The word is also used as a noun, meaning the worthless paper thus employed.

laches The established doctrine of equity that, apart from any question of statutory limitation, its courts will discourage delay and sloth in the enforcement of rights. Equity demands conscience, good faith, and reasonable diligence.

law merchant The custom of merchants, or lex mercatorio, that grew out of the necessity and convenience of business, and that, although different from the general rules of the common law, was engrafted into it and became part of it. It was founded on the custom and usage of merchants.

leading case A case often referred to by the courts and by counsel as having settled and determined a point of law.

leading questions Those questions that suggest to the witness the answer desired, assume a fact to be proved that is not proved, or, embodying a material fact, admit of an answer by a simple negative or affirmative.

lease A contract for the possession and use of land on one side, and a recompense of rent or other income on the other, a conveyance to a person for life, or years, or at will in consideration of a return of rent or other recompense.

legacy A bequest; a testamentary gift of personal property. Sometimes incorrectly applied to a testamentary gift of real property.

legal According to the principles of law; according to the method required by statute; by means of judicial proceedings; not equitable.

legitimacy A person's status embracing his right to inherit from his ancestors, to be inherited from, and to bear the name and enjoy the support of his father.

lemon law A type of state consumer protection law.

letter of credit An instrument containing a request (general or special) to pay to the bearer or person named money, or sell him or her some commodity on credit or give something of value and look to the drawer of the letter for recompense.

levy At common law, a levy on goods consisted of an officer's entering the premises where they were and either leaving an assistant in charge of them or removing them after taking an inventory. Today, courts differ as to what is a valid levy, but by the weight of authority there must be an actual or constructive seizure of the goods. In most states, a levy on land must be made by some unequivocal act of the officer indicating the intention of singling out certain real estate for the satisfaction of the debt.

license A personal privilege to do some act or series of acts on the land of another, without possessing any estate therein. A permit or authorization to do what, without a license, would be unlawful.

lien In its most extensive meaning, it is a charge on property for the payment or discharge of a debt or duty; a qualified right; a proprietary interest that, in a given case, may be exercised over the property of another.

life estate See **estate for life.**

limited liability company A form of organization that is neither corporation nor partnership, but has elements of both.

limited partnership A form of business organization that has one or more general partners who manage the business and have unlimited liability for the obligations of the business and one or more limited partners who do not manage and have limited liability.

lis pendens A pending suit. As applied to the doctrine of lis pendens, it is the jurisdiction, power, or control that courts acquire over property involved in a suit, pending the continuance of the action, and until its final judgment therein.

listing contract A so-called contract whereby an owner of real property employs a broker to procure a purchaser without giving the broker an exclusive right to sell. Under such an agreement, it is generally held that the employment may be terminated by the owner at will, and that a sale of the property by the owner terminates the employment.

litigant A party to a lawsuit.

long arm statute A statute subjecting a foreign corporation to jurisdiction although it may have committed only a single act within the state.

magistrate A word commonly applied to lower judicial officers such as justices of the peace, police judges, town recorders, and other local judicial functionaries. In a broader sense, a magistrate is a public civil officer invested with some part of the legislative, executive, or judicial power given by the Constitution. The president of the United States is the chief magistrate of the nation.

maker A person who makes or executes an instrument, the signer of an instrument.

mala fides Bad faith.

malfeasance The doing of an act that a person ought not to do at all. It is to be distinguished from misfeasance, which is the improper doing of an act that a person might lawfully do.

malicious prosecution An intentional tort designed to protect against the wrongful initiation of criminal proceedings.

malum in se Evil in and of itself. An offense or act that is naturally evil as adjudged by the senses of a civilized community. Acts malum in se are usually criminal acts but not necessarily so.

malum prohibitum An act that is wrong because it is made so by statute.

mandamus We command. It is a command issuing from a competent jurisdiction, in the name of the state or sovereign, directed to some inferior court, officer, corporation, or person, requiring the performance of a particular duty therein specified, which duty results from the official station of the party to whom it is directed, or from operation of law.

margin A deposit by a buyer in stocks with a seller or a stockbroker, as security to cover fluctuations in the market in reference to stocks that the buyer has purchased but for which he has not paid. Commodities are also traded on margin.

marshals Ministerial officers belonging to the executive department of the federal government, who with their deputies have the same powers of executing the laws of the United States in each state as the sheriffs and their deputies in such state may have in executing the laws of that state.

material Important. In securities law, a fact is material if a reasonable person would consider it important in his decision to purchase shares or to vote shares.

mechanic's lien A claim created by law for the purpose of securing a priority of payment of the price of value of work performed and materials furnished in erecting or repairing a building or other structure; as such, it attaches to the land as well as to the buildings erected therein.

mediation A form of dispute resolution in which the disputing parties resolve their dispute with the help of a third party, the mediator.

mens rea A guilty mind, criminal intent.

merchant Under the Uniform Commercial Code, one who regularly deals in goods of the kind sold in the contract at issue, or holds himself out as having special knowledge or skill relevant to such goods, or who makes the sale through an agent who regularly deals in such goods or claims such knowledge or skill.

merchantable Of good quality and salable, but not necessarily the best. As applied to articles sold, the word requires that the article shall be such as is usually sold in the market, of medium quality, and bringing the average price.

merger In corporation law, traditionally, a transaction by which one corporation acquires another corporation, with the acquiring corporation being owned by the shareholders of both corporations and the acquired corporation going out of existence. Today, loosely applied to any negotiated acquisition of one corporation by another.

minitrial A form of dispute resolution in which the disputants voluntarily hear a shortened version of their cases presented by their lawyers, then try to negotiate a settlement.

minor A person who has not reached the age at which the law recognizes a general contractual capacity (called majority), formerly 21 years; recently changed to 18 in many states.

misdemeanor Any crime that is punishable neither by death nor by imprisonment in a state prison.

mistrial An invalid trial due to lack of jurisdiction, error in selection of jurors, or some other fundamental requirement.

mitigation of damages A reduction in the amount of damages due to extenuating circumstances.

moiety One half.

mortgage A conveyance of property to secure the performance of some obligation, the conveyance to be void on the due performance thereof.

motive The cause or reason that induced a person to commit a crime.

movables A word derived from the civil law and usually understood to signify the utensils that are to furnish or ornament a house, but it would seem to comprehend personal property generally.

mutuality Reciprocal obligations of the parties required to make a contract binding on either party.

necessaries With reference to a minor, the word includes whatever is reasonably necessary for his or her proper and suitable maintenance, in view of the income level and social position of the minor's family.

negligence The word has been defined as the omission to do something that a reasonable person, guided by those considerations that ordinarily regulate human affairs, would do, or doing something that a prudent and reasonable person would not do.

negotiable Capable of being transferred by indorsement or delivery so as to give the holder a right to sue in his or her own name and to avoid certain defenses against the payee.

negotiable instrument An instrument that may be transferred or negotiated, so that the holder may maintain an action thereon in his own name.

no arrival, no sale A sale of goods "to arrive" or "on arrival," per or ex a certain ship, has been construed to be a sale subject to a double condition precedent, namely, that the ship arrives in port and that when it arrives the goods are on board, and if either of these conditions fails, the contract becomes nugatory.

nolo contendere A plea in a criminal action that has the same effect as a guilty plea except that it does not bind the defendant in a civil suit on the same wrong.

nominal damages See **damages.**

non compos mentis Totally and positively incompetent. The term denotes a person entirely destitute or bereft of his memory or understanding.

nonfeasance In the law of agency, it is the total omission or failure of an agent to enter on the performance of some distinct duty or undertaking that he or she has agreed with the principal to do.

non obstante veredicto See **judgment non obstante veredicto.**

nonsuit A judgment given against a plaintiff who is unable to prove a case, or when the plaintiff refuses or neglects to proceed to trial.

no par value stock Stock of a corporation having no face or par value.

notice A person has notice of a fact if she knows it, has reason to know it, or has been given proper notification of it.

noting protest The act of making a memorandum on a bill or note at the time of, and embracing the principal facts attending, its dishonor. The object is to have a record from which the instrument of protest may be written, so that a notary need not rely on his memory for the fact.

novation A mutual agreement, between all parties concerned, for the discharge of a valid obligation on the part of the debtor or another, or a like agreement for the discharge of a debtor to his creditor by the substitution of a new creditor.

nudum pactum A naked promise, a promise for which there is no consideration.

nuisance In legal parlance, the word extends to everything that endangers life or health, gives offense to the senses, violates the laws of decency, or obstructs the reasonable and comfortable use of property.

oath Any form of attestation by which a person signifies that he is bound in conscience to perform an act faithfully and truthfully. It involves the idea of calling on God to witness what is averred as truth, and it is supposed to be accompanied with an invocation of His vengeance, or a renunciation of His favor, in the event of falsehood.

obiter dictum That which is said in passing; a rule of law set forth in a court's opinion, but not necessary to decide the case.

objection In the trial of a case, it is the formal remonstrance made by counsel to something that has been said or done, in order to obtain the court's ruling thereon; and when the court has ruled, the alleged error is preserved by the objector's exception to the ruling, which exception is noted in the record.

obligee A person to whom another is bound by a promise or other obligation; a promisee.

obligor A person who is bound by a promise or other obligation; a promisor.

offer A proposal by one person to another that is intended of itself to create legal relations on acceptance by the person to whom it is made.

offeree A person to whom an offer is made.

offeror A person who makes an offer.

opinion The opinion of the court represents merely the reasons for its judgment, while the decision of the court is the judgment itself.

option A contract whereby the owner of property agrees with another person that such person shall have the right to buy the property at a fixed price within a certain time. There are two independent elements in an option contract: First, the offer to sell, which does not become a contract until accepted; second, the completed contract to leave the offer open for a specified time.

order A court decree.

ordinance A legislative enactment of a county or an incorporated city or town.

ostensible authority Such authority as a principal, either intentionally or by want or ordinary care, causes or allows a third person to believe the agent to possess.

ostensible partners Members of a partnership whose names are made known and appear to the world as partners.

overdraft The withdrawal from a bank by a depositor of money in excess of the amount of money he or she has on deposit there.

overplus That which remains; a balance left over.

owner's risk A term employed by common carriers in bills of lading and shipping receipts to signify that the carrier does not assume responsibility for the safety of the goods.

par Par means equal, and par value means a value equal to the face of a bond or a stock certificate.

parol Oral; verbal; by word of mouth; spoken as opposed to written.

parties All persons who are interested in the subject matter of an action and who have a right to make defense, control the proceedings, examine and cross-examine witnesses, and appeal from the judgment.

partition A proceeding the object of which is to enable those who own property as joint tenants or tenants in common to put an end to the tenancy so as to vest in each a sole estate in specific property or an allotment of the lands and tenements. If a division of the estate is impracticable, the estate ought to be sold and the proceeds divided.

partners Those persons who contribute property, money, or services to carry on a joint business for their common benefit, and who own and share the profits thereof in certain proportions; the members of a partnership.

partnership A form of business organization; specifically, an association of two or more persons to carry on as co-owners of a business for profit.

patent A patent for land is a conveyance of title to government lands by the government; a patent of an invention is the right of monopoly secured by statute to those who invent or discover new and useful devices and processes.

pawn A pledge; a bailment of personal property as security for some debt or engagement, redeemable on certain terms, and with an implied power of sale on default.

payee A person to whom a payment is made or is made payable.

pecuniary Financial; pertaining or relating to money; capable of being estimated, computed, or measured by money value.

pendente lite During the litigation.

per curiam By the court; by the court as a whole.

peremptory challenge A challenge to a proposed juror that a defendant in a criminal case may make as an absolute right, and that cannot be questioned by either opposing counsel or the court.

perfection The process or method by which a secured party obtains a priority in certain collateral belonging to a debtor against creditors or claimants of a debtor; it usually entails giving notice of the security interest, such as by taking possession or filing a financial statement.

performance As the word implies, it is such a thorough fulfillment of a duty as puts an end to obligations by leaving nothing to be done. The chief requisite of performance is that it shall be exact.

perjury The willful and corrupt false swearing or affirming, after an oath lawfully administered, in the course of a judicial or quasi-judicial proceeding as to some matter material to the issue or point in question.

per se The expression means by or through itself; simply; as such; in its own relations.

petition In equity pleading, a petition is in the nature of a pleading (at least when filed by a stranger to the suit) and forms a basis for independent action.

plaintiff A person who brings a suit, action, bill, or complaint.

plaintiff in error The unsuccessful party to the action who prosecutes a writ of error in a higher court.

plea A plea is an answer to a declaration or complaint or any material allegation of fact therein that, if untrue, would defeat the action. In criminal procedure, a plea is the matter that the accused, on his arraignment, alleges in answer to the charge against him.

pledge A pawn; a bailment of personal property as security for some debt or engagement, redeemable on certain terms, and with an implied power of sale on default.

pledgee A person to whom personal property is pledged by a pledgor.

pledgor A person who makes a pledge of personal property to a pledgee.

polygraph A mechanical test used to help determine whether someone is telling the truth.

positive law Laws actually and specifically enacted or adopted by proper authority of the government of a jural society, as distinguished from principles of morality or laws of honor.

possession Respecting real property, possession involves exclusive dominion and control such as owners of like property usually exercise over it. Manual control of personal property either as owner or as one having a qualified right in it.

power of attorney A written authorization to an agent to perform specified acts on behalf of his or her principal. The writing by which the authority is evidenced is termed a letter of attorney and is dictated by the convenience and certainty of business.

precedent A previous decision relied on as authority.

preemption A state or local law is stricken when federal legislation dealing with interstate commerce regulates the same activity (expressly) or when Congress has shown an intent to reserve such regulatory power (impliedly).

preference The act of a debtor in paying or securing one or more of his creditors in a manner more favorable to them than to other creditors or to the exclusion of such other creditors. In the absence of statute, a preference is perfectly good, but to be legal it must be bona fide and not a mere subterfuge of the debtor to secure a future benefit to himself or to prevent the application of his property to his debts.

prerogative A special power, privilege, or immunity, usually used in reference to an official or his office.

presumption A term used to signify that which may be assumed without proof, or taken for granted. It is asserted as a self-evident result of human reason and experience.

prima facie At first sight; a fact that is presumed to be true unless disproved by contrary evidence.

principal In agency law, one under whose direction an agent acts and for whose benefit that agent acts.

priority Having precedence or the better right.

privilege A right peculiar to an individual or body.

privity A mutual or successive relationship as, for example, between the parties to a contract.

probate A term used to include all matters of which probate courts have jurisdiction, which in many states are the estates of deceased persons and of persons under guardianship.

proceeds Whatever is received on the sale, exchange, collection, or other disposition of collateral.

process In law, generally the summons or notice of beginning of suit.

proffer To offer for acceptance or to make a tender of.

promisee The person to whom a promise is made.

promisor A person who makes a promise to another; a person who promises.

promissory estoppel An estoppel arising on account of a promise that the promisor should expect to and which does induce an action or forbearance of a substantial nature.

promoters The persons who bring about the incorporation and organization of a corporation.

pro rata According to the rate, proportion, or allowance.

prospectus An introductory proposal for a contract in which the representations may or may not form the basis of the contract actually made; it may contain promises that are to be treated as a sort of floating obligation to take effect when appropriated by persons to whom they are addressed, and amount to a contract when assented to by any person who invests his money on the faith of them.

pro tanto For so much; to such an extent.

proximate cause That cause of an injury that, in natural and continuous sequence, unbroken by any efficient intervening cause, produces the injury, and without which the injury would not have occurred.

qualified acceptance A conditional or modified acceptance. In order to create a contract, an acceptance must accept the offer substantially as made; hence, a qualified acceptance is no acceptance at all, is treated by the courts as a rejection of the offer made, and is in effect an offer by the offeree, which the offeror may, if he chooses, accept and thus create a contract.

quantum meruit As much as is deserved. A part of a common law action in assumpsit for the value of services rendered.

quash To vacate or make void.

quasi contract An obligation arising not from an agreement between the parties but from the voluntary act of one of them or some relation between them that will be enforced by a court.

quasi-judicial Acts of public officers involving investigation of facts and drawing conclusions from them as a basis of official action.

quid pro quo Something for something. The term is used in employment law to describe a form of sexual harassment in which a job benefit is conditioned on sexual favors.

quiet enjoyment A tenant's right to use the leasehold in peace and without disturbance.

quiet title, action to An action to establish a claimant's title in land by requiring adverse claimants to come into court to prove their claim or to be barred from asserting it later.

quitclaim deed A deed conveying only the right, title, and interest of the grantor in the property described, as distinguished from a deed conveying the property itself.

quorum That number of persons, shares represented, or officers who may lawfully transact the business of a meeting called for that purpose.

quo warranto By what authority. The name of a writ (and also of the whole pleading) by which the government commences an action to recover an office or franchise from the person or corporation in possession of it.

ratification The adoption or affirmance by a person of a prior act that did not bind him.

rebuttal Testimony addressed to evidence produced by the opposite party; rebutting evidence.

receiver One appointed by a court to take charge of a business or the property of another during litigation to preserve it and/or to dispose of it as directed by the court.

recognizance At common law, an obligation entered into before some court of record or magistrate duly authorized, with a condition to do some particular act, usually to appear and answer to a criminal accusation. Being taken in open court and entered on the order book, it was valid without the signature or seal of any of the obligors.

recorder A public officer of a town or county charged with the duty of keeping the record books required by law to be kept in his or her office and of receiving and causing to be copied in such books such instruments as by law are entitled to be recorded.

redemption The buying back of one's property after it has been sold. The right to redeem property sold under an order or decree of court is purely a privilege conferred by, and does not exist independently of, statute.

redress Remedy; indemnity; reparation.

release The giving up or abandoning of a claim or right to a person against whom the claim exists or the right is to be enforced or exercised. It is the discharge of a debt by the act of the party, in distinction from an extinguishment that is a discharge by operation of law.

remainderman One who is entitled to the remainder of the estate after a particular estate carved out of it has expired.

remand An action of an appellate court returning a case to the trial court to take further action.

remedy The appropriate legal form of relief by which a remediable right may be enforced.

remittitur The certificate of reversal issued by an appellate court on reversing the order or judgment appealed from.

replevin A common law action by which the owner recovers possession of his own goods.

repudiation Indicating to another party to a contract that the party does not intend to perform his obligations.

res The thing; the subject matter of a suit; the property involved in the litigation; a matter; property; the business; the affair; the transaction.

res adjudicata A matter that has been adjudicated; that which is definitely settled by a judicial decision.

rescind As the word is applied to contracts, to rescind in some cases means to terminate the contract as to future transactions, while in others it means to annul the contract from the beginning.

residue All that portion of the estate of a testator of which no effectual disposition has been made by his will otherwise than in the residuary clause.

respondeat superior *Let the master answer.* Docrine that imposes liability on principals/employers for the injuries their agents/employees cause while working within the scope of their agency/employment.

respondent The defendant in an action; a party adverse to an appellant in an action that is appealed to a higher court. The person against whom a bill in equity was exhibited.

restitution Indemnification.

reversion The residue of a fee simple remaining in the grantor, to commence in possession after the determination of some particular estate granted out by him. The estate of a landlord during the existence of the outstanding leasehold estate.

reversioner A person who is entitled to a reversion.

right When we speak of a person having a right, we must necessarily refer to a civil right, as distinguished from the elemental idea of a right absolute. We must have in mind a right given and protected by law, and a person's enjoyment thereof is regulated entirely by the law that creates it.

riparian Pertaining to or situated on the bank of a river. The word has reference to the bank and not to the bed of the stream.

sale of goods The transfer of ownership to tangible personal property in exchange for money, other goods, or the performance of service.

sanction The penalty that will be incurred by a wrongdoer for the breach of law.

satisfaction A performance of the terms of an accord. If such terms require a payment of a sum of money, then "satisfaction" means that such payment has been made.

scienter In cases of fraud and deceit, the word means knowledge on the part of the person making the representations, at the time when they are made, that they are false. In an action for deceit, it is generally held that scienter must be proved.

seal At common law, a seal is an impression on wax or some other tenacious material, but in modern practice the letters "l.s." (locus sigilli) or the word "seal" enclosed in a scroll, either written or printed, and acknowledged in the body of the instrument to be a seal, are often used as substitutes.

security That which makes the enforcement of a promise more certain than the mere personal obligation of the debtor or promisor, whatever may be his possessions or financial standing. It may be a pledge of property or an additional personal obligation, but it means more than the mere promise of the debtor with property liable to general execution.

security agreement An agreement that creates or provides a security interest or lien on personal property. A term used in the UCC including a wide range of transactions in the nature of chattel mortgages, conditional sales, and so on.

security interest A lien given by a debtor to his creditor to secure payment or performance of a debt or obligation.

seizin In a legal sense, the word means possession of premises with the intention of asserting a claim to a freehold estate therein; it is practically the same thing as ownership; it is a possession of a freehold estate, such as by the common law is created by livery of seizin.

sequester To keep jurors under court supervision, day and night, until the end of a case.

service As applied to a process of courts, the word ordinarily implies something in the nature of an act or proceeding adverse to the party served, or of a notice to him.

setoff A setoff both at law and in equity is that right that exists between two parties, each of whom, under an independent contract, owes an ascertained amount to the other, to set off their respective debts by way of mutual deduction, so that, in any action brought for the larger debt, the residue only, after such deduction, shall be recovered.

severable contract A contract that is not entire or indivisible. If the consideration is single, the contract is entire; but if it is expressly or by necessary implication apportioned, the contract is severable. The question is ordinarily determined by inquiring whether the contract embraces one or more subject matters, whether the obligation is due at the same time to the same person, and whether the consideration is entire or apportioned.

shareholder It is generally held that one who holds shares on the books of the corporation is a shareholder and that one who merely holds a stock certificate is not. Shareholders may become such either by original subscription, by direct purchase from the corporation, or by subsequent transfer from the original holder.

share of stock The right that its owner has in the management, profits, and ultimate assets of the corporation. The tangible property of a corporation and the shares of stock therein are separate and distinct kinds of property and belong to different owners, the first being the property of an artificial person—the corporation; the latter the property of the individual owner.

sight A term signifying the date of the acceptance or that of protest for the nonacceptance of a bill of exchange; for example, 10 days after sight.

sinking fund A fund accumulated by an issuer to redeem corporate securities.

situs Location; local position; the place where a person or thing is, is his situs. Intangible property has no actual situs, but it may have a legal situs and for the purpose of taxation its legal situs is at the place where it is owned and not at the place where it is owed.

sole proprietorship A form of business under which one person owns and controls the business.

sovereign immunity Generally, the idea that the sovereign (or state) may not be sued unless it consents to such a suit.

specific performance Performance of a contract precisely as agreed on; the remedy that arose in equity law to compel the defendant to do what he agreed to do.

stare decisis The doctrine or principle that the decisions of the court should stand as precedents for future guidance.

stated capital Defined specifically in the Model Business Corporation Act; generally, the amount received by a corporation on issuance of its shares except that assigned to capital surplus.

status quo The existing state of things.

statute of limitations A statute that requires that certain classes of lawsuits must be brought within defined limits of time after the right to begin them accrued or the right to bring the lawsuit is lost.

stay To hold an order or decree in abeyance.

stipulation An agreement between opposing counsel in a pending action, usually required to be made in open court and entered on the minutes of the court, or else to be in writing and filed in the action, ordinarily entered into for the purpose of avoiding delay, trouble, or expense in the conduct of the action.

stockholder See **shareholder.**

stoppage in transitu A right that the vendor of goods on credit has to recall them, or retake them, on the discovery of the insolvency of the vendee. It continues so long as the carrier remains in the possession and control of the goods or until there has been an actual or constructive delivery to the vendee, or some third person has acquired a bona fide right in them.

strict liability Legal responsibility placed on an individual for the results of his actions irrespective of whether he was culpable or at fault.

sub judice Before a court.

sub nom Under the name.

subpoena A process the purpose of which is to compel the attendance of a person whom it is desired to use as a witness.

subrogation The substitution of one person in the place of another with reference to a lawful claim or right, frequently referred to as the doctrine of substitution. It is a device adopted or invented by equity to compel the ultimate discharge of a debt or obligation by the person who in good conscience ought to pay it.

sui generis Of its own kind; peculiar to itself.

summary judgment A decision of a trial court without hearing evidence.

summary proceedings Proceedings, usually statutory, in the course of which many formalities are dispensed with. But such proceedings are not concluded without proper investigation of the facts, or without notice, or an opportunity to be heard by the person alleged to have committed the act, or whose property is sought to be affected.

summons A writ or process issued and served on a defendant in a civil action for the purpose of securing his appearance in the action.

supra Above; above mentioned; in addition to.

surety One who by accessory agreement, called a contract of suretyship, binds himself with another, called the principal, for the performance of an obligation with respect to which such other person is already bound and primarily liable for such performance.

T/A Trading as, indicating the use of a trade name.

tacking The adding together of successive periods of adverse possession of persons in privity with each other, in order to constitute one continuous adverse possession for the time required by the statute, to establish title.

tangible Capable of being possessed or realized; readily apprehensible by the mind; real; substantial; evident.

tariff A custom or duty imposed on foreign merchandise imported into a country.

tenancy A tenancy exists when one has let real estate to another to hold of him as landlord. When it is duly created and the tenant is put into possession, he is the owner of an estate for the time being, and has all the usual rights and remedies to defend his possession.

tender An unconditional offer of payment, consisting in the actual production in money or legal tender of a sum not less than the amount due.

tender offer An offer to security holders to acquire their securities in exchange for money or other securities.

tenement A word commonly used in deeds that passes not only lands and other inheritances but also offices, rents, commons, and profits arising from lands. Usually it is applied exclusively to land, or what is ordinarily denominated real property.

tenor The tenor of an instrument is an exact copy of the instrument. Under the rule that an indictment for forgery must set out in the instrument according to its "tenor," the word means an exact copy that the instrument is set forth in the very words and figures.

tenure The manner of holding or occupying lands or offices. The most common estate in land is tenure in "fee simple." With respect to offices, tenure imports time, for example, "tenure for life" or "during good behavior."

testament A last will and testament is the disposition of one's property to take effect after death.

testator A deceased person who died leaving a will.

testatrix Feminine of testator.

testimony In some contexts, the word bears the same import as the word "evidence," but in most connections it has a much narrower meaning. Testimony is the words heard from the witness in court, and evidence is what the jury considers it worth.

time is of the essence A contract clause which allows a court to deem late performance a material breach unless the penalty on the promisor would be unjust. A court may imply time is of the essence if late performance would be of little or no value to the promisee.

tippee A person who is given information by insiders in breach of trust.

title Legal ownership; also, a document evidencing legal rights to real or personal property.

tort An injury or wrong committed, either with or without force, to the person or property of another. Such injury may arise by nonfeasance, or by the malfeasance or the misfeasance of the wrongdoer.

tort-feasor A person who commits a tort; a wrongdoer.

tortious Partaking of the nature of a tort; wrongful; injurious.

trade fixtures Articles of personal property that have been annexed to the freehold and that are necessary to the carrying on of a trade.

trade secret A secret formula, pattern, process, program, device, method, technique, or compilation of information that is used in its owner's business and affords that owner a competitive advantage. Trade secrets are protected by state law.

transcript A copy of a writing.

transferee A person to whom a transfer is made.

transferor A person who makes a transfer.

treasury shares Shares of stock of a corporation that have been issued as fully paid to shareholders and subsequently acquired by the corporation.

treble damages Three times provable damages, as may be granted to private parties bringing an action under the antitrust laws.

trespass Every unauthorized entry on another's property is a trespass and any person who makes such an entry is a trespasser. In its widest signification, trespass means any violation of law. In its most restricted sense, it signifies an injury intentionally inflicted by force either on the person or property of another.

trial An examination before a competent tribunal, according to the law of the land, of the facts or law put in issue in a cause, for the purpose of determining such issue. When the court hears and determines any issue of fact or law for the purpose of determining the rights of the parties, it may be considered a trial.

trover A common law action for damages due to a conversion of personal property.

trust A confidence reposed in one person, who is termed trustee, for the benefit of another, who is called the cestui que trust, respecting property that is held by the trustee for the benefit of the cestui que trust. As the word is used in the law pertaining to unlawful combinations and monopolies, a trust in its original and typical form is a combination formed by an agreement among the shareholders in a number of competing corporations to transfer their shares to an unincorporated board of trustees, and to receive in exchange trust certificates in some agreed proportion to their shareholdings.

trustee A person in whom property is vested in trust for another.

trustee in bankruptcy The federal bankruptcy act defines the term as an officer, and she is an officer of the courts in a certain restricted sense but not in any such sense as a receiver. She takes the legal title to the property of the bankrupt and in respect to suits stands in the same general position as a trustee of an express trust or an executor. Her duties are fixed by statute. She is to collect and reduce to money the property of the estate of the bankrupt.

ultra vires act An act of a corporation that is beyond the powers conferred on the corporation.

unilateral contract A contract formed by an offer or a promise on one side for an act to be done on the other, and a doing of the act by the other by way of acceptance of the offer or promise; that is, a contract wherein the only acceptance of the offer that is necessary is the performance of the act.

unliquidated Undetermined in amount.

usury The taking of more than the law allows on a loan or for forbearance of a debt. Illegal interest; interest in excess of the rate allowed by law.

utter As applied to counterfeiting, to utter and publish is to declare or assert, directly or indirectly, by words or action, that the money or note is good. Thus, to offer it in payment is an uttering or publishing.

valid Effective; operative; not void; subsisting; sufficient in law.

value Under the Uniform Commercial Code (except for negotiable instruments and bank collections), generally any consideration sufficient to support a simple contract.

variance An amendment to a zoning ordinance for a single piece of land on the grounds that the ordinance deprives the owner of reasonable use of the land.

vendee A purchaser of property. The word is more commonly applied to a purchaser of real property, the word "buyer" being more commonly applied to the purchaser of personal property.

vendor A person who sells property to a vendee. The words "vendor" and "vendee" are more commonly applied to the seller and purchaser of real estate, and the words "seller" and "buyer" are more commonly applied to the seller and purchaser of personal property.

venire The name of a writ by which a jury is summoned.

venue The word originally was employed to indicate the county from which the jurors were to come who were to try a case, but in modern times it refers to the county in which a case is to be tried.

verdict The answer of a jury given to the court concerning the matters of fact committed to their trial and examination; it makes no precedent, and settles nothing but the present controversy to which it relates. It is the decision made by the jury and reported to the court, and as such it is an elemental entity that cannot be divided by the judge.

verification The affidavit of a party annexed to his pleadings that states that the pleading is true of his own knowledge except as to matters that are therein stated on his information or belief, and as to those matters, that he believes it to be true. A sworn statement of the truth of the facts stated in the instrument verified.

versus Against.

vest To give an immediate fixed right of present or future enjoyment.

void That which is entirely null. A void act is one that is not binding on either party, and that is not susceptible of ratification.

voidable Capable of being made void; not utterly null but annullable, and hence, that may be either voided or confirmed.

waive To throw away; to relinquish voluntarily, as a right that one may enforce, if he chooses.

waiver The intentional relinquishment of a known right. It is a voluntary act and implies an election by the party to dispense with something of value, or to forgo some advantage that he or she might have demanded and insisted on.

warrant An order authorizing a payment of money by another person to a third person. Also, an option to purchase a security. As a verb, the word means to defend; to guarantee; to enter into an obligation of warranty.

warrant of arrest A legal process issued by competent authority, usually directed to regular officers of the law but occasionally issued to private persons named in it, directing the arrest of a person or persons on grounds stated therein.

warranty In the sale of a commodity, an undertaking by the seller to answer for the defects therein is construed as a warranty. In a contract of insurance, as a general rule, any statement or description, or any undertaking on the part of the insured on the face of the policy or in another instrument properly incorporated in the policy, which relates to the risk, is a warranty.

waste The material alteration, abuse, or destructive use of property by one in rightful possession of it that results in injury to one having an underlying interest in it.

watered stock Stock issued by a corporation as fully paid up, when in fact it is not fully paid up.

whistleblowing The reporting of organizational wrongdoing by someone within the organization to someone who can correct the wrongdoing.

winding up In partnership and corporation law, the orderly liquidation of the business's assets.

writ A commandment of a court given for the purpose of compelling a defendant to take certain action, usually directed to a sheriff or other officer to execute it.

writ of certiorari An order of a court to an inferior court to forward the record of a case for reexamination by the superior court.

Appendix C

Spanish–English Equivalents for Important Legal Terms[1]

abatement of nuisance abolición de un estorbo
abstract of title resumen de título
acceptance aceptación
accession accesión
accommodation paper documento de favor
accord and satisfaction acuerdo y satisfacción
act of state acto de gobierno
adjudicate juzgar, adjudicar
administrator administrador
adverse possession posesión adversa
affirm afirmar
affirmative action acción afirmativa
agent agente
allegation alegato
allege alegar
answer contestación
anticipatory breach infracción anticipadora
appellee apelado
arbitrate arbitrar
assignee cesionario
assignment cesión
assignor cedente
bailee depositario
bailment depósito, entrega
bailor depositante
bankruptcy bancarrota
bearer portador
beneficiary beneficiario
bid oferta
bill of lading conocimiento de embarque
blue sky laws leyes reguladoras del comercio
brief alegato, resumen bursátil
bulk transfer transferencia a granel
burden of proof obligación de la prueba
case law jurisprudencia, precedentes
cashier's check cheque de caja, cheque bancario
cause of action derecho de acción
caveat emptor tenga cuidado el comprador
caveat venditor tenga cuidado el vendedor
certification certificación
certified check cheque certificado
check cheque
C.I.F. costo, seguro y flete
civil action juicio civil
class action litigio entablado en representación de un grupo
C.O.D. "Cash on Delivery" pago contra entrega
code código
codicil codicilo, cambio a un testamento
common carrier transportador público
compensatory (see damages) compensatario
complaint escrito de agravios demanda

[1]Prepared by Roberto Cisnerosa, Jr., Chaviano & Associates, Ltd., Chicago, Illinois.

composition with creditors concordato con acreedores
condition condición
conditional gift regalo condicional
condition precedent condición precedente
condition subsequent condición subsiguiente
consignee consignatario
consignment consignación
consignor consignador
contract contrato
conversion conversión
corporation corporación, sociedad autónoma
counterclaim contrademanda
counteroffer contraoferta
custody custodia
damages daños y perjuicios
D/B/A haciendo negocio como
debtor deudor
deceit engaño
decision decisión
deed escritura, título de propiedad
defendant acusado, demandado
defraud estafar
deliver entregar
de novo, trial juicio de nuevo
deposition deposición
derivative action acción en representación de la sociedad
dictum opinión expresado por un tribunal
directed verdict veredicto dirigido por el juez
discharge in bankruptcy extención de una obligación en bancarrota
dismiss desechar, denegar
donee donatario
donor donante
dower los bienes del esposo fallecido que le corresponden a la viuda
draft letra de cambio
drawee girado
duress coacción
easement servidumbre
en banc en el tribunal
equity equidad, valor líquido
equity of redemption derecho de rescate de una propiedad hipotecada
estoppel impedimento por actas propios
exculpatory clause claúsula disculpable
executor albacea
executory ejecutorio
executrix mujer albacea
ex ship enviar al gasto y riesgo del venededor
F.A.S. franco al costado del vapor
felony felonia, crimen
fiduciary fiduciario
financing statement declaración de seguridad
fixture instalación fijo
F.O.B. franco a bordo
fungible goods bienes fungibles
garnishment embargo
gift regalo
good faith veracidad de intención
guarantor garante
guaranty garantía
heirs herederos
holder in due course tenedor a su debido tiempo
illusory illusorio
implied warranty garantía implícita
incapacity incapacidad
independent contractor contratista independiente
indorsement endoso
injunction interdicto judicial
in personam contra la persona
insolvency insolvencia
in status quo en statu quo
instrument instrumento
jointly conjuntamente
jointly and severally conjunta e independientemente, solidariamente
joint tenancy tenencia conjunta
judgment sentencia
judgment N.O.V. sentencia contraria al veredicto
jurisdiction jurisdicción
law merchant derecho comercial
lease contrato de arrendamiento
legal legal
lien gravamen, derecho de retención
litigant litigante
magistrate juez, magistrado
mechanic's lien gravamen de mecánico
mens rea intención de cometer un delito, mentalidad delictuosa
minitrial mini juicio
minor menor
misdemeanor delito, ofensa menor

mistrial juicio nulo
mitigation of damages mitagación de daños
mortgage hipoteca
necessaries necesidades básicas
negligence negligencia
negotiable negociable
negotiable instrument instrumento negociable
negotiation negociación
no arrival, no sale sino llegan los bienes, no hay pago por ellos
nolo contendere admisión de culpabilidad como estrategia
non compos mentis incapacitado mentalmente
novation novación
oath juramento
obligee obligante
obligor obligado
objection objeción
offer oferta
offeree quien recibe una oferta
offeror oferente
opinion opinión
option opción
ordinance ordenanza
parol evidence prueba verbal
partners socios
payee tenedor, beneficiaro de pago
per curiam por el tribunal
perjury perjurio
petition (bankruptcy) petición de bancarrota
plaintiff demandante
plea alegato
polygraph polígrafo
positive law ley positiva
postdated check cheque a fecha
power of attorney poder, carta de personería
precedent precedente
privity relación de partes de interés común
probate validación de testamento
promise promesa
promisor prometedor
promissory estoppel impedimento promisorio
promoters promotores
prospectus prospecto
proximate cause causa inmediata
quasi contract cuasicontrato
ratification ratificación
rebuttal refutación
recorder registrador, grabador
redemption redención
remand reencarcelar
remedy remedio
res asunto
respondent respondiente
satisfaction satisfacción
scienter a sabiendas
security agreement acuerdo de seguridad
shareholder accionista
sovereign immunity inmunidad soberana
specific performance ejecución de lo estipulado en un contrato
stare decisis doctrina de seguir los precedentas judiciales
stated capital dicha capital
status quo statu quo
stockholder accionista
subpoena orden de aparición
summary judgment sentencia sumaria
summons emplazamiento
testimony testimonio
tort agravio
tortious agravioso
transcript transcripción
treble damages daños triplicados
trial juicio
trustee in bankruptcy síndico concursal
***ultra vires* act** un acto que se realizó sin autoridad legal
unliquidated debt deuda no liquidado
usury usura
venue lugar de jurisdicción
verdict veredicto
versus contra
void nulo
voidable anulable
waive renunciar
waiver renuncia
warranty garantía
whistleblower denunciante
writ orden judicial
writ of certiorari auto de avocación
writ of execution (or garnishment) ejecutoria, mandamiento de ejecución

Index

A

C

S

T

U